PROPER NOUN Speller

2001 Edition

Over 45,000 Entries

UPDATED & UP-TO-DATE

Compiled by Beverly Loeblein Ritter & Patricia Pooser Rhyne

Stenotype Educational Products, Inc.
Phone: 888-StenEd1 • Fax: 352-475-2152
P.O. Box 959, Melrose, Florida 32666

www.stened.com

ISBN 0-938643-67-3
StenEd #PNS101

Foreword

The *Proper Noun Speller* is an invaluable reference for the correct spelling of proper nouns (names of people, places, and things). This updated edition contains over 45,000 entries compiled from well over 4,000 sources.

People

Artists	Scientists
Business leaders	Sports figures
Entertainers	Tribes
Fictional characters	Nationalities
Media figures	US leaders
Mythological figures	World leaders
Religious figures	Writers

Places

Cities	Mountains
Continents	Nations
Countries	Oceans
Deserts	Planets & stars
Famous attractions	Rivers
Lakes	States

Things

Books	Medicines
Brand names	Movies
Businesses	Newspapers
Court cases	Organizations
Current events	Paintings
Government agencies	Plays
Historical events	Religions
Historical periods	Scientific terms
Holidays	Songs
Languages	Space vehicles
Magazines	TV shows

Bonus

To make this the most useful and complete proper noun speller on the market, a brief description is included with most entries to further authenticate that this is the name you're looking for.

> Wolfe, Thomas (Clayton)(US writer; 1900-38)
> Wolfe, Tom (b. Thomas Kennerly Wolfe, Jr.)(US writer; 1931-)
> Wolff, Tobias (US writer; 1945-)
> Woolf, (Adeline) Virginia (Stephen)(Br. writer; 1882-1941)

Introduction

Style of Entries

Most entries include a brief description in addition to the actual name. The description chosen is that which is most inclusive or most well known. For example, an entertainer (ent.) may be an actor, singer, director, etc.; a novel may also be a film or play.

When appropriate, names are cross-referenced.

>Goldberg, Whoopi (b. Caryn Johnson)(ent.; 1950-)
>Whoopi Goldberg (b. Caryn Johnson)(ent.; 1950-)

Proper nouns known by more than one name are further cross-referenced.

>Clemens, Samuel Langhorne (pseud. Mark Twain)(US writer; 1835-1910)
>Mark Twain (aka Samuel Langhorne Clemens)(US writer; 1835-1910)
>Samuel Langhorne Clemens (pseud. Mark Twain)(US writer; 1835-1910)
>Twain, Mark (aka Samuel Langhorne Clemens)(US writer; 1835-1910)

Dates refer to the birth and death dates of people and the date of occurrence for events.

>Battle of the Bulge (WWII; 1944-45)

When giving day/month/year, dates other than the 1900's will be itemized.

>Black Friday (US finan. disasters; 9/24/1869 & 9/19/1873)
>Black Tuesday (US stock market crash; 10/29/29)

Acronyms

Acronyms are included in the body of the text.

Pronunciation Marks

Pronunciation marks have been included for those entries which retain them when Anglicized. Whether you need to include these marks will depend on the nature of your work.

>Perón, Eva Duarte de ("Evita")(b. Maria Eva Duarte)(ex-pres., Argentina; 1919-52)

Italicized Nouns

The following have been italicized:

- Titles of books, magazines, newspapers;
- Names of films, plays, TV and radio shows;
- Names of paintings, sculptures, symphonies, songs, poems; and
- Legal citations.

Erin Brockovich (film, 2000)
Washington Post (DC newspaper)

Spelling Variations

Because of country origins or phonetic translations, some names may have more than one correct spelling. In addition, often the most respected references differ on the preferred spelling of a proper noun.

When one spelling has been generally accepted by the majority of reference sources, only that spelling has been included. When variant spellings are common, most variations have also been included.

Bosnia-Hercegovina (republic, Yug.)(also Bosnia-Herzegovina)

Hyphenating Proper Nouns

Simply stated, it is best not to hyphenate a name. When hyphenation is unavoidable, follow these few rules.

- Do not divide nouns of one syllable.
- Do not divide an acronym unless it has a natural division (e.g., AFL-CIO).
- Do not separate the title from the name.

Alphabetization

Alphabetization is letter by letter with the following qualifications.

Abbreviated designations such as St. and Mt. are alphabetized as though they were spelled out as Saint and Mount. Arabic numbers are alphabetized as though they were spelled out. Symbols such as & are alphabetized by what they represent (e.g., the word "and").

Roman numerals are alphabetized by the actual letters. Punctuation marks, titles such as Sir and Dr., and material in parentheses are ignored for purposes of alphabetization.

Entries with the same first word are listed together before any entries followed by a comma.

> Henry Ford (US bus./auto.; 1863-1947)
> Henry Ford, II (US bus./auto.; 1917-87)
> Henry James (US writer; 1843-1916)
> Henry VIII (king, Eng.; 1491-1547)
> Henry Winkler (ent.; 1945-)
> Henry, John (fict. chara., exceptional strength)
> Henry, Patrick (US pol./orator; 1736-99)
> Henry's law (gas in liquid)

Trademarks/Brand Names

Brand names are generally trademarked and as such are usually capitalized.

> Kleenex
> Xerox

Trademarks may be applied for (™) or registered (®). The trademark symbols ™ and ® rarely occur in print (the main exception being advertising copy) and thus these symbols have not been included in this text.

The word(s) following a trademarked capitalized word is generally not capitalized unless it is part of the brand name or is a proper noun in its own right.

> Godiva chocolates
> Godiva Chocolatier (US bus.)

Unusual Capitalization

Some trademarks of brand and/or company names incorporate special capitalization.

> eBay Inc.
> Jell-O
> pHisoDerm
> ScotTowels
> StenEd

Abbreviations Used in Text

adm.	admiral		CT	Connecticut
admin.	administrator		Czech.	Czechoslovakia(n)
adv.	advertiser, advertising		Dan.	Danish
Afghan.	Afghanistan, Afghan(i)		DC	District of Columbia;
Afr.	Africa(n)			Washington, DC
agcy.	agency		DE	Delaware
agr.	agriculture, agriculturalist		Den.	Denmark
AK	Alaska		dipl.	diplomat
aka	also known as		dir.	director
AL	Alabama		Dom. Rep.	Dominican Republic
Amer.	America(n)		drama.	dramatist
anthrop.	anthropologist, anthropology		E	east
AR	Arkansas		ecol.	ecology, ecologist
arch.	architect(ure)		econ.	economics, economist
archaeol.	archaeologist		educ.	educator, educational
art.	artist		Eg.	Egypt(ian)
assoc.	association		elect.	electronics, electrical
astro.	astronaut		emp.	emperor, empire
astrol.	astrology, astrologer		Eng.	England, English
astron.	astronomy, astronomer		eng.	engineer
astrophyst.	astrophysicist		ent.	entertainer, entertainment
Atl.	Atlantic Ocean			industry
atty.	attorney		environ.	environment(al)(ist)
Aus.	Austria(n)		est.	established
Austl.	Australia(n)		ethnol.	ethnologist
auto.	automobile, automotive		Eur.	Europe(an)
AZ	Arizona		expl.	explorer
b.	born		fict.	fictitious
bacteriol.	bacteriologist		Fin.	Finnish, Finland
BC	before Christ		finan.	financial, financier
biol.	biologist, biology		FL	Florida
biopharm.	biopharmaceutical(s)		fl.	flourished
Br.	British, Britain		Flem.	Flemish
bro.	brother		Fr.	French, France
bus.	business		furn.	furniture
c	circa		GA	Georgia
c.	century		gen.	general
CA	California		genet.	genetics, geneticist
CAmer.	Central America(n)		geol.	geologist, geology
Can.	Canada, Canadian		Ger.	German(y)
capt.	captain		gov.-gen.	governor-general
celeb.	celebrity		gov.	governor
Ch.	China, Chinese		govt.	government
chanc.	chancellor		Gr.	Greek, Greece
chara(s).	character(s)		grp.	group
chem.	chemical, chemist, chemistry		Guat.	Guatemala
CO	Colorado		HI	Hawaii
Co.	Company		hist.	history, historian
Col.	Colonel		Hung.	Hungary, Hungarian
comm.	communications		IA	Iowa
comp.	composer		ID	Idaho
compu.	computers		IL	Illinois
cond.	conductor		illus.	illustrator
cong.	congress		IN	Indiana
cos.	companies		Inc.	Incorporated
cosmo.	cosmonaut		inv.	inventor
crim.	criminology, criminologist		Ir.	Ireland, Irish

Isr.	Israel(i)	photo.	photographer, photography
It.	Italian, Italy	phys.	physician
Jam.	Jamaica(n)	physiol.	physiologist
Jap.	Japan(ese)	physt.	physicist
Jew.	Jewish	PM	prime minister
jour.	journalist	Pol.	Poland, Polish
KS	Kansas	pol.	politician, political, politics
KY	Kentucky	Port.	Portugal, Portuguese
l.c.	lower case	pres.	president
LA	Louisiana	prods.	products
lang(s).	language(s)	pseud.	pseudonym
lit.	literature, literary	psych.	psychiatrist, psychologist,
Lith.	Lithuania(n)		psychoanalyst
m.	married	publ.	publisher, publishing
MA	Massachusetts	rel.	religion, religious, religionist
mag.	magazine	RI	Rhode Island
math.	mathematics, mathematician	rr.	railroad
MD	Maryland	Rus.	Russia(n)
ME	Maine	S Afr.	South Africa (area)
med.	medical, medicine	S	south
meteorol.	meteorologist	SAfr.	South Africa(n)(country)
MI	Michigan	SAmer.	South America(n)
mil.	military, militarist	SC	South Carolina
MN	Minnesota	scien.	scientist
MO	Missouri	Scot.	Scottish, Scotland
MS	Mississippi	SD	South Dakota
MT	Montana	Secy.	Secretary
myth.	mythical, mythology	seismol.	seismologist
N	north	sociol.	sociology, sociologist
NAfr.	North Africa(n)	Sp.	Spanish
NAmer.	North America(n)	St.	Saint
nat.	naturalist	Ste.	Sainte
nav.	navigator	SViet.	South Vietnam
NC	North Carolina	Swed.	Sweden, Swedish
ND	North Dakota	Switz.	Switzerland
NE	Nebraska	sym.	symbol
neurol.	neurologist	TN	Tennessee
neuropharm.	neuropharmacologist	trans.	transportation
NewZeal.	New Zealand	Turk.	Turkey, Turkish
NH	New Hampshire	TX	Texas
NIre.	Northern Ireland	UAE	United Arab Emirates
NJ	New Jersey	UK	United Kingdom
NM	New Mexico	US	United States
Nor.	Norway, Norwegian	USSR	United Soviet Socialist Republic
NV	Nevada	UT	Utah
NViet.	North Vietnam	VA	Virginia
NY	New York	VI	Virgin Islands
ofc.	office	Viet.	Vietnam(ese)
OH	Ohio	virol.	virologist
OK	Oklahoma	VP	vice president
OR	Oregon	VT	Vermont
org.	organization, organized	W	west
orig.	originally	WA	Washington
ornithol.	ornithologist	WGer.	West Germany
PA	Pennsylvania	WI	Wisconsin
Pac.	Pacific Ocean	WSamoa	Western Samoa
Pak.	Pakistan(i)	WV	West Virginia
paleontol.	paleontologist	WY	Wyoming
pathol.	pathologist	Yug.	Yugoslavia(n)
Pers.	Persia, Persian	zool.	zoologist
petro.	petroleum		
pharm.	pharmaceuticals, pharmacology		
Phil.	Philippine(s)		
phil.	philosopher, philosophy		

- A -

AA (Alcoholics Anonymous, American Airlines, Associate of Arts)
AAA (American Automobile Association)
AAA World (mag.)
AAdvantage (finan.)
A(lan) A(lexander) Milne (Br. writer; 1882-1956)
Aaron Neville (ent.; 1941-)
AAS (Associate of Applied Science) degree
Aachen, Germany (also Aix-la-Chapelle)
Aage Bohr (Dan. physt.; 1922-)
Aalborg, Denmark
Aalto, Alvar (Fin. arch.; 1898-1976)
AAMCO Transmission, Inc.
A&E (Arts & Entertainment)(TV channel)
A & P Food Stores (Great Atlantic & Pacific Tea Co.)
A & W Brands, Inc.
A & W root beer
Aare River (also Aar)(Switz.)
Aarhus, Denmark (also Arhus)
Aaron Brothers Art Marts, Inc.
Aaron Burr (ex-US VP; 1756-1836)
Aaron Copland (US comp.; 1900-90)
Aaron Douglas (US artist; 1900-79)
Aaron Montgomery Ward (US bus.; 1843-1913)
Aaron Spelling (ent.; 1928-)
Aaron, Hank (Henry)(baseball; 1934-)
Aaron, Tommy (baseball; 1939-84)
AARP (American Association of Retired Persons)
AARP Bulletin (mag.)
AAU (Amateur Athletic Union)
AAUW (American Association of University Women)
AB (Associate of Business) degree
ABA (American Bar Association, American Booksellers Association)
Aba, Nigeria
Abacha, Sani (ex-ruler, Nigeria; 1943-1998)
Abadan, Iran
Abaddon (also Apollyon)(destroyer, hell)
Abba Eban (b. Aubrey Solomon)(Isr. pol.; 1915-)
Abbado, Claudio (It. ent.; 1933-)
Abbas I ("the Great")(Pers. shah; c1557-1629)
Abbasid dynasty (Islamic ruling family; 750-1258)
Abbe Lane (b. Abigail Francine Lassman)(ent.; 1933-)
Abbe, Cleveland (US meteor.; 1838-1916)
Abbeville Press, Inc.
Abbeville, France
Abbey Road (Beatles album)
Abbey Theatre (Ir.)
Abbie (Abbott H.) Hoffman (US pol. activist; 1936-89)
Abbot, Charles Greeley (US physt.; 1872-1973)
Abbott (slang, Nembutal)
Abbott and Costello (ent.)
Abbott Laboratories USA (US bus.)
Abbott, Bud (William)(ent.; 1898-1974)
Abbott, George (ent.; 1887-1995)

Abbott, Lyman (US rel.; 1835-1922)
Abby Dalton (ent.; 1932-)
Abby, Dear (Abigail Van Buren)(b. Pauline Esther Friedman)(US advice columnist; 1918-)
ABC (Alcoholic Beverage Control Board)
ABC (American Broadcasting Company)(TV channel)
ABC After School Special
ABC Information Radio
ABC News (TV show)
ABC Radio Network News
A. B. (Happy) Chandler (baseball; 1899-1991)
Abd al-Salam al (or Abdul-Salam) Majali (ex-PM, Jordan; 1925-)
Abdel Nasser, Gamal (ex-pres., Eg.; 1918-70)
Abdel-Rahman, Sheik Omar (Muslim rel.; 1938-)
Abdelaziz Bouteflika (pres., Algeria; 1937-)
Abderrahmane El-Youssoufi (PM, Morocco; 1924-)
Abdesalam, Belaid (Algerian pol.; 1928-)
A. B. Dick Co.
Abdiqassim Salad Hassan (head of state, Somalia)
Abdou Diouf (ex-pres., Senegal; 1935-)
Abdou, Muhammad (ex-PM, Comoros)
Abdoulaye Sekou Sow (ex-PM, Mali)
Abdoulaye Wade (pres., Senegal; 1926-)
Abdul Hashim Mutalov (ex-PM, Uzbekistan)
Abdul-Jabbar, Kareem (b. [Ferdinand] Lew[is] Alcindor, Jr.)(basketball; 1947-)
Abdul-Karim al-Iryani (PM, Yemen; 1934-)
Abdul-Salam (or Abd al-Salam al) Majali (ex-PM, Jordan; 1925-)
Abdul, Paula (ent.; 1962-)
Abdullah bin Khalifa al-Thani (PM, Qatar)
Abdullah ibn Hussein (ex-king, Jordan; 1882-1951)
Abdullah II, King (Abdullah ibn Hussein)(king, Jordan; 1962-)
Abdullah, Muhammad ibn (Arab, founded Islam; c570-632)
Abdumalik Abulajanov (ex-PM, Tajikistan)
Abdur Rahman Biswas (ex-pres., Bangladesh; 1926-)
Abdurrahman Wahid (pres., Indonesia; 1940-)
Abe Burrows (US writer; 1910-85)
Abe Fortas (US jurist; 1910-82)
Abe Kobo (Jap. writer; 1924-93)
Abe Vigoda (ent.; 1921-)
Abeche, Chad
Abel (son of Adam & Eve)
Abel (Tendekayi) Muzorewa (Zimbabwean pol./rel.; 1925-)
Abel Janszoon Tasman (Dutch expl./nav.; 1603?-59)
Abelard, Pierre (or Peter)(Fr. phil.; 1079-1142)
Abeokuta, Nigeria
Abercrombie & Fitch (US bus.)
Aberdeen (Black) Angus cattle
Aberdeen Proving Ground, MD (mil.)
Aberdeen, MD, SD, WA
Aberdeen, Scotland
Abernathy Sport (clothing)
Abernathy, Ralph David (US rel./civil rights leader; 1926-90)

A. B. Guthrie (US writer; 1901-91)
Abhidhamma Pitaka (rel.)
Abidjan, Ivory Coast
Abie's Irish Rose (play)
Abigail (Smith) Adams (wife of ex-US pres.;
    1744-1818)
Abigail Van Buren (Dear Abby)(b. Pauline Esther
    Friedman)(US advice columnist; 1918-)
Abilene, TX
Abington Township v. Schempp (US law; 1963)
Abisala, Aleksandras (Lith. pol.)
Abkhazi (Georgian republic)
Abkhazian (people, area)
ABM (antiballistic missile)
Abner Doubleday (US mil., possibly inv.
    baseball; 1819-93)
Abner Louima (US news/assaulted by NY
    police)
Abner, Li'l (fict. chara.)
Abner, Lum and
ABO system (blood classification)
A-bomb (atom bomb; slang, heroin/marijuana
    cigarette)
Abomey, Benin
Abominable Snowman (also l.c.)
Aboriginal Science Fiction
Aborigine, Australian (people)(also l.c.)
Abracadabra, Lady
Abraham & Straus/Jordan Marsh Co.
Abraham Lincoln (16th US pres.; 1809-65)
Abraham (Edmund) Spencer (US secy./ener.;
    1952-)
Abraham, F. Murray (ent.; 1939-)
Abraham, Plains of (Can.)
Abraham's bosom (heaven)
Abrahamson, Brecht v. (US law; 1993)
Abramovitz, Max (US arch.; 1908-)
Abrams v. U.S. (US law; 1919)
Abrams, Creighton (US gen.; 1914-74)
Abruzzi (region, It.)
Abruzzi e Molise, Italy
Abscam scandal (*Ab*dul/Arab *Scam*, US cong.,
    bribes; 1978-80)
Absessalem, Belnid (ex-PM, Algeria)
Absolut (vodka)
Abu Bakr (Islamic pol., 573-634)
Abu Dhabi (state, UAE)
Abu Said Omar Dourda (ex-PM, Libya)
Abuja, Nigeria
Abulajanov, Abdumalik (ex-PM, Tajikistan)
Aburdene, Patricia (US writer)
Abu Said Omar Dourda (ex-PM, Libya)
A(tal) B(ihari) Vajpayee (PM, India; 1924-)
Abyssinia (now Ethiopia)
Abyssinian (cat)
Abzug, Bella (Savitzky)(US pol.; 1920-98)
AC (alternating current)
Ac (chem. sym., actinium)
A/C (air conditioning)
Acacia Winery (US bus.)
Academy Awards (also Oscars)
Academy of Arts, Royal (Br. ; est. 1768)
Academy of Country Music Awards
Academy of Motion Picture Arts and Sciences
Academy of Sciences, National (org. 1863)

Academy of St. Martin-in-the-Fields (music
    ensemble)
Academy of Television Arts and Sciences,
    National (NATAS, Emmy Awards)
Acadia (now Nova Scotia)
Acadia National Park (ME)
Acadian (people)
Acapulco gold (marijuana)
Acapulco, Mexico
Acarigua, Venezuela
Accent, Hyundai (auto.)
Accenture (orig. Andersen Consulting)(US bus.)
Acclaim, Plymouth (auto.)
Accord, Honda (auto.)
Accra, Ghana (also Akka)
Accutane (med.)
AC/DC (electrical current; slang, bisexual)
AC/DC (pop music)
Ace bandage
Ace Hardware Corp.
ACE inhibitors (med.)
Ace Ventura: Pet Detective (film, 1993)
Ace Ventura: When Nature Calls (film, 1995)
Acevedo, California v. (US law; 1991)
Achates (fict. chara., *Aeneid*)
Achebe, Chinua (Nigerian writer; 1930-)
Acheron River ("River of Woe")(myth.)
Acheson, Dean (Gooderham)(US pol.; 1893-1971)
Achieva, Oldsmobile (auto.)
Achille Lauro (hijacked It. cruise ship; 1984)
Achilles (hero of Homer's *Iliad*)
Achilles heel (also Achilles' heel)
Achilles tendon
Achinese (also Atjehnese)(lang./people)
Achmed Sukarno (ex-pres., Indonesia; 1901-70)
Achromycin (med.)
Achtung (Ger., attention)
Achu, Simon Achidi (ex-PM, Cameroon)
ACLU (American Civil Liberties Union)
A. C. Nielsen (US bus./ratings; 1897-1980)
A. C. Nielsen Co. (TV ratings)
Acoma, NM (Pueblo Native Amer. village)
Aconcagua Mountain (Argentina)
Acre, Israel
Acrilan (acrylic fiber)
Acrobat Reader, Adobe (compu.)
Acropolis, the (Athens, Gr.)
ACS (American Cancer Society)
Act (toothpaste)
act of Congress
act of God
Actifed (med.)
Actigall (med.)
Actium, Battle of (Rome, 31 BC)
Actors' Equity Association (also AEA)
Acts, The (aka Acts of the Apostles)(rel., book
    of the New Testament)
Acuff, Roy (Claxton)(ent.; 1903-1992)
Acura (auto.)
Acura 3.2CL coupe (auto.)
Acura 3.2CL Type S (auto.)
Acura 3.2TL sedan (auto.)
Acura 3.5RL sedan (auto.)
Acura CL (auto.)
Acura Integra (auto.)

Acura Integra coupe (auto.)
Acura Integra GS (auto.)
Acura Integra GS-R (auto.)
Acura Integra hatchback (auto.)
Acura Integra LS (auto.)
Acura Integra RS (auto.)
Acura Integra SE (auto.)
Acura Integra sedan (auto.)
Acura Integra Type R (auto.)
Acura Legend (auto.)
Acura MDX (auto.)
Acura NSX (auto.)
Acura NSX Targa (auto.)
Acura NSX-T (auto.)
Acura RL (auto.)
Acura SLX (auto.)
Acura TL (auto.)
Acura Vigor (auto.)
Acutrim (med.)
AD (or A.D.) (anno Domini, in the year of the Lord)
Adalat (med.)
Adam (rel., 1st man)
Adam 12 (TV show)
Adam and Eve (rel.)
Adam Ant (b. Stuart Leslie Goddard)(ent.; 1954-)
Adam Arkin (ent.; 1957-)
Adam Clayton Powell, Jr. (US pol./rel.; 1908-72)
Adam II, Prince Hans- (head of state,
   Liechtenstein; 1945-)
Adam Mickiewicz (Pol. poet; 1798-1855)
Adam Sandler (ent.; 1966-)
Adam Smith (Br. econ.; 1723-90)
Adam Walsh (football; 1902-85)
Adam Willis Wagnalls (US publ.; 1843-1924)
Adami, Edward Fenech (PM, Malta; 1934-)
Adamkus, Valdas (pres., Lith.; 1926-)
Adam's apple (med.)
Adam's needle (plant)
Adam's Rib (film, 1949)
Adams, Abigail (Smith)(wife of ex-US pres.;
   1744-1818)
Adams, Alice (US writer; 1926-99)
Adams, Ansel (US photo.; 1902-84)
Adams, Brooks (US hist.; 1848-1927)
Adams, Bryan (ent.; 1959-)
Adams, Charles Francis (US dipl.; 1807-86)
Adams, Don (ent.; 1926-)
Adams, Edie (b. Elizabeth Edith Enke)(ent.; 1929-)
Adams, Franklin Pierce (US writer; 1881-1960)
Adams, Gerry (Ir. pol. leader; 1948-)
Adams, Grizzly (TV show)
Adams, Life and Times of Grizzly (film, 1974)
Adams, Harriet S. (pseud. Carolyn Keene)(US
   writer; 1803-82)
Adams, Henry (US hist.; 1838-1918)
Adams, Joey (ent.; 1911-99)
Adams, John (2nd US pres.; 1735-1826)
Adams, John Quincy (6th US pres.; 1767-1848)
Adams, Mason (ent.; 1919-)
Adams, Maud (b. Maud Wikstrom)(Swed. ent.;
   1945-)
Adams, Maude (b. Maude Kiskadden)(ent.;
   1872-1953)
Adams, Patch (film, 1999)
Adams, Samuel (US pol.; 1722-1803)

Adams, Scott (cartoonist; 1957-)
Adamson, Joy (naturalist/writer; 1910-80)
Adana, Turkey
Adapa (myth.)
Adapin (med.)
Adar (Jew. month)
Adar Sheni (Jew. month)
ADC (aide-de-camp)
Addams Family, The (TV show; film, 1964, 1991)
Addams, Charles (cartoonist; 1912-88)
Addams, Jane (US reformer; 1860-1935)
Adderley, Cannonball (Julian)(US jazz; 1928-75)
Adderly, Herbert A. (football; 1939-)
Addis Ababa, Ethiopia
Addison, Joseph (Br. writer; 1672-1719)
Addison's disease (med.)
Addressograph
Addyston Pipe and Steel Co. v. U.S. (US law;
   1899)
Ade, George (US writer/humorist; 1866-1944)
Adela Rogers St. Johns (US writer; 1894-1988)
Adelaide, Australia
Adele Astaire (ent.; 1897-1981)
Adelina Patti (It. opera; 1843-1919)
Adeline, Sweet (film, 1926, 1935)
Aden, Gulf of (Yemen/Africa)
Aden, Yemen
Adenauer, Konrad (ex-chanc., WGer.; 1876-1967)
Adha, Eid ul- (Muslim festival)
ADHD (Attention Deficit Hyperactivity Disorder)
Adidas (sportswear)
Adidas USA, Inc.
Adigranth (also Grunth, Grant Sahib, Granth)(rel.)
Adirondack chair
Adirondack Mountains (also the
   Adirondacks)(NY)
Adja (people)
Adjani, Isabelle (ent.; 1955-)
Adjodhia, Jules (Suriname pol.)
Adlai E(wing) Stevenson (US pol.; 1835-1914)
Adlai E(wing) Stevenson II (US ex-VP/IL gov.;
   1900-65)
Adlai E(wing) Stevenson III (US pol.; 1930-)
Adler, Alfred (Aus. psych.; 1870-1937)
Adler, Felix (US phil.; 1851-1933)
Adler, Larry (Lawrence Cecil)(US musician; 1914-)
Adler, Luther (ent.; 1903-84)
Adler, Richard (US comp.; 1921-)
Adler, Stella (US acting teacher; 1901-92)
Adlerian psychotherapy
Admetus (mythical king of Thessaly)
Administration, Office of (US govt.)
Admiral (appliances)
Admiral of the Fleet
Admiralty mile
Admission Day (holiday, AZ/CA/NV)
Adnan Khashoggi
Adobe Acrobat (compu. software)
Adobe Acrobat Reader (compu. software)
Adobe Illustrator (compu. software)
Adobe PageMaker (compu. software)
Adobe Photoshop (compu. software)
Adobe Systems Incorporated
Ado-Ekiti, Nigeria
Adolf Eichmann (Aus./Ger. Nazi; 1906-62)

Adolf Erik Nordenskjöld, (Nils), Baron (Swed. expl.; 1832-1901)
Adolf Hitler (ex-chanc./fuhrer, Ger.; 1889-1945)
Adolf Ogi (ex-pres., Switz.; 1942-)
Adolfas Slezevicius (ex-PM, Lith.; 1948-)
Adolfo Suárez González (ex-PM, Sp.; 1933-)
Adolph Coors Co.
Adolph Green (US lyricist; 1915-)
Adolph Simon Ochs (US publ.; 1858-1935)
Adolph Zukor (ent.; 1873-1976)
Adolphe Joseph Thomas Monticelli (Fr. artist; 1824-86)
Adolphe Menjou (ent.; 1890-1963)
Adolphus Busch (US bus.; 1839-1913)
Adolphus Washington Greely (US mil.; 1844-1935)
Adonai (also Adonoy)(Hebrew, God)
Adonis (myth.)
ADP (automatic data processing)(compu.)
Adrenalin (med.)
Adriaen van Ostade (Dutch artist; 1610-85)
Adriamycin (med.)
Adrian (also Hadrian)(Publius Aelius Hadrianus)(emp., Rome; 76-138)
Adrian (Cedric) Boult, Sir (Br. cond.; 1889-1983)
Adrian Dantley (basketball; 1956-)
Adriatic Sea (arm, Mediterranean)
Adrien Arpel (cosmetics)
Adrien Sibomana (ex-PM, Burundi)
Adrienne Barbeau (ent.; 1945-)
Adrienne Clarkson (gov.-gen., Can.; 1939-)
Adrienne Vittadini (clothing)
Adulyadej, Bhumibol (aka Rama IX)(king, Thailand; 1927-)
Advance, Staten Island (NY newspaper)
Advanced Micro Devices, Inc.
Advanced Translations Technology, Inc.
Advantage Software (US bus.)
Advent (rel.)
Advent Christian Church
Advent Sunday (rel.)
Adventist, Seventh-Day (rel.)
Adventure Road (mag.)
Adventures of Pinocchio, The (C. Collodi fantasy)
Adventures of Sonic the Hedgehog (cartoon)
Adversary, the (the Devil)
Advertiser, Honolulu (HI newspaper)
Advertiser, Montgomery (AL newspaper)
Advertising Age (mag.)
Advil (med.)
Advocate, Baton Rouge (LA newspaper)
Adyebo, George Cosmas (ex-PM, Uganda)
Aeaea (myth.)
Aegean civilization (Gr.)
Aegean Islands (Gr.)
Aegean Sea (arm, Mediterranean)
Aegeus (myth.)
Aegir (myth.)
Aegis (myth., shield)
A(lfred) E(dward) Housman (Br. poet; 1859-1936)
Aeneas (fict. chara., *Aeneid*)
Aeneid (Virgil epic poem)
Aeolian harp (19th c. wind instr.)(also l.c.)
Aeolus (myth.)

Aer Lingus (airline)
AeroBid (med.)
Aeroflot (airline)
Aerolineas Argentinas (airline)
AeroMexico (airline)
Aeronautics and Space Administration, National (NASA)(US govt. agcy.; est. 1958)
Aero Peru (airline)
Aerosmith (pop music)
Aerospace Corp.
Aerostar, Ford (auto.)
Aeschines (Gr. orator; 389-314 BC)
Aeschylus (Gr. drama.; 525-456 BC)
Aesculapius (myth.)
Aesir (myth.)
Aesop (Gr. fabler; c620-c560 BC)
Aesop's fables
Aetna Inc.
Aetna Investment Services, Inc.
Aetna Life Company of America
Aetna Life Insurance and Annuity Company
Aetna Life & Casualty Co.
A(lfred) E(lton) Van Vogt (US writer; 1912-2000)
AF (air force, audio-frequency)
AFA (Air Force Academy)
Afar (lang./people)
AFB (Air Force Base)
AFC (American Football Conference, automatic frequency control)
AFDC (Aid to Families with Dependent Children)
Affleck, Ben (ent.; 1972-)
Affleck, Francis (auto racing; 1951-85)
Afghan (also Afghani)(people)
Afghan hound (dog)
Afghan Mujahedeen (Islamic holy warriors)
Afghanistan (Republic of)(S central Aisa)
AFL (American Federation of Labor, American Football League)
AFL-CIO (American Federation of Labor & Congress of Industrial Organizations)
Afonso de Albuquerque (Port. mil.; 1453-1515)
A-frame (arch.)
Aframerican (also Afro-American, African-American)(people)
Afrasian (people)
Africa
Africa, South (Republic of)
Africa, South-West (now Namibia)
African (people)
African-American (also Aframerican, Afro-American)(people)
African cherry-orange
African daisy (plant)
African elephant
African gray (parrot)
African green monkey
African honeybee (also killer bee)
African lily (also lily-of-the-Nile)
African lion hound (also Rhodesian ridgeback)
African mahogany
African marigold (also Aztec marigold)
African Methodist Episcopal Church
African Methodist Episcopal Zion Church
African millet
African mongoose

African Plate (division of earth's crust)
African Queen (film, 1951)
African sleeping sickness (also African trypanosomiasis)
African Unity, Organization of (OAU)(est. 1963)
African violet
Africanism
Africanist
Afrikaans (lang.)
Afrikander (also Africander)(cattle)
Afrikaner (also Afrikaaner)(formerly Boer)(people)
Afrin (med.)
Afrinol (med.)
Afro (hairstyle)
Afro-American (also Aframerican, African-American)(people)
Afro-Asiatic (also Afroasiatic)(langs.)
Afro-Caribbean (people)
Afro-Cuban (people, music)
After Five (toiletries)
AFTRA (American Federation of Television and Radio Artists)
Afwerki, Isaias (pres., Eritrea; 1946-)
AG (adjutant general, attorney general)
Ag (chem. sym., silver)
Aga Khan IV (Islamic rel.; 1936-)
Agadir, Morocco
Agam, Yaacov (Isr. artist; 1928-)
Agamemnon (myth.)
Agana, Guam
Agapemone (Br. utopian community; 1849)
Agassi, Andre (tennis; 1970-)
Agassiz, (Jean) Louis (Rodolphe)(Swiss nat.; 1807-73)
Agate Technologies (US bus.)
Agatha Christie, Dame (Br. writer; 1891-1976)
Agathocles (Sicilian pol.; 361-289 BC)
Agbeyome Messan Kodjo (PM, Togo; 1954-)
Age Discrimination in Employment Act (US hist.; 1967)
Age of Aquarius (also Aquarian Age)
Age of Enlightenment (18th c. Eur. movement)
Age of Metternich
Age of Reason (phil.)
Age of Reason, The (by Thomas Paine; 1794-96)
Age, Space (also l.c.)
Agee, James (US writer; 1909-55)
Agence France-Press (Eur. news org.; est. 1944)
Agenerase (med.)
Agent Orange (poison, herbicide/defoliant)
Ager, Milton (US comp.; 1893-1979)
Agesilaus II (Spartan king; 444?-360? BC)
Agfa (photo.)
Agfachrome (photo.)
Agfacolor (photo.)
Agfa-Gevaert (photo.)
Aggadah (also Aggada, Agada, Haggadah)(rel.)
Agilent Technologies, Inc.
Agincourt, Battle of (Eng./Fr.; 1415)
Agincourt, France
Agnes Browne (film, 1999)
Agnes De Mille (US dancer/choreographer; 1905-93)
Agnes Moorehead (ent.; 1906-74)

Agnes Nixon (US writer, soap operas; 1927-)
Agnes of God (film, 1985)
Agnes, St. (Christian martyr; ?-304?)
Agnes's Eve, St. (young woman dream of future husband; 1/20)
Agnew, David Hayes (US phys.; 1818-92)
Agnew, Spiro T(heodore)(ex-US VP; 1918-96)
Agni (myth.)
Agnolo Bronzino (It. artist; 1503-72)
Agnon, Shmuel Yosef (b. Samuel Josef Czaczkes)(Isr. writer; 1888-1970)
Agnus Dei (Latin, Lamb of God)
Agonistes, Samson (by J. Milton)
Agostinho Antonio Neto (ex-pres., Angola; 1922-79)
Agostino Carracci (It. artist; 1557-1602)
Agra, India
Agree
Agricola, Gnaeus Julius (Roman mil./pol.; AD 37-93)
Agriculture Organization, Food and (FAO)(UN agcy.)
Agriculture, Department of (US govt.)
Agrippa, Herod (Julius Agrippa)(king, Judea; c10 BC-AD 44)
Agrippa, Marcus Vipsanius (Roman mil./pol.; 63-12 BC)
Agrippina, the Elder (Roman matron; 13? BC-AD 33)
Agrippina, the Younger (Roman empress; AD 15?-59)
Agua Caliente Race Track
Aguascalientes, Mexico
Aguecheek, Sir Andrew (fict. chara., *Twelfth Night*)
Aguilera, Christina (ent.; 1980-)
Aguinaldo, Emilio (Phil. revolutionary; 1869-1964)
Agulhas Cape, Africa
Agulhas Current (also Mozambique Current)
AHA (American Heart Association)
Ahab (Isr. king; c875-854 BC)
Ahab, Captain (fict. chara., *Moby Dick*)
A-head (slang, habitual amphetamine user)
Ahern, Bertie (PM, Ir.; 1951-)
Aherne, Brian (ent.; 1902-86)
Ahmad al-Jaber al-Sabah, Sheik Jaber al-(emir, Kuwait; 1928-)
Ahmad Jamal (b. Frederick Russell Jones)(US jazz; 1930-)
Ahmad Rashad (b. Bobby Moore)(football, sportscaster; 1949-)
Ahmad Tejan Kabbath (pres., Sierra Leone; 1932-)
Ahmadal-Samarrai (ex-PM, Iraq)
Ahmadzai Najibullah (Afghan. pol.; 1947-)
Ahmanson & Co., H. F. (S&L assoc.)
Ahmanson Theater (Los Angeles)
Ahmed Hussein Khudair (Iraq, pol.)
Ahmed I (Turk. sultan; 1589-1617)
Ahmed II (Turk. sultan; 1642-95)
Ahmed III (Turk. sultan; 1673-1736)
Ahmed, Shahabuddin (pres., Bangladesh; 1930-)
Ahmedabad, India (also Ahmadabad)
Ahmet Necdet Sezer (pres., Turk.; 1941-)
Aho, Esko (ex-PM, Fin.; 1954-)

A horizon (geol.)

Ahtna (Native Amer.)(also Ahtena or Atna)

Ahura Mazda (also Ormuzd, Ormazd)(rel.)

Ahvaz, Iran (also Ahwaz)

AI (artificial intelligence)(compu.)

Aida (opera by Verdi)

Aidan Quinn (ent.; 1959-)

Aidid, Muhammad Farad (Somali gen.)

AIDS (acquired immune deficiency syndrome)(med.)

AIDS-related complex (ARC)(med.)

AIDS-related virus (ARV)(med.)

Aiello, Danny (ent.; 1933-)

Aikawa, Japan

Aiken, Conrad Potter (US writer; 1889-1973)

Aiken, Howard H. (US math.; 1900-73)

Aiken, Joan (US writer; 1924-)

Aikman, Troy (football; 1966-)

Ailey, Alvin (choreographer; 1931-89)

AIM (American Indian Movement)

Aim (toothpaste)

Aimee Mann (ent.; 1960-)

Aimee Semple McPherson (US rel.; 1890-1944)

Aimee, Anouk (b. Francoise Soyra Dreyfus)(Fr. ent.; 1932-)

Ain't Misbehavin' (play)

Ainsworth, William Harrison (Br. writer; 1805-82)

Ainu (people)

Air Canada (airline)

Air Express

Air Express International Corp.

Air Force Academy, U.S. (Colorado Springs, CO)(est. 1954)

Air Force Cross

Air Force Magazine

Air Force One (US pres. plane)

Air Force Times (mag.)

Air Force, Department of the (US govt.)

Air Force, U.S. (US mil.)

Air France (airline)

Air India (airline)

Air Jamaica (airline)

Air Malta (airline)

Air Medal

Air New Zealand (airline)

Air Products and Chemicals, Inc.

Air Sedona (airline)

Air Supply (music)

Air Wisconsin, Inc. (airline)

Airbus (trans.)

Airedale terrier (dog)

Airplane II: The Sequel (film, 1982)

Airplane! (film, 1980)

Airport (film, 1970)

Airport '77 (film, 1977)

Airwick (air freshener)

Airwick Stick Ups (air freshener)

Aisha (chief wife of Mohammed; 611-678)

Aisne River (Fr.)

Aiwa (cassette)

Aix-en-Provence, France

Aix-la-Chapelle, Germany (also Aachen)

Ajaccio, Corsica

Ajax (cleanser)

Ajax (myth.)

A(nthony) J(oseph) Foyt (auto racing; 1935-)

Ajman (state, UAE)

A(lexander) J(ames) McLean (ent., Backstreet Boys; 1978-)

Ajodhia, Jules (PM, Suriname)

A(lan) J(ohn) P(ercivale) Taylor (Br. hist.; 1906-89)

AK (Alaska)

AKA (or aka)(also known as)

Akai (stereo)

Akaka, Daniel K(ahikina)(US cong.; 1924-)

Akan (lang./people)

Akayev, Askar (pres., Kyrgyzstan; 1944-)

Akbar Mizoyev (Tajikistan pol.)

Akbar the Great (Mogul emp. of India; 1542-1605)

AKC (American Kennel Club)

Ake v. Oklahoma (US law; 1985)

Akeley, Carl Ethan (US nat./sculptor; 1864-1926)

AK-47 (assault rifle)

Akhenaton (also Ikhnaton, Amenhotep IV)(king/pharaoh, Eg.; 14th c. BC)

Akhmedov, Khan (Turkmenistan pol.)

Akhmatova, Anna (poet; 1889-1966)

Akiba ben Joseph (Jew. rel.; AD 50?-132)

Akihito, Emperor (emp., Jap.; 1933-)

Akil Akilov (PM, Tajikistan; 1944-)

Akim Tamiroff (ent.; 1899-1972)

Akineton (med.)

Akins, Claude (ent.; 1918-94)

Akio Morito (Jap. bus.; 1921-99)

Akira Kurosawa (Jap. ent.; 1910-98)

Akita (dog)

Akita, Japan

Akkadian (lang./people)

Akranes, Iceland

Akron Beacon Journal (OH newspaper)

Akron Center for Reproductive Health, Ohio v. (US law; 1983)

Akron, OH

AK Steel Corp.

Akureyri, Iceland

Akutagawa Ryunosuke (Jap. writer; 1892-1927)

AL (Alabama, American Legion)

Al (chem. sym., aluminum)

Al Capone (Alphonse, "Scarface")(US gangster; 1899-47)

Al Capp (Alfred Gerald Caplin)(cartoonist, *Li'l Abner*; 1909-79)

Al Cohn (US jazz; 1925-88)

Al Cowlings (US news)

Al(fonse M.) D'Amato (US cong..; 1937-)

Al Dubin (US lyricist; 1891-1945)

Al Fatah (also al-Fatah)(PLO guerrilla group)

Al Freeman, Jr. (ent.; 1934-)

Al(bert Arnold) Gore, Jr. (ex-VP/cong., US; 1948-)

Al Green (ent.; 1946-)

Al Hirschfeld (cartoonist; 1903-)

Al Hirt (ent.; 1922-99)

Al Jarreau (ent.; 1940-)

Al Jizah, Egypt (also Gîza or El Gîza)

Al Jizah, Great Pyramids of (also Gîza or El Gîza)(Eg.)

Al Jolson (b. Asa Yoelson)(ent.; 1886-1950)

Al Joyner

Al(bert) Kaline (baseball; 1934-)

Al Kooper (ent.; 1944-)
Al Lopez (baseball; 1908-)
Al McGuire (ent.; 1931-)
Al Michaels (ent.; 1944-)
Al Molinaro (ent.; 1919-)
Al Oerter (discus thrower; 1936-)
Al(berto) Pacino (ent.; 1940-)
Al Roker (TV host/meteorol.; 1954-)
Al Sharpton (clergyman/pol./activist; 1954-)
Al Shean (b. Albert Schoenberg)(ent.; 1868-1949)
Al Simmons (baseball; 1902-56)
Al Unser (auto racing; 1939-)
Al Yankovic, Weird (ent.; 1959-)
ALA (American Library Association)
Alabama (AL)
Alabama River (AL/GA)
Aladdin (film, 1986, 1992)
Aladdin (myth.)
al-Adha, 'Id (Islamic festival)
al-Ahmad al-Jaber al-Sabah, Sheik Jaber (emir, Kuwait; 1928-)
Alain Delon (ent.; 1935-)
Alain LeRoy Locke (US phil./educ.; 1886-1954)
Alain-René Lesage (Fr. writer; 1668-1747)
Alain Resnais (ent.; 1922-)
Alain Robbe-Grillet (Fr. writer; 1922-)
Alamanni (also Alemanni)(Ger. tribes; 3rd-5th c.)
Alameda Naval Air Station (CA)
Alameda, CA
Alamine (med.)
Alamo (car rental)
Alamo, the (TX)
Alamogordo, NM
Alan Alda (b. Alphonso D'Abruzzo)(ent.; 1936-)
Alan Alexander Milne ("A.A.")(Br. writer; 1882-1956)
Alan Ameche (football; 1933-88)
Alan Arkin (ent.; 1934-)
Alan Autry (ent.; 1952-)
Alan Ayckbourn (playwright; 1939-)
Alan Bates (ent.; 1934-)
Alan B(artlett) Shepard, Jr. (astro.; 1923-98)
Alan Dershowitz (US atty.; 1938-)
Alan Greenspan (US chair/Fed. Reserve Brd.; 1926-)
Alan Hale (ent.; 1892-1950)
Alan Hale, Jr. (ent.; 1919-90)
Alan Hovhaness (US comp.; 1911-2000)
Alan Jackson (ent.; 1958-)
Alan Jay Lerner (US lyricist; 1918-86)
Alan J. Pakula (ent.; 1928-98)
Alan K. Simpson (US pol.; 1931-)
Alan King (b. Irwin Alan Kniberg)(ent.; 1927-)
Alan Ladd (ent.; 1913-64)
Alan L(aVern) Bean (astro.; 1932-)
Alan Menken (US comp.; 1949-)
Alan Parker (ent.; 1944-)
Alan Parsons (ent.; 1949-)
Alan Parsons Project (pop music)
Alan (Stewart) Paton (SAfr. writer; 1903-88)
Alan Rachins (ent.; 1947-)
Alan Thicke (ent.; 1947-)
Alan Young (ent.; 1919-)
Al-Anon (alcoholism support grp.)
Alar (pesticide)

Alarcón, Pedro Antonio de (Sp. writer/pol.; 1833-91)
Alaric (Visigoth king; c370-410)
Alaska (AK)
Alaska Airlines (airline)
Alaska Highway (also Alaskan, Alcan Highway)
Alaska Purchase (also Seward's Folly/folly)(1867)
Alaska Range (AK mountains)
Alaska Standard Time
Alaska, baked
Alaskan king crab
Alaskan malamute (dog)
Alaskan Pipeline, Trans- (oil transport; 1977-)
al-Assad, Dr. Bashar (pres., Syria; 1965-)
al-Assad, Hafez (ex-pres., Syria; 1930-2000)
Alassane D. Ouattara (ex-PM, Ivory Coast; 1942-)
al-Attas, Haidar Abu Bakr (ex-PM, Yemen; 1939-)
Alba, Duke of (also Alva; Fernando Alvarez de Toledo)(Sp. gen./pol.; 1508-82)
Alba, Italy (also Alba Longa)
Alban Berg (Aus. comp.; 1885-1935)
Albanese, Licia (soprano; 1913-)
Albania (Republic of)(SE Eur.)
Albanian (lang./people)
Albans, Council of St. (Br. hist.)
Albany Congress (US hist.; 1754)
Albany Convention (Amer. colonies; 1754)
Albany Marine Corps Logistics Base (GA)
Albany Times-Union (NY newspaper)
Albany, Austria
Albany, CA, GA, NY, OR
Alanis Morissette (ent.; 1974-)
al-Bashir, Gen. Omar Hassan Ahmed (pres., Sudan; 1944-)
Albee, Edward (US writer; 1928-)
Albemarle, Duke of (George Monck)(Br. mil./pol.; 1608-70)
Alben William Barkley (ex-US VP; 1877-1956)
Alberghetti, Anna Maria (It./US ent.; 1936-)
Albers, Josef (US artist; 1888-1976)
Albert A(braham) Michelson (US physt.; 1852-1931)
Albert Bierstadt (US artist; 1830-1902)
Albert Brooks (b. Albert Einstein)(ent.; 1947-)
Albert Bruce Sabin (US phys./biol.; 1906-93)
Albert Camus (Fr. writer; 1913-60)
Albert Claude (Belgium biol.; 1899-1983)
Albert Dekker (ent.; 1905-68)
Albert DeSalvo (the Boston Strangler; 1934-73)
Albert Einstein (Ger./US physt.; 1879-1955)
Albert Finney (ent.; 1936-)
Albert Gallatin (US pol.; 1761-1849)
Albert (Léon) Gleizes (Fr. artist; 1881-1953)
Albert II (king, Belgium; 1934-)
Albert Kahn (US arch.; 1869-1942)
Albert King (US jazz; 1923-92)
Albert Lasker (US bus.; 1880-1952)
Albert Museum, Victoria & (London)
Albert Nipon (clothing)
Albert Payson Terhune (US writer; 1872-1942)
Albert Pickham Ryder (US artist; 1847-1917)
Albert Reynolds (ex-PM, Ir.; 1932-)
Albert Schweitzer, Dr. (Ger. phys./phil./rel.; 1875-1965)
Albert Shanker (US educ.; 1928-97)

Albert (Goodwill) Spalding (baseball; 1850-1915)
Albert Speer (Ger. arch./Nazi pol.; 1905-81)
Albert the Great, St. (also St. Albertus
   Magnus)(Ger. rel.; 1193-1280)
Albert von Tilzer (US comp.; 1878-1956)
Albert Warner (ent.; 1884-1967)
Albert Zafy (ex-pres., Madagascar; 1927?-)
Albert, Eddie (b. Edward Albert Heimberger)
   (ent.; 1908-)
Albert, Edward (ent.; 1951-)
Albert, Fat (cartoon chara.)
Albert, Marv (sportscaster; 1941-)
Albert, Prince (Br., husband of Queen Victoria;
   1819-61)
Albert, Prince (prince, Monaco; 1958-)
Alberta (province, Can.)
Alberta R. Gonzales (US White House counsel;
   1955?-)
Alberto (hair care)
Alberto-Culver Co.
Alberto Dahik (Ecuador. pol.)
Alberto Fujimori (ex-pres., Peru; 1938-)
Alberto Giacometti (It. sculptor; 1901-66)
Alberto Juantoreno (track; 1951-)
Alberto Salazar (track; 1958-)
Alberto Santos-Dumont (Fr. aviator; 1873-1932)
Alberto VO5 (hair care)
Albertson, Jack (ent.; 1907-81)
Albertson's, Inc.
Albertsons (food stores)
Albertus Magnus, St. (also St. Albert the
   Great)(Ger. rel.; 1193-1280)
Albrecht Dürer (Ger. artist; 1471-1528)
Albright, Ivan Le Lorraine (US artist; 1897-1983)
Albright, Madeleine K. (US ex-secy./state; 1937-)
Albright, William Foxwell (US archaeol.; 1891-
   1971)
Albuquerque Journal (NM newspaper)
Albuquerque Living
Albuquerque Tribune (NM newspaper)
Albuquerque, Afonso de (Port. conquerer;
   1453-1515)
Albuquerque, NM
Alcaeus (Gr. poet; c611-c580 BC)
Alcan Aluminum, Ltd.
Alcan Highway (also Alaska Highway, Alaskan)
Alcatraz Island (CA)
Alcatraz Prison ("The Rock")(CA)
Alcatraz, The Birdman of (film, 1962)
Alcestis (myth.)
Alcibiades (Gr. pol.; 450-404 BC)
Alcide De Gasperi (It. pol.; 1881-1954)
Alcindor, Lew(is), Jr. (aka Kareem Abdul-
   Jabbar)(basketball; 1947-)
Alcoa Corp. (Aluminum Co. of America)
Alcoholics Anonymous (also AA)
Alcoholism, National Council on (est. 1944)
Alcott, Amy (golf; 1956-)
Alcott, (Amos) Bronson (US educ./phil.; 1799-
   1888)
Alcott, Louisa May (US writer; 1832-88)
Alcuin (also Flaccus Albinus Alcuinus, Ealhwine
   Flaccus, Alchuine, Albinus)(Br. scholar; 735-804)
Alcyone (also Halcyon or Halcyone)(astron.; myth.)
Alda, Alan (b. Alphonso D'Abruzzo)(ent.; 1936-)

Alda, Robert (ent.; 1914-86)
Aldactazide (med.)
Aldactone (med.)
Aldebaran (also Alpha Tauri)(astron.)
Aldeburgh, Baron Britten of (aka Benjamin
   Britten)(Br. comp.; 1913-76)
Alden, John (American Pilgrim; c1599-1687)
Alder, Kurt (Ger. chem.; 1902-58)
Aldington, Richard (Br. poet; 1892-1962)
Aldo Moro (ex-PM, It.; 1916-78)
Aldo Ray (ent.; 1927-91)
Aldomet (med.)
Aldoril (med.)
Aldous Leonard Huxley (Br. writer; 1894-1963)
Aldrich Ames (US traitor)
Aldrich, Henry (Br. rel./logician; 1647-1710)
Aldrich, Nelson Wilmarth (US finan./pol.; 1841-
   1915)
Aldrich, Thomas Bailey (US writer; 1836-1907)
Aldridge, Ira Frederick (ent.; 1804-67)
Aldrin, Edwin Eugene, Jr. ("Buzz")(astro.; 1930-)
Aldus Corp.
Aldus Freehand (compu.)
Aldus PageMaker (now Adobe
   PageMaker)(compu.)
Alec Andrew Templeton (pianist/comp.; 1910-63)
Alec Baldwin (ent.; 1958-)
Alec (Alexander Frederick) Douglas-Home, Sir
   (ex-PM, Br.; 1903-95)
Alec Guinness, Sir (ent.; 1914-2000)
Alec John Jeffreys (Br. geneticist; 1950-)
Alec (Alexander Raban) Waugh (Br. writer;
   1898-1981)
Alegre, Norberto Costa (ex-PM, Saö Tomé/
   Príncipe)
Aleichem, Shalom (or Sholom)(aka Solomon
   Rabinowitz)(Yiddish writer; 1859-1916)
Aleixandre, Vicente (Sp. poet; 1898-1984)
Alejandro Toledo (pres., Peru; 1946-)
Aleksandr Aleksandrovich Blok (Rus. poet;
   1880-1921)
Aleksandr (Feodorovich) Kerensky (Rus. pol.;
   1881-1970)
Aleksandr Kwasniewski (pres., Pol.; 1954-)
Aleksandr Lukashenko (pres., Belarus; 1954-)
Aleksandr Nikolaevich (Alexander II)(emp.,
   Rus.; 1818-81)
Aleksandr Pavlovich (Alexander I)(emp., Rus.;
   1777-1825)
Aleksandr (Sergeyevich) Pushkin (Rus. writer;
   1799-1837)
Aleksandr Samsonov (Rus. mil.; 1859-1914)
Aleksandr S. Yakovlev (Rus. airplane designer;
   1905-89)
Aleksandras Abisala (Lith. pol.)
Aleksei (Arkhipovich) Leonov (cosmo., 1st to
   walk in space; 1934-)
Aleksei Maksimovich Peshkov (pseud. Maxim
   Gorky [or Gorki])(Rus. writer; 1868-1936)
Aleksei Nikolaevich Kosygin (also Alexei
   Nikolaievich)(ex-PM, USSR; 1904-80)
Aleksei Yeliseyev (cosmo.; 1934-)
Alekseyev, Konstantin Sergeyevich (aka
   Konstantin Stanislavsky [or
   Stanislavski])(Rus. theater; 1863-1938)

A. Leland Stanford (US bus./finan.; 1824-93)
Alemán Lacayo, Arnoldo (pres., Nicaragua; 1946-)
Alemanni (also Alamannic)(Ger. tribes; 3rd-5th c.)
Alençon lace (also point d'Alençon)
Aleppo grass (also Johnson grass, Means grass)
Aleppo, Syria
Alero, Oldsmobile (auto.)
Alesana, Tofilau Eti (ex-PM, WSamoa; 1921-99)
Alessandra Ferri (ballet; 1963-)
Alessandria, Italy
Alessandro Farnese (Pope Paul III)(It.; 1468-1549)
Alessandro (Gaspare) Scarlatti, (Pietro)(It. comp.; 1660-1725)
Alessandro Stradella (It. comp.; 1642-82)
Alessandro Volta, Count (It. physt.; 1745-1827)
Aleut (also Aleutian)(Native Amer.)
Aleut, Eskimo- (Native Amer.)
Aleutian Islands (N Pac.)
Aleve (med)
A level (Br. school, advanced level)
Alex Comfort (Br. phys./writer; 1920-2000)
Alex Cord (ent.; 1931-)
Alex Haley (US writer; 1921-92)
Alex Karras (ent.; 1935-)
Alex Peter Delvecchio (hockey; 1931-)
Alex Raymond (cartoonist, *Flash Gordon, Jungle Jim*; 1909-56)
Alex Trebek (ent.; 1940-)
Alex Webster (football; 1931-)
Alexander & Alexander Services, Inc.
Alexander Archipenko (US sculptor; 1887-1964)
Alexander Borodin (Rus. comp.; 1833-87)
Alexander Brailowsky (pianist; 1896-1976)
Alexander Calder (US sculptor; 1898-1976)
Alexander "Alec" (Frederick) Douglas-Home, Sir (ex-PM, Br.; 1903-95)
Alexander Dubcek (Czech. pol.; 1921-92)
Alexander Fleming, Sir (Br. bacteriol.; 1881-1952)
Alexander Godunov (Rus./US ent.; 1949-95)
Alexander Graham Bell (US inv., telephone; 1847-1922)
Alexander Hamilton (US pol.; 1755-1804)
Alexander I ("the Fierce")(king, Scot.; c1078-1124)
Alexander I (Aleksandr Pavlovich)(emp., Rus.; 1777-1825)
Alexander I (king, Epirus; ?-330 BC)
Alexander I (king, Yug.; 1888-1934)
Alexander I (prince, Bulgaria; 1857-93)
Alexander I Obrenovich (king, Serbia; 1876-1903)
Alexander II (Aleksandr Nikolaevich)(emp., Rus.; 1818-81)
Alexander II (king, Epirus; ?-242 BC)
Alexander II (king, Scot.; 1198-1249)
Alexander III (Aleksandr Aleksandrovich)(emp., Rus.; 1845-94)
Alexander III (Alexander the Great)(king, Macedonia; 356-323 BC)
Alexander III (king, Scot.; 1241-86)
Alexander III (Orlando Bandinelli)(pope; 1159-81)
Alexander (or Aleksandr) Isayevich Solzhenitsyn (Rus. writer; 1918-)
Alexander Kipnis (basso; 1891-1978)
Alexander (or Aleksandr) Konstantinovich

Glazunov (Rus. comp.; 1865-1936)
Alexander M. Haig, Jr. (US gen./pol.; 1924-)
Alexander Mackenzie (ex-PM, Can.; 1822-92)
Alexander Mackenzie, Sir (Scot. expl.; 1764-1820)
Alexander Meiklejohn (US educ.; 1872-1964)
Alexander (Gabriel) Meksi (ex-PM, Albania; 1939-)
Alexander Nikolayevich Scriabin (Rus. comp.; 1872-1915)
Alexander Pope (Br. poet; 1688-1744)
Alexander Procofieff de Seversky (US/Rus. aviator/writer; 1894-1974)
Alexander Rutskoi (Rus. pol.)
Alexander (Nikolayevich) Scriabin (Rus. comp.; 1872-1915)
Alexander Selkirk (Scot. sailor; 1676-1721)
Alexander technique (med.)
Alexander the Great (Alexander III)(king, Macedonia; 356-323 BC)
Alexander Vasilievich Kolchak (Rus. adm.; 1875-1920)
Alexander VI (Rodrigo Borgia)(pope; 1431-1503)
Alexander von Humboldt, (Friedrich Heinrich), Baron (Ger. expl.; 1769-1859)
Alexander von Kluck (Ger. gen.; 1846-1934)
Alexander Woollcott (US writer; 1887-1943)
Alexander, brandy (also l.c.)(cocktail)
Alexander, Grover Cleveland (baseball; 1887-1950)
Alexander, Harold (Br. mil.; 1891-1969)
Alexander, Jane (b. Jane Quigley)(ent.; 1939-)
Alexander, Jason (b. Jay Scott Greenspan) (ent.; 1959-)
Alexandra Danilova (Rus. ballet; 1906-97)
Alexandra Feodorovna (empress, Rus.; 1872-1918)
Alexandra Kollontai (Rus. mil./pol./writer; 1872-1952)
Alexandre Dumas (aka Dumas fils)(Fr. writer; 1824-95)
Alexandre Dumas (aka Dumas père)(Fr. writer; 1802-70)
Alexandre-Edmond Becquerel (Fr. physt.; 1820-91)
Alexandre Millerand (ex-pres., Fr.; 1859-1943)
Alexandria Women's Health Clinic, Bray v. (US law; 1993)
Alexandria, Egypt
Alexandria, LA, VA
Alexandria, Library of (Eg.)
Alexandrine (poetry style)
Alexandrine rat
Alexio, Dennis (kickboxing)
Alexion Pharmaceuticals (US bus.)
Alexis (Charles Henri Maurice Clérel) de Tocqueville (Fr. hist.; 1805-59)
Alexis Carrel (US phys.; 1873-1944)
Alexis Emmanuel Chabrier (Fr. comp.; 1841-94)
Alexis (Margaret) Herman (US ex-secy./labor; 1947-)
Alexis Smith (ent.; 1921-93)
Alexis, Jacques-Edouard (PM, Haiti; 1947-)
Alf (TV show)
Alf(red Mossman) Landon (US pol.; 1887-1987)

al-Fadl, Jamal Ahmed (Sudanese informant on Osama bin Laden; 1964-)
Alfa Romeo (auto.)
Alfa Romeo Spider (auto.)
Alfardaws (Muslim paradise)
al-Fayumi, Saadia ben Joseph (aka Saadia Gaon)(Jew. scholar; 882-942)
Alfie (song)
Alfonso Bustamante (ex-PM, Peru)
Alfonso Portillo Cabrera (pres., Guat.; 1951-)
Alfre Woodard (ent.; 1953-)
Alfred Adler (Aus psych.; 1870-1937)
Alfred A(braham) Knopf (US publ.; 1892-1984)
Alfred A. Knopf, Inc.
Alfred Bester (US writer; 1913-87)
Alfred Binet (Fr. psych.; 1857-1911)
Alfred B(ernhard) Nobel (Swed. chem./eng./finan.; 1833-96)
Alfred C. Fuller (US, bus./brushes; 1885-1973)
Alfred Charles Kinsey (US sociol./biol.; 1894-1956)
Alfred Damon Runyon (US writer; 1880-1946)
Alfred de Musset (Fr. writer; 1810-57)
Alfred Drake (b. Alfred Capurro)(ent.; 1914-92)
Alfred Dreyfus (Fr. capt.; 1859-1935)
Alfred Eisenstaedt (news photo.; 1898-1995)
Alfred E. Neuman (fict. chara., *Mad* magazine)
Alfred E(manuel) Smith (NY gov.; 1873-1944)
Alfred (Joseph) Hitchcock, Sir (Br. writer/ent.; 1899-1980)
Alfred Hitchcock Hour, The (TV show)
Alfred Hitchcock Presents (TV show)
Alfred Hitchcock's Mystery Magazine
Alfred Krupp (Ger. armaments maker; 1812-87)
Alfred Krupp (Ger. armaments maker; 1907-67)
Alfred L(ouis) Kroeber (US anthrop.; 1876-1960)
Alfred L(othar) Wegener (Ger. meteor.; 1880-1930)
Alfred Lord Tennyson (Br. poet; 1809-92)
Alfred Lunt (ent.; 1892-1977)
Alfred M. Worden (astro.; 1932-)
Alfred North Whitehead (Br. phil./math.; 1861-1947)
Alfred Noyes (Br. poet; 1880-1958)
Alfred Pritchard Sloan (US bus.; 1875-1966)
Alfred Rosenberg (Ger. Nazi; 1893-1946)
Alfred Russel Wallace (Br. nat.; 1823-1913)
Alfred Sisley (Fr. artist; 1840?-99)
Alfred Stieglitz (US photo.; 1864-1946)
Alfred Thayer Mahan (US naval hist.; 1840-1914)
Alfred the Great (king, Wessex; c848-c900)
Alfred von Tirpitz (Ger. mil.; 1849-1930)
Alfred Wallenstein (US cond.; 1898-1983)
Alfredo Cristiani (ex-pres., El Salvador; 1947-)
Alfredo Stroessner (ex-pres., Paraguay; 1912-)
Algeciras, Gibraltar
Alger Hiss (US pol.; 1904-96)
Alger, Horatio, Jr. (US writer; 1832-99)
Algeria (Democratic and Popular Republic of)(NAfr.)
Algerian ivy (also Canary Island ivy)(plant)
Algernon (Charles) Swinburne (Br. poet; 1837-1909)
al Ghazali (Islamic phil.; 1058-1111)
Algiers, Algeria
Algiers, Battle of (Algeria/Fr.; 1954-62)

Algirdas Brazauskas (pres., Lith.)
Algol (also Beta Persei)(astron.)
Algonquian (langs.)
Algonquin (Native Amer.)
Algonquin Hotel (NYC)
Algren, Nelson (US writer; 1909-81)
al-Hairi, Rafiq (ex-PM, Lebanon)
Alhaji Shehu Shagari (ex-pres., Nigeria; 1925-)
Alhambra (palace in Spain)
Alhambra, CA
al-Hoss, Salim (PM, Lebanon; 1929-)
Ali Abdullah Saleh (pres., Yemen; 1942-)
Ali Abu al-Ragheb (PM, Jordan; 1946-)
Ali Akbar Hashemi Rafsanjani, Hojatolislam (ex-pres., Iran; 1935-)
Ali Baba (fict. chara.)
Ali Baba and the Forty Thieves (fairy tale)
Ali Benflis (PM, Algeria; 1944-)
Ali Hassan Mwinyi (ex-pres., Tanzania; 1925-)
Ali Jinnah, Muhammad (India/Pak. pol.; 1876-1948)
Ali Kafi (ex-pres., Algeria; 1928-)
Ali Khalif Galaid (PM, Somalia; 1941-)
Ali Khamenei, Ayatollah Sayyed (rel. leader, Iran; 1940-)
Ali MacGraw (ent.; 1938-)
Ali Mahdi, Muhammad (ex-pres., Somalia)
Ali Pasha ("the Lion")(Turk. pol.; 1741-1822)
Ali Pasha, Mehmed Emin (Turk. pol.; 1815-71)
Ali Seybou (ex-pres., Niger; 1940-)
Ali, Hyder (also Haidar Ali)(Indian ruler/mil.; 1722-82)
Ali, Muhammad (also Mehemet Ali)(Eg. pol./mil.; 1769-1849)
Ali, Muhammad (b. Cassius Clay, Jr.)(boxing; 1942-)
Ali, Zine el-Abidine Ben (pres., Tunisia; 1936-)
Alia Ramiz (ex-pres., Albania; 1925-)
Alia Royal Jordanian Airlines (airline)
Alice Adams (US writer; 1926-99)
Alice B. Toklas (US writer; 1877-1967)
Alice B. Toklas!, I Love You, (film, 1968)
Alice Cooper (b. Vincent Furnier)(ent.; 1948-)
Alice Doesn't Live Here Anymore (film, 1974)
Alice Dunbar-Nelson (US writer; 1875-1935)
Alice Faye (ent.; 1912-98)
Alice Ghostley (ent.; 1926-)
Alice Hamilton (US phys./reformer; 1869-1970)
Alice in Wonderland (Lewis Carroll book)
Alice Marble (tennis; 1913-90)
Alice Munro (Can. writer; 1931-)
Alice Paul (US women's-rights activist; 1885-1977)
Alice Roosevelt Longworth (US social figure; 1884-1980)
Alice Through the Looking Glass (L. Carroll book)
Alice Town, the Bahamas
Alice Walker (US writer; 1944-)
Alice, Bob & Carol & Ted & (film, 1969)
Alice, Poker (film, 1987)
Alice's Restaurant (film, 1969)
Alicia Alonso (ballet; 1921?-)
Alicia Silverstone (ent.; 1976-)
Alien (film, 1979)
Alien and Sedition Acts (US hist.; 1798)
Aliens (film, 1986)

Alighieri, Dante (It. poet, *Divine Comedy*;
   1265-1321)
Alija Izetbegovic, Dr. (co-pres., Bosnia-
   Hercegovina, Muslim; 1925)
A-line (clothing)
al-Iryani, Abdul-Karim (PM, Yemen; 1934-)
Alison Lurie (US writer; 1926-)
Alistair Cooke (Br./US jour.; 1908-)
Alitalia (airline)
Aliyev, Heydar A. (pres., Azerbaijan; 1923-)
al-Jaber al-Sabah, Sheik Jaber al-Ahmad (emir,
   Kuwait; 1928-)
al-Jazair, Algeria
al-Jubayl, Saudi Arabia
Alka-Seltzer (med.)
Alkeran (med.)
al-Khalifa, Sheik Isa bin Sulman (ex-emir,
   Bahrain; 1933-)
al-Khalifa, Sheik Khalifa bin Sulman (PM,
   Bahrain; 1935-)
al-Khalifa, Shiek Hamad bin Isa (emir, Bahrain;
   1950-)
All About Eve (film, 1950)
All Creatures Great and Small (book, TV show)
All Fools' Day (also April Fools' Day)(April 1)
All in the Family (TV show)
All My Children (TV soap)
All Nippon Airways (ANA)(airline)
All Saints' Day (also Hallowmas, All-Hallows)(rel.)
All Souls' Day (rel.)
al-Ladhiqiyah, Syria
Allah (Islam God)
Allah akbar (rel.)
Allahabad, India
all-American
Allan Carr (ent.; 1939-99)
Allan Dean Feuerbach (track; 1948-)
Allan Nevins (US hist./educ.; 1890-1971)
Allan Pinkerton (US detective; 1819-84)
Allante, Cadillac (auto.)
Allard, Wayne (US cong.; 1943-)
All-Bran (cereal)
Allegany, NY
Allegheny Mountains (PA)(also Alleghenies)
Allegheny National Forest (PA)
Allegheny River (PA)
Allegheny Technologies, Inc.
Allegheny, PA
Allegra (med.)
Allegra Kent (ent.; 1937-)
Allen Funt (ent.; 1914-99)
Allen Ginsberg (US poet; 1926-97)
Allen Ludden (ent.; 1918-81)
Allen radiation belts, Van (regions surrounding
   earth)
Allen screw (constr.)
Allen Tate, (John Orley)(US poet/critic/editor;
   1899-1979)
Allen wrench (constr.)
Allen, Debbie (ent.; 1950-)
Allen, Dick (Richard Anthony)(baseball; 1942-)
Allen, Ethan (US Revolutionary War hero;
   1738-89)
Allen, Fred (b. John Florence Sullivan)(ent.;
   1894-1956)

Allen, George (football; 1918-90)
Allen, George F. (US cong./ex-VA gov.; 1952-)
Allen, Gracie (ent.; 1906-64)
Allen, Inc., Ethan
Allen, Joan (ent.; 1956-)
Allen, Karen (ent.; 1951-)
Allen, Marcus (football; 1960-)
Allen, Mel (b. Melvin Israel)(US sportscaster;
   1913-96)
Allen, Nancy (ent.; 1949-)
Allen, Peter (ent./songwriter; 1944-92)
Allen, Steve (ent.; 1921-2000)
Allen, Tim (b. Timothy Allen Dick)(ent.; 1953-)
Allen, Woody (b. Allen Stewart Konigsberg)
   (ent.; 1935-)
Allenby, Edmund (Br. mil.; 1861-1936)
Allende, Isabel (writer; 1942-)
Allentown Morning Call (PA newspaper)
Allentown, PA
Allerest (med.)
Allergan (eye care)
Allergan Lens Plus (eye care)
Allergan, Inc.
Alley, Gasoline (comic strip)
Alley, Kirstie (ent.; 1951-)
Allhallowmas (also Allhallows, All Saints's Day)
All-Hallows (also Hallowmas, All Saints' Day)(rel.)
Allhallowtide
Allianz Group (US/Eur. bus.)
Allied-Signal, Inc.
Allied Van Lines (US bus.)
Allies, the (of WW I, WW II, NATO)
Alliluyeva, Svetlana (Iosifovna)(daughter of J.
   Stalin; 1927-)
Allison Smith (ent.; 1969-)
Allison, Bobby (Robert Arthur)(auto racing; 1937-)
Allison, Fran (ent.; 1908-89)
All-Knowing (God)
Allman Brothers, the (pop music)
Allman, Duane (ent.; 1946-71)
Allman, Gregg (ent.; 1947-)
All-Pro (sports)
Allsburg, Chris Van (US writer/artist; 1949-)
All-Star Game (baseball)
Allstate Corp.
Allston, Washington (US artist; 1779-1843)
All's Well That Ends Well (Shakespeare comedy)
Alltel Corp.
Ally McBeal (TV show)
Ally Sheedy (ent.; 1962-)
Allyce Beasley (ent.; 1954-)
Allyson, June (b. Ella Geisman)(ent.; 1917-)
ALM Antillean Airlines (airline)
Alma-Ata, Kazakhstan
Almaden (wine)
Almagest (by Ptolemy, 2nd c.)
al Majali, Abd al-Salam (or Abdul-Salam)(ex-
   PM, Jordan; 1925-)
al-Maktoum, Sheik Maktoum bin Rashid (PM,
   UAE; 1946-)
Almay (cosmetics)
Almay, Inc.
Almighty, the (God)
Almond Joy (candy)
Almond, Lincoln C. (RI gov.; 1936-)

al-Nahayan, Sheik Zaid bin Sultan (pres., UAE; 1923-)

al-Nimeiry, Gaafar Muhammad (ex-pres., Sudan; 1930-)

Aloha Airlines (airline)

Aloha Bowl (college football)

Aloha State (nickname, HI)

Alomar, Roberto (baseball; 1968-)

Alonso, Alicia (ballet; 1921?-)

Alonso, Maria Conchita (ent.; 1956-)

Alpert and The Tijuana Brass, Herb (pop music)

Alpert, Herb (ent.; 1935-)

Alpes, Rhône- (region, Fr.)

Alpha Aquilae (also Altair)(astron.)

Alpha Aurigae (also Capella)(astron.)

Alpha Beta Co. (Alpha Beta stores)

Alpha-Bits (cereal)

Alpha Bootis (also Arcturus)(astron.)

Alpha Canis Minoris (also Procyon)(astron.)

Alpha Carinae (also Canopus)(astron.)

Alpha Centauri (also Rigel Kentaurus)(astron.)

Alpha Keri (med.)

Alpha Orionis (also Betelgeuse)(astron.)

Alpha Oumar Konare, (pres., Mali; 1946-)

Alpha Scorpii (also Antares)(astron.)

Alpha Tauri (also Aldebaran)(astron.)

Alphonse Bertillon (Fr. anthrop./criminol.; 1853-1914)

Alphonse de Lamartine (Fr. writer; 1790-1869)

Alphonse, King (mixed drink)

Alpine (cigarette)

Alpine (people)

Alpine skiing (sports)(also l.c.)

Alpo Petfoods, Inc.

Alps, Lunar (mountains, the moon)

Alps, the (mountains, It./Fr./Ger./Aus.)

al-Qaddafi (or Khadafy) Muammar, Colonel (pres., Libya; 1942-)

Al-Qaida (aka al Qaeda)(network of radical groups under Osama bin Laden)

al-Ragheb, Ali Abu (PM, Jordan; 1946-)

A(lfred) L(eslie) Rowse (Br. hist.; 1903-97)

al-Sabah, Sheik Jaber al-Ahmad al-Jaber (emir, Kuwait; 1928-)

al-Sabah, Sheik Saad al-Abdullah al-Salim (PM, Kuwait; 1930-)

Alsace (Fr. wine region)

Alsace-Lorraine (region, Fr.)

Alsatian (dog)

Alsatian (people)

Alsatian German (lang.)

al-Shamikh, Mubarak Abdullah (PM, Libya)

Al-Solh, Rashid (ex-PM, Lebanon)

Alsop, Joseph W., Jr. (jour.; 1910-89)

Alsop, Stewart (jour.; 1914-74)

Alston, Walter (baseball; 1911-84)

Alstyne, Egbert van (US comp.; 1882-1951)

Alt, Carol (model; 1960-)

Altadena, CA

Altair (also Alpha Aquilae)(astron.)

Altamaha-Ocmulgee River (GA)

Altamira, Caves of (also Altamira caves)(Sp. paleolithic paintings)

Altamont (CA racetrack)

Altamont, CA

Altamonte Springs, FL

Alta Vista (Internet search engine)

Altec (speaker)

ALternaGEL (med.)

Alternative Nation (TV show)

al-Thani, Abdullah bin Khalifa (PM, Qatar)

al-Thani, Sheik Hamad bin Khalifa (emir, Qatar; 1950-)

al-Thani, Sheik Khalifa bin Hamad (ex-emir, Qatar; 1932-)

Althea Gibson (tennis; 1927-)

Althing (Iceland parliament)

Altima, Nissan (auto.)

Altman & Co., B.

Altman, Robert (ent.; 1925-)

Altman, Robert (US atty./banker; 1947-)

Altoids (mints)

Alton, IL

Altoona, PA

Altus Air Force Base, OK (mil.)

Aluminum Co. of America (Alcoa Corp.)

Alundum (abrasive prods.)

Alupent (med.)

Alurate (med.)

Alva, Duke of (also Alba, Fernando Alvarez de Toledo)(Sp. gen./pol.; 1508-82)

Alvar Aalto (Fin. arch.; 1898-1976)

Alvarez, Luis Walter (US physt.; 1911-88)

Alvin & the Chipmunks (cartoon)

Alvin Ailey (choreographer; 1931-89)

Alvin Dark (baseball; 1922-)

Alvin F. Poussaint (ent.; 1934-)

Alvin Toffler (US sociol./writer; 1928-)

Always (health)

Alworth, Lance (football; 1940-)

Alysheba (racehorse)

Alyssa Milano (ent.; 1972-)

Alzheimer's disease (med.)

AMA (American Medical Association)

Amadeo Avogadro (It. chem.; 1776-1856)

Amadeo P. Giannini (US, founded Bank of America; 1870-1949)

Amadeus (film, 1984)

Amadeus Quartet

Amadou Cheiffou (ex-PM, Niger)

Amadou Toumani Toure (ex-pres., Mali)

Amadou, Hama (PM, Niger; 1950-)

Amalekite (people)

Amalthea (Jupiter moon; myth.)

Amana (appliances)

Amana Church Society

Amana Refrigeration, Inc.

Amanda Blake (b. Beverly Louise Neill)(ent.; 1929-89)

Amanda Peet (ent.; 1972-)

Amanda Plummer (ent.; 1957-)

Amandine Aurore Lucie Dudevant (b. Dupin) (pseud. George Sand)(Fr. writer; 1804-76)

Amangeldy Muraliev (PM, Kyrgyzstan; 1947-)

Amanita (fungus, usually poisonous)

Amanpour, Christiane (broadcast jour.; 1958-)

Amarcord (film, 1974)

Amarillo Globe-Times (TX newspaper)

Amarillo News-Globe (TX newspaper)

Amarillo, TX

Amata Kabua (pres., Marshall Islands)
Amateur Athletic Union of the United States
  (AAU)
Amati, Andrea (It. violin maker; c1510-?)
Amati, Antonio (It. violin maker; 1555-1638)
Amati, Geronimo (It. violin maker, father of
  Nicolo; 1556-1630)
Amati, Geronimo (It. violin maker, son of
  Nicolo; 1649-1740)
Amati, Nicolo (It. violin maker; 1596-1684)
Amato, Guiliano (PM, It.; 1938-)
Amazing Spider-Man, The (cartoon chara.)
Amazing Stories
Amazon (myth., female warriors)
Amazon River (SAmer.)
Amazon.com (also amazon.com)(US bus.)
Amazonian Highway, Trans- (also
  Transamazonica)(Brazil; 1970-)
Ambersons, The Magnificent (B. Tarkington
  novel)
Ambler, Eric (Br. writer; 1909-98)
Amboise, France
Ambroise, Thomas (Fr. comp.; 1811-96)
Ambrose Everett Burnside (US gen.; 1824-81)
Ambrose Gwinnett Bierce (US writer; 1842-1914)
Ambrose, St. (bishop of Milan; c340-397)
Ambrosian Library (It.)
AMC (American Movie Classics)(TV channel)
AMC Gremlin (auto.)
Ameche, Alan (football; 1933-88)
Ameche, Don (b. Dominic Amici)(ent.; 1908-93)
Amedeo Modigliani (It. artist; 1884-1920)
Amelia Bloomer (US reformer; 1818-94)
Amelia Earhart (US aviator; 1897-1937?)
Amelia Island (FL)
Amen (or Amon), Temple of (Karnak, Eg.; built
  13th-20th c. BC)
Amenhotep (also Amenophis)(four Eg.
  pharaohs)
Amenhotep I (Eg. pharaoh; fl. 1570 BC)
Amenhotep III (Eg. pharaoh; c1400 BC)
Amenhotep IV (also Ikhnaton,
  Akhenaton)(king/pharaoh, Eg.; 14th c. BC)
Amen-Ra (also Amon-Ra)(Eg. myth.)
Amenti (myth., region of the dead)
Amerada Hess Corp.
Amerasian (also Amer-Asian)
America
America, Coming to (film, 1988)
America Online, Inc. (AOL)
America West Airlines
America, Captain (cartoon chara.)
America, Inc., Audi of
America, Latin (S & central Amer.)
America, North
America, South
America, Voice of (US broadcasting service)
America's Cup (yacht racing)
America's Funniest Home Videos (TV show)
America's Most Wanted (TV show)
Americaine (med.)
American (people)
American Airlines, Inc.
American Artist (mag.)
American Association of University Women

(AAUW)
American Ballet Theater
American Bandstand (pop music)
American Banking Association number (ABA
  number)
American Bar Association (ABA)
American Bar Association Journal
American Beauty rose
American beech (tree)
American Book Review
American Brands, Inc.
American Broadcasting Company (ABC)(TV
  channel)
American Broadcasting Cos., Inc. (Capital
  Cities-ABC, Inc.)(ABC)
American Cage Bird (mag.)
American Cancer Society
American Century Services Corporation
American cheese
American Civil Liberties Union (ACLU)
American Civil War (also War of Secession, War
  Between the States)(1861-65)
American Comedy Awards, The
American Cyanamid Co.
American Demographics
American Dream/dream
American eagle
American elm (tree)
American English (also General American)
American Express card
American Express Centurion Bank
American Express Company
American Express Financial Advisors Inc.
American Express Travelers Cheques
American Federation of Labor and Congress of
  Industrial Organizations (AFL-CIO)
American Federation of Television and Radio
  Artists (AFTRA)
American Football Conference (AFC)
American foxhound (dog)
American Graffiti (film, 1973)
American Greetings Corp.
American Health (mag.)
American Heart Association (AHA)
American Heritage (mag.)
American Heritage Dictionary, The
American Heroes & Legends (cartoon)
American Home Products Corporation
American Homestyle (mag.)
American Honda Motor Co., Inc.
American Hunter (mag.)
American Indian (also Native American)(peoples)
American Indian Day
American Indian Movement (AIM)
American Institute of Architects (AIA)
American International Group, Inc.
American Isuzu Motors, Inc.
American Journal (TV show)
American League of Professional Baseball Clubs
American Legion (mag.)
American Legion (war veterans org.)
American Legion Auxiliary (mag.)
American Library Association (ALA)
American lion
American Medical Association (AMA)

American Movie Classics (AMC)(TV channel)
American Museum of Natural History (NYC)
American National Red Cross (US relief agcy.;
   est. 1881)
American Oil Co. (Amoco Oil Co.)
American Opinion Bookstore
American Party of the U.S. (US pol.)
American Photo (mag.)
American pit bull terrier (also American
   Staffordshire terrier)(dog)
American Poetry Review (mag.)
American quarter horse
American Revolution (also Revolutionary War;
   1776-83)
American Rifleman (mag.)
American saddle horse
American Samoa
American serviceberry (also Juneberry)(shrub)
American Sign Lang. (also Ameslan)
American Staffordshire terrier (also American
   pit bull terrier)(dog)
American Standard Code for Information
   Interchange (ASCII)(compu.)
American Standard Companies, Inc.
American Standard Version (of the Bible)
American Standards Association (ASA)(photo.)
American States, Organization of (OAS)(N/
   central/S Amer.; est.; 1948)
American-Statesman, Austin (TX newspaper)
American Stock Exchange (AMEX, Amex)
American Stores Co.
American Suzuki Motor Corporation
American Telephone & Telegraph Co. (AT&T)
American Tobacco Co., The
American Tobacco Co., U.S. v. (US law; 1911)
American Tourister (US bus.)
American trotter (also Standardbred)(horse)
American University (Washington, DC)
American War, Spanish-
American water spaniel (dog)
American West (west of Mississippi River)
American wirehair (cat)
American Woodworker (mag.)
American, Hispanic (also Hispano)(people)
Americana
Americanism
Americans With Disabilities Act (US hist.; 1990)
Americans, Jay and the (pop music)
Americo-Liberians (people)
Americus Vespucius (also Amerigo Vespucci)(It.
   nav./expl.; 1451?-1512)
Amerind (also Amerindian)(Native Amer.,
   dialects/langs.)
Amerindian (lang.)
Ameritech (utilities co.)
Ameritrade, Inc.
Ames Brothers, the (pop music)
Ames Department Stores, Inc.
Ames test (biochemistry)
Ames, Aldrich (US traitor)
Ames, Champion v. (also Lottery Case)(US law;
   1903)
Ames, Ed (b. Edmond Dantes Urick)(ent.; 1927-)
Ames, Leon (ent.; 1903-93)
Ameslan (also American Sign Language)

AMEX (or Amex)(American Stock Exchange)
AM General (auto.)
AM General Hummer (auto.)
AM General Hummer H1 pickup (auto.)
AM General Hummer H1 wagon (auto.)
AM General Hummer H2 (auto.)
Amhara (people)
Amharic (lang./people)
Amherst College (Amherst, MA)
Amherst, Jeffrey, Baron (Br. gen.; 1717-97)
Amherst, MA, OH
Amherst, Nova Scotia, Canada
Amiens, France
Amiens, Treaty of (Br. & Fr./Sp./Batavia; 1802)
AmigaWorld
Amigo, Isuzu (auto.)
Amilcare Ponchielli (It. comp.; 1834-86)
Amin (Dada Oumee), Idi (ex-pres., Uganda;
   1925-)
Amin Gemayel (ex-pres., Lebanon; 1942-)
Amin Tarif, Sheik (Islamic rel.; 1898-1993)
Amis, Kingsley (writer; 1922-95)
Amis, Martin (writer; 1949-)
Amish (Mennonites, Dunkers, Plain People)(rel.)
Amityville Horror, The (book; film, 1979)
Amityville, NY
Amman, Jordan (also Rabbath Ammon)
Ammens (health)
Ammianus (Roman hist.; c330-395 BC)
Ammon (also Amon)(king, Judah; 6th c BC)
Ammonite (people)
Amnesty International (human rights org.)
Amoco Oil Co. (American Oil Co.)
Amon (or Amen), Temple of (Karnak, Eg.; built
   13th-20th c. BC)
Amon (or Ammon)(king, Judah; 6th c BC)
Amon-Ra (also Amen-Ra)(Eg. myth.)
Amorite (lang./people)
Amory, Cleveland (US writer/conservationist;
   1917-98)
Amos (rel., book of the Old Testament)
Amos Alonzo Stagg (football; 1862-1965)
Amos (Freeman F. Gosden)(radio comedian,
   The Amos 'n' Andy Show; 1899-1982)
Amos Bronson Alcott (US educ./phil.; 1799-1888)
Amos Chocolate Chip Cookie, The Famous (US
   bus.)
Amos Sawyer (ex-pres., Liberia; 1945-)
Amos, John (ent.; 1941-)
Amos, Tori (Myra Ellen) (ent.; 1963-)
Amoskaeg (textiles)
Amoxil (med.)
Ampère, André Marie (Fr. physt.; 1775-1836)
Ampère's law (or rule)(elect.)
Amphitrite (myth.)
Amphojel (med.)
AMR Corp.
Amschel Mayer Rothschild (Ger. finan.; 1773-
   1855)
Amsterdam, Morey (ent.; 1908-96)
Amsterdam, NY
Amsterdam, the Netherlands (or Holland)
Amtrak
Amu Darya (Oxus River)(cental Asia)
Amur grape (plant)

Amur River (E. Asia)
AMVETS (American Veterans of WWII, Korea, Vietnam)
Amway Corp.
Amy Alcott (golf; 1956-)
Amy Brenneman (ent.; 1964-)
Amy Carter (ex-US pres.'s daughter; 1967-)
Amy Fisher ("Long Island Lolita")(US news; 1974-)
Amy Grant (ent.; 1960-)
Amy Irving (ent.; 1953-)
Amy Johnson, (Br. aviator; 1903-41)
Amy Lowell (US poet; 1874-1925)
Amy Madigan (ent.; 1950-)
Amy Tan (US writer; 1952-)
Amy Vanderbilt (US writer/manners; 1908-74)
Amy Vanderbilt's Complete Book of Etiquette
Amytal (med.)
An Wang (Ch./US inv./bus.; 1920-90)
An-Shih, Wang (Ch. pol.; 1021-86)
ANA (All Nippon Airways)
ANA (American Nurses Association)
Anabaptist (rel.)
Anacin (med.)
Anacreon (Gr. poet; c582-c485 BC)
Anadir (or Anadyr) Mountains (Siberia)
Anadir (or Anadyr) River (Siberia)
Anafranil (med.)
Anaheim, CA (Disneyland)
Anais Anais (cosmetics)
Anais Nin (US writer; 1903-77)
Analects (rel.)
Anand Panyarachun (ex-PM, Thailand; 1933-)
Anaprox (med.)
Anapurna (also Annapurna, Devi, Parvati)(myth.)
Anaspaz (med.)
Anastas Mikoyan (USSR pol.; 1895-1978)
Anastasia (film, 1956)
Anastasia (Nikolaievna Romanov)(Rus. Grand Duchess; 1901-18)
Anastasio Somoza (Debayle)(ex-pres., Nicaragua; 1925-80)
Anastasio Somoza (Garcia)(ex-pres., Nicaragua; 1896-1956)
Anatole, France (Fr. writer; 1844-1924)
Anatolia (part of Turk.)
Anatolijs Gorbunov (ex-pres., Latvia)
Anatoly (Federovich) Dobrynin (Rus. dipl.; 1919-)
Anatoly Berezovoy (cosmo.)
Anatoly Filipchenko (cosmo.; 1928-)
Anatoly Karpov (Rus., chess; 1951-)
Anatuss (med.)
Anaxagoras (Gr. phil.; c500-428 BC)
Anaximander (Gr. phil./astron.; 611-546 BC)
Anbesol (med.)
Anchorage Daily News (AK newspaper)
Anchorage News (AK newspaper)
Anchorage, AK
Ancient Mystic Order Rosae Crucis (AMORC) (order of Rosicrucian)(phil./rel.)
Ancren Riwle (monastic life rules; 13th c)
Andalusia (also Andalucia)(region, Sp.)
Andalusia, AL
Andalusian (horse)
Andalusian (people)
Andalusian, Blue (chicken)

Andaman Islands (India, Bay of Bengal)
Andaman Sea (part of Bay of Bengal)
Andamanese (also Andaman)(people)
Anders Celsius (Swed. astron.; 1701-44)
Anders (Leonhard) Zorn (Swed. artist; 1860-1920)
Anders, Jonas Angström (Swed. astrophyst.; 1814-74)
Anders, William A. (astro.; 1933-)
Andersen (windows/doors)
Andersen Windows, Inc.
Andersen, Hans Christian (Dan. writer; 1805-75)
Anderson, Brad (cartoonist, *Marmaduke*; 1924-)
Anderson, (Gary) Donny (football; 1949-)
Anderson, Dame Judith (ent.; 1898-1992)
Anderson, Eddie "Rochester" (ent.; 1905-77)
Anderson, Gillian (ent.; 1968-)
Anderson, Harry (ent.; 1952-)
Anderson, Ian (ent., Jethro Tull; 1947-)
Anderson, Ib (ballet; 1954-)
Anderson, IN, SC
Anderson, Jack (US jour.; 1922-)
Anderson, Ken (football; 1949-)
Anderson, Leroy (US comp.; 1908-75)
Anderson, Lindsay (Gordon)(ent.; 1923-94)
Anderson, Loni (ent.; 1946-)
Anderson, Lynn (ent.; 1947-)
Anderson, Marian (ent.; 1902-93)
Anderson, Maxwell (US writer; 1888-1959)
Anderson, Melissa Sue (ent.; 1962-)
Anderson, Pamela (model/ent.; 1967-)
Anderson, Richard (ent.; 1926-)
Anderson, Richard Dean (ent.; 1950-)
Anderson, Robert (playwright; 1917-)
Anderson, Sherwood (US writer; 1876-1941)
Anderson, Sparky (George)(baseball; 1934-)
Anderson, Terry (jour./former hostage; 1947-)
Andersonville National Cemetery (GA)
Andersonville Prison (GA)
Andersson, Bibi (Swed. ent.; 1935-)
Andes Mountains (SAmer.)
Andes, Christ of the (peace monument between Chile/Argentina)
Andie MacDowell (b. Rosalie Anderson MacDowell) (ent.; 1958-)
Ando Hiroshige ("Tokube")(Jap. artist; 1797-1858)
Andorra (Principality of)(Eur.)
Andorra la Vella, Andorra
Andorran (people)
Andranik Markarian (or Margaryan)(PM, Armenia; 1951-)
Andre Agassi (tennis; 1970-)
Andre Braugher (ent.; 1962-)
André Breton (Fr. poet; 1896-1966)
Andre Cold Duck (champagne)
André Courréges (Fr. designer; 1923-)
Andre Dawson (baseball; 1954-)
André Eglevsky (US/Rus. ballet; 1917-77)
André Gide (Fr. writer; 1869-1951)
André Kolingba (gen./ex-pres., Central African Republic; 1936-)
Andre Kostelanetz (ent.; 1901-80)
André Malraux (Fr. writer; 1901-76)
André Marie Ampère (Fr. physt.; 1775-1836)
André Maurois (aka Emile Herzog)(Fr. writer;

1885-1967)
André Milongo (ex-PM, Congo)
André (George) Previn (US cond./comp.; 1929-)
Andre the Giant ((b. Andre Rousimoff)
   wrestling; 1946-93)
Andre Watts (pianist; 1946-)
André, Carl (US sculptor; 1935-)
André, John, Major (Br. spy; 1751-80)
Andrea Amati (It. violin maker; c1510-?)
Andrea Bocelli (ent., opera; 1958-)
Andrea del Castagno (It. artist; c1421-57)
Andrea del Sarto (It. artist; 1486-1530)
Andrea del Verrocchio (b. Andrea di Michele di
   Francesco di Cioni)(It. artist; 1435-88)
Andrea della Robbia (It. sculptor; 1437-1528)
Andrea Doria (It. adm./pol.; 1466-1560)
Andrea Doria, S.S. (steamship; sank 1956)
Andrea Mantegna (It. artist; 1431-1506)
Andrea McArdle (ent.; 1963-)
Andrea Palladio (It. arch.; 1508-80)
Andrea Pisano (b. Andrea da Pontadera)(It.
   sculptor; c1290-c1349)
Andrea Sansovino (It. sculptor; 1460-1529)
Andreas (Bernhard Lyonel) Feininger (US
   photo.; 1906-99)
Andreas (George) Papandreou (ex-PM, Gr.;
   1919-96)
Andreas Vesalius (Flem. anatomist; 1515-64)
Andrei A. Gromyko (ex-pres., Rus.; 1909-89)
Andrei Chesnokov (tennis; 1966-)
Andrei Dmitrievich Sakharov (Rus. physt.;
   1921-89)
Andrei Sangheli (ex-PM, Moldova)
Andrej Bajuk (PM, Slovenia; 1943-)
Andrés Pastrana (Arango)(pres., Colombia; 1954-)
Andrés Rodríguez (ex-pres., Paraguay; 1923-)
Andres Segovia (ent.; 1893-1987)
Andress, Ursula (Swiss ent.; 1936-)
Andretti, Mario (Gabriel)(auto racing; 1940-)
Andrew Aguecheek, Sir (fict. chara., *Twelfth
   Night*)
Andrew Bonar Law (Br. pol.; 1858-1923)
Andrew "Andy" (Hill) Card, Jr. (US White House
   chief of staff; 1947-)
Andrew Carnegie (US bus./finan.; 1835-1919)
Andrew Dice Clay (b. Andrew Clay Silverstein)
   (ent.; 1957-)
Andrew Grove (b. Andras Grof)(bus.,
   computers; 1936-)
Andrew Jackson ("Old Hickory")(7th US pres.;
   1767-1845)
Andrew Jackson Young, Jr. (US dipl./pol.; 1932-)
Andrew Jerkins Co., The
Andrew Johnson (17th US pres.; 1808-75)
Andrew Lloyd Webber (Br. comp.; 1948-)
Andrew Marvell (Br. poet/satirist; 1621-78)
Andrew McCarthy (ent.; 1962-)
Andrew M(ark) Cuomo (US ex-secy./HUD; 1957-)
Andrew N(ewell) Wyeth (US artist; 1917-)
Andrew Shue (ent.; 1967-)
Andrew Stevens (ent.; 1955-)
Andrew Volstead (US pol.; 1860-1947)
Andrew Weil (US phys./writer, alternative med.)
Andrew William Mellon (US finan./bus.; 1855-
   1937)

Andrew Young (US pol./reformer; 1932-)
Andrew, Hurricane (FL/LA; 1992)
Andrew, Merry (slang, adv. chara.)
Andrew, Prince (Andrew Albert Christian Edward)
   (2nd son of Queen Elizabeth II; 1960-)
Andrew, St. (patron saint of Scot.)
Andrew's Cross/cross, St. (X-shaped cross)
Andrews Air Force Base, DC (mil.)
Andrews Sisters (Patty, Maxene, Laverne)(music)
Andrews, Archie (cartoon chara.)
Andrews, Dana (ent.; 1909-92)
Andrews, Joseph (Henry Fielding novel)
Andrews, Julie (b. Julia Wells)(ent.; 1935-)
Andrews, Laverne (ent.; Andrew Sisters; 1911-67)
Andrews, Maxene (ent., Andrews Sisters;
   1916-95)
Andrews, Patty (ent., Andrews Sisters; 1918-)
Andrews, V(irginia) C. (US writer)
Andrian G(rigorievich) Nikolayev (cosmo.; 1929-)
Andrianarivo, Tantely (PM, Madagascar; 1954-)
Andries Pretorius (SAfr. colonizer/mil.; 1799-
   1853)
Andrija Mohorovicic (Yug. physt.; 1857-1936)
Andris Berzins (PM, Latvia; 1951-)
Andrius Kubilius (premier, Lith.; 1956-)
Androcles (also Androclus)(myth., Roman
   slave, befriended lion)
Androcles (Gr. orator; 5th c. BC)
Androcles and the Lion (by G. B. Shaw)
Andromache (Euripides play)
Andromache (myth.)
Andromeda (astron., chained lady; myth.)
Andromeda Strain (M. Crichton novel)
Andronicus, Titus (Shakespeare play)
Andropov, Yuri (ex-pres., Rus.; 1914-84)
Andros Town, the Bahamas
Andrus, Cecil D. (ex-ID gov.; 1931-)
Andy (Charles J. Correll)(radio comedian, *The
   Amos 'n' Andy Show*; 1890-1972)
Andy Capp (comic strip)
Andy (Andrew Hill) Card, Jr. (US White House
   chief of staff; 1947-)
Andy Devine (ent.; 1905-77)
Andy Garcia (ent.; 1956-)
Andy Gibb (ent.; 1958-88)
Andy Griffith (ent.; 1926-)
Andy Griffith Show, The (TV show)
Andy Hardy (fict. chara.)
Andy Kaufman (ent.; 1949-84)
Andy Razaf (US lyricist; 1895-1973)
Andy (Andrew Aitken) Rooney (US TV jour.;
   1919-)
Andy Warhol (b. Andrew Warhola)(US artist;
   1927-87)
Andy Williams (ent.; 1930-)
Andy, Raggedy Ann & (fict. dolls)
Anegada (Br. Virgin Island)
Anerood Jugnauth (PM, Mauritius; 1930-)
Aneurin Bevan (Br. pol.; 1897-1960)
Anfernee "Penny" Hardaway (basketball; 1972-)
Anfinn Kallsberg (PM, Faeroe Islands)
Ang Lee (ent.; 1954-)
Angana, Guam
Angas (lang.)
Ange Patasse (pres., Central African Republic)

Ange-Félix Patassé (pres., Central African
    Republic; 1937-)
Angel Cordero (jockey; 1942-)
Angel Corella (ballet; 1975-)
Angel Falls (Venezuela)(world's highest waterfall)
Angel One (TV channel)
Angel Serafin Seriche Dougan (PM, Equatorial
    Guinea; 1946-)
Angel Soft (paper prods.)
Angel Street (play)
Angela Bassett (ent.; 1958-)
Angela (Yvonne) Davis (US activist/Communist;
    1944-)
Angela Lansbury (ent.; 1925-)
Angeleno (also Los Angeleno)(native of Los
    Angeles)
Angeles, Port (WA)
Angelico, Fra (It. artist; 1400-55)
Angelina Jolie (Voight)(ent.; 1975-)
Angelo Secchi (It. astron.; 1818-78)
Angelo Siciliano (aka Charles Atlas)(US body
    builder; 1894-1972)
Angelou, Maya (b. Marguerite Johnson)(US
    writer; 1928-)
Angels, California (baseball team)
Angelus (prayer, bell)(also l.c.)
Angie Dickinson (b. Angeline Brown)(ent.; 1931-)
Angie Harmon (ent./model; 1972-)
Angkor Wat (also Vat)
Angkor, Cambodia
Anglais, creme (sauce)
Angle (Ger. tribes invaded Br., 5th c.)
Anglican Church (also Church of England)
Anglican Orthodox Church
Anglo-American
Anglo-Australian
Anglo-French
Anglo-Indian
Anglo-Saxon (also Old English)(lang.; c500-1050)
Anglo-Saxon (Ger. tribes invaded Br., 5th and
    7th c.)
Anglo-Saxon Chronicle (Eng. hist.; 55 BC-AD
    1154)
Anglophile
Anglophobia
Angola (People's Republic of)(SW Afr.)
Angolan (people)
Angora cat
Angora goat
Angora rabbit
Angora wool
Angström, Anders Jonas (Swed. physt.; 1814-74)
Anguilla, West Indies
Angus cattle, Red
Angus S. King, Jr. (ME gov.; 1944-)
Anh, Le Duc (ex-pres., Viet.; 1920-)
Anheuser Busch, August, Jr. (US bus.; 1899-
    1989)
Anheuser-Busch, Inc.
Ani DiFranco (ent./songwriter; 1970-)
Aníbal Cavaco Silva (ex-PM, Port.; 1939-)
Anicet Georges Dologuele (PM, Central African
    Republic)
Animal Farm (G. Orwell novel)
Animal House, National Lampoon's (film, 1978)

Animal Planet (TV channel)
Animalia (biol.)
Animals' Voice Magazine
Animals, the (pop music)
Aniston, Jennifer (b. Jennifer Anistonapoulos)
    (ent.; 1969-)
Anita Baker (ent.; 1958-)
Anita Bryant (ent.; 1940-)
Anita Ekberg (Swed./US ent.; 1931-)
Anita Gillette (ent.; 1938-)
Anita Hill (US atty./educ.; 1956-)
Anita Loos (US writer; 1893?-1981)
Anita O'Day (US jazz; 1919-)
Anjelica Huston (ent.; 1951-)
Anjou (region, Fr.)
Anjou pear
Anjou, House of (or Plantagenet)(Br. ruling
    family; 1154-1399)
Anjou, Margaret of (queen, Eng./wife of Henry
    VI; 1430-82)
Anka, Paul (Can./US comp./ent.; 1941-)
Ankara, Turkey
Ann & Andy, Raggedy
Ann Arbor, MI
Ann B. Davis (ent.; 1926-)
Ann Beattie (US writer; 1947-)
Ann Blyth (ent.; 1928-)
Ann doll, Raggedy
Ann Jillian (b. Ann Nauseda)(ent.; 1950-)
Ann Landers (Eppie Lederer)(b. Esther Pauline
    Friedman)(US advice columnist; 1918-)
Ann-Margret (b. Ann-Margret Olsson)(ent.; 1941-)
Ann Miller (b. Lucille Ann Collier)(ent.; 1919-)
Ann M. Veneman (US secy./agr.; 1949-)
Ann (Ward) Radcliffe (Br. writer; 1764-1823)
Ann Reinking (ent.; 1949-)
Ann (Dorothy) Richards (nee Willis)(ex-TX
    gov.; 1933-)
Ann Rutherford (ent.; 1920-)
Ann Rutledge (fianceé of Abraham Lincoln;
    1816-35)
Ann Sheridan (ent.; 1915-67)
Ann Sothern (b. Harriette Lake)(ent.; 1909-)
Ann Taylor (designer)
Anna Akhmatova (poet; 1889-1966)
Anna and the King of Siam (film, 1946)
Anna Chlumsky (ent.; 1980-)
Anna Christie (film, 1923, 1930)
Anna Freud (Aus./Br. psych.; 1895-1982)
Anna Held (ent.; 1873-1918)
Anna Karenina (L. Tolstoy novel)
Anna Kournikova (tennis; 1981-)
Anna Magnani (ent.; 1908-73)
Anna Maria Alberghetti (It./US ent.; 1936-)
Anna May Wong (b. Lu Tsong Wong)(ent.;
    1907-61)
Anna Moffo (ent.; 1927-)
Anna Neagle (b. Marjorie Robertson)(ent.;
    1908-86)
Anna Nicole Smith (US ent.; 1968-)
Anna Pavlova (Rus. ballet; 1885-1931)
Anna Quindlen (US jour.; 1953-)
Anna Sewell (Br. writer; 1820-78)
Anna Sokolow (US dancer/choreographer;
    1915-2000)

Anna, Antonio (López) de Santa (ex-pres./gen., Mex.; 1795?-1876)
Annan, Kofi (dipl., Ghana/UN secy.-gen.; 1938-)
Annana/Bone, Algeria
Annapolis Convention (US hist.; 1786)
Annapolis, MD
Annapurna (also Anapurna, Devi, Parvati)(myth.)
Annapurna (mountain, Himalayas, Nepal)
Anne Archer (ent.; 1947-)
Anne Bancroft (b. Anna Maria Italiano)(ent.; 1931-)
Anne Baxter (ent.; 1923-85)
Anne Boleyn (2nd wife of Henry VIII; 1507-36)
Anne (Dudley) Bradstreet (US poet, c1612-72)
Anne Brontë (aka Acton Bell)(Br. writer; 1820-49)
Anne Francis (ent.; 1930-)
Anne Frank (Ger./Jew. diarist; 1929-45)
Anne Harvey Sexton (US poet; 1928-74)
Anne Hathaway (wife of Shakespeare; 1557?-1623)
Anne Heche (ent.; 1969-)
Anne Jackson (ent.; 1925-)
Anne Jeffreys (ent.; 1923-)
Anne Klein
Anne Klein & Co.
Anne Klein Jewelry (US bus.)
Anne Meara (ent.; 1929-)
Anne (Spencer) Morrow Lindbergh (US writer/ aviator; 1906-2001)
Anne Murray (ent.; 1945-)
Anne of Austria (queen, Fr./mother of Louis XIV; 1601-66)
Anne of Avonlea (film, 1987)
Anne of Brittany (queen, Fr.; 1477-1514)
Anne of Cleves (4th wife of Henry VIII; 1515-57)
Anne of Denmark (queen consort, James VI of Scot.; 1574-1619)
Anne of Green Gables (book; film, 1934, 1985)
Anne Rice (US writer; 1941-)
Anne-Sophie Mutter (violinist; 1963-)
Anne style, Queen (arch./furn.; 1700-20)
Anne Tyler (US writer; 1941-)
Anne, Princess (Anne Elizabeth Alice Louise) (daughter of Queen Elizabeth II; 1950-)
Anne, Queen (queen, Br./Ir.; 1665-1714)
Anne's lace, Queen (plant)
Anne's War, Queen (Br./Fr. in Amer.; 1702-13)
Anne-Marie Johnson (ent.; 1960-)
Annemarie Moser Proell (skiing; 1953-)
Annenberg, Walter (US publ./finan.; 1908-)
Annette Bening (ent.; 1958-)
Annette Funicello (ent.; 1942-)
Annette O'Toole (ent.; 1953-)
Annibale Carracci (It. artist; 1560-1609)
Annie (play)
Annie Besant (Br. theosophist; 1847-1933)
Annie Dillard (US writer; 1945-)
Annie Get Your Gun (film, 1950)
Annie Hall (film, 1977)
Annie Leibovitz (US photo.; 1949-)
Annie Lennox (ent.; 1954-)
Annie Oakley (Phoebe Mozee)(ent./ sharpshooter; 1860-1926)
Annie Potts (ent.; 1952-)
Annie Proulx, E(dna) (US writer; 1935-)

Annie, Little Orphan (fict. chara.)
Annie, Tugboat
anno Domini (also AD)(Latin, in the year of the Lord)
Annunciation (rel.)
Annunciation lily (also Madonna lily)
Annunzio Mantovani (ent.; 1905-80)
Another World (TV soap)
Anouilh, Jean (playwright; 1910-87)
Anouk Aimee (b. Francoise Soyra Dreyfus)(Fr. ent.; 1932-)
Ansaid (med.)
Anschluss (Ger., union)
Ansel Adams (US photo.; 1902-84)
Anselm Feuerbach (Ger. artist; 1829-80)
Anselm, St. (archbishop of Canterbury; c1033-1109)
Anshar (myth.)
Anspach, Susan (ent.; 1939-)
Anspor (med.)
Ant, Adam (b. Stuart Leslie Goddard)(ent.; 1954-)
ANTA (American National Theatre and Academy)
Antabuse (med.)
Antaeus (myth.)
Antal Dorati (Hung. cond.; 1906-88)
Antall, József (ex-PM, Hung.; 1932-)
Antananarivo, Madagascar
Antarctic Circle (South Pole)
Antarctic Peninsula (West Antarctica)
Antarctica (also Antarctic Continent)(South Pole)
Antares (also Alpha Scorpii)(astron.; myth.)
Ante Jelavic (Bosnia-Hercegovina/Bosnian Croat pol.)
Anthony and the Imperials, Little (pop music)
Anthony Armstrong-Jones (Earl of Snowdon)(Br. photo.; 1930-)
Anthony "Tony" A(llen) Williams (DC mayor; 1951-)
Anthony Burgess (Br. writer/comp.; 1917-1993)
Anthony Comstock (US reformer; 1844-1915)
Anthony Eden, Sir (Earl of Avon)(ex-PM, Br.; 1897-1977)
Anthony Edwards (ent.; 1962-)
Anthony "Tony" Franciosa (b. Anthony Papaleo) (ent.; 1928-)
Anthony Geary (ent.; 1947-)
Anthony Gustav de Rothschild (Br. finan.; 1887-1961)
Anthony Hopkins (ent.; 1937-)
Anthony Johnson (rowing; 1940-)
Anthony Joseph Principi (US ex-secy./vet. affairs; 1944-)
Anthony "Tony" Knowles (AK gov.; 1943-)
Anthony "Tony" (William) Lake (US ex-nat'l security advisor; 1939-)
Anthony Lewis (US writer; 1927-)
Anthony Lukas, J. (US writer; 1932-97)
Anthony M. Kennedy (US jurist; 1936-)
Anthony Newley (ent.; 1931-99)
Anthony "Tony" Perkins (ent.; 1932-)
Anthony Quayle (ent.; 1913-89)
Anthony Quinn (ent.; 1915-2001)
Anthony "Fat Tony" Salerno (US Mafia; 1912-92)
Anthony Trollope (Br. writer; 1815-82)
Anthony van Dyck, Sir (Flem. artist; 1599-1641)

Anthony Wayne (Mad Anthony)(US gen.; 1745-96)
Anthony Zerbe (ent.; 1936-)
Anthony, Earl (bowling; 1938-)
Anthony, Kenny D. (PM, St. Lucia; 1951-)
Anthony, Marc (b. Antonio Marco Muniz)(ent.; 1969-)
Anthony, Piers (b. Piers Anthony Jacob)(US writer; 1934-)
Anthony, St. (Eg., founded monasticism; c251-356)
Anthony, Susan B(rownell)(US reformer/ suffragist; 1820-1906)
Anthony's Cross/cross, St. (T-shaped cross)
Anthony's fire, St. (skin disease)(med.)
Antibes, France
Antichrist (opponent of Christ)
Anti-Corn-Law League (Br. hist.; 1839)
Antietam National Battlefield (MD)
Antietam, Battle of (US hist.; 1862)
Antigone (myth.)
Antigua and Barbuda (State of)
Antigua, Guatemala
Antilles, Greater (West Indies)(Cuba, Hispaniola, Jamaica, Puerto Rico)
Antilles, Lesser (West Indies)(Aruba, Netherlands Antilles, Trinidad and Tobago, Windward Islands, Leeward Islands)
Antilles, Netherlands (West Indies)
Anti-Masonic Party (US pol. org.; 1827-1840)
Antioch, CA
Antioch, Turkey (also Antakya)
Antiphon (Gr. speechwriter; c480-411 BC)
Antiques, The Magazine (mag.)
Anti-Saloon League of America (US org.; 1895-)
anti-Semite
anti-Semitism
Antivert (med.)
Antlia (astron., air pump)
Antofagasta, Chile
Antoine (Marie Roger) de Saint-Exupery (Fr. writer/aviator; 1900-44)
Antoine Cadillac (founded Detroit; 1658-1730)
Antoine-César Becquerel (Fr. physt.; 1788-1878)
Antoine-Henri Becquerel (Fr. physt.; 1852-1908)
Antoine Laurent Lavoisier (Fr. chem.; 1743-1794)
Antoine Pevsner (Fr. artist; 1886-1962)
Antoine Watteau (Fr. artist; 1684-1721)
Antoinette, Marie (queen, Fr./wife of Louis XVI; 1755-93)
Anton Bruckner (Austl. comp.; 1824-96)
Anton (Pavlovich) Chekhov (Rus. writer; 1860-1904)
Anton Denikin (Rus. mil.; 1872-1947)
Anton Dolin, Sir (b. Patrick Healey-Kay)(Br. ballet; 1904-83)
Anton Dvorak (also Antonin)(Czech. comp.; 1841-1904)
Anton (Grigoryevich) Rubinstein (Rus. pianist/ comp.)
Anton van Leeuwenhoek (Dutch, father of microbiology; 1632-1723)
Anton, Susan (ent.; 1950-)
Antonia Fraser (Br. writer; 1932-)
Antonia Novello (nee Coello)(US phys., 1st woman/1st Hispanic surgeon gen.; 1944-)

Antonin Dvorak (also Anton)(Czech. comp.; 1841-1904)
Antonin Scalia (US jurist; 1936-)
Antoninus Pius (emp., Rome; AD 86-161)
Antonio Allegri da Correggio (It. artist; 1494-1534)
Antonio Amati (It. violin maker; 1555-1638)
Antonio Banderas (ent.; 1960-)
Antonio de O(liveira) Salazar (ex-PM, Port.; 1899-1970)
Antonio (López) de Santa Anna (ex-pres./gen., Mex.; 1795?-1876)
Antonio dos Santos Ramalho Eanes (ex-pres., Port.; 1935-)
Antonio Gaudí (Sp. arch.; 1852-1926)
Antonio Gualberto do Rosario (PM, Cape Verde)
Antonio Guterres (PM, Port.; 1949-)
Antonio Mascarenhas Monteiro (pres., Cape Verde; 1944-)
Antonio Rossellino (It. sculptor; 1427-79)
Antonio Salieri (It. comp./cond.; 1750-1825)
Antonio Sant'Elia (It. arch.; 1888-1916)
Antonio (Lucio) Vivaldi (It. comp.; 1678-1741)
Antonioni, Michelangelo (ent.; 1912-)
Antonius Stradivarius (also Antonio Stradivari)(It. violin maker; 1644-1737)
Antonius, Marcus (aka Mark Antony)(Roman gen.; 83?-30 BC)
Antonius, Marcus Aurelius (b. Marcus Annius Verus)(emp., Rome; 121-180)
Antony and Cleopatra (Shakespeare play)
Antony Tudor (choreographer; 1909-87)
Antony, Mark (aka Marcus Antonius)(Roman gen.; 83?-30 BC)
Antrobus, Sir Charles (gov.-gen., St. Vincent/ Grenadines)
Antron (nylon)
Antsiranana, Madagascar
Anturane (med.)
Antwerp (province, Belgium)
Antwerp, Belgium
Anu (myth.)
Anubis (myth.)
Anuszkiewicz, Richard (artist; 1930-)
Anvers Island, Antarctica
Anwar (el-) Sadat (ex-pres., Eg.; 1918-81)
Anything But Love (TV show)
Anza, Juan Bautista de (Sp. expl.; 1735-88?)
Anzac Day (Austl. and New Zeal.)
AOL (America Online)
AOL Time Warner
A.1. Steak Sauce
AP (Associated Press)(US news org.; est. 1848)
APA (American Pharmaceutical Association, American Psychiatric Association, American Psychological Association)
Apache (Native Amer.)
Apache, Fort (film, 1948)
Apalachicola National Forest (FL)
Apalachicola River (GA/FL)
Apalachicola, FL
APB (all-points bulletin)
APEC (Asia-Pacific Economic Cooperation Conference; 1989)
Apennine Mountains (It.)

Apgar score (med.)

A(sa) Philip Randolph (US labor leader; 1889-1979)

Aphrodite (myth.)

Aphrodite, Mighty (film, 1995)

API (American Petroleum Institute)

Apia, Western Samoa

APO (Army and Air Force Post Office)

Apocalypse Now (film, 1979)

Apocalypse, the (also l.c.)

Apocrypha (also l.c.)(rel.)

Apollo (also Phoebus)(myth., sun god)

Apollo (US crewed space flights)

Apollo asteroid (astron.)

Apollo at Delphi, oracle of

Apollo Comedy Hour (TV show)

Apollo project (US space flight to moon, 7/20/69)

Apollo-Saturn (US crewed space flights)

Apollo Theater (Harlem, NYC)

Apollodorus (writer; myth.)

Apollonian (adj. = l.c.)

Apollonius of Perga (Gr. math.; c265-170 BC)

Apollonius of Rhodes (Gr. poet; c220-180 BC)

Apollonius of Tyana (Gr. phil.; 1st c AD)

Apollonius of Tyre (fict. Gr. hero)

Apollyon (also Abaddon)(destroyer, hell)

Apolo Nsibambi, Prof. (PM, Uganda; 1938-)

Apostles, Acts of the (also *The Acts*)(rel.)

Apostles' Creed (rel.)

Apostolic Fathers (rel.)

Appalachia (eastern US)

Appalachia, VA

Appalachian Mountains (eastern US)

Appalachian Trail (ME to GA)

Appaloosa (horse)

Appenzell, Switzerland

Appian Way (ancient Roman highway)

Appice, Carmine (ent.; 1946-)

Apple Computer, Inc.

Apple Jacks (cereal)

Apple Macintosh (compu.)

Apple Newtons (cookies)

Apple Pan Dowdy, Shoo-Fly Pie & (song)

Apple, Fiona (b. Fiona Apple McAfee Maggart) (ent.; 1977-)

Appleby, John Francis (US inv.; 1840-1917)

Applegate, Christina (ent.; 1971-)

Applegate, Jesse (US pioneer/pol.; 1811-88)

Appleseed, Johnny (b. John Chapman)(US pioneer; 1774-1845)

Appleton, WI

Applied Materials, Inc.

Appling, Luke (baseball; 1907-90)

Appomattox Court House National Historical Park (VA)

Appomattox, VA

Apra, Guam

Apresazide (med.)

Apresoline (med.)

April Fools' Day (also All Fools' Day)(April 1)

Aptidon, Hassan Gouled (ex-pres., Djibouti; 1916-)

Apuleius, Lucius (Roman satirist/atty.; c124-c170 BC)

Apure River (Venezuela)

Apus (astron., bird of paradise)

APV (all-purpose vehicle)

Aqaba, Gulf of (Jordan)

Aquafresh (toothpaste)

Aqua-Lung (underwater apparatus)

Aquaman (cartoon chara.)

Aqua Net (hair care)

Aqua Velva (toiletries)

Aquarian Age (also Age of Aquarius)

Aquarium Fish (mag.)

Aquarius (zodiac, astron., water bearer)

Aquascutum (raincoat)

Aquila (astron., eagle)

Aquinas, St. Thomas ("the Angelic Doctor")(It. phil./rel.; 1225-74)

Aquino, Corazon (ex-pres., Phil.; 1933-)

Aquitaine (region, Fr.)

Aquitaine, Eleanor of (queen, Louis VII [Fr.] & Henry II [Eng.]; c1122-1204)

AR (Arkansas, army regulation)

Ar (chem. sym., argon)

Ara (astron., altar)

Ara Parseghian (football; 1923-)

Arab (lang./people)

Arab-Berber (people)

Arab Emirates (also United Arab Emirates)

Arab-Israeli Six-Day War (1967)

Arab-Israeli Wars (series of wars since 1948)

Arab League (govt.)

Arab League Day (Arab nations)

Arab Petroleum Exporting Countries, Organization of (OAPEC)(est.; 1968)

Arab, Omani (people)

Arabia (also Arabian Peninsula)

Arabia, (T[homas] E[dward]) Lawrence of (Br. mil.; 1888-1935)

Arabia, Lawrence of (film, 1962)

Arabian camel (dromedary, one hump)

Arabian Desert (Eg.)

Arabian Gulf (also Persian Gulf)(SW Asia)

Arabian horse

Arabian Nights' Entertainments, The (also *The Thousand and One Nights, Arabian Nights*)(myth.)

Arabian Sea (India/Arabia)

Arabic (lang.)

Arabic alphabet

Arabic numerals

Arable, Fern (fict. chara., *Charlotte's Web*)

Arachnophobia (film, 1990)

Arachne (myth.)

Arafat, Yasir (PLO Chairman; 1929-)

Aragon (region, Sp.)

Aragon, Catherine of (1st wife of Henry VIII; 1485-1536)

Araguaia River (Brazil)(also Araguaya)

Arak, Iran

Araks River (Turk.)

Aral Sea (was Lake Aral)(Kazakhstan/ Uzbekistan)

Arallu (also Aralu)(ancient Babylonian world of the dead)

Aram Ilich (or Ill'yich) Khachaturian (Armenian comp.; 1903-78)

Aramaic (lang.)

Arango, Andrés Pastrana (pres., Colombia;

1954-)
Arapaho (Native Amer.)
Arapaho National Forest
Ararat, Mount (Turk.)(Noah's Ark landing)
Araucana chicken (also Easter egg chicken)
Araucanian (also Araucan)(Native SAmer.)
Arawak (Native SAmer.)
Arbitron ratings
Arbor Day
Arbuckle, Fatty (Roscoe)(ent.; 1887-1933)
Arbuthnot, John (Scot. phys./satirist; 1667-1735)
Arby's, Inc.
Arc de Triomphe (Arch of Triumph)(Paris)
Arc, St. Joan of (also Jeanne d'Arc, Maid of
  Orléans)(Fr. rel./mil.; 1412?-31)
Arcadia (ancient Gr. region)
Arcadia, CA, FL
Arcangelo Corelli (It. comp.; 1653-1713)
Arcaro, Eddie (George Edward)(jockey; 1916-97)
Arch Oboler (ent.; 1909-87)
Arch of Constantine (Rome)
Arch of Titus (statue)
Archaeology (mag.)
Archangel Blue (now Russian Blue)(cat)
archangel Gabriel
archbishop of Canterbury (archbishop, Church
  of England)
Archeozoic era (also Archaeozoic)
Archer Daniels Midland Co.
Archer, Anne (ent.; 1947-)
Archerd, Army (US jour.; 1919-)
Arches National Park (UT)
Archibald Cox (US atty./Watergate; 1912-)
Archibald Joseph Cronin ("A.J.")(Br. phys./
  writer; 1896-1981)
Archibald MacLeish (US poet; 1892-1982)
Archibald M. Willard (US artist; 1836-1918)
Archibald (Percival) Wavell (Br. mil.; 1883-1950)
Archie (cartoon)
Archie (Internet search engine)
Archie Andrews (cartoon chara.)
Archie Bunker (fict. chara., *All in the Family*)
Archie Goodwin (fict. chara.)
Archie Moore (boxing; 1913-98)
Archimedean (or Archimedes') screw (pump)
Archimedean water snail
Archimedes (Gr. math.; c287-212 BC)
Archimedes' (or Archimedean) screw (pump)
Archimedes' principle (physics)
Archipenko, Alexander (US sculptor; 1887-1964)
Architectural Digest (mag.)
Archives and Records Administration, National
  (NARA)(US govt. agcy.; est. 1984)
Archives, National (DC)
Arco Products, Inc.
Arcosanti community (AZ)(self-sufficient desert
  community)
Arctic Circle (North Pole)
Arctic Current (also Labrador Current)(cold
  ocean current)
Arctic Ocean (North Pole)
Arctic region (North Pole)
Arctic, the (North Pole)
Arcturus (or Alpha Bootis)(astron.)
Arden Co., Elizabeth

Arden doctrine, Enoch (divorce)
Arden, Elizabeth (b. Florence Nightingale
  Graham)(US bus.; 1884-1966)
Arden, Elizabeth (cosmetics)
Arden, Enoch (missing person presumed dead,
  but is alive)
Arden, Enoch (Tennyson poem)
Arden, Eve (b. Eunice Quedens)(ent.; 1908-90)
Ardenne, Champagne- (region, Fr.)
Ardipithecus ramidus (anthrop., earliest
  hominid, 4.4 million years ago)
ARE (Arab Republic of Egypt, Association for
  Research & Enlightenment)
Are You Being Served (TV show)
Arendt, Hannah (historian; 1906-75)
Arequipa, Peru
Ares (myth., god of war)
Aretha Franklin (ent.; 1942-)
Arezzo, Italy
Argentina (also Argentine Republic)(SAmer.)
Argo (astron., ship)
Argo (myth., Jason's ship in quest of the
  Golden Fleece)
Argonauts (myth.)
Argonauts, Jason and the (film, 1963)
Argonne Forest (Fr.)(also Argonne)
Argos (ancient Gr. city)
Argote, Luis de Gongora y (Sp. writer; 1561-
  1627)
Argus (myth.)
Argyle (diamond-shaped pattern)(also l.c.)
Argyll, Duke of (John D. S. Campbell)(ex-gov.-
  gen., Can.; 1845-1914)
Arhat (rel.)(also Arhant)
Arhus, Denmark (also Aarhus)
Ari Fleischer (US White House press secy.; 1960?-)
Ariadne (myth.)
Arianna Huffington
Arica, Chile
Aricept (med.)
Ariel (Arik) Sharon (PM, Isr. ; 1928-)
Ariel (astron.)
Ariel Durant (US hist.; 1898-1981)
Ariens (lawn care)
Aries (zodiac, astron., ram)
Arima, Trinidad
Aris-Isotoner (gloves)
Aristide Briand (ex-PM, Fr.; 1862-1932)
Aristide Maillol (Fr. sculptor; 1861-1944)
Aristide, Jean-Bertrand (deposed pres., Haiti;
  1953-)
AristoCAT (CAT system)
Aristocort (med.)
Aristophanes (Gr. drama.; c448-380 BC)
Aristotelian logic (also Aristotelean)
Aristotelianism (phil.)
Aristotle (Gr. phil.; 384-322 BC)
Aristotle Socrates Onassis (Gr. bus.; 1900-75)
Arizona (AZ)
Arizona Daily Star (AZ, newspaper)
Arizona Highways (mag)
Arizona Republic (AZ newspaper)
Arizona v. Fulminate (US law; 1991)
Arizona, Miranda vs. (US law; 1966)
Ark of the Covenant (rel.)

Ark, Joan Van (ent.; 1943-)
Arkansas (AR)
Arkansas River (CO-LA)
Arkie (compu. game)
Arkin, Adam (ent.; 1957-)
Arkin, Alan (ent.; 1934-)
Arkwright, Sir Richard (Br. inv.; 1732-92)
Arledge, Roone (US TV exec.; 1931-)
Arlen Specter, (J.) (US cong.; 1930-)
Arlen, Harold (b. Hyman Arluck)(US comp.;
  1905-86)
Arlen, Richard (ent.; 1900-76)
Arlene Dahl (ent.; 1928-)
Arlene Francis (b. Arline Francis Kazanjian)
  (ent.; 1907-2001)
Arles, France
Arlington National Cemetery (VA)
Arlington, MA, NJ, TX, VA
Arlington, VA
Arliss, George (ent.; 1868-1946)
Arlo Guthrie (ent.; 1947-)
ARM (adjustable-rate mortgage)
A.R.M. (allergy relief medicine)(med.)
Armada, Spanish (Invincible Armada)(fleet of
  ships)
Armageddon (rel., final battle)
Armagh, County (NIre.)
Armagnac (brandy)
Armagnac (district, Fr.)
Armand, The Vampire (A. Rice novel)
Armand Assante (ent.; 1949-)
Arm & Hammer (baking powder)
Armand Hammer (US bus.; 1898-1990)
Armand Jean du Plessis Richelieu, Duc de (Fr.
  cardinal/pol.; 1585-1642)
Armando Calderon Sol (ex-pres., El Salvador;
  1948-)
Armani, Giorgio (It. designer; 1934-)
Armatrading, Joan (ent.; 1950-)
Armbruster, Robert (US cond.)
Armbruster, Robert E. (US gen.; 1949-)
Armed Forces Day
Armed Forces Radio
Armenia (Republic of)(formerly part of USSR)
  (W Asia)
Armenian (lang./people)
Armenian Church
Armetale (dinnerware)
Armey, Dick (Richard K.)(US econ./cong.; 1940-)
Armistice Day (now Veterans Day)
Armor All cleaner
Armor All Corp.
Armour (meats)
Armour Swift-Eckrich (US bus.)
Armour, Philip D. (US bus.; 1832-1901)
Arms, College of (also Heralds' College)(Br.
  heraldry)
Armstrong World Industries, Inc.
Armstrong, Henry (boxing; 1912-88)
Armstrong, Lance (US cyclist/Tour de France
  winner; 1971-)
Armstrong, Louis "Satchmo" (US jazz; 1900-71)
Armstrong, Neil A(lden)(astro., 1st to walk on
  moon; 1930-)
Armstrong-Jones, Anthony (Earl of Snowdon)

(Br. photo.; 1930-)
Army Air Forces
Army and Air Force Post Office (APO)
Army Archerd (US jour.; 1919-)
Army Corps of Engineers (US mil.)
Army Magazine
Army of the U.S. (also United States Army)
Army Times (mag.)
Army, Department of the (US govt.)
Army, Red (USSR army until 1946)
Army, Regular (US army maintained in both
  peace and war)
Army, U.S. (US mil.)
Arnage, Bentley (auto.)
Arnaz, Desi (b. Desiderio Alberto Araz y de
  Acha III)(ent.; 1917-86)
Arnaz, Desi, Jr. (ent.; 1953-)
Arnaz, Lucie (ent.; 1951-)
Arne (Helge) Carlson (ex-MN gov.; 1934-)
Arness, James (b. James Aurness)(ent.; 1923-)
Arnie Robinson (track; 1948-)
Arno, Peter (aka Curtis Arnoux
  Peters)(cartoonist, *New Yorker*; 1904-68)
Arnold (Daniel) Palmer (golf; 1929-)
Arnold (Franz Walter) Schoenberg (Aus. comp.;
  1874-1951)
Arnold Lucius Gesell (US psych./educ.; 1880-
  1961)
Arnold Rüütel (ex-pres., Estonia)
Arnold Schwarzenegger (ent.; 1947-)
Arnold Stang (ent.; 1925-)
Arnold (Joseph) Toynbee (Br. hist.; 1889-1975)
Arnold, Benedict (US traitor; 1741-1801)
Arnold, Eddy (ent.; 1918-)
Arnold, Edward (ent.; 1890-1956)
Arnold, Hap (Henry)(US mil.; 1886-1950)
Arnold, Matthew (Br. poet/critic; 1822-88)
Arnold, Tom (ent.; 1959-)
Arnoldo Alemán Lacayo (pres., Nicaragua; 1946-)
Aroostook War (US/Can.; 1838-39)
Arp, Jean (or Hans)(Fr. artist; 1887-1966)
Arpad Goncz (ex-pres., Hung.; 1922-)
Arpel, Adrien (cosmetics)
Arpels, Inc., Van Cleef &
Arquette, Cliff (aka Charlie Weaver)(ent.;
  1905-74)
Arquette, Courteney Cox (ent.; 1964-)
Arquette, Patricia (ent.; 1968-)
Arquette, Rosanna (ent.; 1959-)
Arrau, Claudio (Chilean pianist; 1903-91)
Arrid (anti-perspirant)
Arrid Extra Dry
Arrigo Boito (It. comp./writer; 1842-1918)
Arrindell, Clement Athelston (gov.-gen., St.
  Kitts/Nevis)
Arrowhead Drinking Water Co.
Arrowhead, Lake, CA
Arroyo, Gloria Macapagal- (pres., Phil.; 1947-)
Arroyo, Martina (ent.; 1937-)
Arsenic and Old Lace (play; film, 1942)
Arsenio Hall (ent.; 1955-)
Arsenishvili, Giorgi (secy./state, Georgia)
Arshile (Vosdanig Adoian) Gorky (US artist;
  1905-48)
Art & Antiques (mag.)

Art Blakey (US jazz; 1919-90)
Art Buchwald (US columnist; 1925-)
Art Carney (ent.; 1918-)
Art Deco (also l.c.)
Art Garfunkel (ent.; 1941-)
Art in America (mag.)
Art Institute of Chicago
Art Linkletter (ent.; 1912-)
Art News
Art Nouveau (also l.c.)
Art Pepper (US jazz; 1925-82)
Art Rooney (football; 1901-88)
Art Sansom (cartoonist, *The Born Loser*; 1920-91)
Art Spiegelman (cartoonist; 1948-)
Art(hur) Tatum (US jazz; 1910-56)
Art Young (pol. cartoonist; 1866-1943)
Artagnan, Charles de Baatz d', Seigneur (fict. chara., *Three Musketeers*)
Artane (med.)
Arte Johnson (ent.; 1929-)
Artemia, Inc.
Artemis (myth.)
Artemis (toiletries)
Artemision (also Temple of Artemis at Ephesus)
Artful Dodger (fict. pickpocket, *Oliver Twist*)
Arthropan (med.)
Arthur (film, 1981)
Arthur Ashe (tennis; 1943-93)
Arthur C(harles) Clarke (Br. writer; 1917-)
Arthur (Holly) Compton (US physt.; 1892-1962)
Arthur Conan Doyle, Sir (Br. phys./writer, Sherlock Holmes; 1859-1930)
Arthur Davies (US artist; 1862-1928)
Arthur Dove (US artist; 1880-1946)
Arthur Fiedler (US cond.; 1894-1979)
Arthur Fonzerelli (also "the Fonz" or "Fonzie") (fict chara.)
Arthur Godfrey (ent.; 1903-83)
Arthur Godfrey and Friends (TV show)
Arthur Godfrey's Talent Scouts (TV show)
Arthur Hailey (US writer; 1920-)
Arthur Hays Sulzberger (US publ.; 1881-1968)
Arthur Hill (ent.; 1922-)
Arthur Honegger (Swiss comp.; 1892-1955)
Arthur H(endrick) Vandenberg (US pol.; 1884-1951)
Arthur James Balfour (ex-PM, Br.; 1848-1930)
Arthur Joyce Lunel Cary (Ir. writer; 1888-1957)
Arthur Kennedy (ent.; 1914-90)
Arthur Koestler (Br./Hung. writer; 1905-83)
Arthur Kornberg (US chem.; 1918-)
Arthur Laffer (US econ.; 1940-)
Arthur Laurents (US playwright; 1918-)
Arthur Levitt, Jr. (US bus., ex-chair/SEC; 1931-)
Arthur Lewis, Sir (William)(Br. econ.; 1915-91)
Arthur "Harpo" Marx (ent.; 1888-1964)
Arthur M(eier) Schlesinger (US hist.; 1888-1965)
Arthur M(eier) Schlesinger, Jr. (US hist.; 1917-)
Arthur Miller (US writer; 1915-)
Arthur Murray (US dancer; 1896-1991)
Arthur Murray Dance Studios (US bus.)
Arthur N(apoleon) R. Robinson (pres., Trinidad/Tobago; 1926-)
Arthur Ochs Sulzberger (US publ.; 1926-)
Arthur Penn (ent.; 1922-)

Arthur Rimbaud, (Jean Nicolas)(Fr. poet; 1854-91)
Arthur Rubinstein (Pol./US pianist; 1887-1982)
Arthur Saint Clair (US gen.; 1736-1818)
Arthur Schomberg (bibliophile, black lit./hist.; 1874-1938)
Arthur Schopenhauer (Ger. phil.; 1788-1860)
Arthur Schwartz (US comp.; 1900-84)
Arthur S(eymour) Sullivan, Sir (Br. comp.; 1842-1900)
Arthur Symons (poet/critic; 1865-1945)
Arthur Thomas Quiller-Couch, Sir (aka "Q")(Br. writer; 1863-1944)
Arthur Travers Harris, Sir (Br. mil.; 1895-1984)
Arthur Treacher (ent.; 1894-1975)
Arthur Treacher's Fish & Chips (US bus.)
Arthur Wellesley (Duke of Wellington)(Br. mil.; 1769-1852)
Arthur, Bea (Beatrice)(b. Bernice Frankel)(ent.; 1926-)
Arthur, Chester A(lan)(21st US pres.; 1829-86)
Arthur, Jean (ent.; 1900-91)
Arthur, King (legendary Br. king, 6th c.)
Arthur, Owen (PM, Barbados; 1949-)
Arthur, Port (Ontario, Can.)
Arthur, Port (TX)
Arthurian legend
Arthus reaction/phenomenon (med.)
Articles of Confederation (US hist.; 1781)
Articles of War
Artie Shaw (b. Arthur Arshawsky)(US jazz; 1910-)
Artis Gilmore (basketball; 1949-)
Artist's Magazine
Arts & Entertainment (A&E)(TV channel)
Arts and Humanities, National Endowment on (or for) the (US govt. agcy.; est. 1965)
Artur Rasizade (PM, Azerbaijan; 1935-)
Artur Rodzinski (US cond.; 1894-1958)
Artur Schnabel (pianist/comp.; 1882-1951)
Arturo Toscanini (It. cond.; 1867-1957)
Artweek
Aruba (the Netherlands, Antilles)
Arvin Industries, Inc.
Aryan (langs.)
AS (Associate of Science) degree
As (chem. sym., arsenic)
As the World Turns (TV soap)
As You Like It (Shakespeare play)
Asa Candler (U.S., founded Coca-Cola Co.; 1851-1929)
ASAP (as soon as possible)
Asbury Jukes, Southside Johnny and the (pop music)
Asbury Park Press (NJ newspaper)
Asbury Park, NJ
ASCAP (American Society of Composers, Authors, and Publishers)
Ascension (Br. island[s] in S Atl.)
Ascension Day (also Holy Thursday)(rel.)
ASCII (American Standard Code for Information Interchange)(compu.)
Ascot Heath (race course, Eng.)
Ascot races (Eng.)
Ascriptin (med.)
A. Schulman (US bus.)
Asendin (med.)

Asgard (myth.)
Ash Wednesday (rel.)
Ashburner, Charles (US geol.; 1854-89)
Ashbury, Haight- (district, San Francisco)
Ashcan school (1908-14, art from city life)
Ashcroft, Dame Peggy (ent.; 1907-91)
Ashcroft, John David (US atty. gen.; 1942-)
Ashe, Arthur (tennis; 1943-93)
Asher Brown Durand (US artist; 1796-1886)
Asheville, NC
Ashford, Evelyn (track & field; 1957-)
Ashkenazi (plural = Ashkenazim)(people)
Ashkenazy, Vladimir (Rus. pianist/cond.; 1937-)
Ashkhabad, Turkmenistan
Ashland Oil, Inc.
Ashland, KY, OH, OR, PA, WI
Ashley Judd (ent.; 1968-)
Ashley Montagu, (Montague Francis)(Br./US
   anthrop.; 1905-99)
Ashley Olsen (ent.; 1986-)
Ashley, Elizabeth (b. Elizabeth Cole)(ent.; 1939-)
Ashley, Ellen (clothing)
Ashley, Laura (Br. designer; 1926-85)
Ashley, Laura (US bus.)
Ashman, Howard (US lyricist; 1951-91)
ash-Shariqah (state, UAE)
Ash-Shaytan (rel., Satan)
Ashton-Tate Co.
Ashton, Sir Frederick William Mallandaine
   (choreographer; 1904-88)
Ashwander v. Tennessee Valley Authority (US
   law; 1936)
Asia
Asia Minor (ancient region, Turk.)(now Anatolia)
Asia-Pacific Economic Cooperation Conference
   (APEC; 1989)
Asia Week
Asiago (liqueur)
Asiago, Italy
Asian (people)
Asian-American
A-side (music, hit side)
Asimov, Isaac (US writer/sci-fi; 1920-92)
Asimov's Science Fiction Magazine, Isaac
Ask Jeeves (compu.)
Ask Jeeves, Inc.
Askar Akayev (pres., Kyrgyzstan; 1944-)
Asko (kitchen appliances)
ASL (American sign language)
Asmara, Ethiopia (also Asmera)
Asmodeus (an evil spirit)
Asner, Ed (ent.; 1929-)
ASPCA (American Society for the Prevention of
   Cruelty to Animals)
Aspen Music Festival
Aspen Music School
Aspen, CO
Aspercreme (med.)
Aspergum (med.)
Aspin Les(lie), Jr. (US ex-secy./defense; 1938-
   95)
Aspire, Ford (auto.)
Asquith, Herbert H. (ex-PM, Br.; 1852-1928)
Assab, Ethiopia
Assad, Dr. Bashar al- (pres., Syria; 1965-)

Assad, Hafez al- (ex-pres., Syria; 1930-2000)
as-Salimiyah, Kuwait
Assama (Muslim paradise)
Assamese (lang.)
Assante, Armand (ent.; 1949-)
Assemblies of God (rel.)
Assiniboin (Native Amer.)
Assiniboine River (Can.)
Assiniboine, Mount (Can.)
Assisi, Italy
Assisi, St. Francis of (It. rel., founded
   Franciscans; 1182-1226)
Associated Press (AP)(US news org.; est. 1848)
Associates First Capital Corp.
Association for the Advancement of Colored
   People, National (NAACP)(org. 1909)
Association of Broadcast Employees and
   Technicians, National (also NABET)
Association of Broadcasters, National (also NAB)
Association of Intercollegiate Athletics, National
   (also NAIA)
Association of Manufacturers, National (NAM)
   (est. 1895)
Association of Radio and Television News
   Analysts (ARTNA)
Association of Television and Radio Announcers,
   National (also NATRA)
Association, the (pop music)
Assoumani, Azali (pres., Comoros; 1951-)
Assumption (rel.)
Assumption Day
Assur (myth.)
Assyria (ancient Asian empire)
Assyrian (lang.)
Assyrian art (17-7th c. BC)
AST (Atlantic Standard Time)
Astaire, Adele (ent.; 1897-1981)
Astaire, Fred (b. Frederick Austerlitz)(ent.;
   1899-1987)
Astarte (myth.)
Asti Spumante/spumante (wine)
Astin, John (ent.; 1930-)
Astin, Patty Duke (ent.; 1946-)
Aston Martin (auto.)
Aston Martin DB7 Vantage (auto.)
Aston Martin DB7 Vantage Volante convertible
   (auto.)
Aston Martin Vanquish (auto.)
Aston Martin Vanquish GT coupe (auto.)
Astor, Brooke (socialite/philanthropist; 1905-)
Astor, John Jacob (US bus.; 1763-1848)
Astor, John Jacob, 5th (US/Br. publ.; 1886-1971)
Astor, Mary (b. Lucile Langhanke)(ent.; 1906-87)
Astoria Hotel, Waldorf- (NYC)
Astoria, OR
Astounding Science Fiction
Astro, Chevrolet (auto.)
Astrodome, the (Houston, TX)
Astrophysical Observatory, Special (USSR)
Astros, Houston (baseball team)
Astroturf
Asturian (people)
Asturias (cheese)
Asturias (region, Sp.)
Asturias, Miguel Angel (Guat. writer/dipl.; 1899-

1974)
Asunción, Paraguay
Aswan High Dam (Eg.)
Aswan, Egypt
Asylum/Nonesuch Records, Elektra/ (US bus.)
Ata, Prince Ulukalala Lavaka (PM, Tonga; 1959-)
Atabrine (med.)
Atahualpa (last Incan emp.; c1502-33)
AT&T (American Telephone & Telegraph Co.)
AT&T (comm.)
AT&T/Lucent (comm.)
AT&T Wireless (comm.)
Atari (compu.)
Atari, Inc.
Atatürk, Kemal (b. Mustafa Kemal Pasha)(ex-pres./dictator, Turk.; 1881-1938)
Atbara River (NE Afr.)
A. T. Cross Co.
A-Team (TV show)
Atef Muhammad Ebeid, Dr. (PM, Egypt; 1932-)
Atef Sidqi (ex-PM, Eg.)
Athanasius, St. (bishop of Alexandria; 298-373)
Atharva-Veda (rel.)
Athena (myth.)
Athena Nike, Temple of (Gr.)
Athena Parthenos, Temple of (also Parthenon, Gr.)
Athena, Pallas (myth.)
Athena, Temple of (Gr.)
Athenaeum (Athena temple[s])(also l.c.)
Athenaeus (Gr. scholar/writer; 3rd c. AD)
Athens, AL, GA, OH, PA, TN, TX
Athens, Greece
Athens, School of (by Raphael)
Athens, Timon of (by Shakespeare)
Atherton, Gertrude (Franklin Horn)(US writer; 1857-1948)
Atherton, William (ent.; 1947-)
Athletic Association, National Collegiate (NCAA)(est. 1906)
Athletic Union of the United States, Amateur (AAU)
Athletics, National Association of Intercollegiate (also NAIA)
Athletics, Oakland (also Oakland A's)(baseball team)
Athol (Harold) Fugard (SAfr. playwright; 1932-)
Ativan (med.)
Atjehnese (also Achinese)(lang./people)
Atkins, Chet (Chester)(ent.; 1924-2001)
Atkins, Dr. Robert C. (US, low-carb diet)
Atkins, Tommy (slang, Br. army private)
Atkinson, (Justin) Brooks (US critic; 1894-1984)
Atkinson, Rowan (ent.; 1955-)
Atkov, Oleg (cosmo.)
Atlanta Braves (baseball team)
Atlanta Constitution (GA newspaper)
Atlanta Falcons (football team)
Atlanta Hawks (basketball team)
Atlanta International Airport, Hartsfield (GA)
Atlanta Journal (GA newspaper)
Atlanta, GA
Atlantic & Pacific Tea Co., Great (A&P Food Stores)
Atlantic Beach, FL

Atlantic Charter (WWII, US/Br.)
Atlantic City Press (NJ newspaper)
Atlantic City, NJ
Atlantic Monthly, The (mag.)
Atlantic Ocean (also the Atlantic)
Atlantic Richfield Co.
Atlantic Standard Time
Atlantis (legendary continent)
Atlantis (US space shuttle)
Atlantis, New (utopia, Sir Francis Bacon)
Atlas (astron., myth.)
Atlas Mountains (NW Afr.)
Atlas, Charles (b. Angelo Siciliano)(US body builder; 1894-1972)
Atlas, Mercury- (US crewed space flights)
ATM (automatic teller machine)
Atman (World Soul, rel.)
Atna (Native Amer.)(also Ahtena or Ahtna)
Atna River (also Copper River)(AK)
Atom Egoyan (ent./writer; 1960-)
Atomic Age (usually l.c.)
Atonement, Day of (Yom Kippur)(rel.)
Atopare, Silas (gov.-gen., Papua New Guinea)
Atromid (med.)
Atropos (myth.)
Atrovent (med.)
Attack of the Killer Tomatoes (film, 1977)
Attas, Haidar Abu Bakr al- (ex-PM, Yemen; 1939-)
Attenborough, Sir Richard (ent.; 1923-)
Attends (undergarments)
Attic (lit., Gr.)
Attica (region, Gr.)
Attica, IN, NY
Attila the Hun ("Scourge of God")(King of the Huns; c406-453)
Attlee, Clement R(ichard)(ex-PM, Br.; 1883-1967)
Attucks, Crispus (Amer. Revolutionary patriot; c1723-70)
ATV (all-terrain vehicle)
Atwater, Lee (Harvey Leroy)(US pol.; 1951-91)
Atwood, Margaret (Can. writer; 1939-)
Au (chem. sym., gold)
Auberjonois, Rene (ent.; 1940-)
Aubervilliers, France
Aubrey Smith, Sir C. (ent.; 1863-1948)
Aubrey Solomon "Abba" Eban (Isr. pol.; 1915-)
Aubrey Vincent Beardsley (Br. artist; 1872-98)
Aubrey, John (Br. antiquarian; 1626-97)
Auburn University (AL)
Auburn, AL, CA, IN, MA, ME
Aubusson tapestry/rug
Aubusson, France
Auchincloss, Louis Stanton (US writer; 1917-)
Auckland, New Zealand
Auden, W(ystan) H(ugh) (Br. poet; 1907-73)
Audi (auto.)
Audi A4 (auto.)
Audi A4 Avant (auto.)
Audi A4 Avant 1.8T wagon (auto.)
Audi A4 Avant 2.8 wagon (auto.)
Audi A4 Avant Quattro wagon (auto.)
Audi A4 Avant S4 wagon (auto.)
Audi A4 Quattro (auto.)
Audi A4 Quattro 1.8 (auto.)

Audi A4 Quattro 1.8T (auto.)
Audi A4 Quattro 2.8 (auto.)
Audi A4 S4 (auto.)
Audi A6 (auto.)
Audi A6 Allroad 2.7T Quattro (auto.)
Audi A6 Avant (auto.)
Audi A6 Avant 2.8 Quattro wagon (auto.)
Audi A6 Avant Quattro wagon (auto.)
Audi A6 Quattro (auto.)
Audi A6 Quattro 2.7T (auto.)
Audi A6 Quattro 2.8 (auto.)
Audi A6 Quattro 4.2 (auto.)
Audi A8 (auto.)
Audi A8 Quattro (auto.)
Audi A8 Quattro 4.2 (auto.)
Audi A8 S8 (auto.)
Audi A8L (auto.)
Audi Allroad 2.7T Quattro (auto.)
Audi Allroad Quattro (auto.)
Audi Cabriolet convertible (auto.)
Audi 90CS (auto.)
Audi 90S (auto.)
Audi of America, Inc.
Audi 100 (auto.)
Audi 100CS (auto.)
Audi 100S (auto.)
Audi Quattro (auto.)
Audi S4 (auto.)
Audi S4 Avant wagon (auto.)
Audi S6 (auto.)
Audi S8 (auto.)
Audi TT (auto.)
Audi TT coupe (auto.)
Audi TT roadster (auto.)
Audie Murphy (ent., war hero; 1924-71)
Audio (mag.)
Audio/Video Interiors (mag.)
Audrey Hepburn (ent.; 1929-73)
Audrey Meadows (ent.; 1924-96)
Audrey Rose (film, 1977)
Audubon Society, National (environ. org.)
Audubon, John James (US artist, birds; 1785-1851)
Audubon's warbler (bird)
Auel, Jean M. (US writer; 1936-)
Auer, Leopold (violinist/educ.; 1845-1930)
Auerbach, Red (Arnold)(basketball; 1917-)
Auermann, Nadja (model; 1971-)
auf Wiedersehen (Ger., good-bye, until we meet again)
Augean stables (mythical stables not cleaned for 30 years)
Auger effect (astron.)
Auger shower (cosmic ray shower)
Augmentin (med.)
Augsburg, Germany
August Anheuser Busch, Jr. (US bus.; 1899-1989)
August Belmont (US finan.; 1816-90)
August Macke (Ger. artist; 1887-1914)
August Strindberg (Johan)(Swed. writer; 1849-1912)
August von Wassermann (Ger. phys./bacteriol.; 1866-1925)
August Wilhelm von Schlegel (Ger. writer;

1767-1845)
August Wilson (b. Frederick August Kittel)(US writer; 1945-)
August Wilson (US writer; 1945-)
Augusta Ada Byron (Lady Lovelace)(Br. math./inv., compu.; 1815-52)
Augusta Chronicle (GA newspaper)
Augusta Gregory, Lady (Ir. writer; 1852-1932)
Augusta Herald (GA newspaper)
Augusta, GA, KS, ME
Auguste Comte (Fr. phil.; 1798-1857)
Auguste Escoffier (Fr. chef/writer; 1847-1935)
Auguste (Marie) Lumière (Fr. inv.; 1862-1954)
Auguste Piccard (Swiss physt.; 1884-1962)
Auguste (René) Rodin, (François)(Fr. sculptor; 1840-1917)
Augustin Eugene Scribe (Fr. writer; 1791-1861)
Augustin Fresnel (Fr. physt.; 1788-1827)
Augustine of Hippo, St. (rel.; 354-430)
Augustine, St. (1st archbishop of Canterbury; late 6th c.)
Augusto César Sandino (Nicaraguan mil.; 1893-1934)
Augusto Pinochet (Ugarte)(ex-pres., Chile; 1915-)
Augustus Saint-Gaudens (US artist; 1848-1907)
Augustus, Caesar (aka Gaius Julius Caesar Octavius)(1st Roman emp.; 63 BC-AD 14)
Aukland, New Zealand
Auld Lang Syne (song)
Aulus Gellius (Latin writer; c130-c165)
Aumont, Jean-Pierre (Fr. ent.; 1909-)
Aung San Suu Kyi (human rights activist; 1945-)
Aunt Emma (slang, morphine)
Aunt Jemima (food)
Aunt Jemima (offensive slang, black woman subservient to whites)
Aunt Sally (Br. slang, person set up as easy target)
Auntie Mame (film, 1958)
Auralgan (med.)
Aureomycin (med.)
Auriga (astron., charioteer)
Aurora (myth., goddess of dawn)
Aurora, CO, IL, IN, MO, NE
Aurora, Oldsmobile (auto.)
Auschwitz, Poland
Auslander (Ger., foreigner, outsider)
Ausseil, Jean (Monacan pol.)
Aussie (hair care)
Aussie (native of Austl.)
Austen Chamberlain (Br. pol.; 1863-1937)
Austen, Jane (Br. writer; 1775-1817)
Austin American-Statesman (TX newspaper)
Austin City Limits (TV show)
Austin Powers: International Man of Mystery (film, 1997)
Austin Powers: The Spy Who Shagged Me (film, 1999)
Austin v. U.S. (US law; 1993)
Austin, MN, TX
Austin, Patti (ent.; 1948-)
Austin, Stephen Fuller (Texas colonizer; 1793-1836)
Austin, "Stone Cold" Steve (b. Steven Williams) (wrestling; 1964-)
Austin, Tracy (tennis; 1962-)

Australia (Commonwealth of)
Australia Day (Austl. holiday)
Australia, South (state, Austl.)
Australian (people)
Australian Aborigine (people)
Australian Airlines
Australian Alps
Australian Antarctic Territory
Australian ballot (voting method; used in US since 1888)
Australian Capital Territory (govt. headquarters)
Australian cattle dog (dog)
Australian crawl
Australian heeler (dog)
Australian kelpie (dog)
Australian rye grass
Australian shepherd (dog)
Australian terrier (dog)
Australopithecus (anthrop.)
Australopithecus aethiopicus (anthrop., early hominid, 2.3 to 2.6 million years ago)
Australopithecus afarensis (anthrop., early hominid, 2.8 to 3.7 million years ago)
Australopithecus africanus (anthrop., early hominid, 2 to 3 million years ago)
Australopithecus anamensis (anthrop., early hominid, 3.9 to 4.2 million years ago)
Australopithecus boisei (anthrop., early hominid, 1.1 to 2.1 million years ago)
Australopithecus garhi (anthrop., early hominid, 2.5 million years ago)
Australopithecus robustus (anthrop., early hominid, 1.5 to 2 million years ago)
Australorp (chicken)
Austria (Republic of)(Eur.)
Austria, Anne of (queen, Fr.; mother of Louis XIV; 1601-66)
Austria, Margaret of (regent, Netherlands; 1480-1530)
Austrian Airlines
Austrinius, Piscis (astron., southern fish)
Austro-Prussian War (also Seven Weeks' War) (Aus./Prussia; 1866)
Austronesian (also Malayo-Polynesian)(lang.)
Authorized Version (of the Bible)(also King James Version)
Autodesk, Inc.
Autoharp (music)
Automat
Automatic Data Processing, Inc.
Automobile (mag.)
Automobile Workers of America, United (UAW) (union, est. 1935)
Automundo (mag.)
AutoNation, Inc.
AutoWeek (mag.)
Autry, Alan (ent.; 1952-)
Autry, Gene (ent.; 1907-98)
Auvergne (region, Fr.)
AV (audiovisual)
Av (also Ab)(Jew. month)
Ava Gardner (ent.; 1922-90)
Avalanche, Chevrolet (auto.)
Avalanche-Journal, Lubbock (TX newspaper)
Avalon (myth. utopia)

Avalon, CA, PA
Avalon, Frankie (b. Francis Thomas Avallone) (ent.; 1939-)
Avalon, Toyota (auto.)
Avandia (med.)
Avant Quattro, Audi (auto.)
Avant, Audi (auto.)
Avanti Motor Corp.
Ave Maria (also *Hail Mary*)(prayer)
Avedon, Richard (US photo.; 1923-)
Aveeno (med.)
Avenger, Dodge (auto.)
Avensa Airlines
Aventis, Strasbourg (Fr. pharmaceutical bus.)
Aventyl (med.)
Averback, Hy (ent.; 1920-97)
Averell Harriman, (William)(US pol./dipl.; 1891-1986)
Averill, Earl (baseball; 1915-83)
Avernus (It. lake, myth. entrance to hell)
Averroe (clothing)
Averroes (Islamic phil.; 1126-98)
Avery Brooks (ent.; 1949-)
Avery Dennison Corp.
Avery Label Systems (US bus.)
Avery Schreiber (ent.; 1935-)
Avery, Milton (artist; 1893-1965)
Avery, Steve (baseball; 1970-)
Avery, Tex (cartoonist, *Bugs Bunny, Porky Pig, Daffy Duck*; 1908-80)
Avesta, Zend- (rel.)
Avia Athletic Footwear (US bus.)
Aviation Week and Space Technology (mag.)
Avignon, France
Avis Rent a Car System, Inc.
Avogadro, Amadeo (It. chem.; 1776-1856)
Avogadro's constant/hypothesis/law/number (chem.)
Avon Products, Inc.
Avonlea (TV show)
Awakening, the Great
AWOL (absent without leave)
Ax, Emmanuel (Rus. ent.; 1949-)
Axelrod, George (playwright; 1922-)
Axelrod, Julius (US neuropharmacol.; 1912-)
Axid (med.)
Axiom, Isuzu (auto.)
Axis (of WW II)
Axl Rose (William Bailey)(ent.; 1962-)
Axminster carpet
Axton, Hoyt (ent.; 1938-99)
Ayatollah Ruhollah Khomenei (Iran, rel.; 1900-89)
Ayatollah Sayyed Ali Khamenei (rel. head, Iran; 1940-)
Ayckbourn, Alan (playwright; 1939-)
Ayer, Francis W. (US adv.; 1848-1923)
Aygestin (med.)
Aykroyd, Dan (ent.; 1952-)
Aylesbury (duck)
Aylesbury, England
Aylwin Azócar, Patricio (ex-pres., Chile; 1918-)
Aymara (lang./people)
Ayn Rand (b. Alisa Rosenbaum)(US writer/phil.; 1905-82)

Ayres, Lew (ent.; 1908-96)
Ayrshire (cattle)
Ayurveda (med., ancient)
AZ (Arizona)
Azali Assoumani (pres., Comoros; 1951-)
Azaria, Hank (ent.; 1964-)
Azazel (evil spirit, rel.)
Azerbaijan (Republic of)(formerly part of USSR)
   (W Asia)
Azerbaijani (lang./people)
Azeri (lang./people)
Azinger, Paul (golf; 1960-)
Aziz (al-Saud), King Fahd ibn Abdul (king,
   Saudi Arabia; 1923-)
Aziz Shah, Sultan Salahuddin Abdul
   (paramount ruler, Malaysia; 1926-)
Azlan (Muhibuddin) Shah, (Rajah)(ex-king,
   Malaysia; 1928-)
Azmacort (med.)
Aznar, José María (PM, Spain; 1953-)
Aznavour, Charles (b. Shahnour Varenagh
   Aznourian)(Fr. ent.; 1924-)
Azo Gantrisin (med.)
Azócar, Patricio Aylwin (ex-pres., Chile; 1918-)
Azores Islands (also the Azores)(mid-Atl.)
AZT (azidothymidine)(med.)
Aztec (Native Amer./Mex.)
Aztec marigold (also African marigold)
Aztec two-step (also Montezuma's
   revenge)(traveler's diarrhea)
Aztek, Pontiac (auto.)
Azulfidine (med.)
Azure, Bentley (auto.)
Azuza, CA
Az-Zarqa, Jordon
Azzedine Laraki (ex-PM, Morocco)

-B-

B (chem. sym., boron)
B. Altman & Co.
BA (Bachelor of Arts)
Ba (chem. sym., barium)
Baal (myth.)
Baal Shem-Tov (also Israel ben Eliezer)(Jew. rel.; c1700-60)
Baalbek, Lebanon (ruins of Temple of the Sun)
Ba'ath Party (Iraqi pol. party)
Baba and the Forty Thieves, Ali (fairy tale)
Baba Yaga (myth. monster, eats children)
Baba, Ali (fict. chara.)
Babangida, Ibrahim (ex-pres., Nigeria; 1941-)
Babar the Elephant (fict. chara.)
Babashoff, Shirley (swimming; 1957-)
Babbage, Charles (Br. math., inv., compu.; 1792-1871)
Babbitt (S. Lewis novel)
Babbitt metal (used for bearings)
Babbitt, Bruce E(dward)(US ex-secy./interior; 1938-)
Babbitt, George F(ollansbee)(fict. chara.)
Babbitt, Milton Byron (US comp.; 1916-)
Babe (Mildred) Didrikson Zaharias (US athlete; 1914-56)
Babe (Floyd Caves) Herman (baseball; 1903-87)
Babe (George Herman) Ruth (baseball; 1895-1948)
Babe Ruth league (baseball)
Babe the Blue Ox (Paul Bunyan's)(US folklore)
Babel, Isaac (Rus. writer; 1894-1941)
Babel, Tower of (Babylon, different languages)
Babes in Toyland (film, 1934)
Babes in Toyland (pop music)
Babi (or Babism)(now Baha'i, Baha'ism)(rel.)
Babrak Karmal (ex-pres., Afghan.; 1929-)
Baby Bells (slang, regional phone cos.)
Baby Doc (Jean-Claude Duvalier)(ex-pres., Haiti; 1951-)
Baby Dodds (Warren)(US jazz; 1898-1959)
Baby Face Nelson (film, 1957)
Baby Jane?, Whatever Happened to (film, 1962)
Baby Jessica (US news)
Baby Magic (baby care prods.)
Baby Ruth (candy)
Baby Snooks (fict. chara, radio)
Babyface (Kenneth Edmonds) (ent.; 1958-)
Babylon (ancient capital of Babylonia)
Babylon, Hanging Gardens of (1 of 7 Wonders of the World)
Babylonia (ancient country)
Babylonian captivity (Isr. hist., exile of the Jews)
Bacall, Lauren (b. Betty Perske)(ent.; 1924-)
Bacardi (rum)
Bacardi cocktail (mixed drink)
Baccarat, Inc.
Bacchanalia (ancient feasts)
Bacchus (also Dionysus)(myth.)
Baccio Bandinelli (It. sculptor; 1493-1560)

Bach, Barbara (ent.; 1947-)
Bach, Catherine (b. Catherine Bachman)(ent.; 1954-)
Bach, Johann Ambrosia (Ger. musician, father of J.S.; 1645-95)
Bach, Johann Christian (Ger. comp., son of J.S.; 1735-82)
Bach, Johann Christoph Friedrich (Ger. comp., bro. of J.S.; 1732-95)
Bach, Johann Sebastian (Ger. comp.; 1685-1750)
Bach, Johannes (or Hans)(Ger. musician, great-grandfather of J.S.; 1580-1626)
Bach, Karl (or Carl) Philipp Emanuel (Ger comp.; 1714-88)
Bach, P. D. Q. (aka Peter Schickele)(ent.; 1935-)
Bach, Richard (US writer; 1936-)
Bach, Wilhelm Friedemann (Ger. comp.; 1710-84)
Bacharach, Burt (US comp.; 1928-)
Bachelor of Arts (B.A.)
Bachelor of Fine Arts (B.F.A.)
Bachelor of Science (B.S.)
Back to the Future (film, 1985)
Back to the Future, Part II (film, 1989)
Back to the Future, Part III (film, 1990)
Backstreet Boys (pop music)
Backus, Jim (ent.; 1913-89)
Bacolod, Philippines
Bacon, Delia Salter (US writer; 1811-59)
Bacon, Francis (Br. artist; 1909-92)
Bacon, Henry (US arch.; 1866-1924)
Bacon, Kevin (ent.; 1958-)
Bacon, Nathaniel (US pol.; 1647-76)
Bacon, Roger (Br. phil./scien.; 1214-94)
Bacon, Sir Francis (Br. phil./pol.; 1561-1626)
Bacon's Rebellion (Nathaniel)(VA; 1676)
Bac-Os (food)
Bactine (med.)
Bactocill (med.)
Bactria (ancient Persian province)
Bactrian camel (2 humps)
Bactrim (med.)
Bad Lands (region, NE/SD)
Bad News Bears, The (film, 1976)
Badajoz, Spain
Badalona, Spain
Baden (former Ger. state)
Baden-Baden, Germany
Baden-Powell, Sir Robert (Br. gen., founded Boy Scouts; 1857-1941)
Baden-Württemberg (state, Ger.)
Badenov, Boris (fict. chara.)
Badenov, Natasha (or Fataly)(fict. chara.)
Bader Ginsburg, Ruth (US jurist; 1933-)
Badger State (nickname, WI)
Badlands National Park (SD)
Badran, Mudar (ex-PM, Jordan)
Badu, Erykah (b. Erica Wright)(ent.; 1971-)
Baedeker, Karl (Ger. guidebook publ.; 1801-1959)
Baer, Max (boxing; 1909-59)
Baez, Joan (ent.; 1941-)
Baffin Bay, Canada
Baffin Island, Northwest Territories, Canada
Baffin, William (Br. nav.; 1584-1622)
Bagabandi, Natsagiyn (pres., Mongolia; 1950-)

Bagehot, Walter (Br. econ./jour.; 1826-77)
Baggie (storage bags)
Baggins, Bilbo (fict. chara.)
Baggins, Frodo (fict. chara.)
Baghdad, Iraq (also Bagdad)
Baha'i (also Baha'ism, Bahai)(formerly Babi, Babism)(rel.)
Bahamas (Commonwealth of the)(islands, SE of FL)
Bahamas Air (airline)
Bahasa Indonesian (lang.)
Bahaullah (Mirza Husayn Ali)(Pers., founded Bahaism; 1817-92)
Bahia grass
Bahía Blanca, Argentina
Bahia, Brazil
Bahrain (State of)(also Bahrein)(SW Asia)
Bahraini (people)
Baia Mare, Romania
Baikal, Lake (also Baykal)(Russia)(deepest lake in the world)
Baikonur (Soviet launch site)
Bailey bridge (temporary, prefab bridge)
Bailey Circus, Barnum &
Bailey Circus, Ringling Brothers and Barnum &
Bailey Olter (pres., Micronesia)
Bailey, Beetle (comic strip)
Bailey, DeFord (ent.; 1899-1982)
Bailey, F(rancis) Lee (US atty.; 1933-)
Bailey, Mildred (US jazz; 1907-51)
Bailey, Nathan(iel)(Br. lexicographer; ?-1742)
Bailey, Old (London criminal court)
Bailey, Pearl (Mae)(US jazz; 1918-90)
Bain de Soleil (health)
Bain, Barbara (ent.; 1931-)
Bain, Conrad (Can. ent.; 1923-)
Bainimarama, Commodore Josaia Voreqe (Fiji mil./pol.)
Bainter, Fay (ent.; 1892-1968)
Baio, Scott (ent.; 1961-)
Bairam (rel. festival)
Baird, Bill (William Britton)(US puppeteer; 1904-87)
Baird, John Logie ("Father of Television")(Scot. eng.; 1888-1946)
Baird, Zoë (US atty.; 1952-)
Baiul, Oksana (figure skating; 1977-)
Baizerman, Saul (US/Rus. sculptor; 1899-1957)
Baja California (state, Mex.)
Baja California Sur (state, Mex.)
Bajan (lang.)
Bajuk, Andrej (PM, Slovenia; 1943-)
baked Alaska (dessert)
Bakelite (1st synthetic plastic)
Bake-Off (cooking contest)
Baker v. Carr (US law; 1962)
Baker, Anita (ent.; 1958-)
Baker, Carroll (ent.; 1931-)
Baker, Chet (US jazz; 1929-88)
Baker, George (cartoonist, *The Sad Sack*; 1915-75)
Baker, Ginger (Peter)(ent.; 1940-)
Baker, James A. III (US pol.; 1930-)
Baker, Joe Don (ent.; 1936-)
Baker, Josephine (ent.; 1906-75)
Baker, Mark Linn- (ent.; 1953-)

Baker, Russell (US jour.; 1925-)
Bakersfield Californian (CA newspaper)
Bakersfield, CA
Bakhtaran, Iran (formerly Kermanshah)
Bakili Muluzi (pres., Malawi; 1943-)
Bakke, Regents of the University of California vs. (US law; 1978)
Bakken, Jim (James Leroy)(football; 1940-)
Bakker, Jim (James Orsen)(US evang.; 1940-)
Bakker, Tammy Faye (LaValley)(ex-wife of Jim Bakker; 1942-)
Bakley, Bonnie (US news; ?-2001)
Bakongo (people)
Bakr, Abu (Islamic leader; 573-634)
Bakshi, Ralph (ent.; 1938-)
Bakst, Léon (Rus. artist/designer; 1867-1924)
Baku, Azerbaijan
Bakula, Scott (ent.; 1954-)
Bakunin, Mikhail (Rus. pol.; 1814-76)
Balaguer, Joaquín Ricardo (ex-pres., Dom. Rep.; 1907-)
Balakirev, Mily Alexeyevich (Rus. comp.; 1837-1910)
Balanchine, George (US choreographer; 1904-83)
Balanta (people)
Balboa Heights, Panama
Balboa, CA
Balboa, Vasco Núñez de (Sp. expl., discovered Pac.; 1475-1519)
Baldassare, Castiglione (It. pol.; 1478-1529)
Balder (myth.)
Baldwin (apple)
Baldwin Park, CA
Baldwin, Alec (ent.; 1958-)
Baldwin, Daniel (ent.; 1960-)
Baldwin, James (US writer; 1924-87)
Baldwin, James Mark (US psych.; 1861-1934)
Baldwin, Stephen (ent.; 1966-)
Baldwin, William (ent.; 1963-)
Bale, Christian (ent.; 1974-)
Baleares (province, Sp.)
Balearic Islands (Mediterranean)
Balenciaga, Cristobal (Sp. designer; 1895-1972)
Balfe, Michael (William)(Ir. comp./ent.; 1808-70)
Balfour Declaration (national home for Jews in Palestine)
Balfour, Arthur James (ex-PM, Br.; 1848-1930)
Bali (clothing)
Bali (Indonesian island)
Bali Ha'i (song)
Balikpapan, Indonesia
Balin, Marty (b. Martyn Jerel Buchwald)(ent.; 1943-)
Balinese (cat)
Balinese (lang.)
Balkan Mountains (Bulgaria)
Balkan Peninsula (SE Eur.)
Balkan States (also the Balkans)(countries occupying Balkan Peninsula)
Balkan Wars (1878-1913)
Balkhash, Lake (Kazakhstan)(salt)
Ball Brothers Glass (canning jars)
Ball jar
Ball Mason jar
Ball Park Franks

Ball State University (Muncie, IN)
Ball, Ernest (US comp.; 1878-1927)
Ball, George W(ildman)(US atty./banker/pol.; 1909-94)
Ball, Lucille (ent.; 1911-89)
Balla, Giacomo (It. artist; 1871?-1958)
Balladur, Édouard (ex-PM, Fr.; 1929-)
Ballantine
Ballantine Books (US bus.)
Ballarat, Victoria, Australia
Ballard, Hank (ent./songwriter; 1936-)
Ballard, J(ames) G(raham)(Br. writer; 1930-)
Ballard, Kaye (b. Catherine Gloria Balotta)(ent.; 1926-)
Balleek ware
Ballesteros, Seve (golf; 1957-)
Ballet Folklórico de México
Ballet Russe de Monte Carlo
Ballington Booth (US, founded Volunteers of America; 1859-1940)
Bally Manufacturing Corp.
balm of Gilead (also balm-of-Gilead)
Balmer, Johann (Jakob)(Swiss math./physt.; 1825-98)
Balmoral (clothing)
Balmoral Castle, Scotland
Balnetar (med.)
balsam of Peru (also Peru balsam)
Balsam, Martin (ent.; 1919-96)
Balsas River (Mex.)
Balthazar (one of three Magi)
Balthus (b. Balthasar Klossowski)(Swiss artist; 1909-2001)
Baltic (lang./people)
Baltic Sea (N. Eur.)
Baltic States (Estonia, Latvia, Lith.)
Baltimore chop (baseball)
Baltimore Evening Sun (MD newspaper)
Baltimore method (real estate)
Baltimore oriole (bird)
Baltimore Orioles (baseball team)
Baltimore Ravens (football team)
Baltimore Sun (MD newspaper)
Baltimore, Barron v. (US law; 1833)
Baltimore, Lord (Sir George Calvert)(founded MD; 1606-75)
Baltimore, MD
Baltimore's Inner Harbor (MD)
Baluchi (lang./people)
Baluchistan region (SE Iran/SW Pak.)
Balzac, Honoré de (Fr. writer; 1799-1850)
Balzers, Liechtenstein
Bamako, Mali
Bamangwato (people)
Bamba, La (film, 1987)
Bamba, La (song)
Bambara (lang./people)
Bambi (F. Salten book)
Bambi (fict. deer)
Bambi (film, 1942)
Bamileke (people)
Bamvuginyumvira, Frederic (PM, Burundi)
Ban Roll-On (anti-perspirant)
Banacek (TV show)
Banana Boat (health)

Banana Republic (US bus.)(l.c. when referring to countries)
Banana River (FL)
Bananas (film, 1971)
Banbury (Eng. market town)
Banbury cake (also Banbury bun)(pastry)
Banbury tart
Banc of America Investment Services, Inc.
Bancroft, Anne (b. Anna Maria Italiano)(ent.; 1931-)
Bancroft, George (ent.; 1882-1956)
Bancroft, George (US hist.; 1800-91)
Banda (Indonesian islands)
Banda (people)
Banda Sea (Indonesia)
Banda, (Ngwazi) Hastings Kamuzu (ex-pres., Malawi; 1902-97)
Band-Aid (med.)
Bandar Seri Begawan, Brunei (formerly Brunei Town)
Bandaranaike, Sirimavo (ex-PM, Sri Lanka; 1916-2000)
Bandaranaike, Solomon West Ridgeway Dias (ex-PM, Sri Lanka; 1899-1959)
B & B (bed and breakfast)
B and B (liqueur)
B & E (breaking and entering)
Banderas, Antonio (ent.; 1960-)
Bandinelli, Baccio (It. sculptor; 1493-1560)
Bandit Queen, India's (Phoolan Devi)(Indian bandit/pol.; 1963-2001)
Bandung, Java (Indonesia)(also Bandoeng)
Banff National Park (Can.)
Banff, Alberta, Canada
Banff, Scotland
Bang's disease (of cattle)
Bangalore, India
Bangkok, Thailand
Bangla (also Bengali)(lang.)
Bangladesh (People's Republic of)(S Asia)
Bangor News (ME newspaper)
Bangor Submarine Base (WA)(mil.)
Bangor, ME
Bangui, Central African Republic
Bangwaketse (people)
Bani, John (pres., Vanuatu; 1941-)
Banja, Bosnia-Hercegovina
Banjermasin, Indonesia
Banjul, Gambia
Bank of America Corp.
Bank of Credit and Commerce International (BCCI)(internat'l banking scandal; 1991)
Bank of England
Bank One Corp.
Bankers Trust
Bankhead, Tallulah (ent.; 1902-68)
Bankruptcy Reform Act (US hist.; 1978)
Banks, Ernie (baseball; 1931-)
Banks, Jonathan (ent.; 1947-)
Banks, Tyra (model/ent.; 1973-)
Ban-Lon (also Banlon)(textile)
Banner, Nashville (TN newspaper)
Bannister, Sir Roger (Gilbert)(Br. runner/phys.; 1929-)
Bannon, Jack (ent.; 1940-)

Banon (cheese)
Banquet Foods Corp.
Banquo (fict. chara., *Macbeth*)
Bantam chicken (also l.c.)
Bantam Doubleday Dell Publishing Group, Inc.
Banting, Frederick Grant (physiol.; 1891-1941)
Bantu (lang./people)
Banzai, Buckaroo (fict. chara.)
Bapounon (people)
Baptist (rel.)
Baptist Church
Bar Harbor, ME
Bara, Theda (b. Theodosia Goodman)(ent.;
    1890-1955)
Barabbas (Biblical thief)
Barak T. Sopé (PM, Vanuatu)
Barak, Ehud (ex-PM, Isr.; 1942-)
Baraka, Imamu Amiri (aka LeRoi
    Jones)(playwright; 1934-)
Baranski, Christine (ent.; 1952-)
Barbados (island, British West Indies)
Barbara (Pierce) Bush (US daughter of pres./
    granddaughter of ex-pres.; 1981-)
Barbara A. Mikulski (US cong.; 1936-)
Barbara Ann Cochran (skiing; 1951-)
Barbara Bach (ent.; 1947-)
Barbara Bailey Kennelly (US cong.; 1936-)
Barbara Bain (ent.; 1931-)
Barbara Barrie (ent.; 1931-)
Barbara Bel Geddes (ent.; 1922-)
Barbara Bosson (ent.; 1939-)
Barbara Boxer (nee Levy)(US cong.; 1940-)
Barbara Bush (nee Pierce)(US mother of pres./
    wife of ex-pres.; 1925-)
Barbara Cartland, Dame (Br. writer; 1902-2000)
Barbara Cook (ent.; 1927-)
Barbara Eden (ent.; 1934-)
Barbara Feldon (ent.; 1941-)
Barbara Ferris (ent.; 1940-)
Barbara Frietchie (C. Fitch play)
Barbara Hale (ent.; 1922-)
Barbara Harris (b. Sandra Markowitz)(ent.; 1935-)
Barbara Hepworth (sculptor; 1903-75)
Barbara Hershey (b. Barbara Herzstein)(ent.;
    1948-)
Barbara Hutton (US heiress; 1887-1979)
Barbara (Charline) Jordan (US atty./educ./pol.;
    1936-96)
Barbara Kingsolver (US writer; 1955-)
Barbara Mandrell (ent.; 1948-)
Barbara McClintock (US geneticist; 1902-92)
Barbara Roberts (nee Hughey)(ex-OR gov.; 1936-)
Barbara Rush (ent.; 1930-)
Barbara Stanwyck (ent.; 1907-90)
Barbara Walters (US TV jour.; 1931-)
Barbara Ward (Baroness Jackson of
    Lodsworth)(Br. econ.; 1914-81)
Barbara Woodhouse (Br. dog trainer, writer;
    1910-88)
Barbara W(ertheim) Tuchman (US writer/hist.;
    1912-89)
Barbara, Major (film, 1941)
Barbarella (film, 1968)
Barbarosa (film, 1982)
Barbarossa (Frederick I, "Red Beard")(Holy

Roman emp.; 1123-90)
Barbarossa I (aka Arouj)(Turk. pirate; 1473?-
    1518)
Barbarossa II (aka Khair ed-Din)(Turk. pirate;
    c1466-1546)
Barbary ape
Barbary Coast (NAfr.)
Barbary Coast (San Francisco)
Barbary horse
Barbary sheep
Barbary States (Afr.)
Barbasol (healthcare)
Barbeau, Adrienne (ent.; 1945-)
Barber of Seville, The (Beaumarchais play, G.
    Rossini opera)
Barber, Red (Walter)(ent.; 1908-92)
Barber, Samuel (US comp.; 1910-81)
Barbera (wine)
Barbera, Joe (cartoonist, *Tom & Jerry, Huckleberry
    Hound, Yogi Bear, Flintstones*; 1911-)
Barbers Point Naval Air Station (HI)
Barbers Point, HI (also Kalaeloa Point)
Barbi Benton (US Playmate; 1950-)
Barbie (mag.)
Barbie doll
Barbie, Klaus (Ger. Nazi leader; 1913-91)
Barbirolli, Sir John (Br. cond.; 1899-1970)
Barbizon School (Fr. group of artists)
Barbizon, France
Barbour, John (Scot. poet; 1316?-95)
Barbra Streisand (ent.; 1942-)
Barbuda, Antigua and (State of)
Barcalounger Co.
Barcellona, Italy
Barcelona chair
Barcelona, Spain
Barclay Plager (hockey; 1941-88)
Bard of Avon (Shakespeare)
Bardeen, John (US physt.; 1908-91)
Bardi, Beatrice Portinari de' (inspiration for
    Dante's Beatrice; 1266-90)
Bardolino (wine)
Bardot, Brigitte (b. Camille Javal)(Fr. ent.;
    1934-)
Barefoot in the Park (play)
Barenboim, Daniel (Isr. pianist/cond.; 1942-)
Barents Sea (part of Arctic Ocean)
Baretta (TV show)
Barger, Sonny (Ralph)(founder, Hell's Angels;
    1938-)
Bari, Italy
Bariba (people)
Barkat Gourad Hamadou (PM, Djibouti; 1930-)
Barker, Bob (ent.; 1923-)
Barker, Clive (writer; 1952-)
Barkin, Ellen (ent.; 1954-)
Barkley, Alben William (ex-US VP; 1877-1956)
Barkley, Charles (basketball; 1963-)
Barksdale Air Force Base, LA
Barlach, Ernst (Heinrich)(Ger. sculptor/writer;
    1870-1938)
Barleycorn, John (personification of alcohol)
Barmecide (fict. chara., *Arabian Nights*)
Barmecide feast (false feast with empty dishes)
Barmecides (wealthy, powerful Persian family;

fl. 752-803)

Barnabas Sibusiso Dlamini (PM, Swaziland; 1942-)

Barnabas, St. ("fellow laborer")

Barnard College of Columbia University (NYC)

Barnard Hughes (ent.; 1915-)

Barnard, Dr. Christiaan (SAfr. phys., performed 1st human heart transplant; 1922-2001)

Barnard, Henry (US educ.; 1811-1900)

Barnardo, Thomas (Br. reformer; 1845-1905)

Barnburners v. Hunkers (US pol.; mid 1800s)

Barnes & Noble Booksellers (US bus.)

Barnes & Noble Bookstores, Inc.

Barnes & Noble, Inc.

Barnes, Roy E(ugene)(GA gov.)

Barnett Newman (US artist; 1905-70)

Barnette, West Virginia State Board of Education v. (US law; 1943)

Barnevelder (chicken)

Barney (TV dinosaur)

Barney & Friends (TV show)

Barney Bigard (US jazz; 1906-80)

Barney Frank (US cong.; 1940-)

Barney Google (cartoon)

Barney Kessel (US jazz; 1923-)

Barney Miller (TV show)

Barney (Berna Eli) Oldfield (auto racing; 1878-1946)

Barney Rubble (cartoon chara.)

Barnie's Coffee & Tea Co., Inc.

BarNone (candy)

Barns v. Glen Theater (US law; 1991)

Barnsley, England

Barnum & Bailey Circus

Barnum, P(hineas) T(aylor)(ent., circus; 1810-91)

Barolo (wine)

Baron Philippe de Rothschild (wine)

Baron Vaea (ex-PM, Tonga)

Baroque (style of art/arch.)

Barquisimeto, Venezuela

Barr, Roseanne (ent.; 1952-)

Barr body (also sex chromatin)(med.)

Barr virus, Epstein- (EBV)(med.)

Barr, Murray L. (Can. phys.; 1908-95)

Barranquilla, Colombia

Barré reflex/syndrome, Guillain- (med.)

Barre, MA, VT

Barred Rock (chicken)

Barrès, Maurice (Fr. writer/pol.; 1862-1923)

Barrett Browning, Elizabeth (Br. poet, wife of Robert; 1806-61)

Barrett, Rona (b. Rona Burstein)(US gossip columnist; 1936-)

Barricini/Loft's Candies, Inc.

Barrie Dunsmore (US journ.)

Barrie, Barbara (ent.; 1931-)

Barrie, Ontario, Canada

Barrie, Sir James M. (Br. writer; 1860-1937)

Barris, Chuck (ent.; 1929-)

Barron v. Baltimore (US law; 1833)

Barron's Educational Series, Inc.

Barron's National Business and Financial Weekly

Barrow, Clyde (US criminal; 1900-34)

Barrow, (Ruth) Nita (ex-gov.-gen.; Barbados; 1916-95)

Barrow, Point, AK (northernmost point of US)

Barrow-in-Furness, England

Barry Bonds (baseball; 1964-)

Barry Bostwick (ent.; 1945-)

Barry Corbin (ent.; 1940-)

Barry Fitzgerald (ent.; 1888-1961)

Barry Levinson (ent.; 1932-)

Barry Lyndon (film, 1975)

Barry Manilow (b. Barry Alan Pincus)(ent.; 1946-)

Barry Mann (US comp.; 1939-)

Barry M(orris) Goldwater (US pol.; 1909-98)

Barry M(orris) Goldwater, Jr. (US pol.; 1938-)

Barry Serafin (US TV jour.)

Barry Sonnenfeld (ent.; 1953-)

Barry Sullivan (ent.; 1912-)

Barry White (ent.; 1944-)

Barry, Dave (US writer/humorist; 1947-)

Barry, Gene (ent.; 1919-)

Barry, John (US mil.; 1745-1803)

Barry, Madame (Jeanne Bécu) du (Comtesse, mistress, Louis XV; 1743-93)

Barry, Marion (ex-mayor, Washington DC; 1936-)

Barry, Philip (US writer; 1896-1949)

Barry, Rick (Richard)(basketball; 1944-)

Barry, Sy (Seymour)(cartoonist; 1928-)

Barrymore, Diana (ent.; 1921-60)

Barrymore, Drew (ent.; 1975-)

Barrymore, Ethel (ent.; 1879-1959)

Barrymore, John (Blythe)(ent.; 1882-1942)

Barrymore, John Drew (ent.; 1932-)

Barrymore, Lionel (ent.; 1878-1954)

Barrymore, Maurice (ent.; 1848-1905)

Bars, Stars and (also Southern Cross) (Confederate flag)

Barstow Marine Corps Logistics Base (CA)

Barstow, CA

Bart Simpson (cartoon chara.)

Bart Starr (football; 1934-)

Bart(lett) Giamatti, (Angelo)(US educ./writer/ baseball; 1938-89)

Barth, John (US writer; 1930-)

Barth, Karl (Swed. rel.; 1886-1968)

Barthelme, Donald (writer; 1931-89)

Barthes, Roland (Fr. critic; 1915-80)

Bartholdi, Frederic-Auguste (Fr. sculptor, designed Statue of Liberty; 1834-1904)

Bartholomeu Dias (also Diaz)(Port. expl.; c1450-1500)

Bartholomew, Freddie (ent.; 1925-92)

Bartholomew, St. (apostle)

Bartiromo, Maria (TV finan. jour.; 1967-)

Bartles & Jaymes (wine coolers)

Bartlett pear

Bartlett, John (US publ./editor, *Familiar Quotations*; 1820-1905)

Bartlett's *Familiar Quotations* (book)

Bartók, Béla (Hung. comp.; 1881-1945)

Bartoli, Cecilia (US opera; 1972-)

Bartolomé Estebán Murillo (Sp. artist; 1618-82)

Bartolommeo, Fra (It. artist; 1472-1517)

Bartolommeo, Michelozzo di (aka Michelozzo Michelozzi)(It. sculptor/arch.; 1396-1472)

Barton Silversmiths, Reed & (US bus.)

Barton Yarborough (ent.; 1900-51)

Barton, Clara (U.S., founded American Red Cross; 1821-1912)
Barton, Reed &
Barty, Billy (b. William John Bertanzetti)(ent.; 1924-2000)
Baruch (rel., Apocrypha)
Baruch Spinoza (also Benedict de)(Dutch phil.; 1632-77)
Baruch, Bernard M. (US finan./pol.; 1870-1965)
Baryshnikov, Mikhail (Latvian/US dancer; 1948-)
Basaljel (med.)
Basdeo Panday (PM, Trinidad/Tobago; 1933-)
Base Exchange (BX)
Baseball Clubs, American League of Professional
Baseball Digest (mag.)
Baseball Hall of Fame and Museum, National (est. 1939, Cooperstown, NY)
Basehart, Richard (ent.; 1914-84)
Basel, Switzerland
Basenji (dog)(also l.c.)
BASF Corp.
Bashar al-Assad, Dr. (pres., Syria; 1965-)
Bashir, Gen. Omar Hassan Ahmed al- (pres., Sudan; 1944-)
Bashkir (lang./people)
Bashō Matsuo (aka Matsuo Munefusa)(Jap. poet, haiku; 1644-94)
BASIC (Beginners' All-Purpose Symbolic Instruction Code)(compu.)
Basic English
Basie, Count (William)(US jazz; 1904-84)
Basil Cardinal Hume (Br. rel.; 1923-99)
Basil Rathbone (ent.; 1892-1967)
Basildon, England
Basinger, Kim (ent.; 1953-)
Baskerville (type style)
Baskerville, John (Br. typographer; 1706-75)
Baskervilles, The Hound of the (by A.C. Doyle)
Basket Maker Indian culture
Basketball Association, National (NBA)
Basketball Digest (mag.)
Baskin-Robbins Ice Cream Co.
Basque (also Basque Provinces)(region, Sp.)
Basque (lang./people)
Basra, Iraq
Bass (shoes)
Bass Pro Shops, Inc.
Bass, Lance (ent., 'N Sync; 1979-)
Basse-Normandie (region, Fr.)
Basse-Terre, Guadeloupe
Basseterre, St. Kitts and Nevis
Bassett Furniture Industries, Inc.
Bassett, Angela (ent.; 1958-)
Bassey, Shirley (ent.; 1937-)
Bastille Day (Fr.)
Bastille, the (former castle/prison, Paris)
Bastogne, Belgium
Basutoland (now called Lesotho)(SAfr.)
Bat (William Barclay) Masterson (US marshal; 1853-1921)
Bata, Equatorial Guinea
Bataan Death March (Phil.)
Bataan, Philippines
Batak Toda (lang.)

Batalla, Francesc Badia (covicar, Andorra)
Batangas, Luzon, Philippines
Batchelor, Clarence Daniel (pol. cartoonist; 1888-1977)
Bateke (people)
Bateman, Jason (ent.; 1969-)
Bateman, Justine (ent.; 1966-)
Bates, Alan (ent.; 1934-)
Bates, Katharine Lee (US poet/educ.; 1859-1929)
Bates, Kathy (ent.; 1948-)
Bath chair (type of wheelchair)
Bath, England
Bath, Order of the (Br. order of knighthood)
Bathinette
Bathsheba (rel., wife of King David)
Batista y Zaldivar, Fulgencio (ex-dictator, Cuba; 1901-73)
Batiuk, Tom (cartoonist; 1947-)
Batlle Ibanez, Jorge (pres., Uruguay; 1927-)
Batman (film, cartoon)
Batman and Robin (film, cartoon)
Baton Rouge Advocate (LA newspaper)
Baton Rouge, LA
Battambang, Cambodia
Battenberg cake
Battersea district (old London)
Battle Creek, MI
Battle of Actium (Rome, 31 BC)
Battle of Agincourt (Eng./Fr.; 1415)
Battle of Algiers (Algeria/Fr.; 1954-62)
Battle of Antietam (US hist.; 1862)
Battle of Brandywine (US hist.; 1777)
Battle of Britain (WWII air battle)
Battle(s) of Bull Run (US hist.; 1861 & 1862)
Battle of Bunker Hill (Breed's Hill)(US hist., MA; 1775)
Battle(s) of Cambrai (WWI; 1917)
Battle of Chancellorsville (US hist.; 1863)
Battle(s) of Chattanooga (US hist.; 1863)
Battle of Corregidor (WWII; 1942)
Battle of Dien Bien Phu (also Dienbienphu) (NViet.; 1954)
Battle of Edgehill (Eng.; 1642)
Battle of Fredericksburg (US hist.; 1862)
Battle of Gettysburg (US hist.; 1863)
Battle of Hastings (Br. hist.; 1066)
Battle of Iwo Jima (WWII; 1945)
Battle of Lexington (US hist.; 1775)
Battle of Marathon (Gr./Persia; 490 BC)
Battle of Monmouth (US hist.; 1778)
Battle of New Orleans (US/Br.; 1815)(Amer. Civil War; 1862)
Battle(s) of Saratoga (US hist.; 1777)
Battle of Shiloh (also Pittsburg Landing)(US hist.; 1862)
Battle of the Bulge (WWII; 1944-45)
Battle of the Little Bighorn (also Custer's Last Stand)(US/Sioux Native Amer.; 1876)
Battle of the Wilderness (US hist.; 1864)
Battle of Tippecanoe (US hist.; 1811)
Battle of Trafalgar (Br./Fr.-Sp.; 1805)
Battle of Waterloo (Napoleon's defeat; 1815)
Battle, Kathleen (opera; 1948-)
Battlestar Galactica (film, 1979)
Batumi, Georgia

Bat-Yam, Israel
Baucus, Max (US cong.; 1941-)
Baudelaire, Charles Pierre (Fr. poet; 1821-67)
Baudouin, King (Belgium; 1930-93)
Bauer Expedition Outfitter, Eddie (US bus.)
Bauer, Hank (Henry)(baseball; 1922-)
Baugh, Sammy (Samuel Adrian)(football; 1914-)
Bauhaus (Ger. school of design)
Baule (lang./people)
Baum, L(yman) Frank (US writer; 1856-1919)
Baumeister, Willi (Ger. artist; 1889-1955)
Baumer Candle Co., Inc., Will &
Baumgarten's (US bus.)
Bausch & Lomb (vision care)
Bausch & Lomb, Inc.
Bavaria (state, Ger.)
Bavarian cream (dessert)
Bawoyeu, Jean Alingue (ex-PM, Chad)
Baxter International, Inc.
Baxter, Anne (ent.; 1923-85)
Baxter, Meredith (ent.; 1947-)
Bay City, MI, TX
Bay of Bengal (part of Indian Ocean)
Bay of Biscay (Fr./Sp.)
Bay of Fundy (N Atl., Can.)
Bay of Pigs (Cuban inlet, invasion)
Bay State (nickname, MA)
Bay, Willow (model, TV jour.; 1963-)
Baya (people)
Bayamón, Puerto Rico
Bayard Rustin (US civil rights leader; 1910-87)
Bayard Taylor, (James)(US jour.; 1825-78)
Bayer (med.)
Bayeux Tapestry (Fr., depicting Norman
    Conquest; created 11th c.)
Bayeux, France
Bayh, Evan (US cong./ex-IN gov.; 1955-)
Bayi, Filbert (runner; 1953-)
Baykal, Lake (also Baikal)(Russia)(deepest lake
    in the world)
Baylor University (Waco, TX)
Baylor, Elgin (basketball; 1934-)
Bayonne Military Ocean Terminal (NJ)(mil.)
Bayonne, France
Bayonne, NJ
Bayou State (nickname, MS)
Bayreuth Wagner Festival (Bavaria, Ger.)
Bayreuth, Germany
Bazin, Marc (ex-PM, Haiti)
Baziotes, William (US artist; 1912-63)
Bazooka Joe (bubble gum)
BBA (Bachelor of Business Administration)
BBC (British Broadcasting Corporation)(TV)
BBC America (British Broadcasting Corporation
    America)(TV channel)
B. B. King (b. Riley B. King)(ent.; 1925-)
B-bomb (slang, benzedrine inhaler)
BC (before Christ, British Columbia)
BC (comic strip)
B cell (also beta cell)(med.)
B complex (vitamin)
B. Cribari & Sons Winery (US bus.)
B. Dalton Bookseller (US bus.)
Be (chem. sym., beryllium)
Bea Arthur (Beatrice)(b. Bernice Frankel)(ent.;
    1926-)
Bea Wain (ent.; 1917-)
Beach Boys, the (pop music)
Beacon Journal, Akron (OH newspaper)
Beal, John (ent.; 1909-97)
Beale Air Force Base, CA (mil.)
Beals, Jennifer (ent.; 1963-)
Beam Brands Co., Jim
Beamon, Bob (jumper; 1946-)
Bean, Alan L(aVern)(astro.; 1932-)
Bean, Inc., L. L. (US bus.)
Bean, Judge Roy (US frontier; 1825?-1903)
Bean, Orson (ent.; 1928-)
Beanee Weenee
Beanie Baby
Bear Bryant, (Paul)(football coach; 1913-83)
Bear Co., The Gummy
Bear Mountain(s)(NY & PA)
Bear, Smokey the (fict. chara.)
Bear, Stearns & Co., Inc.
Bear, Yogi (cartoon)
Bear's Jellystone Park Camp-Resort, Yogi (US
    bus.)
Beard, Charles A. (US hist.; 1874-1948)
Beardsley gown (Br. gown; 19th c.)
Beardsley, Aubrey Vincent (Br. artist; 1872-98)
Bears, Chicago (football team)
Beasley, Allyce (ent.; 1954-)
Beast, Beauty and the (fairy tale; TV show;
    film, 1946, 1983, 1991)
Beastie Boys (pop music)
Beat Generation (also Beat
    movement)(beatniks; 1950s-60s)
Beat the Clock (TV show)
Beatitudes (Jesus' blessings, Sermon on the Mount)
Beatles, the (pop music)
Beatles, The Compleat (film, 1982)
Beaton, Sir Cecil (Br. photo.; 1904-80)
Beatrice "Bea" Arthur (b. Bernice Frankel)(ent.;
    1926-)
Beatrice Cos., Inc.
Beatrice Lillie (ent.; 1894-1989)
Beatrice Portinari de' Bardi (inspiration for
    Dante's Beatrice; 1266-90)
Beatrice Straight (ent.; 1918-)
Beatrice Tanner (aka Mrs. Patrick
    Campbell)(ent.; 1865-1940)
Beatrice (Potter) Webb, (Martha)(Br. reformer/
    writer; 1858-1943)
Beatrice, Princess (daughter of Prince Andrew
    and Sarah; 1988-)
Beatrix (Wilhelmina Armgard), Queen (queen,
    Netherlands; 1938-)
Beatrix Potter (Helen)(Br. writer/artist; 1866-
    1943)
Beattie, Ann (US writer; 1947-)
Beatty, Clyde (ent.; 1904-65)
Beatty, Ned (ent.; 1937-)
Beatty, Warren (ent.; 1937-)
Beau Bassin, Mauritius
Beau Bridges (b. Lloyd Vernet Bridges III)(ent.; ;
    1941-)
Beau Brummell (film, 1954)
Beau (George Bryan) Brummell (Br. dandy;
    1778-1840)

Beau Brummell Ties (US bus.)
Beau Geste (film, 1939)
Beau (Richard) Nash (Br. dandy/gambler; 1674-1761)
Beaufort Marine Corps Air Station (SC)
Beaufort scale (wind velocity)
Beaufort Sea (part of the Arctic Ocean)
Beaufort, NC, SC
Beaujolais (wine)
Beaumarchais, Pierre Augustin Caron de (Fr. writer; 1732-99)
Beaumont Enterprise (TX newspaper)
Beaumont, Francis (Br. dramatist; 1584-1616)
Beaumont, TX
Beauport, Quebec, Canada
Beauregard, P(ierre) G(ustave) T(outant)(US gen.; 1818-93)
Beauty and the Beast (fairy tale; TV show; film, 1946, 1983, 1991)
Beauvoir, Simone de (Fr. writer; 1908-86)
Beaver Cleaver ("the Beaver")(fict. chara.)
Beaver Falls, PA
Beaver, Leave It to (TV show; film, 1997)
Beaverbrook, William Maxwell, Baron (aka Lord Beaverbrook)(Br. finan./pol.; 1879-1964)
Beaverton, OR
Beavis and Butt-Head (TV show)
Bebe Daniels (ent.; 1901-71)
Bebe (Beatrice) Neuwirth (ent.; 1958-)
Bechet, Sidney (US jazz; 1897-1959)
Bechuanaland (now Botswana)(SAfr.)
Beck (b. Beck Hansen)(ent.; 1970-)
Beck, C. C. (cartoonist, *Captain Marvel*; 1910-89)
Beck, John (ent.; 1943-)
Beck's (beer)
Becker, Boris (tennis; 1967-)
Becker, Paula Modersohn- (Ger. artist; 1867-1907)
Becket, St. Thomas à (Br. rel./pol.; 1118-70)
Beckett Baseball Card Monthly (mag.)
Beckett, Samuel (Ir. writer; 1906-89)
Beckham, Victoria (aka Posh Spice)(ent.; 1974-)
Becklin-Neugebauer object (astron.)
Beckmann, Max (Ger. artist; 1884-1950)
Becky Sharp (fict. chara., *Vanity Fair*)
Beclovent (med.)
Beconase (med.)
Becquerel rays (now gamma rays)
Becquerel, Alexandre-Edmond (Fr. physt.; 1820-91)
Becquerel, Antoine-César (Fr. physt.; 1788-1878)
Becquerel, Antoine-Henri (Fr. physt.; 1852-1908)
Becton Dickinson Co.
Bede, St. ("the Venerable Bede")(Br. rel./hist.; c673-735)
Bedelia, Bonnie (ent.; 1948-)
Bedford, England (also Bedfordshire, Beds)
Bedford, IN, MA, OH, PA, TX, VA
Bedford-Stuyvesant (Brooklyn neighborhood)
Bedie, Henri Konan (ex-pres., Ivory Coast; 1934-)
Bedivere, Sir (Arthurian legend)
Bedlam (early Eng. mental hospital)
Bedlington terrier (dog)
Bedloe's Island (now Liberty Island)(NY)
Bedouin (or Beduin)(people)

Bedrich Smetana (Czech. comp.; 1824-84)
Bedtime for Bonzo (film, 1951)
Bee Gees, the (pop music)
Bee, Clair (basketball; 1896-1983)
Bee, Fresno (CA newspaper)
Bee, Modesto (CA newspaper)
Bee, Sacramento (CA newspaper)
Beebe, (Charles) William (US nat./expl./writer; 1877-1962)
Beecham, Sir Thomas (Br. cond.; 1879-1961)
Beecham, SmithKline (US bus.)
Beecher, Henry Ward (US rel./abolitionist; 1813-87)
Beech-Nut, Inc.
Beef Tonight (sauce)
beef Bourguignonne
beef Stroganoff (also l.c.)
beef Wellington
Beefaroni
Beefeater (Br. Yeoman of the Guard)
Beefheart, Captain (b. Don Van Vliet)(ent.; 1941-)
Beefsteak Charlie's, Inc.
Beehive State (nickname, UT)
Beelzebub (Satan/a devil)
Beene, Geoffrey (US designer; 1927-)
Beerbohm, Sir Max (Br. critic/caricaturist; 1872-1956)
Beer-Nuts
Beersheba, Israel
Beery, Noah (ent.; 1884-1946)
Beery, Noah, Jr. (ent.; 1913-94)
Beery, Wallace (ent.; 1889-1949)
Beethoven (St. Bernard; film, 1992)
Beethoven, Ludwig van (Ger. comp.; 1770-1827)
Beetle Bailey (comic strip)
Beetle, Volkswagen (auto.)
Beetle, Volkswagen New (auto.)
Beetlejuice (film, 1988)
Begin, Menachem (ex-PM, Isr.; 1913-92)
Begley, Ed (ent.; 1901-70)
Begley, Ed, Jr. (ent.; 1949-)
Begum Khaleda Zia (ex-PM, Bangladesh; 1944-)
Behan, Brendan (Ir. writer; 1923-64)
Behrens, Peter (Ger. arch.; 1868-1940)
Behring, Emil von (Ger. bacteriol.; 1854-1917)
Behrman, S(amuel) N(athaniel)(US writer; 1893-1973)
Beiderbecke, Bix (Leon Bismarck)(US jazz; 1903-31)
Beijing duck (also Peking duck)
Beijing man (also Peking Man)(*Homo erectus*)
Beijing, China (formerly Peking)
Beineix, Jean-Jacques (ent.; 1946-)
Being John Malkovich (film, 1999)
Being There (film, 1979)
Beira, Mozambique
Beirut, Lebanon (also Beyrouth)
Beja (lang./people)
Bejarano, Gustavo Noboa (pres., Ecuador; 1937-)
Bekaa Valley (Lebanon)
Bekins Van Lines Co.
Bel (myth.)
Bel Geddes, Barbara (ent.; 1922-)
Bel Geddes, Norman (US designer; 1893-1958)
Bel Paese (cheese)

Béla Bartók (Hung. comp.; 1881-1945)
Bela Karolyi (gymnastics; 1942-)
Béla Kun (Hung. pol.; 1885-1938)
Bela Lugosi (ent.; 1882-1956)
Belafonte, Harry (ent.; 1927-)
Belafonte, Shari (ent.; 1954-)
Belaid Abdesalam (Algerian pol.; 1928-)
Belarus (people)
Belarus (Republic of)(formerly part of USSR)(E central Eur.)
Belasco, David (US writer/ent.; 1854-1931)
Belau (Republic of)(formerly Palau)(island, Micronesia)
Belch, Sir Toby (fict. chara., *Twelfth Night*)
Belem, Brazil
Belfast, Northern Ireland
Belgaum, India
Belgian (horse)
Belgian Congo (Zaire)(now Democratic Republic of the Congo)
Belgian endive
Belgian hare
Belgian Malinois (dog)
Belgian sheepdog (also Groenendael)(dog)
Belgian Tervuren (dog)
Belgium (Kingdom of)
Belgrade, Serbia
Belgrave Square (London)
Belgravia (district in London)
Belial (Satan, evil personified)
Believe It or Not!, Ripley's
Belinda Carlisle (ent.; 1958-)
Belinda, Johnny (film, 1948)
Beliveau, Jean (hockey; 1931-)
Belize (formerly British Honduras)
Belize City, Belize
Bell & Howell Co.
Bell Atlantic Corp.
Bell for Adano, A (film, 1945)
Bell Laboratories, Inc.
Bell, Alexander Graham (US inv., telephone; 1847-1922)
Bell, Bonne (cosmetics)
Bell, Grove City v. (US law; 1984)
Bell, Inc., Bonne
Bell, Ma (slang, AT&T)
Bell, Quentin (writer/artist; 1910-96)
Bell, Rickey (football; 1949-84)
Bell's palsy (med.)
Bella (Savitzky) Abzug (US pol.; 1920-98)
Bella Spewack (playwright; 1899-1990)
Bellamy, Edward (US writer; 1850-98)
Bellamy, Ralph (ent.; 1904-91)
Bellatrix (astron.)
Belle Isle, Strait of (Labrador/Newfoundland)
Belle Starr (b. Myra Belle Shirley)(US outlaw; 1848-89)
Belleek ware (porcelain)
Bellén, Sixto Durán (ex-pres., Ecuador; 1921-)
Bellergal (med.)
Bellerophon (also Bellerophontes)(myth.)
Belleville, IL, KS, NJ
Belleville, Ontario, Canada
Bellevue Hospital (NYC)
Bellevue, KY, NE, OH, PA, WA

Bellflower, CA
Belli, Melvin (Mouron)(US atty.; 1907-96)
Bellingham, MA, WA
Bellini, Gentile (It. artist; 1426-1507)
Bellini, Giovanni (It. artist; 1426-1516)
Bellini, Jacopo (It. artist; 1400-70)
Bellini, Vincenzo (It. comp.; 1801-35)
Bellisario, Donald P. (US writer/producer; 1936-)
Bellow, Saul (US writer; 1915-)
Bellows, George Wesley (US artist; 1882-1925)
Bellows, Gil (ent.; 1967-)
BellSouth Corp.
Belluschi, Pietro (US arch.; 1899-1994)
Belmondo, Jean-Paul (Fr. ent.; 1933-)
Belmont Park Race Track
Belmont Park, NY
Belmont Stakes (racing)
Belmont, August (US finan.; 1816-90)
Belmont, CA, MA, NC
Belmonts, Dion and the (pop music)
Belmopan, Belize
Belnid Absessalem (ex-PM, Algeria)
Belo Horizonte, Brazil
Beloit, WI
Belorussia (also Byelorussia)(former USSR republic)
Belorussian (lang.)
Belouch (Pers. rug)
Belsen (Ger./Nazi concentration camp)
Belshazzar (rel.)
Beltone Electronics Corp.
Beltsy, Moldova
Beluga Caviar Imports & Exports (US bus.)
Belushi, James "Jim" (ent.; 1954-)
Belushi, John (ent.; 1949-82)
Belvedere Winery (US bus.)
Belvedere, Mr. (TV show)
Belvoir, Fort, VA (mil.)
Belyayev, Pavel I. (cosmo.; 1925-70)
Belzer, Richard (ent.; 1944-)
Beman, Deane (golf; 1938-)
Bemba (lang./people)
Bembo (typeface)
Ben Affleck (ent.; 1972-)
Ben Ali, Zine el-Abidine (pres., Tunisia; 1936-)
Ben & Jerry's Homemade Ice Cream
Ben & Jerry's Homemade, Inc.
Ben Blue (ent.; 1901-75)
Ben Bradlee (US publ.; 1921-)
Ben Cayetano (Benjamin Jerome)(HI gov.; 1939-)
Ben Cohen (Ben & Jerry's)
Ben Crenshaw (golf; 1952-)
Ben Cross (ent.; 1948-)
Ben Franklin Stores (US bus.)
Ben Gazzara (ent.; 1930-)
Ben-Gay (med.)
Ben Grauer (ent.; 1908-77)
Ben-Gurion, David (ex-PM, Isr.; 1886-1973)
Ben Hecht (US writer; 1894-1964)
Ben Hogan (golf; 1912-97)
Ben Hur (film, 1959)
Ben Johnson (Can. runner; 1961-)
Ben Johnson (ent.; 1918-96)
Ben Jonson (Br. writer; 1572-1637)

Ben Kingsley (b. Krishna Bhanji)(ent.; 1943-)
Ben Murphy (ent.; 1942-)
Ben Nelson, (Earl Benjamin)(US cong./ex-NE gov.; 1941-)
Ben Nicholson (Br. artist; 1894-1982)
Ben Nighthorse Campbell (US cong.; 1933-)
Ben Shahn (Benjamin)(US artist; 1898-1969)
Ben Stiller (ent.; 1965-)
Ben Turpin (ent.; 1874-1940)
Ben Vereen (ent.; 1946-)
Ben Webster (US jazz; 1909-73)
ben Joseph, Saadia (Jew. phil./scholar; 882-942)
Benadryl (med.)
Benatar, Pat (b. Pat Andrzejewski)(ent.; 1953-)
Benay Venuta (b. Benvenuta Rose Crooke)(ent.; 1911-95)
Benazir Bhutto (ex-PM, Pak.; 1953-)
Bench, Johnny (baseball; 1947-)
Benchley, Peter (US writer; 1940-)
Benchley, Robert (US writer/humorist; 1889-1945)
Bender Gestalt (psych. test)
Bendery, Moldova
Bendix Corp.
Bendix, William (ent.; 1906-64)
Benedetto Croce (It. phil.; 1866-1952)
Benedict Arnold (US traitor; 1741-1801)
Benedict de Spinoza (also Baruch)(Dutch phil.; 1632-77)
Benedict, Dirk (b. Dirk Niewoehner)(ent.; 1945-)
Benedict, eggs (also l.c.)
Benedict, Ruth (US anthrop.; 1887-1948)
Benedict, St. (It., founded the Benedictines; c480-547)
Benedictine (liqueur)
Benedictine (order of monks/nuns)
Benemid (med.)
Benes, Eduard (Czech. pol.; 1884-1948)
Benét, Stephen Vincent (US poet/novelist; 1898-1943)
Benetton (US bus.)
Benetton, Guiliana (It. designer; 1938-)
Benevolent and Protective Order of Elks (BPOE)(US society, founded 1868)
Benflis, Ali (PM, Algeria; 1944-)
Bengal (former province, India)
Bengal light
Bengal tiger
Bengal, Bay of (part of Indian Ocean)
Bengali (lang./people)
Bengals, Cincinnati (football team)
Bengasi, Libya (also Benghazi)
Benglis, Lynda (US sculptor; 1941-)
Benguela Current
Benguela, Angola
Benicio Del Toro (ent.; 1967-)
Benigni, Roberto (ent./writer; 1952-)
Benihana of Tokyo (US bus.)
Benin (Republic of, formerly Dahomey)(W Afr.)
Bening, Annette (ent.; 1958-)
Benito (Pablo) Juárez (ex-pres., Mex.; 1806-72)
Benito Mussolini (aka Il Duce)(ex-PM, It.; 1883-1945)
Benjamin Bratt (ent.; 1963-)
Benjamin Britten (also Baron Britten of Aldeburgh)(Br. comp.; 1913-76)

Benjamin Disraeli (ex-PM/writer, Br.; 1804-81)
Benjamin (Franklin) Chavis (aka Benjamin Chavis Muhammad)(US rel./leader NAACP; 1948-)
Benjamin Franklin (US publ./writer/inv./dipl.; 1706-90)
Benjamin Franklin Wade (US pol.; 1800-78)
Benjamin Harrison (23rd US pres.; 1833-1901)
Benjamin Harrison (US pol.; 1726?-91)
Benjamin Harrison, Fort, IN (mil.)
Benjamin Henry Latrobe (US arch.; 1764-1820)
Benjamin Lawson Hooks (US civil rights leader; 1925-)
Benjamin Lincoln (US mil./pol.; 1722-1810)
Benjamin Moore & Co.
Benjamin Netanyahu (Isr. pol.; 1949-)
Benjamin Rush (US phys./writer; 1745-1813)
Benjamin "Bugsy" Siegel (US gangster/Las Vegas gambling; 1906-47)
Benjamin (McLane) Spock, Dr. (US phys./writer; 1903-98)
Benjamin West (US artist; 1738-1820)
Benjamin William Mkapa (pres., Tanzania; 1938-)
Benjamin, Private (film, 1980)
Benjamin, Richard (ent.; 1938-)
Benji (dog)
Benji (film, 1974)
Benji the Hunted (film, 1987)
Benji's Moist 'n Chunky (dog food)
Bennett Cerf (US editor/publ.; 1898-1971)
Bennett, Constance (ent.; 1904-65)
Bennett, Cornelius (football; 1966-)
Bennett, Enoch Arnold (Br. writer; 1867-1931)
Bennett, James Gordon (editor; 1795-1872)
Bennett, Joan (ent.; 1910-90)
Bennett, Johnston, J., Jr.(US pol.; 1932-)
Bennett, Robert F. (US cong.; 1933-)
Bennett, Robert Russell (US comp.; 1894-1981)
Bennett, Tony (b. Anthony Dominick Benedetto)(ent.; 1926-)
Bennie Moten (US jazz; 1894-1935)
Benning, Fort, GA (mil.)
Benny Carter (US jazz; 1907-)
Benny (Benjamin David) Goodman (US jazz; 1909-86)
Benny Goodman Story, The (film, 1955)
Benny Hill (ent.; 1925-92)
Benny (Benjamin Leiner) Leonard (boxing; 1896-1947)
Benny, Jack (b. Benjamin Kubelsky)(ent.; 1894-1974)
Benoit Samuelson, Joan (Olympic marathon; 1957-)
Benrus Watch Co.
Benson, Ezra Taft (US pol.; 1900-94)
Benson, George (ent.; 1943-)
Benson, Robby (b. Robert Segal)(ent.; 1956-)
Benten (myth.)
Bentham, Jeremy (Br. jurist/phil./social reformer; 1748-1832)
Bentley (auto.)
Bentley Arnage (auto.)
Bentley Arnage Green Label (auto.)
Bentley Arnage Red Label (auto.)
Bentley Azure convertible (auto.)
Bentley Continental (auto.)

Bentley Continental R (auto.)
Bentley Continental T (auto.)
Bentley Motors, Inc.
Benton Harbor, MI
Benton, Barbi (US Playmate; 1950-)
Benton, Thomas Hart (US artist; 1889-1975)
Benton, Thomas Hart (US pol.; 1782-1858)
Bentsen, Lloyd (US ex-secy./treas.; 1921-)
Bentyl (med.)
Benvenuto Cellini (It. sculptor; 1500-71)
Benylin (med.)
Benz, Mercedes- (auto.)
Benzamycin (med.)
Benzedrex (med.)
Benzedrine (med.)
Beothuk (Native Amer. tribe/Can.)
Beowulf (cartoon chara.)
Beowulf (epic poem; 8th c.)
Berardino, John (ent.; 1917-)
Berber (lang./people)
Berbera, Somalia
Berberati, Central African Republic
Berchtesgaden, Germany
Bercy (sauce)
Beregovoi, Georgi (or Georgy) T. (cosmo.; 1921-)
Bérégovoy, Pierre (ex-PM, Fr.; 1925-93)
Berendt, John (writer; 1939-)
Berenger, Tom (b. Thomas Michael Moore) (ent.; 1950-)
Berenice's Hair (astron.)
Berenices, Coma (astron., Berenice's hair)
Berenson, Bernard (or Bernhard)(US art critic; 1865-1959)
Berenson, Marisa (ent.; 1947-)
Berets, Green (also Special Forces)(US mil.)
Beretta, Chevrolet (auto.)
Berezovoy, Anatoly (cosmo.)
Berg, Alban (Aus. comp.; 1885-1935)
Berg, Gertrude (ent.; 1899-1966)
Berg, Patty (Patricia Jane)(golf; 1918-)
Berg, Paul (US molecular biol.; 1926-)
Bergalis, Kimberly (US AIDS victim; 1968-91)
Bergdorf Goodman (store)
Bergen Brunswig Corp.
Bergen County Record (NJ newspaper)
Bergen, Candice (ent.; 1946-)
Bergen, Edgar (ent.; 1903-78)
Bergen, Norway
Bergen, Polly (b. Nellie Paulina Burgin)(ent.; 1930-)
Berger, Sandy (Samuel Richard)(US ex-nat'l security advisor; 1945-)
Berger, Thomas (US writer; 1924-)
Bergerac (wine)
Bergerac, Cyrano de (Fr. poet/mil.; 1619-55)
Bergerac, Cyrano de (play)
Bergman, Ingmar (Swed. ent.; 1918-)
Bergman, Ingrid (ent.; 1915-82)
Bergson, Henri (Fr. phil.; 1859-1941)
Bergsonian/Bergsonism (phil.)
Bergstrom Air Force Base (TX)(mil.)
Beria, Lavrenti (USSR pol.; 1899-1953)
Berigan, Bunny (US jazz; 1909-42)
Bering Sea (N. Pac., Afr./Siberia)
Bering Strait (Alaska/Siberia)

Berisha, Sali (ex-pres., Albania; 1944-)
Berke Breathed (cartoonist, *Bloom County*; 1957-)
Berkeleian/Berkeleianism (phil.)
Berkeley Laboratory, Lawrence (nuclear research, CA)
Berkeley, Busby (b. William Berkeley Enos) (ent.; 1895-1976)
Berkeley, CA, MO
Berkeley, England
Berkeley, George (Ir. phil.; 1685-1753)
Berkley Publishing Corp.
Berkley, MI
Berkowitz, David ("Son of Sam")(serial killer; 1953-)
Berkshire (county, Eng.)
Berkshire Hathaway, Inc.
Berkshire Music Festival (Tanglewood, MA)
Berkshire swine
Berkshires (also Berkshire Hills)(MA)
Berle, Milton ("Uncle Miltie")(b. Milton Berlinger)(ent.; 1908-)
Berlin (state, Ger.)
Berlin Wall (divided E/W Berlin; 1961-89)
Berlin, CT, NH, WI
Berlin, Germany
Berlin, Irving (b. Israel Baline)(US comp.; 1888-1989)
Berlinger, Warren (ent.; 1937-)
Berlioz, Louis Hector (Fr. comp.; 1803-69)
Berlitz Language Center
Berlusconi, Silvio (ex-PM, It.; 1936-)
Berman, Lazar (pianist; 1930-)
Berman, Shelly (ent.; 1926-)
Bermuda
Bermuda bag (handbag)
Bermuda grass
Bermuda onion
Bermuda shorts
Bermuda Triangle (also Devil's Triangle)
Bern, Switzerland
Bernadette Peters (b. Bernadette Lazzara) (ent.; 1948-)
Bernadette, St. (aka Bernadette of Lourdes) (Fr.; 1844-79)
Bérnaise sauce (also l.c.)
Bernard (or Bernhard) Berenson (US art critic; 1865-1959)
Bernard A. De Voto (US hist.; 1897-1955)
Bernard Dowiyogo (pres., Nauru; 1946-)
Bernard Gimbel (US bus.; 1885-1966)
Bernard Howell Leach (Br. potter; 1887-1969)
Bernard Law Montgomery (Br. mil.; 1887-1976)
Bernard Lovell, Sir (Alfred Charles)(Br. astron.; 1931-)
Bernard Makuza (PM, Rwanda)
Bernard M. Baruch (US finan./pol.; 1870-1965)
Bernard Malamud (US writer; 1914-86)
Bernard Marcel Parent (hockey; 1945-)
Bernard R. Maybeck (US arch.; 1862-1957)
Bernard Shaw, (George)(Ir. writer/critic; 1856-1950)
Bernard, Crystal (ent.; 1961-)
Bernard, St. (dog)
Bernadette, The Song of (film, 1943)
Bernardi, Herschel (ent.; 1923-86)

Bernardin, Joseph Cardinal (US rel.; 1928-96)
Bernardo Bertolucci (It. ent.; 1940-)
Bernardo Rossellino (It. arch./sculptor; 1409-64)
Berne, Dr. Eric (US psych./writer; 1910-70)
Bernese Alps (also Bernese Oberland)(Switz.)
Bernese mountain dog
Bernhard H. Goetz (US news, shot NYC robbers)
Bernhard Riemann, (Georg Friedrich)(Ger. math.; 1826-66)
Bernhard von Bülow, Prince (ex-chanc., Ger.; 1849-1929)
Bernhard, Sandra (ent.; 1955-)
Bernhardt, Sarah (ent.; 1844-1923)
Bernie Kopell (ent.; 1933-)
Bernie Taupin (lyricist; 1950-)
Bernina Sewing Machine Co., Inc.
Berning, Susan Maxwell (golf; 1941-)
Bernini, Giovanni Lorenzo (It. sculptor; 1598-1680)
Bernoulli effect (physics)
Bernoulli, Daniel (Swiss math.; 1700-82)
Bernoulli, Jakob (Swiss math./scien.; 1654-1705)
Bernoulli, Johann (Swiss math./scien.; 1667-1748)
Bernoulli's principle (law of averages)
Bernsen, Corbin (ent.; 1954-)
Bernstein Foods, Inc.
Bernstein, Carl (US jour.; 1944-)
Bernstein, Leonard (US comp./cond.; 1918-90)
Bernstein's
Berotec (med.)
Berov, Lyuben (Borisov)(ex-PM, Bulgaria; 1925-)
Berra, Yogi (Lawrence Peter)(baseball; 1925-)
Berry Gordy, Jr. (US bus./founded Motown; 1929-)
Berry, Bertice (TV show)
Berry, Chuck (Charles)(ent.; 1926-)
Berry, Halle (ent.; 1966-)
Berry, Jim (cartoonist, *Berry's World*; 1932-)
Berry, Ken (ent.; 1933-)
Berry, Raymond (football; 1933-)
Berry, Richard (songwriter; 1935-97)
Berry's World (comic strip)
Berryman, John (US poet; 1914-72)
Bert Convy (ent.; 1934-91)
Bert Lahr (b. Irving Lahrheim)(ent.; 1895-1967)
Bert Lytell (ent.; 1885-1954)
Bert Parks (ent.; 1914-92)
Bertelsmann (US bus.)
Bertha Krupp (Ger. armaments maker; 1886-1957)
Bertha, Big (WWII Ger. cannon)
Berthe Morisot (Fr. artist; 1841-95)
Bertice Berry (TV show)
Bertie Ahern (PM, Ir.; 1951-)
Bertillon system (criminology)
Bertillon, Alphonse (Fr. anthrop./criminol.; 1853-1914)
Bertinelli, Valerie (ent.; 1960-)
Bertolli USA, Inc.
Bertolt Brecht (Ger. writer; 1898-1956)
Bertolucci, Bernardo (It. ent.; 1940-)
Bertram G. Goodhue (US arch.; 1869-1924)
Bertrand (Arthur William) Russell (Br. phil./math.; 1872-1970)
Berzelius, Jöns Jakob, Baron (Swed. chem.; 1779-1848)
Berzins, Andris (PM, Latvia; 1951-)
B horizon (geol.)
Besançon, France (Roman ruins)
Besant, Annie (Br. theosophist; 1847-1933)
Bess (Wallace) Truman (wife of ex-US pres.; 1885-1982)
Bess Myerson (ent./consumer advocate/ex-Miss America; 1924-)
Bess, Porgy and (Gershwin operetta)
Bessemer process (steel)
Bessemer, Sir Henry (Br. eng.; 1813-98)
Besser, Joe (ent.; 1907-88)
Bessie Smith (US jazz; 1894-1937)
Best Buy Co., Inc.
Best Foods Baking Group (US bus.)
Best Little Whorehouse in Texas, The (play; film, 1982)
Bester, Alfred (US writer; 1913-87)
BET (Black Entertainment Television)(TV channel)
Beta fiber
Beta Orionis (also Rigel)(astron.)
Beta Persei (also Algol)(astron.)
Betamax (also Beta)(video format)
Bete (people)
Betelgeuse (also Alpha Orionis)(astron.)
Beth Henley (playwright/ent.; 1952-)
Bethe, Hans Albrecht (US physt.; 1906-)
Bethesda Naval Hospital (MD)
Bethesda, MD
Bethlehem Steel Corp.
Bethlehem, Jordan
Bethlehem, PA
Bethlehem, Star of
Bethlehem, Star-of- (plant)
Bethune, Mary McLeod (US educ./civil rights; 1875-1955)
Beti (lang.)
Betjeman, Sir John (Br. poet laureate; 1906-84)
Betoptic (med.)
Betsy Palmer (ent.; 1929-)
Betsy (Elizabeth Earle) Rawls (golf; 1928-)
Betsy (Griscom) Ross (made 1st US flag; 1752-1836)
Betsy von Furstenberg (ent.; 1935-)
Betsy, The (film, 1978)
Bette Davis (ent.; 1908-89)
Bette Davis Eyes (song)
Bette Midler (ent.; 1945-)
Bettelheim, Bruno (Aus./US psych.; 1903-90)
Better Business Bureau
Better Homes & Gardens Books (US bus.)
Better Homes and Gardens (mag.)
Bettino Craxi (ex-PM, It.; 1934-2000)
Betty Boop (cartoon chara.)
Betty Broderick (US news)
Betty Buckley (ent.; 1947-)
Betty Carter (US jazz/comp.; 1930-98)
Betty Comden (US lyricist/ent.; 1919-)
Betty Crocker
Betty Ford (b. Elizabeth Bloomer Warren)(wife of ex-US pres.; 1918-)
Betty (Naomi Goldstein) Friedan (US feminist/writer; 1921-)
Betty (Elizabeth Mary) Furness (US ent./

consumer activist; 1916-94)
Betty Garrett (ent.; 1919-)
Betty Grable (ent.; 1916-73)
Betty Hutton (ent.; 1921-)
Betty (Sanders) Shabazz (US civil rights
　activist; 1936-97)
Betty White (ent.; 1922-)
Beulah Bondi (ent.; 1892-1981)
Beulah, Land of (*Pilgrim's Progress*)
Beuys, Joseph (Ger. sculptor/ent.; 1921-86)
Bevan, Aneurin (Br. pol.; 1897-1960)
Beverly Cleary (US writer; 1916-)
Beverly Crusher, Dr. (fict. chara., *Star Trek*)
Beverly D'Angelo (ent.; 1954-)
Beverly Garland (ent.; 1926-)
Beverly Hillbillies, The (TV show; film, 1962,
　1993)
Beverly Hills 90210 (TV show)
Beverly Hills Cop (film, 1984)
Beverly Hills Cop II (film, 1987)
Beverly Hills Cop III (film, 1994)
Beverly Hills Hotel
Beverly Hills, CA
Beverly (Adams) Sassoon (US bus.)
Beverly Sassoon & Co.
Beverly Sills (b. Belle Silverman)(US opera; 1929-)
Beverly, MA, NJ
Bevin, Ernest (Br. pol.; 1881-1951)
Bewitched (TV show)
Bexley (borough in London, Eng.)
Bexley, OH
Beyle, Marie Henri (aka Stendhal)(Fr. writer;
　1783-1842)
Beyond Good and Evil (by F. Nietzsche)
Beyrouth, Lebanon (also Beirut)
Bezier curve (compu. graphics)
Bezos, Jeff(rey Preston) (US bus./Amazon.com;
　1964-)
BFA (Bachelor of Fine Arts)
B. F. Goodrich (tires)
B. F. Goodrich Co.
B(urrhus) F(rederic) Skinner (US psych./writer;
　1903-90)
BHA (synthetic antioxidant preservative)
Bhádgáon, Nepal
Bhagavad-Gita (also Gita)(rel.)
Bhagwan (aka Shree [or Osho] Rajneesh)(b.
　Chaadra Mohan Jain)(Indian rel.; 1931-90)
Bhaktapur, Nepal
Bhakti (rel.)
Bharat Natya (dance, India)
Bharrat Jagdeo (pres.; Guyana; 1964-)
Bhavnagar, India (also Bhaunagar)
Bhili (lang.)
Bhiwandi, India
Bhojpuri (lang.)
Bhopal, India
Bhote (people)
BHT (synthetic antioxidant preservative)
Bhumibol Adulyadej (aka Rama IX)(king,
　Thailand; 1927-)
Bhutan (Kingdom of)
Bhutto, Benazir (ex-PM, Pak.; 1953-)
Bhutto, Zulfikar Ali (ex-pres./PM, Pak.; 1928-79)
Bi (chem. sym., bismuth)

BIA (Bureau of Indian Affairs)
Biafra, Bight of (also Bight of Bonny)(bay, Afr.)
Biafra, Republic of (former republic)(Afr.)
Bialik, Mayim (ent.; 1975-)
Bialystok, Poland
Bianca Jagger (b. Bianca Peréz Morena de
　Macîas)(1945-)
Bianrifi Tarmidi (PM, Comoros)
Biarritz, France
Bibb lettuce
Bibi Andersson (Swed. ent.; 1935-)
Bible
Bible Belt
Bibliothèque Nationale (Fr. National Library, Paris)
Bic (pens, razors)
Bic Corp.
Bickford, Charles (ent.; 1889-1967)
Bicol (lang.)
BiCozene (med.)
Bicycle Guide (mag.)
Biddle, John (Br. rel.; 1615-62)
Biddle, Nicholas (US finan.; 1786-1844)
Biden, Joseph R., Jr. (US cong.; 1942-)
Biedermeier (style of art/furniture)
Biel, Jessica (ent./model; 1982-)
Biel, Switzerland (also Bienne)
Bielefeld, Germany
Bienne, Switzerland (also Biel)
Bienville, Jean Baptiste Le Moyne (Fr. colonial
　admin.; 1680-1768)
Bierce, Ambrose Gwinnett (US writer; 1842-
　1914)
Bierstadt, Albert (US artist; 1830-1902)
Bifrost (myth.)
Big Apple (nickname, NYC)
Big Bang theory (astron.)
Big Bear City, CA
Big Ben (London clock)
Big Bend National Park (TX)
Big Bertha (WWII Ger. cannon)
Big Bill (William Tatem) Tilden, Jr. (tennis;
　1893-1953)
Big Bill Broonzy (US jazz; 1893-1958)
Big Bird (fict. chara., *Sesame Street*)
Big Board (New York Stock Exchange)
Big Bopper, the (b. J. P. "Jape"
　Richardson)(ent.; 1930-59)
Big Boy Restaurants (US bus.)
Big Brother (sociology)
Big Daddy (also l.c.)
Big Dipper (also Ursa Major)(astron.)
Big Foot (also Bigfoot or Sasquatch)
Big Joe Turner (ent.; 1911-85)
Big Rapids, MI
Big Rock Candy Mountain, The (W. Stegner
　novel)
Big Sid Catlett (US jazz; 1910-51)
Big Sur region (CA)
Big Sur River (CA)
Big Train (Walter Perry) Johnson (baseball;
　1887-1946)
Big Valley, The (TV show)
Big, Mr. (pop music)
Big, Mr. (slang, man in charge)
Bigard, Barney (US jazz; 1906-80)

Bigelow (carpet)
Bigelow (tea)
Bigelow, Inc., Karastan-
Bighorn Mountains (WY)
Bighorn, Battle of the Little (also Custer's Last Stand)(US/Sioux Native Amer.; 1876)
Bight of Biafra (also Bight of Bonny)(bay, Afr.)
Bihari (people)
Bijan (US bus.)
Bijou Phillips (ent.; 1980-)
Bikel, Theodore (ent.; 1924-)
Bikenibeu Paeniu (ex-PM, Tuvalu; 1956-)
Bikini Atoll (atomic bomb test site-1940s)
Biko, Stephen (b. Stephen Bantu)(SAfr. civil rights leader; 1946-77)
Bikol (lang.)
Bil Keane (cartoonist, *The Family Circus*; 1922-)
Bilbao, Spain
Bilbo Baggins (fict. chara.)
Bildt, Carl (ex-PM, Swed.; 1949-)
Bildungsroman (lit.)
Bileka, Silvestre Siale (ex-PM, Equatorial Guinea)
Biletnikoff, Frederick (football; 1943-)
Bilko, Sergeant (or *Sgt.*)(TV show)
Bill (William Britton) Baird (US puppeteer; 1904-87)
Bill Bixby (ent.; 1934-93)
Bill Blass (US designer; 1922-)
Bill (William Warren) Bradley (US cong../ basketball; 1943-)
Bill "Big Bill" Broonzy, (US jazz; 1893-58)
Bill Burrud (ent.; 1925-90)
Bill (William Jefferson) Clinton (42nd US pres.; 1946-)
Bill Cosby (ent.; 1937-)
Bill (William L.) Cullen (ent.; 1920-90)
Bill (William Michael) Daley (US ex-secy./ commerce; 1948-)
Bill Dana (ent.; 1924-)
Bill Davison, Wild (US jazz; 1906-89)
Bill Evans (US jazz; 1929-80)
Bill (William) Frist (US cong.; 1952-)
Bill (William) Gates (US bus./Microsoft; 1955-)
Bill Graham (b. Wolfgang Grajonca)(rock impresario; 1930-91)
Bill (William Preston) Graves (KS gov.; 1953-)
Bill Haley (ent.; 1925-81)
Bill Haley and the Comets (pop music)
Bill Hanna (cartoonist, *Tom & Jerry, Huckleberry Hound, Yogi Bear, Flintstones*; 1910-2001)
Bill (William) Hartack, Jr. (jockey; 1932-)
Bill Hickok, Wild (b. James Butler Hickok)(US frontier; 1837-76)
Bill (William John) Janklow (SD gov.; 1939-)
Bill (William Orland) Kilmer (football; 1939-)
Bill Macy (ent.; 1922-)
Bill Madlock (baseball; 1951-)
Bill Maher (ent.; 1956-)
Bill (William Henry) Mauldin (US writer/ cartoonist; 1921-)
Bill Moyers (US jour.; 1934-)
Bill Murray (ent.; 1950-)
Bill (Clarence William) Nelson (US cong.; 1942-)
Bill of Rights (1st 10 amendments, US Constitution)

Bill O'Reilly (US TV jour.; 1949-)
Bill (William) Owens (CO gov.; 1950-)
Bill Paxton (ent.; 1955-)
Bill Pullman (ent.; 1953-)
Bill (William Blaine) Richardson (US ex-secy./ ener.; 1947-)
Bill "Bojangles" Robinson (US tap dancer; 1878-1949)
Bill Russell (basketball; 1934-)
Bill Russell (US jazz; 1905-92)
Bill Shoemaker (horse racing; 1931-)
Bill "Moose" Skowron (baseball; 1930-)
Bill "Big Bill" (William Tatem) Tilden, Jr. (tennis; 1893-1953)
Bill Walton (basketball; 1952-)
Bill Watterson (cartoonist, *Calvin and Hobbes*; 1958-)
Bill White (baseball; 1934-)
Bill, Buffalo (aka William F(rederick) Cody)(Amer. scout/ent.; 1846-1917)
Bill, Mr. (fict. chara.)
Bill, Pecos (legendary cowboy)
Billboard (mag.)
Billboard Music Awards
Billie Burke (ent.; 1885-1970)
Billie Holiday (b. Eleanora Fagan)(US jazz; 1915-59)
Billie Jean (Moffitt) King (tennis; 1943-)
Billings, Josh (b. Henry Wheeler Shaw)(US humorist; 1818-85)
Billings, MT
Billingsgate (London fish market, coarse lang.)
Billionaire Boys Club
Bills, Buffalo (football team)
Billy Barty (b. William John Bertanzetti)(ent.; 1924-2000)
Billy Blanks (ent./fitness expert; 1955-)
Billy Bob Thornton (ent.; 1955-)
Billy Bragg (ent./songwriter; 1957-)
Billy Budd (H. Melville story)
Billy Campbell (ent.; 1959-)
Billy (William Aldon) Carter III (US bro. of ex-pres.; 1937-88)
Billy Casper (golf; 1931-)
Billy Corgan (ent.; 1967-)
Billy Crash Craddock (ent.; 1940-)
Billy Crudup (ent.; 1968-)
Billy Crystal (ent.; 1947-)
Billy De Wolfe (ent.; 1907-74)
Billy DeBeck (cartoonist, *Barney Google*; 1890-1942)
Billy Dee Williams (ent.; 1937-)
Billy Eckstine (ent.; 1914-93)
Billy (William Franklin) Graham, Rev. (US rel.; 1918-)
Billy Idol (b. Billy Broad)(ent.; 1955-)
Billy Jack (film, 1971)
Billy Joel (ent.; 1949-)
Billy (Alfred Manuel) Martin (baseball; 1928-89)
Billy Mitchell (US mil.; 1879-1936)
Billy Ocean (b. Leslie Sebastian Charles)(ent.; 1950-)
Billy Packer (ent.; 1940-)
Billy Preston (ent.; 1946-)
Billy Ray Cyrus (ent.; 1961-)

Billy Rose (ent.; 1899-1966)
Billy Sims (football; 1955-)
Billy Smith (hockey; 1950-)
Billy Sol Estes (US bus./scandal)
Billy Strayhorn (US jazz; 1915-67)
Billy Sunday (William Ashley)(US rel.; 1862-1935)
Billy Taylor (US jazz; 1921-)
Billy the Kid (aka William Henry Bonney)(US outlaw; 1859-81)
Billy (Samuel) Wilder (ent./writer; 1906-)
Billy Zane (William George Zane, Jr.)(ent.; 1966-)
Biloxi (Native Amer.)
Biloxi Blues (film, 1988)
Biloxi, MS
Biltmore Estate (Ashville, NC)
Binaca (health)
Binding Corp., General (GBC)
Binet test, Stanford- (intelligence test)
Binet, Alfred (Fr. psych.; 1857-1911)
Bing (Harry Lillis) Crosby (ent.; 1903-77)
Bing cherry
Bing, Dave (basketball; 1943-)
Bing, Sir Rudolf (opera; 1902-97)
Bingaman, Jeff (US cong.; 1943-)
Bingham, George Caleb (US artist; 1811-79)
Binghamton Press & Sun-Bulletin (NY newspaper)
Binghamton, NY
bin Laden, Osama (Saudi terrorist, Islamic, based in Afghanistan; 1957-)
Binoche, Juliette (ent.; 1964-)
Biography Channel, The (TV channel)
Bioko, Cristino Seriche (ex-PM, Equatorial Guinea)
Biondi, Matt (swimming; 1965-)
BioSphere 2 (BS2)(ecological test project)
BIP (*Books in Print* [Bowker])
Biphetamine (med.)
Biratnagar, Nepal
Birch Society, John (US pol.)
Bird Watchers Digest
Bird, Caroline (US writer)
Bird, Larry (basketball; 1956-)
Bird, Lester B(ryant)(PM, Antigua/Barbuda; 1938-)
Bird, Vere C(ornwall)(ex-PM, Antigua and Barbuda; 1910-99)
Birdie (George R.) Tebbetts (baseball; 1914-99)
Birdman of Alcatraz, The (film, 1962)
Birdseye (frozen foods)
Birdseye, Clarence "Bob" (US inv., frozen food; 1886-1956)
Birendra Bir Bikram Shah Dev (king, Nepal; 1945-)
Birganj, Nepal
Birgit Nilsson (Swed., opera; 1918-)
Birkavs, Valdis (ex-PM, Latvia; 1942-)
Birkenhead, England
Birkenstock Footprint Sandals, Inc.
Birkirkara, Malta
Birman (cat)
Birmingham News (AL newspaper)
Birmingham Post-Herald (AL newspaper)
Birmingham, AL, MI
Birmingham, England
Birnam Wood (Scot.)

Birney, David (ent.; 1939-)
Birney, James Gillespie (US reformer; 1792-1857)
Birobizhan (also Birobidjan)(Jew. settlement)
Birth of Venus, The (by Botticelli)
Biscay, Bay of (Fr./Sp.)
Biscayne Bay (Miami, FL)
Biscayne Boulevard (Miami, FL)
Biscayne National Park (FL)
Bishkek, Kyrgyzstan
Bishop, Elizabeth (US poet; 1911-79)
Bishop, Joey (b. Joseph Abraham Gottlieb) (ent.; 1918-)
Bislama (lang.)
Bismarck Archipelago (SW Pac. islands)
Bismarck, ND
Bismarck, Otto (Eduard Leopold) von, Prince ("Iron Chancellor")(ex-chanc., Ger.; 1815-98)
Bismarck, the (Ger. WWII battleship; sunk 1941)
Bisoglio, Val (ent.; 1926-)
Bisquick
Bissau, Guinea- (Republic of)(W Afr.)
Bissau, Guinea-Bissau
Bissell (home appliances)
Bissell (sweeper)
Bissell, Inc.
Bisset, Jacqueline (ent.; 1944-)
Bissinger's, Inc.
Biswas, Abdur Rahman (ex-pres., Bangladesh; 1926-)
Bitterroot Range (also Bitter Root Range)(ID/MT)
Bivar, Rodrigo Diaz de (also El Cid, el Campeador)(Sp. mil.; 1040-99)
Bix Beiderbecke, (Leon Bismarck)(US jazz; 1903-31)
Bixby, Bill (ent.; 1934-93)
Biya, Paul (pres., Cameroon; 1933-)
Biysk, Siberia (also Bisk, Biisk)
Biz (bleach)
Bizerte, Tunisia (also Bizerta)
Bizet, Georges (Fr. comp.; 1838-75)
Bjoerling, Jussi (Swed. tenor; 1911-60)
Björk (Gudmundsdottir) (ent.; 1965-)
Björn Borg (tennis; 1956-)
Bk (chem. sym., berkelium)
B(ernard) Kliban (cartoonist, cats; 1935-91)
Black & Decker (power tools)
Black & Decker Corp., The
Black and Tans (Br. troops; 1920-21)
Black Angus cattle (also Aberdeen Angus)
Black Audio Network (BAN)
Black Beauty (Anna Sewell novel; film, 1946, 1971, 1994)
Black Crowes, the (pop music)
Black Dahlia (Elizabeth Short)(aspiring actress/ murder victim; 1924-47)
Black Death (bubonic plague; 14th c)
Black Enterprise (mag.)
Black Entertainment Television (BET)(TV channel)
black-eyed Susan (plant)
Black Forest (Ger.)
Black Forest cake
Black Friday (US finan. disasters; 9/24/1869 & 9/19/1873)
Black Hand (various pol. & criminal societies)

Black Hawk War (US hist.; 1831-32)
Black Hawk, Chief (Sauk Native Amer.; 1767-1838)
Black Hawks, Chicago (hockey team)
Black Hills (SD/WY mountains)
Black Hole of Calcutta (prison cell; 1756)
Black Maria (patrol wagon)
Black Mass
Black Monday (US stockmarket crash; 10/19/87)
Black Mountains (SE US)
Black Muslims (also Nation of Islam)(rel.)
Black Panther Party (Black separatist group)
Black Prince, Edward the (Prince of Wales; 1330-76)
Black Russian (mixed drink)
Black Sabbath (pop music)
Black Sea (SE Eur.)
Black Tuesday (US stockmarket crash; 10/29/29)
Black Velvet (whiskey)
Black Watch (Br. Royal Highland regiment)
Black, Clint (ent./songwriter; 1962-)
Black, Hugo LaFayette (US jurist; 1886-1971)
Black, Karen (b. Karen Ziegler)(ent.; 1942-)
Black, Lisa Hartman (ent.; 1956-)
Black, Shirley Temple (US ent./dipl.; 1928-)
Black's Law Dictionary
Blackbeard (Edward Teach)(also Thatch, Thach) (pirate; ?-1718)
Blackburn, Mount (AK)
Blackburnian warbler (bird)
Blackett, Patrick Maynard Stuart, Baron (Br. physt.; 1897-1974)
Blackfoot (Native Amer.)
Blackfriars (Elizabethan playhouse, London)
Blackhawk (cartoon chara.)
Blackie, Boston (fict. detective)
Blackmun, Harry A(ndrew)(ex-US jurist; 1908-99)
Blackpool, England
Blackstone, Harry, Jr. (ent.; 1934-97)
Blackstone, Sir William (Br. jurist; 1723-80)
Blackwall hitch (knot)
Blackwater State (nickname, NE)
Blackwell Co., The Crosse &
Blackwell, Elizabeth (1st US woman phys.; 1821-1910)
Blackwell, Mr. (b. Richard Selzer)(fashion)
Blackwood, Lincoln (auto.)
Blackwood, Nina (ent.; 1955-)
Blades, Ruben (ent./songwriter; 1948-)
Blaik, Earl H. (football; 1897-1989)
Blaine, James G(illespie)(US pol.; 1830-93)
Blaine, Vivian (ent.; 1921-95)
Blair Brown (ent.; 1948-)
Blair Underwood (ent.; 1964-)
Blair Witch Project, The (film, 1999)
Blair, Bonnie (speed skating; 1964-)
Blair, Eric A(rthur)(pseud. George Orwell)(Br. writer; 1903-50)
Blair, Linda (ent.; 1959-)
Blair, Tony (PM, Br.; 1953-)
Blaise Compaoré (pres., Burkina Faso; 1951-)
Blaise Pascal (Fr. phil./math.; 1623-62)
Blaize, Herbert (ex-PM, Grenada; 1918-1989)
Blake Edwards (b. William Blake McEdwards) (ent.; 1922-)

Blake, Amanda (b. Beverly Louise Neill)(ent.; 1929-89)
Blake, Eubie (James Hubert)(US jazz pianist/comp.; 1883-1983)
Blake, Robert (b. Michael Gubitosi)(ent.; 1933-)
Blake, Robert, Adm. (Br. mil.; 1599-1657)
Blake, William (Br. poet/artist; 1757-1827)
Blakey, Art (US jazz; 1919-90)
Blanc, (Jean Joseph Charles) Louis (Fr. socialist/hist.; 1811-82)
Blanc, Mel (ent.; 1908-89)
Blanc, Mont (Fr./It.)
Blanca Peak (CO)
Blanche (Lambert) Lincoln (US cong.; 1960-)
Blanche Thebom (mezzo-soprano; 1919-)
Blanchett, Cate (ent.; 1969-)
Bland, Bobby (ent.; 1930-)
Blanda, George (Frederick)(football; 1927-)
Blanding, Sarah G. (US educ.; 1899-1985)
Blandings Builds His Dream House, Mr. (film, 1948)
Blanks, Billy (ent./fitness expert; 1955-)
Blanton, Jimmy (US jazz; 1921-42)
Blantyre, Malawi
Blarney stone (Ir.)
Blass, Bill (US designer; 1922-)
Blaue Reiter, der ("the blue Rider")(Ger. painters)
Blavatsky Hahn, Madame Helena Petrovna (Rus. theosophist; 1831-91)
Blazer, Chevrolet (auto.)
Bledsoe, Tempestt (ent.; 1973-)
Bleeth, Yasmine (ent.; 1968-)
Blenheim spaniel (dog)
Blenheim, Germany
Blenkinsop 'rack (railroad)
Bléroit, Louis (Fr. aviator; 1872-1936)
Blessed Sacrament (rel.)
Blessed Virgin (rel.)
Blige, Mary J. (ent.; 1971-)
Bligh, William (Br. capt., H.M.S. *Bounty*; 1754-1817)
Blimp, Colonel (fict. chara.)
Blind Faith (pop music)
Blind Lemon Jefferson (US jazz; 1897-1930)
Bliss, Fort, TX (mil.)
Blistex (med.)
Blistex, Inc.
Blistik (lip balm)
Blitzkrieg (also the Blitz)(Ger., lightning war) (also l.c.)
Blixen, Karen (pseud. Isak Dinesen)(Dan. writer; 1885-1962)
BLM (Bureau of Land Management)
Blocadren (med.)
Bloch, Ernest (Swiss/US comp.; 1880-1959)
Bloch, Felix (Swiss/US physt.; 1905-83)
Bloch, Konrad (Emil)(US chem.; 1912-2000)
Bloch, Ray (ent.; 1902-82)
Block, Herb(ert Lawrence)("Herblock")(pol. cartoonist; 1909-)
Block, Inc., H & R
Blockbuster Bowl (college football)
Blockbuster Video (US bus.)
Blocker, Dan (ent.; 1928-72)
Bloemfontein, South Africa

Blois, France
Blok, Aleksandr Aleksandrovich (Rus. poet; 1880-1921)
Blondell, Gloria (ent.; 1910-86)
Blondell, Joan (ent.; 1909-79)
Blondie (pop music)
Blondie Bumstead (cartoon chara.)
Blood, Sweat, and Tears (pop music)
Blood of Dracula (film, 1957)
Bloodless Revolution (also English [or Glorious] Revolution)(Br. hist.; 1688-89)
Bloods and Crips (gangs, also pop music group)
Bloodworth-Thomason, Linda (ent.)
Bloody Mary (alcoholic drink)
Bloody Mary (also Mary Tudor, Mary I)(queen, Eng.; 1516-58)
Bloody Sunday (Rus. hist., 1905; NIre. hist., 1972)
Bloom County (comic strip)
Bloom, Claire (ent.; 1931-)
Bloomer, Amelia (US reformer; 1818-94)
Bloomfield, CT, IA, IN, NJ
Bloomfield, Leonard (US linguist; 1887-1949)
Bloomgarden, Kermit (ent.; 1904-76)
Bloomingdale's (also "Bloomies")(stores)
Bloomington, IL, IN, MN
Bloomsbury group (writers/artists, London)
Blossom Dearie (ent.; 1926-)
Blow, Joe (also Joe Doakes)(average guy)
BLT (bacon, lettuce, and tomato)
Blücher, Gebhard von (Ger. gen.; 1742-1819)
Blue Andalusian (chicken)
Blue Angels, the (aviation)
Blue Bonnet (margarine)
Blue Book (auto.)
Blue Cross & Blue Shield Association (med. insurance)
Blue Ice
Blue Jays, Toronto (baseball team)
Blue Mountains (Austl.)
Blue Nile (Ethiopia)
Blue Ridge Mountains (WV to GA)
Blue Shield (med. insurance)
Blue Suede Shoes (song)
Blue Swedish (duck)
Blue, Ben (ent.; 1901-75)
Blue, Vida (baseball; 1949-)
Bluebeard (legendary murderer of wives)
Blueberry Morning (cereal)
Bluegrass State (nickname, KY)
Blues Brothers, The (film, 1980)
Blues, St. Louis (hockey team)
Blum, Léon (Fr. pol.; 1872-1950)
Blume in Love (film, 1973)
Blume, Judy (Sussman)(US writer, young adults; 1938-)
Bly, Nellie (Elizabeth Cochrane Seaman)(US jour./reformer; 1867-1922)
Bly, Robert (US poet/critic; 1926-)
Blyth, Ann (ent.; 1928-)
Blythe Danner (ent.; 1943-)
Blytheville Air Force Base, AR (mil.)
Blytheville, AR
BMC Software, Inc.
BMOC (big man on campus)
BMW (auto.)

BMW (Bayerische Motoren Werke)
BMW 3-series (auto.)
BMW 3-series/M3 (auto.)
BMW 318i (auto.)
BMW 318ti (auto.)
BMW 323Ci (auto.)
BMW 323i (auto.)
BMW 323is (auto.)
BMW 323iT (auto.)
BMW 325Ci (auto.)
BMW 325i (auto.)
BMW 325is (auto.)
BMW 325s (auto.)
BMW 325Xi (auto.)
BMW 328Ci (auto.)
BMW 328i (auto.)
BMW 328is (auto.)
BMW 330Ci (auto.)
BMW 330i (auto.)
BMW 330s (auto.)
BMW 330Xi (auto.)
BMW 5-series (auto.)
BMW 525i (auto.)
BMW 528i (auto.)
BMW 528i Sportwagon (auto.)
BMW 528iT (auto.)
BMW 530Ci (auto.)
BMW 530i (auto.)
BMW 540i (auto.)
BMW 540iT (auto.)
BMW 7-series (auto.)
BMW 740i (auto.)
BMW 740iA (auto.)
BMW 740iL (auto.)
BMW 750iL (auto.)
BMW 840Ci (auto.)
BMW 850Ci (auto.)
BMW M (auto.)
BMW M3 (auto.)
BMW M5 (auto.)
BMW of North America, Inc.
BMW X5 3.0 (auto.)
BMW X5 3.0i (auto.)
BMW X5 4.4 (auto.)
BMW X5 series (auto.)
BMW Z3 (auto.)
BMW Z8 (auto.)
B'nai B'rith (US Jew. org.)
BO (box office, branch office, body odor)
Bo Derek (b. Mary Cathleen Collins)(ent.; 1956-)
Bo Diddley (b. Elias McDaniel)(ent.; 1928-)
Bo Jackson (Vincent)(baseball; 1962-)
Bo Svenson (ent.; 1941-)
Bo, Sierra Leone
Board of Education of Topeka, Kansas, Brown v. (US law; 1954)
Boas, Franz (US anthrop.; 1858-1942)
Boating (mag.)
Bob & Carol & Ted & Alice (film, 1969)
Bob Barker (ent.; 1923-)
Bob Beamon (jumper; 1946-)
Bob Birdseye (Robert Clarence)(US inv., frozen food; 1886-1956)
Bob Clampett (US cartoonist; 1913-84)
Bob Costas (ent.; 1952-)

Bob (Robert Joseph) Cousy (basketball; 1928-)
Bob Crane (ent.; 1928-78)
Bob Cratchit (fict. chara., *A Christmas Carol*)
Bob (George Robert) Crosby (ent.; 1913-93)
Bob Denver (ent.; 1935-)
Bob (Robert Joseph) Dole (US pol.; 1923-)
Bob Dylan (b. Robert Zimmerman)(US comp./ ent.; 1941-)
Bob Elliott (ent.; 1923-)
Bob Eubanks (ent.; 1937-)
Bob Feller (baseball; 1918-)
Bob (Robert Prometheus) Fitzsimmons (boxing; 1862-1917)
Bob Fosse (ent.; 1927-87)
Bob Geldof (ent.; 1954-)
Bob Gibson (baseball; 1935-)
Bob "Bobcat" Goldthwait (ent.; 1962-)
Bob (Robert) Graham (US cong.; 1936-)
Bob (Robert Allen) Griese (football; 1945-)
Bob Guccione (publ., *Penthouse*; 1930-)
Bob (Robert James Lee) Hawke (ex-PM, Austl.; 1929-)
Bob Holden (MO gov.)
Bob Hope (b. Leslie Townes Hope)(ent.; 1903-)
Bob Hoskins (ent.; 1942-)
Bob Jamieson (US jour.)
Bob Jones University (Greenville, SC)
Bob Keeshan (ent.; 1927-)
Bob (Joseph Robert) Kerrey (US pol.; 1943-)
Bob Knight (basketball; 1940-)
Bob Mackie (US fashion designer; 1940-)
Bob (Robert Nesta) Marley (ent.; 1945-81)
Bob (Robert) Martinez (US pol.; 1934-)
Bob Mathias (Olympic star; 1930-)
Bob McAdoo (basketball; 1951-)
Bob Merrill (US lyricist; 1921-98)
Bob (Robert Joseph) Miller (ex-NV gov.; 1945-)
Bob Montana (cartoonist, *Archie*; 1920-75)
Bob Newhart (ent.; 1929-)
Bob Newhart Show, The (TV show)
Bob (Robert William) Packwood (US pol.; 1932-)
Bob Pettit (basketball; 1932-)
Bob Prince (baseball announcer; 1917-85)
Bob Saget (ent.; 1956-)
Bob (Robert Lloyd) Seagren (pole vaulter; 1946-)
Bob Seger (ent./songwriter; 1945-)
Bob "Buffalo Bob" Smith (b. Robert Schmidt) (ent.; 1917-98)
Bob (Robert C.) Smith (US cong.; 1941-)
Bob (Robert Alphonso) Taft II (OH gov.; 1942-)
Bob Thaves (cartoonist, *Frank and Ernest*; 1924-)
Bob Uecker "Mr. Baseball" (ent.; 1935-)
Bob Waterfield (football; 1921-83)
Bob (Robert Ellsworth) Wise, Jr. (WV gov.; 1948-)
Bob Woodward (US jour.; 1943-)
Bobbie Gentry (b. Roberta Streeter)(ent.; 1944-)
Bobbies (Br. police officers)
Bobbitt, John Wayne (US news)
Bobbitt, Lorena (US news)
Bobbsey Twins, The (book series)
Bobby (Robert Arthur) Allison (auto racing; 1937-)
Bobby Bland (ent.; 1930-)
Bobby (Robert) Breen (ent.; 1927-)
Bobby Brown (ent.; 1969-)

Bobby (Robert Earle) Clarke (hockey; 1949-)
Bobby Darin (ent.; 1936-73)
Bobby (Robert James) Fischer (US chess; 1943-)
Bobby Goldsboro (ent.; 1942-)
Bobby Hackett (US jazz; 1915-76)
Bobby (Robert Marvin) Hull (hockey; 1939-)
Bobby (Robert Tyre) Jones, Jr. (golf; 1902-71)
Bobby Layne (football; 1927-86)
Bobby McFerrin (ent.; 1950-)
Bobby (Robert Gordon) Orr (hockey; 1948-)
Bobby Rahal (auto racing; 1953-)
Bobby Riggs (tennis; 1918-95)
Bobby Rydell (ent.; 1942-)
Bobby Seale (cofounded Black Panther Party; 1936-)
Bobby Short (ent.; 1924-)
Bobby Unser (auto racing; 1934-)
Bobby Vee (b. Robert Velline)(ent.; 1943-)
Bobby Vinton (ent.; 1935-)
Bobcat (Bob) Goldthwait (ent.; 1962-)
Bobo-Dioulasso, Burkina Faso
Bobois, Roche- (US bus.)
Bobruisk, Belarus
Boca Raton, FL
Boccaccio, Giovanni (It. writer; 1313-75)
Boccherini, Luigi (It. comp.; 1743-1805)
Boccioni, Umberto (It. artist; 1882-1916)
Bocelli, Andrea (ent., opera; 1958-)
Boch Tableware, Ltd., Villeroy &
Bochco, Steven (ent.; 1943-)
Bochum, Germany
Bock, Jerry (US comp.; 1928-)
Bode, Johann Elert (Ger. astron.; 1747-1826)
Bode's law (astron.)
Bodenheim, Maxwell (US writer; 1892-1954)
Bodhisattva (rel.)
Bodleian Library (Oxford Univ., Eng.)
Bodley, Sir Thomas (Br. scholar/dipl., founded Bodleian Library; 1545-1613)
Bodoni (type style)
Bodoni, Giambattista (It. printer/typographer; 1740-1813)
body English
Boehm, Sydney (screenwriter)
Boehme, Jakob (Ger. theosophist; 1575-1624)
Boeing Company
Boer (now Afrikaner)(people)
Boer War (also South African War)(Boers/Br.; 1899-1902)
Boesky, Ivan F(rederick)(US stock market scandal; 1937-)
Boeslav I ("the Mighty")(king, Pol.; ?-1025)
Boeslav II ("the Bold")(king, Pol.; 1039?-83)
Boeslav III ("Wry-mouthed")(king, Pol.; 1086-1138)
Boeslav IV (king, Pol.; 1127-73)
Boeslav V ("the Chaste")(king, Pol.; 1221-79)
Boethius (Roman scholar; c480-524 BC)
Bogarde, Dirk (ent.; 1921-99)
Bogart, Humphrey ("Bogey")(ent.; 1899-1957)
Bogdanovich, Peter (ent.; 1939-)
Boggs, Dock (Moran Lee)(ent.; 1898-1971)
Boggs, Wade (baseball; 1958-)
Bogor, Java (Indonesia)
Bogosian, Eric (ent./writer; 1953-)

Bogota, Colombia
Bogue, Merwyn (aka Ish Kabibble)(ent.; 1908-94)
Bohème, La (by Puccini)
Bohemia, Czechoslovakia
Bohemian (also l.c.)
Bohlen, Charles E. (US dipl.; 1904-74)
Bohr theory (of atomic structure)
Bohr, Aage (Dan. physt.; 1922-)
Bohr, Niels Henrik David (Dan. physt.; 1885-1962)
Boigny, Félix Houphouët- (ex-pres., Ivory Coast; 1905-93)
Bois Wines, Clos Du (US bus.)
Bois, W(illiam) E(dward) B(urghardt) Du (US educ./writer, NAACP; 1868-1963)
Boise Cascade Corp.
Boise State University (Boise, ID)
Boise, ID
Boitano, Brian (figure skating; 1963-)
Boito, Arrigo (It. comp./writer; 1842-1918)
Bojangles (Bill Robinson)(US tap dancer; 1878-1949)
Bok, Sissela (b. Sissela Ann Myrdal)(US phil./writer; 1934-)
Bokhara (Pers. rug)
Bold and the Beautiful (TV soap)
Bold, Philip the (Fr., duke, Burgundy; 1342-1404)
Bold, Philip the (Philip III)(king, Fr.; 1245-85)
Bolden, (Charles) Buddy (US jazz; 1868-1931)
Boléro (M. Ravel music)
Boleyn, Anne (2nd wife Henry VIII; 1507-36)
Bolger, Jim (James Brendan)(ex-PM, NewZeal.; 1935-)
Bolger, Ray (ent.; 1904-87)
Bolingbroke, Henry of (Henry IV, king, Eng.; 1367-1413)
Bolivar, Simon ("El Libertador")(SAmer. pol.; 1783-1830)
Bolivia (Republic of)(central SAmer.)
Bolkiah Mu'izzaddin Waddaulah, Muda Hassanal (Sultan/PM, Brunei; 1946-)
Böll, Heinrich (Theodor)(Ger. writer; 1917-85)
Bolla Soave (It. wine)
Bolling Air Force Base, DC (mil.)
Bologna, Italy
Bologna, Joseph (ent.; 1934-)
Bolognese (art style)
Bolshevik (also bolshevik)(Rus. pol. party)
Bolshevik Revolution (Rus.; 1917)
Bolshevism (communist doctrine)
Bolshoi Ballet
Bolten, Joshua (US White House staff)
Bolton, England
Boltzmann constant (physics, k)
Boltzmann, Ludwig (Aus. physt.; 1844-1906)
Bolzano, Italy
Boma, Zaire
Bombay duck (fish)
Bombay, India
Bombeck, Erma (US writer/humorist; 1927-96)
BOMC (Book-of-the-Month Club)
b'Omer, Lag (rel.)
Bomu River (also Mbomu)(Africa)
Bon (Jap. holiday)

Bon Appétit (mag.)
Bon Jovi (pop music)
Bon Jovi, Jon (b. John Francis Bongiovi)(ent.; 1962-)
Bon, Simon Le (ent.; 1958-)
Bonaduce, Danny (ent.; 1959-)
Bonaire, the Netherlands Antilles
Bonanza (TV show)
Bonaparte, Jerome (bro. of Napoleon, king, Westphalia; 1784-1860)
Bonaparte, Joseph (bro. of Napoleon, king, Naples/Spain; 1768-1844)
Bonaparte, Louis (bro. of Napoleon, king, Holland; 1778-1846)
Bonaparte, Lucien (bro. of Napoleon, prince, Canino; 1775-1840)
Bonaparte, Napoleon (Napoleon I, "the Little Corporal")(emp., Fr.; 1769-1821)
Bonapartism
Bonar Law, (Andrew)(Br. pol.; 1858-1923)
Bonaventure, St. (also Bonaventura)("the Seraphic Doctor")(It. rel./phil.; 1221-74)
Bond, Carrie Jacobs (US comp.; 1862-1946)
Bond, Christopher S(amuel) "Kit" (US cong.; 1939-)
Bond, James (fict. spy)
Bond, James (ornithol.; 1900-89)
Bond, (Horace) Julian (US reformer/NAACP; 1940-)
Bond, Ward (ent.; 1903-60)
Bondi, Beulah (ent.; 1892-1981)
Bonds, Barry (baseball; 1964-)
Bonds, Gary "U.S." (b. Gary Anderson)(ent.; 1939-)
Bones, Mr. (slang)
Bonet, Lisa (ent.; 1967-)
Bongo, (Albert Bernard) Omar (pres., Gabon; 1935-)
Bonham Carter, Helena (ent.; 1966-)
Bonheur, Rosa (Maria Rosalie)(Fr. artist; 1822-99)
Boniface (name of nine popes)
Boniface, St. (Br. rel. in Ger.; 680-754)
Bonilla, Bobby (baseball; 1963-)
Bonin Islands (Pac.)
Bonine (med.)
Bonior, David E. (US cong.; 1945-)
Bonjour Tristesse (F. Sagan novel)
Bonkers (cartoon)
Bonn, Germany
Bonnard, Pierre (Fr. artist; 1867-1947)
Bonne Bell (cosmetics)
Bonne Bell, Inc.
Bonneville Salt Flats (UT)
Bonneville, Pontiac (auto.)
Bonney, William Henry ("Billy the Kid")(US outlaw; 1859-81)
Bonnie and Clyde (film, 1967)
Bonnie Bakley (US news; ?-2001)
Bonnie Bedelia (ent.; 1948-)
Bonnie Blair (speed skating; 1964-)
Bonnie Franklin (ent.; 1944-)
Bonnie Parker (US criminal; 1911-34)
Bonnie Prince Charles (or Charlie)(Charles Edward Stuart, aka the Young Pretender)(prince, Br.; 1720-88)

Bonnie Raitt (ent.; 1949-)
Bonny, Bight of (also Bight of Biafra)(bay, Afr.)
Bono (b. Paul Hewson) (ent.; 1960-)
Bono, Chastity (daughter of Sonny and Cher; 1969-)
Bono, Mary (US cong.; 1961-)
Bono, Sonny (Salvatore) (ent./pol.; 1935-98)
Bonwit Teller & Co.
Bonzo, Bedtime for (film, 1951)
Boog (John) Powell (baseball; 1941-)
Book Dealers World
Book of Books (Bible)
Book of Changes (also *I Ching*)(rel.)
Book of Common Prayer (Church of England)
Book of Job (rel.)
Book of Kells (rel.)
Book of Kings (rel.)
Book of Mormon (rel.)
Book of Proverbs (rel.)
Book of the Dead (Eg., rel.)
Book of the Dead, The Tibetan (rel.)
Book-of-the-Month Club
Booke, Sorrell (ent.; 1930-94)
Booker T and the MGs (pop music)
Booker T(aliaferro) Washington (US educ./ reformer; 1856-1915)
Books of Chronicles (rel.)
Boole, George (Br. math.; 1815-64)
Boolean algebra (math.)
Boom Boom (Bernie) Geoffrion (hockey; 1931-)
Boomer Esiason (Norman Julius Esiason, Jr.) (football; 1961-)
Boomer State (OK)
Boone Pickens, T. (US bus.; 1928-)
Boone, Daniel (US pioneer; 1734-1820)
Boone, Debbie (ent.; 1956-)
Boone, Pat (ent.; 1934-)
Boone, Richard (ent.; 1917-81)
Boop, Betty (cartoon chara.)
Boorstin, Daniel (hist.; 1914-)
Boosler, Elayne (ent.; 1952-)
Boötes (astron., herdsmen)
Booth Tarkington, (Newton)(US writer; 1869-1946)
Booth, Ballington (US, founded Volunteers of Amer.; 1859-1940)
Booth, Edwin Thomas (US actor, brother of John Wilkes; 1833-93)
Booth, Evangeline Cory (US, Salvation Army; 1865?-1950)
Booth, George (cartoonist, *New Yorker*; 1926-)
Booth, John Wilkes (US, assassinated Lincoln, actor; 1838-65)
Booth, Junius Brutus (US actor, father of John Wilkes; 1796-1852)
Booth, Shirley (ent.; 1907-92)
Booth, William ("General Booth")(Br., founded Salvation Army; 1829-1912)
Boothe Luce, Clare (US drama./pol./dipl.; 1903-87)
Boothe, Powers (ent.; 1949-)
Boothia Peninsula (Can.)
Boothia, Gulf of (Arctic/N Can.)
Bootle, England
Boots Malone (film, 1952)

Bo-Peep, Little (fict. chara.)
Bophuthatswana (S. Africa)
Bopper, the Big (b. J. P. "Jape" Richardson) (ent.; 1930-59)
BOQ (bachelor officers' quarters, base officers' quarters)
Bora-Bora (French Polynesian islands)
Borah, William E. (US pol.; 1865-1940)
Borateem (laundry aid)
Bordeaux (Fr. wine region)
Bordeaux mixture (fungicide)
Bordeaux, France
Bordelaise (sauce)
Borden (dairy prods.)
Borden, Inc.
Borden, Lizzie A. (US, tried/acquitted of ax murders; 1860-1927)
Border States (US Civil War, DE/MD/KY/MO)
Borders (region, Scot.)
Boreanaz, David (ent.; 1971-)
Boren, David Lyle (US pol.; 1941-)
Borg, Björn (tennis; 1956-)
Borge, Victor (b. Boerge Rosenbaum)(Dan./US ent./musician; 1909-2000)
Borges, Jorge Luis (Argentinean writer; 1900-86)
Borghese Gallery (It.)
Borghese, Halston- (US bus.)
Borgia, Cesare (It. mil./pol.; 1476-1507)
Borgia, Lucrezia (It., Duchess of Ferrara; 1480-1519)
Borglum, (John) Gutzon (US sculptor; 1871-1941)
Borgnine, Ernest (b. Ermes Borgnino)(ent.; 1917-)
Boris Badenov (fict. chara.)
Boris Becker (tennis; 1967-)
Boris B. Yegorov (cosmo.; 1937-)
Boris Karloff (William Henry Pratt)(ent.; 1887-1969)
Boris (Fëdorovich) Godunov (Rus. tsar; 1552-1605)
Boris (Leonidovich) Pasternak (Rus. writer; 1890-1960)
Boris Trajkovski (pres., Macedonia; 1956-)
Boris V. Volyanov (cosmo.)
Boris (Nikolayevich) Yeltsin (ex-pres., Rus.; 1931-)
Borman, Frank (astro.; 1928-)
Bormann, Martin (Ger. Nazi leader; 1900-45)
Born Loser, The (comic strip)
Born, Max (Ger. physt.; 1882-1970)
Borneo (island, W Pac.)
Borodin, Alexander (Rus. comp.; 1833-87)
Boros, Julius (golf; 1920-94)
Boross, Peter (ex-PM, Hung.; 1928-)
Borromini, Francesco (It. arch.; 1599-1667)
Bors, Sir (Arthurian knight)
Bosc (pear)
Bosch Corp., Robert (US bus.)
Bosch, Carl (or Karl)(Ger. chem.; 1874-1940)
Bosch, Hieronymus (Dutch artist; 1450-1516)
Bosco, Philip (ent.; 1930-)
Bose (stereo equip.)
Bose Acoustimass
Bose Corp., The
Bose, Satyendranath (Indian physt./chem./ math.; 1894-1974)

Bose, Sir Jagadis Chunder (Indian physt.; 1858-1937)
Boskop (man, skull)
Bosley, Tom (ent.; 1927-)
Bosnia-Hercegovina (republic, Yug.)(also Bosnia-Herzegovina)
Bosnian Muslims (people)
Bosnian Serbs (people)
Bosporus Strait (Turk.)
Boss Tweed (William M[arcy] Tweed)(US pol.; 1823-78)
Bossangoa, Central African Republic
Bosson, Barbara (ent.; 1939-)
Bossy, Mike (hockey; 1957-)
Bostic, Earl (ent.; 1913-65)
Bostitch Inc., Stanley- (US bus.)
Boston bag (luggage)
Boston baked beans
Boston Bay
Boston Blackie (fict. detective)
Boston brown bread
Boston Bruins (hockey team)
Boston bull terrier (also Boston terrier)(dog)
Boston Celtics (basketball team)
Boston cream pie
Boston fern (plant)
Boston Globe (MA newspaper)
Boston Herald (MA newspaper)
Boston ivy (also Japanese Ivy)(plant)
Boston lettuce
Boston Massacre (US hist.; 3/5/1770)
Boston Museum of Fine Arts
Boston National Historical Park (MA)
Boston Pops Orchestra
Boston Red Sox (baseball team)
Boston rocker
Boston Tea Party (US hist.; 12/16/1773)
Boston terrier (also Boston bull terrier)(dog)
Boston, MA
Boston, Ralph (jumper; 1939-)
Bostonian
Bostwick, Barry (ent.; 1945-)
Boswell, James (Scot. biographer; 1740-95)
Bosworth Field (Eng.)
Bosworth, Brian (football; 1965-)
Botany 500 (US bus.)
Botany Bay, Australia (early Br. penal colony)
Botany wool (also botany)
Botha, Louis (ex-PM, SAfr.; 1863-1919)
Botha, Pieter W. (ex-pres., SAfr.; 1916-)
Bothnia, Gulf of (Swed./Fin.)
Botswana (Republic of)(formerly Bechuanaland)(central Afr.)
Botticelli, Sandro (It. artist; 1444-1510)
Bottoms, Timothy (ent.; 1951-)
Bottrop, Germany
Botts dots (auto.)
Bouaké, Ivory Coast
Bouar, Central African Republic   .
Boubacar, Sidi Mohamed Ould (ex-PM, Mauritania)
Boucher, François (Fr. artist; 1703-70)
Bougainville Islands (S Pac.)
Bougainville, Louis-Antoine de (Fr. nav.; 1729-1811)

Bouillon, Godfrey of (also Godefroy de Bouillon) (Fr. crusader; c1060-1100)
Boulanger, Nadia (Fr. cond./educ.; 1887-1979)
Boulder City, NV
Boulder Dam (officially Hoover Dam)(between Nevada and Arizona)
Boulder, CO
Boulez, Pierre (Fr. comp./cond.; 1925-)
Boulogne, France (also Boulogne-sur-Mer)
Boulogne-Billancourt, France (also Boulogne-sur-Seine)
Boult, Sir Adrian (Cedric)(Br. cond.; 1889-1983)
Boulwareism (econ.)
Bountiful, Lady (fict. chara., *Beaux' Strategem*)
Bountiful, UT
Bounty (paper towels)
Bounty, H.M.S. (ship; naval mutiny against Capt. Bligh)
Bounty, Mutiny on the (film, 1935, 1962)
Bourbon dynasty (France)
Bourbon Street (New Orleans)
Bourbonism (extreme political conservatism)
Bourdelle, Emile Antoine (Fr. artist; 1861-1929)
Bourdon(-tube) gauge (chem.)
Bourgeois, Léon Victor Auguste (Fr. pol.; 1851-1925)
Bourgeois, Louise (Fr./US sculptor; 1911-)
Bourgogne (region, Fr., formerly Burgundy)
Bourguignonne sauce
Bourguignonne, beef
Bourke-White, Margaret (US photo./writer; 1906-71)
Bournemouth, England
Bourque, Ray (hockey; 1960-)
Boursin (cheese)
Bouteflika, Abdelaziz (pres., Algeria; 1937-)
Bouvier des Flandres (also bouvier)(dog)
Bovary, Madame (G. Flaubert novel)
Bovary, Madame Emma (fict. chara.)
Bow Church (also St. Mary-le-Bow Church)(London)
Bow, Clara (the "It Girl")(ent.; 1905-65)
Bowdler, Thomas (Shakespeare editor; 1754-1825)
Bowe, Riddick (boxing; 1967-)
Bowen, Catherine Drinker (biographer; 1897-1973)
Bowers v. Hardwick (US law; 1986)
Bowery Boys
Bowery, the (NYC)(cheap hotels, saloons, destitutes)
Bowes' Original Amateur Hour, Major
Bowes, Major Edward (ent.; 1874-1946)
Bowie Kent Kuhn (baseball; 1926-)
Bowie knife (also l.c.)
Bowie, David (b. David Robert Jones)(ent.; 1947-)
Bowie, James "Jim" (US frontier; 1796-1836)
Bowker Co., R. R.
Bowles, Camilla Parker- (Br. news; 1947-)
Bowles, Chester (US dipl.; 1901-86)
Bowling Green State University (Bowling Green, OH)
Bowling Green, KY, OH
BoxCar Willie (b. Lecil Martin) (ent.; 1931-99)
Boxer Rebellion/Uprising (Ch.; 1898-1900)

Boxer, Barbara (nee Levy)(US cong.; 1940-)
Boxing Day (Br. holiday)
Boxleitner, Bruce (ent.; 1950-)
Boxster, Porsche (auto.)
Boy Blue, Little (nursery rhyme)
Boy George (b. George Alan O'Dowd)(ent.; 1961-)
Boy Scouts of America (founded 1910)
Boy's Town of the West (Hanna Boys Center)(CA)
Boyardee, Chef
Boyce, William (comp.; 1710-79)
Boycott, Charles C., Capt. (Br., boycotted by Ir. tenants; 1832-97)
Boyd, Guillermo Ford (Panama, pol.)
Boyd, Stephen (b. Stephen Millar)(ent.; 1928-77)
Boyd, William "Hopalong Cassidy" (ent.; 1898-1972)
Boyer, Charles (ent.; 1899-1978)
Boykin spaniel (dog)
Boyle, Lara Flynn (ent.; 1970-)
Boyle, Peter (ent.; 1933-)
Boyle, Robert (Br. physt./chem.; 1627-91)
Boyle's law (physics)
Boynton greeting cards
Boynton, Sandra (US writer)
Boys Town, NE
Boys' Life (mag.)
Boys, Sir Michael Hardie (gov.-gen., NewZeal.; 1931-)
Boyz II Men (pop music)
Boz (pseud. of Charles Dickens)
Boz (William Royce) Scaggs (ent.; 1944-)
Bozcaada (Turk. island in Aegean Sea)
Bozeman Trail (to MT, gold fields; 1863-65)
Bozeman, John (US pioneer; 1835-67)
Bozeman, MT
B/P (blood pressure)
BPD (also bpd)(barrels per day)
BPI (or bpi)(bytes per inch, bits per inch)
BPOE (Benevolent and Protective Order of Elks)
Br (chem. sym., bromine)
Brabant (province, Belgium)
Brabant Copper (cookware)
Bracco, Lorraine (ent.; 1955-)
Brace Jovanovich, Inc., Harcourt
Brach & Sons, E. J. (US bus.)
Brach's (candy)
Bracken, Eddie (ent.; 1920-)
Bracknell, Lady (fict. chara., *The Importance of Being Earnest*)
Brad Anderson (cartoonist, *Marmaduke*; 1924-)
Brad Pitt (ent.; 1963-)
Brad(ford) Park, (Douglas)(hockey; 1948-)
Brad Renfro (ent.; 1982-)
Bradbury, Ray (US writer/sci fi; 1920-)
Braddock, Edward (Br. gen. in Amer.; 1695-1755)
Bradenton, FL
Bradford Dillman (ent.; 1930-)
Bradford Exchange, Inc.
Bradford, England
Bradford, William (1st gov., Pilgrim colony; 1590-1657)
Bradlee, Ben (US newspaper exec.; 1921-)
Bradley Co., Milton
Bradley, Bill (William Warren)(US cong../basketball; 1943-)

Bradley, Ed (US TV jour.; 1941-)
Bradley, Marion Zimmer (US writer; 1930-99)
Bradley, Milton- (board games)
Bradley, Omar Nelson (US gen.; 1893-1981)
Bradley, Tom (ex-mayor, Los Angeles, CA; 1917-98)
Bradley, Truman (ent.; 1905-74)
Bradshaw, Terry (football; 1948-)
Bradstreet Corp., Dun &
Bradstreet, Anne Dudley (US poet, c1612-72)
Brady Bill (gun control; 1993)
Brady Bunch (TV show)
Brady, James B. ("Diamond Jim")(US finan.; 1856-1917)
Brady, Jim (James S.)(US gun control advocate/Brady Bill; 1940-)
Brady, Mathew B. (US photo.; 1823?-96)
Brady, Sarah (US gun control advocate/Brady Bill; 1942-)
Braganza, Catherine of (Br. queen of Charles II; 1638-1705)
Bragg, Billy (ent./songwriter; 1957-)
Bragg, Fort, NC (mil.)
Bragg, Sir William Henry (Br. physt.; 1862-1942)
Bragg, Sir William Lawrence (Br. physt.; 1890-1971)
Braghis, Dumitru (PM, Moldova; 1957-)
Brahe, Tycho (astron.; 1546-1601)
Brahma (also Brahman)(cattle)
Brahma (chicken)
Brahma (rel.)
Brahman (also Brahmin)(rel.)
Brahmanism (rel.)
Brahmaputra River (Asia)
Brahms, Johannes (Ger. comp.; 1833-97)
Brahui (lang.)
Braila, Romania
Braille (writing system for the blind)
Braille Institute (Los Angeles)
Braille, Louis (Fr., blind inv. of Braille; 1809-52)
Brailowsky, Alexander (pianist; 1896-1976)
Brain Trust (FDR's advisers)
Braithwaite, Nicholas (ex-PM, Grenada; 1925-)
Bram (Abraham) Stoker (Br. writer; 1847-1912)
Bramante, Donato D'Agnolo (It. arch.; 1444-1514)
Brampton, Ontario, Canada
Branagh, Kenneth (ent./writer; 1960-)
Brancacci Chapel (Italy)
Branch Davidians (rel. cult)
Branch Rickey, (Wesley)(baseball; 1881-1965)
Brancusi, Constantin (Romanian artist; 1876-1957)
Brand, Vance (astro.; 1931-)
Brandauer, Klaus Maria (ent.; 1944-)
Brandeis, Louis (Dembitz)(US jurist; 1856-1941)
Brandenburg (state, Ger.)
Brandenburg Concerto (by Johann Sebastian Bach)
Brandenburg Gate
Brandenburg, Germany
Brando, Marlon (ent.; 1924-)
Brandon De Wilde (ent.; 1942-72)
Brandon Tartikoff (ent.; 1949-97)
Brandon, Manitoba, Canada

Brandt, Willy (Herbert Ernst Karl Frahm)(ex-chanc., WGer.; 1913-92)
Brandy (b. Brandy Norwood)(ent.; 1979-)
brandy Alexander (also l.c.)(cocktail)
Brandywine, Battle of (US hist.; 1777)
Branestawm, Professor
Branford Marsalis (ent.; 1960-)
Braniff Airways
Branigan, Laura (ent.; 1957-)
Branko Crvenkovski (ex-PM, Macedonia; 1962)
Branson, MO
Branstad, Terry E(dward)(ex-IA gov.; 1946-)
Brantford, Ontario, Canada
Braque, Georges (Fr. artist; 1882-1963)
Brasco, Donnie (film, 1996)
Brasilia, Brazil
Brasov, Romania
Brasselle, Keefe (ent.; 1923-81)
Brasseur, Isabelle (figure skating; 1971-)
Brathwaite, Chris (track; 1949-84)
Bratislava, Czechoslovakia
Bratt, Benjamin (ent.; 1963-)
Brattain, Walter Houser (US physt./inv.; 1902-87)
Brattleboro, VT
Bratwurst (also l.c.)(sausage)
Braugher, Andre (ent.; 1962-)
Braun (kitchen appliances)
Braun Corp.
Braun principle, Le Chatelier- (also Le Chatelier['s] p.)(chem.)
Braun, Carol Moseley- (US pol.; 1947-)
Braun, Eva (mistress of Adolph Hitler; 1910-45)
Braun, Inc.
Braun, Werner (or Wernher) von (Ger./US eng.; 1912-77)
Braunschweig, Germany (also Brunswick)
Braunschweiger (also braunschweiger)(sausage)
Bravada, Oldsmobile (auto.)
Brave New World (A. Huxley novel)
Braves, Atlanta (baseball team)
Bravo Network (TV channel)
Braxton, Toni (ent.; 1966-)
Bray v. Alexandria Women's Health Clinic (US law; 1993)
Brazauskas, Algirdas (pres., Lith.)
Brazelton, T(homas) Berry II (pediatrician/writer; 1918-)
Brazil (Federative Republic of)(SAmer.)
Brazil nut (tree/nut)
Brazzaville, Republic of the Congo
Brazzi, Rossano (It. ent.; 1916-94)
Brea Tar Pits, La (fossils, CA)
Breaker Morant (film, 1979)
Breakfast at Tiffany's (film, 1961)
Breakstone Sugar Creek Foods (US bus.)
Breakstone's (dairy prods.)
Bream, Julian (Alexander)(ent.; 1933-)
Breasted, James Henry (US archaeol.; 1865-1935)
Breathalyzer (alcohol level)
Breathed, Berke (cartoonist, *Bloom County*; 1957-)
Breathless Mahoney (fict. chara., *Dick Tracy*)
Breaux, John B. (US cong.; 1944-)

Brecht v. Abrahamson (US law; 1993)
Brecht, Bertolt (Ger. writer; 1898-1956)
Breck (hair care)
Breck, Miss (hair care)
Breckinridge, John C(abell)(ex-US VP/gen.; 1821-75)
Breed's Hill (Battle of Bunker Hill)(US hist., MA; 1775)
Breeders' Cup (racing)
Breen, Bobby (Robert)(ent.; 1927-)
Breeze, Plymouth (auto.)
Brel, Jacques (ent./comp.; 1929-78)
Bremen (state, Ger.)
Bremen, Germany
Bremerhaven, Germany
Bremerton, WA
Brenda Lee (b. Brenda Mae Tarpley)(ent.; 1944-)
Brenda Starr (comic strip)
Brenda Vaccaro (ent.; 1939-)
Brendan Behan (Ir. writer; 1923-64)
Brendan Fraser (ent.; 1968-)
Brennan, Eileen (ent.; 1935-)
Brennan, Walter (ent.; 1894-1974)
Brennan, William J(oseph), Jr. (US jurist; 1906-97)
Brenneman, Amy (ent.; 1964-)
Brenner Pass (in Alps, Aus./It.)
Brenner, David (ent.; 1945-)
Brennschluss (astron.)
Brent Musburger (ent.; 1939-)
Brent Scowcroft (US pol.; 1925-)
Brent Spiner (ent.; 1949-)
Brent, George (ent.; 1904-79)
Brentano's Bookstore
Brentwood, CA, MO, PA
Brer Fox (fict. chara., *Uncle Remus*)
Brer Rabbit (fict. chara., *Uncle Remus*)
Brer Rabbit molasses
Brereton C. Jones (ex-KY gov.; 1939-)
Breslin, Jimmy (US writer; 1930-)
Brest, Belarus
Brest, France
Bret Harte, (Francis)(US writer; 1839-1902)
Bret Maverick (fict chara.; *Maverick*)
Bret Saberhagen (baseball; 1964-)
Bretagne, France (also Brittany)
Brethaire (med.)
Brethine (med.)
Breton (headwear, lace)
Breton (lang.)
Breton, André (Fr. poet; 1896-1966)
Brett Butler (ent.; 1958-)
Brett Hull (hockey; 1964-)
Brett, George (baseball; 1953-)
Breuer chair (tubular steel)
Breuer, Marcel (US arch.; 1902-81)
Brewer, Teresa (ent.; 1931-)
Brewers, Milwaukee (baseball team)
Brewster chair
Brewster McCloud (film, 1970)
Brewster Place, The Women of (TV show)
Brewster, Kingman, Jr. (US educ.; 1919-88)
Brewster, Punky (fict. chara.)
Brewster, William (Br., Pilgrim leader; 1567-1644)
Breyer, Stephen G. (US jurist; 1938-)

Breyers ice cream
Brezhnev, Leonid Ilyich (ex-pres., USSR; 1906-82)
Brian Aherne (ent.; 1902-86)
Brian Austin Green (ent.; 1973-)
Brian Boitano (figure skating; 1963-)
Brian Bosworth (football; 1965-)
Brian De Palma (ent.; 1940)
Brian Dennehy (ent.; 1938-)
Brian Donlevy (ent.; 1889-1972)
Brian Eno (ent.; 1948-)
Brian Epstein (ent.; 1935-67)
Brian Gottfried (tennis; 1952-)
Brian Holland (US comp.; 1941-)
Brian Keith (ent.; 1921-97)
Brian Littrell (ent., Backstreet Boys; 1975-)
Brian Mulroney (ex-PM, Can.; 1939-)
Brian Orser (figure skating; 1961-)
Brian Spencer (hockey; 1949-88)
Brian Stuart Goodell (swimming; 1959-)
Brian Williams (US TV jour.)
Brian Wilson (ent.; 1942-)
Brian's Song (film, 1971)
Briand Pact, Kellogg- (also Kellogg Peace Pact)(US/Fr.; 1927)
Briand, Aristide (ex-PM, Fr.; 1862-1932)
Briar Cliff College (Sioux City, IA)
Briard (dog)
Bricanyl (med.)
Brice, Fanny (b. Fannie Borach)(ent.; 1891-1951)
Brick, NJ
Brickell, Edie (ent.; 1966-)
Bride of Frankenstein (film, 1935)
Bride's (mag.)
Brides of Dracula (film, 1960)
Bridey Murphy, The Search for (film, 1956)
Bridge of San Luis Rey, The (film, 1944)
Bridge on the River Kwai, The (film, 1957)
Bridgeport Marine Corps Mountain Warfare Training Center (CA)
Bridgeport Post (CT newspaper)
Bridgeport, AL, CT, IL, OH, PA, TX
Bridger-Teton National Forest
Bridges of Madison County, The (R. J. Waller novel)
Bridges, Beau (b. Lloyd Vernet Bridges III) (ent.; 1941-)
Bridges, Harry (Alfred Renton Bridges)(US labor leader; 1901-90)
Bridges, Jeff (ent.; 1949-)
Bridges, Lloyd (Vernet)(ent.; 1913-98)
Bridges, Todd (ent.; 1965-)
Bridgestone Tire Co. Ltd.
Bridget Fonda (ent.; 1964-)
Bridget Jones's Diary (novel, film)
Bridgeton, NJ
Bridgetown, Barbados
Brie (cheese)
Brigadoon (film, 1954)
Briggs & Stratton Corp.
Briggs, Clare (cartoonist, *Mr. & Mrs.*; 1875-1930)
Brigham Young (US rel./Mormon; 1801-77)
Brigham Young University (Provo, UT; Laie, Oahu, HI)
Bright's disease (med.)

Brighton Beach Memoirs (play)
Brighton Beach Memories (film, 1986)
Brighton, CO
Brighton, England
Brighton, Victoria, Australia
Brigitte Bardot (b. Camille Javal)(Fr. ent.; 1934-)
Brigitte Nielsen (ent.; 1963-)
Brill's disease
Brillo pad
Brimley, Wilford (ent.; 1934-)
Brindisi, Italy
Brinell hardness test (metal)
Brinell, Johann August (Swed. eng.; 1849-1925)
Bringing Up Father (comic strip)
Brink's armored car
Brinker, or the Silver Skates, Hans (children's book)
Brinkley, Christie (US model; 1953-)
Brinkley, David (US TV jour.; 1920-)
Brisbane, Queensland, Australia
Bristol Bay (AK)
Bristol board (cardboard)
Bristol Channel (Eng.)
Bristol, CT, PA, RI, TN, VA
Bristol, England
Bristol-Myers Products (US bus.)
Bristol-Myers Squibb Company
Britain, Battle of (WWII air battle)
Britain, Great (Eng., Scot., and Wales, part of the UK)
Britannia (poetic for Great Britain)
Briticism (also Britishism)(linguistics)
British (people)
British Airways
British Airways Plc
British Antarctic Territory
British Broadcasting Corporation (BCC)(TV)
British Broadcasting Corporation America (BBC America)(TV channel)
British Columbia (province, Can.)
British East India Company (trade; 1600-1873)
British Empire
British English
British Guiana (now Guyana)
British Honduras (now Belize)
British Hong Kong
British Indian Ocean Territory
British Isles
British Knights (US bus.)
British Museum (London)
British North America Act (Can.; 1867)
British Open (golf tournament)
British Somaliland (now part of Somalia)
British thermal unit (BTU, B.T.U., Btu, B.t.u.) (physics)
British Virgin Islands (West Indies)
British West Indies
Britisher (also Brit or Briton)(native of Br.)
Britney Spears (ent.; 1981-)
BritRail Pass
Britt Ekland (Swed./US ent.; 1942-)
Brittany spaniel (dog)
Brittany, Anne of (queen, Fr.; 1477-1514)
Brittany, France
Brittany, Morgan (b. Suzanne Cupito)(ent.; 1951-)

Britten, Benjamin (also Baron Britten of Aldeburgh)(Br. comp.; 1913-76)
Brix scale (chem., sugar content)
Brno, Czechoslovakia
Broad Home Corp., Kaufman and
Broadcast Employees and Technicians, National Association of (also NABET)
Broadcasters, National Association of (also NAB)
Broadcasting Company, National (also NBC)
Broadway (major NYC avenue; theater district, "the Great White Way")
Broadway Danny Rose (film, 1984)
Broadway Joe (aka Joe [Joseph William] Namath)(football; 1943-)
Broadway, Off (also off Broadway)(theater)
Broadway, Off Off (also off off Broadway)(theater)
Brobdingnag (fict. land of giants, *Gulliver's Travels*)
Brock Candy Co.
Brock Peters (ent.; 1927-)
Brock, Lou(is Clark)(baseball; 1939-)
Brocklin, Norm Van (football; 1926-83)
Brockovich, Erin (film, 2000)
Brockton, MA
Broderick Crawford (ent.; 1911-86)
Broderick, Betty (US news)
Broderick, Matthew (ent.; 1962-)
Brodie, The Prime of Miss Jean (film, 1969)
Brodsky, Joseph (US writer; 1940-)
Brody, Jane (US jour.; 1941-)
Broglie, Louis de (Fr. physt.; 1893-1987)
Brokaw, Tom (US TV jour.; 1940-)
Broken Arrow, OK
Brokopondo, Suriname
Brolin, James (b. James Bruderlin)(ent.; 1940-)
Bromfield, Louis (writer; 1896-1956)
Bromo-Seltzer (med.)
Brompton('s) cocktail/mixture (med.)
Bronco Eddie Bauer, Ford (auto.)
Bronco XL, Ford (auto.)
Bronco XLT, Ford (auto.)
Bronco, Ford (auto.)
Broncos, Denver (football team)
Bronica (US bus.)
Bronislaw Malinowski (Pol. anthrop.; 1884-1942)
Bronkaid Mist (med.)
Bronko (Bronislaw) Nagurski (football; 1908-90)
Bronkodyl (med.)
Bronkolixir (med.)
Bronkometer (med.)
Bronkosol (med.)
Bronkotabs (med.)
Bronson Alcott, Amos (US educ./phil.; 1799-1888)
Bronson Pinchot (ent.; 1959-)
Bronson, Charles (b. Charles Buchinsky)(ent.; 1921-)
Brontë sisters (Anne, Charlotte, Emily)
Brontë, Anne (aka Acton Bell)(Br. writer; 1820-49)
Brontë, Charlotte (aka Currer Bell)(Br. writer; 1816-55)
Brontë, Emily (aka Ellis Bell)(Br. writer; 1818-48)
Bronx (borough, NYC)
Bronx cheer (also raspberry)
Bronx cocktail (mixed drink)
Bronx Zoo (NYC)

Bronze Age (anthrop.)
Bronze Star Medal (Bronze Star)
Bronzino, Agnolo (It. artist; 1503-72)
Brook Farm (MA community; 1841-47)
Brook, Peter (ent.; 1925-)
Brooke Astor (socialite/philanthropist; 1905-)
Brooke Shields (ent.; 1965-)
Brooke, Edward William (US pol.; 1919-)
Brooke, Rupert (Br. poet; 1887-1915)
Brookhaven National Laboratory (atomic energy, Long Island NY)
Brookings Institution (econ. org.; DC)
Brookline, MA
Brooklyn (borough, NYC)
Brooklyn Bridge (NYC)
Brooklyn Coast Guard Air Station
Brooklyn Museum of Art
Brooklyn, NY, OH
Brooks Adams (US hist.; 1848-1927)
Brooks Atkinson (Justin)(US critic; 1894-1984)
Brooks Brothers
Brooks Robinson (baseball; 1937-)
Brooks, Albert (b. Albert Einstein)(ent.; 1947-)
Brooks, Avery (ent.; 1949-)
Brooks, (Troyal) Garth (ent.; 1962-)
Brooks, Gwendolyn (US writer; 1917-)
Brooks, James L. (ent.; 1940-)
Brooks, Mel (b. Melvin Kaminsky)(ent.; 1926-)
Brooks, Our Miss (TV show)
Brooks, Van Wyck (US hist.; 1886-1963)
Broom Hilda (comic strip)
Broonzy, Big Bill (US jazz; 1893-1958)
Brosnan, Pierce (ent.; 1953-)
Brotherly Love, City of (Philadelphia)
Brothers Grimm (wrote/collected folk tales)
Brothers Karamazov, The (Dostoevsky novel)
Brothers, Dr. Joyce (b. Joyce Bauer)(US psych./writer; 1928-)
Brothers, Marx (Chico, Harpo, Groucho, Gummo, Zeppo)
Brothers, The Mills (pop music)
Brougham, Cadillac (auto.)
Brougham, Cadillac Fleetwood (auto.)
Broun, Matthew Heywood Campbell (jour.; 1888-1939)
Brown & Co., Inc., Little
Brown & Williamson Tobacco Corp.
Brown Apparel, Inc., Buster
brown-eyed Susan (plant)
Brown-Forman, Inc.
Brown Group, Inc.
Brown Swiss (cattle)
Brown v. Board of Education of Topeka, Kansas (US law; 1954)
Brown, Blair (ent.; 1948-)
Brown, Bobby (ent.; 1969-)
Brown, Buster (cartoon chara.)
Brown, Buster (shoes, collar)
Brown, Charles Brockden (writer; 1771-1810)
Brown, Charlie (fict. chara., *Peanuts*)
Brown, Christy (Ir. writer/artist; 1932-81)
Brown, Clifford (US jazz; 1930-56)
Brown, Corrine (US cong.)
Brown, Edmund Gerald "Jerry," Jr. (ex-CA gov.; 1938-)

Brown, Edmund Gerald "Pat," Sr. (ex-CA gov.; 1905-96)
Brown, Ford Madox (Br. artist; 1821-93)
Brown, Hank (George Hanks)(US pol.; 1940-)
Brown, Helen Gurley (US editor/writer; 1922-)
Brown, James (ent.; 1933-)
Brown, Jesse (US ex-secy./vet. affairs; 1944-)
Brown, Jimmy (James Nathaniel)(football/ent.; 1936-)
Brown, Joe E. (ent.; 1892-1973)
Brown, John (US abolitionist; 1800-59)
Brown, Larry (football; 1947-)
Brown, Lee P. (Houston mayor; 1937-)
Brown, Les (ent.; 1912-2001)
Brown, Margaret Wise (children's writer; 1910-62)
Brown, Melanie (aka Scary Spice)(ent.; 1975-)
Brown, Murphy (fict. chara.)
Brown, Murphy (TV show)
Brown, Nacio Herb (US comp.; 1896-1964)
Brown, Pat (Edmund Gerald), Sr. (ex-gov., CA; 1905-96)
Brown, Paul (football coach; 1908-91)
Brown, Rap (b. Hubert Gerald Brown)(US activist; 1943-)
Brown, Ray (US jazz; 1926-)
Brown, Robert (Scot. botanist; 1773-1858)
Brown, Ron(ald Harmon)(US ex-secy./ commerce; 1941-96)
Brown, The Unsinkable Molly (film, 1964)
Brown, Trisha (choreographer; 1936-)
Brownback, Sam (US cong.; 1956-)
Browne belt, Sam (mil. sword belt)
Browne, Agnes (film, 1999)
Browne, Dik (cartoonist, *Hi & Lois, Hagar the Horrible*; 1917-89)
Browne, Jackson (ent.; 1948-)
Browne, Joy (on-air psychologist; 1950-)
Browne, Roscoe Lee (ent.; 1925-)
Browne, Sylvia (US psychic)
Browner, Carol M. (US ex-adm./EPA; 1955-)
Brownian movement/motion (particles in fluid)
Brownie points
Browning automatic rifle/machine gun
Browning, Elizabeth Barrett (Br. poet, wife of Robert; 1806-61)
Browning, John M(oses)(US inv.; 1955-1926)
Browning, Kurt (figure skating; 1967-)
Browning, Robert (Br. poet, husband of Elizabeth; 1812-89)
Browns Ferry (nuclear power station, AL)
Browns, Cleveland (football team)
Brownsville, FL, PA, TN, TX
Broyhill furniture
Broyhill Furniture Industries, Inc.
Brubaker (film, 1980)
Brubeck, Dave (David Warren)(US jazz; 1920-)
Bruce (Edward) Babbitt (US ex-secy./interior; 1938-)
Bruce Boxleitner (ent.; 1950-)
Bruce Catton (US historian; 1899-1978)
Bruce Dern (ent.; 1936-)
Bruce Furniss (swimming; 1957-)
Bruce G. Sundlun (RI gov.; 1920-)
Bruce Hornsby (ent.; 1954-)
Bruce Jenner (US track/TV jour.; 1949-)

Bruce King (ex-NM gov.; 1924-)
Bruce Lee (ent./martial arts; 1940-73)
Bruce Springsteen (ent.; 1949-)
Bruce Wayne (ent.)
Bruce Weitz (ent.; 1943-)
Bruce Willis (ent.; 1955-)
Bruce Winery, David (US bus.)
Bruce, Lenny (b. Leonard Alfred Schneider) (ent.; 1926-66)
Bruce, Nigel (ent.; 1895-1953)
Brücke, die (Ger. art movement)
Bruckner, Anton (Austl. comp.; 1824-96)
Brudenell, James Thomas (7th Earl of Cardigan) (Br. mil./pol., cardigan sweater; 1797-1868)
Brueghel, Jan (also Breughel)(aka the "Velvet Bruegel")(Flem. artist; 1568-1625)
Brueghel, Pieter, the Elder (also Breughel)(aka "Peasant Bruegel")(Flem. artist; 1525-69)
Brueghel, Pieter, the Younger (also Breughel) (aka "Hell Bruegel")(Flem. artist; 1564-1638)
Bruges, Belgium
Bruhl, Lucien Lévy- (Fr. phil.; 1857-1939)
Bruhn, Erik (b. Belton Evers)(ballet; 1928-86)
Bruins, Boston (hockey team)
Brumel, Valeri (jumper; 1942-)
Brummell Ties, Beau (US bus.)
Brummell, Beau (film, 1954)
Brummell, Beau (George Bryan)(Br. dandy; 1778-1840)
Brundtland, Gro Harlem (ex-PM, Nor.; 1939-)
Brunei (State of)(also Brunei Darussalam)(NW Borneo)
Brunei, Sultan of (Muda Hassanal Bolkiah Mu'izzaddin Waddaulah)
Brunelleschi, Filippo (It. arch.; 1377-1446)
Brunhart, Hans (ex-premier, Liechtenstein; 1945-)
Brunner, Emil (Swed. rel.; 1889-1966)
Bruno Bettelheim (Aus./US psych.; 1903-90)
Bruno Kirby (ent.; 1949-)
Bruno Walter (b. Bruno Walter Schlesinger)(cond.; 1876-1962)
Bruno, Giordano (It. phil.; 1548-1600)
Brunswick black (color, varnish)
Brunswick Corp.
Brunswick green (color)
Brunswick Naval Air Station (ME)
Brunswick stew
Brunswick, Caroline of (Br. queen of George IV; 1768-1821)
Brunswick, GA, ME, MD, OH
Brunswick, Germany
Brussels carpet
Brussels griffon (dog)
Brussels lace
Brussels sprout(s)(vegetable)
Brussels, Belgium
Brut 33 (cologne)
Brut, Fabergé (cologne)
Brutus, Marcus Junius (Roman pol., Caesar assassin; c78-42 BC)
Bryan Adams (ent.; 1959-)
Bryan Trottier (hockey; 1956-)
Bryan, OH, TX
Bryan, Richard H. (Dick)(US pol.; 1937-)
Bryan, William Jennings (US pol./orator; 1860-

1925)
Bryant Gumbel (US TV jour.; 1948-)
Bryant, Anita (ent.; 1940-)
Bryant, Bear (Paul)(football coach; 1913-83)
Bryant, Inc., Lane
Bryant, Kobe (basketball; 1978-)
Bryant, Rosalyn Evette (track; 1956-)
Bryant, William Cullen (US poet/jour.; 1794-
    1878)
Bryce Canyon National Park (UT)
Brylcreem (hair care)
Bryn Mawr College (Bryn Mawr, PA)
Bryn Mawr, PA
Brynmawr, Wales
Brynner, Yul (ent.; 1915-85)
Bryophyta (plant classification)
Bryson, Peabo (ent.; 1951-)
Brzezinski, Zbigniew (US ex-pres. adviser; 1928-)
BS (Bachelor of Science)
BSA (Boy Scouts of America)
B school (business school)
B-side (music)
BTU (also BTU, Btu, B.t.u.)(Br. thermal unit)
Bubba (Charles Aaron) Smith (football; 1945-)
Bubble Yum (gum)
Bubble, Mr. (bubble bath)
Buber, Martin (Isr. phil.; 1878-1965)
Bubi (lang./people)
Bucaramanga, Columbia
Buccaneers, Tampa Bay (football team)
Bucephalus (war horse of Alexander the Great)
Buchanan, James (15th US pres.; 1791-1868)
Buchanan, Liberia
Buchanan, Patrick J. (US pol. commentator/
    candidate; 1938-)
Bucharest, Romania
Buchenwald (Ger. concentration camp)
Bucher, Lloyd M., Commander (US mil.)
Buchholz, Horst (ent.; 1933-)
Buchner funnel (chem.)
Buchner, Eduard (Ger. chem.; 1860-1917)
Buchwald, Art (US columnist; 1925-)
Buck Clayton (US jazz; 1911-)
Buck Owens (ent.; 1929-)
Buck Rogers (fict. chara.)
Buck Rogers in the 21st Century (film, 1979)
Buck, Pearl S(ydenstricker)(US writer; 1892-
    1973)
Buckaroo Banzai (fict. chara.)
Bucket, Charlie (fict. chara.)
Buckeye State (nickname, OH)
Buckingham Palace (London, home of royal family)
Buckingham, England
Buckingham, Lindsey (ent.; 1947-)
Buckingham, Quebec, Canada
Buckinghamshire (county, Eng.)
Buckley v. Fitzsimmons (US law; 1993)
Buckley, Betty (ent.; 1947-)
Buckley, Christopher (US writer; 1952-)
Buckley, Jeff (ent./songwriter; 1966-97)
Buckley, William F., Jr. (US editor/writer; 1925-)
Bucknell University (Lewisburg, PA)
Bucks County Courier-Times (PA newspaper)
Bucks, Milwaukee (basketball team)
Bud (William) Abbott (ent.; 1898-1974)

Bud Collyer (ent.)
Bud Fisher (cartoonist, Mutt & Jeff; 1884-1954)
Bud Powell (US jazz; 1924-66)
Bud (Charles Burnham) Wilkinson (football;
    1916-94)
Bud Yorkin (ent.; 1926-)
Budapest, Hungary
Budd (Wilson) Schulberg (US writer; 1914-)
Budd, Billy (H. Melville story)
Budd, Zola (SAfr. athlete; 1966-)
Buddha (Gautama Siddhartha)(Indian phil.,
    founded Buddhism; c563-c483 BC)
Buddhism (rel.)
Buddhism, Lama(istic)(rel.)
Buddhism, Mahayana (rel.)
Buddhism, Theravada (rel.)
Buddhism, Tibetan
Buddhism, Zen (rel.)
Buddhist (rel.)
Buddig & Co., Carl
Buddig, Carl (meats)
Buddy Bolden, (Charles)(US jazz; 1868-1931)
Buddy De Franco (US jazz; 1933-)
Buddy De Sylva (US lyricist; 1895-1950)
Buddy Ebsen (b. Christian Ebsen, Jr.)(ent.; 1908-)
Buddy (George) Guy (ent.; 1936-)
Buddy Hackett (b. Leonard Hacker)(ent.; 1924-)
Buddy Holly (ent.; 1936-59)
Buddy Holly and the Crickets (pop music)
Buddy Rich (US jazz; 1917-87)
Buddy (Charles) Rogers (ent.; 1904-99)
Budge, Don (tennis; 1915-2000)
Budget (car rental)
Budget Rent A Car Corp.
Budgetel Inns (US bus.)
Budweiser (beer)
Buehler Vineyards (US bus.)
Bueller's Day Off, Ferris (film, 1986)
Buena Park, CA
Buena Vista Pictures
Buena Vista Winery (US bus.)
Buenadventura, Colombia
Bueno, Maria (tennis; 1939-)
Buenos Aires, Argentina
Buff (goose)
Buffalo Bill (William Frederick) Cody (US scout/
    ent.; 1846-1917)
Buffalo Bills (football team)
Buffalo Bob Smith (b. Robert Schmidt) (ent.;
    1917-98)
Buffalo China (chinaware)
Buffalo News (NY newspaper)
Buffalo Sabres (hockey team)
Buffalo Spree Magazine
Buffalo Springfield (pop music)
Buffalo, NY
Bufferin (med.)
Buffett, Jimmy (ent./songwriter; 1946-)
Buffett, Warren (investment expert; 1930-)
Buffy (Beverly) Sainte-Marie (ent.; 1941-)
Buffy the Vampire Slayer (film, 1992)
Buf-Puf
Bugatti (auto.)
Bugatti EB110 (auto.)
Bugatti, Ettore (It. designer; 1881-1947)

Bugatti, Jean (It. designer; 1909-39)
Bugis (lang.)
Bugs (George) Moran (US gangster; 1893-1957)
Bugs Bunny & Looney Tunes Magazine (mag.)
Bugs Bunny (cartoon chara.)
Bugsy (Benjamin) Siegel (US gangster/Las Vegas gambling; 1906-47)
Bugsy Malone Story, The (film, 1976)
Buick (auto.)
Buick Century (auto.)
Buick Century Custom (auto.)
Buick Century Limited (auto.)
Buick Century Special (auto.)
Buick LeSabre (auto.)
Buick LeSabre Custom (auto.)
Buick LeSabre Limited (auto.)
Buick Park Avenue (auto.)
Buick Park Avenue Ultra (auto.)
Buick Regal (auto.)
Buick Regal Custom (auto.)
Buick Regal Gran Sport (auto.)
Buick Regal GS (auto.)
Buick Regal GSE (auto.)
Buick Regal Limited (auto.)
Buick Regal LS (auto.)
Buick Regal LSE (auto.)
Buick Rendezvous (auto.)
Buick Riviera (auto.)
Buick Roadmaster (auto.)
Buick Roadmaster Estate (auto.)
Buick Roadmaster Limited (auto.)
Buick Skylark (auto.)
Buick Skylark Custom (auto.)
Buick Skylark Gran Sport (auto.)
Buick Skylark Limited (auto.)
Buick Starfire (auto.)
Buick, David Dunbar (US bus./auto.; 1854-1929)
Building Design Journal (mag.)
Buji (lang.)
Bujold, Genevieve (ent.; 1942-)
Bujones, Fernando (ballet; 1955-)
Bujumbura, Burundi
Bukavu, Zaire
Bukhara, Uzbekistan
Bukharin, Nikolai (USSR pol.; 1888-1938)
Bulatovic, Momir (ex-PM, Yug.; 1956-)
Bulawayo, Zimbabwe
Bülent Ecevit (PM, Turk.; 1925-)
Bulfinch, Charles (US arch.; 1763-1844)
Bulfinch's Mythology
Bulgakov, Mikhail (Rus. writer; 1891-1940)
Bulganin, Nikolai A(leksandrovich)(ex-PM USSR; 1895-1975)
Bulgaria (Republic of)(SE Eur.)
Bulgarian (lang./people)
Bulgarian Orthodox (rel.)
Bulge, Battle of the (WWII; 1944-45)
Bull Durham (film, 1988)
Bull Frog (healthcare)
Bull Moose Party (US pol.; 1912-17)
Bull Run, Battle(s) of (US hist.; 1861 & 1862)
Bull, John (Br. comp.; 1562-1628)
Bull, John (pamphlets)(Br. hist.; 1712)
Bull, John (synonym for Eng. people)

Bulldog Drummond (film, 1929)
Bullets, Washington (basketball team)
Bullion State (nickname, MO)
Bullitt, William C. (US dipl.; 1891-1967)
Bullock, Sandra (ent.; 1964-)
Bullock's (US bus.)
Bulls, Chicago (basketball team)
Bullwinkle (cartoon)
Bully Hill (US bus.)
Bulova (watches/clocks)
Bulova Corp.
Bülow, Bernhard von, Prince (ex-chanc., Ger.; 1849-1929)
Bulow, Claus von (US news; 1926-)
Bulow, Sunny (Martha) von (US news; 1932-)
Bumble Bee (tuna)
Bumble Bee Seafoods (US bus.)
Bumbry, Grace (ent.; 1937-)
Bumex (med.)
Bumpers, Dale (US pol.; 1925-)
Bumstead, Blondie (cartoon chara.)
Bumstead, Dagwood (cartoon chara.)
BUN (blood urea nitrogen)(med.)
Bunche, Ralph J. (US dipl.; 1904-71)
Bundesrat (Ger. govt.)
Bundt (pan)
Bundy, McGeorge (US educ.; 1919-96)
Bundy, Ted (US serial killer; 1946-89)
Bundy, William Putnam (US editor; 1917-2000)
Bunk Johnson (US jazz; 1879-1949)
Bunker Hill (Boston, MA)
Bunker Hill, Battle of (Breed's Hill)(US hist., MA; 1775)
Bunker, Archie (fict. chara., *All in the Family*)
Bunn (kitchen appliances)
Bunning, Jim (US cong.; 1931-)
Bunny Berigan (US jazz; 1909-42)
Bunny Lake is Missing (film, 1965)
Bunny Wailer (b. Neville O'Riley Livingston)(ent.; 1947-)
Bunny, Bugs (cartoon chara.)
Bunsen burner (chem.)
Bunsen, Robert W. (Ger. chem./inv., Bunsen burner; 1811-99)
Bunshaft, Gordon (US arch.; 1909-90)
Bunton, Emma (aka Baby Spice)(ent.; 1976-)
Bunyan, John (Br. writer/rel.; 1628-88)
Bunyan, Paul (& Babe the Blue Ox)(fict. lumberjack)
Buonarroti, Michelangelo (It. artist/poet; 1475-1564)
Buprenex (med.)
Burbage, Richard (Br. Shakespearean actor; 1567-1619)
Burbank, CA
Burbank, Luther (US horticulturist; 1849-1926)
Burberry (raincoat)
Burck, John Robert II (aka the Naked Cowboy) (ent.; 1971-)
Burdon, Eric (ent./songwriter; 1941-)
Bureau of Customs and Excise (Br.)
Bureau of Indian Affairs (BIA)(US govt. agcy.; est. 1849)
Bureau of Standards, National (NBS)(US govt. agcy.; est. 1901)

Buren, Abigail Van (Dear Abby)(b. Pauline Esther Friedman)(US advice columnist; 1918-)
Buren, Martin Van (8th US pres.; 1782-1862)
Burgas, Bulgaria
Burger King Corp.
Burger, Warren Earl (US jurist; 1907-95)
Burgess Meredith (ent.; 1908-97)
Burgess Shale Site (fossils, Can.)
Burgess, Anthony (Br. writer/comp.; 1917-1993)
Burghers of Calais (by Rodin)
Burghoff, Gary (ent.; 1943-)
Burgoyne, John (Br. gen./writer; 1722-92)
Burgundy (Fr. wine region)
Burgundy (region, Fr., now Bourgogne)
Burgundy, Mary of (heiress of Charles the Bold; 1457-82)
Burhanuddin Rabbani (ex-pres., Afghan.; 1940-)
Burke, Billie (ent.; 1885-1970)
Burke, Delta (ent.; 1956-)
Burke, Edmund (Ir./Br. pol.; 1729-97)
Burke, Johnny (US lyricist; 1908-84)
Burke, Martha Jane (Calamity Jane)(US frontier; c1852-1903)
Burkina Faso (People's Democratic Republic of) (formerly Upper Volta)(W Afr.)
Burkitt, Denis (Br. phys./rel.; 1911-93)
Burkitt's lymphoma (med.)
Burl Ives (Icle Ivanhoe)(ent.; 1909-95)
Burlington Coat Factory Warehouse Corp.
Burlington Free Press
Burlington Industries, Inc.
Burlington Northern Santa Fe Corp.
Burlington, IA, MA, NC, NJ, VT, WI
Burlington, Ontario, Canada
Burma (now Myanmar)
Burma Road (Ch.)
Burma Shave signs
Burman (people)
Burmese (cat)
Burmese (lang./people)
Burnaby, British Columbia, Canada
Burne Hogarth (cartoonist, *Tarzan*; 1911-96)
Burne-Jones, Edward (Br. artist; 1833-98)
Burnett, Carol (ent.; 1933-)
Burnett, Mark (ent./*Survivor* producer)
Burney, Fanny (Frances)(Madame D'Arblay)(Br. writer; 1752-1840)
Burnham Lambert, Drexel (US stock market scandal)
Burnham, Daniel H. (US arch.; 1846-1912)
Burns, Conrad (US cong.; 1935-)
Burns, Ed(ward)(ent./writer; 1968-)
Burns, George (b. Nathan Birnbaum)(ent.; 1896-1996)
Burns, Ken (ent.; 1953-)
Burns, Robert (Scot. poet; 1759-96)
Burnside, Ambrose Everett (US gen.; 1824-81)
Burpee (seeds/plants)
Burpee Co., W. Atlee
Burpee, David (US horticulturist; 1893-1980)
Burr, Aaron (ex-US VP; 1756-1836)
Burr, Raymond (ent.; 1917-93)
Burroughs Corp.
Burroughs Wellcome Co.
Burroughs, Edgar Rice (US writer; 1875-1950)

Burroughs, William S. (US writer; 1914-97)
Burrows, Abe (US writer; 1910-85)
Burrows, Darren E. (ent.; 1966-)
Burrud, Bill (ent.; 1925-90)
Bursa, Turkey
Burstyn, Ellen (b. Edna Rae Gillooly)(ent.; 1932-)
Burt Bacharach (US comp.; 1928-)
Burt Reynolds (ent.; 1936-)
Burt Wolf (US chef/writer)
Burt Young (ent.; 1940-)
Burt(on Stephen) Lancaster (ent.; 1913-94)
Burton Lane (US comp.; 1912-97)
Burton, Dan(iel L.)(US cong..; 1938-)
Burton, LeVar (or Levar)(ent.; 1957-)
Burton, Michael (swimming; 1947-)
Burton, Richard (b. Richard Walter Jenkins) (ent.; 1925-84)
Burton, Sir Richard Francis (Br. expl.; 1821-90)
Burton, Tim (ent.; 1958-)
Burundi (Republic of)(central Afr.)
Bururi, Burundi
Busby Berkeley (b. William Berkeley Enos)(ent.; 1895-1976)
Buscaglia, Leo F. (US writer; 1924-98)
Buscemi, Steve (ent.; 1957-)
Busch (beer)
Busch, Adolphus (US bus.; 1839-1913)
Busch, August Anheuser, Jr. (US bus.; 1899-1989)
Busch, Inc., Anheuser-
Busey, Gary (ent.; 1944-)
Busfield, Timothy (ent.; 1957-)
Bush, Barbara (nee Pierce)(US mother of pres./ wife of ex-pres.; 1925-)
Bush, Barbara (Pierce)(US daughter of pres./ granddaughter of ex-pres.; 1981-)
Bush, Columba Garnica Gallo (US/Mex. wife of FL gov.; 1953-)
Bush, Dorothy (nee Walker)(US grandmother of pres./mother of ex-pres.; 1901-92)
Bush, George Herbert Walker (41st US pres./ father of pres.; 1924-)
Bush, George W(alker)(43rd US pres./son of ex-pres.; 1946-)
Bush, Jeb (John Ellis)(US FL gov., bro. of pres./ son of ex-pres.; 1953-)
Bush, Jenna (Welch)(US daughter of pres./ granddaughter of ex-pres.; 1981-)
Bush, John Ellis "Jeb" (FL gov.; 1953-)
Bush, Laura (nee Welch)(US wife of pres.; 1946-)
Bush, Marvin Pierce (US bro. of pres./son of ex-pres.; 1956-)
Bush, Neil Mallon (US bro. of pres./son of ex-pres.; 1955-)
Bush, Prescott Sheldon (US pol., grandfather of pres./father of ex-pres.; 1895-1972)
Bush, Vannevar (US eng.; 1890-1974)
Bushman, Francis X. (ent.; 1883-1966)
Bushmiller, Ernie (cartoonist, *Nancy*; 1905-82)
Bushnell Associates (US bus.)
Busignani, Patricia (captain-regent; San Marino)
Business Administration, Small (SBA)(US govt. agcy.; est. 1953)
Business Week (mag.)
Busoni, Ferruccio (It. comp.; 1866-1924)

BuSpar (med.)
Bustamante, Alfonso (ex-PM, Peru)
Buster Brown (cartoon chara.)
Buster Brown (shoes, collar)
Buster Brown Apparel, Inc.
Buster Crabbe (ent./swimmer; 1908-83)
Buster (James) Douglas (boxing; 1960-)
Buster (Joseph Frank) Keaton (ent.; 1895-1966)
Buster Poindexter (aka David Johansen)(ent.; 1950-)
Butare, Rwanda
Butch and Sundance: The Early Days (film, 1979)
Butch Cassidy and the Sundance Kid (film, 1969)
Butchart Gardens (Can.)
Butcher's Blend (dog food)
Butisol (med.)
Butkus, Dick (Richard Marvin)(football/ent.; 1942-)
Butler (health)
Butler Derrick (US pol.; 1936-)
Butler, Brett (ent.; 1958-)
Butler, Nicholas Murray (US educ.; 1862-1947)
Butler, Rhett (fict. chara., *Gone With the Wind*)
Butler, Samuel (Br. writer; 1835-1902)
Butler, U.S. v. (US law; 1936)
Butt-Head, Beavis and (TV show)
Buttafuoco, Joey (US news; 1956-)
Butte, MT
Butterfield & Butterfield
Butterfinger (candy)
Butterflies Are Free (play; film, 1972)
Butterfly McQueen (ent.; 1911-95)
Butterfly, Madame (Puccini opera)
Butterick Co., The
Butterick patterns
Butterick, Ebenezer (US inv./tailor; 1826-1903)
Butterworth, Charles (ent.; 1896-1946)
Butterworth's, Mrs.
Button, Dick (Richard)(figure skating/ent.; 1929-)
Buttons, Red (b. Aaron Chwatt)(ent.; 1919-)
Buttram, Pat (ent.; 1916-94)
Buxtehude, Dietrich (Dan. comp.; 1637-1707)
Buyoya, Pierre (pres., Burundi; 1949-)
Buzek, Jerzy (PM, Pol.; 1940-)
Buzz Aldrin (Edwin Eugene, Jr.)(astro.; 1930-)
Buzzards Bay, MA (also Buzzard's Bay)
Buzzi, Ruth (ent.; 1936-)
BVD (underwear)
B.V.D. Co., Inc., The
BVM (Blessed Virgin Mary)
BX (base exchange)
Byambasuren, Dashiyn (ex-PM, Mongolia)
Byas, Don (US jazz; 1912-72)
Bydgoszcz, Poland
Byelorussia (also Belorussia)(former USSR republic)
Byelorussian (lang./people)
Byington, Spring (ent.; 1893-1971)
Bykovsky, Valéry F. (cosmo.; 1934-)
Bynum Winery, Davis (US bus.)
BYO (bring your own)
Byrd, Robert C(arlyle)(US cong.; 1917-)
Byrd, Richard E., Adm. (US expl.; 1888-1957)
Byrd, William (Br. comp.; 1543-1623)

Byrds, the (pop music)
Byrne, David (ent./songwriter; 1952-)
Byrne, Gabriel (ent.; 1950-)
Byrnes, Edd "Kookie" (ent.)
Byron Janis (US pianist; 1928-)
Byron L(eslie) Dorgan (US cong.; 1942-)
Byron Nelson (golf; 1911-)
Byron R(aymond) White ("Whizzer")(US jurist; 1917-)
Byron, Augusta Ada (Lady Lovelace)(Br. math./ inv., compu.; 1815-52)
Byron, George Gordon, Lord (Br. poet; 1788-1824)
Byronic (literature)
Byte (mag.)
Byzantine (style, arch./art/music)
Byzantine Church (also Orthodox Church)(rel.)
Byzantine Empire (390-1453)
Byzantium (later called Constantinople, now Istanbul)

C (chem. sym., carbon)
CA (California)
Ca (chem. sym., calcium)
Caaguazú, Paraguay
Caan, James (ent.; 1939-)
CAB (Civil Aeronautics Board)(US govt.)
Cab Calloway (ent.; 1907-94)
Cabaret (play; film, 1972)
Cabbage Patch dolls
Cabell, James Laurence (US phys.; 1813-89)
Cabernet Sauvignon (grape, wine)
Cable News Network (CNN)(TV channel)
Cabot Lodge, Henry (US pol.; 1850-1924)
Cabot Lodge, Henry, Jr. (US jour./pol.; 1902-85)
Cabot, John (also Giovanni Caboto)(It. nav.; 1450-98)
Cabot, Sebastian (ent.; 1918-77)
Cabot, Sebastian (It. nav./expl.; 1474-1557)
Caboto, Giovanni (also John Cabot)(It. nav.; 1450-98)
Cabrera, Alfonso Portillo (pres., Guat.; 1951-)
Cabrini, Mother (also St. Frances Xavier Cabrini)(US rel./reformer; 1850-1917)
Cabrio, Volkswagen (auto.)
Cabriolet, Audi (auto.)
Caciocavallo (cheese)
CACM (Central American Common Market)
Cactus Flower (play; film, 1969)
CAD (computer-aided design)
Cadbury (candy)
Cadbury Corp., Peter Paul
Caddo (Native Amer.)
Caddylak Systems, Inc.
Cadillac (auto.)
Cadillac Allante (auto.)
Cadillac Brougham (auto.)
Cadillac Catera (auto.)
Cadillac DeVille (auto.)
Cadillac DeVille DHS (auto.)
Cadillac DeVille DTS (auto.)
Cadillac DeVille Sedan d'Elegance (auto.)
Cadillac Eldorado (auto.)
Cadillac Eldorado ESC (auto.)
Cadillac Eldorado ETC (auto.)
Cadillac Escalade (auto.)
Cadillac Fleetwood (auto.)
Cadillac Fleetwood Brougham (auto.)
Cadillac Fleetwood DeVille (auto.)
Cadillac Seville (auto.)
Cadillac Seville SLS (auto.)
Cadillac Seville STS (auto.)
Cadillac, Antoine (founded Detroit; 1658-1730)
Cádiz, Spain
Cadmus, Paul (US artist; 1904-99)
Caelum (astron., chisel)
Caenozoic era (also Cenozoic)(65 million years ago to present)
Caerphilly (cheese)

Caesar Augustus (aka Gaius Julius Caesar Octavius)(1st Roman emp.; 63 BC-AD 14)
Caesar salad
Caesar, Gaius (aka Caligula)(Roman emp.; AD 12-41)
Caesar, Germanicus (Roman gen.; 15 BC-AD 19)
Caesar, Irving (lyricist; 1895-1996)
Caesar, Julius (Gaius Julius)(Roman gen.; 100-44 BC)
Caesar, Julius (Shakespeare play)
Caesar, Sid (ent.; 1922-)
Caesar's Palace (Las Vegas NV hotel/casino)
Caesar's World, Inc.
Caetano N'Tchama (PM, Guinea-Bissau)
Cafergot (med.)
Cage aux Folles 3: The Wedding, La (film, 1986)
Cage aux Folles II, La (film, 1981)
Cage aux Folles, La (play; film, 1978)
Cage, John (Milton)(US comp.; 1912-92)
Cage, Nicholas (b. Nicholas Coppola)(ent.; 1964-)
Cagney & Lacey (TV show)
Cagney, James (ent.; 1899-1986)
Cahn, Sammy (b. Samuel Cohen)(US lyricist; 1913-93)
Caicos Islands, Turks and (Br. West Indies)
Cain (1st son of Adam and Eve, murdered Abel)
Cain, James M(allahan)(US writer; 1892-1977)
Caine Mutiny, The (H. Wouk novel)
Caine, Michael (b. Maurice Joseph Micklewhite, Jr.)(ent.; 1933-)
Cairns, Queensland, Australia
Cairo Museum
Cairo, Egypt
Cairo, The Purple Rose of (film, 1985)
Caius (also Gaius)(Roman jurist; 2nd c. AD)
Caius, St. (also Gaius)(pope; ?-296)
Cajun (people)
Cajun music
Cakebread Cellars (US bus.)
Calabar, Nigeria
Caladryl (med.)
Calafia Winery (US bus.)
Calais, France
Calais, Oldsmobile (auto.)
Calamity Jane (aka Martha Jane Burke)(US frontier; c1852-1903)
Calan (med.)
Calcutta, India
Calcutta!, Oh! (play)
CaldeCORT (med.)
Caldecott Medal/Award (children's lit.)
Caldecott, Randolph (Br. artist; 1846-86)
Calder, Alexander (US sculptor; 1898-1976)
Calderon Sol, Armando (ex-pres., El Salvador; 1948-)
Calderón Fournier, Rafael Angel (ex-pres., Costa Rica; 1949-)
Calderón Guardia, Rafael Angel (ex-pres., Costa Rica; 1900-71)
Caldwell, Erskine (US writer; 1903-87)
Caldwell, Sarah (ent.; 1924-)
Caldwell, Taylor (writer; 1900-85)
Caldwell, Zoe (ent.; 1933-)
Cale(b) Yarborough, (William)(auto racing; 1939-)
Cale, John (ent.; 1942-)

Caledonia (type style)
Calgary Flames (hockey team)
Calgary, Alberta, Canada
Calgon water softener
Calhern, Louis (ent.; 1895-1956)
Calhoun, John C. (ex-US VP; 1782-1850)
Calhoun, Rory (b. Francis Timothy Durgin)
   (ent.; 1922-99)
Cali, Colombia
Caliban (fict. chara., *Tempest*)
Califano, Joseph A., Jr. (US ex-secy./HEW; pres.,
   Nat'l. Ctr. Addiction & Substance Abuse; 1931-)
California (CA)
California Angels (baseball team)
California condor (bird)
California current (cold ocean current)
California Raisin Bowl (college football)
California sunshine (slang, LSD)
California v. Acevedo (US law; 1991)
California, Gulf of (CA/Mex.)
California, Whitney v. (US law; 1927)
Californian, Bakersfield (CA newspaper)
Caligula (aka Gaius Caesar)(Roman emp.; 12-
   41 AD)
Calio, Nicholas (US pres. staff; 1953-)
Calisher, Hortense (US writer; 1911-)
Calista Flockhart (ent.; 1964-)
Callaghan, James (ex-PM, Br.; 1912-)
Callao, Peru
Callas, Charlie (ent)
Callas, Maria (ent.; 1923-77)
Callaway (golf clubs)
Callaway Carpets (US bus.)
Callaway Gardens (GA)
Callaway Vineyard & Winery (US bus.)
Callejas, Rafael Leonardo (ex-pres., Honduras;
   1943-)
Caller, Corpus Christi (TX newspaper)
Caller-Times, Corpus Christi (TX newspaper)
Callicrates (Gr. arch.; 5th c. BC)
Callimachus (Gr. poet; c305-240 BC)
Calliopa Pearlette Louisy (gov.-gen., St. Lucia;
   1946-)
Calliope (myth.)
Callisto (myth.; Jupiter moon)
Callot, Jacques (Fr. engraver; 1592?-1635)
Calloway, Cab (ent.; 1907-94)
Calphalon (cookware)
Calpurnia (Caesar's 3rd wife; 1st c. BC)
Calvados (liqueur)(also l.c.)
Calvary (rel.)
Calvert, Sir George (aka Lord Baltimore)
   (founded MD; 1606-75)
Calvin and Hobbes (comic strip)
Calvin Coolidge (30th US pres.; 1872-1933)
Calvin cycle (photosynthesis)
Calvin Klein (US designer; 1942-)
Calvin Klein Cosmetics Corp.
Calvin Klein, Ltd. (US bus.)
Calvin Murphy (basketball; 1948-)
Calvin Peete (golf; 1943-)
Calvin Trillin (US writer; 1935-)
Calvin, John (Fr. rel.; 1509-64)
Calvin, Melvin (US chemist; 1911-97)
Calvinism (rel.)

Calypso (J. Cousteau's ship)
Calypso (myth., sea nymph)
CAM (computer-aided manufacturing)
Cam red (red, Cambodian marijuana)
Cama Arthritis Reliever (med.)
Camaguey, Cuba
Camaro Z28, Chevrolet (auto.)
Camaro, Chevrolet (auto.)
Cambodia (State of)(SE Asia)
Cambodian (people)
Cambrai, Battle(s) of (WWI; 1917)
Cambrai, Treaty of (Rome/Fr.; 1529)
Cambrian period (570-500 million years ago)
Cambridge Platform (MA rel. statement; 1648)
Cambridge University (Eng.)
Cambridge, England
Cambridge, Godfrey (ent.; 1933-76)
Cambridge, MA, MD, OH
Camden Courier-Post (NJ newspaper)
Camden Yards (Baltimore Orioles stadium)
Camden, AR, ME, NJ, SC
Cameleopardalis (astron., giraffe)
Camelot (film, 1967)
Camelot (King Arthur's utopia)
Camembert cheese
Cameron Diaz (ent./model; 1972-)
Cameron Mitchell (ent.; 1918-94)
Cameron, Candace (ent.; 1976-)
Cameron, James (ent.; 1954-)
Cameron, Kirk (ent.; 1970-)
Cameron, Rod (ent.; 1912-83)
Cameroon (Republic of)(W Afr.)
Camilla Parker-Bowles (Br. news; 1947-)
Camille (Dumas novel)
Camille (Jacob) Pissarro (Fr. artist; 1830-1903)
Camille Flammarion (Fr. astron.; 1842-1925)
Camille Guérin (Fr. bacteriol.; 1872-1961)
Camille Paglia (US writer/social critic; 1947-)
Camille Saint-Saëns (Charles)(Fr. comp.; 1835-
   1921)
Camillo Benso Cavour (It. pol.; 1810-61)
Camillo Golgi (It. biol.; 1843-1926)
Camp Butler Marine Corps Base (Okinawa)
Camp David Accords/Agreements (Isr./Eg.,
   Isr./Palestine)
Camp David, MD (official country home of US
   pres.)
Camp Fire members (formerly Camp Fire girls)
Camp Lejeune Marine Corps Base (NC)
Camp Pendleton Marine Corps Base (CA)
Camp Sea Food Co., Inc., Van
Camp, Rosemary De (ent.; 1910-)
Camp, Walter (football; 1859-1925)
Campaign of Vicksburg (US hist.; 1862-63)
Campanella, Joseph (ent.; 1927-)
Campanella, Roy (baseball; 1921-93)
Campari U.S.A., Inc.
Campath (med./cancer)
Campbell Conference (hockey)
Campbell Soup Co.
Campbell, Ben Nighthorse (US cong.; 1933-)
Campbell, Billy (ent.; 1959-)
Campbell, Carroll A(shmore), Jr. (ex-SC gov.;
   1940-)
Campbell, Earl (football; 1955-)

Campbell, Glen (ent.; 1936-)
Campbell, John D. S. (Duke of Argyll)(ex-gov./
   gen, Can.; 1845-1914)
Campbell, Joseph (US mythologist/folklorist;
   1904-87)
Campbell, Khaki (duck)
Campbell, Kim (ex-PM, Can.; 1947-)
Campbell, Naomi (model; 1970-)
Campbell, Neve (ent.; 1973-)
Campbell, Patrick, Mrs. (aka Beatrice Tanner)
   (ent.; 1865-1940)
Campbell, Tisha (ent.; 1970-)
Campbell's (soup)
Campeador, el (also El Cid, Rodrigo Diaz de
   Bivar)(Sp. mil.; 1040-99)
Campeche, Mexico
Campho-Phenique (med.)
Campine (chicken)
Campion, Jane (ent./writer; 1954-)
Camry, Toyota (auto.)
Camry Solara, Toyota (auto.)
Camryn Manheim (b. Debra Manheim)(ent.;
   1961-)
Camus, Albert (Fr. writer; 1913-60)
Canaan, Promised Land of (rel.)
Canada
Canada Company (for colonization of S. Can.;
   org. 1825)
Canada Day (formerly Dominion Day)
Canada Dry (soft drink)
Canada First movement
Canada goose
Canada jay
Canada lily
Canada lynx
Canada mayflower
Canada thistle (plant)
Canadian (or Laurentian) Plateau/Shield (also
   Precambrian Shield)(Can.)
Canadian (people)
Canadian Airlines
Canadian bacon
Canadian Broadcasting Corp. (CBC)
Canadian English
Canadian Football League (CFL)
Canadian French
Canadian Press (Can. news org.)
Canadian Shield (also Laurentian Plateau)
Canadian whiskey
Canadiens, Montreal (hockey team)
Canal Zone, Panama (CAmer.)
Canaletto (b. Giovanni Antonio Canale)(It.
   artist; 1697-1768)
Canary Island ivy (also Algerian ivy)(plant)
Canary Islands (also Canaries)(NW coast of Afr.)
Canaveral, Cape (FL)(Kennedy Space Center)
Canberra, Australia
Cancer (zodiac, astron., crab)
Cancer Research Institute
Cancer, Tropic of (H. Miller novel)
Cancer, tropic of (23° 27' N of equator)
Cancun, Mexico
Candace Cameron (ent.; 1976-)
Candice Bergen (ent.; 1946-)
Candid Camera (TV show)

Candida (G. B. Shaw comedy)
Candida (genus)
Candida albicans (med.)
Candide (Voltaire satire)
Candido Jacuzzi (It./US eng./inv.; 1903-86)
Candie's Socks (US bus.)
Candlemas (also Candlemas Day)(rel.)
Candler, Asa (U.S., founded Coca-Cola Co.;
   1851-1929)
Candlestick Park (San Francisco, CA)
C & R Clothiers, Inc.
C & W (country & western)
Candy, John (Franklin)(ent.; 1950-94)
Canes Venatici (astron., hunting dogs)
Caniff, Milton (cartoonist, *Terry & the Pirates,
   Steve Canyon*; 1907-88)
Canis Major (astron., great dog, inc. the Dog
   Star, Sirius)
Canis Minor (astron., little [or lesser] dog)
Cannabis indica (marijuana plant)
Cannabis sativa (marijuana plant)
Canned Heat (pop music)
Cannell, Stephen J. (ent.; 1942-)
Cannery Row (film, 1982)
Cannes Film Festival (Cannes, Fr.)
Cannes, France
Cannon (linens)
Cannon (TV show)
Cannon Air Force Base, NM (mil.)
Cannon Beach, OR
Cannon, Dyan (b. Samille Diane Friesen)(ent.;
   1937-)
Cannon, Frank (fict. detective)
Cannon, Inc., Fieldcrest-
Cannonball (Julian) Adderley (US jazz; 1928-75)
Cannonball Express (Casey Jones' train)
Canon (elec.)
Canon USA, Inc.
Canon, Inc.
Canopus (also Alpha Carinae)(astron.)
Canova, Judy (ent.; 1916-83)
Canseco, Jose (baseball; 1964-)
Canterbury bells (also Campanula)(flowering
   plant)
Canterbury Tales, The (by Chaucer)
Canterbury, archbishop of (archbishop, Church
   of England)
Canterbury, England
Canticle for Leibowitz, A
Canticle of Canticles (aka Song of Solomon,
   Song of Songs)(rel., book of the Old
   Testament)
Cantinflas (b. Mario Moreno)(Mex. ent.; 1912-
   1993)
Canton (crepe, enamel)
Canton Repository (OH newspaper)
Canton, China (also Guangzhou or Kuang-chou)
Canton, CT, IL, MA, MS, NC, NY, OH, SD
Cantonese (lang./people)
Cantonese food
Cantor, Eddie (ent.; 1892-1964)
Cantrell, Lana (ent.; 1943-)
Canuck (slang, Fr. Canadian)
Canucks, Vancouver (hockey team)
Canyon de Chelly National Monument (AZ)(cliff-

dweller ruins)
.*Canyon, Steve* (comic strip)
Canyonlands National Park (UT)
CAP (Civil Air Patrol)
Capac, Manco (legendary Inca ruler)
Cape Breton Islands (Nova Scotia)
Cape buffalo
Cape Canaveral, FL (Kennedy Space Center)
Cape Charles Air Force Station, VA (mil.)
Cape Charles, VA
Cape Cod cottage
Cape Cod Times (MA newspaper)
Cape Cod, MA
Cape Codder (mixed drink)
Cape Fear, NC
Cape fox
Cape gooseberry (plant)
Cape Guardafui (also Ras Asir)(cape, Somalia)
Cape Hatteras, NC
Cape Henlopen, DE
Cape Horn (SAmer.)
Cape May Coast Guard Air Station (NJ)
Cape May, NJ
Cape of Good Hope (SAfr)
Cape Province (SAfr)
Cape Town, South Africa
Cape Verde (Republic of)(E Atl.)
Capella (also Alpha Aurigae)(astron.)
Capelli & Company (TV show)
Caperton, W. Gaston (ex-WV gov.; 1940-)
Capetown, South Africa (also Cape Town, Kaapstad)
Capezio (US bus.)
Cap-Haïtien, Haiti
Capital Cities-ABC, Inc. (American Broadcasting Cos., Inc., ABC)
Capital One Financial Corporation
CapitalOne
Capital Times, Madison (WI newspaper)
Capitals, Washington (hockey team)
Capitol Center (Landover, MD)
Capitol Hill (also Capitol, the Hill)(US Congress)
Capitol Records
Capitol Reef National Park (UT)
Capitol, the (US Capitol building)
Capitoline Hill (ancient Roman temple)
Cap'n Crunch (cereal)
Cap'n Crunch's Crunch Berries (cereal)
Capone, Al (Alphonse, "Scarface")(US gangster; 1899-47)
Caponi, Donna Maria (golf; 1945-)
Capote, Truman (US writer; 1924-84)
Capoten (med.)
Capozide (med.)
Capp, Al (Alfred Gerald Caplin)(cartoonist, *Li'l Abner*; 1909-79)
Capp, Andy (comic strip)
Cappelletti, Gino (football; 1934-)
Capra, Frank (ent.; 1897-1991)
Capri (cigarettes)
Capri pants
Capri, Italy
Capriati, Jennifer (tennis; 1976-)
Caprice, Chevrolet (auto.)
Capricorn (also Capricornus)(astron., goat)

Capricorn, Tropic of (H. Miller novel)
Capricorn, tropic of (23°27' S of equator)
Capshaw, Kate (b. Kathleen Sue Nail)(ent.; 1953-)
Captain & Tennille (Daryl Dragon & Toni Tennille)(pop music)
Captain Ahab (fict. chara., *Moby Dick*)
Captain America (cartoon chara.)
Captain Beefheart (b. Don Van Vliet)(ent.; 1941-)
Captain Horatio Hornblower (film, 1951)
Captain Janeway (Star Trek character)
Captain Kangaroo (fict. chara.)
Captain (William) Kidd (Scot. pirate; 1645?-1701)
Captain Marvel (cartoon chara.)
Captain Midnight (cartoon chara.)
Captain Planet (TV show)
Captain Queeg (fict. chara., *The Caine Mutiny*)
Captiva Island, FL
Capucine (b. Germaine Lefebvre)(Fr. ent.; 1933-90)
Capulet and Montague families (*Romeo and Juliet*)
Capulet, Juliet (fict. chara., *Romeo and Juliet*)
Caputo, Phil(ip Joseph) (US writer; 1941-)
Car and Driver (mag.)
Car Audio and Electronics (mag.)
Cara, Irene (ent.; 1959-)
Caracalla (Marcus Aurelius Bassianus)(emp., Rome; 188-217)
Caracas, Venezuela
Carafate (med.)
Caravaggio, Michelangelo da (It. artist; 1573-1610)
Caravan, Dodge (auto.)
Caray, Harry (sportscaster; 1917-98)
Carbondale, IL, PA
Carboniferous period (345-280 million years ago)
Carborundum (hard artificial compound)
Card, Andy (Andrew Hill), Jr. (US White House chief of staff; 1947-)
Cárdenas, Lázaro (ex-pres., Mex.; 1895-1970)
Cardene (med.)
Cardiff by the Sea, CA
Cardiff, Wales
Cardigan, Earl of (James Thomas Brudenell)(Br. mil./pol., cardigan sweater; 1797-1868)
Cardilate (med.)
Cardin, Pierre (Fr. designer; 1922-)
Cardinal de Richelieu ("red eminence")(Fr. pol.; 1585-1642)
Cardinal Health, Inc.
Cardinale, Claudia (ent.; 1939-)
Cardinals, Phoenix (football team)
Cardinals, St. Louis (baseball team)
Cardioquin (med.)
Cardizem (med.)
Cardoso, Fernando Henrique (pres., Brazil; 1931-)
Cardura (med.)
CARE (Cooperative for American Relief Everywhere, Inc.)
Care Bears (cartoon)
Care Bears Adventures in Wonderland, The (film, 1987)
Care Bears Movie II: A New Generation (film,

© 2001 *StenEd*® **Proper Noun Speller**

1986)
Care Bears Movie, The (film, 1985)
Carefree (panty shields)
Caress (soap)
Carew, Rod(ney Cline)(baseball; 1945-)
Carew, Thomas (Br. poet; 1595?-1640?)
Carey, Drew (ent.; 1958-)
Carey, Harry (ent.; 1878-1947)
Carey, Macdonald (ent.; 1913-94)
Carey, Mariah (ent.; 1970-)
Carey, Ron (ex-Teamsters pres.)
Carhartt (clothes)
Carhartt, Inc.
Carib (people, lang.)
Caribbean Community and Common Market
  (CARICOM)
Caribbean Sea
Caribbean Travel & Life (mag.)
Carina (astron., ship's keel)
Carl Andre (US sculptor; 1935-)
Carl August Nielsen (Dan. comp.; 1865-1931)
Carl Bernstein (US jour.; 1944-)
Carl Bildt (ex-PM, Swed.; 1949-)
Carl (or Karl) Bosch (Ger. chem.; 1874-1940)
Carl Buddig & Co.
Carl Buddig (meats)
Carl (or Karl) Czerny (Aus. pianist; 1791-1857)
Carl E. Mundy, Jr. (US gen.)
Carl Ethan Akeley (US nat./sculptor; 1864-1926)
Carl (or Karl) Friedrich Gauss (Ger. math.;
  1777-1855)
Carl Furillo (baseball; 1922-89)
Carl Gustaf Emil von Mannerheim, Baron (Fin.
  gen./pol.; 1867-1951)
Carl Gustav Jung (Swiss psych.; 1875-1961)
Carl Hiaasen (US writer; 1953-)
Carl Hubbell (baseball; 1903-88)
Carl Icahn (US finan./corporate raider)
Carl(eton) Lewis, (Frederick)(track; 1961-)
Carl M. Levin (US cong.; 1934-)
Carl Maria (Friedrich Ernst) von Weber, Baron
  (Ger. comp.; 1786-1826)
Carl Orff (Ger. comp.; 1895-1982)
Carl Perkins (ent.; 1932-98)
Carl (or Karl) Philipp Emanuel Bach (Ger.
  comp.; 1714-88)
Carl Reiner (ent.; 1922-)
Carl (Thomas) Rowan (US jour.; 1925-2000)
Carl R(ansom) Rogers (US psych.; 1902-87)
Carl Ruggles (US comp.; 1876-1971)
Carl (August) Sandburg (US poet; 1878-1967)
Carl (Edward) Sagan (US astron./writer; 1934-
  96)
Carl Schurz (Ger./US pol.; 1829-1906)
Carl Seashore (US psych.; 1866-1949)
Carl Spaatz (US mil.; 1891-1974)
Carl Stokes (US TV jour.; 1927-96)
Carl Van Doren (US writer/educ.; 1885-1950)
Carl von Clausewitz (also Karl)(Ger. mil./writer;
  1780-1831)
Carl Wilson (ent.; 1946-98)
Carl XVI Gustaf (king, Swed.; 1946-)
Carl Yastrzemski (baseball; 1939-)
Carl's Jr.
Carla Fracci (ballet; 1936-)

Carla (Anderson) Hills (US atty./public official;
  1934-)
Carlene Carter (b. Rebecca Carlene Smith)
  (ent.; 1955-)
Carlene Watkins (ent.; 1952-)
Carlin Glynn (ent.; 1940-)
Carlin, George (ent.; 1937-)
Carlisle Barracks, PA (mil.)
Carlisle Tire & Rubber Co.
Carlisle, Belinda (ent.; 1958-)
Carlisle, England
Carlisle, James B(eethoven), Dr. (gov.-gen.,
  Antigua/Barbuda; 1937-)
Carlisle, Kitty (ent.; 1915-)
Carlisle, PA
Carlo Azeglio Ciampi (pres., It.; 1920-)
Carlo Carra (It. artist; 1881-1966)
Carlo Levi (It. artist/writer; 1902-75)
Carlo Ponti (It. ent.; 1913-)
Carlo Rossi Vineyards (US bus.)
Carlo Rubbia (It. physt.; 1934-)
Carlo Sforza, Conte (It. pol./dipl.; 1873-1952)
Carlos Andrés Pérez (ex-pres., Venezuela; 1922-)
Carlos Castaneda (US anthrop./writer; 1925-98)
Carlos Chávez (Mex. comp.; 1899-1978)
Carlos I (king, Port.; 1863-1908)
Carlos I, King Juan (king, Spain; 1938-)
Carlos (Saul) Menem (ex-pres., Argentina; 1935-)
Carlos Montoya (Sp. guitarist; 1903-93)
Carlos Pena Romulo (Phil. dipl./jour./educ.;
  1899-1985)
Carlos Roberto Flores Facusse (pres.,
  Honduras; 1950-)
Carlos Salinas de Gortari (ex-pres., Mex.; 1949-)
Carlos Santana (ent.; 1947-)
Carlos Veiga (ex-PM, Cape Verde)
Carlos, Don (F. von Schiller play, Verdi opera)
Carlos, Don (prince, Spain; 1545-68)
Carlos, John (sprinter; 1945-)
Carlot Korman, Maxime (ex-PM, Vanuatu)
Carlsbad Caverns National Park (NM)
Carlsbad, CA, NM
Carlsberg (beer)
Carlson, Arne (Helge)(ex-MN gov.; 1934-)
Carlton (cigarettes)
Carlton E. Morse
Carlton, Steve(n Norman)(baseball; 1944-)
Carlucci, Frank (Charles)(US ex-secy./defense;
  1930-)
Carly Simon (ent.; 1945-)
Carlyle, Robert (ent.; 1961-)
Carlyle, Thomas (Scot. hist.; 1795-1881)
Carmarthen, Wales
Carmel, CA (also Carmel-by-the-Sea)
Carmel, Mount
Carmel, NY
Carmelite order ("White Friars")
Carmen (opera)
Carmen Cavallaro (US band leader; 1913-89)
Carmen Dragon (cond.; 1914-84)
Carmen Electra (b. Tara Leigh Patrick)(ent.;
  1972-)
Carmen McRae (ent.; 1920-94)
Carmen Miranda (ent.; 1913-55)
Carmen Sandiego (TV show)

Carmen, Eric (ent.; 1949-)
Carmichael, Hoagy (Hoagland Howard)(US comp.; 1899-1981)
Carmichael, Stokely (aka Kwame Ture) (activist; 1941-98)
Carmine Appice (ent.; 1946-)
Carnahan, Jean (Anne)(US cong.; 1933-)
Carnahan, Mel(vin)(Eugene)(US ex-cong./MO gov.; 1934-2000)
Carnap, Rudolph (US phil.; 1891-1970)
Carnation Co.
Carne, Judy (b. Joyce Botterill)(ent.; 1939-)
Carnegie Corp. of New York (philanthropic agcy. est. 1911)
Carnegie Hall (NYC concert hall)
Carnegie-Mellon University (Pittsburgh, PA)
Carnegie Steel Co.
Carnegie, Andrew (US bus./finan.; 1835-1919)
Carnegie, Dale (US writer/educ.; 1888-1955)
Carner, Joanne Gunderson (golf; 1939-)
Carnera, Primo (boxing; 1907-67)
Carneros Creek Winery (US bus.)
Carney, Art (ent.; 1918-)
Carney, Harry (US jazz; 1910-74)
Carnie Wilson (ent.; 1968-)
Carnival Cruise Lines, Inc.
Carnock, Erskine of (aka John Erskine)(Scot. writer, law; 1695-1768)
Carol & Ted & Alice, Bob & (film, 1969)
Carol Alt (model; 1960-)
Carol Burnett (ent.; 1933-)
Carol Channing (ent.; 1923-)
Carol (Friedman) Gilligan (US psych.; 1936-)
Carol Kane (ent.; 1952-)
Carol Lawrence (b. Carol Laraia)(ent.; 1934-)
Carol Leifer (ent.; 1956-)
Carol Mann (golf; 1941-)
Carol M. Browner (US ex-adm./EPA; 1955-)
Carol (Elizabeth) Moseley-Braun (US pol./dipl.; 1947-)
Carol Reed, Sir (ent.; 1906-76)
Carole King (b. Carole Klein)(US comp./ent.; 1942-)
Carole Landis (ent.; 1919-48)
Carole Lombard (b. Jane Alice Peters)(ent.; 1909-42)
Carolina horse nettle (plant)
Carolina Panthers (football team)
Caroline affair (US steamer sank by Can.; 1837)
Caroline Bird (US writer)
Caroline Kennedy Schlossberg (US atty., daughter of JFK; 1957-)
Caroline of Brunswick (queen of George IV; 1768-1821)
Caroline, Princess (princess, Monaco; 1957-)
Carolingian dynasty (Frankish, Fr./Ger.; c800-987)
Carolus Linnaeus (Carl von Linne)(Swed. botanist; 1707-78)
Carolyn Bessette Kennedy (wife of JFK, Jr.; 1966-99)
Carolyn Jones (ent.; 1933-83)
Carolyn Keene (aka Harriet S. Adams)(US writer; 1803-82)
Carolyne Roehm (writer)

Caron, Leslie (Fr./US ent.; 1931-)
Carousel (film, 1956)
Carpathian Mountains (central Eur.)
Carpenter, Karen (ent.; 1950-83)
Carpenter, M(alcolm) Scott (astro.; 1925-)
Carpenter, Mary Chapin (ent.; 1958-)
Carpenter, Richard (ent.; 1946-)
Carpenters, The (pop music)
Carper, Thomas "Tom" R(ichard)(US cong./ex-DE gov.; 1947-)
Carpeteria (US bus.)
Carpio, Ramiro de León (ex-pres., Guat.; 1942-)
Carr, Allan (ent.; 1939-99)
Carr, Baker v. (US law; 1962)
Carr, Gerald P(aul)(astro.; 1932-)
Carr, Vikki (ent.; 1941-)
Carra, Carlo (It. artist; 1881-1966)
Carracci, Agostino (It. artist; 1557-1602)
Carracci, Annibale (It. artist; 1560-1609)
Carracci, Lodovico (or Ludovico)(It. artist; 1555-1619)
Carradine, David (ent.; 1936-)
Carradine, John (ent.; 1906-88)
Carradine, Keith (ent.; 1949-)
Carré, John le (b. David Cornwell)(Br. writer; 1931-)
Carrel, Alexis (Fr. phys.; 1873-1944)
Carreras, José (Sp. tenor; 1947-)
Carrey, Jim (ent.; 1962-)
Carrickmacross (lace)
Carrie (Amelia Moore) Nation (US temperance leader; 1846-1911)
Carrie (film, 1976)
Carrie Chapman Catt (US suffragist; 1859-1947)
Carrie Fisher (ent.; 1956-)
Carrie Jacobs Bond (US comp.; 1862-1946)
Carrie Snodgrass (ent.; 1946-)
Carrillo, Leo (ent./preservationist/conservationist; 1880-1961)
Carrol's Vanities, Earl
Carroll A(shmore) Campbell, Jr. (ex-SC gov.; 1940-)
Carroll Baker (ent.; 1931-)
Carroll Naish, J. (ent.; 1900-73)
Carroll O'Connor (ent.; 1924-2001)
Carroll, Diahann (b. Carol Diahann Johnson) (ent.; 1935-)
Carroll, Leo G. (ent.; 1892-1972)
Carroll, Lewis (aka Charles Dodgson)(Br. writer/math.; 1832-98)
Carroll, Pat (ent.; 1927-)
Carruthers, Kitty (figure skating)
Carruthers, Peter (figure skating)
Cars, the (pop music)
Carson City, NV
Carson Daly (ent.; 1973-)
Carson (Smith) McCullers (US writer; 1917-67)
Carson, CA
Carson, Jack (ent.; 1910-63)
Carson, Johnny (ent.; 1925-)
Carson, Kit (Christopher)(US frontier; 1809-68)
Carson, Rachel (Louise)(US writer/biol.; 1907-64)
Carswell Air Force Base (TX)(mil.)
CART (Communications Access Realtime Translation, Computer-Assisted Realtime

Translation, Computer Assisted RealTime)
Cartagena, Columbia
Cartagena, Spain
Carte, Richard D'Oyly (Br. opera; 1844-1901)
Car-Temps (car rental)
Carter G. Woodson (US hist.; 1875-1950)
Carter Hawley Hale Stores, Inc.
Carter-Wallace, Inc.
Carter, Amy (daughter of ex-US pres.; 1967-)
Carter, Benny (US jazz; 1907-)
Carter, Betty (US jazz/comp.; 1930-98)
Carter, Billy (William Aldon) III (US bro. of ex-
  pres.; 1937-88)
Carter, Carlene (b. Rebecca Carlene
  Smith)(ent.; 1955-)
Carter, Chris (ent./writer; 1957-)
Carter, Dixie (ent.; 1939-)
Carter, Helena Bonham (ent.; 1966-)
Carter, Howard (Br. archaeol.; 1873-1939)
Carter, Jack (ent.; 1923-)
Carter, Jimmy (James Earl, Jr.)(39th US pres.;
  1924-)
Carter, Joe (baseball; 1960-)
Carter, June (ent.; 1929-)
Carter, Lynda (ent.; 1951-)
Carter, "Mother" Maybelle (ent.; 1909-78)
Carter, Nick (ent., Backstreet Boys; 1980-)
Carter, Nick (fict. detective)
Carter, Ron (US jazz; 1937-)
Carter, Rosalynn (Smith)(US wife of ex-pres.;
  1927-)
Carter's Little Pills (med.)
Cartesian coordinates (geometry)
Cartesianism (Descartes phil.)
Carthage (ancient city, NAfr.)
Carthage, IL, MO, NY
Cartier (jewelry)
Cartier-Bresson, Henri (Fr. photo.; 1908-)
Cartier, Inc.
Cartier, Jacques (Fr. explorer; 1491-1557)
Cartoon Network (TV channel)
Cartrol (med.)
Cartland, Barbara (Br. writer; 1901-2000)
Cartwright, Veronica (ent.; 1950-)
Caruso, Enrico (It. tenor; 1873-1921)
Carvel Ice Cream Stores (US bus.)
Carvel, Tom (Ger./US bus.; 1908-90)
Carver chair
Carver, George Washington (US botanist/
  chem.; 1860?-1943)
Carvey, Dana (ent.; 1955-)
Carville, (Chester) James, Jr. (the Ragin'
  Cajun) (US pol.; 1944-)
Cary Grant (b. Archibald Leach)(ent.; 1904-86)
Cary, Arthur Joyce Lunel (Ir. writer; 1888-
  1957)
Caryatids, Porch of the (Gr., female figures
  used for columns)
Caryl Chessman ("Red Light Bandit")(US rapist;
  1921-1960)
Caryn Kadavy (figure skating; 1964-)
Casa Grande, AZ (prehistoric ruins)
Casablanca (film, 1942)
Casablanca Conference (Roosevelt/Churchill;
  1943)

Casablanca, Morocco
Casablance Fan Co.
Casals, Pablo (Sp. musician; 1876-1973)
Casals, Rosemary (tennis; 1948-)
Casanova (film, 1987)
Casanova, Giovanni Jacopo (also Casanova de
  Seingalt)(It. adventurer; 1725-98)
Casbah, the (also Kasbah)
Cascade (dish detergent)
Cascade Range (mountains, OR/WA)
Cascade, Seychelles
CASE (NCRA's Council on Approved Student
  Education)
Case, Steve (Stephen M.)(US bus./AOL; 1958-)
Casey (John Luther) Jones (US railroad eng.;
  1864-1900)
Casey Kasem (ent.; 1933-)
Casey Siemaszko (ent.; 1961-)
Casey (Charles) Stengel (baseball; 1891-1975)
Casey Tibbs (rodeo; 1929-90)
Casey, Robert Patrick (ex-PA gov.; 1932-2000)
Casey, William J(oseph)(ex-dir./FBI; 1914-87)
Cash McCall (film, 1960)
Cash, Johnny (ent.; 1932-)
Cash, Rosanne (ent.; 1955-)
Cashmere (also Kashmir)(goat)
Casimir (or Kasimir) Malevich (Rus. artist;
  1878-1935)
Casimir Oye-Mba (ex-PM, Gabon)
Casimir Pulaski, Count (Pol./Amer.
  Revolutionary gen.; 1748-79)
Casio PhoneMate (comm.)
Casio, Inc.
Caslon (type style)
Caslon, William (Br. typographer; 1692-1766)
Caspar (one of the Magi)
Caspar David Friedrich (Ger. artist; 1774-1840)
Caspar Milquetoast (cartoon chara.)
Casper the Friendly Ghost (cartoon chara.)
Caspar "Cap" W(illard) Weinberger (US ex-
  secy./defense; 1917-)
Casper, Billy (golf; 1931-)
Casper, WY
Caspian Sea (SE Eur./W Asia)
Caspian, Prince (by C.S. Lewis)
Cass Elliot (b. Ellen Naomi Cohen)(ent.; 1941-74)
Cass Gilbert (US arch.; 1859-1934)
Cass, Peggy (ent.; 1924-99)
Cassam Uteem (pres., Mauritius; 1941-)
Cassandra (myth.)
Cassandra Peterson (aka Elvira)(ent.; 1951-)
Cassandra Wilson (US jazz/comp.; 1955-)
Cassatt, Mary (US artist; 1845-1926)
Cassavetes, John (ent.; 1929-89)
Cassegrain (or Cassegrainian) reflector/
  telescope (astron.)
Cassel brown (also Vandyke brown, Cassel
  earth)(color)
Cassel yellow (color)
Cassidy and the Sundance Kid, Butch (film,
  1969)
Cassidy, David (ent.; 1950-)
Cassidy, Hopalong (b. William Boyd)(ent.;
  1898-1972)
Cassidy, Hopalong (TV show)

Cassidy, Jack (ent.; 1927-76)
Cassidy, Joanna (ent.; 1944-)
Cassidy, Shaun (ent.; 1958-)
Cassini (space probe to Saturn)
Cassini, Giovanni Domenico (It./Fr. astron.; 1625-1712)
Cassini, Inc., Oleg
Cassini, Oleg (b. Oleg Cassini Loiewski)(US designer; 1913-)
Cassiopeia (astron., queen; myth.)
Cassius Clay, Jr. (aka Muhammad Ali)(boxing; 1942-)
Cassius, Gaius (Roman leader of conspiracy against Caesar; ?-42 BC)
Castagno, Andrea del (It. artist; c1421-57)
Castaneda, Carlos (US anthrop./writer; 1925-98)
Casterbridge, The Mayor of (T. Hardy novel)
Castiglione Baldassare (It. pol.; 1478-1529)
Castile (region, Sp.)
Castile, Eleanor of (queen, Eng.; c1245-90)
Castilian (lang./people)
Castilian brown (color)
Castilian red (color)
Castle Air Force Base, CA (mil.)
Castle, Irene (Foote)(US dancer; 1893-1969)
Castle, Vernon (US dancer; 1887-1918)
Castlereagh, Robert (Br. pol.; 1769-1822)
Castor and Pollux (astron., myth., Gemini/twins)
Castries, St. Lucia
Castro Convertibles (US bus.)
Castro Ruíz, Fidel (pres., Cuba; 1927-)
Castroism (pol.)
Casual Corner (clothing)
Caswell-Massey Co., Ltd.
CAT (computer-aided translation/transcription)
CAT scan (computerized axial tomography)(also CT scan)(med.)
Cat Ballou (film, 1965)
Cat Fancy (mag.)
Cat Stevens (aka Steven Georgiou, Yusuf Islam)(ent.; 1948-)
Catacombs, the (subterranean burial chambers, ancient Rome)
Catalan (lang./people)
Catalina (sportswear)
Catalina Island, CA (also Catalina, Santa Catalina)
Catalonia (region, Sp.)
Catania, Italy
Catapres (med.)
Catawba (Native Amer.)
Catawba River (NC/SC)
Catch-22 (Joseph Heller novel)
Catcher in the Rye, The (J.D. Salinger novel)
Cate Blanchett (ent.; 1969-)
Catera, Cadillac (auto.)
Caterpillar Tractor Co.
Cates, Phoebe (ent.; 1963-)
Catfish (Jim) Hunter (baseball; 1946-99)
Cathay Pacific Airways (airline)
Cathedral of St. John the Divine (NYC)
Cather, Willa (US writer; 1876-1947)
Catherine Bach (ent.)
Catherine de' Medici (queen, Fr./wife of Henry II; 1518-89)
Catherine Deneuve (b. Catherine Dorleac)(Fr.

ent.; 1943-)
Catherine Drinker Bowen (biographer; 1897-1973)
Catherine Howard (5th wife of Henry VIII; 1520?-42)
Catherine I (Rus. empress, wife of Peter the Great; 1684-1727)
Catherine II (Rus. empress, Catherine the Great; 1729-96)
Catherine Keener (ent.; 1959?-)
Catherine of Aragon (1st wife of Henry VIII; 1585-36)
Catherine of Braganza, (Br., queen of Charles II; 1638-1705)
Catherine of Siena, St. (It. mystic; 1347-80)
Catherine Parr (6th wife of Henry VIII; 1512-48)
Catherine the Great (Rus. empress, Catherine II; 1729-96)
Catherine (Anne) Tizard, Dame (nee Maclean) (ex-gov.-gen., NewZeal.; 1931-)
Catherine Zeta-Jones (ent.; 1969-)
Catholic (rel.)
Catholic Apostolic Church
Catholic Church
Catholic Church, Roman (also Church of Rome)
Catholic Emancipation Act (Br.; 1829)
Catholic Epistles (rel.)
Catholic Foreign Mission Society of America (also Maryknoll Missioners)(rel.)
Catholic Reformation (also Counter Reformation)(Eur. rel./hist.; 16th-17th c.)
Catholic, Roman (rel.)
Catholicism (also Roman Catholicism)(rel.)
Cathy (comic strip)
Cathy Guisewite (cartoonist, *Cathy*; 1950-)
Cathy Lee Crosby (ent.; 1948-)
Cathy Rigby (gymnast/ent.; 1952-)
Catilina (Lucius Sergius)(also Catiline)(Roman pol.; c108-62 BC)
Catlett, Sidney ("Big Sid")(US jazz; 1910-51)
Catlin, George (US artist; 1796-1872)
Cato the Elder (also Cato the Censor, Marcus Porcius Cato)(Roman pol.; 234-149 BC)
Cats (mag.)
Cats (play)
Catskills (also Catskill Mountains)(NY)
Catt, Carrie Chapman (US suffragist; 1859-1947)
Catton, Bruce (US historian; 1899-1978)
Cattrall, Kim (ent.; 1956-)
Catullus (Gaius Catullus)(Roman poet; c84-43 BC)
Caucasoid (also Caucasian)(one of three major races of humans)
Caulfield, Joan (ent.; 1922-91)
Caulkins, Tracy (swimming; 1963-)
Cauthen, Steve (jockey)
cavalier King Charles spaniel (dog)
Cavalier, Chevrolet (auto.)
Cavaliers, Cleveland (basketball team)
Cavallaro, Carmen (US band leader; 1913-89)
Cavendish, Henry (Br. chem./physt.; 1731-1810)
Caves of Altamira (also Altamira caves)(Sp. paleolithic paintings)
Cavett, Dick (ent.; 1936-)
Cavour, Camillo Benso (It. pol.; 1810-61)
Caxton, William (1st English printer; c1422-91)

Cayenne, French Guiana
Cayetano, Ben(jamin)(Jerome)(HI gov.; 1939-)
Cayman Airways
Cayman Islands (Br. West Indies)
Caymus Vineyards, Inc.
Cayuga (Native Amer.)
Cayuga duck
Cayuga Lake (NY)
CB radio
CBC (Canadian Broadcasting Corp.)
CBC (complete blood cell count)
CBS (Columbia Broadcasting System)(TV channel)
CBS Evening News With Dan Rather, The (TV show)
CBS News (TV show)
CBS Records (US bus.)
CBS Sunday Night Movie (TV show)
CBS, Inc. (Columbia Broadcasting System)
C. C. Beck (cartoonist, *Captain Marvel*; 1910-89)
CCC (Civilian Conservation Corps)
CCR (Certified Court Reporter)
CCU (coronary care unit)
CD (certificate of deposit, civil defense, compact disk)
Cd (chem. sym., cadmium)
CD-ROM (Compact Disk-Read Only Memory)(compu.)
CDC (Centers for Disease Control)
CDW Computer Centers, Inc.
CE (chemical engineer, civil engineer)
Ce (chem. sym., cerium)
Ceausescu, Nicolae (ex-pres., Romania; 1918-89)
Cebu, Philippines
Cebuano (lang.)
Cecchetti method (ballet)
Cecchetti, Enrico (ballet; 1850-1928)
Cecil B. De Mille (ent.; 1881-1959)
Cecil Beaton, Sir (Br. photo.; 1904-80)
Cecil D. Andrus (ex-ID gov.; 1931-)
Cecil Day Lewis (Ir. poet; 1904-72)
Cecil H(arland) Underwood (ex-WV gov.; 1922-)
Cecil (John) Rhodes (Br./SAfr. pol., est. Rhodes scholarships; 1853-1902)
Cecil Taylor (US jazz; 1933-)
Cecilia Bartoli (US opera; 1972-)
Cecilia Helena Payne-Gaposchkin (Br./US astron.; 1900-79)
Ceclor (med.)
Cecropia moth (silkworm)
Cecrops (myth.)
Cedar Falls, IA
Cedar Rapids Gazette Post (IA newspaper)
Cedar Rapids, IA
Cedars-Sinai Medical Center
Cedilanid (med.)
Cédras, Lieut. Gen. Raoul (Haitian mil.)
Cedric Hardwicke, Sir (ent.; 1893-1964)
CEEB (College Entrance Examination Board)
CeeNU (med.)
Cefotan (med.)
Ceftin (med.)
Celanese (yarn, fabric)
Celebes (now Sulawesi)(Indonesian island)
Celebrex (med.)
Celeste Holm (ent.; 1919-)

Celestial City (from *Pilgrim's Progress*)
Celestial Seasonings, Inc.
Celestine I, St. (pope; ?-432)
Celestine II, St. (Guido del Castello)(pope; ?-1144)
Celestine III, St. (Giacinto Bobone)(It. pope; 1106?-98)
Celestine IV, St. (Gofredo Castiglioni)(It. pope; ?-1241)
Celestine V, St. (Pietro di Murrone [or Morone]) (pope; 1215-96)
Celestone (med.)
Celica, Toyota (auto.)
Celine Dion (ent.; 1968-)
Cellini, Benvenuto (It. sculptor; 1500-71)
Cellucci, A(rgeo) Paul (MA gov.; 1948-)
Celontin (med.)
Celotex (constr.)
Celsius (also Centigrade)(temperature scale)
Celsius, Anders (Swed. astron.; 1701-44)
Celt (people)
Celtic (lang./people)
Celtic art
Celtic Church
Celtic cross
Celtic Renaissance (also Irish Literary Renaissance, Irish Revival)(lit.)
Celtic Sea (UK)
Celtics, Boston (basketball team)
Cenozoic era (65 million years ago to present)
Centauri, Alpha (also Rigel Kentaurus)(astron.)
Centauri, Proxima (astron.)
Centaurus (astron., centaur [half man/half horse])
Centennial State (nickname, CO)
Centers for Disease Control and Prevention (CDC)
Centigrade (also Celsius)(temperature scale)
Central African Republic
Central America
Central American Common Market (CACM)
Central American States, Organization of (ODECA)(est. 1951/1962)
Central Asian Republics (Kazakhstan, Kyrgyzstan, Tajikistan, and Turkmenistan; Uzbekistan)
Central Highlands
Central Intelligence Agency (CIA)(US govt.)
Central Islip, NY
Central Powers (of WW I)
Central Standard Time (also Central Time)
Centrax (med.)
Centre (region, Fr.)
Centrex Corp.
Centrum (med.)
Centrum Products Co.
Centrum, Jr. (med.)
Century (type style)
Century 21 Real Estate Corp.
Century, Buick (auto.)
CEO (chief executive officer)
Cepacol (med.)
Cepastat (med.)
Cepheid variable(s)(astron.)
Cepheus (astron., king)
Cerberus (myth., 3-headed guard dog)
Cerdic, House of (Br. ruling family; 827-1016,

1042-66)
Cerenkov radiation
Ceres (astron., myth.)
Ceres, CA
Cerf, Bennett (US editor/publ.; 1898-1971)
Cernan, Eugene A(ndrew)(astro.; 1934-)
Cerro Tololo Inter-American Observatory
  (Chile)
Cervantes Saavedra, Miguel de (Sp. writer;
  1547-1616)
Cesamet (med.)
César Auguste Franck (Belg. comp.; 1822-90)
Cesar Chavez (US labor leader; 1927-93)
César Gaviria Trujillo (ex-pres., Colombia; 1947-)
Cesar Romero (ent.; 1907-94)
Cesare Borgia (It. mil./pol.; 1476-1507)
Cesare Siepi (basso; 1923-)
Cessna Aircraft Co.
Cetinje, Montenegro (Yug.)
Cetus (astron., whale)
C. Everett Koop (US ex-surgeon gen./phys.;
  1916-)
Ceylon (now Sri Lanka)
Ceylon tea (tree)
Cézanne, Paul (Fr. artist; 1839-1906)
Cf (chem. sym., californium)
CFI (cost, freight, and insurance)
CFP (Certified Financial Planner)
CFTC (Commodity Futures Trading Commission)
CG (Coast Guard)
Chablis (wine)
Chablis, France
Chabrier, Alexis Emmanuel (Fr. comp.; 1841-94)
Chaco (province, Argentina)
Chaco Culture National Historical Park (NM)
  (formerly Chaco Canyon National Monument)
Chad (Republic of)(N Afr.)
Chad Everett (b. Raymond Lee Cramton)(ent.;
  1936-)
Chad Lowe (ent.; 1968-)
Chad, Lake (Nigeria)
*Chadha, Immigration and Naturalization
  Service v.* (US law; 1983)
Chadwick, Florence (US swimmer; 1918-95)
Chadwick, Sir James (Br. physt.; 1891-1974)
Chadwick's of Boston, Ltd. (clothing)
Chafee, John H. (US pol.; 1922-99)
Chafee, Lincoln (US cong.; 1953-)
Chaffee, Fort, AR (mil.)
Chagall, Marc (Fr. artist; 1887-1985)
Chagas' disease (med.)
Chaim Gross (US artist; 1904-91)
Chaim Herzog (ex-pres., Isr.; 1918-97)
Chaim Potok (US writer; 1929-)
Chaim Soutine (Fr. artist; 1893-1943)
Chaim Weizmann (ex-pres., Isr.; 1874-1952)
Chairman Mao (also Mao Tse-tung, Mao
  Zedong)(Ch. leader; 1893-1976)
Chaka Khan (b. Yvette Marie Stevens)(ent.; 1953-)
Chakma (lang.)
Chakrabarty, Diamond v. (US law; 1980)
Chalcedon, Council of (rel.)
Chaldea (part of Babylonia)
Chaldean (ancient people)
Chaliapin, Feodor Ivanovitch (Rus. bass; 1873-

1938)
Challenger (Br. oceanic expedition; 1872-76)
Challenger (US space shuttle)(exploded after
  takeoff on 1/28/86)
Cham (people)
Chamaeleon (astron., chameleon)
Chamberlain, (Arthur) Neville (ex-PM, Br.;
  1869-1940)
Chamberlain, (Joseph) Austen (Br. pol.; 1863-
  1937)
Chamberlain, Joseph (Br. pol.; 1836-1914)
Chamberlain, Richard (ent.; 1934-)
Chamberlain, Wilt (Norman)(Wilt the Stilt)
  (basketball; 1936-99)
Chambers, Sir William (Br. arch.; 1723-96)
Chamorro (lang.)
Chamorro, Violeta Barrios de (ex-pres.,
  Nicaragua; 1939-)
Champagne (Fr. wine region)
Champagne-Ardenne (region, Fr.)
Champaign, IL
Champion (spark plug)
Champion International Corp.
Champion v. Ames (also Lottery Case)(US law;
  1903)
Champion, Gower (US dancer; 1921-80)
Champion, Marge (US dancer; 1923-)
Champlain, Lake (NY/VT/Can.)
Champlain, Samuel de (Fr. expl.; c1567-1635)
Champollion, Jean François (Fr. archaeol.;
  1790-1832)
Champs Élysées (Paris avenue)
Chan Chan ruins (Peru)
Chan, Charlie (fict. detective)
Chan, Dennis (wakeboarding)
Chan, Jackie (b. Chan Kwong-Sang)(ent.; 1954-)
Chan, Lien (ex-premier; Taiwan)
Chancellor of the Exchequer (Br. govt.)
Chancellor, John (US TV jour.; 1927-96)
Chancellorsville, Battle of (US hist.; 1863)
Chancellorsville, VA
Chandler Pavilion, Dorothy (Los Angeles)
Chandler period (also Chandler wobble)
  (oscillation of earth's axis)
Chandler, A. B. (Happy)(baseball; 1899-1991)
Chandler, Jeff (ent.; 1918-61)
Chandler, Raymond (US writer; 1888-1959)
Chandler, Spud (Spurgeon Ferdinand)(baseball;
  1907-90)
Chandra Levy (US missing intern; 1977-)
Chandrasekhar limit (astron., physics)
Chandrika Bandaranaike Kumaratunga (pres.,
  Sri Lanka; 1945-)
Chanel, Gabrielle "Coco" (Fr. designer; 1883-
  1971)
Chanel, Inc.
Chaney, Lon (ent.; 1883-1930)
Chaney, Lon, Jr. (ent.; 1905-73)
Chang Chun-hsiung (PM, Taiwan; 1938-)
Chang Jiang River (also Yangtze Kiang)(Ch.)
Chang, Lee Hoi (ex-PM; SKorea)
Chang, Michael (tennis; 1972-)
Changchiakow, China (also Zhangjiakou)
Changchun, China (formerly Hsinking)
Changes, Book of (also *I Ching*)

Changing Times (mag.)

Changsha, China

Chanin, Irwin (US arch.; 1892-1988)

Channel Islands (English Channel)

Channel Islands National Park, CA

Channel Tunnel (also Chunnel)(tunnel joining Eng./Fr.)

Channing, Carol (ent.; 1923-)

Channing, Edward (US hist.; 1856-1931)

Channing, Stockard (ent.; 1944-)

Channing, William Ellery (US rel.; 1780-1842)

Chanson de Roland (Fr. epic poem, *Song of Roland*)

Chantilly lace

Chantilly, crème (sauce)

Chantilly, France

Chanukah (also Hanukkah)(rel.)

Chanute Air Force Base, IL (mil.)

Chao, Elaine Lan (US secy./labor; 1953-)

Chaos (myth.)

Chap Stick (med.)

Chapelle Winery, Inc., Ste.

Chapin, Harry (ent.; 1942-81)

Chaplin, Charlie (Sir Charles Spencer)(ent.; 1889-1977)

Chaplin, Geraldine (ent.; 1944-)

Chapman, John (aka Johnny Appleseed)(US pioneer; 1774-1845)

Chapman, Tracy (ent.; 1964-)

Chapot, Frank (equestrian; 1934-)

Chappaqua, NY (Clinton's NY home)

Chappaquiddick bridge (site of Ted Kennedy/ Mary Jo Kopechne accident; 1969)

Chappaquiddick Island, MA

Chapter 11 (of US Bankruptcy Code)

Chapultepec, Mexico

Charbray (cattle)

Charcot, Jean M. (Fr. phys.; 1825-93)

Chardin, Jean-Baptiste-Siméon (Fr. artist; 1699-1779)

Chardonnay (grape, wine)

Chardzhov, Turkmenistan

Charge of the Light Brigade (battle, Crimean War)

Charge of the Light Brigade (poem)

Charger, Dodge (auto.)

Chargers, San Diego (football team)

Charing Cross (London railroad terminal)

Charisse, Cyd (ent.; 1921-)

Charlayne Hunter-Gault (US TV jour./activist; 1942-)

Charlemagne (also Charles the Great, Charles I)(Holy Roman Emperor; 742-814)

Charlene Tilton (ent.; 1958-)

Charleroi, Belgium

Charles A. Beard (US hist.; 1874-1948)

Charles Addams (cartoonist; 1912-88)

Charles A(ugustus) Lindbergh (US aviator; 1902-74)

Charles Anderson Dana (US editor; 1819-97)

Charles Antrobus, Sir (gov.-gen., St. Vincent/ Grenadines)

Charles Arthur Floyd ("Pretty Boy")(US bank robber; 1901-34)

Charles Ashburner (US geol.; 1854-89)

Charles Atlas (aka Angelo Siciliano)(US body builder; 1894-1972)

Charles Augustin de Coulomb (Fr. physt.; 1736-1806)

Charles Aznavour (b. Shahnour Varenagh Aznourian)(Fr. ent.; 1924-)

Charles Babbage (Br. math., inv. precursor of modern compu.; 1792-1871)

Charles Barkley (basketball; 1963-)

Charles Bickford (ent.; 1889-1967)

Charles Bolden ("Buddy")(US jazz; 1868-1931)

Charles Boyer (ent.; 1899-1978)

Charles B. Rangel (US cong.; 1930-)

Charles Brockden Brown (US writer; 1771-1810)

Charles Bronson (b. Charles Buchinsky)(ent.; 1921-)

Charles Bulfinch (US arch.; 1763-1844)

Charles Butterworth (ent.; 1896-1946)

Charles Camille Saint-Saëns (Fr. comp.; 1835-1921)

Charles C. Boycott, Capt. (Br., boycotted by Ir. tenants; 1832-97)

Charles Chips (US bus.)

Charles Coburn (ent.; 1877-1961)

Charles Collingwood (TV jour.; 1917-85)

Charles Conrad, Jr. (astro.; 1930-99)

Charles Cornwallis (Br. gen./pol.; 1738-1805)

Charles Cotesworth Pinckney (US pol.; 1746-1825)

Charles Crocker (US railroad/finan.; 1822-88)

Charles Curtis (ex-US VP; 1860-1936)

Charles Dana Gibson (US artist; 1867-1944)

Charles de Baatz d'Artagnan, Seigneur (fict. chara., *Three Musketeers*)

Charles de Gaulle (ex-pres., Fr.; 1890-1970)

Charles (Maurice) de Talleyrand(-Périgord)(Fr. pol.; 1754-1838)

Charles (John Huffam) Dickens ("Boz")(Br. writer; 1812-70)

Charles Dodgson (pseud. Lewis Carroll)(Br. writer/math.; 1832-98)

Charles Dow (US finan.; 1851-1902)

Charles Durning (ent.; 1923-)

Charles Eames (US arch./designer; 1907-78)

Charles E. Bohlen (US dipl.; 1904-74)

Charles Édouard Jeanneret (aka Le Corbusier)(Fr. arch./artist; 1887-1965)

Charles Edward Stuart (aka the Young Pretender, Bonnie Prince Charles [or Charlie])(prince, Br.; 1720-88)

Charles E. Greene (sprinter; 1945-)

Charles Elton (Br. ecol.; 1900-91)

Charles E. Merrill (US finan.; 1885-1956)

Charles "Chuck" Ernest Grassley (US cong.; 1933-)

Charles E. Schumer (US cong.; 1950-)

Charles Evans Hughes (US jurist; 1862-1948)

Charles Evers, (James)(US reformer/pol./ NAACP; 1922-)

Charles Farrell (ent.; 1902-90)

Charles F. Kettering (US eng./inv.; 1876-1958)

Charles F(ollen) McKim (US arch.; 1847-1909)

Charles Fourier (Fr. social scien.; 1772-1837)

Charles Francis Adams (US dipl.; 1807-86)

Charles Francis Richter (US seismol.; 1900-85)

Charles François Gounod (Fr. comp.; 1818-93)
Charles Frederick Menninger (US psych.; 1862-1953)
Charles Frohman (US theater; 1860-1915)
Charles Fuller (US writer; 1939-)
Charles G. Dawes (US pol./banker; 1865-1951)
Charles G(eorge) Gordon (Br. mil.; 1833-85)
Charles Goodyear (US inv.; 1800-60)
Charles Greeley Abbot (US physt.; 1872-1973)
Charles Grodin (ent.; 1935-)
Charles Hagel (US cong.; 1946-)
Charles Haid (ent.; 1943-)
Charles Hamilton Houston (US civil rights atty.; 1895-1950)
Charles Hard Townes (US physt.; 1915-)
Charles Haughey (ex-PM, Ir.; 1925-)
Charles H. Goren (US contract bridge authority; 1901-91)
Charles Hickcox (swimming; 1947-)
Charles H. Keating, III (US S&L scandal)
Charles H. Keating, Jr. (US S&L scandal; 1923-)
Charles H(orace) Mayo (US surgeon; 1865-1939)
Charles I (aka Charles the Great, Charlemagne)(Holy Roman emp.; 742-814)
Charles I (king, Br./Ir.; 1600-49)
Charles II (aka Charles the Bald)(Holy Roman emp.; 823-877)
Charles II (king, Br./Ir.; 1630-85)
Charles II (king, Sp.; 1661-1700)
Charles III (aka Charles the Fat)(Holy Roman emp.; 839-888)
Charles III (aka Charles the Simple)(king, Fr.; 893-922)
Charles III (king, Sp.; 1716-88)
Charles IV (aka Charles the Fair)(king, Fr.; 1294-1328)
Charles IV (Holy Roman emp.; 1316-78)
Charles IV (king, Sp.; 1748-1819)
Charles (Edward) Ives (US comp.; 1874-1954)
Charles IX (king, Fr.; 1550-74)
Charles IX (king, Swed.; 1550-1611)
Charles Joseph "Joe" Clark (ex-PM, Can.; 1939-)
Charles Krug Winery (US bus.)
Charles Kuralt (US TV jour.; 1934-97)
Charles Lamb ("Elia")(Br. writer; 1775-1834)
Charles Lang Freer (US bus./art collector; 1856-1919)
Charles Laughton (ent.; 1899-1962)
Charles Lewis Tiffany (US bus.; 1912-1902)
Charles Louis Montesquieu (Fr. phil.; 1689-1755)
Charles MacArthur (US playwright; 1895-1956)
Charles Manson (US, mass murderer; 1934-)
Charles McGraw (ent.; 1914-80)
Charles M. Duke, Jr. (astro.; 1935-)
Charles Messier (Fr. astron.; 1730-1817)
Charles Mingus (US jazz; 1922-79)
Charles M. McKim (US arch.; 1920-)
Charles M. Russell (US arch.; 1866-1926)
Charles M(ichael) Schwab (US bus.; 1862-1939)
Charles M(onroe) Schulz (cartoonist, *Peanuts*; 1922-2000)
Charles Nelson Reilly (ent.; 1931-)
Charles O. Finley (US bus./baseball; 1918-96)
Charles of the Ritz Group, Ltd.
Charles Osgood (TV jour.; 1933-)

Charles Pasarell (tennis; 1944-)
Charles Pathé (Fr. bus./films; 1863-1957)
Charles Perrault (Fr. writer; 1628-1703)
Charles Pierre Baudelaire (Fr. poet; 1821-67)
Charles Pinckney (US pol.; 1757-1824)
Charles P(roteus) Steinmetz (Ger./US eng.; 1865-1923)
Charles Rennie Mackintosh (Scot. arch.; 1868-1928)
Charles Revson (US bus.; 1906-75)
Charles Ringling (US circus; 1863-1926)
Charles River Bridge v. Warren Bridge (US law; 1837)
Charles Robert Darwin (Br. scien.; 1809-82)
Charles Robinson (ent.)
Charles Robinson (US pol.; 1818-94)
Charles "Charlie" Ruggles (ent.; 1886-1970)
Charles R. Walgreen (US bus.; 1873-1939)
Charles Schulz (cartoonist, *Peanuts*; 1923-2000)
Charles Schwab & Co.
Charles Schwab Corp., The
Charles Scribner, Jr. (US publ.)
Charles Scribner, Sr. (US publ.)
Charles Scribner's Sons (US bus.)
Charles Sheeler (US artist; 1883-1965)
Charles (Scott) Sherrington, Sir (Br. physiol.; 1857-1952)
Charles spaniel, King (dog)
Charles S(anders) Peirce (US physt./phil.; 1839-1914)
Charles S(pittal) "Chuck" Robb (US pol.; 1939-)
Charles "Casey" Stengel (baseball; 1891-1975)
Charles Stewart Parnell (Ir. pol.; 1846-91)
Charles Strouse (US comp.; 1928-)
Charles Sumner (US pol.; 1811-74)
Charles (Ghankay) Taylor (pres., Liberia; 1948-)
Charles the Great (also Charlemagne, Charles I)(Holy Roman emp.; 742-814)
Charles Town, WV
Charles Townshend (Br. pol., Townshend Acts; 1725-67)
Charles Townshend, Viscount ("Turnip")(Br. pol./agr.; 1675-1738)
Charles T(aze) Russell (US, rel./Jehovah's Witnesses; 1852-1916)
Charles V (aka the Wise)(king, Fr.; 1337-80)
Charles V (Holy Roman emperor; 1500-58)
Charles Van Doren (US educ./TV scandal; 1926-)
Charles VI (aka the Mad, the Well-Beloved)(king, Fr.; 1368-1422)
Charles VI (Holy Roman emperor; 1685-1740)
Charles VII (Holy Roman emperor; 1697-1745)
Charles VII (king, Fr.; 1403-61)
Charles VIII (king, Fr.; 1470-98)
Charles VIII (king, Swed.; 1408-70)
Charles Waddell Chesnutt (US writer; 1858-1932)
Charles W. Colson (US pol./Watergate; 1931-)
Charles W. Fairbanks (ex-US VP; 1852-1918)
Charles "Cootie" Williams (US jazz; 1908-85)
Charles Wilson Peale (US artist; 1741-1827)
Charles W. Mayo (US surgeon; 1898-1968)
Charles X (king, Fr.; 1757-1836)
Charles X (king, Swed.; 1622-60)
Charles XI (king, Swed.; 1655-97)
Charles XII (king, Swed.; 1682-1718)

Charles XIII (king, Swed./Nor.; 1748-1818)
Charles XIV (John Baptiste Jules)(king, Swed./
   Nor.; 1763-1844)
Charles XV (king, Swed./Nor.; 1826-72)
Charles' law (also Gay-Lussac's law)
   (thermodynamics)
Charles (or Charlie), Bonnie Prince (Charles
   Edward Stuart, aka the Young
   Pretender)(prince, Br.; 1720-88)
Charles, Jacques (Alexandre César)(Fr. physt.;
   1746-1823)
Charles, Lake, LA
Charles, Mary Eugenia (ex-PM, Dominica; 1919-)
Charles, Pierre (PM, Dominica; 1954-)
Charles, Prince (Charles Philip Arthur George,
   Prince of Wales)(eldest son of Queen
   Elizabeth II; 1948-)
Charles, Ray (b. Ray Charles Robinson)(ent.;
   1930-)
Charlesbourg, Quebec, Canada
Charleston (dance)
Charleston Air Force Base, SC (mil.)
Charleston Gazette (WV newspaper)
Charleston Gazette-Mail (WV newspaper)
Charleston Mail (WV newspaper)
Charleston Naval Shipyard (SC)
Charleston Naval Station (SC)
Charleston Naval Weapons Station (SC)
Charleston Post & Courier (SC newspaper)
Charleston, IL, MO, SC, WV
Charlie Brown (fict. chara., *Peanuts*)
Charlie Bucket (fict. chara.)
Charlie Callas (ent.)
Charlie Chan (fict. detective)
Charlie Chaplin (Sir Charles Spencer)(ent.;
   1889-1977)
Charlie Christian (US jazz; 1919-42)
Charlie Daniels (ent.; 1936-)
Charlie Gehringer (baseball; 1903-93)
Charlie Jones (ent.; 1930-)
Charlie "Bird" Parker (b. Charles Christopher
   Parker, Jr.)(US jazz; 1920-55)
Charlie Pride (ent.; 1938-)
Charlie Rich (ent.; 1932-)
Charlie Rose (US TV journ.; 1942-)
Charlie (Charles) Ruggles (ent.; 1886-1970)
Charlie Sheen (ent.; 1965-)
Charlie Spivak (ent.)
Charlie Weaver (aka Cliff Arquette)(ent.; 1905-74)
Charlie, Checkpoint (East/West Berlin)
Charlie, Mr. (Black slang, white man)
Charlie's Angels (TV show/film)
Charlie's, Inc., Beefsteak
Charlize Theron (ent./model; 1975-)
Charlotte Amalie, St. Thomas, VI
Charlotte Brontë (aka Currer Bell)(Br. writer;
   1816-55)
Charlotte Corday d'Armont (Fr. patriot; 1768-
   93)
Charlotte Hornets (basketball team)
Charlotte Observer (NC newspaper)
Charlotte Rae (b. Charlotte Lubotsky)(ent.; 1926-)
Charlotte Rampling (ent.; 1946-)
Charlotte, Hush...Hush, Sweet (film, 1965)
Charlotte, NC

*Charlotte-Mecklenburg County Board of
   Education, Swann v.* (US law; 1971)
Charlotte's Web (E.B. White children's book)
Charlottesville, VA
Charlottetown, Prince Edward Island, Canada
Charlton Heston (b. Charles Carter)(ent.; 1924-)
Charmin (bath tissue)
Charming, Prince
Charo (b. Maria Rosario Pilar Martinez Molina
   Baeza)(Sp./US ent.; 1951-)
Charolais (also Charolaise)(cattle)
Charon (myth.)
Charpentier, Gustave (Fr. comp.; 1860-1956)
Chartres Cathedral (Fr., cathedral of Notre Dame)
Chartres, France
Chartreuse (liqueur)
Charybdis (also modern-Galofalo, Garofalo)
Charybdis, Scylla and (myth.)
Chase Manhattan Bank
Chase Manhattan Corp.
Chase Smith, Margaret (US pol.; 1897-1995)
Chase, Chevy (Cornelius Crane)(ent.; 1943-)
Chase, Ilka (US writer/ent.; 1905-78)
Chase, Lucia (founder Ballet Theatre [now
   American Ballet Theatre]; 1907-86)
Chase, Salmon P. (US jurist; 1808-73)
Chasez, J. C. (Joshua Scott)(ent., 'N Sync; 1976-)
Chasid (also Hasid, Hassid)(rel.)
Chasidism (also Hasidism)(rel.)
Chast, Roz (cartoonist, *New Yorker*; 1954-)
Chastity Bono (daughter of Sonny and Cher;
   1969-)
Chateau Haut-Brion (Fr. wine)
Chateau Lafite-Rothschild (Fr. wine)
Chateau Latour (Fr. wine)
Chateau Leoville-Las-Cases (Fr. wine)
Chateau Margaux (Fr. wine)
Chateau Montelena Winery (US bus.)
Chateau Montrose (Fr. wine)
Chateau Mouton-Rothschild (Fr. wine)
Chateau Petrus (Fr. wine)
Chateau St. Jean, Inc.
Chateau Ste. Michelle Vintners (US bus.)
Chateau Souverain (US bus.)
Chateaubriand (steak)
Chateaubriand, François René (Fr. writer;
   1768-1848)
Chateauguay, Quebec, Canada
Chatelaine (mag.)
Chatelier('s) principle, Le (also Le Chatelier-
   Braun p.)(chem.)
Chatham Islands (S Pac.)
Chatham, England
Chatham, Ontario, Canada
Chattahoochee River (GA/AL/FL)
Chattahoochee, FL
Chattanooga Choo Choo (song)
Chattanooga News-Free Press (TN newspaper)
Chattanooga Times (TN newspaper)
Chattanooga, Battle(s) of (US hist.; 1863)
Chattanooga, TN
Chatterley, Lady Constance (fict. chara.)
Chatterley's Lover, Lady (D.H. Lawrence novel)
Chatterton, Thomas (Br. poet; 1752-70)
Chaucer, Geoffrey (Br. poet; c 1340-1400)

Chaudry, Fazal Elahi (ex-pres., Pak.; 1904-88)
Chauncey Olcott (US comp./ent.; 1860-1932)
Chausson, Ernest (Fr. comp.; 1855-99)
Chautauqua movement (US adult educ.)
Chautauqua, NY
Chavannes, Pierre Cecile Puvis de (Fr. artist;
    1824-98)
Chávez Frías, Hugo (Rafael) (pres., Venezuela;
    1954-)
Chavez, Carlos (Mex. comp.; 1899-1978)
Chávez, Cesar (US labor leader; 1927-93)
Chavez, Julio Cesar (boxing; 1962-)
Chavis, Benjamin F(ranklin)(aka Benjamin Chavis
    Muhammad)(US rel./leader NAACP; 1948-)
Chayefsky, Paddy (US writer; 1923-81)
Chazz Palminteri (b. Chalogero Lorenzo
    Palminteri)(ent./writer; 1951-)
Che (Ernesto) Guevara (SAmer. mil.; 1928-67)
Cheadle, Don (ent.; 1964-)
Cheapside district (London, Eng.)
Chechnya, Chechen Republic
Checker cab
Checker Motors Corp.
Checker, Chubby (b. Ernest Evans)(ent.; 1941-)
Checkpoint Charlie (East/West Berlin)
Cheddar cheese (also cheddar)
Cheddar, England
Cheddi (Berrat) Jagan (ex-pres., Guyana; 1918-)
Chee Hwa, Tung (or Tung Chee-hwa)(chief
    exec., Hong Kong; 1937-)
Cheech & Chong (ent.)
Cheech (Richard) Marin (ent.; 1946-)
Cheektowaga, NY
Cheer (detergent)
Cheerios (cereal)
Cheers (TV show)
Cheese Nips
Cheetah Systems (US bus.)
Chee-tos (chips)
Cheever, John (US writer; 1912-82)
Cheever, Susan (US writer; 1943-)
Cheez Doodles
Cheez-It (crackers)
Chef Boyardee
Cheiffou, Amadou (ex-PM, Niger)
Cheikh El Afia Ould Mohamed Khouna (PM,
    Mauritania)
Chekhov, Anton (Pavlovich)(Rus. writer; 1860-
    1904)
Chekiang (also Zhejiang)(province, Ch.)
Chellean (early humans)
Chelsea Clinton (US daughter of ex-pres.; 1980-)
Chelsea Quinn Yarbro (US writer; 1942-)
Chelsea, Kensington and (London borough)
Chelsea, MA, ME
Cheltenham (type style)
Chelyabinsk, Siberia
Chem-Dry (US bus.)(carpet cleaning)
Chemistry, Nobel Prize for
Chemnitz, Germany (formerly Karl-Marx-Stadt)
Chemomyrdin, Viktor S. (ex-PM, Rus.)
Chen Ning Yang (Ch./US physt.; 1922-)
Chen Shui-bian (pres., Taiwan; 1951-)
Cheney, Dick (Richard Bruce) (US VP; 1941-)
Cheney, Lynne (Anne)(US wife of VP; 1941-)

Chengchow, China (also Zhengzhou)
Chengdu, China (also Chengtu)
Chenin Blanc (grape, wine)(also l.c.)
Chennault, Claire Lee (US gen.; 1890-1958)
Cheong, Ong Teng (ex-pres., Singapore; 1936-)
Cheops (or Khufu), Great Pyramid of (Eg.)
Cher (b. Cherilyn Sirkisian)(ent.; 1946-)
Cheracol (med.)
Cherbourg, France
Chernenko, Konstantin (ex-pres., USSR; 1911-85)
Chernobyl, Ukraine (nuclear accident; 1986)
Cherokee (Native Amer.)
Cherokee rose (plant)
Cherokee, Jeep (auto.)
Cherokee, Jeep Grand (auto.)
Cherry Heering
Cherry Hill, NJ
Cherry Orchard, The (play by Chekhov)
Cherry Point Marine Corps Air Station (NC)
Cherry, Neneh (ent./songwriter; 1964-)
Cherubini, Luigi (It. comp.; 1760-1842)
Cheryl Ladd (b. Cheryl Stoppelmoor)(ent.; 1951-)
Cheryl Tiegs (model/ent.; 1947-)
Chesapeake and Ohio Canal National Historical
    Park (MD/WV/DC)
Chesapeake Bay (MD, VA)
Chesapeake Bay retriever (dog)
Chesapeake Beach, MD
Chesapeake, U.S.S. (US frigate, War of 1812)
Chesapeake, VA
Chesebrough-Ponds, Inc.
Cheshire (cheese)
Cheshire (county, Eng.)
Cheshire cat
Chesney, Kenny (ent.; 1968-)
Chesnutt, Charles Waddell (US writer; 1858-
    1932)
Chesnokov, Andrei (tennis; 1966-)
Chessman, Caryl ("Red Light Bandit")(US
    rapist; 1921-1960)
Chester A(lan) Arthur (21st US pres.; 1829-86)
Chester Bowles (US dipl.; 1901-86)
Chester Gould (cartoonist, *Dick Tracy*; 1900-85)
Chester W(illiam) Nimitz (US adm.; 1885-1966)
Chesterfield, Lord Philip (4th Earl of
    Chesterfield, Philip Dormer Stanhope)(Br.
    writer/pol.; 1694-1773)
Chesterton, G(ilbert) K(eith) (writer; 1874-1936)
Chet (Chester) Atkins (ent.; 1924-2001)
Chet Baker (US jazz; 1929-88)
Chet Huntley (US TV jour.; 1912-74)
Chevalier, Maurice (ent.; 1888-72)
Chevette, Chevrolet (auto.)
Cheviot Hills (Scot./Eng.)
Cheviot sheep (Scot./Br./Austl.)
Cheviot, OH
Chevret (cheese)
Chevrolet (auto.)
Chevrolet Astro (auto.)
Chevrolet Astro LS (auto.)
Chevrolet Astro LT (auto.)
Chevrolet Avalanche pickup/SUV (auto.)
Chevrolet Avalanche Z66 (auto.)
Chevrolet Avalanche Z71 (auto.)
Chevrolet Beretta (auto.)

Chevrolet Beretta Z26 (auto.)
Chevrolet Blazer (auto.)
Chevrolet Blazer LS (auto.)
Chevrolet Blazer LT (auto.)
Chevrolet Blazer Trailblazer (auto.)
Chevrolet Blazer Xtreme (auto.)
Chevrolet C1500 (auto.)
Chevrolet Camaro (auto.)
Chevrolet Camaro RS (auto.)
Chevrolet Camaro SS (auto.)
Chevrolet Camaro Z28 (auto.)
Chevrolet Caprice (auto.)
Chevrolet Cavalier (auto.)
Chevrolet Cavalier LS (auto.)
Chevrolet Cavalier RS (auto.)
Chevrolet Cavalier Z24 (auto.)
Chevrolet Chevette (auto.)
Chevrolet Chevy Van (auto.)
Chevrolet Chevy Van 1500 (auto.)
Chevrolet Chevy Van 2500 (auto.)
Chevrolet Chevy Van 3500 (auto.)
Chevrolet Corsica (auto.)
Chevrolet Corvette (auto.)
Chevrolet Corvette Z06 (auto.)
Chevrolet Express 1500 van (auto.)
Chevrolet Express 2500 van (auto.)
Chevrolet Express 3500 van (auto.)
Chevrolet Express LT (auto.)
Chevrolet Express van (auto.)
Chevrolet Geo Prizm (auto.)
Chevrolet Impala (auto.)
Chevrolet Impala LS (auto.)
Chevrolet Impala SS (auto.)
Chevrolet K-Blazer (auto.)
Chevrolet K1500 (auto.)
Chevrolet Lumina (auto.)
Chevrolet Lumina APV van (auto.)
Chevrolet Lumina LS (auto.)
Chevrolet Lumina LTZ (auto.)
Chevrolet Lumina minivan (auto.)
Chevrolet Malibu (auto.)
Chevrolet Malibu LS (auto.)
Chevrolet Metro (auto.)
Chevrolet Metro Lsi (auto.)
Chevrolet Monte Carlo (auto.)
Chevrolet Monte Carlo LS (auto.)
Chevrolet Monte Carlo SS (auto.)
Chevrolet Monte Carlo Z34 (auto.)
Chevrolet Prizm (auto.)
Chevrolet Prizm LSi (auto.)
Chevrolet S-Blazer (auto.)
Chevrolet S10 (auto.)
Chevrolet S10 Blazer (auto.)
Chevrolet S10 LS (auto.)
Chevrolet S10 pickup (auto.)
Chevrolet Silverado (auto.)
Chevrolet Silverado 1500 (auto.)
Chevrolet Silverado 2500 (auto.)
Chevrolet Silverado 3500 (auto.)
Chevrolet Silverado pickup (auto.)
Chevrolet Sportvan (auto.)
Chevrolet Suburban (auto.)
Chevrolet Suburban C1500 (auto.)
Chevrolet Suburban C2500 (auto.)
Chevrolet Suburban K1500 (auto.)

Chevrolet Suburban K2500 (auto.)
Chevrolet Suburban LS (auto.)
Chevrolet Suburban LT (auto.)
Chevrolet Tahoe (auto.)
Chevrolet Tahoe Limited (auto.)
Chevrolet Tahoe LS (auto.)
Chevrolet Tahoe LT (auto.)
Chevrolet Tahoe Z71 (auto.)
Chevrolet Tracker (auto.)
Chevrolet Tracker LT (auto.)
Chevrolet Tracker ZR2 (auto.)
Chevrolet TrailBlazer (auto.)
Chevrolet Vega (auto.)
Chevrolet Venture LS minivan (auto.)
Chevrolet Venture minivan (auto.)
Chevron Corp.
Chevy (Cornelius Crane)Chase (ent.; 1943-)
Chevy (see Chevrolet)(auto.)
Chevy Chase, MD
Chevy Van (auto.)
Chewa (lang./people)
Cheyenne Mountain Complex (CO)
Cheyenne River (WY)
Cheyenne, WY
Cheyne-Stokes respiration/psychosis (med.)
Chiang Ching (also Madame Mao, Jiang Ching,
    Jiang Qing, Lan Ping)(Ch. pol./ent., wife of
    Chairman Mao; 1914-91)
Chiang Kai-shek (also Chiang Chung-cheng)
    (ex-pres., Nationalist China; 1887-1975)
Chiang Kai-shek, Madame (b. Soong Mei-
    ling)(Ch. lecturer/writer; 1898-?)
Chiangmai, Thailand
Chianti (region, It.)
Chianti (wine)
Chiba, Japan
Chic (Murat Bernard) Young (cartoonist,
    Blondie; 1901-73)
Chicago (pop music)
Chicago Bears (football team)
Chicago Black Hawks (hockey team)
Chicago Board of Trade
Chicago Bulls (basketball team)
Chicago Cubs (baseball team)
Chicago Eight, the (US hist.; 1968)
Chicago Fire (also l.c.)(1871)
Chicago Herald (IL newspaper)
Chicago Loop (also "The Loop")(highway)
Chicago Sun-Times (IL newspaper)
Chicago Tribune (IL newspaper)
Chicago White Sox (baseball team)
Chicago, Art Institute of
Chicago, IL
Chicano (Mex.-Amer.)
Chichen Itzá (ancient Mayan ruins)
Chick Corea (US jazz; 1941-)
Chick Webb (US jazz; 1902-39)
Chickadee, My Little (film, 1940)
Chickasaw (horse)
Chickasaw (Native Amer.)
Chicken Little (fict. chara.)
Chicken of the Sea (tuna)
Chicken Tonight (sauce)
chicken Kiev
chicken Marengo (food)

chicken Tetrazzini (food)
Chiclayo, Peru
Chico (Filho Francisco) Mendes (Brazilian
    environ./labor leader; 1944-88)
Chico (Glenn) Resch (hockey; 1948-)
Chico (Leonard) Marx (ent.; 1886-1961)
Chico San (rice cakes)
Chico, CA
Chief (Joseph) Leabua Jonathan (ex-PM,
    Lesotho; 1914-87)
Chief Black Hawk (Sauk Native Amer.; 1767-
    1838)
Chief Cochise (Apache Native Amer.; 1812?-74)
Chief Cornplanter (Seneca Native Amer., half-
    white, aided Br. in Amer. Rev.; c1740-1836)
Chief Crazy Horse (Sioux Native Amer., Little
    Bighorn; 1842-77)
Chief Executive (US pres. title)
Chief Joseph (Nez Percé Native Amer.; c1840-
    1904)
Chief Justice of the United States (US Supreme
    Court)
Chief Little Turtle (Michikinikwa)(Miami Native
    Amer.; 1752?-1812)
Chief Mangas Coloradas (Apache Native Amer.;
    c1797-1863)
Chief Massasoit (Wampanoag Native Amer.,
    peace treaty with Pilgrims; c1590-1661)
Chief of Naval Operations (US mil.)
Chief Osceola (Seminole Native Amer.; 1800?-
    38)
Chief Pontiac (Ottawa Native Amer.; c1720-69)
Chief Red Cloud (Sioux Native Amer.; 1822-1909)
Chief Seattle (also Seatlh)(Suquamish Native
    Amer.; c1790-1866)
Chief Sequoya (aka George Guess)(Cherokee
    Native Amer., scholar; c1766-1843)
Chief Sitting Bull (Tatanka Yotanka)(Sioux
    Native Amer.; c1831-90)
Chief Tecumseh (also Tecumtha)(Shawnee
    Native Amer.; 1768-1813)
Chiefs, Kansas City (football team)
Chiesa, Vivienne Della (ent.; 1920-)
Chihuahua (dog)
Chihuahua, Mexico
Child (mag.)
Child Custody Protection Act (US
Child Life (mag.)
Child, Julia (US chef/writer; 1912-)
Childe Hassam (US artist; 1859-1935)
Children of a Lesser God (film, 1986)
Children's Crusade (Fr-Ger./Jerusalem; 1212)
Children's Fund, United Nations (UNICEF)
    (formerly United Nations International
    Children's Emergency Fund)(est. 1946)
Chile (Republic of)(SAmer.)
Chiles, Lawton (ex-FL gov.; 1930-98)
Chill Wills (ent.; 1903-78)
Chillicothe, MO, OH
Chilliwack, British Columbia, Canada
Chilly Willy (cartoon chara.)
Chiluba (also Luba-Lulua)(lang.)
Chiluba, Frederick (Jacob Titus)(pres., Zambia;
    1943-)
Chin dynasty, Eastern (Ch.; 317-420)

Chin dynasty, Later (Ch.; 1115-1234)
Chin dynasty, Western (Ch.; 265-316)
Chin, Tiffany (figure skating; 1967-)
China (People's Republic of)(mainland China)
China (Republic of)(Nationalist China)
China aster (flower)
China Beach (TV show)
China grass (fiber)
China grasscloth
China hibiscus (plant)
China Lake Naval Weapons Center (CA)
China oil
China rose (plant)
China Sea (also South China Sea)(off SE Asia)
China silk
China Syndrome, The (film, 1979)
China tree
China White (slang for heroin)
China, Great Wall of
China, Red (People's Republic of China)
Chinaglia, Giorgio (soccer; 1947-)
Chinaman
Chinatown
Chinatown (film, 1974)
Chincoteague (pony)
Chincoteague, VA
Ch'in dynasty (also Qin)(Ch.; 221-206 BC)
Chine, crepe de (fabric)
Chinese (goose)
Chinese (lang./people)
Chinese art
Chinese cabbage/celery
Chinese checkers (game)
Chinese chestnut
Chinese date (tree)
Chinese Empire
Chinese gooseberry (also kiwi)(fruit)
Chinese ink (also India ink)
Chinese lantern (also Japanese lantern)
Chinese lantern (plant)
Chinese molasses (slang, opium)
Chinese New Year
Chinese parsley (coriander)
Chinese puzzle
Chinese red (color)
Chinese restaurant
Chinese-restaurant syndrome
Chinese Revolution (1911 & 1949)
Chinese Shar-Pei (dog)
Chinese white (color)
Chinese wisteria (plant)
Ching dynasty (also Manchu)(Ch.; 1644-1912)
Ching, Chiang (also Madame Mao, Jiang Ching,
    Jiang Qing, Lan Ping)(Ch. pol./ent., wife of
    Chairman Mao; 1914-91)
Ching, I (also *Book of Changes*)(rel.)
Ching, Tao-te (rel.)
Chinock (helicopter)
Chinon (movie equip.)
Chinon America, Inc.
Chinook (Native Amer.)
Chinook salmon
Chinook State (nickname, WA)
Chinua Achebe (Nigerian writer; 1930-)
Chip 'N' Dale, The Adventures of (TV show)

Chip Hanauer (boat racing)
Chipata, Zambia
Chipewyan (Native Amer.)
Chipmunks, Alvin & the (cartoon)
Chippendale chair
Chippendale style
Chippendale, Thomas (Br. furniture designer; c1718-79)
Chippewa (also Ojibwa)(Native Amer.)
Chippewa Falls, WI
Chippewa National Forest
CHiPs (TV show)
Chips Ahoy! (cookies)
Chips, Goodbye, Mr. (film, 1939)
Chirac, Jacques (pres., Fr.; 1932-)
Chirico, Giorgio de (It. artist; 1888-1978)
Chisholm Trail (cattle drives)
Chisholm v. Georgia (US law; 1793)
Chisholm, Melanie (aka Sporty Spice)(ent.; 1974-)
Chisholm, MN
Chisholm, Shirley (Anita St. Hill)(US pol.; 1924-)
Chisinau, Moldova (also Kishinev)
Chissano, Joaquim Alberto (pres., Mozambique; 1939-)
Chita Rivera (ent.; 1933-)
Chittagong, Bangladesh
Chitty Chitty Bang Bang (film, 1968)
Chivas Regal (scotch)
Chlamydia (med.)
Chloe Sevigny (ent.; 1974-)
Chloë, Daphnis and (Gr. romance)
Chloraseptic (med.)
Chloris (myth.)
Chloromycetin (med.)
Chlorophyta (green algae phylum)
Chloroptic (med.)
Chlor-Trimeton (med.)
Chlumsky, Anna (ent.; 1980-)
Chocolatier (mag.)
Choctaw (Native Amer.)
Choice Hotels International (US bus.)
Choledyl (med.)
Choloxin (med.)
Chomsky, Noam (US linguist; 1928-)
Chondokyo (rel.)
Chong, Cheech & (ent.)
Chong, Rae Dawn (ent.; 1962-)
Chong, Tommy (Thomas)(ent.; 1938-)
Chongjin, North Korea
Chongqing, China (also Chungking)
Chop, Lamb (S. Lewis puppet)
Chopin, Frédéric (Pol. comp.; 1810-49)
Chopin, Kate O'Flaherty (US writer; 1851-1904)
Chopra, Deepak (Indian phys./writer; 1947-)
Chopsticks (also *The Celebrated Chop Waltz*) (by A. de Lulli)
C horizon (geol.)
Chorus Line, A (play)
Chorzow, Poland
Chosen People (also l.c.)(rel.)
Chou dynasty (Ch. hist.; 1122-255 BC)
Chou En-Lai (also Zhou Enlai)(ex-PM, Ch.; 1898-1976)
Chouteau, Jean Pierre (US pioneer/fur trader; 1758-1849)
Chouteau, Rene Auguste (US pioneer/fur trader; 1749-1829)
Chow, Yun-Fat (ent.; 1955-)
Choybalsan, Mongolia
CHPA (Consumer Healthcare Products Association)
Chretién, (Joseph Jacques) Jean (PM, Can.; 1934-)
Chris Brathwaite (track; 1949-84)
Chris Carter (ent./writer; 1957-)
Chris Columbus (ent./writer; 1958-)
Chris-Craft boats
Chris Craft Boats Corp.
Chris Evert-Lloyd (tennis; 1954-)
Chris Farley (ent.; 1964-97)
Chris Isaak (ent./songwriter; 1956-)
Chris Kirkpatrick (ent., 'N Sync; 1971-)
Chris Lemmon (ent.; 1954-)
Chris Matthews (US TV jour.)
Chris O'Donnell (ent.; 1970-)
Chris Rock (ent.; 1965-)
Chris Sarandon (ent.; 1942-)
Chris Schenkel (ent.; 1923-)
Chris Tucker (ent.; 1971-)
Chris Van Allsburg (US writer/artist; 1949-)
Chrissie Hynde (ent.; 1951-)
Christ of the Andes (peace monument between Chile/Argentina)
Christ, Jesus (known as Jeshua ben Joseph to contemporaries)
Christ, Vicar of (pope)
Christ, Yellow (by Gauguin)
Christa McAuliffe, (Sharon)(nee Corrigan)(US educ., Challenger; 1948-1986)
Christchurch, England
Christchurch, New Zealand
Christendom (rel.)
Christhood
Christiaan Barnard, Dr. (SAfr. phys., performed 1st human heart transplant; 1922-2001)
Christian (rel.)
Christian Bale (ent.; 1974-)
Christian Broadcasting Network (CBN)
Christian Brothers (brandy)
Christian Brothers religious order (also Brother of the Christian Schools)
Christian Coalition
Christian Dior (Fr. designer; 1905-57)
Christian Dior Perfumes Corp.
Christian Doppler (Aus. physt.; 1803-53)
Christian Endeavor Societies (rel.)
Christian Era
Christian Huygens (or Huyghens)(Dutch math./ physt./astron.; 1629-95)
Christian I (king, Den.; 1426-48)
Christian IV (king, Den./Nor.; 1577-1648)
Christian IX (king, Den.; 1818-1906)
Christian name (first [baptismal] name)
Christian Science (also Church of Christ, Scientist)
Christian Science Monitor (Christian Science newspaper)
Christian Slater (b. Christian Hawkins)(ent.; 1969-)
Christian VIII (king, Den.; 1786-1848)
Christian X (king, Den./Iceland; 1870-1947
Christian, Charlie (US jazz; 1919-42)
Christian, Judeo- (beliefs, traditions)

Christiane Amanpour (broadcast jour.; 1958-)
Christianity (rel.)
Christians and Jews, National Conference of
    (est. 1928)
Christiansted, St. Croix
Christie Ann Hefner (US publ.)
Christie Brinkley (US model; 1953-)
Christie Love!, Get (film, 1974)
Christie, Agatha, Dame (Br. writer; 1891-1976)
Christie, Julie (ent.; 1941-)
Christie, Lou (b. Lugee Sacco)(ent.; 1943-)
Christie's (auction)
Christina (Georgina) Rossetti (Br. poet; 1830-94)
Christina (queen, Swed.; 1626-89)
Christina Aguilera (ent.; 1980-)
Christina Applegate (ent.; 1971-)
Christina Onassis (Gr. heiress; 1951-88)
Christina Pickles (ent.; 1935-)
Christina Ricci (ent.; 1980-)
Christina Stead (Austl. writer; 1903-83)
Christina's World (A. Wyeth painting)
Christine Baranski (ent.; 1952-)
Christine Ebersole (ent.; 1953-)
Christine Jorgensen (b. George Jorgensen, Jr.)
    (1st sex-change operation; 1927-89)
Christine Lahti (ent.; 1950-)
Christine "Christie" Todd Whitman (US adm./
    EPA, ex-NJ gov.; 1946-)
Christmas (also Noel, Xmas)(rel.)
Christmas cactus (flowering plant)
Christmas Carol, A (C. Dickens novel)
Christmas club (type of savings account)
Christmas Day (12/25)
Christmas Eve (12/24)
Christmas fern (plant)
Christmas Island (also Gilbert Islands)(site of
    nuclear testing, Pac.)
Christmas Island (Indian Ocean)
Christmas rose (plant)
Christmas tree
Christmas tree (slang for Tuinal)
Christmasberry
Christmastide
Christmastime
Christo (Christo Javacheff)(Bulgarian artist; 1935-)
Christology (rel.)
Christoph W(illibald) von Gluck (Ger. comp.;
    1714-87)
Christopher Buckley (US writer; 1952-)
Christopher Columbus (It./Sp. nav.; 1451-1506)
Christopher Dean (figure skating; 1958-)
Christopher Fry (Br. writer; 1907-)
Christopher Grant LaFarge (US arch.; 1862-1938)
Christopher (Haden-) Guest (ent./writer; 1948-)
Christopher (William Bradshaw) Isherwood (Br.
    writer; 1904-86)
Christopher J. Dodd (US cong.; 1944-)
Christopher Lasch (US hist./social critic; 1932-94)
Christopher Lee (aka Lee Yuen Kam)(ent.; 1922-)
Christopher Lloyd (ent.; 1938-)
Christopher Marlowe (Br. writer; 1564-93)
Christopher (Darlington) Morley (US writer/
    editor; 1890-1957)
Christopher-Nevis, St. (Federation of)(also St.
    Kitts-Nevis)(West Indies)

Christopher Plummer (ent.; 1927-)
Christopher Reeve (ent.; 1952-)
Christopher Robin (fict. chara, Winnie-the-Pooh)
Christopher S(amuel) "Kit" Bond (US cong.;
    1939-)
Christopher Walken (ent.; 1943-)
Christopher Wallace (aka The Notorious
    B.I.G.)(ent.; 1972-97)
Christopher Wren, Sir (Br. arch.; 1632-1723)
Christopher, St. (patron saint of travelers)
Christopher, Warren (US ex-secy./state; 1925-)
Christopher, William (ent.; 1932-)
Christy Brown (Ir. writer/artist; 1932-81)
Christy (Christopher) Mathewson (baseball;
    1880-1925)
Christy Turlington (model; 1969-)
Christy, Edwin P. (ent.; 1815-62)
Christy's Minstrels (music)
Chronicle of Higher Education
Chronicle, Augusta (GA newspaper)
Chronicle, Houston (TX newspaper)
Chronicle, San Francisco (CA newspaper)
Chronicles, Books I&II (rel., book of the Old
    Testament)
Chrysler (auto.)
Chrysler 300M (auto.)
Chrysler Cirrus (auto.)
Chrysler Cirrus LX (auto.)
Chrysler Cirrus LXi (auto.)
Chrysler Concorde (auto.)
Chrysler Concorde LX (auto.)
Chrysler Concorde LXi (auto.)
Chrysler Corp.
Chrysler Fifth Avenue (auto.)
Chrysler Grand Voyager minivan (auto.)
Chrysler Imperial (auto.)
Chrysler Jeep Grand Cherokee (auto.)
Chrysler Jeep Grand Cherokee Laredo (auto.)
Chrysler LeBaron (auto.)
Chrysler LH sedan (auto.)
Chrysler LHS (auto.)
Chrysler New Yorker (auto.)
Chrysler Prowler roadster (was Plymouth)(auto.)
Chrysler PT Cruiser (auto.)
Chrysler PT Cruiser Limited (auto.)
Chrysler Sebring (auto.)
Chrysler Sebring JX (auto.)
Chrysler Sebring JXi (auto.)
Chrysler Sebring JXi Limited (auto.)
Chrysler Sebring LX (auto.)
Chrysler Sebring LXi (auto.)
Chrysler Town & Country Limited minivan
    (auto.)
Chrysler Town & Country LX minivan (auto.)
Chrysler Town & Country LXi minivan (auto.)
Chrysler Town & Country minivan (auto.)
Chrysler Town & Country SX minivan (auto.)
Chrysler Voyager LX minivan (auto.)
Chrysler Voyager minivan (auto.)
Chrysler Voyager SE minivan (auto.)
Chrysler, Walter P(ercy)(US bus./auto.; 1875-
    1940)
Chrysophyta (phylum)
Chuan Leekpai (PM, Thailand; 1938-)
Chubby Checker (b. Ernest Evans)(ent.; 1941-)

Chuck Barris (ent.; 1929-)
Chuck (Charles) Berry (ent.; 1926-)
Chuck Connors (ent.; 1921-92)
Chuck (Charles Ernest) Grassley (US cong.; 1933-)
Chuck Jones (cartoonist, *Bugs Bunny, Porky Pig, Daffy Duck*; 1912-)
Chuck Mangione (ent.; 1940-)
Chuck Noll (football; 1931-)
Chuck Norris (b. Carlos Ray)(ent.; 1940-)
Chuck (Charles Spittal) Robb (US pol.; 1939-)
Chuck (Charles) Scarborough
Chuck Wagon (dog food)
Chuck Woolery (ent.)
Chuck (Charles Elwood) Yeager, Col. (US aviator; 1923-)
Chula Vista, CA
Chun Doo Hwan (ex-pres., SKorea; 1931-)
Chun-hsiun, Chang (PM, Taiwan; 1938-)
Chung King (foods)
Chung King Corp.
Chung Won Shik (ex-PM, SKorea)
Chung, Connie (b. Constance Yu-Hwa Chung) (US TV jour.; 1946-)
Chung, Eye to Eye With Connie (TV show)
Chungking, China (also Chongqing)
Chunky Soup
Chunnel (tunnel joining Eng./Fr.)
Church of Christ (also Christian Science/ Scientist)
Church of England (also Anglican Church)
Church of God
Church of Jesus Christ of the Latter-Day Saints (also Latter-Day Saints, Mormon Church)
Church of Rome (also Roman Catholic Church)
Church of Scientology (rel.)
Church of Scotland
Church of the Brethren (also Dunkers)
Church of the Holy Sepulcher (Jerusalem)
Church of the New Jerusalem (also Swedenborgians)
Church of Tonga
Church Rock (NM)(nuclear accident; 1979)
Church, Frederic (US artist; 1826-1900)
Church's Fried Chicken, Inc.
Churches of Christ in the United States of America, National Council of the (est. 1950)
Churchill, Baroness Clementine Spencer- (wife of ex-Br. PM; 1885-1977)
Churchill, Jennie (Br., mother of Winston; 1854-1921)
Churchill, John (aka Duke of Marlborough)(Br. mil.; 1650-1722)
Churchill, Manitoba, Canada
Churchill, Randolph (Henry Spencer), Lord (Br. pol., father of Winston; 1849-95)
Churchill, Sarah (Br., duchess of Marlboro; 1660-1744)
Churchill, Sir Winston (Leonard Spencer)(ex-PM, Br.; 1874-1965)
Churchill, Winston (US writer; 1871-1947)
Chuvash (lang./people)
Chyna (b. Joanie Laurer)(wrestling; 1969-)
Chyngyshev, Tursenbek (ex-PM, Kyrgyzstan)
Chynna Phillips (ent.; 1968-)

CIA (Central Intelligence Agency)
Ciampi, Carlo Azeglio (pres., It.; 1920-)
Ciano, Galeazzo (It. pol.; 1903-44)
Ciba Consumer Pharmaceuticals (US bus.)
Cibola, Seven Cities of (utopia)
Cicely Tyson (ent.; 1933-)
Cicero, Marcus Tullius ("Tully")(Roman orator/ writer/pol.; 106-43 BC)
Cid, El (also el Campeador, Rodrigo Diaz de Bivar)(Sp. mil.; 1040-99)
Ciera, Oldsmobile (auto.)
CIGNA Corp.
Cilea, Francesco (It. comp.; 1866-1950)
Cilento, Diane (ent.; 1933-)
Ciller, Tansu (PM, Turk.)
Cimabue, Giovanni (It. artist; 1240-1302)
Cimarosa, Domenico (It. comp.; 1749-1801)
Cimarron (early CAT system)
Cimarron, Territory of (now Oklahoma panhandle)
Cimino, Michael (US ent.; 1943-)
Cimmerians (myth. people, lived in darkness)
C in C (also C. in C., C-in-C)(Commander in Chief)
Cincinnati Bengals (football team)
Cincinnati Enquirer (OH newspaper)
Cincinnati Post (OH newspaper)
Cincinnati Reds (baseball team)
Cincinnati, OH
Cinco de Mayo (Mex. holiday)
Cinderella (fairy tale)
Cinderfella (film, 1960)
Cindy Crawford (US model; 1966-)
Cindy Nelson (skiing; 1955-)
Cindy Pickett (ent.; 1947-)
Cindy Williams (ent.; 1947-)
Cinema Corp., General
CinemaScope (wide screen)
Cinemax (MAX)(TV channel)
Cineplex
Cineplex Odeon Theaters
Cinerama (wide screen)
CineTellFilms
Cingular Wireless LLC (US bus.)
Cinobac (med.)
Cinzano USA, Inc.
Cipro (med.)
Circassia (region, Russia)
Circassian (people)
Circassian walnut (wood of the English walnut tree)
Circe (myth.)
Circinus (astron., compasses)
Circle K (store)
Circle K Corp.
Circuit City Stores, Inc.
Circus Flaminius (Roman circus)
Circus Maximus (ancient Roman circus)
Circus, Circus Enterprises, Inc.
Cirrus, Chrysler (auto.)
Cisco Kid (fict. chara.)
Cisco Systems, Inc.
Cisneros, Henry Gabriel (US ex-secy./HUD; 1947-)
CITES (Convention on International Trade in Endangered Species)
Citgo Petroleum (US bus.)

Citibank
Citicorp
Citicorp Diners Club, Inc.
Citigroup, Inc.
Citium, Zeno of (Gr. phil.; late 4th early 3rd c. BC)
Citizen Kane (film, 1941)
Citizen Watch Co. of America, Inc.
Citizens Band (CB)(radio)
Citracal (med.)
Citrucel (med.)
Citrus Bowl (college football)
City of Brotherly Love (Philadelphia)
City of David (also Jerusalem, Bethlehem)
City of God (heaven)
City of God, The (Latin, De Civitate Dei)(by St. Augustine)
City of Light (Paris)
City of Seven Hills (Rome)
Ciudad Bolivar, Venezuela
Ciudad Guzman, Mexico
Ciudad Juarez, Mexico
Ciudad Rodrigo, Spain
Ciudad Trujillo, Santo Domingo
Civic, Honda (auto.)
Civil Aeronautics Board (CAB)(US govt.)
Civil Rights Act, the (US hist.; 1875, 1964)
Civil War, American (also War of Secession, War Between the States)(1861-65)
Civil War, English (1642-47)
Civil War, Spanish (1936-39)
Civilian Conservation Corps (CCC)(US govt.; 1933-42)
Civitan International (service club)
C. J. Van Houten & Zoon, Inc.
Cl (chem. sym., chlorine)
Clabber Girl (baking powder)
Claes (Thure) Oldenburg (US artist; 1929-)
Claiborne Pell (US cong..; 1918-)
Claiborne, Craig (US writer/food; 1920-2000)
Claiborne, Inc., Liz
Claiborne, Liz (clothing)
Claiborne, Liz (US designer; 1929-)
Clair Bee (basketball; 1896-1983)
Clair de Lune (by Debussy)
Clair, Arthur Saint (US gen.; 1736-1818)
Claire Bloom (ent.; 1931-)
Claire Danes (ent.; 1979-)
Claire Lee Chennault (US gen.; 1890-1958)
Claire Trevor (ent.; 1909-2000)
Claire, Ina (b. Ina Fagan)(ent.; 1895-1985)
Clairol (hair care)
Clairol, Inc.
Clamato (juice)
Clampett, Bob (US cartoonist; 1913-84)
Clampett, Elly May (fict. chara.)
Clampett, Jed (fict. chara.)
Clampett, Jethro (fict. chara.)
Clancy, Tom (Ir. ent.; 1923-90)
Clancy, Tom (US writer; 1947-)
Clapton, Eric (b. Eric Clapp)(ent.; 1945-)
Clara Barton (US, founded American Red Cross; 1821-1912)
Clara Bow (the "It Girl")(ent.; 1905-65)
Clara Josephine (Wieck) Schumann (Ger. pianist; 1819-96)

Clare (county, Ir.)
Clare Boothe Luce (US drama./dipl./pol.; 1903-87)
Clare Briggs (cartoonist, *Mr. & Mrs.*; 1875-1930)
Clarence "Bob" Birdseye (US inv., frozen food; 1886-1956)
Clarence (Seward) Darrow (US atty./writer; 1857-1938)
Clarence Daniel Batchelor (pol. cartoonist; 1888-1977)
Clarence Day, Jr. (US writer; 1874-1935)
Clarence Kelley (ex-FBI dir.; 1911-97)
Clarence (Augustus) Seignoret (pres., Dominica)
Clarence "Pinetop" Smith (US jazz; 1904-29)
Clarence S. Stein (US arch.; 1882-1975)
Clarence Thomas (US jurist; 1948-)
Clarendon (also l.c.)(type style)
Clarion, Ltd. (US bus./cosmetics)
Clarion-Ledger, Jackson (MS newspaper)
Claritin (med.)
Clark Clifford (US pol.; 1906-98)
Clark Corp., Kimberly-
Clark Expedition, Lewis and (St. Louis to Pac.; 1804-06)
Clark Gable, (William)(ent.; 1901-60)
Clark National Historical Park, George Rogers (IN)
Clark National Park, Lake (AK)
Clark, Charles Joseph "Joe" (ex-PM, Can.; 1939-)
Clark, Dane (ent.; 1913-)
Clark, Dave (ent.; 1942-)
Clark, Dick (ent.; 1929-)
Clark, George Rogers (US mil.; 1752-1818)
Clark, Helen (PM, NewZeal.; 1950-)
Clark, Inc., Coats &
Clark, Joe (Charles Joseph)(ex-PM, Can.; 1939-)
Clark, Mark (US gen.; 1896-1984)
Clark, Mary Higgins (US writer; 1931-)
Clark, Petula (ent.; 1932-)
Clark, Roy (ent.; 1933-)
Clark, Susan (ent.; 1940-)
Clark, Will (baseball; 1964-)
Clark, William (US explorer; 1770-1838)
Clarke, Arthur C(harles)(Br. sci-fi writer; 1917-)
Clarke, Bobby (Robert Earle)(hockey; 1949-)
Clarke, Kenny (US jazz; 1914-85)
Clarkson, Adrienne (gov.-gen., Can.; 1939-)
Clarksville, AR, IN, TN, TX
Clash, the (pop music)
Classic, U.S. v. (US law; 1941)
Classicism (style, art/music/lit.)
Claude (Henri de Rouvoy) Saint-Simon, Comte de (Fr. phil.; 1760-1825)
Claude Akins (ent.; 1918-94)
Claude Dauphin (ent.; 1903-78)
Claude Debussy (Fr. comp.; 1862-1918)
Claude Garamond (Fr. typographer; c1480-1561)
Claude glass (photo.)
Claude Lévi-Strauss (Fr. anthrop.; 1908-1990)
Claude Lorrain (Fr. artist; 1600-82)
Claude Monet (Fr. artist; 1840-1926)
Claude Pepper (US pol.; 1901-89)
Claude Rains (ent.; 1890-1967)
Claude, Albert (Belgium biol.; 1899-1983)
Claudette Colbert (Fr./US ent.; 1903-96)

Claudia Cardinale (ent.; 1939-)
Claudia "Lady Bird" (Alta Taylor) Johnson (wife
    of ex-US pres.; 1912-)
Claudia Kolb (swimming; 1949-)
Claudia Schiffer (model; 1970-)
Claudian (Roman poet; c370-c404 BC)
Claudio (Giovanni Antonio) Monteverdi (It.
    comp.; 1567-1643)
Claudio Abbado (It. ent.; 1933-)
Claudio Arrau (Chilean pianist; 1903-91)
Claudius I (Tiberius Claudius Drusus Nero
    Germanicus)(emp., Rome; 10 BC-AD 54)
Claudius Nero (Caesar) Tiberius (emp., Rome;
    42 BC-AD 37)
Claus von Bulow (US news; 1926-)
Claus, Santa (also St. Nicholas, Kriss Kringle)
Clausen, Zorach v. (US law; 1952)
Clausewitz, Karl von (Ger. mil.; 1780-1831)
Claussen (pickles)
Claussen Pickle Co.
Clavell, James (Br./US writer; 1924-94)
Clay Johnson (US White House staff)
Clay S. Felker (US publ./editor; 1925-)
Clay, Andrew Dice (b. Andrew Clay Silverstein)
    (ent.; 1957-)
Clay, Cassius, Jr. (aka Muhammad Ali)(boxing;
    1942-)
Clay, Henry (also Great Compromiser, Great
    Pacificator)(US pol.; 1777-1852)
Clay, Lucius D. (US gen.; 1897-1978)
Clayburgh, Jill (ent.; 1944-)
Claymation (animated clay figures)
Clayton Antitrust Act (US hist.; 1914)
Clayton Homes (manufactured homes)
Clayton Moore (ent.; 1914-99)
Clayton, Buck (US jazz; 1911-)
Clean & Clear (cosmetics)
Clean, Mr. (cleaner)
Clean, Mr. (slang, scandal free)
Clear Eyes (med.)
Clearasil (med./skincare)
Clearly Canadian Beverage Corp. (US/Can. bus.)
Clearwater, FL
Cleary, Beverly (US writer; 1916-)
Cleaver, Beaver ("the Beaver")(fict. chara.)
Cleaver, Eldridge (US activist/writer; 1935-98)
Cleavon Little (ent.; 1939-92)
Cleef & Arpels, Inc., Van
Cleef, Lee Van (ent.; 1925-89)
Cleese, John (ent.; 1939-)
Cleland, Max (US cong.; 1942-)
Clemenceau, Georges (ex-PM, Fr.; 1841-1929)
Clemens W(enzel) L(othar) Metternich (Prince
    von Metternich)(ex-chanc., Aus.; 1773-1859)
Clemens, Roger (baseball; 1962-)
Clemens, Samuel Langhorne (pseud. Mark
    Twain)(US writer; 1835-1910)
Clement (name of 14 popes)
Clement Athelston Arrindell (gov.-gen., St.
    Kitts/Nevis)
Clement C(lark) Moore (US poet/educ.; 1779-
    1863)
Clement R(ichard) Attlee (ex-PM, Br.; 1883-1967)
Clement Studebaker (US bus.; 1831-1901)
Clement VII (pope; 1478-1534)

Clement Vineyards, St. (US bus.)
Clemente, Roberto (baseball; 1934-72)
Clementine Spencer-Churchill, Baroness (wife
    of ex-Br. PM; 1885-1977)
Clemson University (Clemson, SC)
Cleo Laine (ent.; 1927-)
Cleocin (med.)
Cleopatra (queen, Eg.; c68-30 BC)
Cleopatra, Antony and (Shakespeare play)
Cleopatra's Needle(s)(Eg. obelisks in NYC and
    London)
Clerides, Glafcos (pres., Cyprus; 1919-)
Cleveland Abbe (US meteor.; 1838-1916)
Cleveland Amory (US writer/conservationist;
    1917-98)
Cleveland bay (horse)
Cleveland Browns (football team)
Cleveland Cavaliers (basketball team)
Cleveland Indians (baseball team)
Cleveland Plain Dealer (OH newspaper)
Cleveland, Grover (22nd & 24th US pres.;
    1837-1908)
Cleveland, MS, OH, OK, TN
Cleves, Anne of (4th wife of Henry VIII; 1515-57)
Cliburn, Van (Harvey Lavan Cliburn, Jr.)(ent.;
    1934-)
Cliff Arquette (aka Charlie Weaver)(ent.; 1905-74)
Cliff Richard (b. Harry Webb)(ent.; 1940-)
Cliff Robertson (ent.; 1925-)
Cliff, Jimmy (b. Jimmy Chambers)(ent./
    songwriter; 1949-)
Clifford Brown (US jazz; 1930-56)
Clifford Darling (ex-gov.-gen., Bahamas)
Clifford Husbands, Sir (gov.-gen., Barbados;
    1926-)
Clifford Odets (US writer; 1906-63)
Clifford, Clark (US pol.; 1906-98)
Cliffs Notes, Inc.
Clift, Montgomery (ent.; 1920-66)
Clifton Davis (ent.; 1945-)
Clifton Fadiman (US writer/editor; 1904-99)
Clifton Webb (ent.; 1891-1966)
Clifton, AZ, NJ
Cline, Patsy (ent.; 1932-63)
Cling Free (fabric softener)
Clingman's Dome (Great Smoky Mts.)
Clinique (skincare)
Clinique Laboratories, Inc.
Clinoril (med.)
Clint Black (ent./songwriter; 1962-)
Clint Eastwood (ent.; 1930-)
Clinton, Bill (William Jefferson)(42nd US pres.;
    1946-)
Clinton, Chelsea (US daughter of ex-pres.; 1980-)
Clinton, DeWitt (US pol.; 1769-1828)
Clinton, George (ex-US VP; 1739-1812)
Clinton, Henry (Br. mil.; 1738-95)
Clinton, Hillary Rodham (US cong.; wife of ex-
    pres.; 1947)
Clinton, Roger, Jr. (US half-brother of ex-pres.;
    1956-)
Clio (myth.)
Clio (TV ad award)
Clippers, Los Angeles (basketball team)
Clive Barker (writer; 1952-)

Clive, Robert (Br. leader in India; 1725-74)
Clockwork Orange, A (film, 1971)
Cloderm (med.)
Cloisters, the (NYC)(museum of medieval art)
Clomid (med.)
Clooney, George (ent.; 1961-)
Clooney, Rosemary (ent.; 1928-)
Clootie (also Cloot, Cloots)(Satan)
Cloris Leachman (ent.; 1926-)
Clorox bleach
Clorox Co., The
Clos Du Bois Wines (US bus.)
Clos du Val Wine Co., Ltd., The
Close Encounters of the Third Kind (film, 1977)
Close-Up (toothpaste)
Close, Glenn (ent.; 1947-)
Clotho (myth.)
Cloud, Chief Red (Sioux Native Amer.; 1822-1909)
Clover, Inside Daisy (film, 1965)
Clovis, NM
Clower, Jerry (ent.; 1926-98)
Cloxapen (med.)
Clozaril (med.)
Club Med (travel)
Club Wagon, Ford (auto.)
Cluj-Napoca, Romania
CLVS (Certified Legal Video Specialist)
Clyde Barrow (US criminal; 1900-34)
Clyde Beatty (ent.; 1904-65)
Clyde McPhatter (ent.; 1932-72)
Clyde Tombaugh (discoverer of Pluto; 1906-97)
Clyde, Bonnie and (film, 1967)
Clyde, Bonnie and (US criminals)
Clydesdale (horse)
Clydesdale terrier (dog)
Clytemnestra (myth.)
CM (Certificate of Merit)
CMRS (Certified Manager of Reporting Services)
CMT (County Music Television)(TV channel)
CNBC (TV channel)
CNN (Cable News Network)(TV channel)
CNN Financial (CNNfn)(TV channel)
CNN Headline News (TV channel)
CNN International (CNNI)(TV channel)
CNNfn (CNN Financial)(TV channel)
CNNI (CNN International)(TV channel)
C(yril) Northcote Parkinson (Br. writer/hist.; 1909-93)
Cnossos (also Knossos)(ruins, palace, Crete)
C-note (also C)(hundred dollar bill)
CO (Colorado)
Co (chem. sym., cobalt)
Coach (TV show)
Coachman Industries, Inc.
CoActifed (med.)
Coactin (med.)
CoAdvil (med.)
Coalinga, CA
Coast Guard Academy, U.S. (New London, CT) (est. 1876)
Coast Guard, U.S. (US mil.)
Coasters, the (pop music)
Coats & Clark, Inc.
Coats, Daniel R. (US pol.; 1943-)

Cobain, Kurt (ent.; 1967-94)
Cobb, Irvin Shrewsbury (US humorist; 1876-1944)
Cobb, Lee J. (ent.; 1911-76)
Cobb, Ty(rus Raymond)(baseball; 1886-1961)
COBE (Cosmic Background Explorer)(US satellite)
COBOL (common business-oriented lang.)(compu.)
COBRA (Consolidated Omnibus Budget Reconciliation Act)(enacted 1985)(health insurance)
Coburg-Gotha, House of Saxe- (Br. ruling family; 1901-10)
Coburn, Charles (ent.; 1877-1961)
Coburn, James (ent.; 1928-)
Coca, Imogene (ent.; 1908-2001)
Coca-Cola
Coca-Cola Co., The
Cocacolonize/Cocacolonization (US trade/ cultural influence on foreign countries)
Cochabamba, Bolivia
Cochin-China chicken (also Cochin-China fowl, cochin)
Cochin-China, South Vietnam
Cochise, Chief (Apache Native Amer.; 1812?-74)
Cochran, Barbara Ann (skiing; 1951-)
Cochran, Eddie (ent.; 1938-60)
Cochran, Johnnie L., Jr. (US atty.; 1937-)
Cochran, Marilyn (skiing; 1950-)
Cochran, Robert (skiing; 1951-)
Cochran, Thad (US cong.; 1937-)
Cochran's Law Lexicon (legal dictionary text)
Cock Robbin
Cockaigne (also Cockayne)(myth. utopia)
Cockcroft, John D. (Br. physt.; 1897-1967)
Cocker, Jarvis (ent./songwriter; 1963-)
Cocker, Joe (John Robert)(ent.; 1944-)
Coco Chanel, (Gabrielle)(Fr. designer; 1883-1971)
Coco, James (ent.; 1929-87)
Cocoa Beach, FL
Cocoa Krispies (cereal)
Cocoa Pebbles (cereal)
Cocoa Puffs (cereal)
Coconino National Forest
Coconut Grove (area, Los Angeles)
Coconut Grove, FL
Cocoon (film, 1985)
Cocos Islands (also Keeling Islands)(Indian Ocean)
Cocteau, Jean (Fr. writer/artist; 1889-1963)
COD (cash [or collect] on delivery, certificate of death)
Code Napoléon (also Napoleonic Code)(Fr. law)
Code, Hammurabi (ancient law)
Cody, William F(rederick) "Buffalo Bill" (US scout/ent.; 1846-1917)
Coe, Sebastian (Newbold)(track; 1956-)
Coen, Ethan (ent.; 1957-)
Coen, Joel (ent.; 1955-)
Coeur d'Alene (Native Amer.)
Coeur d'Alene National Forest (ID)
Coeur d'Alene, ID
Coffee, Mr.
Cogburn, Rooster (film, 1975)
Cogentin (med.)
Co-Gesic (med.)

Cognac (also l.c.)(brandy)
Cognac, France
Cognex (med.)
Cohan, George M(ichael)(US comp.; 1878-1942)
Cohen, Leonard (ent./songwriter/poet; 1934-)
Cohen, Mickey (Meyer Harris)(US gangster; 1913-76)
Cohen, William S(ebastian)(US ex-secy./ defense; 1940-)
Cohn, Al (US jazz; 1925-88)
Cohn, Myron (ent.; 1902-86)
Coimbra, Portugal
Cointreau (liqueur)
Coke
Cokie Roberts (b. Mary Martha Corinne Morrison Claiborne Boggs)(TV jour.; 1943-)
Cola Co., Pepsi-
Colace (med.)
Colavito, Rocky (Rocco Domenico)(baseball; 1933-)
Colbert, Claudette (Fr./US ent.; 1903-96)
Colbert, Jean Baptiste (Fr. pol.; 1619-83)
Cold Sassy Tree (book; film, 1989)
Cold War (US/USSR; 1945-90)
Coldstream Guards (Br. mil., formerly Monck's Regiment)
Coldwell Banker Real Estate
Cole of California (sportswear)
Cole of California, Inc.
Cole Porter (US comp.; 1893-1964)
Cole(man) Younger, (Thomas)(US outlaw; 1844-1916)
Cole, Cozy (US jazz; 1909-81)
Cole, Gary (ent.; 1957-)
Cole, Nat "King" (ent.; 1919-65)
Cole, Natalie (ent.; 1950-)
Cole, Olivia (ent.; 1942-)
Cole, Paula (ent.; 1968-)
Cole, Thomas (US artist; 1801-48)
Cole, U.S.S. (Navy warship bombed in Aden Yemen; 10/12/2000)
Coleman Hawkins (US jazz; 1904-69)
Coleman Young (Detroit mayor; 1918-97)
Coleman, Cy (US comp.; 1929-)
Coleman, Dabney (ent.; 1932-)
Coleman, Derrick (basketball; 1967-)
Coleman, Gary (ent.; 1968-)
Coleman, Ornette (US jazz; 1930-)
Coleraine, Northern Ireland
Coleridge, Samuel Taylor (Br. poet; 1772-1834)
Coleridge-Taylor, Samuel (Br. comp.; 1875-1912)
Colestid (med.)
Colette, Sidonie Gabrielle (Fr. writer; 1873-1954)
Colfax, Schuyler (ex-US VP; 1823-85)
Colgate (dental care)
Colgate-Palmolive Co.
Colgate, William (US bus.; 1783-1857)
Colin Davis (Br. cond.; 1927-)
Colin Firth (ent.; 1960-)
Colin L(uther) Powell, Gen. (US secy./state; 1937-)
Colleen Dewhurst (ent; 1926-1991)
Colleen McCullough (Austl. writer/ neuroscientist; 1937-)
College Entrance Examination Board (CEEB)

College of Arms (also Heralds' College)(Br. heraldry)
College of Cardinals (also Sacred College of Cardinals)(rel.)
College of William and Mary (Williamsburg, VA)
College Park, GA, MD
College Station, Texas
Collegiate Athletic Association, National (NCAA)(est. 1906)
Collingwood, Charles (TV jour.; 1917-85)
Collins, Fort (CO)(city)
Collins, Francis (Sellers)(US genet./human genome; 1950-)
Collins, Herrera v. (US law; 1993)
Collins, Jackie (US writer; 1939-)
Collins, Joan (ent.; 1933-)
Collins, Judy (ent.; 1939-)
Collins, Michael (astro.; 1930-)
Collins, Pauline (ent.; 1940-)
Collins, Phil (ent.; 1951-)
Collins, Susan M. (US cong.; 1952-)
Collins, Tom (mixed drink)
Collis Potter Huntington (US bus.; 1821-1900)
Collyer, Bud (ent.)
Colm Meaney (ent.; 1953-)
Colman, Ronald (ent.; 1891-1958)
Cologne brown (color)
Cologne Cathedral
Cologne, eau de
Cologne, Germany (also Köln)
Coloma, CA
Colombia (Republic of)(SAmer.)
Colombian gold (slang, South American marijuana)
Colombo, Sri Lanka
Colón, Panama
Colonel Blimp (fict. chara.)
Colonel Tom Parker (Elvis Presley's manager; ?-1997)
Colonel (Harland) Sanders (US bus./chicken; 1890-1980)
Colonial architecture
Colonial Dames of America
Colonial Homes (mag.)
Colonial National Historical Park (VA)
Colonial Penn Insurance Co.
Colonies, Thirteen (original US states)
Colonna, Jerry (ent.; 1905-86)
Colonus, Oedipus at (by Sophocles)
Colony, Lost (VA settlement; disappeared 1591)
Color Key (graphic design)
Coloradas, Chief Mangas (Apache Native Amer.; c1797-1863)
Colorado (CO)
Colorado potato beetle
Colorado River (Argentina)
Colorado River (SW US)
Colorado River (TX)
Colorado Rockies (baseball team)
Colorado Springs Gazette Telegraph (CO newspaper)
Colorado Springs, CO
Colosseum of Rome (site of mock battles & Christian sacrifices)
Colossians (rel., book of the New Testament)
Colossians, Epistle to the (rel.)

Colossus of Memnon, (ancient Eg. statue)
Colossus of Rhodes (statue of Apollo; fell in
   224 BC)
Colson, Charles W. (US pol./Watergate; 1931-)
Colt (revolver)
Colt, Dodge (auto.)
Colt, Samuel (US gunsmith; 1814-62)
Coltrane, John (US jazz; 1926-67)
Colts, Indianapolis (football team)
Columba (also Columba Noae)(astron., dove)
Columba (Garnica Gallo) Bush (US/Mex. wife of
   FL gov.; 1953-)
Columbia (US space shuttle, 1st to orbit &
   return to Earth)
Columbia Broadcasting System (CBS)(TV
   channel)
Columbia Pictures (US film co.)
Columbia River (Can.)
Columbia State (SC newspaper)
Columbia University (NYC)
Columbia, District of (Washington, DC, US capital)
Columbia, MD, MO, MS, PA, SC, TN
Columbian Order of NYC (also Tammany
   Society)
Columbine (US news, school shootings; 4/20/
   99)
Columbo (TV show)
Columbo, Mrs. (TV show)
Columbo, Russ (ent.; 1908-34)
Columbus Day (formerly Discovery Day)
   (October 12)
Columbus Dispatch (OH newspaper)
Columbus, Chris (ent./writer; 1958-)
Columbus, Christopher (It./Sp. nav.; 1451-1506)
Columbus, GA, IN, KS, MS, NE, OH, TX, WI
Columbus, Knights of (rel. org.)
Colville N(orbert) Young, Sir (gov.-gen., Belize;
   1932-)
Colvin, Shawn (ent.; 1956-)
Coly-Mycin (med.)
Coma Berenices (astron., Berenice's hair)
Coma cluster (astron.)
Comanche (Native Amer.)
Comaneci, Nadia (gymnast; 1961-)
Combipres (med.)
Combs, Sean "Puffy" (aka Puff Daddy)(ent.;
   1969-)
Comden, Betty (US lyricist/ent.; 1919-)
Comdisco, Inc.
Comédie Française (Fr. national theater)
Comedy Central (COM)(TV channel)
Comedy of Errors, The (Shakespeare play)
Comenius, Johann Amos (Czech. educ.
   reformer; 1592-1670)
Comet (cleanser)
Comet Hale-Bopp
Comets, Bill Haley and the (pop music)
Comfort, Alex (Br. phys./writer; 1920-2000)
Comice (pear)
Coming to America (film, 1988)
Comintern (Third Communist International)
Commager, Henry Steele (US hist./educ.;
   1902-98)
Commerce Commission, Interstate (ICC)(US
   govt. agcy.)

Commerce, Department of (US govt.)
Commercialware (cookware)
Commerical Appeal, Memphis (TN newspaper)
Commish, The (TV show)
Commodity Credit Corporation
   (CCC)(agriculture)
Commodore (compu.)
Commodore International, Ltd.
Common Market (EEC)(also European Economic
   Community, est. 1957)
Common Prayer, Book of (Church of England)
Common Sense (by Thomas Paine; 1776)
Common Sense Oat Bran (cereal)
Commons, House of (Br. & Can. parliaments)
Commons, John R. (US econ./hist.; 1862-1945)
Commonwealth Day (Br. holiday)
Commonwealth of Independent States (CIS)
   (informal successor body to the USSR)
Commonwealth of Nations
Commonwealth, the (voluntary assoc. of past &
   present British Empire countries)
Communion, Holy (also Eucharist, Lord's
   Supper)(rel.)
Communism (usually l.c.)
Communism Peak (also Pik Kommunizma)
   (formerly Mount Garmo, Mount Stalin)(Tajikisyan)
Communist Manifesto (by K. Marx/F. Engels)
Communist Party (pol.)
Como, Perry (ent.; 1912-2001)
Comorian (also Comoran)(people)
Comoros (Federal Islamic Republic of the)
   (Indian Ocean)
Compaoré, Blaise (pres., Burkina Faso; 1951-)
Compaq Computer Corp.
Compaq Information Technologies Group, L.P.
Compazine (med.)
Compleat Beatles, The (film, 1982)
Compoboard (constr.)
Composite column (arch.)
Compound W (med.)
Compoz (med.)
Compromise of 1850 (US hist. re: slaves)
Compromiser, Great (also Great Pacificator)
   (Henry Clay)(US pol.; 1777-1852)
Compton effect (also Compton-Debye effect)(x-
   rays)
Compton, Arthur (Holly)(US physt.; 1892-1962)
Compton, John (George Melvin)(ex-PM, St.
   Lucia; 1926-)
Compton, Karl Taylor (US physt.; 1887-1954)
CompuServe (compu.)
Compute (mag.)
Computer Associates International, Inc.
Computer Chronicles (TV show)
Computer Graphics World
Computer Sciences Corp.
Computer Shopper (mag.)
Computerland Corp.
Computerworld
Comsat (*com*munications *sat*ellite)
Comstock Lode (gold/silver vein, NV)
Comstock, Anthony (US reformer; 1844-1915)
Comstock, Henry T(omkins) P. (US, Comstock
   Lode; 1820-70)
Comstockery (censorship of arts)

Comte, Auguste (Fr. phil.; 1798-1857)
Comtrex (med.)
Comus (also Komos)(myth.)
ConAgra Foods, Inc.
Conair (appliances)
Conair Corp.
Conakry, Guinea
Conan Doyle, Sir Arthur (Br. phys./writer; 1859-1930)
Conan O'Brien (ent.; 1963-)
Conan the Adventurer (TV show)
Conan the Barbarian (film, 1982)
Conan the Destroyer (film, 1984)
Conant, James B. (US chem./educ./dipl.; 1893-1978)
Concepción, Chile
Conceptrol (med.)
Conchata Ferrell (ent.; 1943-)
Concord (grape/wine)
Concord coach (trans.)
Concord Naval Weapons Station (CA)
Concord, CA, MA, NC, NH
Concorde, Chrysler (auto.)
Concorde, Place de la (building/museum, Paris)
Concorde, the (supersonic jet)
Conde Nast (US publ.)
Conde Nast Traveler (mag.)
Condit, Gary A. (US cong..; 1948-)
Condoleezza "Condi" Rice (US nat'l security advisor; 1954-)
Condon, Eddie (US jazz; 1904-73)
Conduct Medal, Distinguished (mil.)
Cone Mills Corp.
Conecuh National Forest
Coneheads, the (fict. charas., *Saturday Night Live*)
Conestoga (Native Amer.)
Conestoga wagon (horse drawn, covered)
Coney Island (NYC)
Confederate Memorial Day
Confederate note (econ.)
Confederate States of America (also Confederacy)(US hist.; 1861-65)
Confederation, Articles of (US hist.; 1781)
Conference of Christians and Jews, National (est. 1928)
Conference on Environment and Development, United Nations (Earth Summit)(June 1992)
Conference on Trade and Development, United Nations (UNCTAD)(est. 1964)
Confessions of Nat Turner, The (W. Styron book)
Confucianism (also called Confucian, Confucius) (phil./rel.)
Confucianist (rel.)
Confucius (Ch., founded Confucianism; 551-479 BC)
Cong, Vo Chi (ex-pres., Viet.)
Conger, Darva (TV's *Who Wants to Marry a Multimillionaire?* bride; 1966-)
Congespirin (med.)
Congo (aka Democratic Republic of the Congo & DRC & Congo-Kinshasa)(was Zaire)(W central Afr.)
Congo-Brazzaville (aka Republic of the Congo & Congo Republic)(W central Afr.)

Congo-Kinshasa (aka Democratic Republic of the Congo & Congo)(was Zaire)(W central Afr.)
Congo red
Congo Republic (aka Republic of the Congo & Congo-Brazzaville)(W central Afr.)
Congo River (also Zaire River)(Afr.)
Congo snake (also l.c.)
Congo, Niger- (langs.)
Congoleum Corp.
Congregational Church
Congregationalism (rel.)
Congress (of the U.S.)(US govt.)
Congress of Industrial Organizations (US labor org.)
Congress of Racial Equality (CORE)(US civil-rights org.)
Congress of Vienna (Eur. hist.; 1814-15)
Congress, Library of (DC)
Congressional Medal of Honor (also Medal of Honor)(mil.)
Congressional Record (US Congress proceedings)
Congreve, William (Br. writer; 1670-1729)
Conigliaro, Tony (baseball; 1945-90)
Connally, John B. (ex-gov., TX; 1917-93)
Connecticut (CT)
Connecticut General Life Insurance Co.
Connecticut Wits (also Hartford Wits)(18th c US lit. grp.)
Connecticut Yankee in King Arthur's Court, A (Mark Twain novel)
Connecticut, Griswold v. (US law; 1965)
Connell, Evan S. (US writer; 1924-)
Connelly, Marc (US playwright; 1890-1980)
Connelly, Michael (US writer; 1956-)
Connemara pony
Conner, Nadine (ent.; 1913-)
Connery, Sean (Scot./US ent.; 1930-)
Connick, Harry, Jr. (ent.; 1967-)
Connie Chung (b. Constance Yu-Hwa Chung)(US TV jour.; 1946-)
Connie Chung, Eye to Eye With (TV show)
Connie Francis (b. Concetta Franconero)(ent.; 1938-)
Connie Mack (b. Cornelius McGillicuddy)(baseball; 1862-1956)
Connie Mack III (US pol.; 1940-)
Connie Sellecca (b. Concetta Sellecchia)(ent.; 1955-)
Connie Stevens (b. Concetta Ann Ingolia)(ent.; 1938-)
Conniff Orchestra, Ray
Conniff, Ray (ent.; 1916-)
Connolly, Maureen ("Little Mo")(tennis; 1934-69)
Connors, Chuck (ent.; 1921-92)
Connors, Jimmy (James Scott)(tennis; 1952-)
Connors, Mike (b. Krekor Ohanian)(ent.; 1925-)
Conoco, Inc.
Conrad (Potter) Aiken (US writer; 1889-1973)
Conrad Bain (Can. ent.; 1923-)
Conrad Burns (US cong.; 1935-)
Conrad I (king, Ger.; ?-918)
Conrad II (king, Ger., Holy Roman emp.; c990-1039)
Conrad III (king, Ger.; 1093-1152)
Conrad IV (king, Ger.; 1228-54)

Conrad Janis (ent.; 1928-)
Conrad Nagel (ent.; 1896-1970)
Conrad N(icholson) Hilton (US bus./hotels; 1888-1979)
Conrad Potter Aiken (US writer; 1889-1973)
Conrad V (also Conradin)(king, Ger.; 1252-68)
Conrad Veidt (ent.; 1893-1943)
Conrad, Charles, Jr. (astro.; 1930-99)
Conrad, Joseph (Br. writer; 1857-1924)
Conrad, Kent (US cong.; 1948-)
Conrad, Paul (pol. cartoonist; 1924-)
Conrad, Robert (ent.; 1935-)
Conrad, William (ent.; 1920-94)
Conried, Hans (ent.; 1917-82)
Conroy, Pat (US writer; 1945-)
Conservative Judaism (rel.)
Conservative Party (UK pol.)
Conservative Party (US pol.)
Conservative Party, Progressive- (Can. pol.)
Consolidated Omnibus Budget Reconciliation Act (COBRA)(enacted 1985)(health insurance)
Constable, John (Br. artist; 1776-1837)
Constance Bennett (ent.; 1904-65)
Constance Cummings (ent.; 1910-)
Constance Talmadge (ent.; 1897-1973)
Constanta, Romania
Constantin Brancusi (Romanian artist; 1876-1957)
Constantine I (aka Constantine the Great)(emp., Rome; 306-337)
Constantine I (king, Gr.; 1868-1923)
Constantine II (deposed king, Gr.; 1940-)
Constantine Karamanlis (ex-pres., Gr.; 1907-98)
Constantine Mitsotakis (ex-PM, Gr.; 1918-)
Constantine the Great (aka Constantine I)(emp., Rome; 306-337)
Constantine, Arch of (Rome)
Constantine, Michael (b. Constantine Joanides)(ent.; 1927-)
Constantinescu, Emil (pres., Romania; 1939-)
Constantinople (formerly Byzantium, now Istanbul)
Constantinos (or Konstantinos) Stephanopoulos (pres., Gr.; 1926-)
Constant-T (med.)
Constitution (of the U.S.)(ratified 1787)
Constitution State (nickname, CT)
Constitution, Atlanta (GA newspaper)
Constitution, The ("Old Ironsides")(US naval ship)
Constitutional Convention (US hist.; 1787)
Consumer Guide (book)
Consumer Price Index
Consumer Reports (mag.)
Consumer Reports Buying Guide (book)
Consumers Digest (mag.)
Consumers Digest, Inc.
Consumers Union (US consumers' org.; est. 1936)
Contac (med.)
Contadina Foods (US bus.)
Conté (art crayon)
Conté Alessandro Volta (It. physt.; 1745-1827)
Conté Lansana (pres., Guinea; 1934-)
Conté, Richard (ent.; 1911-75)
Conti, Tom (Scot. ent.; 1941-)
Continental Airlines, Inc.
Continental Congress (US hist.; 1774-89)

Continental Divide (also the Great Divide)(the Rockies)
Continental, Bentley (auto.)
Continental, Lincoln (auto.)
Contour, Ford (auto.)
Contras, the (Central Amer. guerrilla force; 1979-90)
Control Data Corp.
Convention on International Trade in Endangered Species (CITES)
Convy, Bert (ent.; 1934-91)
Conway Twitty (ent.; 1933-93)
Conway, Tim (ent.; 1933-)
Cooder, Ry (Ryland) (ent./songwriter; 1947-)
Coogan, Jackie (ent.; 1914-84)
Cook Islands (Polynesian)
Cook, Barbara (ent.; 1927-)
Cook, James, Capt. (Br. nav./expl.; 1728-79)
Cook, Jay (US finan.; 1821-1905)
Cook, Peter (ent./writer; 1937-95)
Cook, Robin (ophthalmologist/writer; 1940-)
Cook, Thomas (Br. travel agent; 1808-92)
Cook's tour (travel)
Cooke, Alistair (Br./US jour.; 1908-)
Cooke, Jack Kent (US bus.; 1912-97)
Cooke, Sam (ent.; 1935-64)
Cooke, Sir Howard F. H. (gov.-gen.; Jamaica; 1915-)
Cookie Monster (fict. chara.)
Cookin' USA (TV show)
Cooking Light (mag.)
Cool Hand Luke (film, 1967)
Cool J, LL (pop music)
Cool, Mr. (slang)
Cooley, Denton A(rthur)(US heart surgeon; 1920-)
Cooley, Spade (Donnell Clyde) (ent.; 1910-69)
Coolidge, Calvin (30th US pres.; 1872-1933)
Coolidge, Rita (ent.; 1945-)
Coolio (b. Artis Ivey, Jr.)(ent.; 1963-)
Cooney, Gerry (boxing)
Cooney, Joan Ganz (ent.; 1929-)
Coonts, Stephen (US writer; 1946-)
Cooper-Hewitt Museum (Smithsonian, DC)
Cooper Industries, Inc.
Cooper Tire & Rubber Co.
Cooper, Alice (b. Vincent Furnier)(ent.; 1948-)
Cooper, Dame Gladys (ent.; 1898-1971)
Cooper, Gary (ent.; 1901-62)
Cooper, Jackie (ent.; 1921-)
Cooper, James Fenimore (US writer; 1789-1851)
Cooper, L(eroy) Gordon, Jr. (astro.; 1927-)
Cooper, Peter (US bus.; 1791-1883)
Cooperstown, NY (baseball)
Coors (beer)
Coors Co., Adolph
Coos Bay (OR)
Cootie (Charles) Williams (US jazz; 1908-85)
Coowescoowe (aka John Ross)(Cherokee Native Amer. chief; 1790-1866)
Copacabana (film, 1947)
Copas, Lloyd "Cowboy" (ent.; 1913-63)
Copco, Inc.
Copeland, Kenneth (US rel.)
Copenhagen, Denmark
Copernican physics

Copernican system (movement of solar system)
Copernicus, Nicholas (or Nicolaus)(Pol. astron.;
 1473-1543)
Copland, Aaron (US comp.; 1900-90)
Copley, John Singleton (US artist; 1738-1815)
Coppéliá (ballet by Délibes)
Copper Age (anthrop.)
Copper Bowl (college football)
Copper River (also Atna River)(AK)
Copperfield, David (b. David Kotkin)(ent.; 1956-)
Copperfield, David (C. Dickens novel)
Copperheads (northerners opposing Civil War)
Coppertone (health)
Coppola, Francis Ford (ent.; 1939-)
Copt (people)
Coptic (lang.)
Coptic Christian (rel.)
Copyright Act, Digital Millennium (passed 1998)
coquilles St. Jacques (scallop dish)
Coral Gables, FL
Coral Sea (Pac. /NE Austl.)
Coral Sea Islands Territory (Austl.)
Corazon Aquino (ex-pres., Phil.; 1933-)
Corbett, James "Gentleman Jim" (boxing;
 1866-1933)
Corbin (clothing)
Corbin Bernsen (ent.; 1954-)
Corbin, Barry (ent.; 1940-)
Corbin, Ltd.
Corbusier, Le (aka Charles Édouard Jeanneret)
 (Fr. arch./artist; 1887-1965)
Corby Group, The (US bus.)
Corby, Ellen (ent.; 1911-99)
Cord, Alex (ent.; 1931-)
Cordarone (med.)
Corday d'Armont, (Marie Anne) Charlotte (Fr.
 patriot; 1768-93)
Cordell Hull (US pol.; 1871-1955)
Cordero, Angel (jockey; 1942-)
Cordilleras, the (mountain range, S/CAmer.)
Córdoba, Argentina
Córdoba, Francisco Fernandez de (also
 Cordova)(Sp. expl.; 1475?-1526)
Córdoba, Mexico
Córdoba, Spain (also Cordova)
Cordobés, El (Manuel Benitez Pérez)(Sp.
 matador; 1936?-)
Cordova, AK
Cordovan (leather)
Cordran (med.)
CORE (Congress of Racial Equality)
Corea, Chick (US jazz; 1941-)
Corella, Angel (ballet; 1975-)
Corelli, Arcangelo (It. comp.; 1653-1713)
Corelli, Franco (tenor; 1923-)
Coretta Scott King (US civil rights; 1927-)
Corey Feldman (ent.; 1971-)
Corey Haim (ent.; 1971-)
Corey, Jeff (ent.; 1914-)
Corey, Wendell (ent.; 1914-68)
Corfu (Gr. island)
Corgan, Billy (ent.; 1967-)
Corgard (med.)
Corian (countertop)
Coricidin (med.)

Corin Redgrave (ent.; 1939-)
Corinth, Greece
Corinth, Lovis (Ger. artist; 1858-1925)
Corinth, MS, NY
Corinthian column/order (arch. column)
Corinthians, Books I&II (rel., books of the New
 Testament)
Corinthians, Epistles to the (rel.)
Corinto, Nicaragua
Coriolanus (Shakespeare play)
Coriolanus, Gaius (or Gnaeus) Marcius (Roman
 hero; 5th c)
Coriolis (effect/force/acceleration)(Earth's
 rotation)
Cork (county, Ir.)
Cork, Ireland
Corn Belt (agriculture)
Corn Chex (cereal)
Corn Flakes (cereal)
Corn Laws (Br., regulating grain trade)
Corn Pops (cereal)
Corn Silk (cosmetics)
Corneille, Pierre (Fr. dramatist; 1606-84)
Cornel Wilde (ent; 1915-89)
Cornelia Otis Skinner (US writer/ent.; 1901-79)
Cornelius McGillicuddy (aka Connie Mack)
 (baseball; 1862-1956)
Cornelius Nepos (Roman hist.; c100-c25 BC)
Cornelius Tacitus, (Publius)(Roman hist.; c55-
 c120)
Cornelius Vanderbilt (US bus./finan.; 1794-1877)
Cornelius Vanderbilt (US bus./finan.; 1843-99)
Cornell College (Mount Vernon, IA)
Cornell MacNeil (ent.; 1922-)
Cornell University (Ithaca, NY)
Cornell, Ezra (US, bus.; 1807-74)
Cornell, Katharine (ent.; 1893-1974)
Corner Brook, Newfoundland
Cornhusker State (nickname, NE)
Corniche, Rolls-Royce (auto.)
Corning Fiberglas Corp., Owens-
Corning, Erastus (US finan.; 1794-1872)
Corning, Inc.
Corning, NY
Cornish (lang.)
Cornish hen
Cornish pasty
Cornish Rex (cat)
Cornishman
Cornishwoman
Cornplanter, Chief (Seneca Native Amer., half-
 white, aided Br. in Amer. Rev.; c1740-1836)
Cornwall and Isles of Scilly (county, Eng.)
Cornwall, Ontario, Canada
Cornwallis, Charles (Br. gen./pol.; 1738-1805)
Cornwell, David (pseud. John le Carré)(Br.
 writer; 1931-)
Cornwell, Patricia (aka Patricia Daniels)(writer;
 1956-)
Corolla, Toyota (auto.)
Corona Australis (astron., southern crown)
Corona Borealis (astron., northern crown)
Corona Corp., Smith
Corona, Smith (typewriters)
Coronado Naval Amphibious Base (CA)

Coronado, Francisco Vásquez de (Sp. expl.; c1510-54)
Coronel Oviedo, Paraguay
Coronet (paper prods.)
Corot, Jean-Baptiste-Camille (Fr. artist; 1796-1875)
Corozal, Belize
Corporal, Little (Napoleon Bonaparte)
Corporation for Public Broadcasting (CPB)
Corps of Engineers, Army (US mil.)
Corpus Christi Caller (TX newspaper)
Corpus Christi Caller-Times (TX newspaper)
Corpus Christi day (Catholic festival)
Corpus Christi, TX
Corrado, Volkswagen (auto.)
Correctol (med.)
Correggio, Antonio Allegri da (It. artist; 1494-1534)
Corregidor Island (Phil.)
Corregidor, Battle of (WWII; 1942)
Corriedale sheep
Corrine Brown (US cong.)
Corsica (Fr. island, Mediterranean)
Corsica, Chevrolet (auto.)
Corsica/Beretta, Chevrolet (auto.)
Cortaid (med.)
Cortef (med.)
Cortenema (med.)
Cortez, Hernando (or Ferdinand)(also Cortés) (Sp. expl.; 1485-1547)
Cortifoam (med.)
Cortisporin (med.)
Cortizone (med.)
Cortone (med.)
Cortril (med.)
Corvette, Chevrolet (auto.)
Corvus (astron., crow)
Coryell, John (US writer; 1927-)
Corzine, Jon (US cong.; 1947-)
COS (cash on shipment)
Cosa Nostra (US secret org. crime assoc.)
Cosby Show, The (TV show)
Cosby, Bill (ent.; 1937-)
Cosell, Howard (US sportscaster; 1920-95)
Cosenza, Italy
Cosgrave, Liam (ex-PM, Ir.; 1920-)
Cosgrave, William Thomas (Ir. pol.; 1880-1965)
Cosimo de' Medici (It. pol.; 1389-1464)
Cosimo de' Medici I (It., Duke of Florence; 1519-74)
Cosmic Background Explorer (COBE)(US satellite)
Cosmopolitan (mag.)
Cosmos (Soviet satellites)
Cossack (people)
Costa Brava, Spain
Costa del Sol, Spain
Costa Mesa, CA
Costa Rica (Republic of)(CAmer.)
Costa, Guilherme Posser da (PM, São Tomé/ Príncipe; 1945-)
Costa, Nikka (Dominica) (ent.; 1972-)
Costas (or Kostis) Simitas (PM, Gr.; 1936-)
Costas, Bob (ent.; 1952-)
Costco Wholesale Corp.
Costello, Abbott and (ent.)

Costello, Elvis (Declan McManus)(ent.; 1954-)
Costello, Lou (ent.; 1906-59)
Costner, Kevin (ent.; 1955-)
Cotazym (med.)
Cote d'Ivorie (also Ivory Coast)
Côte d'Azur (Fr. Riviera)
Côtes du Rhône (Fr. wine region)
Coton de Tulear (dog)
Cotonou, Benin
Cotswold Hills, England (also Cotswolds)
Cotswold sheep
Cotten, Joseph (ent.; 1905-94)
Cotti, Flavio (ex-pres., Switz.)
Cottian Alps (It./Fr.)
Cotton Bowl (college football)
Cotton Mather (US rel.; 1663-1728)
Cotton State (nickname, AL)
Cotton, John (Br./US rel.; 1584-1652)
Cotton, King (US hist., early 19th c)
Coty (US bus./cosmetics)
CoTylenol (med.)
Couch, Sir Arthur Thomas Quiller- (aka "Q")(Br. writer; 1863-1944)
Cougar, Mercury (auto.)
Coulomb, Charles Augustin de (Fr. physt.; 1736-1806)
Coulomb's law (elec.)
Coumadin (med.)
Council of Chalcedon (rel.)
Council of Economic Advisers
Council of Economic Advisers (US govt.)
Council of Europe
Council of Lyons
Council of Pisa (Roman Catholic Church; 1409)
Council of St. Albans (Br. hist.)
Council of the Churches of Christ in the United States of America, National (est. 1950)
Council of Trent (rel. hist.; 1545-63)
Council on Alcoholism, National (org. 1944)
Council on Environmental Quality (US govt.)
Council(s) of Nicaea (also Nicene Council)(rel.; 325)
Count Basie (William)(US jazz; 1904-84)
Count Dracula (vampire based on Vlad Tepes, the Impaler)
Count Duckula (cartoon)
Count of Monte Cristo (by Dumas)
Countee Cullen (US poet; 1903-46)
Counter Reformation (also Catholic Reformation)(Eur. rel./hist.; 16th-17th c.)
Country America (mag.)
Country Home (mag.)
Country Living (mag.)
Country Music Association Awards, The
Country Music Awards, Academy of
Country of the Gillikins (from *The Wizard of Oz*)
County Armagh (NIre.)
County Cork (Ir.)
County Kerry (Ir.)
County Music Television (CMT)(TV channel)
County Tipperary (Ir.)
Coupland, Doug (US writer/*Generation X*; 1961-)
Couples, Fred (golf; 1959-)
Courant, Hartford (CT newspaper)
Courbet, Gustave (Fr. artist; 1819-77)

Couric, Katherine "Katie" (US TV jour.; 1957-)
Courier-Journal, Louisville (KY newspaper)
Courier-Post, Camden (NJ newspaper)
Courier-Times, Bucks County (PA newspaper)
Courier, Evansville (IN newspaper)
Courier, Jim (tennis; 1970-)
Cournoyer, Yvan Serge (hockey; 1943-)
Courréges, André (Fr. designer; 1923-)
Court of Arbitration, Permanent (internat'l court; est. 1899)
Court of International Justice, United Nations Permanent (also World Court)(est. 1945)
Court of St. James (Br. royal court)
Court of Star Chamber (Br. hist.; 1487-1641)
Court Reporters Association, National (NCRA)
Court TV (TV channel)
Court, Margaret Smith (tennis; 1942-)
Courtenay, Robert of (Constantinople emp.; 13th c.)
Courtenay, Tom (ent.; 1937-)
Courteney Cox Arquette (ent.; 1964-)
Courtney Love (b. Love Michelle Harrison)(ent.; 1964-)
Courtney Quennell, (Sir) Peter (Br. biographer; 1905-93)
Courtney Thorne-Smith (ent.; 1967-)
Courtois, Jean-Pierre (covicar, Andorra)
Courvoisier (cognac)
Cousin, Cousine (film, 1975)
Cousins, Norman (US editor/writer; 1912-90)
Cousteau, Jacques Yves (Fr. oceanographer; 1910-97)
Cousy, Bob (Robert Joseph)(basketball; 1928-)
Covenant, Ark of the (rel.)
Covent Garden (London)
Coventry, Earl of (card game)
Coventry, England
Cover Girl (cosmetics)
Coverdell, Paul (US cong.; 1939-2000)
Coverly, Sir Roger de (dance)
Covey, Stephen R. (US writer; 1932-)
Covington, GA, IN, KY, LA, TN, VA
Coward, Sir Noel (Br. writer/comp.; 1899-1973)
Cowboy (Lloyd) Copas (ent.; 1913-63)
Cowboys, Dallas (football team)
Cowles, Gardner, Jr. (US publ.; 1903-85)
Cowlings, Al (US news)
Cowper, William (Br. judge; 1665?-1723)
Cowper, William (Br. phys.; 1666-1709)
Cowper, William (Br. poet; 1731-1800)
Cowper's gland (med.)
Cox, Archibald (US atty./Watergate; 1912-)
Cox (Arquette), Courteney (ent.; 1964-)
Cox, Ronny (ent.; 1938-)
Cox, Tricia (Patricia) Nixon (daughter of ex-US pres.; 1946-)
Cox, Wally (ent.; 1924-73)
Coyote State (nickname, SD)
Coyote, Peter (b. Peter Cohon)(ent.; 1942-)
Cozumel, Mexico
Cozy Cole (US jazz; 1909-81)
Cozzens, James Gould (US writer; 1903-78)
CP (command post, Communist Party)
CPA (certified public accountant)
CPC International, Inc.

CPE (Certified Program Evaluator)
CPI (consumer price index)
C(lement) P(hilibert) Leo Delibes (Fr. comp.; 1836-91)
CPO (chief petty officer)
CPR (cardiopulmonary resuscitation)
C(harles) P(ercy) Snow, Baron (Br. writer/physt.; 1905-80)
CPU (central processing unit)(compu.)
Cr (chem. sym., chromium)
Crab Nebula (astron.)
Crabbe, Buster (ent./swimmer; 1908-83)
Crabtree & Evelyn (toiletries)
Crabtree & Evelyn, Ltd.
Crabtree, Lotta (ent.; 1847-1924)
Cracker Jack (US bus.)
Cracker Jacks (snack)
Cracklin' Oat Bran (cereal)
Craddock, Billy "Crash" (ent.; 1940-)
Crafts (mag.)
Craftsman (tools)
Craig Claiborne (US writer/food; 1920-2000)
Craig Kilborn (ent./sportscaster; 1962-)
Craig L. Morton (football; 1943-)
Craig T. Nelson (ent.; 1946-)
Craig Thomas (US cong.; 1933-)
Craig Venter, J(ohn)(US genet./human genome; 1946-)
Craig Weight Loss Centers, Jenny (US bus.)
Craig, Larry E. (US cong.; 1945-)
Crain, Jeanne (ent.; 1925-)
Crain's New York Business (mag.)
Craiova, Romania
Cram, Ralph Adams (US arch.; 1863-1942)
Cranach, Lucas (the elder)(Ger. artist; 1472-1553)
Cranberries, the (pop music)
Crane Co.
Crane, Bob (ent.; 1928-78)
Crane, (Harold) Hart (US poet; 1899-1932)
Crane, Ichabod (fict. chara., *Legend of Sleepy Hollow*)
Crane, Stephen (US writer; 1871-1900)
Cranmer, Thomas (Br. rel./writer; 1489-1556)
Cranston, RI
Crapo, Mike (US cong.; 1951-)
Crash Craddock, Billy (ent.; 1940-)
Crassus, Marcus Licinius (Roman gen.; c108-53 BC)
Cratchit, Bob (fict. chara., *A Christmas Carol*)
Cratchit, Tiny Tim (fict. chara., *A Christmas Carol*)
Crate & Barrel (housewares)
Crate & Barrel (US bus.)
Crater (astron., cup)
Crater Lake National Park (OR)
Crater Mound (AZ)(also Meteor Crater)
Cratinus (Gr. drama.; 520-421 BC)
C ration
Craven, Wes(ley Earl) (ent.; 1939-)
Crawford, Broderick (ent.; 1911-86)
Crawford, Cindy (US model; 1966-)
Crawford, Joan (ent.; 1908-77)
Craxi, Bettino (ex-PM, It.; 1934-2000)
Cray Research, Inc.

Crayola (crayons)
Crazy Eights (also Wild Eights)(card game)
Crazy Guggenheim (aka Frank Fontaine)(ent.;
    1920-78)
Crazy Horse, Chief (Sioux Native Amer., Little
    Bighorn; 1842-77)
Cream (pop music)
Cream of Wheat (cereal)
Creamette (pasta)
Creamette Co., The
Creation (rel.)
Creative Forces (also All That Is, Divine Mind, God)
Creator, the (God)
Cree (Native Amer.)
Creedence Clearwater Revival (pop music)
Creek (Native Amer.)
Creighton Abrams (US gen.; 1914-74)
crema Danica (cheese)
creme Anglais (sauce)
crème Chantilly (sauce)
Cremona (province in Lombardy, It.)
Crenna, Richard (ent.; 1927-)
Crenshaw (melon)
Crenshaw, Ben (golf; 1952-)
Creole (langs., peoples)
Creole, Haitian (lang.)
Creole, Jamaican (lang.)
crepe de Chine (fabric)
crepes Suzette (also l.c.)
Crescent Wrench (constr.)
Crescent, Red (functioning as Red Cross in
    Muslim countries)
Cressida, Troilus and (Shakespeare play)
Cresson, Edith (ex-PM, Fr.; 1934-)
Crest (dental care)
Crestline Capital Corp.
Cretaceous period (136-65 million years ago)
Cretan dittany (plant)
Crete (Gr. island)
Crews, Harry (US writer; 1935-)
CRI (Certified Reporting Instructor)
Cribari & Sons Winery, B.
Cribari (wine)
Crichton, Michael (US writer; 1942-)
Crichton, Robert (US writer; 1925-93)
Crick model, Watson- (3-D structure of DNA)
Crick, Francis H(arry) C(ompton)(Br. physt.;
    1916-)
Cricket Lighters (US bus.)
Crickets, Buddy Holly and the (pop music)
Crime and Punishment (Dostoevski novel)
Crimea (peninsula on the Black Sea)
Crimean War (Turk./Rus.; 1853-56)
Crimes and Misdemeanors (film, 1989)
Crippen, Robert L. (astro.; 1937-)
Cripple Creek, CO (gold mining)
Cripps, Sir Stafford (Br. pol.; 1889-1952)
Crips, Bloods and (gangs, also pop music group)
Crisco (vegetable shortening)
Crisp, Donald (ent.; 1880-1974)
Crispix (cereal)
Crispus Attucks (Amer. Revolutionary patriot;
    c1723-70)
Crist, Judith (US writer; 1922-)
Cristiani, Alfredo (ex-pres., El Salvador; 1947-)

Cristino Seriche Bioko (ex-PM, Equatorial
    Guinea)
Cristobal Balenciaga (Sp. designer; 1895-1972)
Cristobal, Panama
Cristy Lane (ent.; 1940-)
Crito (by Plato)
Crito (Gr. phil.; 5th c BC)
Crittenden Compromise (plan to avert US Civil War)
Croat (people)
Croatia (republic. Yug.)
Croatian (people)
Croatian, Serbo- (lang.)
Croce, Benedetto (It. phil.; 1866-1952)
Croce, Jim (ent.; 1942-73)
Crochet World (mag.)
Crocker, Betty
Crocker, Charles (US railroad/finan.; 1822-88)
Crockett, Davy (David)(US frontier/pol.; 1786-
    1836)
Crockpot (cooking)
Crocodile Dundee (film, 1986)
Crocodile Dundee 2 (film, 1988)
Croesus (king, Lydia, noted for great wealth;
    c560-c546 BC)
Croesus (very rich person)
Crohn's disease (med.)
Croix de Guerre (Fr. mil. award)
Cro-Magnon (prehistoric human)
Cromwell Current (also Equatorial Countercurrent)
Cromwell, Oliver (Br. gen./pol.; 1599-1658)
Cronenberg, David (ent.; 1943-)
Cronin, A(rchibald) J(oseph)(Br. phys./writer;
    1896-1981)
Cronin, Joe (baseball exec.; 1906-84)
Cronkite, Walter (US TV jour.; 1916-)
Cronus (also Kronos)(myth.)
Cronyn, Hume (ent.; 1911-)
Crook and Chase (TV show)
Crookes tube (cathode rays)
Crookes, Sir William (Br. physt./chem.; 1832-
    1919)
Crosby, Bing (Harry Lillis)(ent.; 1903-77)
Crosby, Bob (George Robert)(ent.; 1913-93)
Crosby, Cathy Lee (ent.; 1948-)
Crosby, David (b. David Van Cortland)(ent.;
    1941-)
Crosby, Norm (ent.; 1927-)
Crosby, Stills & Nash (pop music)
Crosby, Stills, Nash & Young (pop music)
Crosman air gun
Crosman Corp.
Cross Co., A. T.
Cross Creek (book by Marjorie Kinnan
    Rawlings, 1942; film, 1983)
cross of Lorraine
cross the Rubicon (take an irrevocable step)
Cross, American National Red (US relief agcy.;
    est. 1881)
Cross, Ben (ent.; 1948-)
Cross, Red (internat'l relief agcy.; est. 1864)
Crosse & Blackwell Co., The
Crossfire (TV show)
Crossing Delancey (film, 1988)
Crothers, Scatman (ent.; 1910-86)
Crouse, Lindsay (ent.; 1948-)

Crouse, Russel (US writer; 1893-1966)
Crow (Native Amer.)
Crow laws, Jim (US hist., pro-segregation; pre-1960s)
Crow, Jim (racial discrimination)(also l.c.)
Crow, Sheryl (ent.; 1962-)
Crowe, Russell (ent.; 1964-)
Crowell, Rodney (ent.; 1950-)
Crowley, John (US writer; 1942-)
Crowley, Patricia (ent.)
Crown Affair, The Thomas (film, 1999)
Crown Books (US bus.)
Crown Cork & Seal Co., Inc.
Crown Royal (whiskey)
Crown Victoria, Ford (auto.)
CRR (Certified Realtime Reporter)
CRT (cathode ray tube)(compu.)
Crucifixion, the (rel.)
Crudup, Billy (ent.; 1968-)
Cruel, Peter the (king, Castile/León; 1334-69)
Cruella DeVille (fict. chara., *101 Dalmatians*)
Cruikshank, George (Br. artist; 1792-1878)
Cruise, Tom (b. Thomas Cruise Mapother, IV) (ent.; 1962-)
Cruising World (mag.)
Crumb, Robert (cartoonist, underground; 1943-)
Crumb?, Who's Harry (film, 1989)
Crunch 'n Munch
Crusade, Children's (Fr./Ger. v. Jerusalem; 1212)
Crusades, the (rel. wars; 11th-13th c)
Crusher, Dr. Beverly (fict. chara., *Star Trek*)
Crusher, Ensign Wesley (fict. chara., *Star Trek*)
Crusoe, Robinson (D. Defoe novel)
Crux (astron., cross)
Cruyff, Johan (soccer; 1947-)
Cruz, Penelope (ent.; 1974-)
Crvenkovski, Branko (ex-PM, Macedonia; 1962)
Cryptophyta (phylum, biology)
Crystal Bernard (ent.; 1961-)
Crystal Brands, Inc.
Crystal Gayle (b. Brenda Webb)(ent.; 1951-)
Crystal Light (beverage mix)
Crystal Palace (London)
Crystal, Billy (ent.; 1947-)
Crystals, the (pop music)
Crystodigin (med.)
C-section (med.)
CSFBdirect (US bus./finan.)
C(ecil) S(cott) Forester (Br. writer; 1899-1966)
C(live) S(taples) Lewis ("Clive Hamilton")(Br. writer; 1898-1963)
Csonka, Larry (Lawrence Richard)(football; 1946-)
C-SPAN (CSP)(TV channel)
C-SPAN2 (CSP)(TV channel)
CSR (Certified Shorthand Reporter)
CST (Central Standard Time)
CSX Corp.
CT (Connecticut)
CT scan (computed tomography)(also CAT scan)(med.)
C. Thomas Howell (ent.; 1966-)
C3PO (fict. chara., *Star Wars*)
C-type (photo.)
Cub Scouts (also l.c.)
Cuba (Republic of)(Caribbean Sea)

Cuba Gooding, Jr. (ent.; 1968-)
Cuba libre (mixed drink)
Cuban heel (footwear)
Cuban missile crisis (1962)
Cuban royal palm
Cuban sandwich
Cubism (art movement)(also l.c.)
Cubs, Chicago (baseball team)
Cuckoo's Nest, One Flew Over the (film, 1975)
Cuéllar, Javier Pérez de (Peruvian/UN dipl.; 1920-)
Cuenca, Ecuador
Cuenca, Spain
Cuernavaca, Mexico
Cuervo Gold (tequila)
Cuervo, Jose (tequila)
Cugat, Xavier (Sp./US cond.; 1920-90)
Cuisenaire rod (colored rods used to teach arithmetic)
Cuisinart (kitchen appliances)
Cuisinart, Inc.
Cujo (S. King novel)
Cukor, George (ent.; 1899-1983)
Culbro Corp.
Culkin, Macaulay (ent.; 1980-)
Cullen, Bill (William L.)(ent.; 1920-90)
Cullen, Countee (US poet; 1903-46)
Culligan (water conditioner)
Culligan International, Inc.
Cullum, John (ent.; 1930-)
Culp, Robert (ent.; 1930-)
Cultural Revolution (Ch.; 1966-69)
Cumberland Gap National Historical Park (KY/TN/VA)
Cumberland Plateau/Mountains (part of Appalachians, VA/KY/TN/GA/AL)
Cumberland River (KY/TN)
Cumberland Road (MD to IL)
Cumberland, MD, RI
Cumbria (county, Eng.)
Cummings, Constance (ent.; 1910-)
Cummings, Edward Estlin (pseud. e.e. cummings)(US poet; 1894-1962)
Cummings, Robert (ent.; 1908-90)
Cummins, Inc.
Cunard Line (ships)
Cunard, Samuel (Can., trans-Atl. navigation; 1787-1865)
Cunningham, Merce (Mercier Philip)(US dancer/choreographer; 1919-)
Cunningham, R. Walter (astro.; 1932-)
Cunningham, Randall (football; 1963-)
Cuomo, Andrew M(ark)(ex-US secy./HUD; 1957-)
Cuomo, Mario M(atthew)(ex-NY gov.; 1932-)
Cupid (myth., god of love)
Curaçao (island, the Netherlands Antilles)
Curad (bandage)
Curepipe, Mauritius
Curia Romana (papal govt.)
Curie point/temperature)(chem.)
Curie, Frédéric Joliot- (Fr. physt.; 1900-58)
Curie, Irène Joliot- (Fr. physt.; 1897-1956)
Curie, Madame Marie (Fr. physt., radium; 1867-1934)
Curie, Pierre (Fr. physt., radium; 1859-1906)

Curie-Weiss law
Curie's law
Curitiba, Brazil
Curly Howard (b. Jerome Horwitz)(ent.; 1903-52)
Current Affair (TV show)
Current Affair: Extra (TV show)
Currier & Ives (US lithography)
Currier, Nathaniel (US lithographer; 1813-88)
Curry, John Steuart (US artist; 1897-1946)
Curry, Tim (ent.; 1946-)
Curt Gowdy (ent.; 1919-)
Curt Jurgens (ent.; 1912-82)
Curtin, Jane (ent.; 1947-)
Curtin, Phyllis (soprano; 1927-)
Curtis Arnoux Peters (aka Peter Arno)
    (cartoonist, *New Yorker*; 1904-68)
Curtis Industries, Helene
Curtis (Emerson) LeMay (US gen.; 1906-90)
Curtis-Mathes Corp.
Curtis Mayfield (ent.; 1942-99)
Curtis Sliwa (founder, Guardian Angels; 1954-)
Curtis Strange (golf; 1955-)
Curtis, Charles (ex-US VP; 1860-1936)
Curtis, Jamie Lee (ent.; 1958-)
Curtis, Keene (ent.; 1923-)
Curtis, Tony (b. Bernard Schwartz)(ent.; 1925-)
Curtiss, Glenn Hammond (US aviator/inv.;
    1878-1930)
Curzon, George Nathaniel (Marquis Kedleston
    of Curzon)(Br. leader in India; 1859-1925)
Cusack, Joan (ent.; 1962-)
Cusack, John (ent.; 1966-)
Cushing, Harvey Williams (US phys.; 1869-1939)
Cushing, Peter (ent.; 1913-94)
Cushing's disease/syndrome (med.)
Custer, George A(rmstrong)(US gen., Little
    Bighorn; 1839-76)
Custer, SD
Custer's Last Stand (also Battle of the Little
    Bighorn)(US/Sioux Native Amer.; 1876)
Customs and Excise, Bureau of (Br.)
Cutex (nail care)
Cuthbert M. Sebastian, Sir (gov.-gen., St. Kitts-
    Nevis; 1921-)
Cuticura (med.)
Cutlass Supreme, Oldsmobile (auto.)
Cutlass, Oldsmobile (auto.)
Cut-Rite (wax paper)
Cutty Sark (liquor)
Cuxhaven, Germany
Cuyahoga Falls, OH
Cuzco, Peru (Incan ruins)
CVS Corp.
CWO (cash with order, chief warrant officer)
Cy (Denton True) Young (baseball; 1867-1955)
Cy Coleman (US comp.; 1929-)
Cy Young Award (baseball)
Cybele (myth.)
Cybill Shepherd (ent.; 1950-)
Cyclades Islands (Gr., Aegean Sea)
Cycle (dog food)
Cycle Plan, The (dog food)
Cyclocort (med.)
Cyclogyl (med.)
Cyclone (fence)

Cyclops (myth.; plural = Cyclopes)
Cyd Charisse (ent.; 1921-)
Cygnus (astron., swan)
Cylert (med.)
Cymbeline (king, Br; 1st c. AD)
Cymbeline (Shakespeare play)
Cymric (also Kymric)(Celtic langs.)
Cyndi Lauper (ent.; 1953-)
Cynicism (phil.)
Cynthia Gregory (ent.; 1946-)
Cynthia Nixon (ent.; 1966-)
Cynthia Ozick (US writer; 1928-)
Cynthia Weil (US comp.; 1937-)
Cynthia Woodhead (swimming; 1964-)
Cypress Gardens, FL
Cypress, CA
Cyprian, St. (rel. in Africa; ?-258)
Cypriot (people)
Cyprus (Republic of)(south, Gr.; north, Turk.)
Cyrano de Bergerac (Fr. poet/mil.; 1619-55)
Cyrano de Bergerac (play; film, 1925, 1950,
    1985, 1990)
Cyrenaic (phil.; 4th c BC)
Cyril Ritchard (ent.; 1898-1977)
Cyrillic alphabet
Cyrus (Hall) McCormick (US inv.; 1809-84)
Cyrus R(oberts) Vance (US pol.; 1917-)
Cyrus West Field (US finan., 1st Atl. cable;
    1819-92)
Cyrus, Billy Ray (ent.; 1961-)
Cytomel (med.)
Cytotec (med.)
Cytovene (med.)
Cytoxan (med.)
Czech (lang./people)
Czechoslovak Airlines
Czechoslovakia (now Czech and Slovakia)
    (central Eur.)
Czerny, Karl (Aus. pianist; 1791-1857)
Czestochowa, Poland

© 2001 *StenEd*® **Proper Noun Speller**

- D -

DA (district attorney)
Dabney Coleman (ent.; 1932-)
da Bologna, Giovanni (sculptor; 1529-1608)
da Caravaggio, Michelangelo (It. artist; 1573-1610)
Dacca, Bangladesh (also Dhaka)
Dachau, Germany (concentration camp)
da Correggio, Antonio Allegri (It. artist; 1494-1534)
da Costa, Guilherme Posser (PM, São Tomé/Príncipe; 1945-)
Dacron (polyester fiber)
Dada (also Dadaism)(art./lit. movement)
Daedalus (myth.)
Daewoo (auto.)
Daewoo Korando (auto.)
Daewoo Lanos (auto.)
Daewoo Lanos S (auto.)
Daewoo Lanos SE (auto.)
Daewoo Lanos SX (auto.)
Daewoo Leganza (auto.)
Daewoo Leganza CDX (auto.)
Daewoo Leganza SE (auto.)
Daewoo Leganza SX (auto.)
Daewoo Motor America
Daewoo Nubira (auto.)
Daewoo Nubira CDX (auto.)
Daewoo Nubira SE (auto.)
Daewoo Nubira SX (auto.)
Dafa, Falun (aka Falun Gong)(phil. group, China)
Daffy Duck (cartoon chara.)
Dafoe, Willem (ent.; 1955-)
Dag (Hjalmar Agne Carl) Hammarskjöld (Swed., UN secy. gen.; 1905-61)
da Gama, Vasco (Port. nav.; c1460-1524)
Dagenhart, Hammer v. (US law; 1918)
Dagomba, Moshi- (people)
Daguerre, Louis Jacques Mande (Fr. photo.; 1789-1851)
Dagwood Bumstead (cartoon chara.)
Dagwood sandwich
Dahik, Alberto (Ecuador. pol.)
Dahl, Arlene (ent.; 1928-)
Dahl, Roald (Br./US writer; 1916-90)
Dahlia, Black (Elizabeth Short)(aspiring actress/murder victim; 1924-47)
Dahmer, Jeffrey (US serial killer; 1960-94)
Dahomey (now Benin)
Daikoku (myth.)
Dailey, Dan (ent.; 1914-78)
Dailey, Janet (US writer; 1944-)
Daily Mirror (Br. newspaper)
Daily News, Anchorage (AK newspaper)
Daily News, Los Angeles (CA newspaper)
Daily News, New York (NY newspaper)
Daily News, Philadelphia (PA newspaper)
Daily Oklahoman, Oklahoma City (OK newspaper)
Daimler, Gottlieb (Ger. eng./inv.; 1834-1900)

DaimlerChrysler AG (auto. co.)
DaimlerChrysler Unimog (auto., universal motorized machine)
Daio, Daniel Lima dos Santos (ex-PM, São Tomé/Príncipe)
Dairy Queen/Brazier
Daisetz Teitaro Suzuki (Jap. rel.; 1870-1966)
Daisy Clover, Inside (film, 1965)
Daisy Duck (cartoon chara.)
Daisy Miller (H. James novel)
Daisy, Driving Miss (film, 1989)
Dakar, Senegal
Dakota (also Sioux)(Native Amer.)
Dakota, Dodge (auto.)
Daladier, Édouard (Fr. pol.; 1884-1970)
Dalai Lama (b. Tenzin Gyatso)(Tibetan rel.; 1935-)
Dalai Lama (spiritual leader of Tibetan Buddhism)
Dale Bumpers (US pol.; 1925-)
Dale Carnegie (US writer/educ.; 1888-1955)
Dale Earnhardt (aka The Intimidator)(auto racing; 1951-2001)
Dale Evans (b. Lucille Wood Smith)(ent.; 1912-2001)
Dale Messick (cartoonist, *Brenda Starr*; 1906-)
Dale Murphy (football; 1956-)
Dale Robertson (ent.; 1923-)
d'Alençon, point (also Alençon lace)
Daley, Richard Joseph (ex-mayor, Chicago; 1902-76)
Daley, Richard M. (Chicago mayor; 1942-)
Daley, William "Bill" M(ichael) (US ex-secy./commerce; 1948-)
Dali, Salvador (Sp. artist; 1904-89)
Dalkon Shield (med.)
Dallas (TV show)
Dallas Cowboys (football team)
Dallas-Fort Worth International Airport (TX)
Dallas Mavericks (basketball team)
Dallas Morning News (TX newspaper)
Dallas, George M. (ex-US VP; 1792-1864)
Dallas, OR, TX
Dallas, Stella (film, 1937)
Dalles, The, OR
Dalloway, Mrs. (V. Woolf novel)
Dalmane (med.)
Dalmatian (dog)
Dalmatians, 101
Daloa, Ivory Coast
Dalton Bookseller, B. (US bus.)
Dalton, Abby (ent.; 1932-)
Dalton, John (Br. chem./physt.; 1766-1844)
Dalton, Timothy (ent.; 1944-)
Dalton's law (of partial pressures)(chem.)
Daltonism (red/green color blindness)
Daltrey, Roger (ent., The Who; 1944-)
Daly, (Ellen) Tyne (ent.; 1946-)
Daly, Carson (ent.; 1973-)
Daly, Chuck (basketball; 1930-)
Daly, John (golf; 1966-)
Daly, John Charles, Jr. (ent./TV news exec.; 1914-91)
Daly, Marcus (US bus.; 1841-1900)
Daly, Timothy (ent.; 1956-)
Damara (people)
Damascus steel (also l.c.)

Damascus, Syria
D'Amato, Al(fonse M.)(US cong.; 1937-)
d'Amboise, Jacques (ballet; 1934-)
Dameron, Tadd (US jazz; 1917-65)
Damian, St. Peter (It. rel.; 1007-72)
Damien: Omen II (film, 1978)
Damietta, Egypt
Dammam, Saudi Arabia
Damme, Jean-Claude Van (b. Jean-Claude Van
    Varenberg)(ent.; 1960-)
Damocles (myth.)
Damocles, Sword/sword of
Damon and Pythias (myth., loyal friendship)
Damon Runyon, (Alfred)(US writer/jour.; 1880-
    1946)
Damon Wayans (ent.; 1960-)
Damon, Matt (ent.; 1970-)
Damone, Vic (b. Vito Farinola)(ent.; 1928-)
Damrosch, Walter Johannes (cond.; 1862-1950)
Dan Aykroyd (ent.; 1952-)
Dan Blocker (ent.; 1928-72)
Dan(iel L.) Burton (US cong.; 1938-)
Dan Dailey (ent.; 1914-78)
Dan Duryea (ent.; 1907-68)
Dan Fogelberg (ent.; 1951-)
Dan Gable (wrestling; 1945-)
Dan Glickman (Daniel Robert)(US ex-secy./
    agr.; 1944-)
Dan Marino (football; 1961-)
Dan McGrew, The Shooting of (R.W. Service
    ballad)
Dan O'Herlihy (ent.; 1919-)
Dan Quayle III, (James Danforth)(ex-VP, US;
    1947-)
Dan Rather (US TV jour.; 1931-)
Dan Rather, The CBS Evening News With (TV
    show)
Dan Rostenkowski (Daniel)(US pol.; 1928-)
Dan Rowan (ent.; 1922-87)
Dan, Steely (pop music)
Dana Andrews (ent.; 1909-1992)
Dana Carvey (ent.; 1955-)
Dana Corp.
Dana Delany (ent.; 1956-)
Dana Scully (fict. chara., *The X-Files*)
Dana, Bill (ent.; 1924-)
Dana, Charles Anderson (US editor; 1819-97)
Danang, Vietnam
Danann, Tuatha Dé (myth.)
Danbury Hatters Case (*Loewe v. Lawler*)(US
    law; 1908)
Danbury, CT
Dance (mag.)
Dance Theater of Harlem
Dancer, Stanley (harness racing; 1927-)
Dances With Wolves (film, 1990)
Dancin' (play)
D & B (Dun & Bradstreet)
D & C (dilation and curettage)(med.)
D & E (dilation and evacuation)(med.)
Dandie Dinmont terrier (dog)
Dandridge, Dorothy (ent.; 1923-65)
Dandridge, Ruby (ent.)
Dane (people)
Dane Clark (ent.; 1913-)

Dane, Great (dog)
Danes, Claire (ent.; 1979-)
Danforth, John Claggett (US pol.; 1936-)
D'Angelo (b. Michael D'Angelo Archer)(ent.; 1974-)
D'Angelo, Beverly (ent.; 1954-)
Danger Cave (UT)
Dangerfield, Rodney (b. Jacob Cohen)(ent.;
    1922-)
Dangriga, Belize
Danica, crema (cheese)
Daniel (rel., book of the Old Testament)
Daniel arap Moi (pres., Kenya; 1924-)
Daniel Baldwin (ent.; 1960-)
Daniel Barenboim (Isr. pianist/cond.; 1942-)
Daniel Bernoulli (Swiss math.; 1700-82)
Daniel Boone (US pioneer; 1734-1820)
Daniel Boorstin (US hist.; 1914-)
Daniel C. Williams, Sir (gov.-gen., Grenada;
    1935-)
Daniel Chester French (US artist; 1850-1931)
Daniel D. Tompkins (ex-US VP; 1774-1825)
Daniel Day-Lewis (ent.; 1957-)
Daniel Defoe (Br. writer; 1660-1731)
Daniel Distillery, Jack (US bus.)
Daniel Ellsberg (US social activist; 1931-)
Daniel Frohman (US writer/ent.; 1851-1940)
Daniel Guggenheim (US finan./bus.; 1856-1930)
Daniel H. Burnham (US arch.; 1846-1912)
Daniel J. Travanti (ent.; 1940-)
Daniel K(ahikina) Akaka (US cong.; 1924-)
Daniel K. Inouye (US cong.; 1924-)
Daniel Lima dos Santos Daio (ex-PM, São
    Tomé/Príncipe)
Daniel Morgan (US mil.; 1736-1802)
Daniel O'Connell ("the Liberator")(Ir. pol.;
    1775-1847)
Daniel Ortega Saavedra, (José)(ex-pres.,
    Nicaragua; 1945-)
Daniel Patrick Moynihan (US pol./dipl.; 1927-)
Daniel R. Coats (US pol.; 1943-)
Daniel S. Goldin (Head/NASA; 1940-)
Daniel Schorr (US jour.; 1916-)
Daniel Shays (US mil./pol.; 1747?-1825)
Daniel Webster (US orator/pol.; 1782-1852)
Daniel Webster, The Devil and (film, 1941)
Daniela Silivas (gymnast; 1970-)
Daniell cell (elec.)
Daniell, Harry (ent.; 1894-1963)
Daniell, John Frederic (Br. chem.; 1790-1845)
Danielle Steel (writer; 1947-)
Daniels, Bebe (ent.; 1901-71)
Daniels, Charlie (ent.; 1936-)
Daniels, Jeff (ent.; 1955-)
Daniels, William (ent.; 1927-)
Danilova, Alexandra (Rus. ballet; 1906-97)
Danino, Roberto (PM, Peru)
Danish (lang.)
Danish blue (cheese)
Danish East India Company (trade; 1729-1801)
Danish ham
Danish pastry
Dannay, Frederick (pseud. Ellery Queen)(US
    writer; 1905-82)
Danner, Blythe (ent.; 1943-)
Dannon Company, Inc., The

Dannon yogurt
D'Annunzio, Gabriele (It. writer; 1863-1938)
Danny Aiello (ent.; 1933-)
Danny and the Juniors (pop music)
Danny Bonaduce (ent.; 1959-)
Danny DeVito (ent. 1944-)
Danny Ferguson (US news)
Danny Glover (ent.; 1947-)
Danny Kaye (ent.; 1913-87)
Danny Rose, Broadway (film, 1984)
Danny Thomas (ent.; 1912-91)
Danny Thomas Show, The (TV show)
Danny Wood (ent.; 1969-)
Danocrine (med.)
Dansk International Designs, Ltd.
Danskin, Inc.
Danson, Ted (ent.; 1947-)
Dante (Alighieri)(It. poet, *Divine Comedy*;
   1265-1321)
Dante (or Savonarola) chair
Dante Gabriel Rossetti (Br. poet/artist; 1828-82)
Dante's Inferno (*Divine Comedy*)
Dantès, Edmund (fict. chara., *Count of Monte
   Cristo*)
Dantine, Helmut (ent.; 1918-82)
Dantley, Adrian (basketball; 1956-)
Danton, Georges (Fr. mil.; 1759-94)
Dantrium (med.)
Danube River (Eur.)
Danville, VA
Danza, Tony (b. Antonio Iadanza)(ent.; 1951-)
Danzig, Poland (also Gdansk)
Dao, Lee Tsung (Ch. physt.; 1926-)
da Palestrina, Giovanni P(ierluigi)(It. comp.;
   c1525-94)
Daphne (myth.)
Daphne Du Maurier (Br. writer; 1907-89)
Daphne Maxwell Reid (ent.; 1948-)
Daphnis and Chloë (Gr. romance)
da Pontormo, Jacopo (It. artist; 1492-1557)
DAR (Daughters of the American Revolution)
Dar es Salaam, Tanzania
D'Arbanville, Patti (ent.; 1951-)
Darby and Joan (fict. happy, elderly, married
   couple)
Darby Lumber Co., U.S. v. (US law; 1941)
Darby, Kim (ent.; 1948-)
D'Arby, Terence Trent (ent.; 1962-)
Darc-to-alpha d'Arc, Jeanne (also St. Joan of
   Arc or Maid of Orléans)(Fr. rel./mil.; 1412?-31)
Dardanelles (Turk. strait)(formerly Hellespont)
Darden Restaurants, Inc.
DARE (Drug Abuse Resistance Education)
Dare, Virginia (1st Eng. child born in Amer.;
   1587-?)
Darhan, Mongolia
Dari (lang.)
Dari Persian (lang.)
Daricon (med.)
Darin, Bobby (ent.; 1936-73)
Darius I ("the Great")(king, Persia; c558-486 BC)
Darius Milhaud (Fr. comp.; 1892-1974)
Darius Rucker (ent./songwriter; 1966-)
Darjeeling tea
Darjeeling, India

Dark Ages (c476-13th c. of the Middle Ages)
Dark Continent (old name for Africa)
Dark, Alvin (baseball; 1922-)
Darkness, Prince of (the Devil)
Darley Arabian (horse)
Darling children (Wendy, John, Michael)(*Peter Pan*)
Darling River, Australia (also Range-Aus)
Darling, Clifford (ex-gov.-gen., Bahamas)
Darling, Jay N. ("Ding")(pol. cartoonist; 1876-
   1962)
d'Armont, (Marie Anne) Charlotte Corday (Fr.
   patriot; 1768-93)
Darnell, Linda (ent.; 1921-65)
Darrell Pace (archery; 1956-)
Darren E. Burrows (ent.; 1966-)
Darren McGavin (ent.; 1922-)
Darren Stephens (fict. chara., *Bewitched*)
Darrow, Clarence (Seward)(US atty./writer;
   1857-1938)
Darryl F(rancis) Zanuck (ent.; 1902-79)
Darryl Strawberry (baseball; 1962-)
d'Artagnan, Charles de Baatz, Seigneur (fict.
   chara., *Three Musketeers*)
Darth Vader (fict. chara., *Star Wars*)
D'Arthur, Le Morte (by T. Malory)
Dartmoor pony
Dartmoor Prison (Eng.)
Dartmoor sheep
Dartmouth College (Hanover, NH)
Dartmouth College Case (*Trustees of Dartmouth
   College v. Woodward*)(US law; 1819)
Dartmouth, Nova Scotia, Canada
Darva Conger (TV's *Who Wants to Marry a
   Multimillionaire?* bride; 1966-)
Darvocet (med.)
Darvon (med.)
Darwin, Australia
Darwin, Charles Robert (Br. scien.; 1809-82)
Darwinism (also Darwin's theory)(evolution)
Darwinism, neo- (evolution theory)
Darwinism, Social/social (sociol.)
Daryl Dragon (ent., The Captain & Tennille; 1942-)
Daryl F. Gates (US news)
Daryl Hall (b. Daryl Hohl)(ent.; 1948-)
Daryl Hannah (ent.; 1960-)
Daryle Lamonica (football; 1941-)
Das Kapital (by Karl Marx)
Daschle, Thomas A(ndrew)(US cong.; 1947-)
Dash, Mrs. (seasoning)
Dashiell Hammett, (Samuel)(US writer; 1894-
   1961)
Dashiyn Byambasuren (ex-PM, Mongolia)
Da Silva, Howard (ent.; 1909-86)
Dassin, Jules (ent.; 1911-)
Data General Corp.
Data, Lt. Commander (*Star Trek*)
DataTimes (compu.)
Dateline NBC (TV show)
Datril (med.)
Daugavpils, Latvia
Daugherty, Brad (basketball; 1965-)
Daughters of the American Revolution (D.A.R.)
   (org. 1890)
Daulton, Darren (baseball; 1962-)
Daumier, Honoré (Fr. artist; 1808-79)

Dauphin, Claude (ent.; 1903-78)
Dauphin, the (title of eldest son of Fr. king until 1830)
Davao, Philippines
Dave Barry (US writer/humorist; 1947-)
Dave Bing (basketball; 1943-)
Dave Brubeck (David Warren)(US jazz; 1920-)
Dave Clark (ent.; 1942-)
Dave Davies (ent., The Kinks; 1947-)
Dave DeBusschere (basketball; 1940-)
Dave Garroway (TV host; 1913-82)
Dave Matthews (ent.; 1966-)
Dave Matthews Band (DMB)
Dave Robinson (basketball; 1965-)
Dave Tough (US jazz; 1908-48)
Dave Winfield (baseball; 1951-)
Dave, Sam and (pop music)
Dave's World (TV show)
Davenport Quad City Times (IA newspaper)
Davenport, IA
Davenport, Lacey (fict. chara., *Doonesbury*)
Davenport, Willie (track; 1943-)
da Verrazano, Giovanni (It. navigator; c1485-1528)
David (Donatello sculpture)
David (king, Isr.; c1060-970 BC)
David (Michelangelo sculpture)
David Alan Grier (ent.; 1955-)
David Alfaro Siqueiros (Mex. artist; 1896-1974)
David and Bathsheba (film, 1951)
David and Goliath (rel.)
David and Lisa (film, 1962)
David Aykroyd (ent.)
David Belasco (US writer/ent.; 1854-1931)
David Ben-Gurion (ex-PM, Isr.; 1886-1973)
David Berkowitz ("Son of Sam")(serial killer; 1953-)
David Birney (ent.; 1939-)
David Boies (US atty.; 1941-)
David Boreanaz (ent.; 1971-)
David Bowie (b. David Robert Jones)(ent.; 1947-)
David Brenner (ent.; 1945-)
David Brinkley (US TV jour.; 1920-)
David Bruce Winery (US bus.)
David Burpee (US horticulturist; 1893-1980)
David Byrne (ent./songwriter; 1952-)
David Carradine (ent.; 1936-)
David Cassidy (ent.; 1950-)
David Copperfield (b. David Kotkin) (ent.; 1956-)
David Copperfield (C. Dickens novel)
David Cornwell (pseud. John le Carré)(Br. writer; 1931-)
David "Davy" Crockett (US frontier/pol.; 1786-1836)
David Cronenberg (ent.; 1943-)
David Crosby (b. David Van Cortland)(ent.; 1941-)
David Dinkins (ex-NYC mayor; 1927-)
David Doyle (ent.; 1929-97)
David Du Bose Gaillard (US mil./eng.; 1859-1913)
David Dubinsky (US labor leader; 1892-1982)
David Duchovny (ent.; 1960-)
David Duke (US pol.; 1950-)
David Dukes (ent.; 1945-2000)
David Dunbar Buick (US bus./auto.; 1854-1929)

David E. Bonior (US cong.; 1945-)
David Eddings (US writer; 1931-)
David E. Kelley (ent.; 1956-)
David Farragut (US adm.; 1801-70)
David Faustino (ent.; 1974-)
David F. Durenberger (US pol.; 1934-)
David Friedkin (ent.; 1912-76)
David Frost (ent.; 1939-)
David Gardner (US finan./Motley Fool; 1966-)
David Garrick (ent.; 1717-79)
David Geffen (ent.; 1943-)
David Gergen (US pol./jour.; 1942-)
David Graham (golf; 1946-)
David Groh (ent.; 1941-)
David Halberstam (writer; 1934-)
David Hampton Pryor (US pol.; 1934-)
David Hartman (ent.; 1935-)
David Hasselhoff (ent.; 1952-)
David Hayes
David Hayes Agnew (US phys.; 1818-92)
David Hemmings (ent.; 1941-)
David Hilbert (Ger. math.; 1862-1943)
David Hockney (Br. artist; 1937-)
David Hollis (clothing)
David Horowitz (writer)
David H(ackett) Souter (US jurist; 1939-)
David Hume (Scot. phil./hist.; 1711-76)
David Hyde Pierce (ent.; 1959-)
David I (king, Scot.; 1084-1153)
David II (king, Scot.; 1324-72)
David Jack (ex-gov.-gen., St. Vincent/Grenadines)
David James Wottle (runner; 1950-)
David Janssen (ent.; 1930-80)
David Johansen (aka Buster Poindexter)(ent.; 1950-)
David J. Stern (basketball; 1942-)
David Keith (ent.; 1954-)
David Kendall (US atty./Clintons' atty.)
David Koresh (b. Vernon Wayne Howell)(US cult leader; 1959-1993)
David (Russell) Lange (ex-PM, NewZeal.; 1942-)
David Lean, Sir (ent.; 1908-91)
David Lee Roth (ent.; 1955-)
David Letterman (ent.; 1947-)
David Letterman, Late Night With (TV show)
David Levine (cartoonist; 1926-)
David Livingstone, Dr. (Scot. rel./expl. in Afr.; 1813-73)
David Lloyd George (ex-PM, Br.; 1863-1945)
David L. Wolper (ent.)
David L. Wolper Productions
David Lyle Boren (US pol.; 1941-)
David Lynch (ent.; 1946-)
David Malcolm Storey (Br. writer; 1933-)
David Mamet (US writer/ent.; 1947-)
David McCallum (ent.; 1933-)
David Merrick (ent.; 1912-2000)
David Niven (ent.; 1909-83)
David Oddsson (PM, Iceland; 1948-)
David Ogden Stiers (ent.; 1942-)
David Ogilvy (Br. writer/adv.; 1911-99)
David Oistrakh (violinist; 1908-74)
David O(liver) Selznick (ent.; 1902-65)
David Packard (US bus.; 1913?-)

David R. Scott (astro.; 1932-)
David Rabe (US writer; 1940-)
David Remnick (US writer; 1958-)
David Ricardo (Br. econ.; 1772-1823)
David Riesman (US sociol./writer; 1909-)
David Rittenhouse (US astron./inv.; 1732-96)
David Rockefeller (US finan.; 1915-)
David Rose (US comp.; 1910-90)
David Ross Locke (aka Petroleum V[esuvius]
  Nasby)(US humorist; 1833-88)
David Sarnoff (US TV pioneer, NBC; 1891-1971)
David Schwimmer (ent.; 1966-)
David Soul (b. David Solberg)(ent.; 1943-)
David Spade (ent.; 1964-)
David (Roland) Smith (US sculptor; 1906-65)
David Steinberg (ent.; 1942-)
David Susskind (US ent.; 1920-87)
David Thompson (basketball; 1954-)
David Walters (ex-OK gov.; 1951-)
David Wayne (ent.; 1914-95)
David, City of (also Jerusalem, Bethlehem)
David, Hal (US lyricist; 1921-)
David, Inc., Harry &
David, Jacques Louis (Fr. artist; 1748-1825)
David, Mogan (or Magen)(also Star of David)(6
  points, Jew. symbol)
David, Mogen (kosher foods)
David, Mogen (wine)
David, Panama
David, Star of (also Magen [or Mogan] David)(6
  points, Jew. symbol)
Davidians, Branch (rel. cult)
Davidson, Inc., Harley
Davidson, John (ent.; 1941-)
Davies, Arthur (US artist; 1862-1928)
Davies, Dave (ent., The Kinks; 1947-)
Davies, Marion (Douras)(ent.; 1897-1961)
Davies, Peter Maxwell (Br. comp./cond.; 1934-)
Davies, Ray (ent., The Kinks; 1944-)
Davies, (William) Robertson (Can. writer;
  1913-96)
da Vinci, Leonardo (It. artist/scien.; 1452-1519)
Davis & Co., Parke
Davis Bynum Winery (US bus.)
Davis Cup (tennis)
Davis Group, Spencer (pop music)
Davis-Monthan Air Force Base, AZ (mil.)
Davis, Al (football; 1929-)
Davis, Angela (Yvonne)(US activist/Communist;
  1944-)
Davis, Ann B. (ent.; 1926-)
Davis, Bette (ent.; 1908-89)
Davis, Clifton (ent.; 1945-)
Davis, Colin (Br. cond.; 1927-)
Davis, Eddie "Lockjaw" (US jazz; 1921-86)
Davis, Geena (ent.; 1957-)
Davis, Gray (Joseph Graham), Jr. (CA gov.;
  1942-)
Davis, Jefferson (US pol./confederate pres.,;
  1808-89)
Davis, Jim (cartoonist, *Garfield*; 1945-)
Davis, Kristin (ent.; 1965-)
Davis, Mac (ent.; 1942-)
Davis, Miles (US jazz; 1926-91)
Davis, Ossie (ent.; 1917-)

Davis, Sammy, Jr. (ent.; 1925-90)
Davis, Skeeter (b. Mary Frances Penick)(ent.;
  1931-)
Davis, Spencer (ent.; 1942-)
Davis, Stuart (US artist; 1894-1964)
Davison, Wild Bill (US jazz; 1906-89)
Davy Crockett (David)(US frontier/pol.; 1786-
  1836)
Davy Jones (personification of sea)
Davy Jones's locker (ocean bottom; grave of
  those who die at sea)
Davy, Sir Humphry (Br. chem.; 1778-1829)
Daw Books, Inc.
Daw, Margery (fict. chara.)
Dawber, Pam (ent.; 1951-)
Dawda Kairaba Jawara, Sir (ex-pres., Gambia;
  1924-)
Dawes plan (Ger. war debts, WWI)
Dawes, Charles G. (US pol./banker; 1865-1951)
Dawn, Tony Orlando and (pop music)
Dawnn Lewis (ent.; 1960-)
Dawson, Andre (baseball; 1954-)
Dawson, Leonard Ray (football; 1935-)
Dawson, Richard (ent.; 1932-)
Dawson, Yukon, Canada
Day-Glo (graphic design)
Day-Glo Color Corp.
Day Lewis, Cecil (Ir. poet; 1904-72)
Day-Lewis, Daniel (ent.; 1957-)
Day of Atonement (Yom Kippur)(rel.)
Day of the Jackal, The (film, 1973)
Day, Clarence, Jr. (US writer; 1874-1935)
Day, Dennis (ent.; 1917-88)
Day, Doris (b. Doris von Kappelhoff)(ent.; 1924-)
Day, Dorothy (US reformer; 1897-1980)
Dayan, Moshe (Isr. pol./gen.; 1915-81)
DayQuil (med.)
Days Inns of America (US bus.)
Days of Our Lives (TV soap)
Daytek Online (US bus.)
Dayton News (OH newspaper)
Dayton Peace Accords (Dayton OH, 11/21/95,
  re: Bosnia-Hercegovina)
Dayton, Mark (US cong.; 1947-)
Dayton, OH
Daytona Beach News-Journal (FL newspaper)
Daytona Beach, FL
Daytona International Speedway (FL)
Daytona, Dodge (auto.)
DBA (also d/b/a)(doing business as)
D(aniel) B(ernard) Sweeney (ent.; 1961-)
DC (direct current, District of Columbia)
D-Con Co., Inc., The
d-Con (pest control)
DDAVP (med.)
D-Day (WW II, invasion of Normandy; 6/6/44)
DDC (Dewey Decimal System)
DDS (diaminodiphenyl sulfone)(med.)
DDS (Doctor of Dental Surgery/Science)
DDT (dichlorodiphenyltrichloroethane)
DE (Delaware)
DEA (Drug Enforcement Administration/agency)
Deacon (David) Jones (football; 1938-)
Dead Poets Society (film, 1989)
Dead Sea (Isr./Jordan)

Dead Sea Scrolls (ancient writings; c150 BC-AD 68)
Dead, Book of the (Eg., rel.)
Dead, The Tibetan Book of the (rel.)
Dead-End Kids
Deadwood, SD
de Alarcón, Pedro Antonio (Sp. writer/pol.; 1833-91)
de Albuquerque, Afonso (Port. conquerer; 1453-1515)
Dean (Gooderham) Acheson (US pol.; 1893-1971)
Dean Jagger (ent.; 1903-91)
Dean Jones (ent.; 1931-)
Dean Martin (ent.; 1917-95)
Dean Meat Co., Jimmy
Dean R(ay) Koontz (US writer; 1945-)
Dean Rusk, (David)(US pol.; 1909-94)
Dean Smith (basketball; 1931-)
Dean Stockwell (ent.; 1936-)
Dean Witter Reynolds Inc.
Dean Witter & Co., Morgan Stanley
Dean Witter Online Inc., Morgan Stanley
Dean Young (cartoonist, *Blondie*)
Dean, Christopher (figure skating; 1958-)
Dean, Dizzy (Jay Hanna)(baseball; 1911-74)
Dean, Howard (VT gov.; 1948-)
Dean, James (ent.; 1931-55)
Dean, Jimmy (ent.; 1928-)
Dean, Jimmy (sausage)
Dean, Morton (US TV jour.)
Deane Beman (golf; 1938-)
Deane, Sir William Patrick (gov.-gen., Austl.; 1931-)
Deanna Durbin (ent.; 1921-)
de Anza, Juan Bautista (Sp. expl.; 1735-88?)
Dear Abby (Abigail Van Buren)(b. Pauline Esther Friedman)(US advice columnist; 1918-)
Dear John letter
Dearborn Heights, MI
Dearborn, MI
Dearie, Blossom (ent.; 1926-)
Death Valley (CA/NV)
Death Valley National Monument (CA/NV)
Deathtrap (play)
Deauville, France
DeBakey, Michael Ellis (US phys.; 1908-)
de Balboa, Vasco Núñez (Sp. expl., discovered Pac.; 1475-1519)
de Balzac, Honoré (Fr. writer; 1799-1850)
de' Bardi, Beatrice Portinari (inspiration for Dante's Beatrice; 1266-90)
DeBarge, El(dra) (ent.; 1961-)
Debbie A. Stabenow (US cong.; 1950-)
Debbie Allen (ent.; 1950-)
Debbie Boone (ent.; 1956-)
Debbie Gibson (ent.; 1970-)
Debbie Reynolds (ent.; 1932-)
de Beaumarchais, Pierre Augustin Caron (Fr. writer; 1732-99)
de Beauvoir, Simone (Fr. writer; 1908-86)
DeBeck, Billy (cartoonist, *Barney Google*; 1890-1942)
de Bergerac, Cyrano (Fr. poet/mil.; 1619-55)
de Bergerac, Cyrano (play)

Debi Thomas (figure skating/phys.; 1967-)
de Bivar, Rodrigo Diaz (also El Cid, el Campeador)(Sp. mil.; 1040-99)
Deborah Harry (ent.; 1945-)
Deborah Kerr (ent.; 1921-)
Deborah Meyer (swimming; 1952-)
Deborah Norville (US TV jour.; 1958-)
Deborah Raffin (ent.; 1953-)
de Bougainville, Louis-Antoine (Fr. nav.; 1729-1811)
Debra Messing (ent.; 1968-)
Debra Winger (ent.; 1955-)
Debrecen, Hungary
de Broglie equation
de Broglie principle (physics)
de Broglie wave/wavelength
de Broglie, Louis (Fr. physt.; 1893-1987)
de Broglie's hypothesis (chem.)
Debs Garms (baseball; 1908-84)
Debs, Eugene V. (US labor leader; 1855-1926)
Debs, In re (US law; 1895)
DeBusschere, Dave (basketball; 1940-)
Debussy, (Achille) Claude (Fr. comp.; 1862-1918)
Déby, Idriss (pres., Chad; 1952-)
Decaderm (med.)
Decadron (med.)
Decalog(ue)(also Ten Commandments)(rel.)
Decalogue Books, Inc.
Decameron, The (Boccaccio tales)
De Camp, Rosemary (ent.; 1910-)
DeCarlo, Yvonne (ent.; 1922-)
Decatur, AL, IL, GA
Decatur, Stephen (US mil.; 1779-1820)
Decca Records, Inc.
Deccan (region, India)
December Bride (TV show)
de Cervantes Saavedra, Miguel (Sp. writer; 1547-1616)
de Chamorro, Violeta Barrios (ex-pres., Nicaragua; 1939-)
de Champlain, Samuel (Fr. expl.; c1567-1635)
de Chavannes, Pierre Cecile Puvis (Fr. artist; 1824-98)
de Chirico, Giorgio (It. artist; 1888-1978)
Decholin (med.)
Decker (or Dekker), Thomas (Br. writer; 1572?-1632?)
Decker Corp., The Black &
Decker Slaney, Mary (US runner; 1958-)
Decker, Black & (power tools)
Declaration of Independence (US; July 4, 1776)
Declaration of Rights (Br.)
Declomycin (med.)
Deconamine (med.)
DeConcini, Dennis (US pol.; 1937-)
Decoration Day (now Memorial Day)
de Córdoba, Francisco Fernandez (Sp. expl.; 1475?-1526)
DeCordova, Fred(erick)(US TV exec.; 1910-)
de Coronado, Francisco Vásquez (Sp. expl.; c1510-54)
DeCorsia, Ted (ent.; 1904-73)
de Coulomb, Charles Augustin (Fr. physt.; 1736-1806)
de Coverly, Sir Roger (dance)

de Cuéllar, Javier Pérez (Peruvian/UN dipl.; 1920-)
Dé Danann, Tuatha (myth.)
Dee Dee (Margaret Jane) Myers (US ex-White House press secy.; 1961-)
Dee, Frances (ent.; 1907-)
Dee, Ruby (ent.; 1924-)
Dee, Sandra (b. Alexandra Zuck)(ent.; 1942-)
Deems Taylor (US comp.; 1885-1966)
Deep Sea Drilling Project
Deep South
Deep Throat (Watergate informant)
Deepak Chopra (Indian phys./writer; 1947-)
Deer Hunter, The (film, 1978)
Deere & Co.
Deere, John (agr. products)
Deere, John (US bus.; 1804-86)
Def Jam Recordings (pop music)
Def Leppard (pop music)
Def, Mos (b. Dante Beze)(ent.)
de Falla, Manuel (Sp. comp.; 1876-1946)
Defender, Land Rover (auto.)
Defense Electronics (mag.)
Defense, Department of (DOD)(US govt.)
de Fermat, Pierre (Fr. math.; 1601-65)
Defoe, Daniel (Br. writer; 1660-1731)
DeFord Bailey (ent.; 1899-1982)
Defore, Don (ent.; 1913-93)
DeForest Kelley (ent.; 1920-99)
de Forest, Lee (US inv., radio/sound films/TV; 1873-1961)
De Franco, Buddy (US jazz; 1933-)
de Frontenac, Louis (Fr./Can. gov.; 1620-98)
Dégas, (Hilaire Germain) Edgar (Fr. artist; 1834-1917)
De Gasperi, Alcide (It. pol.; 1881-1954)
de Gaulle, Charles (ex-pres., Fr.; 1890-1970)
DeGeneres, Ellen (ent.; 1958-)
de Givenchy, Hubert (Fr. designer; 1927-)
de Gortari, Carlos Salinas (ex-pres., Mex.; 1949-)
de Graaf, Regnier (Dutch phys.; 1641-73)
de Graaff generator, Van (also electrostatic generator)
de Graaff, Robert Jemison Van (US physt.; 1901-67)
de Greiff, Monica (Colombian pol.)
Dehaene, Jean-Luc (PM, Belgium; 1940-)
DeHaven, Gloria (ent.; 1925-)
De Havilland, Olivia (ent.; 1916-)
Dehiwala-Mount Lavinia, Sri Lanka
Dei gratia (Latin, by the grace of God)
Dei, Agnus (Latin, Lamb of God)
Deidre Hall (ent.; 1948-)
Deimos (Mars moon)
Deity (in ref. to God)
de Kamp's Frozen Foods, Van (US bus.)
Deke (Donald Kent) Slayton (astro.; 1924-93)
Dekker, Albert (ent.; 1905-68)
Dekker, Desmond (b. Desmond Dacris)(ent./ songwriter; 1942-)
Dekker, Thomas (also Decker)(Br. writer; 1572?-1632?)
de Klerk, Frederik W(illem)(ex-pres., SAfr; 1936-)
de Kooning, Willem (US artist; 1904-97)

del Castagno, Andrea (It. artist; c1421-57)
Del Coronado Hotel (CA)
Del Insko (harness racing; 1931-)
Del Laboratories, Inc.
Del Mar, CA
Del Monte Corp.
Del Monte Foods (US bus.)
Del Pharmaceuticals, Inc.
Del Rey Books
Del Rio, Dolores (ent.; 1908-83)
Del Shannon (ent.; 1940-90)
Del Toro, Benicio (ent.; 1967-)
Del Webb Hotels (US bus.)
Del Williams (football; 1945-84)
del Sarto, Andrea (It. artist; 1486-1530)
del Verrocchio, Andrea (b. Andrea di Michele di Francesco di Cioni)(It. artist; 1435-88)
Delacorte, George T. (US publ.; 1893-1991)
Delacroix, Eugene (Fr. artist; 1789-1863)
de Lafayette, Marquis (aka Marie Joseph Gilbert de Motier Lafayette)(Fr. mil./pol.; 1757-1834)
de la Mare, Walter (Br. poet; 1873-1956)
de Lamartine, Alphonse (Fr. writer; 1790-1869)
Delancey, Crossing (film, 1988)
Delaney Amendment (banned carcinogenic food additives)
Delany, Dana (ent.; 1956-)
de la Renta, Ltd., Oscar
de la Renta, Oscar (US designer; 1932-)
Delaroche, Paul (Fr. hist./artist; 1797-1856)
de la Rúa, Fernando (pres., Argentina; 1937-)
de La Tour, Georges (Fr. artist; 1593-1652)
Delaunay, Robert (Fr. artist; 1885-1941)
Delaware (DE)
Delaware (grape)
Delaware (Native Amer.)(also Lenni Lenape)
Delaware River (NY/PA/NJ/DE)
Delaware, Thomas West, Baron (also De La Warr)(US colonial leader; 1577-1618)
De La Warr, Thomas West, Baron (also Delaware)(US colonial leader; 1577-1618)
De Laurentiis, Dino (It. ent.; 1919-)
DeLay, Tom (Thomas Dale)(US cong.; 1947-)
Delbert McClinton (ent./songwriter; 1940-)
Delbruck, Max (US biol.; 1907-81)
de León, (Juan) Ponce (Sp. expl.; c1460-1521)
de Lesseps, Ferdinand, Vicomte (Fr. dipl./eng.; 1805-94)
Delft, Netherlands
Delhi, India
Delia Salter Bacon (US writer; 1811-59)
Delibes, C(lement) P(hilibert) Leo (Fr. comp.; 1836-91)
Delicious (apple), Golden
Delicious (apple), Red
Delilah, Samson & (rel.)
Delius, Frederick (Br. comp.; 1862-1934)
Deliverance (film, 1972)
Dell Computer Corp.
Dell Publishing Group, Inc., Bantam, Doubleday
Della Chiesa, Vivienne (ent.; 1920-)
Della Reese (b. Deloreese Patricia Early)(ent.; 1931-)
della Francesca, Piero (It. artist; c1415-92)
della Robbia, Andrea (It. sculptor; 1437-1528)

della Robbia, Luca (It. artist; 1400-82)
,Dello Joio, Norman (US comp.; 1913-)
Delmonico steak
Delon, Alain (ent.; 1935-)
De Lorean, John (US bus./auto.; 1925-)
Delos Island (Aegean Sea)
de Lozada, Gonzalo Sánchez (ex-pres., Bolivia; 1930-)
Delphi, Greece
Delphi, Oracle of (also Delphic oracle)(noted for ambiguous answers)
Delphi, oracle of Apollo at
Delphinus (astron., dolphin)
Delray Beach, FL
Delsarte method/system (calisthenics)
Delta 88, Oldsmobile (auto.)
Delta Air Lines, Inc.
Delta Burke (ent.; 1956-)
Delta Connection, The (airline)
Delta-Cortef (med.)
Delta Force (mil.)
Delta Plan
Delta SkyMiles
Delta team (mil.)
Deltasone (med.)
Deluge, the (also the Flood)(rel.)
DeLuise, Dom (ent.; 1933-)
DeLuise, Peter (ent.; 1966-)
Delvaux, Paul (Belgian artist; 1897-1994)
Delvecchio, Alex Peter (hockey; 1931-)
de Machaut, Guillaume (Fr. comp.; 1300-77)
de Marco, Prof. Guido (pres., Malta; 1931-)
Demarest DriCort
Demarest, William (ent.; 1892-1983)
Demaret, Jim (golf; 1910-83)
de Maupassant, (Henri René Albert) Guy (Fr. writer; 1850-93)
de' Medici, Catherine (queen, Fr./wife of Henry II; 1518-89)
de' Medici, Cosimo I (It., Duke of Florence; 1519-74)
de' Medici, Lorenzo ("the Magnificent")(It. poet/pol.; 1449-92)
de' Medici, Marie (queen, Fr./wife of Henry IV; 1573-1642)
de' Medici, Piero (It. pol.; 1416-69)
de Mello, Fernando Collor (ex-pres., Brazil; 1949-)
Demerol (med.)
Demeter (myth.)
Demetrius I (Demetrius Poliorcetes)(king, Macedonia; c337-283 BC)
Demi Moore (b. Demetria Guynes)(ent.; 1962-)
De Mille, Agnes (US dancer/choreographer; 1905-93)
De Mille, Cecil B. (ent.; 1881-1959)
de Milo, Venus (also Venus of Melos, Aphrodite of Melos)(Gr. statue; c.200 BC)
Demirel, Suleyman (ex-PM, Turk.; 1924-)
Demme, Jonathan (ent.; 1944-)
Democracy, National Endowment for (US pol. agcy.)
Democrat (politics)
Democrat & Chronicle, Rochester (NY newspaper)

Democrat-Gazette, Little Rock (AR newspaper)
Democrat, Tallahassee (FL newspaper)
Democratic Party (US pol.)
Democratic Party, New (NDP)(Can. pol.)
Democratic Party, Social (Br. pol.; 1981-90)
Democratic Republic of the Congo (aka DRC, Congo, Congo-Kinshasa)(W central Afr.)(was Zaire)
Democrats, Social (US pol. party)
Democrats, Social and Liberal (Br. pol. party)
Democritus ("the Laughing Philosopher")(Gr. phil.; c460-370 BC)
Demond Wilson (ent.; 1946-)
de Montaigne, Michel (Eyquem)(Fr. writer; 1533-92)
de Montcalm (-Gozon), Louis (-Joseph)(Fr. mil.; 1712-59)
De Mornay, Rebecca (ent.; 1962-)
Demosthenes (Gr. orator/pol.; 384-322 BC)
Demotic Greek (lang.)
Dempsey, Jack (William Harrison)(boxing; 1895-1983)
Demulen (med.)
de Musset, Alfred (Fr. writer; 1810-57)
Denali National Park (formerly Mount McKinley National Park)(AK)
Denali, GMC (auto.)
Dench, Dame Judi (ent.; 1934-)
Dene (people)
Deneb (also Alpha Cygni)(astron.)
de Nemours & Co., E. I. du Pont
de Nemours, E(leuthere) I. du Pont (US bus.; 1771-1834)
Deneuve, Catherine (b. Catherine Dorleac)(Fr. ent.; 1943-)
Deng Xiaoping (also Teng Hsiao-ping)(Ch. pol.; 1904-97)
Denikin, Anton (Rus. mil.; 1872-1947)
De Niro, Robert (ent.; 1943-)
Denis Burkitt (Br. phys./rel.; 1911-93)
Denis Charles Potvin (hockey; 1953-)
Denis Diderot (Fr. phil.; 1713-84)
Denis Leary (ent./writer; 1957-)
Denis Sassou-Nguesso (pres., Rep/Congo; 1943-)
Denise Levertov (Br./US poet; 1923-97)
Denise Nicholas (ent.; 1944-)
Denise Rich (US news, ex-wife of pardoned Marc Rich)
Denise Richards (ent.; 1971-)
Denison, TX
Denmark (Kingdom of)(N Eur.)
Denmark Strait (Greenland/Iceland)
Denmark, Anne of (Queen consort, James VI of Scot.; 1574-1619)
Dennehy, Brian (ent.; 1938-)
Dennis Alexio
Dennis Chan (wakeboarding)
Dennis Day (ent.; 1917-88)
Dennis DeConcini (US pol.; 1937-)
Dennis et al v. U.S. (US law; 1951)
Dennis Franz (ent.; 1944-)
Dennis Gabor (Br. inv., holography; 1900-70)
Dennis Hastert, J(ohn) III (US cong.; 1942-)
Dennis Hopper (ent.; 1936-)
Dennis James (ent.; 1917-97)
Dennis McLain (baseball; 1944-)

Dennis Miller (ent.; 1953-)
Dennis Morgan (ent.; 1910-)
Dennis O'Keefe (ent.; 1908-68)
Dennis Quaid (ent.; 1954-)
Dennis Ralston (tennis; 1942-)
Dennis the Menace (comic strip)
Dennis Weaver (ent.; 1924-)
Dennis, Sandy (ent.; 1937-92)
Dennison Corp., Avery
Dennison Manufacturing Co.
Denny, Reginald (ent.; 1891-1967)
Denny's, Inc.
Denon (audio)
Denon America, Inc.
Denorex (med.)
Denton A(rthur) Cooley (US heart surgeon; 1920-)
Dentyne (gum)
Denver boot (car tire clamp)
Denver Broncos (football team)
Denver Nuggets (basketball team)
Denver Post (CO newspaper)
Denver Pyle (ent.; 1920-97)
Denver Rocky Mountain News (CO newspaper)
Denver, Bob (ent.; 1935-)
Denver, CO
Denver, John (ent.; 1943-97)
Denzel Washington (ent.; 1954-)
Denzil L(lewellyn) Douglas (PM, St. Kitts-Nevis; 1953-)
Deo volente (Latin, God willing)
Dep (hair care)
Depakene (med.)
Depakote (med.)
De Palma, Brian (ent.; 1940)
Depardieu, Gerard (ent.; 1948-)
Department of Agriculture (US govt.)
Department of Commerce (US govt.)
Department of Defense (DOD)(US govt.)
Department of Education (US govt.)
Department of Energy (US govt.)
Department of Health and Human Services (HHS)(US govt.)
Department of Housing and Urban Development (HUD)(US govt.)
Department of Justice (DOJ)(US govt.)
Department of Labor (DOL)(US govt.)
Department of State (US govt.)
Department of the Air Force (US mil.)
Department of the Army (US mil.)
Department of the Interior (US govt.)
Department of the Navy (US mil.)
Department of the Treasury (US govt.)
Department of Transportation (DOT)(US govt.)
Department of Veterans Affairs (US govt.)
Department of War (US govt.)
DePaul University (Chicago, IL)
de Paul, St. Vincent (Fr. rel.; c1581-1660)
DePauw University (Greencastle, IN)
de Perón, Eva Duarte ("Evita")(ex-pres., Argentina; 1919-52)
de Perón, Maria Estela ("Isabel") Martínez (ex-pres., Argentina; 1931-)
Depogen (med.)
Depo-Medrol

Depo-Provera (med.)
Depo-Testosterone (med.)
de Pompadour, Marquise (aka Jeanne Antoinette Poisson Le Normant d'Étioles) (mistress of Louis XV, Fr.; 1721-64)
Depp, Johnny (ent.; 1963-)
Depression glass
Depression, the Great (US hist.; 1930s)
der Blaue Reiter (*"the blue Rider"*)(Ger. painters)
Derby (cheese)
Derby (horse races)
Derby, England
Derbyshire (county, Eng.)
Derbyshire chair (also Yorkshire chair)
Derek Jacobi (ent.; 1938-)
Derek, Bo (b. Mary Cathleen Collins)(ent.; 1956-)
Derek, John (b. Derek Harris) (ent.; 1926-98)
der Fuhrer (also *Fuehrer*)(title adopted by Hitler)
de Richelieu, Cardinal ("red eminence")(Fr. pol.; 1585-1642)
Deringer pistol
Deringer, Henry (US gunsmith; 19th c.)
DeRita, Joe (b. Joseph Wardell)(ent.; 1909-93)
de Rivera, José (US sculptor; 1904-85)
DermaFlex (med.)
Dermarest (med.)
Dermocaine (med.)
Dermoplast (med.)
Dern, Bruce (ent.; 1936-)
Dern, Laura (ent.; 1967-)
de Ronsard, Pierre (Fr. poet; 1524-85)
de Rossi, Portia (b. Amanda Rogers)(ent.; 1973-)
de Rothschild, Anthony Gustav (Br. finan.; 1887-1961)
de Rothschild, Lionel (Br. finan.; 1882-1942)
de Rothschild, Lionel, Baron (Br. pol./finan.; 1808-79)
der Post, Laurens (Jan) Van (SAfr. writer; 1906-96)
Derrel's law
Derrick Thomas (football; 1967-2000)
Derrick, Butler (US pol.; 1936-)
Derrida, Jacques (phil.; 1930-)
der Rohe, Ludwig Mies van (US arch.; 1886-1969)
Derry (county, NIre.)
Derry, Northern Ireland (formerly Londonderry)
Dershowitz, Alan (US atty.; 1938-)
Der Spiegel (*The Mirror,* Ger. news magazine)
der Weyden, Rogier van (Flem. artist; c1400-64)
Des Moines Register (IA newspaper)
Des Moines, IA
Desmond, Johnny (ent./songwriter; 1921-85)
de Sade, Marquis (Donatien)(Fr. mil./writer; 1740-1814)
de Saint-Exupery, Antoine (Marie Roger)(Fr. writer/aviator; 1900-44)
de Santa Anna, Antonio (ex-pres./gen., Mex.; 1795?-1876)
de Saussure, Ferdinand (Swiss linguist; 1857-1913)
Descartes, René (Fr. phil.; 1596-1650)
Deschutes National Forest
Deschutes River (OR)

Desdemona (fict. chara., *Othello*)
·de Seingalt, Casanova (also Giovanni Jacopo Casanova)(It. adventurer; 1725-98)
Desenex (med.)
Desert Culture (anthrop.)
Desert Shield, Operation (Gulf War; 1990-91)
Desert Storm, Operation (Gulf War; 1991)
de Seversky, Alexander Procofieff (Rus./US aviator/writer; 1894-1974)
Desi Arnaz (b. Desiderio Alberto Araz y de Acha III)(ent.; 1917-86)
Desi Arnaz, Jr. (ent.; 1953-)
De Sica, Vittorio (ent.; 1901-74)
Desiderius Erasmus (Dutch scholar; c1466-1536)
Designing Women (TV show)
Desilu Productions (film co.)
Desitin (med.)
Desmond (Mpilo) Tutu (SAfr. rel.; 1931-)
Desmond Dekker (b. Desmond Dacris)(ent./songwriter; 1942-)
Desmond Hoyte, Hugh (ex-pres., Guyana)
Desmond Morris (Br. writer; 1928-)
Desmond, Paul (US jazz; 1924-77)
de Soto, Hernando (or Fernando)(Sp. expl.; c1496-1542)
Desoxyn (med)
Desperately Seeking Susan (film, 1985)
de Spinoza, Benedict (also Baruch)(Dutch phil.; 1632-77)
Des Pres, Josquin (Flem. comp.; c1445-1521)
Dessau, Germany
Dessau, Paul (Ger. comp; 1894-1979)
d'Estaing, Valéry Giscard (ex-pres., Fr.; 1926-)
de Stijl (Dutch art, early 20th c.)
Destiny's Child (pop music)
De Sylva, Buddy (US lyricist; 1895-1950)
Desyrel (med.)
de Talleyrand(-Périgord), Charles (Maurice)(Fr. pol.; 1754-1838)
Detioles-to-alpha d'Étioles, Jeanne Antoinette Poisson Le Normant (Marquise de Pompadour) (mistress of Louis XV, Fr.; 1721-64)
de Tocqueville, Alexis (Charles Henri Maurice Clérel)(Fr. hist.; 1805-59)
de Toulouse-Lautrec, Henri (Marie Raymond) (Fr. artist; 1864-1901)
Detrick, Fort (MD)(mil.)
Detroit Arsenal (MI)(mil.)
Detroit Free Press (MI newspaper)
Detroit Lions (football team)
Detroit Metropolitan Wayne County Airport (MI)
Detroit News (MI newspaper)
Detroit News & Free Press (MI newspaper)
Detroit Pistons (basketball team)
Detroit Red Wings (hockey team)
Detroit Tigers (baseball team)
Detroit, MI
Deukmejian, George (ex-CA gov.; 1928-)
Deuteronomy (rel., book of the Old Testament)
Deutsche mark (also Deutschemark)
Deutschland (Ger. name for Germany)
Dev, Birendra Bir Bikram Shah (king, Nepal; 1945-)
de Valera, Eamon (ex-PM/pres., Ir.; 1882-1975)
Devanagari (also Nagari)(alphabetic script)

Devane, William (ent.; 1939-)
De Varona, Donna (swimming/sportscaster; 1947-)
de Vega (Carpio), Lope (Félix)(Sp. writer; 1562-1635)
Development Program, United Nations (UNDP) (est. 1965)
Devens, Fort, MA (mil.)
Devereux, Robert (Earl of Essex)(Br. mil./pol.; 1567-1601)
Devers, Gail (track; 1966-)
Devi (also Anapurna, Annapurna, Parvati) (myth.)
Devi, Phoolan (aka the Bandit Queen)(Indian bandit/pol.; 1963-2001)
DeVicenzo, Roberto (golf; 1923-)
Devil, the
Devil and Daniel Webster, The (film, 1941)
Devil and Max Devlin, The (film, 1981)
Devil and Miss Jones, The (film, 1941)
Devil's Island (former penal colony, Fr. Guiana)
Devil's Triangle (also Bermuda Triangle)
DeVille, Cadillac (auto.)
DeVille, Cruella (fict. chara., *101 Dalmatians*)
Devils, New Jersey (hockey team)
Devine, Andy (ent.; 1905-77)
DeVito, Danny (ent. 1944-)
de Vlaminck, Maurice (Fr. artist; 1876-1958)
Devlin, The Devil and Max (film, 1981)
De Vol, Frank (US comp.; 1911-99)
Devon (also Devonshire)(county, Eng.)
Devon cattle
Devon sheep
Devon(shire) cream
Devonian period (395-345 million years ago)
Devonshire (also Devon)(county, Eng.)
De Voto, Bernard A. (US hist.; 1897-1955)
De Vries, Hugo (Dutch botanist; 1848-1935)
De Vries, Peter (US writer; 1910-93)
de Waart, Edo (cond.; 1941-)
Dewar flask/vessel (thermos)
Dewar, Sir James (Scot. chem./physt.; 1842-1923)
Dewey decimal system (library classification)
Dewey, George (US adm.; 1837-1917)
Dewey, John (US phil./educ.; 1859-1952)
Dewey, Melvil (US librarian; 1851-1931)
Dewey, Thomas E(dmund)(ex-gov., NY; 1902-71)
Dewhurst, Colleen (ent; 1926-1991)
De Wilde, Brandon (ent.; 1942-72)
DeWine, Mike (US cong.; 1947-)
DeWitt Clinton (US pol.; 1769-1828)
DeWitt Wallace (US publ.; 1889-1981)
DeWitt, Joyce (ent.; 1949-)
DeWolf Hopper (ent.; 1858-1935)
De Wolfe, Billy (ent.; 1907-74)
Dexatrim (med.)
Dexedrine (med.)
Dexter Gordon (US jazz; 1923-90)
Dey, Susan (ent.; 1952-)
de Young Memorial Museum, M. H. (San Francisco)
DFC (Distinguished Flying Cross)
Dhaka, Bangladesh (also Dacca)
Dhamma (rel.)

Dhammapada (rel. work)
DHL (shipper)
D(avid) H(erbert) Lawrence (Br. writer; 1885-1930)
DI (drill instructor)
DiaBeta (med.)
Diabetes Self-Management
Diabinese (med.)
Diablo, Lamborghini (auto.)
Diaghilev, Sergei (Pavlovich)(Rus. ballet; 1872-1929)
Diahann Carroll (b. Carol Diahann Johnson)(ent.; 1935-)
Dial Corp., Greyhound-
Dial Corp., The
Dial Magazine
Dial One service (comm.)
Dialog (compu. database)
Diamante, Mitsubishi (auto.)
Diamond Head, Honolulu
Diamond Jim Brady (US finan.; 1856-1917)
Diamond State (nickname, DE)
Diamond v. Chakrabarty (US law; 1980)
Diamond, Neil (b. Noah Kaminsky)(US comp./ent.; 1941-)
Diamond, Selma (ent.; 1920-85)
Diamox (med.)
Dian Fossey (US zool., gorillas; 1932-85)
Diana (myth.)
Diana Barrymore (ent.; 1921-60)
Diana Hyland (ent.; 1936-77)
Diana Krall (ent.; 1964-)
Diana Lynn (ent.; 1926-71)
Diana Muldaur (ent.; 1938-)
Diana Nyad (swimming/jour.; 1949-)
Diana Rigg (ent.; 1938-)
Diana Ross (ent.; 1944-)
Diana Trilling (US writer; 1905-96)
Diana Vreeland (Fr./US editor/designer; 1903-89)
Diana, Princess (Princess of Wales, Lady Diana Spencer; 1961-97)
Diane Cilento (ent.; 1933-)
Diane English (ent./created Murphy Brown; 1948-)
Diane Keaton (ent.; 1946-)
Diane Ladd (b. Rose Diane Ladner)(ent.; 1932-)
Diane Lane (ent.; 1965-)
Diane Sawyer (US TV jour.; 1945-)
Diane (Halfin) von Furstenberg (US bus.; 1946-)
Diane von Furstenberg Importing Co.
Diane, steak
Dianetics (Scientology therapy, L. Ron Hubbard)
Dianne Feinstein (US cong.; 1933-)
Dianne Wiest (ent.; 1948-)
Diarra, Seydou Elimane (PM, Ivory Coast; 1933-)
Dias, Bartholomeu (also Diaz)(Port. expl.; c1450-1500)
Diaspora (dispersal of Jews outside Isr.)
Diaz, Cameron (ent./model; 1972-)
Diba, Farah
Dibbs, Edward George (tennis; 1951-)
DiCaprio, Leonardo (ent.; 1974-)
Dichter, Misha (pianist; 1945-)
Dick (Richard Anthony) Allen (baseball; 1942-)
Dick (Richard K.) Armey (US econ./cong.; 1940-)
Dick (Richard H.) Bryan (US pol.; 1937-)

Dick (Richard Marvin) Butkus (football/ent.; 1942-)
Dick (Richard) Button (figure skating, ent.; 1929-)
Dick Cavett (ent.; 1936-)
Dick (Richard Bruce) Cheney (US VP; 1941-)
Dick Clark (ent.; 1929-)
Dick Co., A. B.
Dick Ebersole (TV sports exec.)
Dick Enberg (sportscaster; 1935-)
Dick (Richard) Fosbury (jumper; 1947-)
Dick Francis (Br. writer/jockey; 1920-)
Dick Gregory (ent.; 1932-)
Dick Haymes (ent.; 1917-80)
Dick Howser (baseball; 1937-87)
Dick Martin (ent.; 1922-)
Dick Moores (cartoonist, *Gasoline Alley*; 1909-86)
Dick Powell (ent.; 1904-63)
Dick Sargent (ent.; 1933-94)
Dick Schaap (TV sports jour.)
Dick (Francis Richard) Scobee (astro., Challenger; 1939-86)
Dick Smothers (ent.; 1939-)
Dick Tracy (fict. chara.)
Dick (Richard) Turpin (Br. highwayman; 1706-39)
Dick Van Dyke (ent.; 1925-)
Dick Van Dyke Show, The (TV show)
Dick Van Patten (ent.; 1928-)
Dick Vitale (ent.; 1940-)
Dick Wakefield (baseball; 1921-85)
Dick Williams (baseball; 1929-)
Dick York (ent.; 1929-92)
Dick, Moby (H. Melville novel)
Dickens, Charles (John Huffam)("Boz")(Br. writer; 1812-70)
Dickens, Little Jimmy (ent.; 1920-)
Dickenson, Vic (US jazz; 1906-84)
Dickerson, Eric (football; 1960-)
Dickerson, Minnesota v. (US law; 1993)
Dickey, James (US writer; 1923-97)
Dickinson, Angie (b. Angeline Brown)(ent.; 1931-)
Dickinson, Emily (US poet; 1830-86)
Dictaphone
Dictaphone Corp.
Dictator, The Great (film, 1940)
Dictograph
Dictograph Products, Inc.
Diddley, Bo (b. Elias McDaniel)(ent.; 1928-)
Diderot, Denis (Fr. phil.; 1713-84)
Didier Ratsiraka (pres., Madagascar; 1936-)
Didion, Joan (US writer; 1934-)
Dido (myth.)
Didot point system (printing)
Didot, François (Ambrose)(Fr. printer; 1730-1804)
Die Fledermaus (Strauss operetta)
Die Hard (film, 1988)
Die Hard 2 (film, 1990)
Die Walküre (Wagner opera)
die Brücke (Ger. art movement)
Diebenkorn, Richard (US artist; 1922-93)
Diebold, Inc.
Diefenbaker, John George (ex-PM, Can.; 1895-1979)
Diego (Rodríguez de Silva y) Velázquez (Sp. artist; 1599-1660)
Diego Rivera (Mex. artist; 1886-1957)

Diem, Ngo Dinh (ex-pres., SViet.; 1901-63)
Dien Bien Phu, Battle of (also Dienbienphu)
  (NViet.; 1954)
Dien Bien Phu, Vietnam (also Dienbienphu)
Dieppe lace
Dieppe, France
Diesel, Rudolf (Ger. eng.; 1858-1913)
Diesel, Vin (ent.; 1967-)
Diet 7UP
Diet Coke
Diet of Worms (rel. hist.; 1521)
Diet Pepsi
Dietrich Buxtehude (Dan. comp.; 1637-1707)
Dietrich Fischer-Dieskau (baritone; 1925-)
Dietrich, Marlene (b. Maria Magdalene von
  Losch)(ent.; 1901-92)
Dietz, Howard (US lyricist.; 1896-1983)
Dietz, James W. (rowing; 1949-)
Dieu et mon droit (motto, Br. royalty, God and
  my right)
Diflucan (med.)
DiFranco, Ani (ent./songwriter; 1970-)
Di-Gel (med.)
Digger Indians (tribes who dig roots for food)
Diggers (Br. hist.; 1649-60)
Digges, Dudley (ent.; 1879-1947)
Diggs, Taye (ent.; 1971-)
Digital Equipment Corp.
Digital Millennium Copyright Act (passed 1998)
Digitalis lantana (med. plant)
Digory Ketterley (fict. chara., C. S. Lewis'
  Chronicles of Narnia)
Dijon mustard
Dijon, France
Dik Browne (cartoonist, Hi & Lois, Hagar the
  Horrible; 1917-89)
Dikhil, Djibouti
di Lampedusa, Giuseppe (Tomasi)(It. writer;
  1896-1957)
Dilantin (med.)
Dilaudid (med.)
Dilbert (cartoon chara.)
Dillard Department Stores, Inc.
Dillard, Annie (US writer; 1945-)
Diller, Phyllis (b. Phyllis Driver)(ent.; 1917-)
Dillinger, John (US bank robber/murderer;
  1902?-34)
Dillman, Bradford (ent.; 1930-)
Dillon, Matt (ent.; 1964-)
Dillon, Matt, Marshal (fict. chara., Gunsmoke)
DiMaggio, Dom (baseball; 1917-)
DiMaggio, Joe (baseball; 1914-99)
Dimetane (med.)
Dimetapp (med.)
Dimitri Mitropoulos (cond.; 1896-1960)
Dimitri Shostakovich (Rus. comp.; 1906-75)
Dimitri Tiomkin (Rus./US comp.; 1899-1979)
Dimitrov, Filip (ex-PM, Bulgaria)
Dimitrov, Georgi (ex-PM, Bulgaria; 1882-1949)
Dimli (lang.)
Din, Gunga (film, 1939)
Dina Merrill (b. Nedinia Hutton)(ent.; 1925-)
Dinah Manoff (ent.; 1958-)
Dinah Shore (ent.; 1917-94)
Dinah Washington (ent.; 1924-63)

d'Indy, (Paul Marie Théodore) Vincent (Fr.
  comp.; 1851-1931)
Dine, Jim (US artist; 1935-)
Diners Club credit card
Diners Club International (US bus.)
Diners Club, Citicorp (US bus.)
Diners Club, Inc.
Dinesen, Isak (aka Karen Blixen)(Dan. writer;
  1885-1962)
Ding Dong School (TV show)
Dingiri Banda Wijetunge (ex-pres., Sri Lanka;
  1922-)
Dinka (lang./people)
Dinkins, David (ex-NYC mayor; 1927-)
Dino De Laurentiis, (It. ent.; 1919-)
Dinty Moore (stew)
Diocletian window (also Palladian window)
Diodorus (Gr. hist.; 1st c. BC)
Diogenes (Gr. phil.; 4th c. BC)
Diola (people)
Diomedes (myth.)
Dion (DiMucci) (ent.; 1939-)
Dion and the Belmonts (pop music)
Dion, Celine (ent.; 1968-)
Dione (Saturn moon)(myth.)
Dionne quintuplets
Dionne Warwick (b. Marie Warrick)(ent.; 1940-)
Dionne, Marcel (hockey; 1951-)
Dionysius Longinus (Gr. critic; 1st c. AD)
Dionysius, the Elder (Gr. mil.; 432-367 BC)
Dionysius, the Younger (Gr. mil.; c390-344 BC)
Dionysus (myth.)
Dior Perfumes Corp., Christian
Dior, Christian (Fr. designer; 1905-57)
Diouf, Abdou (ex-pres., Senegal; 1935-)
Diphedryl (med.)
Dippity-Do It (US bus.)
Dippity-do (hair care)
Diprosone (med.)
Dire Dawa, Ethiopia
Dire Straits (pop music)
Direct TV (satellite TV)
Directoire (arch. style)
Dirk Benedict (b. Dirk Niewoehner)(ent.; 1945-)
Dirk Bogarde (ent.; 1921-99)
Dirk (Arthur) Kempthorne (ID gov./ex-cong.;
  1951-)
Dirks, Rudolph (cartoonist, Katzenjammer Kids;
  1877-1968)
Dirksen Senate Office Building (DC)
Dirksen, Everett M. (US pol./orator; 1896-1969)
Dirt Devil (home appliances)
Dirty Harry (film, 1971)
Dis (also Dis Pater)(myth.)
Disabilities Act, Americans With (US hist.; 1990)
di Sant'Angelo, Giorgio (designer)
Disarmament Conference
Disciples of Christ (also The Christian Church)
Disciples, Twelve
Discover (mag.)
Discovery (US space shuttle)
Discovery Channel (TV channel)
Discovery Day (now Columbus Day)(October 12)
Discovery Health Channel (TV channel)
Discovery, Land Rover (auto.)

Disease Control and Prevention, Centers for (CDC)
Dish Network (satellite TV)
Dismal Swamp, VA/NC
Disney Adventures (mag.)
Disney Channel (TV channel)
Disney Co., The Walt
Disney Enterprises, Inc.
Disney-MGM Studios Theme Park
Disney World (FL)
Disney, Walt(er) Elias (US bus./ent.; 1901-66)
Disneyland (CA)
Dispatch, Columbus (OH newspaper)
Dispatch, York (PA newspaper)
Di-Spaz (med.)
Disraeli, Benjamin (ex-PM/writer, Br.; 1804-81)
Distinguished Conduct Medal (mil.)
Distinguished Flying Cross (mil.)
Distinguished Service Cross (mil.)
Distinguished Service Medal (mil.)
Distinguished Service Order (Br. mil.)
District of Columbia (Washington, DC, US capital)
District, Lake (region, Eng.)
Distrito Federal, Mexico (also Federal District)
di Suvero, Mark (US artist; 1933-)
Ditka, Mike (football; 1939-)
Ditko, Steve (cartoonist, *Spider-Man*; 1927-)
Ditmars, Ivan (ent./comp.; ?-1997)
Ditmars, Raymond (US zool., writer; 1876-1942)
Ditropan XL (med.)
Ditto machine
Diucardin (med.)
Diupres (med.)
Diurese (med.)
Diuril (med.)
Divehi (lang.)
Divide, Continental (also the Great Divide)(the Rockies)
Divine Comedy, The (by Dante)
Divine Father (God)
Divine Light Mission (rel.)
Divine Liturgy (rel.)
Divine Mind (rel.)
Divine Mother (rel.)
Divine Office (also Liturgy of the Hours)(rel.)
Divine, Major M. J. (also Father Divine)(b. George Baker)(US rel.; 1882-1965)
Divinity, the
Divorce Court (TV show)
Diwali (Hindu rel. festival)
Dix, Dorothea (US educ./reformer; 1802-87)
Dix, Fort, NJ (mil.)
Dix, Otto (Ger. artist; 1891-1969)
Dixie (song)
Dixie Carter (ent.; 1939-)
Dixie Chicks (pop music)
Dixie cup
Dixie Stores, Inc., Winn-
Dixiecrat (politics)
Dixieland (music)
Dixon, Donna (ent.; 1957-)
Dixon, Jeane (Pinckert) (US psychic/writer; 1918-97)
Dixon, U.S. v. (US law; 1993)
Dizzy (John Birks) Gillespie (US jazz; 1917-93)

Dizzy Dean (Jay Hanna)(US baseball; 1911-74)
DJ (disc jockey)
Djakarta, Indonesia (also Jakarta)
Django Reinhardt (US jazz; 1910-53)
Djerma (people)
DJI (Dow-Jones Industrials)
DJIA (Dow-Jones Industrial Average)
Djibouti (Republic of)(E Afr.)
Djibouti, Djibouti
Djindjic, Zoran (PM, Serbia; 1952)
D.J. Jazzy Jeff & the Fresh Prince (pop music)
Djohar, Said Muhammad (ex-pres., Comoros; 1918-)
Djukanovic, Milo (pres., Montenegro; 1962-)
Djurgarden (parkland, Stockholm)
Dlamini, Barnabas Sibusiso (PM, Swaziland; 1942-)
Dlamini, Obed (ex-PM, Swaziland)
D(arryl) L(ynn) Hughley (ent.; 1963-)
DLO (dead letter office)
Dmitri Ivanovich Mendeleyev (Rus. chem., periodic law; 1834-1907)
Dmitri Kabalevsky (Rus. comp.; 1904-87)
Dmitry (Dmitriyevich) Shostakovich (Rus. comp.; 1906-75)
DMSO (dimethylsulfoxide [colorless liquid])
DMV (Department of Motor Vehicles)
DMZ (demilitarized zone)
DNA (deoxyribonucleic acid)(med.)
Dnepr River (also Dnieper)(Rus./Ukraine)
Dnepropetrovsk, Ukraine
Dnieper River (also Dnepr)(Rus./Ukraine)
Dniester River (also Dnestr)(Ukraine)
DO (Doctor of Osteopathy)
DOA (dead on arrival)
Doakes, Joe (also Joe Blow)(average guy)
Doan's pills (med.)
DOB (date of birth)
Dobbins Air Force Base, GA (mil.)
Dobbs, Mattiwilda (soprano; 1925-)
Doberman pinscher (dog)
Dobie Gillis (fict. chara.)
Dobro (music)
Dobrovolsky, Georgi (or Georgy) T. (cosmo.; 1928-71)
Dobrynin, Anatoly (Federovich) (Rus. dipl.; 1919-)
Dobson, Kevin (ent.; 1944-)
Doc (Carl Hilding) Severinsen (ent.; 1927-)
Doc Holliday, (John Henry) (US frontier/dentist; 1851-87)
Doc Hollywood (film, 1991)
Doc Pomus (b. Jerome Felder)(US comp.; 1925-91)
Doc, Baby (Jean-Claude Duvalier)(ex-pres., Haiti; 1951-)
Doc, Papa (François Duvalier)(ex-pres., Haiti; 1907-71)
Dock (Moran Lee) Boggs (ent.; 1898-1971)
Dockers (clothing)
Dr. Atkins (Robert C. Atkins)(US, low-carb diet)
Doctor Doolittle (also *Dr. Doolittle*)(film, 1967, 1998)
Dr. Dre (b. Andre Young)(ent./rap; 1965-)
Dr. Faustus (*The Tragical History of Dr. Faustus*)(Marlowe)

Dr. Frankenstein (fict. chara.)
Dr. Jekyll and Mr. Hyde, The Strange Case of (by R.L. Stevenson)
Dr. John (b. Malcolm Rebennack)(ent./ songwriter; 1941-)
Dr. Kildare (TV show)
Dr. Laura (Schlessinger)(radio talk show host; 1947-)
Dr. No (film, 1962)
Doctor of Dental Surgery/Science (DDS)
Doctor of Juridical Science (also SJD., Scientiae Juridicae Doctor)
Doctor of Laws (also LL.D., Legum Doctor)
Doctor of Letters (also D. Litt., Doctor Litterarum)
Doctor of Medicine (also MD, Medicinae Doctor)
Doctor of Philosophy (also Ph.D., doctorate)
Doctor of Science (also Sc.D., Scientiae Doctor)
Doctor of Theology (also D.Th., D.Theol.)
Dr. Pepper (soda)
Dr Pepper/Seven Up, Inc.
Dr. Quinn, Medicine Woman (TV show)
Dr. Scholl's (footware/care)
Dr. Seuss (aka Theodore Seuss Geisel)(US writer/artist; 1904-91)
Dr. Strangelove: or, How I Learned to Stop Worrying and Love the Bomb (film, 1964)
Dr. Watson (fict. chara. w/Sherlock Holmes)
Doctor Who (TV show; film, 1996)
Doctor Zhivago (B. Pasternak novel)
Doctorow, E(dgar) L(awrence)(US writer; 1931-)
DOD (Department of Defense)(US govt.)
Dodd, Christopher J. (US cong.; 1944-)
Dodd, Mead & Co., Inc.
Dodds, Johnny (US jazz; 1892-1940)
Dodds, Warren "Baby" (US jazz; 1898-1959)
Dodecanese Islands (Aegean Sea)
Dodge (auto.)
Dodge Avenger (auto.)
Dodge Avenger ES (auto.)
Dodge Caravan (auto.)
Dodge Caravan ES (auto.)
Dodge Caravan LE (auto.)
Dodge Caravan SE (auto.)
Dodge Caravan Sport (auto.)
Dodge Charger (auto.)
Dodge City, KS
Dodge Colt (auto.)
Dodge Dakota (auto.)
Dodge Dakota Quad Cab (auto.)
Dodge Dakota R/T (auto.)
Dodge Dakota SLT (auto.)
Dodge Dakota Sport (auto.)
Dodge Daytona (auto.)
Dodge Durango (auto.)
Dodge Durango R/T (auto.)
Dodge Durango SLT (auto.)
Dodge Dynasty (auto.)
Dodge Grand Caravan (auto.)
Dodge Grand Caravan ES (auto.)
Dodge Intrepid (auto.)
Dodge Intrepid ES (auto.)
Dodge Intrepid R/T (auto.)
Dodge Intrepid SE (auto.)
Dodge Neon (auto.)
Dodge Neon ES (auto.)

Dodge Neon Highline (auto.)
Dodge Neon R/T (auto.)
Dodge Omni (auto.)
Dodge Ram (auto.)
Dodge Ram 1500 pickup (auto.)
Dodge Ram 2500 pickup (auto.)
Dodge Ram 3500 pickup (auto.)
Dodge Ram pickup (auto.)
Dodge Ram Van (auto.)
Dodge Ram Van 1500 (auto.)
Dodge Ram Van 2500 (auto.)
Dodge Ram Van 3500 (auto.)
Dodge Ram Van B150 (auto.)
Dodge Ram Wagon (auto.)
Dodge Ram Wagon 1500 (auto.)
Dodge Ram Wagon 2500 (auto.)
Dodge Ram Wagon 3500 (auto.)
Dodge Ram Wagon B150 (auto.)
Dodge Shadow (auto.)
Dodge Spirit (auto.)
Dodge Stealth (auto.)
Dodge Stealth R/T (auto.)
Dodge Stratus (auto.)
Dodge Stratus ES (auto.)
Dodge Stratus R/T (auto.)
Dodge Stratus SE (auto.)
Dodge Viper (auto.)
Dodge Viper GTS coupe (auto.)
Dodge Viper RT/10 roadster (auto.)
Dodge, Mary Abigail (pseud. Gail Hamilton)(US writer; 1833-96)
Dodge, Mary Elizabeth Mapes (US writer/editor; 1831-1905)
Dodge/Plymouth Neon (auto.)
Dodge/Plymouth Neon R/T (auto.)
Dodgem (carnival bumper cars)
Dodger Stadium (Los Angeles)
Dodgers, Los Angeles (baseball team)
Dodgson, Charles (pseud. Lewis Carroll)(Br. writer/math.; 1832-98)
Dodi Al Fayed (Br. news; 1955-97)
Dodoma, Tanzania
Dody (Delores) Goodman (ent.; 1929-)
Doe, Jane (unidentified or "any" woman)
Doe, John (unidentified or "any" man)
Doesburg, Theo van (Dutch artist/writer; 1883-1931)
Doeskin Products (US bus.)
Dog Day Afternoon (film, 1975)
Dog Fancy (mag.)
Dog Star (astron., part of Canis Major [or Great Dog])
Dog World (mag.)
Dog, Great (astron., Canis Major, includes the Dog Star, Sirius)
Dogpatch, U.S.A.
Dogri (lang.)
Doha, Qatar
Doherty, Shannen (ent.; 1971-)
Dohnányi, Ernst (or Ernö) von (Hung. pianist/ comp.; 1877-1960)
Doister, Ralph Roister (Nicholas Udall comedy)
DOJ (Department of Justice)(US govt.)
DOL (Department of Labor)(US govt.)
Dolby Laboratories, Inc.

Dolby sound system
Dolce Vita, La (film, 1960)
Dolcetto (wine)
Dole Foods Co.
Dole, (Mary) Elizabeth "Liddy" (nee Hanford)
  (US pol.; 1936-)
Dole, Bob (Robert Joseph)(US pol.; 1923-)
Dole, Sanford B. (ex-gov., HI; 1844-1921)
Dolin, Anton, Sir (b. Patrick Healey-Kay)(Br.
  ballet; 1904-83)
Doll's House (H. Ibsen play)
Dollar General Corp.
Dollar Rent-A-Car Systems, Inc.
Dolley (Payne Todd) Madison (wife of ex-US
  pres.; 1768-1849)
Dollfuss, Engelbert (ex-chanc. Aus.; 1892-1934)
Dolly Parton (ent.; 1946-)
Dolly Varden (clothing style)
Dolly Varden (fict. chara.)
Dolly Varden trout (colorful fish)
Dolobid (med.)
Dologuele, Anicet Georges (PM, Central African
  Republic)
Dolophine (med./narcotic)
Dolores Del Rio (ent.; 1908-83)
Dolph (Hans) Lundgren (ent.; 1959-)
Dolphins, Miami (football team)
Dolphy, Eric (US jazz; 1928-64)
Dom DeLuise (ent.; 1933-)
Dom DiMaggio (baseball; 1917-)
Dom(inic) Mintoff (ex-PM, Malta; 1916-)
Dom Naroda (aka House of Peoples) (Bosnia-
  Hercegovina)
Dom Pérignon, Curvée (champagne)
Dome of the Rock (Jerusalem)
Domenici, Pete V. (US cong.; 1932-)
Domenico Cimarosa (It. comp.; 1749-1801)
Domenico Scarlatti, (Giuseppe)(It. comp.;
  1685-1757)
Domesday Book (also Doomsday Book)(Br.
  Wm. the Conqueror land surveys)
Domestic Policy Council (US govt.)
Domingo, Placido (Sp. tenor; 1941-)
Domínguez, Hipólita Mejía (pres., 1941-)
Dominic, St. (Sp. rel., founded Dominican
  order; 1170-1221)
Dominica (Commonwealth of)
Dominican order (Catholic friars)
Dominican Republic (West Indies)
Dominick Dunne (US writer; 1926-)
Dominion Day (now Canada Day)
Dominique (also Dominick) chicken
Domino, Fats (Antoine)(ent.; 1928-)
Domino's Pizza, Inc.
Dominquin, Luis Miguel (Sp. matador; 1926-)
Dominus (God)
Dominus vobiscum (Latin, the Lord be with you)
Domoni, Comoros
Don (Sp. & It. male title)
Don Adams (ent.; 1926-)
Don Ameche (b. Dominic Amici)(ent.; 1908-93)
Don Budge (tennis; 1915-2000)
Don Byas (US jazz; 1912-72)
Don Carlos (F. von Schiller play, Verdi opera)
Don Carlos (prince, Spain; 1545-68)

Don Cheadle (ent.; 1964-)
Don Defore (ent.; 1913-93)
Don Drysdale (baseball; 1937-93)
Don (Donald Louis) Evans (US secy./
  commerce; 1946-)
Don Everly (b. Isaac Everly)(ent.; 1937-)
Don Giovanni (by Mozart)
Don Giovanni (Don Juan)(Sp. legend)
Don Henley (ent.; 1947-)
Don Ho (ent.; 1930-)
Don Hudson (football; 1913-)
Don Imus (b. John Donald Imus, Jr.)(radio
  host; 1940-)
Don Johnson (ent.; 1949-)
Don Juan (Don Giovanni)(Sp. legend)
Don King (boxing promoter; 1931-)
Don Knotts (ent.; 1924-)
Don Martin (cartoonist, *Mad* magazine; 1931-
  2000)
Don Mattingly (baseball; 1961-)
Don McLean (ent./songwriter; 1945-)
Don Michael Paul (ent.; 1963-)
Don Murray (ent.; 1929-)
Don Quixote (film, 1935, 1957)
Don Quixote de la Mancha (by Cervantes)
Don Redman (US jazz; 1900-64)
Don Rickles (ent.; 1926-)
Don (Donald Francis) Shula (football; 1930-)
Don Siegelman (Donald Eugene)(AL gov.; 1946-)
Don (Kenneth) Sundquist (TN gov.; 1936-)
Don (Donald Howard) Sutton (baseball; 1945-)
Dona (also Doña)(Sp. female title)
Donahue, Elinor (ent.; 1937-)
Donahue, Heather (ent.; 1973-)
Donahue, Phil (ent.; 1935-)
Donahue, Phil (TV show)
Donahue, Troy (b. Merle Johnson)(ent.; 1936-
  2001)
Donald Barthelme (writer; 1931-89)
Donald Crisp (ent.; 1880-1974)
Donald Duck (cartoon chara.)
Donald E(dward) Newhouse (US publ.; 1929-)
Donald E. Westlake (US writer; 1933-)
Donald Gramm (Grambach)(bass-baritone;
  1927-83)
Donald (Andrew) Hall, (Jr.)(US poet; 1928-)
Donald Henry Rumsfeld (US secy./defense;
  1932-)
Donald Hutson (football; 1913-97)
Donald Kent "Deke" Slayton (astro.; 1924-93)
Donald Lee Nickles (US cong.; 1948-)
Donald Moffat (ent.; 1930-)
Donald O'Connor (ent.; 1925-)
Donald P. Bellisario (US writer/producer; 1936-)
Donald Pleasence (ent.; 1919-95)
Donald Schollander (swimming; 1946-)
Donald Sutherland (ent.; 1934-)
Donald (John) Trump (US bus.; 1946-)
Donald W. Riegle, Jr. (US pol.; 1938-)
Donald's Quack Attack (TV show)
Donaldson, Sam (US TV jour.; 1934-)
Donaldson, Walter (US comp.; 1893-1947)
Donat, Robert (ent.; 1905-58)
Donatella Versace (designer; 1955-)
Donatello (It. sculptor; 1386-1466)

Donatien Alphonse François, Comte de Sade (Marquis de Sade)(Fr. mil./writer; 1740-1814)
Donato D'Agnolo Bramante (It. arch.; 1444-1514)
Donegal (county, Ir.)
Donegal tweed (fabric)
Donegal, Ireland
Donegan (railroad slang)
Donen, Stanley (ent.; 1924-)
Donetsk, Ukraine
Dong (lang.)
Dong, Lee Han (PM, SKorea; 1934-)
Dong, Pham Van (ex-PM, NViet.; 1906-2000)
Donizetti, Gaetano (It. comp.; 1797-1848)
Donlevy, Brian (ent.; 1889-1972)
Donn F. Eisele (astro.; 1930-87)
Donna De Varona (swimming/sportscaster; 1947-)
Donna Dixon (ent.; 1957-)
Donna Douglas (b. Doris Smith)(ent.; 1939-)
Donna E(dna) Shalala (US ex-secy./HHS; 1941-)
Donna Fargo (ent.; 1945-)
Donna Karan (US designer; 1948-)
Donna Maria Caponi (golf; 1945-)
Donna McKechnie (ent.; 1942-)
Donna Mills (ent.; 1942-)
Donna Reed (ent.; 1921-86)
Donna Reed Show, The (TV show)
Donna Rice (US news; 1958-)
Donna Summer (b. LaDonna Gaines)(ent.; 1948-)
Donnatal (med.)
Donne, John (Br. poet; 1573-1631)
Donnelley & Sons, R. R. (US bus.)
Donner Party (CA; 1846-47)
Donner Pass, CA
Donner, Richard (ent.; 1939-)
Donnie Brasco (film, 1996)
Donnie Wahlberg (ent.; 1969-)
Donny Anderson, (Gary)(football; 1949-)
Donny Osmond (ent.; 1958-)
D'Onofrio, Vincent (ent.; 1959-)
Donovan (b. Donovan Leitch)(ent./songwriter; 1946-)
Donovan, William Joseph ("Wild Bill")(US mil.; 1883-1959)
Donovan's Reef (film, 1963)
Doobie Brothers (also the Doobies)(pop music)
Doodles (Winstead) Weaver (ent.; 1912-83)
Doody, Howdy (fict. chara.)
Doogie Howser, M.D. (TV show)
Doohan, James R. (Scotty on *Star Trek*)
Dooley Wilson (ent.; 1894-1953)
Dooley, Thomas A. (US phys.; 1927-61)
Dooley, Tom (song)
Doolittle, Doctor (film, 1967, 1998)
Doolittle, Eliza (fict. chara., *Pygmalion*)
Doolittle, Hilda ("HD")(US poet; 1886-1961)
Doolittle, James Harold (US aviator; 1896-93)
Doomsday Book (also Domesday Book)(Br. Wm. the Conqueror land surveys)
Doone, Lorna (R.D. Blackmore novel)
Doonesbury (comic strip)
Doors, the (pop music)
Dopar (med.)
Doppelgänger (Ger., phantom double)

Doppler effect (physics)(sound/light waves)
Doppler shift (astron.)
Doppler, Christian (Aus. physt.; 1803-53)
Dorado (astron., goldfish)
Dorati, Antal (Hung. cond.; 1906-88)
Dorcas society (church women who help poor)
Dore Schary (US writer/ent./reformer; 1905-80)
Doré, Gustave (Fr. artist; 1832-83)
Doren, Charles Van (US educ./TV scandal)
Doren, Mamie Van (ent.; 1933-)
Dorgan, Byron L(eslie)(US cong.; 1942-)
Doria, Andrea (It. adm./pol.; 1466-1560)
Dorian Gray, The Picture of (O. Wilde novel)
Dorian Harewood (ent.; 1950-)
Dorians (ancient Gk. division/people)
Doric (also Doric order)(arch. column)
Do-Right, Dudley, Mountie (fict. chara.)
Doris (May Taylor) Lessing (Br. writer; 1919-)
Doris Day (b. Doris von Kappelhoff)(ent.; 1924-)
Doris Duke (US finan.; 1913-93)
Doris (Helen) Kearns Goodwin (US hist.; 1943-)
Doris Roberts (ent.; 1929-)
Dorking chicken (Br., 5 toes instead of 4)
Dorland's Medical Dictionary
Dormouse, the (fict. chara.)
Dorn, Michael (ent.; 1952-)
Dorothea Dix (US educ./reformer; 1802-87)
Dorothea Lange (US photo.; 1895-1965)
Dorothy (fict. chara., *Wizard of Oz*)
Dorothy bag (handbag)
Dorothy Bush (nee Walker)(US grandmother of pres./mother of ex-pres.; 1901-92)
Dorothy Chandler Pavilion (Los Angeles)
Dorothy Dandridge (ent.; 1923-65)
Dorothy Day (US reformer; 1897-1980)
Dorothy Fields (US lyricist; 1905-74)
Dorothy Gish (ent.; 1898-1968)
Dorothy Gray Cosmetics, Ltd.
Dorothy (Stuart) Hamill (figure skating; 1956-)
Dorothy Kilgallen (US columnist/ent.; 1913-65)
Dorothy Kirsten (US opera; 1919-92)
Dorothy Lamour (ent.; 1914-96)
Dorothy Loudon (ent.; 1933-)
Dorothy L(eigh) Sayers (Br. writer; 1893-1957)
Dorothy Malone (ent.; 1925-)
Dorothy Mary Crowfoot Hodgkin (Br. chem.; 1910-94)
Dorothy McGuire (ent.; 1919-)
Dorothy (Rothschild) Parker (US writer; 1893-1967)
Dorothy Provine (ent.; 1937-)
Dorothy Sarnoff (ent.; 1917-)
Dorothy Schiff (US publ.; 1903-89)
Dorothy Thompson (US writer; 1894-1961)
Dorothy Wordsworth (Br. writer; 1771-1855)
Dorough, Howie (ent., Backstreet Boys; 1973-)
Dorset (county, Eng.)(also Dorsetshire)
Dorset Horn (sheep)
Dorsett, Tony (football; 1954-)
Dorsey, Jimmy (US cond.; 1904-57)
Dorsey, Thomas Andrew (father of gospel music; 1899-1993)
Dorsey, Tommy (US cond.; 1905-56)
Dortmund, Germany
Dory, John (fish)

DOS (disk operating system)(compu.)
Dos Equis XX (beer)
Dos Passos, John (US writer; 1896-1970)
dos Santos Daio, Daniel Lima (ex-PM, São Tomé/Príncipe)
dos Santos, José Eduardo (pres., Angola; 1942-)
Dostoyevsky, Fyodor (also Dostoevsky)(Rus. writer; 1821-81)
DOT (Department of Transportation)(US govt.)
Dothan, AL
Dotrice, Roy (ent.; 1923-)
Dottie West (ent.; 1932-91)
Dou, Gerard (also Dow or Douw)(Dutch artist; 1613-75)
Douala, Cameroon (also Duala)
Douay Bible (also Douay Version)
Double Dutch
Doubleday & Co., Inc.
Doubleday Book Club
Doubleday Book Shop
Doubleday Dell Publishing Group, Inc., Bantam
Doubleday, Abner (US mil., possibly inv. baseball; 1819-93)
Doubleday, Frank Nelson (US publ.; 1862-1934)
Doubtfire, Mrs. (film, 1993)
doubting Thomas
Doug Coupland (US writer/*Generation X*; 1961-)
Doug Henning (ent.; 1947-2000)
Doug McClure (ent.; 1935-95)
Dougan, Angel Serafin Seriche (PM, Equatorial Guinea; 1946-)
Douglas Corp., McDonnell
Douglas debates, Lincoln- (US hist.; 1858)
Douglas Edwards (US TV jour.; 1917-90)
Douglas Fairbanks, Jr. (ent.; 1909-2000)
Douglas Fairbanks, Sr. (ent.; 1883-1939)
Douglas fir (tree)
Douglas Haig (Br. mil.; 1861-1928)
Douglas-Home, Sir Alexander "Alec" Frederick (ex-PM, Br.; 1903-95)
Douglas-Home, William (Br. writer; 1912-92)
Douglas MacArthur (US gen.; 1880-1964)
Douglas pine (tree)
Douglas spruce (tree)
Douglas Wilder, L(awrence)(ex-VA gov.; 1931-)
Douglas, Aaron (US artist; 1900-79)
Douglas, Buster (James)(boxing; 1960-)
Douglas, Denzil L(lewellyn)(PM, St. Kitts-Nevis; 1953-)
Douglas, Donna (b. Doris Smith)(ent.; 1939-)
Douglas, Illeana (ent.; 1965-)
Douglas, Kirk (b. Issur Danielovich Demsky)(ent.; 1916-)
Douglas, Marjory Stoneman (US writer/environ. activist; 1890-1998)
Douglas, Melvyn (ent.; 1901-81)
Douglas, Michael (ent.; 1944-)
Douglas, Mike (b. Michael D. Dowd, Jr.)(TV jour.; 1925-)
Douglas, Paul (ent.; 1907-59)
Douglas, Stephen A. (US pol./orator; 1813-61)
Douglas, William O(rville)(US jurist; 1898-1980)
Douglass, Frederick (US abolitionist, ex-slave; 1817-95)
Dourda, Abu Said Omar (ex-PM, Libya)

Douw, Gerard (also Dou or Dow)(Dutch artist; 1613-75)
Dove, Arthur (US artist; 1880-1946)
Dove, Rita (US poet; 1952-)
Dover Air Force Base, DE (mil.)
Dover sole (fish)
Dover, DE, NH, NJ, OH, TN
Dover, England
Dover, Strait of (Eng./Fr.)
Dovre wood stove
Dovre, Inc.
Dow Chemical Co., The
Dow Jones & Co.
Dow Jones Average (NY Stock Exchange index)
Dow Jones Index
Dow Jones News/Retrieval (compu. database)
Dow, Charles (US finan.; 1851-1902)
Dow, Gerard (also Dou or Douw)(Dutch artist; 1613-75)
Dow, Herbert H(enry)(US bus./chem.; 1866-1930)
Dow, Tony (ent.; 1945-)
Dowding, Hugh C. (Br. mil.; 1883-1970)
Dowiyogo, Bernard (pres., Nauru; 1946-)
Down (county, NIre)
Down East (mag.)
Down, Leslie-Ann (ent.; 1954-)
Down's (or Down) syndrome (med.)
Downey, Morton, Jr. (ent./writer/comp.; 1933-2001)
Downey, Morton, Sr. (ent./tenor; 1901-85)
Downey, Robert, Jr. (ent.; 1965-)
Downey, Roma (ent.; 1960-)
Downing Street (London, site of Br. govt.)
Downs, Hugh (ent.; 1921-)
Downy (clothes softener)
Downyflake (waffles)
Doxidan (med.)
Doxology, the (rel.)
Doxsee Food Corp.
Doxy-Caps (med.)
Doxy-Tabs (med.)
Doyle, David (ent.; 1929-97)
Doyle, Popeye (fict. chara., *The French Connection*)
Doyle, Sir Arthur Conan (Br. phys./writer, Sherlock Holmes; 1859-1930)
D'Oyly Carte Opera Company (Birmingham, Eng.)
D'Oyly Carte, Richard (Br. opera; 1844-1901)
Dozier, Lamont (US comp.; 1941-)
DP (dew point)
Dr. *(see Doctor)*
Drabble, Margaret (Br. writer; 1939-)
Drackett Products Co.
Draco (astron., dragon)
Draco (Gr. pol.; 7th c. BC)
Draconian laws (severe; 7th c. BC)
Dracula (film, 1931, 1973, 1979)
Dracula, Brides of (film, 1960)
Dracula, Count (vampire based on Vlad Tepes, the Impaler)
Dragnet (TV show)
Dragon, Carmen (cond.; 1914-84)
Dragon, Daryl (ent., The Captain & Tennille; 1942-)
Dragons, Dungeons & (compu. game)
Draize test (Rabbit's eye test)

Drake, Alfred (b. Alfred Capurro)(ent.; 1914-92)
Drake, Larry (ent.)
Drake, Sir Francis (Br. expl.; c1545-96)
Drake, Stan (cartoonist; 1921-97)
Dramamine (med.)
Drambuie (liqueur)
Drang, Sturm und (Storm and Stress)(Ger. lit.; 18th c.)
Drano (plumbing)
Draper, Ruth (ent.; 1889-1956)
Dravidian (lang./people)
DRC (aka Democratic Republic of the Congo, Congo-Kinshasa, Congo)(W central Afr.)(was Zaire)
Dream On (TV show)
Dreamgirls (play)
DreamWorks L.L.C. (US bus./films)
DreamWorks SKG (US bus./films)
Drechsler, Heike (Olympic long jumper/sprinter; 1964-)
Dred Scott (US slave; 1795?-1858)
Dred Scott Case/Decision (US law, pro-slavery; 1856-57)
D region
Dreiser, Theodore (US writer; 1871-1945)
Drescher, Fran (ent.; 1957-)
Dresden china/porcelain/ware (also Meissen)
Dresden, Germany
Dresser Industries
Dresser, Louise (ent.; 1881-1965)
Dressler, Marie (ent.; 1869-1934)
Drew Barrymore (ent.; 1975-)
Drew Carey (ent.; 1958-)
Drew Pearson (US jour.; 1897-1969)
Drew, Ellen (ent.; 1915-)
Drew, John, Mrs. (ent.; 1820-97)
Drew, Nancy (fict. chara.)
Drexel Burnham Lambert (US stock market scandal)
Drexel University (Philadelphia, PA)
Drexler, Clyde (basketball; 1962-)
Dreyer's Grand Ice Cream, Inc.
Dreyfus Affair
Dreyfus Corp., The
Dreyfus, Alfred (Fr. capt.; 1859-1935)
Dreyfus, Julia Louis- (ent.; 1961-)
Dreyfuss, Richard (ent.; 1947-)
Drifters, the (pop music)
D-ring (also D ring)(clothing closure)
Drinkwater, Terry (US TV jour.; 1936-)
Dristan (med.)
Driver, Minnie (ent.; 1970-)
Driving Miss Daisy (film, 1989)
Drixoral (med.)
Drnovsek, Janez (ex-PM, Slovenia; 1950-)
Drogheda, Ireland
Drood, Edwin (fict. chara., C. Dickens)
Droste (chocolate)
Droste USA, Ltd.
Drottningholm (palaces in Swed.)
Dru, Joanne (ent.; 1923-96)
Drucker, Mort (cartoonist, *Mad* magazine; 1929-)
Drudge, Matt (internet/TV jour., *Drudge Report*; 1966-)
Drug Administration, Food and (FDA)(US govt. agcy.)

Drug Control Policy, Office of National (US govt.)
Drug Emporium (US bus.)
Drug Enforcement Agency (DEA)
Drum, Fort (NY)(mil.)
Drummond, Bulldog (film, 1929)
Drummondville, Quebec, Canada
Drumstick (ice cream)
Drumstick Co.
Drury Lane theatre (London)
Druse (also Druze)(rel.)
Druten, John (William) Van (US writer; 1901-57)
Dry Ice
Dry Ice Corp. of America
Dryden Flight Research Center (CA)
Dryden, John (Br. writer; 1631-1700)
Dryden, John Fairchild (US bus./pol.; 1839-1911)
Dryden, Kenneth (hockey; 1947-)
Dryer, Fred (ent.; 1946-)
Drysdale, Don (baseball; 1937-93)
DSAR (Distinguished Service Award Recipient)
DSC (Distinguished Service Cross)
DSM (Distinguished Service Metal)
DSO (Distinguished Service Order)
DST (daylight-saving time)
DT's (delirium tremens)
Dual Alliance
Dual Entente (Fr./Rus. alliance; 1893-1917)
Duala, Cameroon (also Douala)
Duane Allman (ent.; 1946-71)
Duane Eddy (ent.; 1938-)
Duane Hanson (US sculptor; 1925-)
Duarte, José Napoleon (ex-pres., El Salvador; 1925-90)
Dubai (state, UAE)
du Barry, Madame (Jeanne Bécu)(Comtesse, mistress, Louis XV; 1743-93)
Dubavy, United Arab Emirates
Dubcek, Alexander (Czech. pol.; 1921-92)
Dubin, Al (US lyricist; 1891-1945)
Dubinsky, David (US labor leader; 1892-1982)
Dublin, Ireland
Du Bois Wines, Clos (US bus.)
Du Bois, W(illiam) E(dward) B(urghardt)(US educ./writer, NAACP; 1868-1963)
Dubonnet (wine)
DuBose Heyward (US lyricist; 1885-1940)
Dubrovnik, Croatia
Dubuffet, Jean (Fr. artist; 1902-85)
Dubuque, IA
Dubya (George W. Bush's nickname)
Duce, Il (aka Benito Mussolini)(ex-PM, It.; 1883-1945)
Duchamp, Marcel (Fr. artist; 1887-1968)
Duchamp-Villon, Raymond (Fr. artist; 1876-1918)
Duchin, Eddy (ent.; 1909-51)
Duchin, Peter (US pianist/band leader; 1937-)
Duchovny, David (ent.; 1960-)
Duck Soup (film, 1933)
Duck, Daffy (cartoon chara.)
Duck, Daisy (cartoon chara.)
Duck, Donald (cartoon chara.)
Dudelange, Luxembourg
Dudevant, Amandine Aurore Lucie (b. Dupin) (pseud. George Sand)(Fr. writer; 1804-76)
Dudley Digges (ent.; 1879-1947)

Dudley Do-Right, Mountie (fict. chara.)
Dudley Moore (ent.; 1935-)
Dudley Robert Herschbach (US chem.; 1932-)
Duel in the Sun (film, 1946)
Dufay, Guillaume (Flemish comp.; c1400-74)
Duff, Howard (ent.; 1914-90)
Duffy, Julia (ent.; 1951-)
Duffy, Patrick (ent. 1949-)
Dufour, Val (ent.; 1927-2000)
Dufy, Raoul (Fr. artist; 1877-1953)
DUI (driving under the influence)
Duisburg, Germany (formerly Duisburg-Hamborn)
Dukakis, Kitty (Katharine)(nee Dickson)(US wife of ex-MA gov.; 1937-)
Dukakis, Michael S(tanley)(ex-MA gov.; 1933-)
Dukakis, Olympia (ent.; 1931-)
Dukas, Paul (Fr. comp.; 1865-1935)
Duke Astin, Patty (ent.; 1946-)
Duke Ellington (Edward Kennedy)(US comp./US jazz; 1899-1974)
Duke Energy (US bus.)
Duke Kahanamoku (Olympic swimmer; 1890-1968)
Duke of Alba (also Alva, Fernando Alvarez de Toledo)(Sp. pol.; 1508-82)
Duke of Albemarle (George Monck)(Br. mil./pol.; 1608-70)
Duke of Argyll (John D. S. Campbell)(ex-gov.-gen., Can.; 1845-1914)
Duke of Edinburgh, (Philip Mountbatten, Lt., Prince of the UK and NIre.; 1921-)
Duke of Marlborough (John Churchill)(Br. mil.; 1650-1722)
Duke of Paducah (aka Whitey [Edward Charles] Ford)(baseball; 1928-)
Duke of Wellington (Arthur Wellesley)(Br. mil.; 1769-1852)
Duke of Windsor (Edward VIII)(abdicated Br. throne; 1894-1972)
Duke (Edwin) Snider (baseball; 1926-)
Duke University (Durham, NC)
Duke, Charles M., Jr. (astro.; 1935-)
Duke, David (US pol.; 1950-)
Duke, Doris (US finan.; 1913-93)
Duke, James (US bus.; 1856-1925)
Duke, the (nickname, John Wayne)
Duke, Vernon (US comp.; 1903-69)
Dukes, David (ent.; 1945-2000)
Dukham, Qatar
Dukhobors (people)
Dulcolax (med.)
Dullea, Keir (ent.; 1936-)
Dulles International Airport (DC/VA)
Dulles, John Foster (US pol.; 1888-1959)
Duluth News-Tribune (MN newspaper)
Duluth, MN
Dumas, Alexandre (aka Dumas fils)(Fr. writer; 1824-95)
Dumas, Alexandre (aka Dumas peré)(Fr. writer; 1802-70)
Du Maurier, Daphne (Br. writer; 1907-89)
du Maurier, George Louis Palmella Busson (Br. writer/artist; 1834-96)
Dumbarton Oaks (estate in Washington DC)
Dumbbell Nebula/nebula (astron.)

Dumbo (fict. flying elephant)
Dumbo's Circus (TV show)
Dumitru Braghis (PM, Moldova; 1957-)
Dumont, Alberto Santos- (Fr. aviator; 1873-1932)
Dumont, Margaret (ent.; 1889-1965)
Dumpster (refuse container)
Dun & Bradstreet Corp.
Dun's (mag.)
Dunaway, Faye (ent.; 1941-)
Dunbar, Paul Laurence (US poet/novelist; 1872-1906)
Dunbar-Nelson, Alice (US writer; 1875-1935)
Duncan Phyfe (Scot./US furniture maker; c1768-1854)
Duncan, Isadora (US dancer; 1878-1927)
Duncan, Michael Clarke (ent.; 1957-)
Duncan, Sandy (ent.; 1946-)
Dundalk, MD
Dundee, Major (film, 1965)
Dundee, Crocodile (film, 1986)
Dundee 2, Crocodile (film, 1988)
Dundee, Scotland
Dunedin, New Zealand
Dunem, Fernando Jose de Franca Dias van (ex-PM, Angola)
Dunem, Fernando van (PM, Angola)
Dungeness crab
Dungeons & Dragons (compu. game)
Dunham, Katherine (ent.; 1910-)
Dunkers (also Church of the Brethren, Amish, Mennonites, Plain People)(rel.)
Dunkin' Donuts of America, Inc.
Dunkirk, France
Dunkirk, IN, NY
Dunlap, Inc., Grosset &
Dunlop (cheese)
Dunlop Sports Corp.
Dunlop Tire Corp.
Dunn, James (ent.; 1905-67)
Dunne, Dominick (US writer; 1926-)
Dunne, Griffin (ent.; 1955-)
Dunne, Irene (ent.; 1898-1990)
Dunne, John Gregory (US writer; 1932-)
Duns Scotus, John ("Doctor Subtilis")(Scot. rel; 1265?-1308)
Dunsinane (hill in Scot.)
Dunsmore, Barrie (US jour.)
Dunst, Kirsten (ent.; 1982-)
Du Pont chemicals
Du Pont Circle (DC traffic circle)
du Pont de Nemours & Co. E. I.
du Pont de Nemours, E(leuthere) I. (US bus.; 1771-1834)
Du Pont fibers
du Pont Pharmaceuticals (US bus.)
du Pont, Henry (Belin)(US bus.; 1899-1970)
du Pont, Henry (US bus.; 1812-89)
du Pont, Henry Algernon (US mil./pol.; 1838-1926)
Dupont, Jacques (minister/state, Monaco)
Du Pont, Pierre Samuel (Fr. econ./pol.; 1739-1817)
du Pont, Pierre Samuel (US bus.; 1870-1954)
du Pont, Samuel Francis (US mil.; 1803-65)
du Pont, Thomas Coleman (US bus./pol.; 1863-

1930)
Duquesne University (Pittsburgh, PA)
Duracell (batteries)
Duracell Co. USA, The
Duramorph (med.)
Duran Duran (pop music)
Durán Bellén, Sixto (ex-pres., Ecuador; 1921-)
Duran, Roberto (boxing; 1951-)
Durand, Asher Brown (US artist; 1796-1886)
Durango, Dodge (auto.)
Durango, Mexico
Durant, Ariel (US hist.; 1898-1981)
Durant, Thomas C. (US bus./finan.; 1820-85)
Durant, Will (US hist.; 1885-1981)
Durant, William C. (US bus., GM; 1861-1947)
Durante, Jimmy (James Francis)(ent.; 1893-1980)
Duraphyl (med.)
Duraquin (med.)
Duras, Marguerite (Donnadieu)(writer; 1914-96)
Duration (med.)
Durban, South Africa
D'Urbervilles, Tess of the (T. Hardy novel)
Durbin, Deanna (ent.; 1921-)
Durbin, Richard J. (US cong.; 1944-)
Durenberger, David F. (US pol.; 1934-)
Dürer, Albrecht (Ger. artist; 1471-1528)
Durga (Hindu goddess)
Durham (county, Eng.)
Durham, Bull (film, 1988)
Durham, England
Durham, NC, NH
Duricef (med.)
Durkee
Durkee French Foods (US bus.)
Durkheim, Emile (Fr. sociol.; 1858-1917)
Durning, Charles (ent.; 1923-)
Durocher, Leo (baseball; 1906-91)
Durr, Francois (tennis; 1942-)
Durrell, Lawrence (Br. writer; 1912-90)
Durres, Albania
Durward Kirby (ent.; 1912-2000)
Duryea, Dan (ent.; 1907-68)
Dusan Mihajlovic (Serbian pol.)
Duse, Eleonora (ent.; 1858-1924)
Dushanbe, Tajikistan
Dussault, Nancy (ent.; 1936-)
Düsseldorf, Germany
Dust Bowl (KS/OK/TX/NM/CO)
Dustin Hoffman (ent.; 1937-)
Dustin Nguyen (ent.; 1962-)
Dusty Springfield (b. Mary O'Brien) (ent.;
    1939-99)
Dutch (lang./people)
Dutch Belted cattle
Dutch bob (hair style)
Dutch Borneo (now Kalimantan)
Dutch cap (headwear)
Dutch door
Dutch East India Company (trade; 1602-1798)
Dutch East Indies (now Indonesia)
Dutch elm disease
Dutch-Flemish (lang.)
Dutch Guiana (now Suriname)
Dutch oven
Dutch Reformed Church

Dutch treat (share expenses)
Dutch uncle
Dutch West India Co. (1621-1794)
Dutchman's-breeches (plant)
Dutchman's-pipe (plant)
Dutton, E(dward) P(ayson)(US publ.; 1831-1923)
Duvalier, François (aka Papa Doc)(ex-pres.,
    Haiti; 1907-71)
Duvalier, Jean-Claude (aka Baby Doc)(ex-pres.,
    Haiti; 1951-)
Duvall, Robert (ent.; 1931-)
Duvall, Shelley (ent.; 1949-)
Duvall's Bedtime Stories, Shelley (TV show)
du Val Wine Co., Ltd., The Clos
Duvoid (med.)
DVM (Doctor of Veterinary Medicine)
Dvorak, Anton (also Antonin)(Czech. comp.;
    1841-1904)
Dweezil Zappa (ent.; 1969-)
D(avid) W(ark) Griffith (ent.; 1875-1948)
DWI (driving while intoxicated)
Dwight D(avid) Eisenhower (34th US pres.;
    1890-1969)
Dwight Edwin Stones (track; 1953-)
Dwight Gooden (baseball; 1964-)
Dwight Hemion (ent.)
Dwight Lyman Moody (US rel.; 1837-99)
Dwight Yoakam (ent.; 1956-)
Dy (chem. sym., dysprosium)
Dyan Cannon (b. Samille Diane Friesen)(ent.;
    1937-)
Dyazide (med.)
Dyck, Sir Anthony van (Flem. artist; 1599-1641)
Dyerma (lang.)
Dyke Show, Dick Van (TV show)
Dyke, Dick Van (ent.; 1925-)
Dyke, Jerry Van (ent.; 1931-)
Dykstra, Lenny (baseball; 1963-)
Dylan (Marlais) Thomas (Welsh poet; 1914-53)
Dylan McDermott (ent.; 1961-)
Dylan, Bob (b. Robert Zimmerman)(US comp./
    ent.; 1941-)
Dylan, Jakob (ent.; 1969-)
Dymelor (med.)
DynaCirc (med.)
Dynamic Cooking System (kitchen appliances)
Dynapen (med.)
Dynasty, Dodge (auto.)
Dynel
Dyrenium (med.)
Dysart, Richard (ent.; 1929-)
Dzongkha (lang.)
Dzurinda, Mikuláš (PM, Slovakia; 1955-)

Ea (Babylonian god)
Eadweard Muybridge (aka Edward James Muggeridge)(US photo.; 1830-1904)
Eagle (auto.)
Eagle (potato chips)
Eagle Talon (auto.)
Eagle Vision (auto.)
Eagle Vision TSi (auto.)
Eagle, Reading (PA newspaper)
Eagle, Wichita (KS newspaper)
Eagles, Philadelphia (football team)
Eagles, the (pop music)
Eakins, Thomas (US artist; 1844-1916)
Eames (chair)
Eames, Charles (US arch./designer; 1907-78)
Eamon de Valera (ex-PM/pres., Ir.; 1882-1975)
E & J Gallo Winery (US bus.)
Eanes, Antonio dos Santos Ramalho (ex-pres., Port.; 1935-)
Earhart, Amelia (Mary)(US aviator; 1897-1937?)
Earl Anthony (bowling; 1938-)
Earl Averill (baseball; 1915-83)
Earl Bostic (ent.; 1913-65)
Earl Campbell (football; 1955-)
Earl Carrol's Vanities
Earl Grey (tea)
Earl H. Blaik (football; 1897-1989)
Earl "Fatha" Hines (US jazz; 1905-83)
Earl Holliman (ent.; 1928-)
Earl Morrall (football; 1934-)
Earl of Albemarle (George Monk [also Monck])(Br. mil./pol.; 1608-70)
Earl of Cardigan (James Thomas Brudenell (Br. mil./pol., cardigan sweater; 1797-1868)
Earl of Coventry (card game)
Earl of Essex (Robert Devereux)(Br. mil./pol.; 1566-1601)
Earl of Sandwich (John Montagu)(Br. pol.; 1718-92)
Earl of Shaftesbury (A. A. Cooper)(Br. reformer; 1801-85)
Earl of Southhampton (Henry Wriothesley)(Br. scholar; 1573-1624)
Earl Scheib (auto painting)
Earl Scheib, Inc.
Earl Scruggs (ent.; 1924-)
Earl Warren (US jurist; 1891-1974)
Earl Weaver (baseball; 1930-)
Earle Hyman (ent.; 1926-)
Earle, Steve (ent./songwriter; 1955-)
Early Modern English (lang.; c1550-1700)
Early, Jubal Anderson (US gen.; 1816-94)
Earnhardt, Dale (auto racing; 1951-2001)
Earp, Wyatt (Berry Stapp)(US frontier; 1848-1929)
Earth (planet)(also l.c.)
Earth Journal (mag.)
Earth Summit (UN Conference on Environment and Development)(June 1992)
Earth, Wind, and Fire (pop music)
Eartha Kitt (ent.; 1927-)
Earthlink, Inc.
Earthly Delights, Garden of (Bosch)
Earthwatch
Ease Sport (clothing)
Easley, Mike (Michael F.), Sr. (NC gov.; 1950-)
Easprin (med.)
East Berlin (now part of united Berlin, Ger.)
East China Sea (also Dong Hai)
East Flanders (province, Belgium)
East Germany (now part of united Germany)
East Goths (also Ostrogoths)(ancient Germans)
East India Company, British (trade; 1600-1873)
East India Company, Danish (trade; 1729-1801)
East India Company, Dutch (trade; 1602-1798)
East India Company, French (trade; 1664-1794)
East Indian (people)
East Indies (formerly SE Asia, now only Malay Archipelago)
East Lansing, MI
East London, South Africa
East Lynne, or The Elopement (E.P. Wood novel)
East of Eden (John Steinbeck novel)
East Orange, NJ
East Pakistan (now Bangladesh)
East Side Kids (film, 1940)
East Sussex (county, Eng.)
Easter (rel. holiday)
Easter egg
Easter Island (also Rapa Nui)(S Pac.)
Easter lily
Easter Rebellion (also Easter Rising)(Ir.; 1916)
Eastern Conference (basketball)
Eastern Hamitic (people)
Eastern Hemisphere
Eastern Orthodox Church (also Orthodox Eastern Church)(rel.)
Eastern Standard Time
Eastern Tsin (or Chin) dynasty (Ch.; 317-420)
Easterner
Eastertide
Eastman Kodak Company
Eastman, George (US inv./photo.; 1854-1932)
Easton, Sheena (b. Sheena Orr)(ent.; 1959-)
Eastwick, The Witches of (film, 1987)
Eastwood, Clint (ent.; 1930-)
Easy Rider (film, 1969)
Easy Street
Easy-Off (oven cleaner)
Eating Raoul (film, 1982)
Eating Well (mag.)
Eaton Corp.
Eaton Paper Co.
eau de Cologne
Eban, Aubrey Solomon "Abba" (Isr. pol.; 1915-)
eBay Inc.
Ebbets Field
Ebeid, Dr. Atef Muhammad (PM, Egypt; 1932-)
Ebenezer Butterick (US inv./tailor; 1826-1903)
Ebenezer Scrooge (fict. chara., *A Christmas Carol*)
Eber, José (hairstylist)
Ebersole, Christine (ent.; 1953-)
Ebersole, Dick (TV sports exec.)

Ebert, Friedrich (Ger. pol.; 1871-1925)
Ebert, Roger (US critic; 1942-)
Ebert, Siskel & (US critics)
Ebing, Richard von Krafft-, Baron (Ger. phys.; 1840-1902)
Ebony (mag.)
Ebony Man (mag.)
Ebsen, Buddy (b. Christian Ebsen, Jr.)(ent.; 1908-)
EBV (Epstein-Barr virus)(med.)
E(lwyn) B(rooks) White (US writer; 1899-1985)
EC (European Community)(pol./econ. alliance)
Ecclesiastes (rel., book of the Old Testament)
Ecclesiasticus (rel., Apocrypha)
Ecevit, Bülent (PM, Turk.; 1925-)
ECG (electrocardiogram)(also EKG)(med.)
Echeverría, Miquel Angel Rodríguez (pres., Costa Rica; 1940-)
Echlin, Inc.
Echo (myth.)
Echo (US space satellite)
Echo, Toyota (auto.)
EchoStar Communications Corporation
Eckerd (drug stores)
Eckersley, Dennis (baseball; 1954-)
E. C. Knight Co., U.S. v. (US law; 1895)
Eckrich meats
Eckrich, Armour Swift- (US bus.)
Eckstine, Billy (ent.; 1914-93)
Eclipse (CAT system)
Eclipse, Mitsubishi (auto.)
E. coli (med.)
Econoline, Ford (auto.)
Economic Advisers, Council of (US govt.)
Economic Community of West African States (ECOWAS)(est. 1975)
Economic Cooperation and Development, Organization for (OECD)(internat'l; est. 1961)
Economic Policy Council (US govt.)
Economic World
Ecotrin (med.)
Ecuador (Republic of)(SAmer.)
Ecuatoriana Airlines
Ecumedia News Service
Ed Ames (b. Edmond Dantes Urick)(ent.; 1927-)
Ed Asner (ent.; 1929-)
Ed Begley (ent.; 1901-70)
Ed Begley, Jr. (ent.; 1949-)
Ed Bradley (US TV jour.; 1941-)
Ed Burns (ent.; 1968-)
Ed Flanders (ent.; 1934-95)
Ed Gallagher (ent.)
Ed Giacomin (hockey; 1939-)
Ed Harris (ent.; 1950-)
Ed Herlihy (US radio/TV announcer; 1909-99)
Ed "Too Tall" Jones (football; 1951-)
Ed Lauter (ent.; 1940-)
Ed Marinaro (football/ent.; 1950-)
Ed McMahon (ent.; 1923-)
Ed(win Corley) Moses (US track; 1955-)
Ed Nelson (ent.; 1928-)
Ed O'Neill (ent.; 1946-)
Ed (Edward Vincent) Sullivan (ent.; 1902-74)
Ed Sullivan Show, The (TV show)
Ed(ward Davis) Wood, Jr. (ent.; 1924-78)
Ed Wynn (ent.; 1886-1966)

Ed, Mr. (fict. horse)
EDA (Economic Development Administration)
Edam cheese
Edam, Netherlands
Edberg, Stefan (tennis; 1966-)
EDD (Doctor of Education)
Edd "Kookie" Byrnes (ent.)
Edd Roush (baseball; 1893-1988)
Edd, Fred (US lyricist; 1936-)
Edda (also *Prose Edda*)(Icelandic folk tales)
Eddie Albert (b. Edward Albert Heimberger)(ent.; 1908-)
Eddie Anderson ("Rochester")(ent.; 1905-77)
Eddie Arcaro (George Edward)(jockey; 1916-97)
Eddie Bauer Expedition Outfitter (US bus.)
Eddie Bracken (ent.; 1920-)
Eddie Cantor (ent.; 1892-1964)
Eddie Cochran (ent.; 1938-60)
Eddie Condon (US jazz; 1904-73)
Eddie Davis ("Lockjaw")(US jazz; 1921-86)
Eddie Fisher (ent.; 1928-)
Eddie Floyd (ent./songwriter; 1935-)
Eddie Foy (ent.; 1857-1928)
Eddie Foy, Jr. (ent.; 1905-83)
Eddie Heywood (US jazz; 1916-89)
Eddie Holland (US comp.; 1939-)
Eddie Lopat (baseball; 1918-92)
Eddie Mathews (baseball; 1931-2001)
Eddie Merckx ("the Cannibal")(Belgian cyclist; 1945-)
Eddie Money (b. Eddie Mahoney)(ent.; 1949-)
Eddie Murphy (ent.; 1961-)
Eddie Murphy: Raw (film, 1987)
Eddie (Edward Thomas) Rabbitt (ent.; 1944-98)
Eddie (Edward Vernon) Rickenbacker, Capt. (US aviator; 1890-1973)
Eddie Shore (hockey; 1902-85)
Eddie Van Halen (ent.; 1957-)
Eddings, David (US writer; 1931-)
Eddy Arnold (ent.; 1918-)
Eddy Duchin (ent.; 1909-51)
Eddy, Duane (ent.; 1938-)
Eddy, Mary Baker (US, founder Christian Science; 1821-1910)
Eddy, Nelson (ent.; 1901-67)
Ede, Nigeria
Edecrin (med.)
Edel, Leon (US writer; 1907-97)
Edelman, Herb (ent.; 1933-96)
Edelman, Marian Wright (US social activist; 1939-)
Edelpilzkäse (cheese)
Eden, Barbara (ent.; 1934-)
Eden, Garden of (rel.)
Eden, (Sir) Anthony (Earl of Avon)(ex-PM, Br.; 1897-1977)
Eden, Villa Mt. (US bus.)
Ederle, Gertrude (swimming; 1906-)
Edgar Allan Poe (US writer; 1809-49)
Edgar Bergen (ent.; 1903-78)
Edgar Dégas (Fr. artist; 1834-1917)
Edgar D. Mitchell (astro.; 1930-)
Edgar (Albert) Guest (US writer; 1881-1959)
Edgar Lee Masters (US writer; 1869-1950)
Edgar Rice Burroughs (US writer; 1875-1950)

Edgar the Peaceful (king, Eng.; 944-975)
Edgar Winter (ent.; 1946-)
Edgar, Jim (James)(ex-IL gov.; 1946-)
Edgehill, Battle of (Eng.; 1642)
Edict of Nantes (Fr. hist.; 1598)
Edie Adams (b. Elizabeth Edith Enke)(ent.; 1929-)
Edie Brickell (ent.; 1966-)
Edie Falco (ent.; 1963-)
Edie McClurg (ent.; 1951-)
Edinburg, IN, TX
Edinburgh fog (dessert)
Edinburgh, Duke of (Philip Mountbatten, Lt.,
   Prince of the UK and NIre.; 1921-)
Edinburgh, Scotland
Edison Co., McGraw-
Edison effect (physics)
Edison, NJ
Edison, Thomas Alva (US inv.; 1847-1931)
Edith Cresson (ex-PM, Fr.; 1934-)
Edith Evans, Dame (ent.; 1888-1976)
Edith Hamilton (Ger./US educ./writer; 1867-1963)
Edith Head (US designer; 1898?-1981)
Edith Piaf (b. Edith Giovanna Gassion)(Fr. ent.;
   1915-63)
Edith Sitwell, Dame (Br. writer; 1887-1964)
Edith (Newbold Jones) Wharton (US writer;
   1862-1937)
Edmond O'Brien (ent.; 1915-85)
Edmond Rostand (Fr. writer; 1868-1918)
Edmond, OK
Edmonds, Kenneth "Babyface" (ent.; 1958-)
Edmonton Oilers (hockey team)
Edmonton, Alberta, Canada
Edmund Allenby (Br. mil.; 1861-1936)
Edmund Burke (Ir./Br. pol.; 1729-97)
Edmund Dantès (fict. chara., Count of Monte
   Cristo)
Edmund Gerald "Jerry" Brown, Jr. (ex-CA gov.;
   1938-)
Edmund Gerald "Pat" Brown, Sr. (ex-CA gov.;
   1905-96)
Edmund Gwenn (ent.; 1875-1959)
Edmund Halley (Br. astron.; 1656-1742)
Edmund Ho (chief exec., Macau, Ch.)
Edmund Husserl (Ger. phil.; 1859-1938)
Edmund II ("Ironside")(king, Eng.; c989-1016)
Edmund Kean (ent.; 1787-1833)
Edmund Muskie (US pol.; 1914-96)
Edmund P. Hillary, (Sir)(NewZeal. expl., Mt.
   Everest; 1919-)
Edmund (Jennings) Randolph (US atty.; 1753-
   1813)
Edmund Ruffin (US agriculturist; 1794-1865)
Edmund Spenser (Br. poet; 1552-99)
Edmund White (US writer; 1940-)
Edmund Wilson (US writer/critic; 1895-1972)
Edna Ferber (US writer; 1887-1968)
Edna St. Vincent Millay (US poet; 1892-1950)
Edna Valley Vineyard (US bus.)
Edo (lang.)
Edo de Waart (cond.; 1941-)
Édouard Balladur (ex-PM, Fr.; 1929-)
Édouard Daladier (Fr. pol.; 1884-1970)
Édouard Frank (ex-PM, Central African Republic)
Édouard Herriot (ex-PM/pres., Fr.; 1872-1957)

Édouard Lalo, (Victor Antoine)(Fr. comp.;
   1823-92)
Édouard Manet (Fr. artist; 1832-83)
Édouard Vuillard, (Jean)(Fr. artist; 1868-1940)
Edsel (Bryant) Ford (US bus./auto.; 1893-1943)
Edsel, Ford (auto.)
EDT (Eastern Daylight Time)
EDTA (crystalline solid used as food preservative)
Eduard A. Shevardnadze (pres., Georgia; 1928-)
Eduard Benes (Czech. pol.; 1884-1948)
Eduard Buchner (Ger. chem.; 1860-1917)
Eduardo Paolozzi (Br. sculptor; 1924-)
Educating Rita (film, 1983)
Education Association of the United States,
   National (NEA)(est. 1906)
Education Testing Service
Education, Department of (US govt.)
Educational Broadcasting Corp.
Educational, Scientific, and Cultural Organization,
   United Nations (UNESCO)(est. 1945)
Edvard (Hagerup) Grieg (Nor. comp.; 1843-1907)
Edvard Munch (Nor. artist; 1863-1944)
Edward A. Filene (US bus.; 1860-1937)
Edward Albee (US writer; 1928-)
Edward Albert (ent.; 1951-)
Edward Alexander MacDowell (US comp.; 1861-
   1908)
Edward Arnold (ent.; 1890-1956)
Edward Bellamy (US writer; 1850-98)
Edward Bennett Williams (US atty.; 1920-88)
Edward Bowes, Major (ent.; 1874-1946)
Edward Braddock (Br. gen. in Amer.; 1695-1755)
Edward Burne-Jones (Br. artist; 1833-98)
Edward Burns (ent./writer; 1968-)
Edward Channing (US hist.; 1856-1931)
Edward Charles "Whitey" Ford ("Duke of
   Paducah")(baseball; 1928-)
Edward Charles Pickering (US astron./physt.;
   1846-1919)
Edward Craven Walker (Br. inventor, Lava
   lamp; 1918-2000)
Edward Durell Stone (US arch.; 1902-75)
Edward Eggleston (US writer; 1837-1902)
Edward (William) Elgar, (Sir)(Br. comp.; 1857-
   1934)
Edward Estlin Cummings (pseud. e.e.
   cummings)(US poet; 1894-1962)
Edward Everett Hale (US writer/rel.; 1822-1909)
Edward Everett Horton (ent.; 1886-1970)
Edward Fenech Adami (PM, Malta; 1934-)
Edward Fitzgerald (Br. poet; 1809-83)
Edward George Dibbs (tennis; 1951-)
Edward G. Gibson (astro.; 1936-)
Edward Gibbon (Br. hist.; 1737-94)
Edward (St. John) Gorey (US illustrator/writer;
   1925-)
Edward G. Robinson (ent.; 1893-1973)
Edward (Richard George) Heath (ex-PM, Br.;
   1916-)
Edward Herrmann (ent.; 1943-)
Edward H(enry) Harriman (US bus.; 1848-1909)
Edward Hicks (US artist; 1780-1849)
Edward Hopper (US artist; 1882-1967)
Edward H(iggins) White, II (astro., 1st Amer. to
   walk in space; 1930-67)

Edward I (king, Eng.; 1239-1307)
Edward II (king, Eng.; 1284-1327)
Edward III (king, Eng.; 1312-77)
Edward IV (king, Eng.; 1442-83)
Edward J(ames) "Ted" Hughes (Br. poet; 1930-98)
Edward James Olmos (ent.; 1947-)
Edward Jenner (Br. phys., smallpox vaccine; 1749-1823)
Edward (Irving) Koch (ex-NYC mayor; 1924-)
Edward Koren (cartoonist; *New Yorker*; 1935-)
Edward Lawrie Tatum (US chem.; 1909-75)
Edward Lear (Br. artist/humorist; 1812-88)
Edward M. House (US dipl.; 1858-1938)
Edward McDowell (US comp.; 1861-1908)
Edward M(oore) "Ted" Kennedy (US cong., bro. of ex-pres.; 1932-)
Edward Mulhare (ent.; 1923-97)
Edward Norton (ent.; 1969-)
Edward O. Wilson (US zool.; 1929-)
Edward R(oscoe) Murrow (US TV jour.; 1908-65)
Edward R. Stettinius, Jr. (US bus./pol.; 1900-49)
Edward Sapir (Ger./US anthrop.; 1884-1939)
Edward Scissorhands (film, 1990)
Edward (Wyllis) Scripps (US publ.; 1854-1926)
Edward S. Harkness (US bus.; 1874-1940)
Edward Steichen (US photo.; 1879-1973)
Edward Stratemeyer (US writer; 1862-1930)
Edward Teach (also Thatch, Thach; Blackbeard) (pirate; ?-1718)
Edward Teller, Dr. (US physt., A-bomb/H-bomb; 1908-)
Edward the Black Prince (Prince of Wales; 1330-76)
Edward the Confessor (king, Eng.; 1003-66)
Edward the Elder (king, W Saxons; c870-924)
Edward the Martyr (king, Eng.; c963-978)
Edward T. Schafer (ex-ND gov.; 1946-)
Edward V (king, Eng.; 1470-83)
Edward Vernon "Eddie" Rickenbacker, Capt. (US aviator; 1890-1973)
Edward VI (king, Eng.; 1537-53)
Edward VII (king, Br.; 1841-1910)
Edward VIII, Duke of Windsor (abdicated Br. throne; 1894-1972)
Edward Villella (ballet; 1936-)
Edward William Brooke (US pol.; 1919-)
Edward Woodward (ent.; 1930-)
Edward, John (US psychic/medium)
Edward, Prince (Edward Anthony Richard Louis, Prince of the UK)(3rd son of Queen Elizabeth II; 1964-)
Edwards Air Force Base, CA (mil.)
Edwards, Anthony (ent.; 1962-)
Edwards, Blake (b. William Blake McEdwards)(ent.; 1922-)
Edwards, Douglas (US TV jour.; 1917-90)
Edwards, Edwin (Washington), Jr. (ex-LA gov.; 1927-)
Edwards, Gus (US comp.; 1879-1945)
Edwards, John (US cong.; 1953-)
Edwards, Jonathan (US rel.; 1703-58)
Edwards, Ralph (ent.; 1913-)
Edwards, Sherman (US comp.; 1919-81)
Edwards, Vincent (b. Vincent Edward Zoino) (ent.; 1928-96)
Edwin (Herbert) Land (US inv., Polaroid Land camera; 1910-91)
Edwin Arlington Robinson (US poet; 1869-1935)
Edwin Drood (fict. chara., C. Dickens)
Edwin (Washington) Edwards, Jr. (ex-LA gov.; 1927-)
Edwin Eugene "Buzz" Aldrin, Jr. (astro.; 1930-)
Edwin Markham (US poet; 1852-1940)
Edwin Meese III (US pol./ex-atty gen; 1931-)
Edwin M(cMasters) Stanton (US mil./pol.; 1814-69)
Edwin Newman (US writer; 1919-)
Edwin P. Christy (ent.; 1815-62)
Edwin P(owell) Hubble (US astron.; 1889-1953)
Edwin Thomas Booth (US actor, bro. of John Wilkes; 1833-93)
EEA (European Economic Area)(est. 1994)
EEC (European Economic Community)(also Common Market, est. 1957)
e. e. cummings (b. Edward Estlin Cummings) (US poet; 1894-1962)
EEG (electroencephalogram)(med.)
E! Entertainment Television (TV channel)
EEOC (Equal Employment Opportunity Commission)
Eero Saarinen (US arch.; 1910-61)
Eeyore (fict. chara., *Winnie-the-Pooh*)
Effect of Gamma Rays on Man-in-the-Moon Marigolds, The (film, 1972)
Efferdent (health)
Efik (lang.)
Efrem Kurtz (cond.; 1900-95)
Efrem Zimbalist, Jr. (ent.; 1923-)
Efrem Zimbalist, Sr. (US violinist/comp.; 1889-1985)
EFT (electronic fund transfer)
EFTA (European Free Trade Area)(est. 1960)
Egbert van Alstyne (US comp.; 1882-1951)
Eggar, Samantha (ent.; 1939-)
Eggleston, Edward (US writer; 1837-1902)
Eggo (waffles)
eggs Benedict (also l.c.)
Eglevsky, André (Rus./US ballet; 1917-77)
Eglin Air Force Base, FL (mil.)
E. G. Marshall (ent.; 1910-98)
Egon Schiele (Aus. artist; 1890-1918)
Egoyan, Atom (ent./writer; 1960-)
Egypt (Arab Republic of)(NE Afr.)
Egyptair (airline)
Egyptian (lang./people)
Egyptian archeology
Egyptian architecture (mainly ancient Egypt)
Egyptian art (mainly ancient Egypt)
Egyptian Mau (cat)
Egyptology (study of ancient Eqypt)
Ehime Maru (Japanese fishing vessel that collided with US sub near Hawaii, 2/9/2001)
Ehrenburg, Ilya G. (Rus. writer; 1891-1967)
Ehrlich, Paul (Ger. bacteriol.; 1854-1915)
Ehrlichman, John Daniel (US pol./Watergate; 1925-99)
Ehud Barak (ex-PM, Isr.; 1942-)
Eichhorn, Lisa (ent.; 1952-)
Eichmann, Adolf (Aus./Ger. Nazi; 1906-62)

Eid ul-Adha (Muslim festival)
Eid ul-Fitr (Muslim festival)
E(leuthere) I. du Pont de Nemours (US bus.; 1771-1834)
E. I. du Pont de Nemours & Co.
Eielson Air Force Base, AK (mil.)
Eiffel Tower (Paris, Fr.)
Eiffel, (Alexandre) Gustave (Fr. eng.; 1832-1923)
Eight Immortals (myth.)
Eight, the (group of US artists, Ashcan school)
Eightfold Path (rel.)
Eikenberry, Jill (ent.; 1947-)
Eilat, Israel (also Elath)
Eileen Brennan (ent.; 1935-)
Eileen Farrell (ent.; 1920-)
Eileen Heckart (ent.; 1919-)
Eindhoven, the Netherlands (or Holland)
Eine kleine Nachtmusik (by Mozart)
Einstein, Albert (Ger./US physt.; 1879-1955)
Eire (Republic of Ireland)(NW Eur.)
Eisaku Sato (ex-PM, Jap.; 1901-75)
Eisele, Donn F. (astro.; 1930-87)
Eisenhower, Dwight D(avid)(34th US pres.; 1890-1969)
Eisenhower, Julie Nixon (daughter of ex-US pres.; 1948-)
Eisenhower, Mamie (Doud)(wife of ex-US pres.; 1896-1979)
Eisenhower, Milton S. (US educ.; 1899-1985)
Eisenstaedt, Alfred (news photo.; 1898-1995)
Eisler, Lloyd (figure skating; 1964-)
Eisner, Michael (US bus.; 1942-)
Eizenstat, Stuart Elliot (US atty./pol.; 1943-)
E. J. Brach & Sons (US bus.)
E. J. Gitano (US bus.)
Ejup Ganic (Bosnia-Hercegovina, pol.)
Ekaterinburg (formerly Sverdlovsk)
Ekberg, Anita (Swed./US ent.; 1931-)
Ekco (kitchenware)
EKCO Housewares, Inc.
EKG (electrocardiogram)(also ECG)(med.)
Ekland, Britt (Swed./US ent.; 1942-)
el-Abidine Ben Ali, Zine (pres., Tunisia; 1936-)
Elaine Hiesey Pagels (rel. scholar; 1943-)
Elaine Lan Chao (US secy./labor; 1953-)
Elaine Malbin (ent.; 1932-)
Elaine May (b. Elaine Berlin)(ent.; 1932-)
Elaine Stritch (ent.; 1926-)
Elaine Zayak (US figure skating; 1965-)
El Al Israel Airlines
Elam, Jack (ent.; 1916-)
Elantra, Hyundai (auto.)
Elath, Israel (also Eilat)
Elavil (med.)
E layer (also Kennelly-Heaviside layer)(in lower regions, ionosphere)
Elayne Boosler (ent.; 1952-)
Elba Island (Mediterranean Sea)
Elbasan, Albania
Elbe River (Ger.)
Elbert H. Gary (US steel exec.; 1846-1927)
El Bluff, Nicaragua
Elbridge Gerry (ex-US VP, gerrymander; 1744-1814)
Elburz Mountain (Eur.)

El Cajon, CA
El Camino Real
El Cid (also el Campeador, Rodrigo Diaz de Bivar)(Sp. mil.; 1040-99)
El Cid (film, 1961)
El Cordobés (Manuel Benitez Pérez)(Sp. matador; 1936?-)
El(dra) DeBarge (ent.; 1961-)
Eldepryl (med.)
Elder Beerman Stores
Elder, Lee (golf; 1934-)
Elder, Sons of Katie (film, 1965)
Elderhostel (econ. accommodations for elderly)
Elders, Joycelyn (nee Minnie Lee Jones)(US phys./ex-surgeon gen.; 1933-)
El Djazair, Algeria
E(dgar) L(awrence) Doctorow (US writer; 1931-)
Eldon Industries, Inc.
El Dorado (fabled city of gold)
El Dorado, AR, KS
Eldorado ESC (auto.)
Eldorado ETC (auto.)
Eldorado, Cadillac (auto.)
Eldorado, IL, OK
Eldridge Cleaver (US activist/writer; 1935-98)
Eldridge, Roy (US jazz; 1911-89)
Elea, Zeno of (Gr. phil./math.; c490-430 BC)
Eleanor & Franklin (film, 1976)
Eleanor Holmes Norton (US pol.; 1937-)
Eleanor of Aquitaine (queen, Louis VII [Fr.] & Henry II [Eng.]; c1122-1204)
Eleanor of Castile (queen, Eng.; c1245-90)
Eleanor Parker (ent.; 1922-)
Eleanor Powell (ent.; 1912-82)
Eleanor Roosevelt, (Anna)(wife of US pres., UN dipl.; 1884-1962)
Eleanor Steber (soprano; 1916-90)
Eleaticism (Gr. phil.;6th & 5th c BC)
Election Day (US)
Electra (myth.)
Electra (type style)
Electra complex (psych.)
Electra, Carmen (b. Tara Leigh Patrick)(ent.; 1972-)
Electra-Park Avenue, Buick (auto.)
Electric Co., General
Electric Light Orchestra
Electrolux (home appliances)
Electrolux vacuum
Electronic Data Systems Corp.
Electronic Realty Associates, Inc.
Elektra/Asylum/Nonesuch Records (US bus.)
Eleonora Duse (ent.; 1858-1924)
Elephant Man, the (B. Pomerance play)
Elephant Man, the (b. John Merrick)(?-1890)
Eleusinian Mysteries (rel.)
Eleutherios Venizelos (Gr. pol.; 1864-1936)
Elfman, Jenna (b. Jennifer Butala)(ent.; 1971-)
Elgar, (Sir) Edward (William)(Br. comp.; 1857-1934)
Elgart, Larry (band leader; 1922-)
Elgin Baylor (basketball; 1934-)
Elgin marbles (ancient Gr. sculptures)
Elgin Watch International (US bus.)
Elgin, IL

El Gîza, Egypt (also Gîza or Al Jizah)
El Gîza, Great Pyramids of (also Gîza or Al Jizah)(Eg.)
El Greco (aka Domenikos Theotocopoulos)(Sp. artist; 1541-1614)
Eli Lilly & Company
Eli Wallach (ent.; 1915-)
Eli Whitney (US inv./bus.; 1765-1825)
Elia Kazan (ent.; 1909-)
Elian Gonzalez (US/Cuban news; 1993-)
Elias Howe (US inv., sewing machine; 1819-67)
Elias Hrawi (ex-pres., Lebanon; 1926-)
Elias Ramaema, Col. (Lesotho, mil.)
Elias Sarkis (ex-pres., Lebanon)
Elias, St. Mount (mountain, AK/Can.)
Elías, Jorge Serrano (ex-pres., Guat.)
Eliel Saarinen, (Gottlieb)(US arch.; 1873-1950)
Elie(zer) Wiesel (US writer/reformer; 1928-)
Eliezer, Israel ben (also Baal Shem-Tov)(Jew. rel.; c1700-60)
Elihu Root (US atty./pol.; 1845-1937)
Elihu Yale (US bus./finan.; 1649-1721)
Elijah (prophet; 9th c. BC)
Elijah Muhammad (b. Elijah Poole)(US rel.; 1897-1975)
Elijah Wood (ent.; 1981-)
Elinor Donahue (ent.; 1937-)
Elinor Wylie (US poet; 1885-1928)
Elion, Gertrude Belle (US physiol.; 1918-99)
Eliot Janeway (US econ.; 1913-93)
Eliot, George (aka Mary Ann [or Marian] Evans)(Br. writer; 1819-80)
Eliot, T(homas) S(terns)(US/Br. poet; 1888-1965)
Eliott Ness (US FBI agent; 1902-57)
Eliphalet Remington (US inv./bus.; 1793-1861)
Elisabeth Kübler-Ross (Swiss/US phys./writer; 1926-)
Elisabeth Schwarzkopf (Ger. opera; 1915-)
Elisabeth Shue (ent.; 1963-)
Elise, Lotus (auto.)
Elisha (Graves) Otis (US inv., elevator; 1811-61)
Elixophyllin (med.)
Eliza Doolittle (fict. chara., *Pygmalion*)
Elizabeth "Liddy" Dole, (Mary)(nee Hanford)(US pol.; 1936-)
Elizabeth "Sister" Kenny (Austl. nurse; 1886-1952)
Elizabeth (empress, Rus.; 1709-62)
Elizabeth Ann (Bayley) Seton, St. (also Mother Seton)(US rel.; 1774-1821)
Elizabeth Arden (b. Florence Nightingale Graham)(US bus.; 1884-1966)
Elizabeth Arden (cosmetics)
Elizabeth Arden Co.
Elizabeth Ashley (b. Elizabeth Cole)(ent.; 1939-)
Elizabeth Barrett Browning (Br. poet, wife of Robert; 1806-61)
Elizabeth Bishop (US poet; 1911-79)
Elizabeth Blackwell (1st US woman phys.; 1821-1910)
Elizabeth Cady Stanton (US suffragist; 1815-1902)
Elizabeth Hurley (ent./model; 1965-)
Elizabeth I (queen, Eng.; 1533-1603)

Elizabeth II (Elizabeth Alexandra Mary Windsor) (queen, Eng./UK; 1926-)
Elizabeth Janeway (US writer; 1913-)
Elizabeth McGovern (ent.; 1961-)
Elizabeth Montgomery (ent.; 1933-95)
Elizabeth Perkins (ent.; 1961-)
Elizabeth P. Peabody (US educ.; 1804-94)
Elizabeth Spelke (US psych.; 1949-)
Elizabeth Swados (US comp./playwright; 1951-)
Elizabeth (Rosemond) Taylor (ent.; 1932-)
Elizabeth Wilson (ent.; 1925-)
Elizabeth, NJ
Elizabethan architecture/style
Elizabethan literature (1558-1603)
Elizabethan sonnet
Elizabethton, TN
Elizabethtown, KY, NY, PA
Elizondo, Hector (ent.; 1936-)
Elk (member, BPOE)
Elkay Products Co., Inc.
Elke Sommer (b. Elke Schletz)(ent.; 1940-)
Elkhart, IN
Elkin, Stanley (US writer; 1930-)
Elko, NV
Elks (mag.)
Elks, Benevolent and Protective Order of (BPOE)(US society, founded 1868)
Elkton, MD
Ella Fitzgerald (US jazz; 1918-96)
Ella Raines (ent.; 1920-88)
Ella Tambussi Grasso (US pol.; 1919-81)
Ella Wheeler Wilcox (US poet; 1850-1919)
Elle (mag.)
Elle Decor (mag.)
Elle MacPherson (b. Eleanor Gow)(model/ent.; 1964-)
Ellen Ashley (clothing)
Ellen Barkin (ent.; 1954-)
Ellen Burstyn (b. Edna Rae Gillooly)(ent.; 1932-)
Ellen Corby (ent.; 1911-99)
Ellen DeGeneres (ent.; 1958-)
Ellen Drew (ent.; 1915-)
Ellen (Alicia) Terry, Dame (ent.; 1847-1928)
Ellen (Kean) Tree (ent.; 1806-80)
Ellen Winery, Glen (US bus.)
Ellen, Vera- (ent.; 1926-81)
Ellerbee, Linda (US jour.; 1944-)
Ellery Queen (pseud. for US writers: Frederick Dannay, 1905-82; Manfred B. Lee, 1905-71)
Ellery Queen (TV show)
Ellery Queen's Mystery Magazine
Ellington, Duke (Edward Kennedy)(US comp./ US jazz; 1899-1974)
Elliot L. Richardson (US, ex-atty.-gen.; 1920-99)
Elliot, Cass (b. Ellen Naomi Cohen)(ent.; 1941-74)
Elliot, Sam (ent.; 1944-)
Elliott Gould (b. Elliott Goldstein)(ent.; 1938-)
Elliott Nugent (ent.; 1899-1980)
Elliott, Bob (ent.; 1923-)
Elliott, Sumner Locke (Austl. writer; 1917-91)
Ellis Island (NY Harbor)
Ellis Rabb (ent.; 1930-98)
Ellis Sportswear, Inc., Perry
Ellis, (Henry) Havelock (Br. psych.; 1859-1939)
Ellis, Perry (US designer)

Ellison syndrome/tumor, Zollinger-(med.)
Ellison, Harlan (US writer; 1934-)
Ellison, Lawrence J. (US bus./computers; 1944-)
Ellison, Ralph (Waldo)(US writer; 1914-94)
Ellroy, James (US writer; 1948-)
Ellsberg, Daniel (US social activist; 1931-)
Ellsworth Air Force Base, SD (mil.)
Elly May Clampett (fict. chara.)
Elman, Mischa (ent.; 1891-67)
Elman, Ziggy (b. Harry Finkelman)(1914-68)
El Mansura, Egypt (also Mansura)
Elmendorf Air Force Base, AK (mil.)
Elmer Ambrose Sperry (US eng./inv.; 1860-1930)
Elmer Fudd (fict. chara.)
Elmer Gantry (S. Lewis novel)
Elmer (Leopold) Rice (US writer; 1892-1967)
Elmer's (glue)
Elmer's Adhesives (US bus.)
Elmira Minita Gordon, Dame (ex-gov.-gen.,
   Belize)
Elmira, NY
Elmo R(ussell) Zumwalt, Jr. (US adm.; 1920-
   2000)
Elmo's fire/light, St. (visible electrical discharge)
El Monte, CA
Elmore Leonard (US writer; 1925-)
El Niño (unusually warm ocean current,
   Equatorial Pacific)
Eloah (God)
Elohim (God)
Elopement, East Lynne, or The (E.P. Wood novel)
El Paso Herald-Post (TX newspaper)
El Paso Times (TX newspaper)
El Paso, TX
el-Sadat, Anwar (also Anwar Sadat)(ex-pres.,
   Eg.; 1918-81)
Elsa Lanchester (ent.; 1902-82)
Elsa Schiaparelli (Fr. designer; 1890-1973)
El Salvador (Republic of)(CAmer.)
Elsinore, Denmark (also Helsingor)
Elston Howard (baseball; 1929-80)
Elton (Hercules) John (b. Reginald Kenneth
   Dwight)(ent.; 1947-)
Elton, Charles (Br. ecol.; 1900-91)
Elul (Jew. month)
Elvin Hayes (basketball; 1945-)
Elvin Jones (US jazz; 1927-)
Elvira (aka Cassandra Peterson)(ent.; 1951-)
Elvis Costello (Declan McManus)(ent.; 1954-)
Elvis (Aron) Presley (ent.; 1935-77)
Elway, John (football; 1960-)
El-Youssoufi, Abderrahmane (PM, Morocco;
   1924-)
Elyria, OH
Elysée Palace (Fr. pres. residence)
Elysian Fields (also Elysium)(also Elysian
   fields)(myth. heaven)
Elzie C. Segar (cartoonist, *Popeye*; 1894-1938)
eMachines (compu.)
Emancipation Proclamation (freed Southern
   slaves; 1862)
Emanuel Leutze (US artist; 1816-68)
Emanuel Swedenborg (Swed. phil./mystic;
   1688-1772)
Embargo Act of 1807 (US hist., limit trade)

Embassy Row (DC)
Embassy Suites, Inc.
Embden (goose)
EMCOF (European Monetary Cooperation Fund)
   (econ.)
Emcyt (med.)
Emerald Isle (Ir.)
Emeraude (perfume)
Emergency Broadcast System (radio)
Emeril Lagasse (US chef/writer/ent.; 1959-)
Emerson Electric Co.
Emerson Fittipaldi (auto racing; 1946-)
Emerson, Lake and Palmer (pop music)
Emerson, Ralph Waldo (US writer/phil.; 1803-82)
Emerson, Roy (tennis; 1936-)
Emery Air Freight Corp.
Emery Worldwide (shipper)
E(dward) M(organ) Forster (Br. writer; 1879-
   1970)
EMG (electromyogram)(med.)
Emil Brunner (Swed. rel.; 1889-1966)
Emil Constantinescu (pres., Romania; 1939-)
Emil Erlenmeyer (Ger. chem.; 1825-1909)
Emil (Grigoryevich) Gilels (Rus. pianist; 1916-85)
Emil Hermann Fischer (Ger. chem.; 1852-1919)
Emil Nolde (b. Emil Hansen)(Ger. artist; 1867-
   1956)
Emil von Behring (Ger. bacteriol.; 1854-1917)
Emile Antoine Bourdelle (Fr. artist; 1861-1929)
Emile Durkheim (Fr. sociol.; 1858-1917)
Emile Herzog (pseud. André Maurois)(Fr.
   writer; 1885-1967)
Emile Jonassaint (pres., Haiti; 1914-)
Emile Lahoud (pres., Lebanon; 1936-)
Émile (Édouard Charles Antoine) Zola (Fr.
   writer; 1840-1902)
Emiliano Zapata (Mex. mil./agr.; c1879-1919)
Emilio Aguinaldo (Phil. revolutionary; 1869-1964)
Emilio Estevez (ent.; 1962-)
Emilio Guglielmo Winery (US bus.)
Emilio Pucci (It. designer; 1914-92)
Emilio Pucci Perfumes International, Inc.
Emily Brontë (aka Ellis Bell)(Br. writer; 1818-48)
Emily Dickinson (US poet; 1830-86)
Emily Lloyd (ent.; 1970-)
Emily (Price) Post (US writer, social etiquette;
   1873?-1960)
Emily Watson (ent.; 1967-)
Eminem (b. Marshall Mathers, III)(ent.; 1972-)
Eminence, Your (title)
Emlyn Williams (ent./playwright; 1905-87)
Emma (Jane Austen novel)
Emma Bovary, Madame (fict. chara.)
Emma Bunton (aka Baby Spice)(ent.; 1976-)
Emma Goldman (Rus./US reformer; 1869-1940)
Emma Hamilton, Lady (b. Amy Lyon)(Br. lady;
   1765?-1815)
Emma Lazarus (US poet; 1849-87)
Emma Peel (fict. chara., *The Avengers)*
Emma Samms (ent.; 1960-)
Emma Thompson (ent.; 1959-)
Emma (Hart) Willard (US educ.; 1787-1870)
Emmanuel Ax (Rus. ent.; 1949-)
Emmanuel Lewis (ent.; 1971-)
Emmeline (Goulden) Pankhurst (Br. suffragist;

1858-1928)
Emmenthaler (cheese)
Emmett Kelly, (Leo)(US clown; 1898-1979)
Emmy Awards
Emmylou Harris (ent.; 1947-)
Emory University (Atlanta, GA)
Empedocles (Gr. phil.; c490-430 BC)
Empire architecture/style (fl. 1804-15)
Empire State (nickname, NY)
Empire State Building (NYC, built 1931)
Empire State of the South (nickname, GA)
Empire Strikes Back, The (film, 1980)
Empirin (med.)
Empty Nest (TV show)
EMS (European Monetary System)(est. 1979)
EMU (European Monetary Union)(econ.)
E-Mycin (med.)
Enberg, Dick (sportscaster; 1935-)
Encarnación, Paraguay
Enceladus (Saturn moon)(myth.)
Encore (TV channel)
Encyclopaedia Britannica
Encyclopedism (also Encyclopaedism)(also
l.c.)(phil.)
Endara, Guillermo (ex-pres., Panama; 1936-)
Endeavor (US space shuttle)
Endep (med.)
Ender, Kornelia (swimming; 1958-)
Enderby Land (region, Antarctica)
Enders, John F. (US virol.; 1897-1985)
Endless Vacation (mag.)
Endowment for Democracy, National (US pol.
agcy.)
Endowment on (or for) the Arts and Humanities,
National (US govt. agcy.; est. 1965)
Enduron (med.)
Enduronyl (med.)
Endust (cleaner)
Endymion (myth.)
Energizer (battery, bunny)
Energy, Department of (US govt.)
Enesco (or Enescu), Georges (Romanian cond./
comp.; 1881-1955)
Enfamil (med.)
Enfield rifle (also Lee-Enfield rifle)
Engelbert Dollfuss (ex-chanc. Aus.; 1892-1934)
Engelbert Humperdinck (b. Arnold Dorsey)
(ent.; 1936-)
Engelbert Humperdinck (Ger. comp.; 1854-1921)
Engels, Friedrich (Ger. pol. writer; 1820-95)
Engineers, Army Corps of (US mil.)
England (largest part of Great Britain and the UK)
England Air Force Base, LA (mil.)
England, Church of (also Anglican Church)
Engler, John (Mathias)(MI gov.; 1948-)
English (lang./people)
English (type style)
English bulldog (dog)
English Channel (Eng./Fr.)
English Civil War (1642-47)
English cocker spaniel (dog)
English foxhound (dog)
English Game, Old (chicken)
English horn (instrument)
English ivy (plant)

English law (legal system)
English Leather (toiletries)
English muffin
English Revolution (also Bloodless [or Glorious]
Revolution)(Br. hist.; 1688-89)
English Revolution (Eng. hist.; 1640-60)
English rye grass
English saddle
English setter (dog)
English sheepdog, Old
English shepherd (dog)
English sonnet (Shakespearean sonnet)
English sparrow (house sparrow)
English springer spaniel (dog)
English toy spaniel (dog)
English walnut (tree)
English, Diane (ent./created Murphy Brown;
1948-)
English, Early Modern (lang.; c1550-1700)
English, Late Modern (lang.; c1700-present)
English, Middle (lang.; c1050-1550)
English, Old (also Anglo-Saxon)(lang.; c500-1050)
English, Old (type style)
Englishman
Englishwoman
Englund, Robert (ent.; 1949-)
Enid, OK
Enigma (WWII decoder)
Eniwetok atoll (nuclear bomb tests, W Pac.)
Enkhbayar, Nambaryn (PM, Mongolia; 1958-)
Enkidu (myth.)
Enlai, Zhou (also Chou En-Lai)(ex-PM, Ch.;
1898-1976)
Enlightenment, Age of (18th c. Eur. movement)
Enlil (myth.)
Enlon (med.)
Ennio Morricone (It. comp.; 1928-)
Enniskillen, Northern Ireland
Ennius (Latin poet; 239-170 BC)
Eno, Brian (ent.; 1948-)
Enoch (rel.)
Enoch Arden (missing person presumed dead,
but is alive)
Enoch Arden (Tennyson poem)
Enoch Arden doctrine (divorce)
Enoch Arnold Bennett (Br. writer; 1867-1931)
Enoch Derant Lakoue (ex-PM, Central African
Republic)
Enola Gay (US mil. B-29 bomber that dropped
1st atomic bomb in 1945)
Enovid (med.)
Enquirer, Cincinnati (OH newspaper)
Enrico Caruso (It. tenor; 1873-1921)
Enrico Cecchetti (ballet; 1850-1928)
Enrico Fermi (It. physt.; 1901-54)
Enrique Iglesias (ent.; 1975-)
Enriquez, Rene (ent.; 1932-90)
Enron Corp.
Ensenada, Mexico
Ensign Pulver (film, 1964)
Ensign, John (US cong.; 1958-)
Ensor, James, Baron (Belgian artist; 1860-1949)
Ensure (med.)
ENT (ear, nose, and throat)(med.)
Entebbe, Uganda

Entente Cordiale (Br./Fr.; 1904)
Enterprise Rent-A-Car (US bus.)
Enterprise, Beaumont (TX newspaper)
Entertainment Tonight (TV show)
Entertainment Weekly (mag.)
Entex (med.)
Entremont, Philippe (pianist; 1934-)
Entrepreneur (mag.)
Entrepreneurial Women (mag.)
Enugu, Nigeria
Environmental Protection Agency (EPA)(US govt.)
Environmental Quality, Council on (US govt.)
Envoy, GMC (auto.)
Enya (b. Eithne Ni Bhraona)(ent.; 1962-)
Enzi, Michael B. (US cong.; 1944-)
Enzo Ferrari (It. bus./auto.; 1898-1988)
Eocene epoch (54-38 million years ago)
Eolithic Age (also l.c.)
Eos (myth.)
EPA (Environmental Protection Agency)(US govt.)
Epaminondas (Gr. mil./pol.; 418?-362 BC)
E(dward) P(ayson) Dutton (US publ.; 1831-1923)
Ephesians (rel., book of the New Testament)
Ephesus, Temple of Artemis at (also Artemision)
Ephron, Nora (US writer/ent.; 1941-)
EPI Products (US bus.)
Epic of Gilgames (myth.)
Epicharmus (Gr. drama.; c530-440 BC)
Epictetus (Gr. phil.; c55-c135 BC)
Epicureanism (phil.)
Epicurus (Gr. phil.; 341-270 BC)
Epifrin (med.)
Epiphany (rel.)
Epirus (region, Gr.)
Episcopal Church
Episcopalian (rel.)
Epistle of James (rel.)
Epistle to the Colossians (rel.)
Epistle to the Ephesians (rel.)
Epistles to the Corinthians (rel.)
Epoisses (cheese)
Eppie Lederer (aka Ann Landers)(b. Esther Pauline Friedman)(US advice columnist; 1918-)
Eppy/N (med.)
Epsom Downs (Br. racetrack)
Epsom salts (med.)
Epsom, England
Epson (compu.)
Epson America, Inc.
Epstein-Barr virus (EBV)(med.)
Epstein, Brian (ent.; 1935-67)
Epstein, Jacob (Br. sculptor; 1880-1959)
Epstein's disease/nephrosis/pearls/syndrome (med.)
Equagesic (med.)
Equal (sweetener)
Equal Employment Opportunity Commission
Equal Rights Amendment
Equality State (nickname, WY)
Equanil (med.)
Equatorial Countercurrent
Equatorial Current
Equatorial Guinea (Republic of)(formerly

Spanish Guinea)(W Afr.)
Equitable Life Assurance Society of the United States
Equuleus (astron., little horse)
Equus (P. Shaffer play)
ER (emergency room)
Er (chem. sym., erbium)
ERA (detergent)
ERA (Equal Rights Amendment)
Erasistratus (Gr. phys.; 3rd c. BC)
Erasmus, Desiderius (Dutch scholar; c1466-1536)
Erastianism (rel.)
Erastus Corning (US finan.; 1794-1872)
Eratosthenes (Gr. geographer/math.; c276-194 BC)
Erb's palsy (med.)
Erdrich, (Karen) Louise (US writer; 1954-)
Erebus (myth., darkness)
Erebus, Mount (volcano, Antarctica)
Erechtheum (Gr. temple, Acropolis)
Erector Set (building toy)
E region (lower ionosphere region)
Erewhon (S. Butler novel)
Ergamisol (med.)
Ergostat (med.)
Ergotrate (med.)
Erhard, Ludwig (ex-chanc., WGer.; 1897-1977)
Eric A(rthur) Blair (pseud. George Orwell)(Br. writer; 1903-50)
Eric Ambler (Br. writer; 1909-98)
Eric Berne, Dr. (US psych./writer; 1910-70)
Eric Bogosian (ent./writer; 1953-)
Eric Burdon (ent./songwriter; 1941-)
Eric Carmen (ent.; 1949-)
Eric Clapton (b. Eric Clapp)(ent.; 1945-)
Eric Dickerson (football; 1960-)
Eric Dolphy (US jazz; 1928-64)
Eric Heiden (speed skating; 1958-)
Eric (Honeywood) Partridge (Br. lexicographer; 1894-1979)
Eric Roberts (ent.; 1956-)
Eric Sevareid (US TV jour.; 1913-92)
Eric Stoltz (ent.; 1961-)
Eric the Red (Norse expl., Greenland; 940-1010)
Erica (Mann) Jong (US writer; 1942-)
Erica Morini (violinist; 1904-95)
Erich Fromm (Ger. psych.; 1900-80)
Erich Leinsdorf (ent.; 1912-93)
Erich Maria Remarque (Ger./US writer; 1898-1970)
Erich Segal (US writer; 1937-)
Erich Von Stroheim (ent.; 1885-1957)
Erickson, Leif (ent.; 1911-86)
Ericsson, Leif (Norse expl.; c.1000)
Eridanus (astron., river)
Erie (Native Amer.)
Erie Canal (NY)
Erie News (PA newspaper)
Erie Times (PA newspaper)
Erie, Lake (NY/OH/PA/Can.)
Erie, PA
Erik Bruhn (b. Belton Evers)(ballet; 1928-86)
Erik Estrada (ent.; 1949-)
Erik Menendez (US news, killed parents)
Erik (Alfred Leslie) Satie (Fr. comp.; 1866-1925)

Erika & Co. (clothes)
Erika Slezak (ent.; 1946-)
Erika Studio (clothes)
Erin (also Ireland)
Erin Brockovich (film, 2000)
Erin Gray (ent.; 1950-)
Erin Moran (ent.; 1961-)
Eriq Lasalle (ent.; 1962-)
Eris (myth.)
Eritrea (province, Ethiopia)
Erle Stanley Gardner (US writer; 1889-1970)
Erlenmeyer flask (chem.)
Erlenmeyer, Emil (Ger. chem.; 1825-1909)
Erma Bombeck (US writer/humorist; 1927-96)
Ermanno Wolf-Ferrari (It. comp.; 1876-1948)
Ernest Ball (US comp.; 1878-1927)
Ernest Bevin (Br. pol.; 1881-1951)
Ernest Bloch (Swiss/US comp.; 1880-1959)
Ernest Borgnine (b. Ermes Borgnino)(ent.; 1917-)
Ernest Chausson (Fr. comp.; 1855-99)
Ernest F. Hollings (US cong.; 1922-)
Ernest Gallo (US winemaker)
Ernest (Heinrich) Haeckel (Ger. zool.; 1834-1919)
Ernest (Miller) Hemingway (US writer; 1899-1961)
Ernest J(oseph) King (US mil.; 1878-1956)
Ernest O(rlando) Lawrence (US physt.; 1901-58)
Ernest "Ernie" Pyle (US jour.; 1900-45)
Ernest Rutherford, Baron (Br. physt.; 1871-1937)
Ernest (Henry) Shackleton, (Sir)(Br. expl.; 1874-1922)
Ernest Solvay (Belgian chem.; 1838-1922)
Ernest Truex (ent.; 1890-1973)
Ernest Tubb (ent.; 1914-84)
Ernest, Frank and (comic strip)
Ernestine Schumann-Heink (ent.; 1861-1936)
Ernesto "Che" Guevara (SAmer. mil.; 1928-67)
Ernie Banks (baseball; 1931-)
Ernie Bushmiller (cartoonist, *Nancy*; 1905-82)
Ernie Ford, Tennessee (ent.; 1919-91)
Ernie Kovacs (ent.; 1919-62)
Ernie Nevers (football; 1903-76)
Ernie (Ernest) Pyle (US jour.; 1900-45)
Erno Rubik (Hung. arch. 1944-)
Ernst & Young, Inc.
Ernst (Heinrich) Barlach (Ger. sculptor/writer; 1870-1938)
Ernst Kaltenbrunner (Aus. Nazi; 1901-46)
Ernst Lubitsch (Ger. ent.; 1892-1947)
Ernst Ludwig Kirchner (Ger. artist; 1880-1938)
Ernst Mach (Aus. physt./psych./phil.; 1838-1916)
Ernst Röhm (Ger. Nazi; 1887-1934)
Ernst (or Ernö) von Dohnányi (Hung. pianist/comp.; 1877-1960)
Ernst, Max (Ger. artist; 1891-1976)
Eros (astron.)
Eros (myth., god of love)
Errol Flynn (ent.; 1909-59)
Erroll Garner (US jazz; 1921-77)
Ershad, Hussain Mohammad (ex-pres., Bangladesh; 1930-)
Erskine Caldwell (US writer; 1903-87)
Erskine Lloyd Sandiford (ex-PM, Barbados; 1937-)
Erskine of Carnock (aka John Erskine)(Scot. writer, law; 1695-1768)

Erté (Romain de Tirtoff)(Rus. designer; 1893-1990)
Ervin, Sam, Jr. (US pol.; 1896-1985)
Erving, Julius "Dr J" (basketball; 1950-)
Erwin Rommel (aka "Desert Fox")(Ger. gen. in NAfr.; 1891-1944)
Erwin Schrödinger (Ger. physt.; 1887-1961)
EryDerm (med.)
Erykah Badu (b. Erica Wright)(ent.; 1971-)
EryPed (med.)
Ery-Tab (med.)
Es (chem. sym., einsteinium)
ESA (Eur. Space Agency)(est. 1975)
Esa-Pekka Salonen (Fin. comp.; 1958-)
Esbjerg, Denmark
Escalade, Cadillac (auto.)
Escape, Ford (auto.)
Escher, M(aurits) C(ornelis)(Dutch artist; 1902-72)
Escobar, Ricardo Lagos (pres., Chile; 1938-)
Escoffier, (Georges) Auguste (Fr. chef/writer; 1847-1935)
Escondido, CA
Escort, Ford (auto.)
Esdraelon Plain (also Plain of Jezreel)(Isr.)
Esdras, I&II (rel., Apocrypha)
Esfahan, Iran
Esiason, "Boomer" (Norman Julius Esiason, Jr.) (football; 1961-)
Esimil (med.)
Eskalith (med.)
Eskimo (people)
Eskimo dog (dog)
Eskimo Pie Corp.
Eskimo-Aleut (Native Amer.)
Eskisehir, Turkey
Esko Aho (ex-PM, Fin.; 1954-)
ESP (extrasensory perception)
Esperante, Panoz (auto.)
Esperanto (artificial internat'l lang.)
Espinosa, Nino (baseball; 1953-88)
ESPN (TV channel)
ESPN Classic Sports Network (TV channel)
ESPN2 (TV channel)
ESPNEWS (TV channel)
Esposito, Phil(ip Anthony)(hockey; 1942-)
Esprit (clothing)
Esprit, Lotus (auto.)
Espy, Mike (US ex-secy./agr.; 1953-)
Esquimalt, British Columbia, Canada
Esquire (mag.)
Esquivel, Manuel (ex-PM, Belize; 1940-)
Essen, Germany
Essence (mag.)
Essene (rel.)
Essex (county, Eng.)
Essex, CT, MD, VT
Essex, Earl of (Robert Devereux)(Br. mil./pol.; 1566-1601)
Essex, Ontario, Canada
Estar (med.)
Estée Lauder (cosmetics)
Estee Lauder (designer; 1908-)
Estée Lauder, Inc.
Esteem, Suzuki (auto.)
Estefan, Gloria (b. Gloria Fajardo)(ent.; 1958-)

Estelle Getty (ent.; 1924-)
Estelle Parsons (ent.; 1927-)
Estenssoro, Victor Paz (ex-pres., Bolivia; 1907-)
Estèphe, St.- (also Saint-Estèphe)(Fr. wine region)
Estes Kefauver, (Carey)(US pol.; 1903-63)
Estes, Billy Sol (US bus./scandal)
Estevez, Emilio (ent.; 1962-)
Esther (rel., book of the Old Testament)
Esther Ralston (ent.; 1902-94)
Esther Rolle (ent.; 1920-98)
Esther Williams (ent./swimming; 1923-)
Estinyl (med.)
Estonia (Republic of)(formerly part of the
    USSR)(N Eur.)
Estonian (lang./people)
Estrace (med.)
Estrada Winery, Joe P. (US bus.)
Estrada, Erik (ent.; 1949-)
Estrada, Joseph (ex-pres., Phil.; 1937-)
Estraderm (med.)
Estratab (med.)
Estrovis (med.)
Estwing hammer
Eszterhas, Joe (ent./writer; 1944-)
E.T.: The Extra-Terrestrial (film, 1982)
ETA (estimated time of arrival)
Etah, Greenland
Etah, India
ETD (estimated time of departure)
Eteocles (myth., Seven against Thebes)
Ethan Allen (US Revolutionary War hero; 1738-
    89)
Ethan Allen, Inc.
Ethan Coen (ent.; 1958-)
Ethan Frome (E. Wharton novel)
Ethan Hawke (ent./writer; 1970-)
Ethel Barrymore (ent.; 1879-1959)
Ethel (Skakel) Kennedy (US wife of ex-atty.
    gen.; 1928-)
Ethel Merman (ent.; 1908-84)
Ethel (Greenglass) Rosenberg (US, executed
    for treason; 1915-53)
Ethel Smyth, Dame (Br. comp.; 1858-1944)
Ethel Waters (ent.; 1900-77)
Ethelred II ("the Unready")(king, Eng.; c968-
    1016)
Etheridge, Melissa (ent.; 1961-)
Ethiopia (People's Democratic Republic of)
    (formerly Abyssinia)(E Afr.)
Ethiopian (lang./people)
Ethmozine (med.)
Ethyl Corp.
Etienne Tshisekedi (premier, Zaire)
Etna, Mount (volcano, Sicily)
Etobicoke, Ontario, Canada
Eton collar (clothing)
Eton College (Br. public school)
Eton jacket
Eton, England
E-Trade (US bus.)
Etrafon (med.)
Etruria (now Tuscany and W. Umbria)
Etruscan (ancient civilization; fl. 7th-5th c BC)
Etta James (b. Jamesetta Hawkins)(ent.; 1938-)
Etting, Ruth (ent.; 1897-1978)

Ettore Bugatti (It. designer; 1881-1947)
Ettore Maserati (It. bus./auto.; 1894-1990)
EU (European Union)(est. 1994)
Eu (chem. sym., europium)
Eubanks, Bob (ent.; 1937-)
Eubie Blake, (James Hubert)(US jazz pianist/
    comp.; 1883-1983)
Euboea (Gr. island)
Eucharist (also Holy Communion, Lord's
    Supper)(rel.)
Euclid (Gr. math.; c330-c260 BC)
Euclidean geometry (math.)
Eudora Welty (US writer; 1909-2001)
Euell Gibbons (US writer, wild edible plants;
    1911-75)
Eugene A(ndrew) Cernan (astro.; 1934-)
Eugene Delacroix (Fr. artist; 1789-1863)
Eugene Field (US poet; 1850-95)
Eugene Fodor (US travel guide writer; 1906-91)
Eugene Fodor (US violinist; 1950-)
Eugène Ionesco (Fr. writer; 1912-94)
Eugene J. Keogh (US pol.; 1907-89)
Eugene Loring (b. LeRoy Kerpestein)(dancer/
    choreographer; 1911-82)
Eugene (Joseph) McCarthy (US pol.; 1916-)
Eugene (Gladstone) O'Neill (US writer; 1888-
    1953)
Eugene Ormandy (US cond.; 1899-1985)
Eugene Register-Guard (OR newspaper)
Eugene Roche (ent.; 1928-)
Eugène Scribe, (Augustin)(Fr. writer; 1791-1861)
Eugene V. Debs (US labor leader; 1855-1926)
Eugene, OR
Eugenia Charles, (Mary)(ex-PM, Dominica; 1919-)
Eugénie, Empress (Comtesse de Teba, wife of
    Napoleon III; 1826-1920)
Eugénie, Marie Ignace Augustine de Montijo
    (empress, Fr.; 1826-1920)
Eugenie, Princess (daughter of Prince Andrew
    and Sarah; 1990-)
Eugenio Montale (It. poet; 1896-1981)
Eulenspiegel, Till (Ger. legend/practical jokes;
    14th c.)
Euler, Leonhard (Swiss math./physt.; 1707-83)
Euler's diagram (logic)
Euler's formula/phi-function (math.)
Eulexin (med.)
Eumenides (myth.)
Eunice Kennedy Shriver (US wife of pol.; 1921-)
Euphrates River (Turk.)
Eurailpass
Eurasia
Eurasian (people)
Eurasian Plate
Eureka (vacuum cleaner)
Eureka Co., The
Eureka, CA, KS, UT
Euripides (Gr. drama.; c484-406 BC)
Eurobond (econ.)
Euroclydon wind
Eurocurrency (also Euromoney)
Eurodollar (econ.)
Europa (Jupiter moon, myth.)
Europe
Europe, Council of

European (people)
European Atomic Energy Commission
  (Eurotom)(est. 1957)
European Community (EC)(pol./econ. alliance)
European Court of Justice (court of EC)
European Economic Area (EEA)(est. 1994)
European Economic Community (EEC)(also
  Common Market, est. 1957)
European Free Trade Area (EFTA)(est. 1960)
European Monetary Cooperation Fund (EMCOF)
  (econ.)
European Monetary System (EMS)(est. 1979)
European Monetary Union (EMU)(econ.)
European Parliament (EC parliament)
European Recovery Program (also Marshall
  Plan)(after WWII)
European Space Agency (ESA)(est. 1975)
European Telecommunications Satellite
  Organization (Eutelsat)
European Union (EU)(est. 1994)
Eurotom (European Atomic Energy
  Commission)(est. 1957)
EuroVan, Volkswagen (auto.)
Eurydice (myth.)
Eurythmics, the (pop music)
Eustis, Fort, VA (mil.)
Eutelsat (European Telecommunications
  Satellite Organization)
Euterpe (myth., muse of music)
Euthoid (med.)
Eva Braun (mistress of Adolph Hitler; 1910-45)
Eva Evdokimova (ballet)
Eva Gabor (ent.; 1919?-95)
Eva Le Gallienne (ent.; 1899-91)
Eva Marie Saint (ent.; 1924-)
Eva Duarte "Evita" de Perón (b. Maria Eva
  Duarte)(ex-pres., Argentina; 1919-52)
Eva Tanguay (ent.; 1878-1947)
Eva, Little (b. Eva Narcissus Boyd)(ent.; 1945-)
Evan Bayh (US cong./ex-IN gov.; 1955-)
Evan Mecham (ex-AZ gov.: 1924-)
Evan Picone
Evan-Picone, Inc.
Evan S. Connell (US writer; 1924-)
Evander Holyfield (boxing; 1962-)
Evangel (rel.)
Evangelical (rel.)
Evangelical Alliance (Christian assoc.; est. 1846)
Evangelical Lutheran Church
Evangeline Cory Booth (US, Salvation Army;
  1865?-1950)
Evangelist (rel.)
Evangelista, Linda (model; 1965-)
Evans, Bill (US jazz; 1929-80)
Evans, Dale (b. Lucille Wood Smith)(ent.;
  1912-2001)
Evans, Don(ald) Louis (US secy./commerce;
  1946-)
Evans, Edith, Dame (ent.; 1888-1976)
Evans, Gil (US jazz; 1912-88)
Evans, Greg (cartoonist, *Luann*)
Evans, Janet (swimming; 1971-)
Evans, Lee (runner; 1947-)
Evans, Linda (b. Linda Evanstad)(ent.; 1942-)
Evans, Mary Ann (or Marian)(pseud. George

Eliot)(Br. writer; 1819-80)
Evans, Maurice (ent.; 1901-89)
Evans, Robert (ent.; 1930-)
Evans, Ronald E. (astro.; 1933-)
Evanston, IL, WY
Evansville Courier (IN newspaper)
Evansville Press (IN newspaper)
Evansville, IN
Evdokimova, Eva (ballet)
Eve (rel., 1st woman)
Eve Arden (b. Eunice Quedens)(ent.; 1908-90)
Eve Queler (US cond.; 1936-)
Eve, Adam and (rel.)
Eve, All About (film, 1950)
Eve, The Three Faces of (film, 1957)
Evel (Robert Craig) Knievel (US daredevil; 1938-)
Evelyn Ashford (track & field; 1957-)
Evelyn Keyes (ent.; 1919-)
Evelyn (Shulman) Lear (soprano; 1926-)
Evelyn (Arthur St. John) Waugh (Br. writer;
  1903-66)
Evelyn Wood Reading Dynamics (US bus.)
Evelyn Wood speed-reading method
Evelyn, Crabtree & (toiletries)
Evelyn, Ltd., Crabtree &
Evenflo (baby bottle)
Evening at the Improv (TV show)
Evening Shade (TV show)
Evening Sun, Baltimore (MD newspaper)
Evensong (also l.c.)(evening prayer)
Eveready (battery)
Eveready Battery Company, Inc.
Everest, Mount (highest mountain, Himalayas)
Everett Koop, C. (US ex-surgeon gen./phys.;
  1916-)
Everett M. Dirksen (US pol./orator; 1896-1969)
Everett, Chad (b. Raymond Lee Cramton)(ent.;
  1936-)
Everett, MA, WA
Everett, Rupert (ent./model; 1959-)
Everglades (S FL)
Everglades National Park (FL)
Evergreen State (nickname, WA)
Everly Brothers, the (pop music)
Everly, Don (b. Isaac Everly)(ent.; 1937-)
Everly, Phil (ent.; 1939-)
Evers-Williams, Myrlie (US civil rights leader;
  1933-)
Evers, (James) Charles (US reformer/pol./
  NAACP; 1922-)
Evers, Medgar Wiley (US reformer/NAACP;
  1925-63)
Evert-Lloyd, Chris (tennis; 1954-)
Everybody Loves Raymond (TV show)
Everyman (Eng. play; 15th c.)
Evian Waters of France (US bus.)
Evigan, Greg (ent.; 1953-)
Evinrude (boat/engine)
Evita (play)
Evita (Eva Duarte) de Perón (b. Maria Eva
  Duarte)(ex-pres., Argentina; 1919-52)
Evonne Goolagong (Cawley)(tennis; 1951-)
Evyan Perfumes, Inc.
Ewan McGregor (ent.; 1971-)
Ewbank, Weeb (Wilbur Charles)(football; 1907-

98)
Ewe (lang./people)
Ewell, Tom (ent.; 1909-94)
Ewing, J. R. (fict. chara., *Dallas*)
Ewing, Patrick (basketball; 1962-)
Ewok (fict. chara., *Star Wars*)
Ewry, Ray (Olympics; 1873-1937)
E. W. Scripps Co.
EWTN (TV channel)
Examiner, San Francisco (CA newspaper)
Excalibur (Arthurian magic sword)
Excalibur (film, 1981)
Excedrin (med.)
Excel, Hyundai (auto.)
Excel, Microsoft (compu.)
Excellency, Your (title)
Excelsior State (nickname, NY)
Exchange Rate Mechanism (ERM)(European
    Community)
Exchequer, Chancellor of the (Br. finance
    minister)
Excursion, Ford (auto.)
Execution of Private Slovik, The (film, 1974)
Executive Female (mag.)
Exelderm (med.)
Exercycle
Exercycle Corp.
Exeter, CA, NH, PA
Exeter, England
Ex-Lax (med.)
Exodus (L. Uris novel)
Exodus (rel., Israelites deliverance from Eg.)
Exodus (rel., book of the Old Testament)
Exon, J. James (US pol.; 1921-)
Exorcist II: The Heretic (film, 1977)
Exorcist, The (W.P. Blatty novel; film, 1973)
Ex parte McCardle (US law; 1869)
Ex parte Merryman (US law; 1861)
Ex parte Milligan (US law; 1866)
Expedia, Inc.
Expedition, Ford (auto.)
Explorer (mag.)
Explorer (US space satellite)
Explorer, Ford (auto.)
Expos, Montreal (baseball team)
Express Mail (USPS service)
Express News, San Antonio (TX newspaper)
Express, Chevrolet (auto.)
Expressionism (art/lit.)
Exupery, Antoine (Marie Roger) de, Saint- (Fr.
    writer/aviator; 1900-44)
Exxon Mobil Corp.
Exxon Valdez (US tanker, oil spill; 1989)
Eyadéma, Gnassingbe (pres., Togo; 1937-)
Eyck, Hubert (or Huybrecht) van (Flem. artist;
    1366-1426)
Eyck, Jan van (Flem. artist; 1380-1441)
Eydie Gorme (ent.; 1932-)
Eye to Eye With Connie Chung (TV show)
E. Y. "Yip" Harburg (US lyricist; 1898-1981)
Eyre, Jane (C. Brontë novel)
Eyre, Lake (Austl.)
Eysenck, Hans Jurgen (Br. psych.; 1916-97)
Ezekiel (rel., book of the Old Testament)
Ezer Weizman (ex-pres., Isr.; 1924-)

Ezio Pinza (ent.; 1892-1957)
Ezra (rel., book of the Old Testament)
Ezra Cornell (US bus.; 1807-74)
Ezra Loomis Pound (US poet; 1885-1972)
Ezra Taft Benson (US pol.; 1900-94)

-F-

F (chem. sym., fluorine)
FAA (Federal Aviation Administration)(DOT agcy.)
Fabares, Shelley (ent.; 1944-)
Faberge Co.
Fabergé Brut
Fabergé egg
Fabergé, Peter Carl (Rus. jeweler; 1846-1920)
Fabian (Forte)(ent.; 1943-)
Fabian Society (Br. socialist org.)
Fabianism (pol.)
Fabio (b. Fabio Lanzoni)(model; 1961-)
Fabius Maximus Verrucosus, Quintus
    ("Cunctator")(Roman pol./mil.; 275-03 BC)
Fabius, Laurent (ex-PM, Fr.; 1946-)
Fabray, Nanette (b. Ruby Nanette Fabares)
    (ent.; 1920-)
FACE (Freedom of Access to Abortion Clinics)
Face the Nation (TV show)
Factor & Co., Max
Factor, Max (cosmetics)
Factor, Max (US bus.; 1877-1938)
Facts of Life (TV show)
Facusse, Carlos Roberto Flores (pres.,
    Honduras; 1950-)
Fadiman, Clifton (US writer/editor; 1904-99)
Fadl, Jamal Ahmed al- (Sudanese informant on
    Osama bin Laden; 1964-)
Faeroe Islands (also Faroe)(N Atl.)
Fafnir (myth.)
Fagatogo, American Samoa
Fagin (fict. chara., *Oliver Twist*, crim., fence)
Fahd ibn Abdul Aziz (al-Saud)(king, Saudi
    Arabia; 1923-)
Fahrenheit (temperature scale)
Fahrenheit 451 (R. Bradbury novel)
Fahrenheit, Gabriel D(aniel)(Ger. physt.; 1686-
    1736)
Fain, Sammy (US comp.; 1902-89)
Fair Deal (Pres. Truman policy)
Fair Labor Standards Act (also Wages and
    Hours Act; 1938)
Fair, Philip the (Philip IV)(king, Fr.; 1268-1314)
Fairbanks, AK
Fairbanks, Charles W. (ex-US VP; 1852-1918)
Fairbanks, Douglas, Jr. (ent.; 1909-2000)
Fairbanks, Douglas, Sr. (ent.; 1883-1939)
Fairchild Air Force Base, WA (mil.)
Fairchild Corp.
Fairchild, Morgan (b. Patsy McClenny)(ent.; 1950-)
Faircloth, Lauch (Duncan McLaunchlin)(US pol.;
    1928-)
Fairfax, VA
Fairweather, Mount (AK)
Faisal I (also Feisal I)(ex-king, Iraq; 1885-1933)
Faisal ibn Abdul Aziz (ex-king/PM, Saudi
    Arabia; 1905-75)
Faisal II (also Feisal I)(ex-king, Iraq; 1935-58)
Faisalabad, Pakistan
Faith Hill (ent.; 1967-)

Faith Popcorn (b. Faith Plotkin)(writer/trend
    analyst; 1943-)
Faith, Percy (cond.; 1908-76)
Faithfull, Marianne (ent.; 1946-)
Falana, Lola (Loletha Elaine)(ent.; 1943-)
Falasha (people)
Falcam, Leo A. (pres., Micronesia; 1935-)
Falco, Edie (ent.; 1963-)
Falcons, Atlanta (football team)
Faldo, Nick (golf; 1957-)
Falk, Lee (cartoonist; 1911-99)
Falk, Peter (ent.; 1927-)
Falkenburg, Jinx (Eugenia)(ent.; 1919-)
Falkland Islands (Br., S Atl.)
Falklands War (Argentina/Br.; 1982)
Fall of the House of Usher, The (E.A. Poe story)
Fall River, MA
Falla, Manuel de (Sp. comp.; 1876-1946)
Falling Water (also Kaufman house)(F.L. Wright
    house)
Fallon Naval Air Station (NV)
Fallon, NV
Falstaff, (Sir) John (fict. chara., Shakespeare)
Faludi, Susan (US writer; 1959-)
Falun Gong (aka Falun Dafa)(phil. group, China)
Falwell, Jerry, Rev. (US rel.; 1933-)
Famagusta, Cyprus (Turk.)
Fame Bowl, Hall of (college football)
Fame, Hall of (NY)(erected 1990)
Familiar Quotations, Bartlett's (book)
Family Affair (TV show)
Family Channel, The (FAM)(cable TV)
Family Circle (mag.)
Family Circus, The (comic strip)
Family Feud (TV show)
Family Handyman, The (mag.)
Family Matters (TV show)
Family Stone, Sly and the (pop music)
Family Ties (TV show)
Family Fun (mag.)
Famous Amos Chocolate Chip Cookie, The (US
    bus.)
Fang (lang./people)
Fangio, Juan (auto racing; 1911-95)
Fannie (Frances) Farmer (ent.; 1914-70)
Fannie (Merritt) Farmer (US chef/educ./writer;
    1857-1915)
Fannie Hurst (US writer; 1889-1968)
Fannie Mae (also Federal National Mortgage
    Association, FNMA)
Fanning, Shawn (aka Napster; 1981-)
Fanny Brice (b. Fannie Borach)(ent.; 1891-1951)
Fanny (Frances) Burney (Madame D'Arblay)(Br.
    writer; 1752-1840)
Fanny (Francis Anne) Kemble (Br. writer/ent.;
    1809-93)
Fantasia (film, 1940)
Fantastic Four, The (cartoon charas.)
Fantastic Sam's Family Haircutters (US bus.)
Fantastik (cleaner)
Fantasy Island (TV show)
Fantin-Latour, (Ignace) Henri (Joseph
    Théodore)(Fr. artist; 1836-1904)
FAO (Food and Agriculture Organization)(UN agcy.)
FAO Schwarz (toy store/mail order)

FAPR (Fellow of the Academy of Professional
Reporters)
Far East (all of Asia E of the Indian
subcontinent)
Far Niente Winery (US bus.)
Far Side, The (cartoon)
Farad Aidid, Muhammad (Somali gen.)
Faraday cage (shield)
Faraday, Michael (Br. chem./physt; 1791-1867)
Faraday's constant (elec.)
Faraday's laws (elec.)
Farah Diba
Farah, Inc.
Farberware, Inc.
Farentino, James (ent.; 1938-)
Farge, John La (US artist; 1835-1910)
Fargo & Co., Wells
Fargo, Donna (ent.; 1945-)
Fargo, ND
Fargo, William George (US bus.; 1818-81)
Farley Granger (ent.; 1925-)
Farley, Chris (ent.; 1964-97)
Farm Journal
Farmer, Fannie (Frances)(ent.; 1914-70)
Farmer, Fannie (Merritt)(US chef/educ./writer;
1857-1915)
Farmer, James (US civil rights leader; 1920-99)
Farmer's Almanac, The
Farmer's Loan and Trust Co., Pollock v. (US
law; 1895)
Farmington, CT, ME, MI, MO, NH, NM
Farmland Industries, Inc.
Farner, Mark (ent., Grand Funk Railroad; 1948-)
Farnese Palace (Rome)
Farnese, Alessandro (Pope Paul III)(It.; 1468-
1549)
Farnsworth, Philo T. (US physt./TV pioneer;
1906-71)
Farnsworth, Richard (ent.; 1920-)
Faro, Portugal
Faroe Islands (also Faeroe)(N Atl.)
Faroese (lang.)
Faron Young (ent.; 1932-96)
Farooq Leghari (ex-pres., Pak.; 1940-)
Farouk I (king, Eg.; 1920-65)
Farr, Jamie (b. Jameel Joseph Farah)(ent.; 1934-)
Farragut, David (US adm.; 1801-70)
Farrah Aidid, Mohammed (Somali gen.)
Farrah Fawcett (ent.; 1947-)
Farrakhan, Louis (b. Louis Eugene Walcott)
(Islam/US rel.; 1933-)
Farrar, Geraldine (ent.; 1882-1967)
Farrar, Straus & Girous, Inc.
Farrell, Charles (ent.; 1902-90)
Farrell, Eileen (ent.; 1920-)
Farrell, James T(homas)(US writer; 1904-79)
Farrell, Mike (ent.; 1939-)
Farrell, Perry (b. Perry Bernstein)(ent.; 1959-)
Farrell, Suzanne (b. Roberta Sue Ficker)(ballet;
1945-)
Farrow, Mia (ent.; 1945-)
Fars (province, Iran)
Farsi (lang.)
Fasanella, Ralph (US artist; 1914-97)
Fassbinder, Rainer Werner (Ger. ent.; 1946-82)

Fast Times at Ridgemont High (film, 1982)
Fast, Howard (US writer; 1914-)
Fasteeth (med.)
FasText (stenoscription system)
Fat Albert (cartoon chara.)
Fat Boy's Bar-B-Q (US bus.)
Fat City
Fata Morgana (Arthurian)
Fatah, Al (also al-Fatah)(PLO guerrilla group)
Fatal Attraction (film, 1987)
Fate (mag.)
Fates, three (Clotho, Lachesis, Atropos)(myth.)
Father (God)
Father Divine (also Major M. J. Divine)(b.
George Baker)(US rel.; 1882-1965)
Father Dowling Mysteries (TV show)
Father Goose (film, 1964)
Father Time (personification of time)
Father, Life With (play; film, 1947)
Father's Day (3rd Sunday in June)
Fatiha (rel.)
Fátima (fict. chara., *Arabian Nights*)
Fátima (wife of Ali, daughter of Mohammed;
606?-632)
Fátima, Miracle of
Fátima, Portugal
Fatman, Jake & the (TV show)
Fatone, Joey (ent., 'N Sync; 1977-)
Fats (Antoine) Domino (ent.; 1928-)
Fats (Theodore) Navarro (US jazz; 1923-50)
Fats (Thomas Wright) Waller (US comp./jazz;
1904-43)
Fatty (Roscoe) Arbuckle (ent.; 1887-1933)
Faubus, Orval E(ugene)(ex-gov., AR; 1910-94)
Faulkner, William (US writer; 1897-1962)
Fauntleroy suit, Little Lord
Fauntleroy, Little Lord (book by F. H. Burnett)
Faunus (myth.)
Fauré, Gabriel (Fr. comp.; 1845-1924)
Faust (by Goethe)
Faust (legendary magician, sold his soul to the
Devil)
Faust (or Faustus), Johann (Ger. fortuneteller/
magician; 1480?-1540?)
Faustin Twagiramungu (ex-PM, Rwanda; 1945-)
Faustino, David (ent.; 1974-)
Faustus, Doctor (also *The Tragical of Doctor
Faustus*)(by C. Marlowe)
Fauves, Les (also l.c.)(Fauvist artists)
Fauvism (also l.c.)(style of painting)
Fauvist (also l.c.)(grp. of Fr. artists)
Favreau, Jon (ent.; 1966-)
Fawcett Books (US bus.)
Fawcett, Farrah (ent.; 1947-)
Fawkes Day, Guy (Br.)
Fawkes, Guy (Br. conspirator; 1570-1606)
Fawlty Towers (TV show)
Fawn Hall (US news; 1959-)
Fay Bainter (ent.; 1892-1968)
Fay Separates, Leslie (US bus.)
Fay Wray (ent.; 1907-)
Fay, Inc., Leslie
Fay, Morgan le (also Morgain le Fay)(King
Arthur's fairy sister)
Fayard Nicholas (ent.; 1914-)

Faye Dunaway (ent.; 1941-)
Faye Wattleton (US reformer; 1943-)
Faye, Alice (ent.; 1912-98)
Fayed, Dodi Al (Br. news; 1955-97)
Fayette, Marie Madeleine Pioche de la Vergne La
    (Comtesse de La Fayette)(Fr. writer; 1634-93)
Fayetteville Observer-Times (NC newspaper)
Fayetteville, AR, NC, TN
Fayumi, Saadia ben Joseph al- (aka Saadia
    Gaon)(Jew. scholar; 882-942)
Fazal Elahi Chaudry (ex-pres., Pak.; 1904-88)
Fazio, Vic(tor Herbert), Jr. (US pol.; 1942-)
FBI (Federal Bureau of Investigation)(DOJ agcy.)
FCC (Federal Communications Commission)(US
    govt. agcy.)
FDA (Food and Drug Administration)(US govt.
    agcy.)
FDIC (Federal Deposit Insurance Corporation)
    (banking)
February Revolution (Fr.; 1848)
February Revolution (Russian Revolution; 1917)
Fedders Corp.
Federal Aviation Administration (FAA)(DOT agcy.)
Federal Bureau of Investigation (FBI)(DOJ agcy.)
Federal Communications Commission (FCC)(US
    govt. agcy.)
Federal Constitutional Convention
Federal Deposit Insurance Corporation (FDIC)
    (banking)
Federal Emergency Management Agency
    (FEMA)
Federal Express (shipping)
Federal Express Corp. (FedEx)
Federal Home Loan Mortgage Corporation
    (FHLMC, Freddie Mac)
Federal Insurance Contributions Act (FICA)
Federal Land Bank(s)(US govt.)
Federal National Mortgage Association (FNMA,
    Fannie Mae)
Federal Reserve Bank
Federal Reserve note
Federal Reserve System (also the "Fed")(US
    banking)
Federal Security Service (FSB)(ex-KGB, Russia)
Federal Trade Commission (FTC)(US govt. agcy.)
Federalist (US pol. party; late 1700s)
Federated Department Stores, Inc.
Federated Malay States
Federico F. Pena (US ex-secy./trans., secy./
    ener.; 1947-)
Federico Fellini (It. ent.; 1920-93)
Federico Salas Guevara (ex-PM, Peru; 1950-)
FedEx (Federal Express Corp.)
Feen-a-Mint (med.)
Fehling, Hermann (Ger. chem.; 1812-85)
Fehling's test/solution (sugar)
Feiffer, Jules (cartoonist; 1929-)
Fein, Sinn (Ir. pol. party)
Feingold, Russell (US cong.; 1953-)
Feininger, Andreas (Bernhard Lyonel)(US
    photo.; 1906-99)
Feininger, Lyonel (Charles Adrian)(US artist;
    1871-1956)
Feinstein, Dianne (US cong.; 1933-)
Feisal I (also Faisal I)(king, Iraq; 1885-1933)

Feisal II (also Faisal II)(king, Iraq; 1935-58)
Felber, Réne (ex-pres., Switz.)
Feldene (med.)
Feldman, Corey (ent.; 1971-)
Feldman, Marty (ent.; 1933-82)
Feldon, Barbara (ent.; 1941-)
Feldshuh, Tovah (ent.; 1952-)
Feliciano, Jose (ent.; 1945-)
Felipe González Márquez (ex-PM, Spain; 1942-)
Felix Adler (US phil.; 1851-1933)
Felix Bloch (Swiss/US physt.; 1905-83)
Felix Frankfurter (US jurist; 1882-1965)
Félix Houphouët-Boigny (ex-pres., Ivory Coast;
    1905-93)
Felix Mendelssohn (-Bartholdy), (Jakob Ludwig)
    (Ger. comp.; 1809-47)
Felix Salten (b. Siegmund Salzman)(Aus.
    writer; 1869-1945)
Felix the Cat (cartoon chara.)
Felix Wankel (Ger., inv.; 1902-88)
Felker, Clay S. (US publ./editor; 1925-)
Fell, Norman (ent. 1924-98)
Feller, Bob (baseball; 1918-)
Fellini, Federico (It. ent. ; 1920-93)
Fellowes Manufacturing Co.
Feltsman, Vladimir (Rus. pianist; 1952-)
FEMA (Federal Emergency Management Agency)
Feminist Majority Foundation
Femiron (med.)
Femstat (med.)
Fender, Freddie (b. Baldemar Huerta)(ent.; 1937-)
Fenech Adami, Edward (PM, Malta; 1934-)
Fenian movement (Ir./Amer.; 1858-67)
Fenland (also the Fens)(fertile agricultural area, Eng.)
Fenneman, George (ent.; 1919-97)
Fenway Park (Boston)
Fenwick, Millicent (US pol.; 1900-92)
Feodor Ivanovitch Chaliapin (Rus. basso; 1873-
    1938)
Feoktistov, Konstantin P. (cosmo.)
Ferber, Edna (US writer; 1887-1968)
Ferde Grofe (US comp.; 1892-1972)
Ferdinand (king, Bulgaria; 1861-1948)
Ferdinand Cortés (or Hernando)(also Cortez)
    (Sp. expl.; 1485-1547)
Ferdinand de Lesseps, Vicomte (Fr. dipl./eng.;
    1805-94)
Ferdinand de Saussure (Swiss linguist; 1857-
    1913)
Ferdinand E(dralin) Marcos (ex-pres., Phil.;
    1917-89)
Ferdinand Foch (Fr. mil.; 1851-1929)
Ferdinand I (Ferdinand the Great)(king, Castile;
    c1016-65)
Ferdinand II (Holy Roman emp.; 1578-1637)
Ferdinand III (Holy Roman emp.; 1608-57)
Ferdinand Magellan (Port. nav.; c1480-1521)
Ferdinand Porsche (Ger. eng./auto.; 1875-1951)
Ferdinand the Great (Ferdinand I)(king, Castile;
    c1016-65)
Ferdinand V (king, Castile; 1452-1516)
Ferdinand von Zeppelin, Graf (or Count)(Ger.
    mil./aeronaut; 1838-1917)
Ferdinand, Franz (or Francis)(archduke, Aus.;
    1863-1914)

Ferenc Mádl (pres., Hung.; 1931-)
Ferenc Molnár (Hung. writer; 1878-1952)
Ferenc Nagy (ex-PM, Hung.; 1903-79)
Ferghana, Uzbekistan
Fergie (Sarah Margaret) Ferguson (Br.,
    Duchess of York; 1959-)
Ferguson Arthur Jenkins (baseball; 1943-)
Ferguson, Danny (US news)
Ferguson, Inc., Massey- (US bus.)
Ferguson, Maynard (ent.; 1928-)
Ferguson, Plessy v. (US law; 1896)
Ferguson, Sarah Margaret "Fergie" (Br.,
    Duchess of York; 1959-)
Ferlin Husky (ent.; 1927-)
Ferlinghetti, Lawrence (US writer/publ.; 1919-)
Fermanagh (county, NIre.)
Fermat, Pierre de (Fr. math.; 1601-65)
Fermi, Enrico (It. physt.; 1901-54)
Fermilab (Fermi National Accelerator Lab.)
Fern Arable (fict. chara., *Charlotte's Web*)
Fernand Leger (Fr. artist; 1881-1955)
Fernandel (b. Fernand Joseph Desire
    Contandin)(ent.; 1903-71)
Fernando Bujones (ballet; 1955-)
Fernando Collor de Mello (ex-pres., Brazil; 1949-)
Fernando de la Rúa (pres., Argentina; 1937-)
Fernando Henrique Cardoso (pres., Brazil; 1931-)
Fernando Jose de Franca Dias van Dunem (ex-
    PM, Angola)
Fernando Lamas (ent.; 1915-82)
Fernando Valenzuela (baseball; 1960-)
Fernando van Dunem, (PM, Angola)
Ferrante & Teicher (US piano duo)
Ferrari (auto.)
Ferrari 355 Modena (auto.)
Ferrari 360 Modena (auto.)
Ferrari 360 Modena F1 (auto.)
Ferrari 360 Spider (auto.)
Ferrari 456 (auto.)
Ferrari 456GT (auto.)
Ferrari 456M (auto.)
Ferrari 456M GTA (auto.)
Ferrari 550 Barchetta Pininfarina (auto.)
Ferrari 550 Maranello (auto.)
Ferrari North America (US bus.)
Ferrari, Enzo (It. bus./auto.; 1898-1988)
Ferrari, Ermanno Wolf- (It. comp.; 1876-1948)
Ferraris, Galileo (It. physt./eng.; 1847-97)
Ferraro, Geraldine (US pol./1st major US
    female VP candidate; 1935-)
Ferrell, Conchata (ent.; 1943-)
Ferrell, Will (US ent./SNL; 1967-)
Ferrer, Jose (ent.; 1912-92)
Ferrer, Mel (ent.; 1917-)
Ferrer, Miguel (ent.; 1954-)
Ferri, Alessandra (ballet; 1963-)
Ferrigno, Lou (bodybuilder/ent.; 1952-)
Ferris Bueller's Day Off (film, 1986)
Ferris State University (Big Rapids, MI)
Ferris wheel
Ferris, Barbara (ent.; 1940-)
Ferris, George Washington Gale (US eng./inv.;
    1859-96)
Ferruccio Busoni (It. comp.; 1866-1924)
Ferruccio Lamborghini (It. bus.; 1917-93)

Fertile Crescent (Middle East)
Fess Parker (ent.; 1925-)
Festiva, Ford (auto.)
Festus Mogae (pres., Botswana; 1939-)
Fetchit, Stepin (b. Lincoln Perry)(ent.; 1898-1985)
Fetzer Vineyards (US bus.)
Feuerbach, Allan Dean (track; 1948-)
Feuerbach, Anselm (Ger. artist; 1829-80)
Feynman, Richard (Phillips)(US physt.; 1918-88)
Fez, Morocco (also Fès)
FFA (Future Farmers of America)
FFP (fresh frozen plasma)
FHA (Farmers Home Administration, Federal
    Housing Administration)
FHLMC (also Federal Home Loan Mortgage
    Corporation, Freddie Mac)
FHMA (Federal Home Mortgage Corp. [Freddie
    Mac])
Fianarantsoa, Madagascar
Fianna (also Fians)(Ir. hist.; 2nd-3rd c)
Fianna Fáil (Irish pol. party; 20th c)
Fians (also Fianna)(Ir. hist.; 2nd-3rd c)
Fiat USA, Inc.
Fibber McGee and Molly (radio comedy)
Fiberall (med.)
FiberCon (med.)
Fiberglas (constr.)
Fibonacci numbers/sequence (math.)
Fibonacci, Leonardo (It. math.; c1175-c1250)
Fibranne
Fibreboard Corp.
FICA (Federal Insurance Contributions Act)
Fichte, Johann (Ger. phil.; 1762-1814)
Fiddler on the Roof (play)
Fidel Castro Ruíz (pres., Cuba; 1927-)
Fidel V. Ramos (ex-pres., Phil.; 1928-)
Fidèle Moungar (ex-PM, Chad)
Fidelism (also Fidelismo)
Fidelity Investments (aka FMR Corp.)
Fiedler, Arthur (US cond.; 1894-1979)
Fiedler, John (ent.; 1925-)
Field & Stream (mag.)
Field, Cyrus West (US finan., 1st Atl. cable;
    1819-92)
Field, Eugene (US poet; 1850-95)
Field, Marshall (US merchant; 1834-1906)
Field, Sally (ent.; 1946-)
Fieldcrest-Cannon, Inc.
Fielder, Cecil (baseball; 1963-)
Fielding, Henry (Br. writer; 1707-54)
Fields, Dorothy (US lyricist; 1905-74)
Fields, Gracie (ent.; 1898-1979)
Fields, Inc., Mrs.
Fields, Kim (ent.; 1969-)
Fields, Totie (ent.; 1931-78)
Fields, W. C. (b. William Claude Dukenfield)(US
    ent.; 1880-1946)
Fiennes, Joseph (ent.; 1970-)
Fiennes, Ralph (ent.; 1962-)
Fierstein, Harvey (ent./writer; 1954-)
Fiesta Bowl (college football)
Fiesta ware
Fife (region, Scot.)
Fife Symington (ex-AZ gov.; 1945-)
FIFO (first in, first out)

Fifth Avenue, Chrysler (auto.)
.Fifty-four-forty or Fight (US hist.)
Fig Newtons (cookies)
Figgis, Mike (ent./writer/comp.; 1948-)
Fighting Sullivans, The (film, 1942)
Fiji (Republic of)(SW Pac.)
Fijian (lang./people)
Filbert Bayi (runner; 1953-)
Filene, Edward A. (US bus.; 1860-1937)
Filene's department store (Boston)
Filho, Oscar Niemeyer Soares (Brazilian arch.; 1907-)
Filip Dimitrov (ex-PM, Bulgaria)
Filipchenko, Anatoly (cosmo.; 1928-)
Filipino (also Pilipino)(lang.)
Filipino (people)
Filippo (or Filippino) Lippi (It. artist; 1457-1504)
Filippo Brunelleschi (It. arch.; 1377-1446)
Filippo Lippi, (Fra)(It. artist; 1406-69)
Filippo, Fra Lippi (It. artist; 1406-69)
Fillmore, Millard (13th US pres.; 1800-74)
Final Solution (Nazi annihilation policy)
Final/Last Judgment (rel.)
Finance Committee, Senate (US govt.)
Financial World (mag.)
Finch, Peter (ent.; 1916-77)
Finder (compu.)
Fine, Larry (b. Louis Feinberg)(ent.; 1902-75)
Finesse (hair care)
Fingal's Cave (by Mendelssohn)
Fingal's Cave (Scot.)
Finger Lakes region (NY)
Finian's Rainbow (film, 1968)
Finland (Republic of)(N Eur.)
Finland, Gulf of (arm of Baltic Sea)
Finlandia
Finley, Charles O. (US bus./baseball; 1918-96)
Finn, Huckleberry (fict. chara., Mark Twain)
Finn, Huckleberry (M. Twain novel)
Finn, Mickey (drugged drink)
Finnair (airline)
Finnbogadóttir, Vigdís (ex-pres., Iceland; 1930-)
Finnegan Begin Again (film, 1984)
Finnegan's Wake (film, 1963)
Finney, Albert (ent.; 1936-)
Finney, Joan (Marie)(nee McInroy)(ex-KS gov.; 1925-)
Finnish (lang./people)
Finnish War, Russo- (Rus./Fin.; 1939-40)
Finno-Ugric (family of langs.)
Finns (people)
Fiona Apple (b. Fiona Apple McAfee Maggart)(ent.; 1977-)
Fiorello (Henry) La Guardia (ex-mayor, NYC; 1882-1947)
Fiorentino, Linda (b. Clorinda Fiorentino)(ent.; 1960-)
Fiorinal (med.)
Firebird, Pontiac (auto.)
Firebird, The (by Stravinsky)
Firestone (tires)
Firestone Tire & Rubber Co.
Firestone, Harvey (Samuel)(US bus.; 1868-1938)
Firing Line (TV show)
Firkusny, Rudolf (pianist; 1912-94)

First Cause (rel.)
First Data Corp.
First Legal Tender Case (*Hepburn v. Griswold*)(US law; 1870)
First Reich (Holy Roman Empire; 962-1806)
First State (nickname, DE)
First Temple (rel.)
First Triumvirate (ancient Rome ruling board)
First Union Corp.
First World War (also World War I, WWI)(1914-18)
Firth of Forth (also Firth of Forth Bridge)(Scot., arm of North Sea)
Firth, Colin (ent.; 1960-)
Firth, Peter (ent.; 1953-)
Fischbacher, Siegfried (illusionist, Siegfried and Roy; 1939-)
Fischer (skis)
Fischer-Dieskau, Dietrich (baritone; 1925-)
Fischer, Bobby (Robert James)(US chess; 1943-)
Fischer, Emil Hermann (Ger. chem.; 1852-1919)
Fischer, Hans (Ger. chem.; 1881-1945)
Fish Called Wanda, A (film, 1988)
Fish, Hamilton (US pol.; 1808-93)
Fish, Hamilton, III (US pol.; 1899-1991)
Fish, Hamilton, Jr. (US cong.; 1926-)
Fishburne, Laurence (ent.; 1962-)
Fisher (nuts)
Fisher Nut Co.
Fisher-Price Toys (US bus.)
Fisher USA Corp., Sanyo
Fisher, Amy ("Long Island Lolita")(US news; 1974-)
Fisher, Bud (cartoonist, *Mutt & Jeff*; 1884-1954)
Fisher, Carrie (ent.; 1956-)
Fisher, Eddie (ent.; 1928-)
Fisher, Fred (US comp.; 1875-1942)
Fisher, Ham (US cartoonist, *Joe Palooka*; 1900-55)
Fisher, Irving (US econ.; 1867-1947)
Fisher, Joely (ent.; 1967-)
Fisher, Mary Frances Kennedy (M.F.K.)(US writer; 1909-92)
Fisher, Mel (maritime treasure hunter; 1922-98)
Fiske, John (US hist.; 1842-1901)
Fiske, Minnie Maddern (ent.; 1865-1932)
Fitch, Abercrombie & (US bus.)
Fitch, John (US inv.; 1743-98)
Fitchburg, MA
Fitr, Eid ul- (Muslim festival)
Fittipaldi, Emerson (auto racing; 1946-)
Fitzgerald, Barry (ent.; 1888-1961)
Fitzgerald, Edward (Br. poet; 1809-83)
Fitzgerald, Ella (US jazz; 1918-96)
Fitzgerald, F(rancis) Scott (Key)(US writer; 1896-1940)
Fitzgerald, Geraldine (Ir./US ent.; 1913-)
Fitzgerald, Pegeen (radio broadcaster; 1910-89)
Fitzgerald, Peter G. (US cong.; 1960-)
FitzRoy (James Henry) Somerset Raglan, Baron (Br. gen., raglan sleeve; 1788-1855)
Fitzsimmons Army Medical Center (CO)(mil.)
Fitzsimmons, Bob (Robert Prometheus)(boxing; 1862-1917)
Fitzsimmons, Buckley v. (US law; 1993)
Fitzwater, Marlin (US pol./ex-press secy.; 1942-)
Five Civilized Tribes/Nations

Five Dynasties
Five Dynasties and Ten Kingdoms
Five Satins, the (pop music)
Five-Year Plan (USSR hist., Stalin)
Fixit, Mr. (slang)
Fixx, James "Jim" S. (US runner; 1932-84)
F. Korbel & Brothers, Inc.
FL (Florida)
Flaccus Albinus Alcuinus (also Alcuin, Ealhwine
    Flaccus, Alchuine, Albinus)(Br. scholar; 735-804)
Flack, Roberta (ent.; 1939-)
Flag Day (unofficial holiday)
Flagg, James Montgomery (US cartoonist, Uncle
    Sam; 1877-1960)
Flagler, Henry M(orrison)(US finan.; 1830-1913)
Flagstad, Kirsten (Wagnerian soprano; 1895-
    1962)
Flagstaff, AZ
Flagyl (med.)
Flaherty, Robert (ent.; 1884-1951)
Flame Glow (toiletries)
Flames, Calgary (hockey team)
Flamingo Kid, The (film, 1984)
Flammarion, Camille (Fr. astron.; 1842-1925)
Flanders field
Flanders, Ed (ent.; 1934-95)
*Flanders, The Fortunes and Misfortunes of the
    Famous Moll* (D. Defoe)
Flannagan, John Bernard (US sculptor; 1895-
    1942)
Flannery O'Connor, (Mary)(US writer; 1925-64)
Flash Gordon (comic strip)
Flash, Grandmaster (b. Joseph Saddler)(ent.;
    1958-)
Flash, Jumpin' Jack (song; film, 1986)
Flat Earth Research Society International
Flathead (also Salish)(Native Amer.)
Flatley, Michael (dance; 1958-)
Flatt, Lester (Raymond)(ent.; 1914-79)
Flaubert, Gustave (Fr. writer; 1821-80)
Flavio Cotti (ex-pres., Switz.)
Flavius Sabinus Vespasianus (aka Titus)(Roman
    emp.; AD 39-81)
F(rancis) Lee Bailey (US atty.; 1933-)
Fleet enema (med.)
Fleet Street (London, publishing)
Fleet, Jo Van (ent.; 1919-96)
FleetBoston Financial Corp.
Fleetwood Brougham, Cadillac (auto.)
Fleetwood DeVille, Cadillac (auto.)
Fleetwood Enterprises, Inc.
Fleetwood Mac (pop music)
Fleetwood, Cadillac (auto.)
Fleetwood, Mick (ent.; 1942-)
Fleischer, Ari (US White House press secy.;
    1960?-)
Fleischer, Max (US cartoonist, *Betty Boop,
    Popeye*; 1883-1972)
Fleischmann's Yeast, Inc.
Fleiss, Heidi (US news)
Fleming (people)
Fleming Companies, Inc.
Fleming, Ian (Lancaster)(Br. writer ; 1908-64)
Fleming, Peggy (Gale)(figure skating; 1948-)
Fleming, Rhonda (ent.; 1923-)

Fleming, (Sir) Alexander (Br. bacteriol.; 1881-
    1952)
Flemish (lang./people)
Flemish architecture
Flemish art
Flensburg, Germany
Flesh Gordon (film, 1972)
Fletch (film, 1985)
Fletcher Henderson (US jazz; 1898-1952)
Fletcher v. Peck (US law; 1810)
Fletcher, Jessica (fict. chara., *Murder, She Wrote*)
Fletcher, John (Br. dramatist; 1579-1625)
Fletcher, Louise (ent.; 1934-)
Fletcher's Castoria (med.)
Flexeril (med.)
Flexon (med.)
Flicka, My Friend ((film, 1943)
Flickertail State (nickname, ND)
Flim-Flam Man, The (film, 1967)
Flinders Petrie, (Sir William Matthew)(Br.
    archaeol.; 1853-1942)
Flint Journal (MI newspaper)
Flint, MI
Flint, Our Man (film, 1966)
Flintstone, Fred (cartoon chara.)
Flintstones vitamins
Flintstones, The (cartoon; film, 1960, 1994)
Flip (Clerow) Wilson (ent.; 1933-98)
Flip-Top (cigarette box)
Flippen, Jay C. (ent.; 1900-71)
Flipper (TV show)
FLIX (TV channel)
Flo Jo (Florence Griffith) Joyner (sprinter;
    1959-98)
Flo(renz) Ziegfeld (ent.; 1869-1932)
Flockhart, Calista (ent.; 1964-)
Flood, the (also the Deluge)(rel.)
Flora (myth.)
Florence Chadwick (US swimmer; 1918-95)
Florence fennel (also finocchio)(herb)
Florence Griffith Joyner ("Flo Jo")(track; 1959-
    98)
Florence Henderson (ent.; 1934-)
Florence Nightingale (Br., founded modern
    nursing; 1820-1910)
Florence, AL, CO, SC
Florence, Italy (also Firenze)
Flores Pérez, Francisco Guillermo (pres., El
    Salvador; 1959-)
Florida (FL)
Florida Keys (FL)
Florida Marlins (baseball team)
Florida Panhandle (NW FL)
Florio, James "Jim" J(oseph)(ex-NJ gov.; 1937-)
Florists' Transworld Delivery (FTD)
Florsheim Shoe Co., The
Flotow, Friedrich von (Ger. comp.; 1812-83)
Floyd Caves (Babe) Herman (baseball; 1903-87)
Floyd Douglas Little (football; 1942-)
Floyd Patterson (boxing; 1935-)
Floyd, Charles Arthur ("Pretty Boy")(US bank
    robber; 1901-34)
Floyd, Eddie (ent./songwriter; 1935-)
Floyd, Pink (pop music)
Floyd, Pretty Boy (Charles Arthur)(US bank

robber; 1901-34)
Floyd, Ray (golf; 1942-)
FLSA (Fair Labor Standards Act)
Flubber (film, 1997)
Flumadine (med.)
Flushing Meadow, NY (tennis center)
Flushing, NY
Fly, The (cartoon chara.)
Fly, The (film, 1958, 1986)
Fly, The Human (cartoon chara.)
Flyers, Philadelphia (hockey team)
Flying (mag.)
Flying Cross, Distinguished (mil.)
Flying Dutchman (legendary mariner)
Flying Fortress (B-17 bomber)
Flying Tiger Line
Flying Tigers
Flying Wallendas
Flynn, Errol (ent.; 1909-59)
Flynt, Larry (Claxton)(US publ./*Hustler*; 1942-)
FMC Corp.
FMR Corp. (aka Fidelity Investments)
F. Murray Abraham (ent.; 1939-)
FNMA (also Federal National Mortgage
   Association [Fannie Mae])
FO (foreign office)
Foch, Ferdinand (Fr. mil.; 1851-1929)
Foch, Nina (ent.; 1924-)
Focus, Ford (auto.)
Fodor, Eugene (US travel guide writer; 1906-91)
Fodor, Eugene (US violinist; 1950-)
Fodor's Travel Guides (US bus.)
FOE (Fraternal Order of Eagles)(FoE, Friends of
   the Earth [Br. environ. grp., est. 1971])
Fogarty, Tom (ent.; 1942-90)
Fogelberg, Dan (ent.; 1951-)
Fogerty, John (ent.; 1945-)
Fogg Art Museum (Harvard Univ.)
Foghorn Leghorn (cartoon chara.)
Fokin, Vitold (Ukrainian pol.)
Fokine, Michel (Rus. ballet/choreographer;
   1880-1942)
Folex (med.)
Foley catheter (med.)
Foley, Red (ent.; 1910-68)
Foley, Thomas S. (US pol.; 1929-)
Foley's department store
Folger Coffee Co., The
Folger Shakespeare Library (DC)
Folgers Coffee Singles
Folies-Bergère (Paris music hall)
Folkestone, England
Follett Publishing Co.
Follett, Ken(neth Martin)(Br. writer; 1949-)
Follette, Robert Marion La (ex-gov., WI; 1855-
   1925)
Follette, Robert Marion La, Jr. (US pol./publ.,
   WI; 1895-1953)
Folsom culture (anthrop., NM)
Folsom Prison (CA)
Fon (lang./people)
Foncard (comm.)
Fonda, Bridget (ent.; 1964-)
Fonda, Henry (ent.; 1905-82)
Fonda, Jane (ent.; 1937-)

Fonda, Peter (ent.; 1939-)
Fontaine, Frank (aka Crazy Guggenheim)(ent.;
   1920-78)
Fontaine, Jean de la (Fr. poet; 1621-95)
Fontaine, Joan (b. Joan de Beauvoir de
   Havilland)(ent.; 1917-)
Fontainebleau school (Fr., art)
Fontainebleau, France
Fontainebleau, palace at
Fontanne, Lynn (ent.; 1887-1983)
Fonteyn, Margot, Dame (ballet; 1919-91)
Fontvieille, Monaco
Fonzerelli, Arthur (also "the Fonz" or "Fonzie")
   (fict chara.)
Food and Agriculture Organization (FAO)(UN
   agcy.)
Food and Drug Act, Pure (US hist.; 1906)
Food and Drug Administration (FDA)(US govt.
   agcy.)
Food Network (TV channel)
Food & Wine (mag.)
Foods USA, General (US bus.)
Football Foundation and Hall of Fame, National
   (NFFHF)(est. 1947)
Football League, National (NFL)
Foote, Shelby (US hist.; 1916-)
For Better or Worse (comic strip)
Forbes (mag.)
Forbes, Malcolm (US publ.; 1919-90)
Forbes, Jr., (Malcolm) Steve(nson)(US publ.,
   pol.; 1947-)
Forbidden City (Peking, Ch.)
Ford (auto.)
Ford Aerostar (auto.)
Ford Aerostar XLT van (auto.)
Ford Aspire (auto.)
Ford Bronco (auto.)
Ford Bronco Eddie Bauer (auto.)
Ford Bronco XL (auto.)
Ford Bronco XLT (auto.)
Ford C. Frick (baseball; 1894-1978)
Ford Club Wagon (auto.)
Ford Contour (auto.)
Ford Contour GL (auto.)
Ford Contour LX (auto.)
Ford Contour SE (auto.)
Ford Contour SE Sport (auto.)
Ford Contour SVT (auto.)
Ford Crown Victoria (auto.)
Ford Crown Victoria LX (auto.)
Ford Econoline Club Wagon (auto.)
Ford Econoline Club Wagon Chateau (auto.)
Ford Econoline Club Wagon XL (auto.)
Ford Econoline Club Wagon XLT (auto.)
Ford Econoline Van (auto.)
Ford Econoline Van E-150 (auto.)
Ford Econoline Van E-250 (auto.)
Ford Econoline Van E-350 (auto.)
Ford Econoline Wagon (auto.)
Ford Econoline Wagon E-150 (auto.)
Ford Econoline Wagon E-250 (auto.)
Ford Econoline Wagon E-350 (auto.)
Ford Edsel (auto.)
Ford Escape (auto.)
Ford Escape XLS (auto.)

© 2001 *StenEd*® **Proper Noun Speller**

Ford Escape XLT (auto.)
Ford Escort (auto.)
Ford Escort GT (auto.)
Ford Escort LX (auto.)
Ford Escort SE (auto.)
Ford Escort ZX2 (auto.)
Ford Excursion (auto.)
Ford Excursion Limited (auto.)
Ford Excursion XLT (auto.)
Ford Expedition (auto.)
Ford Expedition Eddie Bauer (auto.)
Ford Expedition XLT (auto.)
Ford Explorer (auto.)
Ford Explorer Eddie Bauer (auto.)
Ford Explorer Limited (auto.)
Ford Explorer Sport (auto.)
Ford Explorer Sport Trac (auto.)
Ford Explorer XL (auto.)
Ford Explorer XLS (auto.)
Ford Explorer XLT (auto.)
Ford F-150 (auto.)
Ford F-150 Lariat pickup (auto.)
Ford F-150 pickup (auto.)
Ford F-150 SuperCrew pickup (auto.)
Ford F-150 SVT Lightning pickup (auto.)
Ford F-150 XL pickup (auto.)
Ford F-150 XLT pickup (auto.)
Ford F-250 pickup (auto.)
Ford F-350 pickup (auto.)
Ford F-450 pickup (auto.)
Ford F-550 pickup (auto.)
Ford F-750 (auto.)
Ford F-series (auto.)
Ford F-series Super Duty pickup (auto.)
Ford Festiva (auto.)
Ford Focus (auto.)
Ford Focus LX (auto.)
Ford Focus SE (auto.)
Ford Focus ZTS (auto.)
Ford Focus ZX3 (auto.)
Ford Foundation
Ford Madox Brown (Br. artist; 1821-93)
Ford Madox Ford (b. Ford Herman Heuffer)(Br.
    writer; 1873-1939)
Ford Mercury Villager (auto.)
Ford Mondeo (auto.)
Ford Motor Co. (auto.)
Ford Mustang (auto.)
Ford Mustang Cobra (auto.)
Ford Mustang GT (auto.)
Ford Mustang SVT Cobra convertible (auto.)
Ford Pinto (auto.)
Ford Probe (auto.)
Ford Probe GT (auto.)
Ford Probe SE (auto.)
Ford Ranger (auto.)
Ford Ranger Edge pickup (auto.)
Ford Ranger pickup (auto.)
Ford Ranger Splash pickup (auto.)
Ford Ranger XL pickup (auto.)
Ford Ranger XLT pickup (auto.)
Ford Taurus (auto.)
Ford Taurus G (auto.)
Ford Taurus GL (auto.)
Ford Taurus LX (auto.)

Ford Taurus SE (auto.)
Ford Taurus SEL (auto.)
Ford Taurus SES (auto.)
Ford Taurus SHO (auto.)
Ford Taurus wagon (auto.)
Ford Tempo (auto.)
Ford Thunderbird (T-Bird)(auto.)
Ford Thunderbird LX (T-Bird)(auto.)
Ford Van (auto.)
Ford Windstar GL minivan (auto.)
Ford Windstar Limited minivan (auto.)
Ford Windstar LX minivan (auto.)
Ford Windstar minivan (auto.)
Ford Windstar SE minivan (auto.)
Ford Windstar SE sport minivan (auto.)
Ford Windstar SEL minivan (auto.)
Ford ZX2 (auto.)
Ford, Betty (b. Elizabeth Bloomer Warren)(wife
    of ex-US pres.; 1918-)
Ford, Edsel (Bryant)(US bus./auto.; 1893-
    1943)
Ford, Gerald R(udolph)(b. Leslie Lynch King,
    Jr.)(38th US pres.; 1913-)
Ford, Glenn (ent.; 1916-)
Ford, Harrison (ent.; 1942-)
Ford, Henry (US bus./auto.; 1863-1947)
Ford, Henry, II (US bus./auto.; 1917-87)
Ford, John (ent.; 1895-1973)
Ford, Les Paul & Mary (ent.)
Ford, Mary (ent.; 1928-77)
Ford, Tennessee Ernie (ent.; 1919-91)
Ford, Wendell Hampton (US pol.; 1924-)
Ford, Whitey (Edward Charles)("Duke of
    Paducah")(baseball; 1928-)
Ford's Theater
Fordham University (New York, NY; Bronx, NY)
Fordham University Press (US bus.)
Fordice, (Daniel) Kirk(wood), Jr. (ex-MS gov.;
    1934-)
Forego (champion horse)
Foreign Legion (mil.)
Foreign Wars of the United States, Veterans of
    (VFW)(est. 1899)
Foreman, George (boxing; 1949-)
Forest Hills, NY
Forest Lawn Memorial Park (Glendale, CA)
Forest Whitaker (ent.; 1961-)
Forest, Lake, IL
Forest, Lee de (US inv., radio/sound films/TV;
    1873-1961)
Forester, C(ecil) S(cott)(Br. writer; 1899-1966)
Forester, Subaru (auto.)
Forman, Milos (Czech. ent.; 1932-)
Formby, Inc., Thompson &
Formby's
Formfit Rogers (US bus.)
Formica Corp.
Formosa (now Taiwan)
Formosa Strait (now Taiwan Strait)
Formosan (people)
Formula 409 (cleaner)
Fornax (astron., furnace)
Forrest E(dward) Mars (US bus.; 1904-99)
Forrest Gump (film, 1994)
Forrest Tucker (ent.; 1919-86)

Forrest, Nathan Bedford (US gen.; 1821-77)
.Forrest, Steve (ent.; 1924-)
Forrestal, James V(incent)(ex-secy./navy/
    defense; 1892-1949)
Forrester, Maureen (contralto; 1930-)
Forster, E(dward) M(organ)(Br. writer; 1879-
    1970)
Forstner bit (constr.)
Forsyth, Frederick (Br. writer; 1938-)
Forsythe, John (b. John Lincoln Freund)(ent.;
    1918-)
Fort Apache (film, 1948)
Fort Belvoir, VA (mil.)
Fort Benning, GA (mil.)
Fort Bliss, TX (mil.)
Fort Bragg, CA (city)
Fort Bragg, NC (mil.)
Fort Chaffee (AR)(mil.)
Fort Collins, CO (city)
Fort-de-France, Martinique
Fort Detrick (MD)(mil.)
Fort Devens, MA (mil.)
Fort Dix, NJ (mil.)
Fort Drum (NY)(mil.)
Fort Eustis, VA (mil.)
Fort George G. Meade (MD)(mil.)
Fort Gillern (GA)(mil.)
Fort Gordon, GA (mil.)
Fort Hamilton, NY (mil.)
Fort (Benjamin) Harrison, IN (mil.)
Fort Hood, TX (mil.)
Fort (Sam) Houston, TX (mil.)
Fort Huachuca, AZ (mil.)
Fort Hunter Liggett (CA)(mil.)
Fort Irwin, CA (mil.)
Fort Jackson, SC (mil.)
Fort James Corp.
Fort Knox, KY (mil., gold depository)
Fort Laramie (WY)
Fort Laramie National Historic Site (WY)
Fort Lauderdale News (FL newspaper)
Fort Lauderdale Sun-Sentinel (FL newspaper)
Fort Lauderdale, FL (city)
Fort Leavenworth, KS (mil.)
Fort Lee, NJ (city)
Fort Lee, VA (mil.)
Fort Leonard Wood, MO (mil.)
Fort McClellan, AL (mil.)
Fort McCoy (WI)
Fort McHenry (MD)(*Star Spangled Banner*)
Fort (Lesley J.) McNair (DC)(mil.)
Fort McPherson, GA (mil.)
Fort (George G.) Meade (MD)(mil.)
Fort Monmouth, NJ (mil.)
Fort Monroe, VA (mil.)
Fort Myer, VA (mil.)
Fort Myers News-Press (FL newspaper)
Fort Myers, FL (city)
Fort Ord, CA (mil.)
Fort Pierce, FL (city)
Fort Polk, LA (mil.)
Fort Richardson, AK (mil.)
Fort Riley, KS (mil.)
Fort Ritchie, MD (mil.)
Fort Rucker, AL (mil.)

Fort Sam Houston, TX (mil.)
Fort Shafter, HI (mil.)
Fort Sheridan, IL (mil.)
Fort Sill, OK (mil.)
Fort Smith, AR (city)
Fort Story, VA (mil.)
Fort Sumter, SC (fort)
Fort Ticonderoga, NY (fort)
Fort Wainwright (AK)(mil.)
Fort Walton Beach, FL (city)
Fort Wayne Journal-Gazette (IN newspaper)
Fort Wayne News-Sentinel (IN newspaper)
Fort Wayne, IN (city)
Fort Worth International Airport, Dallas- (TX)
Fort Worth Star-Telegram (TX newspaper)
Fort Worth, TX (city)
Fort Yukon, AK (city)
Fortaleza, Brazil
Fortas, Abe (US jurist; 1910-82)
Forth River (Scot.)
FORTRAN (formula translator)(compu. lang.)
Fortrel (fabric)
Fortune (mag.)
Fortune 500 (500 largest publicly-owned US
    indust. cos.)
Fortune Brands, Inc.
Forty Hours (rel.)
48 Hours (TV show)
49ers, San Francisco (football team)
42rd Street (play/movie)
Fosbury flop (track & field)
Fosbury, Dick (Richard)(jumper; 1947-)
Foscavir (med.)
Fosdick, Harry Emerson (US rel./writer; 1878-
    1969)
Fosse, Bob (ent.; 1927-87)
Fossey, Dian (US zool., gorillas; 1932-85)
Foster Parents Plan, Inc.
Foster, Hal (US cartoonist; *Tarzan, Prince
    Valiant*; 1892-1982)
Foster, Jodie (ent.; 1962-)
Foster, Meg (ent.; 1948-)
Foster, Mike (Murphy James), Jr. (LA gov.;
    1930-)
Foster, Preston (ent.; 1901-70)
Foster, Stephen Collins (US comp.; 1826-64)
Foster, Vincent, Jr. (US atty./pol.; 1945-93)
Fostex (med.)
Fotomat (photo.)
Fotomat Corp.
Foulah (also Fulah)(people)
Founding Fathers (Constitutional Convention
    delegates)
Fountain of Youth (fabled fountain)
Fountain, Pete (US jazz; 1930-)
Four Aces, The (pop music)
Four Corners (point where 4 states meet, AZ/
    UT/CO/NM)
Four Freedoms of FDR (of speech, of worship,
    from want, from fear; 1941)
Four-H Club (4-H)(agriculture)
Four Horsemen of the Apocalypse
Four Lads, The (pop music)
Four Noble Truths (Buddhism)
Four Seasons Hotel (NYC)

Four Seasons Solar Products, Corp.
Four Seasons, the (pop music)
Four Tops, the (pop music)
Four Wheeler (mag.)
Fourier, Charles (Fr. social scien.; 1772-1837)
Fourier, Jean B(aptiste) J(oseph)(Fr. math.; 1768-1830)
Fourierism (social phil.)
Fournier, Rafael Angel Calderón (ex-pres., Costa Rica; 1949-)
4Runner, Toyota (auto.)
Fourth of July (also July Fourth, Independence Day)
Fowles, John (Br. writer; 1926-)
FOX (FX)(TV channel)
Fox (Native Amer.)
Fox Family Channel (TV channel)
Fox Film Co., 20th Century-
Fox Indians, Sac (or Sauk) and
Fox Movie Channel (TV channel)
Fox Mulder (fict. chara., *The X-Files*)
Fox News Channel (TV channel)
Fox Record Corp., 20th Century-
Fox Sports Net (TV channel)
Fox Sports World (TV channel)
Fox Story, The Terry (film, 1983)
Fox, Brer (fict. chara., *Uncle Remus*)
Fox, George (Br. rel.; 1624-91)
Fox, James (ent.; 1939-)
Fox, Katherine (Can./US spiritualist)
Fox, Margaret (Can./US spiritualist; 1833-93)
Fox, Matthew (ent.; 1966-)
Fox, Michael J. (ent.; 1961-)
Fox, Nellie (Jacob Nelson)(baseball; 1927-75)
Fox, Samantha (ent.; 1966-)
Fox (Quesada), Vicente (pres., Mex.; 1942-)
Fox, Vivica A. (ent.; 1964-)
Foxworth, Robert (ent.; 1941-)
Foxworthy, Jeff (ent.; 1958-)
Foxx, Jamie (b. Eric Bishop)(ent.; 1967-)
Foxx, Jimmy (James Emory)(baseball; 1907-67)
Foxx, Redd (b. John Elroy Sandford)(ent.; 1922-91)
Foy, Eddie (ent.; 1857-1928)
Foy, Eddie, Jr. (ent.; 1905-83)
Foyt, A(nthony) J(oseph)(auto racing; 1935-)
Fozzie Bear (Muppet)
FPC (Federal Power Commission)
FPO (U.S. Navy Fleet Post Office)
Fr (chem. sym., francium)
Fra Angelico (It. artist; 1400-55)
Fra Bartolommeo (It. artist; 1472-1517)
Fra Filippo Lippi (It. artist; 1406-69)
Fracci, Carla (ballet; 1936-)
Fraggle Rock (cartoon)
Fragonard, Jean Honoré (Fr. artist; 1732-1806)
Frakes, Jonathan (ent.; 1952-)
Fraktur (type style)
Framingham, MA
Frampton, Peter (ent.; 1950-)
Fran & Ollie, Kukla, (TV show)
Fran Allison (ent.; 1908-89)
Fran Drescher (ent.; 1957-)
Fran(cis Asbury) Tarkenton (football; 1940-)
Francaise, Comédie (Fr. national theater)

France (French Republic)(Eur.)
France-Albert René (pres., Seychelles; 1935-)
France-Press, Agence (Eur. news org.; est. 1944)
France, Anatole (Fr. writer; 1844-1924)
France, Besançon (Roman ruins)
France, Tour de (Fr. bicycle race)
Frances "Fanny" Anne Kemble (Br. writer/ent.; 1809-93)
Frances Dee (ent.; 1907-)
Frances E(lizabeth Caroline) Willard (US educ./reformer; 1839-98)
Frances "Fannie" Farmer (ent.; 1914-70)
Frances Langford (ent.; 1913-)
Frances McDormand (ent.; 1957-)
Frances Parkinson Keyes (US writer; 1885-1970)
Frances Perkins (US sociol./pol.; 1882-1965)
Frances Sternhagen (ent.; 1930-)
Frances Xavier Cabrini, St. (also Mother Cabrini)(US rel./reformer; 1850-1917)
Francesc Badia Batalla (covicar, Andorra)
Francesca, Piero della (It. artist; c1415-92)
Francescatti, Zino (Fr. violinist; 1902-91)
Francesco Borromini (It. arch.; 1599-1667)
Francesco Cilea (It. comp.; 1866-1950)
Francesco Guicciardini (It. hist.; 1483-1540)
Francesco Petrarca (It. poet; 1304-74)
Francesco Scavullo (photo.; 1929-)
Francesco Sforza (It. pol.; 1401-66)
Franche-Comté (region, Fr.)
Franchi, Sergio (ent.; 1933-90)
Franchot Tone (ent.; 1903-68)
Francie Larrieu (track; 1952-)
Francine Pascal (writer; 1938-)
Franciosa, Anthony "Tony" (b. Anthony Papaleo)(ent.; 1928-)
Francis Affleck (auto racing; 1951-85)
Francis Bacon (Br. artist; 1909-92)
Francis Bacon, (Sir)(Br. phil./pol.; 1561-1626)
Francis Beaumont (Br. dramatist; 1584-1616)
Francis Billy Hilly (ex-PM, Solomon Islands)
Francis (Sellers) Collins (US genet./human genome; 1950-)
Francis Drake, (Sir)(Br. expl.; c1545-96)
Francis E(verett) Townsend (US phys./reformer; 1867-1960)
Francis (or Franz) Ferdinand (archduke, Aus.; 1863-1914)
Francis Ford Coppola (ent.; 1939-)
Francis Gary Powers (US mil./U-2 spy pilot shot down over USSR in 1960; 1929-77)
Francis H(arry) C(ompton) Crick (Br. physt.; 1916-)
Francis I (king, Fr.; 1492-1547)
Francis II (Holy Roman emp.; 1768-1835)
Francis II (king, Fr.; 1544-60)
Francis (or Franz) Joseph (Aus./Hung., emp.; 1830-1916)
Francis L. Sullivan (ent.; 1903-56)
Francis Lear (US publ.; 1923-)
Francis Lightfoot Lee (US pol.; 1734-97)
Francis Marion ("the Swamp Fox")(US mil./pol. c1732-95)
Francis of Assisi, St. (It. rel., founded Franciscans; 1182-1226)
Francis Parkman (US hist.; 1823-93)

Francis (Jean Marcel) Poulenc (Fr. comp.; 1899-1963)

Francis Quarles (Br. poet; 1592-1644)

Francis Richard "Dick" Scobee (astro., Challenger; 1939-86)

Francis Scott Key (US atty., wrote *The Star Spangled Banner*; 1780-1843)

Francis Steegmuller (biographer; 1906-94)

Francis the Talking Mule (film, 1949)

Francis W. Ayer (US adv.; 1848-1923)

Francis Xavier, St. (Francisco Javier)("the Apostle of the Indies")(Sp. rel.; 1506-52)

Francis X. Bushman (ent.; 1883-1966)

Francis, Anne (ent.; 1930-)

Francis, Arlene (b. Arline Francis Kazanjian) (ent.; 1907-2001)

Francis, Connie (b. Concetta Franconero)(ent.; 1938-)

Francis, Dick (Br. writer/jockey; 1920-)

Francis, Emile (hockey; 1926-)

Francis, Genie (ent.; 1962-)

Franciscan order (of friars)

Franciscan Vineyards (US bus.)

Francisco (José) de Goya y Lucientes (Sp. artist; 1746-1828)

Francisco Fernandez de Córdoba (also Cordova) (Sp. expl.; 1475?-1526)

Francisco Franco, Generalissimo (dictator, Sp.; 1892-1975)

Francisco Guillermo Flores Pérez (pres., El Salvador; 1959-)

Francisco Macías Nguema (ex-pres., Equatorial Guinea; 1924-79)

Francisco Pizarro (Sp. mil./expl.; 1475?-1541)

Francisco Vásquez de Coronado (Sp. expl.; c1510-54)

Franciscus, James (ent.; 1934-91)

Francisque Ravony (ex-PM, Madagascar)

Francistown, Botswana

Franck, César Auguste (Belg. comp.; 1822-90)

Franck, James (Ger./US physt.; 1882-1964)

Franco-American (foods)

Franco Corelli (tenor; 1923-)

Franco Harris (football; 1950-)

Franco-Prussian War (also Franco-German War)(Fr./Ger.-Prussia; 1870-71)

Franco Zeffirelli (ent.; 1923-)

Franco, Buddy De (US jazz; 1933-)

Franco, Generalissimo Francisco (dictator, Sp.; 1892-1975)

Franco, Itamar (ex-pres., Brazil; 1930-)

François (Fr. form of Francis)

François Boucher (Fr. artist; 1703-70)

François (Ambrose) Didot (Fr. printer; 1730-1804)

Francois Durr (tennis; 1942-)

François Duvalier (aka Papa Doc)(ex-pres., Haiti; 1907-71)

François Girardon (Fr. sculptor; 1628-1715)

François La Rochefoucauld, Duc de (Fr. writer; 1613-80)

François Mansard (or Mansart), (Nicolas)(Fr. arch.; 1598-1666)

François Mauriac (Fr. writer; 1885-1970)

François Mitterrand (ex-pres., Fr.; 1916-96)

François Quesnay (Fr. econ.; 1694-1774)

François Rabelais (Fr. writer; 1495-1553)

François René Chateaubriand (Fr. writer; 1768-1848)

François Rochefoucauld, Duc de La (Fr. writer; 1613-80)

François Toussaint L'Ouverture (Haitian pol.; c1744-1803)

François Truffaut (Fr. ent.; 1932-84)

François Villon (Fr. poet; 1431-63?)

François, Donatien Alphonse, Comte de Sade (Marquis de Sade)(Fr. mil./writer; 1740-1814)

Françoise Sagan (b. Françoise Quoirez)(Fr. writer; 1935-)

Francophile

Francophobe

Franjo Greguric (ex-PM, Croatia)

Franjo Tudjman (ex-pres., Croatia; 1922-99)

Frank (ancient people; 3rd-9th c.)

Frank and Ernest (comic strip)

Frank and Ollie (film, 1995)

Frank B(illings) Kellogg (US pol.; 1856-1937)

Frank B. Kelso, II (US adm.)

Frank Borman (astro.; 1928-)

Frank Cannon (fict. detective)

Frank Capra (ent.; 1897-1991)

Frank (Charles) Carlucci (US ex-secy./defense; 1930-)

Frank Chapot (equestrian; 1934-)

Frank De Vol (US comp.; 1911-99)

Frank Ernest Gannett (US newspaper publ.; 1876-1957)

Frank F. Mankiewicz (US jour.; 1924-)

Frank Fontaine (aka Crazy Guggenheim)(ent.; 1920-78)

Frank G. Slaughter (US writer; 1908-)

Frank Gifford (ent./football; 1930-)

Frank Gilroy (US writer; 1925-)

Frank Gorshin (ent.; 1934-)

Frank H. Murkowski (US cong.; 1933-)

Frank James (US outlaw; 1843-1915)

Frank (Francis Anthony) Keating (OK gov.; 1944-)

Frank King (cartoonist; *Gasoline Alley*; 1883-1969)

Frank (Frantisek) Kupka (Czech. artist; 1871-1957)

Frank Langella (ent.; 1940-)

Frank Lloyd Wright (US arch.; 1867-1959)

Frank Loesser (US comp.; 1910-69)

Frank Lorenzo (US bus./airlines)

Frank Lovejoy (ent.; 1912-62)

Frank (Francis William) Mahovlich (hockey; 1938-)

Frank McCloskey (US cong.; 1939-)

Frank McCourt (US writer; 1930-)

Frank Nelson Doubleday (US publ.; 1862-1934)

Frank Norris (US writer; 1870-1902)

Frank (Lewis) O'Bannon (IN gov.; 1930-)

Frank Oz (Muppet puppeteer; 1944-)

Frank R. Lautenberg (US pol.; 1924-)

Frank Reynolds (US jour.; 1923-83)

Frank Rich (US drama critic)

Frank Rizzo (ex-mayor, Phila.; 1921-91)

Frank Robinson (baseball; 1935-)

Frank Rosollino (US jazz; 1926-78)

Frank Selke (hockey; 1893-1985)
Frank Shorter (runner; 1947-)
Frank (Francis Albert) Sinatra (ent.; 1915-98)
Frank Stella (US artist; 1936-)
Frank (Francis Richard) Stockton (US writer; 1834-1902)
Frank (Francis John) Sullivan (US humorist; 1892-1976)
Frank (Wright) Tuttle (ent.; 1892-1963)
Frank Viola (baseball; 1960-)
Frank Willard (cartoonist, *Moon Mullins*; 1893-1958)
Frank W. Taussig (US econ./educ.; 1859-1940)
Frank W(infield) Woolworth (US bus.; 1852-1919)
Frank Yerby (US writer; 1916-92)
Frank Zappa (ent.; 1940-1993)
Frank, Anne (Ger./Jew. diarist; 1929-45)
Frank, Barney (US cong.; 1940-)
Frank, Édouard (ex-PM, Central African Republic)
Frankenheimer, John (ent.; 1930-)
Frankenstein (by Mary Shelley)
Frankenstein (film, 1931, 1973, 1982, 1993)
Frankenstein Meets the Wolf Man (film, 1943)
Frankenstein, Bride of (film, 1935)
Frankenstein, Dr. (fict. chara.)
Frankenstein, House of (film, 1944)
Frankenstein, The Revenge of (film, 1958)
Frankenstein, Young (film, 1974)
Frankenthaler, Helen (US artist; 1928-)
Frankfort, IN, KY, NY
Frankfurt, Germany
Frankfurt-am-Main, Germany
Frankfurter, Felix (US jurist; 1882-1965)
Frankie and Johnny (film, 1936, 1965, 1991)
Frankie Avalon (b. Francis Thomas Avallone) (ent.; 1939-)
Frankie Laine (b. Francisco Paolo LoVecchio) (ent.; 1913-)
Frankie Lymon (ent.; 1942-68)
Frankie Muniz (ent.; 1985-)
Frankie Valli (b. Frank Castelluccio)(ent.; 1937-)
Frankl, Victor E. (US psych.; 1905-97)
Franklin D(elano) Roosevelt (FDR)(32nd US pres.; 1882-1945)
Franklin D(elano) Roosevelt, Jr. (US pol.; 1914-88)
Franklin Gothic (type style)
Franklin Pierce (14th US pres.; 1804-69)
Franklin Pierce Adams (US writer; 1881-1960)
Franklin Stores, Ben (US bus.)
Franklin stove
Franklin Templeton Distributors, Inc.
Franklin Templeton Investments
Franklin, Aretha (ent.; 1942-)
Franklin, Benjamin (US publ./writer/inv./dipl.; 1706-90)
Franklin, Bonnie (ent.; 1944-)
Franklin, Eleanor & (film, 1976)
Franklin, Joe (ent.; 1929-)
Franklin, John Hope (US hist.; 1915-)
Frann, Mary (ent.; 1943-98)
Frans Hals (Dutch artist; c1580-1666)
Frans Snyders (Flem. artist; 1579-1657)
Frantisek (Frank) Kupka (Czech. artist; 1871-

1957)
Franz Boas (US anthrop.; 1858-1942)
Franz (or Francis) Ferdinand (archduke, Aus.; 1863-1914)
Franz (or Francis) Joseph (Aus./Hung. emp.; 1830-1916)
Franz Joseph Haydn (Aus. comp.; 1732-1809)
Franz Joseph II (ruler, Liechtenstein; 1906-89)
Franz Joseph Strauss (WGer. pol.; 1915-88)
Franz Kafka (Ger. writer; 1889-1961)
Franz Lehar (Hung. comp.; 1870-1948)
Franz Liszt (Hung. comp.; 1811-86)
Franz Marc (Ger. artist; 1880-1916)
Franz (or Friedrich Anton) Mesmer (Ger. phys.; 1734-1815)
Franz (Peter) Schubert (Aus. comp.; 1797-1828)
Franz von Papen (Ger. pol.; 1879-1969)
Franz Vranitzky (ex-chanc., Aus.; 1937-)
Franz Waxman (Ger./US comp.; 1906-67)
Franz Werfel (Aus. writer; 1890-1945)
Franz Xaver Gabelsberger (Ger. stenographer; 1789-1849)
Franz, Dennis (ent.; 1944-)
Franzia Brothers Winery (US bus.)
Frascati (wine)
Frasch process (sulfur extraction)
Fraser River (British Columbia, Can.)
Fraser, Antonia (Br. writer; 1932-)
Fraser, Brendan (ent.; 1968-)
Frasier (TV show, fict. chara.)
Fratianne, Linda (figure skating; 1960-)
Frau (Ger., married woman)
Fräulein (Ger., unmarried woman)
Fraunhofer lines/spectrum (dark lines of the sun)
Fraunhofer, Joseph von (Ger. optician/physt.; 1787-1826)
Frawley, William (ent.; 1887-1966)
Frazer, (Sir) James George (Scot. anthrop.; 1854-1941)
Frazier, Joe (boxing; 1944-)
Frazier, Walt (basketball; 1945-)
FSB (Federal Security Service, Russia)
Freberg, Stan (ent.; 1926-)
Fred & Barney (cartoon)
Fred Allen (b. John Florence Sullivan)(ent.; 1894-1956)
Fred Astaire (b. Frederick Austerlitz)(ent.; 1899-1987)
Fred(erick) DeCordova (US TV exec.; 1910-)
Fred Dryer (ent.; 1946-)
Fred D. Thompson (US cong.; 1942-)
Fred Edd (US lyricist; 1936-)
Fred Fisher (US comp.; 1875-1942)
Fred Flintstone (cartoon chara.)
Fred Grandy (ent./pol.; 1948-)
Fred Gwynne (ent.; 1926-93)
Fred(erick) Hoyle (Br. astron./writer; 1915-)
Fred Lasswell (cartoonist)
Fred Lawrence Whipple (US astron.; 1906-)
Fred Lawrence Whipple Observatory (AZ)
Fred MacMurray (ent.; 1908-91)
Fred M. Waring (US cond., designed Waring blender; 1900-84)
Fred Rogers (ent.; 1928-)
Fred Savage (ent.; 1976-)

Fred Shero (hockey; 1945-90)
Fred Silverman (ent.; 1937-)
Fred(erick) Timakata (ex-pres., Vanuatu; 1936-)
Fred Ward (ent.; 1942-)
Fred W(allace) Haise, Jr. (astro.; 1933-)
Fred (Frederick) Zinnemann (ent.; 1907-97)
Freddie Bartholomew (ent.; 1925-92)
Freddie Fender (b. Baldemar Huerta)(ent.; 1937-)
Freddie Mac (also FHLMC, Federal Home Loan
    Mortgage Corporation)
Freddie Mercury (b. Farookh Bulsara)(ent.;
    1946-91)
Freddie Prinze (ent.; 1954-77)
Freddie Prinze, Jr. (ent.; 1976-)
Frederic-Auguste Bartholdi (Fr. sculptor,
    designed Statue of Liberty; 1834-1904)
Frederic Bamvuginyumvira (PM, Burundi)
Frederic Chopin (Pol. comp.; 1810-49)
Frederic Church (US artist; 1826-1900)
Frederic Eugene Ives (US inv.; 1856-1937)
Frederic Joliot-Curie (Fr. physt.; 1900-58)
Frederic Michael Lynn (baseball; 1952-)
Frederic Mistral (Fr. poet; 1830-1914)
Frederic Remington (US artist; 1861-1909)
Frederica Von Stade (ent.; 1945-)
Frederick & Nelson department store
Frederick Biletnikoff (football; 1943-)
Frederick Burr Opper (cartoonist, *Happy
    Hooligan*; 1857-1937)
Frederick (Jacob Titus) Chiluba (pres., Zambia;
    1943-)
Frederick Dannay (pseud. Ellery Queen)(US
    writer; 1905-82)
Frederick Delius (Br. comp.; 1862-1934)
Frederick Douglass (US abolitionist, ex-slave;
    1817-95)
Frederick Forsyth (Br. writer; 1938-)
Frederick Grant Banting (physiol.; 1891-1941)
Frederick I (Barbarossa, "Red Beard")(Holy
    Roman emp.; 1123-90)
Frederick II ("Frederick the Great")(king,
    Prussia; 1712-86)
Frederick II ("the Wonder of the World")(Holy
    Roman emp.; 1194-1250)
Frederick III (king, Prussia; emp., Ger.; 1831-
    88)
Frederick IX (king, Den.; 1899-1972)
Frederick J(ackson) Turner (US hist./educ.;
    1861-1932)
Frederick L(aw) Olmsted (US landscaper; 1822-
    1903)
Frederick Loewe (US comp.; 1901-88)
Frederick North (ex-PM, Br.; 1732-92)
Frederick Sanger (Br. chem.; 1918-)
Frederick Soddy (Br. chem.; 1877-1956)
Frederick the Great (Frederick II)(king, Prussia;
    1712-86)
Frederick Tluway Sumaye (PM, Tanzania; 1950-)
Frederick V ("the Winter King")(king, Bohemia
    for one winter; 1596-1632)
Frederick William I (king, Prussia; 1688-1740)
Frederick William II (king, Prussia; 1744-97)
Frederick William III (king, Prussia; 1770-1840)
Frederick William IV (king, Prussia; 1795-1861)
Frederick William Mallandaine Ashton, (Sir)

(choreographer; 1904-88)
Frederick Winslow Taylor (US inv.; 1856-1915)
Frederick, Pauline (US radio/TV jour.; 1918-90)
Frederick's of Hollywood, Inc.
Fredericksburg, Battle of (US hist.; 1862)
Fredericksburg, TX, VA
Fredericktown, MO
Frederico Garcia Lorca (Sp. poet/dramatist;
    1898-1936)
Fredericton, New Brunswick, Canada
Frederik Pohl (US writer, sci-fi; 1919-)
Frederik W(illem) de Klerk (ex-pres., SAfr; 1936-)
Fredric March (ent.; 1897-1975)
Free Church of Tonga (rel.)
Free Press, Detroit (MI newspaper)
Free-Soil (pol. party)
Free State (nickname, MD)
Free Wesleyan (rel.)
Free Willy (film, 1993)
Free Willy 2: The Adventure (film, 1995)
Free Willy 3: The Rescue (film, 1997)
Freebie and the Bean (film, 1974)
Freebies (mag.)
Freed, James Ingo (US arch.; 1930-)
Freedom Bowl (college football)
Freedom of Information Act
Freedom, Presidential Medal of (US, highest
    civilian honor)
Freeh, Louis Joseph (US ex-dir./FBI; 1950-)
Freehand, Aldus (compu.)
Freelander, Land Rover (auto.)
Freeman Gosden (ent., Amos of *Amos 'n' Andy
    Show*; 1899-1982)
Freeman, Al, Jr. (ent.; 1934-)
Freeman, Morgan (ent.; 1937-)
Freemark Abbey Winery (US bus.)
Freemason (member, fraternal organization)
Freemasonry (Freemason phil.)
Freenet (compu.)
Freeport, IL, ME, NY, PA, TX
Freeport, the Bahamas
Freer Gallery of Art (Smithsonian, DC)
Freer, Charles Lang (US bus./art collector;
    1856-1919)
Freetown, Sierra Leone
Frege, Friedrich Ludwig Gottlob (Ger. phil.;
    1848-1925)
Freiberga, Vaira Vike- (pres., Latvia; 1937-)
Freiburg, Germany
Freixenet (champagne)
Freixenet USA, Inc.
Fremont, CA, NE
Fremont, John Charles (US mil.; 1813-90)
French (lang./people)
French Alpine (goat)
French and Indian War (NAmer./Br.; 1754-63)
French bed
French braid (hairstyle)
French bread
French bulldog (dog)
French Canadian
French coach horse
French connection (mixed drink)
French Creole (lang.)
French cuff (clothing)

French curve (drafting instrument)
French doors
French dressing
French East India Company (trade; 1664-1794)
French endive
French Equatorial Africa (former county)
French fries
French Guiana (SAmer.)
French heel (footwear)
French horn (musical inst.)
French kiss
French knot (also Fr. twist)(hairstyle)
French leave
French letter (slang, condom)
French patois (lang.)
French Polynesia (S Pac.)
French provincial/Provincial style
French Revolution (Fr. hist.; 1789-99)
French Revolutionary calendar
French Riviera
French roll
French seam (clothing)
French Sudan (now Republic of Mali)(NW Afr.)
French telephone
French toast
French twist (also Fr. knot)(hairstyle)
French West Africa (Senegal, Mauritania, Sudan,
   Burkina Faso, Guinea, Niger, Ivory Coast, Benin)
French windows
French, Daniel Chester (US artist; 1850-1931)
French, Norman (lang.)
French's Dijon mustard
Frenchman
Frenchwoman
Freon
Fresh Prince, D.J. Jazzy Jeff & the (pop music)
Fresh Start (detergent)
Fresh Step (cat litter)
Fresnel lens (lighthouses)
Fresnel, Augustin (Fr. physt.; 1788-1827)
Fresno Bee (CA newspaper)
Fresno, CA
Freud, Anna (Aus./Br., founder of child
   psychoanalysis; 1895-1982)
Freud, Sigmund (Aus. phys., founder of
   psychoanalysis; 1856-1939)
Freudian slip
Frey (also Freyr)(myth.)
Frey, Glen (ent.; 1948-)
Freya (also Frigga)(myth.)
Friar John (fict. chara., *Gargantua, Pantagruel*)
Friar Tuck (fict. chara., *Robin Hood*)
Friars Club
Frías, Hugo (Rafael) Chávez (pres., Venezuela;
   1954-)
Frick Collection (art museum, NYC)
Frick Winery (US bus.)
Frick, Ford C. (baseball; 1894-1978)
Frick, Henry Clay (US bus.; 1849-1919)
Frick, Mario (PM, Liechtenstein; 1965-)
Friday, girl/man
Fridtjof Nansen (Nor. expl; 1861-1930)
Friedan, Betty (Naomi Goldstein)(US feminist/
   writer; 1921-)
Friedkin, David (ent.; 1912-76)

Friedkin, William (ent.; 1939-)
Friedman, Milton (US econ.; 1912-)
Friedman, Pauline Esther (pseud. Abigail Van
   Buren, "Dear Abby")(US advice columnist; 1918-)
Friedrich Alfred Krupp (Ger. armaments maker;
   1854-1902)
Friedrich Anton (or Franz) Mesmer (Ger. phys.;
   1734-1815)
Friedrich Ebert (Ger. pol.; 1871-1925)
Friedrich Engels (Ger. pol. writer; 1820-95)
Friedrich Froebel (Ger. educ., orig.
   kindergarten; 1782-1852)
Friedrich Hund (Ger. physt.; 1896-1997)
Friedrich Krupp, (Ger. armaments maker;
   1787-1826)
Friedrich Ludwig Gottlob Frege (Ger. phil.;
   1848-1925)
Friedrich (Ernst Daniel) Schleiermacher (Ger.
   rel.; 1768-1834)
Friedrich von Flotow (Ger. comp.; 1812-83)
Friedrich von Schiller, (Johann Christoph)(Ger.
   writer/hist.; 1759-1805)
Friedrich von Schlegel (Ger. phil./writer; 1772-
   1829)
Friedrich Wilhelm (Ludolf Gerhard Augustin) von
   Steuben, Baron (Prussian/US gen.; 1730-94)
Friedrich Wilhelm Joseph von Schelling (Ger.
   phil.; 1775-1854)
Friedrich Wilhelm Nietzsche (Ger. phil.; 1844-
   1900)
Friedrich, Caspar David (Ger. artist; 1774-1840)
Friendly Ice Cream Corp.
Friendly Islands (also Tonga)(SW Pac.)
Friends of the Earth (FoE, FOE)(Br. environ.
   grp., est. 1971)
Friends, Society of (also Quakers)(rel.)
Friendship 7 (US spacecraft)
Frietchie, Barbara (Clyde Fitch play)
Frigga (also Freya)(myth.)
Frigid Zone (also l.c.)
Frigidaire (appliances)
Frigidaire Co.
Frigo Cheese Corp.
Friml, Rudolf (US comp.; 1879-1972)
Frisbee (game disk)
Frisco
Frisco Kid, The (film, 1979)
Frisian (lang.)
Friskies (cat food)
Friskies Buffet (cat food)
Friskies Petcare Co.
Frist, William "Bill" (US cong.; 1952-)
Frito-Lay, Inc.
Frito Lay's (chips)
Fritos (chips)
Fritz Haber (Ger. chem.; 1868-1934)
Fritz Kreisler (Aus. comp.; 1875-1962)
Fritz Lang (Aus. ent.; 1890-1976)
Fritz Reiner (Hung. cond.; 1888-1963)
Fritz the Cat (film, 1972)
Fritz Weaver (ent.; 1926-)
Frizzle chicken
Frobisher, (Sir) Martin (Br. nav./expl.; 1535-94)
Frodo Baggins (fict. chara.)
Froebel, Friedrich (Ger. educ., orig.

kindergarten; 1782-1852)
Frog's Leap Winery (US bus.)
Frohman, Charles (US theater; 1860-1915)
Frohman, Daniel (US writer/ent.; 1851-1940)
Froman, Jane (ent.; 1907-80)
Frome, Ethan (E. Wharton novel)
Fromm, Erich (Ger. psych.; 1900-80)
Fromme, Squeaky (Lynette)(US, shot Pres. Ford)
Frontenac, Louis de (Fr./Can. gov.; 1620-98)
Frontier, Nissan (auto.)
Frookie Cookie
Frookie, R. W. (US bus.)
Froot Loops (cereal)
Frost, David (ent.; 1939-)
Frost, Jack (personification of frost)
Frost, Robert (Lee)(US poet; 1874-1963)
Frosted Flakes (cereal)
Frosted Mini-Wheats (cereal)
Frosted Wheat Bites (cereal)
FRS (Federal Reserve System)
Fructuoso Rivera, (José)(ex-pres., Uruguay;
    1784-1854)
Fruehauf Trailer Corp.
Frugal Gourmet (TV show)
Fruit of The Loom (underwear)
Fruit of the Loom, Inc.
Fruity Pebbles (cereal)
Fry, Christopher (Br. writer; 1907-)
FS (forest service)
F(rancis) Scott (Key) Fitzgerald (US writer;
    1896-1940)
FTC (Federal Trade Commission)(US govt. agcy.)
FTD (Florists' Transworld Delivery)
F Troop (TV show)
Fu Hsing (myth.)
Fu Manchu (fict. criminal)
Fu: The Legend Continues, Kung (TV show)
Fu: The Movie, Kung (film, 1986)
Fu, Tu (Ch. poet; 710-770)
Fuad I (king, Eg.; 1868-1936)
Fuchs, Klaus (Emil Julius)(Ger. spy; 1911-88)
Fudd, Elmer (fict. chara.)
Fudgsicle
Fugard, Athol (Harold)(SAfr. playwright/ent.;
    1932-)
Fugger, Jakob (Jakob the Rich)(Ger. banker;
    1459-1525)
Fuhrer, der (also *Fuehrer*)(title adopted by Hitler)
Fujairah (state, UAE)
Fuji Electric Co., Ltd.
Fuji film (also Fujifilm)
Fuji Photo Film USA, Inc.
Fuji, Japan
Fuji, Mount (also Fujiyama)(Jap. dormant volcano)
Fujian (also Fukien)(province, Ch.)
Fujicolor
Fujimori, Alberto (ex-pres., Peru; 1938-)
Fujiyama (also Mount Fuji)(Jap. volcano)
Fukien (also Fujian)(province, Ch.)
Fukuoka, Japan
Fula (lang./people)
Fulakunda (lang.)
Fulani (lang./people)
Fulbright Act (scholarships)
Fulbright, J(ames) William (US pol.; 1905-95)

Fulgencio Batista y Zaldivar (ex-dictator, Cuba;
    1901-73)
Full House (TV show)
Full Monty, The (film, 1996)
Fuller Brush Co., The
Fuller Brush man
Fuller, Alfred C. (US, bus./brushes; 1885-1973)
Fuller, Charles (US writer; 1939-)
Fuller, Margaret (US writer/reformer; 1810-50)
Fuller, Melville Weston (US jurist; 1833-1910)
Fuller, R(ichard) Buckminster (US eng./arch.;
    1895-1983)
Fullerton, CA
Fullilove v. Klutznick (US law; 1980)
Fulminate, Arizona v. (US law; 1991)
Fulton Fish Market
Fulton J(ohn) Sheen, Bishop (US rel./writer/
    educ.; 1895-1979)
Fulton, Robert (US gunsmith/artist/eng./inv.
    steamship; 1745-1815)
Fulvicin (med.)
Fumimaro Konoe, Prince (ex-PM, Jap.; 1891-
    1946)
Funafuti, Tuvalu
Funchal, Madeira
Functionalism (arch./design)
Fundy, Bay of (N Atl., Can.)
Fungizone (med.)
Funicello, Annette (ent.; 1942-)
Funkadelic, Parliament- (pop music)
Funk & Wagnalls Corp.
Funk & Wagnalls encyclopedias
Funky Winkerbean (comic strip)
Funny Girl (play)
Funt, Allen (ent.; 1914-99)
Furadantin (med.)
Furies (also the Erinyes)(myth.)
Furillo, Carl (baseball; 1922-89)
Furness, Betty (Elizabeth Mary)(US ent./
    consumer activist; 1916-94)
Furniss, Bruce (swimming; 1957-)
Furniture Brands International, Inc.
Furstenberg Importing Co., Diane von
Furstenberg, Diane (Halfin) von (US bus.; 1946-)
Futuna Islands, Wallis and (SW Pac.)
Futura (type style)
Future Farmers of America (FFA)
Futurism (art./lit. movement; 1909-14)
Futurist
Fuzzbuster
Fuzzy (Frank Urban) Zoeller (golf; 1951-)
F(riedrich) W(ilhelm Plumpe) Murnau (Ger.
    ent.; 1889-1931)
F. W. Woolworth Co.
FX (FOX)(TV channel)
FYA (for your attention)
FYI (for your information)
Fyodor Dostoyevsky (or Dostoevsky)(Rus.
    writer; 1821-81)

– G –

GA (Georgia)
Ga (chem. sym., gallium)
Ga (people)
Ga-Adangme (lang.)
Gaafar Muhammad al-Nimeiry (ex-pres., Sudan; 1930-)
Gabby (George) Hayes (ent.; 1885-1969)
Gabel, Martin (ent.; 1912-)
Gabelsberger, Franz Xaver (Ger. stenographer; 1789-1849)
Gabin, Jean (ent.; 1904-76)
Gable, (William) Clark (ent.; 1901-60)
Gable, Dan (wrestling; 1945-)
Gable, John Clark (ent.; 1961-)
Gabler, Hedda (H. Ibsen play)
Gabo, Naum (b. Naum Pevsner)(US sculptor; 1890-1977)
Gabon (Gabonese Republic)(central Afr.)
Gabor, Dennis (Br. inv., holography; 1900-70)
Gabor, Eva (ent.; 1919?-95)
Gabor, Zsa Zsa (Sari)(ent.; 1917?-)
Gaborone, Botswana
Gabriel (rel., archangel)
Gabriel Byrne (ent.; 1950-)
Gabriel D(aniel) Fahrenheit (Ger. physt.; 1686-1736)
Gabriel Fauré (Fr. comp.; 1845-1924)
Gabriel Kaplan (ent.; 1945-)
Gabriel, Jacques Ange (Fr. arch.; 1689?-1782)
Gabriel, John (ent.; 1931-)
Gabriel, Peter (ent.; 1950-)
Gabriel, Roman (football; 1940-)
Gabriela Mistral (aka Lucilla Godoy de Alcayaga)(Chilean poet; 1889-1957)
Gabriela Sabatini (tennis; 1970-)
Gabriele D'Annunzio (It. writer; 1863-1938)
Gabrieli, Giovanni (It. comp.; c1557-1612)
Gabrielle Chanel ("Coco")(Fr. designer; 1883-1971)
Gad (rel.)
Gaddis, William (US writer; 1922-98)
Gadsden Purchase (AZ/NM; 1853)
Gadsden, AL
Gadsden, James (US mil./dipl.; 1788-1858)
Gaea (also Ge)(myth.)
Gaelic (lang.)
Gaetano Donizetti (It. comp.; 1797-1848)
Gagarin, Yuri A(lexeyevich)(cosmo.; 1st to orbit earth; 1934-68)
Gage, Thomas (Br. gen./colonial gov.; 1721-87)
Gahan Wilson (US cartoonist; 1930-)
Gail Godwin (US writer; 1937-)
Gail Goodrich (basketball; 1943-)
Gail Hamilton (aka Mary Abigail Dodge)(US writer; 1833-96)
Gail Russell (ent.; 1924-61)
Gail Sheehy (US writer; 1937-)
Gail, Max (ent.; 1943-)
Gaillard Cut (section of Panama Canal)

Gaillard, David Du Bose (US mil./eng.; 1859-1913)
Gaillard, Slim (Bulee)(ent.; 1916-91)
Gaines, William M. (US publ.; 1922-92)
Gainesville Sun (FL newspaper)
Gainesville, FL, GA, TX, VA
Gainsborough, Thomas (Br. artist; 1727-88)
Gaitskell, Hugh (Br. pol.; 1906-63)
Gaius (also Caius)(Roman jurist; 2nd c. AD)
Gaius (or Gnaeus) Marcius Coriolanus (Roman hero; 5th c)
Gaius Caesar (aka Caligula)(Roman emp.; AD 12-41)
Gaius Cassius Longinus (Roman leader, conspired against Caesar; ?-42 BC)
Gaius Julius Caesar Octavius (aka Caesar Augustus)(1st Roman emp.; 63 BC-AD 14)
Gaius Lucilius (Roman poet; c180-c102 BC)
Gaius Petronius ("Arbiter Elegantiae")(Roman writer; ?-AD 66)
Gaius, St. (also Caius)(pope; ?-296)
Galactica, Battlestar (film, 1979)
Galahad, Sir (Arthurian knight)
Galaid, Ali Khalif (PM, Somalia; 1941-)
Galanos, James (US designer; 1925-)
Galant, Mitsubishi (auto.)
Galápagos Islands (also Archipiélago de Colón) (Pac.)
Galatea (Pygmalion's statue)(myth.)
Galati, Romania
Galatians (rel., book of the New Testament)
Galavision (TV channel)
Galbraith, John Kenneth (US/Can. econ.; 1908-)
Gale Ann Norton (US secy./interior; 1954-)
Gale Gordon (ent.; 1906-95)
Gale Sayers (football; 1943-)
Gale Storm (b. Josephine Owaissa Cottle)(ent.; 1922-)
Gale, Zona (US writer; 1874-1938)
Galeazzo Ciano (It. pol.; 1903-44)
Galeazzo Maria Sforza (It. pol.; 1444-76)
Galen (Gr. phys./writer; c129-199)
Galicia (region, Sp.)
Galician (lang./people)
Galilean satellites (astron.)
Galilean telescope (astron.)
Galilee (region, Isr.)
Galilee, Man of (Jesus)
Galilee, Sea of (also Lake Tiberias)(Isr.)
Galilei, Galileo (It. astron./physt./math.; 1564-1642)
Galileo (US uncrewed space probe)
Galileo Ferraris (It. physt./eng.; 1847-97)
Galileo Galilei (It. astron./physt./math.; 1564-1642)
Galina Ulanova (ballet; 1910-98)
Galina Vishnevskaya (soprano; 1926-)
Galla (lang./people)
Gallagher & (Al) Shean, (Ed)(ent.)
Gallagher (clothing)
Gallagher, Ed (ent.)
Gallagher, Liam (ent., Oasis; 1972-)
Gallagher, Michael Donald (skiing; 1941-)
Gallagher, Peter (ent.; 1955-)
Gallatin, Albert (US pol.; 1761-1849)

Gallaudet University (DC)
Gallaudet, Thomas (Hopkins)(US educ. for the
    deaf; 1787-1851)
Gallaudet, Thomas (US rel./educ. for the deaf;
    1822-1902)
Galle, Sri Lanka
Gallery Magazine
Galliano (liqueur)
Gallic Wars
Gallico, Paul (William)(US writer; 1897-1976)
Gallienne, Eva Le (ent.; 1899-91)
Gallienne, Richard Le (US/Br. writer; 1866-1947)
Gallo Winery, E & J (US bus.)
Gallo, Ernest (US winemaker)
Gallo, Julio (US winemaker; 1910-93)
Gallo, Robert Charles (US scien.; 1937-)
Galloping Gourmet (aka Graham Kerr)(Br. chef;
    1934-)
Galloway (district, SW Scot.)
Galloway cattle
Gallup poll
Gallup, George (Horace)(US jour./statistician;
    1901-84)
Gallup, NM
Galoob (toys)
Galoob, Inc., Lewis
Galsworthy, John (Br. writer; 1867-1933)
Galt MacDermot (comp.; 1928-)
Galt, John (fict. chara.; *Atlas Shrugged*)
Galt, John (Scot. writer; 1779-1839)
Galtieri, Leopoldo (ex-pres., Argentina; 1926-)
Galvani, Luigi (It. phys./physt.; 1737-98)
Galveston, TX
Galway (county, Ir.)
Galway, James (Ir./US ent.; 1939-)
Gama, Vasco da (Port. nav.; c1460-1524)
Gamal Abdel Nasser (ex-pres., Eg.; 1918-70)
Gamay (wine, grape)
Gambetta, Léon (Fr. pol.; 1838-82)
Gambia (Republic of)(W Afr.)
Gambia River (W Afr.)
Gamble Co., Procter &
Gambling Times
Game (chicken)
Game Show Network (TV channel)
Gammelost (cheese)
Gamsakhurdia, Zviad (ex-pres., Georgia)
Gan (lang.)
Ganda (also Luganda)(lang.)
Gandhi, Indira (b. Nehru)(ex-PM, India; 1917-84)
Gandhi, Mahatma (Mohandas Karamchand)
    (Indian pol./pacifist; 1869-1948)
Gandhi, Rajiv (ex-PM, India; 1944-91)
Gandolfini, James (ent.; 1961-)
Ganesha (myth.)
Ganges River (also Ganga)(India/Bangladesh)
Ganic, Ejup (Bosnia-Hercegovina pol.)
Ganilau, Ratu (Sir) Penaia (ex-pres., Fiji; 1918-)
Gann, Paul (US reformer; 1912-89)
Gannett Co., Inc.
Gannett, Frank Ernest (US publ.; 1876-1957)
Gansu (also Kansu)(province, Ch.)
Gant, Ron (baseball; 1965-)
Gantanol (med.)
Gantrisin (med.)

Gantry, Elmer (S. Lewis novel)
Ganymede (Jupiter moon; myth.)
GAO (Government Accounting Office)
Gap Stores, Inc., The
Gaposchkin, Cecilia Helena Payne- (Br./US
    astron.; 1900-79)
Garagiola, Joe (ent.; 1926-)
Garamond (type style)
Garamond, Claude (Fr. typographer; c1480-1561)
Garamycin (med.)
Garand (or M-1) rifle (semiautomatic)
Garbage (mag.)
Garbo, Greta (b. Greta Lovisa Gustafsson)(ent.;
    1905-90)
Garcia Lorca, Frederico (Sp. poet/dramatist;
    1898-1936)
*Garcia v. San Antonio Metropolitan Transit
    Authority* (US law; 1985)
Garcia, Andy (ent.; 1956-)
Garcia, Jerry (ent.; 1942-95)
Garden Design (mag.)
Garden Grove, CA
Garden of Earthly Delights (by Bosch)
Garden of Eden (also Paradise)(rel.)
Garden of Gethsemane (rel.)
Garden of Irem (myth.)
Garden State (NJ)
Garden, Mary (soprano; 1874-1967)
Garden, The Victory (TV show)
Gardena, CA
Gardenia, Vincent (ent.; 1921-92)
Gardiner, Reginald (ent.; 1903-80)
Gardner Cowles, Jr. (US publ.; 1903-85)
Gardner, Ava (ent.; 1922-90)
Gardner, David (US finan./Motley Fool; 1966-)
Gardner, Erle Stanley (US writer; 1889-1970)
Gardner, Tom (US finan./Motley Fool)
Garfield (comic strip)
Garfield, James A(bram)(20th US pres.; 1831-81)
Garfield, John (ent.; 1913-52)
Garfunkel, Art (ent.; 1941-)
Garfunkel, Simon and (pop music)
Gargantua (F. Rabelais satire)
Gargas, William C. (US phys.; 1854-1920)
Garibaldi, Giuseppe (aka Peppino)(It. mil.;
    1879-1950)
Garibaldi, Giuseppe (It. mil.; 1807-82)
Garland, Beverly (ent.; 1926-)
Garland, Judy (b. Frances Gumm)(ent.; 1922-69)
Garland, Red (US jazz; 1923-1984)
Garland, TX
Garms, Debs (baseball; 1908-84)
Garner, Erroll (US jazz; 1921-77)
Garner, James (b. James Baumgarner)(ent.;
    1928-)
Garner, John Nance (ex-US VP; 1868-1967)
Garnet Hill, Inc.
Garofalo, Janeane (ent.; 1964-)
Garoua, Cameroon
Garp, The World According to (J. Irving novel)
Garr, Teri (ent.; 1949-)
Garret A(ugustus) Hobart (ex-US VP; 1844-99)
Garrett, Betty (ent.; 1919-)
Garrett, Pat(rick Floyd), Sheriff (US sheriff,
    shot "Billy the Kid"; 1850-1908)

Garrick Ohlsson (pianist; 1948-)
Garrick Utley (TV jour.)
Garrick, David (ent.; 1717-79)
Garriott, Owen K. (US physt./astro.; 1930-)
Garrison Keillor (US humorist/writer; 1942-)
Garrison, Jim (US atty.; 1922-92)
Garrison, William Lloyd (US reformer; 1805-79)
Garrison, Zina (tennis; 1963-)
Garroway, Dave (TV host; 1913-82)
Garry Marshall (ent./screenwriter; 1934-)
Garry Moore (ent.; 1915-93)
Garry Shandling (ent.; 1949-)
Garry Trudeau (Can./US cartoonist,
    Doonesbury; 1948-)
Garson Kanin (US writer; 1912-99)
Garson, Greer (ent.; 1908-96)
Garter, Order of the (Br., knighthood)
Garth Brooks, (Troyal)(ent.; 1962-)
Garth, Jennie (ent.; 1972-)
Garuda Indonesia Airways (airline)
Garvey, Marcus (Jamaican/US reformer; 1887-
    1940)
Garvey, Steve (baseball; 1948-)
Gary A. Condit (US cong.; 1948-)
Gary "U.S." Bonds (b. Gary Anderson)(ent.;
    1939-)
Gary Burghoff (ent.; 1943-)
Gary Busey (ent.; 1944-)
Gary Cole (ent.; 1957-)
Gary Coleman (ent.; 1968-)
Gary Cooper (ent.; 1901-62)
Gary E. Johnson (NM gov.; 1953-)
Gary Glitter (b. Paul Gadd)(ent.; 1940-)
Gary Hall (swimming; 1951-)
Gary (or Garry) Kasparov (Rus., chess; 1963-)
Gary Larson (US cartoonist, The Far Side; 1950-)
Gary Locke (WA gov.; 1950-)
Gary Morton (ent.; 1921?-99)
Gary Oldman (ent.; 1958-)
Gary Player (golf; 1935-)
Gary Post-Tribune (IN newspaper)
Gary Puckett and the Union Gap (pop music)
Gary Sandy (ent.; 1945-)
Gary Sinise (ent.; 1955-)
Gary, Elbert H. (US bus.; 1846-1927)
Gary, IN
Gascony (region, Fr.)
Gasoline Alley (comic strip)
Gasperi, Alcide De (It. pol.; 1881-1954)
Gasset, Jose Ortega y (Sp. phil.; 1883-1955)
Gassman, Vittorio (ent.; 1922-2000)
Gaston Caperton, W. (ex-WV gov.; 1940-)
Gaston Lachaise (US sculptor; 1882-1935)
Gastonia, NC
Gastrocrom (med.)
Gas-X (med.)
Gates McFadden (ent.; 1949-)
Gates of Paradise (by Ghiberti)
Gates of the Artic National Park (AK)
Gates Rubber Co., The
Gates, Bill (William)(US bus./Microsoft; 1955-)
Gates, Daryl F. (US news)
Gates, Horatio (US gen.; 1728-1806)
Gates, Robert M. (US ex-dir./CIA; 1943-)
Gateway Bookstore (US bus.)

Gateway, Inc.
Gatlin Brothers, The (pop music)
Gatlin, Larry (ent.; 1948-)
Gatling gun (early machine gun)
Gatling, Richard (Jordan)(US inv.; 1818-1903)
Gator Bowl (college football)
Gatorade (beverage)
Gatsby, Jay (fict. chara., The Great Gatsby)
Gatsby, The Great (F.S. Fitzgerald novel)
GATT (General Agreement on Tariffs and
    Trade)(UN org.)
Gauche, Rive (also Left Bank)(Paris)
Gaudí, Antonio (Sp. arch.; 1852-1926)
Gauguin, (Eugène Henri) Paul (Fr. artist; 1848-
    1903)
Gaul (ancient Fr./Belgium, people)
Gaulle, Charles de (ex-pres., Fr.; 1890-1970)
Gault, In re (US law; 1967)
Gault, Willie (football; 1960-)
Gaunt, John of (Br. pol.; 1340-99)
Gauss, Carl (or Karl) Friedrich (Ger. math.;
    1777-1855)
Gaussian curve (also normal curve, probability
    curve)(a bell curve)
Gaussian distribution (also normal distribution)
Gaussian image (also Gaussian image point)
Gaussian integer
Gautama (Buddha) Siddhartha (Indian phil.,
    founded Buddhism; c563-c483 BC)
Gavin MacLeod (b. Allan See)(ent.; 1930-)
Gavin Rossdale (ent., Bush; 1967-)
Gavin, John (ent./dipl.; 1935-)
Gavras, Konstantinos (ent.; 1933-)
Gawain, Sir (Arthurian knight)
Gay, Enola (US mil. B-29 bomber that dropped
    1st atomic bomb in 1945)
Gay, John (Br. writer; 1685-1732)
Gay-Lussac, Joseph (Louis)(Fr. chem./physt.;
    1778-1850)
Gay-Lussac's law (also Charles' law)
    (thermodynamics)
Gaye, Marvin (ent.; 1939-84)
Gayle, Crystal (b. Brenda Webb)(ent.; 1951-)
Gaylord Perry (baseball; 1938-)
Gaylord, Mitch (gymnast; 1961-)
Gaynor, Janet (ent.; 1906-84)
Gaynor, Mitzi (b. Francesca Marlene Von
    Gerber)(ent.; 1930-)
Gayoom, Maumoon Abdul (pres., Maldives;
    1937-)
Gaza Strip (on Mediterranean Sea)(occupied by
    Isr.; 1967)
Gazette Journal, Reno (NV newspaper)
Gazette-Mail, Charleston (WV newspaper)
Gazette Post, Cedar Rapids (IA newspaper)
Gazette Telegraph, Colorado Springs (CO
    newspaper)
Gazette, Charleston (WV newspaper)
Gazette, Kalamazoo (MI newspaper)
Gazette, Phoenix (AZ newspaper)
Gazette, Texarkana (AR newspaper)
Gazzara, Ben (ent.; 1930-)
GB (Great Britain)
GCT (Greenwich Conservatory Time)
Gd (chem. sym., gadolinium)

Gdansk, Poland (also Danzig)
Gdynia, Poland
GE (General Electric)
Ge (also Gaea)(myth.)
Ge (chem. sym., germanium)
Geary, Anthony (ent.; 1947-)
Geb (rel.)
Gebaur Air Force Base, Richards- (MO)
Gebel-Williams, Gunther (Ger. animal trainer)
Gebhard von Blücher (Ger. gen.; 1742-1819)
GED (general equivalency diploma [high school])
Gedda, Nicolai (tenor; 1925-)
Geddes, Barbara Bel (ent.; 1922-)
Geddes, Norman Bel (US designer; 1893-1958)
Geena Davis (ent.; 1957-)
Geer, Will (ent.; 1902-78)
Geffen, David (ent.; 1943-)
Gehenna (hell)
Gehrig, (Henry) Lou(is)(baseball; 1903-41)
Gehrig's disease, Lou (med.)
Gehringer, Charlie (baseball; 1903-93)
GEICO Corp.
Geidar Aliyev (pres., Azerbaijan)
Geiger(-Müller) counter (detects radiation)
Geiger(-Müller) tube
Geiger, Hans (Ger. physt.; 1882-1945)
Geils, J(erome)(ent.; 1946-)
Geingob, Hage G. (PM, Namibia; 1941-)
Geisel, Theodore Seuss (pseud. Dr. Seuss)(US
    writer/artist; 1904-91)
Geissler pump (air pump)
Geissler tube (elect.)
Geissler, Heinrich (Ger. inv./glassblower; 1814-
    79)
Gelderland (also Guelders)(province,
    Netherlands)
Geldof, Bob (ent.; 1954-)
Gellar, Sarah Michelle (ent./model; 1977-)
Geller, Uri (Israeli psychic; 1946-)
Gellius, Aulus (Latin writer; c130-c165)
Gell-Mann, Murray (US physt.; 1929-)
Gelsenkirchen, Germany
Gelsey Kirkland (ent.; 1953-)
Gelusil (med.)
Gem State (nickname, ID)
Gemayel, Amin (ex-pres., Lebanon; 1942-)
Gemeinschaft and Gesellschaft (Ger.,
    community and association)
Gemini (A. Innaurato play)
Gemini (US crewed space flights)
Gemini (zodiac; astron., twins)
Gemini-Titan (US crewed space flights)
Geminids (also Geminid)(meteor shower, c
    December 13)
Gemonil (med.)
Gemütlichkeit (also Gemuetlichkeit)(Ger.,
    good-natured)
Gena Rowlands (ent.; 1934-)
Gencorp (US bus.)
Gene Anthony Ray (ent.; 1963-)
Gene Autry (ent.; 1907-98)
Gene Barry (ent.; 1919-)
Gene Hackman (ent.; 1930-)
Gene Kelly (ent.; 1912-96)
Gene Krupa (US jazz; 1909-73)

Gene Littler (golf; 1930-)
Gene Lockhart (ent.; 1891-1957)
Gene Raymond (ent.; 1908-98)
Gene (Eugene Wesley) Roddenberry (writer/
    producer, Star Trek; 1921-91)
Gene Saks (ent.; 1921-)
Gene Sarazen (golf; 1902-99)
Gene Shalit (US critic; 1932-)
Gene Simmons (b. Chaim Witz)(ent.; 1949-)
Gene Siskel (US critic; 1946-99)
Gene Tierney (ent.; 1920-91)
Gene Tunney (b. James Joseph
    Tunney)(boxing; 1898-1978)
Gene Vincent (ent.; 1935-71)
Gene Wilder (ent.; 1935-)
Genentech, Inc.
General Accounting Office (GAO)(US govt.)
General Agreement on Tariffs and Trade (GATT)
    (UN org.)
General Assembly (UN)
General Binding Corp. (GBC)
General Cinema Corp.
General Dynamics Corp.
General Electric Co.
General Foods (US bus.)
General Foods International Coffees
General Foods USA (US bus.)
General Hospital (TV soap)
General Mills, Inc.
General Motors (GM)(auto.)
General Motors Corp. (GM Corp.)
General Nutrition Corp. (GNC)
General Tire, Inc.
Generra Sportswear (US bus.)
Genesco, Inc.
Genesis (pop music)
Genesis (rel., 1st book of the Old Testament)
Genet, Jean (Fr. writer; 1911-86)
Geneva bands (clerical neckwear)
Geneva Conference (US/Br./Jap.; 1927)
Geneva Convention(s)(treatment of war
    wounded and POWs; 1864, 1868, 1906, 1929,
    1949, 1977)
Geneva gown (clerical wear)
Geneva Protocol (arbitration of internat'l
    disputes; 1924)(agreement to prohibit
    chemical warfare; 1974)
Geneva, AL, IL, NY, OH)
Geneva, Lake of (also Lake Leman)(Switz./Fr.)
Geneva, Switzerland
Genevieve Bujold (ent.; 1942-)
Genghis Khan (also Jenghiz, Chinghiz Khan,
    Temujin)(Mongol conqueror; c1167-1227)
GEnie (compu. database)
Genie Co., The
Genie Francis (ent.; 1962-)
Genie remote control
Genji (also Minamoto)(Jap. hist.; 1192-1219)
Genoa salami
Genoa, Italy
Genoptic (med.)
Genovese, Vito (US Mafia; 1898-1969)
Genscher, Hans-Dietrich (Ger. pol.; 1927-)
Gentile Bellini (It. artist; 1426-1507)
Gentile, Giovanni (It. phil./educ.; 1875-1944)

Gentleman Jim (James) Corbett (boxing; 1866-1933)

Gentleman Jim Reeves (ent.; 1923-64)

Gentry, Bobbie (b. Roberta Streeter)(ent.; 1944-)

Gentry, Ruby (film, 1952)

Gen X (also GenX, Gen-X)(US generation born beginning 1960)

Gen Xers (also GenXers, Gen-Xers)

Geo (Chevrolet)(auto.)

Geo (Chevrolet) Metro (auto.)

Geo (Chevrolet) Prizm (auto.)

Geo (Chevrolet) Tracker (auto.)

Geoffrey Beene (US designer; 1927-)

Geoffrey Chaucer (Br. poet; c 1340-1400)

Geoffrey Holder (dancer; 1930-)

Geoffrey of Monmouth (Br. writer/chronicler; c1100-54)

Geoffrey Rush (ent.; 1951-)

Geoffrion, Boom Boom (Bernie)(hockey; 1931-)

Geographic Society, National (est. 1888)

Geological Survey, U.S. (US agcy.)

Geopen (med.)

Georg F. K. Wittig (Ger. chem.; 1897-1987)

Georg (Simon) Ohm (Ger. physt.; 1789-1854)

Georg Philipp Telemann (Ger. comp.; 1681-1767)

Georg Solti, (Sir)(Br. cond.; 1912-97)

Georg W(ilhelm Friedrich) Hegel (Ger. phil.; 1770-1831)

George (magazine)

George Abbott (ent.; 1887-1995)

George A(rmstrong) Custer (US gen., Little Bighorn; 1839-76)

George Ade (US writer/humorist; 1866-1944)

George A. Hormel & Co.

George Air Force Base, CA (mil.)

George Allen (football; 1918-90)

George Arliss (ent.; 1868-1946)

George Axelrod (playwright; 1922-)

George Baker (cartoonist, *The Sad Sack*; 1915-75)

George Balanchine (US choreographer; 1904-83)

George Bancroft (ent.; 1882-1956)

George Bancroft (US hist.; 1800-91)

George Benson (ent.; 1943-)

George Berkeley (Ir. phil.; 1685-1753)

George Bernard Shaw (Ir. writer/critic; 1856-1950)

George (Frederick) Blanda (football; 1927-)

George B(rinton) McClellan (US gen.; 1826-85)

George Boole (Br. math.; 1815-64)

George Booth (cartoonist, *New Yorker*; 1926-)

George Brent (ent.; 1904-79)

George Brett (baseball; 1953-)

George Browne Post (US arch.; 1837-1913)

George Burns (b. Nathan Birnbaum)(ent.; 1896-1996)

George Caleb Bingham (US artist; 1811-79)

George Calvert, (Sir)(aka Lord Baltimore)(founded MD; 1606-75)

George Carlin (ent.; 1937-)

George Catlin (US artist; 1796-1872)

George Clinton (ex-US VP; 1739-1812)

George Clooney (ent.; 1961-)

George C(atlett) Marshall (US gen.; 1880-1959)

George Cosmas Adyebo (ex-PM, Uganda)

George Cruikshank (Br. artist; 1792-1878)

George C(ampbell) Scott (ent.; 1927-99)

George Cukor (ent.; 1899-1983)

George C(orley) Wallace (ex-gov., AL; 1919-98)

George Deukmejian (ex-CA gov.; 1928-)

George Dewey (US adm.; 1837-1917)

George Eastman (US inv./photo.; 1854-1932)

George Eliot (aka Mary Ann [or Marian] Evans)(Br. writer; 1819-80)

George E. Moore (Br. phil.; 1873-1958)

George E(lmer) Pataki (NY gov.; 1945-)

George E(dward) Pickett (US gen.; 1825-75)

George F(ollansbee) Babbitt (fict. chara.)

George F. Allen (US cong./ex-VA gov.; 1952-)

George Fenneman (ent.; 1919-97)

George F. Kennan (US dipl.; 1904-)

George Foot Moore (US rel.; 1851-1931)

George Foreman (boxing; 1948-)

George Foster Peabody Radio and Television Awards

George Fox (Br. rel.; 1624-91)

George Frederic Watts (Br. artist; 1817-1904)

George Frederick (also Georg Friedrich) Handel (Ger./Br. comp.; 1685-1759)

George F. Will (US jour.; 1941-)

George (Horace) Gallup (US jour./statistician; 1901-84)

George Gaylord Simpson (US paleontol.; 1902-84)

George Gershwin (US comp.; 1898-1937)

George Gervin (basketball; 1952-)

George Gobel (ent.; 1921-91)

George Gordon Byron, Lord (Br. poet; 1788-1824)

George Grenville (ex-PM, Br.; 1712-70)

George Grizzard (ent.; 1928-)

George (Stanley) Halas (football; 1895-1983)

George Hamilton (ent.; 1939-)

George Harrison (ent.; 1943-)

George Hearn (ent.; 1935-)

George Hepplewhite (Br. furniture designer; ?-1786)

George Herbert (Br. rel./poet; 1593-1633)

George Herbert Walker Bush (41st US pres.; 1924-)

George Herman "Babe" Ruth (baseball; 1895-1948)

George Herriman (US cartoonist, *Krazy Kat*; 1881-1944)

George H. Meade (US phil.; 1863-1931)

George H(omer) Ryan (IL gov.; 1934-)

George H(enry) Thomas (US mil.; 1816-70)

George I (Christian William Ferdinand Adolphus George)(king, Gr.; 1845-1913)

George I (George Louis)(king, Br./Ir.; 1660-1727)

George II (George Augustus)(king, Br.; 1683-1760)

George II (king, Gr.; 1890-1947)

George III (George William Frederick)(king, Br./Ir.; 1738-1820)

George Inness (US artist; 1825-94)

George IV (George Augustus Frederick)(king, Br./Ir.; 1762-1830)

George Jean Nathan (US writer; 1882-1958)

George Jessel (ent.; 1898-1981)
George J. Mitchell (US pol.; 1933-)
George Jones (ent.; 1931-)
George Kennedy (ent.; 1925-)
George Kirby (ent.; 1923-95)
George Lepping (ex-gov.-gen.; Solomon Islands)
George L. Murphy, (US ent./pol.; 1902-92)
George London (baritone; 1920-85)
George Louis Palmella Busson du Maurier (Br. writer/artist; 1834-96)
George (Benjamin) Luks (US artist; 1867-1933)
George Macaulay Trevelyan (Br. hist.; 1876-1962)
George Macready (ent.; 1909-73)
George Mason (US pol.; 1725-92)
George Mason University (Fairfax, VA)
George McManus (US cartoonist, *Bringing Up Father*; 1884-1954)
George M(ichael) Cohan (US comp.; 1878-1942)
George M. Dallas (ex-US VP; 1792-1864)
George (Gordon) Meade (US gen.; 1815-72)
George Meany (US labor leader; 1894-1980)
George Meredith (Br. writer; 1828-1909)
George Michael (b. Georgios Kyriacou Panayiotou)(ent. 1963-)
George Mikan (basketball; 1924-)
George Monck (Duke of Albemarle)(Br. mil./pol.; 1608-70)
George Montgomery (ent.; 1916-2000)
George Moore (Ir. writer; 1852-1933)
George "Bugs" Moran (gang killed in St. Valentine's Day massacre)
George Nathaniel Curzon (Marquis Kedleston of Curzon)(Br. leader in India; 1859-1925)
George N. Papanicolaou (Gr./US cytologist, Pap test; 1883-1962)
George of the Jungle (film, 1997)
George Orwell (aka Eric A[rthur] Blair)(Br. writer; 1903-50)
George Papadopoulos (ex-pres., Gr.; 1919-99)
George Papandreou (ex-PM, Gr.; 1888-1968)
George Peabody (US bus./finan.; 1795-1869)
George Peppard (ent.; 1928-94)
George Plimpton (US writer; 1927-)
George (Cadle) Price (ex-PM, Belize; 1919-)
George Price (US cartoonist, *New Yorker*; 1901-95)
George P(ratt) Shultz (US pol./ex-secy./state; 1920-)
George (Mortimer) Pullman (US inv./bus.; 1831-97)
George Raft (ent.; 1895-1980)
George Reeves (ent.; 1914-59)
George Rogers Clark (US mil.; 1752-1818)
George Rogers Clark National Historical Park (IN)
George Romney (Br. artist; 1734-1802)
George Romney (US pol./bus.; 1907-95)
George Roy Hill (ent.; 1922-)
George Russell (US jazz; 1923-)
George Saitoti (Kenya pol.)
George Sand (aka Amandine Aurore Lucie Dupin)(Fr. writer; 1804-76)
George Sanders (ent.; 1906-72)

George Santayana (Sp./US writer/phil.; 1863-1952)
George Schaefer (ent.; 1920-)
George Schlatter (ent.)
George Segal (ent.; 1934-)
George Segal (US sculptor; 1924-2000)
George Shearing (US jazz; 1919-)
George Simmel (Ger. sociol./phil.; 1858-1918)
George S. Irving (ent.; 1922-)
George (Harold) Sisler (baseball; 1893-1973)
George S(imon) Kaufman (US writer; 1889-1961)
George S(tanley) McGovern (US pol.; 1922-)
George S. Mickelson (ex-gov., SD; 1941-93)
George S(mith) Patton (US gen.; 1885-1945)
George (Michael) Steinbrenner, III (US bus./baseball; 1930-)
George Stephanopoulos (US pol./jour.; 1961-)
George Strait (ent.; 1952-)
George Stubbs (Br. artist; 1724-1806)
George Szell (US cond.; 1897-1970)
George Takei (ent.; 1939-)
George T. Delacorte (US publ.; 1893-1991)
George Tenet (US dir./CIA; 1953-)
George Thorogood (ent.; 1951-)
George Town, the Bahamas
George Townshend, Marquis (Br. mil.; 1724-1807)
George (Otto) Trevelyan, (Sir)(Br. hist.; 1838-1928)
George V (George Frederick Ernest Albert) (king, Br.; 1865-1936)
George Vassilou (ex-pres., Cyprus; 1931-)
George VI (Albert Frederick Arthur George)(king, Br.; 1895-1952)
George (Victor) Voinovich (US cong./ex-OH gov.; 1936-)
George Washington (1st US pres.; 1732-99)
George Washington Carver (US botanist/chem.; 1860?-1943)
George Washington Gale Ferris (US eng./inv.; 1859-96)
George Washington University (DC)
George W(ildman) Ball (US atty./banker/pol.; 1909-94)
George W(alker) Bush (43rd US pres./son of ex-pres.; 1946-)
George Weiss (baseball exec.; 1895-1972)
George Wendt (ent.; 1948-)
George Wesley Bellows (US artist; 1882-1925)
George Westinghouse (US bus.; 1846-1914)
George W(ashington) Goethals (US mil./eng.; 1858-1928)
George Wilbur Peck (US writer; 1840-1916)
George Will (US jour.; 1941-)
George William Norris (US pol.; 1861-1944)
George Willig (ent.; 1949-)
George W. Lucas, Jr. (ent.; 1944-)
George Wythe (US jurist; 1726-1806)
George, Boy (b. George Alan O'Dowd)(ent.; 1961-)
George, David Lloyd (ex-PM, Br.; 1863-1945)
George, Henry (US econ., advocate of a single tax; 1839-97)
George, Phyllis (US 1st woman sportscaster, ex-Miss America; 1949-)
George, St. (by Donatello)

George, St. (patron saint of Eng., legendary dragon slayer; ?-c303)
Georges Bizet (Fr. comp.; 1838-75)
Georges Braque (Fr. artist; 1882-1963)
Georges Clemenceau (ex-PM, Fr.; 1841-1929)
Georges Danton (Fr. mil.; 1759-94)
Georges de La Tour (Fr. artist; 1593-1652)
Georges Edouard Lemaître (Belgium astron.; 1894-1966)
Georges Enesco (or Enescu)(Romanian cond./comp.; 1881-1955)
Georges (Jean Raymond) Pompidou (ex-pres., Fr.; 1911-74)
Georges (Henri) Rouault (Fr. artist; 1871-1958)
Georges Seurat (Fr. artist; 1859-91)
Georges Simenon (Georges Sim)(mystery writer; 1903-89)
Georgetown (area in DC)
Georgetown University (DC)
Georgetown, Gambia
Georgetown, Guyana
Georgetown, KY, SC
Georgetown, Malaysia (also Penang)
Georgette crepe (fabric)
Georgi Dimitrov (ex-PM, Bulgaria; 1882-1949)
Georgi (Valentinovich) Plekhanov (Rus. phil., "Father of Russian Marxism"; 1857-1918)
Georgi S. Shonin (cosmo.; 1935-97)
Georgi (or Georgy) T. Beregovoi (cosmo.; 1921-)
Georgi (or Georgy) T. Dobrovolsky (cosmo.; 1928-71)
Georgi (Konstantinovich) Zhukov (USSR mil.; 1895-1974)
Georgia (GA)
Georgia (Republic of)(formerly part of the USSR)(SE Eur.)
Georgia O'Keeffe (US artist; 1887-1986)
Georgia on my Mind (song)
Georgia-Pacific Corp.
Georgia, Chisholm v. (US law; 1793)
Georgian (lang./people)
Georgian style (arch.)
Georgievski, Ljupco (PM, Macedonia; 1966-)
Georgy Girl (film, 1966)
Gepetto (Pinocchio's creator)
Gephardt, Richard A. (US cong.; 1941-)
Geradus (or Gerhardus) Mercator (aka Gerhard Kremer)(Flem. geographer; 1512-94)
Gerald Grosvenor (6th Duke of Westminster, England; 1951-)
Gerald Manley Hopkins (Br. poet; 1844-89)
Gerald McRaney (ent.; 1948-)
Gerald P(aul) Carr (astro.; 1932-)
Gerald R(udolph) Ford (b. Leslie Lynch King, Jr.)(38th US pres.; 1913-)
Geraldine Chaplin (ent.; 1944-)
Geraldine Farrar (ent.; 1882-1967)
Geraldine Ferraro (US pol./1st major US female VP candidate; 1935-)
Geraldine Fitzgerald (Ir./US ent.; 1913-)
Geraldine Page (ent.; 1924-87)
Geraldo (TV show)
Geraldo Rivera (ent.; 1943-)
Gerard Depardieu (ent.; 1948-)
Gerard Swope (US bus./econ.; 1872-1957)

Gerber (baby prods.)
Gerber Products Co.
Gere, Richard (ent.; 1949-)
Gergen, David (US pol./jour.; 1942-)
Gerhard Henrik Armauer Hansen (Nor. phys.; 1841-1912)
Gerhard Schröder (chanc., Ger.; 1944-)
Gerhardus (or Geradus) Mercator (aka Gerhard Kremer)(Flem. geographer; 1512-94)
Geri Halliwell (aka Ginger Spice)(ent.; 1972-)
Geringer, James "Jim" (WY gov.; 1944-)
Geritol (med.)
Germaine Greer (Austl. writer/feminist; 1939-)
German (lang./people)
German coach horse
German measles (rubella)
German shepherd (also Alsatian, German police dog)(dog)
German shorthaired pointer (dog)
German silver (silvery alloy of nickel/copper/zinc)
German wirehaired pointer (dog)
Germanic languages
Germanic law
Germanic religion
Germanicus Caesar (Roman gen.; 15 BC-AD 19)
Germanophile
Germanophobe
Germantown (carriage)
Germany (Federal Republic of)(formerly East and West Germany)(Eur.)
Germiston, South Africa
Geron Corp.
Geronimo (Chiricahua Apache chief; 1829-1909)
Geronimo Amati (It. violin maker, father of Nicolo; 1556-1630)
Geronimo Amati (It. violin maker, son of Nicolo; 1649-1740)
Geronimo, OK
Gerry Adams (Ir. pol. leader; 1948-)
Gerry Cooney (boxing)
Gerry Goffin (US lyricist; 1939-)
Gerry Mulligan (US jazz; 1927-)
Gerry, Elbridge (ex-US VP, gerrymander; 1744-1814)
Gershwin, George (US comp.; 1898-1937)
Gershwin, Ira (US lyricist; 1896-1983)
Gertrude Atherton (Franklin Horn)(US writer; 1857-1948)
Gertrude Belle Elion (US physiol.; 1918-99)
Gertrude Berg (ent.; 1899-1966)
Gertrude Ederle (swimmer; 1906-)
Gertrude Lawrence (ent.; 1898-1952)
Gertrude "Ma" Rainey (US jazz; 1886-1939)
Gertrude Stein (US writer; 1874-1946)
Gerulaitis, Vitas (tennis; 1954-94)
Gervin, George (basketball; 1952-)
Gesamtkunstwerk (Ger., performing arts)
Gesell, Arnold Lucius (US psych./educ.; 1880-1961)
Gesellschaft, Gemeinschaft and (Ger., community, association)
Gestalt (Ger., unified whole)(usually l.c.)
Gestalt psychology/therapy (also l.c.)
Gestalt, Bender (psych. test)
Gestapo (Ger. Nazi secret police)

Geste, Beau (film, 1939)
Gesundheit (Ger., good health to you)(also l.c.)
Get Christie Love! (film, 1974)
Get Shorty (film, 1995)
Get Smart (TV show)
Gethsemane cheese (also Trappist cheese)
Gethsemane, Garden of (rel.)
Getty Petroleum Corp.
Getty, Estelle (ent.; 1924-)
Getty, J(ean) Paul (US bus.; 1892-1976)
Gettysburg Address (by Pres. Lincoln; 11/19/63)
Gettysburg military campaign
Gettysburg National Military Park (PA)
Gettysburg, Battle of (US hist.; 1863)
Gettysburg, PA
Getz, Stan(ley)(US jazz; 1927-91)
Geulleh, Ismail Omar (pres., Djibouti; 1947-)
Gewürztraminer (wine)
Geyser Peak Winery (US bus.)
G-force (gravity force)
G. Gordon Liddy (US pol./Watergate; 1930-)
Ghalib, Umar Arteh (ex-PM, Somalia)
Ghana (Republic of)(W Afr.)
Ghannouchi, Mohamed (PM, Tunisia; 1941-)
Ghazali, al (Islamic phil.; 1058-1111)
Ghent Altarpiece (by J. van Eyck)
Ghent, Belgium
Ghent, Treaty of (US/Br.; 1814)
Gheorghe Zamfir (Romanian ent./panflutist; 1941-)
Gherman (or Herman) S(tepanovich) Titov (cosmo.; 1935-)
Ghibellines (It. pol.; 12th-15th c.)
Ghiberti, Lorenzo (It. sculptor; 1378-1455)
Ghirardelli Chocolate Co.
Ghirardelli Square (San Francisco)
Ghost (film, 1992)
Ghost and Mrs. Muir, The (film, 1947)
Ghost Rider (cartoon chara.)
Ghostbusters (film, 1984)
Ghostbusters II (film, 1989)
Ghostley, Alice (ent.; 1926-)
Ghulam Ishaq Khan (ex-pres., Pak.)
GI (gastrointestinal, government issue)
GI Bill
GI Jane (US female soldier)
GI Joe (US male soldier)
Giacometti, Alberto (It. sculptor; 1901-66)
Giacomin, Ed (hockey; 1939-)
Giacomo Balla (It. artist; 1871?-1958)
Giacomo Meyerbeer (b. Jakob Liebmann Beer) (Ger. comp.; 1791-1864)
Giacomo (Antonio Domenico Michele Secondo Maria) Puccini (It. comp.; 1858-1924)
Giamatti, (Angelo) Bart(lett)(US educ./writer/ baseball; 1938-89)
Giambattista Bodoni (It. printer/typographer; 1740-1813)
Giambattista Piranesi (It. artist; 1720-78)
Giancana, Sam "Momo" (US gangster; 1908-75)
Giancarlo Giannini (ent.; 1942-)
Gian-Carlo Menotti (It./US comp.; 1911-)
Gianni Versace (It. fashion designer; 1946-97)
Giannini, Amadeo P. (US, founded Bank of America; 1870-1949)

Giannini, Giancarlo (ent.; 1942-)
Giant Food, Inc.
Giants, New York (football team)
Giants, San Francisco (baseball team)
Gibb, Andy (ent.; 1958-88)
Gibbon, Edward (Br. hist.; 1737-94)
Gibbons v. Ogden (US law; 1924)
Gibbons, Euell (US writer, wild edible plants; 1911-75)
Gibbons, Leeza (ent.; 1957-)
Gibbons, Orlando (Br. comp.; 1583-1625)
Gibbs free energy (also Gibbs function, thermodynamic potential)
Gibbs, Josiah W(illard)(US physt./chem.; 1839-1903)
Gibbs, Marla (b. Margaret Bradley)(ent.; 1931-)
Gibraltar (Br. dependency, S Sp.)
Gibraltar, Rock of (S coast Sp.)
Gibralter, Strait of (NAfr./Sp.)
Gibran, Kahlil (Lebanese writer/mystic/artist; 1883-1931)
Gibson (cocktail)
Gibson girl
Gibson, Althea (tennis; 1927-)
Gibson, Bob (baseball; 1935-)
Gibson, Charles Dana (US artist; 1867-1944)
Gibson, Debbie (ent.; 1970-)
Gibson, Edward G. (astro.; 1936-)
Gibson, Henry (ent.; 1935-)
Gibson, Hoot (ent.; 1892-1962)
Gibson, Kirk (baseball; 1957-)
Gibson, Mel (ent.; 1956-)
Gidada, Negasso (pres., Ethiopia; 1943-)
Gide, André (Fr. writer; 1869-1951)
Gideon v. Wainwright (US law; 1963)
Gideon Welles (US pol./jour.; 1802-78)
Gideon(s) Bible
Gideon's Trumpet (US film, 1980)
Gideons International, The
Gidget (film, 1959)
Gielgud, (Sir Arthur) John (ent.; 1904-2000)
Giffard, Henri (Fr. inv.; 1825-82)
Gifford, Frank (ent./football; 1930-)
Gifford, Kathie Lee (b. Kathie Epstein)(ent.; 1953-)
Gig Young (b. Byron Ellsworth Barr)(ent.; 1913-78)
Gigantes (myth.)
Gigi (film, 1958)
Gigli's saw/operation (med.)
GIGO (garbage in, garbage out)
Gil Bellows (ent.; 1967-)
Gil Evans (US jazz; 1912-88)
Gil Hodges (baseball; 1924-72)
Gil Kane (comic book artist, Spider-Man; 1926-2000)
Gil Lamb (ent.; 1906-95)
Gil Shaham (violinist; 1971-)
Gila monster (poisonous lizard)
Gilaki (lang.)
Gilbert & Sullivan (created comic operas)
Gilbert (Hovey) Grosvenor (US geographer/ writer/editor; 1875-1966)
Gilbert Islands (now Kiribati)(central Pac.)
Gilbert M. Grosvenor (US publ.; 1931-)

Gilbert Roland (b. Luis Antonio Damaso de Alonso)(ent.; 1905-94)
Gilbert (Charles) Stuart (US artist; 1755-1828)
Gilbert, Cass (US arch.; 1859-1934)
Gilbert, Melissa (ent.; 1964-)
Gilbert Newton Lewis (US chem.; 1875-1946)
Gilbert, Rod(rique)(hockey; 1941-)
Gilbert, (Sir) William (Br. physt./phys.; 1540-1603)
Gilbert, (Sir) W(illiam) S(chwenck)(Br. writer; 1836-1911)
Gilbert, Walter (US chem.; 1932-)
Gilbertese (lang.)
Gilbey's International (US bus.)
Gilda Marx Swimwear (US bus.)
Gilda Radner (ent.; 1946-89)
Gildersleeve, The Great (film, 1943)
Gilels, Emil (Grigoryevich)(Rus. pianist; 1916-85)
Giles system, Wade- (Eng. representation of Ch.)
Giles, Warren (baseball exec.; 1896-1979)
Gilgamesh (myth.)
Gilgamesh, Epic of (myth.)
Gill, Vince (ent.; 1957-)
Gillern, Fort (GA)(mil.)
Gillespie, Dizzy (John Birks)(US jazz; 1917-93)
Gillette Co., The
Gillette, Anita (ent.; 1938-)
Gillette, King Camp (US bus., razor; 1855-1932)
Gilley, Mickey (ent.; 1936-)
Gillian Anderson (ent.; 1968-)
Gilligan, Carol (Friedman)(US psych.; 1936-)
Gilligan's Island (TV show)
Gillikins, Country of the
Gillis, Dobie (fict. chara.)
Gillooly, Jeff (US news)
Gilmore, Artis (basketball; 1949-)
Gilmore, James "Jim" S(tuart) III (VA gov.; 1949-)
Gilpin, Peri (ent.; 1961-)
Gilroy, Frank (US writer; 1925-)
Gimbel, Bernard (US bus.; 1885-1966)
Gimbel, Inc., J.
Gina Lollobrigida (It. ent.; 1927-)
Ginger (Peter) Baker (ent.; 1940-)
Ginger Rogers (ent.; 1911-95)
Gingold, Hermione (ent.; 1897-1987)
Gingrich, Newt(on Leroy)(US pol.; 1943-)
Ginnie Mae (also Government National Mortgage Association, GNMA)
Gino Cappelletti (football; 1934-)
Gino Severini (It. artist; 1883-1966)
Ginsberg, Allen (US poet; 1926-97)
Ginsburg, Ruth Bader (US jurist; 1933-)
Ginty, Robert (ent.; 1948-)
Ginza (district, Tokyo)
Gioacchino (Antonio) Rossini (It comp.; 1792-1868)
Gioconda, La (aka *Mona Lisa*)(da Vinci painting)
Giordano Bruno (It. phil.; 1548-1600)
Giordano, Luca ("Luca Fapresto")(It. artist; 1632-1705)
Giordano, Umberto (It. comp.; 1867-1948)
Giorgi Arsenishvili (secy./state, Georgia)
Giorgio Armani (It. designer; 1934-)
Giorgio Beverly Hills (US bus.)

Giorgio Chinaglia (soccer; 1947-)
Giorgio de Chirico (It. artist; 1888-1978)
Giorgio di Sant'Angelo (designer)
Giorgio, Yes, (film, 1982)
Giorgione (del Castelfranco)(It. artist; c1475-1510)
Giotto (di Bondone)(It. artist; 1267-1337)
Giotto (space probe)
Giovanni Battista Pergolesi (It. comp.; 1710-36)
Giovanni Battista Tiepolo (It. artist; 1696-1770)
Giovanni Bellini (It. artist; 1426-1516)
Giovanni Boccaccio (It. writer; 1313-75)
Giovanni Caboto (also John Cabot)(It. nav.; 1450-98)
Giovanni Cimabue (It. artist; 1240-1302)
Giovanni da Bologna (sculptor; 1529-1608)
Giovanni da Verrazano (It. navigator; c1485-1528)
Giovanni Domenico Cassini (It./Fr. astron.; 1625-1712)
Giovanni Gabrieli (It. comp.; c1557-1612)
Giovanni Gentile (It. phil./educ.; 1875-1944)
Giovanni Jacopo Casanova (also Casanova de Seingalt)(It. adventurer; 1725-98)
Giovanni Lorenzo Bernini (It. sculptor; 1598-1680)
Giovanni Martinelli (tenor; 1885-1969)
Giovanni P(ierluigi) da Palestrina (It. comp.; c1525-94)
Giovanni Pisano (It. artist; c1250-c1314)
Giovanni (Virginio) Schiaparelli (It. astron.; 1835-1910)
Giovanni (Battista) Vico (It. hist./phil.; 1668-1744)
Giovanni, Don (by Mozart)
Giovanni, Don (Don Juan)(Sp. legend)
Giovanni, Nikki (b. Yolande Cornelia Giovanni, Jr.)(US poet; 1943-)
Girard, Stephen (US finan.; 1750-1831)
Girardon, Francois (Fr. sculptor; 1628-1715)
Giraudoux, Jean (Fr. writer/dipl.; 1882-1944)
Girija Prasad Koirala (PM, Nepal; 1925-)
Girl Guides (Br.)
Girl Scouts (US)
girl/man Friday
Girolamo Savonarola (It. rel./reformer; 1452-98)
Girondin (also Girondist)(Fr. hist.)
Giscard d'Estaing, Valéry (ex-pres., Fr.; 1926-)
Gisele MacKenzie (ent.; 1927-)
Giselle (Coralli, Perrot, Adam ballet)
Gish, Dorothy (ent.; 1898-1968)
Gish, Lillian (ent.; 1895-1993)
Gita (also Bhagavad-Gita)(rel.)
Gitano, E. J. (US bus.)
Gitega, Burundi
Gitlow v. New York (US law; 1925-)
Giuliani, Rudy (Rudolph W.)(mayor, NYC; 1944-)
Giulio Natta (It. chem./eng.; 1903-79)
Giuseppe (Tomasi) di Lampedusa, (It. writer; 1896-1957)
Giuseppe Garibaldi (aka Peppino)(It. mil.; 1879-1950)
Giuseppe (Fortunino Francesco) Verdi (It. comp.; 1813-
Giussepe Mazzini (It. reformer; 1805-72)

Givenchy, Hubert de (Fr. designer; 1927-)
Givens, Robin (ent.; 1964-)
Giverny, France
Gîza, Egypt (also El Gîza or Al Jizah)
Gîza, Great Pyramids of (also El Gîza or Al Jizah)(Eg.)
Gjetost (cheese)
G(ilbert) K(eith) Chesterton (writer; 1874-1936)
Glace Bay, Nova Scotia, Canada
Glacier Bay National Park (AK)
Glacier National Park (MT)
Glackens, William (James)(US artist; 1870-1938)
Glad Cling Wrap
Glad-Lock (plastic bags)
Gladsheim (myth.)
Gladstone bag (luggage)
Gladstone, William E(wart)(ex-PM, Br.; 1809-98)
Gladys Cooper, Dame (ent.; 1898-1971)
Gladys Knight (ent.; 1944-)
Gladys Knight & the Pips (pop music)
Gladys Swarthout (US opera; 1904-69)
Glafcos Clerides (pres., Cyprus; 1919-)
Glamour (mag.)
Glance, Harvey (track; 1957-)
Glaser, Paul Michael (ent.; 1943-)
Glasgow, Scotland
Glass Menagerie, The (T. Williams play)
Glass Plus (cleaner)
Glass, Philip (US comp.; 1937-)
Glass, Ron (ent.; 1945-)
Glastonbury chair
Glastonbury, England
Glauber's salt (med.)
Glavine, Tom (baseball; 1966-)
Glaxo Wellcomm Inc.
GlaxoSmithKline (US bus.)
Glazunov, Alexander (or Aleksandr) Konstantinovich (Rus. comp.; 1865-1936)
Gleason, Jackie (Herbert John)(ent.; 1916-87)
Gleason, James (ent.; 1886-1959)
Gleason, Joanna (ent.; 1950-)
Gleem (toothpaste)
Gleevec (med./cancer)
Gleizes, Albert (Léon)(Fr. artist; 1881-1953)
Glen Campbell (ent.; 1936-)
Glen Canyon Dam (AZ)
Glen Ellen Winery (US bus.)
Glen Frey (ent.; 1948-)
Glen Theater, Barns v. (US law; 1991)
Glenda Jackson (ent.; 1936-)
Glendale, AZ, CA
Glendening, Parris N(elson)(MD gov.; 1942-)
Glenlivet scotch
Glenn (Herbert) Gould (Can. comp.; 1932-82)
Glenn Close (ent.; 1947-)
Glenn Ford (ent.; 1916-)
Glenn Frey (ent./songwriter; 1948-)
Glenn Hammond Curtiss (US aviator/inv.; 1878-1930)
Glenn Miller (US jazz; 1904-44)
Glenn Miller Story, The (film, 1954)
Glenn T(heodore) Seaborg, Dr. (US chem./ chair, AEC; 1912-99)
Glenn Yarborough (ent.; 1930-)
Glenn, John H(erschel), Jr. (US ex-cong./

astro.; 1921-)
Glenn, Scott (ent.; 1942-)
Glenview Naval Air Station (IL)
Gless, Sharon (ent.; 1943-)
Glickman, Dan(iel)(Robert)(US ex-secy./agr.; 1944-)
Glidden Co., The
Glidden paint
Gligorov, Kiro (ex-pres., Macedonia; 1917-)
Glinka, Mikhail Ivanovitch (Rus. comp.; 1804-57)
Glitter, Gary (b. Paul Gadd)(ent.; 1940-)
Globe (mag.)
Globe & Mail, Toronto (Can. newspaper)
Globe Theatre (London, Shakespeare; fl. 16th-17th c.)
Globe-Times, Amarillo (TX newspaper)
Globe, Boston (MA newspaper)
Globetrotters, Harlem (basketball team; founded 1927)
Gloria Blondell (ent.; 1910-86)
Gloria DeHaven (ent.; 1925-)
Gloria Estefan (b. Gloria Fajardo)(ent.; 1958-)
Gloria Grahame (ent.; 1925-81)
Gloria . . . Happy at Last, Little (TV miniseries)
Gloria in Excelsis Deo (also great[er] doxology)(rel.)
Gloria Loring (ent.; 1946-)
Gloria Macapagal-Arroyo (pres., Phil.; 1947-)
Gloria Marshall Figure Salon (US bus.)
Gloria Reuben (ent.; 1965-)
Gloria Steinem (US jour./feminist; 1934-)
Gloria Swanson (ent.; 1899-1983)
Gloria Vanderbilt (perfume/clothing)
Gloria Vanderbilt (US bus.; 1924-)
Glorious Revolution (also English [or Bloodless] Revolution)(Br. hist.; 1688-89)
Gloucester (also Gloucestershire)(county, Eng.)
Gloucester (cheese)
Gloucester, England
Gloucester, MA
Gloucestershire (also Gloucester)(county, Eng.)
Glover, Danny (ent.; 1947-)
Glover, Savion (dancer/choreographer; 1973-)
Gluck, Christoph W(illibald) von (Ger. comp.; 1714-87)
Glucotrol (med.)
Glucovance (med.)
Gluyas Williams (US cartoonist; 1888-1982)
Glyndebourne Opera Festival (Eng.)
Glynis Johns (ent.; 1923-)
Glynn, Carlin (ent.; 1940-)
GM (general manager)
GM (General Motors)(auto.)
GM Corp. (General Motors Corp.)
GM Heavy Truck Corp., Volvo
GMAC (auto.)
GMAC Commercial Mortgage
G-man (FBI agent)
GMC (auto.)
GMC Denali (auto.)
GMC Denali XL (auto.)
GMC Envoy (auto.)
GMC Jimmy (auto.)
GMC Jimmy SL (auto.)
GMC Jimmy SLE (auto.)

GMC Jimmy SLS (auto.)
GMC Jimmy SLT (auto.)
GMC S-15 Jimmy (auto.)
GMC S-15 Sonoma pickup (auto.)
GMC Safari (auto.)
GMC Safari SL van (auto.)
GMC Safari SLE van (auto.)
GMC Safari SLT van (auto.)
GMC Safari SLX van (auto.)
GMC Savana (auto.)
GMC Savana 1500 van (auto.)
GMC Savana 2500 van (auto.)
GMC Savana 3500 van (auto.)
GMC Sierra (auto.)
GMC Sierra 1500 (auto.)
GMC Sierra 2500 (auto.)
GMC Sierra 3500 (auto.)
GMC Sierra C1500 pickup (auto.)
GMC Sierra C3 (auto.)
GMC Sierra K1500 (auto.)
GMC Sonoma (auto.)
GMC Sonoma crew cab (auto.)
GMC Sonoma extended cab (auto.)
GMC Suburban (auto.)
GMC Truck (US bus.)
GMC Yukon (auto.)
GMC Yukon Denali (auto.)
GMC Yukon SL (auto.)
GMC Yukon SLE (auto.)
GMC Yukon SLT (auto.)
GMC Yukon XL (auto.)
GMC Yukon XL Denali (auto.)
GMT (Greenwich Mean Time)
Gnaeus (or Gaius) Marcius Coriolanus (Roman
    hero; 5th c)
Gnaeus Julius Agricola (Roman mil./pol.; AD
    37-93)
Gnassingbe Eyadéma (pres., Togo; 1937-)
Gnosticism (rel.)
GNP (gross national product)
Guiliano Amato, (ex-PM, Italy; 1938-)
Gobel, George (ent.; 1921-91)
Gober, Hershel W. (US ex-secy./vet. affairs;
    1936-)
Gobi Desert (Mongolia/Ch.)
God (the supreme being)
God Almighty (God)
God the Father (God)
God the Son (Jesus Christ)
God, City of (heaven)
God, Kingdom of (heaven)
God, Lamb of (Jesus)
God, man of (saint, clergy, priest, etc.)
God, Mother of (rel.)
God, Party of (also Hezbollah)(rel./mil.)
God, The City of (Latin, De Civitate Dei)(by St.
    Augustine)
God, the Word of
God's acre (cemetery)
God's Little Acre (E. Caldwell novel)
Godard, Jean-Luc (Fr. ent.; 1930-)
Goddard Space Flight Center (MD)
Goddard, Paulette (ent.; 1905-90)
Goddard, Robert H. (US physt., father of
    modern rocketry; 1882-1945)

Godden, (Margaret) Rumer (Br. writer; 1907-98)
Goddess, The Great (also The Great
    Mother)(rel.)
Gödel's incompleteness theorem (math.)
Godey, Louis Antoine (US publ.; 1804-78)
Godey's Lady's Book (1st US women's magazine)
Godfather, The (M. Puzo novel)
Godfather's Pizza (US bus.)
Godfrey Cambridge (ent.; 1933-76)
Godfrey of Bouillon (also Godefroy de Bouillon)
    (Fr. crusader; c1060-1100)
Godfrey, Arthur (ent.; 1903-83)
Godfrey, My Man (film, 1936, 1957)
Godhavn, Greenland
Godhead (rel.)
Godiva chocolates
Godiva Chocolatier (US bus.)
Godiva, Lady (Br. noblewoman ; c1040-80)
Godmanis, Ivars (ex-PM, Latvia)
Godot, Waiting for (S. Beckett play)
Godoy, Virgilio (Nicaragua pol.)
Godspell (play)
Godthaab, Greenland (also Godthåb)
Godunov, Alexander (Rus./US ent.; 1949-95)
Godunov, Boris (Fëdorovich)(Rus. tsar; 1552-
    1605)
Godwin, Gail (US writer; 1937-)
Godzilla (film, 1985)
Goebbels, (Paul) Joseph (Ger. Nazi
    propagandist; 1897-1945)
Goering (or Göring), Hermann Wilhelm (Ger.
    Nazi; 1893-1946)
Goethals, George W(ashington)(US mil./eng.;
    1858-1928)
Goethe, Johann Wolfgang von (Ger. writer/
    phil.; 1749-1852)
Goetz, Bernhard H. (US news, shot NYC
    robbers)
Gog and Magog (rel.)
Gogh, Vincent van (Dutch artist; 1853-90)
Gogo (lang.)
Go-Jo Industries, Inc.
Gogol, Nikolai (Vasilievich)(Rus. writer; 1809-52)
Goh Chok Tong (PM, Singapore; 1941-)
Go Kart
Golan Heights (plateau on Isr./Syrian border)
Golconda (ruined city known for diamond
    cutting, India)
Gold Star Medal
Gold, Tracey (ent.; 1969-)
Golda Meir (also Goldie Mabovitch, Goldie
    Myerson)(ex-PM, Isr.; 1898-1979)
Goldberg (aka Bill Goldberg)(wrestling; 1966-)
Goldberg, Rube (complex/impractical inventions)
Goldberg, Rube (Reuben Lucius)(US cartoonist,
    Boob McNutt; 1883-1970)
Goldberg, Whoopi (b. Caryn Johnson)(ent.;
    1950-)
Goldblum, Jeff (ent.; 1952-)
Golden Age (Gr./Roman myth.)
Golden Age of Spain
Golden Ass, The (also Metamorphoses)(L.
    Apuleius novel)
Golden Books
golden Cadillac (mixed drink)

Golden Delicious (apple)
Golden Dipt (marinade)
Golden Dipt Co.
Golden Fleece (myth., stolen by Jason and the Argonauts)
Golden Gate Bridge (San Francisco)
Golden Gate Park (San Francisco)
Golden Girls (TV show)
Gloden Globe Awards (aka Golden Globes)(film & TV)
Golden Gloves (boxing)
Golden Horde, Empire of the
Golden Horn
Golden Rule
Golden Sebright bantam (chicken)
Golden State (nickname, CA)
Golden State Warriors (basketball team)
Golden Temple (Sikh temple, India)
Golden Years (TV show)
Golden, Harry (b. Harry Goldhurst)(US writer; 1902-81)
Goldfinger (film, 1964)
Goldie Hawn (ent.; 1945-)
Goldilocks (fict. chara.)
Goldin, Daniel S. (head/NASA; 1940-)
Golding, William (Gerald)(US writer; 1912-93)
Goldman Sachs Group, Inc.
Goldman, Emma (Rus./US reformer; 1869-1940)
Goldman, William (US writer; 1931-)
Goldmark, Karl (Hung. comp.; 1830-1915)
Goldsboro, Bobby (ent.; 1942-)
Goldsboro, NC
Goldsmith, Oliver (Br./Ir. writer; 1730?-74)
Goldstar (kitchen appliances)
Goldstar Electronics International, Inc.
Goldthwait, Bob "Bobcat" (ent.; 1962-)
Goldwater, Barry M(orris), Jr. (US pol.; 1938-)
Goldwater, Barry M(orris)(US pol.; 1909-98)
Goldwyn Girls (ent.)
Goldwyn Follies, The (film, 1938)
Goldwyn, Samuel (b. Samuel Goldfish)(ent.; 1882-1974)
Golf (mag.)
Golf Channel, The (TV channel)
Golf Digest (mag.)
Golf Illustrated (mag.)
Golf, Volkswagen (auto.)
Golgi apparatus/complex/tendon organ (med.)
Golgi, Camillo (It. biol.; 1843-1926)
Golgi's cells (med.)
Golgotha (hill where Jesus was crucified)
Goliards (Eur. minstrels; 12th-13th c.)(also l.c.)
Goliath (Biblical giant)
Goliath, David and (rel.)
Golliwogg (also Golliwog)(grotesque doll)(also l.c.)
GoLYTELY (or GoLytely)(med.)
Gomel, Belarus
Gomer Pyle (fict. chara.)
Gomorrah, Sodom and (ancient cities destroyed for wickedness)
Gompers, Samuel (US labor leader; 1850-1924)
Gonaïves, Haiti
Goncz, Arpad (ex-pres., Hung.; 1922-)
Gondi (lang.)
Gone With the Wind (M. Mitchell novel; film, 1939)
Goneril (*King Lear*)
Gong, Falun (aka Falun Dafa)(phil. group, China)
Gongora y Argote, Luis de (Sp. writer; 1561-1627)
Gongorism (lit. style)
González, Adolfo Suárez (ex-PM, Sp.; 1933-)
Gonzales, Alberta R. (US White House counsel; 1955?-)
Gonzalez, Elian (US/Cuban news; 1993-)
Gonzalez, Juan (baseball; 1969-)
González Márquez, Felipe (ex-PM, Spain; 1942-)
Gonzalez, Pancho (Richard Alonzo)(tennis; 1928-95)
Gonzalo Sánchez de Lozada (ex-pres., Bolivia; 1930-)
Gonzo journalism (also l.c.)
Good Book, the (Bible)
Good Friday (rel., Friday before Easter)
Good Hope, Cape of (SAfr)
Good Housekeeping (mag.)
Good Humor (ice cream)
Good Humor bar
Good Humor Corp., The
Good Humor man
Good King Wenceslas (also *Wenceslaus*)(song)
Good King Wenceslaus (also St. Wenceslaus)
Good Morning (TV show)
Good Morning, America (TV show)
Good Morning, Vietnam (film, 1987)
Good Neighbor Policy (govt.)
Good News, Gillette (razor)
Good Samaritan
Good Seasons (salad dressing)
Good Shepherd (Jesus Christ)
good-time Charlie
Good Will Hunting (film, 1997)
Goodall, Jane (Br. animal behaviorist/writer; 1934-)
Goodbar, Looking for Mr. (film, 1977)
Goodbar, Mr. (candy)
Goodbye Girl, The (film, 1977)
Goodbye, Columbus (P. Roth novel)
Goodbye, Mr. Chips (film, 1939)
Goodell, Brian Stuart (swimming; 1959-)
Gooden, Dwight (baseball; 1964-)
Goodfellow, Robin (also Puck, Hobgoblin)(fict. chara., *A Midsummer Night's Dream*)
Goodhue, Bertram G. (US arch.; 1869-1924)
Gooding, Cuba, Jr. (ent.; 1968-)
Goodman Story, The Benny (film, 1955)
Goodman, Benny (Benjamin David)(US jazz; 1909-86)
Goodman, Bergdorf (store)
Goodman, Dody (Delores)(ent.; 1929-)
Goodman, John (ent.; 1953-)
Goodrich Co., B. F.
Goodrich Tire Co., Uniroyal
Goodrich, Gail (basketball; 1943-)
Goodson, Mark (ent.; 1915-92)
Goodwill Industries
Goodwin, Archie (fict. chara.)
Goodwin, Doris (Helen) Kearns (US hist.; 1943-)
Goodwrench, Mr.
Goody (hair care)

Goodyear Tire & Rubber Co.
Goodyear, Charles (US inv.; 1800-60)
Google (Internet search engine)
Google, Barney (cartoon)
Goolagong (Cawley), Evonne (tennis; 1951-)
Goose and Grimm, Mother (comic strip)
Goose (Rich) Gossage (baseball; 1951-)
Goose Tales, Mother (fairy tales, C. Perrault)
Goose (Reese) Tatum (basketball; 1921-67)
Goose, Father (film, 1964)
Goose, Mother (fict. author of fairy tales)
GOP (Grand Old Party [Republican])
Gopher (Internet search engine)
Gopher State (nickname, MN)
Goran Visnijc (Croatian ent.; 1972-)
Göran Persson (PM, Swed.; 1949-)
Gorbachev, Mikhail (Sergeyevich)(ex-pres.;
  Rus. 1931-)
Gorbachev, Raisa (Maksimova Titorenko)(wife
  of ex-Rus. pres./educ.; 1932-99)
Gorbatko, Viktor V(asilyevich)(cosmo.; 1934-)
Gorbunov, Anatolijs (ex-pres., Latvia)
Gorcey, Leo (ent.; 1915-69)
Gordian knot (myth.)
Gordie (Gordon) Howe (hockey; 1928-)
Gordimer, Nadine (SAfr. writer; 1923-)
Gordon Bunshaft (US arch.; 1909-90)
Gordon Cooper, L(eroy), Jr. (astro.; 1927-)
Gordon Jump (ent.; 1932-)
Gordon Liddy, G. (US pol./Watergate; 1930-)
Gordon Lightfoot (ent.; 1938-)
Gordon MacRae (ent.; 1921-86)
Gordon Parks (ent.; 1912-)
Gordon R. Sullivan (US mil.; 1937-)
Gordon setter (dog)
Gordon Smith (US cong.; 1952-)
Gordon, Charles G(eorge)(Br. mil.; 1833-85)
Gordon, Dexter (US jazz; 1923-90)
Gordon, Flash (comic strip)
Gordon, Flesh (film, 1972)
Gordon, Fort, GA (mil.)
Gordon, Gale (ent.; 1906-95)
Gordon, Jeff (auto racing; 1971-)
Gordon, Mack (Pol./US lyricist; 1905-59)
Gordon, Mary (US writer; 1949-)
Gordon, Dame (Elmira) Minita (ex-gov.-gen.,
  Belize)
Gordon, Richard F., Jr. (astro.; 1929-)
Gordon, Ruth (ent.; 1896-1985)
Gordy, Berry, Jr. (US bus./founded Motown;
  1929-)
Gore Vidal (b. Eugene Luther Vidal)(US writer/
  critic; 1925-)
Gore, Albert A(rnold), Jr. (ex-VP/cong., US;
  1948-)
Gore, Lesley (ent.; 1946-)
Gore, Tipper (b. Mary Elizabeth Aitcheson)(US
  wife of ex-VP; 1948-)
Goren, Charles H. (US contract bridge
  authority; 1901-91)
Gore-Tex (fabric laminate)
Gorey, Edward (St. John)(US illustrator/writer;
  1925-)
Gorgon (myth.)
Gorgonzola cheese

Gorham (silverware)
Gorham (US bus.)
Gorilla, Magilla (cartoon)
Göring, Hermann Wilhelm (also Goering)(Ger.
  Nazi; 1893-1946)
Gorky (or Gorki), Maxim (aka Aleksei Maksimovich
  Peshkov)(Rus. writer; 1868-1936)
Gorky Park (M.C. Smith novel)
Gorky, Arshile (Vosdanig Adoian)(US artist;
  1905-48)
Gorky, Russia (now Nizhni-Novgorod)
Gorme, Eydie (ent.; 1932-)
Gorshin, Frank (ent.; 1934-)
Gortari, Carlos Salinas de (ex-pres., Mex.; 1949-)
Gorton, Slade (US cong.; 1928-)
Gorton's (fish prods.)
Gosden, Freeman (ent., Amos of *Amos 'n' Andy
  Show*; 1899-1982)
Goshen (Biblical fertile land)
Goshen, IN
Gospel(s)(rel.)
Gospels, Synoptic/synoptic
Gosport, England
Gossage, Goose (Rich)(baseball; 1951-)
Gossett, Louis, Jr. (ent.; 1936-)
Göteborg, Sweden
Goth (people)
Gotha, House of Saxe-Coburg- (Br. ruling
  family; 1901-10)
Gotham (nickname for NYC)
Gotham City (Batman's)
Gotham, England
Gothic (arch./art/lit.)(Eur.; 12th-15th c)
Gothic novel/romance
Gothic revival (arch.; 19th c)
Goths, East (also Ostrogoths)(ancient Germans)
Gotland (island, Baltic Sea)
Götterdämmerung (also Ragnarök)(myth.)
Gottfried Wilhelm von Leibnitz, Baron (Ger.
  phil./math; 1646-1716)
Gottfried, Brian (tennis; 1952-)
Gotthold (Ephraim) Lessing (Ger. writer; 1729-
  81)
Gotti, John (US mobster; 1940-)
Gottlieb Daimler (Ger. eng./inv.; 1834-1900)
Gottschalk, Louis Moreau (US comp.; 1829-69)
Gottwald, Klement (Czech. pol.; 1896-1953)
Goucher College (Towson, MD)
Gouda (cheese)
Gouda, the Netherlands
Goudy (type style)
Gould, Chester (cartoonist, *Dick Tracy*; 1900-85)
Gould, Elliott (b. Elliott Goldstein)(ent.; 1938-)
Gould, Glenn (Herbert)(Can. comp.; 1932-82)
Gould, Harold (ent.; 1923-)
Gould, Jay (US finan., railroad; 1836-92)
Gould, Morton (ent.; 1913-96)
Gould, Stephen Jay (US paleontol./writer; 1941-)
Goulet, Robert (b. Stanley Applebaum)(ent.;
  1933-)
Gounod, Charles François (Fr. comp.; 1818-93)
Gourmet (mag.)
Gourmet, Galloping (aka Graham Kerr)(Br.
  chef; 1934-)
Gouveja, U.S. v. (US law; 1984)

Gouverneur Morris (US pol./dipl.; 1752-1816)
Government National Mortgage Association
(also Ginnie Mae, GNMA)
Government Printing Office (US govt. agcy.)
Gowdy, Curt (ent.; 1919-)
Gower Champion (US dancer; 1921-80)
Goya y Lucientes, Francisco (José) de (Sp.
artist; 1746-1828)
GPO (general post office, Government Printing
Office)
GQ (mag.)
Graaf, Regnier de (Dutch phys.; 1641-73)
Graaff generator, Van de (also electrostatic
generator)
Graaff, Robert Jemison Van de (US physt.;
1901-67)
Graafian follicle (med.)
Grable, Betty (ent.; 1916-73)
Grace & Co., W. R.
Grace Bumbry (ent.; 1937-)
Grace Jones (ent.; 1952-)
Grace (Patricia) Kelly (US actress; princess,
Monaco; 1929-82)
Grace Metalious (b. Marie Grace
DeRepentigny)(US writer; 1924-64)
Grace Mirabella (publ.; 1929-)
Grace Moore (soprano; 1901-47)
Grace Paley (US writer; 1922-)
Grace Slick (b. Grace Wing)(ent.; 1939-)
Grace Under Fire (TV show)
Grace, Princess (b. Grace Patricia Kelly)(US
actress; princess, Monaco; 1929-82)
Grace, Will and (TV show)
Grace, Your (title)
Graceland (Elvis Presley's home)
Graces (3 goddesses)(myth.)
Gracie Allen (ent.; 1906-64)
Gracie Fields (ent.; 1898-1979)
Graco (baby prods.)
Graf (Ger./Aus./Swed. title, a count)
Graf Zeppelin (Ger. airship)
Graf, Steffi (Stephanie Maria)(tennis; 1969-)
Graham Greene (Henry)(Br. writer; 1904-91)
Graham Kerr (aka Galloping Gourmet)(Br. chef;
1934-)
Graham Nash (ent.; 1942-)
Graham (Vivian) Sutherland (Br. artist; 1903-80)
Graham, Bill (b. Wolfgang Grajonca)(rock
impresario; 1930-91)
Graham, Billy (William Franklin), Rev. (US rel.;
1918-)
Graham, Bob (Robert)(US cong.; 1936-)
Graham, David (golf; 1946-)
Graham, Heather (ent./model; 1970-)
Graham, Katharine (US newspaper exec.;
1917-2001)
Graham, Martha (US dancer/choreographer;
1894-1991)
Graham, Otto (football; 1921-)
Graham, Sheilah (gossip columnist; 1904-88)
Graham, Thomas (Scot. chem.; 1805-69)
Graham, Virginia (ent.; 1912-98)
Graham's law (diffusion of gases)
Grahame, Gloria (ent.; 1925-81)
Grahame, Kenneth (Scot. writer; 1859-1932)

Grail, the Holy (legendary cup used by Jesus at
the Last Supper)
Grainger, Percy Aldridge (Austl. pianist/comp.;
1882-1961)
Gram Parsons (b. Cecil Ingram Connor III)
(ent.; 1946-73)
Gram, Hans Christian Joachim (Dan. phys.;
1853-1938)
Gram's method (med.)
Gram's stain (med.)
Gramercy Park (NYC)
Gramm (Grambach), Donald (bass-baritone;
1927-83)
Gramm, Phil (US cong.; 1942-)
Grammer, Kelsey (ent.; 1955-)
Grammy Awards (music)
Gran Quivira (utopia)
Granada, Nicaragua
Granada, Spain
Granby, Quebec, Canada
Grand Alliance (Fr. hist.; 1689, 1701)
Grand Am, Pontiac (auto.)
Grand Army of the Republic (G.A.R.)(US hist.;
founded 1865)
Grand Canal (Ch.)
Grand Canyon National Park (AZ)
Grand Canyon State (nickname, AZ)
Grand Caravan, Dodge (auto.)
Grand Cherokee Laredo, Jeep (auto.)
Grand Cherokee, Jeep (auto.)
Grand Coulee Dam (WA)
Grand Duke Henri (ruler, Luxembourg; 1955-)
Grand Duke Jean (ex-pres., Luxembourg; 1921-)
Grand Forks Air Force Base, ND (mil.)
Grand Forks, ND
Grand Funk Railroad (pop music)
Grand Guignol (theater)
Grand Island, NE
Grand Junction, CO
Grand Marnier (liqueur)
Grand Marquis, Mercury (auto.)
Grand Old Party (GOP, Republican Party)
Grand Ole Opry
Grand Ole Opry Live (TV show)
Grand Prix (racing)
Grand Prix, Pontiac (auto.)
Grand Rapids Press (MI newspaper)
Grand Rapids, MI
Grand Slam (golf, tennis)
Grand Teton National Park (WY)
Grand Vitara, Suzuki (auto.)
Grand Voyager, Plymouth (now Chrysler)(auto.)
Grandma Moses (b. Anna Mary Robertson)(US
artist; 1860-1961)
Grandmaster Flash (b. Joseph Saddler)(ent.;
1958-)
Grandpa Jones (b. Lewis Marshall Jones)(ent.;
1913-98)
Grandy, Fred (ent./pol.; 1948-)
Grange (or Granger) Movement, the (US hist.;
1867-c1878)
Grange, Red (Harold)(football; 1903-91)
Granger, (James) Stewart (ent.; 1913-93)
Granger, Farley (ent.; 1925-)
Granite State (nickname, NH)

Granny Smith (apple)
Granolith (concrete)
Grant Sahib (also Grunth, Granth, Adigranth)(rel.)
Grant Tinker (ent.; 1926-)
Grant Wood (US artist; 1891-1942)
Grant, Amy (ent.; 1960-)
Grant, Cary (b. Archibald Leach)(ent.; 1904-86)
Grant, Hugh (ent.; 1960-)
Grant, Lee (b. Lyova Rosenthal)(ent.; 1927-)
Grant, Ulysses S(impson)(18th US pres.; 1822-85)
Granth (also Grunth, Grant Sahib, Adigranth)(rel.)
Grantland Rice (US sports writer; 1880-1954)
Granville, France
Grape-Nuts (cereal)
Grapes of Wrath, The (J. Steinbeck novel)
Graphic Arts Monthly (mag.)
Grappelli, Stephane (US jazz; 1908-97)
Grass, Günter (Wilhelm)(Ger. writer/artist; 1927-)
Grassley, Charles "Chuck" Ernest (US cong.; 1933-)
Grasso, Ella Tambussi (US pol.; 1919-81)
Grateful Dead (pop music)
Grau, Shirley Ann (US writer; 1929-)
Grauer, Ben (ent.; 1908-77)
Graves (Fr. wine district)
Graves, Bill (William Preston)(KS gov.; 1953-)
Graves, Nancy (Stevenson)(US artist; 1940-96)
Graves, Peter (b. Peter Aurness)(ent.; 1926-)
Graves, Robert (Ranke)(Br. writer/hist.; 1895-1985)
Graves' disease (med.)
Gravy Train (dog food)
Gray Cosmetics, Ltd., Dorothy
Gray (Joseph Graham) Davis, Jr. (CA gov.; 1942-)
Gray Lady (Amer. Red Cross volunteer)
Gray, Erin (ent.; 1950-)
Gray, Harold (US cartoonist, *Little Orphan Annie*; 1894-1968)
Gray, Linda (ent.; 1940-)
Gray, Macy (b. Natalie McIntyre)(ent.; 1967-)
Gray, The Picture of Dorian (O. Wilde novel)
Gray, Thomas (Br. poet; 1716-71)
Gray's Anatomy (med. text)
Grayson, Kathryn (ent.; 1922-)
Grayson (Louis) Kirk (US educ.; 1903-97)
Graz, Austria
Graziano, Rocky (Thomas Rocco Barbella)(boxing, 1919-90)
Grease (play; film, 1978)
Great Atlantic & Pacific Tea Co. (A&P Food Stores)
Great Awakening, the
Great Barrier Reef (coral reefs/islands off E Austl.)
Great Basin (region, W US)
Great Basin National Park (NV)
Great Britain (Eng., Scot., and Wales; part of the UK)
Great Chefs of Chicago (TV show)
Great Chefs of New Orleans (TV show)
Great Chefs of New York (TV show)
Great Chefs of San Francisco (TV show)
Great Compromiser (also Great Pacificator)

(Henry Clay)(US pol.; 1777-1852)
Great Dane (dog)
Great Depression, the (US hist.; 1930s)
Great Dictator, The (film, 1940)
Great Divide (also Continental Divide)(the Rockies)
Great Dog (astron., Canis Major, includes the Dog Star, Sirius)
Great Falls, MT
Great Gatsby, The (F.S. Fitzgerald novel)
Great Gildersleeve, The (film, 1943)
Great Goddess, The (also The Great Mother) (rel.)
Great Lake State (nickname, MI)
Great Lakes Naval Training Center (IL)(mil)
Great Lakes, the (US/Can. border: Erie, Huron, Michigan, Ontario, Superior)
Great Mosque of Samarra
Great Mother, The (also The Great Goddess)(rel.)
Great Ouse River (also Ouse)(Eng.)
Great Pacificator (also Great Compromiser) (Henry Clay)(US pol.; 1777-1852)
Great Plains region (E of Rockies: TX/OK/KS/NE/SD/ND)
Great Pyramid of Khufu (or Cheops)(Eg.)
Great Pyramids of Gîza (also El Gîza or Al Jizah) (Eg.)
Great Pyrenees (dog)
Great Rift Valley (SW Asia/SE Afr.)
Great River Winery, Windsor Vineyards & (US bus.)
Great Salt Lake (UT)
Great Santini, The (film, 1980)
Great Schism (also the Schism of the West)(rel.)
Great Slave Lake (Northwest Territories, Can.)
Great Smoky Mountains (NC/TN)
Great Smoky Mountains National Park (NC/TN)
Great Sphinx, the (Eg.; c2500 BC)
Great Turtle (myth.)
Great Wall (astron.)
Great Wall of China (1,450 miles; built 214 BC)
Great War (also World War I, First World War, War of the Nations)(1914-18)
Great White Way, the (Broadway theatre district)
Greater Antilles, West Indies (Cuba, Hispaniola, Jamaica, Puerto Rico)
Greater Pittsburgh International Airport (PA)
Greatest Show on Earth, The (film, 1952)
Greatest Show on Earth, The (P.T. Barnum's circus)
Grecian bend
Grecian profile
Greco-Roman wrestling
Greco, El (aka Domenikos Theotocopoulos)(Sp. artist; 1541-1614)
Greco, El (art style)
Greece (Hellenic Republic)(SE Eur.)
Greek (lang./people)
Greek Church (also Greek Orthodox Church)
Greek fire (ignites with water)
Greek gods/goddesses
Greek modes (music)
Greek Orthodox Church (also Greek Church)
Greek Revival (arch.)
Greeley, Horace (US publ./pol.; 1811-72)
Greely, Adolphus Washington (US mil.; 1844-

1935)
Green Bay Packers (football team)
Green Bay Press-Gazette (WI newspaper)
Green Bay, WI
Green Berets (also Special Forces)(US mil.)
Green Giant (food)
Green Giant Co.
Green Lantern (cartoon chara.)
Green Mountain Boys (US mil.; late 1700s)
Green Mountain State (nickname, VT)
Green Party, International (pol.)
Green River (WY/UT)
Green River ordinance/law (bans door-to-door selling)
Green, Adolph (US lyricist; 1915-)
Green, Al (ent.; 1946-)
Green, Brian Austin (ent.; 1973-)
Green, Gretna ("any" town for eloping couples)
Green, Hamilton (ex-PM, Guyana)
Green, Hetty (US finan., "witch of Wall Street"; 1834-1916)
Green, Hubert (golf; 1946-)
Green, Tom (ent.; 1971-)
Green, William (US labor leader; 1873-1952)
Greenaway, Kate (Catherine)(Br. artist/writer; 1846-1901)
Greenback-Labor Party (US hist.; 1878-c1884)
Greenback Party (US hist.; 1875-78)
Greene, Charles E. (sprinter; 1945-)
Greene, (Henry) Graham (Br. writer; 1904-91)
Greene, "Mean" Joe (football; 1946-)
Greene, Lorne (ent.; 1915-87)
Greene, Michele (ent.; 1962-)
Greene, Nathanael (US mil.; 1742-86)
Greene, Shecky (b. Sheldon Greenfield)(ent.; 1926-)
Greeneville, USS (US sub that collided with Japanese fishing vessel near Hawaii, 2/9/2001)
Greenland (also Kalaallit Nunaat)(island, N Atl.)
Greenlandic (lang.)
Greenough, Horatio (US sculptor; 1805-52)
Greenpeace (environ. grp.; founded 1971)
Greensboro News & Record (NC newspaper)
Greensboro, NC
Greensburg, PA
Greensburg Tribune-Review (PA newspaper)
Greenspan, Alan (US chair/Fed. Reserve Brd.; 1926-)
Greenstreet, Sydney (ent.; 1879-1954)
Greenville News (SC newspaper)
Greenville Piedmont (SC newspaper)
Greenville, Liberia
Greenville, MS, NC, OH, SC, TX
Greenwich (London borough)
Greenwich Mean Time (GMT)(also Greenwich Time, coordinated universal time [UTC])
Greenwich meridian (0° longitude, Greenwich, London)
Greenwich Observatory, Royal (London)(also Old Royal Observatory)
Greenwich Village (NYC)
Greenwich Village Theatre (NYC)
Greenwich, CT
Greer Garson (ent.; 1908-96)
Greer, Germaine (Austl. writer/feminist; 1939-)

Greg Evans (cartoonist, *Luann*)
Greg Evigan (ent.; 1953-)
Greg Gumbel (ent.; 1946-)
Greg Kinnear (ent.; 1963-)
Greg LeMond (US cyclist; 1961-)
Greg(ory) Louganis (US diver; 1960-)
Greg Morris (ent.; 1934-96)
Greg(ory) Norman (golf; 1955-)
Gregg Allman (ent.; 1947-)
Gregg, John Robert (inv. shorthand system; 1868-1948)
Gregg, Judd (US cong.; 1947-)
Gregg, William (US bus.; 1800-67)
Gregor J(ohann) Mendel (Aus. biol.; 1822-84)
Gregor Piatigorsky (Rus./US cellist; 1903-76)
Gregorian calendar
Gregorian chant (music, rel.)
Gregory Harrison (ent.; 1950-)
Gregory Hines (ent.; 1946-)
Gregory I, St. ("the Great")(It., pope; c540-604)
Gregory II, St. (It., pope; ?-731)
Gregory III, St. (Syrian, pope; ?-741)
Gregory Peck, (Eldred)(ent.; 1916-)
Gregory VII, St. (aka Hildebrand)(It., pope; c1023-85)
Gregory XIII (Ugo Buoncompagno)(It., pope; 1502-85)
Gregory, Cynthia (ent.; 1946-)
Gregory, Dick (ent.; 1932-)
Gregory, James (ent.; 1911-)
Gregory, Lady Augusta (Ir. writer; 1852-1932)
Greguric, Franjo (ex-PM, Croatia)
Greiff, Monica de (Colombian pol.)
Gremlin, AMC (auto.)
Gremlins (film, 1984)
Grenada, West Indies
Grenadines, St. Vincent and the (island nation) (West Indies)
Grendel (fict. chara., *Beowulf*)
Grenoble, France
Grenville (or Greynville), (Sir) Richard (Br. mil.; 1541-91)
Grenville, George (ex-PM, Br.; 1712-70)
Grenville, Grenada
Grenville, William Wyndham, Baron (Br. pol.; 1759-1834)
Gresham, OR
Gresham, (Sir) Thomas (Br. finan.; 1519?-79)
Gresham's law (econ.)
Greta Garbo (b. Greta Lovisa Gustafsson)(ent.; 1905-90)
Grete (Andersen) Waitz (runner; 1953-)
Gretel, Hänsel and (folktale)
Gretna Green ("any" town for eloping couples)
Gretna Green, Scotland (Scot./Eng. border town where couples eloped)
Gretzky, Wayne (hockey; 1961-)
Greuze, Jean-Baptiste (Fr. artist; 1725-1805)
Grey Cup (Can. football)
Grey Poupon (mustard)
Grey, Earl (tea)
Grey, Jennifer (ent.; 1960-)
Grey, Joel (b. Joel Katz)(ent.; 1932-)
Grey, Lady Jane (Dudley)(queen, Eng. [10 days]; 1537-54)

Grey, Zane (US writer; 1875-1939)
Greyhound bus
Greyhound-Dial Corp.
Greynville (or Grenville), (Sir) Richard (Br. mil.; 1541-91)
Greystoke, Lord (fict. chara., *Tarzan*)
Greystoke: The Legend of Tarzan, Lord of the Apes (film, 1984)
Grieg, Edvard (Hagerup)(Nor. comp.; 1843-1907)
Grier, David Alan (ent.; 1955-)
Grier, Pam (ent.; 1949-)
Grier, Roosevelt "Rosey" (ent./football; 1932-)
Griese, Bob (Robert Allen)(football; 1945-)
Griffey, Ken, Jr. (baseball; 1969-)
Griffin Act, Landrum- (US hist.; 1959)
Griffin Dunne (ent.; 1955-)
Griffin, Merv (ent.; 1925-)
Griffiss Air Force Base, NY (mil.)
Griffith Joyner, Florence ("Flo Jo")(track; 1959-98)
Griffith Park (Los Angeles)
Griffith, Andy (ent.; 1926-)
Griffith, D(avid) W(ark)(ent.; 1875-1948)
Griffith, Hugh (ent.; 1912-80)
Griffith, Melanie (ent.; 1957-)
Griffith, Nanci (ent./comp.; 1953-)
Grifulvin (med.)
Grigori Efimovich Rasputin ("Rasputin")(Rus. rel.; c1865-1916)
Grigory Aleksandrovich Potemkin, Prince (Rus. pol.; 1739-91)
Grim Reaper
Grimes, Tammy (ent.; 1934-)
Grimm, Brothers (wrote/collected folk tales)
Grimm, Jakob (Ludwig Karl)(Ger. writer/ linguist; 1785-1863)
Grimm, Mother Goose and (comic strip)
Grimm, Wilhelm (Karl)(Ger. writer/linguist; 1786-1859)
Grimm's Fairy Tales (by the Brothers Grimm)
Grimm's law (linguistics)
Grimsby, England
Grímsson, Olafur Ragnar (pres., Iceland; 1943-)
Gris, Juan (b. José Vittoriano Gonzales)(Sp. artist; 1887-1927)
Grisactin (med.)
Griselda
Grisham, John (US writer; 1955-)
Grissom Air Force Base (IN)(mil.)
Grissom, Virgil I. "Gus" (astro.; 1926-67)
Griswold v. Connecticut (US law; 1965)
Griswold, Hepburn v. (US law; 1870)
Grizzard, George (ent.; 1928-)
Grizzly Adams (TV show)
Grizzly Adams, Life and Times of (film, 1974)
Gro Harlem Brundtland (ex-PM, Nor.; 1939-)
Grodin, Charles (ent.; 1935-)
Grodno, Belarus
Groebli, "Mr. Frick" (Werner)(ice skating; 1915-)
Groenendael (also Belgian sheepdog)(dog)
Groening, Matt(hew Akbar)(US cartoonist, *The Simpsons*; 1954-)
Grofe, Ferde (US comp.; 1892-1972)
Groh, David (ent.; 1941-)

Grolier, Inc.
Gromyko, Andrei A. (ex-pres., Rus.; 1909-89)
Groningen (province, Netherlands)
Grooms, Red (Charles Roger)(US artist; 1937-)
Gropius, Walter (Adolf)(US arch.; 1883-1969)
Gropper, William (US artist; 1897-1977)
Gross, Chaim (US artist; 1904-91)
Gross, Mary (ent.; 1953-)
Gross, Michael (ent.; 1947-)
Grosse Point, MI
Grosset & Dunlap, Inc.
Grosvenor, Gerald (6th Duke of Westminster, England; 1951-)
Grosvenor, Gilbert (Hovey)(US geographer/ writer/editor; 1875-1966)
Grosvenor, Gilbert M. (US publ.; 1931-)
Groucho Marx, (Julius)(ent.; 1890-1977)
Groundhog Day (Feb. 2)
Group W. Productions
Grove City v. Bell (US law; 1984)
Grove, Andrew (b. Andras Grof)(bus., computers; 1936-)
Grove, Lefty (Robert Moses)(baseball; 1900-75)
Grover Cleveland (22nd & 24th US pres.; 1837-1908)
Grover Cleveland Alexander (baseball; 1887-1950)
Growing Pains (TV show)
Groza, Lou (football; 1924-2000)
Grrravy, Purina (dog food)
Grub Street (lit., London)
Grumbacher, Inc., M.
Grumman Corp.
Grundy (narrow-minded person)
Grundy, Mrs. (fict. chara., *Speed the Plough*)
Grünewald, Matthias (or Mathäus)(Ger. artist; 1480-1528)
Grunth (also Granth, Grant Sahib, Adigranth)(rel.)
Grus (astron., crane)
Gruyère (district, Switz.)
Gruyère cheese
GSA (General Services Administration, Girl Scouts of America)
G spot (also G-spot, Grafenberg spot)
GST (Greenwich Sidereal Time)
Gstaad, Switzerland
G-string (also gee-string, gee string)
G-suit (also g-suit, G suit, anti-G suit) (antigravity suit)
GTE Communications Systems, Inc.
GTE Corp.
Guadalajara, Mexico
Guadalajara, Spain
Guadalcanal Diary
Guadalcanal Island (SW Pac.)
Guadalupe Hidalgo, Treaty of (ended Mexican War; 1848)
Guadalupe Mountains National Park (TX)
Guadalupe Victoria (b. Manuel Félix Fernández)(1st pres., Mex.; 1789-1843)
Guadeloupe (West Indies)(Fr.)
Guam (US territory, W Pac.)
Guangdong (also Kwangtung)(province, Ch.)
Guangxi (also Kwangsi-Chuang)(region, Ch.)

Guangzhou, China (also Canton or Kuang-chou)
Guantánamo Bay (Cuba)
Guantánamo, Cuba
Guaraní (lang./people)
Guardafui, Cape (also Ras Asir)(cape, Somalia)
Guardia, Rafael Angel Calderón (ex-pres.,
    Costa Rica; 1900-71)
Guardian (Br. newspaper)
Guardian Angels
Guardino, Harry (ent.; 1925-)
Guare, John (US writer; 1938-)
Guatemala (City), Guatemala
Guatemala (Republic of)(CAmer.)
Guatemalan (people)
Guayaquil, Ecuador
Guaymas, Mexico
Guaymi (Costa Rican Native Amer.)
Gub-Gub the pig (fict. chara., *The Story of*
    Doctor Dolittle)
Gucci (fashion)
Gucci America, Inc.
Guccione, Bob (publ., *Penthouse*; 1930-)
Guderian, Heinz (Ger. gen.; 1888-1953)
Guéi, Gen. Robert (pres., Ivory Coast; 1941-)
Guelders (also Gelderland)(province,
    Netherlands)
Guelph, Ontario, Canada
Guelphs (It. pol.; 12th-15th c.)
Guérin, Camille (Fr. bacteriol.; 1872-1961)
Guerlain, Inc.
Guernica (Picasso)
Guernica, Spain
Guernsey cattle
Guernsey, Isle of (island, English Channel)
Guerrero (state, Mex.)
Guess (jeans)
Guess? Inc.
Guest Quarters, Inc.
Guest, Christopher (Haden-)(ent./writer; 1948-)
Guest, Edgar (Albert)(US writer; 1881-1959)
Guevara, Ernesto "Che" (SAmer. mil.; 1928-67)
Guevara, Federico Salas (ex-PM, Peru; 1950-)
Guggenheim Museum, Solomon R. (NYC)
Guggenheim, Crazy (aka Frank Fontaine)(ent.;
    1920-78)
Guggenheim, Daniel (US bus./finan.; 1856-1930)
Guggenheim, Harry F. (US bus./finan.; 1890-
    1971)
Guggenheim, Meyer (US bus./finan.; 1828-1905)
Guggenheim, Peggy (US finan.; 1898-1979)
Guggenheim, Simon (US bus./finan.; 1867-1941)
Guggenheim, Solomon R(obert)(US bus./finan.;
    1861-1949)
Guglielmo Marconi (It. eng./inv., radio; 1874-
    1937)
Guglielmo Winery, Emilio (US bus.)
Guiana (SAmer., inc. Fr. Guiana/Guyana/Surinam)
Guiana, Dutch (now Suriname)
Guicciardini, Francesco (It. hist.; 1483-1540)
Guideposts (mag.)
Guidi (Masaccio), Tommaso (It. artist; 1401-28?)
Guiding Light (TV soap)
Guido de Marco, Prof. (pres., Malta; 1931-)
Guidry, Ronald Ames (baseball; 1950-)
Guildenstern (fict. chara., *Hamlet*)

Guildenstern, Rosencrantz & (T. Stoppard play)
Guilherme Posser da Costa (PM, São Tomé/
    Príncipe; 1945-)
Guiliana Benetton (It. designer; 1938-)
Guiliano Amato (PM, It.; 1938-)
Guilin, China (also Kweilin)
Guillain-Barré reflex/syndrome (med.)
Guillaume de Machaut (Fr. comp.; 1300-77)
Guillaume Dufay (Flem. comp.; c1400-74)
Guillaume, Robert (b. Robert Williams)(ent.;
    1937-)
Guillermo Endara (ex-pres., Panama; 1936-)
Guillermo Ford Boyd (Panama, pol.)
Guillermo Vilas (tennis; 1952-)
Guinea (Republic of)(W Afr.)
Guinea, Equatorial (Republic of)(formerly
    Spanish Guinea)(W central Afr.)
Guinea, Spanish (now Equatorial Guinea)
Guinea-Bissau (Republic of)(W Afr.)
Guinevere, Queen (King Arthur's wife, Sir
    Lancelot's love)
Guinier, Lani (US atty./educ.)
Guinn, Kenny C. (NV gov.; 1936-)
Guinness Book of World Records
Guinness, (Sir) Alec (ent.; 1914-2000)
Guiomar Novaes (pianist; 1895-1979)
Guiscard, Robert (Robert de Hauteville)
    (Norman /It. mil.; c1015-85)
Guise, Mary of (queen to James V, Scot.; 1515-
    60)
Guisewite, Cathy (cartoonist, *Cathy*; 1950-)
Guitry, Sacha (Alexandre)(Fr. ent./dramatist;
    1885-1957)
Guiyang (also Kweiyang), China
Guizhou (also Kweichow)(province, Ch.)
Gujarat (also Gujerat)(state, India)
Gujarati (lang./people)
Gula (myth.)
GULAG (USSR prison system)(also gulag)
Gulbuddin Hekmatyar (ex-PM, Afghan.)
Gulden's mustard
Gulf of Aden (Yemen/Africa)
Gulf of Aqaba (Jordan)
Gulf of Boothia (Arctic/N Can.)
Gulf of Bothnia (Swed./Fin.)
Gulf of California (CA/Mex.)
Gulf of Finland (arm of Baltic Sea)
Gulf of Lions
Gulf of Mexico (US/Mex.)
Gulf of Oman (Oman/Iran)
Gulf of Siam (or Thailand)
Gulf of Suez (Eg.)
Gulf of Tadjoura (Djibouti)
Gulf of Thailand (or Siam)
Gulf of Tonkin (also Tonkin Gulf)(Viet./Ch.)
Gulf Oil Corp.
Gulf States, Persian (Bahrain/Iran/Iraq/Kuwait/
    Oman/Qatar/Saudi Arabia/UAE)
Gulf States, U.S. (AL/FL/LA/MS/TX)
Gulf Stream (warm ocean current, Gulf of Mexico)
Gulf War (28 nations [inc. US]/Iraq; 1991)
Gulf War (also Iran-Iraq War)(1980-88)
Gulfport, FL, MS
Gullah (lang./people)
Gulliver's Travels (J. Swift satire)

Gulu, Uganda
Gumbel, Bryant (US TV commentator; 1948-)
Gumbel, Greg (ent.; 1946-)
Gummi Bears, The (cartoon)
Gummo Marx, (Milton)(ent.; 1893-1977)
Gummy Bear Co., The
Gump, Forrest (film, 1994)
Gump's store
Gunfight at the O.K. Corral (film, 1957)
Gunga Din (film, 1939)
Gunn effect
Gunn, Peter (TV show)
Gunnar (myth.)
Gunnar Martens (High Comm., Greenland)
Gunnar Myrdal (Swed. econ.; 1898-1987)
Gunpowder Plot (Br. hist.; 1605)
Guns 'N Roses (pop music)
Guns of Navarone, The (film, 1961)
Gunsmoke (TV show)
Gunter (Wilhelm) Grass (Ger. writer/artist; 1927-)
Gunter, Nancy Richey (tennis; 1942-)
Gunter's chain (surveyor's measure/chain)
Gunther Gebel-Williams (Ger. animal trainer)
Gunther, John (US jour./writer; 1901-70)
Guntis Ulmanis (ex-pres., Latvia)
Guofeng (or Kuo-feng), Hua (ex-PM, Ch.; 1920?-)
Guomindang (also Kuomintang)(Ch. pol. party)
Gupta (Indian dynasty/empire)
Gur languages
Gurkha (soldier, people)
Gurung (lang.)
Gus Edwards (US comp.; 1879-1945)
Gus (Virgil I.) Grissom (astro.; 1926-67)
Gus Kahn (US lyricist; 1886-1941)
Gush Emunim (Isr. pol. grp.; founded 1973)
Gusii (lang.)
Gustaf, Carl XVI (king, Swed.; 1946-)
Gustafsons Dairy, Inc.
Gustav (Theodore) Holst (Br. comp.; 1874-1934)
Gustav Klimt (Aus. artist; 1862-1918)
Gustav Mahler (Aus. comp.; 1860-1911)
Gustav Stresemann (ex-chanc., Ger.; 1878-1929)
Gustave Charpentier (Fr. comp.; 1860-1956)
Gustave Courbet (Fr. artist; 1819-77)
Gustave Doré (Fr. artist; 1832-83)
Gustave Eiffel, (Alexandre)(Fr. eng.; 1832-1923)
Gustave Flaubert (Fr. writer; 1821-80)
Gustave Moreau (Fr. artist; 1826-98)
Gustavo Noboa Bejarano (pres., Ecuador; 1937-)
Gustavo Thoeni (skiing; 1951-)
Gustavus I (Gustavus Vasa [or Eriksson])(king, Swed.; 1496-1560)
Gustavus II (Gustavus Adolphus)("Snow King," "Lion of the North")(king, Swed.; 1594-1632)
Gustavus III (king, Swed.; 1746-92)
Gustavus IV (Gustavus Adolphus)(king, Swed.; 1778-1837)
Gustavus Swift (US pioneer meat packer; 1839-1903)
Gustavus V (Gustaf)(king, Swed.; 1858-1950)
Gustavus VI (king, Swed.; 1882-1973)
Gutenberg Bible (also Mazarin Bible)
Gutenberg, Johann (Ger. printer; c1400-68)
Guterres, Antonio (PM, Port.; 1949-)

Guthrie, A. B. (US writer; 1901-91)
Guthrie, Arlo (ent.; 1947-)
Guthrie, (Sir) Tyrone (William)(Br. ent.; 1900-71)
Guthrie, Woody (Woodrow Wilson)(ent.; 1912-67)
Guttenberg, Steve (ent.; 1958-)
Gutzon Borglum, (John)(US sculptor; 1871-1941)
Guy de Maupassant, (Henri René Albert)(Fr. writer; 1850-93)
Guy Fawkes (Br. conspirator; 1570-1606)
Guy Fawkes Day (Br.)
Guy Hunt, (Harold)(ex-AL gov.; 1933-)
Guy Kibbee (ent.; 1886-1956)
Guy Lafleur (hockey; 1951-)
Guy (Albert) Lombardo (ent.; 1902-77)
Guy Mollet (Fr. pol.; 1905-75)
Guy (Willy) Razanamasy (ex-PM, Madagascar)
Guy Ritchie (ent.; Madonna's husband)
Guy Verhofstadt (PM, Belgium; 1953-)
Guy Williams (ent.; 1924-89)
Guy, Buddy (George)(ent.; 1936-)
Guy, Jasmine (ent.; 1964-)
Guyana (Cooperative Republic of)(formerly British Guiana)(SAmer.)
Guyana Airways (airline)
Guys and Dolls (play; film, 1955)
Gwaltney of Smithfield, Ltd.
Gwelo, Zimbabwe (also Gweru)
Gwen Stefani (ent.; 1969-)
Gwen Verdon (ent.; 1925-2000)
Gwendolyn Brooks (US writer; 1917-)
Gwenn, Edmund (ent.; 1875-1959)
Gwent (county, Wales)
Gweru, Zimbabwe (also Gwelo)
Gwyn (or Gwynne), Nell (Eleanor)(ent.; 1651-87)
Gwynedd (county, Wales)
Gwyneth Paltrow (ent.; 1972-)
Gwynn, Tony (baseball; 1960-)
Gwynne, Fred (ent.; 1926-93)
Gyandzha, Azerbaijan
Gyne-Lotrimin (med.)
Gyne-Moistrin (med.)
Gynt, Peer (H. Ibsen play)
Gyo Obata (US arch.; 1923-)
Gypsy (people/lang.)(lang. also Romany)
Gypsy Rose Lee (b. Rose Louise Hovick)(ent.; 1914-70)

– H –

H (chem. sym., hydrogen)
Häagen-Dazs Co., Inc., The
Häagen-Dazs ice cream
Haarlem, the Netherlands
Habakkuk (rel., book of the Old Testament)
Haber process (chem.)
Haber, Fritz (Ger. chem.; 1868-1934)
Habib Thiam (ex-PM, Senegal)
Habitrol (med.)
Habyarimana, Juvénal (ex-pres., Rwanda;
    1937-94)
Hackensack Record (NJ newspaper)
Hackensack, NJ
Hackett, Bobby (US jazz; 1915-76)
Hackett, Buddy (b. Leonard Hacker)(ent.; 1924-)
Hackman, Gene (ent.; 1930-)
Hackney (horse)
Hadassah (Jew. org.)
Hadassah Lieberman (US wife of pol.; 1948-)
Hades (myth., Hell)
Hadiyya (lang.)
Hadrian (also Adrian)(Publius Aelius Hadrianus)
    (emp., Rome; 76-138)
Hadrian's Wall (Roman hist.; 122-383)
Haeckel, Ernest (Heinrich)(Ger. zool.; 1834-1919)
Haemophilus (med.)
Hafez al-Assad (ex-pres., Syria; 1930-2000)
Haflinger (horse)
Haganah (Isr. army)
Hagar the Horrible (comic strip)
Hage G. Geingob (PM, Namibia; 1941-)
Hagel, Charles (US cong.; 1946-)
Hagen, Germany
Hagen, Uta (ent.; 1919-)
Hagen, Walter (golf; 1892-1969)
Hagerstown, MD
Haggadah (also *Haggada*)(rel.)
Haggai (rel., book of the Old Testament)
Haggar Co.
Haggar slacks
Haggard, Merle (ent.; 1937-)
Hagia Sophia (also Saint [or Santa] Sophia)
    (museum, Istanbul)
Hagin, Joseph (US White House staff)
Hagiographa, the (also *Ketuvim, Ketubim*)(rel.)
Hagler, Marvelous Marvin (boxing; 1954-)
Hagman, Larry (ent.; 1931-)
Hague Conferences (internat'l; late 18th/early
    19th c.)
Hague Tribunal (also Permanent Court of
    Arbitration)(internat'l court)
Hague, (The), the Netherlands (or Holland)
Hahn, Jessica (US news)
Hahn, Madame Helena Petrovna Blavatsky
    (Rus. theosophist; 1831-91)
Hahn, Otto (Ger. chem.; 1879-1968)
Hai Duong, Vietnam
Haid, Charles (ent.; 1943-)
Haida (Native Amer.)

Haidar (or Hyder) Ali (Indian ruler/mil.; 1722-82)
Haidar Abu Bakr al-Attas (ex-PM, Yemen; 1939-)
Haifa, Israel
Haig, Alexander M., Jr. (US gen./pol.; 1924-)
Haig, Douglas (Br. mil.; 1861-1928)
Haight-Ashbury (district, San Francisco)
Hail Mary (also *Ave Maria*)(prayer)
Haile Mariam Mengistu (ex-pres., Ethiopia; 1937-)
Haile Selassie (Ras [Prince] Tafari, "the Lion of
    Judah")(emp., Eth.; 1891-1975)
Hailey, Arthur (US writer; 1920-)
Haim, Corey (ent.; 1971-)
Hain Pure Food Co., Inc.
Hainaut (province, Belgium)
Haiphong, Vietnam
Hair (play; film, 1979)
Hairi, Rafiq al- (ex-PM, Lebanon)
Haise, Fred W(allace), Jr. (astro.; 1933-)
Haiti (Republic of)(Caribbean Sea)
Haiti Trans Air (airline)
Haitian Centers Council, Sale v. (US law; 1993)
Haitian Creole (lang.)
Hakka (lang.)
Hal David (US lyricist.; 1921-)
Hal Foster (US cartoonist; *Tarzan, Prince
    Valiant*; 1892-1982)
Hal Holbrook (ent.; 1925-)
Hal Linden (b. Hal Lipschitz)(ent.; 1931-)
Hal Roach (ent.; 1892-92)
Hal (Harold Brent) Wallis (ent.; 1899-1986)
Hal Williams (ent.; 1938-)
Halakhah (also Halakah, Halachah, Halacha)
    (Jew. law/tradition)
Halas, George (Stanley)(football; 1895-1983)
Halberstam, David (writer; 1934-)
Halcion (med.)
Halcyon (also Halcyone)(astrol., myth.)
Haldeman, H. R. "Bob" (US pol.; 1926-93)
Haldol (med.)
Hale-Bopp (comet)
Hale Irwin (golf; 1945-)
Hale Stores, Inc., Carter Hawley
Hale, Alan (ent.; 1892-1950)
Hale, Alan, Jr. (ent.; 1919-90)
Hale, Barbara (ent.; 1922-)
Hale, Edward Everett (US writer/rel.; 1822-1909)
Hale, Nathan (US mil.,; 1755-76)
Haleakala National Park (HI)
Halen, Eddie Van (ent.; 1957-)
ha-Levi (also Halevi), Judah (Judah ben Samuel
    Halevi)(Sp. rabbi/phys./poet/phil.; 1085-1140)
Haley and the Comets, Bill (pop music)
Haley, Alex (US writer; 1921-92)
Haley, Bill (ent.; 1925-81)
Haley, Jack (ent.; 1899-1979)
Haley's M-O (med.)
Half Moon Bay, CA
Haliburton, Thomas Chandler (pseud. Sam
    Slick)(Can. writer/judge/hist.; 1796-1865)
Halicarnassus (SW Asia Minor)
Halicarnassus, Mausoleum at (1 of 7 Wonders
    of the World)
Halifax, England
Halifax, Nova Scotia, Canada
Hall & Oates (pop music)

Hall of Fame (NY)(erected 1990)
Hall of Fame Bowl (college football)
Hall, Annie (film, 1977)
Hall, Arsenio (ent.; 1955-)
Hall, Daryl (b. Daryl Hohl)(ent.; 1948-)
Hall, Deidre (ent.; 1948-)
Hall, Donald (Andrew, Jr.)(US poet; 1928-)
Hall, Fawn (US news; 1959-)
Hall, Gary (swimming; 1951-)
Hall, Huntz (ent.; 1919-99)
Hall, Jerry (model; 1956-)
Hall, Monty (b. Monty Halparin)(ent.; 1923-)
Hall, Peter (Reginald Frederick)(Br. theater; 1930-)
Hall, Tom T. (ent.; 1936-)
Hall's honeysuckle (plant)
Halle Berry (ent.; 1966-)
Halle, Germany (also Halleander Saale)
Halleander Saale, Germany (also Halle)
Halley, Edmund (Br. astron.; 1656-1742)
Halley's Comet (astron.)
Halliwell, Geri (aka Ginger Spice)(ent.; 1972-)
Hallmark Cards, Inc.
Halloween (10/31)
Hallowmas (also All Saints' Day, All-Hallows)(rel.)
Halls Mentho-Lyptus (med.)
Halog (med.)
Halonen, Tarja (pres., Fin.; 1943-)
Halotex (med.)
Halpern, Steven (ent./writer; 1947-)
Hals, Frans (Dutch artist; c1580-1666)
Halsey, William F(rederick)(US mil.; 1882-1959)
Halston (clothing)
Halston (Roy Halston Frowick)(US designer; 1932-90)
Halston-Borghese (US bus.)
Haltran (med.)
Ham Fisher (US cartoonist, *Joe Palooka*; 1900-55)
Hama Amadou (PM, Niger; 1950-)
Hamad bin Isa al-Khalifa, Shiek (emir, Bahrain; 1950-)
Hamad bin Khalifa al-Thani, Sheik (emir, Qatar; 1950-)
Hamadou, Barkat Gourad (PM, Djibouti; 1930-)
Hambletonian (horse, race)
Hamburg (chicken)
Hamburg (state, Ger.)
Hamburg, Germany
Hamburg, NY
Hamburger Helper
Hamden, CT
Hamed Karoui (ex-PM, Tunisia; 1927-)
Hamel, Veronica (ent.; 1943-)
Hamill, Dorothy (Stuart)(figure skating; 1956-)
Hamill, Mark (ent.; 1951-)
Hamilton, Alice (US phys./reformer; 1869-1970)
Hamilton Beach/Proctor-Silex, Inc.
Hamilton Fish (US pol.; 1808-93)
Hamilton Fish, III (US pol.; 1899-1991)
Hamilton Fish, Jr. (US cong.; 1926-)
Hamilton Green (ex-PM, Guyana)
Hamilton River (Can.)
Hamilton, Alexander (US pol.; 1755-1804)
Hamilton, Bermuda

Hamilton, Edith (Ger./US educ./writer; 1867-1963)
Hamilton, Fort, NY (mil.)
Hamilton, Gail (aka Mary Abigail Dodge)(US writer; 1833-96)
Hamilton, George (ent.; 1939-)
Hamilton, Lady Emma (b. Amy Lyon)(Br. lady; 1765?-1815)
Hamilton, Linda (ent.; 1956-)
Hamilton, New Zealand
Hamilton, OH
Hamilton, Ontario, Canada
Hamilton, Scotland
Hamilton, Scott (figure skating; 1958-)
Hamites (people)
Hamitic (lang./people)
Hamitic, Nilo (lang.)
Hamito-Semitic (langs.)
Hamlet (Prince of Denmark)(Shakespeare play)
Hamlin, Hannibal (ex-US VP; 1809-91)
Hamlin, Harry (ent.; 1951-)
Hamlisch, Marvin (US comp.; 1944-)
Hamm Brewing Co.
Hamm, Germany
Hamm's
Hammacher, Schlemmer & Co., Inc.
Hammarskjöld, Dag (Hjalmar Agne Carl)(Swed., UN secy. gen.; 1905-61)
Hammer v. Dagenhart (US law; 1918)
Hammer, Arm & (baking powder)
Hammer, Armand (US bus.; 1898-1990)
Hammer, M. C. (b. Stanley Kirk Burrell)(ent.; 1962-)
Hammer, Mike (fict. chara., Mickey Spillane)
Hammermill Paper Co.
Hammerstein, Oscar (ent.; 1847-1919)
Hammerstein, Oscar, II (US lyricist; 1895-1960)
Hammett, (Samuel) Dashiell (US writer; 1894-1961)
Hammond Organ Co.
Hammond, IN, LA
Hammond, Kathy (runner; 1951-)
Hammurabi (also Hammurapi)(king, Babylonia; c20th c. BC)
Hammurabi Code (ancient law)
Hampshire (also Hampshire Down)(sheep)
Hampshire (also Hants)(county, Eng.)
Hampshire (hog)
Hampton Court (palace, London)
Hampton Court Conference (Br. hist.; 1604)
Hampton Inn & Suites
Hampton Institute (VA)
Hampton Roads Channel (VA/Chesapeake Bay)
Hampton, Lionel (US jazz; 1908-)
Hampton, VA
Hamsun, Knut (Norwegian writer; 1859-1952)
Han (people)
Han Chinese (people)
Han Cities, China (also Wuhan)
Han dynasty (Ch. hist.; 202 BC-AD 220)
Han River (Ch.)
Han Solo (fict. chara., *Star Wars*)
Hana Mandlikova (tennis; 1962-)
Hanafi (Islamic law)
Hanauer, Chip (boat racing)
Hanbali (Islamic law)

Hancock Bowl, John (college football)
Hancock Mutual Life Insurance Co., John
Hancock, Herbie (US jazz; 1940-)
Hancock, John (one's signature)
Hancock, John (US pol.; 1737-93)
Hand, Learned (Billings)(US jurist; 1872-1961)
Handel, George Frederick (also Georg Friedrich) (Ger./Br. comp.; 1685-1759)
Handi-Wrap
H & R Block tax service
H & R Block, Inc.
Handy, W(illiam) C(hristopher)(US jazz; 1873-1958)
Hanes Hosiery, Inc.
Hanes Underwear (US bus.)
Hangchow, China (now Hangzhou)
Hanging Gardens of Babylon (1 of 7 Wonders of the World)
Hangtown Fry (oyster omelet)
Hangul (Korean alphabet)
Hangzhou, China (formerly Hangchow)
Hani (lang.)
Hanimex (movie equipment)
Hanimex USA, Inc.
Hank (Henry) Aaron (baseball; 1934-)
Hank Azaria (ent.; 1964-)
Hank Ballard (ent./songwriter; 1936-)
Hank (Henry) Bauer (baseball; 1922-)
Hank (George Hanks) Brown (US pol.; 1940-)
Hank Ketcham (US cartoonist, *Dennis the Menace*; 1920-2001)
Hank Snow (ent.; 1914-99)
Hank Williams (ent.; 1923-53)
Hank Williams, Jr. (ent.; 1949-)
Hanks, Tom (ent.; 1956-)
Hanna-Barbera Productions, Inc.
Hanna Boys center (Boys' Town of the West)(CA)
Hanna Suchocka (ex-PM, Pol.)
Hanna, Bill (cartoonist, *Tom & Jerry, Huckleberry Hound, Yogi Bear, Flintstones*; 1910-2001)
Hannaford Brothers Co.
Hannah and Her Sisters (film, 1986)
Hannah Arendt (historian; 1906-75)
Hannah More (Br. writer; 1745-1833)
Hannah, Daryl (ent.; 1960-)
Hanni Wenzel (skiing; 1956-)
Hannibal (Carthaginian gen.; 247-182 BC)
Hannibal (film, 2001)
Hannibal Hamlin (ex-US VP; 1809-91)
Hannibal Lecter (fict. chara.)
Hannibal, MO
Hanns Kornell Champagne Cellars (US bus.)
Hanoi Hilton (film, 1987)
Hanoi, Vietnam
Hanover, Germany
Hanover, House of (Br. ruling family; 1714-1901)
Hans (or Jean) Arp (Fr. artist; 1887-1966)
Hans-Adam II, Prince (head of state, Liechtenstein; 1945-)
Hans Albrecht Bethe (US physt.; 1906-)
Hans (or Johannes) Bach (Ger. musician, great-grandfather of J.S.; 1580-1626)
Hans Brinker, or the Silver Skates (children's book)
Hans Brunhart (ex-premier, Liechtenstein; 1945-)

Hans Christian Andersen (Dan. writer; 1805-75)
Hans Christian Joachim Gram (Dan. phys.; 1853-1938)
Hans Conried (ent.; 1917-82)
Hans-Dietrich Genscher (Ger. pol.; 1927-)
Hans Fischer (Ger. chem.; 1881-1945)
Hans Geiger (Ger. physt.; 1882-1945)
Hans Holbein, the Elder (Ger. artist; 1460-1524)
Hans Holbein, the Younger (Ger. artist; 1497-1543)
Hans Jurgen Eysenck (Br. psych.; 1916-97)
Hans (Adolf) Krebs, (Sir)(Ger./Br. chem.; 1900-81)
Hans (Christian) Oersted (Dan. physt.; 1777-1851)
Hans Sachs (Ger. writer; 1494-1576)
Hans Zinsser (US bacteriol.; 1878-1940)
Hansa League (also Hanseatic)(Ger. hist.)
Hansard (verbatim published reports of Br. Parliament)
Hansard, Luke (Br. Parliament reporter; 1752-1828)
Hansberry, Lorraine (US writer; 1930-65)
Hanscom Air Force Base (MA)
Hanseatic League (also Hansa)(Ger. hist.)
Hänsel and Gretel (folktale)
Hansen, Gerhard Henrik Armauer (Nor. phys.; 1841-1912)
Hansen, Sally (US bus./cosmetics)
Hansen's disease (leprosy)(med.)
Hansom, J. A. (Br. arch., hansom cab; 1803-82)
Hanson, Duane (US sculptor; 1925-)
Hanson, Howard (US comp.; 1896-1981)
Hanukkah (also Chanukah)(rel.)
Hanuman (myth.)
Hanzell Vineyards (US bus.)
Hap (Henry) Arnold (US mil.; 1886-1950)
Happy (A. B.) Chandler (baseball; 1899-1991)
Happy Days (TV show)
Happy Hooligan (comic strip)
Happy Valley (utopia, S. Johnson)
Happy Valley-Goose Bay, Newfoundland, Canada
Hapsburg family (also Habsburg)(Eur./Ger. royal family)
Haq, Muhammad Zia ul- ("President Zia")(ex-pres., Pak.; 1924-88)
Har Gobind Khorana (India/US chem.; 1922-)
Harald V (also Harold)(king, Nor.; 1936-)
Harappa
Harare, Zimbabwe
Harbin, China (also Haerhpin, Pinkiang)
Harburg, (E. Y.) Yip (US lyricist; 1898-1981)
Harcourt Brace Jovanovich, Inc.
Harcourt, Port (Nigeria)
Hard Copy (TV show)
Hardaway, Anfernee "Penny" (basketball; 1972-)
Hardaway, Tim (basketball; 1966-)
Hardball with Chris Matthews (TV show)
Hardee's Food Systems, Inc.
Harding, John Wesley (US outlaw; 1853-95)
Harding, Tonya (figure skating/US news; 1970-)
Harding, Warren G(amaliel)(29th US pres.; 1865-1923)
Hardwick, Bowers v. (US law; 1986)

Hardwicke, (Sir) Cedric (ent.; 1893-1964)
Hardy Boys (Joe & Frank)
Hardy-Weinberg principle/law/distribution
 (genetics)
Hardy, Laurel & (Stan & Oliver)(US comedy team)
Hardy, Oliver (ent.; 1892-1957)
Hardy, Thomas (Br. writer; 1840-1928)
Hare Krishna (rel.)
Harewood, Dorian (ent.; 1950-)
Hargreaves, James (Br. inv.; c1720-1778)
Hari, Mata (b. Gertrud Margarete Zelle)(Dutch
 dancer, executed as spy by Fr.; 1876-1917)
Harijans (also Scheduled Castes, formerly
 Untouchables)(India)
Harkin, Thomas R. (US cong.; 1939-)
Harkness, Edward S. (US bus.; 1874-1940)
Harlan Ellison (US writer; 1934-)
Harlan Fiske Stone (US jurist; 1872-1946)
Harlan Mathews (US pol.; 1927-)
Harlan, John Marshall (US jurist; 1833-1911)
Harlan, John Marshall (US jurist; 1899-1971)
Harlem (NYC)
Harlem Globetrotters (basketball team;
 founded 1927)
Harlem Renaissance (also Black
 Renaissance)(post-WWI)
Harlem River (NY)
Harlequin (comic chara.)(also l.c.)
Harlequin Enterprises, Ltd.
Harley Davidson, Inc.
Harley-Davidson motorcycle
Harlingen, TX
Harlow Shapley (US astron.; 1885-1972)
Harlow, Jean (b. Harlean Carpenter)(ent.;
 1911-37)
Harlow, Shalom (model/ent.; 1973-)
Harman-Kardon stereo
Harman-Kardon, Inc.
Harmon Killebrew (baseball; 1936-)
Harmon, Angie (ent./model; 1972-)
Harmon, Mark (ent.; 1951-)
Harmonic Convergence (astron./astrol.)
Harmonicats, The (ent.)
Harmonyl (med.)
Harnick, Sheldon (US lyricist; 1924-)
Harold Alexander (Br. mil.; 1891-1969)
Harold and Maude (film, 1971)
Harold Arlen (b. Hyman Arluck)(US comp.;
 1905-86)
Harold C. Urey (US chem.; 1893-1981)
Harold Gould (ent.; 1923-)
Harold "Red" Grange (football; 1903-91)
Harold Gray (US cartoonist, *Little Orphan
 Annie*; 1894-1968)
Harold Guy Hunt (ex-AL gov.; 1933-)
Harold (Le Claire) Ickes (US atty./pol.; 1874-
 1952)
Harold (McEwen) Ickes (US atty./Clinton
 deputy chief of staff); 1939-)
Harold Lloyd (ent.; 1893-1971)
Harold Macmillan, (Maurice)(ex-PM, Br.; 1895-
 1987)
Harold Nicholas (ent.; 1921-2000)
Harold Pinter (Br. writer; 1930-)
Harold Ramis (ent.; 1944-)

Harold Robbins (US writer; 1916-97)
Harold Rome (US comp.; 1908-93)
Harold Solomon (tennis; 1952-)
Harold (Edward) Stassen (US pol.; 1907-2001)
Harold V (also Harald)(king, Nor.; 1936-)
Harold Washington (ex-mayor, Chicago; 1922-
 87)
Harold Wilson, (Sir James)(ex-PM, Br.; 1916-95)
Harper & Row Publishers, Inc.
Harper Valley P.T.A. (song, film, 1978)
Harper, Jessica (ent.; 1949-)
Harper, Tess (b. Tessie Jean Washam)(ent.;
 1950-)
Harper, Valerie (ent.; 1940-)
Harper's Bazaar (mag.)
Harper's Magazine (mag.)
Harpers (or Harper's) Ferry (WV)
Harpers (or Harper's) Ferry National Historical
 Park (MD/WV)
Harpo Marx, (Arthur)(ent.; 1888-1964)
Harpy (myth.)
Harrah's Entertainment, Inc.
Harrell, Lynn (US cellist; 1944-)
Harrelson, Woody (ent.; 1961-)
Harriet (Hilliard) Nelson (ent.; 1909-94)
Harriet Beecher Stowe (US writer/abolitionist;
 1811-96)
Harriet Nelson, Ozzie & (TV couple)
Harriet S. Adams (pseud. Carolyn Keene)(US
 writer; 1803-82)
Harriet Tubman (b. Araminta Ross)(US
 reformer; c1820-1913)
Harriman, (William) Averell (US pol./dipl.;
 1891-1986)
Harriman, Edward H(enry)(US bus., railroad;
 1848-1909)
Harriman, Pamela (Digby Churchill
 Hayward)(US dipl.; 1920-97)
Harrington, Michael (US reformer/writer; 1928-
 89)
Harrington, Pat, Jr. (ent.; 1929-)
Harris Poll
Harris Tweed (fabric)
Harris Wofford (US educ./pol.; 1926-)
Harris, Barbara (b. Sandra Markowitz)(ent.;
 1935-)
Harris, Ed (ent.; 1950-)
Harris, Emmylou (ent.; 1947-)
Harris, Franco (football; 1950-)
Harris, Jean (Struven)(US educ., shot Dr. H.
 Tarnower)
Harris, Joel Chandler (US writer; 1848-1908)
Harris, Julie (ent.; 1925-)
Harris, Katherine (FL pol.)
Harris, Louis (US pollster/writer; 1921-)
Harris, Neil Patrick (ent.; 1973-)
Harris, Phil (ent.; 1904-95)
Harris, Richard (ent.; 1933-)
Harris, Rosemary (ent.; 1930-)
Harris, Roy (US comp.; 1898-1979)
Harris, (Sir) Arthur Travers (Br. mil.; 1895-
 1984)
Harris, Thomas (US writer, *Silence of the
 Lambs*; 1940-)
Harrisburg News (PA newspaper)

Harrisburg Patriot (PA newspaper)
Harrisburg, PA
Harrison E. Salisbury (US jour.; 1908-93)
Harrison Ford (ent.; 1942-)
Harrison Hahen (Jack) Schmitt (US pol./astro.;
   1935-)
Harrison, Benjamin (23rd US pres.; 1833-1901)
Harrison, Benjamin (US pol.; 1726?-91)
Harrison, Fort (Benjamin), IN (mil.)
Harrison, George (ent.; 1943-)
Harrison, Gregory (ent.; 1950-)
Harrison, Peter (US arch.; 1716-75)
Harrison, Rex (Reginald Carey)(ent.; 1908-90)
Harrison, Wallace K. (US arch.; 1895-1981)
Harrison, William Henry (9th US pres.; 1773-
   1841)
Harrods store (London)
Harrow (London borough)
Harrow(-on-the-Hill)(London school; founded
   1571)
Harry A(ndrew) Blackmun (ex-US jurist; 1908-
   99)
Harry & David, Inc.
Harry Anderson (ent.; 1952-)
Harry and Tonto (film, 1974)
Harry Belafonte (ent.; 1927-)
Harry Blackstone, Jr. (ent.; 1934-97)
Harry Brakmann Helmsley (US bus.; 1909-97)
Harry Bridges, (Alfred Renton Bridges)(US labor
   leader; 1901-90)
Harry Caray (sportscaster; 1917-98)
Harry Carey (ent.; 1878-1947)
Harry Carney (US jazz; 1910-74)
Harry Chapin (ent.; 1942-81)
Harry Connick, Jr. (ent.; 1967-)
Harry Crews (US writer; 1935-)
Harry Crumb?, Who's (film, 1989)
Harry Daniell (ent.; 1894-1963)
Harry Dean Stanton (ent.; 1926-)
Harry Diamond Laboratories (MD)(mil.)
Harry Emerson Fosdick (US rel./writer; 1878-
   1969)
Harry F. Guggenheim (US finan./bus.; 1890-1971)
Harry Golden (b. Harry Goldhurst)(US writer;
   1902-81)
Harry Guardino (ent.; 1925-)
Harry Hamlin (ent.; 1951-)
Harry Hershfield (US cartoonist, *Abie the
   Agent*; 1885-1974)
Harry Houdini (Erich Weiss)(US magician;
   1874-1926)
Harry James (ent.; 1916-83)
Harry Met Sally, When (film, 1989)
Harry Morgan (ent.; 1915-)
Harry M. Reid (US cong.; 1939-)
Harry M(orris) Warner (ent.; 1881-1958)
Harry Nilsson (ent./songwriter; 1941-94)
Harry Potter (fict. chara.)
Harry Potter and the Chamber of Secrets (J.K.
   Rowling series, Book 2)
Harry Potter and the Goblet of Fire (J.K.
   Rowling series, Book 4)
Harry Potter and the Prisoner of Azkaban (J.K.
   Rowling series, Book 3)
Harry Potter and the Sorcerer's Stone (J.K.

Rowling series, Book 1)
Harry Reasoner (US TV jour.; 1923-91)
Harry Reems (b. Herbert Streicher)(ent.; 1947-)
Harry Rono (track; 1952-)
Harry Ruby (US comp.; 1895-1974)
Harry Smith (TV jour.; 1951-)
Harry Stack Sullivan (US psych.; 1892-1949)
Harry S Truman (33rd US pres.; 1884-1972)
Harry Thomason (ent.)
Harry Von Zell (ent.; 1906-81)
Harry von Tilzer (US comp.; 1872-1946)
Harry Warren (US comp.; 1893-1981)
Harry Winston (US bus./diamonds; ?-1978)
Harry Winston, Inc.
Harry, Deborah (ent.; 1945-)
Harry of Wales, Prince (Henry Charles Albert
   David Windsor)(youngest son of Prince
   Charles & Princess Diana; 1984-)
Harsco Corp.
Hart Crane, (Harold)(US poet; 1899-1932)
Hart to Hart (TV show)
Hart, Johnny (US cartoonist, *BC, Wizard of Id*;
   1931-)
Hart, Lorenz (US lyricist; 1895-1943)
Hart, Mary (ent.; 1951-)
Hart, Melissa Joan (ent.; 1976-)
Hart, Moss (US writer; 1904-61)
Hart, Rodgers & (comp./lyricist team)
Hart, William S(hakespeare)(ent.; 1870?-1946)
Hartack, Bill (William), Jr. (jockey; 1932-)
Harte, (Francis) Bret (US writer; 1839-1902)
Hartex, Leggett & Platt/ (US bus.)
Hartford Courant (CT newspaper)
Hartford Financial Services Group, Inc.
Hartford Whalers (hockey team)
Hartford Wits (also Connecticut Wits)(18th c.
   US lit. grp.)
Hartford, CT
Hartford, John (ent.; 1937-)
Hartley Act, Taft (Labor-Management Relations
   Act of 1947)
Hartley, Mariette (ent.; 1940-)
Hartman Black, Lisa (ent.; 1956-)
Hartman, David (ent.; 1935-)
Hartman, Lisa (ent.; 1956-)
Hartman, Phil (ent.; 1948-98)
Hartsfield Atlanta International Airport (GA)
Haruki Murakami (Jap. writer; 1949-)
Harum, Procol (pop music)
Harunobu, Suzuki (Jap. artist; 1725-70)
Harvard Business Review
Harvard Magazine
Harvard University (Cambridge, MA)
Harvard, John (Br./US rel.; 1607-38)
Harvard's Kennedy School of Government
Harvey (play; film, 1950)
Harvey Fierstein (ent./writer; 1954-)
Harvey (Samuel) Firestone (US bus.; 1868-
   1938)
Harvey Glance (track; 1957-)
Harvey Keitel (ent.; 1939-)
Harvey Korman (ent.; 1927-)
Harvey Kuenn (baseball; 1930-88)
Harvey Kurtzman (cartoonist, *Mad* magazine;
   1925-93)

Harvey Milk (San Francisco pol., murdered; 1930-78)
Harvey Wallbanger (mixed drink)
Harvey Williams Cushing (US phys.; 1869-1939)
Harvey, Laurence (ent.; 1928-73)
Harvey, Paul (US news commentator; 1918-)
Harvey, Steve (ent.; 1960-)
Harvey, William (Br. phys.; 1578-1657)
Harveys Bristol Cream
Harwood, Vanessa (ballet)
Hasaniya Arabic (lang.)
Hasbro (toys)
Hasbro, Inc.
Hashanah, Rosh (High Holy Day, Yom Kippur, High Holiday)
Hashemi Rafsanjani, Hojatolisiam Ali Akbar (pres., Iran; 1934-)
Hashemite Kingdom of Jordan (SW Asia)
Hasid (also Hassid, Chasid)(rel.)
Hasidic Jews (rel.)
Hasidic movement (rel.)
Hasidism (also Chasidism)(rel.)
Hasina Wazed, Sheik (PM, Bangladesh; 1947-)
Hasmonaean (also Maccabee)(rel.)
Hass, Robert (Louis)(US ex-poet laureate; 1941-)
Hassam, Childe (US artist; 1859-1935)
Hassan Gouled Aptidon (ex-pres., Djibouti; 1916-)
Hassan II (king, Morocco; 1929-99)
Hassan, Abdiqassim Salad (head of state, Somalia)
Hassanal Bolkiah Mu'izzaddin Waddaulah, Muda (Sultan/PM, Brunei; 1946-)
Hassanali, Noor (Mohammed)(ex-pres., Trinidad/Tobago; 1918-)
Hassanya Arabic (lang.)
Hasselblad camera
Hasselblad, Inc., Victor
Hasselhoff, David (ent.; 1952-)
Hanssen, Robert (Philip)(US traitor; 1944-)
Hasso, Signe (Swed. ent.; 1910-)
Hastert, J(ohn) Dennis III (US cong.; 1942-)
Hastings Center for Bioethics (NY)
Hastings Kamuzu Banda, (Ngwazi)(ex-pres., Malawi; 1902-97)
Hastings, Battle of (Br. hist.; 1066)
Hastings, England
Hastings, MN, NE
Hastings, Thomas (US arch.; 1860-1929)
Hatch Act (US hist.; 1939)
Hatch, Orrin G(rant)(US cong.; 1934-)
Hatch, Richard (US TV "Survivor"; 1961-)
Hatcher, Teri (ent.; 1964-)
Hatfield-McCoy Feud (opposite sides, Amer. Civil War)
Hatfield, Mark O. (US pol.; 1922-)
Hathaway, Anne (wife of Shakespeare; 1557?-1623)
Hatlo, Jimmy (US cartoonist, *Little Iodine*; 1898-1963)
Hatshepsut (queen, Eg.; c1540-c1481 BC)
Hatteras, Cape (NC)
Hattie McDaniel (ent.; 1895-1952)
Hattiesburg, MS
Hau Pei-tsum (ex-PM, Taiwan)

Hauer, Rutger (Neth. ent.; 1944-)
Haughey, Charles (ex-PM, Ir.; 1925-)
Haughton, William (harness racing; 1923-86)
Hausa (lang./people)
Hausa States (NW Afr.)
Haut-Brion, Chateau (Fr. wine)
Haute-Normandie (region, Fr.)
Hava Nagilah (Isr. dance/song)
Havana (cigar)
Havana brown (cat)
Havana, Cuba
Havarti (cheese)
Havasu City, Lake, AZ
Havatampa Co.
Have Gun, Will Travel (TV show)
Havel, Václav (pres./writer, Czech; 1936-)
Havelock Ellis, (Henry)(Br. psych.; 1859-1939)
Havens, Richie (ent./songwriter; 1941-)
Haver, June (ent.; 1926-)
Haverhill, MA
Havilland, Olivia De (ent.; 1916-)
Havlicek, John (basketball; 1940-)
Havoc, June (ent; 1916-)
Havre de Grace, MD
Hawaii (HI)
Hawaii Five-O (TV show)
Hawaii Volcanoes National Park (HI)
Hawaiian Airlines, Inc.
Hawaiian guitar
Hawaiian Punch (drink)
Hawaiian shirt
Hawaiian Tropic (health)
Hawalli, Kuwait
Hawke, Bob (Robert James Lee)(ex-PM, Austl.; 1929-)
Hawke, Ethan (ent./writer; 1970-)
Hawken, Paul (US bus./writer)
Hawkes, John (US writer; 1925-98)
Hawkeye State (nickname, IA)
Hawking, Stephen (William)(Br. physt./math./writer; 1942-)
Hawkins Day, Sadie
Hawkins, Coleman (US jazz; 1904-69)
Hawkins, Jack (ent.; 1910-73)
Hawks, Atlanta (basketball team)
Hawley Hale Stores, Inc., Carter
Hawley-Smoot Tariff Act (US hist.; 1930)
Hawn, Goldie (ent.; 1945-)
Haworth, Jill (ent.; 1945-)
Hawthorne, Nathaniel (US writer; 1804-64)
Hay, John (Milton)(US pol.; 1838-1905)
Haya (lang.)
Hayakawa, S(amuel) I(chiye)(US educ./pol./linguist; 1906-92)
Hayakawa, Sessue (ent.; 1890-1973)
Hayatou, Sadou (ex-PM, Cameroon)
Hayden Planetarium (NYC)
Hayden, Sterling (ent.; 1916-86)
Hayden, Tom (Thomas E.)(US pol.; 1941-)
Hayden, William George (ex-gov.-gen., Austl.; 1933-)
Haydn, Franz Joseph (Aus. comp.; 1732-1809)
Hayek, Salma (ent.; 1966-)
Hayes, Elvin (basketball; 1945-)
Hayes, Gabby (George)(ent.; 1885-1969)

Hayes (Brown McArthur), Helen (ent.; 1900-93)
Hayes, Isaac (ent.; 1942-)
Hayes, Peter Lind (ent.; 1915-98)
Hayes, Robert (ent.; 1947-)
Hayes, Rutherford B(irchard)(19th US pres.; 1822-93)
Hayes, Woody (football; 1913-87)
Hayley Mills (ent.; 1946-)
Haym Salomon (Am. Revolution finan.; 1740-85)
Haymarket Square riot (Chicago; 1886)
Haymes, Dick (ent.; 1917-80)
Haynes, Roy (US jazz; 1925-)
Haynie, Sandra (golf; 1943-)
Hays, Wayne L. (US pol.; 1912-89)
Hayward, CA
Hayward, Susan (ent.; 1917-75)
Haywood, William Dudley (US labor leader; 1869-1928)
Hayworth, Rita (b. Margarita Carmen Cansino) (ent.; 1918-87)
Hazara (people)
Hazel (cartoon)
Hazel R. O'Leary (US ex-secy./ener.; 1937-)
HBC (hepatitis C virus)(med.)
HBO (Home Box Office)(TV channel)
HBO Comedy (TV channel)
HBO Family (TV channel)
HBO Plus (TV channel)
HBO Signature (TV channel)
H-bomb (hydrogen bomb)
HBV (hepatis B virus)(med.)
HCA - The Healthcare Co.
HDL (high-density lipoprotein, the "good" cholesterol)
HDTV (high definition television)
He (chem. sym., helium)
Head & Shoulders (med.)
Head of the Class (TV show)
Head Sports Wear, Inc.
Head Sports, Inc.
Head Start, Project (educ.)
Head, Edith (US designer; 1898?-1981)
Headline News, CNN (TV channel)
Headroom, Max (fict. chara.)
Health (mag.)
Health and Human Services, Department of (HHS)(US govt.)
Health Care Financing Administration (HCFA) (US govt.)
Health Valley (food)
Health Valley Natural Foods (US bus.)
Health-Tex, Inc.
Healthy Choice (food)
Healy, Ted (b. Charles Earnest Nash)(ent.; 1896-1937)
Heard, John (ent.; 1945-)
Hearn, George (ent.; 1935-)
Heaney, Seamus (Ir. poet; 1939-)
Hearns, Thomas ("Hit Man")(boxing; 1958-)
Hearst Castle (San Simeon, CA)
Hearst, Patty (Patricia)(US heiress, kidnapped/ imprisoned; 1954-)
Hearst, William Randolph (US publ.; 1863-1951)
Hearst, William Randolph, Jr. (US publ.; 1908-

93)
Heart of Atlanta Motel, Inc. v. U.S. (US law; 1964)
Heart of Dixie (nickname, AL)
Heartbreakers, Tom Petty and the (pop music)
Hearts, Queen of
Heat of the Night (TV show)
Heat, Miami (basketball team)
Heath, Edward (Richard George)(ex-PM, Br.; 1916-)
Heathcliff (cartoon)
Heather Donahue (ent.; 1973-)
Heather Graham (ent./model; 1970-)
Heather Locklear (ent.; 1961-)
Heather O'Rourke (ent.; 1975-88)
Heatherton, Joey (ent.; 1944-)
Heathrow Airport (London)
Heatilator, Inc.
Heaven (rel.)
Heaven Knows, Mr. Allison (film, 1957)
Heaven, King of (God)
Heaven, Kingdom of (heaven)
Heaven, Queen of (Virgin Mary)
Heaven's Gate (mass suicide cult; 1997)
Heaviside layer, (Kennelly)(also E layer)(in lower regions, ionosphere)
Hebe (myth., astron.)
Hebrew (lang./people)
Hebrew-Aramaic
Hebrew Bible/Scriptures (rel.)
Hebrew calendar (also Jewish calendar)
Hebrew National (meats)
Hebrew school (rel.)
Hebrews (rel., book of the New Testament)
Hebrides, Inner (islands, W Scot.)
Hebrides, New (now Vanuatu)
Hebrides, Outer (islands, W Scot.)
Hecate (myth.)
Hecatoncheires (myth.)
Heche, Anne (ent.; 1969-)
Hecht, Ben (US writer; 1894-1964)
Hecht's (department store)
Heckart, Eileen (ent.; 1919-)
Hector (myth.)
Hector (or Louis-Hector) Berlioz (Fr. comp.; 1803-69)
Hector Elizondo (ent.; 1936-)
Hecuba (myth., queen of Troy)
Hedda Gabler (H. Ibsen play)
Hedda Hopper (US columnist/ent.; 1890-1966)
Hedren, Tippi (Nathalie)(ent.; 1928-)
Hedrick Smith (US writer; 1933-)
Hedy Lamarr (b. Hedwig Eva Maria Kiesler) (ent.; 1913-2000)
Hee, Park Chung (ex-pres., SKorea; 1917-79)
Heep, Uriah (villain, *David Copperfield*)
Heflin, Howell Thomas (US pol.; 1921-)
Heflin, Van (ent.; 1910-71)
Hefner, Christie Ann (US publ.)
Hefner, Hugh (US publ.; 1926-)
Hefner, Kimberley (US, ex-wife of Hugh H.)
Hefty Cinch Sak
Hegel, Georg W(ilhelm Friedrich)(Ger. phil.; 1770-1831)
Hegelian dialectic (phil.)

Hegira (rel.)
Heian period (Jap. hist.; 794-1185)
Heidegger, Martin (Ger. phil.; 1889-1976)
Heidelberg jaw (anthrop.)
Heidelberg man (anthrop.)
Heidelberg, Germany
Heiden, Eric (speed skating; 1958-)
Heidi (by J. Spyri)
Heidi Fleiss (US news)
Heidi Klum (model; 1973-)
Heidsieck, Inc., Piper-
Heidt, Horace (ent.; 1901-86)
Heifetz, Jascha (Rus./US violinist; 1901-87)
Heigh-Ho (song, *Snow White and the Seven Dwarf*s)
Heihachiro, Marquis Togo (Jap. mil.; 1847-1934)
Heike Drechsler (Olympic long jumper/sprinter; 1964-)
Heike monogatari (Jap. written hist.; 14th c.)
Heimlich maneuver (med.)
Heine, Heinrich (Harry)(Ger. poet/writer; 1797-1856)
Heineken (beer)
Heink, Ernestine Schumann- (ent.; 1861-1936)
Heinlein, Robert A(nson)(US writer, sci-fi; 1907-88)
Heinrich (Theodor) Böll (Ger. writer; 1917-85)
Heinrich Geissler (Ger. inv./glassblower; 1814-79)
Heinrich (Harry) Heine (Ger. poet/writer; 1797-1856)
Heinrich (Rudolf) Hertz (Ger. physt.; 1857-94)
Heinrich Himmler (Ger. Nazi; 1900-45)
Heinrich Lenz (Estonian physt.; 1804-65)
Heinrich Muhlenberg (Ger. rel.; 1711-87)
Heinrich Schliemann (Ger. archaeol.; 1822-90)
Heinrich von Kleist (Ger. writer; 1777-1811)
Heinz (food)
Heinz Co., H. J.
Heinz Guderian (Ger. gen.; 1888-1953)
Heinz Pet Products Co.
Heinz, Henry J(ohn)(US food exec.; 1844-1919)
Heisei era (Japan)
Heisenberg uncertainty (or indeterminacy) principle
Heisenberg, Werner Carl (Ger. physt.; 1901-76)
Heisman Trophy (also Heisman Memorial Trophy)(football)
Heitor Villa-Lobos (Brazilian comp.; 1881-1959)
Heitz Wine Cellars (US bus.)
Hekmatyar, Gulbuddin (ex-PM, Afghan.)
Helbros Watches (US bus.)
Held, Anna (ent.; 1873-1918)
Held, John, Jr. (US cartoonist; 1889-1958)
Helen (myth.)
Helen Brooke Taussig (US phys.; 1898-1986)
Helen Clark (PM, NewZeal.; 1950-)
Helen Fielding (Br. writer)
Helen Frankenthaler (US artist; 1928-)
Helen Gurley Brown (US editor/writer; 1922-)
Helen (Brown McArthur) Hayes (ent.; 1900-93)
Helen Hunt (ent.; 1963-)
Helen Hunt Jackson (pseud. H. H.)(US writer; 1830-85)

Helen (Adams) Keller (US writer/educ., blind/deaf; 1880-1968)
Helen (Clark) MacInnes (Scot. writer; 1907-85)
Helen Mirren (b. Ilynea Lydia Mironoff)(ent.; 1945-)
Helen Newington Wills (Moody)(tennis; 1906-98)
Helen O'Connell (ent.; 1921-)
Helen of Troy (myth.)
Helen Reddy (ent.; 1941-)
Helen Slater (ent.; 1965-)
Helen Traubel (US opera; 1903-72)
Helen Vinson (ent.; 1907-)
Helena Bonham Carter (ent.; 1966-)
Helena Modjeska (ent.; 1844-1909)
Helena Petrovna Blavatsky Hahn, Madame (Rus. theosophist; 1831-91)
Helena Rubinstein (cosmetics)
Helena Rubinstein (US bus.; 1871-1965)
Helena, MT
Helene Curtis (cosmetics)
Helene Curtis Industries
Heliopolis (ancient Eg. city)
Helios (myth.)
Helios space probe
Hell's Kitchen (NYC)
Hellenic languages (also Greek)
Hellenic period (Gr.; 776-323 BC)
Hellenism (Gr. hist.)
Hellenist (Greek-like)
Hellenistic period (Gr.; 323-27 BC)
Heller, Joseph (US writer; 1923-99)
Hellespont, the (now the Dardanelles)(strait, Eur./Asia)
Helling v. McKinney (US law; 1993)
Hellman, Lillian (Florence)(US writer; 1905-84)
Hello, Dolly (play; film, 1969)
Hellzapoppin (play; film, 1941)
Helmholtz, Hermann (Ludwig Ferdinand) von (Ger. physt.; 1821-94)
Helmond, Katherine (ent.; 1934-)
Helmont, Jean Baptiste van (Belgian physt.; 1577-1644)
Helms, Jesse Alexander (US cong.; 1921-)
Helms, Richard (McGarrah)(US ex-dir/CIA; 1913-)
Helmsley, Harry Brakmann (US bus.; 1909-97)
Helmsley, Leona (US bus./hotel; c1920-)
Helmut (Heinrich Waldemar) Schmidt (ex-chanc., WGer.; 1918-)
Helmut Dantine (ent.; 1918-82)
Helmut Kohl (ex-chanc., Ger.; 1930-)
Helmuth von Moltke (Ger. mil.; 1800-91)
Heloise (b. Ponce Kiah Marchelle Heloise Cruse) (US writer; 1951-)
Héloïse (Fr., rel., Abelard's love; 1101-64)
Helprin, Mark (US writer; 1947-)
Helsingör, Denmark (also Elsinore)
Helsinki Conference (internat'l mtg.; 1975)
Helsinki, Finland
Helvetica (type style)
Hemingway, Ernest (Miller)(US writer; 1899-1961)
Hemingway, Margaux (ent.; 1955-96)
Hemingway, Mariel (ent.; 1961-)
Hemion, Dwight (ent.)
Hemisphere, Eastern
Hemisphere, Northern

Hemisphere, Southern
Hemisphere, Western
Hemmings, David (ent.; 1941-)
Hemsley, Sherman (ent.; 1938-)
Hencken, John (swimming; 1954-)
Henderson, Fletcher (US jazz; 1898-1952)
Henderson, Florence (ent.; 1934-)
Henderson, NV
Henderson, Ray (US comp.; 1896-1970)
Henderson, Rickey (baseball; 1958-)
Henderson, Skitch (US cond.; 1918-)
Hendrick Terbrugghen (Dutch artist; 1588-1629)
Hendricks, Thomas A(ndrews)(ex-US VP; 1819-85)
Hendrik F. Verwoerd (ex-PM, SAfr; 1901-66)
Hendrix, Jimi (James Marshall)(ent.; 1942-70)
Henie, Sonja (figure skating/ent.; 1912-69)
Henlein, Konrad (Ger. Nazi; 1898-1945)
Henley, Beth (playwright/ent.; 1952-)
Henley, Don (ent.; 1947-)
Henner, Marilu (ent.; 1952-)
Henning, Doug (ent.; 1947-2000)
Henny Youngman (ent.; 1906-98)
Henredon Furniture Industries, Inc.
Henreid, Paul (ent.; 1908-92)
Henri Bergson (Fr. phil.; 1859-1941)
Henri Cartier-Bresson (Fr. photo.; 1908-)
Henri (Marie Raymond) de Toulouse-Lautrec (Fr. artist; 1864-1901)
Henri (Joseph Théodore) Fantin-Latour, (Ignace)(Fr. artist; 1836-1904)
Henri Giffard (Fr. inv.; 1825-82)
Henri Konan Bedie (ex-pres., Ivory Coast; 1934-)
Henri Laurens (Fr. sculptor; 1885-1954)
Henri Matisse (Fr. artist; 1869-1954)
Henri Philippe Pétain (Fr. mil.; 1856-1951)
Henri Poincaré (Fr. math./physt.; 1854-1912)
Henri, Robert (US artist; 1865-1926)
Henri (Julien Félix) Rousseau ("Le Douanier")(Fr. artist; 1844-1910)
Henri, Grand Duke (ruler, Luxembourg; 1955-)
Henrietta Maria (queen, Eng.; 1609-69)
Henrik (Johan) Ibsen (Nor. writer; 1828-1906)
Henriksen, Lance (ent./writer; 1940-)
Henry "Hank" Aaron (baseball; 1934-)
Henry "Hap" Arnold (US mil.; 1886-1950)
Henry Adams (US hist.; 1838-1918)
Henry Aldrich (fict. chara.)
Henry Algernon du Pont (US mil./pol.; 1838-1926)
Henry Armstrong (boxing; 1912-88)
Henry A(gard) Wallace (ex-US VP; 1888-1965)
Henry Bacon (US arch.; 1866-1924)
Henry Barnard (US educ.; 1811-1900)
Henry Bessemer, (Sir)(Br. eng.; 1813-98)
Henry Cabot Lodge (US pol.; 1850-1924)
Henry Cabot Lodge, Jr. (US jour./pol.; 1902-85)
Henry Cavendish (Br. chem./physt.; 1731-1810)
Henry (Gabriel) Cisneros (US ex-secy./HUD; 1947-)
Henry Clay (also Great Compromiser, Great Pacificator)(US pol.; 1777-1852)
Henry Clay Frick (US bus.; 1849-1919)
Henry Clinton (Br. mil.; 1738-95)

Henry David Thoreau (US writer/phil./nat.; 1817-62)
Henry Deringer (US gunsmith; 19th c.)
Henry du Pont (US bus.; 1812-89)
Henry (Belin) du Pont (US bus.; 1899-1970)
Henry E. Huntington Library and Art Gallery (CA)
Henry Engelhard Steinway (b. Steinweg)(US piano manufacturer; 1797-1871)
Henry Fielding (Br. writer; 1707-54)
Henry Fonda (ent.; 1905-82)
Henry Ford (US bus./auto.; 1863-1947)
Henry Ford, II (US bus./auto.; 1917-87)
Henry George (US econ., advocate of a single tax; 1839-97)
Henry Gibson (ent.; 1935-)
Henry H. Richardson (US arch.; 1838-86)
Henry Hudson (Br. expl.; c1565-c1611)
Henry I ("the Fowler")(king, Ger.; c876-936)
Henry I ("the Scholar")(king, Eng.; 1068-1135)
Henry I (king, Fr.; 1008-60)
Henry II ("the Saint")(king, Ger./Holy Roman emp.; 973-1024)
Henry II (king, Eng.; 1133-89)
Henry II (king, Fr.; 1519-59)
Henry III ("the Black")(king, Ger./Holy Roman emp.; 1017-56)
Henry III (king, Eng.; 1207-72)
Henry III (king, Fr.; 1551-89)
Henry IV ("the Great")(king, Fr.; 1553-1610)
Henry IV (Bolingbroke)(king, Eng.; 1367-1413)
Henry IV (king, Ger./Holy Roman emp.; 1050-1106)
Henry IV (Rom emp.; 1050-1106)
Henry James (US writer; 1843-1916)
Henry J(ohn) Kaiser (US bus.; 1882-1967)
Henry John Temple Palmerston, Viscount (ex-PM, Br.; 1784-1865)
Henry Jones (ent.; 1912-)
Henry (Alfred) Kissinger, Dr. (US ex-secy./ state; 1923-)
Henry Laurens (US pol.; 1724-92)
Henry "Light-Horse Harry" Lee (Amer. gen.; 1756-1818)
Henry L(ewis) Stimson (US pol.; 1867-1950)
Henry Mancini (US comp.; 1924-94)
Henry Martyn Robert (US eng., wrote Robert's Rules of Order; 1837-1923)
Henry M(orrison) Flagler (US finan.; 1830-1913)
Henry Miller (US writer; 1891-1980)
Henry Moore (Br. sculptor; 1898-1986)
Henry More (Br. phil.; 1614-87)
Henry Morgan (ent.; 1915-94)
Henry Morgan, (Sir)(Welsh buccaneer in Amer.; 1635?-88)
Henry Morgenthau (US finan./dipl.; 1856-1946)
Henry Morgenthau, Jr. (US publ./pol.; 1891-1967)
Henry M(orton) Stanley, (Sir)(aka John Rowlands)(Br. jour./expl.; 1841-1904)
Henry Orient, The World of (film, 1964)
Henry Percy, (Sir)(aka Hotspur)(Br. mil.; 1366-1403)
Henry Purcell (Br. comp.; 1658?-95)

Henry R. Kravis (US bus.; 1944-)
Henry Robinson Luce (US publ.; 1898-1967)
Henry Roth (US writer; 1906-95)
Henry Royce, (Frederick)(Br. eng./Rolls-Royce; 1863-1933)
Henry Steele Commager (US hist./educ.; 1902-98)
Henry the Fowler (Henry I)(king, Ger.; c876-936)
Henry the Lion (Roman duke/mil.; 1129-95)
Henry the Navigator (Port. prince/nav.; 1394-1460)
Henry T(omkins) P. Comstock (US, Comstock Lode; 1820-70)
Henry V (king, Eng.; 1387-1422)
Henry V (king, Ger./Holy Roman emp.; 1081-1125)
Henry VI (king, Eng./Fr.; 1421-71)
Henry VI (king, Ger./Holy Roman emp.; 1165-97)
Henry VII (Henry Tudor)(king, Eng.; 1457-1509)
Henry VII (of Luxemburg)(king, Ger./Holy Roman emp.; 1275?-1313)
Henry VIII (king, Eng.; 1491-1547)
Henry Villard (US bus.; 1835-1900)
Henry Wadsworth Longfellow (US poet; 1807-82)
Henry Ward Beecher (US rel./abolitionist; 1813-87)
Henry Wheeler Shaw (pseud. Josh Billings)(US humorist; 1818-85)
Henry Wilson (ex-US VP; 1812-75)
Henry Winkler (ent.; 1945-)
Henry W. Kendall (US physt.; 1926-99)
Henry Wriothesley (Earl of Southhampton)(Br. scholar; 1573-1624)
Henry, John (fict. chara., exceptional strength)
Henry, Joseph (US phys./inv.; 1797-1878)
Henry, O. (aka. William Sydney Porter)(US writer; 1862-1910)
Henry, Patrick (US pol./orator; 1736-99)
Henry, William (Br. chem.; 1774-1836)
Henry's law (gas in liquid)
Henson, Jim (James Maury)(US puppeteer/ Muppets; 1936-90)
Henze, Hans Werner (Ger. comp.; 1926-)
Hepburn v. Griswold (US law; 1870)
Hepburn, Audrey (ent.; 1929-93)
Hepburn, Katharine (ent.; 1907-)
Hephaestus (myth.)
Hepplewhite, George (Br. furniture designer; ?-1786)
Hepworth, Barbara (sculptor; 1903-75)
Hera (myth.)
Heracles (also Hercules)(myth.)
Heraclitus ("the Obscure")(Gr. phil.; c535-c475 BC)
Heraclius (Byzantine emp.; c575-641)
Herald-American, Syracuse (NY newspaper)
Herald Examiner, Los Angeles (CA newspaper)
Herald-Journal, Syracuse (NY newspaper)
Herald-Leader, Lexington (KY newspaper)
Herald-Post, El Paso (TX newspaper)
Herald-Tribune, Sarasota (FL newspaper)
Herald, Augusta (GA newspaper)
Herald, Boston (MA newspaper)
Herald, Chicago (IL newspaper)

Herald, Miami (FL newspaper)
Heralds' College (also College of Arms)(Br. heraldry)
Herat, Afghanistan
Herb Alpert (ent.; 1935-)
Herb Alpert and The Tijuana Brass (pop music)
Herb(ert Lawrence) Block (aka Herblock) (US pol. cartoonist; 1909-)
Herb Edelman (ent.; 1933-96)
Herb(ert) Kohl (US cong.; 1935-)
Herb-Ox (bouillon cubes)
Herb Shriner (ent.; 1918-70)
Herbalife International (US bus.)
Herbert A. Adderly (football; 1939-)
Herbert Bayard Swope (US jour.; 1882-1958)
Herbert Beerbohm Tree, (Sir)(ent.; 1853-1917)
Herbert Blaize (ex-PM, Grenada; 1918-1989)
Herbert C(lark) Hoover (31st US pres.; 1874-1964)
Herbert, George (Br. rel./poet; 1593-1633)
Herbert H. Asquith (ex-PM, Br.; 1852-1928)
Herbert H(enry) Dow (US bus./chem.; 1866-1930)
Herbert Marcuse (US phil.; 1898-1979)
Herbert Marshall (ent.; 1890-19676)
Herbert "Zeppo" Marx (ent.; 1901-79)
Herbert Spencer (Br. phil.; 1820-1903)
Herbert Tree, (Sir)(b. Herbert Beerbohm)(ent.; 1853-1917)
Herbert von Karajan (Aus. cond.; 1908-89)
Herbert, Victor (Ir./US comp./cond.; 1859-1924)
Herbie Hancock (US jazz; 1940-)
Herbie Mann (US jazz; 1930-)
Herbie Rides Again (film, 1974)
Herblock (aka Herbert [Lawrence] Block)(US pol. cartoonist; 1909-)
Hercegovina, Bosnia- (republic. Yug.)(also Bosnia-Herzegovina)
Herceptin (med./cancer)
Hercule Poirot (fict. detective, Agatha Christie)
Hercules (also Heracles)(myth.)
Hercules (astron.)
Hercules, Pillars of (rocks/entrance, Strait of Gibralter)
Herder, Johann G(ottfried von)(Ger. phil.; 1744-1803)
Here's Lucy (TV show)
Hereford (cattle, hogs)
Hereford and Worcester (county, Eng.)
Herero (people)
Heritage USA (rel., PTL)
Herlihy, Ed (US radio/TV announcer; 1909-99)
Herman Jansen Knickerbocker (Dutch settler in NY; 1650?-1716?)
Herman Melville (US writer; 1819-91)
Herman Miller (furniture)
Herman Miller, Inc. (furniture)
Herman (or Gherman) S(tepanovich) Titov (cosmo.; 1935-)
Herman Tarnower (US phys., Scarsdale Diet; 1911-80)
Herman Wouk (US writer; 1915-)
Herman, Alexis (Margaret)(US ex-secy./labor; 1947-)
Herman, Floyd Caves (Babe)(baseball; 1903-87)

Herman, Jerry (US comp.; 1932-)
Herman, Pee-Wee (aka Paul Rubens)(ent.; 1952-)
Herman, Woody (Woodrow)(US jazz; 1913-87)
Hermann Fehling (Ger. chem.; 1812-85)
Hermann Hesse (Ger. writer; 1877-1962)
Hermann Oberth (Ger. physt./rocketry pioneer; 1894-1989)
Hermann Staudinger (Ger. chem.; 1881-1965)
Hermann Wilhelm Goering (or Göring)(Ger. Nazi; 1893-1946)
Hermaphroditus (myth.)
Hermes (myth.)
Hermione Gingold (ent.; 1897-1987)
Hermione Granger (fict. chara., *Harry Potter*)
Hermitage museum (Leningrad, USSR)
Hernandez, Keith (baseball; 1953-)
Hernandez, Orlando (El Duque)(baseball; 1969-)
Hernando Cortés (or Ferdinand)(also Cortez)(Sp. expl.; 1485-1547)
Hernando (or Fernando) de Soto (Sp. expl.; c1496-1542)
Herndon v. Lowry (US law; 1937)
Herndon, VA
Herne, Germany
Hero and Leander (myth.)
Herod Agrippa I (b. Marcus Julius Agrippa)(king, Palestine; c10 BC-AD 44)
Herod Agrippa II (king, Chalcis; c40-93)
Herod Antipas (gov., Galilee; 21 BC-AD 39)
Herod the Great (king, Judea; 74-4 BC)
Herodotus (Gr. hist.; c484-420 BC)
Herrera v. Collins (US law; 1993)
Herrera, Luis Alberto Lacalle (ex-pres., Uruguay; 1941-)
Herrera, Omar Torrijos (Panamanian gen./pol.; 1929-81)
Herrick, Robert (Br. poet; 1591-1674)
Herriman, George (US cartoonist, *Krazy Kat*; 1881-1944)
Herriot, Édouard (ex-PM/pres., Fr.; 1872-1957)
Herriot, James (Br. writer; 1916-95)
Herrmann, Edward (ent.; 1943-)
Herschbach, Dudley Robert (US chem.; 1932-)
Herschel Bernardi (ent.; 1923-86)
Herschel, Caroline Lucretia (Br. astron.; 1750-1848)
Herschel, John Frederick William (Br. astron.; 1792-1871)
Herschel, William (Br. astron.; 1738-1822)
Hersey, John (US writer; 1917-93)
Hershel W. Gober (US ex-secy./vet. affairs; 1936-)
Hershey Bar
Hershey Chocolate USA (US bus.)
Hershey Foods Corp.
Hershey, Barbara (b. Barbara Herzstein)(ent.; 1948-)
Hershey, Milton (Snavely)(US, bus./chocolate; 1857-1945)
Hershey, PA
Hershey's chocolate
Hershfield, Harry (US cartoonist, *Abie the Agent*; 1885-1974)
Hershiser, Orel (baseball; 1958-)
Hersholt, Jean (ent.; 1886-1956)

Hertfordshire (county, Eng.)
Hertz (car rental)
Hertz Corp.
Hertz, Heinrich (Rudolf)(Ger. physt.; 1857-94)
Hertzog, James Barry Munnik (ex-PM, SAfr.; 1866-1942)
Hertzsprung-Russell diagram (astron.)
Herve Villechaize (ent.; 1943-93)
Herzegovina, Bosnia- (republic. Yug.)(also Bosnia-Hercegovina)
Herzl, Theodor (Aus. pol.; 1860-1904)
Herzog (S. Bellow novel)
Herzog, Chaim (ex-pres., Isr.; 1918-97)
Herzog, Emile (pseud. André Maurois)(Fr. writer; 1885-1967)
Herzog, Werner (Ger. ent.; 1942-)
Hesburgh, Theodore M. (US educ.; 1917-)
Heshvan (Jew. month)
Hesiod (Gr. poet; 8th c. BC)
Hesperides (myth.)
Hesperus, The Wreck of the (by. H.W. Longfellow)
Hess, (Walther Richard) Rudolf (Ger. Nazi; 1894-1987)
Hess, Victor Franz (Aus. physt.; 1883-1964)
Hess's law (chem.)
Hesse (state, Ger.)
Hesse, Hermann (Ger. writer; 1877-1962)
Hesseman, Howard (ent.; 1940-)
Hessian boots
Hessian troops (mercenaries, Amer. Rev.)
Hestia (myth.)
Heston, Charlton (b. Charles Carter)(ent.; 1924-)
Hetty Green (US finan., "witch of Wall Street"; 1834-1916)
Heublein Fine Wine Group (US bus.)
Heublein, Inc.
Heusen Corp., Phillips-Van (US bus.)
Heusen, Jimmy (James) Van (US comp.; 1913-90)
HEW (Department of Health, Education, and Welfare)
Hewitt Museum, Cooper- (Smithsonian, DC)
Hewitt, Jennifer Love (ent.; 1979-)
Hewlett-Packard Co. (HP)
Heydar A. Aliyev (pres., Azerbaijan; 1923-)
Heydrich, Reinhard (Ger. Nazi; 1904-42)
Heyerdahl, Thor (Nor. expl./anthrop.; 1914-)
Heyward, DuBose (US writer/lyricist; 1885-1940)
Heywood, Eddie (US jazz; 1916-89)
Hezbollah (also Party of God)(rel./mil.)
HF (high frequency)
Hf (chem. sym., hafnium)
H. F. Ahmanson & Co. (S&L assoc.)
Hg (chem. sym., mercury)
HGTV (Home & Garden Television)(TV channel)
H(erbert) G(eorge) Wells (Br. writer; 1866-1946)
HH (Her/His Highness)
H. H. (aka Helen Hunt Jackson)(US writer; 1830-85)
H(enry) L(ouis) Mencken (US writer/editor; 1880-1956)
H(ector) H(ugh) Munro (pseud. Saki)(Br.

writer; 1870-1916)
H-hour (mil., time of attack)
HHS (Department of Health and Human
  Services)(US govt.)
HI (Hawaii)
Hiaasen, Carl (US writer; 1953-)
Hialeah Park Racetrack (FL)
Hialeah, FL
Hi & Lois (comic strip)
Hiawatha, Chief (Native Amer./educ.; 16th c.)
Hiawatha, The Song of (Longfellow poem)
Hi-C (drink)
Hickam Air Force Base, HI (mil.)
Hickcox, Charles (swimming; 1947-)
Hickel, Wally (Walter Joseph)(ex-AK gov./ex-
  secy./interior; 1919-)
Hickok, Wild Bill (James Butler)(US frontier/
  law; 1837-76)
Hickory Farms, Inc.
Hickory, NC
Hicks, Edward (US artist; 1780-1849)
Hicks, St. Mary's Honor Center v. (US law; 1993)
Hidalgo (state, Mex.)
Hidalgo y Costilla, Miguel (Mex. rel.; 1753-1811)
Hidatsa Indians/lang.)
Hidden Valley (food)
Hide-A-Bed
Hideki, Tojo (ex-PM, Jap.; 1884-1948)
Hieronymus Bosch (Dutch artist; 1450-1516)
Higby's Yogurt & Treat Shoppe, J. (US bus.)
Higginbotham, Jay C. (US jazz; 1906-73)
Higgins, William R. (US mil./murdered by
  Lebanese terrorists; 1945-90)
Higgledy-Piggledy (play, Mother Goose rhyme)
High Anxiety (film, 1977)
High Church
High German
High Holy Day (Rosh Hashanah, Yom Kippur,
  High Holiday)
High Mass (rel.)
High Noon (film, 1952)
High Point, NC (furniture)
High Renaissance
High Society (film, 1956)
High Times
Highland fling (Scot. dance)
Highland Park, MI
Highland Region (Scot.)
Highlander, Toyota (auto.)
Highlands (Scot. area)
Highlights for Children (mag.)
Highness, Your (title)
Highway to Heaven (TV show)
Hi Ho (crackers)
Hijrah (also Hegira)(rel.)
Hilary Swank (ent.; 1974-)
Hilbert, David (Ger. math.; 1862-1943)
Hilda Doolittle ("HD")(US poet; 1886-1961)
Hilda, Broom (comic strip)
Hildegarde (b. Hildegarde Loretta Sell)(ent.; 1906-)
Hildegarde Neff (ent.; 1925-)
Hilfiger, Tommy (designer; 1951-)
Hiligaynon, Panay- (lang.)
Hill Book Co., McGraw-
Hill Street Blues (TV show)

Hill Winery, William (US bus.)
Hill, Anita (US atty./educ.; 1956-)
Hill, Arthur (ent.; 1922-)
Hill, Benny (ent.; 1925-92)
Hill, Faith (ent.; 1967-)
Hill, George Roy (ent.; 1922-)
Hill, Inc., McGraw-
Hill, James J. (US bus.; 1838-1916)
Hill, Lauryn (ent.; 1975-)
Hill, Steven (ent.; 1922-)
Hill, the (also Capitol, Capitol Hill)(US Congress)
Hillary Rodham Clinton (US cong., wife of ex-
  pres.; 1947-)
Hillary, (Sir) Edmund P(ercival)(NewZeal. expl.,
  Mt. Everest; 1919-)
Hillel (Jew. rel./educ.; fl. 30 BC-AD 9)
Hillel Foundation
Hiller, Wendy, Dame (ent.; 1912-)
Hillerman, John (ent.; 1932-)
Hillman, Sidney (US labor leader; 1887-1946)
Hills Bros (coffee)
Hills Brothers Coffee, Inc.
Hills, Carla (Anderson)(US atty./public official;
  1934-)
Hillsborough, Grenada
Hillshire Farm Co.
Hilly, Francis Billy (ex-PM, Solomon Islands)
Hilo, HI
Hilton Head Island, SC
Hilton HHonors
Hilton Hospitality, Inc.
Hilton Hotels Corp.
Hilton, Conrad N(icholson)(US bus./hotels;
  1888-1979)
Himalayan (cat)
Himalayas (also Himalaya[n] Mountains)(India)
Himmler, Heinrich (Ger. Nazi; 1900-45)
Hinayana Buddhism (also Theravada
  Buddhism)(rel.)
Hinckley, John (Warnock), Jr. (US, shot R.
  Reagan; 1955-)
Hindemith, Paul (Ger./US comp.; 1895-1963)
Hindenburg (dirigible disaster)
Hindenburg, Paul (Ludwig Hans) von
  (Beneckendorf und)(ex-pres., Ger.; 1847-1932)
Hindenburg, Poland (also Zabrze)
Hindi (lang.)
Hinds, Samuel (PM, Guyana; 1943-)
Hindu (people)
Hindu Kush Mountains (Asia)
Hinduism (rel.)
Hindustan ("land of the Hindus," India)
Hindustani (people/lang.)
Hines, Duncan (US travel writer/publ.; 1880-1959)
Hines, Earl "Fatha" (US jazz; 1905-83)
Hines, Gregory (ent.; 1946-)
Hines, James (sprinter; 1946-)
Hines, Jerome (ent.; 1921-)
Hingle, Pat (ent.; 1924-)
Hinton, S. E. (US writer; 1948-)
Hipólita Mejía Domínguez (pres., 1941-)
Hipparchus (Gr. astron.; c190-c120 BC)
Hipparcos (*hi*gh *p*recision *pa*rallax *c*ollecting
  *s*atellite)(Eur. satellite; 1989)
Hippo, St. Augustine of (rel.; 354-430)

Hippocrates (Gr. phys.; c460-377 BC)
Hippocratic oath (med.)
Hippolyta (queen of Amazons)(myth.)
Hippolyte (Adolphe) Taine (Fr. hist.; 1828-93)
Hippolytus (myth.)
Hiprex (med.)
Hirabayashi v. U.S. (US law; 1943)
Hiram Powers (US sculptor; 1805-73)
Hiram Stevens Maxim, (Sir)(US/Br. inv.; 1840-1916)
Hiram Walker & Sons, Inc.
Hiraoka Kimitake (pseud. Mishima Yukio)(Jap. writer; 1925-70)
Hirobumi Ito, Prince (ex-PM, Jap.; 1841-1909)
Hirohito ("Showa")(emp., Jap.; 1902-89)
Hiroshige, Ando ("Tokube")(Jap. artist; 1797-1858)
Hiroshima, Japan
Hirsch, Judd (ent.; 1935-)
Hirschfeld, Al (cartoonist; 1903-)
Hirshhorn Museum and Sculpture Garden (Smithsonian, DC)
Hirshhorn, Joseph H. (US bus./finan.; 1899-1981)
Hirt, Al (ent.; 1922-99)
Hismanal (med.)
Hispanic (mag.)
Hispanic American (also Hispano)(people)
Hispaniola, Greater Antilles (Haiti, Dom Rep.)
Hispano (also Hispanic American)(people)
Hiss, Alger (US pol.; 1904-96)
History Channel, The (TV channel)
Hitachi
Hitachi Home Electronics America, Inc.
Hitachi, Ltd. (US bus.)
Hitachi-Maxell, Ltd. (US bus.)
Hitchcock Hour, The Alfred (TV show)
Hitchcock Presents, Alfred (TV show)
Hitchcock, (Sir) Alfred (Joseph)(ent.; 1899-1980)
Hitchcock's Mystery Magazine, Alfred
Hitchhiker's Guide to the Galaxy, The (book; film, 1981)
Hite, Shere (US writer; 1942-)
Hitler, Adolf (Schicklgruber)(*der Führer*)(ex-chanc./dictator, Ger.; 1889-1945)
Hittite (lang./people)
HIV (human immunodeficiency virus)(med.)
H. J. Heinz Co.
HM (Her/His Majesty)
HMO (health maintenance organization)
HMS (also H.M.S.)(Her/His Majesty's Service/ Ship/Steamer)
H.M.S. Bounty (ship, naval mutiny against Capt. Bligh)
H.M.S. Pinafore (or The Lass that Loved a Sailor)(Gilbert/Sullivan opera)
Hnatyshyn, Ramon (ex-gov.-gen., Can.; 1934)
H. Norman Schwarzkopf, Jr. ("Stormin' Norman")(US gen.; 1934-)
Ho (chem. sym., holmium)
Ho (lang.)
Ho Chi Minh (b. Nguyen That Tan)(ex-pres., NViet; 1890-1969)
Ho Chi Minh City, Vietnam (formerly Saigon)
Ho Chi Minh Trail (Vietnam)
Ho, Don (ent.; 1930-)

Ho, Edmund (chief exec., Macau, Ch.)
Hoagy (Hoagland Howard) Carmichael (US comp.; 1899-1981)
Hoban, James (US arch.; 1762-1831)
Hobart, Australia
Hobart, Garret A(ugustus)(ex-US VP; 1844-99)
Hobbes, Calvin and (comic strip)
Hobbes, Thomas (Br. writer/phil.; 1588-1679)
Hobbit, The (by J.R.R. Tolkien)
Hobbs Takes a Vacation, Mr. (film, 1962)
Hobbs, NM
Hobby, Oveta Culp (US publ./pol.; 1905-95)
Hobgoblin (also Robin Goodfellow, Puck)(fict. chara., *A Midsummer Night's Dream*)
Hobie Cat Co.
Hobson-Jobson (linguistics)
Hobson, Laura Z(ametkin)(US writer; 1900-86)
Hobson, Thomas (Br. bus.; 1544-1631)
Hobson's choice (take choice given or nothing)
Hockey League, National (also NHL)
Hockney, David (Br. artist; 1937-)
Hodges, Gil (baseball; 1924-72)
Hodges, James "Jim" (Hovis)(SC gov.; 1956-)
Hodges, Johnny (US jazz; 1906-71)
Hodgkin, Dorothy Mary Crowfoot (Br. chem.; 1910-94)
Hodgkin's disease (med.)
Hodiak, John (ent.; 1914-55)
Hódmezővásárhely, Hungary
Hoechst Celanese Corp.
Hoeven, John (ND gov.)
Hoffa, Jimmy (James R(iddle)(US labor leader; 1913-75?)
Hoffa, Portland (ent.)
Hoffman, Abbie (Abbott)(US pol. activist; 1936-89)
Hoffman, Dustin (ent.; 1937-)
Hoffman, Phillip Seymour (ent.; 1968-)
Hoffmann, Roald (chem.; 1937-)
Hoffmann, The Tales of (Jacques Offenbach opera)
Hofmann, Hans (US artist; 1880-1966)
Hofstadter, Richard (US hist.; 1916-70)
Hofstadter, Robert (US physt.; 1915-90)
Hofstra University (Hempstead, NY)
Hogan, Ben (golf; 1912-97)
Hogan, Hulk (b. Terry Gene Bollea)(wrestling; 1953-)
Hogan, Paul (ent.; 1939-)
Hogan's Heroes (TV show)
Hogarth, Burne (cartoonist, *Tarzan*; 1911-96)
Hogarth, William (Br. artist; 1697-1764)
Hogg, James ("the Ettrick Shepherd")(Scot. poet; 1770-1835)
Hogwarts School of Witchcraft (fict., *Harry Potter*)
Hohhot, China
Hojatolislam Ali Akbar Hashemi Rafsanjani (ex-pres., Iran; 1935-)
HoJo (Howard Johnson)
Hokinson, Helen (US cartoonist; 1900-49)
Hokkaido (Jap. island)
Hokusai, (Katsushika)(Jap. artist; 1760-1849)
Holbein, the Elder, Hans (Ger. artist; 1460-1524)
Holbein, the Younger, Hans (Ger. artist; 1497-1543)

Holbrook, Hal (ent.; 1925-)
Holden, Bob (MO gov.)
Holden, William (ent.; 1918-81)
Holder, Geoffrey (dancer; 1930-)
Holetown, Barbados
Holi (Hindu festival)
Holiday Bowl (college football)
Holiday Inn
Holiday, Billie (b. Eleanora Fagan)(US jazz; 1915-59)
Holiness, Your (title)
Holland (the Netherlands)
Holland, Brian (US comp.; 1941-)
Holland, Eddie (US comp.; 1939-)
Holland, MI
Holland's Opus, Mr. (film, 1995)
Hollander, Nicole (US cartoonist, *Sylvia*; 1939-)
Holliday, (John Henry) "Doc" (US frontier/dentist; 1851-87)
Holliday, Judy (ent.; 1922-65)
Holliday, Polly (ent.; 1937-)
Holliman, Earl (ent.; 1928-)
Hollings, Ernest F. (US cong.; 1922-)
Hollis, David (clothing)
Holloman Air Force Base, NM (mil.)
Holloway, Sterling (ent.; 1905-1992)
Holly Farm Foods, Inc.
Holly Hunter (ent.; 1958-)
Holly Robinson Peete (ent.; 1964-)
Holly, Buddy (ent.; 1936-59)
Holly, Buddy and the Crickets (pop music)
Holly, Lauren (ent.; 1963-)
Hollywood bed
Hollywood Park
Hollywood Reporter, The
Hollywood Squares (TV show)
Hollywood, CA, FL
Hollywood, Doc (film, 1991)
Holm, Celeste (ent.; 1919-)
Holmes, Katie (ent.; 1978-)
Holmes, Larry (boxing; 1949-)
Holmes, Oliver Wendell (US writer/phys.; 1809-94)
Holmes, Oliver Wendell, Jr. (US jurist; 1841-1935)
Holmes, Sherlock (fict. detective)
Holocaust Memorial Museum, United States (DC)
Holocaust, the (Nazi annihilation of Jews; 1933-45)
Holocene epoch (geological time, began 10,000 years ago)
Holon, Israel
Holst, Gustav(us Theodore von)(Br. comp.; 1874-1934)
Holstein(-Friesian) cattle
Holstein, Schleswig- (state, Ger.)
Holt, John (US educ./writer; 1924-85)
Holt, Tim (ent.; 1918-73)
Holtz, Lou (football; 1937-)
Holtzman technique (personality evaluation, inkblots)
Holy Alliance ("Christian Union of Charity, Peace, and Love")(Rus./Eur. hist.; 1815-1823)
Holy Ark

Holy Bible
Holy City
Holy Communion (also Eucharist, Lord's Supper)(rel.)
Holy Cross, AK
Holy Cross, Mount of the (CO)
Holy Father (Pope's title)
Holy Ghost (also Holy Spirit)(part of Christian Trinity)
Holy Grail, the (legendary cup used by Jesus at the Last Supper)
Holy Land (Isr.)
Holy Mother (also the Madonna, Mary, Our Lady, Virgin Mary)(rel.)
Holy One
Holy Roller (rel.)
Holy Roman Empire (Ger. empire; 962-1806)
Holy Saturday
Holy Scripture(s)(rel.)
Holy See (also See of Rome)(Vatican)
Holy Sepulcher (Jesus' tomb)
Holy Spirit (also Holy Ghost)(part of Christian Trinity)
Holy Thursday (also Ascension Day)(rel.)
Holy Trinity, the (also Trinity)(Father, Son, Holy Ghost/Spirit)(rel.)
Holy Week (week before Easter)
Holy Writ (Bible)
Holyfield, Evander (boxing; 1962-)
Holyoke, MA
Hombre, Isuzu (auto.)
Home (mag.)
Home Alone (film, 1990)
Home Box Office (HBO)(TV channel)
Home Depot, Inc.
Home Improvement (TV show)
Home Mechanix (mag.)
Home Office Computing (mag.)
Home Rule (Irish/English)(DC)
Home Shopping Network, The (TV channel)
Home, (Sir) Alexander "Alec" Frederick Douglas- (ex-PM, Br.; 1903-95)
Home, William Douglas- (Br. writer; 1912-92)
Home & Away (mag.)
Home & Garden Television (HGTV)(TV channel)
Homefront (TV show)
Homeier, Skippy (ent.)
Homelite (US bus.)
Homelite saw
Homer & Jethro (ent.)
Homer (Gr. poet; c850 BC)
Homer Simpson (cartoon chara.)
Homer, Winslow (US artist; 1836-1910)
Homeric Hymns (wrongly attributed to Homer)
Homestead Act (US hist.; 1862)
Homestead Air Force Base, FL (mil.)
Homestead, FL, PA
Homo (anthrop.)
Homo erectus (anthrop.)
Homo habilis (anthrop.)
Homo sapien(s)(anthrop.)
Homoiousian (rel.)
Homoousian (rel.)
Homs, Syria
Hon Industries (US bus.)

Honda (auto.)
Honda Accord (auto.)
Honda Accord DX (auto.)
Honda Accord EX (auto.)
Honda Accord LX (auto.)
Honda Accord SE (auto.)
Honda Civic (auto.)
Honda Civic CX (auto.)
Honda Civic del Sol (auto.)
Honda Civic del Sol S (auto.)
Honda Civic del Sol Si (auto.)
Honda Civic del Sol VTEC (auto.)
Honda Civic DX (auto.)
Honda Civic EX (auto.)
Honda Civic EXA (auto.)
Honda Civic HX (auto.)
Honda Civic LX (auto.)
Honda Civic LXA (auto.)
Honda Civic LXO (auto.)
Honda Civic Si (auto.)
Honda Civic VP (auto.)
Honda CR-V (auto.)
Honda CR-V EX (auto.)
Honda CR-V LX (auto.)
Honda CR-V SE (auto.)
Honda Insight (auto.)
Honda Motor Co., Inc., American
Honda Motor Co., Ltd
Honda Odyssey (auto.)
Honda Odyssey EX minivan (auto.)
Honda Odyssey LX minivan (auto.)
Honda Passport (auto.)
Honda Passport DX (auto.)
Honda Passport EX (auto.)
Honda Passport EX-L (auto.)
Honda Passport LX (auto.)
Honda Prelude (auto.)
Honda Prelude S (auto.)
Honda Prelude SH (auto.)
Honda Prelude Si (auto.)
Honda S2000 convertible (auto.)
Hondo, Soichiro (Jap. bus./auto.; 1907-91)
Honduras (Republic of)(CAmer.)
Honegger, Arthur (Fr. comp.; 1892-1955)
Honey Bunches of Oats (cereal)
Honey-Comb (cereal)
Honey Maid (crackers)
Honeymooners, The (TV show)
Honeywell International, Inc.
Honeywell, Inc.
Hong Kong (SE Ch.)
Hong Song Nam (PM, NKorea)
Honiara, Soloman Islands
Honokohau National Historical Park, Kaloko-
    (HI)
Honolulu Advertiser (HI newspaper)
Honolulu International Airport (HI)
Honolulu Star-Bulletin (HI newspaper)
Honolulu, HI
Honor, Legion of (Fr.)
Honor, Medal of (also Congressional Medal of
    Honor)(mil.)
Honor, Your (title)
Honorat, Jean-Jacques (ex-PM, Haiti)
Honoré Daumier (Fr. artist; 1808-79)

Honoré de Balzac (Fr. writer; 1799-1850)
Honoré Gabriel (Riqueti) Mirabeau, Comte de
    (Fr. pol.; 1749-91)
Honshu (Jap. island)
Honus Wagner, (John Peter)(baseball; 1867-1955)
Hooch, Turner and (film, 1989)
Hood, Fort, TX (mil.)
Hood, Prince of Thieves, Robin (film, 1991)
Hood, Raymond (US arch.; 1881-1934)
Hood, Robin (legendary Eng. hero/outlaw;
    13th-14th c.)
Hook, Sidney (US phil.; 1902-89)
Hooke, Robert (Br. physt./inv.; 1635-1703)
Hooke's law (of elasticity)
Hooker, John Lee (ent./songwriter; 1917-2001)
Hooker, Joseph (US gen.; 1814-79)
Hooker, (Sir) Joseph Dalton (Br. botanist;
    1817-1911)
Hooker, Thomas (US rel.; 1586-1647)
Hooks, Benjamin Lawson (US civil rights
    leader; 1925-)
Hooks, Jan (ent.; 1957-)
Hooks, Robert (ent.; 1937-)
Hooligan, Happy (comic strip)
Hooper (film, 1978)
Hoosier cabinet
Hoosier State (nickname, IN)
Hoot Gibson (ent.; 1892-1962)
Hoover (home appliances)
Hoover Co., The
Hoover Dam (also Boulder Dam)(AZ/NV)
Hoover, Herbert C(lark)(31st US pres.; 1874-
    1964)
Hoover, J(ohn) Edgar (ex-dir., FBI; 1895-1972)
Hoover, William Henry (US bus./vacuum
    cleaner; 1849-1932)
Hopalong Cassidy (b. William Boyd)(ent.;
    1898-1972)
Hopalong Cassidy (TV show)
Hope Lange (ent.; 1931-)
Hope Town, the Bahamas
Hope, Bob (b. Leslie Townes Hope)(ent.; 1903-)
Hopi (Native Amer.)
Hopkins Hospital, Johns (Baltimore, MD)
Hopkins Observatory, Mount (now Fred
    Lawrence Whipple Observatory)(AZ)
Hopkins University, Johns (Baltimore, MD)
Hopkins, Anthony (ent.; 1937-)
Hopkins, Gerald Manley (Br. poet; 1844-89)
Hopkins, Harry L. (US pol.; 1890-1946)
Hopkins, Johns (US bus./finan.; 1795-1873)
Hopkins, Mark (US educ./rel.; 1802-87)
Hopkins, Sam "Lightnin" (US jazz; 1912-82)
Hopkins, Samuel (US rel.; 1721-1803)
Hopkins, Telma (ent.; 1948-)
Hopkinsville, KY
Hopnoodle's Haven of Bliss, Ollie (film, 1988)
Hopper, Dennis (ent.; 1936-)
Hopper, DeWolf (ent.; 1858-1935)
Hopper, Edward (US artist; 1882-1967)
Hopper, Hedda (US columnist/ent.; 1890-1966)
Horace (b. Quintus Horatius Flaccus)(Latin
    poet; 65-8 BC)
Horace Greeley (US publ./pol.; 1811-72)
Horace Heidt (ent.; 1901-86)

Horace Mann (US pol./educ.; 1796-1859)
Horace Silver (US jazz; 1928-)
Horace (Horatio) Walpole (Earl of Oxford)(Br.
    writer; 1717-97)
Horatio Alger, Jr. (US writer; 1832-99)
Horatio Gates (US gen.; 1728-1806)
Horatio Greenough (US sculptor; 1805-52)
Horatio H. Kitchener (Br. mil.; 1850-1916)
Horatio Hornblower, Capt. (fict. chara., C.S.
    Forester)
Horatio Hornblower, Captain (film, 1951)
Horatio Nelson, Viscount (Br. admiral; 1758-
    1805)
Horchow (home furnishings)
Horizon Air Industries (airline)
Horizon, Plymouth (auto.)
Hormel (meats)
Hormel & Co., George A.
Hormel Corp.
Hormuz (also Ormuz)(island, Iran)
Hormuz (also Ormuz), Strait of (Iran)
Horn, Cape (Chile)
Horn, Roy Uwe Ludwig (illusionist, Siegfried
    and Roy; 1944-)
Hornblower, Capt. Horatio (fict. chara., C.S.
    Forester)
Hornblower, Captain Horatio (film, 1951)
Hornby, Leslie "Twiggy" (model; 1946-)
Horne, Lena (ent.; 1917-)
Horne, Marilyn (ent.; 1934-)
Horner, Little Jack (nursery rhyme)
Hornets, Charlotte (basketball team)
Horney, Karen Danielsen (Ger./US psych./
    writer; 1885-1952)
Hornie (the Devil)
Hornsby, (Rajah) Rogers (baseball; 1896-1963)
Hornsby, Bruce (ent.; 1954-)
Hornung, Paul (football; 1935-)
Horologium (astron., clock)
Horowitz, David (writer)
Horowitz, Vladimir (Rus./US pianist; 1904-89)
Horse Guards (Br.)
Horsehead Nebula (astron.)
Horsley, Lee (ent.; 1955-)
Horst Buchholz (ent.; 1933-)
Hortense Calisher (US writer; 1911-)
Horton, Edward Everett (ent.; 1886-1970)
Horton, Willie (William R.), Jr. (US murd. in
    1988 pol. ad)
Horus (Eg. deity)
Hosea (rel., book of the Old Testament)
Hoskins, Bob (ent.; 1942-)
Hosni Mubarak, Mohammed (pres., Egypt; 1928-)
Hosokawa, Morihiro (ex-PM, Jap.; 1938-)
Hoss, Salim al- (PM, Lebanon; 1929-)
Host International Corp.
Hot Lips (Oran Thaddeus) Page (ent.; 1908-54)
Hot Lips Houlihan (fict. chara., *M*A*S*H*)
Hot Rod (mag.)
Hot Springs National Park (AR)
Hot Wheels (toys)
Hotchner, A. E. (US writer/bus.; 1920-)
Hotel New Hampshire, The (J. Irving novel)
Hotpoint (US bus.)
Hotspur (aka Sir Henry Percy)(Br. mil.; 1366-1403)

Hottentot (also Khoikhoi)(people)
Hottentot's bread (plant)
Houdin, Eugène "Jean" Robert (Fr. magician;
    1805-71)
Houdini, Harry (b. Erich Weiss)(US magician;
    1874-1926)
Houghton Mifflin Co.
Houk, Ralph (baseball; 1919-)
Houlihan, Hot Lips (fict. chara., *M*A*S*H*)
Houma, LA
Hound of the Baskervilles, The (by A.C. Doyle)
Hound, Huckleberry (cartoon)
Houphouët-Boigny, Félix (ex-pres., Ivory
    Coast; 1905-93)
Hours, Book of (rel.)
Hours, Liturgy of the (also Divine Office)(rel.)
House Beautiful (mag.)
House Committee on Un-American Activities
    (HUAC)(US govt. comm.; 1938-75)
House of Almonds (US bus.)
House of Anjou (or Plantagenet)(Br. ruling
    family; 1154-1399)
House of Burgesses
House of Cerdic (Br. ruling family; 827-1016,
    1042-66)
House of Commons (Br. & Can. parliaments)
House of Frankenstein (film, 1944)
House of Hanover (Br. ruling family; 1714-1901)
House of Lancaster (Br. ruling family; 1399-
    1461, 1470-71)
House of Lords (Br. parliament)
House of Normandy (Br. ruling family; 1066-1154)
House of Orange (Br. ruling family; 1689-1702)
House of Orange (royal family, Netherlands)
House of Plantagenet (or Anjou)(Br. ruling
    family; 1154-1399)
House of Representatives (US govt.)
House of Saxe-Coburg-Gotha (Br. ruling family;
    1901-10)
House of Stuart (Br. ruling family; 1603-49,
    1660-88, 1702-14)
House of the Skjoldungs of Denmark (Br. ruling
    family; 1016-42)
House of Tudor (Br. ruling family; 1485-1603)
House of Usher (film, 1960)
House of Usher, The Fall of the (E.A. Poe short
    story)
House of Windsor (Br. ruling family; 1910-
    present)
House of York (Br. ruling family; 1461-70,
    1471-85)
House Un-American Activities Committee
    (HUAC)(US govt.; est. 1938)
House Ways and Means Committee (US govt.)
House(s) of Parliament (Br. govt.)
House, Edward M(andell)(US pol./dipl.; 1858-
    1938)
Houseman, John (ent.; 1902-88)
Housing and Urban Development, Department
    of (HUD)(US govt.)
Housman, A(lfred) E(dward)(Br. poet; 1859-
    1936)
Houston Astros (baseball team)
Houston Chronicle (TX newspaper)
Houston Intercontinental Airport (TX)

Houston Oilers (football team)
Houston Post (TX newspaper)
Houston Rockets (basketball team)
Houston, Charles Hamilton (US civil rights atty.; 1895-1950)
Houston, Fort Sam (TX)(mil.)
Houston, Sam(uel)(US gen./pol.; 1793-1863)
Houston, TX
Houston, Whitney (ent.; 1963-)
Houten & Zoon, Inc., C. J. Van
Houyhnhnm (fict. race of horses; *Gulliver's Travels*)
Hovercraft
Hovhaness, Alan (US comp.; 1911-2000)
How the Grinch Stole Christmas (book; film, 1965)
Howard Ashman (US lyricist; 1951-91)
Howard Carter (Br. archaeol.; 1873-1939)
Howard Cosell (US sportscaster; 1920-95)
Howard Da Silva (ent.; 1909-86)
Howard Dean (VT gov.; 1948-)
Howard Dietz (US lyricist; 1896-1983)
Howard Duff (ent.; 1914-90)
Howard Fast (US writer; 1914-)
Howard F. H. Cooke, (Sir)(gov.-gen.; Jamaica; 1915-)
Howard H. Aiken (US math.; 1900-73)
Howard Hanson (US comp.; 1896-1981)
Howard Hesseman (ent.; 1940-)
Howard (Robard) Hughes (US bus./ent./aviator; 1905-76)
Howard Johnson (US bus.; 1896-1972)
Howard Johnson Co.
Howard Johnson Lodge & Restaurant
Howard Keel (b. Harold Clifford Leek)(ent.; 1919-)
Howard K. Smith (US TV jour.; 1914-)
Howard Lindsay (US playwright; 1889-1968)
Howard M(orton) Metzenbaum (US pol.; 1917-)
Howard Morris (ent.; 1925-)
Howard Nemerov (US writer; 1920-91)
Howard Rollins (ent.; 1950-)
Howard Stern (ent.; 1954-)
Howard University (DC)
Howard W. Hunter (US atty./rel.; 1907-)
Howard, Catherine (5th wife of Henry VIII; 1520?-42)
Howard, Curly (b. Jerome Horwitz)(ent.; 1903-52)
Howard, Elston (baseball; 1929-80)
Howard, Jane (Temple)(US writer; 1935-96)
Howard, Joe (ent.; 1867-1961)
Howard, John (PM, Austl.; 1939-)
Howard, Ken (ent.; 1944-)
Howard, Leslie (ent.; 1890-1943)
Howard, Melvin and (film, 1980)
Howard, Moe (b. Moses Horwitz)(ent.; 1897-1975)
Howard, Ron (ent.; 1953-)
Howard, Shemp (b. Samuel Horwitz)(ent.; 1895-1955)
Howard, Trevor (Wallace)(ent.; 1916-88)
Howard's End (E.M. Forster novel; film, 1992)
Howdy Doody (fict. chara.)
Howdy Doody Show, The
Howe, Elias (US inv./sewing machine; 1819-67)
Howe, Gordie (Gordon)(hockey; 1928-)

Howe, Irving (US literary critic; 1920-93)
Howe, Julia Ward (US reformer/writer; 1819-1910)
Howe, Richard, Earl (Br. mil.; 1726-99)
Howe, Samuel G(ridley)(US educ./reformer; 1801-76)
Howe, (Sir) William (Br. mil.; 1729-1814)
Howell Edmunds Jackson (US jurist; 1832-95)
Howell Thomas Heflin (US pol.; 1921-)
Howell, C. Thomas (ent.; 1966-)
Howell, Jim Lee (football; 1915-95)
Howells, William Dean (US writer; 1837-1920)
Howes, Sally Ann (ent.; 1930-)
Howie Dorough (ent., Backstreet Boys; 1973-)
Howie Mandell (ent.; 1955-)
Howie Morenz (hockey; 1902-37)
Howser, Dick (baseball; 1937-87)
Howser, M.D., Doogie (TV show)
Hoyer, Steny H(amilton)(US cong.; 1939-)
Hoyle, Edmund (Br. writer/card game rules; 1672-1769)
Hoyle, Fred(erick)(Br. astron./writer; 1915-)
Hoyt Axton (ent.; 1938-99)
Hoyte, Hugh Desmond (ex-pres., Guyana)
HP (horse power)
HP (Hewlett-Packard)
HP DeskJet (compu.)
H(oward) P(hillips) Lovecraft (US writer; 1890-1937)
HP OfficeJet (compu.)
HQ (headquarters)
HR (home run)
Hrawi, Elias (ex-pres., Lebanon; 1926-)
H. R. "Bob" Haldeman (US pol.; 1926-93)
H. Ross Perot (US bus./pol.; 1930-)
HS (high school)
Hsia dynasty (also Xia)(Ch.; 2205-1766 BC)
Hsiao-ping, Teng (also Deng Xiaoping)(Ch. pol.; 1904-97)
HTLV (human T-cell leukemia virus)
HTML (Hypertext Markup Language)(compu.)
Hua Kuo-feng (or Guofeng)(ex-PM, Ch.; 1920?-)
HUAC (House Un-American Activities Committee)
Huachuca, Fort, AZ (mil.)
Huambo, Angola
Huang Hai (also Yellow Sea)(Ch./Korea)
Huang He (also Yellow River)(Ch.)
Hubbard, L(afayette) Ron(ald)(US writer/rel., Scientology; 1911-86)
Hubbard, Mother (fict. chara., nursery rhyme)
Hubbard, Mother (loose gown; railroad engine)
Hubbell, Carl (Owen)(baseball; 1903-88)
Hubbell, Webster (US atty., Whitewater)
Hubble classification scheme (astron.)
Hubble Space Telescope (HST)(US/Eur. uncrewed space probe)
Hubble, Edwin P(owell)(US astron.; 1889-1953)
Hubble's constant (astron.)
Hubble's law (astron.)
Hubert A. Ingraham (PM, Bahamas; 1947-)
Hubert de Givenchy (Fr. designer; 1927-)
Hubert Green (golf; 1946-)
Hubert H(oratio) Humphrey (ex-US VP; 1911-78)
Hubert (or Huybrecht) van Eyck (Flem. artist;

1366-1426)
Huckabee, Mike (Michael Dale)(AR gov.; 1955-)
Huckleberry Finn (fict. chara., Mark Twain)
Huckleberry Finn (M. Twain novel)
Huckleberry Hound (cartoon)
HUD (Department of Housing and Urban
    Development)(US govt.)
Hud (film, 1963)
Huddie "Leadbelly" Ledbetter (US jazz; 1888-
    1949)
Huddle House, Inc.
Hudibrastic verse (lit.)
Hudson Bay (Can.)
Hudson Bay blanket
Hudson River (NY)
Hudson River School (grp. of artists; early 19th c.)
Hudson, Don (football; 1913-)
Hudson, Henry (Br. expl.; c1565-c1611)
Hudson, Kate (ent.; 1979-)
Hudson, Rock (b. Roy Scherer, Jr.)(ent.; 1925-
    85)
Hudson's Bay Company (Can./Native Amer.,
    trade; founded 1670)
Hue, Vietnam
Huey Lewis (b. Hugh Cregg III)(ent.; 1950-)
Huey Lewis and the News (pop music)
Huey P(ierce) Long ("the Kingfish")(ex-gov.,
    LA; 1893-1935)
Huey P. Newton (US, cofounded Black
    Panthers; 1942-89)
Huff, Sam (Robert Lee)(football; 1934-)
Huffy Corp.
Huggies (diapers)
Huggins, Nathan Irvin (US hist.; 1927-89)
Hugh C. Dowding (Br. mil.; 1883-1970)
Hugh Desmond Hoyte (ex-pres., Guyana)
Hugh Downs (ent.; 1921-)
Hugh Gaitskell (Br. pol.; 1906-63)
Hugh Grant (ent.; 1960-)
Hugh Griffith (ent.; 1912-80)
Hugh Hefner (US publ.; 1926-)
Hugh Lofting (Br. writer; 1886-1947)
Hugh MacDiarmid (b. Christopher Murray
    Grieve)(Scot. poet; 1892-1978)
Hugh Masekela (ent., trumpet; 1939-)
Hugh O'Brian (b. Hugh J. Krampe)(ent.; 1925-)
Hugh Rodham (US atty./bro. of Hillary)
Hugh (Ellsworth) Rodham (US father of Hillary;
    1911-93)
Hughes Aircraft Corp.
Hughes Markets, Inc.
Hughes, Barnard (ent.; 1915-)
Hughes, Charles Evans (US jurist; 1862-1948)
Hughes, Edward J(ames) "Ted" (Br. poet;
    1930-98)
Hughes, Howard (Robard)(US bus./ent./
    aviator; 1905-76)
Hughes, John (Joseph)(US rel.; 1797-1864)
Hughes, Karen P.(nee Parfill)(US White House
    pol. adviser; 1957?-)
Hughes, Langston (US writer; 1902-67)
Hughes, Ted (Edward James)(Br. poet; 1930-
    98)
Hughley, D(arryl) L(ynn)(ent.; 1963-)
Hugo (Rafael) Chávez Frías (pres., Venezuela;

1954-)
Hugo Banzer Suárez (pres., Bolivia; 1926-)
Hugo De Vries (Dutch botanist; 1848-1935)
Hugo L(aFayette) Black (US jurist; 1886-1971)
Hugo the Hippo (film, 1976)
Hugo Wolf (Aus. comp.; 1860-1903)
Hugo, Hurricane (E US; 1989)
Hugo, Victor (Marie)(Fr. writer; 1802-85)
Huguenots (rel.)
Hui (lang./people)
Huitzilopochtli (also Uitzilopochtli)(myth.)
Hula Hoop
Hulce, Tom (ent.; 1953-)
Huldreich (or Ulrich) Zwingli (Swiss rel.; 1484-
    1531)
Hulk Hogan (b. Terry Gene Bollea)(wrestling;
    1953-)
Hulk, The Incredible (cartoon chara.)
Hull House (Chicago settlement house)
Hull, Bobby (hockey; 1939-)
Hull, Brett (hockey; 1964-)
Hull, Cordell (US pol.; 1871-1955)
Hull, England (officially Kingston-upon-Hull)
Hull, Isaac (US mil.; 1773-1843)
Hull, Jane Dee (nee Bowersock)(AZ gov.; 1935-)
Hull, Josephine (ent.; 1886-1957)
Hull, Quebec, Canada
Hull, Robert Marvin "Bobby" (hockey; 1939-)
Human Fly, The (cartoon chara.)
Human Genome Sciences, Inc.
Human Rights Day (UN)
Human Torch, The (cartoon chara.)
Humana, Inc.
Humbert I (king, It.; 1844-1900)
Humboldt Current (now Peru Current)(cold
    ocean current)
Humboldt, (Friedrich Heinrich) Alexander von,
    Baron (Ger. expl.; 1769-1859)
Hume, Basil Cardinal (Br. rel.; 1923-99)
Hume Cronyn (ent.; 1911-)
Hume, David (Scot. phil./hist.; 1711-76)
Hume, Kirsty (model; 1976-)
Hummel figurines
Hummel, Johann Nepomuk (Ger. comp.; 1778-
    1837)
Hummer, AM General (auto.)
Humorsol (med.)
Humperdinck, Engelbert (b. Arnold Dorsey)
    (ent.; 1936-)
Humperdinck, Engelbert (Ger. comp.; 1854-1921)
Humphrey Bogart ("Bogey")(ent.; 1899-1957)
Humphrey, Hubert H(oratio)(ex-US VP; 1911-
    78)
Humphry Davy, (Sir)(Br. chem.; 1778-1829)
Humpty Dumpty (fict. chara.)
Humpty Dumpty's (mag.)
Humulin (med.)
Humvee (auto.)
Hun (ancient people)
Hun Sen (PM, Cambodia; 1950-)
Hun, Attila the ("Scourge of God")(king of the
    Huns; c406-453)
Hunan (province, Ch.)
Hunchback of Notre Dame, The (V. Hugo novel)
Hund, Friedrich (Ger. physt.; 1896-1997)

Hund's rule (chem.)
Hundred Days (FDR/Congress; 1933)
Hundred Flowers (Ch. hist.; 1957)
Hundred Years' War (also Hundred Years War)
    (Br./Fr.; 1337-1453)
Hung, Sammo (b. Samo Hung Kam-Bo)(ent.;
    1952-)
Hungarian (lang./people)
Hungarian uprising (Hung. hist.; 1956)
Hungary (Republic of)(Eur.)
Hungnam, North Korea
Hungry Jack (pancake mix)
Hunkers, Barnburners v. (US pol.; mid 1800s)
Huns, the (people)
Hunsa (lang.)
Hunt, Harold Guy (ex-AL gov.; 1933-)
Hunt, H. L. (US bus./oil; 1889-1974)
Hunt, Helen (ent.; 1963-)
Hunt, James B(axter), Jr. (ex-NC gov.; 1937-)
Hunt, Linda (ent.; 1945-)
Hunt, Richard M(orris)(US arch.; 1827-95)
Hunt's (ketchup)
Hunter Army Airfield (GA)
Hunter College of the City University of New
    York (NY)
Hunter Fans Co.
Hunter-Gault, Charlayne (US TV jour./activist;
    1942-)
Hunter Liggett, Fort (CA)(mil.)
Hunter S. Thompson (US jour.; 1939-)
Hunter, Catfish (Jim)(baseball; 1946-99)
Hunter, Holly (ent.; 1958-)
Hunter, Howard W. (US atty./rel.; 1907-)
Hunter, Jeffrey (ent.; 1925-69)
Hunter, Kim (ent.; 1922-)
Hunter, Reed (clothing)
Hunter, Ross (ent.; 1921-)
Hunter, Tab (b. Arthur Gelien)(ent.; 1931-)
Hunter's Lessee, Martin v. (US law; 1816)
Huntington Beach, CA
Huntington Library and Art Gallery, Henry E.
    (CA)
Huntington Park, CA
Huntington, Collis P(otter)(US bus.; 1821-1900)
Huntington, Henry E(dwards)(US bus.; 1850-
    1927)
Huntington, IN, WV
Huntington's chorea/disease (med.)
Huntley, Chet (US TV jour.; 1912-74)
Huntley, Joni (track; 1956-)
Huntsville News (AL newspaper)
Huntsville Times (AL newspaper)
Huntsville, AL, TX
Hunt-Wesson, Inc.
Huntz Hall (ent.; 1919-99)
Huppert, Isabelle (ent.; 1955-)
Hurley, Elizabeth (ent./model; 1965-)
Hurok, Sol(omon)(Rus./US impresario; 1884-1974)
Huron (Native Amer.)
Huron-Manistee National Forest
Huron, Lake (MI/Can.)
Huron, Port (MI)
Hurricane Andrew (FL/LA; 1992)
Hurricane Hugo (E US; 1989)
Hurst, Fannie (US writer; 1889-1968)

Hurston, Zora Neale (US writer; 1901-60)
Hurt, John (ent.; 1940-)
Hurt, Mary Beth (b. Mary Beth Supinger)(ent.;
    1948-)
Hurt, William (ent.; 1950-)
Husák, Gustav (ex-pres., Czech.; 1913-91)
Husayn, Bahaullah Ali Mirza (Pers., founded
    Baha'i faith; 1817-92)
Husbands, (Sir) Clifford (gov.-gen., Barbados;
    1926-)
Huseynov, Surat (ex-PM, Azerbaijan)
Hush Puppies (shoes)
Hush...Hush, Sweet Charlotte (film, 1965)
Husing, Ted (US sportscaster; 1901-62)
Husky, Ferlin (ent.; 1927-)
Hussain Mohammad Ershad (ex-pres.,
    Bangladesh; 1930-)
Hussein (al-Tikriti), Saddam (pres., Iraq; 1937-)
Hussein I (ibn Talal)(king, Jordan; 1935-99)
Hussein, Abdullah ibn (ex-king, Jordan; 1882-
    1951)
Hussein, Kamil (or Kemal)(Eg. sultan; 1850?-
    1917)
Husserl, Edmund (Gustav Albercht)(Ger. phil.;
    1859-1938)
Hussey, Olivia (ent.; 1951-)
Hussey, Ruth (ent.; 1914-)
Hustler (mag.)
Huston, Anjelica (ent.; 1951-)
Huston, John (US ent./writer; 1906-87)
Huston, Walter (ent.; 1884-1950)
Hutchins, Robert M. (US educ.; 1899-1977)
Hutchinson, Anne (Marbury)(US rel.; 1591-1643)
Hutchinson, Kathyrn Bailey "Kay" (US cong.;
    1943-)
Hutchinson, KS
Hutchinson, Tim (US cong.; 1949-)
Hutson, Donald (football; 1913-97)
Hutton, Barbara (US heiress; 1887-1979)
Hutton, Betty (ent.; 1921-)
Hutton, James (Scot. geol.; 1726-97)
Hutton, Lauren (ent./model; 1943-)
Hutton, Timothy (ent.; 1960-)
Hutu (people)
Hutzler Manufacturing Co.
Huxley, Aldous (Leonard)(Br. writer; 1894-1963)
Huxley, (Sir) Julian (Br. biol.; 1887-1975)
Huxley, Thomas (Henry)(Br. phil./educ.; 1825-
    95)
Huybrecht (or Hubert) van Eyck (Flem. artist;
    1366-1426)
Huygens (or Huyghens), Christian (Dutch
    math./physt./astron.; 1629-95)
Huygens eyepiece
Huygens principle
Hwa, Tung Chee (or Tung Chee-hwa)(chief
    exec., Hong Kong; 1937-)
Hwan, Chun Doo (ex-pres., SKorea; 1931-)
Hwange, Zimbabwe
Hy Averback (ent.; 1920-97)
Hyannis Port, MA (Kennedy Compound)
Hyatt Hotels and Resorts
Hyatt Hotels Corp.
Hycodan (med.)
Hycomine (med.)

Hyde Park (London)
Hyde Park, NY
Hyde Pierce, David (ent.; 1959-)
Hyde, Jekyll and (dual personality, one good/
  one evil)
Hyde, The Strange Case of Dr. Jekyll and Mr.
  (by R.L. Stevenson)
Hyder (or Haidar) Ali (Indian ruler/mil.; 1722-82)
Hyderabad, India
Hyderabad, Pakistan
Hydergine (med.)
Hydra (myth., astron., water snake [female])
Hydrea (med.)
Hydrocortone (med.)
HydroDIURIL (med.)
Hydromox (med.)
Hydrox (cookies)
Hydrus (astron., water snake [male])
Hygieia (myth.)
Hygroton (med.)
Hyksos (ancient Eg. kings; 1680-1580 BC)
Hyland, Diana (ent.; 1936-77)
Hylorel (med.)
Hylton v. U.S. (US law; 1796)
Hylutin (med.)
Hyman George Rickover, Adm. (US mil./A-
  bomb; 1900-86)
Hyman, Earle (ent.; 1926-)
Hymen (myth.)
Hynde, Chrissie (ent.; 1951-)
Hyperion (astron.; myth.)
Hypnus (myth.)
Hyponex (agriculture)
Hyponex Corp.
Hytone (med.)
Hytrin (med.)
Hyundai (auto.)
Hyundai Accent (auto.)
Hyundai Accent GL (auto.)
Hyundai Accent GS (auto.)
Hyundai Accent GSi (auto.)
Hyundai Accent GT (auto.)
Hyundai Accent L (auto.)
Hyundai Elantra (auto.)
Hyundai Elantra GL (auto.)
Hyundai Elantra GLS (auto.)
Hyundai Excel (auto.)
Hyundai Motor America (US bus.)
Hyundai Santa Fe (auto.)
Hyundai Scoupe (auto.)
Hyundai Sonata (auto.)
Hyundai Sonata GL (auto.)
Hyundai Sonata GLS (auto.)
Hyundai Tiburon (auto.)
Hyundai Tiburon FX (auto.)
Hyundai XG300 (auto.)
Hyundai XG300 L (auto.)

– I –

I (chem. sym., iodine)
IA (Iowa)
Iacocca, Lee A. (US auto exec.; 1924-)
Iago (fict. chara., *Othello*)
Ian Anderson (ent., Jethro Tull; 1947-)
Ian (Lancaster) Fleming (Br. writer ; 1908-64)
Ian McKellen (ent.; 1939-)
Ian (Douglas) Smith (ex-PM, Rhodesia; 1919-)
Ian, Janis (b. Janis Fink)(ent.; 1951-)
IAS (indicated airspeed)
Ib Anderson (ballet; 1954-)
Ibadan, Nigeria
Ibadhi Moslem (rel.)
Iban (lang.)
Ibanez, Jorge Batlle (pres., Uruguay; 1927-)
Iberia (also Iberian Peninsula)(Sp./Port.)
Iberia (now Georgia)
Iberia Air Lines of Spain (airline)
Iberian (lang./people)
Iberian Peninsula (also Iberia)(Sp./Port.)
Ibiza (Balearic Island)
Ibizan hound (also Ibizan Podenco)
Iblis (rel., evil spirit)
IBM
IBM Corp. (International Business Machines Corp.)
Ibn Saud (also Abdul-Azaz Ibn-Saud)(king,
    Saudi Arabia; 1880-1953)
Ibo (also Igbo)(lang./people)
IBP, Inc.
Ibrahim Babangida (ex-pres., Nigeria; 1941-)
Ibsen, Henrik (Johan)(Nor. writer; 1828-1906)
Icahn, Carl (US finan./corporate raider)
I Can't Believe It's Not Butter
I Can't Believe It's Yogurt, Inc.
ICAO (International Civil Aviation Organization)
Icarus (astron.; myth.)
ICBM (intercontinental ballistic missile)
ICC (Interstate Commerce Commission)(US govt.)
Ice Cube (b. O'Shea Jackson)(ent.; 1969-)
Ice-T (b. Tracy Morrow)(ent.; 1959-)
Iceland (Republic of)(N Atl.)
Icelandair (airline)
Icelandic (lang.)
Ichabod Crane (fict. chara., *Legend of Sleepy
    Hollow*)
I'chaim (Hebrew, to your health)
I Ching (also *Book of Changes*)(rel.)
Ichiro Ozawa (Jap. pol./writer; 1942-)
Ichiro Suzuki (baseball; 1973-)
Ickes, Harold (Le Claire)(US atty./pol.; 1874-
    1952)
Ickes, Harold (McEwen)(US atty./Clinton
    deputy chief of staff); 1939-)
ICU (intensive care unit)(med.)
ID (Idaho, identity document)
Id, Wizard of (comic strip)
Ida Bell (Barnett) Wells (US jour./civil rights
    leader; 1862-1931)
Ida Lupino (ent.; 1918-95)

Ida Minerva Tarbell (US writer; 1857-1944)
Idaho (ID)
Idaho Falls, ID
Idaho Supreme Potatoes, Inc.
'Id al-Adha (Islamic festival)
Ideals Publishing Co.
Ides (15th day of Mar., May, July, Oct.)(also l.c.)
Ides of March (3/15)
Idi Amin (Dada Oumee)(ex-pres., Uganda; 1925-)
Iditarod Trail Sled Dog Race
Idol, Billy (ent.; 1955-)
I Dream of Jeannie (TV show)
Idriss Déby (pres., Chad; 1952-)
Ife, Nigeria
I formation (football)
IFR (instrument flight rules)
I. F. Stone (US jour.; 1908-89)
IG (inspector general)
Igbo (also Ibo)(lang./people)
Iggy Pop (b. James Osterburg)(ent.; 1947-)
Iglesias, Enrique (ent.; 1975-)
Iglesias, Julio (Sp./US ent.; 1943-)
Igloo cooler
Igloo Corp.
Ignace Henri (Joseph Théodore) Fantin-Latour,
    (Fr. artist; 1836-1904)
Ignace Jan Paderewski (ex-PM, Pol./comp.;
    1860-1941)
Ignatius of Loyola, St. (aka (Iñigo de Oñez y
    Loyola)(Sp. rel.; 1491-1556)
Ignazio Silone (Secondo Tranquilli)(It. writer;
    1900-78)
Igor F(ederovich) Stravinsky (Rus./US comp.;
    1882-1971)
Igor I. Sikorsky (Rus./US aeronautical eng.;
    1889-1972)
Igor Kipnis (harpsichordist; 1930-)
IGY (International Geophysical Year)
Iloilo, Ratu Josefa (Fiji pol.)
Ijaw (lang.)
Ike Turner (ent.; 1931-)
Ikhnaton (also Akhenaton, Amenhotep
    IV)(king/pharaoh, Eg.; 14th c. BC)
IKON Office Solutions, Inc.
IL (Illinois)
Il Duce (aka Benito Mussolini)(ex-PM, It.;
    1883-1945)
Il Tintoretto ("the little dyer")(b. Jacopo
    Robusti)(It. artist; 1518-94)
Il Trovatore (Verdi opera)
Ila, Nigeria
Ildebrando Pizzetti (It. comp./hist.; 1880-1968)
Ile-de-France (now Mauritius)
Ile-de-France (region, Fr.)
Ilesha, Nigeria
ILGWU (International Ladies Garment Workers
    Union)
Iliad (Homer epic poem)
Ilie Nastase (tennis; 1946-)
Iliescu, Ion (ex-pres., Romania; 1930-)
Ilir Meta (PM, Albania; 1969-)
Ilka Chase (US writer/ent.; 1905-78)
Ileana Douglas (ent.; 1965-)
I'll Fly Away (TV show)
Illinois (IL)

Illinois (Native Amer.)
Illinois Tool Works, Inc.
Illinois, Inc., Owens-
Illinois, Munn v. (US law; 1877)
Illustrator, Adobe (compu.)
ILO (International Labor Organization)
Ilocano (also Ilokano)(lang./people)
Iloilo, Philippines
Ilorin, Nigeria
Ilosone (med.)
Ilotycin (med.)
I Love Lucy (TV show)
I Love You, Alice B. Toklas! (film, 1968)
Ilya G. Ehrenburg (Rus. writer; 1891-1967)
iMac (compu.)
I. Magnin (retail stores)
Imamu Amiri Baraka (aka LeRoi Jones)
   (playwright; 1934-)
Iman (b. Iman Abdul Majid)(model; 1955-)
Imbruglia, Natalie (ent.; 1975-)
Imelda (Romualdez) Marcos (Phil. pol., wife of
   ex-pres.; 1929-)
IMF (International Monetary Fund)
Imhotep (Eg. phys.; c2800 BC)
Immaculate Conception (rel.)
Immanuel (rel.)
Immanuel Kant (Ger. phys./phil.; 1724-1804)
Immelmann turn (airplace maneuver)
Immigration and Naturalization Service v.
   Chadha (US law; 1983)
Imodium (med.)
Imogene Coca (ent.; 1908-2001)
Imomali Rakhmonov (pres., Tajikistan; 1952-)
Impala, Chevrolet (auto.)
Impe, Jack Van (TV show)
I(eoh) M(ing) Pei (US arch.; 1917-)
Imperial conference
Imperial Highness (title)
Imperial Majesty (title)
Imperial margarine
Imperial Valley, CA
Imperial, Chrysler-Plymouth (auto.)
Imperials, Little Anthony and the (pop music)
Importance of Being Earnest, The (Oscar Wilde
   comedy)
Impressionism (art movement; fl. 1860-c1900)
Impreza, Subaru (auto.)
Imre Nagy (ex-PM, Hung.; c1895-1958)
Imus, Don (John Donald Imus, Jr.)(radio host;
   1940-)
IN (Indiana)
Ina Claire (b. Ina Fagan)(ent.; 1895-1985)
Inauguration Day
Inc. (mag.)
Inca empire (Peru; fl. 1200-c1530)
Inchon, South Korea (formerly Chemulpo)
Increase Mather (US rel.; 1639-1723)
Incredible Hulk, The (cartoon chara.)
Incredible Mr. Limpet, The (film, 1964)
Independence Bowl (college football)
Independence Day (also Fourth of July, July 4th)
Independence Hall (Philadelphia, PA)
Independence National Historical Park (PA)
Independence, Declaration of (US; July 4, 1776)
Independence, KS, MO

Independent Film Channel, The (TV channel)
Independent Order of Odd Fellows (fraternal
   society; est. 1918)
Inderal (med.)
Inderide (med.)
Index Expurgatorius (rel.)
Index Librorum Prohibitorum (rel.)
India (Republic of)(S Asia)
India ink (also Chinese ink)
India paper
India-Pakistan wars
India-rubber tree
Indian (langs., peoples)
Indian Affairs, Bureau of (BIA)(US govt. agcy.;
   est. 1849)
Indian corn (grass)
Indian cress (plant)
Indian currant (also snowberry)(plant)
Indian fig (plant)
Indian hawthorn (plant)
Indian hemp (plant)
Indian mulberry (tree)
Indian Mutiny (also Sepoy Rebellion/Mutiny)
   (India/Br.; 1857-58)
Indian Ocean (Afr./Austl.)
Indian paintbrush (plant)
Indian pipe (plant)
Indian pudding (dessert)
Indian red (color)
Indian strawberry (also mock strawberry)(plant)
Indian Territory (part of OK; 1829-1907)
Indian War, French and (NAmer./Br.; 1754-63)
Indian warrior (plant)
Indian yellow (color)
Indian, American (also Native American)(peoples)
Indiana (IN)
Indiana Jones (fict. chara.)
Indiana Jones and the Last Crusade (film, 1989)
Indiana Jones and the Temple of Doom (film,
   1984)
Indiana Pacers (basketball team)
Indianapolis 500 (racing)
Indianapolis Colts (football team)
Indianapolis News (IN newspaper)
Indianapolis Star (IN newspaper)
Indianapolis, IN
Indians, Cleveland (baseball team)
Indic (also Indo-Aryan)(lang[s], people)
Indira Gandhi (b. Nehru)(ex-PM, India; 1917-84)
Individual Investor (mag.)
Individual Retirement Account (IRA)
Indo-Aryan languages (also Indo-European)
Indochina (now Cambodia, Laos, and Viet.)
Indochinese (langs., peoples)
Indocin (med.)
Indo-European languages (also Indo-Aryan)
Indo-Germanic languages (now Indo-European)
Indo-Heriz (Pers. rug)
Indo-Iranian languages
Indonesia (Republic of)(SE Asia)
Indonesian (lang.)
Indonesian, Malay- (lang./people)
Indo-Tabriz (Pers. rug)
Indra (Hindu god)
Indus (astron., Indian)

Indus River (India)
Indus Valley civilization (India, c2500 BC)
Industrial Development Organization, United Nations (UNIDO)(est. 1966)
Industrial Recovery Act, National (NIRA)(US law; 1933)
Industrial Revolution (US/Eur. hist.; c1830-c1925)
Industrial Workers of the World (IWW, "Wobblies")(labor movement; 1905-1917)
Industrial World
Industry Week
Indy, (Paul Marie Théodore) Vincent d' (Fr. comp.; 1851-1931)
Infinite, the (also the Infinite Being)
Infiniti (auto.)
Infiniti Division of Nissan North America, Inc.
Infiniti G20 (auto.)
Infiniti I30 (auto.)
Infiniti J30 (auto.)
Infiniti Q45 (auto.)
Infiniti Q45t (auto.)
Infiniti QX4 (auto.)
Information Act, Freedom of
Information America (compu. database)
Information Week
InfoWorld
Inga Swenson (ent.; 1932-)
Inge, William (Motter)(US writer; 1913-73)
Inge, William (Ralph)(Br. rel.; 1860-1954)
Ingels, Marty (ent.; 1936-)
Ingemar Johansson (Swed. boxing; 1932-)
Ingemar Stenmark (skiing; 1956-)
Inger Stevens (ent.; 1934-70)
Ingersoll-Rand Co.
Inglenook (wine)
Inglewood, CA
Ingmar Bergman (Swed. ent.; 1918-)
In God We Trust
Ingraham, Hubert A. (PM, Bahamas; 1947-)
Ingram Micro, Inc.
Ingres, Jean Auguste Dominique (Fr. artist; 1780-1867)
Ingrid Bergman (ent.; 1915-82)
Inhofe, James M. (US cong.; 1934-)
Inigo Jones (Br. arch.; 1573-c1652)
Initial Teaching Alphabet (also augmented Roman)
Ink Spots, The (pop music)
Inkatha (SAfr. pol. org.; 1975-)
Inner Hebrides (islands, W Scot.)
Inner Mongolia (NE Ch.)
Inness, George (US artist; 1825-94)
Inns of Court (Br. law)
Innsbruck, Austria
Inouye, Daniel K. (US cong.; 1924-)
Inquirer, Philadelphia (PA newspaper)
Inquisition (rel.)
In re Debs (US law; 1895)
In re Gault (US law; 1967)
In Search of... (TV show)
Inside Daisy Clover (film, 1965)
Inside Edition (TV show)
Inside Sports (mag.)
Inside Washington (TV show)

Insight, Honda (auto.)
Insko, Del (harness racing; 1931-)
Inspector Gadget (cartoon)
Instamatic camera
Institute for Training and Research, United Nations (UNITAR)(est. 1963)
Institutes of Health, National (NIH)(US govt. agcy.; est. 1930)
Insulatard (med.)
Intal (med.)
Integra, Acura (auto.)
Integrated Services Digital Network (ISDN) (internat'l telecommunications)
Intel (compu. chip)
Intel Corp.
IntelliCAT (CAT system)
Intelligencer-Journal, Lancaster (PA newspaper)
Intelsat (also INTELSAT, International Telecommunications Satellite)(comm.)
Interco, Inc.
Intercollegiate Athletics, National Association of (NAIA)
Interior, Department of the (US govt.)
Interlaken, Switzerland
Intermediate Nuclear Forces Treaty (US/USSR; 1987)
Internal Revenue Service (IRS)(US govt. agcy.; est. 1862)
International Bank for Reconstruction and Development (World Bank)(UN; est. 1945)
International Brotherhood of Teamsters, Chauffeurs, Warehousemen, and Helpers of America (Teamsters Union)(trade union; est. 1903)
International Business Machines Corp. (IBM Corp.)
International Court of Justice (also World Court)(UN; founded 1945)
International Criminal Police Organization (Interpol)
International Date Line (IDL)(180° longitude)
International Development Association (IDA) (UN; est. 1960)
International Green Party (US pol.)
International Harvester Co.
International Labour Organization (ILO)(UN; est. 1919)
International Monetary Fund (IMF)(UN; est. 1944)
International Paper Co.
International Phonetic Alphabet (also IPA)
International Standard Book Number (ISBN)
International Style (arch.)
International System of Units (also SI, Système Internationale d'Unités)
International Telephone and Telegraph Corp (ITT)
Internet (compu.)
Interpol (International Criminal Police Organization)
Interstate Commerce Commission (ICC)(US govt. agcy.)
Interview (mag.)
In the Heat of the Night (TV show)
Intifada (Liberation Army of Palestine; founded 1987)

Intolerable Acts (US/Br. hist.; 1774)
Intracoastal Waterway (SE US)
Intrepid, Dodge (auto.)
Intrigue, Oldsmobile (auto.)
Intuit (US bus.)
Inuit (lang./people)
Inuktitut (lang.)(also Inuktituut)
Invar (iron alloy)
Invasion of the Body Snatchers (film, 1956, 1978)
Inverness, Scotland
Investor's Business Daily (mag.)
Invincible Armada (Spanish Armada)(fleet of ships; 1588)
Invitation Tournament, National (NIT) (basketball)
INXS (pop music)
Io (Jupiter moon; myth.)
Iodine, Little (comic strip)
Iolani Palace (HI)
Iolanthe (Gilbert and Sullivan)
Iomega (US bus.)
Ion Iliescu (ex-pres., Romania; 1930-)
Ionatana Ionatana (PM, Tuvalu)
Ionesco, Eugène (Fr. writer; 1912-94)
Ionia (ancient Asia Minor)
Ionian (people)
Ionian Islands (Ionian/Mediterranean seas)
Ionian Sea (arm of Mediterranean)
Ionic (type style)
Ionic order (arch., lang.)
IOOF (Independent Order of Odd Fellows)
IOU (I owe you)
Iowa (IA)
Iowa City, IA
I Pagliacci (R. Leoncavallo opera)
Iphigene Ochs Sulzberger (US publ.; 1883-1990)
Ipoh, Malaysia
Ipswich, Australia
Ipswich, England
Ipswich, MA
IQ (intelligence quotient)
Iquique, Chile
Iquitos, Peru
Ir (chem. sym., iridium)
IRA (Individual Retirement Account)
IRA (Irish Republican Army)(mil.; est. 1919)
Ira Frederick Aldridge (ent.; 1804-67)
Ira Gershwin (US lyricist; 1896-1983)
Ira Levin (US writer; 1929-)
Iráklion, Greece
Iran (Islamic Republic of)(formerly Persia)(SW Asia)
Iran-Contra scandal (also Irangate)(US pol. scandal; 1987)
Irangate (also Iran-Contra scandal)(US pol. scandal; 1987)
Iranian (lang./people)
Iran-Iraq War (also Gulf War)(1980-88)
Iraq (Republic of)(SW Asia)
Iraq War , Iran- (also Gulf War)(1980-88)
Irbid, Jordan
IRBM (intermediate range ballistic missile)
Ireland (Republic of)(also Erie)(NW Eur.)

Ireland, Jill (ent.; 1936-90)
Ireland, John (ent.; 1914-92)
Ireland, Kathy (model/bus.; 1963-)
Ireland, Northern (part of the UK)
Ireland, Patricia (US feminist/reformer, pres./ NOW; 1945-)
Irem, Garden of (myth.)
Irene Cara (ent.; 1959-)
Irene (Foote) Castle (US dancer; 1893-1969)
Irene Dunne (ent.; 1898-1990)
Irène Joliot-Curie (Fr. physt.; 1897-1956)
Irene Papas (ent.; 1926-)
Irene Ryan (ent.; 1903-73)
Irianese (people)
Iris (myth.)
Iris Murdoch (Br. writer; 1919-99)
Iris, Stanley and (film, 1990)
Irish (lang./people)
Irish coffee (mixed drink)
Irish Gaelic (lang.)
Irish harp (music)
Irish knit (sweater)
Irish Literary Renaissance (also Irish Revival, Celtic Renaissance)
Irish Mist (liqueur)
Irish Republican Army (IRA)(mil.; est. 1919)
Irish setter (dog)
Irish terrier (dog)
Irish water spaniel (dog)
Irish wolfhound (dog)
Irma La Douce (film, 1963)
Irma, My Friend (film, 1949)
Iron Age (c2000 BC to present)
Iron Chancellor (Prince Otto [Eduard Leopold] von Bismarck)(ex-chanc., Ger.; 1815-98)
Iron Cross, the (Ger. war medal)
Iron Curtain (imaginary boundary between capitalist/communist Eur.)
Iron Guard (Romanian hist.; 1930's)
Iron Maiden (rock group)
Iron, Ralph (aka Olive Schreiner)(SAfr. writer; 1855-1920)
Irons, Jeremy (ent.; 1948-)
Ironsides, Old (Constitution, The)(US naval ship)
Iroquois (Native Amer.)
Iroquois Confederacy/League (Native Amer.)
Irrawaddy River (Myanmar/Burma)
IRS (Internal Revenue Service)
Irvin, Michael (football; 1966-)
Irvine, CA
Irving Berlin (b. Israel Baline)(US comp.; 1888-1989)
Irving Caesar (lyricist; 1895-1996)
Irving Fisher (US econ.; 1867-1947)
Irving Howe (US literary critic; 1920-93)
Irving Langmuir (US chem.; 1881-1957)
Irving R. Levine (US TV jour.; 1922-)
Irving Stone (US writer; 1903-89)
Irving (Grant) Thalberg (ent.; 1899-1936)
Irving Wallace (US writer; 1916-90)
Irving, Amy (ent.; 1953-)
Irving, George S. (ent.; 1922-)
Irving, John (US writer; 1942-)
Irving, TX
Irving, Washington (US writer/hist.; 1783-1859)

Irwin Chanin (US arch.; 1892-1988)
Irwin Shaw (US writer; 1913-84)
Irwin Shrewsbury Cobb (US humorist; 1876-1944)
Irwin, Fort, CA (mil.)
Irwin, Hale (golf; 1945-)
Irwin, James B. (astro.; 1930-91)
Iryani, Abdul-Karim al- (PM, Yemen; 1934-)
Isa bin Sulman al-Khalifa, Sheik (ex-emir, Bahrain; 1933-)
Isa Town, Bahrain
Isaac (rel.)
Isaac Asimov (US writer/sci-fi; 1920-92)
Isaac Asimov's Science Fiction Magazine
Isaac Babel (Rus. writer; 1894-1941)
Isaac B(ashevis) Singer (Pol./US writer; 1904-91)
Isaac Hayes (ent.; 1942-)
Isaac M(errit) Singer (US inv./sewing machine; 1811-75)
Isaac Newton, (Sir)(Br. physt./math., gravity; 1642-1727)
Isaac Pitman, (Sir)(Br., inv. shorthand system; 1813-97)
Isaac Stern (Rus. violinist; 1920-)
Isaacs, Susan (US writer; 1943-)
Isaak, Chris (ent./songwriter; 1956-)
Isabel Allende (writer; 1942-)
Isabel de Perón (b. Maria Estela Martínez)(ex-pres., Argentina; 1931-)
Isabel Sanford (ent.; 1917-)
Isabella I ("the Catholic")(queen, Sp.; 1451-1504)
Isabella II (queen, Sp.; 1830-1904)
Isabella Rossellini (It. ent.; 1952-)
Isabelle Adjani (ent.; 1955-)
Isabelle Brasseur (figure skating; 1971-)
Isabelle Huppert (ent.; 1955-)
Isabelle, Therese & (film, 1967)
Isadora (film, 1969)
Isadora Duncan (US dancer; 1878-1927)
Isaiah (Hebrew prophet; 8th c. BC)
Isaiah (rel., book of the Old Testament)
Isaias Afwerki (pres., Eritrea; 1946-)
Isak Dinesen (aka Karen Blixen)(Dan. writer; 1885-1962)
Isamu Noguchi (Jap./US artist; 1904-88)
Isaresci, Mugur (PM, Romania; 1949-)
ISBN (International Standard Book Number)
Iscariot, Judas (betrayer of Jesus; ?-c28)
Isenheim Altarpiece (Grünewald)
Iseult, Tristan and (also Tristam, Isolde)(Celtic legend)
Isfahan, Iran
Ish Kabibble (aka Merwyn Bogue)(ent.; 1908-94)
Isherwood, Christopher (William Bradshaw)(Br. writer; 1904-86)
Ishiguro, Kazuo (Jap./US writer; 1954-)
Ishihara('s) test (for color blindness)
Ishmael (rel.)
Ishmael Reed (US writer; 1938-)
Ishtar (film, 1987)
Ishtar (myth.)
Isiah Thomas (basketball; 1961-)

Isidor Isaac Rabi (US physt.; 1899-1988)
Isis (Eg. goddess)
Islam (rel.)
Islam A. Karimov (pres., Uzbekistan; 1938-)
Islam, Nation of (also Black Muslims)(rel.)
Islamabad, Pakistan
Islamic Jihad (Islamic Holy War)(Middle East terrorist movement)
Islamic New Year's Day
Islamic Resistance Movement
Islamic Taliban movement (mil., Afghan.)
Island of Dr. Moreau (film, 1977, 1996)
Island of La Grande Jatte, A Sunday Afternoon on the (by Seurat)
Islanders, New York (hockey team)
Islands (mag.)
Isle of Guernsey (island, English Channel)
Isle of Man (island, Irish Sea)
Isle of Wight (island/county, Eng.)
Isle Royale National Park (MI)
Isles of Scilly, Cornwall and (county, Eng.)
islets of Langerhans (med.)
Isley Brothers, The (pop music)
Islip, NY
Isma'ili (rel.)
Ismail I (also Ismail Pasha)(ex-gov., Eg.; 1830-95)
Ismail I (shah, Persia; 1486-1524)
Ismail Merchant (b. Ismail Noormohamed Abdul Rehman)(ent.; 1936-)
Ismail Omar Guelleh (pres., Djibouti; 1947-)
Ismailia, Egypt
Ismelin (med.)
Isocrates (Gr. orator; 436-338 BC)
Isolde, Tristan and (also Tristam, Iseult)(Celtic legend)
Isoptin (med.)
Isordil (med.)
Isotoner (gloves/slippers)
I Spy (TV show)
Israel (State of)(SW Asia)
Israel ben Eliezer (also Baal Shem-Tov)(Jew. rel.; c1700-60)
Israel, Tribes of
Israeli (people)
Israeli Wars, Arab- (series of wars since 1948)
Israelite (people)
Issa (lang./people)
Issoufou, Mahamadou (ex-PM, Niger)
Istanbul, Turkey (previously called Byzantium and Constantinople)
Isuprel (med.)
Isuzu (auto.)
Isuzu Amigo (auto.)
Isuzu Amigo S (auto.)
Isuzu Axiom (auto.)
Isuzu Hombre pickup (auto.)
Isuzu Motors Inc., American
Isuzu Oasis (auto.)
Isuzu Oasis LS (auto.)
Isuzu Oasis S (auto.)
Isuzu Rodeo (auto.)
Isuzu Rodeo LS (auto.)
Isuzu Rodeo LSE (auto.)
Isuzu Rodeo S (auto.)

Isuzu Rodeo Sport (auto.)
Isuzu Trooper (auto.)
Isuzu Trooper LE (auto.)
Isuzu Trooper Limited (auto.)
Isuzu Trooper LS (auto.)
Isuzu Trooper S (auto.)
Isuzu VehiCROSS (auto.)
Isuzu, Joe (fict. chara.)
Itaipu (dam, Brazil)
Italia (grape)
Italian (lang./people)
Italian aster (flowering plant)
Italian dressing
Italian greyhound (dog)
Italian ice (dessert)
Italian jasmine (plant)
Italian sausage
Italian sonnet (also Petrarchan sonnet)(lit.)
Italy (Republic of)(S Eur.)
Itamar Franco (ex-pres., Brazil; 1930-)
ITAR-Tass (Rus. news org.)
Ithaca (Gr. island)
Ithaca, NY
ITO (International Trade Organization)
Ito, Hirobumi, Prince (ex-PM, Jap.; 1841-1909)
Ito, Midori (figure skating; 1969-)
It's a Living (TV show)
It's A Mad, Mad, Mad, Mad World (film, 1963)
Itsy Bitsy Teenie Weenie Yellow Polka Dot Bikini
    (song)
ITT Corp.
Iturbi, Jose (Sp. cond.; 1895-1980)
Itzhak Perlman (Isr./US violinist; 1945-)
IUD (intrauterine device)(med.)
I.V. (also IV) (intravenous)(med.)
I.V. port (also IV port) (med.)
Ivan Ditmars (ent./comp.; ?-1997)
Ivan F(rederick) Boesky (US stock market
    scandal; 1937-)
Ivan III ("the Great")(ex-tsar, Muscovy; 1440-
    1505)
Ivan IV ("the Terrible")(ex-tsar, Muscovy;
    1530-84)
Ivan Kostov (PM, Bulgaria; 1949-)
Ivan Le Lorraine Albright (US artist; 1897-1983)
Ivan Lendl (tennis; 1960-)
Ivan Nagy (ballet; 1943-)
Ivan (Petrovich) Pavlov (Rus. physiol.; 1849-
    1936)
Ivan Tors (ent.; 1916-83)
Ivan (Sergeievich) Turgenev (Rus. writer;
    1818-83)
Ivana Trump (Mazzucchelli)(nee Zelnicek)(US
    bus./ex-wife of D. Trump; 1949-)
Ivanhoe (Sir Walter Scott novel)
Ivars Godmanis (ex-PM, Latvia)
I've Got a Secret (TV show)
Ives, Burl (Icle Ivanhoe)(ent.; 1909-95)
Ives, Charles (Edward)(US comp.; 1874-1954)
Ives, Currier & (US lithography)
Ives, Frederic Eugene (US inv.; 1856-1937)
Ives, James (Merritt)(US lithographer; 1824-
    95)
Ives, St. (toiletries)
Ivey, Judith (ent.; 1951-)

IVF (in vitro fertilization)(med.)
Ivica Racan (PM, Croatia; 1944-)
Ivins, Molly (US jour.; 1944-)
Ivor Novello (ent./playwright/comp.; 1893-1951)
Ivory Coast (Republic of)(W Afr.)
Ivory Liquid (detergent)
Ivory Snow (soap)
Ivry-sur-Seine, France
Ivy League colleges (Brown/Columbia/Cornell/
    Dartmouth/Harvard/Pennsylvania/Princeton/Yale)
I Witness Video (TV show)
Iwo Jima (also U.S. Marine Corps War
    Memorial)(VA)
Iwo Jima (island, W Pac.)
Iwo Jima, Battle of (WWII; 1945)
Iwo, Nigeria
Iwo Jima, Sands of (film, 1949)
IWW (Industrial Workers of the World)
Ixion (myth.)
Ixtapa, Mexico
Iyar (also Iyyar)(Jew. month)
Izaak Walton (Br. writer; 1593-1683)
Izanagi and Izanami (Jap. myth.)
Izetbegovic, Dr. Alija (co-pres., Bosnia-
    Hercegovina, Muslim; 1925)
Izmir, Turkey (formerly Smyrna)
Iznik, Turkey (formerly Nicaea)
Izzy & Moe (film, 1985)

– J –

JA (judge advocate)
Jabberwocky (L. Carroll poem)
Jaber al-Ahmad al-Jaber al-Sabah, Sheik (emir, Kuwait; 1928-)
Jack Albertson (ent.; 1907-81)
Jack Anderson (US jour.; 1922-)
Jack and Jill (nursery rhyme)
Jack and the Beanstalk (fairy tale)
Jack Bannon (ent.; 1940-)
Jack Benny (b. Benjamin Kubelsky)(ent.; 1894-1974)
Jack Carson (ent.; 1910-63)
Jack Carter (ent.; 1923-)
Jack Cassidy (ent.; 1927-76)
Jack Daniel Distillery (US bus.)
Jack Daniel's
Jack Dempsey, (William Harrison)(boxing; 1895-1983)
Jack Elam (ent.; 1916-)
Jack Flash, Jumpin' (song; film, 1986)
Jack Frost (personification of frost)
Jack Haley (ent.; 1899-1979)
Jack Hawkins (ent.; 1910-73)
Jack Horner, Little (nursery rhyme)
Jack-in-the-pulpit (plant)
Jack (John Arthur) Johnson (boxing; 1878-1946)
Jack Jones (ent.; 1938-)
Jack Kelly (ent.; 1927-92)
Jack Kemp (US pol.; 1935-)
Jack (John Fitzgerald) Kennedy (35th US pres.; 1917-63)
Jack Kent Cooke (US bus.; 1912-97)
Jack (Jean-Louis Lebris de) Kerouac (US writer; 1922-69)
Jack Ketch (Br. slang, official hangman)
Jack (Murad) Kevorkian (US phys.; 1928-)
Jack Klugman (ent.; 1922-)
Jack Kramer (tennis; 1921-)
Jack LaLanne (US, fitness educ.; 1914-)
Jack LaLanne Health Spas (US bus.)
Jack Lemmon (ent.; 1925-2001)
Jack Lescoulie (ent.; 1917-)
Jack (John Griffith) London (US writer; 1876-1916)
Jack Lord (ent.; 1922-98)
Jack L(eonard) Warner (ent.; 1892-1978)
Jack (John) Lynch (ex-PM, Ir.; 1917-99)
Jack McDowell (baseball; 1966-)
Jack Nicholson (ent.; 1937-)
Jack (William) Nicklaus (golf; 1940-)
Jack Norworth (US lyricist; 1879-1959)
Jack Oakie (ent.; 1903-78)
Jack Paar (ent.; 1918-)
Jack Palance (b. Walter Vladimir Palanuik)(ent.; 1920-)
Jack Reed (US cong.; 1949-)
Jack R(obert) Lousma (astro.; 1936-)
Jack Rose (mixed drink)
Jack Ruby (US, murdered L.H. Oswald; 1911-67)

Jack Russell terrier (dog)
Jack Schaefer (US writer; 1908-91)
Jack (Harrison Hahen) Schmitt (US pol./astro.; 1935-)
Jack Sharkey (boxing; 1902-94)
Jack (Weldon John) Teagarden (US jazz; 1905-64)
Jack the Ripper (London murderer; 1888)
Jack Valenti (US writer/ent.; 1921-)
Jack Van Impe (TV show)
Jack Warden (b. Jack Warden Lebzelter)(ent.; 1920-)
Jack Webb (ent.; 1920-82)
Jack Welch (US bus.; 1935-)
Jack Weston (ent.; 1924-96)
Jack Wrather (US bus.; 1918-84)
Jack Yellen (US lyricist; 1892-1991)
Jack, Billy (film, 1971)
Jack, David (ex-gov.-gen., St. Vincent/Grenadines)
Jack, Union (Br. flag)(also l.c.)
Jack, Wolfman (b. Robert Weston Smith)(disc jockey, *American Graffiti*; 1939-95)
Jackee (b. Jackee Harry)(ent.; 1957-)
Jacket, Red (Sagoyewatha)(Seneca Native Amer. leader; c1756-1830)
Jackie Chan (b. Chan Kwong-Sang)(ent.; 1954-)
Jackie Collins (US writer; 1939-)
Jackie Coogan (ent.; 1914-84)
Jackie (Herbert John) Gleason (ent.; 1916-87)
Jackie Gleason Show, The (TV show)
Jackie (Sigmund) Jackson (ent., The Jacksons; 1951-)
Jackie Joyner-Kersee (track; 1962-)
Jackie Mason (b. Yacov Moshe Maza)(ent.; 1934-)
Jackie (Jacqueline Lee Bouvier Kennedy) Onassis (US editor/photo.; wife of ex-US pres.; 1929-94)
Jackie Presser (US labor leader; 1927-88)
Jackie (John Roosevelt) Robinson (baseball; 1919-72)
Jackie Stewart (auto racing; 1939-)
Jackie Wilson (ent.; 1934-84)
Jackson & Perkins (plants/seeds)
Jackson & Perkins Co.
Jackson Browne (ent.; 1948-)
Jackson Clarion-Ledger (MS newspaper)
Jackson 5, the (pop music)
Jackson Hole National Monument (WY)
Jackson Pollock, (Paul)(US artist; 1912-56)
Jackson Winery, Kendall- (US bus.)
Jackson Young, Jr., Andrew (US dipl./pol.; 1932-)
Jackson, Alan (ent.; 1958-)
Jackson, Andrew ("Old Hickory")(7th US pres.; 1767-1845)
Jackson, Anne (ent.; 1925-)
Jackson, Bo (Vincent)(baseball; 1962-)
Jackson, Fort (SC)(mil.)
Jackson, Glenda (ent.; 1936-)
Jackson, Helen Hunt (pseud. H. H.)(US writer; 1830-85)
Jackson, Howell Edmunds (US jurist; 1832-95)
Jackson, Jackie (Sigmund)(ent., The Jacksons; 1951-)
Jackson, Janet (ent.; 1966-)
Jackson, Jermaine (ent.; 1954-)

Jackson, Jesse L(ouis), Jr. (US cong.; 1965-)
Jackson, Jesse L(ouis), Sr. (US rel./pol./civil
    rights activist; 1941-)
Jackson, Joe (ent./songwriter; 1955-)
Jackson, Joshua (ent.; 1978-)
Jackson, Kate (ent.; 1948-)
Jackson, Keith (sportscaster; 1928-)
Jackson, La Toya (ent.; 1956-)
Jackson, Mahalia (US jazz; 1911-72)
Jackson, Marlon (ent., The Jacksons; 1957-)
Jackson, MI, MS, TN, WY
Jackson, Michael (ent.; 1958-)
Jackson, Milt (US jazz; 1923-99)
Jackson, Reggie (baseball; 1946-)
Jackson, Samuel L. (ent.; 1948-)
Jackson, Shirley (US writer; 1916-65)
Jackson, Stonewall (ent.; 1932-)
Jackson, Stonewall (Thomas Jonathan)(US
    gen.; 1824-63)
Jackson, Thomas Penfield (US atty./judge)
Jackson, Tito (Toriano)(ent.; The Jacksons; 1953-)
Jackson, Victoria (ent.; 1959-)
Jacksonville Jaguars (football team)
Jacksonville Times-Union (FL newspaper)
Jacksonville, FL
Jaclyn Smith (ent.; 1947-)
Jacob (rel.)
Jacob Epstein (Br. sculptor; 1880-1959)
Jacob J. Shubert (US theater; 1880-1963)
Jacob Javits (US pol.; 1904-86)
Jacob Lawrence (US artist; 1917-2000)
Jacob Marley, the ghost of (fict. chara., *The
    Christmas Carol*)
Jacob Nena (ex-pres., Micronesia; 1941-)
Jacob (August) Riis (US reformer; 1849-1914)
Jacob (Isaackszoon) van Ruisdael (Dutch artist;
    c1628-82)
Jacob's-ladder (plant)
Jacobean style/literature (Br.; early 17th c.)
Jacobi, Derek (ent.; 1938-)
Jacobin (Fr. hist.; 1789-94)
Jacobite (Br. hist.; 1688-1746)
Jacobite Church (rel.)
Jacobs, Jane (US urbanologist; 1916-)
Jacobs, Walter L. (US bus.; 1898-1985)
Jacopo Bellini (It. artist; 1400-70)
Jacopo da Pontormo (It. artist; 1492-1557)
Jacopo Robusti (aka Tintoretto)(It. artist;
    1518-94)
Jacopo Sansovino (It. sculptor; 1486-1570)
Jacqueline Bisset (ent.; 1944-)
Jacqueline "Jackie" Lee Bouvier Kennedy
    Onassis (US editor/photo.; wife of ex-US
    pres.; 1929-94)
Jacqueline Susann (US writer; 1921-74)
Jacques Ange Gabriel (Fr. arch.; 1689?-1782)
Jacques Brel (ent./comp.; 1929-78)
Jacques Callot (Fr. engraver; 1592?-1635)
Jacques Cartier (Fr. explorer; 1491-1557)
Jacques (Alexandre César) Charles (Fr. physt.;
    1746-1823)
Jacques Chirac (pres., Fr.; 1932-)
Jacques d'Amboise (ballet; 1934-)
Jacques Derrida (phil.; 1930-)
Jacques Dupont (minister/state, Monaco)

Jacques-Edouard Alexis (PM, Haiti; 1947-)
Jacques Étienne Montgolfier (Fr. hot-air
    balloonist; 1745-99)
Jacques-Joachim Yhombi-Opango (ex-PM,
    Congo; 1940-)
Jacques Lipchitz (US sculptor; 1891-1973)
Jacques Louis David (Fr. artist; 1748-1825)
Jacques Maritain (Fr. phil.; 1882-1973)
Jacques Marquette (Fr. expl./rel. in Amer.;
    1637-75)
Jacques Necker (Fr. pol.; 1732-1804)
Jacques (Levy) Offenbach (Fr. comp.; 1819-80)
Jacques Plante (hockey; 1929-86)
Jacques Santer (ex-PM, Luxembourg; 1937-)
Jacques Villon (b. Gaston Duchamp)(Fr. artist;
    1875-1963)
Jacques Yves Cousteau (Fr. oceanographer;
    1910-97)
Jacques, coquilles St. (scallop dish)
Jacuzzi Whirlpool Bath (US bus.)
Jacuzzi, Candido (It./US eng./inv.; 1903-86)
Jada Pinkett Smith (ent.; 1971-)
Jaeckel, Richard (ent.; 1926-97)
Jaffe, Sam (ent.; 1891-1984)
Jaffna, Sri Lanka
JAG (Judge Advocate General)
Jagadis Chunder Bose, (Sir)(Indian physt.;
    1858-1937)
Jagan, Cheddi (Berrat)(ex-pres., Guyana; 1918-)
Jagdeo, Bharrat (pres.; Guyana; 1964-)
Jagger, Bianca (b. Bianca Peréz Morena de
    Macîas)(1945-)
Jagger, Dean (ent.; 1903-91)
Jagger, Mick (Michael Phillip)(ent.; 1943-)
Jaguar (auto.)
Jaguar S-type (auto.)
Jaguar X-type (auto.)
Jaguar XJ Vanden Plas (auto.)
Jaguar XJ Vanden Plas SC (auto.)
Jaguar XJ12 (auto.)
Jaguar XJ6 (auto.)
Jaguar XJ6 Vanden Plas (auto.)
Jaguar XJ6L (auto.)
Jaguar XJ8 (auto.)
Jaguar XJ8L (auto.)
Jaguar XJR (auto.)
Jaguar XJS (auto.)
Jaguar XK8 (auto.)
Jaguar XKR (auto.)
Jaguar XKR Silverstone (auto.)
Jaguars, Jacksonville (football team)
J. A. Hansom (Br. arch., hansom cab; 1803-82)
Jahweh (also Jehovah, God)
Jaime Paz Zamora (ex-pres., Bolivia)
Jainism (rel.)
Jaipur, India
Jakarta, Indonesia (also Djakarta)
Jake & the Fatman (TV show)
Jake (Giacobe) La Motta (boxing; 1921-)
Jake Lloyd (ent.; 1989-)
Jake Siewert (US ex-White House press secy.)
Jakes, John (William)(US writer; 1932-)
Jakob (Ludwig Karl) Grimm (Ger. writer/
    linguist; 1785-1863)
Jakob Bernoulli (Swiss math./scien.; 1654-1705)

Jakob Boehme (Ger. theosophist; 1575-1624)

Jakob Dylan (ent.; 1969-)

Jakob Fugger (Jakob the Rich)(Ger. banker; 1459-1525)

Jalalabad, Afghanistan

Jaleel White (ent.; 1976-)

Jalisco (Mex. state)

Jamaica (island, Caribbean)

Jamaican Creole (lang.)

Jamal Ahmed al-Fadl (Sudanese informant on Osama bin Laden; 1964-)

Jamal Warner, Malcolm- (ent.; 1970-)

Jamal, Ahmad (b. Frederick Russell Jones)(US jazz; 1930-)

James (rel., book of the New Testament)

James A. Baker III (US pol.; 1930-)

James A(bram) Garfield (20th US pres.; 1831-81)

James Agee (US writer; 1909-55)

James Alfred Van Allen (US space physt.; 1914-)

James A. Lovell, Jr. (astro.; 1928-)

James A(lton) McDivitt (astro.; 1929-)

James A(lbert) Michener (US writer; 1907-97)

James & the Shondells, Tommy (pop music)

James A(lbert) Pike, Bishop (US rel.; 1913-69)

James Arness (b. James Aurness)(ent.; 1923-)

James Baldwin (US writer; 1924-87)

James B. Brady ("Diamond Jim")(US finan.; 1856-1917)

James B(eethoven) Carlisle, Dr. (gov.-gen.; Antigua and Barbuda; 1937-)

James B. Conant (US chem./educ./dipl.; 1893-1978)

James "Jim" Belushi (ent.; 1954-)

James B(axter) Hunt, Jr. (ex-NC gov.; 1937-)

James B. Irwin (astro.; 1930-91)

James (Brendan) Bolger (Jim)(ex-PM, NewZeal.; 1935-)

James Bond (fict. spy)

James Bond (ornithol.; 1900-89)

James Boswell (Scot. biographer; 1740-95)

James "Jim" Bowie (US frontier; 1796-1836)

James Brolin (b. James Bruderlin)(ent.; 1940-)

James Brown (ent.; 1933-)

James (Nathaniel) "Jimmy" Brown (football/ ent.; 1936-)

James Browning Wyeth (US artist; 1946-)

James B. Sikking (ent.; 1934-)

James Buchanan (15th US pres.; 1791-1868)

James Caan (ent.; 1939-)

James Cagney (ent.; 1899-1986)

James Callaghan (ex-PM, Br.; 1912-)

James Cameron (ent.; 1954-)

James Carville, Jr., (Chester)(the Ragin' Cajun) (US pol.; 1944-)

James Chadwick, (Sir)(Br. physt.; 1891-1974)

James Clark Ross, (Sir)(Br. expl.; 1800-62)

James Clavell (Brit./US writer; 1924-94)

James Clerk Maxwell (Scot. physt.; 1831-79)

James Coburn (ent.; 1928-)

James Coco (ent.; 1929-87)

James Cook, Capt. (Br. nav./expl.; 1728-79)

James "Gentleman Jim" Corbett (boxing; 1866-1933)

James C(ash) Penney (US bus.; 1875-1971)

James Dean (ent.; 1931-55)

James Dewar, (Sir)(Scot. chem/physt.; 1842-1923)

James Dewey Watson (US biol.; 1928-)

James Dickey (US writer; 1923-97)

James Duke (US bus.; 1856-1925)

James Dunn (ent.; 1905-67)

James Earl "Jimmy" Carter, Jr. (39th US pres.; 1924-)

James Earl Jones (ent.; 1931-)

James Earl Ray (US, assassinated M.L. King; 1928-98)

James "Jim" Edgar (ex-IL gov.; 1946-)

James Edmund Scripps (US publ.; 1835-1906)

James (Francis) Edward Stuart ("Old Pretender")(prince, Br.; 1688-1766)

James Ellroy (US writer; 1948-)

James Ensor, Baron (Belgian artist; 1860-1949)

James E(dward) Oglethorpe (Br. gen., founded Georgia; 1696-1785)

James E. Watt (Scot. eng./inv.; 1736-1819)

James Exon, J. (US pol.; 1921-)

James Farentino (ent.; 1938-)

James Farmer (US civil rights leader; 1920-99)

James Fenimore Cooper (US writer; 1789-1851)

James Fox (ent.; 1939-)

James Franciscus (ent.; 1934-91)

James Franck (Ger./US physt.; 1882-1964)

James Gadsden (US mil./dipl.; 1788-1858)

James Galanos (US designer; 1925-)

James Galway (Ir./US ent.; 1939-)

James Gandolfini (ent.; 1961-)

James Garner (b. James Baumgarner)(ent.; 1928-)

James G(illespie) Blaine (US pol.; 1830-93)

James George Frazer, (Sir)(Scot. anthrop.; 1854-1941)

James "Jim" Geringer (WY gov.; 1944-)

James Gillespie Birney (US reformer; 1792-1857)

James Gleason (ent.; 1886-1959)

James Gordon Bennett (US jour.; 1795-1872)

James Gould Cozzens (US writer; 1903-78)

James Gregory (ent.; 1911-)

James G. Watt (US ex-secy./interior; 1938-)

James Hargreaves (Br. inv.; c1720-1778)

James Harold Doolittle (US aviator; 1896-93)

James Henry Breasted (US archaeol.; 1865-1935)

James Herriot (Br. writer; 1916-95)

James Hines (sprinter; 1946-)

James (Hovis) "Jim" Hodges (SC gov.; 1956-)

James Hogg ("the Ettrick Shepherd")(Scot. poet; 1770-1835)

James H. Robinson (US hist./educ.; 1863-1936)

James I ("the Conqueror")(king, Aragon; 1208-76)

James I (also James VI, Scot.)(king, Eng.; 1566-1625)

James I (king, Scot.; 1394-1437)

James II ("the Just")(king, Aragon; 1260-1327)

James II (also James VII, Scot.)(king, Eng.; 1633-1701)

James II (king, Scot.; 1430-60)

James III (aka James [Francis] Edward Stuart, Old Pretender)(Br. prince; 1688-1766)

James III (king, Scot.; 1451-88)

James Ingo Freed (US arch.; 1930-)
James IV (king, Scot.; 1473-1513)
James (Merritt) Ives (US lithographer; 1824-95)
James J(oseph) "Jim" Florio (ex-NJ gov.; 1937-)
James J. Jeffries (boxing; 1875-1953)
James Jones (US writer; 1922-77)
James (Prescott) Joule (Br. physt.; 1818-89)
James Joyce (Ir. writer; 1882-1941)
James Kirke Paulding (US writer/pol.; 1778-1860)
James Knox Polk (11th US pres.; 1795-1849)
James Laurence Cabell (US phys.; 1813-89)
James L. Brooks (ent.; 1940-)
James Lee Witt (US ex-dir./FEMA; 1944-)
James Levine (ent.; 1943-)
James L(awrence) Laughlin (US econ.; 1850-1933)
James Longstreet (US gen.; 1821-1904)
James MacArthur (ent.; 1937-)
James Madison (4th US pres.; 1751-1836)
James Madison University (Harrisburg, VA)
James Mark Baldwin (US psych.; 1861-1934)
James Mason (ent.; 1909-84)
James M. Barrie, (Sir)(Br. writer; 1860-1937)
James M(allahan) Cain (US writer; 1892-1977)
James McCracken (dramatic tenor; 1926-88)
James McDougal (Whitewater; 1940-1998)
James McGill (Can. trader/finan.; 1744-1813)
James (Abbott) McNeill Whistler (US artist; 1834-1903)
James Meredith (US writer/civil rights leader; 1923-)
James M. Inhofe (US cong.; 1934-)
James M. Jeffords (US cong.; 1934-)
James Mill (Scot. phil.; 1773-1836)
James Mitchell (ent.; 1920-)
James Mitchell, (Sir)(PM, St. Vincent/Grenadines; 1931-)
James Monroe (5th US pres.; 1758-1831)
James Montgomery Flagg (US cartoonist, Uncle Sam; 1877-1960)
James Naismith (Can., inv. basketball; 1861-1939)
James Naughton (ent.; 1945-)
James Noble (ent.; 1922-)
James (Alvin) Palmer (baseball; 1945-)
James P. Johnson (US jazz; 1891-1955)
James P(rescott) Joule (Br. physt.; 1818-89)
James P(aul) Mitchell (US bus./pol.; 1900-64)
James Ralph "Jim" Sasser (US pol.; 1936-)
James R. Doohan (Scotty on *Star Trek*)
James Renwick, Jr. (US arch.; 1818-95)
James (Barrett) "Scotty" Reston (US jour.; 1909-95)
James R(iddle) "Jimmy" Hoffa (US labor leader; 1913-75?)
James River (VA)
James River Corp.
James Rothschild (Ger./Fr. finan.; 1792-1868)
James Russell Lowell (US poet/editor; 1819-91)
James S. "Jim" Fixx (US runner; 1932-84)
James S(tuart) "Jim" Gilmore, III (VA gov.; 1949-)
James Spader (ent.; 1960-)
James S(choolcraft) Sherman (ex-US VP; 1855-1912)

James Stephens (ent.; 1951-)
James Stephens (Ir. writer; 1882-1950)
James "Jimmy" Stewart (ent.; 1908-97)
James Taylor (ent.; 1948-)
James T(homas) Farrell (US writer; 1904-79)
James Thomas Brudenell (7th Earl of Cardigan) (Br. mil./pol., cardigan sweater; 1797-1868)
James Thomson (US scien./stem cells; 1958-)
James Thomson Shotwell (Can/US hist.; 1874-1965)
James (Grover) Thurber (US writer/humorist; 1894-1961)
James T. Kirk, Capt. (fict. chara., *Star Trek*)
James Tobin (US econ.; 1918-)
James V (king, Scot.; 1512-42)
James Van Der Beek (ent.; 1977-)
James "Jimmy" Van Heusen (US comp.; 1913-90)
James V(incent) Forrestal (ex-secy., navy/defense; 1892-1949)
James VI (also James I, Eng.)(king, Scot.; 1566-1625)
James VII (also James II, Eng.)(king, Scot.; 1633-1701)
James Walter Thompson (US bus.; 1847-1928)
James Warren "Jim" Jones (US/Guyana cult leader; 1931-78)
James W. Dietz (rowing; 1949-)
James Weldon Johnson (US writer, NAACP; 1871-1938)
James Whitcomb Riley (US poet; 1849-1916)
James Whitmore (ent.; 1921-)
James Wilson Morrice (Can. artist; 1865-1924)
James Woods (ent.; 1947-)
James Woolsey, R. (US ex-dir./CIA; 1941-)
James, Court of St. (Br. royal court)
James, Dennis (ent.; 1917-97)
James, Epistle of (rel.)
James, Etta (b. Jamesetta Hawkins)(ent.; 1938-)
James, Frank (US outlaw; 1843-1915)
James, Harry (ent.; 1916-83)
James, Henry (US writer; 1843-1916)
James, Jesse (Woodson)(US outlaw; 1847-82)
James, Rick (b. James Johnson, Jr.)(ent.; 1948-)
James, Stanislaus (ex-gov.-gen., St. Lucia)
James, William (US phil./psych.; 1842-1910)
Jameson Parker (ent.; 1947-)
Jameson, (Margaret) Storm (writer; 1897-1986)
Jamestown, ND, NY, VA
Jamie Farr (b. Jameel Joseph Farah)(ent.; 1934-)
Jamie Foxx (b. Eric Bishop)(ent.; 1967-)
Jamie Lee Curtis (ent.; 1958-)
Jamieson, Bob (US jour.)
Jammeh, Colonel Yahya (pres., Gambia; 1965-)
Jammu and Kashmir (state, India)
Jan Brueghel (also Breughel)(aka the "Velvet Bruegel")(Flem. artist; 1568-1625)
Jan C(hristian) Smuts (ex-PM, SAfr.; 1870-1950)
Jan H(endrik) Oort (Dutch astron.; 1900-92)
Jan Kiepura (tenor; 1902-66)
Jan Kodes (tennis; 1946-)
Jan (Garrigue) Masaryk (Czech. pol.; 1886-1948)

Jan-Michael Vincent (ent.; 1945-)
Jan Peerce (ent.; 1904-84)
Jan (Havickszoon) Steen (Dutch artist; 1626-79)
Jan Stenerud (football; 1942-)
Jan Swammerdam (Dutch biol./nat.; 1637-80)
Jan van Eyck (Flem. artist; 1385?-1441?)
Jan Vermeer (Dutch artist; 1632-75)
J&B (scotch)
Jane Addams (US reformer; 1860-1935)
Jane Alexander (b. Jane Quigley)(ent.; 1939-)
Jane Austen (Br. writer; 1775-1817)
Jane Brody (US jour.; 1941-)
Jane Bryant Quinn (US jour./finan.; 1939-)
Jane Campion (ent./writer; 1954-)
Jane Curtin (ent.; 1947-)
Jane Dee Hull (nee Bowersock)(AZ gov.; 1935-)
Jane Doe (unidentified or "any" woman)
Jane Eyre (Charlotte Brontë novel)
Jane Fonda (ent.; 1937-)
Jane Froman (ent.; 1907-80)
Jane Goodall (Br. animal behaviorist/writer; 1934-)
Jane (Dudley) Grey, Lady (queen, Eng. [10 days]; 1537-54)
Jane (Temple) Howard (US writer; 1935-96)
Jane Jacobs (US urbanologist; 1916-)
Jane Krakowski (ent.; 1968-)
Jane Pauley, (Margaret)(US TV jour.; 1950-)
Jane Pittman, The Autobiography of Miss (film, 1974)
Jane Powell (ent.; 1928-)
Jane Russell (ent.; 1921-)
Jane Seymour (b. Joyce Frankenberg)(ent.; 1951-)
Jane Seymour (queen, Eng., 3rd wife of Henry VIII; 1509?-37)
Jane Withers (ent.; 1926-)
Jane Wyatt (ent.; 1912-)
Jane Wyman (b. Sarah Jane Fulks)(ent.; 1914-)
Jane, Calamity (b. Martha Jane Burke)(US frontier heroine; c1852-1903)
Jane, GI (US female soldier)
Jane?, Whatever Happened to Baby (film, 1962)
Janeane Garofalo (ent.; 1964-)
Janesville, WI
Janet Dailey (US writer; 1944-)
Janet D. Steiger (US ex-chair/FTC; 1939-)
Janet Gaynor (ent.; 1906-84)
Janet Jackson (ent.; 1966-)
Janet Leigh (b. Jeannette Helen Morrison)(ent.; 1927-)
Janet Lynn (figure skating; 1953-)
Janet Margolin (ent.; 1943-)
Janet McTeer (ent.; 1961-)
Janet Reno (US ex-atty. gen.; 1938-)
Janeway, Eliot (US econ.; 1913-93)
Janeway, Elizabeth (US writer; 1913-)
Janez Drnovsek (ex-PM, Slovenia; 1950-)
Janice Merrill (track; 1962-)
Jani-King International, Inc.
Janine Turner (ent.; 1962-)
Janis Ian (b. Janis Fink)(ent.; 1951-)
Janis Joplin (ent.; 1943-70)
Janis Paige (ent.; 1922-)

Janis, Byron (US pianist; 1928-)
Janis, Conrad (ent.; 1928-)
Janklow, William "Bill" J(ohn)(SD gov.; 1939-)
Jann Wenner (US publ., *Rolling Stone*; 1946-)
János Kádár, (ex-PM, Hung.; 1912-89)
Jansenism (rel.)
Janson (type style)
Janssen, David (ent.; 1930-80)
J. Anthony Lukas (US writer; 1932-97)
Janus (astron., myth.)
Janus Book Publishers (US bus.)
Janus-faced (two-faced)
Japan (also Nippon)(NE Asia)
Japan Airlines
Japan, Sea of (Jap./Pac.)
Japanese (lang./people)
Japanese bantam (chicken)
Japanese beetle (insect)
Japanese Chin (formerly Japanese spaniel)(dog)
Japanese creeper (plant)
Japanese fleeceflower (plant)
Japanese garden
Japanese knotweed (also Mexican bamboo) (plant)
Japanese lawn grass (also Korean lawn grass)
Japanese spaniel (now Japanese Chin)(dog)
Japanese War(s), Sino- (Jap./Ch.; 1894-95, 1931-45)
Japanese War, Russo- (Rus./Jap.; 1904-05)
Japanese wisteria (plant)
Japlish (linguistics)
Jared Leto (ent.; 1971-)
Jared Sparks (US hist./educ.; 1789-1866)
J. Arlen Specter (US cong.; 1930-)
Jarlsberg (cheese)
Jaroslav Seifert (Czech. poet; 1902-86)
Jarreau, Al (ent.; 1940-)
Jarrett, Keith (US jazz; 1945-)
Jarriel, Tom (TV jour.; 1934-)
Jaruzelski, Wojceich (ex-pres., Pol.; 1923-)
Jarvis Cocker (ent./songwriter; 1963-)
Jascha Heifetz (Rus./US violinist; 1901-87)
Jasmine Guy (ent.; 1964-)
Jason (myth.)
Jason Alexander (b. Jay Scott Greenspan)(ent.; 1959-)
Jason and the Argonauts (film, 1963)
Jason Bateman (ent.; 1969-)
Jason (John) Miller (US playwright/ent.; 1939-)
Jason Patric (ent.; 1966-)
Jason Priestley (ent.; 1969-)
Jason Robards, Jr. (ent.; 1922-2000)
Jason Robards, Sr. (ent.; 1892-1963)
Jasper Johns (US artist; 1930-)
Jaspers, Karl (Ger. phil.; 1883-1969)
Jasray, Puntsagiyn (ex-PM, Mongolia)
Jat (people)
Jataka (rel.)
Java man (fossil remains of *Homo erectus*)
Java, Indonesia
Javanese (lang./people)
Javier Pérez de Cuéllar (Peruvian/UN dipl.; 1920-)
Javits, Jacob (US pol.; 1904-86)
Jawaharlal Nehru (ex-PM, India; 1889-1964)

Jawara, (Sir) Dawda Kairaba (ex-pres., Gambia; 1924-)
Jaworski, Leon (US atty.; 1905-82)
Jaws (P. Benchley novel, film, 1975)
Jaws of Life (auto.)
Jay and the Americans (pop music)
Jay C. Flippen (ent. 1900-71)
Jay Cook (US finan.; 1821-1905)
Jay Gatsby (fict. chara., *The Great Gatsby*)
Jay Gould (US finan., railroad; 1836-92)
Jay Leno (ent.; 1950-)
Jay McInerney (US writer; 1955-)
Jay Mohr (ent.; 1971-)
Jay N. Darling ("Ding")(pol. cartoonist; 1876-1962)
Jay (John Davison) Rockefeller, IV (US cong.; 1937-)
Jay Sandrich (ent.; 1932-)
Jay Silverheels (b. Harry Jay Smith)(ent.; 1919-80)
Jay Silvester (discus thrower; 1937-)
Jay Thomas (ent.; 1948-)
Jay, John (US jurist/dipl.; 1745-1829)
Jay's Treaty (US/Eng.; 1795)
Jaycees (Junior Chambers of Commerce members)
Jayhawker State (KS)
Jaymes, Bartles & (wine coolers)
Jayne Kennedy-Overton (ent.; 1951-)
Jayne Mansfield (ent.; 1932-67)
Jayne Meadows (b. Jayne Cotter)(ent.; 1920-)
Jayne Torvill (figure skating; 1957-)
Jay-Z (b. Shawn Carter)(ent.; 1970-)
Jazz, Utah (basketball team)
Jazzercise (US bus.)
Jazzy Jeff & the Fresh Prince, D.J. (pop music)
J. Bennett, Johnston, Jr. (US pol.; 1932-)
J(ohn) B(oynton) Priestley (Br. writer; 1894-1984)
JC (Jesus Christ)
J. Carroll Naish (ent.; 1900-73)
J. C. (Joshua Scott) Chasez (ent., 'N Sync; 1976-)
JC Penney (stores)
J. C. Penney Co.
J(ohn) Craig Venter (US genet./human genome; 1946-)
JD (Justice Department, Doctor of Jurisprudence, juvenile delinquent)
J(ames) Danforth "Dan" Quayle III (ex-VP, US; 1947-)
JDL (Jewish Defense League)
J(erome) D(avid) Salinger (US writer; 1919-)
Jean Alingue Bawoyeu (ex-PM, Chad)
Jean Ann Smith (nee Kennedy)(US dipl., sister of ex-pres.; 1928-)
Jean Anouilh (Fr. playwright; 1910-87)
Jean Antoine Watteau (Fr. artist; 1684-1721)
Jean (or Hans) Arp (Fr. artist; 1887-1966)
Jean Arthur (ent.; 1900-91)
Jean Auguste Dominique Ingres (Fr. artist; 1780-1867)
Jean Ausseil (Monacan pol.)
Jean-Baptiste-Camille Corot (Fr. artist; 1796-1875)
Jean Baptiste Colbert (Fr. pol.; 1619-83)

Jean-Baptiste Greuze (Fr. artist; 1725-1805)
Jean Baptiste Le Moyne Bienville (Fr. colonial administrator; 1680-1768)
Jean Baptiste Lully (Fr. comp.; 1639-87)
Jean Baptiste Molière (Fr. writer; 1622-73)
Jean Baptiste Ouedraogo (ex-pres., Upper Volta; 1932-)
Jean-Baptiste-Siméon Chardin (Fr. artist; 1699-1779)
Jean Beliveau (hockey; 1931-)
Jean-Bertrand Aristide (deposed pres., Haiti; 1953-)
Jean B(aptiste) J(oseph) Fourier (Fr. math.; 1768-1830)
Jean B(aptiste) Lamarck (Fr. nat.; 1744-1829)
Jean Brodie, The Prime of Miss (film, 1969)
Jean Bugatti (It. designer; 1909-39)
Jean (Anne) Carnahan (US cong.; 1933-)
Jean Chretién, (Joseph Jacques)(PM, Can.; 1934-)
Jean-Claude Duvalier (aka Baby Doc)(ex-pres., Haiti; 1951-)
Jean-Claude Juncker (PM, Luxembourg; 1954-)
Jean-Claude Killy (Fr. skier; 1943-)
Jean-Claude Van Damme (b. Jean-Claude Van Varenberg)(ent.; 1960-)
Jean Cocteau (Fr. writer/artist; 1889-1963)
Jean de la Fontaine (Fr. poet; 1621-95)
Jean Dubuffet (Fr. artist; 1902-85)
Jean Félix Piccard (Swiss chem./eng.; 1884-1963)
Jean François Champollion (Fr. archaeol.; 1790-1832)
Jean François Millet (Fr. artist; 1814-75)
Jean-François Ntoutoume-Emane (PM, Gabon; 1939-)
Jean Gabin (ent.; 1904-76)
Jean Genet (Fr. writer; 1911-1986)
Jean Giraudoux (Fr. writer/dipl.; 1882-1944)
Jean Harlow (b. Harlean Carpenter)(ent.; 1911-37)
Jean (Struven) Harris (US educ., shot Dr. H. Tarnower)
Jean Hersholt (ent.; 1886-1956)
Jean Honore Fragonard (Fr. artist; 1732-1806)
Jean (Eugène Robert) Houdin (Fr. magician; 1805-71)
Jean-Jacques Beineix (ent.; 1946-)
Jean-Jacques Honorat (ex-PM, Haiti)
Jean Jacques Rousseau (Fr. phil./writer; 1712-78)
Jean Kerr (US writer; 1923-)
Jean Laffite National Historical Park (LA)
Jean Lafitte (or Laffite)(Fr. mil./pirate; c1780-c1825)
Jean Louis Rodolphe Agassiz (Swiss nat.; 1807-73)
Jean-Luc Dehaene (PM, Belgium; 1940-)
Jean-Luc Godard (Fr. ent.; 1930-)
Jean-Luc Picard, Capt. (fict. chara., *Star Trek*)
Jean-Marie Le Pen (Fr. pol.; 1928-)
Jean Marsh (ent.; 1934-)
Jean M. Auel (US writer; 1936-)
Jean M. Charcot (Fr. phys.; 1825-93)
Jean Naté (toiletries)
Jean Naté, Inc.

Jean Parker (ent.; 1912-)
Jean-Paul Belmondo (Fr. ent.; 1933-)
Jean Paul Marat (Fr. pol.; 1743-93)
Jean Paul Riopelle (Can. artist; 1923-)
Jean-Paul Sartre (Fr. phil./writer; 1905-80)
Jean Peters (ent.; 1926-)
Jean Philippe Rameau (Fr. comp.; 1683-1764)
Jean Picard (Fr. astron.; 1620-82)
Jean-Pierre Aumont (Fr. ent.; 1909-)
Jean Pierre Chouteau (US pioneer/fur trader;
    1758-1849)
Jean-Pierre Rampal (Fr. flutist; 1922-2000)
Jean (Baptiste) Racine (Fr. writer; 1639-99)
Jean Ratelle, (Joseph Gilbert Yvon)(hockey;
    1953-)
Jean Renoir (Fr. ent./writer; 1894-1979)
Jean R. Yawkey (US bus./baseball; 1908-92)
Jean Seberg (ent.; 1938-79)
Jean (Julius Christian) Sibelius (Fin. comp.;
    1865-1957)
Jean Simmons (ent.; 1929-)
Jean Stapleton (b. Jeanne Murray)(ent.; 1923-)
Jean Valjean (fict. chara., *Les Miserables*)
Jean, Grand Duke (ex-pres., Luxembourg; 1921-)
Jean, Inc., Chateau St.
Jean, Wyclef (ent.; 1969-)
Jeane (Pinckert) Dixon (US psychic/writer;
    1918-97)
Jeane (Jordan) Kirkpatrick (US pol./dipl.; 1926-)
Jeanette MacDonald (ent.; 1903-65)
Jeanne Antoinette Poisson Le Normant d'Étioles
    (Marquise de Pompadour)(mistress of Louis
    XV, Fr.; 1721-64)
Jeanne Bécu du Barry, Madame (Comtesse,
    mistress, Louis XV; 1743-93)
Jeanne Crain (ent.; 1925-)
Jeanne d'Arc (also St. Joan of Arc, Maid of
    Orléans)(Fr. rel./mil.; 1412?-31)
Jeanne Moreau (ent.; 1928-)
Jeanne Shaheen, (Cynthia)(NH gov.; 1947-)
Jeanneret, Charles Édouard (aka Le
    Corbusier)(Fr. arch./artist; 1887-1965)
Jeannette Rankin (US pol.; 1880-1973)
Jeannie C. Riley (ent.; 1945-)
Jeannie, I Dream of (TV show)
Jeb (John Ellis) Bush (US FL gov., bro. of pres./
    son of ex-pres.; 1953-)
J(ames) E(well) B(rown) Stuart (US mil.; 1833-
    64)
Jeb Stuart Magruder (US pol./Watergate; 1934-)
Jed Clampett (fict. chara.)
Jedi, Return of the (film, 1983)
Jeep (auto)
Jeep Cherokee (auto.)
Jeep Cherokee Classic
Jeep Cherokee Country
Jeep Cherokee KJ
Jeep Cherokee Limited
Jeep Cherokee SE (auto.)
Jeep Cherokee Sport
Jeep Grand Cherokee (auto.)
Jeep Grand Cherokee Laredo (auto.)
Jeep Grand Cherokee Limited (auto.)
Jeep Grand Cherokee Tsi (auto.)
Jeep Wrangler (auto.)

Jeep Wrangler Sahara (auto.)
Jeep Wrangler SE (auto.)
Jeep Wrangler Sport (auto.)
Jeeves, Ask (compu.)
Jeeves, the butler (fict. chara.)
Jeff & the Fresh Prince, D.J. Jazzy (pop music)
Jeff(rey Preston) Bezos (US bus./Amazon.com;
    1964-)
Jeff Bingaman (US cong.; 1943-)
Jeff Bridges (ent.; 1949-)
Jeff Buckley (ent./songwriter; 1966-97)
Jeff Chandler (ent.; 1918-61)
Jeff Corey (ent.; 1914-)
Jeff Daniels (ent.; 1955-)
Jeff Foxworthy (ent.; 1958-)
Jeff Gillooly (US news)
Jeff Goldblum (ent.; 1952-)
Jeff Gordon (auto racing; 1971-)
Jeff MacNelly (cartoonist, *Shoe*; 1947-2000)
Jeff Sessions (US cong.; 1946-)
Jeff Smith (US chef/writer; 1939-)
Jeff, Mutt & (comic strip)
Jeffers, (John) Robinson (US writer; 1887-1962)
Jefferson Airplane (pop music)
Jefferson City, MO
Jefferson Davis (US pol./confederate pres.;
    1808-89)
Jefferson Memorial, (Thomas)(DC)
Jefferson Starship (pop music)
Jefferson, Blind Lemon (US jazz; 1897-1930)
Jefferson, Thomas (3rd US pres.; 1743-1826)
Jeffersons, The (TV show)
Jeffires, Haywood (football; 1964-)
Jeffords, James M. (US cong.; 1934-)
Jeffrey Amherst, Baron (Br. gen.; 1717-97)
Jeffrey Dahmer (US serial killer; 1960-94)
Jeffrey D. Sachs (US econ./educ.; 1954-)
Jeffrey Katzenberg (US bus.; 1950-)
Jeffrey Lynn (ent.; 1909-95)
Jeffreys, Alec John (Br. geneticist; 1950-)
Jeffreys, Anne (ent.; 1923-)
Jeffries, James J. (boxing; 1875-1953)
Jeffries, Lionel (ent.; 1926-)
J(ohn) Edgar Hoover (ex-dir., FBI; 1895-1972)
Jehoshaphat (king, Judah; ?-851? BC)
Jehoshaphat, jumping
Jehovah (also Jahweh, God)
Jehovah's Witnesses (rel.)
Jehovah's Witnesses, Kingdom Hall of
Jekyll and Hyde (dual personality, one good/
    one evil)
Jekyll and Mr. Hyde, The Strange Case of Dr.
    (by R.L. Stevenson)
Jelavic, Ante (Bosnia-Hercegovina/Bosnian
    Croat pol.)
Jelgava, Latvia
Jell-O
Jelly Roll Morton (b. Ferdinand Joseph La
    Menthe)(US jazz; 1885-1941)
Jellystone Park Camp-Resort, Yogi Bear's (US
    bus.)
Jemima Puddleduck
Jemison, Mae C. (US astro./phys.; 1956-)
Jenkin's Ear, War of (Br./Sp.; 1739-41)
Jenkins' Art Workshop (TV show)

Jenkins, Fergusin Arthur (baseball; 1943-)
Jenkins, Snuffy (DeWitt)(ent.; 1908-90)
Jenn-Air (appliances)
Jenn-Air Corp.
Jenna (Welch) Bush (US daughter of pres./
  granddaughter of ex-pres.; 1981-)
Jenna Elfman (b. Jennifer Butala)(ent.; 1971-)
Jenner, Bruce (US track/TV jour.; 1949-)
Jenner, Edward (Br. phys., smallpox vaccine;
  1749-1823)
Jenner, William (Br. phys.; 1815-98)
Jennie Churchill (mother of Winston; 1854-
  1921)
Jennie Garth (ent.; 1972-)
Jennifer Aniston (b. Jennifer
  Anistonapoulos)(ent.; 1969-)
Jennifer Beals (ent.; 1963-)
Jennifer Capriati (tennis; 1976-)
Jennifer Grey (ent.; 1960-)
Jennifer Jason Leigh (b. Jennifer Leigh Morrow)
  (ent.; 1962-)
Jennifer Jones (b. Phyllis Isley)(ent.; 1919-)
Jennifer Lopez (ent.; 1970-)
Jennifer Love Hewitt (ent.; 1979-)
Jennifer O'Neal (ent.; 1948-)
Jennifer Smith (premier, Bermuda)
Jennifer Warnes (ent.; 1947-)
Jennings, Peter (US TV jour.; 1938-)
Jennings, Waylon (ent.; 1937-)
Jenny Craig Weight Loss Centers (US bus.)
Jenny Lind (Johanna Maria Lind Goldschmidt,
  "The Swedish Nightingale")(ent.; 1820-87)
Jeno's pizza
Jeno's, Inc.
Jens Stoltenberg (PM, Nor.; 1959-)
Jeopardy (TV show)
Jeremiah (rel., book of the Old Testament)
Jeremiah (Hebrew prophet; 7th-6th c. BC)
Jeremy Bentham (Br. jurist/phil./social
  reformer; 1748-1832)
Jeremy Irons (ent.; 1948-)
Jergens (skin care)
Jergens Co., The Andrew
Jeri Ryan (b. Jeri Lynn Zimmerman)(ent.; 1968-)
Jericho, Jordan (ancient walled city)
Jericho, NY
Jericho, rose of (plant)
Jermaine Jackson (ent.; 1954-)
Jeroboam I (king, Isr.; ?-912? BC)
Jeroboam II (king, Isr.; ?-744? BC)
Jerome Bonaparte (bro. of Napoleon, king,
  Westphalia; 1784-1860)
Jerome (David) Kern (US comp.; 1885-1945)
Jerome Robbins (US ballet; 1918-98)
Jerry Bock (US comp.; 1928-)
Jerry (Edmund Gerald) Brown, Jr. (ex-CA gov.;
  1938-)
Jerry Clower (ent.; 1926-98)
Jerry Colonna (ent.; 1905-86)
Jerry Falwell, Rev. (US rel.; 1933-)
Jerry Garcia (ent.; 1942-95)
Jerry Hall (model; 1956-)
Jerry Kramer (football; 1936-)
Jerry Lee Lewis (ent.; 1935-)
Jerry Leiber (US comp.; 1933-)

Jerry (Gerald M.) Levin (US bus./AOL Time
  Warner)
Jerry Lewis (b. Joseph Levitch)(ent.; 1926-)
Jerry Martin Koosman (baseball; 1942-)
Jerry Mathers (ent.; 1948-)
Jerry Maguire (film, 1996)
Jerry Orbach (ent.; 1935-)
Jerry (John) Rawlings (pres., Ghana; 1947-)
Jerry Reed (ent.; 1937-)
Jerry Rice (football; 1962-)
Jerry Seinfeld (ent.; 1954-)
Jerry Siegel (cartoonist, *Superman*; 1914-96)
Jerry (Gerald) Springer (ent./pol.; 1944-)
Jerry Stiller (ent.; 1929-)
Jerry Vale (b. Genaro Louis Vitaliano)(ent.; 1932-)
Jerry Van Dyke (ent.; 1931-)
Jerry West (basketball; 1938-)
Jerry, Tom and (cartoon)
Jerry, Tom and (cocktail)
Jerry's Homemade, Inc., Ben &
Jersey (cattle)
Jersey (island, English Channel)
Jersey City, NJ
Jersey Giant (chicken)
Jersey Joe Walcott (b. Arnold Raymond Cream)
  (boxing; 1914-94)
Jerusalem artichoke (plant)
Jerusalem, Church of the New (also
  Swedenborgians)
Jerusalem, Israel
Jerusalem, Temple of (rel.)
Jerzy (Nikodem) Kosinski (or Kozinski)(Pol./US
  writer; 1933-91)
Jerzy Buzek (PM, Pol.; 1940-)
Jessamyn West (US writer; 1903-84)
Jesse Alexander Helms (US cong.; 1921-)
Jesse Applegate (US pioneer/pol.; 1811-88)
Jesse Brown (US ex-secy./vet. affairs; 1944-)
Jesse (Woodson) James (US outlaw; 1847-82)
Jesse L(ouis) Jackson, Jr. (US cong.; 1965-)
Jesse L(ouis) Jackson, Sr. (US rel./pol./civil
  rights activist; 1941-)
Jesse (James Cleveland) Owens (track; 1913-
  80)
Jesse Ventura (b. James George Janos)(MN
  gov.; 1951-)
Jesse White (ent.; 1919-97)
Jessel, George (ent.; 1898-1981)
Jessica Biel (ent./model; 1982-)
Jessica Fletcher (fict. chara., *Murder, She Wrote*)
Jessica Hahn (US news)
Jessica Harper (ent.; 1949-)
Jessica Lange (ent.; 1949-)
Jessica (Beth) Savitch (US TV jour.; 1947-83)
Jessica Simpson (ent.; 1980-)
Jessica Tandy (ent.; 1909-94)
Jessica Walter (ent.; 1944-)
Jessica, Baby (US news)
Jessup, Philip C. (US dipl.; 1897-1986)
Jessye Norman (ent.; 1945-)
Jesuit (also Society of Christ)(rel.)
Jesus Christ (also Jesus, Christ Jesus, Jesus of
  Nazareth)(known as Jeshua ben Joseph to
  contemporaries)
Jesus Christ, Superstar (play; film, 1973)

Jesus Christ, Vicar of (pope)
Jesus freak
Jet (mag.)
Jet Li (b. Li Lian-jie)(ent./martial arts; 1963-)
Jet Propulsion Laboratory (JPL)(NASA
    installation; Pasadena, CA)
Jethro Clampett (fict. chara.)
Jethro Tull (Br. agr.; 1674-1741)
Jethro Tull (pop music)
Jets, New York (football team)
Jets, Winnipeg (hockey team)
Jetsons, The (cartoon)
Jett, Joan (b. Joan Larkin)(ent.; 1960-)
Jetta, Volkswagen (auto.)
Jew (people)
Jew's harp (music)
Jewel (b. Jewel Kilcher)(ent.; 1974-)
Jewish (people, rel.)
Jewish calendar (also Hebrew calendar)
Jewison, Norman (ent.; 1926-)
Jewry (Jewish people)
Jews, National Conference of Christians and
    (est. 1928)
Jezebel (film, 1938)
Jezebel (rel.)
Jezek, Linda (swimming; 1960-)
Jezreel, Plain of (also Esdraelon Plain)(Isr.)
J. F. Kennedy International Airport (NY)
J. Fred Muggs (TV chimp; c1952)
J(ames) G(raham) Ballard (Br. writer; 1930-)
J(erome) Geils (ent.; 1946-)
J. Gimbel, Inc.
Jheri Redding Products, Inc.
J. Higby's Yogurt & Treat Shoppe (US bus.)
Jhirmack (hair care)
Jiang Ching (also Madame Mao, Chiang Ching,
    Jiang Qing, Lan Ping)(Ch. pol./ent., wife of
    Chairman Mao; 1914-91)
Jiang Zemin (pres., Ch.; 1926-)
Jiangsu (also Kiangsu)(province, Ch.)
Jiangxi (also Kiangsi)(province, Ch.)
Jidd Hafs, Bahrain
Jiddah, Saudi Arabia (also Jidda)
Jif peanut butter
Jiffy Lube (US bus.)
Jiggs, Maggie and (comic strip)
Jigme Singye Wangchuk (king, Bhutan; 1955-)
Jilin (also Kirin)(province, Ch.)
Jill Clayburgh (ent.; 1944-)
Jill Eikenberry (ent.; 1947-)
Jill Haworth (ent.; 1945-)
Jill Ireland (ent.; 1936-90)
Jill St. John (b. Jill Oppenheim)(ent.; 1940-)
Jill Trenary (figure skating; 1968-)
Jill, Jack and (nursery rhyme)
Jillian, Ann (b. Ann Nauseda)(ent.; 1950-)
Jillie Mack (ent.; 1957-)
Jim Backus (ent.; 1913-89)
Jim (James Leroy) Bakken (football; 1940-)
Jim (James Orsen) Bakker (US evang.; 1940-)
Jim Beam Brands Co.
Jim (James) Belushi (ent.; 1954-)
Jim Berry (cartoonist, *Berry's World*; 1932-)
Jim (James Brendan) Bolger (ex-PM, NewZeal.;
    1935-)

Jim (James) Bowie (US frontier; 1796-1836)
Jim (James S.) Brady (US gun control
    advocate/Brady Bill; 1940-)
Jim Brady, Diamond (US finan.; 1856-1917)
Jim Bunning (US cong.; 1931-)
Jim Carrey (ent.; 1962-)
Jim Croce (ent.; 1942-73)
Jim Crow (racial discrimination)(also l.c.)
Jim Crow laws (US hist., pro-segregation; pre-
    1960's)
Jim Davis (cartoonist, *Garfield*; 1945-)
Jim Demaret (golf; 1910-83)
Jim Dine (US artist; 1935-)
Jim (James) Edgar (ex-IL gov.; 1946-)
Jim (James S.) Fixx (US runner)
Jim (James Joseph) Florio (ex-NJ gov.; 1937-)
Jim Garrison (US atty.; 1922-92)
Jim (James) Geringer (WY gov.; 1944-)
Jim (James Stuart) Gilmore, III (VA gov.; 1949-)
Jim (James) Guy Tucker, Jr. (ex-AR gov.; 1943-)
Jim (James Maury) Henson (US puppeteer/
    Muppets; 1936-90)
Jim (James Hovis) Hodges (SC gov.; 1956-)
Jim (James Warren) Jones (US/Guyana cult
    leader; 1931-78)
Jim Kaat (baseball; 1938-)
Jim Lee Howell (football; 1915-95)
Jim Lehrer (US news jour.; 1934-)
Jim McKay (sportscaster; 1921-)
Jim Messina (ent.; 1947-)
Jim Montgomery (swimming; 1955-)
Jim Morrison (ent.; 1943-71)
Jim Nabors (ent.; 1932-)
Jim Nance (football; 1943-92)
Jim Palmer (baseball; 1945-)
Jim Perry (baseball; 1936-)
Jim Plunkett (football; 1947-)
Jim Reeves, "Gentleman" (ent.; 1923-64)
Jim Rice (baseball; 1953-)
Jim Ryun (James Ronald)(runner; 1947-)
Jim (James Ralph) Sasser (US pol.; 1936-)
Jim Stafford (ent.; 1944-)
Jim (James Francis) Thorpe (Olympics; 1888-
    1953)
Jim Walter Corp.
Jim, Jungle (comic strip)
Jim, Lord (J. Conrad novel)
Jima, Iwo (island, W Pac.)
Jimi (James Marshall) Hendrix (ent.; 1942-70)
Jimmie Lunceford (US jazz; 1902-47)
Jimmie (James Charles) Rodgers (ent./
    songwriter; 1897-1933)
Jimmy Blanton (US jazz; 1921-42)
Jimmy Breslin (US writer; 1930-)
Jimmy Brown (James Nathaniel)(football/ent.;
    1936-)
Jimmy Buffett (ent./songwriter; 1946-)
Jimmy (James Earl) Carter, Jr. (39th US pres.;
    1924-)
Jimmy Cliff (b. Jimmy Chambers)(ent./
    songwriter; 1949-)
Jimmy Connors (James Scott)(tennis; 1952-)
Jimmy Dean (ent.; 1928-)
Jimmy Dean (sausage)
Jimmy Dean Meat Co.

Jimmy Dickens, Little (ent.; 1920-)
Jimmy Dorsey (US cond.; 1904-57)
Jimmy (James Francis) Durante (ent.; 1893-
    1980)
Jimmy (James Emory) Foxx (baseball; 1907-67)
Jimmy Hatlo (US cartoonist, *Little Iodine*;
    1898-1963)
Jimmy Hoffa (James Riddle)(US labor leader;
    1913-75?)
Jimmy McHugh (US comp.; 1894-1969)
Jimmy McPartland (US jazz; 1907-91)
Jimmy Page (ent.; 1944-)
Jimmy Rodgers (ent.; 1933-)
Jimmy Smits (ent.; 1955-)
Jimmy "the Greek" Snyder (oddsmaker; 1919-
    96)
Jimmy (James) Stewart (ent.; 1908-97)
Jimmy Swaggart, Rev. (US rel.; 1935-)
Jimmy (James) Van Heusen (US comp.; 1913-
    90)
Jimmy (James John) Walker (ex-mayor, NYC;
    1881-1946)
Jimmy Webb (US comp.; 1946-)
Jimmy Yancey (US jazz; 1894-1951)
Jimmy, GMC (auto.)
Jinja, Uganda
Jinnah, Muhammad Ali (India/Pak. pol.; 1876-
    1948)
Jinsha Jiang River (Ch.)
Jinx (Eugenia) Falkenburg (ent.; 1919-)
Jivaro (lang./people)
J. James Exon (US pol.; 1921-)
J. J. Johnson (US jazz; 1924-)
J(oseph) J(ohn) Thomson, (Sir)(Br. physt.;
    1856-1940)
J(ames) J(oseph Jacques) Tissot (Fr. artist;
    1836-1902)
J(oanne) K(athleen) Rowling (writer; 1965-)
J. L. Plum (clothing)
J. Lohr Winery (US bus.)
J. M. Saleh (gov., Netherlands Antilles)
J. M. Smucker Co., The
J(oseph) M(allord) W(illiam) Turner (Br. artist;
    1774-1851)
Jo Anne Worley (ent.; 1937-)
Jo Jones (US jazz; 1911-85)
Jo Stafford (ent.; 1918-)
Jo Van Fleet (ent.; 1919-96)
Joachim Murat (king, Naples; 1767-1815)
Joachim von Ribbentrop (Ger. Nazi pol.; 1893-
    1946)
Joachim Yhombi-Opango, Jacques- (ex-PM,
    Congo; 1940-)
Joan Aiken (US writer; 1924-)
Joan Allen (ent.; 1956-)
Joan Armatrading (ent.; 1950-)
Joan Baez (ent.; 1941-)
Joan Bennett (ent.; 1910-90)
Joan Benoit Samuelson (Olympic marathon;
    1957-)
Joan Blondell (ent.; 1909-79)
Joan Caulfield (ent.; 1922-91)
Joan Collins (ent.; 1933-)
Joan Crawford (ent.; 1908-77)
Joan Cusack (ent.; 1962-)

Joan Didion (US writer; 1934-)
Joan (Marie) Finney (nee McInroy)(ex-KS gov.;
    1925-)
Joan Fontaine (b. Joan de Beauvoir de
    Havilland)(ent.; 1917-)
Joan Ganz Cooney (ent.; 1929-)
Joan Jett (b. Joan Larkin)(ent.; 1960-)
Joan Leslie (ent.; 1925-)
Joan Lunden (US TV jour.; 1950-)
Joan Miró (Sp. artist; 1893-1983)
Joan of Arc, St. (also Jeanne d'Arc, Maid of
    Orléans)(Fr. rel./mil.; 1412?-31)
Joan Plowright (ent.; 1929-)
Joan Rivers (ent.; 1933-)
Joan Sutherland (opera; 1926-)
Joan Van Ark (ent.; 1943-)
Joan, Darby and (fict. happy, elderly, married
    couple)
Joan, Pope (card game)
Joanna Cassidy (ent.; 1944-)
Joanna Gleason (ent.; 1950-)
Joanna Kerns (b. Joanna De Varona)(ent.; 1953-)
Joanne Dru (ent.; 1923-96)
Joanne Gunderson Carner (golf; 1939-)
Joanne Woodward (ent.; 1930-)
João Bernardo Vieira (ex-pres., Guinea-Bissau;
    1939-)
Joaquim Alberto Chissano (pres., Mozambique;
    1939-)
Joaquin Phoenix (b. Joaquin Rafael
    Bottom)(ent.; 1974-)
Joaquín Ricardo Balaguer (ex-pres., Dom Rep.;
    1907-)
Job (aka Book of Job)(rel., book of the Old
    Testament)
Job Corps
Job's-tears (grass)
JoBeth Williams (ent.; 1948-)
Jobs, Steve(n)(US bus./Apple; 1955-)
Jocasta (myth.)
Jock Scot (or Scott)(fishing)
Jockey International, Inc.
Jockey shorts (underwear)
Jodhpur, India (also Marwar)
Jodie Foster (ent.; 1962-)
Jody Watley (ent.; 1959-)
Joe Barbera (cartoonist, *Tom & Jerry, Huckleberry
    Hound, Yogi Bear, Flintstones*; 1911-)
Joe Besser (ent.; 1907-88)
Joe Blow (also Joe Doakes)(average guy)
Joe (Charles Joseph) Clark (ex-PM, Can.; 1939-)
Joe (John Robert) Cocker (ent.; 1944-)
Joe College (average college student)
Joe Cronin (baseball exec.; 1906-84)
Joe DeRita (b. Joseph Wardell)(ent.; 1909-93)
Joe DiMaggio (baseball; 1914-99)
Joe Doakes (also Joe Blow)(average guy)
Joe Don Baker (ent.; 1936-)
Joe E. Brown (ent.; 1892-1973)
Joe E. Lewis (ent.; 1902-71)
Joe Eszterhas (ent./writer; 1944-)
Joe Franklin (ent.; 1929-)
Joe Frazier (boxing; 1944-)
Joe Garagiola (ent.; 1926-)
Joe Greene, "Mean" (football; 1946-)

Joe Howard (ent.; 1867-1961)
Joe Isuzu (fict. chara.)
Joe Jackson (ent./songwriter; 1955-)
Joe Jones, Philly (US jazz; 1923-85)
Joe Klein (US writer/*Primary Colors*)
Joe Louis (b. Joseph Louis Barrow)(boxing; 1914-81)
Joe Mantegna (ent.; 1947-)
Joe (Joseph Vincent) McCarthy (baseball; 1887-1978)
Joe McIntyre (ent.; 1972-)
Joe Miller (familiar joke/book of jokes)
Joe Montana (football; 1956-)
Joe (Leonard) Morgan (baseball; 1943-)
Joe Morton (ent.; 1947-)
Joe (Joseph William) Namath ("Broadway Joe")(football; 1943-)
Joe Palooka (comic strip)
Joe Pass (b. Joseph Anthony Passalaqua)(US jazz; 1929-94)
Joe Pesci (ent.; 1943-)
Joe P. Estrada Winery (US bus.)
Joe Piscopo (ent.; 1951-)
Joe Sewell (baseball; 1898-1990)
Joe Shuster (cartoonist, *Superman*; 1914-92)
Joe Slovo (b. Yossel Mashel)(SAfr. pol.; 1926-95)
Joe Spano (ent.; 1946-)
Joe Theismann (football; 1946-)
Joe Turner, Big (ent.; 1911-85)
Joe Tynan, The Seduction of (film, 1979)
Joe Venuti (US jazz; 1904-78)
Joe Walcott, Jersey (b. Arnold Raymond Cream)(boxing; 1914-94)
Joe Walsh (ent.; 1947-)
Joe Williams (b. Joseph Goreed)(ent.; 1918-99)
Joe, Broadway (aka Joe [Joseph William] Namath)(football; 1943-)
Joe, GI (US male soldier)
Joel (rel., book of the Old Testament)
Joel Chandler Harris (US writer; 1848-1908)
Joel Coen (ent.; 1955-)
Joel Grey (b. Joel Katz)(ent.; 1932-)
Joel Klein (US atty., DOJ/antitrust; 1946-)
Joel McCrea (ent.; 1905-90)
Joel Schumacher (ent./writer; 1939-)
Joel, Billy (ent.; 1949-)
Joely Fisher (ent.; 1967-)
Joey Adams (ent.; 1911-99)
Joey Bishop (b. Joseph Abraham Gottlieb)(ent.; 1918-)
Joey Buttafuoco (US news; 1956-)
Joey Fatone (ent., 'N Sync; 1977-)
Joey Heatherton (ent.; 1944-)
Joey, Pal (film, 1957)
Joffre, Joseph (Jacques Césaire)(Fr. mil.; 1852-1931)
Joffrey Ballet
Joffrey, Robert (Abdullah Jaffa Bey Khan)(US ballet; 1930-88)
Johan Cruyff (soccer; 1947-)
Johann Ambrosia Bach (Ger. musician, father of J.S.; 1645-95)
Johann Amos Comenius (Czech. educ. reformer; 1592-1670)

Johann August Brinell (Swed. eng.; 1849-1925)
Johann (Jakob) Balmer (Swiss math./physt.; 1825-98)
Johann Bernoulli (Swiss math./scien.; 1667-1748)
Johann Christian Bach (Ger. comp., son of J.S.; 1735-82)
Johann Christoph Friedrich Bach (Ger. comp., bro. of J.S.; 1732-95)
Johann David Wyss (Swiss writer; 1743-1818)
Johann Elert Bode (Ger. astron.; 1747-1826)
Johann Faust (also Faustus)(Ger. fortuneteller/magician; 1480?-1540?)
Johann Fichte (Ger. phil.; 1762-1814)
Johann Gutenberg (Ger. printer; c1400-68)
Johann Pachelbel (Ger. comp.; 1653-1706)
Johann Pestalozzi (Swiss educ. reformer; 1746-1827)
Johann Rudolf Wyss (Swiss writer; 1782-1830)
Johann Sebastian Bach (Ger. comp.; 1685-1750)
Johann Strauss (the Elder)(Aus.comp./cond.; 1804-49)
Johann Strauss (the Younger)("The Waltz King")(Aus. comp.; 1825-99)
Johann Wolfgang von Goethe (Ger. writer/phil.; 1749-1852)
Johanna Spyri (Swiss writer; 1827-1901)
Johannes (or Hans) Bach (Ger. musician, great-grandfather of J.S.; 1580-1626)
Johannes Brahms (Ger. comp.; 1833-97)
Johannes Evangelista Purkinje (Czech. physiol.; 1787-1869)
Johannes (or Johann) Kepler (Ger. astron./math.; 1571-1630)
Johannes Rau (pres., Ger.; 1931-)
Johannesburg, South Africa
Johannisberg Riesling (wine)
Johanns, Mike (Michael O.)(NE gov.; 1950-)
Johansen, David (aka Buster Poindexter)(ent.; 1950-)
Johansson, Ingemar (Swed. boxing; 1932-)
John (rel., book of the New Testament)
John Adams (2nd US pres.; 1735-1826)
John A(lbert) Kitzhaber (OR gov.; 1947-)
John Alden (American Pilgrim; c1599-1687)
John Alexander Macdonald, (Sir)(ex-PM, Can.; 1815-91)
John Amos (ent.; 1941-)
John and Leeza (TV show)
John André, Major (Br. spy; 1751-80)
John Arbuthnot (Scot. phys./satirist; 1667-1735)
John (David) Ashcroft (US atty. gen; 1942-)
John Astin (ent.; 1930-)
John A(ugustus) Sutter (US pioneer, gold; 1803-80)
John Aubrey (Br. antiquarian; 1626-97)
John Bani (pres., Vanuatu; 1941-)
John Barbirolli, (Sir)(Br. cond.; 1899-1970)
John Barbour (Scot. poet; 1316?-95)
John Bardeen (US physt.; 1908-91)
John Barleycorn (personification of alcohol)
John Barry (US mil.; 1745-1803)
John Barth (US writer; 1930-)
John Bartlett (US publ./editor, *Familiar*

Quotations; 1820-1905)
John (Blythe) Barrymore (ent.; 1882-1942)
John Baskerville (Br. typographer; 1706-75)
John Bassett Moore (US jurist; 1860-1947)
John B. Breaux (US cong.; 1944-)
John B. Connally (ex-gov., TX; 1917-93)
John Beal (ent.; 1909-97)
John Beck (ent.; 1943-)
John Belushi (ent.; 1949-82)
John Berardino (ent.; 1917-)
John Berendt (US writer; 1939-)
John Bernard Flannagan (US sculptor; 1895-1942)
John Berryman (US poet; 1914-72)
John Betjeman, (Sir)(Br. poet; 1906-84)
John Biddle (Br. rel.; 1615-62)
John Birch Society (politics)
John Bozeman (US pioneer; 1835-67)
John Brown (US abolitionist; 1800-59)
John B(atterson) Stetson (US bus.; 1830-1906)
John B. Stetson Co.
John Bull (Br. comp.; 1562-1628)
John Bull (synonym for Eng. people)
John Bull pamphlets (Br. hist.; 1712)
John Bunyan (Br. writer/rel.; 1628-88)
John Burgoyne (Br. gen./writer; 1722-92)
John Cabell Breckinridge (ex-US VP/gen.; 1821-75)
John Cabot (also Giovanni Caboto)(It. nav.; 1450-98)
John (Milton) Cage (US comp.; 1912-92)
John Cale (ent.; 1942-)
John Calvin (Fr. rel.; 1509-64)
John Cameron Swayze (US TV jour.; 1906-95)
John (Franklin) Candy (ent.; 1950-94)
John Carlos (sprinter; 1945-)
John Carradine (ent.; 1906-88)
John Cassavetes (ent.; 1929-89)
John C. Calhoun (ex-US VP; 1782-1850)
John Chancellor (US TV jour.; 1927-96)
John Chapman (aka Johnny Appleseed)(US pioneer; 1774-1845)
John Charles Daly, Jr. (ent./TV news exec.; 1914-91)
John Charles Frémont (US mil.; 1813-90)
John Cheever (US writer; 1912-82)
John Churchill (aka Duke of Marlborough)(Br. mil.; 1650-1722)
John Claggett Danforth (US pol; 1936-)
John Clark Gable (ent.; 1961-)
John Cleese (ent.; 1939-)
John Coltrane (US jazz; 1926-67)
John (George Melvin) Compton, (ex-PM, St. Lucia; 1926-)
John Constable (Br. artist; 1776-1837)
John Coryell (US writer; 1927-)
John Cotton (Br./US rel.; 1584-1652)
John Cougar Mellencamp (ent.; 1951-)
John Crowley (US writer; 1942-)
John Cullum (ent.; 1930-)
John Cusack (ent.; 1966-)
John Dalton (Br. chem./physt.; 1766-1844)
John David Podesta (US ex-White House chief of staff; 1949-)
John Davidson (ent.; 1941-)

John D. Cockcroft (Br. physt.; 1897-1967)
John De Lorean (US bus./auto.; 1925-)
John Deere (agr. products)
John Deere (US bus.; 1804-86)
John Denver (ent.; 1943-97)
John Derek (b. Derek Harris)(ent.; 1926-98)
John Dewey (US phil./educ.; 1859-1952)
John Dillinger (US bank robber/murderer; 1902?-34)
John D. MacDonald (US writer; 1916-86)
John Doe (unidentified or "any" man)
John Donne (Br. poet; 1573-1631)
John Dory (fish)
John Dos Passos (US writer; 1896-1970)
John Drew Barrymore (ent.; 1932-)
John Drew, Mrs. (ent.; 1820-97)
John D(avison) "Jay" Rockefeller, IV (US cong.; 1937-)
John D(avison) Rockefeller (US bus./finan.; 1839-1937)
John D(avison) Rockefeller, III (US finan.; 1906-78)
John D(avison) Rockefeller, Jr. (US bus./finan.; 1874-1960)
John Dryden (Br. writer; 1631-1700)
John D. S. Campbell (Duke of Argyll)(ex-gov.-gen., Can.; 1845-1914)
John Dudley Northumberland, Duke (Br. pol.; c1502-53)
John Duns Scotus ("Doctor Subtilis")(Scot. rel.; 1265?-1308)
John D(avid) Waihee III (ex-HI gov.; 1946-)
John Edgar Wideman (US writer; 1941-)
John Edward (US psychic/medium)
John Edwards (US cong.; 1953-)
John (Daniel) Ehrlichman (US pol./Watergate; 1925-99)
John Ellis Bush (Jeb)(US FL gov., bro. of pres./son of ex-pres.; 1953-)
John (Mathias) Engler (MI gov.; 1948-)
John Ensign (US cong.; 1958-)
John Erskine ("Erskine of Carnock")(Scot. writer, law; 1695-1768)
John E. Sununu (US cong.; 1964-)
John Fairchild Dryden (US bus./pol.; 1839-1911)
John Falstaff, (Sir)(fict. chara., Shakespeare)
John F. Enders (US virol.; 1897-1985)
John Fiedler (ent.; 1925-)
John Fiske (US hist.; 1842-1901)
John Fitch (US inv.; 1743-98)
John F(itzgerald) "Jack" Kennedy (35th US pres.; 1917-63)
John F(itzgerald) Kennedy, Jr. (US publ./son of ex-US pres.; 1960-99)
John F. Kennedy Center for the Performing Arts (DC)
John F. Kennedy Space Center (FL)
John Fletcher (Br. dramatist; 1579-1625)
John F. McWethy (TV jour.)
John Fogerty (ent.; 1945-)
John Ford (ent.; 1895-1973)
John Forsythe (b. John Lincoln Freund)(ent.; 1918-)
John Foster Dulles (US pol.; 1888-1959)
John Fowles (Br. writer; 1926-)

John F. Poindexter (US pol.)
John Francis Appleby (US inv.; 1840-1917)
John Frankenheimer (ent.; 1930-)
John Frederic Daniell (Br. chem.; 1790-1845)
John F(rench) Sloan (US artist; 1871-1951)
John F. Street (Phila. mayor; 1943-)
John Gabriel (ent.; 1931-)
John Galsworthy (Br. writer; 1867-1933)
John Galt (fict. chara.; *Atlas Shrugged*)
John Galt (Scot writer; 1779-1839)
John Garfield (ent.; 1913-52)
John Gavin (ent./dipl.; 1935-)
John Gay (Br. writer; 1685-1732)
John George Diefenbaker (ex-PM, Can.; 1895-1979)
John Gielgud, (Sir Arthur)(ent.; 1904-2000)
John Goodman (ent.; 1953-)
John Gotti (US mobster; 1940-)
John Greenleaf Whittier (US poet/jour.; 1807-92)
John Gregory Dunne (US writer; 1932-)
John Grisham (US writer; 1955-)
John G(rosvenor) Rowland (CT gov.; 1957-)
John G. Tower (US pol.; 1926-91)
John Guare (US writer; 1938-)
John Gunther (US jour./writer; 1901-70)
John Hancock (one's signature)
John Hancock (US pol., Declaration of Independence; 1737-93)
John Hancock Bowl (college football)
John Hancock Mutual Life Insurance Co.
John Hanning Speke (Br. expl. in Afr.; 1827-64)
John Hartford (ent.; 1937-)
John Harvard (Br./US rel.; 1607-38)
John Havlicek (basketball; 1940-)
John Hawkes (US writer; 1925-98)
John (Milton) Hay (US pol.; 1838-1905)
John Hay Whitney (US publ./finan.; 1905-82)
John H. Chafee (US pol.; 1922-99)
John Heard (ent.; 1945-)
John Hencken (swimming; 1954-)
John Henry (fict. chara., exceptional strength)
John Hersey (US writer; 1917-93)
John H(erschel) Glenn, Jr. (US ex-cong./astro.; 1921-)
John (Warnock) Hinckley, Jr. (US, shot R. Reagan; 1955-)
John H(enry) Newman (Br. rel.; 1801-90)
John Hodiak (ent.; 1914-55)
John Hoeven (ND gov.)
John Hope Franklin (US hist.; 1915-)
John Houseman (ent.; 1902-88)
John Howard (PM, Austl.; 1939-)
John H. Sununu (US pol./ex-White House chief of staff; 1939-)
John (Joseph) Hughes (US rel.; 1797-1864)
John Hunt Morgan (US confed. gen.; 1826-64)
John Inni Lapli (gov.-gen., Solomon Islands)
John Ireland (ent.; 1914-92)
John Irving (US writer; 1942-)
John Jacob Astor (US bus.; 1763-1848)
John Jacob Astor, 5th (US/Br. publ.; 1886-1971)
John (William) Jakes (US writer; 1932-)
John James Audubon (US artist, birds; 1785-1851)
John Jay (US jurist/dipl.; 1745-1829)

John Jay College of Criminal Justice of the City University of New York (NY)
John J. McCloy (US atty./banker; 1895-1989)
John J(oseph) Pershing ("Blackjack")(US gen.; 1860-1948)
John Kander (US comp.; 1927-)
John Karlen (ent.; 1933-)
John Keats (Br. poet; 1795-1821)
John Kenneth Galbraith (US/Can. econ.; 1908-)
John Kerr (ent.; 1931-)
John Kerry (US cong.; 1943-)
John Ketch (Br. executioner; 1663?-86)
John Kieran (US writer; 1892-1981)
John Kinsella (swimming; 1952-)
John Knowles (US writer; 1926-)
John Knox (Scot. rel.; 1505-72)
John La Farge (US artist; 1835-1910)
John Labatt, Ltd.
John Landis (ent.; 1950-)
John Landis Mason (US inv., Mason jar; 1832-1902)
John Landy (runner; 1930-)
John Larroquette (ent.; 1947-)
John le Carré (b. David Cornwell)(Br. writer; 1931-)
John Lee Hooker (ent./songwriter; 1917-2001)
John Leguizamo (ent.; 1964-)
John Lennon (Br. comp./ent.; 1940-80)
John Lewis (US jazz; 1920-)
John Lily (or Lyly, Lilly)(Br. writer; 1554?-1606)
John (Vliet) Lindsay (ex-NYC mayor; 1921-2000)
John Lithgow (ent.; 1945-)
John L(lewellyn) Lewis (US labor leader; 1880-1969)
John Locke (Br. phil.; 1632-1704)
John Logie Baird ("Father of Television")(Scot. eng.; 1888-1946)
John Loudon McAdam (Scot. eng.; 1756-1836)
John Lovitz (ent.; 1957-)
John L(awrence) Sullivan (boxing; 1858-1918)
John L. (Jack) Swigert, Jr. (astro.; 1931-82)
John Luther "Casey" Jones (US railroad eng.; 1864-1900)
John Lyly (or Lily, Lilly)(Br. writer; 1554?-1606)
John Mackey (football; 1941-)
John Madden (football/ent.; 1936-)
John Mahoney (ent.; 1940-)
John Major (ex-PM, Br.; 1943-)
John Malecela (ex-PM, Tanzania)
John Malkovich (ent.; 1953-)
John Malkovich, Being (film, 1999)
John Marin (US artist; 1870-1953)
John Marshall (US jurist; 1755-1835)
John Marshall Harlan (US jurist; 1833-1911)
John Marshall Harlan (US jurist; 1899-1971)
John Masefield (Br. poet; 1878-1967)
John Matuszak (football; 1950-89)
John Mayall (ent.; 1933-)
John Maynard Keynes (Br. econ.; 1883-1946)
John Maynard Smith (Br. biol.; 1920-)
John M(oses) Browning (US inv.; 1955-1926)
John McAllister Schofield (US mil.; 1831-1906)
John McCormack (Ir./US tenor; 1884-1945)
John (Patrick) McEnroe (tennis; 1959-)

John (Joseph) McGraw (baseball; 1873-1934)
John McIntire (ent.; 1907-91)
John McLaughlin (ent.; 1942-)
John McLean (US jurist; 1785-1861)
John Mellencamp (ent.; 1951-)
John Michael Montgomery (ent.; 1965-)
John Mills (ent.; 1908-)
John Milton (Br. poet; 1608-74)
John Mitchell (US labor leader; 1870-1919)
John (Newton) Mitchell (US pol./Watergate; 1913-88)
John Montagu (Earl of Sandwich)(Br. pol.; 1718-92)
John Morrell (meats)
John Morrell & Co.
John Mortimer (Br. writer/atty.; 1923-)
John M(arlan) Poindexter (US adm.; 1936-)
John M(illington) Synge (Ir. writer; 1871-1909)
John Muir (US environ.; 1838-1914)
John Naber (swimming; 1956-)
John Nance Garner (ex-US VP; 1868-1967)
John Napier (Scot. math.; 1550-1617)
John Newbery (Br. publ.; 1713-67)
John Newcombe (tennis; 1943-)
John Oates (ent.; 1948-)
John (Joseph) O'Connor, Cardinal (US rel.; 1920-2000)
John of Gaunt (Br. pol.; 1340-99)
John O'Hara (US writer; 1905-70)
John (James) Osborne (Br. writer; 1929-94)
John (McAuley) Palmer (US gen./pol.; 1817-1900)
John Paul I (Albino Luciani)(It. pope; 1912-78)
John Paul II (b. Karol Wojtyla)(Pol. pope; 1920-)
John Paul Jones (US mil.; 1747-92)
John Paul Mitchell Systems (US bus.)
John Paul Stevens (US jurist; 1920-)
John Payne (ent.; 1912-89)
John Philip Sousa (US comp.; 1854-1932)
John Portman (US arch.; 1934-)
John Pym (Br. pol.; 1583?-1643)
John Q. Public (average US citizen)
John Quincy Adams (6th US pres.; 1767-1848)
John Rae (Scot. expl.; 1813-93)
John Raitt (ent.; 1917-)
John (Bennett) Ramsey (US news; 1943-)
John Randolph (ent.; 1915-)
John Randolph (of Roanoke)(US pol.; 1773-1833)
John Ratzenberger (ent.; 1947-)
John Ray (Br. nat.; 1627-1705)
John Ringling North (US circus dir.; 1903-85)
John Ritter (ent.; 1948-)
John R(obert) Lewis (US cong.; 1940-)
John R(ettie) McKernan, Jr. (ex-ME gov.; 1948-)
John Robert Burck II (aka the Naked Cowboy)(ent.; 1971-)
John Robert Gregg (inv. shorthand system; 1868-1948)
John Rolfe (Br. colonist in VA, husband of Pocahontas; 1585-1622)
John Ross (aka Coowescoowe)(Cherokee Native Amer. chief; 1790-1866)
John Ross, (Sir)(Br. expl.; 1777-1856)
John Rubinstein (ent.; 1946-)

John Ruskin (Br. writer/social reformer; 1819-1900)
John Russell (ex-PM, Br.; 1792-1878)
John Russell Pope (US arch.; 1874-1937)
John R. Wooden (basketball; 1910-)
John R. Wooden Award (basketball)
John Saxon (ent.; 1935-)
John Sayles (ent.; 1950-)
John Schneider (ent.; 1954-)
John Sculley (US bus.; 1939-)
John Sebastian (ent.; 1944-)
John Shea (ent.; 1949-)
John Sherman (US pol.; 1823-1900)
John Sholto Douglas Queensberry (Marquis of Queensberry; 1844-1900)
John Silver's Seafood Shoppes, Long (US bus.)
John Singer Sargent (US artist; 1856-1925)
John Singleton (ent./writer; 1968-)
John Singleton Copley (US artist; 1738-1815)
John Sirica (US judge; 1904-92)
John S. Knight (US publ.; 1894-1981)
John Slidell (US pol.; 1793-1871)
John Smith (Br. colonist in Amer., Pocahontas; 1580-1631)
John Spencer (ent.; 1946-)
John Stamos (ent.; 1963-)
John Steed (fict. chara., *The Avengers*)
John (Ernst) Steinbeck (US writer; 1902-68)
John Steuart Curry (US artist; 1897-1946)
John Stossel (TV jour.; 1947-)
John Stuart McCain (US cong.; 1936-)
John Stuart Mill (Br. phil./econ.; 1806-73)
John Sturges (ent.; 1910-92)
John Suckling, (Sir)(Br. poet; 1609-42)
John Sullivan (US mil./pol.; 1740-95)
John Swan (ex-premier, Bermuda; 1935-)
John Taliaferro Thompson (US mil./inv.; 1860-1940)
John Tenniel, (Sir)(Br. artist; 1820-1914)
John Tesh (ent.; 1952-)
John the Baptist, St. (Judean rel.; c6 BC-AD 27)
John the Divine, Cathedral of St. (NYC)
John Travolta (ent.; 1954-)
John Trumbull (US artist; 1756-1843)
John Trumbull (US poet/atty.; 1750-1831)
John T(homas) Scopes (US educ./evolution; 1901-70)
John (Napier) Turner (ex-PM, Can.; 1929-)
John Turturro (ent.; 1957-)
John Tyler (10th US pres.; 1790-1862)
John (Hoyer) Updike (US writer; 1932-)
John Vanderlyn (US artist; 1775-1852)
John (William) Van Druten (US writer; 1901-57)
John Wanamaker (US bus.; 1838-1922)
John Wanamaker, Inc.
John Waters (ent./writer; 1946-)
John Wayne (b. Marion Michael Morrison, aka "the Duke")(ent.; 1907-79)
John Wayne Bobbitt (US news)
John Werner Kluge (US bus.; 1914-)
John Wesley (Br. rel., founded Methodism; 1703-91)
John Wesley Harding (US outlaw; 1853-95)
John Wesley Powell (US geol./ethnol.; 1834-1902)

John Wilkes Booth (US, assassinated Lincoln, actor; 1838-65)
John Williams (US comp./cond.; 1932-)
John Winthrop (Br./Amer., ex-gov., MA; 1588-1649)
John Winthrop (ex-gov., CT; 1606-76)
John (or Fitz-John) Winthrop (ex-gov., CT; 1638-1707)
John Winthrop (US astron./math./physt.; 1714-79)
John Witherspoon (US rel.; 1723-94)
John W(illiam) McCormack (US pol.; 1891-1980)
John Woo (ent./writer; 1946-)
John W. Warner (US cong.; 1927-)
John Wycliffe (Br. rel.; c1320-84)
John W(atts) Young (astro.; 1930-)
John XXII (Jacques d'Euse)(Fr., pope; 1249-1334)
John XXIII (Angelo Giuseppe Roncalli)(It., pope; 1881-1963)
John XXIII (It., [anti]pope; 1370?-1419)
John, Elton (Hercules)(b. Reginald Kenneth Dwight)(ent.; 1947-)
John, Friar (fict. chara., *Gargantua, Pantagruel*)
John, I&II&III (rel., books of the New Testament)
John, Little (fict. chara., *Robin Hood*)
John, Olivia Newton- (ent.; 1947-)
John, Prester (legendary priest-king; 12th-16th c.)
John's-bread, St. (herb/spice, tree)
Johnnie L. Cochran, Jr. (US atty.; 1937-)
Johnnie Ray (ent.; 1927-90)
Johnnie Walker (whiskey)
Johnny and the Asbury Jukes, Southside (pop music)
Johnny Appleseed (b. John Chapman)(US pioneer; 1774-1845)
Johnny Belinda (film, 1948, 1982)
Johnny Bench (baseball; 1947-)
Johnny Burke (US lyricist; 1908-84)
Johnny Carson (ent.; 1925-)
Johnny Cash (ent.; 1932-)
Johnny-come-lately
Johnny Depp (ent.; 1963-)
Johnny Desmond (ent./songwriter; 1921-85)
Johnny Dodds (US jazz; 1892-1940)
Johnny Hart (US cartoonist, *BC, Wizard of Id*; 1931-)
Johnny Hodges (US jazz; 1906-71)
Johnny-jump-up
Johnny Lee (ent.; 1946-)
Johnny Longden (horse racing; 1907-)
Johnny Mathis (ent.; 1935-)
Johnny Mercer (US lyricist; 1909-76)
Johnny Miller (golf; 1947-)
Johnny Mnemonic (film, 1995)
Johnny-on-the-spot
Johnny Paycheck (b. Donald Eugene Lytle)(ent.; 1941-)
Johnny Reb (Confederate soldier, southerner)
Johnny Rivers (b. John Ramistella)(ent.; 1942-)
Johnny Rodriquez (ent.; 1951-)
Johnny Rutherford (auto racing; 1938-)
Johnny (John Constantine) Unitas (football;

1933-)
Johnny (Peter John) Weissmuller (US swimmer/ent.; 1903-84)
Johnny Winter (ent.; 1944-)
Johnny, Frankie and (film, 1936, 1965, 1991)
Johns Hopkins Hospital (Baltimore, MD)
Johns Hopkins University (Baltimore, MD)
Johns Manville International, Inc.
Johns, Glynis (ent.; 1923-)
Johns, Jasper (US artist; 1930-)
Johnson bar (railroad)
Johnson City, NY, TN
Johnson Co., Howard
Johnson Controls, Inc.
Johnson grass (also Aleppo grass, Means grass)
Johnson National Historical Park, Lyndon B. (TX)
Johnson Robb, Lynda Bird (US daughter ex-pres.; 1944-)
Johnson Space Center, Lyndon B. (TX)
Johnson, Amy (Br. aviator; 1903-41)
Johnson, Andrew (17th US pres.; 1808-75)
Johnson, Anne-Marie (ent.; 1960-)
Johnson, Anthony (rowing; 1940-)
Johnson, Arte (ent.; 1929-)
Johnson, Ben (Can. runner; 1961-)
Johnson, Ben (ent.; 1918-96)
Johnson, Bunk (US jazz; 1879-1949)
Johnson, Clay (US White House staff)
Johnson, Don (ent.; 1949-)
Johnson, Dr. Virginia E(shelman)(US psych., Masters & Johnson; 1925-)
Johnson, Drs. Masters and (sexual behavior study)
Johnson, Gary E. (NM gov.; 1953-)
Johnson, Howard (US bus.; 1896-1972)
Johnson, Jack (John Arthur)(boxing; 1878-1946)
Johnson, James P. (US jazz; 1891-1955)
Johnson, James Weldon (US writer, NAACP; 1871-1938)
Johnson, Jimmy (football; 1943-)
Johnson, J. J. (US jazz; 1924-)
Johnson, Kevin (basketball; 1966-)
Johnson, Lady Bird (b. Claudia Alta Taylor)(US wife of ex-pres.; 1912-)
Johnson, Larry (basketball; 1969-)
Johnson, Luci Baines (US daughter ex-pres.; 1947-)
Johnson, Lyndon Baines (36th US pres.; 1908-73)
Johnson, Magic (Earvin)(basketball; 1959-)
Johnson, Philip C(ortelyou)(US arch.; 1906-)
Johnson, Rafer (decathlon; 1935-)
Johnson, Richard M(entor)(ex-US VP; 1780-1850)
Johnson, Samuel ("Dr. Johnson")(Br. lexicographer/writer; 1709-84)
Johnson, Samuel (US educ.; 1696-1772)
Johnson, Tim (US cong.; 1946-)
Johnson, Van (ent.; 1916-)
Johnson, Walter (Perry) "Big Train" (baseball; 1887-1946)
Johnson & Co., Mead
Johnson & Johnson (US bus.)
Johnson & Johnson Consumer Products, Inc.

Johnson & Johnson/Merck Consumer
  Pharmaceuticals Co.
Johnson & Son, Inc., S. C.
Johnston, J. Bennett, Jr. (US pol.; 1932-)
Johnston, Joseph Eggleston (US confed. gen.;
  1807-91)
Johnston, Lynn (cartoonist; *For Better or
  Worse*; 1947-)
Johnstown flood (PA; 1889)
Johnstown, PA
Johor Baharu, Malaysia
Joint Chiefs of Staff (US govt.)
Joio, Norman Dello (US comp.; 1913-)
Joker's Wild (TV show)
Jolie (Voight), Angelina (ent.; 1975-)
Joliet (or Jolliet), Louis (Fr./Can. expl.; 1645-
  1700)
Joliet Army Ammunition Plant (IL)
Joliet, IL
Joliot-Curie, Frédéric (Fr. physt.; 1900-58)
Joliot-Curie, Irène (Fr. physt.; 1897-1956)
Jolly Roger (pirate flag)
Jolson, Al (b. Asa Yoelson)(ent.; 1886-1950)
Jomo Kenyatta (b. Kamau Ngengi)(ex-pres.,
  Kenya; 1893?-1978)
Jon Bon Jovi (b. John Francis Bongiovi)(ent.;
  1962-)
Jon Corzine (US cong.; 1947-)
Jon Favreau (ent.; 1966-)
Jon Kyl (US cong.; 1942-)
Jon Stewart (b. Jonathan Stewart
  Leibowitz)(ent.; 1962-)
Jon Vickers (ent.; 1926-)
Jon Voight (ent.; 1938-)
Jonah (Hebrew prophet; 8th c. BC)
Jonah (rel., book of the Old Testament)
Jonas Angström Anders (Swed. astrophyst.;
  1814-74)
Jonas Savimbi (Angolan mil.; 1934-)
Jonas (Edward) Salk (US phys./biol.; 1914-95)
Jonassaint, Emile (pres., Haiti; 1914-)
Jonathan (apple)
Jonathan Banks (ent.; 1947-)
Jonathan Demme (ent.; 1944-)
Jonathan Edwards (US rel.; 1703-58)
Jonathan Frakes (ent.; 1952-)
Jonathan Knight (ent.; 1968-)
Jonathan Livingston Seagull (R. Bach novel)
Jonathan Logan, Inc.
Jonathan Motzfeldt (Premier, Greenland)
Jonathan M(ayhew) Wainwright (US gen.;
  1883-1953)
Jonathan Pryce (ent.; 1947-)
Jonathan Swift (b. Isaac Bickerstaff)(Br. writer;
  1667-1745)
Jonathan Taylor Thomas (b. Jonathan
  Weiss)(ent.; 1981-)
Jonathan Trumbull (US pol.; 1710-85)
Jonathan Winters (ent.; 1925-)
Jonathan, Chief (Joseph) Leabua (ex-PM,
  Lesotho; 1914-87)
JonBenet (Patricia) Ramsey (US news; 1990-96)
*Jones and Laughlin Steel Co., National Labor
  Relations Board v.* (US law; 1937)
Jones and the Last Crusade, Indiana (film,

1989)
Jones and the Temple of Doom, Indiana (film,
  1984)
Jones Apparel Group, Inc.
Jones Index, Dow
Jones News/Retrieval, Dow (compu. database)
Jones, Anthony Armstrong- (Earl of Snowdon)
  (Br. photo.; 1930-)
Jones, Bobby (golf; 1902-71)
Jones, Brereton C. (ex-KY gov.; 1939-)
Jones, Carolyn (ent.; 1933-83)
Jones, Charlie (ent.; 1930-)
Jones, Chuck (cartoonist, *Bugs Bunny, Porky
  Pig, Daffy Duck*; 1912-)
Jones, Davy (personification of sea)
Jones, Deacon (David)(football; 1938-)
Jones, Dean (ent.; 1931-)
Jones, The Devil and Miss (film, 1941)
Jones, Ed "Too Tall" (football; 1951-)
Jones, Edward Burne- (Br. artist; 1833-98)
Jones, Elvin (US jazz; 1927-)
Jones, George (ent.; 1931-)
Jones, Grace (ent.; 1952-)
Jones, Grandpa (b. Lewis Marshall Jones)(ent.;
  1913-98)
Jones, Indiana (fict. chara.)
Jones, Inigo (Br. arch.; 1573-c1652)
Jones, Jack (ent.; 1938-)
Jones, James (US writer; 1922-77)
Jones, James Earl (ent.; 1931-)
Jones, Jennifer (b. Phyllis Isley)(ent.; 1919-)
Jones, Jim (James Warren)(US/Guyana cult
  leader; 1931-78)
Jones, Jo (US jazz; 1911-85)
Jones, John Luther "Casey" (US railroad eng.;
  1864-1900)
Jones, John Paul (US mil.; 1747-92)
Jones, Marion (US runner; 1975-)
Jones, Mother (mag.)
Jones, Mother (Mary Harris Jones)(US labor
  leader; 1830-1930)
Jones, Paula (US news)
Jones, Philly Joe (US jazz; 1923-85)
Jones, Quincy (US jazz; 1933-)
Jones, Rickie Lee (ent./songwriter; 1954-)
Jones, Robert "Bobby" (Tyre), Jr. (golf; 1902-71)
Jones, Shirley (ent.; 1934-)
Jones, Spike (ent.; 1911-1965)
Jones, Thad (US jazz; 1923-86)
Jones, Tom (b. Thomas Jones Woodward)(ent.;
  1940-)
Jones, Tom (H. Fielding novel)
Jones, Tommy Lee (ent.; 1946-)
Jones's locker, Davy (ocean bottom; grave of
  those who die at sea)
Jonestown mass suicide (Guyana; 1978)
Jonestown, Guyana
Jong II, Kim (pres., NKorea; 1942-)
Jong, Erica (Mann)(US writer; 1942-)
Joni Huntley (track; 1956-)
Joni Mitchell (b. Roberta Joan Anderson)(ent.;
  1943-)
Jonny Quest (cartoon)
Jonquière, Quebec, Canada
Jöns Jakob Berzelius, Baron (Swed. chem.;

1779-1848)
Jonson, Ben (Br. writer; 1572-1637)
Jooss, Kurt (Ger. ballet; 1901-79)
Joplin, Janis (ent.; 1943-70)
Joplin, MO
Joplin, Scott (US jazz; 1868-1917)
Jordache
Jordache Enterprises, Inc.
Jordan (Hashemite Kingdom of)(SW Asia)
Jordan almonds
Jordan Knight (ent.; 1970-)
Jordan Marsh Co., Abraham & Straus/
Jordan River (UT)
Jordan Vineyard & Winery (US bus.)
Jordan, Barbara (Charline)(US atty./educ./pol.;
    1936-96)
Jordan, Michael "Mike" (basketball/baseball;
    1963-)
Jordan, Neil (ent.; 1950-)
Jordan, Richard (ent.; 1938-)
Jordan, River (Pak.)
Jordan, Vernon E., Jr. (US atty.)
Jorge Batlle Ibanez (pres., Uruguay; 1927-)
Jorge Luis Borges (Argentinean writer; 1900-86)
Jorge Sampaio (pres., Port.; 1939-)
Jorge Serrano Elías (ex-pres., Guat.)
Jorgensen, Christine (b. George Jorgensen,
    Jr.)(1st sex-change operation; 1927-89)
Jory, Victor (ent.; 1902-82)
Josaia Voreqe Bainimarama, Commodore (Fiji
    mil./pol.)
José Canseco (baseball; 1964-)
José Carreras (Sp. tenor; 1947-)
José Clemente Orozco (Mex. artist; 1883-1949)
Jose Cuervo (tequila)
José de Rivera (US sculptor; 1904-85)
José Eber (hairstylist)
José Eduardo dos Santos (pres., Angola; 1942-)
José Feliciano (ent.; 1945-)
José Ferrer (ent. 1912-92)
José Francisco Merino (El Salvador, pol.)
José Iturbi (Sp. cond.; 1895-1980)
José Limón (Mex./US dancer; 1908-72)
José Limón Dance Company
José María Aznar (PM, Spain; 1953-)
José Maria Olazabal (golf; 1966-)
José (Julian) Marti (Cuban pol./poet; 1853-95)
José Napoleon Duarte (ex-pres., El Salvador;
    1925-90)
José Ortega y Gasset (Sp. phil.; 1883-1955)
Josef Albers (US artist; 1888-1976)
Josef A. Pasternack (ent.; 1881-1940)
Josef Mengele, Dr. ("angel of death")(Ger.
    Nazi; ?-1979?)
Josef Strauss (Aus. comp.; 1827-70)
Josef Suk (Czech. comp.; 1874-1935)
Joseph (of Nazareth)(husband of the Virgin Mary)
Joseph A. Califano, Jr. (US ex-secy./HEW; pres.,
    Nat'l. Ctr. Addiction & Substance Abuse; 1931-)
Joseph Addison (Br. writer; 1672-1719)
Joseph Andrews (Henry Fielding novel)
Joseph A. Yablonski (US labor leader; ?-1969)
Joseph Banks Rhine (US psych.; 1895-1980)
Joseph Beuys (Ger. sculptor/ent.; 1921-86)
Joseph Bologna (ent.; 1934-)

Joseph Bonaparte (bro. of Napoleon, king,
    Naples/Sp.; 1768-1844)
Joseph Brodsky (US writer; 1940-)
Joseph Campanella (ent.; 1927-)
Joseph Campbell (US mythologist/folklorist;
    1904-87)
Joseph Cardinal Bernardin (US rel.; 1928-96)
Joseph Chamberlain (Br. pol.; 1836-1914)
Joseph Cold Tablets, St. (med.)
Joseph Conrad (Br. writer; 1857-1924)
Joseph Cotten (ent.; 1905-94)
Joseph Dalton Hooker, (Sir)(Br. botanist; 1817-
    1911)
Joseph Eggleston Johnston (US gen.; 1807-91)
Joseph E. Levine (ent.; 1905-87)
Joseph E. Seagram & Sons, Inc.
Joseph Estrada (ex-pres., Phil.; 1937-)
Joseph Fiennes (ent.; 1970-)
Joseph (Louis) Gay-Lussac (Fr. chem./physt.;
    1778-1850)
Joseph Goebbels, (Paul)(Ger. Nazi
    propagandist; 1897-1945)
Joseph Hagin (US White House staff)
Joseph Hayne Rainey (US pol.; 1832-87)
Joseph Heller (US writer; 1923-99)
Joseph Henry (US phys./inv.; 1797-1878)
Joseph H. Hirshhorn (US bus./finan.; 1899-1981)
Joseph Hooker (US gen.; 1814-79)
Joseph I. Lieberman (US cong.; 1942-)
Joseph (Jacques Césaire) Joffre (Fr. mil.; 1852-
    1931)
Joseph Kabila (Congo pres.; 1969-)
Joseph Kokou Koffigoh (ex-PM, Togo)
Joseph (Louis) Lagrange (Fr. astron./math.;
    1736-1813)
Joseph Lister, Baron (Br. phys./antiseptic
    surgery; 1827-1912)
Joseph L(eo) Mankiewicz (US ent./writer; 1909-
    93)
Joseph Meyer (US comp.; 1894-1987)
Joseph Michel Montgolfier (Fr. hot-air
    balloonist; 1740-1810)
Joseph Mollicone, Jr. (US bank scandal)
Joseph Papp (ent.; 1921-91)
Joseph Patrick Kennedy II (US pol.; 1952-)
Joseph Patrick Kennedy, Jr. (US bro. of ex-
    pres., killed in WWII; 1915-44)
Joseph Patrick Kennedy, Sr. (US bus./dipl.,
    father of ex-pres.; 1888-1969)
Joseph Patrick Lockhard (US ex-White House
    press secy.; 1959-)
Joseph Phelps Vineyards (US bus.)
Joseph Pilsudski (Pol. dictator; 1867-1935)
Joseph P(eter) Kerwin (astro.; 1932-)
Joseph Priestley (Br. chem./writer; 1733-1804)
Joseph Pulitzer (US jour./publ./finan.; 1847-1911)
Joseph Pulitzer, Jr. (US publ.; 1913-93)
Joseph R. Biden, Jr. (US cong.; 1942-)
Joseph R(aymond) McCarthy (US pol.; 1908-57)
Joseph Robert Kerrey (Bob)(US pol.; 1943-)
Joseph Schildkraut (ent.; 1895-1964)
Joseph (Alois) Schumpeter (US econ.; 1883-
    1950)
Joseph Smith (US rel./founded Mormons;
    1805-44)

Joseph Stalin (b. Iosif Vissarionovich Dzhugashvili)(ex-dictator, USSR; 1879-1953)
Joseph Story (US jurist; 1779-1845)
Joseph von Fraunhofer (Ger. optician/physt.; 1787-1826)
Joseph W. Alsop, Jr. (jour.; 1910-89)
Joseph Wambaugh (US writer; 1937-)
Joseph Wapner, Judge (*People's Court*; 1919-)
Joseph W(arren) Stilwell ("Vinegar Joe")(US gen.; 1883-1946)
Joseph, Akiba ben (Jew. rel. leader; AD 50?-132)
Joseph, Chief (Nez Percé Native Amer.; c1840-1904)
Joseph, Franz (or Francis)(Aus./Hung., emp.; 1830-1916)
Joseph, Franz, II (ruler, Liechtenstein; 1906-89)
Joseph, Saadia ben (Jew. phil./scholar; 882-942)
Josephine (Marie Joséphe Rose Tascher de la Pagerie, Joséphine de Beauharnais) (empress, Fr., wife of Napoleon I; 1763-1814)
Josephine Baker (ent.; 1906-75)
Josephine Hull (ent.; 1886-1957)
Josey Wales, The Outlaw (film, 1976)
Josh Billings (b. Henry Wheeler Shaw)(US humorist; 1818-85)
Joshua (rel., book of the Old Testament)
Joshua Bolten (US White House staff)
Joshua Jackson (ent.; 1978-)
Joshua Lederberg (US geneticist; 1925-)
Joshua Logan (US writer/ent.; 1908-88)
Joshua Nkomo (Zimbabwean pol.; 1917-99)
Joshua Reynolds, (Sir)(Br. artist; 1723-92)
Joshua tree (tree)
Joshua Tree National Monument (CA)
Joshua Tree, CA
Josiah (king, Judah; ?-608? BC)
Josiah Royce (US phil.; 1855-1916)
Josiah Spode (Br. potter, father; 1733-97)
Josiah Spode (Br. potter, son; 1754-1827)
Josiah W(illard) Gibbs (US physt./chem.; 1839-1903)
Josiah Wedgwood (Br. potter; 1730-95)
Josip Broz Tito (ex-pres., Yug.; 1892-1980)
Jospin, Lionel (PM, Fr.; 1937-)
Josquin Des Pres (Flem. comp.; c1445-1521)
Jost van Dykes (Br. Virgin Island)
Jostens, Inc.
Jotul USA, Inc.
Jotul wood stove
Jotun (also Jotunn)(myth.)
Joule-Kelvin effect (temperature drop in gases)
Joule-Thomson effect (thermodynamics)
Joule, James P(rescott)(Br. physt.; 1818-89)
Joule's law (physics)
Jourdan, Louis (b. Louis Gendre)(Fr. ent.; 1919-)
Journal of Medicine, New England (mag.)
Journal Star, Peoria (IL newspaper)
Journal, Albuquerque (NM newspaper)
Journal, Atlanta (GA newspaper)
Journal, Flint (MI newspaper)
Journal, Lincoln (NE newspaper)
Journal, Milwaukee (WI newspaper)
Journal, Montgomery (AL newspaper)
Journal, Providence (RI newspaper)

Journal, Winston-Salem (NC newspaper)
Journal-Bulletin, Providence (RI newspaper)
Journal-Gazette, Fort Wayne (IN newspaper)
Jovan
Jovanovich, Inc., Harcourt Brace
Jovi, Jon Bon (b. John Francis Bongiovi)(ent.; 1962-)
Jovian planet (Jupiter/Saturn/Neptune/Uranus)
Jovovich, Milla (ent./model; 1975-)
Joy Adamson (naturalist/writer; 1910-80)
Joy Browne (on-air psychologist; 1950-)
Joy of Cooking (cookbook)
Joyce Brothers, Dr. (b. Joyce Bauer)(US psych./writer; 1928-)
Joyce Carol Oates (US writer; 1938-)
Joyce Kilmer, (Alfred)(US poet; 1886-1918)
Joyce Randolph (ent. 1925-)
Joyce, James (Ir. writer; 1882-1941)
Joycelyn Elders (b. Minnie Lee Jones)(US phys./ex-surgeon gen.; 1933-)
Joyner, Al
Joyner, Florence Griffith ("Flo Jo")(track; 1959-98)
Joyner-Kersee, Jackie (track & field; 1962-)
József Antall (ex-PM, Hung.; 1932-)
JP (justice of the peace)
J(ean) Paul Getty (US bus.; 1892-1976)
J. Pedroncelli Winery (US bus.)
JPL (Jet Propulsion Laboratory)
J(ohn) P(hillips) Marquand (US writer; 1893-1960)
J(ohn) P(ierpont) Morgan (US finan.; 1837-1913)
J.P. Morgan Chase & Co.
J(ames) Ramsay MacDonald (ex-PM, Br.; 1866-1937)
J. R. Ewing (fict. chara., *Dallas*)
J(ulius) Robert Oppenheimer (US physt., atomic bomb; 1904-67)
J(ohn) R(onald) R(euel) Tolkien (Br. writer/educ.; 1892-1973)
J(ames) Strom Thurmond (US cong.; 1902-)
J(ames) Thomas Talbot (US finan./insider trading)
Juan Bautista de Anza (Sp. expl.; 1735-88?)
Juan Carlos I (king, Spain; 1938-)
Juan Carlos Wasmosy (ex-pres., Paraguay; 1942-)
Juan de Fuca, Strait of (also Juan de Fuca Strait)(WA/Can.)
Juan Domingo Perón (ex-pres., Argentina; 1895-1974)
Juan Fangio (auto racing; 1911-95)
Juan Gris (b. José Vittoriano Gonzales)(Sp. artist; 1887-1927)
Juan Marichal (baseball; 1937-)
Juan Ponce de León (Sp. expl.; c1460-1521)
Juan, Don (Don Giovanni)(Sp. legend)
Juantoreno, Alberto (track; 1951-)
Juárez, Benito (Pablo)(ex-pres., Mex.; 1806-72)
Juba River (E Afr.)
Juba, Sudan
Jubal Anderson Early (US gen.; 1816-94)
Judaea, Palestine (also Judea, Judah)
Judah (also Judea, Judaea)(now part of Palestine)
Judah ha-Levi (also Halevi), (Judah ben Samuel

Halevi)(Sp. rabbi/phys./poet/phil.; 1085-1140)
Judaica (books, objects re: Jew. life/customs)
Judaism (rel.)
Judas hole (door peephole)
Judas Iscariot (betrayer of Jesus; ?-c28)
Judas Priest (pop music)
Judas tree (tree)
Judd Gregg (US cong.; 1947-)
Judd Hirsch (ent.; 1935-)
Judd Nelson (ent.; 1959-)
Judd, Ashley (ent.; 1968-)
Judd, Naomi (ent.; 1946-)
Judd, Wynonna (b. Christina Claire Ciminella)
    (ent.; 1964-)
Judds, the (pop music)
Jude (rel., book of the New Testament)
Jude Law, (David)(ent.; 1972-)
Jude, St. (also St. Judas)(rel.; 1st c. AD)
Judea (also Judaea, Judah)(now part of Palestine)
Judeo-Christian (beliefs, traditions)
Judge Judy (Judith Sheindlin, aka Judy
    Blum)(TV judge; 1942-)
Judge (Edward Ernest) Reinhold (ent.; 1956-)
Judge Roy Bean (US frontier; 1825?-1903)
Judge, Mike (ent.; 1962-)
Judgment at Nuremberg (film, 1961)
Judges (rel., book of the Old Testament)
Judgment Day (rel.)
Judi Dench, Dame (ent.; 1934-)
Judith (rel., Apocrypha)
Judith Anderson, Dame (ent.; 1898-1992)
Judith Crist (US writer; 1922-)
Judith Ivey (ent.; 1951-)
Judith Krantz (US writer; 1928-)
Judith Light (ent.; 1949-)
Judith Sheindlin (aka Judge Judy, Judy
    Blum)(TV judge; 1942-)
Judy (Sussman) Blume (US writer, young
    adults; 1938-)
Judy Canova (ent.; 1916-83)
Judy Carne (b. Joyce Botterill)(ent.; 1939-)
Judy Collins (ent.; 1939-)
Judy Garland (b. Frances Gumm)(ent.; 1922-69)
Judy H. Martz (MT gov.; 1943-)
Judy Holliday (ent.; 1922-65)
Judy (Torluemke) Rankin (golf; 1945-)
Judy show, Punch-and- (Br. puppet show)
Judy Woodruff (US TV jour.; 1946-)
Judy, Judge (Judith Sheindlin, aka Judy
    Blum)(TV judge; 1942-)
Jugendstil (art)(also l.c.)
Jugnauth, Anerood (PM, Mauritius; 1930-)
Juha Widing (hockey; 1948-85)
Juilliard School of Music (NYC)
Jule Styne (Br./US comp.; 1905-94)
Jules Ajodhia (PM, Suriname)
Jules Dassin (ent.; 1911-)
Jules Feiffer (cartoonist; 1929-)
Jules (Émile Frédéric) Massenet (Fr. comp.;
    1842-1912)
Jules Mazarin (b. Giulo Mazarini)(Fr. rel./pol.;
    1602-61)
Jules Verne (Fr. writer; 1828-1905)
Julia Child (US chef/writer; 1912-)
Julia Duffy (ent.; 1951-)

Julia Louis-Dreyfus (ent.; 1961-)
Julia Ormond (ent.; 1965-)
Julia Roberts (ent.; 1967-)
Julia Ward Howe (US reformer/writer; 1819-
    1910)
Julia, Raul (ent.; 1940-94)
Julian "Cannonball" Adderley (US jazz; 1928-75)
Julian Bond, (Horace)(US reformer/NAACP;
    1940-)
Julian (Alexander) Bream (ent.; 1933-)
Julian calendar
Julian Day (astron.)
Julian Huxley, (Sir)(Br. biol.; 1887-1975)
Julian Lennon (ent.; 1963-)
Julian (Seymour) Schwinger (US physt.; 1918-
    94)
Juliana (ex-queen, Netherlands; 1909-)
Julianna Margulies (ent.; 1966-)
Julianne Moore (b. Julie Anne Smith)(ent.; 1960-)
Julie Andrews (b. Julia Wells)(ent.; 1935-)
Julie Christie (ent.; 1941-)
Julie Harris (ent.; 1925-)
Julie Kavner (ent.; 1951-)
Julie Kent (US dancer; 1971-)
Julie London (ent.; 1926-2000)
Julie Newmar (b. Julie Chalane Newmeyer)
    (ent.; 1935-)
Julie Nixon Eisenhower (daughter of ex-US
    pres.; 1948-)
Julien, St.- (also Saint-Julien)(Fr. wine region)
Juliet Capulet (fict. chara., *Romeo and Juliet*)
Juliet Mills (ent.; 1941-)
Juliet Prowse (ent.; 1936-96)
Juliet, Romanoff and (film, 1961)
Juliet, Romeo and (Shakespeare play)
Juliette Lewis (ent.; 1973-)
Juliette (Gordon) Low (US, founded Girl Scouts;
    1860-1927)
Juliette Binoche (ent.; 1964-)
Juliette Récamier (b. Jeanne Françoise Julie
    Adélaide Bernard)(Fr. society; 1777-1849)
Julio Gallo (US winemaker; 1910-93)
Julio Iglesias (Sp./US ent.; 1943-)
Julius Axelrod (US neuropharmacologist; 1912-)
Julius Boros (golf; 1920-94)
Julius Caesar (Gaius Julius)(Roman gen.; 100-
    44 BC)
Julius Caesar (Shakespeare play)
Julius "Dr J" Erving (basketball; 1950-)
Julius La Rosa (ent.; 1930-)
Julius "Groucho" Marx (ent.; 1890-1977)
Julius (Kambarage) Nyerere (ex-pres.,
    Tanzania; 1922-99)
Julius Rosenberg (US, executed for treason;
    1918-53)
Julius Rudel (cond.; 1921-)
Julius Streicher (Ger. Nazi/publ.; 1885-1946)
July Fourth (also Fourth of July, Independence
    Day)
July Revolution (Fr.; 1830)
Jumanji (film, 1995)
Jump, Gordon (ent.; 1932-)
Jumpin' Jack Flash (song; film, 1986)
jumping Jehoshaphat
Juncker, Jean-Claude (PM, Luxembourg; 1954-)

June Allyson (b. Ella Geisman)(ent.; 1917-)
June bug (also Junebug, May beetle)
June Carter (ent.; 1929-)
June Haver (ent.; 1926-)
June Havoc (ent; 1916-)
June Lockhart (ent.; 1925-)
June Valli (ent.; 1930-93)
Juneau, AK
Juneberry (also American serviceberry)(shrub)
Jung, Carl Gustav (Swiss psych.; 1875-1961)
Jung, Kim Dae (pres., SKorea; 1925-)
Jungian psychology
Jungle Jim (comic strip)
Junior Scholastic (mag.)
Junípero, Miguel José Serra, Father (Sp. rel.;
    1713-84)
Junius Brutus Booth (US actor, father of John
    Wilkes; 1796-1852)
Juno (astron.; myth.)
Junot, Philippe
Jupiter (also Jove)(myth.)
Jupiter (planet)
Jupiter, FL
Jurassic Park (M. Crichton book; film, 1993)
Jurassic period (195-136 million years ago)
Jurgens, Curt (ent.; 1912-82)
Jurgensen, Sonny (football; 1934-)
Juridical Science, Doctor of (also S.J.D.,
    Scientiae Juridicae Doctor)
Jurmala, Latvia
Jurong, Singapore
Jussi Bjoerling (Swed. tenor; 1911-60)
Just Cross Stitch (mag.)
Just My Size
Justerini & Brooks, Ltd. (J&B)
Justice Department (aka Department of Justice,
    DOJ)(US govt.)
Justice, David (baseball; 1966-)
Justice, Department of (DOJ)(US govt.)
Justin Kaplan (US writer; 1925-)
Justin Martyr, St. (It. rel.; 100?-165)
Justin Timberlake (ent., 'N Sync; 1981-)
Justine Bateman (ent.; 1966-)
Justinian Code (law)
Justinian I ("the Great")(Flavius Anicius [or
    Petrus Sabbatius] Justinianus)(emp.,
    Byzantine; 483-565)
Justus von Liebig, Baron (Ger. chem.; 1803-73)
Jute (people)
Juvenal (Roman satirist; c60-c127)
Juvénal Habyarimana (ex-pres., Rwanda;
    1937-94)
Juventas (myth.)
JVC (elec.)
JVC Co. of America
JWB (Jewish Welfare Board)
JWV (Jewish War Veterans)
J(ames) William Fulbright (US pol.; 1905-95)
J. William Klime (US adm.)

-K-

K (chem. sym., potassium)
K (kilobyte)(compu.)
Kaaawa, HI
Kaaba (also Ka'ba, Ka'bah, Ka'abah)(rel.)
Kaat, Jim (baseball; 1938-)
Kaba (also Kabah, Kaabah)(rel. bldg., Mecca)
Kabalevsky, Dmitri (Rus. comp.; 1904-87)
Kabbath, Ahmad Tejan (pres., Sierra Leone;
    1932-)
Kabibble, Ish (aka Merwyn Bogue)(ent.; 1908-94)
Kabila, Joseph (pres., Congo; 1969-)
Kabila, Laurent-Desire (ex-pres., Congo; 1939-
    2001)
Kabua, Amata (pres., Marshall Islands)
Kabuki (Jap. drama; 16th-18th c.)(also l.c.)
Kabul, Afghanistan
Kabwe, Zambia
Kabyle (lang./people)
Kaczynski, Theodore "Ted" (US news,
    Unabomber)
Kádár, János (ex-PM, Hung.; 1912-89)
Kadavy, Caryn (figure skating; 1964-)
Kaddish (rel.)
Kadré Desiré Ouedraogo (ex-PM, Burkina Faso;
    1953-)
Kaduna, Nigeria
Kaédi, Mauritania
Kafi, Ali (ex-pres., Algeria; 1928-)
Kafka, Franz (Ger. writer; 1889-1961)
Kafre (or Khafre), Pyramid of (Eg.)
Kagame, Paul (pres., Rwanda; 1957-)
Kahan, Meir (or Martin)(Jew. activist; 1932-90)
Kahanamoku, Duke (swimming; 1890-1968)
Kahlil Gibran (Lebanese writer/mystic/artist;
    1883-1931)
Kahlúa (liqueur)
Kahn, Albert (US arch.; 1869-1942)
Kahn, Gus (US lyricist; 1886-1941)
Kahn, Louis (US arch.; 1901-74)
Kahn, Madeline (ent.; 1942-99)
Kai Winding (US jazz; 1922-83)
Kaifu Toshiki (ex-PM, Jap.; 1931-)
Kailua, HI
Kain, Karen (ballet; 1951-)
Kaiser (former title, Ger./Aus.)
Kaiser Aluminum & Chemical Corp.
Kaiser-Permanente Foundation (Kaiser
    Foundation Health Plan)
Kaiser-Permanente Medical Group
Kaiser, Henry J(ohn)(US bus.; 1882-1967)
Kai-shek, Chiang (also Chiang Chung-cheng)
    (ex-pres., Nationalist China; 1887-1975)
Kai-shek, Madame Chiang (b. Soong Mei-ling)
    (Ch. lecturer/writer; 1898-)
Kakuei Tanaka (ex-PM, Jap.; 1918-93)
Kal Kan (pet food)
Kal Kan Foods, Inc.
Kalaallit Nunaat (also Greenland)(island, N Atl.)
Kalahari Desert (S Afr)

Kalakaua Ave., Honolulu, HI
Kalamazoo Gazette (MI newspaper)
Kalamazoo, MI
Kalanga (people)
Kalaupapa leper colony
Kalaupapa National Historic Park (HI)
Kali (myth.)
Kali-Yuga (rel.)
Kalimantan (province, Indonesia)
Kaline, Al(bert)(baseball; 1934-)
Kalki (rel.)
Kallikaks (fict. family name, sociological study)
Kallsberg, Anfinn (PM, Faeroe Islands)
Kaloko-Honokohau National Historical Park (HI)
Kaltenbrunner, Ernst (Aus. Nazi; 1901-46)
Kama Sutra (also Kamasutra)(Indian/Sanskrit
    treatise on love)
Kamakura (Jap. art; 13th-15th c)
Kamakura period
Kamakura shogunate
Kamakura, Japan
Kamasutra (also Kama Sutra)(Indian/Sanskrit
    treatise on love)
Kamba (lang./people)
Kamchatka (region, Siberia)
Kamchatka peninsula (NE Asia)
Kamehameha I (ex-king, Hawaii; c1758-1819)
Kamp's Frozen Foods, Van de (US bus.)
Kampala, Uganda
Kampgrounds of America (US bus.)
Kampuchea (now State of Cambodia)
Kamuta Laatasi (ex-PM, Tuvalu)
Kanaka (Hawaiian for native)
Kanakaredes, Melina (ent.; 1967-)
Kanaly, Steve (ent.; 1946-)
Kananga, Zaire
Kanawa, Kiri Te (soprano; 1944-)
Kandahar, Afghanistan
Kander, John (US comp.; 1927-)
Kandinsky, Wassily (or Vasili, Vasily)(Rus.
    artist; 1866-1944)
Kandy, Sri Lanka
Kane, Carol (ent.; 1952-)
Kang Song San (ex-PM, NKorea)
Kangaroo, Captain (fict. chara.)
Kaniksu National Forest
Kanin, Garson (US writer; 1912-99)
Kankakee (IL)
Kankan, Guinea
Kannada (lang.)
Kannon (also Kwannon)(rel.)
Kano (Jap. school of painters)
Kano, Nigeria
Kanpur, India
Kansas (KS)
Kansas City Chiefs (football team)
Kansas City Royals (baseball team)
Kansas City Star (MO newspaper)
Kansas City, KS, MO
Kansas-Nebraska Act/Bill (US hist.; 1854)
Kansu (also Gansu)(province, Ch.)
Kant, Immanuel (Ger. phil./phys.; 1724-1804)
Kantor, MacKinlay (US writer; 1904-77)
Kantor, Mickey (Michael)(US ex-secy./
    commerce; 1939-)

Kantrex (med.)
Kanuri (lang.)
Kanuzi-Dongola (lang.)
Kaohsiung, Taiwan
Kaolack, Senegal
Kaopectate (med.)
Kaplan, Gabriel (ent.; 1945-)
Kaplan, Justin (US writer; 1925-)
Kaposi's sarcoma (med.)
Karabakh, Nagorno- (region, Azerbaijan)
Karachi, Pakistan
Karaganda, Kazakhstan
Karajan, Herbert von (Aus. cond.; 1908-89)
Karakul (sheep)
Karamanlis, Constantine (ex-pres., Gr.; 1907-98)
Karamazov, The Brothers (Dostoevsky novel)
Karan, Donna (US designer; 1948-)
Karastan (carpet)
Karastan-Bigelow, Inc.
Karbe, Myanmar
Kardon, Harman- (stereo)
Kardon, Inc., Harman-
Kareem Abdul-Jabbar (b. Ferdinand) Lew(is)
    Alcindor, Jr.)(basketball; 1947-)
Karen (lang./people)
Karen Allen (ent.; 1951-)
Karen Black (b. Karen Ziegler)(ent.; 1942-)
Karen Blixen (pseud. Isak Dinesen)(Dan.
    writer; 1885-1962)
Karen Carpenter (ent.; 1950-83)
Karen Kain (ballet; 1951-)
Karen P. Hughes (nee Parfill)(US White House
    pol. adviser; 1957?-)
Karen Silkwood (US nuclear safety advocate;
    1946-74)
Karen Valentine (ent.; 1947-)
Karen Young (ent.)
Karenina, Anna (L. Tolstoy novel)
Kariba dam (Zimbabwe)
Kariba, Lake (Zimbabwe)
Karim Lamrani, Mohammed (ex-PM, Morocco)
Karimov, Islam A. (pres., Uzbekistan; 1938-)
Karl A(ugustus) Menninger (US psych.; 1893-
    1990)
Karl Baedeker (Ger. guidebook publ.; 1801-1959)
Karl Barth (Swed. rel.; 1886-1968)
Karl (or Carl) Bosch (Ger. chem.; 1874-1940)
Karl Czerny (Aus. pianist; 1791-1857)
Karl Friedrich Hieronymus Munchhausen, Baron
    von (Ger. soldier/adventurer/anecdotist;
    1720-97)
Karl Goldmark (Hung. comp.; 1830-1915)
Karl Jaspers (Ger. phil.; 1883-1969)
Karl Lagerfeld (designer; 1938-)
Karl Malden (b. Mladen Sekulovich)(ent.; 1913-)
Karl Mannheim (Hung. sociol./hist.; 1893-1947)
Karl (Heinrich) Marx (Ger. phil.; 1818-83)
Karl-Marx-Stadt, Germany (now Chemnitz)
Karl Millöcker (Aus. comp.; 1842-99)
Karl (or Carl) Philipp Emanuel Bach (Ger.
    comp.; 1714-88)
Karl Rove (US White House pol. adviser; 1950-)
Karl (Jay) Shapiro (US poet/editor; 1913-2000)
Karl Taylor Compton (US physt.; 1887-1954)
Karl von Clausewitz (Ger. mil.; 1780-1831)

Karl Wallenda (Ger. circus; 1905-78)
Karl Ziegler (Ger. chem.; 1898-1973)
Karlen, John (ent.; 1933-)
Karlheinz Stockhausen (Ger. comp.; 1928-)
Karloff, Boris (William Henry Pratt)(ent.; 1887-
    1969)
Karlsruhe, Germany
Karmal, Babrak (ex-pres., Afghan.; 1929-)
Karnak, Egypt
Karnak, temples of (Eg., built 21st-1st c. BC)
Karo (syrup)
Karo-Dairi (lang.)
Karol Wojtyla (Pope John Paul II)(Pol. pope;
    1920-)
Karolyi, Bela (gymnastics; 1942-)
Karoui, Hamed (ex-PM, Tunisia; 1927-)
Karpov, Anatoly (Rus., chess; 1951-)
Karras, Alex (ent.; 1935-)
Karsavina, Tamara (Rus. ballet; 1885-1978)
Kasdan, Lawrence (ent./writer; 1948-)
Kasem, Casey (ent.; 1933-)
Kashmir (also Cashmere)(goat)
Kashmir (area, Pak.)
Kashmir, Jammu and (state, India)
Kashmiri (lang.)
Kasimir (or Casimir) Malevich (Rus. artist;
    1878-1935)
Kaspar Schwenkfeld von Ossig (Ger. rel.; 1490-
    1561)
Kasparov, Gary (or Garry)(Rus., chess; 1963-)
Kassebaum, Nancy Landon (US pol.; 1932-)
Kassel, Germany
Kasyanov, Mikhail M. (PM, Rus.; 1957-)
Kasymzhomart Tokayev (PM, Kazakhstan; 1953-)
Kaszner, Kurt (ent.)
Kat Club, Kit- (also Kit-Cat)(London pol. grp.;
    1703-20)
Kat, Krazy (comic strip)
Katanga (now Shaba)
Katarina Witt (Ger. figure skating; 1965-)
Kate (Catherine) Greenaway (Br. artist/writer;
    1846-1901)
Kate Capshaw (b. Kathleen Sue Nail)(ent.; 1953-)
Kate Hudson (ent.; 1979-)
Kate Jackson (ent.; 1948-)
Kate Michelman (US reformist/NARAL pres.)
Kate Millett (US writer/feminist; 1934-)
Kate Moss (model; 1974-)
Kate Mulgrew (ent.; 1955-)
Kate Nelligan (ent.; 1951-)
Kate O'Flaherty Chopin (US writer; 1851-1904)
Kate (Kathryn) Smith (ent.; 1909-86)
Kate Winslet (ent.; 1975-)
Katey Sagal (ent.; 1954-)
Katharine Cornell (ent.; 1893-1974)
Katharine Dukakis (Kitty)(nee Dickson)(US wife
    of ex-MA gov.; 1937-)
Katharine Graham (US newspaper exec.; 1917-
    2001)
Katharine Hepburn (ent.; 1907-)
Katharine Lee Bates (US poet/educ.; 1859-1929)
Katharine Ross (ent.; 1942-)
Käthe (Schmidt) Kollwitz (Ger. artist; 1867-1945)
Katherine Anne Porter (US writer; 1890-1980)
Katherine "Katie" Couric (TV commentator;

1957-)
Katherine Dunham (ent.; 1910-)
Katherine Fox (Can./US spiritualist)
Katherine Harris (FL pol.)
Katherine Mansfield (Br. writer; 1888-1923)
Kathie Lee Gifford (b. Kathie Epstein)(ent.; 1953-)
Kathie Lee, Regis & (TV show)
Kathleen Battle (opera; 1948-)
Kathleen Kennedy (Cavendish)(US sister of ex-pres., died in plane crash; 1920-48)
Kathleen Nesbitt (ent.)
Kathleen (Thompson) Norris (US writer; 1880-1966)
Kathleen Quinlan (ent.; 1954-)
Kathleen Sullivan (ent.)
Kathleen Turner (ent.; 1954-)
Kathleen Woodiwiss (writer; 1939-)
Kathmandu, Nepal (also Katmandu)
Kathryn Grayson (ent.; 1922-)
Kathryn Kuhlman (faith healer; 1907-76)
Kathryn Murray (dance; 1906-99)
Kathy Bates (ent.; 1948-)
Kathy Hammond (runner; 1951-)
Kathy Ireland (model/bus.; 1963-)
Kathy Laverne McMillan (track; 1957-)
Kathy Whitworth (golf; 1939-)
Kathyrn "Kay" (Bailey) Hutchinson (US cong.; 1943-)
Katie (Katherine) Couric (TV commentator; 1957-)
Katie Elder, Sons of (film, 1965)
Katie Holmes (ent.; 1978-)
Katmai National Park (AK)
Katmandu, Nepal (also Kathmandu)
Katowice, Poland
Katsav, Moshe (pres., Isr.; 1945-)
Katt, William (ent.; 1950-)
Katyn Forest (Rus.)
Katzenberg, Jeffrey (US bus.; 1950-)
Katzenjammer Kids (comic strip)
Kauai (island, HI)
Kauai, HI
Kaufman and Broad Home Corp.
Kaufman house (also Falling Water)(F.L.Wright house)
Kaufman, Andy (ent.; 1949-84)
Kaufman, George S(imon)(US writer; 1889-1961)
Kaukauna Cheese (US bus.)
Kaunas, Lithuania
Kaunda, Kenneth (David)(ex-pres., Zambia; 1924-)
Kavango (people)
Kavner, Julie (ent.; 1951-)
Kawasaki disease
Kawasaki Heavy Industries Ltd.
Kawasaki Motors Corp.
Kawasaki Steel Corp.
Kawasaki, Japan
Kawasaki's disease/syndrome (med.)
Kay-Bee Food Products, Inc.
Kay Ciel (med.)
Kay (Kathyrn Bailey) Hutchinson (US cong.; 1943-)
Kay Jewelers, Inc.

Kay Kendall (ent.; 1926-59)
Kay (James Kern) Kyser (US cond.; 1906-85)
Kay Kyser's Kollege of Musical Knowledge
Kay Starr (ent.; 1922-)
Kay Swift (US comp.; 1908-93)
Kaye Ballard (b. Catherine Gloria Balotta)(ent.; 1926-)
Kaye, Danny (ent.; 1913-87)
Kaye, M(ary) M(argaret)(writer; 1911-)
Kaye, Sammy (US band leader; 1910-87)
Kaye, Stubby (ent.; 1918-97)
Kayes, Mali
Kaypro Corp.
Kayseri, Turkey
Kaysone Phomvihan (ex-PM, Laos; 1920-92)
Kazakh (lang./people)
Kazakhstan (Republic of)(formerly part of USSR)(central Asia)
Kazan, Elia (ent.; 1909-)
Kazan, Lainie (ent.; 1942-)
Kazan, Russia
Kazantzakis, Nikos (Gr. writer; 1883-1957)
Kazuo Ishiguro (Jap./US writer; 1954-)
Kazvin, Iran (also Qazvin)
K-Blazer, Chevrolet (auto.)
k. d. lang (b. Katherine Dawn Lang)(ent.; 1961-)
K-Dur (med.)
Keach, Stacy (ent.; 1941-)
Kealakekua (Bay), HI
Kean University (Union, NJ)
Kean, Edmund (ent.; 1787-1833)
Keane, Bil (cartoonist, *The Family Circus*; 1922-)
Keanu (Charles) Reeves (ent.; 1964-)
Kearney, NE
Kearny, NJ
Kearny, Philip (US mil.; 1814-62)
Kearny, Stephen (Watts)(US mil.; 1794-1848)
Keating, Charles H., III (US S&L scandal)
Keating, Charles H., Jr. (US S&L scandal; 1923-)
Keating, Frank (Francis Anthony)(OK gov.; 1944-)
Keating, Paul (ex-PM, Austl.; 1954-)
Keaton, Buster (Joseph Frank)(ent.; 1895-1966)
Keaton, Diane (b. Diane Hall)(ent.; 1946-)
Keaton, Michael (b. Michael Douglas)(ent.; 1951-)
Keats, John (Br. poet; 1795-1821)
Kebich, Vyacheslav F. (ex-PM, Belarus)
Kecskemét, Hungary
Kedleston, Marquis Curzon of (b. George Nathaniel Curzon)(Br. leader in India; 1859-1925)
Kedron (also Kidron)(rel.)
Keds (shoes)
Keds Corp.
Keebler Co.
Keebler elves
Keefe Brasselle (ent.; 1923-81)
Keel, Howard (b. Harold Clifford Leek)(ent.; 1919-)
Keeler, Ruby (ent.; 1909-93)
Keeling Islands (also Cocos Islands)(Indian Ocean)
Keelung, Taiwan
Keely Smith (ent.; 1935-)
Keenan Ivory Wayans (ent.; 1958-)
Keenan Winery, Robert (US bus.)
Keenan Wynn (ent.; 1916-86)

Keene Curtis (ent.; 1923-)
Keene, Carolyn (aka Harriet S. Adams)(US writer; 1803-82)
Keene, NH
Keener, Catherine (ent.; 1959?-)
Keeshan, Bob (ent.; 1927-)
Keesler Air Force Base, MS (mil.)
Kefauver, (Carey) Estes (US pol.; 1903-63)
Keflex (med.)
Keftab (med.)
Keillor, Garrison (US humorist/writer ; 1942-)
Keino, Kipchoge (runner; 1940-)
Keir Dullea (ent.; 1936-)
Keitel, Harvey (ent.; 1939-)
Keith Carradine (ent.; 1949-)
Keith C. Mitchell, Dr. (PM, Grenada; 1946-)
Keith Hernandez (baseball; 1953-)
Keith Jackson (sportscaster; 1928-)
Keith Jarrett (US jazz; 1945-)
Keith Richard (ent.; 1943-)
Keith, Brian (ent.; 1921-97)
Keith, David (ent.; 1954-)
Keith, Minor C. (US bus.; 1848-1929)
Keizo Obuchi (ex-PM, Japan; 1937-2000)
Kelenjin (people)
Keller, Helen (Adams)(US writer/educ., blind/deaf; 1880-1968)
Kellerman, Sally (ent.; 1937-)
Kelley, Clarence (US ex-FBI dir.; 1911-97)
Kelley, David E. (ent.; 1956-)
Kelley, DeForest (ent.; 1920-99)
Kelley, Kitty (US writer; 1942-)
Kellogg-Briand Pact (also Kellogg Peace Pact)(US/Fr.)
Kellogg Co., The
Kellogg, Frank B(illings)(US pol.; 1856-1937)
Kellogg, Will K. (US bus.; 1860-1951)
Kellogg's (cereal)
Kells, Book of (rel.)
Kellwood Co.
Kelly Air Force Base, TX (mil.)
Kelly McGillis (ent.; 1957-)
Kelly Services, Inc.
Kelly, Emmett (Leo)(US clown; 1898-1979)
Kelly, Gene (ent.; 1912-96)
Kelly, Grace (Patricia)(US actress; princess, Monaco; 1929-82)
Kelly, Jack (ent.; 1927-92)
Kelly, Jim (football; 1960-)
Kelly, Leroy (football; 1942-)
Kelly, R. (Robert)(ent.; 1969-)
Kelly, Red (Leonard Patrick)(hockey; 1927-)
Kelly, Sharon Pratt (ex-DC mayor; 1944-)
Kelly, Walt (cartoonist, Pogo; 1913-73)
Kelly's Blues, Pete (film, 1955)
Kelsey Grammer (ent.; 1955-)
Kelso (champion horse)
Kelso, Frank B., II (US adm.)
Kelthane (pesticide)
Kelvin effect, Joule- (temperature drop in gases)
Kelvin scale (temperature)(also l.c.)
Kelvin, William Thomson, Lord (Br. physt./math.; 1824-1907)
Kelvinator (appliances)
Kelvinator, Inc.

Kemadrin (med.)
Kemal Ataturk (aka Mustafa Kemal)(Turk. soldier/dipl.; 1881-1938)
Kemble, Francis "Fanny" Anne (Br. writer/ent.; 1809-93)
Kemp, Jack (US pol.; 1935-)
Kemp, Shawn (basketball; 1969-)
Kempis, Thomas à (Gr. rel.; c1380-1471)
Kempthorne, Dirk (Arthur)(ID gov.; 1951-)
Ken Anderson (football; 1949-)
Ken Berry (ent.; 1933-)
Ken Burns (ent.; 1953-)
Ken Griffey, Jr. (baseball; 1969-)
Ken Kercheval (ent.; 1935-)
Ken Kesey (US writer; 1935-)
Ken(neth Martin) Follett (Br. writer; 1949-)
Ken Murray (ent.; 1903-88)
Ken Olin (ent.; 1954-)
Ken Rosewall (tennis; 1934-)
Ken Russell (ent.; 1927-)
Ken(neth Winston) Starr (US atty./Clinton hearings; 1946-)
Ken Wahl (ent. 1956-)
Kenacort (med.)
Kenai Fjords National Park (AK)
Kenalog (med.)
Kenalog in Orabase (med.)
Kendal green (color, fabric)
Kendal sneck bent (fishing)
Kendall-Jackson Winery (US bus.)
Kendall, David (US atty./Clintons' atty.)
Kendall, Henry W. (US physt.; 1926-99)
Kendall, Kay (ent.; 1926-59)
Keneally, Thomas (Michael)(Austl. writer; 1935-)
Kenema, Sierra Leone
Kenesaw Mountain Landis (US jurist/baseball exec.; 1866-1944)
Kenmore (appliances)
Kennan, George F. (US dipl.; 1904-)
Kennebunkport, ME
Kennedy A(lphonse) Simmonds (ex-PM, St. Kitts-Nevis; 1936-)
Kennedy Center for the Performing Arts, John F. (DC)
Kennedy Compound (Hyannis Port, MA)
Kennedy International Airport, J. F. (NY)
Kennedy Onassis, Jacqueline "Jackie" Lee Bouvier (US editor/photo.; wife of ex-US pres.; 1929-94)
Kennedy Schlossberg, Caroline (US atty., daughter of JFK; 1957-)
Kennedy Shriver, Eunice (US wife of pol.; 1921-)
Kennedy Space Center, (John F.)(FL)
Kennedy, Anthony M. (US jurist; 1936-)
Kennedy, Arthur (ent.; 1914-90)
Kennedy, Carolyn Bessette (wife of JFK, Jr.; 1966-99)
Kennedy, Edward M(oore) "Ted" (US cong.; 1932-)
Kennedy, Ethel (Skakel)(US wife of ex-atty. gen.; 1928-)
Kennedy, George (ent.; 1925-)
Kennedy, John "Jack" F(itzgerald)(35th US pres.; 1917-63)

Kennedy, John F(itzgerald), Jr. (US publ./son of ex-US pres.; 1960-99)
Kennedy, Joseph Patrick, II (US pol.; 1952-)
Kennedy, Joseph Patrick, Jr. (US bro. of ex-pres., killed in WWII; 1915-44)
Kennedy, Joseph Patrick, Sr. (US bus./dipl., father of ex-pres.; 1888-1969)
Kennedy (Cavendish), Kathleen (US sister of ex-pres., died in plane crash; 1920-48)
Kennedy (Lawford), Patricia (US sister of ex-pres.; 1924-)
Kennedy, Patrick Joseph (US bus., grandfather of ex-pres.; 1858-1929)
Kennedy, Patrick Joseph (US pol.; 1967-)
Kennedy, Robert F(rancis)(US pol., bro. of ex-pres.; 1925-68)
Kennedy, Rose Elizabeth (nee Fitzgerald)(US mother of ex-pres.; 1890-1995)
Kennedy, Rosemary (US sister of ex-pres.; 1918-)
Kennedy, Ted (Edward Moore)(US cong., bro. of ex-pres.; 1932-)
Kennedy, William (US writer; 1928-)
Kennedy-Overton, Jayne (ent.; 1951-)
Kennelly-Heaviside layer (also E layer)(in lower regions, ionosphere)
Kennelly, Barbara Bailey (US cong.; 1936-)
Kennerly, Thomas, Jr. (pseud. Tom Wolfe)(US writer; 1931-)
Kennesaw University (Marietta, GA)
Kenneth Branagh (ent./writer; 1960-)
Kenneth Copeland (US rel.)
Kenneth Dryden (hockey; 1947-)
Kenneth "Babyface" Edmonds (ent.; 1958-)
Kenneth Grahame (Scot. writer; 1859-1932)
Kenneth (David) Kaunda (ex-pres., Zambia; 1924-)
Kenneth Millar (pseud. Ross Macdonald)(US writer; 1915-83)
Kenneth Noland (US artist; 1924-)
Kenneth R(oy) Thomson (Can. bus.; 1923-)
Kenneth Stabler (football; 1945-)
Kenny C. Guinn (NV gov.; 1936-)
Kenny Chesney (ent.; 1968-)
Kenny Clarke (US jazz; 1914-85)
Kenny D. Anthony (PM, St. Lucia; 1951-)
Kenny G (Kenneth Gorelick)(US jazz; 1956-)
Kenny Loggins (ent.; 1948-)
Kenny Rogers (ent.; 1938-)
Kenny, Sister (Elizabeth)(Austl. nurse; 1886-1952)
Kenosha, WI
Kensington and Chelsea (London borough)
Kent (county, Eng.)
Kent Conrad (US cong.; 1948-)
Kent Family Chronicles (J. Jakes novels)
Kent State University (Kent, OH)
Kent, Allegra (ent.; 1937-)
Kent, Julie (US dancer; 1971-)
Kent, Rockwell (US artist; 1882-1971)
Kentaurus, Rigel (also Alpha Centauri)(astron.)
Kenton, Stan (US jazz; 1912-79)
Kentucky (KY)
Kentucky and Virginia Resolutions (US hist.; 1798)
Kentucky bluegrass (grass)

Kentucky coffee beans
Kentucky coffee tree
Kentucky Derby (horse racing)
Kentucky Fried Chicken Corp. (KFC Corp.)
Kentucky Fried Movie (film, 1977)
Kenwood Vineyards (US bus.)
Kenworth Truck Co.
Kenya (Republic of)(E Afr)
Kenya Airlines
Kenya, Mount (also Kirinyaga)(extinct volcano)
Kenyatta, Jomo (b. Kamau Ngengi)(ex-pres., Kenya; 1893?-1978)
Keobounphan, Sisavat (PM, Laos; 1928-)
Keogh plan (econ.)
Keogh, Eugene J. (US pol.; 1907-89)
Kepler telescope
Kepler, Johannes (or Johann)(Ger. astron./math.; 1571-1630)
Kepler's laws (planetary motion)
Kerala (state, India)
Kercheval, Ken (ent.; 1935-)
Kérékou, Mathieu (pres., Benin; 1933-)
Kerensky, Aleksandr (Feodorovich)(Rus. pol.; 1881-1970)
Keri Russell (ent.; 1976-)
Kerkorian, Kirk (ent./MGM; 1917-)
Kerlone (med.)
Kermanshah (also Kirman, Kirmanshah)(Pers. rug)
Kermit Bloomgarden (ent.; 1904-76)
Kermit the Frog (Muppet)
Kern, Jerome (David)(US comp.; 1885-1945)
Kerns, Joanna (b. Joanna De Varona)(ent.; 1953-)
Kerouac, Jack (Jean-Louis Lebris de)(US writer; 1922-69)
Kerr-McGee Corp.
Kerr, Deborah (ent.; 1921-)
Kerr, Graham (aka Galloping Gourmet)(Br. chef; 1934-)
Kerr, Jean (US writer; 1923-)
Kerr, John (ent.; 1931-)
Kerr, Walter F. (US writer/critic; 1913-96)
Kerrey, (Joseph) Robert "Bob" (US pol.; 1943-)
Kerrigan, Nancy (US figure skater; 1969-)
Kerry (county, Ir.)
Kerry blue terrier (dog)
Kerry, John (US cong.; 1943-)
Kersee, Jackie Joyner- (track; 1962-)
Kerwin, Joseph P(eter)(astro.; 1932-)
Kesey, Ken (US writer; 1935-)
Keshia Knight Pulliam (ent.; 1979-)
Kessai Note (pres., Marshall Islands)
Kessel, Barney (US jazz; 1923-)
Ketch, Jack (Br. slang, official hangman)
Ketch, John (Br. executioner; 1663?-86)
Ketcham, Hank (US cartoonist, *Dennis the Menace*; 1920-2001)
Ketchikan, AK
Kettering Institute for Cancer Research, Sloan- (NYC)
Kettering, Charles F. (US eng./inv.; 1876-1958)
Ketterley, Digory (fict. chara., C. S. Lewis' *Chronicles of Narnia*)
Kettle, Ma & Pa (fict. charas.)
Ketuvim (also *Ketubim, the Hagiographa*)(rel.)
Kevin Bacon (ent.; 1958-)

Kevin Costner (ent.; 1955-)
Kevin Dobson (ent.; 1944-)
Kevin Kline (ent.; 1947-)
Kevin McCarthy (ent.; 1914-)
Kevin Nealon (ent.; 1953-)
Kevin Richardson (ent., Backstreet Boys; 1972-)
Kevin Roche (US arch.; 1922-)
Kevin Sorbo (ent.; 1958-)
Kevin Spacey (ent.; 1959-)
Kevin Williamson (ent./screenwriter, *Dawson's Creek*; 1965-)
Kevorkian, Jack (Murad)(US phys.; 1928-)
Kew Gardens (Eng.)(also Royal Botanic Gardens)
Kew, England
Kewpie doll
Key Biscayne, FL
Key Largo, FL
Key lime pie
Key West Naval Air Station (FL)
Key West, FL
Key, Francis Scott (US atty., wrote *The Star Spangled Banner*; 1780-1843)
Key, Ted (cartoonist, *Hazel*; 1912-)
Keyes, Evelyn (ent.; 1919-)
Keyes, Frances Parkinson (US writer; 1885-1970)
Keynes, John Maynard (Br. econ.; 1883-1946)
Keynesian economics
Keystone Kops (or Cops)
Keystone State (nickname, PA)
KFC Corp. (Kentucky Fried Chicken Corp.)
KGB (USSR secret police; disbanded 1991; replaced by FSB [Federal Security Service, Russia])
Khachaturian, Aram Ilich (or Ill'yich)(Armenian comp.; 1903-78)
Khadafy (or Qaddafi), Muammar al-, Colonel (pres., Libya; 1942-)
Khafre (or Kafre), Pyramid of (Eg.)
Khai, Phan Dinh (aka Le Duc Tho)(NViet pol.; 1911-90)
Khai, Phan Van (PM, Viet.; 1933-)
Khaki Campbell (duck)
Khaleda Zia, Begum (PM, Bangladesh; 1944-)
Khalifa al-Thani, Abdullah bin (PM, Qatar)
Khalifa bin Hamad al-Thani, Sheik (ex-emir, Qatar; 1932-)
Khalifa bin Sulman al-Khalifa, Shiek (PM, Bahrain; 1935-)
Khalifa, Sheik Isa bin Sulman al-, (emir, Bahrain; 1933-)
Khalka (lang.)
Khalsa (rel.)
Khama, Seretse (ex-pres., Botswana; 1921-80)
Khamenei, Ayatollah Sayyed Ali (rel. head, Iran; 1940-)
Khamtai Siphandon (pres., Laos; 1924-)
Khan Akhmedov (Turkmenistan pol.)
Khan IV, Aga (Islamic rel.; 1936-)
Khan, Chaka (b. Yvette Marie Stevens)(ent.; 1953-)
Khan, Genghis (also Jenghiz, Chinghiz Khan, Temujin)(Mongol conqueror; c1167-1227)
Khan, Ghulam Ishaq (ex-pres., Pak.)
Khan, Kublai (also Kubla Khan)(Mongol/Ch. emp.; 1216-94)

Khan, Liaquat Ali (ex-PM, Pak.; 1895-1951)
Khan, Princess Yasmin (Aga)(1949-)
Khardungla Pass (India)
Kharkov, Ukraine
Khartoum, Sudan (also Khartum)
Khashoggi, Adnan
Khatami, Seyed Mohammed (pres., Iran; 1943-)
Khayyám, Omar (Persian poet/math.; c1028-1122)
Khayyám, The Rubáiyát of Omar (book of verses)
Khíos Island (Gr.)
Khirbet Qumran (Dead Sea Scrolls site)
Khmer (lang./people)
Khmer Empire (ancient Cambodia and Laos)
Khmer Republic (now Cambodia)
Khmer Rouge (Cambodian communist movement)
Khodzhent, Tajikistan
Khoikhoi (lang./people)
Khoisan (langs.)
Khomenei, Ayatollah Ruhollah (Iran, rel.; 1900-89)
Khorana, Har Gobind (India/US chem.; 1922-)
Khouna, Cheikh El Afia Ould Mohamed (PM, Mauritania)
Khrunov, Yevgeny V(asilyevich)(cosmo.; 1933-)
Khrushchev, Nikita S(ergeyevich)(ex-premier, USSR; 1894-1971)
Khudair, Ahmed Hussein (Iraq, pol.)
Khufu (king, Eg.; c2600 BC)
Khufu (or Cheops), Great Pyramid of (Eg.)
Khulna, Bangladesh
Khyber Pass (also Khaibar Pass)(Pak./Afghan.)
Kia (auto.)
Kia Optima (auto.)
Kia Optima LX (auto.)
Kia Optima SE (auto.)
Kia Rio (auto.)
Kia Sephia (auto.)
Kia Sephia GS (auto.)
Kia Sephia LS (auto.)
Kia Sephia RS (auto.)
Kia Spectra (auto.)
Kia Spectra GS (auto.)
Kia Spectra GSX (auto.)
Kia Sportage (auto.)
Kia Sportage EX (auto.)
Kia Sportage Limited (auto.)
Kiangsi (also Jiangxi)(province, Ch.)
Kiangsu (also Jiangsu)(province, Ch.)
Kibbee, Guy (ent.; 1886-1956)
Kibbles 'N Bits (pet food)
Kibbles And Chunks (pet food)
Kickapoo (Native Amer.)
Kid (or Kyd), Thomas (Br. writer; c1557-95)
Kid Ory (US jazz; 1886-1973)
Kid Rock (b. Robert James Ritchie)(ent.; 1972-)
Kidd, Michael (b. Milton Greenwald)(US choreographer; 1919-)
Kidd, William (aka Captain Kidd)(Scot. pirate; 1645?-1701)
Kidder, Margot (ent.; 1948-)
Kidder, Peabody & Co., Inc.
Kidman, Nicole (ent.; 1967-)

Kidron (also Kedron)(rel.)
Kids in the Hall (TV show)
Kiefer Sutherland (ent.; 1966-)
Kiel, Germany
Kiepura, Jan (tenor; 1902-66)
Kieran, John (US writer; 1892-1981)
Kierkegaard, Sören (or Søren)(Dan. phil.;
   1813-55)
Kiesinger, Kurt Georg (ex-chancellor, W. Ger.;
   1904-88)
Kiet, Vo Van (ex-PM, Viet.; 1922-)
Kiev, chicken
Kiev, Ukraine
Kigali, Rwanda
Kiichi Miyazawa (ex-PM, Jap.; 1919-)
Kikkoman International, Inc.
Kikkoman soy sauce
Kikuyu (lang./people)
Kilauea (volcanic crater, HI)
Kilborn, Craig (ent./sportscaster; 1962-)
Kilbride, Percy (ent.; 1888-1964)
Kildare (county, Ir.)
Kildare, Dr. (TV show)
Kiley, Richard (ent.; 1922-99)
Kilgallen, Dorothy (US columnist/ent.; 1913-65)
Kilimanjaro, Mount (Afr.)
Kilimanjaro, The Snows of (film, 1952)
Kilkenny (county, Ir.)
Kilkenny cats
Kilkenny, Ireland
Killarney, Lakes of (Ir.)
Killebrew, Harmon (baseball; 1936-)
Killeen, TX
Killer Tomatoes, Attack of the (film, 1977)
Killian's Red (beer)
Killy, Jean-Claude (Fr. skier; 1943-)
Kilmer, Bill (William Orland)(football; 1939-)
Kilmer, (Alfred) Joyce (US poet; 1886-1918)
Kilmer, Val (ent.; 1959-)
Kilroy was here (WWII saying)
Kim Basinger (ent.; 1953-)
Kim Campbell (ex-PM, Can.; 1947-)
Kim Cattrall (ent.; 1956-)
Kim Dae Jung (pres., SKorea; 1925-)
Kim Darby (ent.; 1948-)
Kim Fields (ent.; 1969-)
Kim Il Sung (ex-pres., NKorea; 1912-94)
Kim Jong II (pres., NKorea; 1942-)
Kim Linehan (swimming; 1962-)
Kim Novak (ent.; 1933-)
Kim Stanley (ent.; 1925-)
Kim Young Sam (ex-pres., SKorea; 1927-)
Kim Zimmer (ent.; 1955-)
Kimba Wood (US atty.; 1944-)
Kimball International, Inc.
Kimball pianos
Kimberley Hefner (US, ex-wife of Hugh H.)
Kimberly Bergalis (US AIDS victim; 1968-91)
Kimberly-Clark Corp.
Kimberly Mays (US news, switched at birth)
Kimbrough, Charles (ent.)
Kimbundu (lang./people)
Kimitake, Hiraoka (pseud. Mishima Yukio)(Jap.
   writer; 1925-70)
Kinco Manufacturing Co.

Kiner, Ralph (baseball; 1922-)
King (Joseph) Oliver (US jazz; 1885-1938)
King (Wallis) Vidor (ent.; 1895-1982)
King Abdullah II (Abdullah ibn Hussein)(king,
   Jordan; 1962-)
King Albert II (king, Belgium; 1934-)
King Alphonse (mixed drink)
King and I, The (play; film, 1956)
King Arthur (legendary Br. king, 6th c.)
King Azlan (Muhibuddin) Shah, (Rajah)(ex-
   king, Malaysia; 1928-)
King Bhumibol Adulyadej (aka King Rama
   IX)(king, Thailand; 1927-)
King Birendra Bir Bikram Shah Dev (king,
   Nepal; 1945-)
King Camp Gillette (US bus./razor; 1855-1932)
King Carl XVI Gustaf (king, Swed.; 1946-)
King Charles spaniel (dog)
King Cotton (US hist., early 19th c)
King Fahd ibn Abdul Aziz (al-Saud)(king, Saudi
   Arabia; 1923-)
King Harald V (also Harold)(king, Nor.; 1936-)
King Hassan II (king, Morocco; 1929-99)
King Hussein I (ibn Talal)(king, Jordan; 1935-99)
King International, Inc., Jani-
King James Bible (also King James Version,
   Authorized Version)
King Juan Carlos I (king, Spain; 1938-)
King Kong (film, 1933, 1976)
King Lear (Shakespeare play)
King Letsie III (king, Lesotho; 1963-)
King Ludd (also Liudd, Nudd, Ned Ludd)(Welsh
   legend)
King Menelaus (myth.)
King Midas (myth.)
King Minos (myth.)
King Mohammed IV (king, Morocco; 1963-)
King Mswati III (king, Swaziland; 1968-)
King Norodom Sihanouk (king, Cambodia; 1922-)
King of Heaven (God)
King of Kings/kings (God, Jesus)
King Philip (aka Metacomet)(Wampanoag
   Indian chief; 1640-76)
King Rama IX (b. Bhumibol Adulyadej)(king,
   Thailand; 1927-)
King Solomon's Mines (film, 1937, 1950, 1985)
King Taufa'ahau Tupou IV (king, Tonga; 1918-)
King Tut (Tutankhamen)(king, Eg.; 1343-25 BC)
King Wenceslas, Good (also *Wenceslaus*)(song)
King Wenceslaus (also St. Wenceslas)(duke,
   Bohemia; 907-929)
king crab, Alaskan
King, Alan (b. Irwin Alan Kniberg)(ent.; 1927-)
King, Albert (US jazz; 1923-92)
King, Angus S., Jr. (ME gov.; 1944-)
King, B. B. (b. Riley B. King)(ent.; 1925-)
King, Billie Jean (Moffitt)(tennis; 1943-)
King, Bruce (ex-NM gov.; 1924-)
King, Carole (b. Carole Klein)(US comp./ent.;
   1942-)'
King, Coretta Scott (US civil rights; 1927-)
King, Don (boxing promoter; 1931-)
King, Ernest J(oseph)(US mil.; 1878-1956)
King, Frank (cartoonist; *Gasoline Alley*; 1883-
   1969)

King, Larry (b. Lawrence Harvey Zeiger)(ent.; 1933-)
King, Pee Wee (Frank)(US comp.; 1914-2000)
King, Perry (ent.; 1948-)
King, Rev. Dr. Martin Luther, Jr. (US civil rights leader; 1929-68)
King, Richard (US rancher; 1825-85)
King, Rodney (US news; 1965-)
King, Rufus (US pol.; 1755-1827)
King, Stephen (US writer; 1947-)
King, William Lyon Mackenzie (ex-PM, Can.; 1874-1950)
King, William R(ufus De Vane)(ex.-US VP; 1786-1853)
King's (or Queen's) Bench (Br. law)
King's (or Queen's) Counsel (Br. law)
king's (or queen's) English (correct English)
Kingdom Hall of Jehovah's Witnesses (rel.)
Kingdom of God (heaven)
Kingdom of Heaven (heaven)
Kingdom, Middle (Eg. hist.; c2040-1670 BC) (Ch. term for China until 1912)
Kingdoms period, Three (Korean hist.; began 3rd c.)
Kingman Brewster, Jr. (US educ.; 1919-88)
Kingman, AZ
Kings Canyon National Park (CA)
Kings of the Orient, Three (also Wise Men of the East, Magi, Three Wise Men)(rel.)
Kings, I&II (aka Book of Kings)(rel., books of the Old Testament)
Kings, Los Angeles (hockey team)
Kings, Sacramento (basketball team)
Kingsley Amis (writer; 1922-95)
Kingsley, Ben (b. Krishna Bhanji)(ent.; 1943-)
Kingsley, Sidney (b. Sidney Kirschner)(US playwright; 1906-95)
Kingsolver, Barbara (US writer; 1955-)
Kingsport, TN
Kingston Trio (folk music)
Kingston, Jamaica
Kingston, Maxine Hong (US writer; 1940-)
Kingston, NY, PA
Kingston, Ontario, Canada
Kingston-upon-Hull, England (also Hull)
Kingstown, Saint Vincent and the Grenadines
Kingsville Naval Air Station (TX)
Kinigi, Sylvie (ex-PM, Burundi)
Kinkade, Thomas (US art.,"Painter of Light")
Kinko's Ventures, Inc.
Kinko's, Inc.
Kinks, The (pop music)
Kinnear, Greg (ent.; 1963-)
Kinney Shoe Corp.
Kinsella, John (swimming; 1952-)
Kinsey Report (officially Sexual Behavior in the Human Male/Female, 2 books by A.C. Kinsey)
Kinsey scale (of sexual orientation)
Kinsey, Alfred Charles (US sociol./biol.; 1894-1956)
Kinshasa, (Democratic Republic of the) Congo
Kinski, Nastassja (b. Nastassja Nakszynski) (ent.; 1961-)
Kinte, Kunta (fict. chara., Roots)

Kiowa (Native Amer.)
Kipchoge Keino (runner; 1940-)
Kipling, (Joseph) Rudyard (Br. writer; 1865-1936)
Kiplinger's Personal Finance (mag.)
Kipnis, Alexander (basso; 1891-1978)
Kipnis, Igor (harpsichordist; 1930-)
Kippur, Yom (Day of Atonement)(rel.)
Kir (mixed drink)
Kir royale (mixed drink)
Kiraly, Karch (volleyball; 1960-)
Kirby Puckett (baseball; 1961-)
Kirby vacuum
Kirby, Bruno (ent.; 1949-)
Kirby, Durward (ent.; 1912-2000)
Kirby, George (ent.; 1923-95)
Kirchner, Ernst Ludwig (Ger. artist; 1880-1938)
Kirghiz (people)
Kiri Te Kanawa (soprano; 1944-)
Kiribati (Republic of)(formerly Gilbert Islands) (central Pac.)
Kirin (also Jilin)(province, Ch.)
Kirin Brewery Co., Ltd.
Kirinyaga, Mount (also Kenya)(extinct volcano)
Kirk Cameron (ent.; 1970-)
Kirk Douglas (b. Issur Danielovich Demsky) (ent.; 1916-)
Kirk(wood) Fordice, (Daniel), Jr. (ex-MS gov.; 1934-)
Kirk Gibson (baseball; 1957-)
Kirk Kerkorian (ent./MGM; 1917-)
Kirk Stieff Co.
Kirk, Grayson (Louis)(US educ.; 1903-97)
Kirk, James T., Capt. (fict. chara., Star Trek)
Kirkland, Gelsey (ballet; 1953-)
Kirkpatrick, Chris (ent., 'N Sync; 1971-)
Kirkpatrick, Jeane (Jordan)(US pol./dipl.; 1926-)
Kirkpatrick, Ralph (US harpsichordist; 1911-84)
Kirksville, MO
Kirlian photography (captures images of energy or "aura")
Kirman (also Kirmanshah, Kermanshah)(Pers. rug)
Kiro Gligorov (ex-pres., Macedonia; 1917-)
Kirov Ballet
Kirov, Russia (now Vyatka)
Kirov, Sergei Mironovich (Rus. pol.; 1886-1934)
Kirsch blinds
Kirsch Co.
Kirstein, Lincoln (ent.; 1907-96)
Kirsten Dunst (ent.; 1982-)
Kirsten Flagstad (Wagnerian soprano; 1895-1962)
Kirsten, Dorothy (US opera; 1919-92)
Kirstie Alley (ent.; 1951-)
Kirsty Hume (model; 1976-)
Kirtland Air Force Base, NM (mil.)
Kirundi (also Rundi)(lang.)
Kisangani, Zaire
Kisatchie National Forest
K. I. Sawyer Air Force Base (MI)
Kishinev, Moldova (also Chisinau)
Kislev (Jew. month)
Kismayu, Somalia
Kismet (play; film, 1920, 1930, 1944, 1955)
Kiss (pop music)
Kiss Me Kate (film, 1953)
Kiss of the Spider Woman (film, 1985)

Kissimmee, FL

Kissinger, Dr. Henry A(lfred)(US pol./ex-secy./ state; 1923-)

Kisumu, Kenya

Kiswahili (also Swahili)(lang.)

Kit (Christopher Samuel) Bond (US cong.; 1939-)

Kit Carson, (Christopher)(US frontier; 1809-68)

Kit Kat bar (candy)

Kit-Kat Club (also Kit-Cat)(London pol. grp.; 1703-20)

Kitaj, Ron B. (US artist; 1932-)

Kitakyushu, Japan

Kitaro (b. Masanori Takahashi)(New Age multiinstrumentalist; 1953-)

Kitchen Cabinet (US hist., Pres. A. Jackson advisers; 1829-33)

KitchenAid (kitchen appliances)

Kitchenaid (US bus.)

Kitchener, Ontario, Canada

Kite, Tom (golf; 1949-)

Kitt Peak National Observatory (AZ)

Kitt, Eartha (ent.; 1927-)

Kitts-Nevis, St. (officially Federation of St. Christopher-Nevis)(West Indies)

Kitty Carlisle (ent.; 1915-)

Kitty Carruthers (figure skating)

Kitty Dukakis (Katharine)(nee Dickson)(US wife of ex-MA gov.; 1937-)

Kitty Hawk, NC

Kitty Kelley (US writer; 1942-)

Kitty Wells (b. Muriel Deason)(ent.; 1919-)

Kituba (lang.)

Kitwe, Zambia

Kitzhaber, John A(lbert)(OR gov.; 1947-)

Kiwanis

Kix (cereal)

Kizim, Leonid (cosmo.)

K ration (US mil. food rations)

KKK (Ku Klux Kan)

Klaipeda, Lithuania

Klamath Falls, OR

Klan, Ku Klux (also KKK, the Klan)(US racist society; founded 1866)

Klaus (Emil Julius) Fuchs (Ger. spy; 1911-88)

Klaus Barbie (Ger. Nazi leader; 1913-91)

Klaus Maria Brandauer (ent.; 1944-)

Klaus, Václav (ex-PM, Czech; 1941-)

Klee, Paul (Swiss artist; 1879-1940)

Kleenex

Klein & Co., Anne

Klein Cosmetics Corp., Calvin

Klein Jewelry, Anne (US bus.)

Klein, Calvin (US designer; 1942-)

Klein, Joe (US writer/*Primary Colors*)

Klein, Joel (US atty., DOJ/antitrust; 1946-)

Klein, Ltd., Calvin (US bus.)

Klein, Melanie (Aus. psych.; 1882-1960)

Klein, Robert (ent.; 1942-)

Kleist, Heinrich von (Ger. writer; 1777-1811)

Klemens W. N. L. Metternich (Aus. pol.; 1773-1859)

Klement Gottwald (Czech. pol.; 1896-1953)

Klemperer, Otto (Ger. cond.; 1885-1973)

Klemperer, Werner (Ger. ent.; 1920-2000)

Klerk, Frederik W(illem) de (ex-pres., SAfr; 1936-)

Klestil, Thomas (pres., Austria; 1932-)

Kliban, B(ernard)(cartoonist, cats; 1935-91)

Klime, J. William (US adm.)

Klimt, Gustav (Aus. artist; 1862-1918)

Kline test (for syphilis)

Kline, Kevin (ent.; 1947-)

Klinefelter's syndrome (genetics)(med.)

Klingon (*Star Trek*)

KLM Royal Dutch Airlines

Klondike (region, Yukon, gold found 1896)

Klondike Gold Rush National Historical Park (AK/WA)

Klondike River

Klonopin (med.)

K-Lor (med.)

Klorvess (med.)

Klotrix (med.)

Kluck, Alexander von (Ger. gen.; 1846-1934)

Kluge, John Werner (US bus.; 1914-)

Klugman, Jack (ent.; 1922-)

Klum, Heidi (model; 1973-)

Kluszewski, Ted (baseball; 1924-88)

Klute (film, 1971)

Klutznick, Fullilove v. (US law; 1980)

K-Lyte (med.)

Kmart Corp.

Knesset (Isr. parliament)

Knickerbocker, Herman Jansen (Dutch settler in NY; 1650?-1716?)

Knickerbockers (Dutch settlers in NY)

Knicks, New York (basketball team)

Knievel, Evel (Robert Craig)(US daredevil; 1938-)

Knievel, Robbie (US daredevil; 1960-)

Knight & the Pips, Gladys (pop music)

Knight, Bob (Robert Montgomery)(basketball; 1940-)

Knight, Gladys (ent.; 1944-)

Knight, John S. (US publ.; 1894-1981)

Knight, Jonathan (ent.; 1968-)

Knight, Jordan (ent.; 1970-)

Knight, Michael E. (ent.; 1959-)

Knight, Ted (ent.; 1923-86)

Knight, Wayne (ent.; 1955-)

Knight-Ridder Financial News

Knight-Ridder, Inc.

Knights of Columbus (rel. org.)

Knights of Labor (US labor org.; 1869-1917)

Knights of Pythias (US benevolent secret society; founded 1864)

Knights of the Round Table (legendary King Arthur knights)

Knights of the Temple of Solomon (also Templar)(rel./mil. order; 1119-1307)

Knights of the Teutonic Order (also Teutonic Knights)(Ger. mil./rel.; est. 1190)

Knights Templars (rel./mil. order; 1119-1307)

Knightsbridge (London)

Knokke-Heist, Belgium

Knopf, Alfred A(braham)(US publ.; 1892-1984)

Knopf, Inc., Alfred A.

Knopfler, Mark (ent., Dire Straits; 1949-)

Knorr Beeswax Products, Inc.

Knossos (also Cnossos)(ruins, palace, Crete)

Knots Landing (TV show)

Knott's Berry Farm (US bus.)
Knotts, Don (ent.; 1924-)
Knowles, John (US writer; 1926-)
Knowles, Tony (Anthony)(AK gov.; 1943-)
Know-Nothings (US pol. party; 1852-60)
Knox gelatin
Knox, Fort, KY (mil., gold depository)
Knox, John (Scot. rel.; 1505-72)
Knoxville News-Sentinel (TN newspaper)
Knoxville, TN
Knud Johan Victor Rasmussen (Dan. expl.;
   1879-1933)
Knudsen & Sons, Inc.
Knudsen (food)
Knudsen Dairy Products (US bus.)
Knudsen, William S. (US bus.; 1879-1848)
Knut Hamsun (Norwegian writer; 1859-1952)
Knute (Kenneth) Rockne (football; 1888-1931)
KO (knock out)
Koala Blue (sportswear)
Koala Blue, Inc.
Koala Springs International (US bus.)
Kobe beef (extremely tender)
Kobe Bryant (basketball; 1978-)
Kobe, Japan
Kobo, Abe (Jap. writer; 1924-93)
Kobuk Valley National Park (AK)
Koch, Edward (Irving)(ex-NYC mayor; 1924-)
Koch, Robert (Ger. phys./bacteriol.; 1843-1910)
Kodachrome (photo.)
Kodacolor (photo.)
Kodak (photo.)
Kodak Co., Eastman
Kodály, Zoltán (Hung. comp.; 1882-1967)
Kodamatic (photo.)
Kodel (fabric, polyester fiber)
Kodes, Jan (tennis; 1946-)
Kodiak bear
Kodiak Island (AK)
Kodjo, Agbeyome Messan (PK, Togo; 1954-)
Koenig, Walter (ent./writer; 1936-)
Koestler, Arthur (Br./Hung. writer; 1905-83)
Koffigoh, Joseph Kokou (ex-PM, Togo)
Kofi Annan (dipl., Ghana/UN secy.-gen.; 1938-)
Kohinoor diamond (also Koh-i-noor)
Kohl, Helmut (ex-chanc., Ger.; 1930-)
Kohl, Herb(ert)(US cong.; 1935-)
Kohler (plumbing fixtures)
Kohoutek (comet; 1973-74)
Kohtla-Jarve, Estonia
Koidu, Sierra Leone
Koirala, Girija Prasad (PM, Nepal; 1925-)
Koivisto, Mauno (Henrik)(ex-pres., Fin.; 1923-)
Kojak (TV show)
Kok, Wim (PM, Netherlands; 1938-)
Kokomo, IN
Kokoschaka, Oscar (Aus. artist; 1886-1980)
Kol Nidre (rel.)
Kolb, Claudia (swimming; 1949-)
Kolchak, Alexander Vasilievich (Rus. adm.;
   1875-1920)
Kolingba, André (gen./ex-pres., Central African
   Republic; 1936-)
Kollontai, Alexandra (Rus. mil./pol./writer;
   1872-1952)

Kollwitz, Käthe (Schmidt)(Ger. artist; 1867-1945)
Komarov, Vladimir M(ikhalovich)(cosmo.;
   1927-67)
Kommunizma, Pik (also Communism Peak)
   (formerly Mount Garmo, Mount Stalin)(Tajikistan)
Komodo dragon (large lizard, Indonesia)
Komondor (dog)
Komos (also Comus)(myth.)
Kompong Som, Cambodia
Komsomol (communist org.)
Kon-Tiki (myth.)
Kon Tiki (T. Heyerdahl raft used to cross Pac.;
   1947)
Konare, Alpha Oumar (pres., Mali; 1946-)
Kongo (lang.)
Konica (copier)
Konica USA, Inc.
Konitz, Lee (US jazz; 1927-)
Konkani (lang.)
Konoe, Fumimaro, Prince (ex-PM, Jap.; 1891-
   1946)
Konrad Adenauer (ex-chanc., WGer.; 1876-1967)
Konrad (Emil) Bloch (US chem.; 1912-2000)
Konrad Lorenz (Aus. ethologist; 1903-89)
Konstantin Chernenko (ex-pres., USSR; 1911-85)
Konstantin E. Tsiolkovsky (Rus., father of
   cosmonautics; 1857-1935)
Konstantin P. Feoktistov (cosmo.)
Konstantin (Sergeivich) Stanislavsky (Rus.
   ent.; 1863-1938)
Konstantinos Gavras (ent.; 1933-)
Konstantinos (or Constantinos) Stephanopoulos
   (pres., Gr.; 1926-)
Kontic, Radoje (ex-PM; Yug.; 1937-)
Koo Stark (Br. news)
Kookie (Edd) Byrnes (ent.)
Kool-Aid
Kooning, Willem de (US artist; 1904-97)
Koontz, Dean R(ay)(US writer; 1945-)
Koop, C. Everett (US ex-surgeon gen./phys.;
   1916-)
Kooper, Al (ent.; 1944-)
Koosman, Jerry Martin (baseball; 1942-)
Kootenay National Park (Can.)
Kootenay River (also Kootenai)(Can.)
Kopechne, Mary Jo (US, died at
   Chappaquiddick; 1941-69)
Kopell, Bernie (ent.; 1933-)
Koppel, Ted (US TV jour.; 1940-)
Kopy Kat Instant Kopy-Printing Centers (US
   bus.)
Koran (also Quran)(rel.)
Korando, Daewoo (auto.)
Korat (cat)
Korbel & Brothers, Inc., F.
Korbel champagne
Korbut, Olga (Soviet gymnast; 1955-)
Kordite (trash bags)
Korea Strait (S Korea/SW Jap.)
Korea, North (Democratic People's Republic of)
   (E Asia)
Korea, South (Republic of Korea)(E Asia)
Korean (lang./people)
Korean Air (airline)
Korean lawn grass (also Japanese lawn grass)

Korean War (NKorea, Ch./SKorea, UN; 1950-53)
Korematsu v. U.S. (US law; 1944)
Koren, Edward (cartoonist; *New Yorker*; 1935-)
Koresh, David (b. Vernon Wayne Howell)(US cult leader; 1959-1993)
Koret North America (US bus.)
Korman, Harvey (ent.; 1927-)
Korman, Maxime Carlot (ex-PM, Vanuatu)
Kornberg, Arthur (US chem.; 1918-)
Kornelia Ender (swimming; 1958-)
Kornell Champagne Cellars, Hanns (US bus.)
Korsakov, Nicolay (Andreyevich) Rimsky- (Rus. comp.; 1844-1908)
Kosciusko, Thaddeus (Tadeusz Andrzej Bonawentura Kosciuszko)(Pol./US mil.; 1746-1817)
Kosciusko, Mount (Austl.)
Kosinski (or Kozinski), Jerzy (Nikodem)(Pol./US writer; 1933-91)
Kosovo (province, Serbia)
Kossuth, Lajos (Hung. pol./editor; 1802-94)
Kostelanetz, Andre (ent.; 1901-80)
Kosti, Sudan
Kostis (or Costas) Simitas (PM, Gr.; 1936-)
Kostov, Ivan (PM, Bulgaria; 1949-)
Kostunica, Vojislav (Yug. pres.; 1944-)
Kosygin, Aleksei Nikolaevich (also Alexei Nikolaievich)(ex-PM, USSR; 1904-80)
Kota Kinabalu, Malaysia
Kotex (healthcare)
Kotter, Welcome Back (TV show)
Kotto, Yaphet (ent.; 1937-)
Koudougou, Burkina Faso
Koufax, Sandy (Sanford)(baseball; 1935-)
Kournikova, Anna (tennis; 1981-)
Kourou River (French Guiana)
Kourou, French Guiana
Koussevitsky, Serge (Sergei Alexandrovich)(Rus. cond.; 1874-1951)
Kovac, Michal (ex-pres., Slovakia; 1930-)
Kovacs, Ernie (ent.; 1919-62)
Kowloon, Hong Kong
Kozinski (or Kosinski), Jerzy (Nikodem)(Pol./US writer; 1933-91)
Kozlowski, Linda (ent.)
KozyKitten (cat food)
KP (kitchen police)
Kpalimé, Togo
Kr (chem. sym., krypton)
Krafft-Ebing, Richard von, Baron (Ger. phys.; 1840-1902)
Kraft General Foods, Inc.
Kraft, Inc.
Kragujevac, Serbia
Krakatoa (also Krakatau, Krakatao)(volcanic island, Java/Sumatra)
Kraken (myth.)
Kraków, Poland (also Cracow)
Krakowski, Jane (ent.; 1968-)
Kraljevo, Yugoslavia
Krall, Diana (ent.; 1964-)
Kramden, Ralph (fict. chara., *The Honeymooners*)
Kramer v. Kramer (film, 1979)
Kramer, Jack (tennis; 1921-)
Kramer, Jerry (football; 1936-)

Kramer, Stanley (ent.; 1913-2001)
Krantz, Judith (US writer; 1928-)
Kraprayoon, Suchinda (Thailand gen.)
Krasnovodsk, Turkmenistan
Kraus, Lili (pianist; 1905-86)
Kravchuk, Leonid (ex-pres., Ukraine; 1934-)
Kravis, Henry R. (US bus.; 1944-)
Kravitz, Lenny (ent.; 1964-)
Krazy Glue (adhesive)
Krazy Glue, Inc.
Krazy Kat (comic strip)
Krebs cycle (food converted into energy)
Krebs, (Sir) Hans (Adolf)(Ger./Br. chem.; 1900-81)
Kreisler, Fritz (Aus. comp.; 1875-1962)
Kremer, Gerhard (aka Geradus [or Gerhardus] Mercator)(Flem. geographer; 1512-94)
Kremlin, the (former USSR govt.)(also l.c.)
Kremlinology (sociol.)
Kresge, S. S. (US bus.; 1867-1966)
Kress, Samuel H. (US bus.; 1863-1955)
Kreutzer, Rodolphe (Fr. comp.; 1766-1831)
Kringle, Kriss (also Santa Claus, St. Nicholas)
Kris Kristofferson (ent.; 1936-)
Krishna (rel.)
Krishna, Hare (rel.)
Krispy Kreme Doughnut (US bus.)
Kriss Kringle (also Santa Claus, St. Nicholas)
Kristallnacht ("night of [broken] glass")(Nazi/ Jew.; 11/9-10/38)
Kristi Yamaguchi (figure skating; 1971-)
Kristin Davis (ent.; 1965-)
Kristin Scott Thomas (ent.; 1960-)
Kristofferson, Kris (ent.; 1936-)
Kristy McNichol (ent.; 1962-)
Krivoi Rog, Ukraine
K(ocheril) R(aman) Narayanan (pres., India; 1920-)
Kroc, Ray(mond A.)(US bus., founded McDonald's; 1902-84)
Kroch's & Brentano's
Kroeber, Alfred L(ouis)(US anthrop.; 1876-1960)
Krofft, Marty (puppeteer; 1939-)
Krofft, Sid (puppeteer; 1931-)
Kroft, Steve (TV jour.; 1945-)
Kroger Co.
Kronborg Castle (Hamlet's)
Kronos (also Cronus)(myth.)
Kropotkin, Piotr (or Pyotr, Peter)(Alekseevich), Prince (Rus. anarchist; 1842-1921)
Kru (lang./people)
Krug Winery, Charles (US bus.)
Kruger, Otto (ent.; 1885-1974)
Krugerrand (also l.c.)(SAfr. money)
Kruk, John (baseball; 1961-)
Krupa, Gene (US jazz; 1909-73)
Krupp von Bohlen und Halbach (Ger. armaments maker; 1870-1950)
Krupp, Alfred (Ger. armaments maker; 1812-87)
Krupp, Alfred (Ger. armaments maker; 1907-67)
Krupp, Bertha (Ger. armaments maker; 1886-1957)
Krupp, Friedrich (Ger. armaments maker; 1787-1826)
Krupp, Friedrich Alfred Krupp (Ger. armaments

maker; 1854-1902)
Krups (appliances)
Krups North America, Robert (US bus.)
Krypton (fict. planet)
Krzysztof Penderecki (Pol. comp.; 1933-)
Krzyzewski, Mike (basketball; 1947-)
KS (Kansas)
K-Tab (med.)
K. T. Oslin (ent.; 1942-)
Ku Klux Klan (also KKK, the Klan)(US racist
    society; founded 1866)
Ku Kluxer (Klan member)
Kuala Belait, Brunei
Kuala Lumpur, Malaysia
Kuang-chou, China (also Canton or Guangzhou)
Kuanyin (myth.)
Kubasov, Valery N(ikolayevich)(cosmo.; 1935-)
Kubelik, Rafael (cond.; 1914-96)
Kubera (myth.)
Kubilius, Andrius (premier, Lith.; 1956-)
Kublai Khan (also Kubla Khan)(Mongol/Ch.
    emp.; 1216-94)
Kübler-Ross, Elisabeth (Swiss/US phys./writer;
    1926-)
Kubota riding mower
Kubrick, Stanley (ent.; 1928-99)
Kucan, Milan (pres., Slovenia; 1941-)
Kuching, Malaysia
Kuchma, Leonid D(anylovich)(pres., Ukraine;
    1938-)
Kudos (snack bars)
Kudrow, Lisa (ent.; 1963-)
Kuenn, Harvey (baseball; 1930-88)
Kufic (early Arabic alphabet)
Kuhlman, Kathryn (faith healer; 1907-76)
Kuhn, Bowie Kent (baseball; 1926-)
Kukla, Fran & Ollie (TV show)
Kulp, Nancy (ent.; 1921-91)
Kulyab, Tajikistan
Kumaratunga, Chandrika Bandaranaike (pres.,
    Sri Lanka; 1945-)
Kumasi, Ghana
Kumayri, Armenia
Kumba Yalá (pres., Guinea-Bissau; 1953?)
Kumminost (cheese)
Kun, Béla (Hung. pol.; 1886-c1939)
Kung (people)
Kung Fu: The Legend Continues (TV show)
Kung Fu: The Movie (film, 1986)
Kunitz, Stanley (Jasspon)(US poet laureate;
    1905-)
Kuniwo Nakamura (pres., Palau; 1943-)
Kunming, China (formerly Yunnan)
Kunstler, William (US atty.; 1919-95)
Kunta Kinte (fict. chara., *Roots*)
Kuo-feng (or Guofeng), Hua (ex-PM, Ch.; 1920?-)
Kuomintang (also Guomindang)(Ch. pol. party)
Kupka, Frank (Frantisek)(Czech. artist; 1871-
    1957)
Kupka, Frantisek (Czech. artist; 1871-1957)
Kuralt, Charles (US TV jour.; 1934-97)
Kurd (people)
Kurdish (lang.)
Kurdistan (Persian-style rug)
Kurdistan (region, SW Asia)

Kurgan-Tyube, Tajikistan
Kurosawa, Akira (Jap. ent.; 1910-98)
Kurt Alder (Ger. chem.; 1902-58)
Kurt Browning (figure skating; 1967-)
Kurt Cobain (ent.; 1967-94)
Kurt Georg Kiesinger (ex-chancellor, W. Ger.;
    1904-88)
Kurt Jooss (Ger. ballet; 1901-79)
Kurt Kaszner (ent.)
Kurt Lewin (US psych.; 1890-1947)
Kurt Masur (Ger. cond.; 1928-)
Kurt Russell (ent.; 1951-)
Kurt Schwitters (Ger. artist; 1887-1948)
Kurt von Schuschnigg (ex-chanc., Aus.; 1897-
    1977)
Kurt Vonnegut, Jr. (US writer; 1922-)
Kurt Waldheim (ex-pres., Aus./UN dipl.; 1918-)
Kurt (Julian) Weill (Ger./US comp.; 1900-50)
Kurtz, Efrem (cond.; 1900-95)
Kurtz, Swoosie (ent.; 1944-)
Kurtzman, Harvey (cartoonist, *Mad* magazine;
    1925-93)
Kutaisi, Georgia
Kutuzov, Mikhail (Larionovich)(Rus. mil.; 1745-
    1813)
Kuvasz (dog)(also l.c.)
Kuwait (State of)(SW Asia)
Kuwait, Kuwait (also Kuwait City)(formerly Qurein)
Kuwaiti (people)
Kuybyshev, Russia (now Samara)
Kwa (lang.)
Kwai, The Bridge on the River (film, 1957)
Kwajalein Island (Marshall Islands atoll)
Kwakiutl (Native Amer.)
Kwalik, Ted (Thaddeus John)(football; 1947-)
Kwame Nkrumah (ex-PM, Ghana; 1909-72)
Kwangchow, China (also Guangzhou, Canton)
Kwangchu, South Korea (also Kwangju)
Kwangju, South Korea (also Kwangchu)
Kwangsi-Chuang (also Guangxi)(region, Ch.)
Kwangtung (also Guangdong)(province, Ch.)
Kwannon (also Kannon)(rel.)
Kwanzaa (also Kwanza)(Afr.-Amer. festival)
Kwasniewski, Aleksander (pres., Pol.; 1954-)
Kwatah, Pakistan (also Quetta)
KwaZulu-Natal, South Africa
Kweichow (also Guizhou)(province, Ch.)
Kweilin, China (also Guilin)
Kweisi Mfume (b. Frizzell Gray)(US pol./NAACP
    leader; 1948-)
Kweiyang (also Guiyang), China
Kwekwe, Zimbabwe (also Que Que)
Kwell (med. lotion/shampoo)
Kwik-Kopy Copy (US bus.)
KY (Kentucky)
Kyd (or Kid), Thomas (Br. writer; c1557-95)
Kyi, Aung San Suu (human rights activist,
    Burma; 1945-)
K-Y jelly (med.)
Kyl, Jon (US cong.; 1942-)
Kyle MacLachlan (ent.; 1959-)
Kyle Rote (football; 1928-)
Kyodo News Agency (Jap. news org.)
Kyoto, Japan
Kyra Sedgwick (ent.; 1965-)

Kyrenia, Cyprus
Kyrghiz (people)
Kyrgystan (Republic of)(formerly part of USSR)
   (central Asia)
Kyrgyz (lang.)
Kyrie (music/rel.)
Kyrie eleison (Lord have mercy)
Kyser, James Kern "Kay" (US cond.; 1906-85)
Kyser's, Kay Kollege of Musical Knowledge
Kyushu (Jap. island)
Kyzyl-Kiya, Kyrgyzstan

– L –

LA (Louisiana, Los Angeles)
La (chem. sym., lanthanum)
Laar, Mart (PM, Estonia; 1960-)
Laarne, Belgium
Laatasi, Kamuta (ex-PM, Tuvalu)
La Bamba (song; film, 1987)
Laban, Rudolf von (Hung. ballet; 1879-1958)
Labanotation (dance)
Labatt, Ltd., John
Labé, Guinea
LaBelle, Patti (b. Patricia Holt)(ent.; 1944-)
La Bohème (Puccini)
Labor and Human Resources Committee (US govt.)
Labor Day (1st Monday in September)
Labor Party (Austl. pol.)
Labor Party (Isr. pol.)
Labor Party, Greenback- (US hist.; 1878-c1884)
Labor Relations Act, National (NLRA)(US law; 1935)
Labor Relations Board, National (NLRB)(US govt. agcy.; est. 1935)
Labor, Department of (DOL)(US govt.)
Labor, Knights of (US labor org.; 1869-1917)
Laborism
Labour Day (Br.)
Labour Party (Br. pol.)
Labrador (NE Can.)
Labrador Current (also Arctic Current)(cold ocean current)
Labrador retriever (dog)
La Brea Tar Pits (fossils, CA)
La Cage aux Folles (play; film, 1978)
La Cage aux Folles 2 (film, 1981)
La Cage aux Folles 3: The Wedding (film, 1986)
Lacalle Herrera, Luis Alberto (ex-pres., Uruguay; 1941-)
Lacayo, Arnoldo Alemán (pres., Nicaragua; 1946-)
Lacedaemon (also Sparta)(ancient Gr.)
La Ceiba, Honduras
Lacerta (astron., lizard)
Lacey Davenport (fict. chara., *Doonesbury*)
Lacey, Cagney & (TV show)
Lachaise, Gaston (US sculptor; 1882-1935)
Lachesis (myth.)
Lachine, Quebec, Canada
La Choy Chinese foods
La Choy Food Products (US bus.)
Lachryma Christi (It. wine, tear of Christ)
Lackawanna, NY
Lackland Air Force Base, TX (mil.)
La Condamine (area, Monaco)
Lacrisert (med.)
La Crosse, WI
LACSA Airline of Costa Rica
Lactaid (med.)
Ladd, Alan (ent.; 1913-64)
Ladd, Cheryl (b. Cheryl Stoppelmoor)(ent.; 1951-)

Ladd, Diane (b. Rose Diane Ladner)(ent.; 1932-)
Laden, Osama bin (Saudi terrorist, Islamic, based in Afghanistan; 1957-)
Ladies' Home Journal (mag.)
La Dolce Vita (film, 1960)
Lady Abracadabra
Lady and the Tramp (Disney classic; film, 1955)
Lady Augusta Gregory (Ir. writer; 1852-1932)
Lady Baltimore cake
Lady Bird Johnson (b. Claudia Alta Taylor)(wife of ex-US pres.; 1912-)
Lady Bountiful (fict. chara., *Beaux' Strategem*)
Lady Bracknell (fict. chara., *The Importance of Being Earnest*)
Lady Chatterley's Lover (D.H. Lawrence novel)
Lady Day (Billie Holiday)
Lady Godiva (Br. noblewoman ; c1040-80)
Lady Jane (Dudley) Grey (queen, Eng. [10 days]; 1537-54)
Lady Lovelace (aka Augusta Ada Byron)(Br. math./inv., compu.; 1815-52)
Lady Luck (personification of luck)
Lady Macbeth (fict. chara., *Macbeth*)
Lady Macduff (fict. chara., *Macbeth*)
Lady Manhattan Co., The
Lady Mary (Wortley) Montagu (aka Mary Pierrepont)(Br. writer; 1689-1762)
Lady of Mercy, Order of Our (rel.)
Lady of Shalott (Tennyson poem)
Lady of the Lake, The (Arthurian chara.)
Lady of the Lake, The (by Sir Walter Scott)
Lady or the Tiger?, The (F.R. Stockton short story)
Lady, Gray (Amer. Red Cross volunteer)
Lady, Our (also the Madonna, Holy Mother, Mary, Virgin Mary)(rel.)
Lady's Circle (mag.)
Lae, Papua New Guinea
Laertes (fict. chara., *Hamlet*; myth.)
LaFarge, Christopher Grant (US arch.; 1862-1938)
La Farge, John (US artist; 1835-1910)
Lafayette College (Easton, PA)
Lafayette, IN, LA
La Fayette, Marie Madeleine Pioche de la Vergne (Comtesse de La Fayette)(Fr. writer; 1634-93)
Lafayette, Marquis de (aka Marie Joseph Gilbert de Motier Lafayette)(Fr. mil./pol.; 1757-1834)
La Femme Nikita (film, 1991)
Laffer curve (econ.)
Laffer, Arthur (US econ.; 1940-)
Laffit Pincay, Jr. (jockey; 1946-)
Lafite-Rothschild, Chateau (Fr. wine)
Lafitte (or Laffite), Jean (Fr. mil./pirate; c1780-c1825)
Lafleur, Guy (hockey; 1951-)
La Follette, Robert Marion (ex-gov., WI; 1855-1925)
La Follette, Robert Marion, Jr. (US pol./publ., WI; 1895-1953)
LaFontaine, Pat (hockey; 1965-)
Lag b'Omer (rel.)
Lagasse, Emeril (US chef/writer/ent.; 1959-)
L. A. Gear (shoes)

L. A. Gear, Inc.
Lagerfeld, Karl (designer; 1938-)
La Gioconda (aka *Mona Lisa*)(da Vinci painting)
Lagos Escobar, Ricardo (pres., Chile; 1938-)
Lagos, Nigeria
La Grange, Georgia
Lagrange, Joseph (Louis)(Fr. astron./math.;
    1736-1813)
Lagrangian points (in space)
La Guaira, Venezuela
La Guardia Airport (NY)
La Guardia, Fiorello (Henry)(ex-mayor, NYC;
    1882-1947)
Laguna Beach, CA
Lahore, Pakistan
Lahoud, Emile (pres., Lebanon; 1936-)
Lahr, Bert (b. Irving Lahrheim)(ent.; 1895-1967)
Lahti, Christine (ent.; 1950-)
Lahti, Finland
Lailat ul-Barah (rel., "Night of Forgiveness")
Lailat ul-Isra Wal Mi'raj (rel.)
Lailat ul-Qadr (rel., "Night of Power")
Laine, Cleo (ent.; 1927-)
Laine, Frankie (b. Francisco Paolo LoVecchio)
    (ent.; 1913-)
Laing, R(onald) D(avid)(Scot. psych./writer;
    1927-89)
Lainie Kazan (ent.; 1942-)
Laird, Melvin (ex-US secy. of defense; 1922-)
Laisenia Qarase (Fiji pol.; 1941-)
Lajos Kossuth (Hung. pol./editor; 1802-94)
Lake and Palmer, Emerson, (pop music)
Lake Arrowhead, CA
Lake Baikal (also Baykal)(Russia)(deepest lake
    in the world)
Lake Balkhash (Kazakhstan)(salt)
Lake Chad (Nigeria)
Lake Champlain (NY/VT/Can.)
Lake Charles, LA
Lake Clark National Park (AK)
Lake County Times (IN newspaper)
Lake District (region, Eng.)
Lake Erie (NY/OH/PA/Can.)
Lake Eyre (Austl.)
Lake Forest, IL
Lake Havasu City, AZ
Lake Kariba (Zimbabwe)
Lake Leman (also Lake of Geneva)(Switz./Fr.)
Lake Louise (Can.)
Lake Malawi (SE Afr.)
Lake Manitoba (Can.)
Lake Maracaibo (Venezuela)
Lake Mead (Hoover Dam, AZ/NV)
Lake Michigan (N central US)
Lake Natron (Tanzania)
Lake Nipigon (Ontario, Can.)
Lake Nipissing (Can.)
Lake Nyasa (now Lake Malawi)
Lake of Geneva (also Lake Leman)(Switz./Fr.)
Lake of the Ozarks (MO)
Lake of the Woods (Ontario, Can.)
Lake Okeechobee (FL)
Lake Onega (NW Russia)
Lake Onondaga (NY)
Lake Ontario (US/Can.)

Lake Oswego, OR
Lake Peipus (NE Eur.)
Lake Placid, NY
Lake Ponchartrain (LA)
Lake Powell (AZ/UT)
Lake Superior (US/Can.)
Lake Tahoe (CA/NV)
Lake Tanganyika (E Afr.)
Lake Titicaca (SAmer.)
Lake Victoria (Afr.)
Lake Windermere (Eng.)
Lake Winnebago (WI)
Lake Winnipeg (Can.)
Lake Wobegon (fict. town, G. Keillor)
Lake, Ricki (ent.; 1968-)
Lake, The Lady of the (Arthurian chara.)
Lake, The Lady of the (by Sir Walter Scott)
Lake, Tony (William Anthony)(US ex-nat'l
    security advisor; 1939-)
Lake, Veronica (ent.; 1919-73)
Lakeland Ledger (FL newspaper)
Lakeland terrier (dog)
Lakeland, FL
Lakenvelder (chicken)
Lakers, Los Angeles (basketball team)
Lakes of Killarney (Ir.)
Lakewood, OH
Lakoue, Enoch Derant (ex-PM, Central African
    Republic)
Lakshmi (myth.)
Lal Bahadur Shastri (Shri)(ex-PM, India; 1904-66)
La Leche League
LaLanne Health Spas, Jack (US bus.)
LaLanne, Jack (US, fitness educ.; 1914-)
L .A. Law (TV show)
Lalique crystal
Lalique, René (Fr. designer; 1860-1945)
Lalitpur, Nepal (formerly Patan)
Lally column (constr.)
Lalo, (Victor Antoine) Édouard (Fr. comp.;
    1823-92)
Lam, Wilfredo (Cuban artist; 1902-82)
Lama(istic) Buddhism (rel.)
Lama, Dalai (b. Tenzin Gyatso)(Tibetan rel.;
    1935-)
Lama, Panchen (Tibetan rel.; 1939-89)
Lamaism (rel.)
La Mancha (district, Sp.)
La Mancha, Man of (play)
Lamarck, Jean B(aptiste)(Fr. nat.; 1744-1829)
la Mare, Walter de (Br. poet; 1873-1956)
Lamarr, Hedy (b. Hedwig Eva Maria
    Kiesler)(ent.; 1913-2000)
La Marseillaise, (Fr. anthem)
Lamartine, Alphonse de (Fr. writer; 1790-1869)
Lamas, Fernando (ent.; 1915-82)
Lamas, Lorenzo (ent.; 1958-)
Lamaze method (childbirth)
Lamb Chop (S. Lewis puppet)
Lamb Chop's Play-Along (TV show)
Lamb of God (Jesus)
Lamb, Charles ("Elia")(Br. writer; 1775-1834)
Lamb, Gil (ent.; 1906-95)
Lamb, Mary (Br. writer; 1764-1847)
Lambert Co., Warner-

Lambert Corp., Norton-
Lambert-St. Louis International Airport (MO)
Lambert, Drexel Burnham (US stock market
	scandal)
Lambeth walk (dance)
Lamborghini (auto.)
Lamborghini Diablo (auto.)
Lamborghini Diablo VT (auto.)
Lamborghini, Ferruccio (It. bus.; 1917-93)
Lambrusco (wine)
Lamentations (rel., book of the Old Testament)
Lamine Sidimé (PM, Guinea; 1944-)
Lamisil (med.)
Lammas (rel.)
Lamonica, Daryle (football; 1941-)
Lamont Dozier (US comp.; 1941-)
LaMontagne, Margaret (US White House staff)
La Motta, Jake (Giacobe)(boxing; 1921-)
Lamour, Dorothy (ent.; 1914-96)
L'Amour, Louis (Dearborn)(US writer; 1908-88)
Lampedusa, Giuseppe (Tomasi) di (It. writer;
	1896-1957)
Lamrani, Mohammed Karim (ex-PM, Morocco)
LAN (local area network)(compu.)
Lana Cantrell (ent.; 1943-)
Lana Turner (ent.; 1920-95)
Lanai, HI
Lancashire (cheese)
Lancaster (also Lancashire)(county, Eng.)
Lancaster Intelligencer-Journal (PA newspaper)
Lancaster New Era (PA newspaper)
Lancaster News (PA newspaper)
Lancaster, Burt(on Stephen)(ent.; 1913-94)
Lancaster, CA, NY, OH, PA, TX
Lancaster, House of (Br. ruling family; 1399-
	1461, 1470-71)
Lance Alworth (football; 1940-)
Lance Armstrong (US cyclist/Tour de France
	winner; 1971-)
Lance Bass (ent., 'N Sync; 1979-)
Lance Henriksen (ent./writer; 1940-)
Lancelot (of the Lake)(Arthurian knight)
Lanchester, Elsa (ent.; 1902-82)
LanChile Airlines
Lancome (US bus.)
Lancôme cosmetics
Land Cruiser, Toyota (auto.)
Land O' Lakes (butter)
Land O' Lakes, Inc.
Land of Beulah (*Pilgrim's Progress*)
Land of Enchantment (nickname, NM)
Land of Lincoln (nickname, IL)
Land of Opportunity (nickname, AR)
Land of Oz
Land of the Leal (heaven)
Land Rover (auto.)
Land Rover Defender 90 (auto.)
Land Rover Discovery (auto.)
Land Rover Discovery II (auto.)
Land Rover Discovery II SD (auto.)
Land Rover Discovery II SD7 (auto.)
Land Rover Discovery LE (auto.)
Land Rover Discovery LSE (auto.)
Land Rover Discovery SD (auto.)
Land Rover Discovery SE (auto.)

Land Rover Discovery SE7 (auto.)
Land Rover Discovery XD (auto.)
Land Rover Freelander (auto.)
Land Rover North America, Inc.
Land Rover Range Rover (auto.)
Land Rover Range Rover 4.6HSE (auto.)
Land Rover Range Rover 4.6SE (auto.)
Land Rover Range Rover HSE (auto.)
Land Rover Range Rover S (auto.)
Land Rover Range Rover SE (auto.)
Land Rover Range Rover Vitesse (auto.)
land of Nod (myth. land of sleep)
Land, Edwin (Herbert)(US inv., Polaroid Land
	camera; 1910-91)
Land's End (cape, Eng.)
Landau, Martin (ent.; 1931-)
Landers, Ann (Eppie Lederer)(b. Esther Pauline
	Friedman)(US advice columnist; 1918-)
Landis, Carole (ent.; 1919-48)
Landis, John (ent.; 1950-)
Landis, Kenesaw Mountain (US jurist/baseball
	exec.; 1866-1944)
Landon, Alf(red Mossman)(US pol.; 1887-1987)
Landon, Michael (ent.; 1936-91)
Landrieu, Mary L. (US cong.; 1955-)
Landrum-Griffin Act (US hist.; 1959)
Landry, Tom (football; 1924-2000)
Lands' End (clothes, etc.)
Lands' End, Inc.
Landsat (US satellite)
Landsbergis, Vytautas (ex-pres., Lith.; 1932-)
Landy, John (runner; 1930-)
Lane (furniture)
Lane Bryant, Inc.
Lane Co., Inc., The
Lane Smith (US illus./writer; 1959-)
Lane, Abbe (b. Abigail Francine Lassman)(ent.;
	1933-)
Lane, Burton (US comp.; 1912-97)
Lane, Cristy (ent.; 1940-)
Lane, Diane (ent.; 1965-)
Lane, Nathan (Joseph)(ent.; 1956-)
Lane, Priscilla (ent.; 1915-95)
Lanford Wilson (US writer; 1937-)
Lang, Fritz (Aus. ent.; 1890-1976)
Lang, Stephen (ent.; 1952-)
lang, k. d. (b. Katherine Dawn Lang)(ent.; 1961-)
Lange, David (Russell)(ex-PM, NewZeal.; 1942-)
Lange, Dorothea (US photo.; 1895-1965)
Lange, Hope (ent.; 1931-)
Lange, Jessica (ent.; 1949-)
Langella, Frank (ent.; 1940-)
Langerhans, islets of (med.)
Langford, Frances (ent.; 1913-)
Langley Air Force Base, VA (mil.)
Langmuir, Irving (US chem.; 1881-1957)
Langtry, Lillie ("the Jersey Lily")(b. Emily
	Charlotte le Breton)(Br. ent.; 1853-1929)
Lani Guinier (US atty./educ.)
Lanier (bus. machines)
Lanier Voice Products, Inc.
Lanier, Sidney (US poet; 1842-81)
La Niña (unusually cold ocean current,
	Equatorial Pacific)
Lanne Health Spas, Jack La (US bus.)

Lanny McDonald (hockey; 1953-)
Lanos, Daewoo (auto.)
Lanoxicaps (med.)
Lanoxin (med.)
Lansana, Conté (pres., Guinea; 1934-)
Lansbury, Angela (ent.; 1925-)
Lansing State-Journal (MI newspaper)
Lansing, IL, MI
Lansing, Robert (b. Robert Howell Brown)(ent.; 1928-94)
Lansing, Robert (US atty./pol.; 1864-1928)
Lansing, Sherry Lee (ent.; 1944-)
Lanson, Snooky (b. Roy Landman)(ent.; 1914-90)
Lantz, Walter (cartoonist, *Woody Woodpecker*; 1900-94)
Lanza, Mario (opera; 1921-1959)
Lanzhou, China (also Lanchow)
Lao (lang./people)
Laocoön (myth.)
Laodamia (myth.)
Laodice (myth.)
Laomedon (myth.)
Laos (Lao People's Democratic Republic)(SE Asia)
Laotian (people)
Lao-Tzu (also Lao-tzu)(Ch. phil.; c570-490 BC)
La Paz (margarita mix)
La Paz Products (US bus.)
La Paz, Bolivia
La Paz, Mexico
L.A.P.D. (Los Angeles Police Department)
Laplace, Pierre S(imon)(aka Marquis de Laplace)(Fr. astron./math.; 1749-1827)
Lapland (region, N Eur.)
La Plata, Argentina
Lapli, John Inni (gov.-gen., Solomon Islands)
Lapps (also Laplanders)(people)
Lapsang souchong tea
Laputa Island (fict. place, *Gulliver's Travels*)
La Quinta Motor Inns, Inc.
Lara Flynn Boyle (ent.; 1970-)
Laraki, Azzedine (ex-PM, Morocco)
Laramie, Fort (WY)
Laramie, WY
LaRaza Unida Party (US pol.)
Lardner, Ring(gold Wilmer)(US writer; 1885-1933)
Laredo, Ruth (ent.; 1937-)
Laredo, TX
la Renta, Oscar de (US designer; 1932-)
Lares (myth.)
Large Electron Positron Collider (LEP)(particle accelerator)
Large Magellanic Cloud (astron.)
Largo Entertainment
Largo, Key, FL
La Rioja (region, Sp.)
Larissa, Greece
Larkin, Barry (baseball; 1964-)
Larkin, Philip (Br. poet; 1922-85)
Lar Lubovitch (US dance; 1945-)
Larnaca, Cyprus
La Rochefoucauld, François, Duc de (Fr. writer; 1613-80)
Larodopa (med.)
La Rosa, Julius (ent.; 1930-)
LaRouche, Lyndon H., Jr. (US pol./econ.; 1922-)

Larrieu, Francie (track; 1952-)
Larroquette, John (ent.; 1947-)
Larry (Lawrence Cecil) Adler (US musician; 1914-)
Larry Bird (basketball; 1956-)
Larry Brown (football; 1947-)
Larry (Lawrence Richard) Csonka (football; 1946-)
Larry Drake (ent.)
Larry E. Craig (US cong.; 1945-)
Larry Elgart (band leader; 1922-)
Larry Fine (b. Louis Feinberg)(ent.; 1902-75)
Larry (Claxton) Flynt (US publ./*Hustler*; 1942-)
Larry Gatlin (ent.; 1948-)
Larry Hagman (ent.; 1931-)
Larry Holmes (boxing; 1949-)
Larry King (b. Lawrence Harvey Zeiger)(ent.; 1933-)
Larry King Live (TV show)
Larry Mahan (rodeo; 1943-)
Larry McMurtry, (Jeff)(US writer; 1936-)
Larry (Lee) Pressler (US pol.; 1942-)
Larry Rivers (b. Vitzroch Loiza Grossberg)(US artist; 1923-)
Larry Robinson (hockey; 1951-)
Larry Sanders Show, The (TV show)
Larry Storch (ent.; 1923-)
Larry (Lawrence Henry) Summers (US ex-secy./treas.; 1954-)
Larsen, Vibeke (High Comm., Faeroe Islands)
Larson, Gary (US cartoonist, *The Far Side*; 1950-)
Larson, Nicolette (ent.; 1952-97)
LaRue, Lash (Alfred)(ent.; 1917-96)
Lasalle, Eriq (ent.; 1962-)
La Salle, IL
La Salle, Quebec, Canada
La Salle, (René) Robert Cavelier (aka Sieur de La Salle)(Fr. expl.; 1643-87)
La Scala (opera house, It.)
Lascaux Cave (Fr., prehistoric wall paintings)
Lasch, Christopher (US hist./social critic; 1932-94)
Las Cruces, NM
LaserWriter (compu. printer)
Lash (Alfred) LaRue (ent.; 1917-96)
Lasher (A. Rice novel)
Lasix (med.)
Lasker, Albert (US bus.; 1880-1952)
Lasorda, Tommy (baseball/ent.; 1927-)
Las Palmas (de Gran Canaria), Canary Islands
Lassa fever (med.)
Lasse Viren (track; 1949-)
Lassen Peak (also Mount Lassen)(CA volcano)
Lassen Volcanic National Park (CA)
Lasser, Louise (ent.; 1939-)
Lassie (dog)
Lassie (TV show; film, 1994)
Lassie Come Home (film, 1943)
Lassiter (film, 1984)
Lasswell, Fred (cartoonist)
Last (or Final) Judgment (rel.)
Last Frontier (nickname, AK)
Last of the Mohicans, The (J.F. Cooper novel)
Last Supper (rel.)
Last Supper, The (da Vinci)

Lastex (elastic fiber)
La Sueur (peas)
Las Vegas Airlines
Las Vegas Review-Journal (NV newspaper)
Las Vegas Sun (NV newspaper)
Las Vegas, NM, NV
La Sylphide (ballet)
Latakia tobacco
Latakia, Syria
Late Modern English (lang.; c1700-present)
Late Night (TV show)
Late Night With David Letterman (TV show)
Later Tsin (or Chin) dynasty (also Chin)(Ch.;
    936-46)
Lateran basilica (also Basilica of the
    Savior)(Rome)
Lateran Treaty(ies)(It./Vatican; 1929)
Latifah, Queen (b. Dana Owens)(ent.; 1970-)
Latin (lang.)
Latin alphabet (also Roman alphabet)
Latin America (S & Central Amer.)
Latin cross
Latin school
Latino (slang)
La Tour, Georges de (Fr. artist; 1593-1652)
Latour, Chateau (Fr. wine)
Latour, (Ignace) Henri (Joseph Théodore)
    Fantin- (Fr. artist; 1836-1904)
La Toya Jackson (ent.; 1956-)
La Traviata (G. Verdi opera)
Latrobe, Benjamin Henry (US arch.; 1764-1820)
Latter-Day Saints (also Church of Jesus Christ
    of the Latter-Day Saints, Mormon
    Church)(rel.)
Latvia (Republic of)(formerly part of USSR)(N Eur.)
Latvian (lang./people)
Lauch (Duncan McLaunchlin) Faircloth (US pol.;
    1928-)
Lauder, Estee (designer; 1908-)
Lauder, Estée (cosmetics)
Lauder, Inc., Estée
Lauderdale, Fort, FL (city)
Lauer, Matt (TV host; 1957-)
Laugh-In, Rowan and Martin's (TV show)
Laughlin Air Force Base, TX (mil.)
Laughlin, James L(awrence)(US econ.; 1850-1933)
Laughton, Charles (ent.; 1899-1962)
Laundromat
Lauper, Cyndi (ent.; 1953-)
Laura Ashley (Br. designer; 1925-85)
Laura Ashley (US bus.)
Laura Branigan (ent.; 1957-)
Laura Bush (nee Welch)(US wife of pres.;
    1946-)
Laura D'Andrea Tyson (US ex-chair/council
    econ. advisers; 1947-)
Laura Dern (ent.; 1967-)
Laura Ingalls Wilder (US writer; 1867-1957)
Laura Linney (ent.; 1964-)
Laura Nyro (ent.; 1947-97)
Laura San Giacomo (ent.; 1962-)
Laura Schlessinger, Dr. (radio talk show host;
    1947-)
Laura Z(ametkin) Hobson (US writer; 1900-86)
Laurance S(pelman) Rockefeller (US bus./

finan.; 1910-)
Laurel & Hardy (Stan & Oliver)(US comedy team)
Laurel, MS
Laurel, Stan (b. Arthur Stanley Jefferson)(ent.;
    1890-1965)
Lauren Bacall (b. Betty Perske)(ent.; 1924-)
Lauren Holly (ent.; 1963-)
Lauren Hutton (ent./model; 1943-)
Lauren Leathergoods, Polo/Ralph (US bus.)
Lauren, Ralph (b. Ralph Lifshitz)(US designer;
    1939-)
Lauren, Ralph (US bus.)
Laurence (Kerr) Olivier, (Sir)(ent.; 1907-89)
Laurence Fishburne (ent.; 1962-)
Laurence Harvey (ent.; 1928-73)
Laurence Luckinbill (ent.; 1934-)
Laurence Sterne (Ir. writer; 1713-68)
Laurens (Jan) Van der Post (SAfr. writer; 1906-
    96)
Laurens, Henri (Fr. sculptor; 1884-?)
Laurens, Henry (US pol.; 1724-92)
Laurent-Desire Kabila (ex-pres., Congo; 1939-
    2001)
Laurent Fabius (ex-PM, Fr.; 1946-)
Laurent SA., Yves St.- (US bus.)
Laurent, Louis S(tephen) St. (ex-PM, Can.;
    1882-1973)
Laurent, Yves (Henri Donat Mathieu) Saint- (Fr.
    designer; 1936-)
Laurentian (or Canadian) Plateau/Shield (also
    Precambrian Shield)(Can.)
Laurentiis, Dino De (It. ent.; 1919-)
Laurents, Arthur (US playwright; 1918-)
Laurette Taylor (b. Laurette Cooney)(ent.;
    1884-1946)
Laurie Metcalf (ent.; 1955-)
Laurie, Piper (b. Rosetta Jacobs)(ent.; 1932-)
Lauris Norstad (US mil./ex-commander, NATO;
    1907-88)
Lauritz Melchior (ent.; 1890-1973)
Lauro, Achille (hijacked It. cruise ship; 1984)
Lauryn Hill (ent.; 1975-)
Lausanne, Switzerland
Lautenberg, Frank R. (US pol.; 1924-)
Lauter, Ed (ent.; 1940-)
Lauti, Toaripi (ex-gov.-gen., Tuvalu)
Lautoka, Fiji
Lautrec, Henri (Marie Raymond) de Toulouse-
    (Fr. artist; 1864-1901)
LAVA (also LAVA LITE)(lamp)
Laval, Pierre (ex-PM, Fr.; 1883-1945)
Laval, Quebec, Canada
Laver, Rod(ney George)(tennis; 1938-)
Laverne & Shirley (TV show)
Laverne Andrews (ent.; Andrew Sisters; 1911-
    67)
La Victoria Foods, Inc.
Lavin, Linda (ent.; 1937-)
Lavoisier, Antoine Laurent (Fr. chem.; 1743-94)
Lavoris (mouthwash)
Lavrenti Beria (USSR pol.; 1899-1953)
Law & Order (TV show)
Law of Moses (rel.)
Law of the Twelve Tables (Roman law; est.
    451-50 BC)

Law School Admission Test (LSAT)
Law, (Andrew) Bonar (Br. pol.; 1858-1923)
Law, (David) Jude (ent.; 1972-)
LaWanda Page (ent.; 1920-)
Lawford, Peter (ent.; 1923-84)
Lawler, Loewe v. (US law; 1908)
Lawless, Lucy (ent.; 1968-)
Lawn Chief (lawn care)
Lawn-Boy (lawn care)
Lawn-Boy (US bus.)
Lawrence (Larry) B. Lindsey (White House staff, econ. adv.)
Lawrence Berkeley Laboratory (nuclear research, CA)
Lawrence Durrell (Br. writer; 1912-90)
Lawrence Ferlinghetti (US writer/publ.; 1919-)
Lawrence "Larry" H(enry) Summers (US ex-secy./treas.; 1954-)
Lawrence J. Ellison (US bus./computers; 1944-)
Lawrence Kasdan (ent./writer; 1948-)
Lawrence Livermore Laboratory (nuclear research, CA)
Lawrence of Arabia (film, 1962)
Lawrence Sanders (US writer; 1920-98)
Lawrence Spivak (ent.; 1900-94)
Lawrence (Mervil) Tibbett (ent.; 1896-1960)
Lawrence Welk (US cond.; 1903-92)
Lawrence, Carol (b. Carol Laraia)(ent.; 1934-)
Lawrence, D(avid) H(erbert)(Br. writer; 1885-1930)
Lawrence, Ernest O(rlando)(US physt.; 1901-58)
Lawrence, Gertrude (ent.; 1898-1952)
Lawrence, IN, KS, MA
Lawrence, Jacob (US artist; 1917-2000)
Lawrence, Martin (ent.; 1965-)
Lawrence, Sharon (ent.; 1962-)
Lawrence, Steve (ent.; 1935-)
Lawrence, T(homas) E(dward)(aka Lawrence of Arabia)(Br. mil.; 1888-1935)
Lawrence, (Sir) Thomas (Br. artist; 1769-1830)
Lawrence, Vicki (ent.; 1949-)
Lawry's Foods, Inc.
Laws, Doctor of (also LL.D., Legum Doctor)
Lawton Chiles (ex-FL gov.; 1930-98)
Lawton, OK
Layne, Bobby (football; 1927-86)
Layne, Tamirat (ex-PM, Ethiopia)
La-Z-Boy (chair)
La-Z-Boy Chair Co.
Lazar Berman (pianist; 1930-)
Lázaro Cárdenas (ex-pres., Mex.; 1895-1970)
Lazarus (rel.)
Lazarus, Emma (US poet; 1849-87)
Lazarus, Mell (cartoonist, *Momma, Miss Peach*; 1929-)
Lazio (region, It.)
Lazio, Rick (Enrico Anthony)(US pol.; 1958-)
LC (landing craft, Library of Congress)
LCD (liquid crystal display)(compu.)
LCD/LED (liquid crystal display/light-emitting diode)(compu.)
LCV (landing craft vehicle)
LDL (low density lipoprotein, the "bad" cholesterol)
L-dopa (med.)
Lea & Perrins (sauces)

Lea & Perrins, Inc.
Lea Thompson (ent.; 1961-)
Leach, Bernard Howell (Br. potter; 1887-1969)
Leach, Penelope (Balchin)(child psych./writer; 1937-)
Leach, Robin (ent.; 1941-)
Leachman, Cloris (ent.; 1926-)
Leacock, Stephen (Butler)(Can. writer/humorist; 1868-1944)
Leadbelly (Huddie) Ledbetter (US jazz; 1888-1949)
League of Nations (internat'l govt. org.; 1920-)
League of Women Voters
Leahy, Pat(rick Joseph)(US cong.; 1940-)
Leahy, William Daniel (US adm.; 1875-1959)
Leakey, Louis S(eymour) B(azett)(Br. archaeol.; 1903-72)
Leakey, Mary (Douglas)(Br. archaeol.; 1913-96)
Leakey, Richard (Br. archaeol.; 1944-)
Leal, Land of the (heaven)
Lean Cuisine, Stouffer's
Lean, (Sir) David (Br. ent.; 1908-91)
Leaning Tower of Pisa (It.)
Leann Rimes (ent.; 1982-)
Lear Corp.
Lear jet (trans.)
Lear, Edward (Br. artist/humorist; 1812-88)
Lear, Evelyn (Shulman)(soprano; 1926-)
Lear, Francis (US publ.; 1923-)
Lear, King (Shakespeare play)
Lear, Norman (ent.; 1922-)
Learned (Billings) Hand (US jurist; 1872-1961)
Learned, Michael (ent.; 1939-)
Learning Channel, The (TLC)(TV channel)
Leary, Denis (ent./writer; 1957-)
Leary, Timothy (US educ./writer; 1920-96)
Leave It to Beaver (TV show; film, 1997)
Leavenworth prison (KS)
Leavenworth, Fort, KS (mil.)
Leavenworth, KS
Leavitt, Mike (Michael Okerlund)(UT gov.; 1951-)
Lebanon (Republic of)(W Asia)
Lebanon, PA
LeBaron, Chrysler (auto.)
Lebedev, Valentin (Vitalyevich)(cosmo.; 1942-)
Lebensraum (Ger., expansion)
Leblanc, Matt (ent.; 1967-)
Le Bon, Simon (ent.; 1958-)
le Carré, John (b. David Cornwell)(Br. writer; 1931-)
Lech Walesa (ex-pres., Pol.; 1943-)
Le Chatelier('s) principle (also Le Chatelier-Braun p.)(chem.)
Leclercq, Patrick (PM, Monaco; 1938-)
Le Corbusier (aka Charles Édouard Jeanneret)(Fr. arch./artist; 1887-1965)
Le Creuset of America, Inc.
LED (light-emitting diode)(compu.)
Led Zeppelin (pop music)
Leda (myth.)
Ledbetter, Huddie "Leadbelly" (US jazz; 1888-1949)
Lederberg, Joshua (US geneticist; 1925-)
Lederer, Eppie (aka Ann Landers)(b. Esther Pauline Friedman)(US advice columnist; 1918-)

Ledger, Lakeland (FL newspaper)
Ledoyen, Virginie (ent./model; 1976-)
Le Duc Anh (ex-pres., Viet.; 1920-)
Le Duc Tho (aka Phan Dinh Khai)(NViet pol.; 1911-90)
Lee A. Iacocca (US bus./auto.; 1924-)
Lee and Yang (Ch. physicists)
Lee (Harvey Leroy) Atwater (US pol.; 1951-91)
Lee Corp., Sara
Lee de Forest (US inv., radio/sound films/TV; 1873-1961)
Lee Elder (golf; 1934-)
Lee-Enfield rifle (also Enfield rifle)
Lee Evans (runner; 1947-)
Lee Falk (cartoonist; 1911-99)
Lee Grant (b. Lyova Rosenthal)(ent.; 1927-)
Lee Han Dong (PM, SKorea; 1934-)
Lee Harvey Oswald (assassinated JFK; 1939-63)
Lee Hoi Chang (ex-PM; SKorea)
Lee Horsley (ent.; 1955-)
Lee J. Cobb (ent.; 1911-76)
Lee jeans
Lee Konitz (US jazz; 1927-)
Lee Majors (b. Harvey Lee Yeary)(ent.; 1939-)
Lee Marvin (ent.; 1924-87)
Lee P. Brown (Houston mayor; 1937-)
Lee (Bouvier) Radziwill (Ross), (Caroline)(sister of Jackie Kennedy Onassis; 1933-)
Lee Remick (ent.; 1935-91)
Lee Salk (US psych.; 1927-92)
Lee Shepherd (auto racing; 1945-85)
Lee Shubert (US theater; 1875-1953)
Lee Strasberg (US ent./educ.; 1901-82)
Lee Tenghui (ex-pres., Taiwan; 1923-)
Lee Trevino (golf; 1939-)
Lee Tsung Dao (Ch. physt.; 1926-)
Lee University, Washington and (VA)
Lee Van Cleef (ent.; 1925-89)
Lee, Ang (ent.; 1954-)
Lee, Brenda (b. Brenda Mae Tarpley)(ent.; 1944-)
Lee, Bruce (ent./martial arts; 1940-73)
Lee, Christopher (aka Lee Yuen Kam)(ent.; 1922-)
Lee, Fort (NJ)(city)
Lee, Fort (VA)(mil)
Lee, Francis Lightfoot (US pol.; 1734-97)
Lee, Gypsy Rose (b. Rose Louise Hovick)(ent.; 1914-70)
Lee, Henry "Light-Horse Harry" (US gen.; 1756-1818)
Lee, Johnny (ent.; 1946-)
Lee, Manfred B(ennington)(pseud. Ellery Queen)(US writer; 1905-71)
Lee, Michele (ent.; 1942-)
Lee, Peggy (b. Norma Egstrom)(ent.; 1920-)
Lee, Pinky (b. Pinkus Leff)(ent.; 1908-93)
Lee, Regis & Kathie (TV show)
Lee, Robert E(dward)(US confed. gen.; 1807-70)
Lee, Spike (Shelton Jackson)(ent.; 1957-)
Lee, Stan (b. Stanley Lieber)(cartoonist, Marvel Comics; 1922-)
Lee, Tommy (b. Thomas Lee Bass)(ent.; 1962-)
Lee, Wen Ho (Taiwan/US eng./scien., nuclear weapons; 1939-)
Leeds, England
Leekpai, Chuan (PM, Thailand; 1938-)

Leelee Sobieski (ent./model; 1982-)
Leeuwenhoek, Anton van (Dutch, father of microbiology; 1632-1723)
Leeward Islands (S. Pac.)
Leeward Islands, Lesser Antilles (Montserrat, Antigua, St. Christopher [St. Kitts]-Nevis, Barbuda, Anguilla, St. Martin, British Virgin Islands, U.S. Virgin Islands)
Leeza Gibbons (ent.; 1957-)
Leeza, John and (TV show)
LeFaro, Scott (US jazz; 1936-61)
le Fay, Morgan (also Morgain le Fay)(King Arthur's fairy sister)
Left Bank (also Rive Gauche)(Paris)
Lefty (Robert Moses) Grove (baseball; 1900-75)
Legacy Outback, Subaru (auto.)
Legacy, Subaru (auto.)
Le Gallienne, Eva (ent.; 1899-91)
Le Gallienne, Richard (US/Br. writer; 1866-1947)
Leganza, Daewoo (auto.)
Legend of Sleepy Hollow, The (W. Irving tale)
Legend, Acura (auto.)
Léger, Fernand (Fr. artist; 1881-1955)
Leggett & Platt, Inc.
Leggett & Platt/Hartex (US bus.)
L'eggs (hosiery)
L'eggs Products, Inc.
Leghari, Farooq (ex-pres., Pak.; 1940-)
Leghorn (chicken)
Leghorn, Foghorn (cartoon chara.)
Legion of Honor (Fr.)
Legion of Merit (US)
Legionnaire (member Amer. Legion)
Legionnaires' disease (also l.c.)(med.)
Lego (toys)
Legree, Simon (fict. chara., Uncle Tom's Cabin)
LeGuin, Ursula (US writer; 1929-)
Leguizamo, John (ent.; 1964-)
Lehár, Franz (Hung. comp.; 1870-1948)
Le Havre, France
Lehman Brothers Holdings, Inc.
Lehmann, Lilli (Ger. opera; 1848-1929)
Lehmann, Lotte (Ger. opera; 1888-1976)
Lehrer News Hour, MacNeil, (former TV show)
Lehrer, Jim (US news jour.; 1934-)
Leiber, Jerry (US comp.; 1933-)
Leibman, Ron (ent.; 1937-)
Leibnitz, Gottfried Wilhelm von, Baron (Ger. phil./math; 1646-1716)
Leibnitzianism (phil.)
Leibovitz, Annie (US photo.; 1949-)
Leica (camera)
Leica USA, Inc.
Leicester (cheese)
Leicester (sheep)
Leicester, England
Leicestershire (also Leicester)(county, Eng.)
Leif Erickson (ent.; 1911-86)
Leif Ericsson (Norse expl.; c.1000)
Leifer, Carol (ent.; 1956-)
Leigh, Janet (b. Jeannette Helen Morrison)(ent.; 1927-)
Leigh, Jennifer Jason (b. Jennifer Leigh Morrow)(ent.; 1962-)
Leigh, Mike (ent./writer; 1943-)

Leigh, Mitch (US comp.; 1928-)
Leigh, Vivien (ent.; 1913-67)
Leighton, Margaret (ent.; 1922-76)
Leinsdorf, Erich (ent.; 1912-93)
Leinster (province, Ir.)
Leipzig, Germany
Le Journal de Montreal
Le Journal de Quebec
Leland Stanford, A(masa)(US bus./finan./pol.;
    1824-93)
LEM (lunar excursion module)
Lem, Stanislaw (Pol. writer; 1921-)
Lemaître, Georges Edouard (Belgium astron.;
    1894-1966)
Leman, Lake (also Lake of Geneva)(Switz./Fr.)
Le Mans, France (auto racing)
LeMans, Pontiac (auto.)
Le Marche (region, It.)
LeMay, Curtis (Emerson)(US gen.; 1906-90)
Lemieux, Mario (hockey; 1965-)
Le Misanthrope (Molière comedy)
Lemmon, Chris (ent.; 1954-)
Lemmon, Jack (ent.; 1925-2001)
Lemnitzer, Lyman (US gen.; 1899-1988)
Lemon Jefferson, Blind (US jazz; 1897-1930)
Lemond, Greg (cyclist; 1961-)
Lemoore Naval Air Station (CA)
Le Morte D'Arthur (by T. Malory)
Lemuralia (ancient Roman rite)
Lena Horne (ent.; 1917-)
Lena Olin (ent.; 1955-)
Lenape, Lenni (Native Amer.)(also Delaware)
Lender's Bagel Bakery (of Kraft, Inc.)
Lendl, Ivan (tennis; 1960-)
L'Enfant, Pierre Charles (Fr./US arch./eng.;
    1754-1825)
L'Engle, Madeleine (US writer; 1918-)
Lenin Library (Moscow)
Lenin Peak (Kyrgyzstan/Tajikistan)
Lenin, Vladimir Ilyich (Ulyanov)(USSR pol.;
    1870-1924)
Leningrad, Russia (now St. Petersburg)
Leninism (pol.)
Lennart Meri (pres., Estonia; 1929-)
Lenni Lenape (Native Amer.)(also Delaware)
Lennie Tristano (US jazz; 1919-78)
Lennie Wilkins (basketball; 1937-)
Lennon Sisters, the (pop music)
Lennon, John (Br. comp./ent.; 1940-80)
Lennon, Julian (ent.; 1963-)
Lennon, Sean (ent.; 1975-)
Lennox, Annie (ent.; 1954-)
Lenny Bruce (b. Leonard Alfred
    Schneider)(ent.; 1926-66)
Lenny Kravitz (ent.; 1964-)
Leno, Jay (ent.; 1950-)
Lenox China, Inc.
Lenox Crystal, Inc.
Lens Plus (eye care)
Lent (rel., period of fasting)
Lente Iletin (med.)
Lenya, Lotte (ent.; 1898-1981)
Lenz, Heinrich (Estonian physt.; 1804-65)
Lenz's law (physics)
Leo (zodiac; astron., lion)

Leo A. Falcam (pres., Micronesia; 1935-)
Leo Carrillo (ent./preservationist/
    conservationist; 1880-1961)
Leo Delibes, C(lement) P(hilibert)(Fr. comp.;
    1836-91)
Leo Durocher (baseball; 1906-91)
Leo F. Buscaglia (US writer; 1924-98)
Leo G. Carroll (ent.; 1892-1972)
Leo Gorcey (ent.; 1915-69)
Leo Minor (astron.; little lion)
Leo Robin (US lyricist; 1900-84)
Leo (Calvin) Rosten (pseud. Leonard Q.
    Ross)(US humorist/sociol.; 1908-97)
Leo (Gerard) Sayer (ent./songwriter; 1948-)
Leo Szilard (US/Hung. physt.; 1898-1964)
Leo (Nikolaievich) Tolstoy, Count (Rus. writer;
    1828-1910)
Leominster, MA
Leon Ames (ent.; 1903-1993)
Léon Bakst (Rus. artist/designer; 1867-1924)
Léon Blum (Fr. pol.; 1872-1950)
Leon Edel (US writer; 1907-97)
Leon E. Panetta (US ex-white house chief of
    staff; 1938-)
Léon Gambetta, (Fr. pol.; 1838-82)
Leon Jaworski (US atty.; 1905-82)
Leon Russell (b. Hank Wilson)(ent./songwriter;
    1941-)
Leon Spinks (boxing; 1953-)
Leon Uris (US writer; 1924-)
Léon Trotsky (b. Lev Davidovich
    Bronstein)(USSR pol.; 1879-1940)
Léon Victor Auguste Bourgeois (Fr. pol.; 1851-
    1925)
Léon, Mexico
Léon, Nicaragua
Léon, (Juan) Ponce de (Sp. expl.; c1460-1521)
Léon, Spain
Leona Helmsley (US bus./hotel; c1920-)
Leonard Bernstein (US comp./cond.; 1918-90)
Leonard Bloomfield (US linguist; 1887-1949)
Leonard Cohen (ent./songwriter/poet; 1934-)
Leonard Maltin (film critic; 1950-)
Leonard "Chico" Marx (ent.; 1886-1961)
Leonard Nimoy (ent.; 1931-)
Leonard Q. Ross (aka Leo [Calvin] Rosten)(US
    humorist/sociol.; 1908-97)
Leonard Ray Dawson (football; 1935-)
Leonard Roscoe Tanner, III (tennis; 1951-)
Leonard Rose (US cellist; 1918-84)
Leonard Sidney Woolf (Br. writer; 1880-1969)
Leonard Slatkin (US cond.; 1944-)
Leonard Wood, Fort, MO (mil.)
Leonard, Benny (Benjamin Leiner)(boxing;
    1896-1947)
Leonard, Elmore (US writer; 1925-)
Leonard, Sheldon (ent.; 1907-97)
Leonard, Sugar Ray (boxing; 1956-)
Leonardo da Vinci (It. artist/scien.; 1452-1519)
Leonardo DiCaprio (ent.; 1974-)
Leonardo Fibonacci (It. math.; c1175-c1250)
Leoncavallo, Ruggiero (It. comp.; 1857-1919)
Leonhard Euler (Swiss math./physt.; 1707-83)
Leoni, Tea (b. Elizabeth Tea Pantaleoni)(ent.;
    1966-)

Leonid D(anylovich) Kuchma (pres., Ukraine; 1938-)

Leonid Ilyich Brezhnev (ex-pres., USSR; 1906-82)

Leonid Kizim (cosmo.)

Leonid Kravchuk (ex-pres., Ukraine; 1934-)

Leonids meteor shower (Nov.)

Leonie Rysanek (dramatic soprano; 1928-98)

Leonine Wall (Vatican)

Leonov, Aleksei (Arkhipovich)(cosmo., 1st to walk in space; 1934-)

Leontyne Price, (Mary)(opera; 1927-)

Leopold Auer (violinist/educ.; 1845-1930)

Leopold (Antoni Stanislaw) Stokowski (US cond.; 1882-1977)

Leopoldo Galtieri (ex-pres., Argentina; 1926-)

Leopoldville (now Kinshasa)

Le Pen, Jean-Marie (Fr. pol.; 1928-)

Le Petit Trianon, (built for Mme. de Pompadour by Louis XV)

Lepisma (insect)

Leppard, Def (pop music)

Lepping, George (ex-gov.-gen.; Solomon Islands)

Lepus (astron., hare)

Lerner & Loewe (US song writing team)

Lerner, Alan Jay (US lyricist; 1918-86)

Lerner, Max (jour.; 1902-92)

Leroy Anderson (US comp.; 1908-75)

Leroy Kelly (football; 1942-)

Leroy (Robert) "Satchel " Paige (baseball; 1906-82)

LeRoy, Mervyn (ent.; 1900-87)

Les(lie) Aspin, Jr. (US ex-secy./defense; 1938-95)

Les Brown (ent.; 1912-2001)

Les Cayes, Haiti

Les Escaldes, Andorra

Les Fauves (also l.c.)(Fauvist artists)

Les Miserables (V. Hugo novel)

Les Paul & Mary Ford (ent.)

Les Paul (b. Lester Polfus)(US inv./ent.; 1915-)

Les Sylphides (ballet)

Les Tremayne (ent.; 1913-)

LeSabre, Buick (auto.)

Lesage, Alain-René (Fr. writer; 1668-1747)

Lesbos Island (now Lesvos)(Gr.)

Lescoulie, Jack (ent.; 1917-)

Leskovac, Yugoslavia

Leslie-Ann Down (ent.; 1954-)

Lesley Ann Warren (ent.; 1946-)

Lesley Gore (ent.; 1946-)

Lesley J. McNair, Fort (DC)(mil.)

Lesley Stahl (US TV jour.; 1941-)

Leslie Caron (Fr./US ent.; 1931-)

Leslie Fay, Inc.

Leslie Nielsen (ent.; 1926-)

Leslie Uggams (ent.; 1943-)

Leslie, Joan (ent.; 1925-)

Lesotho (Kingdom of)(formerly Basutoland)(S Afr.)

Lesseps, Ferdinand de, Vicomte (Fr. dipl./eng.; 1805-94)

Lesser Antilles, West Indies (Aruba, Netherlands Antilles, Trinidad and Tobago, Windward Islands, Leeward Islands)

Lesser Dog (also Little Dog, Canis Minor)

(astron.)

Lessing, Doris (May Taylor)(Br. writer; 1919-)

Lessing, Gotthold (Ephraim)(Ger. writer; 1729-81)

Lestat, The Vampire (A. Rice novel)

Lester B(ryant) Bird (PM, Antigua/Barbuda; 1938-)

Lester (Raymond) Flatt (ent.; 1914-79)

Lester (Garfield) Maddox (ex-GA gov.; 1915-)

Lester (Bowles) Pearson (ex-PM, Can.; 1897-1972)

Lester "Pres" (Willis) Young (US jazz; 1909-59)

Lesvos Island (formerly Lesbos)(Gr.)

Le Tartuffe (Molière comedy)

Lethal Weapon (film, 1987)

Lethal Weapon 2 (film, 1989)

Lethal Weapon 3 (film, 1992)

Lethal Weapon 4 (film, 1998)

Lethbridge, Alberta, Canada

Lethe (myth.)

Leto, Jared (ent.; 1971-)

Letsie III (king, Lesotho; 1963-)

Let's Make a Deal (TV show)

Letterkenny Army Depot (PA)(mil.)

Letterman, David (ent.; 1947-)

Letterman, Late Night With David (TV show)

Lettermen, the (pop music)

Letters, Doctor of (also D. Litt., Doctor Litterarum)

Leukeran (med.)

Leutze, Emanuel (US artist; 1816-68)

Leuven, Belgium (also Louvain)

Levant leather/morocco

Levant, Oscar (ent.; 1906-72)

LeVar Burton (also Levar)(ent.; 1957-)

Levatol (med.)

Levene, Sam (ent.; 1905-80)

Levenson, Sam (US humorist; 1911-80)

Lever Brothers Co., Inc.

Levertov, Denise (Br./US poet; 1923-97)

Lévesque, René (ex-premier, Quebec, Can.; 1922-87)

Levi (Isr. tribe)

Levi P(arsons) Morton (ex-US VP; 1824-1920)

Levi Strauss (US bus.; c1829-1902)

Levi Strauss Co.

Lévi-Strauss, Claude (Fr. anthrop.; 1908-1990)

Levi, Carlo (It. artist/writer; 1902-75)

Levi's (jeans)

Leviathan (rel.)

Levin, Carl M. (US cong.; 1934-)

Levin, Ira (US writer; 1929-)

Levin, Jerry (Gerald M.)(US bus./AOL Time Warner)

Levine, David (cartoonist; 1926-)

Levine, Irving R. (US TV jour.; 1922-)

Levine, James (ent.; 1943-)

Levine, Joseph E. (ent.; 1905-87)

Levinson, Barry (ent.; 1932-)

Levites (people)

Leviticus (rel., book of the Old Testament)

Levitt, Arthur, Jr. (US bus., ex-chair/SEC; 1931-)

Levittown, NY

Levo-Dromoran (med.)

Levolor blinds

Levolor, Inc.

Levon Ter-Petrosyan (ex-pres., Armenia; 1943-)

Levsin (med.)
Levuka, Fiji
Lévy-Bruhl, Lucien (Fr. phil.; 1857-1939)
Levy, Chandra (US missing intern; 1977-)
Lew(is) Alcindor, Jr. (aka Kareem Abdul-Jabbar)(basketball; 1947-)
Lew Ayres (ent.; 1908-96)
Lew Wasserman (ent.; 1913-)
Lewin, Kurt (US psych.; 1890-1947)
Lewinsky, Monica (US news; 1973-)
Lewis and Clark Expedition (St. Louis to Pac.; 1804-06)
Lewis and the News, Huey (pop music)
Lewis Carroll (aka Charles Dodgson)(Br. writer/math.; 1832-98)
Lewis F(ranklin) Powell, Jr. (US jurist; 1907-98)
Lewis Galoob, Inc.
Lewis Mumford (US writer/sociol.; 1895-1990)
Lewis structure/symbol (chem.)
Lewis, Anthony (US writer; 1927-)
Lewis, (Sir William) Arthur (Br. econ.; 1915-91)
Lewis, (Frederick) Carl(eton)(track; 1961-)
Lewis, Cecil Day (Ir. poet; 1904-72)
Lewis, C(live) S(taples)("Clive Hamilton")(Br. writer; 1898-1963)
Lewis, Daniel Day- (ent.; 1957-)
Lewis, Dawnn (ent.; 1960-)
Lewis, Emmanuel (ent.; 1971-)
Lewis, Gilbert Newton (US chem.; 1875-1946)
Lewis, Huey (b. Hugh Cregg, III)(ent.; 1950-)
Lewis, Jerry (b. Joseph Levitch)(ent.; 1926-)
Lewis, Jerry Lee (ent.; 1935-)
Lewis, Joe E. (ent.; 1902-71)
Lewis, John (US jazz; 1920-)
Lewis, John L(lewellyn)(US labor leader; 1880-1969)
Lewis, John R(obert)(US cong.; 1940-)
Lewis, Juliette (ent.; 1973-)
Lewis, Lennox (boxing; 1965-)
Lewis, Mel (US jazz; 1929-90)
Lewis, Meriwether (US expl.; 1774-1809)
Lewis, Ramsey (US jazz; 1935-)
Lewis, Reggie (basketball; 1966-93)
Lewis, Richard (ent.; 1947-)
Lewis, Robert Q. (ent.; 1920-91)
Lewis, Shari (ent.; 1934-98)
Lewis, (Harry) Sinclair (US writer; 1885-1951)
Lewis, (Percy) Wyndham (Br./US artist/writer; 1884-1957)
Lewiston, ME
Lexington Blue Grass Army Depot (KY)
Lexington Herald-Leader (KY newspaper)
Lexington, Battle of (US hist.; 1775)
Lexington, KY, MA, NC
Lexis (compu. database, law)
Lexmark (compu.)
Lexmark International, Inc.
Lexus
Lexus (auto.)
Lexus ES300 sedan (auto.)
Lexus GS300 sedan (auto.)
Lexus GS400 sedan (auto.)
Lexus GS430 (auto.)
Lexus IS300 (auto.)
Lexus LS400 sedan (auto.)

Lexus LS430 (auto.)
Lexus LX450 wagon (auto.)
Lexus LX470 wagon (auto.)
Lexus RX300 wagon (auto.)
Lexus SC300 coupe (auto.)
Lexus SC400 coupe (auto.)
Lexus SC430 convertible (auto.)
Ley, Willie (science writer; 1906-69)
Leyden jar (elec.)
L(yman) Frank Baum (US writer; 1856-1919)
L(eroy) Gordon Cooper, Jr. (astro.; 1927-)
Lhasa apso (dog)
Lhasa, Tibet, China
Li (chem. sym., lithium)
Li (Tai) Po (Ch. poet; 705-62)
Li Peng (ex-PM, Ch.; 1928-)
Li'l Abner (fict. chara.)
Li, Jet (b. Li Lian-jie)(ent./martial arts; 1963-)
Liam Cosgrave (ex-PM, Ir.; 1920-)
Liam Gallagher (ent., Oasis; 1972-)
Liam Neeson (ent.; 1952-)
Liam O'Flaherty (Ir. writer; 1897-1984)
Liaoning (province, Ch.)
Liaquat Ali Khan (ex-PM, Pak.; 1895-1951)
Libbey Glass (US bus.)
Liber (It. myth.)
Liberace (b. Wladziu Valentino)(US pianist; 1919-87)
Liberal Party (Br. pol.; 1830-)
Liberal Party (US pol.; 1944-)
Liberal Party, Australian (Austl. pol.)
Liberal Republican Party (US pol.)
Liberation Army of Palestine (also Intifada)(est. 1987)
Liberia (Republic of)(W Afr.)
Libertarian Party (US pol.)
Liberty Bell (Philadelphia)
Liberty Bell 7 (also Mercury-Redstone 3)(1st US crewed space flight; May 5, 1961)
Liberty Bowl (college football)
Liberty Island (formerly Bedloe's or Bedloe Island)(NY)
Liberty Mutual Insurance Co.
Liberty Party (US pol.; 1840-48)
Liberty Valance, The Man Who Shot (film, 1962)
Liberty, Sons of (US hist.; 1765-66)
Liberty, Statue of (NYC)
Libra (zodiac; astron., balance)
Library of Alexandria (Eg.)
Library of Congress (DC)
Librax (med.)
Libreville, Gabon
Librium (med.)
Libya (Socialist People's Libyan Arab Jamahiriya)(N Afr.)
Libyan Desert (N Afr.)
Lichtenstein, Roy (US artist; 1923-97)
Licia Albanese (soprano; 1913-)
Liddy, G. Gordon (US pol./Watergate; 1930-)
Lidex (med.)
Lidice, Czechoslovakia
Lie, Trygve H(alvdan)(Nor. pol./UN; 1896-1968)
Lieberman, Hadassah (US wife of pol.; 1948-)
Lieberman, Joseph I. (US cong.; 1942-)

Lieberman-Cline, Nancy (basketball; 1958-)
Liebermann, Max (Ger. artist; 1847-1935)
Liebfraumilch (wine)
Liebig condenser (chem.)
Liebig, Justus von, Baron (Ger. chem.; 1803-73)
Liechtenstein (Principality of)(W Eur.)
Liederkranz (cheese)
Liège (province, Belgium)
Liege, Belgium
Lien Chan (ex-premier; Taiwan)
Liepaja, Lativa
Liepzig, Germany
Life (mag.)
Life and Times of Grizzly Adams (film, 1974)
Life Books, Time- (US bus.)
Life Guards (Br.)
Life of Riley, The (TV show, film)
Life With Father (play; film, 1947)
Lifebuoy (soap)
LifeSavers
LifeSavers Co., Planters
Lifestyles of the Rich and Famous (TV show)
Lifetime (TV channel)
Lifetime Movie Network (TV channel)
Liggett, Fort Hunter (CA)(mil.)
Light, City of (Paris)
Light, Judith (ent.; 1949-)
Light, San Antonio (TX newspaper)
Light-Horse Harry (Henry) Lee (US gen.; 1756-1818)
Lightfoot, Gordon (ent.; 1938-)
Lightning, Tampa Bay (hockey team)
Lihue, HI
Likud (Isr. pol.)
Lila Wallace (Acheson)(US publ.; 1889-1984)
Lili Kraus (pianist; 1905-86)
Lilian's Story (film, 1995)
Lilic, Zoran (ex-pres., Yug.)
Lilith (myth.)
Liliuokalani (Lydia Kamekeha)(queen, Hawaii; 1838-1917)
Lille, France
Lillehammer, Norway
Lilli Lehmann (Ger. opera; 1848-1929)
Lilli Palmer (ent.; 1914-86)
Lillian Gish (ent.; 1895-1993)
Lillian (Florence) Hellman (US writer; 1905-84)
Lillian Russell (b. Helen Louise Leonard)(ent.; 1861-1922)
Lillian Vernon Corp.
Lillie Langtry ("the Jersey Lily")(b. Emily Charlotte le Breton)(Br. ent.; 1853-1929)
Lillie, Beatrice (ent.; 1894-1989)
Lilliput (fict. land, *Gulliver's Travels*)
Lilliputian (fict. charas., *Gulliver's Travels*)
Lilly & Company, Eli
Lilly (or Lyly, Lily), John (Br. writer; 1554?-1606)
Lilongwe, Malawi
Lilt (hair care)
Lily Pons (ent.; 1904-76)
Lily Tomlin (ent.; 1939-)
Lily (or Lyly, Lilly), John (Br. writer; 1554?-1606)
Lily(e), William (Br. scholar; c1468-1522)
Lima, OH
Lima, Peru

Limassol, Cyprus
Limbaugh, III, Rush (Hudson)(US radio commentator; 1951-)
Limbitrol (med.)
Limbo (rel.)
Limburg (province, Belgium)
Limburg (province, Netherlands)
Limburger (also Limburg)(cheese)
Limehouse district (London)
Limerick (county, Ir.)
Limited, Inc., The
Limoges china/ware
Limoges, France
Limón Dance Company, José
Limón, Costa Rica (also Puerto Limón)
Limón, José (Mex./US dancer; 1908-72)
Limousin (region, Fr.)
Limousine Liberal
Limpet, The Incredible Mr. (film, 1964)
Lin Yutang (Ch. writer; 1895-1976)
Lin, Maya (US arch./sculptor; 1959-)
Lina Wertmüller (It. ent.; 1926?-)
Lincocin (med.)
Lincoln (auto.)
Lincoln Blackwood pickup (auto.)
Lincoln C. Almond (RI gov.; 1936-)
Lincoln Center for the Performing Arts
Lincoln Chafee (US cong.; 1953-)
Lincoln Continental (auto.)
Lincoln-Douglas debates (US hist.; 1858)
Lincoln Financial Group
Lincoln green (color)
Lincoln Journal (NE newspaper)
Lincoln Kirstein (ent.; 1907-96)
Lincoln LS (auto.)
Lincoln Mark VIII (auto.)
Lincoln Mark VIII LSC (auto.)
Lincoln Memorial (DC)
Lincoln Monument (IL)
Lincoln National Corp.
Lincoln Navigator (auto.)
Lincoln Star (NE newspaper)
Lincoln Steffens, (Joseph)(US writer; 1866-1926)
Lincoln Town Car (auto.)
Lincoln Town Car Cartier (auto.)
Lincoln Town Car Executive (auto.)
Lincoln Town Car Signature (auto.)
Lincoln Town Car Touring (auto.)
Lincoln, Abraham (16th US pres.; 1809-65)
Lincoln, Benjamin (US mil./pol.; 1722-1810)
Lincoln, Blanche (Lambert)(US cong.; 1960-)
Lincoln, England
Lincoln, IL, NE, RI
Lincoln, Mary Todd (wife of A. Lincoln; 1818-82)
Lincoln, Robert Todd (US atty., A. Lincoln's son; 1843-1926)
Lincolnshire (county, Eng.)(also Lincoln)
Lind, Jenny (Johanna Maria Lind Goldschmidt, "The Swedish Nightingale")(ent.; 1820-87)
Linda Blair (ent.; 1959-)
Linda Bloodworth-Thomason (ent.)
Linda Darnell (ent.; 1921-65)
Linda Eastman McCartney (US photo./ent.; 1941-98)
Linda Ellerbee (US jour.; 1944-)

Linda Evangelista (model; 1965-)
Linda Evans (b. Linda Evanstad)(ent.; 1942-)
Linda Fiorentino (b. Clorinda Fiorentino)(ent.; 1960-)
Linda Fratianne (figure skating; 1960-)
Linda Gray (ent.; 1940-)
Linda Hamilton (ent.; 1956-)
Linda Hunt (ent.; 1945-)
Linda Jezek (swimming; 1960-)
Linda Kozlowski (ent.)
Linda Lavin (ent.; 1937-)
Linda Myers (archery; 1947-)
Linda Richman (comedian, *SNL*)
Linda Ronstadt (ent.; 1946-)
Linda Rose Tripp (nee Carotenuto)(US news; 1949-)
Linda Wertheimer (radio jour.; 1943-)
Lindal Cedar Homes, Inc.
Lindbergh kidnapping
Lindbergh, Anne (Spencer) Morrow (US writer/aviator; 1906-2001)
Lindbergh, Charles A(ugustus)(US aviator; 1902-74)
Linden, Hal (b. Hal Lipschitz)(ent.; 1931-)
Lindros, Eric (hockey; 1973-)
Lindsay (Gordon) Anderson (ent.; 1923-94)
Lindsay Boatbuilders, Mark (US bus.)
Lindsay Crouse (ent.; 1948-)
Lindsay International (US bus.)
Lindsay Olive Growers (US bus.)
Lindsay Wagner (ent.; 1949-)
Lindsay, Howard (US playwright; 1889-1968)
Lindsay, John (Vliet)(ex-NYC mayor; 1921-)
Lindsay, (Nicholas) Vachel (US poet; 1879-1931)
Lindsey Buckingham (ent.; 1947-)
Lindy Hop (dance)(also l.c.)
Linehan, Kim (swimming; 1962-)
Lingala (lang.)
Lingayat (rel.)
Lingayata (rel.)
Linkletter, Art (ent.; 1912-)
Linnaeus, Carolus (Carl von Linne)(Swed. botanist; 1707-78)
Linn-Baker, Mark (ent.; 1954-)
Linney, Laura (ent.; 1964-)
Linotype (publ.)
Linus (fict. chara., *Peanuts*)
Linus (myth.)
Linus C(arl) Pauling (US chem.; 1901-94)
Linux
Linzer torte (pastry)
Lion King, The (film, 1994)
Lion, William the (king, Scot.; 1143-1214)
Lionel Barrymore (ent.; 1878-1954)
Lionel de Rothschild (Br. finan.; 1882-1942)
Lionel Hampton (US jazz; 1908-)
Lionel Jeffries (ent.; 1926-)
Lionel Jospin (PM, Fr.; 1937-)
Lionel Nathan Rothschild, Baron de ("Lord Natty")(Br. finan./pol.; 1808-79)
Lionel Richie (ent.; 1949-)
Lionel Stander (ent.; 1908-94)
Lionel Trilling (US writer/educ.; 1905-75)
Lion-Hearted, Richard the (or Coeur de Lion, Richard I)(king, Eng.; 1157-99)

Lions Club (US org.; est. 1917)
Lions, Detroit (football team)
Lions, Gulf of (S Fr.)
Lioresal (med.)
Liotta, Ray (ent.; 1955-)
Lipari Islands (It.)
Lipchitz, Jacques (US sculptor; 1891-1973)
Lipinski, Tara (figure skating; 1982-)
Lipitor (med.)
Lipizaner horse
Lippi, Filippo (or Filippino)(It. artist; 1457-1504)
Lippi, Fra Filippo (It. artist; 1406-69)
Lippmann, Walter (US jour.; 1889-1974)
Lipponen, Paavo Tapio (PM, Fin.; 1941-)
Liptauer (cheese)
Lipton tea
Lipton, Inc., Thomas J.
Lipton, Peggy (ent.; 1947-)
Lipton, (Sir) Thomas J(ohnstone)(Scot. bus., tea; 1850-1931)
Liquid Paper Corp.
Liquid-plumr
Liquiprin (med.)
Liquori, Marty (runner; 1949-)
Lisa Bonet (ent.; 1967-)
Lisa Eichhorn (ent.; 1952-)
Lisa Hartman Black (ent.; 1956-)
Lisa Kudrow (ent.; 1963-)
Lisa Loeb (ent.; 1968-)
Lisa Lopes (ent.; 1971-)
Lisa Marie Presley (daughter of Elvis and Priscilla Presley; 1968-)
Lisa, Mona (aka *La Gioconda*)(da Vinci painting)
Lisbon, Portugal
Lisieux, St. Thérèse of (Fr. rel.; 1873-97)
Lissouba, Pascal (ex-pres., Congo; 1931-)
Lister, Joseph, Baron (Br. phys., antiseptic surgery; 1827-1912)
Listerine (med.)
Listermint (med.)
Liston, Sonny (Charles)(boxing; 1933-71)
Liszt, Franz (Hung. comp.; 1811-86)
Literary Guild, The
Literary Magazine Review
Literature, Nobel Prize for
Lithgow, John (ent.; 1945-)
Lithobid (med.)
Lithotabs (med.)
Lithuania (Republic of)(formerly part of USSR) (N Eur.)
Lithuanian (lang./people)
Little Anthony and the Imperials (pop music)
Little Bighorn, Battle of the (also Custer's Last Stand)(US/Sioux Native Amer.; 1876)
Little Bo-Peep (fict. chara.)
Little Boy Blue (nursery rhyme)
Little Chickadee, My (film, 1940)
Little Corporal (Napoleon Bonaparte)
Little Dipper (also Ursa Minor)(astron.)
Little Dog (also Lesser Dog, Canis Minor)(astron.)
Little Eva (b. Eva Narcissus Boyd)(ent.; 1945-)
Little Gloria . . . Happy at Last (TV miniseries)
Little House on the Prairie (TV show)
Little Iodine (comic strip)
Little Jack Horner (nursery rhyme)

Little Jimmy Dickens (ent.; 1920-)
Little John (fict. chara., *Robin Hood*)
Little King (comic strip)
Little League (baseball)
Little Leaguer (baseball)
Little Lord Fauntleroy (F. H. Burnett book)
Little Lord Fauntleroy suit
Little Mermaid, The (film, 1978, 1984, 1989)
Little Miss Marker (film, 1934, 1980)
Little Miss Muffett (nursery rhyme)
Little Orphan Annie (fict. chara.)
Little Professor Book Centers, Inc.
Little Rascals (TV show)
Little Red Ridinghood (fairy tale)
Little Richard (b. Richard Penniman)(ent.; 1932-)
Little Rock Air Force Base (AR)(mil.)
Little Rock Democrat-Gazette (AR newspaper)
Little Rock, AR
Little Shop of Horrors (film, 1960, 1986)
Little Turtle, Chief (Michikinikwa)(Miami Native
    Amer.; 1752?-1812)
Little Women (Meg, Jo, Beth & Amy March)
    (L.M. Alcott novel)
Little, Brown & Co., Inc.
Little, Chicken (fict. chara.)
Little, Cleavon (ent.; 1939-92)
Little, Floyd Douglas (football; 1942-)
Little, Lou (football; 1893-1979)
Little, Malcolm (aka Malcolm X)(US black-rights
    activist; 1926-65)
Little, Rich (ent.; 1938-)
Little, Stuart (E.B. White novel)
Littler, Gene (golf; 1930-)
Litton Industries, Inc.
Littrell, Brian (ent., Backstreet Boys; 1975-)
Liturgy of the Hours (also Divine Office)(rel.)
Litvinov, Maxim (USSR pol.; 1876-1951)
Liu Shaoqi (also Liu Shao-chi)(Ch. pol.; 1898?-
    1969?)
Liu, Lucy (ent.; 1967-)
Liv Tyler (ent.; 1977-)
Liv Ullmann (ent.; 1939-)
Livarot (cheese)
Livermore Laboratory, Lawrence (nuclear
    research, CA)
Livermore, CA
Liverpool, England
Living Theatre (NYC/Eur.)
Livingston, Robert (US pol.; 1654-1728)
Livingston, Robert R. (US pol.; 1746-1813)
Livingstone, Dr. David (Scot. rel./expl. in Afr.;
    1813-73)
Livingstone, (Sir Henry) Stanley and (Dr.
    David)
Livingstone, Zambia
Livonia, MI
Livy, Titus Livius (Roman hist.; 59 BC-AD 17)
Liz Claiborne (clothing)
Liz Claiborne (US designer; 1929-)
Liz Claiborne, Inc.
Liz Phair (ent./songwriter; 1967-)
Liz Smith (US jour.; 1923-)
Liza Minnelli (ent.; 1946-)
Lizabeth Scott (b. Emma Matzo)(ent.; 1922-)
Lizzie A. Borden (US, tried/acquitted of ax

murders; 1860-1927)
Ljubljana, Slovenia
Ljupco Georgievski (PM, Macedonia; 1966-)
LL Cool J (b. James Todd Smith)(ent.; 1968-)
Lladro USA, Ltd.
Lladró porcelain
LL.B. (Legum Baccalaureus [Bachelor of Laws])
L. L. Bean (clothing)
L. L. Bean, Inc.
LL.D. (Legum Doctor [Doctor of Laws])
Llewellyn, Richard (b. Richard David Vivian
    Llewellyn Lloyd)(Welsh writer; 1906-83)
Llewelyn I (king, Wales; 1173-1240)
Llewelyn II (king, Wales; c1225-1282)
LL.M. (Legum Magister [Master of Laws])
Lloyd Bentsen (US ex-secy./treas.; 1921-)
Lloyd (Vernet) Bridges (ent.; 1913-98)
Lloyd "Cowboy" Copas (ent.; 1913-63)
Lloyd Eisler (figure skating; 1964-)
Lloyd George, David (ex-PM, Br.; 1863-1945)
Lloyd M. Bucher, Commander (US mil.)
Lloyd Nolan (ent.; 1902-85)
Lloyd Price (ent.; 1933-)
Lloyd Webber, Andrew (Br. comp.; 1948-)
Lloyd, Chris Evert- (tennis; 1954-)
Lloyd, Christopher (ent.; 1938-)
Lloyd, Emily (ent.; 1970-)
Lloyd, Harold (ent.; 1893-1971)
Lloyd, Jake (ent.; 1989-)
Lloyd's Electronics, Inc.
Lloyd's of London
LMT (local mean time)
LNG (liquefied natural gas)
Lobito, Angola
Lobos, Heitor Villa- (Brazilian comp.; 1881-1959)
lobster Newburg (food)
Loc, Tone (pop music)
Local Group (of galaxies)(astron.)
Loch Lomond (Scot. lake)
Loch Ness (lake, Scot.)
Loch Ness monster (Scot.)
Lochaber ax (Scot. weapon; 16th c.)
Lochinvar (fict. chara, *Marmion*)
Lochner v. New York (US law; 1905)
Locke, Alain LeRoy (US phil./educ.; 1886-1954)
Locke, David Ross (aka Petroleum V(esuvius)
    Nasby)(US humorist; 1833-88)
Locke, Gary (WA gov.; 1950-)
Locke, John (Br. phil.; 1632-1704)
Locke, Sondra (ent.; 1947-)
Lockhard, Joseph Patrick (US ex-White House
    press secy.; 1959-)
Lockhart, Gene (ent.; 1891-1957)
Lockhart, June (ent.; 1925-)
Lockheed Corp.
Lockheed Martin Corp.
Locklear, Heather (ent.; 1961-)
Lockport, NY
Lodge, Henry Cabot (US pol.; 1850-1924)
Lodge, Henry Cabot, Jr. (US jour./pol.; 1902-85)
Lodi, CA, NJ
Lodi, Italy
Lodovico (or Ludovico) Carracci (It. artist;
    1555-1619)
Lódz, Poland

Loeb, Lisa (ent.; 1968-)
Loesser, Frank (US comp.; 1910-69)
Loestrin (med.)
Loewe v. Lawler (US law; 1908)
Loewe, Frederick (US comp.; 1901-88)
Loewe, Lerner & (US song writing team)
Loews Corp.
Lofgren, Nils (ent.; 1951-)
Loft's Candies, Inc., Barricini/
Logan International Airport (Boston MA)
Logan's Run (film, 1976)
Logan, Inc., Jonathan
Logan, Joshua (US writer/ent.; 1908-88)
Logan, UT
Loggia, Robert (ent.; 1930-)
Loggins & Messina (pop music)
Loggins, Kenny (ent.; 1948-)
Lohengrin (Wagner opera)
Lohr Winery, J. (US bus.)
Loire River (Fr.)
Loire Valley (Fr. wine region)
Lois, Hi & (comic strip)
Lojze Peterle (Slovenian pol.)
Loki (myth.)
Lola (Loletha Elaine) Falana (ent.; 1943-)
Lola Montez (ent.; 1818?-61)
Lolita (seductive young girl)
Lolita (V. Nabokov novel)
Lollobrigida, Gina (It. ent.; 1927-)
Loman, Willy (fict. chara., *Death of a Salesman*)
Lomb, Bausch & (eye care)
Lomb, Inc., Bausch &
Lombard (banker/moneylender)
Lombard (people)
Lombard, Carole (b. Jane Alice Peters)(ent.; 1909-42)
Lombardi, Vince(nt Thomas)(football; 1913-70)
Lombardo, Guy (Albert)(ent.; 1902-77)
Lombardy (region, It.)
Lomé, Togo
Lomond, Loch (Scot. lake)
Lomotil (med.)
Lompoc, CA
Lomwe (lang./people)
Lon Chaney (ent.; 1883-1930)
Lon Chaney, Jr. (ent.; 1905-73)
London Bridge (now in AZ)
London broil
London Fog (raincoat)
London, England
London, George (baritone; 1920-85)
London, Jack (John Griffith)(US writer; 1876-1916)
London, Julie (ent.; 1926-2000)
London, Ontario, Canada
London, Tower of (fortress; built 1078)
London, Treaty of (Br./Fr./Rus./It.; 1915)
Londonderry (county, NIre.)
Londonderry, Northern Ireland (now Derry)
Lone Ranger & Tonto (fict charas.)
Lone Star State (nickname, TX)
Lonette McKee (ent.; 1957-)
Long Beach Press-Telegram (CA newspaper)
Long Beach, CA, NY
Long Branch, NJ

Long Island Expressway (NYC)
Long Island iced tea (mixed drink)
Long Island Newsday (NY newspaper)
Long Island Sound (NY/CT)
Long Island, NY
Long John Silver's Seafood Shoppes (US bus.)
Long March (Ch. hist.; 1934-35)
Long Tom (WWII weapon)
Long, Huey P(ierce)("the Kingfish")(ex-gov., LA; 1893-1935)
Long, Richard (ent.; 1927-77)
Long, Shelley (ent.; 1949-)
Longboat Key, FL
Longden, Johnny (horse racing; 1907-)
Longevity (mag.)
Longfellow, Henry Wadsworth (US poet; 1807-82)
Longford (county, Ir.)
Longhorn (cattle)
Longinus, Dionysius (Gr. critic; 1st c. AD)
Longmont, CO
Longs Drug Stores, Inc.
Longs Drugs
Longstocking, Pippi (fict. chara.)
Longstreet, James (US gen.; 1821-1904)
Longueuil, Quebec, Canada
Longview, TX, WA
Longworth, Alice Roosevelt (US social figure; 1884-1980)
Loni Anderson (ent.; 1946-)
Loniten (med.)
Look Who's Talking (film, 1989)
Look Who's Talking Too (film, 1990)
Looking for Mr. Goodbar (film, 1977)
LOOM (Loyal Order of Moose)
Looney Tunes (cartoon)
Loos, Anita (US writer; 1888?-1981)
Lo/Ovral (med.)
Lopat, Eddie (baseball; 1918-92)
Lope (Félix) de Vega (Carpio)(Sp. writer; 1562-1635)
Lopes, Lisa (ent.; 1971-)
Lopez, Al (baseball; 1908-)
Lopez, Jennifer (ent.; 1970-)
Lopez, Nancy (golf; 1957-)
Lopez, Trini (ent.; 1937-)
Lopez, Vincent (US band leader; 1895-1975)
Lopid (med.)
Lopressor (med.)
Loprox (med.)
Lorado Taft (US sculptor; 1860-1936)
Lorain, OH
Lord & Taylor (US bus.)
Lord (God, Jesus)
Lord Baltimore (aka Sir George Calvert)(founded MD; 1606-75)
Lord Beaverbrook, Baron (aka William Maxwell Beaverbrook)(Brit. finan./pol.; 1879-1964)
Lord Byron (George Gordon)(Br. poet; 1788-1824)
Lord Fauntleroy, Little (book by F. H. Burnett)
Lord Fauntleroy suit, Little
Lord Greystoke (fict. chara., *Tarzan*)
Lord High Chancellor (Br.)(also Lord Chancellor)

Lord Jim (J. Conrad novel)
Lord of hosts (God)
Lord of lords (Jesus Christ)
Lord of Misrule (former Christmas revelry
    director, Br.)
Lord of the Flies (W. Golding novel)
Lord of the Rings (J.R.R. Tolkien book)
Lord Peter Wimsey (fict. chara., D. Sayers)
Lord Tennyson, Alfred (Br. poet; 1809-92)
Lord Voldemort (fict. villain)
Lord, Jack (ent.; 1922-98)
Lord's day, the (Sunday)
Lord's Prayer (also Our Father, Paternoster
    [Pater Noster])(prayer)
Lord's Supper (also Holy Communion,
    Eucharist)(rel.)
Lords, House of (Br. parliament)
Lords, Traci (b. Nora Louise Kuzma)(ent.; 1968-)
L'Oréal Cosmetics (US bus.)
L'Oréal Hair Care (US bus.)
Lorelei (Ger. folklore)
Loren, Sophia (b. Sophia Scicoloni)(It. ent.;
    1934-)
Lorena Bobbitt (US news)
Lorenz curve (econ.)
Lorenz Hart (US lyricist; 1895-1943)
Lorenz, Konrad (Aus. ethologist; 1903-89)
Lorenzo de' Medici ("the Magnificent")(It. poet/
    pol.; 1449-92)
Lorenzo Ghiberti (It. sculptor; 1378-1455)
Lorenzo Lamas (ent.; 1958-)
Lorenzo, Frank (US bus./airlines)
Loretta Lynn (Webb)(ent.; 1935-)
Loretta Swit (ent.; 1937-)
Loretta Young (ent.; 1913-2000)
Lorimar (US bus.)
Lorin Maazel (cond.; 1930-)
Loring Air Force Base, ME (mil.)
Loring, Eugene (b. LeRoy Kerpestein)(dancer/
    choreographer; 1911-82)
Loring, Gloria (ent.; 1946-)
Lorna Doone (R.D. Blackmore novel)
Lorna Luft (ent.; 1952-)
Lorne Greene (ent.; 1915-87)
Lorne Michaels (ent.; 1944-)
Lorrain, Claude (Fr. artist; 1600-82)
Lorraine (region, Fr.)
Lorraine Bracco (ent.; 1955-)
Lorraine Hansberry (US writer; 1930-65)
Lorraine, cross of
Lorraine, quiche
Lorraine, Sweet (film, 1987)
Lorre, Peter (b. Lázló Löwenstein)(ent.; 1904-64)
Lorrie Morgan (b. Loretta Lynn Morgan)(ent.;
    1959-)
Lorus (US bus.)
Lorus watch
Los Alamos Scientific Laboratory (NM)
Los Alamos, NM
Los Angeleno (also Angeleno)(native of Los
    Angeles)
Los Angeles (mag.)
Los Angeles Basin
Los Angeles Clippers (basketball team)
Los Angeles County Museum

Los Angeles Dodgers (baseball team)
Los Angeles International Airport (CA)
Los Angeles Kings (hockey team)
Los Angeles Lakers (basketball team)
Los Angeles News (CA newspaper)
Los Angeles Raiders (football team)
Los Angeles Rams (football team)
Los Angeles Times (CA newspaper)
Los Angeles Times Book Review
Los Angeles, CA
Losec (med.)
Lost Colony (VA settlement; disappeared 1591)
Lost Generation, the (US lit.; 1920s)
Lot (rel.)
Lothario (also l.c.)(seducer/deceiver of women)
Lothian (region, Scot.)
Lotophagi (lotus-eaters)(myth.)
Lotos-Eaters, The (by Tennyson)
Lotrimin (med.)
Lott, Ronnie (football; 1959-)
Lott, Trent (US cong.; 1941-)
Lotta Crabtree (ent.; 1847-1924)
Lotte Lehmann (Ger. opera; 1888-1976)
Lotte Lenya (ent.; 1898-1981)
Lottery Case (also Champion v. Ames)(US law;
    1903)
Lotus (auto.)
Lotus 1-2-3 (compu. software)
Lotus Development Corp.
Lotus Elise (auto.)
Lotus Elise Sport 190 (auto.)
Lotus Esprit (auto.)
Lotus Sutra (rel.)
Lotus/Cars USA, Inc.
Lou Christie (b. Lugee Sacco)(ent.; 1943-)
Lou(is Clark) Brock (baseball; 1939-)
Lou Costello (b. Louis Francis Cristillo)(ent.;
    1906-59)
Lou Diamond Phillips (b. Lou Upchurch)(ent.;
    1962-)
Lou Ferrigno (bodybuilder/ent.; 1952-)
Lou(is) Gehrig, (Henry)(baseball; 1903-41)
Lou Gehrig's disease (med.)
Lou Grant (TV show, fict. chara.)
Lou Groza (football; 1924-2000)
Lou Little (football; 1893-1979)
Lou Rawls (ent.; 1936-)
Lou Reed (b. Louis Firbank)(ent.; 1942-)
Loubomo, Congo
Loudon, Dorothy (ent.; 1933-)
Louella Parsons (US gossip columnist; 1881?-
    1972)
Louganis, Greg(ory)(US diver; 1960-)
Lough Neagh (lake, NIre.)
Louima, Abner (US news/assaulted by NY police)
Louis (Rodolphe) Agassiz, (Jean)(Swiss nat.;
    1807-73)
Louis-Antoine de Bougainville (Fr. nav.; 1729-
    1811)
Louis Antoine Godey (US publ.; 1804-78)
Louis "Satchmo" Armstrong (US jazz; 1900-71)
Louis Blanc, (Jean Joseph Charles)(Fr. socialist/
    hist.; 1811-82)
Louis Blériot (Fr. aviator; 1872-1936)
Louis Bonaparte (bro. of Napoleon, king,

Holland; 1778-1846)
Louis Botha (ex-PM, SAfr.; 1863-1919)
Louis Braille (Fr., blind inv. of Braille; 1809-52)
Louis (Dembitz) Brandeis (US jurist; 1856-1941)
Louis Bromfield (US writer; 1896-1956)
Louis Calhern (ent.; 1895-1956)
Louis de Broglie (Fr. physt.; 1893-1987)
Louis de Frontenac (Fr./Can. gov.; 1620-98)
Louis(-Joseph) de (Montcalm-Gozon) Montcalm
  (Fr. mil.; 1712-59)
Louis de Rouvroy Saint-Simon, Duc de (Fr.
  mil./writer; 1675-1755)
Louis Farrakhan (b. Louis Eugene
  Walcott)(Islam/US rel.; 1933-)
Louis Gossett, Jr. (ent.; 1936-)
Louis Harris (US pollster/writer; 1921-)
Louis Hector Berlioz (Fr. comp.; 1803-69)
Louis Henry Sullivan (US arch.; 1856-1924)
Louis I ("the Pious)(Holy Roman emp.; 788-840)
Louis III ("the Child")(king, Ger.; 893-911)
Louis III (king, Fr.; 863-82)
Louis IV (d'Outremer)(king, Fr.; 921-54)
Louis Jacques Mande Daguerre (Fr. photo.;
  1789-1851)
Louis Joliet (or Jolliet)(Fr./Can. expl.; 1645-1700)
Louis Joseph Freeh (US ex-dir./FBI; 1950-)
Louis Jourdan (b. Louis Gendre)(Fr. ent.; 1919-)
Louis Kahn (US arch.; 1901-74)
Louis (Dearborn) L'Amour (US writer; 1908-88)
Louis (Jean) Lumière (Fr. inv.; 1864-1948)
Louis Malle (Fr. ent.; 1932-95)
Louis B(urt) Mayer (ent.; 1885-1957)
Louis M. Martini Winery (US bus.)
Louis Moreau Gottschalk (US comp.; 1829-69)
Louis Mountbatten, Lord (Br. adm./earl; 1900-79)
Louis Nizer (atty./writer; 1902-94)
Louis Nye (ent.; 1920-)
Louis Pasteur (Fr. chem.; 1822-95)
Louis Philippe ("Philippe Egalité" "the Citizen
  King")(king, Fr.; 1773-1850)
Louis Prima (ent.; 1911-78)
Louis Quatorze style (Louis XIV, classic)
Louis Quinze style (Louis XV)(rococo)
Louis Rich (meats)
Louis Rich Co.
Louis S(eymour) B(azett) Leakey (Br.
  archaeol.; 1903-72)
Louis Seize style (Louis XVI, classic revival)
Louis S(tephen) St. Laurent (ex-PM, Can.;
  1882-1973)
Louis Stanton Auchincloss (US writer; 1917-)
Louis (Comfort) Tiffany (US artist/glassmaker;
  1848-1933)
Louis Treize style (Louis XIII, baroque)
Louis Untermeyer (US anthologist/poet; 1885-
  1977)
Louis VII (king, Fr.; c1120-80)
Louis Whitley Strieber (US writer; 1945-)
Louis X ("the Stubborn")(king, Fr.; 1289-1316)
Louis XI (king, Fr.; 1423-83)
Louis XII (king, Fr.; 1462-1515)
Louis XIII (king, Fr.; 1601-43)
Louis XIII style (Louis Treize, baroque)
Louis XIV ("the Sun King" "the Great")(king,
  Fr.; 1638-1715)

Louis XIV style (Louis Quatorze, classic)
Louis XV (king, Fr.; 1710-74)
Louis XV style (Louis Quinze, rococo)
Louis XVI (king, Fr.; 1754-93)
Louis XVI style (Louis Seize, classic revival)
Louis XVIII (king, Fr.; 1755-1824)
Louis, Joe (b. Joseph Louis Barrow)(boxing;
  1914-81)
Louis, Morris (US artist; 1912-62)
Louis, Port (Mauritius)
Louis-Dreyfus, Julia (ent.; 1961-)
Louisa May Alcott (US writer; 1832-88)
Louise Bourgeois (Fr./US sculptor; 1911-)
Louise Dresser (ent.; 1881-1965)
Louise Erdrich, (Karen)(US writer; 1954-)
Louise Fletcher (ent.; 1934-)
Louise Lasser (ent.; 1939-)
Louise Mandrell (ent.; 1954-)
Louise Nevelson (Rus./US sculptor; 1900-88)
Louise, Lake (Can.)
Louise, Marie (empress, Fr.; 1791-1847)
Louise, Thelma & (film, 1991)
Louise, Tina (ent.; 1937-)
Louisiana (LA)
Louisiana French (Cajun)
Louisiana Purchase (US hist.; 1803)
Louisiana Territory
Louisville Courier-Journal (KY newspaper)
Louisville, KY
Louisy, (Calliopa) Pearlette (gov.-gen., St.
  Lucia; 1946-)
Lourdes, France
Lousma, Jack R(obert)(astro.; 1936-)
Louth (county, Ir.)
Louvain, Belgium (also Leuven)
L'Ouverture, François Toussaint (Haitian pol.;
  c1744-1803)
Louvre (Paris art museum)
Love and War (TV show)
Love at First Bite (film, 1979)
Love Connection (TV show)
Love Story (E. Segal's novel)
Love, American Style (TV show)
Love, Courtney (b. Love Michelle Harrison)
  (ent.; 1964-)
Love!, Get Christie (film, 1974)
Love, Susan (US phys./activist; 1948-)
Love's Baby Soft
Love's Labour's Lost (Shakespeare comedy)
Lovecraft, H(oward) P(hillips)(US writer; 1890-
  1937)
Lovejoy, Frank (ent.; 1912-62)
Lovelace, Lady (aka Augusta Ada Byron)(Br.
  math./inv., compu.; 1815-52)
Lovelace, Richard (Br. poet; 1618-58)
Loveland, CO
Loveless, Patty (ent.; 1957-)
Lovell, James A, Jr. (astro.; 1928-)
Lovell, (Sir Alfred Charles) Bernard (Br.
  astron.; 1931-)
Lovett, Lyle (ent./songwriter; 1956-)
Lovin' Spoonful (pop music)
Loving (TV soap)
Loving v. Virginia (US law; 1967)
Lovis Corinth (Ger. artist; 1858-1925)

Lovitz, John (ent.; 1957-)
Low Church (rel.)
Low Countries (region, Eur.: Belgium/
Netherlands/Luxembourg)
Low Sunday (also Quasimodo)(1st Sunday after
Easter)
Low, Juliette (Gordon)(US, founded Girl Scouts;
1860-1927)
Lowe, Chad (ent.; 1968-)
Lowe, Rob (ent.; 1964-)
Lowe's Companies, Inc.
Lowell National Historical Park (MA)
Lowell North (yachting; 1929-)
Lowell Palmer Weicker, Jr. (ex-CT gov.; 1931-)
Lowell Thomas (US newscaster/expl.; 1892-
1981)
Lowell, Amy (US poet; 1874-1925)
Lowell, James Russell (US poet/editor; 1819-91)
Lowell, MA
Lowell, Percival (US astron.; 1855-1916)
Lowell, Robert (US poet; 1917-77)
Lower California (also Baja California)
Lower Paleolithic period (early Old Stone Age;
200,000 to 2 million years ago)
Lower Saxony (state, Ger.)
Lowestoft porcelain
Lowestoft, England
Lowlands (Scot. area)
Lowry, Mike (Michael Edwards)(ex-WA gov.;
1939-)
LOX (liquid oxygen)
Loxitane (med.)
Loy, Myrna (ent.; 1905-93)
Loyal Order of Moose
Loyola College in Maryland (Baltimore, MD)
Loyola Marymount University (Los Angeles, CA)
Loyola University of Chicago (Chicago, IL)
Loyola University of New Orleans (New Orleans,
LA)
Loyola, St. Ignatius of (aka Iñigo de Oñez y
Loyola)(Sp. rel.; 1491-1556)
Lozada, Gonzalo Sánchez de (ex-pres., Bolivia;
1930-)
LPG (liquefied petroleum gas)
LPGA (Ladies Professional Golfers Association)
LPM (lines per minute)
LPN (licensed practical nurse)
Lr (chem. sym., lawrencium)
L(afayette) Ron(ald) Hubbard (US writer/rel.,
Scientology; 1911-86)
L.S. (locus sigilli [the place of the seal])
LSAT (Law School Admission Test)
LSD (lysergic acid diethylamide, least
significant digit)
LSI Logic Corp.
LSS Holdings Corp.
LTV Corp.
Luanda, Angola (formerly Loanda)
Luang Prabang, Laos
Luann (cartoon chara.)
Luann Ryon (archery; 1953-)
Luanshya, Zambia
Luba-Lulua (also Chiluba)(lang.)
Lubango, Angola
Luba-Shaba (lang.)

Lubbers, Rudd (Rudolph Franz Marie)(ex-PM,
Netherlands; 1939-)
Lubbock Avalanche-Journal (TX newspaper)
Lubbock, TX
Lübeck, Germany
Lubitsch, Ernst (Ger. ent.; 1892-1947)
Lublin, Poland
Lubovitch, Lar (US dance; 1945-)
Lubriderm (skin care)
Lubu (lang.)
Lubumbashi, Zaire
Luby's Cafeterias, Inc.
Luca (d'Egidio di Ventura de') Signorelli (It.
artist; c1445-1523)
Luca della Robbia (It. artist; 1400-82)
Luca Giordano ("Luca Fapresto")(It. artist;
1632-1705)
Lucan (aka Marcus Annaeus Lucanus)(Roman
poet; 39-65)
Lucas Cranach (the elder)(Ger. artist; 1472-1553)
Lucas Industries, Inc.
Lucas Samaras (US sculptor; 1936-)
Lucas, George W., Jr. (ent.; 1944-)
Lucci, Susan (ent.; 1948-)
Luce, Clare Boothe (US drama./dipl./pol.;
1903-87)
Luce, Henry Robinson (US publ.; 1898-1967)
Lucent Technologies, Inc.
Lucerne, Switzerland, (also Luzern)
Luci Baines Johnson (US daughter ex-pres.;
1947-)
Lucia Chase (founder Ballet Theatre [now
American Ballet Theatre]; 1907-86)
Lucian (Gr. writer; c125-c190)
Luciano Pavarotti (It. opera; 1935-)
Luciano, Lucky (Salvatore)(US Mafia; 1899-1962)
Lucie Arnaz (ent.; 1951-)
Lucien Bonaparte (bro. of Napoleon, prince,
Canino; 1775-1840)
Lucien Lévy-Bruhl (Fr. phil.; 1857-1939)
Lucientes, Francisco (José) de Goya y (Sp.
artist; 1746-1828)
Lucifer (the devil)
Lucilius, Gaius (Roman poet; c180-c102 BC)
Lucille Ball (ent.; 1911-89)
Lucinschi, Petru (pres., Moldova; 1940-)
Lucite (plastic)
Lucius Apuleius (Roman satirist/atty.; c124-
c170 BC)
Lucius D. Clay (US gen.; 1897-1978)
Lucius Licinius Lucullus (Roman gen.; 110-56
BC)
Luckinbill, Laurence (ent.; 1934-)
Luckman, Sid (football; 1916-98)
Lucknow, India
Lucky Charms (cereal)
Lucky (Salvatore) Luciano (US Mafia; 1899-1962)
Lucky, Mr. (film, 1943)
Lucretia (Coffin) Mott (US suffragist; 1793-1880)
Lucretia (legendary Roman heroine)
Lucretius (Carus), Titus (Roman poet/phil.;
c99-c55 BC)
Lucrezia Borgia (It., Duchess of Ferrara; 1480-
1519)
Lucullus, Lucius Licinius (Roman gen.; 110-56 BC)

Lucy (fict. chara., *Peanuts*)
Lucy (skeletal remains of female hominid found in Ethiopia)
Lucy Lawless (ent.; 1968-)
Lucy Liu (ent.; 1967-)
Lucy Show, The (TV show)
Lucy Stone (US suffragist; 1818-93)
Lucy Stoner (married woman who keeps maiden name)
Lüda, China (also Hüta)
Ludd, Ned (also Lludd, Nudd, King Ludd)(Welsh legend)
Ludden, Allen (ent.; 1918-81)
Luden's, Inc.
Ludiomil (med.)
Ludlum, Robert (US writer; 1927-2001)
Ludovico (or Lodovico) Carracci (It. artist; 1555-1619)
Ludovico Sforza ("The Moor")(It. pol.; 1451-1508)
Ludwig Boltzmann (Aus. physt.; 1844-1906)
Ludwig Erhard (ex-chanc., WGer.; 1897-1977)
Ludwig Mies van der Rohe (US arch.; 1886-1969)
Ludwig van Beethoven (Ger. comp.; 1770-1827)
Ludwig (Josef Johann) Wittgenstein (Aus. phil.; 1889-1951)
Ludwigshafen am Rhein, Germany
Luening, Otto (US comp.; 1900-96)
Luft, Lorna (ent.; 1952-)
Lufthansa German Airline
Luftwaffe (Ger. air force, WWI & WWII)
Lufyllin (med.)
Lug (myth.)
Luganda (also Ganda)(lang.)
Lugansk, Ukraine
Lugar, Richard G(reen)(US cong.; 1932-)
Luger (pistol)
Lugosi, Bela (ent.; 1882-1956)
Luhya (lang./people)
Luigi Boccherini (It. comp.; 1743-1805)
Luigi Cherubini (It. comp.; 1760-1842)
Luigi Galvani (It. phys./physt.; 1737-98)
Luigi Nono (It. comp.; 1924-90)
Luigi Pirandello (It. writer; 1867-1936)
Luis Alberto Lacalle Herrera (ex-pres., Uruguay; 1941-)
Luis Angel Gonzáles Macchi (pres., Paraguay; 1947-)
Luis de Gongora y Argote (Sp. writer; 1561-1627)
Luis Miguel Dominquin (Sp. matador; 1926-)
Luis Somozo (Debayle)(ex-pres., Nicaragua; 1922-67)
Luis Walter Alvarez (US physt.; 1911-88)
Luisa Tetrazzini (It. opera; 1874-1940)
Luka, Bosnia-Hercegovina
Lukas, J. Anthony (US writer; 1932-97)
Lukas, Paul (ent.; 1895-1971)
Lukashenko, Aleksandr (pres., Belarus; 1954-)
Luke (rel., book of the New Testament)
Luke Air Force Base, AZ (mil.)
Luke Appling (baseball; 1907-90)
Luke Hansard (Br. Parliament reporter; 1752-1828)
Luke Perry (ent.; 1966-)

Luke Skywalker (fict. chara., *Star Wars*)
Luke, Cool Hand (film, 1967)
Luke, St. (rel.; 1st c. AD)
Luks, George (Benjamin)(US artist; 1867-1933)
Lull diagram (logic)
Lully, Jean Baptiste (Fr. comp.; 1639-87)
Lulu (b. Marie McDonald McLaughlin Lawrie) (ent.; 1948-)
Lum and Abner
Lumet, Sidney (ent.; 1924-)
Lumière, Auguste (Marie)(Fr. inv.; 1862-1954)
Lumière, Louis (Jean)(Fr. inv.; 1864-1948)
Lumina LS, Chevrolet (auto.)
Lumina, Chevrolet (auto.)
Luminal (med.)
Lumpenproletariat (lowest class, Marxism)
Lumumba, Patrice (Emergy)(ex-PM, Congo/Zaire; 1926-61)
Luna (myth.)
Luna (USSR uncrewed space probes)
Lunar Alps (mountains, the moon)
Lunar Excursion Module (LEM)
Lunar Orbiter (US uncrewed space probe)
Lunar Rover (also l.c.)(also lunar roving vehicle)
Lunceford, Jimmie (US jazz; 1902-47)
Lunch Bucket (meals)
Lunchables (snacks)
Lunden, Joan (US TV jour.; 1950-)
Lundgren, Dolph (Hans)(ent.; 1959-)
Lunik (USSR space probe)
Lunn teacake, Sally
Lunt, Alfred (ent.; 1892-1977)
Luo (lang./people)
Luong, Tran Duc (pres., Viet.; 1937-)
Lupicare (med./skin care)
Lupino, Ida (ent.; 1918-95)
LuPone, Patti (ent.; 1949-)
Lupus (astron., wolf)
Luray Caverns (VA)
Lurex (metallic fabric)
Luri (lang.)
Lurie, Alison (US writer; 1926-)
Lusaka, Zambia
Lusitania, S.S. (Br. ship sunk by Ger.; 1915)
Lussac, Joseph (Louis) Gay- (Fr. chem./physt.; 1778-1850)
Luther Adler (ent.; 1903-84)
Luther Burbank (US horticulturist; 1849-1926)
Luther Vandross (ent.; 1951-)
Luther, Martin (Ger. rel./writer; 1483-1546)
Lutheran (rel.)
Lutheran Church (rel.)
Lutheranism (also Lutherism)(rel.)
Luvs (diapers)
Lu-Wang School (Ch. phil.)
Lux (soap)
Luxembourg (Grand Duchy of)(Eur.)
Luxembourg (province, Belgium)
Luxembourg, Luxembourg
Luxembourgish (lang.)
Luxor, Egypt (ancient ruins)
Luzern, Switzerland (also Lucerne)
Luzon (island, Philippines)
Lviv, Ukraine
LVN (licensed vocational nurse)

Lwena (lang.)
LWM (low-water mark)
LWV (League of Women Voters)
Lyceum, the (Athens gymnasium where
    Aristotle taught)
Lycopodiophyta
Lycos (Internet search engine)
Lycra (brand of spandex)
Lydia (ancient kingdom; 7th-6th c. BC)
Lydia E(stes) Pinkham (US bus.; 1819-83)
Lydia E. Pinkham's Vegetable Compound, Mrs.
    (med.)
Lydia Sokolova (Br. ballet; 1896-1974)
Lykes Brothers, Inc.
Lyle Lovett (ent./songwriter; 1956-)
Lyle Menendez (US news, killed parents)
Lyle Waggoner (ent.; 1935-)
Lyly (or Lily, Lilly), John (Br. writer; 1554?-1606)
Lyman Abbott (US rel.; 1835-1922)
Lyman Lemnitzer (US gen.; 1899-1988)
Lyme disease (tick-borne virus)(med.)
Lymon, Frankie (ent.; 1942-68)
Lyn Nofzinger (US pol./writer; 1924-)
Lynch & Co., Inc., Merrill
Lynch, David (ent.; 1946-)
Lynch, Jack (John)(ex-PM, Ir.; 1917-99)
Lynch, Merrill & (finan.)
Lynchburg, VA
Lynda Benglis (US sculptor; 1941-)
Lynda Bird Johnson Robb (US daughter ex-
    pres.; 1944-)
Lynda Carter (ent.; 1951-)
Lynde, Paul (ent.; 1926-82)
Lynden (Oscar) Pindling (ex-PM, Bahamas;
    1930-2000)
Lyndon B(aines) Johnson (36th US pres.; 1908-
    73)
Lyndon B. Johnson National Historical Park (TX)
Lyndon B. Johnson Space Center (TX)
Lyndon H. LaRouche, Jr. (US pol./econ.; 1922-)
Lyndon, Barry (film, 1975)
Lynette "Squeaky" Fromme (US, shot Pres. Ford)
Lynn Anderson (ent.; 1947-)
Lynn Fontanne (ent.; 1887-1983)
Lynn Harrell (US cellist; 1944-)
Lynn Johnston (cartoonist; *For Better or Worse*;
    1947-)
Lynn Martin (nee Morley)(US pol.; 1939-)
Lynn Redgrave (ent.; 1943-)
Lynn Seymour (Can. ballet; 1939-)
Lynn Swann (football; 1952-)
Lynn, Diana (ent.; 1926-71)
Lynn, Frederic Michael (baseball; 1952-)
Lynn, Janet (figure skating; 1953-)
Lynn, Jeffrey (ent.; 1909-95)
Lynn (Webb), Loretta (ent.; 1935-)
Lynn, MA
Lynne (Anne) Cheney (US wife of VP; 1941-)
Lynne, Shelby (ent.; 1968-)
Lynx (astron., lynx)
Lynyrd Skynyrd (pop music)
Lyon, France
Lyondell Petrochemical Co.
Lyonel (Charles Adrian) Feininger (US artist;
    1871-1956)

Lyonnesse (legendary Arthurian country)
Lyons, Council of
Lyons, France
Lyra (astron., lyre)
Lysander (Spartan gen.; 5th c BC)
Lysippus (also Lysippos)(Gr. sculptor; 4th c. BC)
Lysol (cleaner)
Lytell, Bert (ent.; 1885-1954)
Lytton Springs Winery (US bus.)
Lytton Strachey, (Giles)(Br. writer; 1880-1932)
Lyuben Berov (Borisov)(ex-PM, Bulgaria; 1925-)

– M –

MA (Massachusetts, Master of Arts)
Ma & Pa Kettle (fict. charas.)
Ma (Gertrude) Rainey (US jazz; 1886-1939)
Ma, Yo-Yo (US cellist; 1955-)
Maalox (med.)
Maaouya Ould Sidi Ahmed Taya (pres., Mauritania; 1943-)
Maastricht, the Netherlands (or Holland)
Maazel, Lorin (cond.; 1930-)
Mab, Queen (Ir./Eng. folklore)
Mabaruma, Guyana
Mabel Mercer (ent.; 1900-84)
Mabel Normand (ent.; 1894-1930)
Ma Bell (AT&T nickname)
Mac (compu.)
Mac Davis (ent.; 1942-)
Mac Maurice Wilkens (track; 1950-)
Mac, Fleetwood (pop music)
MacAddict (mag.)
Macao (Port. province adjoining Ch.)
Macapagal-Arroyo, Gloria (pres., Phil.; 1947-)
Macarena, the (dance)
MacArthur, Charles (US playwright; 1895-1956)
MacArthur, Douglas (US gen.; 1880-1964)
MacArthur, James (ent.; 1937-)
Macaulay Culkin (ent.; 1980-)
Macauley, Thomas B(abington), Baron (Br. hist./pol.; 1800-59)
Macbeth (king; Scot.; ?-1057)
Macbeth (Shakespeare play)
Macbeth, Lady (fict. chara., *Macbeth*)
Maccabee (also Hasmonaean)(rel.)
Maccabees, I&II (rel., Apocrypha)
Macchi, Luis Angel Gonzáles (pres., Paraguay; 1947-)
Macchio, Ralph (ent.; 1962-)
MacDermot, Galt (comp.; 1928-)
MacDiarmid, Hugh (b. Christopher Murray Grieve)(Scot. poet; 1892-1978)
MacDill Air Force Base, FL
Macdonald Carey (ent.; 1913-94)
MacDonald, Jeanette (ent.; 1903-65)
MacDonald, J(ames) Ramsay (ex-PM, Br.; 1866-1937)
MacDonald, John D. (US writer; 1916-86)
Macdonald, Norm (ent.; 1962-)
Macdonald, Ross (aka Kenneth Millar)(US writer; 1915-83)
Macdonald, (Sir) John Alexander (ex-PM, Can.; 1815-91)
MacDonald's Farm, Old (nursery song)
MacDowell, Andie (b. Rosalie Anderson MacDowell)(ent.; 1958-)
MacDowell, Edward Alexander (US comp.; 1861-1908)
Macduff, Lady (fict. chara., *Macbeth*)
Mace (also Chemical Mace)
Macedonia (republic. Yug.)(SE Eur.)
Macedonian (lang./people)

MacGraw, Ali (ent.; 1938-)
MacGyver (TV show)
Mach number (speed of a body/speed of sound ratio)
Mach, Ernst (Aus. physt./psych./phil.; 1838-1916)
Machaut, Guillaume de (Fr. comp.; 1300-77)
Machel, Samora (ex-pres., Mozambique; 1933-86)
Machiavelli, Niccolo (di Bernardo)(It. pol./writer/phil.; 1469-1527)
Machiavellian deed (deceitful political manipulation)
Machu Picchu, Peru (Inca ruins)
Machungo, Mário da Graça (ex-PM, Mozambique)
MacInnes, Helen (Clark)(Scot. writer; 1907-85)
Macintosh computer
Macintosh Performa (compu.)
Mack (Thomas Franklin) McLarty, III (US ex-White House chief of staff; 1946-)
Mack Gordon (Pol./US lyricist; 1905-59)
Mack Sennett (b. Michael Sinnott)(ent.; 1880-1960)
Mack Sennett Studios (old Hollywood)
Mack the Knife (song)
Mack Trucks, Inc.
Mack, Connie (b. Cornelius McGillicuddy)(baseball; 1862-1956)
Mack, Connie, III (US pol.; 1940-)
Mack, Jillie (ent.; 1957-)
Macke, August (Ger. artist; 1887-1914)
MacKenzie Phillips (ent.; 1959-)
Mackenzie River (Can.)
Mackenzie, Alexander (ex-PM, Can.; 1822-92)
MacKenzie, Gisele (ent.; 1927-)
Mackenzie, (Sir) Alexander (Scot. expl.; 1764-1820)
MacKenzie, Spuds (dog)
Mackey, John (football; 1941-)
Mackie, Bob (US fashion designer; 1940-)
Mackinac, Straits of (Lake Huron/Lake Michigan)
Mackinaw blanket
Mackinaw boat
Mackinaw coat (also l.c.)
MacKinlay Kantor (US writer; 1904-77)
Mackintosh, Charles Rennie (Scot. arch.; 1868-1928)
MacLachlan, Kyle (ent.; 1959-)
MacLaine, Shirley (ent.; 1934-)
Maclean's (mag.)
MacLeish, Archibald (US poet; 1892-1982)
MacLeod, Gavin (b. Allan See)(ent.; 1930-)
Macmillan, (Maurice) Harold (ex-PM, Br.; 1895-1987)
MacMurray, Fred (ent.; 1908-91)
Macnee, Patrick (ent.; 1922-)
MacNeil, Cornell (ent.; 1922-)
MacNeil, Lehrer News Hour (former TV show)
MacNeil, Robert (jour.; 1931-)
MacNelly, Jeff (cartoonist, *Shoe*; 1947-2000)
Macnicol, Peter (ent.; 1958-)
Macon (wine)
Macon Telegraph (GA newspaper)
Macon, GA
MacPherson struts (auto.)
MacPherson, Elle (b. Eleanor Gow)(model/ent.;

1964-)
MacRae, Gordon (ent.; 1921-86)
MacRae, Sheila (ent.; 1924-)
Macready, George (ent.; 1909-73)
Macrodantin (med.)
MacUser (mag., defunct)
Macworld (mag.)
Macy & Co., Inc., R. H.
Macy Gray (b. Natalie McIntyre)(ent.; 1967-)
Macy, Bill (ent.; 1922-)
Macy, William H. (ent.; 1950-)
Macy's (department store)
Mad (mag.)
Mad About You (TV show)
Mad Hatter, the (fict. chara., *Alice in Wonderland*)
Mad Max (film, 1980)
Mad Tea Party (*Alice in Wonderland*)
Madagascar (Democratic Republic of)(island, E Afr.)
Madalyn Murray O'Hair (US atheist/activist; 1919-95?)
Madam, Mayflower (film, 1987)
Madame Bovary (G. Flaubert novel)
Madame Butterfly (Puccini opera)
Madame Chiang Kai-shek (b. Soong Mei-ling) (Ch. lecturer/writer; 1898-)
Madame (Marie) Curie (Fr. physt., radium; 1867-1934)
Madame (Jeanne Bécu) du Barry (Comtesse, mistress, Louis XV; 1743-93)
Madame Helena Petrovna Blavatsky Hahn (Rus. theosophist; 1831-91)
Madame Mao (aka Jiang Ching, Jiang Qing, Chiang Ching, Lan Ping)(Ch. pol./ent., wife of Chairman Mao; 1914-91)
Madame (Marie Grosholtz) Tussaud (Swiss wax modeler; 1760-1850)
Madame Tussaud's Exhibition (wax museum, London)
Madang, Papua New Guinea
MADD (Mothers Against Drunk Driving)
Madden, John (football/ent.; 1936-)
Maddox, Lester (Garfield)(ex-GA gov.; 1915-)
Madeira (wine)
Madeira embroidery
Madeira Island(s)(region, Port.)
Madeira River (Brazil)
Madeira topaz
Madeleine K. Albright (US ex-secy./state; 1937-)
Madeleine L'Engle (US writer; 1918-)
Madeleine Stowe (ent.; 1958-)
Madeline (L. Bemelman book)
Madeline Kahn (ent.; 1942-99)
Madeline Manning (running; 1948-)
Mademoiselle (mag.)
Madhya Pradesh (state, India)
Madigan, Amy (ent.; 1950-)
Madison Avenue (NYC)
Madison Capital Times (WI newspaper)
Madison County, The Bridges of (R. J. Waller novel)
Madison Square Garden (NYC)
Madison Square Park (NYC)

Madison State Journal (WI newspaper)
Madison, CT, IN, NJ, WI
Madison, Dolley (Payne Todd)(wife of ex-US pres.; 1768-1849)
Madison, James (4th US pres.; 1751-1836)
Madison, Marbury v. (US law; 1803)
Madlock, Bill (baseball; 1951-)
Madlyn Rhue (ent.; 1934-)
Madonna (b. Madonna Louise Veronica Ciccone)(ent.; 1958-)
Madonna lily (also Annunciation lily)
Madonna, the (also Holy Mother, Mary, Our Lady, Virgin Mary)(rel.)
Madras, India
Madrid, Spain
Madurese (lang.)
Madwoman of Chaillot, The (by J. Giraudoux)
Mae C. Jemison (US astro./phys.; 1956-)
Mae West (ent.; 1892?-1980)
Mae West (life jacket)
Maelstrom (hazardous whirlpool off Nor. coast)
Maestro (CAT system)
Maeterlinck, Count Maurice (Belgian writer; 1962-1947)
Mafeteng, Lesotho
Mafia (secret criminal society)
Mafia don
Mafia princess
Mafioso
Magadha (ancient kingdom, India)
Magdalene, Mary (rel.; 1st c. AD)
Magdeburg, Germany
Magee, Patrick (ent.; 1924-82)
Magellan (US uncrewed space probe)
Magellan, Ferdinand (Port. nav.; c1480-1521)
Magellan, Strait of (tip of SAmer.)
Magellanic clouds (astron.)
Magen David (also Star of David)(6 points, Jew. symbol)
Maggie and Jiggs (comic strip)
Maggie Smith (ent.; 1934-)
Magh (lang.)
Maghreb (name for NW Afr.)
Magi (also Wise Men of the East, Three Kings of the Orient, Three Wise Men)(rel.)
Magi (rel., the wise men)
Magic Chef (kitchen appliances)
Magic Chef, Inc.
Magic Johnson, (Earvin)(basketball; 1959-)
Magic Marker
Magic Show, The (play)
Magic, Orlando (basketball team)
Magilla Gorilla (cartoon)
Magindanaon (lang.)
Maginot line (Fr. mil.)
Magna Carta (Br. hist.; 1215)
Magnani, Anna (ent.; 1908-73)
Magnavox (elec.)
Magnavox Co.
Magnificat (rel. song)
Magnificent Ambersons, The (B. Tarkington novel)
Magnin, I. (retail stores)
Magnolia State (nickname, MS)
Magnoliophyta (plant division)

Magnum, P.I. (TV show)
Magnus hitch (knot)
Magnus, Albertus, St. (also St. Albert the
    Great)(Ger. rel.; 1193-1280)
Magog, Gog and (rel.)
Magoo, Mr. (cartoon)
Magritte, René (Belgian artist; 1898-1967)
Magruder, Jeb Stuart (US pol./Watergate; 1934-)
Maguire, Jerry (film, 1996)
Maguire, Tobey (ent.; 1975-)
Maguires, Molly (also Mollies)(US/Ir. secret
    society; c1854-77)
Maguires, The Molly (film, 1970)
Magyar (lang./people)
Mahabad, Azerbaijan
Mahabharata (rel.)
Mahadeva (rel.)
Mahakala (myth.)
Mahalapye, Botswana
Mahalia Jackson (US jazz; 1911-72)
Mahamadou Issoufou (ex-PM, Niger)
Mahamane Ousmane (ex-pres., Niger; 1950-)
Mahan, Alfred Thayer (US naval hist.; 1840-
    1914)
Mahan, Larry (rodeo; 1943-)
Maharashtra (state, India)
Maharishi Mahesh Yogi (Hindu guru)
Mahathir bin Muhamad (PM, Malaysia; 1925-)
Mahatma Gandhi, (Mohandas K[aramchand])
    (Indian pol./pacifist; 1869-1948)
Mahavira, Vardhamana (legendary educ./rel.;
    ?-480? BC)
Mahayana Buddhism (rel.)
Mahdi (rel.)
Mahdi, Muhammad Ali (ex-pres., Somalia)
Maher, Bill (ent.; 1956-)
Mahfouz, Naguib (Eg. writer; 1911-)
Mah-Jongg (game)
Mahler, Gustav (Aus. comp.; 1860-1911)
Mahmoud Zubi (ex-PM, Syria)
Mahmud I (sultan, Turk.; 1696-1754)
Mahmud II (sultan, Turk.; 1785-1839)
Mahoney, Breathless (fict. chara., *Dick Tracy*)
Mahoney, John (ent.; 1940-)
Mahovlich, Frank (Francis William)(hockey;
    1938-)
Mahre, Phil(lip)(US skier; 1957-)
Mahre, Steve(n)(US skier; 1957-)
Maid Marian (Robin Hood's sweetheart)
Maid of Orléans (also St. Joan of Arc, Jeanne
    d'Arc)(Fr. rel./mil.; 1412?-31)
Maidenform bra
Maidstone, England
Maiduguri, Nigeria
Mail Boxes Etc. USA, Inc.
Mail, Charleston (WV newspaper)
Mailer, Norman (US writer; 1923-)
Mailgram
Maillol, Aristide (Fr. sculptor; 1861-1944)
Maimonides, Moses (ben Maimon), Rabbi (aka
    RaMBaM)(Jew. rel./phil.; 1135-1204)
Main Street (central street of any town)
Main, Marjorie (ent.; 1890-1975)
Mainbocher (Main Rousseau Bocher)(US
    designer; 1891-1976)

Maine (ME)
Maine coon cat
Maine, to hell with Spain," "Remember the
    (Sp.-Amer. War; 1898)
Mairzy Doats (song)
Maitreya (also Mi-lo-fo, Miroku)(rel.)
Majali, Abd al-Salam (or Abdul-Salam)(ex-PM,
    Jordan; 1925-)
Majerle, Dan (basketball; 1965-)
Majesty, Your (title)
Major Barbara (film, 1941)
Major Bowes' Original Amateur Hour
Major Dad (TV show)
Major Dundee (film, 1965)
Major Edward Bowes (ent.; 1874-1946)
Major M. J. Divine (also Father Divine)(b.
    George Baker)(US rel.; 1882-1965)
Major, John (ex-PM, Br.; 1943-)
Major, Ursa (astron., great bear; part of Big
    Dipper)
Majorca (a Balearic island, Sp.)
Majors, Lee (b. Harvey Lee Yeary)(ent.; 1939-)
Majuro, Marshall Islands
Makarios III (ex-pres., Cyprus; 1913-77)
Makarova, Natalia (Rus. ballet; 1940-)
Makassar (lang.)
Makeba, Miriam (ent.; 1932-)
Makeni, Sierra Leone
Maker (God)
Maktoum bin Rashid al-Maktoum, Sheik (PM,
    UAE; 1946-)
Makua (lang./people)
Makuza, Bernard (PM, Rwanda)
Malabo, Equatorial Guinea
Malacca (also Melaka)(state, Malaysia)
Malacca, Strait of (Indian Ocean/China Sea)
Malachi (rel., book of the Old Testament)
Malachy, St. (Irish rel.; 1095-1148)
Malaga (wine)
Malaga grapes
Málaga, Spain
Malagasy (lang./people)
Malamud, Bernard (US writer; 1914-86)
Malaprop, Mrs. (fict. chara. *The Rivals*;
    malapropism)
Malatya, Turkey
Malawi (Republic of)(SE Afr.)
Malawi, Lake (SE Afr.)
Malay (lang./people)
Malay Archipelago (islands, between Asia/Austl.)
Malay-Indonesian (lang./people)
Malay Peninsula (also Malaysia)
Malayalam (lang.)
Malayan-Indonesian (people)
Malayo-Polynesian (also Austronesian)(lang.)
Malaysia (also Malay Peninsula)
Malaysia (country, SE Afr.)
Malaysian Airline System (airline)
Malbin, Elaine (ent.; 1932-)
Malcolm Forbes (US publ.; 1919-90)
Malcolm Little (aka Malcolm X)(US black-rights
    activist; 1926-65)
Malcolm McDowell (ent.; 1943-)
Malcolm-Jamal Warner (ent.; 1970-)
Malcolm Muggeridge (Br. jour.; 1903-90)

Malcolm Muir (US publ.; 1885-1979)
Malcolm Wallop (US pol.; 1933-)
Malcolm X (b. Malcolm Little)(US black-rights
    activist; 1926-65)
Malden, Karl (b. Mladen Sekulovich)(ent.; 1913-)
Maldives (Republic of)(islands, N Indian Ocean)
Malé, Maldives
Malecela, John (ex-PM, Tanzania)
Malek, Redha (ex-PM, Algeria)
Malev Hungarian Airlines
Malevich, Kasimir (or Casimir)(Rus. artist;
    1878-1935)
Mali (Republic of)(NW Afr.)(formerly French Sudan)
Malibu, CA
Malibu, Chevrolet (auto.)
Malielegaoi, Tuilaepa Sailele (PM, Samoa; 1945-)
Malietoa Tanumafili II (head of state, Samoa;
    1913-)
Maliki (Islamic law)
Malikites (rel.)
Malinke (lang./people)
Malinois (dog)
Malinowski, Bronislaw (Pol. anthrop.; 1884-1942)
Malkovich, John (ent.; 1953-)
Malkovich, Being John (film, 1999)
Mallarmé, Stéphane (Fr. poet; 1842-98)
Malle, Louis (Fr. ent.; 1932-95)
Malmaison (Napoleon I estate, Fr.)
Malmö, Sweden
Malmstrom Air Force Base, MT
Malone Story, The Bugsy (film, 1976)
Malone, Dorothy (ent.; 1925-)
Malone, Karl (basketball; 1963-)
Malone, Moses (basketball; 1955-)
Malory, (Sir) Thomas (Br. writer; c1400-71)
Malraux, André (Fr. writer; 1901-76)
Malta (Republic of)(island, Mediterranean Sea)
Maltese (dog, cat)
Maltese (lang.)
Maltese cross
Maltese Falcon, The (D. Hammett novel)
Malthus theory (population growth)
Malthus, Thomas R(obert)(Br. econ.; 1766-1834)
Malthusian (supporter, population theory)
Malthusian parameter (rate of population growth)
Malthusianism (population theory)
Maltin, Leonard (film critic; 1950-)
Malt-O-Meal (cereal)
Malval, Robert (Haitian pol.)
Mamadou, Tandja (pres., Niger; 1938-)
Mamaloni, Solomon (ex-PM, Soloman Islands;
    1943-)
Mamas and the Papas, the (pop music)
Mame, Auntie (play; film, 1958)
Mamet, David (US writer/ent.; 1947-)
Mamie (Doud) Eisenhower (wife of ex-US pres.;
    1896-1979)
Mamie Van Doren (b. Joan Lucile Olander)(ent.;
    1933-)
Mammalia (biological class)
Mammon (rel.)
Mammoth Cave National Park (KY)
Mammoth Lakes, CA
Man From U.N.C.L.E., The (TV show)
Man of Galilee (Jesus)

Man of La Mancha (play)
Man of Sorrows (Jesus)
Man O'War (race horse)
Man Ray (b. Emmanuel Radnitsky)(US artist;
    1890-1976)
man Friday/girl Friday
man of God (saint, clergyman, priest, etc.)
Man Who Shot Liberty Valance, The (film, 1962)
Man, Isle of (island, Irish Sea)
Man, Ivory Coast
Management and Budget, Office of (OMB)(US
    govt.)
Managua, Nicaragua
Manama, Bahrain (also Bahrain, Bahrain)
Manassas, VA
Manasseh Sogavare (PM, Solomon Islands; 1954-)
Manasses, Prayer of (rel., Apocrypha)
Manaus, Brazil
Mancha, Don Quixote de la (by Cervantes)
Mancha, La (district, Sp.)
Mancha, Man of La (play)
Manchester terrier (dog)
Manchester, CT, NH
Manchester, England
Manchester, Melissa (ent.; 1951-)
Manchester, William (US writer; 1922-)
Manchu (lang./people)
Manchu dynasty (Ch.; 1644-1912)
Manchu, Fu (fict. criminal)
Manchuria (NE region, Ch.)
Manchurian Candidate, The (film, 1962)
Mancini, Henry (US comp.; 1924-94)
Mancini, Ray "Boom Boom" (US boxer; 1961-)
Manco Capac (legendary Inca ruler)
Mandalay, Myanmar
Mandan (Native Amer.)
Mandarin (lang.)
Mandarin Chinese (lang.)
Mande (lang./people)
Mande Sidibe (PM, Mali)
Mandela, Nelson (Rolihlahla)(ex-pres., SAfr.;
    1918-)
Mandela, Winnie (Nomzamo)(SAfr. pol./
    reformer; 1934-)
Mandelamine (med.)
Mandell, Howie (ent.; 1955-)
Mandelstam, Osip ([Y]Emilevich)(Rus. poet;
    1891-1938?)
Mandingo (people)
Mandinka (lang./people)
Mandja (people)
Mandlikova, Hana (tennis; 1962-)
M & M's (candy)
Mandrell, Barbara (ent.; 1948-)
Mandrell, Louise (ent.; 1954-)
Mandy Moore (ent.; 1984-)
Mandy (Mandel) Patinkin (ent.; 1952-)
Manet, Édouard (Fr. artist; 1832-83)
Manfred B(ennington) Lee (pseud. Ellery
    Queen)(US writer; 1905-71)
Manganin (copper/manganese/nickel alloy)
Mangas Coloradas, Chief (Apache Native
    Amer.; c1797-1863)
Mangione, Chuck (ent.; 1940-)
Mangusta, Qvale (auto.)

Manhattan (cocktail)
Manhattan (island, NYC borough)
Manhattan clam chowder
Manhattan Project (atomic bomb)
Manhattan Shirt Co., The
Manhattan Transfer, The (pop music)
Manheim, Camryn (b. Debra Manheim)(ent.; 1961-)
Manicheanism (rel.)
Manifest Destiny (govt.)
Manila hemp/rope
Manila paper
Manila, Philippines
Manilow, Barry (b. Barry Alan Pincus)(ent.; 1946-)
Manipur (state, India)
Manitoba (province, Can.)
Manitoba, Lake (Can.)
Manjaca (people)
Mankiewicz, Frank F. (US jour.; 1924-)
Mankiewicz, Joseph L(eo)(US ent./writer; 1909-93)
Manley, Michael (Norman)(ex-PM, Jamaica; 1924-97)
Manley, Norman (ex-PM, Jamaica; 1892-1969)
Mann Act (also White Slave Traffic Act)(US hist.; 1910)
Mann, Aimee (ent.; 1960-)
Mann, Barry (US comp.; 1939-)
Mann, Carol (golf; 1941-)
Mann, Herbie (US jazz; 1930-)
Mann, Horace (US pol./educ.; 1796-1859)
Mann, Murray Gell- (US physt.; 1929-)
Mann, Thomas (Ger. writer; 1875-1955)
Mann's Chinese Theater
Manne, Shelly (US jazz; 1920-84)
Mannerheim Line/line
Mannerheim, Carl Gustaf Emil von, Baron (Fin. gen./pol.; 1867-1951)
Mannerism (art style)
Mannes, Marya (US writer; 1904-90)
Mannheim School
Mannheim, Germany
Mannheim, Karl (Hung. sociol./hist.; 1893-1947)
Manning, Danny (basketball; 1966-)
Manning, Madeline (runner; 1948-)
Manning, Patrick A. M. (ex-PM, Trinidad/ Tobago; 1946-)
Mannington (flooring)
Mannington Mills, Inc.
Mannix (TV show)
Manoff, Dinah (ent.; 1958-)
Manpower Temporary Services
Manpower, Inc.
Mansard (or Mansart), (Nicolas) François (Fr. arch.; 1598-1666)
Mansard roof
Mansfield, CT, OH
Mansfield, England
Mansfield, Jayne (ent.; 1932-67)
Mansfield, Katherine (Br. writer; 1888-1923)
Mansôa, Guinea-Bissau
Manson, Charles (US, mass murderer; 1934-)
Manson, Marilyn (b. Brian Hugh Warner)(ent.; 1969-)
Manson, Shirley (ent.; 1966-)

Mansura, Egypt (also El Mansura)
Mantegna, Andrea (It. artist; 1431-1506)
Mantegna, Joe (ent.; 1947-)
Mantle, Mickey (Charles)(baseball; 1931-95)
Mantoux test (med./TB)
Mantovani, Annunzio (ent.; 1905-80)
Mantua, Italy
Manu (myth.)
Manuel de Falla (Sp. comp.; 1876-1946)
Manuel Esquivel (ex-PM, Belize; 1940-)
Manuel Luis Quezon y Molina (ex-pres. Phil.; 1878-1944)
Manuel (Antonio) Noriega (Morena), Gen. (ex-dictator, Panama; imprisoned for drug trafficking; 1938-)
Manuel Orantes (tennis; 1949-)
Manuel Santana (Martinez)(tennis; 1938-)
Manufacturers, National Association of (NAM) (est. 1895)
Manukau, New Zealand
Manx cat (also l.c.)
Manzanillo, Cuba
Manzini, Swaziland
MAO inhibitors (med.)
Mao jacket
Mao Tse-tung (also Mao Zedong, Chairman Mao)(Ch. pol.; 1893-1976)
Mao, Madame (aka Jiang Ching, Jiang Qing, Chiang Ching, Lan Ping)(Ch. pol./ent., wife of Chairman Mao; 1914-91)
Maoism (pol. phil.)
Maori (lang./people)
Maple Leafs, Toronto (hockey team)
Maples, Marla (US, ex-wife of D. Trump/ actress; 1963-)
Mapp v. Ohio (US law; 1961)
Mapplethorpe, Robert (US photo.; 1946-89)
Maputo, Mozambique (formerly Lourenço Marques)
Mara (rel.)
Maracaibo, Lake (Venezuela)
Maracaibo, Venezuela
Maradi, Niger
Marat, Jean Paul (Fr. pol.; 1743-93)
Marathi (lang.)
Marathon (ancient plain/village, Gr.)
Marathon, Battle of (Gr./Persia; 490 BC)
Maravich, Pistol Pete (Peter)(basketball; 1948-88)
Marax (med.)
Marble, Alice (tennis; 1913-90)
Marboro Books, Inc.
Marbury v. Madison (US law; 1803)
Marc Anthony (b. Antonio Marco Muniz)(ent.; 1969-)
Marc Bazin (ex-PM, Haiti)
Marc Chagall (Fr. artist; 1887-1985)
Marc Connelly (US playwright; 1890-1980)
Marc Forné Molné (PM, Andorra; 1946-)
Marc Racicot (ex-MT gov.; 1948-)
Marc Rich (b. Marc David Reich)(exiled US finan., pardoned in 2001; 1934-)
Marc, Franz (Ger. artist; 1880-1916)
Marceau, Marcel (b. Marcel Mangel)(Fr. ent.; 1923-)

Marceau, Sophie (ent.; 1966-)
Marcel Breuer (US arch.; 1902-81)
Marcel Dionne (hockey; 1951-)
Marcel Duchamp (Fr. artist; 1887-1968)
Marcel Marceau (b. Marcel Mangel)(Fr. ent.; 1923-)
Marcel Proust (Fr. writer; 1871-1922)
Marcello Mastroianni (It. ent.; 1924-96)
March Air Force Base, CA
March on Rome, the (It. hist.; 1922)
March, Fredric (ent.; 1897-1975)
Marchand, Nancy (ent.; 1928-2000)
Marche, Le (region, It.)
Marcia Jones Smoke (canoeing; 1941-)
Marciano, Rocky (b. Rocco Francis Marchegiano)(boxing; 1923-69)
Marco Polo (It. expl.; c1254-1324)
Marco, Prof. Guido de (pres., Malta; 1931-)
Marcolino José Carlos Moco (ex-PM, Angola)
Marconi, Guglielmo (It. eng./inv., radio; 1874-1937)
Marcos, Ferdinand E(dralin)(ex-pres., Phil.; 1917-89)
Marcos, Imelda (Romualdez)(Phil. pol., wife of ex-pres.; 1929-)
Marcus Annaeus Lucanus (aka Lucan)(Roman poet; 39-65)
Marcus Antonius (aka Mark Antony)(Roman gen.; 83?-30 BC)
Marcus Aurelius Antonius (b. Marcus Annius Verus)(emp., Rome; 121-180)
Marcus Cocceius Nerva (emp., Rome; c35-98)
Marcus Daly (US bus.; 1841-1900)
Marcus Garvey (Jamaican/US reformer; 1887-1940)
Marcus Junius Brutus (Roman pol., Caesar assassin; c78-42 BC)
Marcus Licinius Crassus (Roman gen.; c108-53 BC)
Marcus Tullius Cicero ("Tully")(Roman orator/ writer/pol.; 106-43 BC)
Marcus Vipsanius Agrippa (Roman mil./pol.; 63-12 BC)
Marcus Welby, M.D. (TV show)
Marcus, Neiman- (retail)
Marcus, Rudolph Arthur (chem.; 1923-)
Marcuse, Herbert (US phil.; 1898-1979)
Mardi Gras ("fat Tuesday")(festival)
Marduk (myth.)
Mare Imbrium (lunar sea)
Mare Island Naval Shipyard (CA)
Mare Winningham (ent.; 1959-)
Mare, Walter de la (Br. poet; 1873-1956)
Maren Seidler (track; 1962-)
Marengo, chicken (food)
Margaret (queen, Den.; 1353-1412)
Margaret (Rose)(princess, UK; 1930-)
Margaret Atwood (Can. writer; 1939-)
Margaret Bourke-White (US photo./writer; 1906-71)
Margaret Chase Smith (US pol.; 1897-1995)
Margaret Drabble (Br. writer; 1939-)
Margaret C. "Meg" Whitman (US bus./eBay; 1957-)
Margaret D. Tutwiler (US ambassador/Morocco; 1950-)
Margaret Dumont (ent.; 1889-1965)
Margaret E. Rey (writer; 1906-96)
Margaret Fox (Can./US spiritualist; 1833-93)(and sister Katherine)
Margaret Fuller (US writer/reformer; 1810-50)
Margaret LaMontagne (US White House staff)
Margaret Leighton (ent.; 1922-76)
Margaret Maid of Norway (queen, Scot.; 1283-90)
Margaret Mead (US anthrop.; 1901-78)
Margaret Mitchell (US writer; 1900-49)
Margaret O'Brien (ent.; 1937-)
Margaret of Anjou (queen, Eng./wife of Henry VI; 1430-82)
Margaret of Austria (regent, Netherlands; 1480-1530)
Margaret of Navarre (also Margaret of Angoulême)(queen, Navarre; 1492-1549)
Margaret of Parma (Sp. regent, Netherlands; 1522-86)
Margaret of Valois (also Queen Margot)(Fr.; 1553-1615)
Margaret Rutherford, Dame (ent.; 1892-1972)
Margaret (Higgins) Sanger (US reformer; 1883-1966)
Margaret Smith Court (tennis; 1942-)
Margaret Sullavan (ent.; 1911-60)
Margaret (Hilda Roberts) Thatcher (ex-PM, Br.; 1925-)
Margaret Trudeau (Can., ex-wife of ex-PM)
Margaret Truman, (Mary)(daughter of ex-US pres.; 1924-)
Margaret Tudor (Eng., wife of James IV, Scot.; 1489-1541)
Margaret Webster (ent.; 1905-73)
Margaret Whiting (ent.; 1924-)
Margaret Wise Brown (children's writer; 1910-62)
Margarita (mixed drink)
Margaritaville
Margaux (Fr. wine district)
Margaux, Chateau (Fr. wine)
Margaux Hemingway (ent.; 1955-96)
Marge Champion (US dancer; 1923-)
Marge Piercy (US writer; 1936-)
Margery Daw (fict. chara.)
Margolin, Janet (ent.; 1943-)
Margot Fonteyn, Dame (ballet; 1919-91)
Margot Kidder (ent.; 1948-)
Margret, Ann- (Swed./US ent.; 1941-)
Margrethe II (queen, Den.; 1940-)
Marguerite (Donnadieu) Duras (writer; 1914-96)
Marguerite Piazza (soprano; 1926-)
Margulies, Julianna (ent.; 1966-)
Maria Bartiromo (TV finan. jour.; 1967-)
Maria Bueno (tennis; 1939-)
Maria Callas (ent.; 1923-77)
Maria Conchita Alonso (ent.; 1956-)
Maria Estela ("Isabel") Martínez de Perón (ex-pres., Argentina; 1931-)
Maria Goeppert Mayer (Ger./US physt.; 1906-72)
Maria Mitchell (US astron.; 1818-89)
Maria Montessori (It. educ.; 1870-1952)
Maria Rilke, Rainer (Ger. poet; 1875-1926)
Maria Schell (ent.; 1926-)

Maria Schneider (ent.; 1952-)
Maria Shriver (US TV jour.; 1955-)
Maria Taglioni (It. ballet; 1804-84)
Maria Tallchief (US ballet; 1925-)
Maria Theresa (empress, Austria; 1717-80)
Maria Von Trapp, Baroness (b. Maria Augusta Kutschera)(Aus. singer; 1905-87)
Maria, Ave (also *Hail Mary*)(prayer)
Mariah Carey (ent.; 1970-)
Marian Anderson (ent.; 1902-1993)
Marian (or Mary Ann) Evans (pseud. George Eliot)(Br. writer; 1819-80)
Marian McPartland (US jazz; 1920-)
Marian Mercer (ent.; 1935-)
Marian Wright Edelman (US social activist; 1939-)
Marian, Maid (Robin Hood's sweetheart)
Mariana Islands (also Marianas)(NW Pac.)
Mariana Trench (deep depression, NW Pac.)
Marianne Faithfull (ent.; 1946-)
Marianne (Craig) Moore (US poet; 1887-1972)
Marichal, Juan (baseball; 1937-)
Marie (queen, Romania; 1875-1938)
Marie Antoinette (queen, Fr./wife of Louis XVI; 1755-93)
Marie Curie, Madame (Fr. physt., radium; 1867-1934)
Marie de' Medici (queen, Fr./wife of Henry IV; 1573-1642)
Marie Dressler (ent.; 1869-1934)
Marie Henri Beyle (aka Stendhal)(Fr. writer; 1783-1842)
Marie Ignace Augustine de Montijo Eugenie (empress, Fr.; 1826-1920)
Marie Louise (empress, Fr.; 1791-1847)
Marie Madeleine Pioche de la Vergne La Fayette (Comtesse de La Fayette)(Fr. writer; 1634-93)
Marie Osmond (ent.; 1959-)
Marie Rambert, Dame (b. Cyvia Rambam)(Br. ballet; 1888-1982)
Marie (Grosholtz) Tussaud, Madame (Anne)(Swiss wax modeler; 1760-1850)
Marie Wilson (ent.; 1917-72)
Marie, Rose (ent.; 1925-)
Mariel Hemingway (ent.; 1961-)
Marietta Corp., Martin
Marietta, GA, OH
Marietta, Naughty (play; film, 1935)
Mariette Hartley (ent.; 1940-)
Marigot, Dominica
Marilu Henner (ent.; 1952-)
Marilyn Cochran (skiing; 1950-)
Marilyn Horne (ent.; 1934-)
Marilyn Manson (b. Brian Hugh Warner)(ent.; 1969-)
Marilyn McCoo (ent.; 1943-)
Marilyn Monroe (b. Norma Jean Baker [or Mortenson])(ent.; 1926-62)
Marilyn Quayle (US atty., wife of ex-VP ; 1949-)
Marin, Cheech (Richard)(ent.; 1946-)
Marin, John (US artist; 1870-1953)
Marina del Rey, CA
Marina Sirtis (ent.; 1959-)
Marinaro, Ed (football/ent.; 1950-)
Marine Corps War Memorial, U.S. (also Iwo Jima)(VA)

Marine Corps, U.S. (US mil.)
Marine Fisheries Service, National (US govt. agcy.; est. 1970)
Mariner (US uncrewed space probes)
Mariners, Seattle (baseball team)
Marino, Dan (football; 1961-)
Marinol (med.)
Mario (Gabriel) Andretti (auto racing; 1940-)
Mário da Graça Machungo (ex-PM, Mozambique)
Mario Frick (PM, Liechtenstein; 1965-)
Mario Lemieux (hockey; 1965-)
Mario M(atthew) Cuomo (ex-NY gov.; 1932-)
Mario Molina (chem.; 1943-)
Mario Puzo (US writer; 1920-99)
Mário (Alberto Nobre Lopes) Soares (ex-pres., Port.; 1924-)
Mário Lanza (opera; 1921-1959)
Marion (Douras) Davies (ent.; 1897-1961)
Marion Barry (ex-mayor, Washington, DC; 1936-)
Marion Jones (US runner; 1975-)
Marion Ross (ent.; 1928-)
Marion Zimmer Bradley (US writer; 1930-99)
Marion, Francis ("the Swamp Fox")(US mil./ pol.; c1732-95)
Marion, IN, OH
Maris, Roger (Eugene)(baseball; 1934-85)
Marisa Berenson (ent.; 1947-)
Marisa Tomei (ent.; 1964-)
Marisol (Escubar)(Venezuelan artist; 1930-)
Maritain, Jacques (Fr. phil.; 1882-1973)
Maritime Provinces (Can.: New Brunswick, Nova Scotia, Prince Edward Island)
Mariupol, Ukraine
Marjorie Kinnan Rawlings (US writer; 1896-1953)
Marjorie Main (ent.; 1890-1975)
Marjorie Morningstar (H. Wouk novel)
Marjorie Rambeau (ent.; 1889-1970)
Marjorie Reynolds (b. Marjorie Goodspeed) (ent.; 1921-97)
Marjory Stoneman Douglas (US writer/environ. activist; 1890-1998)
Mark (rel., book of the New Testament)
Mark Antony (aka Marcus Antonius)(Roman gen.; 83?-30 BC)
Mark Burnett (ent./*Survivor* producer)
Mark Clark (US gen.; 1896-1984)
Mark David Chapman (killed John Lennon)
Mark Dayton (US cong.; 1947-)
Mark di Suvero (US artist; 1933-)
Mark Farner (ent., Grand Funk Railroad; 1948-)
Mark Goodson (ent.; 1915-92)
Mark Hamill (ent.; 1951-)
Mark Harmon (ent.; 1951-)
Mark Hopkins Hotel (San Francisco)
Mark IV Industries, Inc.
Mark Knopfler (ent., Dire Straits; 1949-)
Mark Lindsay Boatbuilders (US bus.)
Mark Linn-Baker (ent.; 1954-)
Mark McGwire (baseball; 1963-)
Mark Messier (hockey; 1961-)
Mark O. Hatfield (US pol.; 1922-)
Mark Rothko (Rus./US artist; 1903-70)
Mark Russell (ent.; 1932-)
Mark (Andrew) Spitz (swimming; 1950-)

Mark Taper Forum (in Los Angeles)
Mark Twain (aka Samuel Langhorne Clemens)(US writer; 1835-1910)
Mark Udall (US cong.; 1950-)
Mark VIII, Lincoln (auto.)
Mark Wahlberg (ent./model; 1971-)
Mark, St. (b. John Mark)(rel.; 1st c. AD)
Mark, Top of the (Mark Hopkins Hotel, San Francisco)
Mark's Basilica, St. (Venice, It.)
Mark's fly, St. (insect)
Markarian (or Margaryan), Andranik (PM, Armenia; 1951-)
Marker, Little Miss (film, 1934, 1980)
Markham, Edwin (US poet; 1852-1940)
Markie Post (ent.; 1950-)
Markovic, Mirjana (Serbian atty./educ./pol., wife of S. Milosevic; 1942-)
Marks & Spencer (bus.)
Marla Gibbs (b. Margaret Bradley)(ent.; 1931-)
Marla Maples (US, ex-wife of D. Trump/actress; 1963-)
Marlboro (cigarette)
Marlboro Man (Marlboro cigarettes)
Marlboro Music Festival
Marlborough, Duke of (aka John Churchill)(Br. mil.; 1650-1722)
Marlee Matlin (ent.; 1965-)
Marlene Dietrich (b. Maria Magdalene von Losch)(ent.; 1901-92)
Marley, Bob (Robert Nesta)(ent.; 1945-81)
Marley, the ghost of Jacob (fict. chara., *The Christmas Carol*)
Marley, Ziggy (David)(ent.; 1968-)
Marlin Fitzwater (US pol./ex-press secy.; 1942-)
Marlins, Florida (baseball team)
Marlo (Margaret) Thomas (ent.; 1938-)
Marlon Brando (ent.; 1924-)
Marlon Jackson (ent., The Jacksons; 1957-)
Marlowe, Christopher (Br. writer; 1564-93)
Marlowe, Philip (fict. detective, R.T. Chandler)
Marmaduke (comic strip)
Marmara, Sea of (Turk.)
Marner, Silas (G. Eliot novel)
Maroilles (cheese)
Maronite (people)
Marple, Miss (fict. chara., A. Christie)
Marquand, J(ohn) P(hillips)(US writer; 1893-1960)
Marquesas Islands (Fr. Polynesia)
Marquette University (Milwaukee, WI)
Marquette, Jacques (Fr. expl./rel. in Amer.; 1637-75)
Marquette, MI
Márquez, Felipe González (ex-PM, Spain; 1942-)
Marquis de Lafayette (aka Marie Joseph Gilbert de Motier Lafayette)(Fr. mil./pol.; 1757-1834)
Marquis de Sade (b. Donatien Alphonse François, Comte de Sade)(Fr. mil./writer; 1740-1814)
Marquis of Queensberry rules (also Queensberry rules)(boxing)
Marquise de Pompadour (aka Jeanne Antoinette Poisson Le Normant d'Étioles)(mistress of Louis XV, Fr.; 1721-64)
Marrakesh, Morocco

Married...With Children (TV show)
Marriner, Neville (ent.; 1924-)
Marriott Corp.
Marriott Hotel(s)
Marriott, Steve (ent.; 1947-)
Mars (candy)
Mars (planet, myth.)
Mars (US uncrewed space probes)
Mars brown (color)
Mars Observer (US uncrewed space probe)
Mars red (color)
Mars, Forrest E(dward)(US bus.; 1904-99)
Mars, Inc.
Marsala (wine)
Marsala, Sicily, Italy
Marsalis, Branford (ent.; 1960-)
Marsalis, Wynton (US jazz; 1961-)
Marsaxlokk, Malta
Marseillaise, La (Fr. anthem)
Marseille, France
Marsh Co., Abraham & Straus/Jordan
Marsh, (Edith) Ngaio, Dame (NewZeal. writer; 1899-1982)
Marsh, Jean (ent.; 1934-)
Marsh, Reginald (US artist; 1898-1954)
Marsha Mason (ent.; 1942-)
Marsha (Williams) Norman (US playwright; 1947-)
Marshal Tito (b. Josip Broz)(ex-pres., Yug.; 1892-1980)
Marshall Field (US merchant; 1834-1906)
Marshall Field's store
Marshall Figure Salon, Gloria (US bus.)
Marshall Islands (Republic of the)(W Pac.)
Marshall Mathers, III (Eminem)(ent.; 1972-)
Marshall McLuhan, (Herbert)(Can. educ./writer; 1911-80)
Marshall Plan (also European Recovery Program)(after WWII)
Marshall Space Flight Center (AL)
Marshall University (Huntington, WV)
Marshall Warren Nirenberg (US chem.; 1927-)
Marshall, E. G. (ent.; 1910-98)
Marshall, Garry (ent./screenwriter; 1934-)
Marshall, George C(atlett)(US gen.; 1880-1959)
Marshall, John (US jurist; 1755-1835)
Marshall, Penny (ent.; 1943-)
Marshall, Peter (b. Pierre La Cock)(ent.; 1927-)
Marshall, Thomas R(iley)(ex-US VP; 1854-1925)
Marshall, Thurgood (US jurist; 1908-93)
Marshall, TX
Marshallese (lang./people)
Marston Morse (US math.; 1892-1977)
Mart Laar (PM, Estonia; 1960-)
Martello tower (mil.)(also l.c.)
Martens, Gunnar (High Comm., Greenland)
Martens, Wilfried (ex-PM, Belgium; 1936-)
Martha (Dandridge) Washington (wife of ex-US pres.; 1732-1802)
Martha and the Vandellas (pop music)
Martha Graham (US dancer/choreographer; 1894-1991)
Martha Jane Burke (Calamity Jane)(US frontier heroine; c1852-1903)
Martha Plimpton (ent.; 1970-)

Martha Quinn (ent.; 1959-)
Martha Rae Watson (track; 1946-)
Martha Raye (ent.; 1916-94)
Martha Rockwell (skiing; 1944-)
Martha Scott (ent.; 1914-)
Martha Stewart (US bus.; 1941-)
Martha White Foods, Inc.
Martha Wright (ent.; 1926-)
Martha's Vineyard (island, MA)
Marthinus (Wessels) Pretorius (SAfr. mil./pol.; 1819-1901)
Marti, Jose (Julian)(Cuban pol./poet; 1853-95)
Martial (b. Marcus Valerius Martialis)(Roman poet; 41-104)
Martian
Martian Chronicles, The (R. Bradbury novel)
Martin (or Meir) Kahan (Jew. activist; 1932-90)
Martin Amerique, Inc., Remy
Martin Amis (writer; 1949-)
Martin Balsam (ent.; 1919-96)
Martin Bormann (Ger. Nazi leader; 1900-45)
Martin Buber (Isr. phil.; 1878-1965)
Martin Frobisher, (Sir)(Br. nav./expl.; 1535-94)
Martin Gabel (ent.; 1912-)
Martin Landau (ent.; 1931-)
Martin Lawrence (ent.; 1965-)
Martin Luther (Ger. rel./writer; 1483-1546)
Martin Luther King Day (Mon. closest to 1/15)
Martin Luther King, Jr., Rev. Dr. (US civil rights leader; 1929-68)
Martin Marietta Corp.
Martin Milner (ent.; 1927-)
Martin Mull (ent.; 1943-)
Martin Riessen (tennis; 1941-)
Martin Scorsese (ent.; 1942-)
Martin Sheen (ent.; 1940-)
Martin Short (ent.; 1950-)
Martin v. Hunter's Lessee (US law; 1816)
Martin Van Buren (8th US pres.; 1782-1862)
Martin, Billy (Alfred Manuel)(baseball; 1928-89)
Martin, Dean (ent.; 1917-95)
Martin, Dick (ent.; 1922-)
Martin, Don (cartoonist, *Mad* magazine; 1931-2000)
Martin, Lynn (nee Morley)(US pol.; 1939-)
Martin, Mary (ent.; 1913-90)
Martin, Pamela Sue (ent.; 1953-)
Martin, Rick (Richard Lionel)(hockey; 1951-)
Martin, Ricky (b. Enrique Jose Martin Morales)(ent.; 1971-)
Martin, St. (Fr. rel.; c316-401)
Martin, Steve (ent.; 1945-)
Martin, Tony (b. Alvin Morris)(ent.; 1913-)
Martin's Laugh-In, Rowan and (TV show)
Martin's Press, Inc., St. (bus.)
Martina Arroyo (ent.; 1937-)
Martina McBride (ent.; 1966-)
Martina Navratilova (tennis; 1956-)
Martindale-Hubbell
Martindale, Wink (Winston Conrad)(ent.; 1934-)
Martine van Hamel (ballet; 1945-)
Martinelli, Giovanni (tenor; 1885-1969)
Martinez, Bob (Robert)(US pol.; 1934-)
Martinez, Mel(quiades)(Rafael)(US secy./HUD; 1946-)

Martini & Prati Wines, Inc.
Martini & Rossi Asti Spumante
Martini Winery, Louis M. (US bus.)
Martinique (Fr. island, West Indies)
Martinizing Dry Cleaning, One Hour (US bus.)
Martinmas (rel.)
Martins, Peter (US dancer; 1946-)
Martinsburg, WV
Martinsville, VA
Martti Talvela (basso; 1935-89)
Marty (film, 1955)
Marty Balin (b. Martyn Jerel Buchwald)(ent.; 1943-)
Marty Feldman (ent.; 1933-82)
Marty Ingels (ent.; 1936-)
Marty Krofft (puppeteer; 1939-)
Marty Liquori (runner; 1949-)
Marty Robbins (ent.; 1925-82)
Martyr, St. Justin (It. rel.; 100?-165)
Martz, Judy H. (MT gov.; 1943-)
Maru, Ehime (Japanese fishing vessel that collided with US sub near Hawaii, 2/9/2001)
Marv Albert (sportscaster; 1941-)
Marvel, Captain (comic strip)
Marvelettes, the (pop music)
Marvell, Andrew (Br. poet/satirist; 1621-78)
Marvelous Marvin Hagler (boxing; 1954-)
Marvin (Pierce) Bush (US bro. of pres./son of ex-pres.; 1956-)
Marvin Gaye (ent.; 1939-84)
Marvin Hagler, Marvelous (boxing; 1954-)
Marvin Hamlisch (US comp.; 1944-)
Marvin Mitchelson (US atty.)
Marvin Windows & Doors (US bus.)
Marvin, Lee (ent.; 1924-87)
Marx Brothers (Chico, Harpo, Groucho, Gummo, Zeppo)
Marx Swimwear, Gilda (US bus.)
Marx, Arthur "Harpo" (ent.; 1888-1964)
Marx, Gilda
Marx, Herbert "Zeppo" (ent.; 1901-79)
Marx, Julius "Groucho" (ent.; 1890-1977)
Marx, Karl (Heinrich)(Ger. phil.; 1818-83)
Marx, Leonard "Chico" (ent.; 1886-1961)
Marx, Milton "Gummo" (ent.; 1893-1977)
Marx, Richard (ent.; 1963-)
Marxism (phil.)
Mary (also the Madonna, Holy Mother, Our Lady, Virgin Mary)(rel.)
Mary Abigail Dodge (pseud. Gail Hamilton)(US writer; 1833-96)
Mary Ann (or Marian) Evans (pseud. George Eliot)(Br. writer; 1819-80)
Mary Astor (b. Lucile Langhanke)(ent.; 1906-87)
Mary Baker Eddy (US, founder Christian Science; 1821-1910)
Mary Beth Hurt (b. Mary Beth Supinger)(ent.; 1948-)
Mary Bono (US cong.; 1961-)
Mary Cassatt (US artist; 1845-1926)
Mary Chapin Carpenter (ent.; 1958-)
Mary Decker Slaney (US runner; 1958-)
Mary Elizabeth Mapes Dodge (US writer/editor; 1831-1905)
Mary Elizabeth Mastrantonio (ent.; 1958-)

Mary Eugenia Charles (ex-PM, Dominica; 1919-)
Mary Ford (ent.; 1928-77)
Mary Ford, Les Paul & (ent.)
Mary Frances Kennedy Fisher (M.F.K.)(US writer; 1909-92)
Mary Frann (ent.; 1943-98)
Mary Garden (soprano; 1874-1967)
Mary Gordon (US writer; 1949-)
Mary Gross (ent.; 1953-)
Mary Hart (ent.; 1951-)
Mary Higgins Clark (US writer; 1931-)
Mary I (also Mary Tudor, "Bloody Mary") (queen, Eng.; 1516-58)
Mary II (queen, Eng./Scot./Ir.; 1662-94)
Mary J. Blige (ent.; 1971-)
Mary Jane (also maryjane)(slang, marijuana)
Mary Janes (candy sprinkles)
Mary Janes (shoes)
Mary Jo Kopechne (US, died at Chappaquiddick; 1941-69)
Mary-Kate Olsen (ent.; 1986-)
Mary Kay Cosmetics, Inc.
Mary Lamb (Br. writer; 1764-1847)
Mary (Douglas) Leakey (Br. archaeol.; 1913-96)
Mary L. Landrieu (US cong.; 1955-)
Mary Lou Retton (US gymnast; 1968-)
Mary Lou Williams (US jazz; 1914-81)
Mary Magdalene (rel.; 1st c. AD)
Mary Martin (ent.; 1913-90)
Mary Matalin (US pol. commentator/activist; 1953-)
Mary McAleese (pres., Ir.; 1951-)
Mary (Therese) McCarthy (US writer; 1912-89)
Mary (Ludwig Hays) McCauley ("Molly Pitcher") (US heroine; 1754-1832)
Mary McLeod Bethune (US educ./civil rights; 1875-1955)
Mary (Wortley) Montagu, Lady (aka Mary Pierrepont)(Br. writer; 1689-1762)
Mary of Burgundy (heiress of Charles the Bold; 1457-82)
Mary of Guise (queen to James V, Scot.; 1515-60)
Mary Pickford (b. Gladys Marie Smith)(ent.; 1893-1979)
Mary Poppins (P. Travers novel)
Mary Quant (Br. designer; 1934-)
Mary Roberts Rinehart (US writer; 1876-1958)
Mary Robinson (ex-pres., Ir.; 1944-)
Mary Steenburgen (ent.; 1953-)
Mary (Slattery) Stolz (US writer; 1920-)
Mary Stuart (aka Mary, Queen of Scots)(queen, Scot.; 1542-87)
Mary Stuart Masterson (ent.; 1966-)
Mary Todd Lincoln (wife of A. Lincoln; 1818-82)
Mary Travers (ent.; 1936-)
Mary Tudor (also Mary I, "Bloody Mary")(queen, Eng.; 1516-58)
Mary Tyler Moore (ent.; 1936-)
Mary Tyler Show, The (TV show, fict. chara.)
Mary Wells (ent.; 1943-92)
Mary Wollstonecraft (Br. reformer; 1759-97)
Mary Wollstonecraft Shelley (Br. writer/ Frankenstein; 1797-1851)
Mary Worth (cartoon chara.)

Mary Wortley (Pierrepont) Montagu, Lady (Br. writer; 1689-1762)
Mary, Bloody (also Mary I, Mary Tudor)(queen, Eng.; 1516-58)
Mary, College of William and (Williamsburg, VA)
Mary, Hail (also Ave Maria)(prayer)
Mary, Mary (play)
Mary, Queen of Scots (aka Mary Stuart)(queen, Scot.; 1542-87)
Mary, Typhoid (b. Mary Mallon)(Ir. cook, typhoid carrier; ?-1938)
Marya Mannes (US writer; 1904-90)
Maryknoll Missioners (also Catholic Foreign Mission Society of America)(rel.)
Mary-le-Bow Church, St. (also Bow Church) (London)
Maryland (MD)
Maryland, McCulloch vs. (US law; 1819)
Masaccio (b. Tomaso [di Giovanni di Simone] Guidi)(It. artist; 1401-28)
Masada fortress (Isr. hist.; c70)
Masai (lang./people)
Masaka, Uganda
Masaki, Tanzania
Masako (Owada)(princess, Jap.; 1964-)
Masaryk, Jan (Garrigue)(Czech. pol.; 1886-1948)
Masaryk, Thomas G(arrigue)(ex-pres., Czech.; 1850-1937)
Masayoshi, Ohira (ex-PM, Jap.; 1910-80)
Mascagni, Pietro (It. comp.; 1863-1945)
Mascarenhas Monteiro, Antonio (pres., Cape Verde; 1944-)
Masco Corp., Inc.
Masefield, John (Br. poet; 1878-1967)
Masekela, Hugh (ent., trumpet; 1939-)
Maserati (auto.)
Maserati Automobiles, Inc.
Maserati, Ettore (It. bus./auto.; 1894-1990)
Maseru, Lesotho
M*A*S*H (film, 1970; TV show)
Mashburn, Jamal (basketball; 1972-)
Mashhad, Iran
Mashraq (E Mediterranean Arab countries: Egypt/Jordan/Lebanon/Sudan/Syria)
Masire, Quett (Ketumile Joni)(ex-pres., Botswana; 1925-)
Masland Carpets (US bus.)
Mason Adams (ent.; 1919-)
Mason City, IA
Mason-Dixon Line (between MD/PA, North/ South)
Mason jar (also l.c.)
Mason, George (US pol.; 1725-92)
Mason, Jackie (b. Yacov Moshe Maza)(ent.; 1934-)
Mason, James (ent.; 1909-84)
Mason, John Landis (US inv., Mason jar; 1832-1902)
Mason, Marsha (ent.; 1942-)
Mason, Perry (fict. atty.)
Masonite Corp.
Mass (rel.)
Mass, Red (rel., Catholic blessing for legal profession)
Massachuset (also Massachuset)(Native Amer.)
Massachusetts (MA)

Massachusetts Bay (MA)
Massachusetts Bay Company (Br. co., founded Boston; 1630)
Massachusetts Institute of Technology (MIT)
Massacre of St. Bartholomew's Day (Fr. hist.; 1572)
Massapequa, NY
Massasoit, Chief (Wampanoag Native Amer., peace treaty with Pilgrims; c1590-1661)
Massawa, Eritrea
Massenet, Jules (Émile Frédéric)(Fr. comp.; 1842-1912)
Massengill (med.)
Massey Co., Ltd., Caswell-
Massey-Ferguson, Inc.
Massey, Raymond (ent.; 1896-1993)
Massif Central (plateau, Fr.)
Masson Vineyards, Paul (US bus.)
Masson, Paul
Massys (or Matsys), Quentin (Flem. artist; 1466?-1530)
MAST (Military Anti-Shock Trousers)
Master of Arts (also M.A.)
Master of Science (also M.S.)
Master P (b. Percy Miller)(ent.; 1969-)
MasterCard (credit card)
Masterpiece Theatre (TV show)
Masters and Johnson, Drs. (sexual behavior study)
Masters Golf Tournament
Masters, Dr. William H(owell)(US phys./writer; 1915-2001)
Masters, Edgar Lee (US writer; 1869-1950)
Masters, the (golf tournament)
Masterson, Bat (William Barclay)(US marshal; 1853-1921)
Masterson, Mary Stuart (ent.; 1966-)
Mastrantonio, Mary Elizabeth (ent.; 1958-)
Mastroianni, Marcello (It. ent.; 1924-96)
Mastroianni, Umberto (It. artist; 1910-98)
Masur, Kurt (Ger. cond.; 1928-)
Mata Hari (b. Gertrud Margarete Zelle)(Dutch dancer, executed as spy by Fr.; 1876-1917)
Matabele (also Ndebele)(people)
Matadi, Zaire
Matalin, Mary (US pol. commentator/activist; 1953-)
Matamoros, Mexico
Match Light (charcoal)
Matchbox Toys USA (US bus.)
Mathäus (or Matthias) Grünewald (Ger. artist; 1480-1528)
Mather Air Force Base, CA
Mather, Cotton (US rel.; 1663-1728)
Mather, Increase (US rel.; 1639-1723)
Mathers, Jerry (ent.; 1948-)
Mathers, III, Marshall (Eminem)(ent.; 1972-)
Matheson, Tim (ent.; 1947-)
Mathew B. Brady (US photo.; 1823?-96)
Mathews, Eddie (baseball; 1931-2001)
Mathews, Harlan (US pol.; 1927-)
Mathewson, Christy (Christopher)(baseball; 1880-1925)
Mathias, Bob (athlete; 1930-)
Mathieu Kérékou (pres., Benin; 1933-)

Mathis, Johnny (ent.; 1935-)
Matisse, Henri (Fr. artist; 1869-1954)
Matlin, Marlee (ent.; 1965-)
Matlock (TV show)
Mats Wilander (tennis; 1964-)
Matson, Randy (shot putter; 1945-)
Matsuo, Bashō (aka Matsuo Munefusa)(Jap. poet, haiku; 1644-94)
Matsuoka, Yosuke (Jap. pol.; 1880-1946)
Matsys (or Massys), Quentin (Flem. artist; 1466?-1530)
Matt Biondi (swimming; 1965-)
Matt Damon (ent.; 1970-)
Matt Dillon (ent.; 1964-)
Matt Dillon, Marshal (fict. chara., *Gunsmoke*)
Matt Drudge (internet/TV jour., *Drudge Report*; 1966-)
Matt(hew Akbar) Groening (US cartoonist, *The Simpsons*; 1954-)
Matt Lauer (TV host; 1957-)
Matt Leblanc (ent.; 1967-)
Mattel (toys)
Mattel, Inc.
Matterhorn (mountain peak, Alps)
Matthau, Walter (ent.; 1920-2000)
Matthew (rel., book of the New Testament)
Matthew Arnold (Br. poet/critic; 1822-88)
Matthew Broderick (ent.; 1962-)
Matthew Bunker Ridgway (US gen.; 1895-1993)
Matthew Fox (ent.; 1966-)
Matthew Heywood Campbell Broun (US jour.; 1888-1939)
Matthew McConaughey (ent.; 1969-)
Matthew Modine (ent.; 1959-)
Matthew Perry (ent.; 1969-)
Matthew Vassar (Br./US bus./educ.; 1792-1868)
Matthew Walker (knot)
Matthew, St. (rel.; 1st c. AD)
Matthias (or Mathäus) Grünewald (Ger. artist; 1480-1528)
Matthias Corvinus (king, Hung.; 1440-90)
Matthias, St. (chosen to replace Judas Iscariot)
Mattingly, Don (baseball; 1961-)
Mattingly, Thomas K. (astro.; 1936-)
Mattiwilda Dobbs (soprano; 1925-)
Matulane (med.)
Mature, Victor (ent.; 1913-99)
Matuszak, John (football; 1950-89)
Mau Mau (Kenyan mil. movement; 1952-60)
Maud Adams (b. Maud Wikstrom)(Swed. ent.; 1945-)
Maud Land, Queen (region, Antarctica)
Maud Range, Queen (Antarctica)
Maude (TV show)
Maude Adams (b. Maude Kiskadden)(ent.; 1872-1953)
Maude, Harold and (film, 1971)
Maude, Micki & (film, 1984)
Maugham, W(illiam) Somerset (Br. writer; 1874-1965)
Maui (island, HI)
Maui (myth.)
Maui wowie (slang, Hawaiian marijuana)
Maui, HI
Mauldin, Bill (William Henry)(US writer/

cartoonist; 1921-)
Maumoon Abdul Gayoom (pres., Maldives; 1937-)
Mauna Kea (dormant volcano, HI)
Mauna Loa (active volcano, HI)
Maundy Thursday (also Holy Thursday)(rel., Thursday before Easter)
Mauno (Henrik) Koivisto (ex-pres., Fin.; 1923-)
Maupassant, (Henri René Albert) Guy de (Fr. writer; 1850-93)
Maureen Connolly ("Little Mo")(tennis; 1934-69)
Maureen Forrester (contralto; 1930-)
Maureen McGovern (ent.; 1949-)
Maureen O'Hara (b. Maureen FitzSimons)(ent.; 1920-)
Maureen O'Sullivan (ent.; 1911-98)
Maureen Stapleton (ent.; 1925-)
Mauriac, François (Fr. writer; 1885-1970)
Maurice Barrès (Fr. writer/pol.; 1862-1923)
Maurice Barrymore (ent.; 1848-1905)
Maurice B(razil) Prendergast (US artist; c1860-1924)
Maurice Chevalier (ent.; 1888-1972)
Maurice de Vlaminck (Fr. artist; 1876-1958)
Maurice Evans (ent.; 1901-89)
Maurice Maeterlinck, Count (Belgian writer; 1962-1947)
Maurice (Joseph) Ravel (Fr. comp.; 1875-1937)
Maurice (Joseph Henri) Richard ("the Rocket")(hockey; 1921-2000)
Maurice (Bernard) Sendak (US writer; 1928-)
Maurice Utrillo (Fr. artist; 1883-1955)
Maurier, Daphne Du (Br. writer; 1907-89)
Mauritania (Islamic Republic of)(NW Afr.)
Mauritius (Republic of)(island, Indian Ocean)
Maurois, André (aka Emile Herzog)(Fr. writer; 1885-1967)
Maury (Maurice Richard) Povich (US TV jour.; 1939-)
Maury Wills (baseball; 1932-)
Mauser (rifle/gun/pistol)
Mauser, Peter Paul (Ger. inv.; 1838-1914)
Mauser, Wilhelm (Ger. inv.; 1834-82)
Mausoleum at Halicarnassus (1 of 7 Wonders of the World)
Maverick (TV show)
Maverick, Bret (fict. chara.; Maverick)
Mavericks, Dallas (basketball team)
Mawlid (rel.)
M(aurits) C(ornelis) Escher (Dutch artist; 1902-72)
MAX (Cinemax)(TV channel)
Max Abramovitz (US arch.; 1908-)
Max Baer (boxing; 1909-1959)
Max Baucus (US cong.; 1941-)
Max Beckmann (Ger. artist; 1884-1950)
Max Beerbohm, (Sir)(Br. critic/caricaturist; 1872-1956)
Max Born (Ger. physt.; 1882-1970)
Max Cleland (US cong.; 1942-)
Max Delbruck (US biol.; 1907-81)
Max Devlin, The Devil and (film, 1981)
Max Ernst (Ger. artist; 1891-1976)
Max Factor (cosmetics)
Max Factor (US bus.; 1877-1938)
Max Factor & Co.

Max Fleischer (US cartoonist, Betty Boop, Popeye; 1883-1972)
Max Gail (ent.; 1943-)
Max Headroom (fict. chara.)
Max Lerner (jour.; 1902-92)
Max Liebermann (Ger. artist; 1847-1935)
Max (Karl Ernst Ludwig) Planck (Ger. physt.; 1858-1947)
Max Reinhardt (b. Max Goldmann)(ent.; 1873-1943)
Max Roach (US jazz; 1925-)
Max Schmeling (Ger. boxing; 1905-)
Max Shulman (US writer; 1919-88)
Max Von Sydow (Swed. ent.; 1929-)
Max Weber (Ger. sociol.; 1864-1920)
Max Weber (US artist; 1881-1961)
Max Wertheimer (Czech. psych./phil.; 1880-1943)
Max, Mad (film, 1980)
Maxair (med.)
Maxell, Ltd., Hitachi- (US bus.)
Maxene Andrews (ent., Andrews Sisters; 1916-95)
Maxfield Parrish, (Frederick)(US artist; 1870-1966)
Maxidex (med.)
Maxie Rosenbloom (boxing; 1904-76)
Maxim Gorky (or Gorki)(aka Aleksei Maksimovich Peshkov)(Rus. writer; 1868-1936)
Maxim Litvinov (USSR pol.; 1876-1951)
Maxim, (Sir) Hiram Stevens (US/Br. inv.; 1840-1916)
Maxima, Nissan (auto.)
Maxime Carlot Korman (ex-PM, Vanuatu)
Maximilian (emp., Mex.; 1832-67)
Maximilian I (Holy Roman emp.; 1459-1519)
Maximilian Schell (ent.; 1930-)
Maximilien (François Marie Isidore de) Robespierre (Fr. mil./pol.; 1758-94)
Maximus Verrucosus, Quintus Fabius ("Cunctator")(Roman pol./mil.; 275-03 BC)
Maxine Hong Kingston (US writer; 1940-)
Maxtor Corp.
Maxwell Air Force Base, AL
Maxwell Anderson (US writer; 1888-1959)
Maxwell Bodenheim (US writer; 1892-1954)
Maxwell Davenport Taylor (US gen.; 1901-87)
Maxwell House (coffee)
Maxwell House (US bus.)
Maxwell Smart (fict. chara., I Spy)
Maxwell, James Clerk (Scot. physt.; 1831-79)
Maxwell, (Ian) Robert (b. Jan Ludvik Hock) (Czech./Br. publ.; 1923-91)
Maxzide (med.)
May apple (med. plant)
May beetle (also June bug, Junebug)
May Day (May 1)
Mayday (distress signal)
May Department Stores Co., The
May queen
May wine
May, Elaine (b. Elaine Berlin)(ent.; 1932-)
May, Rollo (US psych.; 1909-94)
Maya (lang./people)
Maya (Native CAmer.)
Maya Angelou (b. Marguerite Johnson)(US writer; 1928-)

Maya Lin (US arch./sculptor; 1959-)
Maya Mikhaylovna Plisetskaya (Rus. ballet; 1925-)
Mayacamas Vineyards (US bus.)
Mayaguana, Bahamas
Mayagüez, Puerto Rico
Mayakovsky, Vladimir (Rus. writer; 1893-1930)
Mayall, John (ent.; 1933-)
Mayan art (C Amer.; 200-900)
Mayan ruins
Mayaquiche (Native Amer./Guatemala)
Maybeck, Bernard R. (US arch.; 1862-1957)
Maybelle Carter, "Mother" (ent.; 1909-78)
Maybelline (cosmetics)
Maybelline Co.
Mayberry R.F.D. (TV show)
Mayer Foods Corp., Oscar
Mayer, Louis B(urt)(ent.; 1885-1957)
Mayer, Maria Goeppert (Ger./US physt.; 1906-72)
Mayer, Oscar (meats)
Mayfair district (London)
Mayfield, Curtis (ent.; 1942-99)
Mayflower (Pilgrim ship; 1620)
Mayflower Compact
Mayflower Madam (film, 1987)
Mayflower Transit, Inc.
Mayim Bialik (ent.; 1975-)
Maynard Ferguson (ent.; 1928-)
Maynard Smith, John (Br. biol.; 1920-)
Mayo (county, Ir.)
Mayo Clinic (med.)
Mayo, Charles H(orace)(US surgeon; 1865-1939)
Mayo, Charles W. (US surgeon; 1898-1968)
Mayo, Virginia (ent.; 1920-)
Mayo, William J(ames)(US surgeon; 1861-1939)
Mayor of Casterbridge, The (Thomas Hardy novel)
Mayotte (a Comoro Island, Fr.)
Maypole (also l.c.)
Mayron, Melanie (ent.; 1952-)
Mays, Kimberly (US news, switched at birth)
Mays, Willie (Howard)(baseball; 1931-)
Maytag (appliances)
Maytag Co., The
Maytag Corp.
Maytag repairman, the
Mayumi Moriyama (Jap. pol.)
Mazandarani (lang.)
Mazar-i-Sharif, Afghanistan
Mazarin Bible (also Gutenberg Bible)
Mazarin, Jules (b. Giulo Mazarini)(Fr. rel./pol.; 1602-61)
Mazatlán, Mexico
Mazda (auto.)
Mazda 626 (auto.)
Mazda 626 DX (auto.)
Mazda 626 ES (auto.)
Mazda 626 LX (auto.)
Mazda 626 sedan (auto.)
Mazda B-series pickup (auto.)
Mazda B2500 pickup (auto.)
Mazda B3000 pickup (auto.)

Mazda B4000 pickup (auto.)
Mazda Miata (auto.)
Mazda Miata LS (auto.)
Mazda Miata M-Edition (auto.)
Mazda Miata SE (auto.)
Mazda Millenia (auto.)
Mazda Millenia L (auto.)
Mazda Millenia S (auto.)
Mazda Motors of America, Inc.
Mazda MPV DX minivan (auto.)
Mazda MPV ES minivan (auto.)
Mazda MPV LX minivan (auto.)
Mazda MPV minivan (auto.)
Mazda MX-5 Miata (auto.)
Mazda MX-6 (auto.)
Mazda MX-6 LS (auto.)
Mazda MX-6 M-Edition (auto.)
Mazda North American Operations (auto.)
Mazda Protege (auto.)
Mazda Protege DX (auto.)
Mazda Protege ES (auto.)
Mazda Protege LX (auto.)
Mazda Tribute (auto.
Mazda Tribute DX (auto.)
Mazda Tribute ES (auto.)
Mazda Tribute LX (auto.)
Mazdaism (also Zoroastrianism)(rel.)
Mazola (margarine/oil)
Mazowiecki, Tadeusz (ex-PM, Pol.; 1927-)
Mazursky, Paul (ent.; 1930-)
Mazzini, Giussepe (It. reformer; 1805-72)
MB (also mb)(megabyte)
MBA (Master of Business Administration)
Mba, Casimir Oye- (ex-PM, Gabon)
Mbabane, Swaziland
Mbala, Zambia
Mbale, Uganda
Mbandaka, Zaire
Mbasogo, Teodoro Obiang Nguema (pres., Equatorial Guinea; 1942-)
Mbeki, Thabo (pres. SAfr; 1942-)
Mbilini, Prince (ex-PM, Swaziland)
Mbini, Equatorial Guinea
Mboya, Tom (Kenyan pol.; 1930-69)
Mbundu (lang.)
MC (master of ceremonies, Marine Corps, Medical Corps)
McAdam, John Loudon (Scot. eng.; 1756-1836)
McAdoo, Bob (basketball; 1951-)
McAleese, Mary (pres., Ir.; 1951-)
McAllen, TX
McAn Shoe Co., Thom
McArdle, Andrea (ent.; 1963-)
McAuliffe, (Sharon) Christa (nee Corrigan)(US educ., Challenger; 1948-1986)
McAuliffe, Terry (US finan./pol.; 1957?-)
McBeal, Ally (TV show)
McBride, Martina (ent.; 1966-)
McBride, Patricia (ballet; 1942-)
McCabe & Mrs. Miller (film, 1971)
McCain, John Stuart (US cong.; 1936-)
McCall Pattern Co.
McCall's (mag.)
McCall's Crochet Patterns (mag.)
McCall's Needlework (mag.)

McCallum, David (ent.; 1933-)
McCambridge, Mercedes (ent.; 1918-)
McCardle, Ex parte (US law; 1869)
McCarran International Airport (Las Vegas NV)
McCarthy, Andrew (ent.; 1962-)
McCarthy, Eugene (Joseph)(US pol.; 1916-)
McCarthy, Joe (Joseph Vincent)(baseball; 1887-1978)
McCarthy, Joseph R(aymond)(US pol.; 1908-57)
McCarthy, Kevin (ent.; 1914-)
McCarthy, Mary (Therese)(US writer; 1912-89)
McCarthyism (US hist.)
McCartney, Linda Eastman (US photo./ent.; 1941-98)
McCartney, (James) Paul (ent.; 1942-)
McCartney, Stella (Br. designer; 1971-)
McCarver, Tim (ent.; 1941-)
McCauley, Mary (Ludwig Hays)("Molly Pitcher") (US heroine; 1754-1832)
McChord Air Force Base, WA
McClanahan, Rue (Eddi-Rue)(ent.; 1935-)
McClellan Air Force Base, CA
McClellan, Fort, AL (mil.)
McClellan, George B(rinton)(US gen.; 1826-85)
McClendon, Sarah (US jour.; 1910-)
McClintock, Barbara (US geneticist; 1902-92)
McClinton, Delbert (ent./songwriter; 1940-)
McCloskey, Frank (US cong.; 1939-)
McCloy, John J. (US atty./banker; 1895-1989)
McClure, Doug (ent.; 1935-95)
McClure, (Sir) Robert John le Mesurier (Br. expl.; 1807-73)
McClurg, Edie (ent.; 1951-)
McConaughey, Matthew (ent.; 1969-)
McConnell Air Force Base, KS
McConnell, Mitch (US cong.; 1942-)
McCoo, Marilyn (ent.; 1943-)
McCormack, John (Ir./US tenor; 1884-1945)
McCormack, John W(illiam)(US pol.; 1891-1980)
McCormick & Co., Inc.
McCormick (spices)
McCormick harvester
McCormick, Cyrus (Hall)(US inv.; 1809-84)
McCourt, Frank (US writer; 1930-)
McCovey, Willie (baseball; 1938-)
McCoy Feud, Hatfield- (opposite sides, Amer. Civil War)
McCoy Tyner (US jazz; 1938-)
McCoy, Fort (WI)
McCracken, James (dramatic tenor; 1926-88)
McCrea, Joel (ent.; 1905-90)
McCullers, Carson (Smith)(US writer; 1917-67)
McCulloch vs. Maryland (US law; 1819)
McCullough, Colleen (Austl. writer/ neuroscientist; 1937-)
McCurry, Mike (Michael Demaree)(US ex-White House press secy.; 1954-)
McD.L.T (McDonald's)
McDaniel, Hattie (ent.; 1895-1952)
McDermott, Dylan (ent.; 1961-)
McDivitt, James A(lton)(astro.; 1929-)
McDonald House, Ronald
McDonald, Lanny (hockey; 1953-)
McDonald, Ronald (fict. chara.)
McDonald's Corp.

McDonaldland cookies
McDonnell Douglas Corp.
McDormand, Frances (ent.; 1957-)
McDougal, James (Whitewater; 1940-98)
McDougal, Susan (Whitewater)
McDowall, Roddy (ent.; 1928-98)
McDowell, Edward (US comp.; 1861-1908)
McDowell, Jack (baseball; 1966-)
McDowell, Malcolm (ent.; 1943-)
McDuck, Scrooge (cartoon chara.)
McEnroe, John (Patrick)(tennis; 1959-)
McEntire, Reba (ent.; 1954-)
McFadden, Gates (ent.; 1949-)
McFarland, Spanky (George)(ent.; 1928-93)
McFerrin, Bobby (ent.; 1950-)
McGavin, Darren (ent.; 1922-)
McGee and Molly, Fibber (radio comedy)
McGee Corp., Kerr-
McGeorge Bundy (US educ.; 1919-96)
McGill University (Quebec, Can.)
McGill, James (Can. trader/finan.; 1744-1813)
McGillicuddy, Cornelius (aka Connie Mack) (baseball; 1862-1956)
McGillis, Kelly (ent.; 1957-)
McGinley, Phyllis (US poet/writer; 1905-78)
McGoohan, Patrick (ent.; 1928-)
McGovern, Elizabeth (ent.; 1961-)
McGovern, George S(tanley)(US pol.; 1922-)
McGovern, Maureen (ent.; 1949-)
McGowan, William G. (US bus.; 1928-92)
McGraw, Charles (ent.; 1914-80)
McGraw, John (Joseph)(baseball; 1873-1934)
McGraw, Quick Draw (fict. chara.)
McGraw, Tim (ent.; 1966-)
McGraw-Edison Co.
McGraw-Hill Book Co.
McGregor, Ewan (ent.; 1971-)
McGrew, The Shooting of Dan (R.W. Service ballad)
McGriff, Fred (baseball; 1963-)
McGuane, Thomas (US writer; 1939-)
McGuffey, William H(olmes)(US educ.; 1800-73)
McGuinn, Roger "Jim" (ent.; 1942-)
McGuire Air Force Base, NJ
McGuire Sisters, The (pop music)
McGuire, Al (ent.; 1931-)
McGuire, Dorothy (ent.; 1919-)
McGwire, Mark (baseball; 1963-)
McHale's Navy (TV show)
M. C. Hammer (b. Stanley Kirk Burrell)(ent.; 1962-)
McHenry, Fort (MD)(*Star Spangled Banner*)
McHugh, Jimmy (US comp.; 1894-1969)
MCI Communications Corp.
McIlhenny Co.
McIlhenny Tabasco sauce
McInerney, Jay (US writer; 1955-)
McIntire, John (ent.; 1907-91)
McIntosh (apple)
McIntyre, Joe (ent.; 1972-)
McKay, Jim (sportscaster; 1921-)
McKechnie, Donna (ent.; 1942-)
McKee, Lonette (ent.; 1957-)
McKeesport, PA
McKellen, Ian (ent.; 1939-)

McKernan, John R(ettie), Jr. (ex-ME gov.; 1948-)
McKesson HBOC, Inc.
McKim, Charles F(ollen)(US arch.; 1847-1909)
McKim, Charles M. (US arch.; 1920-)
McKinley National Park, Mount (now Denali National Park)(AK)
McKinley, Mount (also Denali)(AK)
McKinley, William (25th US pres.; 1843-1901)
McKinney, Helling v. (US law; 1993)
McKuen, Rod (US writer/comp.; 1933-)
McLachlan, Sarah (ent.; 1968-)
McLaglen, Victor (ent.; 1907-71)
McLain, Dennis (baseball; 1944-)
McLarty, Mack (Thomas Franklin, III)(US ex-White House chief of staff; 1946-)
McLaughlin Group (TV show)
McLaughlin, John (ent.; 1942-)
McLaughlin's One on One (TV show)
McLean Stevenson (ent.; 1929-96)
McLean, A(lexander) J(ames)(ent., Backstreet Boys; 1978-)
McLean, Don (ent./songwriter; 1945-)
McLean, John (US jurist; 1785-1861)
McLintock! (film, 1963)
McLuhan, (Herbert) Marshall (Can. educ./writer; 1911-80)
McMahon, Ed (ent.; 1923-)
McManus, George (US cartoonist, *Bringing Up Father*; 1884-1954)
McMillan Book Co., Inc.
McMillan, Kathy Laverne (track; 1957-)
McMurtry, Larry (Jeff)(US writer; 1936-)
McNair, Fort Lesley J., DC (mil.)
McNally World Atlas, Rand
McNamara, Robert (Strange)(US bus./pol.; 1916-)
McNamara, Tank (cartoon chara,)
McNichol, Kristy (ent.; 1962-)
McPartland, Jimmy (US jazz; 1907-91)
McPartland, Marian (US jazz; 1920-)
McPeak, Merrill A. (US mil./pol.; 1936-)
McPhatter, Clyde (ent.; 1932-72)
McPherson, Aimee Semple (US rel.; 1890-1944)
McPherson, Fort, GA (mil.)
McQueen, Butterfly (ent.; 1911-95)
McQueen, (Terrence) Steve(n)(ent.; 1930-80)
McRae, Carmen (ent.; 1920-94)
McRaney, Gerald (ent.; 1948-)
MCRI (Master Certified Reporting Instructor)
McTeer, Janet (ent.; 1961-)
McVeigh, Timothy (James)(Oklahoma City bomber; 1968-2001)
McWethy, John F. (TV jour.)
McWherter, Ned R(ay)(ex-TN gov.; 1930-)
MD (Maryland, Medicinae Doctor [Doctor of Medicine])
MD Magazine
ME (Maine)
Me and My Gal (play)
Me Decade (sociol.)
Mead & Co., Inc., Dodd
Mead (paper prods.)
Mead Corp., The
Mead Data General (compu. databases)
Mead Johnson & Co.

Mead Johnson Nutritionals (US bus.)
Mead Johnson Pharmaceuticals (US bus.)
Mead, Lake (Hoover Dam, AZ/NV)
Mead, Margaret (US anthrop.; 1901-78)
Meade, Fort (MD)
Meade, George (Gordon)(US gen.; 1815-72)
Meade, George H. (US phil.; 1863-1931)
Meadows, Audrey (ent.; 1924-96)
Meadows, Jayne (b. Jayne Cotter)(ent.; 1920-)
Mean (Joe) Greene (football; 1946-)
Meaney, Colm (ent.; 1953-)
Means grass (also Johnson grass, Aleppo grass)
Meany, George (US labor leader; 1894-1980)
Meara, Anne (ent.; 1929-)
Meat Loaf (b. Marvin Lee Aday)(ent.; 1951-)
Meath (county, Ir.)
Mebaral (med.)
Mecca, Saudi Arabia
Mecham, Evan (ex-AZ gov.; 1924-)
Mechanix Illustrated (mag.)
Mechlin (lace)
Meciar, Vladimir (ex-pres., Slovakia; 1942-)
Mecklenburg-Western Pomerania (state, Ger.)
Meclomen (med.)
Med Tamoxifen (med.)
Medal of Honor (also Congressional Medal of Honor)(mil.)
Medan, Indonesia
Medea (myth.)
Medellín cartel
Medellín, Colombia
Medfly (Mediterranean fruit fly)(also l.c.)
Medford, MA, OR
Medgar Wiley Evers (US reformer/NAACP; 1925-63)
Media General, Inc.
Medicaid (govt. health insurance)(also l.c.)
Medicare (govt. health insurance)(also l.c.)
Medici Chapel (also New Sacristy)(Florence, It.)
Medici collar (clothing)
Medici family (Florence, It.; 1434-1737)
Medici, Catherine de' (queen, Fr./wife of Henry II; 1518-89)
Medici, Cosimo de' (It. pol.; 1389-1464)
Medici, Lorenzo de' ("the Magnificent")(It. pol./poet; 1449-92)
Medici, Marie de' (queen, Fr./wife of Henry IV; 1573-1642)
Medici, Piero de' (It. pol.; 1416-69)
Medici I, Cosimo de' (It., Duke of Florence; 1519-74)
Medicine Hat, Alberta, Canada
Medicine, Doctor of (also M.D., Medicinae Doctor)
Medicine, Nobel Prize for Physiology or
Medihaler-Iso (med.)
Medina, Saudi Arabia
Medipren (med.)
Medis (compu. database, med.)
Mediterranean fruit fly (also Medfly, medfly)
Mediterranean Sea (between Eur./Afr./Asia)
Médoc (Fr. wine district)
Medrol (med.)
Medtronic, Inc.
Medusa (myth.)

Medvedev, Vadim (Rus. pol.)
Meeker, Ralph (ent.; 1920-88)
Meese, Edwin, III (US pol./ex-atty. gen.; 1931-)
Meet the Press (TV show)
Meg Foster (ent.; 1948-)
Meg Ryan (b. Margaret Hyra)(ent.; 1963-)
Meg Tilly (ent.; 1960-)
Meg (Margaret C.) Whitman (US bus./eBay;
     1957-)
Megace (med.)
Meghalaya (state, India)
Mehemet Ali (also Muhammad Ali)(Eg. pol./
     mil.; 1769-1849)
Mehmed Emin Ali Pasha (Turk. leader; 1815-71)
Mehta, Zubin (India, cond.; 1936-)
Mei Xiang (panda)
Meier, Richard (US arch.; 1934-)
Meiji, Mutsuhito (Jap. emp.; 1852-1912)
Meiklejohn, Alexander (US educ.; 1872-1964)
Mein Kampf (Hitler's book/phil.)
Meineke Discount Muffler Shops, Inc.
Meir, Golda (also Goldie Mabovitch, Goldie
     Myerson)(ex-PM, Isr.; 1898-1978)
Meir (or Martin) Kahan (Jew. activist; 1932-90)
Meissen porcelain (also called Dresden china/
     porcelain/ware)
Meissen, Germany
Meister Braü (beer)
Meister Braü, Inc.
Meistersinger (Ger. minstrels; 14th-16th c.)
Meithei (lang.)
Mejdani, Rexhep (pres., Albania; 1944-)
Mejía Domínguez, Hipólita (pres., 1941-)
Mekere Morauta, (Sir)(PM, Papua New Guinea;
     1946-)
Meknès, Morocco
Mekong Delta, Vietnam
Mekong River (SE Asia)
Meksi, Alexander (Gabriel)(ex-PM, Albania; 1939-)
Mel Allen (b. Melvin Israel)(US sportscaster;
     1913-96)
Mel Blanc (ent.; 1908-89)
Mel Brooks (b. Melvin Kaminsky)(ent.; 1926-)
Mel(vin)(Eugene) Carnahan (US ex-cong./MO
     gov.; 1934-2000)
Mel Ferrer (ent.; 1917-)
Mel Fisher (maritime treasure hunter; 1922-98)
Mel Gibson (ent.; 1956-)
Mel Lewis (US jazz; 1929-90)
Mel(quiades)(Rafael) Martinez (US secy./HUD;
     1946-)
Mel Ott (baseball; 1909-58)
Mel Tillis (ent.; 1932-)
Mel Torme (ent.; 1925-99)
Melaka (also Malacca)(state, Malaysia)
Melanchthon (b. Philipp Schwarzert)(Ger. rel.;
     1497-1560)
Melanesia (islands, SW Pac.)
Melanesian (lang./people)
Melanesian-Polynesian (people)
Melanie Brown (aka Scary Spice)(ent.; 1975-)
Melanie Chisholm (aka Sporty Spice)(ent.; 1974-)
Melanie Griffith (ent.; 1957-)
Melanie Klein (Aus. psych.; 1882-1960)
Melanie Mayron (ent.; 1952-)

Melba Moore (b. Beatrice Hill)(ent.; 1945-)
Melba toast
Melba, Nellie, Dame (aka Helen Porter Mitchell)
     (Austl. opera; 1861-1931)
Melba, peach (also l.c.)
Melbourne Today (FL newspaper)
Melbourne, Australia
Melbourne, FL
Melcher, Terry (ent.; 1942-)
Melchior (1 of Magi)
Melchior Ndadaye (ex-pres., Burundi; ?-1994)
Melchior, Lauritz (ent.; 1890-1973)
Melchite (rel.)
Meles Zenawi (PM., Ethiopia; 1955-)
Melina Kanakaredes (ent.; 1967-)
Melina Mercouri (Gr. ent.; 1925-1994)
Melior (type style)
Melissa Etheridge (ent.; 1961-)
Melissa Gilbert (ent.; 1964-)
Melissa Joan Hart (ent.; 1976-)
Melissa Manchester (ent.; 1951-)
Melissa Sue Anderson (ent.; 1962-)
Melitta (coffeemaker)
Melitta USA, Inc.
Mell Lazarus (cartoonist, *Momma, Miss Peach*;
     1929-)
Mellaril (med.)
Mellencamp, John Cougar (ent.; 1951-)
Mello, Fernando Collor de (ex-pres., Brazil;
     1949-)
Mellon University, Carnegie- (Pittsburgh, PA)
Mellon, Andrew William (US finan./bus.; 1855-
     1937)
Mellon, Paul (US philanthropist; 1907-99)
Melpomene (myth., muse)
Melrose Avenue (Los Angeles)
Melrose Place (TV show)
Melrose, FL, MA
Melrose, Scotland
Melvil Dewey (US librarian; 1851-1931)
Melville Corp.
Melville Weston Fuller (US jurist; 1833-1910)
Melville, Herman (US writer; 1819-91)
Melvin and Howard (film, 1980)
Melvin (Mouron) Belli (US atty.; 1907-96)
Melvin Calvin (US chem.; 1911-97)
Melvin Laird (ex-US secy. of defense; 1922-)
Melvin Van Peebles (US playwright; 1932-)
Melvyn Douglas (ent.; 1901-81)
Memnoch the Devil (A. Rice novel)
Memnon (myth.)
Memnon, Colossus of (ancient Eg. statue)
Memorial Day (formerly Decoration Day)(last
     Monday in May)
Memorial Stadium (Baltimore, MD)
Memphis (city, ancient Egypt)
Memphis Commercial Appeal (TN newspaper)
Memphis Maniax (football team)
Memphis, TN
Men's Fitness (mag.)
Men's Health (mag.)
Men's Journal (mag.)
Mena Suvari (ent.; 1979-)
Menace, Dennis the (comic strip)
Menachem Begin (ex-PM, Isr.; 1913-92)

Menander (Gr. writer; 342-191 BC)
Mencius (also Mengtzu, Mengtse)(Ch. phil.;
  372?-289 BC)
Mencken, H(enry) L(ouis)(US writer/editor;
  1880-1956)
Mende (lang./people)
Mendel, Gregor J(ohann)(Aus. biol.; 1822-84)
Mendel's law (also Mendelism)(genetics)
Mendeleyev, Dmitri Ivanovich (Rus. chem.,
  periodic law; 1834-1907)
Mendelism (also Mendel's law)(genetics)
Mendelssohn (-Bartholdy), (Jakob Ludwig) Felix
  (Ger. comp.; 1809-47)
Mendes, Chico (Filho Francisco)(Brazilian
  environ./labor leader; 1944-88)
Mendes, Sergio (ent.; 1941-)
Mendoza, Argentina
Menelaus, King (myth.)
Menem, Carlos (Saul)(ex-pres., Argentina;
  1935-)
Menendez, Erik (US news, killed parents)
Menendez, Lyle (US news, killed parents)
Menest (med.)
Mengele, Dr. Josef ("angel of death")(Ger.
  Nazi; ?-1979?)
Mengistu, Haile Mariam (ex-pres., Ethiopia;
  1937-)
Mengtse (also Mencius, Mengtzu)(Ch. phil.;
  372?-289 BC)
Meniere's disease/syndrome (med.)
Menjou, Adolphe (ent.; 1890-1963)
Menken, Alan (US comp.; 1949-)
Menlo Park, CA, NJ
Mennen Co., The
Mennin, Peter (b. Peter Mennini)(US comp.;
  1923-83)
Menninger Clinic (psych.)(Topeka, KS)
Menninger Foundation for Psychiatric Education
  and Research
Menninger, Charles Frederick (US psych.;
  1862-1953)
Menninger, Karl A(ugustus)(US psych.; 1893-
  1990)
Menninger, William Claire (US psych.; 1899-
  1966)
Menno Simons (Dutch rel.; c1496-c1561)
Mennonite (rel.)
Mennonite Church
Mennonites (Amish, Dunkers, Plain People)(rel.)
Menorca (or Minorca) Island (Balearic Island,
  Mediterranean)
Menotti, Gian-Carlo (It./US comp.; 1911-)
Mensa (astron., table)
Mensa (high IQ group)
Mensk, Belarus (also Minsk)
Mentadent (med.)
Mentholatum rub (med.)
Mentho-Lyptus, Halls (med.)
Menuhin, (Sir) Yehudi (Br. violinist; 1916-99)
Menzies, Robert Gordon (ex-PM, Austl.; 1894-
  1978)
Meo (people)
Meow Mix (cat food)
Mephistopheles (also Mephisto)(the devil)
Mephyton (med.)

Meprospan (med.)
Mercalli scale (measures intensity of earthquake)
Mercator map projection (also Mercator's
  projection)
Mercator, Geradus (or Gerhardus)(aka Gerhard
  Kremer)(Flem. geographer; 1512-94)
Merce (Mercier Philip) Cunningham (US dancer/
  choreographer; 1919-)
Merced River (CA)
Mercedes-Benz (auto.)
Mercedes-Benz AMG (auto.)
Mercedes-Benz C-class (auto.)
Mercedes-Benz C220 (auto.)
Mercedes-Benz C230 (auto.)
Mercedes-Benz C230 SE (auto.)
Mercedes-Benz C240 (auto.)
Mercedes-Benz C280 (auto.)
Mercedes-Benz C280 SE (auto.)
Mercedes-Benz C36 (auto.)
Mercedes-Benz C320 (auto.)
Mercedes-Benz C43 (auto.)
Mercedes-Benz CL-class (auto.)
Mercedes-Benz CL55 (auto.)
Mercedes-Benz CL500 (auto.)
Mercedes-Benz CL600 (auto.)
Mercedes-Benz CLK-class (auto.)
Mercedes-Benz CLK55 (auto.)
Mercedes-Benz CLK55 AMG (auto.)
Mercedes-Benz CLK320 (auto.)
Mercedes-Benz CLK430 (auto.)
Mercedes-Benz E-class (auto.)
Mercedes-Benz E300 (auto.)
Mercedes-Benz E300D (auto.)
Mercedes-Benz E300TD (auto.)
Mercedes-Benz E320 (auto.)
Mercedes-Benz 400E (auto.)
Mercedes-Benz E420 (auto.)
Mercedes-Benz E430 (auto.)
Mercedes-Benz E55 (auto.)
Mercedes-Benz E55 AMG (auto.)
Mercedes-Benz E500 (auto.)
Mercedes-Benz Geländewagen (auto.)
Mercedes-Benz Geländewagen G500 (auto.)
Mercedes-Benz Geländewagen G500 Cabriolet
  (auto.)
Mercedes-Benz M-class (auto.)
Mercedes-Benz ML320 (auto.)
Mercedes-Benz ML430 (auto.)
Mercedes-Benz ML55 (auto.)
Mercedes-Benz ML55 AMG (auto.)
Mercedes-Benz of North America, Inc.
Mercedes-Benz S-class (auto.)
Mercedes-Benz S320 (auto.)
Mercedes-Benz S350 (auto.)
Mercedes-Benz S420 (auto.)
Mercedes-Benz S430 (auto.)
Mercedes-Benz S55 (auto.)
Mercedes-Benz S55 AMG (auto.)
Mercedes-Benz S500 (auto.)
Mercedes-Benz S600 (auto.)
Mercedes-Benz SL-class (auto.)
Mercedes-Benz SL320 (auto.)
Mercedes-Benz SL500 (auto.)
Mercedes-Benz SL600 (auto.)
Mercedes-Benz SLK-class (auto.)

Mercedes-Benz SLK230 (auto.)
Mercedes-Benz SLK320 (auto.)
Mercedes-Benz USA, LLC (US bus.)
Mercedes McCambridge (ent.; 1918-)
Mercedes Ruehl (ent.; 1948-)
Mercer, Johnny (US lyricist; 1909-76)
Mercer, Mabel (ent.; 1900-84)
Mercer, Marian (ent.; 1935-)
Merchant Marine Academy, U.S. (Kings Point, NY)
Merchant Marine, U.S. (US bus./mil.)
Merchant, Ismail (b. Ismail Noormohamed Abdul Rehman)(ent.; 1936-)
Merchant, Natalie (ent.; 1963-)
Merck & Co., Inc.
Merck Manual, The (med. text)
Merckx, Eddie ("the Cannibal")(Belgian cyclist; 1945-)
Mercouri, Melina (Gr. ent.; 1925-1994)
Mercurochrome (med.)
Mercury (auto.)
Mercury (planet; myth.)
Mercury (US crewed space flights)
Mercury-Atlas (US crewed space flights)
Mercury Cougar (auto.)
Mercury Cougar S (auto.)
Mercury Cougar XR7 (auto.)
Mercury Grand Marquis (auto.)
Mercury Grand Marquis GS (auto.)
Mercury Grand Marquis LS (auto.)
Mercury Mountaineer (auto.)
Mercury Mystique (auto.)
Mercury Mystique GS (auto.)
Mercury Mystique LS (auto.)
Mercury-News, San Jose (CA newspaper)
Mercury-Redstone (US crewed space flights)
Mercury-Redstone 3 (also Liberty Bell 7)(1st US crewed space flight; May 5, 1961)
Mercury Sable (auto.)
Mercury Sable G (auto.)
Mercury Sable GS (auto.)
Mercury Sable LS (auto.)
Mercury Topaz (auto.)
Mercury Tracer (auto.)
Mercury Tracer GS (auto.)
Mercury Tracer LS (auto.)
Mercury Villager Estate minivan (auto.)
Mercury Villager GS minivan (auto.)
Mercury Villager LS minivan (auto.)
Mercury Villager minivan (auto.)
Mercury Villager Sport minivan (auto.)
Mercury Villager Van Nautica minivan (auto.)
Mercury Villager, Ford (auto.)
Mercury, Freddie (b. Farookh Bulsara)(ent.; 1946-91)
Mercy College (Dobbs Ferry, NY)
Meredith Baxter (ent.; 1947-)
Meredith Corp.
Meredith Monk (comp./choreographer/ent.; 1942-)
Meredith Willson (US comp.; 1902-84)
Meredith, Burgess (ent.; 1908-97)
Meredith, George (Br. writer; 1828-1909)
Meredith, James (US writer/civil rights leader; 1923-)

Mergenthaler, Ottmar (Ger./US inv.; 1854-99)
Meri, Lennart (pres., Estonia; 1929-)
Mérida, Mexico
Meriden, CT
Meridia (med.)
Meridian Naval Air Station (MS)
Meridian, MS
Mérimée, Prosper (Fr. writer; 1803-70)
Merina (people)
Merino (sheep)
Merino, José Francisco (El Salvador, pol.)
Merit, Legion of (US)
Meriwether Lewis (US expl.; 1774-1809)
Merkel, Una (ent.; 1903-86)
Merle Haggard (ent.; 1937-)
Merle Norman Cosmetics (US bus.)
Merle Norman Cosmetic Studios (US bus.)
Merle Oberon (ent.; 1911-79)
Merle Travis (ent.; 1917-83)
Merlin (legendary magician)
Merlin (Jay) Olsen (football/ent.; 1940-)
Merlot (grape)
Mermaid, The Little (film, 1978, 1984, 1989)
Merman, Ethel (ent.; 1908-84)
Merovingian dynasty (Fr.; 481-751)
Merriam-Webster, Inc.
Merriam-Webster's Collegiate Dictionary
Merriam-Webster's Dictionary
Merrick, David (ent.; 1912-2000)
Merrie Melodies (cartoon)
Merrie Olde England
Merrill A. McPeak (US mil./pol.; 1936-)
Merrill & Lynch (finan.)
Merrill Lynch & Co., Inc.
Merrill Lynch, Pierce, Fenner & Smith Inc.
Merrill, Bob (US lyricist; 1921-98)
Merrill, Charles E. (US finan.; 1885-1956)
Merrill, Dina (b. Nedinia Hutton)(ent.; 1925-)
Merrill, Janice (track; 1962-)
Merrill, Robert (b. Moishe Miller)(ent.; 1919-)
Merrill, Steve (Stephen)(ex-NH gov.; 1946-)
Merrimack v. Monitor (US hist.; 1862)
Merry Andrew (slang, adv. chara.)
Merryman, Ex parte (US law; 1861)
Mersey beat (pop music; mid-1960s)
Mersey River (Eng.)
Merseyside (county, Eng.)
Merthiolate (med.)
Merton, Thomas (US rel.; 1915-68)
Meru (lang.)
Merv Griffin (ent.; 1925-)
Mervyn LeRoy (ent.; 1900-87)
Merwyn Bogue (aka Ish Kabibble)(ent.; 1908-94)
Mervyn's department store
Meryl Streep (ent.; 1949-)
Mesa Verde National Park (prehistoric ruins)(CO)
Mesa, AZ
Mesantoin (med.)
Mesic, Stipe (or Stjephan)(pres., Croatia; 1934-)
Mesmer, Friedrich Anton (or Franz)(Ger. phys.; 1734-1815)
Mesolithic period (Middle Stone Age; 15,000 to 10,000 years ago)
Mesopotamia (ancient civilization, SW Asia)

Mesozoic era (225-65 million years ago)
Mesquite, TX
Messalina, Valeria (Roman empress; c22-48)
Messenia (ancient region, Gr.)
Messerschmitt plane (Ger. fighter aircraft, WWII)
Messerschmitt, Willy (Wilhelm)(Ger. airplane
    designer; 1898-1978)
Messiah (by Handel)
Messiah (rel. savior, Jesus)
Messick, Dale (cartoonist, *Brenda Starr*; 1906-)
Messier catalog/number/object (astron.)
Messier, Charles (Fr. astron.; 1730-1817)
Messier, Mark (hockey; 1961-)
Messina, Italy
Messina, Jim (ent.; 1947-)
Messina, Loggins & (pop music)
Messina, Strait of (channel, Mediterranean)
Messing, Debra (ent.; 1968-)
Mesta, Perle (US dipl.; 1889-1975)
Meta, Ilir (PM, Albania; 1969-)
Metacomet (aka King Philip)(Wampanoag
    Indian chief; 1640-76)
Metalious, Grace (b. Marie Grace
    DeRepentigny)(US writer; 1924-64)
Metallica (pop music)
Metamorphosis, The (Kafka)
Metamucil (med.)
Metaprel (med.)
Metcalf, Laurie (ent.; 1955-)
Methedrine (med.)
Metheny, Pat(rick Bruce)(ent.; 1954-)
Methergine (med.)
Method (style of acting)
Methodism (rel.)
Methodist (rel.)
Methodist Church (rel.)
Methodist University, Southern (SMU)(Dallas,
    TX)
Methuselah (rel.; said to have lived 969 years)
Metis (myth.)
Metonic cycle (astron.)
Metrazol
Metro-Goldwyn-Mayer (MGM)
Metro, Geo (Chevrolet)(auto.)
Metrodome Stadium (Minneapolis, MN)
Metropolitan Community Church (rel.)
Metropolitan Home (mag.)
Metropolitan Life Insurance Co.
Metropolitan Museum of Art (NYC)
Metropolitan Opera Co.
Mets, New York (baseball team)
Metternich, Age of
Metternich, Clemens W(enzel) L(othar), Prince
    von (ex-chanc., Aus.; 1773-1859)
Metzenbaum, Howard M(orton)(US pol.; 1917-)
Meursault wine
Meuse River (Eur.)
Mevacor (med.)
Mex, Tex- (lang., culture/food/music)
Mexicali, Mexico
Mexican bamboo (also Japanese knotweed)(plant)
Mexican bean beetle
Mexican coffee (mixed drink)
Mexican fruit fly/fruitfly
Mexican hairless (dog)

Mexican hat dance
Mexican stand-off
Mexican War (US/Mex.; 1846-48)
Mexicana Airlines (airline)
Mexico (United Mexican States)(CAmer.)
Mexico City, Mexico
Mexico, Gulf of (US/Mex.)
Mexitil (med.)
MexSp (abbrev. of Mexican-Spanish)
Meyer A(nselm) Rothschild (Ger. finan.; 1744-
    1812)
Meyer Guggenheim (US finan./bus.; 1828-1905)
Meyer Schapiro (US art hist.; 1904-96)
Meyer, Deborah (swimming; 1952-)
Meyer, Joseph (US comp.; 1894-1987)
Meyerbeer, Giacomo (b. Jakob Liebmann Beer)
    (Ger. comp.; 1791-1864)
MFA (Master of Fine Arts)
M-14 (automatic rifle)
Mfume, Kweisi (b. Frizzell Gray)(US pol./NAACP
    leader; 1948-)
Mg (chem. sym., magnesium)
MGM (Metro-Goldwyn-Mayer)
MGM Grand Hotel (Las Vegas)
MGM Records (US bus.)
MGM/UA (US bus.)
M. Grumbacher, Inc.
MGs, Booker T and the (pop music)
MH (Medal of Honor)
M. H. de Young Memorial Museum (San
    Francisco)
MI (Michigan, military intelligence)
MIA (also M.I.A.)(missing in action)
Mia Farrow (ent.; 1945-)
Miami (Native Amer.)
Miami Beach, FL
Miami Dolphins (football team)
Miami Heat (basketball team)
Miami Herald (FL newspaper)
Miami International Airport (FL)
Miami Sound Machine (pop music)
Miami University (Oxford, OH)
Miami Vice (TV show)
Miami, FL
Miao (lang.)
Miata, Mazda (auto.)
Micah (rel., book of the Old Testament)
Micatin (med.)
Michael (William) Balfe (Ir. comp./ent.; 1808-
    70)
Michael B. Enzi (US cong.; 1944-)
Michael Burton (swimming; 1947-)
Michael Caine (b. Maurice Joseph Micklewhite,
    Jr.)(ent.; 1933-)
Michael Chang (tennis; 1972-)
Michael Cimino (US ent.; 1943-)
Michael Clarke Duncan (ent.; 1957-)
Michael Collins (astro.; 1930-)
Michael Connelly (US writer; 1956-)
Michael Constantine (b. Constantine Joanides)
    (ent.; 1927-)
Michael Crichton (US writer; 1942-)
Michael Donald Gallagher (skiing; 1941-)
Michael Dorn (ent.; 1952-)
Michael Douglas (ent.; 1944-)

© 2001 *StenEd*® **Proper Noun Speller**

Michael E. Knight (ent.; 1959-)
Michael Eisner (US bus.; 1942-)
Michael Ellis DeBakey (US phys.; 1908-)
Michael Faraday (Br. chem./physt.; 1791-1867)
Michael Flatley (dance; 1958-)
Michael (or Mikhail) Fyodorovich Romanov
    (emp., Rus.; 1596-1645)
Michael Gross (ent.; 1947-)
Michael Hardie Boys, (Sir)(gov.-gen.,
    NewZeal.; 1931-)
Michael Harrington (US reformer/writer; 1928-
    89)
Michael (Dale) "Mike" Huckabee (AR gov.; 1955-)
Michael Jackson (ent.; 1958-)
Michael "Mick" (Phillip) Jagger (ent.; 1943-)
Michael J. Fox (ent.; 1961-)
Michael John "Mike" Sullivan (ex-WY gov.; 1939-)
Michael "Mike" Jordan (basketball/baseball;
    1963-)
Michael J. Pollard (ent.; 1939-)
Michael "Mickey" Kantor (US ex-secy./
    commerce; 1939-)
Michael Keaton (b. Michael Douglas)(ent.; 1951-)
Michael Kidd (b. Milton Greenwald)(US
    choreographer; 1919-)
Michael Landon (ent.; 1936-91)
Michael Learned (ent.; 1939-)
Michael (Okerlund) "Mike" Leavitt (UT gov.;
    1951-)
Michael (Edwards) "Mike" Lowry (ex-WA gov.;
    1939-)
Michael (Norman) Manley (ex-PM, Jamaica;
    1924-97)
Michael (Demaree) "Mike" McCurry (US ex-
    White House press secy.; 1954-)
Michael Milken (US finan., stock fraud; 1946-)
Michael Moriarty (ent.; 1941-)
Michael Murphy (ent.; 1938-)
Michael O. "Mike" Johanns (NE gov.; 1950-)
Michael Ovitz (ent.; 1946-)
Michael Palin (ent.; 1943-)
Michael (Scudamore) Redgrave, (Sir)(ent.;
    1908-85)
Michael Rennie (ent.; 1909-71)
Michael Richards (ent.; 1949-)
Michael Sarrazin (ent.; 1940-)
Michael S(tanley) Dukakis (ex-MA gov.; 1933-)
Michael Somes (ballet; 1917-94)
Michael Spinks (boxing; 1956-)
Michael Stipe (ent., R.E.M.; 1960-)
Michael Tilson Thomas (cond.; 1944-)
Michael (Kemp) Tippett, (Sir)(Br. comp.; 1905-
    98)
Michael Todd (ent.; 1909-58)
Michael Tucker (ent.; 1944-)
Michael Wigglesworth (US rel./writer; 1631-1705)
Michael Wilding (ent.; 1912-79)
Michael William Balfe (Ir. comp./singer; 1808-
    70)
Michael York (ent.; 1942-)
Michael, George (b. Georgios Kyriacou
    Panayiotou)(ent.; 1963-)
Michaelmas Day (rel.; Sept. 29)
Michaels, Al (ent.; 1944-)
Michaels, Lorne (ent.; 1944-)

Michal Kovac (ex-pres., Slovakia; 1930-)
Michel (Eyquem) de Montaigne (Fr. writer;
    1533-92)
Michel Fokine (Rus. ballet/choreographer;
    1880-1942)
Michel Ney (Fr. mil.; 1769-1815)
Michel, Robert H(enry)(US pol.; 1923-)
Michelangelo Antonioni (ent.; 1912-)
Michelangelo Buonarroti (It. artist/poet; 1475-
    1564)
Michelangelo da Caravaggio (It. artist; 1573-
    1610)
Michele Greene (ent.; 1962-)
Michele Lee (ent.; 1942-)
Michelin Man (tire mascot)
Michelin Tire Corp.
Michelle Pfeiffer (ent.; 1957-)
Michelle Phillips (b. Holly Gilliam)(ent.; 1944-)
Michelle Williams (ent.; 1980-)
Michelman, Kate (US reformist/NARAL pres.)
Michelob (beer)
Michelozzo Michelozzi (also Michelozzo di
    Bartolommeo)(It. sculptor/arch.; 1396-1472)
Michelson, Albert A(braham)(US physt.; 1852-
    1931)
Michener, James A(lbert)(US writer; 1907-97)
Michigan (MI)
Michigan City, IN
Michigan, Lake (N central US)
Michikinikwa (aka Chief Little Turtle)(Miami
    Native Amer.; 1752?-1812)
Mick Fleetwood (ent.; 1942-)
Mick (Michael Phillip) Jagger (ent.; 1943-)
Mickelson, George S. (ex-gov., SD; 1941-93)
Mickey (Meyer Harris) Cohen (US gangster;
    1913-76)
Mickey Finn (drugged drink)
Mickey Gilley (ent.; 1936-)
Mickey (Michael) Kantor (US ex-secy./
    commerce; 1939-)
Mickey (Charles) Mantle (baseball; 1931-95)
Mickey Mouse (cartoon chara.)
Mickey Mouse (mag.)
Mickey Mouse Club (TV show)
Mickey Rooney (b. Joseph Yule, Jr.)(ent.; 1920-)
Mickey Rourke (b. Philip Andre Rourke, Jr.)
    (ent.; 1956-)
Mickey Spillane (b. Frank Morrison Spillane)(US
    writer; 1918-)
Mickey (Mary Kathryn) Wright (golf; 1935-)
Micki & Maude (film, 1984)
Mickiewicz, Adam (Pol. poet; 1798-1855)
Micmac (Native Amer.)
Micro Warehouse, Inc.
Micro-K Extencaps (med.)
Micronase (med.)
Micronesia (Federated States of)(islands, W Pac.)
Micronesian (people)
Micronor (med.)
Microscopium (astron., microscope)
Microsoft (compu.)
Microsoft Corp.
Microsoft Excel (compu.)
Microsoft Windows (compu.)
Microsoft Word (compu.)

Microsoft Works (compu.)
Mid Glamorgan (county, Wales)
Midamor (med.)
Midas International Corp.
Midas muffler
Midas touch
Midas, King (myth.)
Mid-Atlantic Ridge (ocean ridge)
Middle Ages (Eur. hist.; 5th-15th c.)
Middle America
Middle American Indians
Middle Atlantic States (US)(also Middle States)
Middle East (Asia/Africa)(also Mideast)
Middle English (lang.; c1050-1550)
Middle French
Middle Greek (also Medieval Greek)
Middle High German
Middle Irish
Middle Kingdom (Eg. hist.; c2040-1670 BC)(Ch.
   term for China until 1912)
Middle Latin (also Medieval Latin)
Middle Low German
Middle Paleolithic period (200,000-40,000 years
   ago)
Middle Path (rel.)
Middle Stone Age (Mesolithic period; 15,000 to
   10,000 years ago)
Middle Way (rel.)
Middle West (also Midwest)(N central US)
Middlesex (county, Eng.)
Middlesex, NJ
Middletown Record (NY newspaper)
Middletown Times Herald (NY newspaper)
Middletown, CT, NY, OH
Midgard serpent (myth.)
Midianites (ancient people)
Midi-Pyrénées (region, Fr.)
Midland, MI, TX
Midler, Bette (ent.; 1945-)
Midnight Cowboy (film, 1969)
Midnight, Captain (cartoon chara.)
Midol (med.)
Midori (liqueur)
Midori Ito (figure skating; 1969-)
Midrash (rel.)
Midsummer Day (also St. John's Day)(June 24)
Midsummer Night's Dream, A (Shakespeare
   play)
Midway Islands (N Pac.)
Midwest (also Middle West)(N central US)
Midwest City, OK
Midwest Express (airline)
Midwest Living (mag.)
Mien (lang.)
Mies van der Rohe, Ludwig (Ger./US arch.;
   1886-1969)
Mifeprex (RU 486, mifepristone)(med.)
Mifflin Co., Houghton
Mifune Toshiro (Jap. actor; 1920-97)
MIG jet fighter (also MiG, Mig)
Mighty Aphrodite (film, 1995)
Mighty Mouse (cartoon)
Miguel A. Pourier (PM, Netherlands Antilles)
Miguel Angel Asturias (Guat. writer/dipl.; 1899-
   1974)

Miguel de Cervantes Saavedra (Sp. writer;
   1547-1616)
Miguel Ferrer (ent.; 1954-)
Miguel José Serra Junípero, Father (Sp. rel.;
   1713-84)
Miguel Trovoada (pres., São Tomé/Príncipe;1936-)
Mihajlovic, Dusan (Serbian pol.)
Mika Waltari (writer; 1903-79)
Mikado, The (Gilbert and Sullivan)
Mikan, George (basketball; 1924-)
Mikasa Co.
Mike Bossy (hockey; 1957-)
Mike Connors (b. Krekor Ohanian)(ent.; 1925-)
Mike Crapo (US cong.; 1951-)
Mike DeWine (US cong.; 1947-)
Mike Ditka (football; 1939-)
Mike Douglas (b. Michael D. Dowd, Jr.)(TV
   jour.; 1925-)
Mike (Michael F.) Easley, Sr. (NC gov.; 1950-)
Mike Espy (US ex-secy./agr.; 1953-)
Mike Farrell (ent.; 1939-)
Mike Figgis (ent./writer/comp.; 1948-)
Mike (Murphy James) Foster, Jr. (LA gov.; 1930-)
Mike Hammer (fict. chara., Mickey Spillane novels)
Mike (Michael Dale) Huckabee (AR gov.; 1955-)
Mike (Michael O.) Johanns (NE gov.; 1950-)
Mike (Michael) Jordan (basketball/baseball;
   1963-)
Mike Judge (ent.; 1962-)
Mike (Michael Okerlund) Leavitt (UT gov.; 1951-)
Mike Leigh (ent./writer; 1943-)
Mike (Michael Edwards) Lowry (ex-WA gov.;
   1939-)
Mike (Michael Demaree) McCurry (US ex-White
   House press secy.; 1954-)
Mike Myers (ent.; 1962-)
Mike Nichols (ent.; 1931-)
Mike Peters (cartoonist, *Mother Goose &
   Grimm*; 1943-)
Mike Powell (track; 1963-)
Mike Royko (US jour.; 1932-97)
Mike Schmidt (baseball; 1949-)
Mike (Michael John) Sullivan (ex-WY gov.; 1939-)
Mike (Michael Gerald) Tyson (US boxer; 1966-)
Mike Wallace (US TV jour.; 1918-)
Mike, Pat and (film, 1952)
Mikhail Bakunin (Rus. pol.; 1814-76)
Mikhail Baryshnikov (Latvian/US dancer; 1948-)
Mikhail Bulgakov (Rus. writer; 1891-1940)
Mikhail (or Michael) Fyodorovich Romanov
   (emp., Rus.; 1596-1645)
Mikhail Ivanovitch Glinka (Rus. comp.; 1804-57)
Mikhail (Larionovich) Kutuzov (Rus. mil.; 1745-
   1813)
Mikhail M. Kasyanov (PM, Rus.; 1957-)
Mikhail Mordkin (Rus. ballet; 1881-1944)
Mikhail S(ergeyevich) Gorbachev (ex-pres.;
   Rus. 1931-)
Mikhail (Aleksandrovich) Sholokhov (Rus.
   writer; 1906-84)
Mikis Theodorakis (comp.; 1925-)
Mikita, Stan (hockey; 1940-)
Miklos Nemeth (ex-PM, Hung.)
Miklos Rozsa (US comp.; 1907-95)
Mikoyan, Anastas (USSR pol.; 1895-1978)

Mikulás Dzurinda (PM, Slovakia; 1955-)
Mikulski, Barbara A. (US cong.; 1936-)
Milan Kucan (pres., Slovenia; 1941-)
Milan Panic (ex-PM, Yug.)
Milan point (lace)
Milan, Italy
Milan, Victor (aka Richard Austin, Robert
    Baron)(writer; 1954-)
Milano, Alyssa (ent.; 1972-)
Milanov, Zinka (Kunc)(Yug. opera; 1906-89)
Milburn Stone (ent.; 1904-80)
Milburn, Rodney, Jr. (hurdler; 1950-)
Mildred Bailey (US jazz; 1907-51)
Mildred Natwick (ent.; 1908-94)
Mildred Pierce (J.M. Cain novel)
Milenkovic (also Milenkovich), Stefan (violinist;
    1977-)
Miles Davis (US jazz; 1926-91)
Miles Nervine (med.)
Miles Pharmaceuticals (US bus.)
Miles Standish (Br./Amer. settler/mil.; c1584-
    1656)
Miles, Sarah (ent.; 1941-)
Miles, Sylvia (ent.; 1934-)
Miles, Vera (b. Vera Ralston)(ent.; 1930-)
Milford, CT, MA
Milhaud, Darius (Fr. comp.; 1892-1974)
Military Academy, U.S. (West Point, NY)(est.
    1802)
Milk-Bone (dog biscuits)
Milk Duds (candy)
Milk of Magnesia, Phillips' (med.)
Milk, Harvey (San Francisco pol., murdered;
    1930-78)
Milken, Michael (US, "junk bond" king; 1946-)
Milky Way (candy)
Milky Way galaxy (astron.)
Mill, James (Scot. phil.; 1773-1836)
Mill, John Stuart (Br. phil./econ.; 1806-73)
Milla Jovovich (ent./model; 1975-)
Milland, Ray (ent.; 1905-86)
Millar, Kenneth (pseud. Ross Macdonald)(US
    writer; 1915-83)
Millard Fillmore (13th US pres.; 1800-74)
Millay, Edna St. Vincent (US poet; 1892-1950)
Mille Fleur bantam (chicken)
Mille, Agnes De (US dancer/choreographer;
    1905-93)
Mille, Cecil B. De (ent.; 1881-1959)
Millenia, Mazda (auto.)
Millenial Church (also United Society of Believers in
    Christ's Second Coming[Appearing], Shakers)
Millennium Copyright Act, Digital (passed 1998)
Miller (beer)
Miller Brewing Co.
Miller Lite
Miller Story, The Glenn (film, 1954)
Miller, Ann (b. Lucille Ann Collier)(ent.; 1919-)
Miller, Arthur (US writer; 1915-)
Miller, Barney (TV show)
Miller, Bob (Robert Joseph)(ex-NV gov.; 1945-)
Miller, Cheryl (basketball; 1964-)
Miller, Daisy (Henry James novelette)
Miller, Dennis (ent.; 1953-)
Miller, Glenn (US jazz; 1904-44)

Miller, Henry (US writer; 1891-1980)
Miller, Herman (furniture)
Miller, Inc., Herman
Miller, Jason (John)(US playwright/ent.; 1939-)
Miller, Joe (familiar joke/book of jokes)
Miller, Johnny (golf; 1947-)
Miller, McCabe & Mrs. (film, 1971)
Miller, Mitch (ent.; 1911-)
Miller, Perry G. (US hist.; 1905-63)
Miller, Reggie (basketball; 1965-)
Miller, Roger (ent.; 1936-92)
Miller, Shannon (gymnast; 1977-)
Miller, Walter D(ale)(ex-SD gov.; 1925-)
Miller, Zell (US cong./ex-GA gov.; 1932-)
Miller's Outpost (store)
Millerand, Alexandre (ex-pres., Fr.; 1859-1943)
Millet, Jean François (Fr. artist; 1814-75)
Millett, Kate (US writer/feminist; 1934-)
Milli Vanilli (pop music/lip-sync)
Millicent Fenwick (US pol.; 1900-92)
Millie, Thoroughly Modern (film, 1967)
Milligan, Ex parte (US law; 1866)
Millikan, Robert A(ndrews)(US physt.; 1868-1953)
Millöcker, Karl (Aus. comp.; 1842-99)
Mills Brothers, The (pop music)
Mills, Donna (ent.; 1942-)
Mills, Hayley (ent.; 1946-)
Mills, John (ent.; 1908-)
Mills, Juliet (ent.; 1941-)
Mills, Robert (US arch.; 1781-1855)
Mills, Wilbur D. (US pol.; 1910-92)
Millville, NJ
Milne, A(lan) A(lexander)(Br. writer; 1882-1956)
Milner, Martin (ent.; 1927-)
Milnes, Sherrill (ent.; 1935-)
Milo Djukanovic (pres., Montenegro; 1962-)
Milo, Venus de (also *Venus of Melos, Aphrodite
    of Melos)*(Gr. statue; c.200 BC)
Mi-lo-fo (also Maitreya, Miroku)(rel.)
Milongo, André (ex-PM, Congo)
Milos Forman (Czech. ent.; 1932-)
Milos Zeman (PM, Czech; 1944-)
Milos, Greece (also Milo, Melos)(Venus de Milo
    found)
Milosevic, Slobodan (Serbian pol.; 1941-)
Milquetoast (a timid person)(also l.c.)
Milquetoast, Caspar (cartoon chara.)
Milsap, Ronnie (ent.; 1944-)
Milstein, Nathan (violinist; 1904-92)
Milt Jackson (US jazz; 1923-99)
Milton Ager (US comp.; 1893-1979)
Milton Avery (artist; 1893-1965)
Milton Berle ("Uncle Miltie")(b. Milton Berlinger)
    (ent.; 1908-)
Milton-Bradley (board games)
Milton Bradley Co.
Milton Byron Babbitt (US comp.; 1916-)
Milton Caniff (cartoonist, *Terry & the Pirates,
    Steve Canyon*; 1907-88)
Milton Friedman (US econ.; 1912-)
Milton (Snavely) Hershey (US, founded
    chocolate co.; 1857-1945)
Milton "Gummo" Marx (ent.; 1893-1977)
Milton Obote, (Apollo)(ex-pres., Uganda; 1925-)
Milton S. Eisenhower (US educ.; 1899-1985)

Milton Sills (ent.; 1882-1930)
Milton, John (Br. poet; 1608-74)
Miltown (med./tranquilizer)
Milwaukee Brewers (baseball team)
Milwaukee Bucks (basketball team)
Milwaukee Journal (WI newspaper)
Milwaukee Sentinel (WI newspaper)
Milwaukee, WI
Milwaukee's Best (beer)
Mily Alexeyevich Balakirev (Rus. comp.; 1837-1910)
Mimas (Saturn moon, myth)
Mimeograph
Mimetics (software)
Mimi Rogers (ent.; 1956-)
Mimieux, Yvette (ent.; 1939?-)
Mimolette (cheese)
Min (lang.)
Mina (people)
Mina Sulman, Bahrain
Minamata disease (mercury poisoning)(med.)
Minamoto (also Genji)(Jap. hist.; 1192-1219)
Minangkabau (lang.)
Mindanao (island, Philippines)
Mindelo, Cape Verde
Mindy, Mork and (TV show)
Mine Workers of America, United (UMWA) (union, est. 1890)
Mineo, Sal (ent.; 1939-76)
Minerva (myth.)
Mineta, Norman Y(oshio)(US secy./trans, ex-secy./commerce; 1931)
Minetics Corp.
Ming dynasty (Ch. hist.; 1368-1644)
Ming porcelain
Mingo, Norman (cartoonist; 1896-1980)
Mingus, Charles (US jazz; 1922-79)
Minié ball (bullet; 19th c.)
Minimalism (art/music movement)(also l.c.)
Minipress (med.)
Minita Gordon, Dame (Elmira)(ex-gov.-gen., Belize)
Minitran (med.)
Miniver, Mrs. (film, 1942)
Minizide (med.)
Minneapolis Star-Tribune (MN newspaper)
Minneapolis-St. Paul International Airport (MN)
Minneapolis, MN
Minnehaha (fict. chara., Hiawatha's wife)
Minnelli, Liza (ent.; 1946-)
Minnelli, Vincente (ent.; 1910-86)
Minner, Ruth Ann (DE gov.; 1935-)
Minnesota (MN)
Minnesota Fats (b. Rudolf Wanderone, Jr.)(pool hustler; 1913-96)
Minnesota Mining & Manufacturing Co. (3M)
Minnesota Multiphasic Personality Inventory (also MMPI)(psych.)
Minnesota North Stars (hockey team)
Minnesota Timberwolves (basketball team)
Minnesota Twins (baseball team)
Minnesota v. Dickerson (US law; 1993)
Minnesota Vikings (football team)
Minnesota, Near v. (US law; 1931-)
Minnie Driver (ent.; 1970-)

Minnie Maddern Fiske (ent.; 1865-1932)
Minnie Pearl (Sarah Ophelia Cannon)(ent.; 1912-96)
Minoan civilization (Crete; 3000-1100 BC)
Minocin (med.)
Minolta (photo)
Minor C. Keith (US bus.; 1848-1929)
Minor Prophets
Minor, Leo (astron.; little lion)
Minor, Ursa (astron., little/lesser bear; part of Little Dipper)
Minorca (chicken)
Minorca (or Menorca) Island (Balearic Island, Mediterranean)
Minoru Yamasaki (US arch.; 1912-86)
Minos, King (myth.)
Minot Air Force Station, ND
Minot, ND
Minotaur (myth.)
Minoxidil (med.)
Minseito (Jap. pol. party)
Minsk, Belarus (also Mensk)
Mintezol (med.)
Mintoff, Dom(inic)(ex-PM, Malta; 1916-)
Minuit, Peter (Dutch admin. in Amer.; c1580-1638)
Minute Maid (juice)
Minute Maid Foodservice Group (US bus.)
Minute Man National Historical Park (MA)
Minute rice
Minuteman (US mil.; 1770s)(also US missile, mil. org.)
Miocene epoch (26-10 million years ago)
Miostat (med.)
Miquel Angel Rodríguez Echeverría (pres., Costa Rica; 1940-)
Miquelon, St. Pierre and (Fr. islands, Newfoundland)
Mir (USSR space station)
Mira Nair (ent./writer; 1957-)
Mira Sorvino (ent.; 1967-)
Mira variable (also Omicron Ceti)(astron.)
Mirabeau, Honoré Gabriel (Riqueti), Comte de (Fr. pol.; 1749-91)
Mirabella (mag.)
Mirabella, Grace (publ.; 1929-)
Miracle of Fátima
Miracle Whip
Miracle-Ear Hearing Aid Center
Miracle-Ear, Inc.
Miracle-Gro (agr.)
Miracles, Smokey Robinson and the (pop music)
Mirage, Mitsubishi (auto.)
Miramax Films
Miranda (Uranus moon)
Miranda vs. Arizona (US law; 1966)
Miranda warnings (US law)
Miranda, Carmen (ent.; 1913-55)
Mirassou Vineyards (US bus.)
Mircea (Ion) Snegur (ex-pres., Moldova; 1940-)
Mireya Elisa Moscoso Rodriguez (pres., Panama; 1946-)
Miriam Makeba (ent.; 1932-)
Mirjana Markovic (Serbian atty./educ./pol., wife of S. Milosevic; 1942-)
Miro, Dr. Mohammad Mostafa (PM, Syria; 1941-)

Miró, Joan (Sp. artist; 1893-1983)
Miroku (also Maitreya, Mi-lo-fo)(rel.)
Mirren, Helen (b. Ilynea Lydia Mironoff)(ent.; 1945-)
Mirro (cookware)
MIRV (multiple independently targeted reentry vehicle)
Misanthrope, Le (Molière comedy)
Mischa Elman (ent.; 1891-1967)
Miserables, Les (V. Hugo novel)
Misere, Seychelles
Misha Dichter (pianist; 1945-)
Mishawaka, IN
Mishima Yukio (aka Hiraoka Kimitake)(Jap. writer; 1925-70)
Mishna(h) Law (also Oral)(rel.)
Miskolc, Hungary
Misrule, Lord of (former Christmas revelry director, Br.)
Miss America
Miss America Pageant, The
Miss Breck (hair care)
Miss Brooks, Our (TV show)
Miss Clairol (hair care)
Miss Daisy, Driving (film, 1989)
Miss Jean Brodie, The Prime of (film, 1969)
Miss Marple (fict. chara., A. Christie)
Miss Muffett, Little (nursery rhyme)
Miss Peach (comic strip)
Miss Piggy (Muppet)
Miss Sadie Thompson (film, 1953)
Miss Saigon (play)
Miss/Ms. Right (slang)
Missing Persons (TV show)
Mission Viejo, CA
Mission, TX
Missionary Ridge, GA, TN
Mississauga, Ontario, Canada
Mississippi (MS)
Mississippi River (US, between Appalachian/ Rocky Mts.)
Mississippian period (345-320 million years ago)
Missoula, MT
Missouri (MO)
Missouri Compromise (US hist.; 1820-21)
Missouri River (central US)
Mister Roberts (film, 1955)
Mister Rogers' Neighborhood (TV show)
Mister Softee, Inc.
Mistral, Frédéric (Fr. poet; 1830-1914)
Mistral, Gabriela (aka Lucilla Godoy de Alcayaga)(Chilean poet; 1889-1957)
Misty Harbour (raincoat)
Misurata, Libya
MIT (Massachusetts Institute of Technology)
Mita Copystar America, Inc.
Mitch Gaylord (gymnast; 1961-)
Mitch Leigh (US comp.; 1928-)
Mitch McConnell (US cong.; 1942-)
Mitch Miller (ent.; 1911-)
Mitch Pileggi (ent.; 1952-)
Mitch Ryder (b. William Levise, Jr.)(ent.; 1945-)
Mitch Snyder (US reformer/homeless; 1944-90)
Mitchell Parish (US comp.; 1901-93)
Mitchell Systems, John Paul (US bus.)

Mitchell, Billy (US mil.; 1879-1936)
Mitchell, Cameron (ent.; 1918-94)
Mitchell, Edgar D. (astro.; 1930-)
Mitchell, George J. (US pol.; 1933-)
Mitchell, James (ent.; 1920-)
Mitchell, James P(aul)(US bus./pol.; 1900-64)
Mitchell, (Sir) James (PM, St. Vincent/ Grenadines; 1931-)
Mitchell, John (Newton)(US pol./Watergate; 1913-88)
Mitchell, John (US labor leader; 1870-1919)
Mitchell, Joni (b. Roberta Joan Anderson)(ent.; 1943-)
Mitchell, (Dr.) Keith C. (PM, Grenada; 1946-)
Mitchell, Margaret (US writer; 1900-49)
Mitchell, Maria (US astron.; 1818-89)
Mitchell, Paul (hair care)
Mitchell, Thomas (ent.; 1892-1962)
Mitchell, Wisconsin v. (US law; 1993)
Mitchelson, Marvin (US atty.)
Mitchum (anti-perspirant)
Mitchum, Robert (ent.; 1917-97)
Mithraism (also Mithraicism)(rel.)
Mithras (myth.)
Mitrolan (med.)
Mitropoulos, Dimitri (cond.; 1896-1960)
Mitsotakis, Constantine (ex-PM, Gr.; 1918-)
Mitsubishi (auto.)
Mitsubishi 3000GT (auto.)
Mitsubishi 3000GT SL (auto.)
Mitsubishi Diamante (auto.)
Mitsubishi Diamante ES (auto.)
Mitsubishi Diamante LS (auto.)
Mitsubishi Eclipse (auto.)
Mitsubishi Eclipse GS (auto.)
Mitsubishi Eclipse GS-T (auto.)
Mitsubishi Eclipse GSX (auto.)
Mitsubishi Eclipse GT (auto.)
Mitsubishi Eclipse RS (auto.)
Mitsubishi Eclipse Spyder (auto.)
Mitsubishi Eclipse Spyder GS (auto.)
Mitsubishi Eclipse Spyder GS-T (auto.)
Mitsubishi Eclipse Spyder GT (auto.)
Mitsubishi Electric Sales America, Inc.
Mitsubishi Fuso Truck of America, Inc.
Mitsubishi Galant (auto.)
Mitsubishi Galant DE (auto.)
Mitsubishi Galant ES (auto.)
Mitsubishi Galant GTZ (auto.)
Mitsubishi Galant LS (auto.)
Mitsubishi Galant S (auto.)
Mitsubishi International Corp.
Mitsubishi Mirage (auto.)
Mitsubishi Mirage DE (auto.)
Mitsubishi Mirage ES (auto.)
Mitsubishi Mirage LS (auto.)
Mitsubishi Mirage S (auto.)
Mitsubishi Montero (auto.)
Mitsubishi Montero Limited (auto.)
Mitsubishi Montero LS (auto.)
Mitsubishi Montero Sport (auto.)
Mitsubishi Montero Sport ES (auto.)
Mitsubishi Montero Sport Limited (auto.)
Mitsubishi Montero Sport LS (auto.)
Mitsubishi Montero Sport XLS (auto.)

Mitsubishi Montero SR (auto.)
Mitsubishi Montero XLS (auto.)
Mitsubishi Motor Sales of America, Inc.
Mitsubishi Motors (auto.)
Mitterrand, François (ex-pres., Fr.; 1916-96)
Mitty, The Secret Life of Walter (J. Thurber
  short story)
Mitzi Gaynor (b. Francesca Marlene Von
  Gerber)(ent.; 1930-)
Mix, Tom (Thomas Edwin)(ent.; 1880-1940)
Mixtard (med.)
Mixtec (Native Amer./Mex.)
Miyazawa, Kiichi (ex-PM, Jap.; 1919-)
Mizoram (state, India)
Mizoyev, Akbar (Tajikistan pol.)
MJB Co.
MJB coffee
M. J. Divine, Major (also Father Divine)(b.
  George Baker)(US rel.; 1882-1965)
Mkapa, Benjamin William (pres., Tanzania;
  1938-)
Mme. (abbreviation for Madame)
Mmes. (abbreviation for Madames)
M(ary) M(argaret) Kaye (writer; 1911-)
MN (Minnesota)
Mn (chem. sym., manganese)
M'Naghten rule (or law)(US law)
Mnemonic, Johnny (film, 1995)
Mnemosyne (myth.)
MO (Missouri, money order)
Mo (chem. sym., molybdenum)
Mo Ti (also Mo-tze, Mo Tzu, Mo-tse, Mo Tse)
  (Ch. phil.; 5th c. BC)
Moab (ancient kingdom, Jordan)
Moabite (people)
Moabite Stone/stone (Moab hist.; 9th c. BC)
Moban (med.)
Mobil Chemical Co.
Mobil Corp.
Mobil Oil Corp.
Mobile Press (AL newspaper)
Mobile Register (AL newspaper)
Mobile, AL
Möbius strip/band
Mobutu Sese Seko (Kuku Ngbendu wa Zabanga)
  (b. Joseph Désiré Mobutu)(ex-pres., Congo/
  Zaire; 1930-97)
Moby Dick (by Herman Melville)
Moco, Marcolino José Carlos (ex-PM, Angola)
Mocumbi, Dr. Pascoal Manuel (PM, Mozambique;
  1941-)
Model A Ford (auto.)
Model T Ford (auto.)
Modena (pigeon)
Modena, Italy
Modern Bride (mag.)
Modern Electronics (mag.)
Modern English (also New English)(lang.)
Modern English, Early (lang.; c1550-1700)
Modern English, Late (lang.; c1700-present)
Modern Greek (also New Greek)
Modern Hebrew (also New Hebrew)
Modern Latin
Modern Maturity (mag.)
Modernism (art, rel.)

Modersohn-Becker, Paula (Ger. artist; 1867-
  1907)
Modest Petrovich Moussorgsky (Rus. comp.;
  1839-81)
Modesto Bee (CA newspaper)
Modesto, CA
Modigliani, Amedeo (It. artist; 1884-1920)
Modine, Matthew (ent.; 1959-)
Modjeska, Helena (ent.; 1844-1909)
Modoc (Native Amer.)
Modred (also Mordred)(King Arthur's killer)
Moduretic (med.)
Moe Howard (b. Moses Horwitz)(ent.; 1897-1975)
Moe, Izzy & (film, 1985)
Moen (US bus.)
Moerae (also Moirai)(myth.)
Moët & Chandon champagne
Moffat, Donald (ent.; 1930-)
Moffets, The (pop music)
Moffo, Anna (ent.; 1927-)
Mogadishu, Somalia (also Mogadisho)
Mogae, Festus (pres., Botswana; 1939-)
Mogambo (film, 1953)
Mogen (or Magen) David (also Star of David)
Mogen David (kosher foods)
Mogen David (wine)
Mogen David Wine Corp.
Mogilev, Belarus
Mogul art/architecture
Mogul Empire (dynasty, India; 1526-1857)
Mohamed Ghannouchi (PM, Tunisia; 1941-)
Mohammad Mostafa Miro, Dr. (PM, Syria; 1941-)
Mohammad Omar, Mullah (Afghan. pol.)
Mohammad Rafiq Tarar (pres., Pak.; 1929-)
Mohammed Hosni Mubarak (pres., Egypt; 1928-)
Mohammed IV (king, Morocco; 1963-)
Mohammed Karim Lamrani (ex-PM, Morocco)
Mohammed Khatami, Seyed (pres., Iran; 1943-)
Mohammedanism (misnomer for Islam rel.)
Mohandas K(aramchand) "Mahatma" Gandhi
  (Indian pol./pacifist; 1869-1948)
Moharram (also Muharram)(rel.)
Mohave (also Mojave)(Native Amer.)
Mohave (or Mojave) Desert (S CA)
Mohawk (Native Amer.)
Mohawk Airlines
Mohawk Carpet Mills (US bus.)
Mohawk haircut (also l.c.)
Mohawk Industries, Inc.
Mohawk River (NY)
Mohegan (or Mohican)(Native Amer.)
Mohenjo-Daro (Pak. archeological site)
Mohican (or Mohegan)(Native Amer.)
Mohicans, The Last of the (J.F. Cooper novel)
Mohorovicic discontinuity (also Moho, M-
  discontinuity)(geol.)
Mohorovicic, Andrija (Yug. physt.; 1857-1936)
Mohr, Jay (ent.; 1971-)
Mohs' scale (hardness of minerals)
Moi, Daniel arap (pres., Kenya; 1924-)
Moira (myth.)
Moira Shearer (ent.; 1926-)
Moirai (also Moerae)(myth.)
Moise K(apenda) Tshombe (ex-PM, Congo/
  Zaire; 1919-69)

Moiseyev Dance Company
Mojave (or Mohave) Desert (S CA)
Mojave Indians (also Mohave)(AZ/CA)
Mokhehle, Ntsu (ex-PM, Lesotho; 1918-99)
Moldavia (now Moldova and Romania)
Moldavian (lang.)
Moldova (Republic of)(formerly part of USSR)
(E central Eur.)
Moldovian (people)
Molière (b. Jean Baptiste Poquelin)(Fr. writer;
1622-73)
Molina, Manuel Luis Quezon y (ex-pres. Phil.;
1878-1944)
Molina, Mario (chem.; 1943-)
Molina, Rafael L. Trujillo (ex-pres., Dom. Rep.;
1891-1961)
Molinaro, Al (ent.; 1919-)
Moline, IL
Molinism (rel.)
Molise (region, It.)
Molitor, Paul (baseball; 1956-)
*Moll Flanders, The Fortunes and Misfortunes of
the Famous* (D. Defoe)
Moll, Richard (ent.; 1943-)
Mollet, Guy (Fr. pol.; 1905-75)
Mollicone, Joseph, Jr. (US bank scandal)
Mollie Parnis (US designer; 1905-92)
Mollweide (or homolographic) projection
Molly bolt (constr.)
Molly Brown, The Unsinkable (film, 1964)
Molly Ivins (US jour.; 1944-)
Molly Maguires (also Mollies)(US/Ir. secret
society; c1854-77)
Molly Maguires, The (film, 1970)
Molly McButter (food)
Molly Picon (ent.; 1898-1992)
Molly Pitcher (b. Mary [Ludwig Hays] McCauley)
(US heroine; 1754-1832)
Molly Ringwald (ent.; 1968-)
Molly Yard, (Mary Alexander)(US reformer, ex-
pres./NOW; 1912-)
Molly, Fibber McGee and (radio comedy)
Molnár, Ferenc (Hung. writer; 1878-1952)
Molné, Marc Forné (PM, Andorra; 1946)
Molokai (island, HI)
Molotov cocktail (homemade bomb)
Molotov, Vyacheslav M(ikhailovich)(ex-PM,
Rus.; 1890-1986)
Moluccas (also Spice Islands)(Indonesia)
Mombasa, Kenya
Momir Bulatovic (ex-PM, Yug.; 1956-)
Momma (comic strip)
Mommie Dearest (film, 1981)
Mommsen, Theodor (Ger. hist.; 1817-1903)
Mona Lisa (aka *La Gioconda*)(da Vinci painting)
Monaco (Principality of)(Eur.)
Monaco, Monaco
Monaco-Ville, Monaco
Monaghan (county, NIre.)
Mönchengladbach, Germany (formerly
München-Gladbach)
Monck, George (Duke of Albemarle)(Br. mil./
pol.; 1608-70)
Monck's Regiment (Br. mil., now Coldstream
Guards)

Moncton, New Brunswick, Canada
Mondale, Walter F(rederick) "Fritz" (US pol.;
1928-)
Mondavi Winery, Robert (US bus.)
Mondavi, Robert
Monday Night Football, NFL (TV show)
Mondeo, Ford (auto.)
Mondrian, Piet (b. Pieter Cornelis Mondriaan)
(Dutch artist; 1872-1944)
Mondo Cane (film, 1963)
M-1 (or Garand) rifle (semiautomatic)
Monegasque (people)
Monet (jewelry)
Monet, Claude (Fr. artist; 1840-1926)
Monetgo Bay, Jamaica
Money (mag.)
Money, Eddie (b. Eddie Mahoney)(ent.; 1949-)
Moneyline (TV show)
Moneysworth (mag.)
Mongar, Bhutan
Mongo (lang.)
Mongol (or Yüan) dynasty (Ch. ruling house;
1279-1368)
Mongol (people)
Mongol Empire (Rus./Ch. hist.; 1206-c1380)
Mongolia (State of)(formerly Outer Mongolia,
People's Republic of Mongolia)(E central Asia)
Mongolia, Inner (NE Ch.)
Mongolia, Outer (now State of Mongolia)
Mongolian (lang./people)
Mongoloid (now Down's syndrome)(med.)
Mongoloid (one of three major races of humans)
Monica (b. Monica Arnold)(ent.; 1980-)
Monica de Greiff (Colombian pol.)
Monica Lewinsky (US news; 1973-)
Monica Seles (tennis; 1973-)
Monica Vitti (ent.; 1931-)
Monistat (med.)
Monistat 7 (med.)
Monitor, Merrimack v. (US hist.; 1862)
Monk, Art (football; 1957-)
Monk, Meredith (comp./choreographer/ent.;
1942-)
Monk, Thelonious (Sphere)(US jazz; 1920-82)
Monkees, the (pop music)
Mon-Khmer (lang.)
Monmouth Beach, NJ
Monmouth, Battle of (US hist.; 1778)
Monmouth, Fort, NJ (mil.)
Monmouth, Geoffrey of (Br. writer/chronicler;
c1100-54)
Mono Lake (CA)
Monoceros (astron., unicorn)
Monongahela River (PA/WV)
Monophysite (rel.)
Monopoly (game)
Monotheletism (also Monothelism)(rel.)
Monotype (graphics)
Monroe Auto Equipment Co.
Monroe Doctrine (US hist.; 1823)
Monroe shocks
Monroe, Fort, VA (mil.)
Monroe, James (5th US pres.; 1758-1831)
Monroe, LA
Monroe, Marilyn (b. Norma Jean Baker [or

Mortenson])(ent.; 1926-62)
Monroe, Vaughn (ent.; 1911-73)
Monrovia, Liberia
Mons, Belgium
Monsanto Acrilan (carpet)
Monsanto Co.
Monsarrat, Nicholas (Br. writer; 1910-79)
Monseigneur (Fr. title)
Monsieur (Fr. for Mr.)
Monsignor (rel. title)
Montagnais (Native Amer./lang.)
Montagu, (Montague Francis) Ashley (Br./US
    anthrop.; 1905-99)
Montagu, John (Earl of Sandwich)(Br. pol.;
    1718-92)
Montagu, Mary (Wortley), Lady (aka Mary
    Pierrepont)(Br. writer; 1689-1762)
Montague families, Capulet and (*Romeo and
    Juliet*)
Montague, Romeo (fict. chara., *Romeo & Juliet*)
Montaigne, Michel (Eyquem) de (Fr. writer;
    1533-92)
Montalban, Ricardo (ent.; 1920-)
Montale, Eugenio (It. poet; 1896-1981)
Montana (MT)
Montana, Bob (cartoonist, *Archie*; 1920-75)
Montana, Joe (football; 1956-)
Montana, Pontiac (auto.)
Montand, Yves (Fr. ent.; 1921-91)
Montauk (Native Amer.)
Montauk Point (NY)
Mont Blanc (Alps, Fr./It.)
Montcalm, Louis(-Joseph) de (Montcalm-Gozon)
    (Fr. mil.; 1712-59)
Montclair State University (Upper Montclair, NJ)
Monte Carlo method (statistics)
Monte Carlo, Chevrolet (auto.)
Monte Carlo, Monaco
Monte Cristo sandwich
Monte Cristo, Count of (by Dumas)
Montego Bay, Jamaica
Monteil Paris (US bus.)
Monteiro, Antonio Mascarenhas (pres., Cape
    Verde; 1944-)
Montel Williams (ent.; 1956-)
Montelena Winery, Chateau (US bus.)
Montenegro (republic, Yug.)
Monterey Bay, CA
Monterey Jack (cheese)
Monterey Vineyard (US bus.)
Monterey, CA
Montero, Mitsubishi (auto.)
Monterrey, Mexico
Montesquieu, Charles Louis (Fr. phil.; 1689-1755)
Montessori method/system/school (educ.)
Montessori, Maria (It. educ.; 1870-1952)
Monteux, Pierre (cond.; 1875-1964)
Monteverdi, Claudio (Giovanni Antonio)(It.
    comp.; 1567-1643)
Montevideo, Uruguay
Montez, Lola (ent.; 1818?-61)
Montezuma I (Aztec emp., Mex.; 1390?-1464?)
Montezuma II (Aztec emp., Mex.; 1466?-1520)
Montezuma's revenge (also Aztec two-step)
    (traveler's diarrhea)

Montgolfier, Jacques Étienne (Fr. hot-air
    balloonist; 1745-99)
Montgolfier, Joseph Michel (Fr. hot-air
    balloonist; 1740-1810)
Montgomery Advertiser (AL newspaper)
Montgomery Clift (ent.; 1920-66)
Montgomery Journal (AL newspaper)
Montgomery Ward
Montgomery Ward & Co., Inc.
Montgomery Ward, Aaron (US bus.; 1843-1913)
Montgomery, AL, OH
Montgomery, Bernard Law (Br. mil.; 1887-1976)
Montgomery, Elizabeth (ent.; 1933-95)
Montgomery, George (ent.; 1916-2000)
Montgomery, Jim (swimming; 1955-)
Montgomery, John Michael (ent.; 1965-)
Montgomery, Robert (ent.; 1904-81)
Montgomery, Ruth (US writer/psychic; 1912-)
Montgomery, Wes (US jazz; 1925-68)
Monthan Air Force Base, Davis-, AZ (mil.)
Monticelli, Adolphe Joseph Thomas (Fr. artist;
    1824-86)
Monticello (T. Jefferson's home)(VA)
Monticello Carpet Mills (US bus.)
Montmartre (area, Paris)
Montoya, Carlos (Sp. guitarist; 1903-93)
Montparnasse (area, Paris)
Montpelier, VT
Montrachet cheese
Montrachet wine
Montreal Canadiens (hockey team)
Montreal Expos (baseball team)
Montreal-Nord, Quebec, Canada (also Montreal
    North)
Montreal, Quebec, Canada
Montreuil, France
Montreux International Jazz Festival
Mont-Royal, Quebec, Canada
Montserrat (a Leeward island, Br. West Indies)
Monty Hall (b. Monty Halparin)(ent.; 1923-)
Monty Python and the Holy Grail (film, 1975)
Monty Python's Flying Circus (TV show)
Monty Python's Life of Brian (film, 1979)
Monty Woolley (ent.; 1888-1963)
Monty, The Full (film, 1996)
Moody Air Force Base, GA
Moody Blues (pop music)
Moody, Dwight Lyman (US rel.; 1837-99)
Moody, Helen (Newington) Wills (tennis; 1906-
    98)
Moody, Raymond (writer, near-death experiences;
    1944-)
Moody, Ron (ent.; 1924-)
Moog Electronics, Inc.
Moog synthesizer (music)
Moon (Aubrey Wilson) Mulligan (ent.; 1909-67)
Moon Mullins (comic strip)
Moon Unit Zappa (ent.; 1967-)
Moon, Sun Myung, Rev. (Korean rel.; 1920-)
Moon, Warren (football; 1956-)
Moonie (follower of Rev. Moon, Unification
    Church; est. 1954)
Moonlighting (TV show)
Moor (people)
Moor of Venice, The Tragedy of Othello, The

© 2001 *StenEd*® Proper Noun Speller

(Shakespeare play)
Moore & Co., Benjamin
Moore, Archie (boxing; 1913-98)
Moore, Clayton (ent.; 1914-99)
Moore, Clement C(lark)(US poet/educ.; 1779-
　　1863)
Moore, Demi (b. Demetria Guynes)(ent.; 1962-)
Moore, Dudley (ent.; 1935-)
Moore, Garry (ent.; 1915-93)
Moore, George (Ir. writer; 1852-1933)
Moore, George E. (Br. phil.; 1873-1958)
Moore, George Foot (US rel.; 1851-1931)
Moore, Grace (soprano; 1901-47)
Moore, Henry (Br. sculptor; 1898-1986)
Moore, John Bassett (US jurist; 1860-1947)
Moore, Julianne (b. Julie Anne Smith)(ent.; 1960-)
Moore, Mandy (ent.; 1984-)
Moore, Marianne (Craig)(US poet; 1887-1972)
Moore, Mary Tyler (ent.; 1936-)
Moore, Melba (b. Beatrice Hill)(ent.; 1945-)
Moore, Roger (ent.; 1927-)
Moore, Terry (b. Helen Koford)(aka Judy Ford,
　　Jan Ford)(ent.; 1929-)
Moore, Thomas (Ir. poet; 1779-1852)
Moore, Victor (ent.; 1876-1962)
Moorehead, Agnes (ent.; 1906-74)
Moores, Dick (cartoonist, *Gasoline Alley*; 1909-
　　86)
Moorhead, MN
Moorish arch (Sp.; 11-14th c.)
Moorish idol (fish)
Moors (people)
Moose Jaw, Saskatchewan, Canada
Moose, Loyal Order of (US org.)
Moosehead Lake (ME)
Mootsies Tootsies (shoes)
Mootsies Tootsies (US bus.)
Mop & Glo (floor cleaner)
Mopti, Mali
Moral Majority
Moran, Bugs (George)(US gangster; 1893-1957)
Moran, Erin (ent.; 1961-)
Moráng, Nepal
Moranis, Rick (ent.; 1953-)
Morant, Breaker (film, 1979)
Morauta, (Sir) Mekere (PM, Papua New Guinea;
　　1946-)
Moravia (regions, Czech.)
Moravian (rel.)
Moravian Church (also Renewed Church of the
　　Brethren, Unitas Fratrum)
Mordecai (rel.)
Mordkin, Mikhail (Rus. ballet; 1881-1944)
Mordred (also Modred)(King Arthur's killer)
Mordvin (lang./people)
More (cigarettes)
More (lang.)
Moré, Hannah (Br. writer; 1745-1833)
More, Henry (Br. phil.; 1614-87)
More, (Sir) Thomas (Br. writer/pol.; 1478-1535)
Moreau, Dr. (fict. villain)
Moreau, Gustave (Fr. artist; 1826-98)
Moreau, Island of Dr. (film, 1977, 1996)
Moreau, Jeanne (Fr. ent.; 1928-)
Morehead State University (Morehead, KY)

MoreMAX (TV channel)
Moreno Valley, CA
Moreno, Rita (b. Rosita Dolores Alverio)(ent.;
　　1931-)
Moresby, Port (Papua New Guinea)
Morey Amsterdam (ent.; 1908-96)
Morgan (horse)
Morgan Brittany (b. Suzanne Cupito)(ent.; 1951-)
Morgan Fairchild (b. Patsy McClenny)(ent.; 1950-)
Morgan Freeman (ent.; 1937-)
Morgan le Fay (also Morgain le Fay)(King
　　Arthur's fairy sister)
Morgan Stanley & Co. Inc.
Morgan Stanley Dean Witter & Co.
Morgan Stanley Dean Witter Online Inc.
Morgan Stanley DW Inc.
Morgan State University (Baltimore, MD)
Morgan, Daniel (US mil.; 1736-1802)
Morgan, Dennis (ent.; 1910-)
Morgan, Harry (ent.; 1915-)
Morgan, Henry (ent.; 1915-94)
Morgan, Joe (Leonard)(baseball; 1943-)
Morgan, John Hunt (US mil.; 1826-64)
Morgan, J(ohn) P(ierpont)(US finan.; 1837-1913)
Morgan, Lorrie (b. Loretta Lynn Morgan)(ent.;
　　1959-)
Morgan, (Sir) Henry (Welsh buccaneer in
　　Amer.; 1635?-88)
Morgan, Thomas Hunt (US geneticist; 1866-1945)
Morgana, Fata (Arthurian)
Morgantown, WV
Morgenthau, Henry (US finan./dipl.; 1856-1946)
Morgenthau, Henry, Jr. (US publ./pol.; 1891-
　　1967)
Mori, Yoshiro (PM, Jap.; 1937-)
Moriarty, Michael (ent.; 1941-)
Moriarty, Professor (fict. chara., *Sherlock Holmes*)
Morihiro Hosokawa (ex-PM, Jap.; 1938-)
Morini, Erica (violinist; 1904-95)
Morison, Samuel Eliot (US hist.; 1887-1976)
Morisot, Berthe (Fr. artist; 1841-95)
Morissette, Alanis (ent.; 1974-)
Morita, Pat (ent.; 1932-)
Morito, Akio (Jap. bus.; 1921-99)
Moritz Chocolatier, St. (US bus.)
Moriyama, Mayumi (Jap. pol.)
Mork and Mindy (TV show)
Morley Safer (US TV jour.; 1931-)
Morley, Christopher (Darlington)(US writer/
　　editor; 1890-1957)
Morley, Robert (Br. ent.; 1908-92)
Mormon Church (also Latter-Day Saints, Church
　　of Jesus Christ of the Latter-Day Saints)(rel.)
Mormon State (nickname, UT)
Mormon Tabernacle Choir
Mormon, Book of (rel.)
Mornay sauce (also l.c.)
Mornay, Rebecca De (ent.; 1962-)
Morning Call, Allentown (PA newspaper)
Morning News, Dallas (TX newspaper)
Morningstar (finan.)
Morningstar, Marjorie (H. Wouk novel)
Moro, Aldo (ex-PM, It.; 1916-78)
Morocco (Kingdom of)(NW Afr.)
Morocco, Road to (film, 1942)

Moroni, Comoros
Morpheus (myth.)
Morphou, Cyprus
Morrall, Earl (football; 1934-)
Morrell & Co., John
Morrell, John (meats)
Morrice, James Wilson (Can. artist; 1865-1924)
Morricone, Ennio (It. comp.; 1928-)
Morris Agency, Inc., William
Morris K(ing) "Mo" Udall (US pol.; 1922-98)
Morris Louis (US artist; 1912-62)
Morris, Desmond (Br. writer; 1928-)
Morris, Gouverneur (US pol./dipl.; 1752-1816)
Morris, Greg (ent.; 1934-96)
Morris, Inc., Philip
Morris, Robert (US pol./bus.; 1734-1806)
Morris, William (Br. designer; 1834-96)
Morris, Wright (US writer; 1910-98)
Morrison, Jim (ent.; 1943-71)
Morrison, Toni (b. Chloe Anthony Wofford)(US
    writer/poet; 1931-)
Morrison, Van (ent.; 1945-)
Morristown National Historical Park (NJ)
Morristown, NJ
Morro Bay, CA
Morrow, Rob (ent.; 1962-)
Morrow, Vic (ent.; 1932-82)
Mors (myth.)
Morse code (comm.)
Morse, Carlton E.
Morse, Marston (US math.; 1892-1977)
Morse, Robert (ent.; 1931-)
Morse, Samuel (Finley Breese)(US inv.,
    telegraph; 1791-1872)
Morse, Wayne (US pol.; 1900-74)
Mort Drucker (cartoonist, *Mad* magazine; 1929-)
Mort Sahl (ent.; 1927-)
Mort Walker (cartoonist; *Beetle Bailey*; 1923-)
Morte D'Arthur, Le (by T. Malory)
Mortgage Guarantee Insurance Corporation
    (also Maggie Mae)
Mortimer, John (Br. writer/atty.; 1923-)
Morton Dean (US TV jour.)
Morton Downey, Jr. (ent./writer/comp.; 1933-
    2001)
Morton Downey, Sr. (ent./tenor; 1901-85)
Morton Gould (ent.; 1913-96)
Morton International, Inc.
Morton salt
Morton, Craig L. (football; 1943-)
Morton, Gary (ent.; 1921?-99)
Morton, Jelly Roll (b. Ferdinand Joseph La
    Menthe)(US jazz; 1885-1941)
Morton, Joe (ent.; 1947-)
Morton, Levi P(arsons)(ex-US VP; 1824-1920)
Mos Def (b. Dante Beze)(ent.)
Mosaic law (pertaining to Moses)
Mosconi, Willie (billiards; 1913-93)
Moscoso Rodríguez, Mireya Elisa (pres.,
    Panama; 1946-)
Moscow Art Theater
Moscow mule (mixed drink)
Moscow, ID
Moscow, Russia
Moseley-Braun, Carol (Elizabeth)(US pol./dipl.;

1947-)
Moselle (wine)
Moser Proell, Annemarie (skiing; 1953-)
Moses (ben Maimon) Maimonides, Rabbi (aka
    RaMBaM)(Jew. rel./phil.; 1135-1204)
Moses (Hebrew rel.; c13th c BC)
Moses Lake, WA
Moses Malone (basketball; 1955-)
Moses, Ed(win Corley)(US track; 1955-)
Moses, Grandma (b. Anna Mary Robertson)(US
    artist; 1860-1961)
Moses, Law of (rel.)
Moses, Robert (US urban planner; 1888-1981)
Moses, William (ent.; 1959-)
Moshe Dayan (Isr. pol./gen.; 1915-81)
Moshe Katsav (pres., Isr.; 1945-)
Moshi-Dagomba (people)
Mosisili, Pakalitha Bethuel (PM, Lesotho; 1945-)
Moslem (see Muslim)
Mosquito Coast (area, CAmer.)
Moss Hart (US writer; 1904-61)
Moss Town, Bahamas
Moss, Kate (model; 1974-)
Mossadegh, Muhammad (ex-PM, Iran; 1880-
    1967)
Mössbauer effect (physics)
Mössbauer, Rudolf (Ger. physt.; 1929-)
Mossi (lang./people)
Mostar, Bosnia-Hercegovina
Mostel, Zero (Samuel Joel)(ent.; 1915-77)
Mosul, Iraq
Mot (myth.)
Motel 6, Inc.
Moten, Bennie (US jazz; 1894-1935)
Mother Cabrini (also St. Frances Xavier Cabrini)
    (US rel./reformer; 1850-1917)
Mother Earth
Mother Earth News (mag.)
Mother Goose & Grimm (comic strip)
Mother Goose (fict. author of fairy tales)
Mother Goose Tales (fairy tales, C. Perrault)
Mother Hubbard (fict. chara., nursery rhyme)
Mother Hubbard (loose gown; railroad engine)
Mother Jones (mag.)
Mother Jones (Mary Harris Jones)(US labor
    leader; 1830-1930)
Mother Lode (gold belt, CA)
Mother Maybelle Carter (ent.; 1909-78)
Mother Nature
Mother of God (rel.)
Mother Seton (also St. Elizabeth Ann [Bayley]
    Seton)(US rel.; 1774-1821)
Mother Superior (head nun of convent)
Mother Teresa (of Calcutta)(b. Agnes Gonxha
    Bojaxhiu)(Albanian rel.; 1910-97)
Mother, Holy (also the Madonna, Mary, Our
    Lady, Virgin Mary)(rel.)
Mother, The Great (also The Great
    Goddess)(rel.)
Mother's Day (2nd Sunday in May)
Mothers Today (mag.)
Motherwell and Wishaw (Scot.)
Motherwell, Robert (Burns)(US artist; 1915-91)
Motion Picture Association of America
Motley Crue (pop music)

Motley Fool, The (finan.)
Motofen (med.)
Motor Boating & Sailing (mag.)
Motor Trend (mag.)
Motorland (mag.)
Motorola, Inc.
Motors Corp., General
Motown (nickname, Detroit, MI)
Motown Corp.
Motrin (med.)
Mott, Lucretia (Coffin)(US suffragist; 1793-1880)
Mott, Nevill Francis (Br. physt.; 1905-96)
Mott's apple juice
Mott's USA (US bus.)
Motta, Jake (Giacobe) La (boxing; 1921-)
Mottola, Tommy (ent.; 1949-)
Motzfeldt, Jonathan (Premier, Greenland)
Moulin Rouge (film, 1952, 2001)
Moulin Rouge (Paris dancehall)
Moulins, France
Moulmein, Myanmar
Mound Builders (Native Amer.)
Moundou, Chad
Mounds (candy)
Moungar, Fidèle (ex-PM, Chad)
Mount Ararat (Turk.)(Noah's Ark landing)
Mount Baker-Snoqualmie National Forest (WA)
Mount Blackburn (AK)
Mount Clemens, MI
Mt. Eden Vineyards (US bus.)
Mt. Eden, Villa (US bus.)
Mount Erebus (volcano, Antarctica)
Mount Etna, (volcano, Sicily)
Mount Everest (highest mountain, Himalayas)
Mount Fairweather (AK)
Mount Fuji (also Fujiyama)(Jap. dormant volcano)
Mount Holyoke College (South Hadley, MA)
Mount Hopkins Observatory (now Fred
   Lawrence Whipple Observatory)(AZ)
Mount Kenya (also Kirinyaga)(extinct volcano)
Mount Kilimanjaro (Afr.)
Mount Kirinyaga (also Kenya)(extinct volcano)
Mount Kosciusko (Austl.)
Mount Laguna Air Force Station (CA)
Mount Lassen (also Lassen Peak)(CA volcano)
Mount McKinley (also Denali)(AK)
Mount McKinley National Park (now Denali
   National Park)(AK)
Mount Olivet (also Mount of Olives)(Jerusalem)
Mount Olympus (Gr.)
Mount Olympus (WA)
Mount Orizaba (also Citlaltepetl)(dormant
   volcano, Mex.)
Mount Palomar (CA)
Mount Parnassus (Gr.)
Mount Pearl, Newfoundland
Mount Pelée (volcano, Martinique)
Mount Pinatubo (active volcano; Philippines)
Mount Popocatépetl (volcano, Mex.)
Mount Rainier National Park (WA)
Mount Redoubt (active volcano, AK)
Mount Rushmore National Memorial (SD)
Mount Shasta (dormant volcano, CA)
Mount Sinai (NE Eg., Moses/10
   Commandments)

Mount St. Elias (mountain, AK/Can.)
Mount St. Helens (active volcano, WA)
Mount Suribachi (marine flag raising on Iwo Jima)
Mt. Veeder Winery (US bus.)
Mount Vernon (G. Washington's home)(VA)
Mount Vernon, NY
Mount Vesuvius (active volcano, It.)
Mount Whitney (CA)
Mount Zion (Jerusalem)
Mountain Dew (beverage)
Mountain Home Air Force Base, ID
Mountain Standard Time (also Mountain Time)
Mountain State (nickname, WV)
Mountain States
Mountaineer, Mercury (auto.)
Mountbatten, Lord Louis (Br. adm./earl; 1900-79)
Mountbatten, Philip, Lt. (Duke of Edinburgh,
   Prince of the UK and NIre.; 1921-)
Mounted Police, Royal Canadian (RCMP,
   Mounties)(Can. police; est. 1873)
Mounties (Royal Canadian Mounted Police;
   1950-81)
Mourning, Alonzo (basketball; 1970-)
Mouse, Mickey (cartoon chara.)
Mouse, Mickey (mag.)
Mouse, Mighty (cartoon)
Mouskouri, Nana (ent.; 1936-)
Moussorgsky, Modest Petrovich (Rus. comp.;
   1839-81)
Moustapha Niasse (PM, Senegal; 1939-)
Movie Channel, The (TMC)(TV channel)
Movieline (mag.)
Movieola (film editing machine)
Moyers, Bill (US jour.; 1934-)
Moynihan, Daniel Patrick (US pol./dipl.; 1927-)
Mozambique (Republic of)(SE Afr.)
Mozambique Current (also Agulhas Current)
Mozart, Wolfgang Amadeus (Aus. comp.; 1756-
   91)
MP (military police, mounted police)
MP3 (compu. music format)
MPV (multi-purpose vehicle)
Mr. Belvedere (TV show)
Mr. Big (pop music)
Mr. Big (slang, man in charge)
Mr. Bill (fict. chara.)
Mr. Blackwell (b. Richard Selzer)(fashion)
Mr. Blandings Builds His Dream House (film,
   1948)
Mr. Bones (slang)
Mr. Bubble bubble bath
Mr. Charlie (black slang, white man)
Mr. Chips, Goodbye, (film, 1939)
Mr. Clean (cleaner)
Mr. Clean (slang)
Mr. Coffee (kitchen appliances)
Mr. Coffee, Inc.
Mr. Cool (slang)
Mr. Ed (fict. horse)
Mr. Fixit (slang)
Mr. Frick (Werner) Groebli (ice skating; 1915-)
Mr. Goodbar (candy)
Mr. Goodbar, Looking for (film, 1977)
Mr. Goodwrench
Mr. Hobbs Takes a Vacation (film, 1962)

Mr. Holland's Opus (film, 1995)
Mr. Hyde, The Strange Case of Dr. Jekyll and (by R.L. Stevenson)
Mr. Lucky (film, 1943)
Mr. Magoo (cartoon)
Mr. Nice Guy (slang)
Mr. Novak (TV show)
Mr. Right (slang)
Mr. Ripley, The Talented (film, 1999)
Mr. Smith Goes to Washington (film, 1939)
Mr. Spock (fict. chara., *Star Trek*)
Mr. T (Lawrence Tero)(ent.; 1952-)
Mr. Tambo (slang)
Mr. Wizard's World (TV show)
MRI (magnetic resonance imaging)(med.)
Mrs. America
Mrs. Butterworth's
Mrs. Columbo (TV show)
Mrs. Dalloway (V. Woolf novel)
Mrs. Dash
Mrs. Doubtfire (film, 1993)
Mrs. Fields, Inc.
Mrs. Malaprop (fict. chara, *The Rivals*; malapropism)
Mrs. Miller, McCabe & (film, 1971)
Mrs. Miniver (film, 1942)
Mrs. Muir, The Ghost and (film, 1947)
Mrs. Paul's (fish)
Mrs. Paul's Kitchen (US bus.)
Mrs. Smith's (pies)
Mrs. Tiggy-Winkle, The Tale of (B. Potter story)
Mrs. Wiggs of the Cabbage Patch (film, 1942)
Mrs. Winterbourne (film, 1996)
MS (Mississippi, Master of Science, multiple sclerosis)
Ms. (mag.)
MS Contin (med.)
MS-DOS (Microsoft Disc Operating System)(compu.)
MSG (monosodium glutamate)
M-16 (automatic rifle)
Ms./Miss Right (slang)
MSN (Microsoft Network)
MSNBC (Microsoft & National Broadcasting Company)(TV channel)
MST (Mountain Standard Time)
Mstislav Rostropovich (Rus. cellist/cond.; 1927-)
Mswati III (king, Swaziland; 1968-)
MT (Montana)
MTV (Music Television)(TV channel)
MTV Unplugged (TV show)
MTV2 (Music Television 2)(TV channel)
Muammar al-Qaddafi (or Khadafy), Colonel (pres., Libya; 1942-)
Mubarak Abdullah al-Shamikh (PM, Libia)
Mubarak, Mohammed Hosni (pres., Egypt; 1928-)
Much Ado About Nothing (Shakespeare play)
Muda Hassanal Bolkiah Mu'izzaddin Waddaulah (Sultan/PM, Brunei; 1946-)
Mudar Badran (ex-PM, Jordan)
Mudd, Roger (TV jour.; 1928-)
Muddy Waters (aka McKinley Morganfield)(ent.; 1915-83)
Mueller, III, Robert (Swan)(US FBI dir.; 1944-)

Mueller's (noodles)
Muenster cheese (also Munster, also l.c.)
Müeslix (cereal)
Muffett, Little Miss (nursery rhyme)
Mufulira, Zambia
Mugabe, Robert (Gabriel)(pres., Zimbabwe; 1925-)
Muggeridge, Malcolm (Br. jour.; 1903-90)
Muggles (fict. people (mortals), *Harry Potter)*
Muggs, J. Fred (TV chimp; c1952)
Muggsy (Francis Joseph) Spanier (US jazz; 1906-67)
Mughal (also Mogul)(Muslim empire)
Mugur Isaresci (PM, Romania; 1949-)
Muhajirun (rel.)
Muhamad, Mahathir bin (PM, Malaysia; 1925-)
Muhammad Abdou (ex-PM, Comoros)
Muhammad Ali (also Mehemet Ali)(Eg. pol./ mil.; 1769-1849)
Muhammad Ali (b. Cassius Clay, Jr.)(boxing; 1942-)
Muhammad Ali Jinnah (India/Pak. pol.; 1876-1948)
Muhammad Ali Mahdi (ex-pres., Somalia)
Muhammad Djohar, Said (ex-pres., Comoros; 1918-)
Muhammad Farad Aidid (Somali gen.)
Muhammad ibn Abdullah (Arab, founded Islam; c570-632)
Muhammad II ("The Conqueror")(sultan, Turk.; 1432-81)
Muhammad Mossadegh (ex-PM, Iran; 1880-1967)
Muhammad Riza Pahlavi (shah, Iran; 1919-80)
Muhammad Zia ul-Haq ("President Zia")(ex-pres., Pak.; 1924-88)
Muhammad, Elijah (b. Elijah Poole)(US rel.; 1897-1975)
Muhammad, Mahathir bin (PM, Malaysia; 1925-)
Muhammadanism (misnomer for Islam rel.)
Muharram (also Moharram)(rel.)
Muharraq, Bahrain
Muir Woods National Monument (CA)
Muir, John (US environ.; 1838-1914)
Muir, Malcolm (US publ.; 1885-1979)
Muir, The Ghost and Mrs. (film, 1947)
Mujaheddin (Islamic mil.)
Mujahedeen, Afghan (Islamic holy warriors)
Mujibur Rahman (aka Sheik Mujib)(ex-PM, Bangladesh; 1920-75)
Muk, Yon Hyong (ex-premier, NKorea)
Mukalla, Yemen
Mukden (now Shenyang)
Muldaur, Diana (ent.; 1938-)
Mulder, Fox (fict. chara., *The X-Files*)
Muldoon, (Sir) Robert (David)(ex-PM, NewZeal.; 1921-92)
Mulgrew, Kate (ent.; 1955-)
Mulhare, Edward (ent.; 1923-97)
Mülheim (an der Ruhr), Germany
Mulholland Drive (Los Angeles)
Mull, Martin (ent.; 1943-)
Mullah Mohammad Omar (Afghan. pol.)
Muller v. Oregon (US law; 1908-)
Müller counter, Geiger- (also Geiger counter) (detects radiation)

Mulligan, Gerry (US jazz; 1927-)
Mulligan, Moon (Aubrey Wilson)(ent.; 1909-67)
Mulligan, Richard (ent.; 1932-2000)
Mulliken, Robert Sanderson (US chem./physt.;
     1896-1986)
Mullin, Chris (basketball; 1963-)
Mullins, Moon (comic strip)
Mulroney, Brian (ex-PM, Can.; 1939-)
Multan, Pakistan
Multigraph (graphics)
Multilith (graphics)
Muluzi, Bakili (pres., Malawi; 1943-)
Mum (anti-perspirant)
Mumford, Lewis (US writer/sociol.; 1895-1990)
Munch, Edvard (Nor. artist; 1863-1944)
Munchausen syndrome (med./psych.)
München-Gladbach (now Mönchengladbach)
Munchhausen, Karl Friedrich Hieronymus,
     Baron von (Ger. soldier/adventurer/
     anecdotist; 1720-97)
Muncie, IN
Munda (people)
Mundari (lang.)
Mundy, Carl E., Jr. (US gen.)
Munefusa, Matsuo (pseud. Bashō Matsuo)(Jap.
     poet, haiku; 1644-94)
Mungo, Van Lingo (baseball; 1911-85)
Muni, Paul (b. Muni Weisenfreund)(ent.; 1895-
     1967)
Munich Agreement/Pact (UK/Fr./Ger./It.; 1938)
Munich, Germany
Muniz, Frankie (ent.; 1985-)
Munn v. Illinois (US law; 1877)
Munro, Alice (Can. writer; 1931-)
Munro, H(ugh) H(ector)(pseud. Saki)(Br.
     writer; 1870-1916)
Munsel, Patrice (ent.; 1925-)
Munson (Berman), Ona (b. Owena Wolcott)
     (ent.; 1906-55)
Munson, Thurman (baseball; 1947-79)
Munster (province, Ir.)
Munster cheese (also Muenster)(also l.c.)
Münster, Germany
Munsters, The (TV show)
Muong (people)
Muppet Babies (cartoon)
Muppets, the (puppets)
Murakami, Haruki (Jap. writer; 1949-)
Muraliev, Amangeldy (PM, Kyrgyzstan; 1947-)
Murasaki, Shikibu, Lady (Jap. writer; c978-
     1031?)
Murat, Joachim (king, Naples; 1767-1815)
Murcia (region, Sp.)
Murder on the Orient Express (film, 1974)
Murder, Inc. (US prof. killers; 1930s)
Murder, She Wrote (TV show)
Murders in the Rue Morgue, The (E.A. Poe story)
Murdoch, Iris (Br. writer; 1919-99)
Murdoch, (Keith) Rupert (Austl./US publ.; 1931-)
Murfreesboro, TN
Muriel Rukeyser (US poet; 1913-80)
Muriel Spark (writer; 1918-)
Murillo, Bartolomé Esteban (Sp. artist; 1618-82)
Murine (med.)
Murine Co.

Murjani (clothes)
Murjani International (US bus.)
Murkowski, Frank H. (US cong.; 1933-)
Murmansk, Russia
Murnau, F(riedrich) W(ilhelm Plumpe)(Ger.
     ent.; 1889-1931)
Murphy Bed Co., Inc.
Murphy bed (stores in the wall)
Murphy Brown (TV show)
Murphy, Audie (ent., war hero; 1924-71)
Murphy, Ben (ent.; 1942-)
Murphy, Calvin (basketball; 1948-)
Murphy, Dale (football; 1956-)
Murphy, Eddie (ent.; 1961-)
Murphy: Raw, Eddie (film, 1987)
Murphy, George L. (US ent./pol.; 1902-92)
Murphy, Michael (ent.; 1938-)
Murphy, The Search for Bridey (film, 1956)
Murphy, Turk (Melvin Edward Alton)(US jazz;
     1915-87)
Murphy's Law
Murphy's Romance (film, 1985)
Murray cod (fish)
Murray Dance Studios, Arthur (US bus.)
Murray Gell-Mann (US physt.; 1929-)
Murray L. Barr (Can. phys.; 1908-95)
Murray Perahia (US pianist; 1947-)
Murray River (Austl.)
Murray Abraham, F. (ent.; 1939-)
Murray, Anne (ent.; 1945-)
Murray, Arthur (US dancer; 1896-1991)
Murray, Bill (ent.; 1950-)
Murray, Don (ent.; 1929-)
Murray, Kathryn (dance; 1906-99)
Murray, Ken (ent.; 1903-88)
Murray, Patty (US cong.; 1950-)
Murray, Philip (US labor leader; 1886-1952)
Murrow, Edward R(oscoe)(US TV jour.; 1908-65)
Musa, Said (PM, Belize; 1944-)
Musante, Tony (ent.; 1936-)
Musburger, Brent (ent.; 1939-)
Musca (astron., fly)
Muscadet (grape, wine)
Muscat (wine, grape)
Muscat, Oman (also Masqat)
Muscle Beach (Los Angeles)
Muscovite
Muscovy (also Grand Duchy of Muscovy)
     (founded c1271, Rus. empire)
Muscovy Company (also Russia Company)
     (Rus./Eng. trading)
Muscovy duck (also musk duck)
Muses (myth., nine goddesses)
Museum of American Art, National (DC)
Museum of Fine Arts (Boston)
Museum of Modern Art (MOMA)(NYC)
Museveni, Yoweri Kaguta (pres., Uganda; 1944-)
Musgrove, Ronnie (MS gov.; 1956-)
Musharraf, Gen. Pervez (PM, Pak.; 1943-)
Mushin, Nigeria
Musial, Stan(ley Frank)("Stan the Man")
     (baseball; 1920-)
Music Corp. of America (MCA)
Music Man, The (play)
Music Television (MTV)(TV channel)

Musician (mag.)
Musicians, Three (by Picasso)
Musil, Robert (Aus. writer; 1880-1942)
Muskegon, MI
Musketeers, The Three (A. Dumas novel)
Musketeers, The Three (Athos, Porthos, Aramis)
Musketeers, Three (candy bar)
Muskie, Edmund (US pol.; 1914-96)
Muskogee, OK
Muskol (insect repellant)
Muslim (rel.)
Muslim Brotherhood (rel.)
Muslim League
Muslim, Shiite (rel.)
Muslim, Sunni (rel.)
Muslim-Croat Federation (Bosnia-Hercegovina entity)
Muslims, Black (also Nation of Islam)(rel.)
Musonga, Peter Mafani (PM, Cameroon; 1942-)
Musset, Alfred de (Fr. writer; 1810-57)
Mussolini, Benito (aka *Il Duce*)(ex-PM, It.; 1883-1945)
Mustang, Ford (auto.)
Mustargen (med.)
Mutalov, Abdul Hashim (ex-PM, Uzbekistan)
Mutare, Zimbabwe
Muti, Riccardo (It. cond.; 1941-)
Mutiny on the Bounty (film, 1935, 1962)
Mutsamudu, Comoros
Mutsuhito Meiji (Jap. emp.; 1852-1912)
Mutt & Jeff (comic strip)
Mutter, Anne-Sophie (violinist; 1963-)
Mutual of America Life Insurance Company
Mutual of Omaha Insurance Co.
Muybridge, Eadweard (aka Edward James Muggeridge)(US photo.; 1830-1904)
Muyinga, Burundi
Muzak (music)
Muzorewa, Abel (Tendekayi)(Zimbabwean pol./ rel.; 1925-)
Mwanza, Tanzania
Mwinyi, Ali Hassan (ex-pres., Tanzania; 1925-)
MX missile (aka "Peacekeeper")
My Cousin Vinny (film, 1992)
My Fair Lady (play)
My Friend Flicka ((film, 1943)
My Friend Irma (film, 1949)
My Lai massacre (US/SViet.; 1968)
My Little Chickadee (film, 1940)
My Man Godfrey (film, 1936, 1957)
My Two Dads (TV show)
Myadec (multivitamins)
Myanmar (Union of)(formerly Burma)(SE Asia)
Mycelex (med.)
Mycenae (city, ancient Gr.)
Mycenaean civilization (Gr.; 4000-1000 BC)
Mycifradin (med.)
Mycitracin (med.)
Mycobacterium (med.)
Mycolog (med.)
Mycostatin (med.)
Myer, Fort, VA (mil.)
Myers Rum Co., Ltd.
Myers Squibb Co., Bristol-
Myers, Fort (FL)(city)

Myers, Linda (archery; 1947-)
Myers, "Dee Dee" Margaret Jane (US ex-White House press secy.; 1961-)
Myers, Mike (ent.; 1962-)
Myers, Russell (cartoonist, *Broom Hilda*; 1938-)
Myers's rum
Myerson, Bess (ent./consumer advocate/ex-Miss America; 1924-)
Mykonos Island, Greece (also Mikonos Island)
Mylanta (med.)
Mylar (polyester film)
Myleran (med.)
Mylicon (med.)
Myrdal, Gunnar (Swed. econ.; 1898-1987)
Myrlie Evers-Williams (US civil rights leader; 1933-)
Myrna Loy (ent.; 1905-93)
Myron (Gr. sculptor; c500-440 BC)
Myron Cohn (ent.; 1902-86)
Myrtle Beach Air Force Base, SC
Myrtle Beach, SC
Mysoline (med.)
Mystic, CT
Mystique, Mercury (auto.)
Mzuzu, Malawi

© 2001 *StenEd*® Proper Noun Speller

N (chem. sym., nitrogen)
N/A (not applicable, not available)
Na (chem. sym., sodium)
NAACP (National Association for the Advancement of Colored People)(org. 1909)
Naas, Ireland
NAB (National Association of Broadcasters, naval air base)
Naber, John (swimming; 1956-)
NABET (National Association of Broadcast Employees and Technicians)
Nabis (Fr. art; 1889-99)
Nabisco Brands, Inc.
Nabisco Foods (US bus.)
Nabisco, RJR (US bus.)
Nabokov, Vladimir (Vladomirovich)(Rus./US writer; 1899-1977)
Nabors, Jim (ent.; 1932-)
Nacio Herb Brown (US comp.; 1896-1964)
Nacogdoches, TX
Nader, Ralph (US atty./consumer advocate; 1934-)
Nadia Boulanger (Fr. cond./educ.; 1887-1979)
Nadia Comaneci (gymnast; 1961-)
Nadine Conner (ent.; 1913-)
Nadine Gordimer (SAfr. writer; 1923-)
Nadja Auermann (model; 1971-)
NAFTA (North American Free Trade Agreement)(US/Can./Mex.; 1993)
Naftin (med.)
Nagaland (state, India)
Nagari (also Devanagari)(alphabetic script)
Nagasaki, Japan (bombed in WWII; 8/9/45)
Nagel, Conrad (ent.; 1896-1970)
Nagorno-Karabakh (region, Azerbaijan)
Nagoum Yamassoum (PM, Chad)
Nagoya, Japan
Nagpur, India
Naguib Mahfouz (Eg. writer; 1911-)
Nagurski, Bronko (Bronislaw)(football; 1908-90)
Nagy, Ferenc (ex-PM, Hung.; 1903-79)
Nagy, Imre (ex-PM, Hung.; c1895-1958)
Nagy, Ivan (ballet; 1943-)
Nahayan, Sheik Zaid bin Sultan al- (pres., UAE; 1923-)
Nahuatl (lang./people)
Nahum (rel., book of the Old Testament)
NAIA (National Association of Intercollegiate Athletics)
Nair (hair remover)
Nair, Mira (ent./writer; 1957-)
Nairobi, Kenya
Naish, J. Carroll (ent.; 1900-73)
Naismith, James (Can., inv. basketball; 1861-1939)
Najibullah, Ahmadzai (Afghan. pol.; 1947-)
Nakamura, Kuniwo (pres., Palau; 1943-)
Nakasone Yasuhiro (ex-PM, Jap.; 1917-)

Naked Cowboy, the (John Robert Burck, II) (ent.; 1971-)
Nakuru, Kenya
Nala (fict. chara., *The Lion King*)
Naldecon (med.)
Nalfon (med.)
Nalley's Fine Foods (US bus.)
NAM (National Association of Manufacturers) (est. 1895)
Nam, Hong Song (PM, NKorea)
Nam Dinh, North Vietnam
Nama (people)
Namaliu, Rabbie (ex-PM, Papua New Guinea; 1947-)
Namangan, Uzbekistan
Namath, Joe (Joseph William)("Broadway Joe") (football; 1943-)
Nambaryn Enkhbayar (PM, Mongolia; 1958-)
Namib Desert (Namibia)
Namibia (Republic of)(formerly South-West Africa)(SW Afr.)
Nampa, ID
Nampo, North Korea
Nampula, Mozambique
Namur (province, Belgium)
Namur, Belgium
Nana Mouskouri (ent.; 1936-)
Nanaimo, British Columbia, Canada
Nanak (Ind. rel.; 1469-c1539)
Nance, Jim (football; 1943-92)
Nanchang, China
Nanchong, China (also Nanchung)
Nanci Griffith (ent./comp.; 1953-)
Nancy (comic strip)
Nancy Allen (ent.; 1949-)
Nancy Drew (fict. chara.)
Nancy Dussault (ent.; 1936-)
Nancy (Stevenson) Graves (US artist; 1940-96)
Nancy Kerrigan (US figure skater; 1969-)
Nancy Kulp (ent.; 1921-91)
Nancy Landon Kassebaum (US pol.; 1932-)
Nancy Lieberman-Cline (basketball; 1958-)
Nancy Lopez (golf; 1957-)
Nancy Marchand (ent.; 1928-2000)
Nancy Reagan (b. Anne Francis Robbins, aka Nancy Davis)(wife of ex-US pres.; 1923-)
Nancy Richey Gunter (tennis; 1942-)
Nancy Walker (ent.; 1922-92)
Nancy Willard (writer/artist; 1936-)
Nancy Wilson (ent.; 1937-)
Nancy, France
Nancy, Sid and (film, 1986)
Nanette Fabray (b. Ruby Nanette Fabares) (ent.; 1920-)
Nanjing, China (formerly Nanking)
Nanning, China
Nannygate (US hist.; 1993)
Nansen bottle (oceanographic instrument)
Nansen passport
Nansen, Fridtjof (Nor. expl; 1861-1930)
Nanterre, France
Nantes, Edict of (Fr. hist.; 1598)
Nantes, France
Nanticoke (Native Amer.)
Nanticoke Homes, Inc.

Nanticoke River (MD)
Nantucket Island (MA)
Nantucket Sound (MA)
Nantucket, MA
Naomi Campbell (model; 1970-)
Naomi Judd (ent.; 1946-)
Napa (county, CA)
Napa Creek Winery (US bus.)
Napa Valley (CA wine region)
Napa Valley Wines (US bus.)
Napa Wine Cellars (US bus.)
Napa, CA
Napalese (people)
Naperville, IL
Napier, John (Scot. math.; 1550-1617)
Napier, New Zealand
Naples yellow (color)
Naples, FL
Naples, Italy (also Napoli)
Naples, Kingdom of (also Kingdom of the Two
    Sicilies)(S. It.)
Napoleon I (Napoleon Bonaparte, "the Little
    Corporal")(emp., Fr.; 1769-1821)
Napoleon II (François Charles Joseph
    Bonaparte)(titular king, Rome; 1811-32)
Napoleon III (Charles Louis-Napoleon
    Bonaparte)(emp., Fr.; 1808-73)
Napoleonic Code (also Code Napoléon)(Fr. law)
Napoleonic Wars (Eur. hist.; 1799-15)
Naprosyn (med.)
Napster (compu. music)
NARA (National Archives and Records
    Administration)(US govt. agcy.; est. 1984)
Nara, Japan
Naraka (rel.)
NARAL (National Abortion [and Reproductive]
    Rights Action League)
Narasimha Rao, P(amulaparti) V(enkata)(ex-
    PM, India; 1921-)
Narayanan, K(ocheril) R(aman)(pres., India;
    1920-)
Narayanganj, Bangladesh
Narbonne, France
Narcissus (myth.)
Nardil (med.)
Narmada River (India)
Narragansett (Native Amer.)
Narragansett Bay (RI)
Narrows (strait, SE NYC)
Narrows Bridge, Verrazano- (NYC)
Naruhito (prince, Jap.; 1960-)
Narva, Estonia
NASA (National Aeronautics and Space
    Administration)(US govt. agcy.; est. 1958)
NASA (TV channel)
Nasalcrom (med.)
Nasalide (med.)
Nasby, Petroleum V(esuvius)(pseud. David
    Ross Locke)(US humorist; 1833-88)
Nasca (also Nazca)(ancient Native Amer./Peru
    culture)
NASCAR (car racing)
NASCAR's Winston Cup
NASDAQ (also Nasdaq)(finan.)
Nash, Beau (Richard)(Br. dandy/gambler;

    1674-1761)
Nash, Graham (ent.; 1942-)
Nash, Ogden (US writer/humorist; 1902-71)
Nashe, Thomas (Br. writer; 1567-1601)
Nashua, NH
Nashville Banner (TN newspaper)
Nashville Network, The (TNN)(TV channel)
Nashville Now (TV show)
Nashville Tennessean (TN newspaper)
Nashville, TN
Nasik, India
Naskapi (Indians/lang.)
Nasrin, Taslima (phys./writer; 1962-)
Nassau, Germany
Nassau, the Bahamas
Nasser, Gamal Abdel (ex-pres., Eg.; 1918-70)
Nast, Conde (US publ.)
Nast, Thomas (US artist/cartoonist; 1840-1902)
Nastase, Ilie (tennis; 1946-)
Nastassja Kinski (b. Nastassja Nakszynski)
    (ent.; 1961-)
Nastrond (myth.)
Nat "King" Cole (ent.; 1919-65)
Nat Turner (US slave/reformer; 1800-31)
Nat Turner, The Confessions of (W. Styron book)
Natal (province, SAfr.)
Natal, Brazil
Natalia Makarova (Rus. ballet; 1940-)
Natalie Cole (ent.; 1950-)
Natalie Imbruglia (ent.; 1975-)
Natalie Merchant (ent.; 1963-)
Natalie Portman (ent./model; 1981-)
Natalie Wood (ent.; 1938-81)
NATAS (National Academy of Television Arts
    and Sciences, Emmy Awards)
Natasha (or Fataly) Badenov (fict. chara.)
Natasha Richardson (ent.; 1963-)
Natchez (Native Amer.)
Natchez National Historical Park (MS)
Natchez Trace (road from Nashville, TN to
    Natchez, MS)
Natchez, MS
Natchitoches settlement (LA, 1st permanent
    settlement in LA Purchase)
Naté, Inc., Jean
Naté, Jean (toiletries)
Nathan Bedford Forrest (US gen.; 1821-77)
Nathan F. Twining (US Air Force gen.; 1897-1982)
Nathan Hale (US mil.; 1755-76)
Nathan Irvin Huggins (US hist.; 1927-89)
Nathan (Joseph) Lane (ent.; 1956-)
Nathan Mayer Rothschild (Ger./Br. finan.;
    1777-1836)
Nathan Mayer Rothschild, (Sir)(Br. pol./baron;
    1840-1915)
Nathan Milstein (violinist; 1904-92)
Nathan Strauss (Ger./US bus./finan.; 1848-1931)
Nathan(iel) Bailey (Br. lexicographer; ?-1742)
Nathan, George Jean (US writer; 1882-1958)
Nathan, S. R. (pres., Singapore; 1924-)
Nathanael Greene (US mil.; 1742-86)
Nathanael West (aka Nathan Wallenstein
    Weinstein)(US writer; 1904-40)
Nathaniel Bacon (US colonial leader; 1647-76)
Nathaniel Currier (US lithographer; 1813-88)

Nathaniel Hawthorne (US writer; 1804-64)
Natick Research and Development Center (MA)
Natick, MA
Nation of Islam (also Black Muslims)(rel.)
Nation's Business (mag.)
Nation, Carrie (Amelia Moore)(US temperance
 leader; 1846-1911)
National Abortion [and Reproductive] Rights
 Action League (NARAL)
National Academy of Recording Arts & Sciences
National Academy of Sciences (org. 1863)
National Academy of Television Arts and
 Sciences (NATAS, Emmy Awards)
National Aeronautics and Space Administration
 (NASA)(US govt. agcy.; est. 1958)
National Air and Space Museum (Smithsonian,
 DC)
National Arbor Day Foundation, The
National Archives (DC)
National Archives and Records Administration
 (NARA)(US govt. agcy.; est. 1984)
National Association for the Advancement of
 Colored People (NAACP)(org. 1909)
National Association of Broadcast Employees
 and Technicians (NABET)
National Association of Broadcasters (NAB)
National Association of Intercollegiate Athletics
 (NAIA)
National Association of Manufacturers (NAM)
 (est. 1895)
National Association of Real Estate Brokers
National Association of Realtors
National Association of Television and Radio
 Announcers (NATRA)
National Audubon Society (environ. org.)
National Automobile Dealers Association
National Ballet of Canada
National Baseball Hall of Fame and Museum
 (est. 1939, Cooperstown, NY)
National Basketball Association (NBA)
National Broadcasting Company (NBC)(TV
 channel)
National Bureau of Standards (NBS)(US govt.
 agcy.; est. 1901)
National Business Woman (mag.)
National Cancer Institute
National Car Rental System, Inc.
National Christian Network
National Collegiate Athletic Association (NCAA)
 (est. 1906)
National Conference of Christians and Jews
 (est. 1928)
National Congress of Parents and Teachers
 (also National Parent-Teacher Association)
 (PTA)(est. 1897)
National Council of the Churches of Christ in
 the United States of America (est. 1950)
National Council on Alcoholism (org. 1944)
National Court Reporters Association (NCRA)
National Court Reporters Foundation (NCRF)
National Day (Ch., Sp., Viet.)
National Drug Control Policy, Office of (US govt.)
National Education Association of the United
 States (NEA)(est. 1906)
National Endowment for Democracy (US pol.

agcy.)
National Endowment for the Arts (NEA)
National Endowment on (or for) the Arts and
 Humanities (US govt. agcy.; est. 1965)
National Enquirer (mag.)
National Examiner
National Football Conference (NFC)
National Football Foundation and Hall of Fame
 (NFFHF)(est. 1947)
National Football League (NFL)
National Gallery (London)
National Gallery of Art (Smithsonian, DC)
National Geographic (mag.)
National Geographic Explorer (TV show)
National Geographic Society (est. 1888)
National Governors' Association
National Guard of the United States (US mil.)
National Highway Traffic Safety Administration
 (NHTSA)
National Hockey League (NHL)
National Honor Society
National Industrial Recovery Act (NIRA)(US
 law; 1933)
National Institutes of Health (NIH)(US govt.
 agcy.; est. 1930)
National Invitation Tournament (NIT)(basketball)
National Labor Relations Act (NLRA)(US law;
 1935)
National Labor Relations Board (NLRB)(US
 govt. agcy.; est. 1935)
*National Labor Relations Board v. Jones and
 Laughlin Steel Co.* (US law; 1937)
National Lampoon
National Lampoon's Animal House (film, 1978)
National League (baseball)
National League of Professional Baseball Clubs
National Marine Fisheries Service (US govt.
 agcy.; est. 1970)
National Medical Enterprises, Inc. (healthcare)
National Museum of American Art
 (Smithsonian, DC)
National Museum of American History
 (Smithsonian, DC)
National Museum of Natural History
 (Smithsonian, DC)
National Naval Medical Center (also Bethesda
 Naval Hospital)(Bethesda, MD)
National Network, The (TNN)(TV channel)
National Oceanic and Atmospheric
 Administration (NOAA)(US govt. agcy.; est.
 1970)
National Organization for Women (NOW)
National Parent-Teacher Association (also
 National Congress of Parents and Teachers)
 (PTA)(est. 1897)
National Park Service (US govt. bureau)
National Party, Australian (Austl. pol.)
National Portrait Gallery (Smithsonian, DC)
National Public Radio (NPR)
National Red Cross, American (US relief agcy.;
 est. 1881)
National Republican Party (US pol.)
National Review (mag.)
National Rifle Association of America (NRA)
National Safety Council (est. 1913)

National Science Foundation (NSF)(US govt. agcy.; est. 1950)
National Security Council (NSC)(US govt. agcy.; est. 1947)
National Semiconductor Corp.
National Seurity Agency (NSA)(US govt.)
National Socialism (also Nazism)(Ger.)
National Socialist German Workers' Party (also Nazi Party)
National States Rights Party (US pol.)
National Theatre of Great Britain
National Transportation Safety Board (US govt. agcy.; est. 1975)
National Unity Day (It.)
National Unity Party (US pol.)
National University (San Diego, CA)
National Urban League (org. 1910)
National Weather Service (US govt.; est. 1870)
National Wildlife (mag.)
National Woman's Christian Temperance Union (WCTU)
National Zoological Park (Smithsonian, DC)
Nations, Commonwealth of
Nations, League of (internat'l govt. org.; 1920-)
Nations, United (internat'l org.; est. 1945)
Nationwide Insurance Co.
Natitingou, Benin
Native American (also American Indian)(peoples)
Native Dancer (champion horse)
Nativity (rel.)
NATO (North Atlantic Treaty Organization)
NATRA (National Association of Television and Radio Announcers)
Natron, Lake (Tanzania)
Natsagiyn Bagabandi (pres., Mongolia; 1950-)
Natta, Giulio (It. chem./eng.; 1903-79)
Natural Bridges National Monument (UT)
Natural Health (mag.)
Natural History (mag.)
Naturalizer (shoes)
NaturalTouch (contact lenses)
Nature Made (vitamins)
Nature Valley (food)
Nature's Remedy (med.)
Naturetin (med.)
Natwick, Mildred (ent.; 1908-94)
Natya, Bharat (dance, India)
Naugahyde (fabric)
Naugatuck, CT
Naughton, James (ent.; 1945-)
Naughty Marietta (play; film, 1935)
Naum Gabo (b. Naum Pevsner)(US sculptor; 1890-1977)
Nauru (Republic of)(island, SW Pac.)
Nauruan (lang./people)
Nautilus (fitness)
Nautilus Industries (US bus.)
Nautilus Marine Engineering (US bus.)
Navajo (or Navaho)(Native Amer.)
Navajo (or Navaho) rug
Naval Academy, U.S. (Annapolis, MD)(est. 1845)
Naval Jelly Co., Inc.
Naval Medical Center, National (also Bethesda Naval Hospital)(Bethesda, MD)
Naval Observatory (DC)

Navane (med.)
Navarone, The Guns of (film, 1961)
Navarra (also Navarre)(province, Sp.)
Navarra Vineyards (US bus.)
Navarre, Margaret of (also Margaret of Angoulême)(queen, Navarre; 1492-1549)
Navarro, Fats (Theodore)(US jazz; 1923-50)
Navigation Acts (Br. hist.; 17th-16th c.)
Navigator, Lincoln (auto.)
Navistar International Corp.
Navratilova, Martina (tennis; 1956-)
Navy Cross (mil.)
Navy, Department of the (US mil.)
Navy, U.S. (US mil.)
Nawaz Sharif (ex-PM, Pak.; 1948-)
Nazarbayev, Nursultan A. (pres., Kazakhstan; 1940-)
Nazarene (rel.)
Nazarenes (grp. Ger. art.; 19th c.)
Nazareth, Israel
Nazarite (rel.)
Nazca (also Nasca)(ancient Native Amer./Peru culture)
Nazi (Nazi Party member)
Nazi Party (also National Socialist German Workers' Party)
Nazism (also National Socialism)(Ger.)
Nb (chem. sym., niobium)
NBA (National Basketball Association)
NBC (National Broadcasting Company)(TV channel)
NBC News (TV show)
NBS (National Bureau of Standards)(US govt. agcy.; est. 1901)
NC (North Carolina)
NCAA (National Collegiate Athletic Association) (est. 1906)
NCR Corp.
NCRA (National Court Reporters Association)
NCRF (National Court Reporters Foundation)
N(ewel) C(onvers) Wyeth (US artist; 1882-1945)
ND (North Dakota)
Nd (chem. sym., neodymium)
Ndadaye, Melchior (ex-pres., Burundi; ?-1994)
NDE (near-death experience)
Ndebele (also Matabele)(people)
N'Djamena, Chad (also Ndjamena)
Ndola, Zambia
NE (Nebraska)
Ne (chem. sym., neon)
Ne Win (b. Maung Shu Maung)(ex-pres., Myanmar; 1911-)
NEA (National Education Association)
NEA (National Endowment for the Arts)
NEA Today (mag.)
Neagh, Lough (lake, NIre.)
Neagle, Anna (b. Marjorie Robertson)(ent.; 1908-86)
Neal, Patricia (ent.; 1926-)
Nealon, Kevin (ent.; 1953-)
Neanderthal (*Homo sapiens neanderthalensis*) (lived 100,000 to 35,000 years ago)
Neapolitan (Naples citizen)
Neapolitan ice cream
Neapolitan mastiff (dog)
Near v. Minnesota (US law; 1931-)

Nebco Evans Holding Co.
Nebit-Dag, Turkmenistan
Nebraska (NE)
Nebraska Act/Bill, Kansas- (US hist.; 1854)
Nebuchadnezzar (or Nebuchadrezzar)(king, Babylonia; 604?-561? BC)
Nebula, Ring (astron.)
NebuPent (med.)
NEC Corp.
NEC Technologies, Inc.
Neckar River (Ger.)
Necker, Jacques (Fr. pol.; 1732-1804)
Ned Beatty (ent.; 1937-)
Ned Ludd (also Lludd, Nudd, King Ludd)(Welsh legend)
Ned Rorem (US comp.; 1923-)
Ned R(ay) McWherter (ex-TN gov.; 1930-)
Needham, MA
Needles, CA
Neenah, WI
Neeson, Liam (ent.; 1952-)
Neet (hair remover)
Nefertiti (also Nefretete)(queen, Eg.; 14th c.)
Neff, Hildegarde (ent.; 1925-)
Negasso Gidada (pres., Ethiopia; 1943-)
Negev (also Negeb)(desert, Isr.)
NegGram (med.)
Negombo, Sri Lanka
Negri, Pola (ent.; 1900-87)
Negro (also black, African-American, Aframerican, Afro-American)(people)
Negro College Fund, United
Negroid (one of three major races of humans)
Negros (island, Philippines)
Nehemiah (rel., book of the Old Testament)
Nehemiah, Renaldo (track; 1959-)
Nehru jacket
Nehru, Jawaharlal (ex-PM, India; 1889-1964)
Neiafu, Tonga
Neijiang, China (also Neikiang, Nei-chaing)
Neil A(lden) Armstrong (astro., 1st to walk on moon; 1930-)
Neil (Mallon) Bush (US bro. of pres./son of ex-pres.; 1955-)
Neil Diamond (b. Noah Kaminsky)(US comp./ent.; 1941-)
Neil Jordan (ent.; 1950-)
Neil Patrick Harris (ent.; 1973-)
Neil Sedaka (ent.; 1939-)
Neil Simon, (Marvin)(US writer; 1927-)
Neil Young (ent.; 1945-)
Neill, Sam (b. Nigel Neill)(ent.; 1947-)
Neiman-Marcus, Inc.
Neisse River (N central Eur.)
Nell (Eleanor) Gwyn (or Gwynne)(ent.; 1651-87)
Nellie Bly (Elizabeth Cochrane Seaman)(US jour./reformer; 1867-1922)
Nellie (Jacob Nelson) Fox (baseball; 1927-75)
Nellie Melba, Dame (aka Helen Porter Mitchell) (Austl. opera; 1861-1931)
Nelligan, Kate (ent.; 1951-)
Nellis Air Force Base, NV
Nelly (Leonie) Sachs (Ger. writer; 1891-1970)
Nelova (med.)
Nelson A(ldrich) Rockefeller (ex-US VP; 1908-79)

Nelson Algren (US writer; 1909-81)
Nelson Eddy (ent.; 1901-67)
Nelson (Rolihlahla) Mandela (ex-pres., SAfr.; 1918-)
Nelson Riddle (US cond.; 1921-85)
Nelson River (Can.)
Nelson Wilmarth Aldrich (US finan./legislator; 1841-1915)
Nelson, Alice Dunbar-
Nelson, Bill (Clarence William)(US cong.; 1942-)
Nelson, Byron (golf; 1911-)
Nelson, Cindy (skiing; 1955-)
Nelson, Craig T. (ent.; 1946-)
Nelson, E(arl) Ben(jamin)(US cong./ex-NE gov.; 1941-)
Nelson, Ed (ent.; 1928-)
Nelson, Harriet (Hilliard)(ent.; 1909-94)
Nelson, Horatio, Viscount (Br. admiral; 1758-1805)
Nelson, Judd (ent.; 1959-)
Nelson, New Zealand
Nelson, Ozzie (ent.; 1906-75)
Nelson, Ozzie & Harriet (TV couple)
Nelson, Rick(y)(ent.; 1940-85)
Nelson, Tracy (ent.; 1963-)
Nelson, Willie (ent.; 1933-)
Nembutal (med.)
Nemean lion (myth.)
Nemerov, Howard (US writer; 1920-91)
Nemesis (myth.)
Nemeth, Miklos (ex-PM, Hung.)
Nemours & Co., E. I. du Pont de
Nemours, E(leuthere) I. du Pont de (US bus.; 1771-1834)
Nena, Jacob (ex-pres., Micronesia; 1941-)
Neneh Cherry (ent./songwriter; 1964-)
Nenni, Pietro (It. socialist leader/writer; 1891-1980)
neo-Darwinism (evolution theory)
Neolithic period (New Stone Age; 10,000 to 4,500 years ago)
Neon, Dodge (auto.)
Neon, Plymouth (auto.)
Neoplatonism (phil.)
Neoptolemus (myth.)
Neosho River (KS)
Neosporin (med.)
Neosporin Ophthalmic (med.)
Neo-Synephrine (med.)
Nepal (Kingdom of)(S Asia)
Nepalese (people)
Nepali (lang.)
Nephelococcygia (Aristophanes' utopia)
Nepos, Cornelius (Roman hist.; c100-c25 BC)
Neptune (planet; myth.)
Neptune, NJ
Nereid (Neptune moon; myth.)
Nereus (myth.)
Nero (b. Lucius Domitius Ahenobarbus, aka Nero Claudius Caesar Drusus Germanicus) (emp., Rome; 37-68)
Nero Germanicus, Tiberius Claudius Drusus (Claudius I)(emp., Rome; 10 BC-AD 54)
Nero (Caesar) Tiberius, Claudius (emp., Rome; 42 BC-AD 37)

Nero Wolfe (fict. detective)
Nero, Peter (US pianist; 1934-)
Neruda, Pablo (aka Neftali Ricardo Reyes y Basoalto)(Chilean poet; 1904-73)
Nerva, Marcus Cocceius (emp., Rome; c35-98)
Nervi, Pier Luigi (It. arch.; 1891-1979)
Nesbitt, Kathleen (ent.)
Nescafé (beverages)
Ness monster, Loch (Scot.)
Ness, Eliott (US FBI agent; 1902-57)
Ness, Loch (lake, Scot.)
Nesselrode mix (fruits/nuts, sauce)
Nestea (beverages)
Nestle Beverage Co.
Nestle USA (US bus.)
Nestlé Foods (US bus.)
Nestlé Quik
Nestlé Toll House cookies
Nestor (myth.)
Net (Internet)
Netanya, Israel
Netanyahu, Benjamin (Isr. pol.; 1949-)
Netherlands (Kingdom of the)(also Holland)(W Eur.)
Netherlands Antilles (West Indies)
Neto, Agostinho Antonio (ex-pres., Angola; 1922-79)
Nets, New Jersey (basketball team)
Netscape Communications (US bus.)
Network Solutions, Inc.
Netzahualcóyotl, Mexico
Neuchâtel, Switzerland
Neufchâtel cheese
Neugebauer object, Becklin- (astro.)
Neuman, Alfred E. (fict. chara., *Mad*)
Neutra, Richard (Joseph)(US arch.; 1892-1970)
Neutrogena (med./skincare)
Neutrogena Corp.
Neuwirth, Bebe (Beatrice)(ent.; 1958-)
Nevada (NV)
Neve Campbell (ent.; 1973-)
Nevelson, Louise (Rus./US sculptor; 1900-88)
Never-Never Land (Peter Pan's)
Nevers, Ernie (football; 1903-76)
Neves, Brazil
Nevi'im (also Prophets)(rel.)
Nevil Shute (Br. writer/eng.; 1899-1960)
Nevill Francis Mott (Br. physt.; 1905-96)
Neville Chamberlain (ex-PM, Br.; 1869-1940)
Neville Marriner (ent.; 1924-)
Neville, Aaron (ent.; 1941-)
Nevins, Allan (US hist./educ.; 1890-1971)
Nevis, St. Christopher- (Federation of)(also St. Kitts-Nevis)(West Indies)
Nevis, St. Kitts- (officially Federation of St. Christopher-Nevis)(West Indies)
New Age (music)
New Age Journal (mag.)
New Albany, IN
New American Bible
New Amsterdam (now New York City)
New Atlantis (utopia, Sir Francis Bacon)
New Balance
New Balance Athletic Shoes (US bus.)
New Bedford, MA

New Beetle, Volkswagen (auto.)
New Berlin, WI
New Bern, NC
New Britain Island (Papua New Guinea)
New Britain, CT
New Brunswick (province, Can.)
New Brunswick, NJ
New Caledonia (Fr. islands, S Pac.)
New Castle, IN, PA
New Choices for Retirement Living (mag.)
New Criticism (lit.)
New Cumberland Army Depot (PA)
New Deal (US hist./FDR; 1933)
New Delhi, India
New Democratic Party (NDP)(Can. pol.)
New England (region, NE US: CT/MA/ME/NH/RH/VT)
New England boiled dinner
New England clam chowder
New England Confederation
New England Journal of Medicine (mag.)
New England Patriots (football team)
New England Primer (18th c. schoolbook)
New England, United Colonies of (New England Confederation)(US his.)
New English (also Modern English)(lang.)
New English Bible
New Era, Lancaster (PA newspaper)
New Freedom (health)
New General Catalog (NGC)(astron.)
New Glasgow, Nova Scotia, Canada
New Granada (NW SAmer.)
New Guinea (island, SW Pac.)
New Guinea, Territory of (Papua New Guinea)
New Hampshire (NH)
New Hampshire chicken
New Harmony (utopian community, IN)
New Harmony, IN
New Haven Register (CT newspaper)
New Haven, CT
New Hebrides (now Vanuatu)
New Humanism (lit.)
New Iberia, LA
New Ireland (island, Papua New Guinea)
New Jersey (NJ)
New Jersey Devils (hockey team)
New Jersey Nets (basketball team)
New Jerusalem (heaven)
New Jerusalem, Church of the (also Swedenborgians)
New Kids on the Block (pop music)
New Kowloon, Hong Kong
New Left (pol.)
New London, CT
New Mexico (NM)
New Orleans lugger (boat)
New Orleans Saints (football team)
New Orleans Times-Picayune (LA newspaper)
New Orleans, Battle of (US/Br.; 1815)(Amer. Civil War; 1862)
New Orleans, LA
New Party (US pol.)
New Providence Island, Bahamas
New Providence, Bahamas
New Republic, The (mag.)

New Right (pol.)
New Rochelle, NY
New Sacristy (also Medici Chapel)(Florence, It.)
New Scotland Yard (Br. police)
New South Wales (state, Austl.)
New Stone Age (Neolithic period; 10,000 to
    4,500 years ago)
New Testament (rel.)
New Thought (phil./rel.; mid 19th c.)
New Wave (Fr. lit.; 1950s)
New Wave (pop music; 1970s-)
New Westminster, British Columbia, Canada
New WKRP in Cincinnati (TV show)
New Woman (mag.)
New World (the Americas)
New Year's Day (January 1)
New Year's Eve (December 31)
New York (NY)
New York City Ballet (NYCB)
New York City, NY (NYC)
New York Daily News (NY newspaper)
New York fern (plant)
New York Giants (football team)
New York Islanders (hockey team)
New York Jets (football team)
New York Knicks (basketball team)
New York Life Insurance Co.
New York Magazine (mag.)
New York Mets (baseball team)
New York Post (NY newspaper)
New York Public Library (NYC)
New York Rangers (hockey team)
New York Review of Books, the
New York school (art; mid-20th c.)
New York Shakespeare Festival
New York steak (also New York strip)
New York Stock Exchange (also Big Board)
New York Times (NY newspaper)
New York Times Book Review
New York Times Co.
New York Times v. Sullivan (US law; 1964)
New York Yankees (baseball team)
New York, Gitlow v. (US law; 1925-)
New York, Lochner v. (US law; 1905)
New Yorker, Chrysler (auto.)
New Yorker, The (mag.)
New Zealand (SW Pac.)
Newark Air Force Station (OH)
Newark International Airport (NJ)
Newark Star-Ledger (NJ newspaper)
Newark, DE, NJ, OH
Newbery Award (children's lit.)
Newbery, John (Br. publ.; 1713-67)
Newburg (sauce)
Newburg, lobster (food)
Newburgh, NY
Newburyport, MA
Newcastle disease (birds/fowl)
Newcastle, Australia
Newcastle, Ontario, Canada
Newcastle, Thomas Pelham-Holles (ex-PM, Br.;
    1693-1768)
Newcastle-under-Lyme, England
Newcastle-upon-Tyne, England (also
    Newcastle)

Newcombe, John (tennis; 1943-)
Newell Convers Wyeth (US artist; 1882-1945)
Newell Rubbermaid, Inc.
Newfoundland (dog)
Newfoundland (province, Can.)
Newfoundland Time
Newgate prison (London; razed 1902)
Newhart, Bob (ent.; 1929-)
Newhouse, Donald E(dward)(US publ.; 1929-)
Newhouse, Samuel I(rving), Jr. (US publ.;
    1895-1979)
Newington, CT
Newley, Anthony (ent.; 1931-99)
Newman, Barnett (US artist; 1905-70)
Newman, Edwin (US writer; 1919-)
Newman, John H(enry)(Br. rel.; 1801-90)
Newman, Paul (ent.; 1925-)
Newman, Randy (ent.; 1943-)
Newmar, Julie (b. Julie Chalane Newmeyer)
    (ent.; 1935-)
Newmarket, England
Newmarket, Ontario, Canada
Newport Beach, CA
Newport Jazz Festival (RI)
Newport News, VA
Newport, KY, RI
Newport, Wales
Newry, Northern Ireland
News & Free Press, Detroit (MI newspaper)
News & Observer, Raleigh (NC newspaper)
News & Record, Greensboro (NC newspaper)
News & World Report, U.S. (mag.)
News-Free Press, Chattanooga (TN newspaper)
News-Globe, Amarillo (TX newspaper)
News-Journal, Daytona Beach (FL newspaper)
News-Journal, Pensacola (FL newspaper)
News Journal, Wilmington (DE newspaper)
News-Leader, Springfield (MO newspaper)
News-Press, Fort Myers (FL newspaper)
News-Sentinel, Fort Wayne (IN newspaper)
News-Sentinel, Knoxville (TN newspaper)
News-Tribune, Duluth (MN newspaper)
News-Tribune, Tacoma (WA newspaper)
News, Anchorage (AK newspaper)
News, Bangor (ME newspaper)
News, Birmingham (AL newspaper)
News, Buffalo (NY newspaper)
News, Dayton (OH newspaper)
News, Detroit (MI newspaper)
News, Erie (PA newspaper)
News, Fort Lauderdale (FL newspaper)
News, Greenville (SC newspaper)
News, Harrisburg (PA newspaper)
News, Huntsville (AL newspaper)
News, Indianapolis (IN newspaper)
News, Lancaster (PA newspaper)
News, Los Angeles (CA newspaper)
News, Savannah (GA newspaper)
News, York (PA newspaper)
Newsday, Long Island (NY newspaper)
NewsHour with Jim Lehrer (TV show)
Newsnet (compu. database)
Newsweek (mag.)
Newsweek, Inc.
Newt(on Leroy) Gingrich (US pol.; 1943-)

Newton-John, Olivia (ent.; 1948-)
Newton, Huey P. (US, cofounded Black Panthers; 1942-89)
Newton, IA, KS, MA
Newton, (Sir) Isaac (Br. physt./math., gravity; 1642-1727)
Newton, Wayne (ent.; 1942-)
Newton's law(s) of motion (also Newtonian law) (physics)
Newton's rings (photo.)
Newtonian physics
Newtonian reflector (astron.)
Newtownabbey, Northern Ireland
Nexis (compu. database, news)
Nexium (med.)
NeXt, Inc.
Nextel Communications, Inc.
Nexxus (hair care)
Nexxus Products Co.
Ney, Michel (Fr. mil.; 1769-1815)
Nez Percé (Native Amer.)
Nez Percé National Historical Park (ID)
NFC (National Football Conference)
NFL (National Football League)
NFL Monday Night Football (TV show)
Ngaio Marsh, (Edith), Dame (NewZeal. writer; 1899-1982)
Ngalops (people)
NGC (New General Catalog [astron.])
Ngo Dinh Diem (ex-pres., SViet.; 1901-63)
Ngozi, Burundi
Nguema, Francisco Macías (ex-pres., Equatorial Guinea; 1924-79)
Nguesso, Denis Sassou- (pres., Rep/Congo; 1943-)
Ngugi wa Thiong'o (Kenyan writer; 1938-)
Ngulu (lang.)
Nguyen Van Thieu (ex-pres., SViet; 1923-)
Nguyen, Dustin (ent.; 1962-)
Ngwazi Hastings Kamuzu Banda (ex-pres., Malawi; 1902-)
NH (New Hampshire)
Nha Trang, Vietnam
NHL (National Hockey League)
NHTSA (National Highway Traffic Safety Administration)
Ni (chem. sym., nickel)
Niagara Falls, NY
Niagara Falls, Ontario, Canada
Niagara green (color)(also l.c.)
Niagara River (NY/Ontario)
Niamey, Niger
Niasse, Moustapha (PM, Senegal; 1939-)
Niaux Cave (prehistoric paintings, Fr.)
Nibelung, The Ring of the (Richard Wagner tetralogy)
Nibelungenlied (13th c. Ger. epic poem)
Nibelungs (myth.)
Nicaea (ancient cities: now Iznik, Turk. and Nice, Fr.)
Nicaea, Council(s) of (also Nicene Council)(rel.; 325)
Nicaea, Turkey (now Iznik)
Nicaragua (Republic of)(CAmer.)
Nicaraguan Revolution (1978-79)

Niccolo (di Bernardo) Machiavelli (It. pol./ writer/phil.; 1469-1527)
Niccolo Paganini (It. comp.; 1782-1840)
Nice Guy, Mr. (slang)
Nice, France
Nicene Council (also Council(s) of Nicaea)(rel.; 325)
Nicene Creed (rel.)
Nicéphore Soglo (ex-pres., Benin; 1934-)
Nichelle Nichols (ent.; 1933-)
Nicholas Biddle (US finan.; 1786-1844)
Nicholas Braithwaite (ex-PM, Grenada; 1925-)
Nicholas Cage (b. Nicholas Coppola)(ent.; 1964-)
Nicholas Calio (US pres. staff; 1953-)
Nicholas Copernicus (also Nicolaus)(Pol. astron.; 1473-1543)
Nicholas I (Nicolai Pavlovich)(emp., Rus.; 1796-1855)
Nicholas I, St. (Nicholas the Great)(pope; 800?-67)
Nicholas II (Nikolai Aleksandrovich)(emp., Rus.; 1868-1918)
Nicholas III (Giovanni Gaetano Orsini)(It. pope; 1210?-80)
Nicholas Monsarrat (Br. writer; 1910-79)
Nicholas Murray Butler (US educ.; 1862-1947)
Nicholas Nickleby (C. Dickens novel)
Nicholas V (Tomaso Parentucelli)(It. pope; 1397-1455)
Nicholas, Denise (ent.; 1944-)
Nicholas, Fayard (ent.; 1914-)
Nicholas, Harold (ent.; 1921-2000)
Nicholas, St. (also Santa Claus, Kriss Kringle)
Nicolo Amati (It. violin maker; 1596-1684)
Nichols, Mike (ent.; 1931-)
Nichols, Nichelle (ent.; 1933-)
Nichols, Red (US jazz; 1905-65)
Nichols, Terry (Lynn)(Oklahoma City bombing; 1955-)
Nicholson, Ben (Br. artist; 1894-1982)
Nicholson, Jack (ent.; 1937-)
Nichrome (alloy)
Nick at Nite (TV channel)
Nick Carter (ent., Backstreet Boys; 1980-)
Nick Carter (fict. detective)
Nick Faldo (golf; 1957-)
Nick Nolte (ent.; 1940-)
Nickelodeon (NIK)(TV channel)
Nicklaus, Jack (William)(golf; 1940-)
Nickleby, Nicholas (C. Dickens novel)
Nickles, Donald Lee (US cong.; 1948-)
Nicks, Stevie (ent.; 1948-)
Nicobar Islands (Indian Ocean)
Nicodemus (rel.)
Nicoderm (med.)
Nicol prism (physics/optics)
Nicol Williamson (ent.; 1938-)
Nicola Pisano (It. artist; c1220-84)
Nicolae Ceausescu (ex-pres., Romania; 1918-89)
Nicolae Vacarolu (ex-PM, Romania)
Nicolai Gedda (tenor; 1925-)
Nicolai, (Carl) Otto (Ehrenfried)(Ger. comp.; 1810-49)
Nicolar (med.)
Nicolas Poussin (Fr. artist; 1594-1665)

Nicolas Roeg (ent.; 1928-)
Nicolay (Andreyevich) Rimsky-Korsakov (Rus. comp.; 1844-1908)
Nicole (Brown) Simpson (US news; 1959-94)
Nicole Hollander (US cartoonist, *Sylvia*; 1939-)
Nicole Kidman (ent.; 1967-)
Nicolette Larson (ent.; 1952-97)
Nicollette Sheridan (ent./model; 1963-)
Nicorette (med.)
Nicosia, Cyprus
Nicotinex (med.)
Nicotrol (med.)
Nidre, Kol (rel.)
Niebuhr, Reinhold (US rel.; 1892-1971)
Niekro, Phil (baseball; 1939-)
Niels Henrik David Bohr (Dan. physt.; 1885-1962)
Nielsen Co., A. C. (TV ratings)
Nielsen ratings (TV)
Nielsen, A. C. (US bus./ratings; 1897-1980)
Nielsen, Brigitte (ent.; 1963-)
Nielsen, Carl August (Dan. comp.; 1865-1931)
Nielsen, Leslie (ent.; 1926-)
Niemeyer Soares Filho, Oscar (Brazilian arch.; 1907-)
Niente Winery, Far (US bus.)
Nietzsche, Friedrich Wilhelm (Ger. phil.; 1844-1900)
Nieuw Amsterdam, Suriname
Nieuw Nickerie, Suriname
Nifleheim (also Niflheim)(myth.)
Nigel Bruce (ent.; 1895-1953)
Niger (Republic of)(NW Afr.)
Niger-Congo (langs.)
Niger River (W Afr.)
Nigeria (Federal Republic of)(W Afr.)
Night Court (TV show)
Night Journey (also al-Miraj)(rel.)
Nightingale, Florence (Br., founded modern nursing; 1820-1910)
Nightline (TV show)
Niigata, Japan
Niihua (island, HI)
Nijinsky, Vaslav (or Waslaw)(Rus. ballet; 1890-1950)
Nijmegen, Netherlands
NIK (Nickelodeon)(TV channel)
Nike (myth.)
Nike (shoes)
Nike missile
Nike, Inc.
Niki Taylor (model; 1975-)
Nikica Valentic (ex-PM, Croatia)
Nikita S(ergeyevich) Khrushchev (ex-premier, USSR; 1894-1971)
Nikita, La Femme (film, 1991)
Nikka (Dominica) Costa (ent.; 1972-)
Nikkei Average/Index
Nikki Giovanni (b. Yolande Cornelia Giovanni, Jr.)(US poet; 1943-)
Nikko Audio (US bus.)
Nikko National Park (Jap.)
Nikko, Japan
Nikola Tesla (Croatia/US elec. eng.; 1856-1943)
Nikolaevich, Aleksandr (Alexander II)(emp.,

Rus.; 1818-81)
Nikolai A(leksandrovich) Bulganin (ex-PM USSR; 1895-1975)
Nikolai Bukharin (USSR, pol.; 1888-1938)
Nikolai (Vasilievich) Gogol (Rus. writer; 1809-52)
Nikolai Patrushev (Rus. FSB chief; 1951-)
Nikolai Sokoloff (Rus./US cond.; 1886-1965)
Nikolay Viktorovich Podgorny (USSR pol.; 1903-83)
Nikolayev, Andrian G(rigorievich)(cosmo.; 1929-)
Nikolayev, Ukraine
Nikon (photo)
Nikon, Inc.
Nikos Kazantzakis (Gr. writer; 1883-1957)
Nile green (color)
Nile River (Eg.)
Niles, IL, OH
Nilo-Hamitic (lang.)
Nilote (lang./people)
Nilotic (lang./people)
Nils Lofgren (ent.; 1951-)
Nilsson, Birgit (Swed., opera; 1918-)
Nilsson, Harry (ent./songwriter; 1941-94)
Nilstat (med.)
Nimeiry, Gaafar Muhammad al- (ex-pres., Sudan; 1930-)
Nîmes, France
Nimitz, Chester W(illiam)(US adm.; 1885-1966)
Nimotop (med.)
Nimoy, Leonard (ent.; 1931-)
Nimrod (great-grandson of Noah)
Nin, Anais (US writer; 1903-77)
Niña (C. Columbus ship; 1492)
Nina Blackwood (ent.; 1955-)
Nina Foch (ent.; 1924-)
Nina Ricci Jewelry (US bus.)
Nina Simone (ent.; 1933-)
Nina Totenberg (US jour.; 1944-)
Niña, La (unusually cold ocean current)
9 Lives (pet food)
Ninety-Five Theses (rel.)
Nineveh (ancient Assyrian capital)
Ning, Yang Chen (Ch. physt.; 1922-)
Ningbo, China (also Ning-po)
Ningxia (also Ningxia Hui)(region, Ch.)
Ninja Turtles (cartoon)
Ninja Turtles, Teenage Mutant (cartoon; film, 1990)
Nino Espinosa (baseball; 1953-88)
Niño, El (unusually warm ocean current)
Ninotchka (film, 1939)
Nintendo (video games)
Nintendo Co. Ltd.
Nintendo of America, Inc.
Niobe (myth.)
Nipigon, Lake (Ontario, Can.)
Nipissing, Lake (Can.)
Nipon, Albert (clothing)
Nippon (Japanese for Japan)
Nippon Electric Co. (NEC)
Nippon Kogaku USA, Inc.
Nippon Steel Corp.
Nipponese (Japanese)
Nipsey Russell (ent.; 1924-)
Nirenberg, Marshall Warren (US chem.; 1927-)

Niro, Robert De (ent.; 1943-)
Nirvana (pop music)
Nirvana Foundation (psychic research)
Nis, Serbia
Nisan (also Nissan)(Jew. mo.)
Nisei (Amer. of Jap. descent)(also l.c.)
Nishapur, Iran
Nishinomiya, Japan
Nissan (auto.)
Nissan 200SX (auto.)
Nissan 200SX SE (auto.)
Nissan 200SX SE-R (auto.)
Nissan 240SX (auto.)
Nissan 240SX LE (auto.)
Nissan 300 ZX Turbo (auto.)
Nissan Altima (auto.)
Nissan Altima GLE (auto.)
Nissan Altima GXE (auto.)
Nissan Altima SE (auto.)
Nissan Altima SE Limited (auto.)
Nissan Altima XE (auto.)
Nissan Frontier Desert Runner (auto.)
Nissan Frontier pickup (auto.)
Nissan Frontier SC (auto.)
Nissan Frontier SE (auto.)
Nissan Frontier XE (auto.)
Nissan Maxima (auto.)
Nissan Maxima GLE (auto.)
Nissan Maxima GXE (auto.)
Nissan Maxima SE (auto.)
Nissan Maxima SE Limited (auto.)
Nissan Motor Corp. USA.
Nissan North America, Inc.
Nissan Pathfinder (auto.)
Nissan Pathfinder LE (auto.)
Nissan Pathfinder SE (auto.)
Nissan Pathfinder XE (auto.)
Nissan Quest (auto.)
Nissan Quest GLE minivan (auto.)
Nissan Quest GXE minivan (auto.)
Nissan Quest minivan (auto.)
Nissan Quest SE minivan (auto.)
Nissan Quest XE minivan (auto.)
Nissan Sentra (auto.)
Nissan Sentra GLE (auto.)
Nissan Sentra GXE (auto.)
Nissan Sentra SE (auto.)
Nissan Sentra SE Limited (auto.)
Nissan Sentra SE-R (auto.)
Nissan Sentra XE (auto.)
Nissan Stanza (auto.)
Nissan Xterra (auto.)
Nissan Xterra SE (auto.)
Nissan Xterra XE (auto.)
Nissen hut (also Quonset hut)
Nissin Foods USA Co., Inc.
Nita Barrow, (Ruth)(ex-gov.-gen.; Barbados; 1916-95)
Niterói, Brazil
Nitro-Bid (med.)
Nitrocap (med.)
Nitrodisc (med.)
Nitro-Dur (med.)
Nitrogard (med.)
Nitrol (med.)

Nitrolingual (med.)
Nitrong (med.)
Nitrospan (med.)
Nitrostat (med.)
Nitty Gritty Dirt Band, The
Niue Island, New Zealand (also Savage Island)
Nivea (skin care)
Niven, David (ent.; 1909-83)
Nix Creme Rinse (med.)
Nixon Cox, Tricia (Patricia)(daughter of ex-US pres.; 1946-)
Nixon Eisenhower, Julie (daughter of ex-US pres.; 1948-)
Nixon, Agnes (US writer, soap operas; 1927-)
Nixon, Cynthia (ent.; 1966-)
Nixon, Pat (b. Thelma Catherine Ryan)(wife of ex-US pres.; 1912-93)
Nixon, Richard Milhous (37th US pres.; 1913-94)
Nixon, U.S. v. (US law; 1974)
Niyazov, Saparmurad A. (pres., Turkmenistan; 1940-)
Nizam (obsolete title, ruler of India)
Nizer, Louis (atty./writer; 1902-94)
Nizhny Novgorod, Russia (formerly Gorky)
Nizhny Tagil, Russia
Nizoral (med.)
Nizwa, Oman
NJ (New Jersey)
Njord (myth.)
N'Kayi, Congo
Nkole (lang.)
Nkomo, Joshua (Zimbabwean pol.; 1917-99)
Nkongsamba, Cameroon
Nkrumah, Kwame (ex-pres., Ghana; 1909-72)
NLRB (National Labor Relations Board)
NM (New Mexico)
No (chem. sym., nobelium)
No (Jap. drama)
No Nonsense Fashions, Inc.
No, Dr. (film, 1962)
No. 10 Downing Street (London)(PM residence)
Noah (rel.)
Noah Beery (ent.; 1884-1946)
Noah Beery, Jr. (ent.; 1913-94)
Noah Webster (US lexicographer; 1758-1843)
Noah Wyle (ent.; 1971-)
Noah's Ark
Noam Chomsky (US linguist; 1928-)
Nob Hill (San Francisco)
Nobel Peace Prize
Nobel Prize for Chemistry
Nobel Prize for Literature
Nobel Prize for Physics
Nobel Prize for Physiology or Medicine
Nobel, Alfred B(ernhard)(Swed. chem./eng./finan.; 1833-96)
Noble Bookstores, Inc., Barnes &
Noble, James (ent.; 1922-)
Noboa Bejarano, Gustavo (pres., Ecuador; 1937-)
Noboru Takeshita (ex-PM, Jap.; 1924-2000)
Noctec (med.)
Nod, land of (myth. land of sleep)
NoDoz (med.)
Noel (also Christmas, Xmas)(rel.)
Noel Coward, (Sir)(Br. writer/comp.; 1899-1973)

Nofzinger, Lyn (US pol./writer; 1924-)
Nogales, AZ
Nogales, Mexico
Noggin (TV channel)
Noguchi, Isamu (Jap./US artist; 1904-88)
Nokia (US bus.)
Nolan Ryan (baseball; 1947-)
Nolan, Lloyd (ent.; 1902-85)
Noland, Kenneth (US artist; 1924-)
Nolde, Emil (b. Emil Hansen)(Ger. artist; 1867-
   1956)
Noll, Chuck (football; 1931-)
Nolte, Nick (ent.; 1940-)
Nolvadex (med.)
Nome, AK
Nonesuch Records, Elektra/Asylum/ (US bus.)
Nono, Luigi (It. comp.; 1924-90)
Nonpartisan League (US pol. org.; 1915-24)
noodles Romanoff
Noone, Peter (ent.; 1947-)
Noor (Mohammed) Hassanali (ex-pres.,
   Trinidad/Tobago; 1918-)
Nora Ephron (US writer/ent.; 1941-)
Norbert Weiner (US math.; 1894-1964)
Norberto Costa Alegre (ex-PM, Saö Tomé/
   Príncipe)
Norcept-E (med.)
Norcross, Inc.
Nordenskjöld, (Nils) Adolf Erik, Baron (Swed.
   expl.; 1832-1901)
Nordenskjöld, (Nils) Otto Gustaf (Swed. expl.;
   1869-1928)
Nordhausen, Germany
Nordic (people)
Nordic countries (Den./Fin./Iceland/Nor./Swed.)
Nordic Ski Imports, Inc.
NordicTrack (fitness)
NordicTrack, Inc.
Nordiques, Quebec (hockey team)
Nord-Pas-de-Calais (region, Fr.)
Nordstrom (US bus.)
Nordstrom store
Norelco (shavers)
Norelco Consumer Products Co.
Norell, Norman (b. Norman Levinson)(US
   fashion designer; 1900-72)
Norflex (med.)
Norfolk (county, Eng.)
Norfolk Island (Austl.)
Norfolk Island pine
Norfolk jacket/coat
Norfolk Naval Air Station (VA)
Norfolk Naval Shipyard (VA)
Norfolk Southern Corp.
Norfolk terrier (dog)
Norfolk Virginian-Pilot (VA newspaper)
Norfolk, NE, VA
Norge (appliances)
Norge Co.
Norgesic (med.)
Noriega (Morena), Manuel (Antonio), Gen. (ex-
   dictator, Panama; imprisoned for drug
   trafficking; 1938-)
Norinyl (med.)
Noritake (china)

Noritake Co., Inc.
Norlestrin (med.)
Norlutate (med.)
Norlutin (med.)
Norm Crosby (ent.; 1927-)
Norm Macdonald (ent.; 1962-)
Norm Van Brocklin (football; 1926-83)
Norma (astron., square)
Norma Rae (film, 1979)
Norma Shearer (ent.; 1902-83)
Norma Talmadge (ent.; 1893-1957)
Normal, IL
Norman (people)
Norman architecture (Eur.; 12-13th c.)
Norman Bel Geddes (US designer; 1893-1958)
Norman Conquest (Eng. hist.; 1066)
Norman Cosmetic Studios, Merle (Merle
   Norman cosmetics)(US bus.)
Norman Cosmetics, Merle (US bus.)
Norman Cousins (US editor/writer; 1912-90)
Norman Dello Joio (US comp.; 1913-)
Norman Fell (ent. 1924-98)
Norman French (lang.)
Norman Jewison (ent.; 1926-)
Norman Lear (ent.; 1922-)
Norman Mailer (US writer; 1923-)
Norman Manley (ex-PM, Jamaica; 1892-1969)
Norman Mingo (cartoonist; 1896-1980)
Norman M(attoon) Thomas (US pol.; 1884-1968)
Norman Norell (b. Norman Levinson)(US
   fashion designer; 1900-72)
Norman Podhoretz (US writer; 1930-)
Norman Rockwell (US artist; 1894-1978)
Norman Schwarzkopf, H., Jr. ("Stormin'
   Norman")(US gen.; 1934-)
Norman Vincent Peale, Rev. (US rel./writer;
   1898-93)
Norman Y(oshio) Mineta (US secy./trans, ex-
   secy./commerce; 1931)
Norman, Greg(ory)(golf; 1955-)
Norman, Jessye (ent.; 1945-)
Norman, Marsha (Williams)(US playwright; 1947-)
Norman, Merle (cosmetics)
Norman, OK
Normand, Mabel (ent.; 1894-1930)
Normandie, Basse- (region, Fr.)
Normandie, Haute- (region, Fr.)
Normandy (regions, Fr.)
Normandy campaign
Normandy landings (also D-Day)
Normandy, House of (Br. ruling family; 1066-
   1154)
Normodyne (med.)
Norodom Ranariddh (ex-PM, Cambodia; 1944-)
Norodom Sihanouk (king, Cambodia; 1922-)
Noroxin (med.)
Norpace (med.)
Norplant (med.)
Norpramin (med.)
Norris, Chuck (b. Carlos Ray)(ent.; 1940-)
Norris, Frank (US writer; 1870-1902)
Norris, George William (US pol.; 1861-1944)
Norris, Kathleen (Thompson)(US writer; 1880-
   1966)
Norristown, PA

Norrköping, Sweden
Norse (also Norseman)(ancient people)
Norse, Old (ancient lang.)
Norstad, Lauris (US mil./ex-commander, NATO;
 1907-88)
Nortel Networks (US bus.)
North America
North American Free Trade Agreement (NAFTA)
 (US/Can./Mex.; 1993)
North American Philips Co.
North American Rockwell Corp.
North American Soccer League (also NASL)
North Atlantic Current (also North Atlantic
 Drift)(warm ocean current)
North Atlantic Treaty (4/4/49)
North Atlantic Treaty Organization (NATO)
 (internat'l org.; est. 1949)
North Battleford, Saskatchewan, Canada
North Bay, Ontario, Canada
North Bergen, NJ
North Brabant (province, Netherlands)
North Cape (Nor.)
North Carolina (NC)
North Cascades National Park (WA)
North Charleston, SC
North Chicago, IL
North Dakota (ND)
North Dartmouth, MA
North Haven, CT
North Highlands, CA
North Holland (province, the Netherlands)
North Korea (Democratic People's Republic of)
 (E Asia)
North Las Vegas, NV
North Little Rock, AR
North Miami, FL
North Miami Beach, FL
North Olmsted, OH
North Platte, NE
North Platte River (W central US)
North Pole (northern point of Earth)
North Rhine-Westphalia (state, Ger.)
North Richland Hills, TX
North Sea (NW Eur.)
North Star (also Polaris, Polestar)(astron.)
North Star State (nickname, MN)
North Stars, Minnesota (hockey team)
North Tipperary (county, Ir.)
North Tonawanda, NY
North Vancouver, British Columbia, Canada
North Yemen (now part of Yemen)
North York, Ontario, Canada
North Yorkshire (county, Eng.)
North, Frederick (ex-PM, Br.; 1732-92)
North, John Ringling (US circus dir.; 1903-85)
North, Lowell (yachting; 1929-)
North, Oliver "Ollie," Lt. Col. (US mil./pol.; 1943-)
North, Sheree (ent.; 1933-)
Northampton, England
Northampton, MA
Northamptonshire (county, Eng.)
Northanger Abbey (film, 1987)
Northbrook, IL
Northeast Passage (Eur./Asia)
Northeastern (Oklahoma) State University

(Tahlequah, OK)
Northeastern University (Boston, MA)
Northeastern (Illinois) University (Chicago, IL)
Northern Exposure (TV show)
Northern Hemisphere
Northern Ireland (part of the UK)
Northern Mariana Islands (Commonwealth of
 the)(Pac.)
Northern Rhodesia (now Zambia)
Northern Securities Co. v. U.S. (US law; 1904)
Northern Territory (territory, Austl.)
Northerner
Northglenn, CO
Northrop Corp.
Northrop Grumman Corp.
Northumberland (county, Eng.)
Northumberland, John Dudley, Duke of (Br.
 pol.; c1502-53)
Northumbria (Anglo-Saxon kingdom; 6th-9th c.)
Northwest Airlines, Inc.
North-West Frontier Province (province, Pak.)
Northwest Passage (AK/Can.)
Northwest Territories (territory, Can.)
Northwest Territory (US hist.: IL/IN/MI/MN/OH/
 WI; 1783)
Northwestern (Oklahoma) State University
 (Alva, OK)
Northwestern Mutual Life Insurance Co., The
Northwestern State University (Natchitoches, LA)
Northwestern University (Evanston, IL)
Norton AntiVirus (compu)
Norton Computing, Inc., Peter
Norton-Lambert Corp.
Norton Simon (US bus.; 1907-93)
Norton Simon Museum of Art (CA)
Norton SystemWorks (compu)
Norton Utilities (compu.)
Norton, Edward (ent.; 1969-)
Norton, Eleanor Holmes (US pol.; 1937-)
Norton, Gale Ann (US secy./interior; 1954-)
Norville, Deborah (US TV jour.; 1958-)
Norvo, Red (Kenneth)(US jazz; 1908-99)
Norwalk, CA, CT, OH
Norway (Kingdom of)(NW Eur.)
Norway maple (tree)
Norway pine
Norway rat
Norway spruce
Norwegian (lang./people)
Norwegian current
Norwegian elkhound (dog)
Norwegian Sea
Norwich terrier (dog)
Norwich, CT
Norwich, England
Norwood, MA, OH
Norworth, Jack (US lyricist; 1879-1959)
Nostradamus (b. Michel de Nostredame)(Fr.
 astrol./phys./seer; 1503-66)
Nostrand Reinhold Co., Inc., Van
Nosy/nosy Parker (slang, busybody)
Note, Kessai (pres., Marshall Islands)
Notre Dame Cathedral (also Notre Dame de Paris)
Notre Dame, The Hunchback of (by V. Hugo)
Notre Dame, University of (South Bend, IN)

Nottingham, England
Nottingham, Sheriff of (*Robin Hood*)
Nottinghamshire (also Notts)(county, Eng.)
Nouadhibou, Mauritania
Nouakchott, Mauritania
Nouhak Phoumsavan (ex-pres., Laos; 1914-)
Nouméa, New Caledonia
Nova (also Nova Salmon)(smoked Pacific salmon)
Nova Iguaçu, Brazil
Nova Scotia (province, Can.)
Nova Scotia salmon
Nova University (Fort Lauderdale, FL)
Novaes, Guiomar (pianist; 1895-1979)
Novahistine (med.)
Novak, Kim (ent.; 1933-)
Novak, Mr. (TV show)
Novara, Italy
Novarro, Ramon (ent.; 1899-1968)
Novato, CA
Novaya Zemlya (islands, NW Russia)
Novell (US bus.)
Novello, Antonia (nee Coello)(US phys., 1st
    woman/1st Hispanic surgeon gen.; 1944-)
Novello, Ivor (ent./playwright/comp.; 1893-1951)
Novgorod, Russia
Novi Sad, Yugoslavia
Novocain (med.)
Novokuznetsk, Russia
Novolin (med.)
Novosibirsk, Russia
NOW (National Organization for Women)
Nox (myth.)
Noxzema (med./skincare)
Noyce, Robert N. (US inv.; 1927-89)
Noyes, Alfred (Br. poet; 1880-1958)
NP (nurse practitioner)
Np (chem. sym., neptunium)
NPH Iletin (med.)
NPH insulin (med.)
NPV (no par value)
NQB (no qualified bidders)
NRA (also N.R.A.)(National Rifle Association)
NRC (Nuclear Regulatory Commission)
NSAID (nonsteroidal anti-inflammatory drug)
    (med.)
Nsanzimana, Sylvestre (ex-PM, Rwanda)
NSC (National Security Council)
NSF (non/not sufficient funds)
Nsibambi, Prof. Apolo (PM, Uganda; 1938-)
'N Sync (pop music)
N'Tchama, Caetano (PM, Guinea-Bissau)
Ntoutoume-Emane, Jean-François (PM, Gabon;
    1939-)
Ntozake Shange (b. Paulette Williams)(US
    writer; 1948-)
NTP (normal temperature and air pressure)
Ntsu Mokhehle (ex-PM, Lesotho; 1918-99)
NTT Data Corp.
Nu, U (Thakin)(ex-PM, Myanmar; 1907-95)
Nuba (people)
Nubain (med.)
Nubia (region, NE Afr.)
Nubian (lang./people)
Nubian Desert (NE Afr.)
Nubian goat

Nubira, Daewoo (auto.)
Nuclear Regulatory Commission (NRC)
Nucor Corp.
Nude Descending a Staircase (M. Duchamp
    painting)
Nuer (lang./people)
Nueva San Salvador, El Salvador
Nuevo Laredo, Mexico
Nuevo Léon (state, Mex.)
Nugent, Elliott (ent.; 1899-1980)
Nugent, Ted (ent.; 1948-)
Nuggets, Denver (basketball team)
Nujoma, Sam (pres., Namibia; 1929-)
Nuku'alofa, Tonga
Numazu, Japan
Numbers (aka Book of Numbers)(rel., book of
    the Old Testament)
Numorphan (med.)
Nung (lang.)
Nunn-Bush Shoe Co.
Nunn, Sam(uel Augustus)(US pol.; 1938-)
Ñuñoa, Chile
Nupe (lang./people)
Nupercainal (med.)
Nuprin (med.)
Nuremberg Trials (Nazi war crimes)(1945-46)
Nuremberg, Germany
Nuremberg, Judgment at (film, 1961)
Nureyev, Rudolf (Rus. ballet; 1938-93)
Nurmi, Paavo (running; 1897-1973)
Nursultan A. Nazarbayev (pres., Kazakhstan;
    1940-)
Nut (myth.)
Nutcracker Suite, The (Tchaikovsky)
Nutley, NJ
Nutmeg State (nickname, CT)
Nutone (US bus.)
NutraSweet Co., The
Nutri/System, Inc.
Nutrition Corp., General (GNC)
Nutter Butter (cookies)
NV (Nevada)
NY (New York)
Nyad, Diana (swimming/jour.; 1949-)
Nyamwezi-Sukuma (lang.)
Nyanja (lang./people)
Nyasa, Lake (now Lake Malawi)
Nyasaland (now Malawi)
NYC (New York City)
Nye, Louis (ent.; 1920-)
Nyerere, Julius (Kambarage)(ex-pres.,
    Tanzania; 1922-99)
Nyers, Rezso (Hung. pol.; 1923-)
Nyíregyháza, Hungary
Nylint Toy Corp.
Nynex Corp. (also NYNEX)
NYPD Blue (TV show)
NyQuil (med.)
Nyro, Laura (ent.; 1947-97)
NYSE (New York Stock Exchange)
Nytol (med.)
Nyx (myth.)
Nzérékoré, Guinea

– O –

O (chem. sym., oxygen)
O cedar Angler (broom)
Oahu (island, HI)
Oak Forest, IL
Oak Lawn, IL
Oak Park, IL, MI
Oak Ridge Boys, The
Oak Ridge Vineyards (US bus.)
Oak Ridge, TN
Oakie, Jack (ent.; 1903-78)
Oakland Army Base (CA)
Oakland Athletics (also Oakland A's)(baseball
   team)
Oakland Tribune (CA newspaper)
Oakland University (Rochester, MI)
Oakland, CA, NJ
Oakley, Annie (Phoebe Mozee)(ent./
   sharpshooter; 1860-1926)
Oakville, Ontario, Canada
OAPEC (Organization of Arab Petroleum
   Exporting Countries)(est.; 1968)
OAS (Organization of American States)(N/
   central/S Amer.; est. 1948)
Oasis, Isuzu (auto.)
Oates, Hall & (pop music)
Oates, John (ent.; 1948-)
Oates, Joyce Carol (US writer; 1938-)
OAU (Organization of African Unity)(est. 1963)
Oaxaca, Mexico
OB (obstetrics)(med.)
Ob River (Rus.)
o.b. (tampons)
Obadiah (rel., book of the Old Testament)
O'Bannon, Frank (Lewis)(IN gov.; 1930-)
Obasanjo, Olusegun (pres., Nigeria; 1935-)
Obata, Gyo (US arch.; 1923-)
OBE (out-of-body experience)
Obed Dlamini (ex-PM, Swaziland)
Oberammergau, Germany
Oberhausen, Germany
Oberlin College (Oberlin, OH)
Oberon (Uranus moon; myth.)
Oberon, Merle (ent.; 1911-79)
Oberth, Hermann (Ger. physt./rocketry
   pioneer; 1894-1989)
Ob/Gyn (also OB/GYN)(obstretrics/gynecology)
Obidos, Brazil
Óbidos, Portugal
Obie award (off Broadway)
Obock, Djibouti
Oboler, Arch (ent.; 1909-87)
Obote, (Apollo) Milton (ex-pres., Uganda; 1925-)
O'Brian, Hugh (b. Hugh J. Krampe)(ent.; 1925-)
O'Brien, Conan (ent.; 1963-)
O'Brien, Dan (decathlon; 1966-)
O'Brien, Edmond (ent.; 1915-85)
O'Brien, Margaret (ent.; 1937-)
O'Brien, Pat (ent.; 1899-1983)
O'Brien, Tim (US writer; 1946-)

Observer, Charlotte (NC newspaper)
Observer-Times, Fayetteville (NC newspaper)
Obuchi, Keizo (ex-PM, Japan; 1937-2000)
OC (officer commanding)
Ocala, FL
Ocasek, Ric (ent.; 1949-)
O'Casey, Sean (Ir. writer; 1884-1964)
Occam's razor (phil.)
Occam, William of (Br. phil.; c1285-c1349)
Occident (Eur. + W. Hemisphere countries)
Occidental Petroleum Corp.
Occupational Safety and Health Administration
   (OSHA)(US govt. agcy.; est. 1970)
OCD (Office of Civil Defense)
Ocean City, MD, NJ
Ocean Spray Cranberries, Inc.
Ocean State (nickname, RI)
Ocean, Billy (b. Leslie Sebastian Charles)(ent.;
   1950-)
Oceania (collective name for Pac. islands)
Oceanic and Atmospheric Administration,
   National (NOAA)(US govt. agcy.; est. 1970)
Oceanic art
Oceanside, CA, NY
Oceanus (myth.)
Ochirbat, Punsalmaagiyn (ex-pres., Mongolia;
   1943-)
Ocho Rios, Jamaica
Ochs, Adolph Simon (US publ.; 1858-1935)
Oconee National Forest (GA)
O'Connell, Daniel ("the Liberator")(Ir. pol.;
   1775-1847)
O'Connor, Carroll (ent.; 1924-2001)
O'Connor, Donald (ent.; 1925-)
O'Connor, (Mary) Flannery (US writer; 1925-64)
O'Connor, John (Joseph), Cardinal (US rel.;
   1920-2000)
O'Connor, Sandra Day (US jurist; 1930-)
O'Connor, Sinéad (ent.; 1966-)
O'Connor, Tay Pay (Thomas Power)(Ir. jour./
   pol.; 1848-1929)
OCR (optical character reader/
   recognition)(compu.)
OCS (Officer Candidate School)
Octans (astron., octant)
Octavia (Roman empress; c40-62)
Octavia (Roman, wife of M. Anthony; ?-11 BC)
Octavius, Gaius Julius Caesar (aka Caesar
   Augustus, Octavian)(1st Roman emp.; 63
   BC-AD 14)
October Revolution (part of Russian Revolution;
   1917)
Octoberfest (also Oktoberfest)(Ger. beer festival)
Octopussy (film, 1983)
Ocufen (med.)
Ocusert Pilo (med.)
OD (overdose)
O'Day, Anita (US jazz; 1919-)
Odd Couple, The (film, TV show)
Odd Fellows, Independent Order of (fraternal
   society; est. 1918)
Oddsson, David (PM, Iceland; 1948-)
ODECA (Organization of Central American
   States)(est. 1951/1962)
Odense, Denmark

Oder (or Odra) River (N central Eur.)
Odessa, TX
Odessa, Ukraine
Odets, Clifford (US writer; 1906-63)
Odetta (b. Odetta Holmes)(ent.; 1930-)
Odilon Redon (Fr. artist; 1840-1916)
Odin (also Woden, Wotan, Wodan)(myth.)
Odio, Rodrigo Carazo (ex-pres., Costa Rica)
O'Donnell, Chris (ent.; 1970-)
O'Donnell, Rosie (ent.; 1962-)
Odra (or Oder) River (N central Eur.)
Odysseus (fict. chara., Homer's *Odyssey, Illiad*)
Odyssey, Honda (auto.)
Odyssey, the (by Homer)
OE (Old English)
OECD (Organization for Economic Cooperation
    & Development)
Oedipus (myth.)
Oedipus at Colonus (by Sophocles)
Oedipus complex (psych.)
Oedipus Rex (also *Oedipus Tyrannus*)(by
    Sophocles)
OEO (Office of Economic Opportunity)(US govt.)
Oersted, Hans (Christian)(Dan. physt.; 1777-
    1851)
Oerter, Al (discus thrower; 1936-)
Off Broadway (also off Broadway)(theater)
Offaly (county, Ir.)
Offenbach (am Main), Germany
Offenbach, Jacques (Levy)(Fr. comp.; 1819-80)
Office Act, Tenure of (US hist.; 1867)
Office Depot, Inc.
Office of Administration (US govt.)
Office of Economic Opportunity (OEO)(US govt.)
Office of High Commissioner for Refugees,
    United Nations (UNHCR)(est. 1951)
Office of Management and Budget (OMB)(US
    govt.)
Office of National Drug Control Policy (US govt.)
Office of Personnel Management (OPM)(US
    govt. agcy.; est. 1979)
Office of Policy Development (US govt.)
Office of Science and Technology Policy (US
    govt.)
Office of the President and Vice President (US
    govt.)
Office of the U.S. Trade Representative (US
    govt.)
OfficeMax (US bus.)
Off-Off Broadway (also off-off Broadway)(theater)
Offutt Air Force Base, NE
O'Flaherty, Liam (Ir. writer; 1897-1984)
Ogaden (region, Ethiopia)
Ogbomosho, Nigeria
Ogden Corp.
Ogden Nash (US writer/humorist; 1902-71)
Ogden, Gibbons v. (US law; 1924)
Ogden, UT
Ogdensburg, NY
Ogen (med.)
Ogi, Adolf (ex-pres., Switz.; 1942-)
Ogilvy, David (Br. writer/adv.; 1911-99)
Oglethorpe, James E(dward)(Br. gen., founded
    Georgia; 1696-1785)
O'Grady, Sweet Rosie (film, 1943)

Ogun (state, Nigeria)
OH (Ohio)
Oh Boy Corp.
Oh Boy! pizza
Oh! Calcutta! (play)
Oh! Susanna (song)
O'Hair, Madalyn Murray (US atheist activist;
    1919-95?)
O'Hara, John (US writer; 1905-70)
O'Hara, Maureen (b. Maureen FitzSimons)(ent.;
    1920-)
O'Hara, Scarlett (fict. chara., *Gone With the Wind*)
O'Hare International Airport (Chicago IL)
O Henry (aka William Sydney Porter)(US
    writer; 1862-1910)
O'Herlihy, Dan (ent.; 1919-)
Ohio (OH)
Ohio buckeye (tree)
Ohio River (E central US)
Ohio v. Akron Center for Reproductive Health
    (US law; 1983)
Ohio, Mapp v. (US law; 1961)
Ohira Masayoshi (ex-PM, Jap.; 1910-80)
Ohlsson, Garrick (pianist; 1948-)
Ohm, Georg (Simon)(Ger. physt.; 1789-1854)
Ohm's law (elec.)
O(rville) H(itchock) Platt (US pol.; 1827-1905)
Ohrid Lake (SE Eur.)
Ohsumi (Jap. space satellite)
Oil of Olay (skin care)
Oilers, Edmonton (hockey team)
Oilers, Houston (football team)
Oingo Boingo (pop music)
Oise River (W Eur.)
Oistins, Barbados
Oistrakh, David (violinist; 1908-74)
Oita, Japan
Ojai, CA
Ojibwa (also Chippewa)(Native Amer.)
O(renthal) J(ames) Simpson (football; 1947-)
OK (Oklahoma, oll korrect [all right])
OK Corral (Tombstone, AZ; gunfight; 1881)
Oka River (W Russia)
Okayama, Japan
Okazaki, Japan
O.K. Corral, Gunfight at the (film, 1957)
Okeechobee, FL
Okeechobee, Lake (FL)
O'Keefe, Dennis (ent.; 1908-68)
O'Keeffe, Georgia (US artist; 1887-1986)
Okefenokee Swamp (GA/FL)
Okhotsk, Sea of (N Pac.)
Okidata Corp.
Okie (slang)
Okinawa (island, Jap.)
Okker, Tom (tennis; 1944-)
Oklahoma (OK)
Oklahoma City Oklahoman (OK newspaper)
Oklahoma City, OK
Oklahoma! (play; film, 1955)
Oklahoma panhandle (formerly Territory of
    Cimarron)
Oklahoma, Ake v. (US law; 1985)
Oklahoman, Oklahoma City (OK newspaper)
Okmulgee, OK

Oksana Baiul (figure skating; 1977-)
Oktoberfest (also Octoberfest)(Ger. beer festival)
Olaf (or Olav) I (Tryggvesson)(king, Nor.; 969-1000)
Olaf (or Olav) II (Haraldsson)(St. Olaf)(king, Nor.; 995-1030)
Olaf (or Olav) III ("the Quiet")(king, Nor.; ?-1093)
Olaf (or Olav) V (b. Alexander Edward Christian Frederik of Glücksburg)(king, Nor.; 1903-91)
Olafur Ragnar Grímsson (pres., Iceland; 1943-)
Olajuwon, Hakeem (basketball; 1963-)
Oland, Warner (ent.; 1880-1938)
Olathe, KS
Olaus (or Ole) Roemer (Dan. astron.; 1644-1710)
Olay, Oil of (skin care)
Olazabal, Jose Maria (golf; 1966-)
Olcott, Chauncey (US comp./ent.; 1860-1932)
Old Bailey (London criminal court)
Old Bay (seasoning)
Old Bay Co., Inc.
Old Colony State (nickname, MA)
Old Dominion (nickname, VA)
Old Dominion University (Norfolk, VA)
Old El Paso Foods Co.
Old English (also Anglo-Saxon)(lang.; c500-1050)
Old English (type style)
Old English Game (chicken)
Old English sheepdog
Old Faithful geyser (Yellowstone National Park)
Old Glory (also Stars and Stripes)(US flag)
Old-House Journal (mag.)
Old Ironsides (Constitution, The)(US naval ship)
Old Left (pol.)
Old Line State (nickname, MD)
Old MacDonald's Farm (nursery song)
Old Man River (Mississipi River)
Old Norse (ancient lang.)
Old North State (nickname, NC)
Old Pretender (aka James III, James [Francis] Edward Stuart)(Br. prince; 1688-1766)
Old Royal Observatory (London)(also Royal Greenwich Observatory)
Old Saybrook, CT
Old Scratch (the Devil)
Old Spice (men's cologne)
Old Stone Age (Paleolithic period; 2 million to 15,000 years ago)
Old Testament (rel.)
Old Vic Theatre (also Royal Victoria Hall)(London)
Old World (Eur./Asia/Africa)
Old Yeller (F. Gipson novel)
Oldenburg, Claes (Thure)(US artist; 1929-)
Oldenburg, Germany
Oldfield cinquefoil (plant)
Oldfield, Barney (Berna Eli)(auto racing; 1878-1946)
Oldham, England
Oldman, Gary (ent.; 1958-)
Olds (see Oldsmobile)(auto.)
Olds, Ransom Eli (US bus./auto.; 1864-1950)
Oldsmobile (auto.)
Oldsmobile 88 (auto.)
Oldsmobile 88 LS (auto.)

Oldsmobile 88 LSS (auto.)
Oldsmobile 98 (auto.)
Oldsmobile Achieva (auto.)
Oldsmobile Achieva SL (auto.)
Oldsmobile Alero (auto.)
Oldsmobile Alero GL (auto.)
Oldsmobile Alero GLS (auto.)
Oldsmobile Alero GX (auto.)
Oldsmobile Aurora (auto.)
Oldsmobile Bravada (auto.)
Oldsmobile Calais (auto.)
Oldsmobile Ciera (auto.)
Oldsmobile Cutlass (auto.)
Oldsmobile Cutlass Ciera (auto.)
Oldsmobile Cutlass Ciera SL (auto.)
Oldsmobile Cutlass GL (auto.)
Oldsmobile Cutlass GLS (auto.)
Oldsmobile Cutlass Supreme (auto.)
Oldsmobile Delta 88 (auto.)
Oldsmobile Intrigue (auto.)
Oldsmobile Intrigue GL (auto.)
Oldsmobile Intrigue GLS (auto.)
Oldsmobile Intrigue GX (auto.)
Oldsmobile Regency (auto.)
Oldsmobile Silhouette
Oldsmobile Silhouette GL minivan (auto.)
Oldsmobile Silhouette GLS minivan (auto.)
Oldsmobile Silhouette GS minivan (auto.)
Oldsmobile Silhouette minivan (auto.)
Oldsmobile Silhouette Premier minivan (auto.)
Oldsmobile Toronado (auto.)
Olduvai Culture (500,000-2 million years ago)
Olduvai Gorge (archeo. site, Tanzania)
Ole (John Sigvard) Olsen (ent.; 1892-1963)
Ole (or Olaus) Roemer (Dan. astron.; 1644-1710)
O'Leary, Hazel R. (US ex-secy./ener.; 1937-)
Oleg Atkov (cosmo.)
Oleg Cassini (b. Oleg Cassini Loiewski)(US designer; 1913-)
Oleg Cassini, Inc.
Olerud, John (baseball; 1968-)
O level (Br. educ., ordinary level)
Olga (clothing)
Olga Co.
Olga Korbut (Soviet gymnast; 1955-)
Olga Petrova
Oligocene epoch (38-26 million years ago)
Olin Corp.
Olin, Ken (ent.; 1954-)
Olin, Lena (ent.; 1955-)
Olinda, Brazil
Oliphant, Pat (US pol. cartoonist; 1935-)
Oliva, Tony (Pedro)(baseball; 1940-)
Olive Garden (US bus.)
Olive Oyl (fict. chara., Popeye)
Olive Schreiner (pseud. Ralph Iron)(SAfr. writer; 1855-1920)
Oliver! (film, 1968)
Oliver Cromwell (Br. gen./pol.; 1599-1658)
Oliver Goldsmith (Br./Ir. writer; 1730?-74)
Oliver Hardy (ent.; 1892-1957)
Oliver "Ollie" North, Lt. Col. (US mil./pol.; 1943-)
Oliver (Hazard) Perry (US mil.; 1785-1819)
Oliver Reed (ent.; 1938-99)
Oliver Stone (ent.; 1946-)

Oliver Tambo (SAfr. pol.; 1917-93)
Oliver Twist (Dickens novel)
Oliver Wendell Holmes (US writer/phys.; 1809-94)
Oliver Wendell Holmes, Jr. (US jurist; 1841-1935)
Oliver, King (Joseph)(US jazz; 1885-1938)
Oliver, Sy (US jazz; 1910-88)
Olives, Mount of (also Mt. Olivet)(Jerusalem)
Olivetti Corp.
Olivia Cole (ent.; 1942-)
Olivia De Havilland (ent.; 1916-)
Olivia Hussey (ent.; 1951-)
Olivia Newton-John (ent.; 1948-)
Olivier, (Sir) Laurence (Kerr)(ent.; 1907-89)
Ollie Hopnoodle's Haven of Bliss (film, 1988)
Ollie, Frank and (film, 1995)
Ollie, Kukla, Fran & (TV show)
Olmec (ancient Native Amer./Mex.)
Olmos, Edward James (ent.; 1947-)
Olmsted v. U.S. (US law; 1928)
Olmsted, Frederick L(aw)(US landscaper; 1822-1903)
Olomouc, Czechoslovakia
Olsen twins (Mary-Kate & Ashley)
Olsen, Ashley (ent.; 1986-)
Olsen, Mary-Kate (ent.; 1986-)
Olsen, Merlin (Jay)(football/ent.; 1940-)
Olsen, Ole (John Sigvard)(ent.; 1892-1963)
Olsten Corp.
Olsztyn, Poland
Olter, Bailey (pres., Micronesia)
Olusegun Obasanjo (pres., Nigeria; 1935-)
Olvera Street (Los Angeles)
Olympia (ancient Gr. center)
Olympia Dukakis (ent.; 1931-)
Olympia J. Snowe (US cong.; 1947-)
Olympia oyster (also l.c.)
Olympia, WA
Olympiad (Gr., 4-year period between games)
Olympian (Gr. god; participant in games; native of Olympia)
Olympian Games (Gr.; 776 BC-AD 394)
Olympic Airways (airline)
Olympic Games (internat'l; 1896-)
Olympic Mountains (WA)
Olympic National Park (WA)
Olympic Peninsula (WA)
Olympics
Olympics, Summer
Olympics, Winter
Olympus (myth.)
Olympus (photo.)
Olympus Corp.
Olympus, Mount (Gr.)
Olympus, Mount (WA)
Om (rel.)
Omagh, Northern Ireland
Omaha (Native Amer.)
Omaha Steaks International (US bus.)
Omaha World-Herald (NE newspaper)
Omaha, NE
O'Malley, Walter (baseball exec.; 1903-79)
Oman (Sultanate of)(SW Asia)
Oman, Gulf of (Oman/Iran)
Omani Arab (people)

Omar (Islamic leader; c581-644)
Omar Abdel-Rahman, Sheik (Muslim rel.; 1938-)
Omar Bongo, (Albert Bernard)(pres., Gabon; 1935-)
Omar Hassan Ahmed al-Bashir, Gen. (Pres., Sudan; 1944-)
Omar Khayyám (Persian poet/math.; c1028-1122)
Omar Khayyám, The Rubáiyát of (book of verses)
Omar Nelson Bradley (US gen.; 1893-1981)
Omar Sharif (b. Michel Shalhoub)(ent.; 1932-)
Omar Torrijos Herrera (Panamanian gen./pol.; 1929-81)
Omar, Mullah Mohammad (Afghan. pol.)
Omarr, Sydney (b. Zelig Kimmelman)(astrol.)
OMB (Office of Management of Budget)(US govt.)
Omdurman, Sudan
Omega Watch Corp.
Omicron Ceti (also Mira variable)(astron.)
Omisoka (Jap. New Year's Eve)
Omiya, Japan
Omni (mag.)
Omni, Dodge (auto.)
Omnibus
OmniCAT (CAT system)
Omnipen (med.)
Omniscient, the (God)
Omsk, Russia
Ona Munson (Berman)(b. Owena Wolcott)(ent.; 1906-55)
Onassis, Aristotle Socrates (Gr. shipping magnate; 1900-75)
Onassis, Christina (Gr. heiress; 1951-88)
Onassis, Jacqueline "Jackie" Lee Bouvier Kennedy (US editor/photo.; wife of ex-US pres.; 1929-94)
Ondine (J. Genet play)
One Day at a Time (TV show)
One Flew Over the Cuckoo's Nest (film, 1975)
One Hour Martinizing Dry Cleaning (US bus.)
One Life to Live (TV soap)
One-A-Day (med./vitamins)
O'Neal, Jennifer (ent.; 1948-)
O'Neal, Patrick (ent.; 1927-94)
O'Neal, Ryan (ent.; 1941-)
O'Neal, Shaquille (basketball; 1972-)
O'Neal, Tatum (ent.; 1963-)
Onega, Lake (NW Russia)
101 Dalmatians
Oneida (Native Amer.)
Oneida (silverware)
Oneida Community (NY rel. society; 1848)
Oneida Lake (NY)
Oneida, Ltd. (US bus.)
Oneida, NY
O'Neill, Ed (ent.; 1946-)
O'Neill, Eugene (Gladstone)(US writer; 1888-1953)
O'Neill, Paul Henry (US secy./treas.; 1935-)
O'Neill, Tip (Thomas P.), Jr. (US pol.; 1912-94)
Ong Teng Cheong (ex-pres., Singapore; 1936-)
Onitsha, Nigeria
Onkyo (stereo)
Onkyo USA Corp.
Online Access Guide

Ono (Lennon), Yoko (ent.; 1933-)
Onondaga (Native Amer.)
Onondaga, Lake (NY)
Ontario (province, Can.)
Ontario, CA
Ontario, Lake (US/Can.)
Oort cloud (astron.)
Oort, Jan H(endrik)(Dutch astron.; 1900-92)
Oostende, Belgium (also Ostend)
Op Art (1960s)(also l.c.)
Opango, Jacques-Joachim Yhombi- (ex-PM,
    Congo; 1940-)
OPEC (Organization of Petroleum-Exporting
    Countries)(est. 1960)
Open Door policy
Operation Desert Shield (Gulf War; 1990-91)
Operation Desert Storm (Gulf War; 1991)
Operation Overlord (WWI Normandy invasion;
    6/6/44)
Ophelia (*Hamlet* chara.)
Ophiuchus (astron., serpent bearer)
Ophthochlor (med.)
Opium War, First (Br./Ch.; 1839-42)
Opium War, Second (Br./Ch.; 1856-60)
Opole (province, Pol.)
Opole, Poland
Oporto, Portugal (also Porto)
Oppenheimer Funds Distributor, Inc.
Oppenheimer, J(ulius) Robert (US physt.,
    atomic bomb; 1904-67)
Opper, Frederick Burr (cartoonist, *Happy
    Hooligan*; 1857-1937)
Oprah Winfrey (ent.; 1954-)
Opryland USA
Opticrom (med.)
Optima (type style)
Optima, Kia (auto.)
Opus Dei (rel.)
O Sole Mio (song)
OR (operating room, Oregon)
Orabase (med.)
Oracle Corp.
Oracle of Delphi (also Delphic oracle, oracle of
    Apollo at Delphi)(noted for ambiguous
    answers)
Oradea, Romania
Orajel (med.)
Oral-B (med.)
Oral Law (also Mishna[h])(rel.)
Oral Roberts (US rel.; 1918-)
Oran, Algeria (also Wahran)
Orange Bowl (college football)
Orange County Register (CA newspaper)
Orange Free State (province, SAfr.)
Orange River (S Afr.)
Orange Society (Ir.; est. 1795)
Orange Walk, Belize
Orange, CA, NJ, TX
Orange, House of (Br. ruling family; 1689-1702)
Orange, House of (royal family, Netherlands)
Orangemen (member, Orange Society)
Orantes, Manuel (tennis; 1949-)
Orbach, Jerry (ent.; 1935-)
Orbison, Roy (ent.; 1936-88)
ORC (Officers Reserve Corps)

Orcus (myth.)
Ord, Fort, CA (mil.)
Order of Lenin (Soviet award)
Order of Odd Fellows, Independent (fraternal
    society; est. 1918)
Order of Our Lady of Mercy (rel.)
Order of the Bath (Br. order of knighthood)
Order of the Purple Heart (US mil.)
Ordovician period (500-430 million years ago)
Ore-Ida Foods, Inc.
Ore-Ida Tater Tots
Örebro, Sweden
Oreck (home appliances)
Oregon (OR)
Oregon cedar (also Port Orford cedar)
Oregon fir (also Douglas fir)(tree)
Oregon grape (plant)
Oregon myrtle (also California laurel)
Oregon pine (tree)
Oregon Trail (from MO to OR; 1800s)
Oregon, Muller v. (US law; 1908)
Oregonian, Portland (OR newspaper)
O'Reilly Factor, The (TV show)
Orel Hershiser (baseball; 1958-)
Orël, Russia (also Oryol)
Orem, UT
Orenburg, Russia
Orense, Spain
Oreo (cookies)
Orestes (Euripides drama)
Orestes (myth.)
Oretic (med.)
Orff, Carl (Ger. comp.; 1895-1982)
Organic Gardening (mag.)
Organization for Economic Cooperation and
    Development (OECD)(internat'l; est. 1961)
Organization for Women, National (NOW)
Organization of African Unity (OAU)(est. 1963)
Organization of American States (OAS)(N/
    central/S Amer.; est.; 1948)
Organization of Arab Petroleum Exporting
    Countries (OAPEC)(est.; 1968)
Organization of Central American States
    (ODECA)(est. 1951/1962)
Organization of Petroleum-Exporting Countries
    (OPEC)(est. 1960)
Organogenesis Inc.
Orient Express (also Orient-Express)(Eur.
    passenger train since 1883)
Orient Express, Murder on the (film, 1974)
Orient, The World of Henry (film, 1964)
Oriental rug/carpet
Orientale basin (astron.)
Orinase (med.)
O-ring (space shuttle gasket)
Orinoco River (SAmer.)
Orioles, Baltimore (baseball team)
Orion (astron., hunter; myth.)
Orion (US Navy plane)
Orion nebula (astron.)
Orion Pictures Corp.
Orionis, Beta (also Rigel)(astron.)
Orissa (state, India)
Oriya (lang.)
Orizaba, Mexico

Orizaba, Mount (also Citlaltepetl)(dormant volcano, Mex.)
Orkin Pest Control (US bus.)
Orkney Island(s)(Scot.)
Orlando (El Duque) Hernandez (baseball; 1969-)
Orlando and Dawn, Tony (pop music)
Orlando Gibbons (Br. comp.; 1583-1625)
Orlando International Airport (FL)
Orlando Magic (basketball team)
Orlando Sentinel (FL newspaper)
Orlando, FL
Orlando, Tony (b. Michael Anthony Orlando Cassivitis)(ent.; 1944-)
Orléans, France
Orléans, Maid of (also St. Joan of Arc, Jeanne d'Arc)(Fr. rel./mil.; 1412?-31)
Orlon (fiber)
Orly, France
Orman, Suze (finan. writer; 1951-)
Ormandy, Eugene (US cond.; 1899-1985)
Ormazd (also Ormuzd, Ahura Mazda)(rel.)
Ormoc, Philippines
Ormond, Julia (ent.; 1965-)
Ormuz (also Hormuz)(island, Iran)
Ormuz (or Hormuz), Strait of (Iran)
Ormuzd (also Ormazd, Ahura Mazda)(rel.)
Ornade (med.)
Ornette Coleman (US jazz; 1930-)
Oromo (lang./people)
Orontes River (SW Asia)
O'Rourke, Heather (ent.; 1975-88)
Oroweat
Oroweat Foods Co.
Orozco, José Clemente (Mex. artist; 1883-1949)
Orphan Annie, Little (fict. chara.)
Orpheus (myth.)
Orpheus (Stravinsky ballet)
Orphic Mysteries (also Orphism)(rel., ancient Gr.)
Orphism (rel./myth., ancient Gr.)
Orpington (chicken)
Orr, Bobby (Robert Gordon)(hockey; 1948-)
Orrin G(rant) Hatch (US cong.; 1934-)
Orser, Brian (figure skating; 1961-)
Orsk, Russia
Orson Bean (ent.; 1928-)
Orson Welles, (George)(ent.; 1915-85)
Ortega (salsa/Mex. foods)
Ortega Saavedra, (José) Daniel (ex-pres., Nicaragua; 1945-)
Ortho Pharmaceutical Corporation
Orthodox (rel.)
Orthodox Christian (rel.)
Orthodox Church, Greek
Orthodox Eastern Church (also Eastern Orthodox Church)(rel.)
Orthodox Judaism
Ortho-Novum (med.)
Orudis (med.)
Oruro, Bolivia
Orval E(ugene) Faubus (ex-gov., AR; 1910-94)
Orvieto (wine)
Orvieto, Italy
Orville A(lton)Turnquest, (Sir)(gov.-gen., Bahamas; 1929-)
Orville Redenbacher (popcorn)

Orville Redenbacher (US bus.; 1907-95)
Orville Wright (US aviator/inv.; 1871-1948)
Orwell, George (aka Eric A[rthur] Blair)(Br. writer; 1903-50)
Ory, Kid (US jazz; 1886-1973)
Os (chem. sym., osmium)
Osage (Native Amer.)
Osage orange (tree)
Osage River (MO)
Osaka, Japan
Osama bin Laden (Saudi terrorist, Islamic, base in Afghanistan; 1957-)
Osasco, Brazil
Osbert Sacheverell Sitwell, (Sir Francis)(Br. writer; 1892-1969)
Osborne Computer Corp.
Osborne, John (James)(Br. writer; 1929-94)
Osbourne, Ozzy (John Michael)(ent.; 1946-)
Os-Cal (med./calcium tablets)
Oscar (Academy Award statuette)
Oscar Arias Sanchez (ex-pres., Costa Rica; 1941-)
Oscar de La Renta, Ltd. (US bus.)
Oscar de la Renta (US designer; 1932-)
Oscar Hammerstein (ent.; 1847-1919)
Oscar Hammerstein, II (US lyricist; 1895-1960)
Oscar Kokoschaka (Aus. artist; 1886-1980)
Oscar Levant (ent.; 1906-72)
Oscar Luigi Scalfaro (ex-pres., It.; 1918-)
Oscar Mayer (meats)
Oscar Mayer Foods Corp.
Oscar Niemeyer Soares Filho (Brazilian arch.; 1907-)
Oscar Peterson (US jazz; 1925-)
Oscar Pettiford (US jazz; 1922-60)
Oscar Robertson (basketball; 1938-)
Oscar the Grouch (cartoon chara.)
Oscar (Fingal O'Flahertie Wills) Wilde (Ir. writer; 1854-1900)
Oscars (also Academy Awards)
Osceola National Forest
Osceola, Chief (Seminole Native Amer.; 1800?-38)
OSG (Office of Secretary General [UN])
Osgood, Charles (TV jour.; 1933-)
Osh, Kyrgyzstan
OSHA (Occupational Safety and Health Administration)
Oshawa, Ontario, Canada
OshKosh (children's clothing)
OshKosh B'Gosh, Inc.
Oshkosh, WI
Osho (or Shree) Rajneesh (aka Bhagwan)(b. Chaadra Mohan Jain)(Indian rel.; 1931-90)
Oshogbo, Nigeria
Osijek, Croatia
Osip ([Y]Emilevich) Mandelstam (Rus. poet; 1891-1938?)
Osiris (myth.)
Oskar Straus (Aus. comp.; 1870-1954)
Oskar Werner (b. Josef Schliessmayer)(ent.; 1922-84)
Osler, (Sir) William (Can. phys./educ.; 1849-1919)
Oslin, K. T. (ent.; 1942-)
Oslo Fjord (or Fiord), Norway
Oslo, Norway

Osmond, Donny (ent.; 1958-)
Osmond, Marie (ent.; 1959-)
Osnabrück, Germany
Osorno, Chile
Ossetian (people)
Ossie Davis (ent.; 1917-)
Ossig, Kaspar Schwenkfeld von (Ger. rel.;
    1490-1561)
Ossining, NY
Ossip Zadkine (Rus. artist; 1890-1967)
Ostade, Adriaen van (Dutch artist; 1610-85)
Ostend Manifesto (US/Sp. re: Cuba; 1854)
Ostend, Belgium (also Oostende)
Oster Corp.
Oster Corp., Sunbeam
Osterizer blender
Ostpolitik (WGer. hist.; 1971-90)
Ostrava, Czechoslovakia
Ostrogoths (also East Goths)(ancient Germans)
Ostwald, Wilhelm (Ger. chem.; 1853-1932)
O'Sullivan, Maureen (ent.; 1911-98)
Oswald Spengler (Ger. phil./hist.; 1880-1936)
Oswald, Lee Harvey (assassin of JFK; 1939-63)
Oswego River (NY)
Oswego tea (plant)
Oswego, Lake (OR)
Oswego, NY, OR
Otago (district, NewZeal.)
O Tannenbaum (Ger., Christmas tree)
O Tannenbaum (song)
Otar Patsatsia (PM, Georgia)
OTB (off-track betting)
OTC (over-the-counter [stock trading, drugs])
OTEC (ocean thermal energy conversion)
Othello, The Moor of Venice, The Tragedy of
    (Shakespeare play)
Otis Air Force Base, MA
Otis Elevator Co.
Otis Redding (ent.; 1941-67)
Otis Skinner (US writer/ent.; 1858-1942)
Otis, Elisha (Graves)(US inv., elevator; 1811-
    61)
O'Toole, Annette (ent.; 1953-)
O'Toole, Peter (ent.; 1932-)
Otrivin (med.)
Otsu, Japan
Ott, Mel (baseball; 1909-58)
Ottawa (Native Amer.)
Ottawa River (SE Can.)
Ottawa Senators (hockey team)
Ottawa, IL
Ottawa, Ontario, Canada
Ottmar Mergenthaler (Ger./US inv.; 1854-99)
Otto Dix (Ger. artist; 1891-1969)
Otto Graham (football; 1921-)
Otto Gustaf Nordenskjöld, (Nils)(Swed. expl.;
    1869-1928)
Otto Hahn (Ger. chem.; 1879-1968)
Otto Klemperer (Ger. cond.; 1885-1973)
Otto Kruger (ent.; 1885-1974)
Otto Luening (US comp.; 1900-96)
Otto (Ehrenfried) Nicolai, (Carl)(Ger. comp.;
    1810-49)
Otto (Ludwig) Preminger (ent.; 1905-86)
Otto Soglow (US cartoonist, Little King; 1900-75)

Otto Stich (ex-pres., Switz.; 1927-)
Otto (Eduard Leopold) von Bismarck, Prince
    ("Iron Chancellor")(ex-chanc., Ger.; 1815-98)
Ottoman Empire (Turk.; 1300-1920)
Ottorino Respighi (It. comp.; 1879-1936)
Ottumwa, IA
Ouachita Mountains (S central US)
Ouachita River (S central US)
Ouagadougou, Burkina Faso (also Wagadugu)
Ouahran/Oran, Algeria
Ouattara, Alassane D. (ex-PM, Ivory Coast;
    1942-)
Oud, (Jacobus Johannes) Pieter (Dutch arch.;
    1890-1963)
Ouedraogo, Jean Baptiste (ex-pres., Upper
    Volta; 1932-)
Ouedraogo, Kadré Desiré (ex-PM, Burkina
    Faso; 1953-)
Ouedraogo, Youssouf (ex-PM, Burkina Faso)
Ouija board
Oujda, Morocco
Oulu, Finland
Our Father (also Lord's Prayer, Paternoster
    [Pater Noster])(prayer)
Our Lady (also the Madonna, Holy Mother,
    Mary, Virgin Mary)(rel.)
Our Lady of Mercy, Order of (rel.)
Our Man Flint (film, 1966)
Our Miss Brooks (TV show)
Ouse River (also Great Ouse)(Eng.)
Ousmane, Mahamane (ex-pres., Niger; 1950-)
Outback, Subaru (auto.)
Outboard Marine Corp.
Outcault, Richard (US cartoonist, Buster Brown;
    1863-1928)
Outdoor Channel, The (TV channel)
Outdoor Life (mag.)
Outdoor Photographer (mag.)
Outer Hebrides (islands, W Scot.)
Outer Mongolia (now State of Mongolia)
Outlaw Josey Wales, The (film, 1976)
Outremont, Quebec, Canada
Outside (mag.)
Oval Office (US pres. office)
Ovaltine Food Products (US bus.)
Ovambo (people)
Ovcon-35 (med.)
Ovcon-50 (med.)
Overeaters Anonymous
Overijssel (province, Netherlands)
Overland Park, KS
Overlord, Operation (WWI Normandy invasion;
    6/6/44)
Overton, Jayne Kennedy- (ent.; 1951-)
Oveta Culp Hobby (US publ./pol.; 1905-95)
Ovett, Steve (track; 1955-)
Ovid (b. Publius Ovidius Naso)(Roman poet; 43
    BC-AD 17)
Oviedo, Spain
Ovimbundu (people)
Ovitz, Michael (ent.; 1946-)
Ovral (med.)
Ovrette (med.)
Owen Arthur (PM, Barbados; 1949-)
Owen K. Garriott (US physt./astro.; 1930-)

Owen, Robert (Br. phil./reformer; 1771-1858)
Owens, Bill (William)(CO gov.; 1950-)
Owens, Buck (ent.; 1929-)
Owens, Jesse (James Cleveland)(track; 1913-80)
Owens-Corning Fiberglas Corp.
Owens-Illinois, Inc.
Owensboro, KY
Owsley (b. Augustus Owsley Stanley, III)(US
    amateur chem./hallucinogens; fl. 1960s)
Owsley (slang, LSD)
Oxbridge (Oxford and Cambridge, Br. universities)
Oxford bags (trousers)
Oxford Industries, Inc.
Oxford University (Eng.)
Oxford, England
Oxford, MS
Oxfordshire (county, Eng.)(also Oxon)
Oxistat (med.)
Oxmoor House, Inc.
Oxnard, CA
Oxsoralen (med.)
Oxus River (Amu Darya)(central Asia)
Oxy (med./skin care)
Oxy10 (med.)
Oxy5 (med.)
OxyContin (med.)
Oye-Mba, Casimir (ex-PM, Gabon)
Oyl, Olive (fict. chara., *Popeye*)
Oyster Bay, NY
oysters Rockefeller
OZ (CAT system)
Oz (myth.)
Oz Munchkins
Oz, Frank (Muppet puppeteer; 1944-)
Oz, Land of
Oz, The Wizard of (by L.F. Baum)
Ozal, Turgut (ex-pres., Turk.; 1927-93)
Ozalid (photo.)
Ozark Mountains (also Ozarks)(central US)
Ozarks, Lake of the (MO)
Ozawa, Ichiro (Jap. pol./writer; 1942-)
Ozawa, Seiji (Jap./US cond.; 1935-)
Ozick, Cynthia (US writer; 1928-)
OZpc (CAT system)
Ozzie & Harriet Nelson (TV couple)
Ozzie Nelson (ent.; 1906-75)
Ozzy (John Michael) Osbourne (ent.; 1946-)

-P-

P (chem. sym., phosphorus)
PA (Pennsylvania, power of attorney, public-
  address system)
Paar, Jack (ent.; 1918-)
Paavo Nurmi (Olympic runner; 1897-1973)
Paavo Tapio Lipponen (PM, Fin.; 1941-)
PABA (para-aminobenzoic acid)
Pablo (Ruiz y) Picasso (Sp. artist; 1881-1973)
Pablo Casals (Sp. musician; 1876-1973)
Pablo Neruda (aka Neftali Ricardo Reyes y
  Basoalto)(Chilean poet; 1904-73)
Pabst Brewing Co.
PAC (political action committee)
Pace Foods, Inc.
Pace, Darrell (archery; 1956-)
Pacers, Indiana (basketball team)
Pachelbel, Johann (Ger. comp.; 1653-1706)
Pachelbel's Canon (J. Pachelbel music)
Pachuca (de Soto), Mexico
Pacific Bell (comm.)
Pacific Coast Airline
Pacific Corp., Georgia-
Pacific Islanders (people)
Pacific Missile Test Center (CA)
Pacific Northwest
Pacific Ocean
Pacific Palisades (district, Los Angeles)
Pacific Rim National Park Reserve (Can.)
Pacific scandal (Can. hist.; 1873)
Pacific Standard Time (also Pacific Time)
Pacific Tea Co., Great Atlantic & (A&P Food
  Stores)
Pacific Telesis Group (phone co.)
Pacific Time (also Pacific Standard Time)
Pacific War (Bolivia, Peru/Chile; 1879-83)
Pacific yew (tree)
Pacific, War of the (Chile/Bolivia, Peru; 1879-83)
Pacifica, CA
Pacificator, Great (also Great Compromiser)
  (Henry Clay)(US pol.; 1777-1852)
Pacino, Al(berto)(ent.; 1940-)
Packard Co., Hewlett- (HP)
Packard, Vance (US writer; 1914-96)
Packer, Billy (ent.; 1940-)
Packers, Green Bay (football team)
Packwood, Bob (Robert William)(US pol.; 1932-)
Pac-Man defense (econ.)
Pactiv Corp.
Padang, Indonesia
Paddington (area, Westminster, Eng.)
Paddy (slang, Irishman)
Paddy Chayefsky (US writer; 1923-81)
Paderborn, Germany
Paderewski, Ignace Jan (ex-PM, Pol./comp.;
  1860-1941)
Padre Island (Gulf of Mexico)
Padres, San Diego (baseball team)
Padua, Italy (also Padova)
Paducah, Duke of (aka Whitey [Edward

Charles] Ford)(baseball; 1928-)
Paducah, KY
Paeniu, Bikenibeu (ex-PM, Tuvalu; 1956-)
Paganini, Niccolò (It. comp.; 1782-1840)
Page Boy (maternity clothes)
Page Boy Co., Inc.
Page, Geraldine (ent.; 1924-87)
Page, Hot Lips (Oran Thaddeus)(ent.; 1908-54)
Page, Jimmy (ent.; 1944-)
Page, LaWanda (ent.; 1920-)
Page, Patti (b. Clara Ann Fowler)(ent.; 1927-)
Page, Robert Morris (US physt.; 1903-92)
Pagels, Elaine Hiesey (rel. scholar; 1943-)
PageMaker, Aldus (compu.)
Paglia, Camille (US writer/social critic; 1947-)
Pagliacci, I (R. Leoncavallo opera)
Pago Pago, American Samoa (formerly Pango
  Pango)
Pahang (state, Malaysia)
Pahlavi, Muhammad Riza (shah, Iran; 1919-80)
Pahlavi, Riza (shah, Iran; 1877-1944)
Paias Wingti (ex-PM, Papua New Guinea; 1951-)
Paige, Janis (ent.; 1922-)
Paige, Rod(erick Raynor)(US secy./educ.; 1933-)
Paige, Satchel (Leroy Robert)(baseball; 1906-82)
Paine, Tom (Thomas)(US writer; 1737-1809)
PaineWebber Group, Inc.
PaineWebber, Inc.
Painted Desert, AZ
Painter, Sweatt v. (US law; 1950)
Paisley, Scotland (thread factories)
Paiute (or Piute)(Native Amer.)
Pak, Se Ri (golf; 1977-)
Pakalitha Bethuel Mosisili (PM, Lesotho; 1945-)
Pakistan (Islamic Republic of)(S Asia)
Pakistan International Airlines
Pakistan wars, India-
Pakistani (people)
Pakse, Laos (also Pakxé)
Pakula, Alan J. (ent.; 1928-98)
Pal Joey (film, 1957)
Palace of Versailles (Fr.)
Paladin (TV show)
Palance, Jack (b. Walter Vladimir Palanuik)
  (ent.; 1920-)
Palantine, IL
Palatinate, Rhineland- (state, Ger.)
Palatino (type style)
Palau (now Belau)
Palau Islands (W Pac.)
Palaung-Wa (lang.)
Palembang, Indonesia
Paleocene epoch (65-54 million years ago)
Paleolithic period (Old Stone Age; 2 million to
  15,000 years ago)
Paleozoic era (570-225 million years ago)
Palermo, Sicily (Italy)
Palestine (aka Holy Land, Canaan)(region, SW
  Asia)
Palestine Liberation Organization (PLO)(Arab,
  est. 1964)
Palestine National Liberation Movement (also
  al-Fatah)
Palestinian (people)
Palestinian Authority

Palestinian Popular Resistance Forces
Palestrina, Giovanni P(ierluigi) da (It. comp.; c1525-94)
Paley, Grace (US writer; 1922-)
Paley, William (Br. rel.; 1743-1805)
Paley, William S. (US TV exec.; 1901-90)
Pali (lang.)
Pali Canon (also Tripitaka)(rel.)
Palin, Michael (ent.; 1943-)
Palisades Interstate Park (NJ/NY)
Pall Mall (cigarettes)
Pall Mall (London street famed for clubs)
Palladian style (arch.)
Palladian window (also Diocletian window)
Palladio, Andrea (It. arch.; 1508-80)
Palladium (myth.)
Pallas (astron.)
Pallas Athena (myth.)
Pallas's cat
Palm (compu.)
Palm Beach, FL
Palm Springs, CA
Palm Sunday (Sunday before Easter)
Palm, Inc.
Palma, Brian De (ent.; 1940-)
Palma, Spain (also Palma de Mallorca)
Palmdale, CA
Palmer House (Chicago)
Palmer, AK, MA
Palmer, Arnold (Daniel)(golf; 1929-)
Palmer, Betsy (ent.; 1929-)
Palmer, James (Alvin)(baseball; 1945-)
Palmer, Jim (baseball; 1945-)
Palmer, John (McAuley)(US gen./pol.; 1817-1900)
Palmer, Lilli (ent.; 1914-86)
Palmer, Reginald (ex-gov.-gen., Grenada)
Palmerston, Henry John Temple, Viscount (ex-PM, Br.; 1784-1865)
Palmerston North, New Zealand
Palmetto State (nickname, SC)
Palminteri, Chazz (b. Chalogero Lorenzo Palminteri)(ent./writer; 1951-)
Palmiro Togliatti (It. pol.; 1893-1964)
Palmolive Co., Colgate-
Palmyra (also Tadmor)(ancient city, Syria)
Palmyra, NY
Palo Alto, CA
Paloma Picasso (US bus.; 1949-)
Palomar Observatory (also Palomar Mountain Observatory)(CA)
Palomar, Mount (CA)
Palooka, Joe (comic strip)
Palos Verdes Estates, CA
Paltrow, Gwyneth (ent.; 1972-)
Pam (cooking spray)
Pam Dawber (ent.; 1951-)
Pam Grier (ent.; 1949-)
Pam Shriver (tennis; 1962-)
Pam Tillis (ent.; 1957-)
Pamela Anderson (model/ent.; 1967-)
Pamela (Digby Churchill Hayward) Harriman (US dipl. 1920-97)
Pamela Sue Martin (ent.; 1953-)
Pamelor (med.)
Pamine (med.)

Pampangan (lang.)
Pampers (diapers)
Pamprin (med.)
Pan (myth.)
Pan Am (airline)
Pan Am Corp.
PanAm Express (airline)
Pan Am Flight 103 (1988 disaster)
Pan American Day
Pan American Games
Pan-American Union (now Organization of American States)
Pan collar, Peter
Pan Industries, Peter
Pan, Peter (fict. chara.)
Pan, Peter (J. Barrie play)
Panadol (med.)
Panama (Republic of)(CAmer.)
Panama Canal (CAmer.)
Panama Canal Zone (CAmer.)
Panama City, FL
Panama City, Panama (also Panama, Panama)
Panama hat
Panama Jack (health)
Panama red (slang, marijuana from Panama)
Panasonic (elec.)
Panasonic Co.
Panay (island, Philippines)
Panay-Hiligaynon (lang.)
Pancaldi (shoes)
Pancaldi (US bus.)
Panchatantra (Sanskrit lit.; 4th c. BC)
Panchen Lama (Tibetan rel.; 1939-89)
Pancho (Richard Alonzo) Gonzalez (tennis; 1928-95)
Pancho Villa (b. Doroteo Arango)(Mex. gen.; c1877-1923)
Pancrease (med.)
Pandaemonium (capital of hell in *Paradise Lost*)
Panday, Basdeo (PM, Trinidad/Tobago; 1933-)
Pandemonium (film, 1982)
Pandit (title of respect, India)
Pandit, Vijaya Lakshmi (dipl., India; 1900-90)
P and L (also P. and L., P.&L.)(profit and loss)
Pandora (myth.)
Pandora's box (myth.)
Panetta, Leon E. (US ex-white house chief of staff; 1938-)
Panevezys, Lithuania
Pangai, Tonga
Pangasinan (lang.)
Pangloss (fict. chara., *Candide*)
Panhellenism
Paniagua, Valentin (Peruvian pol.)
Panic, Milan (ex-PM, Yug.)
Panipat, India
Pankhurst, Emmeline (Goulden)(Br. suffragist; 1858-1928)
Panmunjom, Korea (also Panmunjon)(Korean War truce talks)
Panoz (auto.)
Panoz AIV roadster (auto.)
Panoz Esperante (auto.)
Pantages Theater (Los Angeles)
Pantagruel (F. Rabelais satire)

Pantaloon (also Pantalone)(fict. chara.)
Pantene (hair care)
Pantheon (temple, Rome)
Panthers, Carolina (football team)
Pantone Matching System (PMS)(colors/graphics)
Pantopon (med.)
Panyarachun, Anand (ex-PM, Thailand; 1933-)
Panza, Sancho (fict. chara., *Don Quixote*)
Paolo Soleri (US arch.; 1919-)
Paolo Uccello (b. Paolo di Dono)(It. artist;
    1397-1475)
Paolo Veronese (It. artist; 1528-88)
Paolozzi, Eduardo (Br. sculptor; 1924-)
Pap smear/test (Papanicolaou test)(med.)
Papa Doc (François Duvalier)(ex-pres., Haiti;
    1907-71)
Papadopoulos, George (ex-pres., Gr.; 1919-99)
Papago (Indians/lang.)
Papal States (It.)
Papandreou, Andreas (George)(ex-PM, Gr.;
    1919-96)
Papandreou, George (ex-PM, Gr.; 1888-1968)
Papanicolaou, George N. (Gr./US cytologist,
    Pap test; 1883-1962)
Papas, Irene (ent.; 1926-)
Papas, the Mamas and the (pop music)
Papeete on Tahiti, French Polynesia
Papen, Franz von (Ger. pol.; 1879-1969)
Paper Mate (pens)
Paper Mate Co., The
Paphos, Cyprus (Gk.)
Papillon (film, 1973)
Papp, Joseph (ent.; 1921-91)
Pappagallo (shoes)
Pappagallo (US bus.)
Papua New Guinea (SW Pac.)
Papua New Guinean (people)
Papuan (lang./people)
Paracel Islands (S Ch.)
Paracelsus, Philippus Aureolus (b. Theophrastus
    Bombastus von Hohenheim)(Swiss phys./
    chem.; 1493-1541)
Paraclete (Holy Spirit)
Parade (Sunday mag.)
Paradise (also Garden of Eden)(rel.)
Paradise Lost (Milton epic poem)
Paradise Regained (Milton epic poem)
Parafon Forte (med.)
Paraguay (Republic of)(SAmer.)
Parakou, Benin
Paramango Ernest Yonli (PM, Burkina Faso)
Paramaribo, Suriname
Paramount Communications, Inc.
Paramount Pictures Corp.
Paramount Records (US bus.)
Paramount, CA
Paramus, NJ
Paraná, Argentina
Parcel Service, United (UPS)
Parcheesi (game)
Parducci Winery, Ltd.
Parent-Teacher Association, National (also
    National Congress of Parents and Teachers)
    (PTA)(est. 1897)
Parent, Bernard Marcel (hockey; 1945-)

Parenting (mag.)
Parents (mag.)
Parents and Teachers, National Congress of
    (also National Parent-Teacher Association)
    (PTA)(est. 1897)
Pariah (rel., member of lowest caste)
Parian ware (porcelain)
Paris (myth.)
Paris green
Paris Opéra
Paris Pacts (1954)
Paris Peace Conference (1919)
Paris Review, The
Paris, France
Paris, plaster of (synthetic gypsum)
Paris, School/school of (art)
Paris, TN, TX
Paris, Treaty of (various peace treaties)
Paris, University of (aka Sorbonne)
Parish, Mitchell (US comp.; 1901-93)
Parisian (people of Paris)
Parisienne (females of Paris)
Park Avenue (NYC)
Park Avenue, Buick (auto.)
Park Chung Hee (ex-pres., SKorea; 1917-79)
Park Place Entertainment Corp.
Park Service, National (US govt. bureau)
Park, (Douglas) Brad(ford)(hockey; 1948-)
Parkay (margarine)
Parke Bernet Gallery (NY art auction, now with
    Sotheby's)
Parke, Davis & Co.
Parke-Davis (US bus.)
Parker-Bowles, Camilla (Br. news; 1947-)
Parker Brothers (games)
Parker Brothers (US bus.)
Parker Hannifin Corp.
Parker House (rolls)
Parker House Hotel (Boston)
Parker Posey (ent.; 1968-)
Parker Stevenson (ent.; 1952-)
Parker, Alan (ent.; 1944-)
Parker, Bonnie (US criminal; 1911-34)
Parker, Charlie "Bird" (b. Charles Christopher
    Parker, Jr.)(US jazz; 1920-55)
Parker, Colonel Tom (Elvis Presley's manager;
    ?-1997)
Parker, Dorothy (Rothschild)(US writer; 1893-
    1967)
Parker, Eleanor (ent.; 1922-)
Parker, Fess (ent.; 1925-)
Parker, Jameson (ent.; 1947-)
Parker, Jean (ent.; 1912-)
Parker, Nosy/nosy (slang, busybody)
Parker, Sarah Jessica (ent.; 1965-)
Parker, Suzy (model/ent.; 1933-)
Parkersburg, WV
Parkinson, C(yril) Northcote (Br. writer/hist.;
    1909-93)
Parkinson's disease (med.)
Parkinson's Law/law (work expands to fill the
    time allotted)
Parkman, Francis (US hist.; 1823-93)
Parks, Bert (ent.; 1914-92)
Parks, Gordon (ent.; 1912-)

Parks, Rosa (US civil rights activist; 1913-)
Parliament, Houses of (Br. govt.)
Parliament-Funkadelic (pop music)
Parlodel (med.)
Parma, Italy
Parma, Margaret of (Sp. regent, Netherlands; 1522-86)
Parma, OH
Parmesan cheese
Parnassian (lit.)
Parnassus, Mount (Gr.)
Parnate (med.)
Parnell, Charles Stewart (Ir. pol.; 1846-91)
Parnis, Mollie (US designer; 1905-92)
Pärnu, Estonia
Paro Dzong, Bhutan
Paro, Bhutan
Parr, Catherine (6th wife of Henry VIII; 1512-48)
Parramatta, Australia
Parris N(elson) Glendening (MD gov.; 1942-)
Parrish, (Frederick) Maxfield (US artist; 1870-1966)
Parry, (Sir) William Edward (Br. expl.; 1790-1855)
Parsee (also Parsi)(rel. community, India)
Parseghian, Ara (football; 1923-)
Parsidol (med.)
Parsifal, (Sir) (also Percivale)(Arthurian knight)
Parsons Project, Alan (pop music)
Parsons table
Parsons, Alan (ent.; 1949-)
Parsons, Estelle (ent.; 1927-)
Parsons, Gram (b. Cecil Ingram Connor, III) (ent.; 1946-73)
Parsons, Louella (US gossip columnist; 1881?-1972)
Parthenon (also Temple of Athena Parthenos, Gr.)
Parthia (ancient country, S Asia)
Parthian horsemen
Parthian shot
Parton, Dolly (ent.; 1946-)
Partridge Family, The (TV show)
Partridge, Eric (Honeywood)(Br. lexicographer; 1894-1979)
Party of God (also Hezbollah)(rel./mil.)
Parvati (also Anapurna, Annapurna, Devi)(myth.)
Pasadena Community Playhouse
Pasadena Tournament of Roses
Pasadena, CA, TX
Pasarell, Charles (tennis; 1944-)
Pasay, Philippines
Pascagoula, MS
Pascal (compu. lang.)
Pascal Lissouba (ex-pres., Congo; 1931-)
Pascal, Blaise (Fr. phil./math.; 1623-62)
Pascal, Francine (writer; 1938-)
Pascal's law/principle (physics)
Pascal's theorem (geometry)
Paschen's law (elec.)
Pasco, WA
Pascoal Manuel Mocumbi, Dr. (PM, Mozambique; 1941-)
Paseo, Toyota (auto.)
Pasha, Ali ("the Lion")(Turk. pol.; 1741-1822)
Pasha, Mehmed Emin Ali (Turk. pol.; 1815-71)

Pashto (also Pushtu)(lang.)
Paslode (power tools)
Paslode Co.
Paso (horse)
Pass, Joe (b. Joseph Anthony Passalaqua)(US jazz; 1929-94)
Passaic River (NJ)
Passaic, NJ
Passamaquoddy (Native Amer.)
Passamaquoddy Bay (ME/Can.)
Passat, Volkswagen (auto.)
Passat GLX, Volkswagen (auto.)
Passion Sunday
Passion Week
Passiontide
Passos, John Dos (US writer; 1896-1970)
Passover (also Pesach)(rel.)
Passport, Honda (auto.)
Pasternak, Josef A. (ent.; 1881-1940)
Pasternak, Boris (Leonidovich)(Rus. writer; 1890-1960)
Pasteur vaccine (med.)
Pasteur, Louis (Fr. chem.; 1822-95)
Pasteur's effect (med.)
Pasto, Colombia
Pastor, Tony (Antonio)(ent.; 1837-1908)
Pastrana (Arango), Andrés (pres., Colombia; 1954-)
Pat and Mike (film, 1952)
Pat Benatar (b. Pat Andrzejewski)(ent.; 1953-)
Pat Boone (ent.; 1934-)
Pat (Edmund Gerald) Brown, Sr. (ex-CA gov.; 1905-96)
Pat(rick J.) Buchanan (US pol. commentator/candidate; 1938-)
Pat Buttram (ent.; 1916-94)
Pat Carroll (ent.; 1927-)
Pat Conroy (US writer; 1945-)
Pat(rick Floyd) Garrett, Sheriff (US sheriff, shot "Billy the Kid"; 1850-1908)
Pat Harrington, Jr. (ent.; 1929-)
Pat(rick Joseph) Leahy (US cong.; 1940-)
Pat(rick Bruce) Metheny (ent.; 1954-)
Pat Morita (ent.; 1932-)
Pat Nixon (b. Thelma Catherine Ryan)(wife of ex-US pres.; 1912-93)
Pat O'Brien (ent.; 1899-1983)
Pat Oliphant (US pol. cartoonist; 1935-)
Pat(rick L.) Paulsen (US bus./ent.; 1927-97)
Pat Paulsen Vineyards (US bus.)
Pat Roberts (US cong.; 1936-)
Pat (Marion Gordon) Robertson (US pol./rel.; 1930-)
Pat Sajak (ent.; 1947-)
Pat Summerall (US sportscaster; 1930-)
Pat Suzuki (ent.; 1931-)
Patagonia (region, Argentina)
Pataki, George E(lmer)(NY gov.; 1945-)
Patan, Nepal (now Lalitpur)
Patassé, Ange-Félix (pres., Central African Republic; 1937-)
Patch Adams (film, 1999)
Pater, Walter (Horatio)(Br. writer; 1839-94)
Paternoster (or Pater Noster)(also Lord's Prayer, Our Father)(prayer)

Paterson, NJ
Pathan (people)
Pathé Gazette (newsreel)
Pathé Journal (newsreel)
Pathe, Charles (Fr. bus./films; 1863-1957)
Pathfinder, Nissan (auto.)
Pathocil (med.)
Patiala, India
Patinkin, Mandy (Mandel)(ent.; 1952-)
Patna, India
Paton, Alan (Stewart)(SAfr. writer; 1903-88)
Patras, Greece (also Patrái)
Patric, Jason (ent.; 1966-)
Patrice (Emergy) Lumumba (ex-PM, Congo/
   Zaire; 1926-61)
Patrice Munsel (ent.; 1925-)
Patricia Aburdene (US writer)
Patricia Arquette (ent.; 1968-)
Patricia Busignani (captain-regent; San Marino)
Patricia Cornwell (aka Patricia Daniels)(writer;
   1956-)
Patricia Crowley (ent.)
Patricia Ireland (US feminist/reformer, pres./
   NOW; 1945-)
Patricia Kennedy (Lawford)(US sister of ex-
   pres.; 1924-)
Patricia McBride (ballet; 1942-)
Patricia Neal (ent.; 1926-)
Patricia (Scott) Schroeder (US pol.; 1940-)
Patricia Stevens International, Inc.
Patricio Aylwin Azócar (ex-pres., Chile; 1918-)
Patrick Air Force Base, FL
Patrick A. M. Manning (ex-PM, Trinidad/Tobago;
   1946-)
Patrick Campbell, Mrs. (aka Beatrice Tanner)
   (ent.; 1865-1940)
Patrick Duffy (ent. 1949-)
Patrick Ewing (basketball; 1962-)
Patrick Henry (US pol./orator; 1736-99)
Patrick Joseph Kennedy (US bus., grandfather
   of ex-pres.; 1858-1929)
Patrick Joseph Kennedy (US pol.; 1967-)
Patrick Leclercq (PM, Monaco; 1938-)
Patrick Macnee (ent.; 1922-)
Patrick Magee (ent.; 1924-82)
Patrick Maynard Stuart Blackett, Baron (Br.
   physt.; 1897-1974)
Patrick McGoohan (ent.; 1928-)
Patrick Moynihan, Daniel (US pol./dipl.; 1927-)
Patrick O'Neal (ent.; 1927-94)
Patrick Steptoe (US phys.; 1914-88)
Patrick Stewart (ent.; 1940-)
Patrick Swayze (ent.; 1952-)
Patrick, St. (Ir. rel.; 389?-461?)
Patrick's Day, St. (3/17)
Patriot (antiaircraft missile)
Patriot, Harrisburg (PA newspaper)
Patriot-Ledger, Quincy (MA newspaper)
Patriots, New England (football team)
Patrushev, Nikolai (Rus. FSB chief; 1951-)
Patsatsia, Otar (PM, Georgia)
Patsayev, Viktor I(vanovich)(cosmo.; 1933-71)
Patsy Cline (ent.; 1932-63)
Patsy Ramsey (b. Patricia Ann Paugh)(US
   news; 1956-)

Patten, Dick Van (ent.; 1928-)
Patterson Air Force Base, Wright (OH)
Patterson, Floyd (boxing; 1935-)
Patterson, Percival J(ames) (PM, Jamaica; 1935-)
Patti Austin (ent.; 1948-)
Patti D'Arbanville (ent.; 1951-)
Patti LaBelle (b. Patricia Holt)(ent.; 1944-)
Patti LuPone (ent.; 1949-)
Patti Page (b. Clara Ann Fowler)(ent.; 1927-)
Patti Smith (ent.; 1946-)
Patti, Adelina (It. opera; 1843-1919)
Patton, George S(mith)(US gen.; 1885-1945)
Patton, Paul E. (KY gov.; 1937?-)
Patty (Patricia Jane) Berg (golf; 1918-)
Patty (Patricia) Hearst (US heiress, kidnapped/
   imprisoned; 1954-)
Patty Andrews (ent., Andrews Sisters; 1918-)
Patty Duke Astin (ent.; 1946-)
Patty Loveless (ent.; 1957-)
Patty Murray (US cong.; 1950-)
Patty Smyth (ent.; 1957-)
Patty, Sandi (ent.; 1957-)
Pauguk (myth.)
Pauillac (Fr. wine region)
Paul & Mary Ford, Les (ent.)
Paul Anka (Can./US comp./ent.; 1941-)
Paul A(nthony) Samuelson (US econ.; 1915-)
Paul A. Volcker (US econ.; 1927-)
Paul Azinger (golf; 1960-)
Paul Berg (US biol.; 1926-)
Paul Biya (pres., Cameroon; 1933-)
Paul Brown (football coach; 1908-91)
Paul "Bear" Bryant (football coach; 1913-83)
Paul Bunyan (& Babe the Blue Ox)(fict. lumberjack)
Paul Cadmus (US artist; 1904-99)
Paul Cellucci, A(rgeo) (MA gov.; 1948-)
Paul Cézanne (Fr. artist; 1839-1906)
Paul Conrad (pol. cartoonist; 1924-)
Paul Coverdell (US pol.; 1939-2000)
Paul Delaroche (Fr. hist./artist; 1797-1856)
Paul Delvaux (Belgian artist; 1897-1994)
Paul Desmond (US jazz; 1924-77)
Paul Dessau (Ger. comp; 1894-1979)
Paul Douglas (ent.; 1907-59)
Paul Dukas (Fr. comp.; 1865-1935)
Paul E. Patton (KY gov.; 1937?-)
Paul Ehrlich (Ger. bacteriol.; 1854-1915)
Paul Francis Webster (US lyricist; 1907-84)
Paul (William) Gallico (US writer; 1897-1976)
Paul Gann (US reformer; 1912-89)
Paul Gauguin, (Eugène Henri)(Fr. artist; 1848-
   1903)
Paul Harvey (US news commentator; 1918-)
Paul Hawken (US bus./writer)
Paul Henri Spaak (Belgium pol.; 1899-1972)
Paul Henry O'Neill (US secy./treas.; 1935-)
Paul Hindemith (Ger./US comp.; 1895-1963)
Paul I (king, Gr.; 1901-64)
Paul III (b. Alessandro Farnese)(pope; 1468-1549)
Paul IV (b. Gian Pietro Carafa)(pope; 1476-1559)
Paul J. Weitz (astro.; 1932-)
Paul Julius Reuter, Baron von (Ger. founded
   news agcy.; 1816-99)
Paul Junger Witt (ent.; 1943-)
Paul Kagame (pres., Rwanda; 1957-)

Paul Keating, (ex-PM, Austl.; 1954-)
Paul Klee (Swiss artist; 1879-1940)
Paul Lukas (ent.; 1895-1971)
Paul Lynde (ent.; 1926-82)
Paul Masson Vineyards (US bus.)
Paul Mazursky (ent.; 1930-)
Paul McCartney, (James)(ent.; 1942-)
Paul Mellon (US philanthropist; 1907-99)
Paul Mitchell (hair care)
Paul Michael Glaser (ent.; 1943-)
Paul Mitchell Systems, John (US bus.)
Paul Molitor (baseball; 1956-)
Paul Muni (b. Muni Weisenfreund)(ent.; 1895-1967)
Paul Newman (ent.; 1925-)
Paul Prudhomme (US chef; 1940-)
Paul Reiser (ent.; 1956-)
Paul Revere (Amer. patriot/silversmith; 1735-1818)
Paul Revere and the Raiders (pop music)
Paul Reynaud (ex-PM, Fr.; 1878-1966)
Paul Robeson (ent.; 1898-1976)
Paul Rubens (b. Paul Rubenfeld)(aka Pee-Wee Herman)(ent.; 1952-)
Paul (Marvin) Rudolph (US arch.; 1918-97)
Paul Scofield (ent.; 1922-)
Paul Sebastian, Inc.
Paul Shaffer (ent.; 1949-)
Paul Signac (Fr. artist; 1863-1935)
Paul Simon (ent.; 1942-)
Paul (Martin) Simon (US pol.; 1928-)
Paul Sorvino (ent.; 1939-)
Paul S(pyros) Sarbanes (US cong.; 1933-)
Paul Stookey (ent.; 1937-)
Paul Terry (cartoonist, *Mighty Mouse*; 1887-1971)
Paul Theroux (US writer; 1941-)
Paul Tillich (US rel./phil.; 1886-1965)
Paul Tsongas (US pol.; 1941-97)
Paul V (b. Camillo Borghese)(It., pope; 1552-1621)
Paul (Ambroise) Valéry (Fr. writer; 1871-1945)
Paul Verlaine (Fr. poet; 1844-96)
Paul VI (b. Giovanni Battista Montini)(It., pope; 1897-1978)
Paul (David) Wellstone (US cong.; 1944-)
Paul "Pops" Whiteman (US cond.; 1891-1967)
Paul Williams (ent.; 1940-)
Paul Winfield (ent.; 1941-)
Paul Zindel (US writer; 1936-)
Paul, Alice (US women's-rights activist; 1885-1977)
Paul, Don Michael (ent.; 1963-)
Paul, Les (b. Lester Polfus)(US inv./ent.; 1915-)
Paul, St. (rel.; c3-c67)
Paul, St. Vincent de (Fr. rel.; c1581-1660)
Paul's Kitchen, Mrs. (US bus.)
Paul's, Mrs. (frozen fish)
Paula Abdul (ent.; 1962-)
Paula Cole (ent.; 1968-)
Paula Jones (US news)
Paula Modersohn-Becker (Ger. artist; 1867-1907)
Paula Poundstone (ent.; 1959-)
Paula Prentiss (b. Paula Ragusa)(ent.; 1939-)
Paula Zahn (US TV jour.; 1956-)
Paulding, James Kirke (US writer/pol.; 1778-

1860)
Paulette Goddard (ent.; 1905-90)
Pauley, (Margaret) Jane (US TV jour.; 1950-)
Pauli exclusion principle (physics)
Pauli, Wolfgang (Aus. physt.; 1900-58)
Paulie (film, 1998)
Paulina Porizkova (model; 1965-)
Pauline Collins (ent.; 1940-)
Pauline Esther Friedman (pseud. Abigail Van Buren, "Dear Abby")(US advice columnist; 1918-)
Pauline Frederick (US radio/TV jour.; 1918-90)
Pauline Trigère (US designer; 1912-)
Pauline, The Perils of (film, 1947)
Pauling, Linus C(arl)(US chem.; 1901-94)
Paulsen Vineyards, Pat (US bus.)
Paulsen, Pat(rick L.) (US bus./ent.; 1927-97)
Pauly Shore (ent.; 1968-)
Pavarotti, Luciano (It. opera; 1935-)
Pavel I. Belyayev (cosmo.; 1925-70)
Pavel R(omanovich) Popovich (cosmo.; 1930-)
Pavlov, Ivan (Petrovich)(Rus. physiol.; 1849-1936)
Pavlov's reflex (med.)
Pavlova, Anna (Rus. ballet; 1885-1931)
Pavlovich, Aleksandr (Alexander I)(emp., Rus.; 1777-1825)
Pavo (astron., peacock)
Pawlak, Waldemar (ex-PM, Pol.; 1959-)
Pawleys Island rope hammock
Pawnee (Native Amer.)
Pawtucket, RI
PAX TV (TV channel)
Pax (period of peace)
Pax Romana (peace imposed by strong nation on weaker one; e.g., ancient Rome over its dominions)
Paxil (med.)
Paxipam (med.)
Paxton, Bill (ent.; 1955-)
Paycheck, Johnny (b. Donald Eugene Lytle) (ent.; 1941-)
Payette National Forest (ID)
Payette River (ID)
Payless Car Rental System, Inc.
Pay Less Drug Stores Northwest, Inc.
Payless Shoe Source (US bus.)
Payne, John (ent.; 1912-89)
Payne-Gaposchkin, Cecilia Helena (Br./US astron.; 1900-79)
Pays de la Loire (region, Fr.)
Paysandú, Uruguay
Payton, Walter (football; 1954-99)
Paz Estenssoro, Victor (ex-pres., Bolivia; 1907-)
PBS (Public Broadcasting System)(TV channel)
PBX (private branch exchange)
PC GlassBlock
PC Magazine (mag.)
PC Today (mag.)
PC World (mag.)
PC/Computing (mag.)
PCB (polychlorinated biphenyl)
PCP (phenylcyclohexylpiperidine)
PCV (positive crankcase ventilation [valve])
PD (per diem, police department, postal district)

Pd (chem. sym., palladium)
PDA (personal digital assistant)(compu.)
PDF files (Adobe Portable Document
  Format)(compu.)
PDQ (pretty damn quick)
P. D. Q. Bach (aka Peter Schickele)(ent.; 1935-)
PDR (*Physicians' Desk Reference*)
PE (physical education)
Peabo Bryson (ent.; 1951-)
Peabody & Co., Inc., Kidder,
Peabody Radio and Television Awards, George
  Foster
Peabody, Elizabeth P. (US educ.; 1804-94)
Peabody, George (US bus./finan.; 1795-1869)
Peabody, MA
Peace Corps (US org.; est. 1961)
Peace Prize, Nobel
Peace River (W Can.)
Peace, Prince of (Jesus)
Peacemaker missile
Peach Bowl (college football)
Peach State (nickname, GA)
peach Melba (also l.c.)
Peach, Miss (comic strip)
Peachtree Doors, Inc.
Peachtree Softwear, Inc.
Peale, Charles Wilson (US artist; 1741-1827)
Peale, Norman Vincent, Rev. (US rel./writer;
  1898-93)
Peale, Rembrandt (US artist; 1778-1860)
Peanut Factory, Inc., The
Peanuts (comic strip)
pear William (liqueur)
Pearl (Mae) Bailey (US jazz singer; 1918-90)
Pearl Harbor, HI (WWII Jap. attack; 12/7/41)
Pearl Jam (pop music)
Pearl S(ydenstricker) Buck (US writer; 1892-
  1973)
Pearl, Minnie (Sarah Ophelia Cannon) (ent.;
  1912-96)
Pearle Vision
Pearle Vision, Inc.
Pearlette Louisy, (Calliopa) (gov.-gen., St.
  Lucia; 1946-)
Pearly Gates (entrance to heaven)
Pears, Peter (tenor; 1910-86)
Pearson, Drew (US jour.; 1897-1969)
Pearson, Lester (Bowles)(ex-PM, Can.; 1897-
  1972)
Peary, Robert E(dwin)(US Arctic expl.; 1856-
  1920)
Pease Air Force Base, NH
Peavy, Queenie (by Robert Burch)
Peck, (Eldred) Gregory (ent.; 1916-)
Peck, Fletcher v. (US law; 1810)
Peck, George Wilbur (US writer; 1840-1916)
Peck's Bad Boy (from G.W. Peck's newspaper
  stories)
Peckinpah, Sam (ent.; 1925-85)
Pecorino (cheese)
Pecos Bill (legendary cowboy)
Pecos National Historical Park (NM)
Pecos River (SW US)
Pecos, TX
Pécs, Hungary

Pedi (lang.)
PediaCare (med.)
Pedialyte (med.)
Pediazole (med.)
Pedro Antonio de Alarcón (Sp. writer/pol.;
  1833-91)
Pedro Juan Caballero, Paraguay
Pedroncelli Winery, J. (US bus.)
Peds (footwear)
Peds Products (US bus.)
Pee-Wee Herman (aka Paul Rubens)(ent.; 1952-)
Pee Wee (Frank) King (US comp.; 1914-2000)
Pee Wee (Harold) Reese (baseball; 1918-99)
Pee Wee Russell (US jazz; 1906-69)
Pee-Wee's Big Adventure (film, 1985)
Pee-Wee's Playhouse (TV show)
Peekskill, NY
Peel, Emma (fict. chara., *The Avengers*)
Peel, (Sir) Robert (ex-PM, Br.; 1788-1850)
Peeping Tom
Peer Gynt (H. Ibsen play)
Peer Gynt Suite (by E. Grieg)
Peerce, Jan (ent.; 1904-84)
Peet, Amanda (ent.; 1972-)
Peete, Calvin (golf; 1943-)
Peete, Holly Robinson (ent.; 1964-)
Peganone (med.)
Pegasus (astron., flying horse; myth.)
Peg-Board
Pegeen Fitzgerald (radio broadcaster; 1910-89)
Peggy Ashcroft, Dame (ent.; 1907-91)
Peggy Cass (ent.; 1924-99)
Peggy (Gale) Fleming (figure skating; 1948-)
Peggy Guggenheim (US finan.; 1898-1979)
Peggy Lee (b. Norma Egstrom)(ent.; 1920-)
Peggy Lipton (ent.; 1947-)
Peggy Ryan (ent.; 1924-)
Peggy Sue Got Married (film, 1986)
Peggy Wood (ent.; 1892-1978)
Pegler, (James) Westbrook (US jour.; 1894-
  1969)
Peg O' My Heart (song; film, 1922)
Pegu, Myanmar
Pei, I(eoh) M(ing)(US arch.; 1917-)
Peipus, Lake (NE Eur.)
Peirce, Charles S(anders)(US physt./phil.;
  1839-1914)
Pei-tsum, Hau (ex-PM, Taiwan)
Pekalongan, Indonesia
Pekin, IL
Peking duck (also Beijing duck)
Peking Man (also Beijing man)(*Homo erectus*)
Peking, China (now Beijing)
Pekingese (Ch. dialect)
Pekingese (dog)
Pelagian (rel.)
Pelagianism (rel.)
Pelagius (Br. rel.; 360-420)
Pelasgian (ancient Gr. people)
Pelé (b. Edson Arantes do
  Nascimento)(Brazilian soccer; 1940-)
Pelée, Mount (volcano, Martinique)
Pelham One Two Three, The Taking of (film,
  1974)
Pelican Publishing Co.

Pelican State (nickname, LA)
Pell grant (educ.)
Pell, Claiborne (US cong.; 1918-)
Pella Windows & Doors (US bus.)
Pelle the Conqueror (film, 1988)
Peloponnese (also Peloponnesos)(Gr. peninsula)
Peloponnesian War (Athens/Sparta; 431-404 BC)
Peltier effect (elec./physics)
Peltier heat (physics)
Pembroke Pines, FL
Pen, Jean-Marie Le (Fr. pol.; 1928-)
Pena, Federico F. (US ex-secy./trans., secy./
    ener.; 1947-)
Penaia Ganilau, (Sir) Ratu (ex-pres., Fiji; 1918-)
Penang (also Pinang)(state, Malaysia)
Penang, Malaysia
Penates (myth.)
Pendaflex (files)
Penderecki, Krzysztof (Pol. comp.; 1933-)
Pendergrass, Teddy (ent.; 1950-)
Pendleton blanket
Pendleton Woolen Mills (US bus.)
Pendleton, Terry (baseball; 1960-)
Pendragon, Uther (King Arthur's father)
Penelope (myth.)
Penelope Cruz (ent.; 1974-)
Penelope (Balchin) Leach (child psych./writer;
    1937-)
Peng, Li (ex-PM, Ch.; 1928-)
Penguin Inc., Viking
Penguins, Pittsburgh (hockey team)
Penicillium (med.)
Penn (tennis balls)
Penn Central Corp., The
Penn, Arthur (ent.; 1922-)
Penn, Robin Wright (ent.; 1966-)
Penn, Sean (ent.; 1960-)
Penn, William (Br. Quaker, founded PA; 1644-
    1718)
Penney Co., J. C.
Penney, James C(ash)(US bus.; 1875-1971)
Pennine Alps (Switz./It.)
Pennine Chain (hills, N. Eng.)
Pennsauken, NJ
Pennsylvania (PA)
Pennsylvania Dutch (SE PA)
Pennsylvania State University Press, The (US
    bus.)
Pennsylvania, Prigg v. (US law; 1842)
Pennsylvanian period (upper Carboniferous
    period)
Penny Arcade (US bus.)
Penny (Anfernee) Hardaway (basketball; 1972-)
Penny Marshall (ent.; 1943-)
Penny Singleton (ent.; 1908-)
Pennzoil Co.
Penobscot (Native Amer.)
Penobscot Bay (ME)
Penobscot River (ME)
Penquin Records, Inc.
Pensacola Naval Air Station (FL)
Pensacola News-Journal (FL newspaper)
Pensacola, FL
Pentagon Papers Case (US law; 1971)
Pentagon, The (VA)(US mil.)

Pentateuch (also Torah)(1st 5 books of Bible)
Pentax (photo.)
Pentax Corp.
Pentecost (also Whitsunday)(rel.)
Pentecostal Church(es)(rel.)
Pentecostalism (rel.)
Pentel Co., Ltd.
Pentel pen
Penthouse (mag.)
Pentids (med.)
Pentium PC microprocessor chip (compu.)
Pentothal (also sodium pentothal)(med.)
Pen-Vee K (med.)
Penzance, England
Penzance, The Pirates of (Gilbert & Sullivan
    operetta)
People Weekly (mag.)
People's Choice Awards, The
People's Court (TV show)
People's Party (also Populist Party)(US pol.;
    1891-1908)
Peoples Drug Stores, Inc.
Peoria Journal Star (IL newspaper)
Peoria, AZ, IL
Pep Boys—Manny, Moe, & Jack (US bus.)
Pepcid (med.)
Pepe's Mexican Restaurant
Peppard, George (ent.; 1928-94)
Pepper/Seven-Up Cos., Dr
Pepper, Art (US jazz; 1925-82)
Pepper, Claude (US pol.; 1901-89)
Pepper, Dr (soda)
Pepper's Lonely Hearts Club Band, Sgt. (Beatles
    album)
Pepperdine University (Los Angeles, CA)
Pepperdine University–Seaver College (Malibu,
    CA)
Pepperell Mill Store, West Point- (US bus.)
Pepperidge Farm (baked goods)
Pepperidge Farm, Inc.
Pepsi (soda)
Pepsi Bottling Group, Inc.
PepsiCo, Inc.
Pepsi-Cola (soda)
Pepsi-Cola Co.
Pepsodent (toothpaste)
Pepto-Bismol (med.)
Pepys' Diary (by S. Pepys; London life; 1600s)
Pepys, Samuel (Br. writer; 1633-1703)
Pequot (Native Amer.)
Pequot War (Pequot/Br.; 1637)
Perahia, Murray (US pianist; 1947-)
Percheron draft horse (also Percheron Norman)
Percival J(ames) Patterson (PM, Jamaica; 1935-)
Percival Lowell (US astron.; 1855-1916)
Percivale, Sir (also Parsifal)(Arthurian knight)
Percocet (med.)
Percodan (med.)
Percogesic (med.)
Percy Aldridge Grainger (Austl. pianist/comp.;
    1882-1961)
Percy Bysshe Shelley (Br. poet; 1792-1822)
Percy Faith (cond.; 1908-76)
Percy Kilbride (ent.; 1888-1964)
Percy Sledge (ent.; 1941-)

Percy Wenrich (US comp.; 1887-1952)
Percy, (Sir) Henry (aka Hotspur)(Br. mil.; 1366-1403)
Perdiem (med.)
Perdue Farms (US bus.)
Père David's deer
Pereira, Columbia
Pereira, William (US arch.; 1909-85)
Perelman, S(idney) J(oseph)(US writer; 1904-79)
Peres, Shimon (ex-PM, Isr.; 1923-)
Pérez de Cuéllar, Javier (Peruvian/UN dipl.; 1920-)
Pérez, Carlos Andrés (ex-pres., Venezuela; 1922-)
Pérez, Francisco Guillermo Flores (pres., El Salvador; 1959-)
Perez, Rosie (ent./choreographer; 1966-)
Performa, Macintosh (compu.)
Perga, Apollonius of (Gk. math.; c265-170 BC)
Pergolesi, Giovanni Battista (It. comp.; 1710-36)
Peri Gilpin (ent.; 1961-)
Periactin (med.)
Pericles (Gr. pol.; c490-429 BC)
Pérignon, Curvée Dom (champagne)
Perilous, Siege (Arthurian)
Perils of Pauline, The (film, 1947)
Periostat (med.)
Peripatetic (phil.)
Peritrate (med.)
Perkin Warbeck (Flem. pretender to Br. throne; 1474-99)
Perkins Co., Jackson &
Perkins Family Restaurant (US bus.)
Perkins, Carl (ent.; 1932-98)
Perkins, Elizabeth (ent.; 1961-)
Perkins, Frances (US sociol./pol.; 1882-1965)
Perkins, Jackson & (plants/seeds)
Perkins, Tony (Anthony)(ent.; 1932-92)
Perle Mesta (US dipl.; 1889-1975)
Perlman, Itzhak (Isr./US violinist; 1945-)
Perlman, Rhea (ent.; 1948-)
Perlman, Ron (ent.; 1950-)
Perm, Russia (formerly Molotov)
Permanent Court of Arbitration (internat'l court; est. 1899)
Permanent Court of International Justice, United Nations (also World Court)(est. 1945)
PermaSoft
Permax (med.)
Permian period (280-225 million years ago)
Pernell Roberts (ent.; 1930-)
Pernod (liqueur)
Perón, Eva Duarte de ("Evita")(b. Maria Eva Duarte)(ex-pres., Argentina; 1919-52)
Perón, Juan Domingo (ex-pres., Argentina; 1895-1974)
Perón, Maria Estela ("Isabel") Martínez de (ex-pres., Argentina; 1931-)
Perot, H. Ross (US bus./pol.; 1930-)
Perrault, Charles (Fr. writer; 1628-1703)
Perrier (water)
Perrier Group of America, The (US bus.)
Perrine, Valerie (ent.; 1943-)
Perrins, Inc., Lea &
Perry Como (ent.; 1912-2001)

Perry Drug Stores, Inc.
Perry Ellis (designer)
Perry Ellis Sportswear, Inc.
Perry Farrell (b. Perry Bernstein)(ent.; 1959-)
Perry G. Miller (US hist.; 1905-63)
Perry King (ent.; 1948-)
Perry Mason (fict. atty.)
Perry, Gaylord (baseball; 1938-)
Perry, Jim (baseball; 1936-)
Perry, Luke (ent.)
Perry, Matthew (ent.; 1969-)
Perry, Oliver (Hazard)(US mil.; 1785-1819)
Perry, Rick (TX gov.; 1950?-)
Perry, William J. (US ex-secy./defense; 1927-)
Persantine (med.)
Perseids meteor shower (astron.)
Persephone (also Proserpina)(myth.)
Persepolis (capital, ancient Persia)
Perseus (astron., hero; myth.)
Pershing, John J(oseph)("Blackjack")(US gen.; 1860-1948)
Persia (now Iran)
Persian (lang./people)
Persian berry (shrub)
Persian cat
Persian Empire (c539-c312 BC)
Persian Gulf (also Arabian Gulf)(SW Asia)
Persian Gulf States (Bahrain/Iran/Iraq/Kuwait/ Oman/Qatar/Saudi Arabia/UAE)
Persian Gulf War (Kuwait, UN allies/Iraq; 1991)
Persian Gulf War syndrome (med.)
Persian knot (also Sehna knot)
Persian lamb
Persian lilac
Persian melon
Persian red (color)
Persian rug/carpet
Persian violet
Persian walnut (also English walnut)
Persian War, Turko-
Persian wars (Gr./Persia; 499-449 BC)
Persius (aka Aulus Persius Flaccus)(Roman satirist; 34-62)
Personnel Management, Office of (OPM)(US govt. agcy.; est. 1979)
Perspex (constr.)
Persson, Göran (PM, Swed.; 1949-)
Pert/Plus (hair care)
Perth, Australia
Perth, Scotland
Peru (Republic of)(SAmer.)
Peru Current (formerly Humboldt Current)(cold ocean current)
Perugino, Pietro (de Cristoforo Vannucci)(It. artist; 1446-1523)
Peruvian perfume (slang, cocaine)
Pervez Musharraf, Gen. (PM, Pak.; 1943-)
Pesach (also Passover)(rel.)
Pesci, Joe (ent.; 1943-)
Peshawar, Pakistan
Peshkov, Aleksei Maksimovich (pseud. Maxim Gorky [or Gorki])(Rus. writer; 1868-1936)
Pestalozzi, Johann (Swiss educ. reformer; 1746-1827)
PET (positron emission tomography)(med.)

Pet, Inc.
PETA (People for the Ethical Treatment of
  Animals)
Petach Tikva, Israel
Petaluma, CA
Petar Stoyanov (pres., Bulgaria; 1952-)
Pete Fountain (US jazz; 1930-)
Pete Kelly's Blues (film, 1955)
Pete Maravich (basketball; 1948-88)
Pete 'N' Tillie (film, 1972)
Pete(r Dennis Blandford) Townshend (ent./The
  Who; 1945-)
Pete(r Edward) Rose (baseball; 1941-)
Pete (Alvin Ray) Rozelle (football exec.; 1926-
  96)
Pete(r) R. Seeger (ent.; 1919-)
Pete Sampras (tennis; 1971-)
Pete V. Domenici (US cong.; 1932-)
Pete(r Barton) Wilson (ex-CA gov.; 1933-)
Pete's Dragon (film, 1977)
Peter, I&II (rel., books of the New Testament)
Peter (or Pierre) Abelard (Fr. phil.; 1079-1142)
Peter (or Piotr, Pyotr)(Alekseevich) Kropotkin,
  Prince (Rus. anarchist; 1842-1921)
Peter Allen (ent./songwriter; 1944-92)
Peter Arno (aka Curtis Arnoux Peters)
  (cartoonist, *New Yorker*; 1904-68)
Peter Behrens (Ger. arch.; 1868-1940)
Peter Benchley (US writer; 1940-)
Peter Bogdanovich (ent.; 1939-)
Peter Boross (ex-PM, Hung.; 1928-)
Peter Boyle (ent.; 1933-)
Peter Brook (ent.; 1925-)
Peter Carl Fabergé (Rus. jeweler; 1846-1920)
Peter Carruthers (figure skating)
Peter Cook (ent./writer; 1937-95)
Peter Cooper (US bus.; 1791-1883)
Peter Courtney Quennell, (Sir)(Br. biographer;
  1905-93)
Peter Coyote (b. Peter Cohon)(ent.; 1942-)
Peter Cushing (ent.; 1913-94)
Peter Damian, St. (It. rel.; 1007-72)
Peter DeLuise (ent.; 1966-)
Peter De Vries (US writer; 1910-93)
Peter Duchin (US pianist/band leader; 1937-)
Peter Falk (ent.; 1927-)
Peter Finch (ent.; 1916-77)
Peter Firth (ent.; 1953-)
Peter Fonda (ent.; 1939-)
Peter Frampton (ent.; 1950-)
Peter Gabriel (ent.; 1950-)
Peter Gallagher (ent.; 1955-)
Peter G. Fitzgerald (US cong.; 1960-)
Peter Graves (b. Peter Aurness)(ent.; 1926-)
Peter Gunn (TV show)
Peter Hall (Reginald Frederick)(Br. theater; 1930-)
Peter Harrison (US arch.; 1716-75)
Peter I (Peter the Great)(ex-tzar, Rus.; 1672-
  1725)
Peter I(lyich) Tchaikovsky (Rus. comp.; 1840-93)
Peter Jennings (US TV jour.; 1938-)
Peter Lawford (ent.; 1923-84)
Peter Lind Hayes (ent.; 1915-98)
Peter Lorre (b. Lázló Löwenstein)(ent.; 1904-64)
Peter Macnicol (ent.; 1958-)

Peter Mafani Musonga (PM, Cameroon; 1942-)
Peter Marshall (b. Pierre La Cock)(ent.; 1927-)
Peter Martins (US dancer; 1946-)
Peter Maxwell Davies (Br. comp./cond.; 1934-)
Peter Mennin (b. Peter Mennini)(US comp.;
  1923-83)
Peter Minuit (Dutch admin. in Amer.; c1580-1638)
Peter Nero (US pianist; 1934-)
Peter Noone (ent.; 1947-)
Peter Norton Computing, Inc.
Peter O'Toole (ent.; 1932-)
Peter Pan (fict. chara.)
Peter Pan (J. Barrie play)
Peter Pan collar
Peter Pan Industries
Peter Pan peanut butter
Peter Paul Almond Joy (candy)
Peter Paul Cadbury Corp.
Peter Paul Mauser (Ger. inv.; 1838-1914)
Peter Paul Rubens (Flem. artist; 1577-1640)
Peter Pears (tenor; 1910-86)
Peter Piper (fict. chara.)
Peter Principle (econ./bus.)
Peter Proud, The Reincarnation of (film, 1975)
Peter Rabbit (fict. chara.)
Peter Riegert (ent.; 1947-)
Peter (Mark) Roget (Br. phys./lexicographer,
  Roget's Thesaurus; 1779-1869)
Peter Schickele (pseud. P. D. Q. Bach)(ent.;
  1935-)
Peter Scolari (ent.; 1954-)
Peter Sellers (ent.; 1925-80)
Peter Serkin (US pianist; 1947-)
Peter Straub (US writer; 1943-)
Peter Strauss (ent.; 1947-)
Peter Stuyvesant (Dutch gov. of NY; 1592-1672)
Peter Taylor (US writer; 1917-94)
Peter the Cruel (king, Castile/León; 1334-69)
Peter the Great (Peter I)(ex-tzar, Rus.; 1672-
  1725)
Peter Ueberroth (US bus./sports; 1937-)
Peter (Alexander) Ustinov, (Sir)(ent.; 1921-)
Peter Vidmar (US gymnast; 1961-)
Peter Weir (ent.; 1944-)
Peter Wimsey, Lord (fict. chara., D. Sayers)
Peter Yarrow (ent.; 1938-)
Peter, Paul and Mary (pop music)
Peter, St. (also Simon Peter)(rel.; ?-AD c64)
Peter's Church, St. (also St. Peter's Basilica)
  (Rome)
Peterbilt Motors Co.
Peterborough, England
Peterborough, Ontario, Canada
Peterle, Lojze (Slovenian pol.)
Peters, Bernadette (b. Bernadette Lazzara)
  (ent.; 1948-)
Peters, Brock (ent.; 1927-)
Peters, Curtis Arnoux (aka Peter
  Arno)(cartoonist, *New Yorker*; 1904-68)
Peters, Jean (ent.; 1926-)
Peters, Mike (cartoonist, *Mother Goose &
  Grimm*; 1943-)
Peters, Roberta (ent.; 1930-)
Petersburg, VA
Peterson, Cassandra (aka Elvira)(ent.; 1951-)

Peterson, Oscar (US jazz; 1925-)
Peterson, Roger Tory (US nat./artist; 1908-96)
Petit Trianon, Le (built for Mme. de Pompadour by Louis XV)
Petit, Roland (Fr. ballet; 1924-)
Petition of Right (Br. hist.; 1628)
Petrarch (aka Francesco Petrarca)(It. poet; 1304-74)
Petrarchan sonnet (also Italian sonnet)(lit.)
Petri dish (also l.c.)
Petrie Stores Corp.
Petrie, (Sir William Matthew) Flinders (Br. archaeol.; 1853-1942)
Petrified Forest National Park (AZ)
Petrified Forest, The (film, 1836)
Petrograd, Russia (now St. Petersburg)
Petroleum V(esuvius) Nasby (pseud. David Ross Locke)(US humorist; 1833-88)
Petroleum-Exporting Countries, Organization of (OPEC)(est. 1960)
Petronius, Gaius ("Arbiter Elegantiae")(Roman writer; ?-AD 66)
Petropavlovsk, Kazakhstan
Petrópolis, Brazil
Petrosyan, Levon Ter- (ex-pres., Armenia; 1943-)
Petrova, Olga
Petrovo Selo, Yugoslavia
Petru Lucinschi (pres., Moldova; 1940-)
Petruchio (fict. chara., *Taming of the Shrew*)
Pettiford, Oscar (US jazz; 1922-60)
Pettit, Bob (basketball; 1932-)
Petty and the Heartbreakers, Tom (pop music)
Petty, Richard (Lee)(auto racing; 1937-)
Petty, Tom (ent.; 1953-)
Petula Clark (ent.; 1932-)
Peugeot (auto.)
Peugeot Motors of America, Inc.
Peul (lang./people)
Pevsner, Antoine (Fr. artist; 1886-1962)
Peyton Place (G. Metalious novel)
Peyton Rous, (Francis)(US phys.; 1879-1970)
Pez Candy, Inc.
Pfaff American Sales Corp.
Pfaff sewing machine
Pfaltzgraff Co., Susquehanna
Pfeiffer, Michelle (ent.; 1957-)
Pfizer Inc. (med.)
PG&E Corp.
PGA (Professional Golfers Association)
P(ierre) G(ustave) T(outant) Beauregard (US gen.; 1818-93)
P(elham) G(renville) Wodehouse, (Sir)(US writer/humorist; 1881-1975)
P(ercival) J. Patterson (PM, Jamaica; 1935-)
Phaedo (by Plato)
Phaedra (myth.)
Phaethon (myth.)
Phair, Liz (ent./songwriter; 1967-)
Phalangist (Lebanese mil.)
Pham Van Dong (ex-PM, NViet.; 1906-2000)
Phan Dinh Khai (aka Le Duc Tho)(NViet pol.; 1911-90)
Phan Van Khai (PM, Viet.; 1933-)
Phanerozoic eon (most recent 570 million years)

Phantom of the Opera (play)
Phar Lap (film, 1983)
Phar Lap (race horse)
Pharaoh (Eg. title)
Pharaoh (or Pharaoh's) ant
Pharisees & Sadducees (opposing Hebrew grps; 2nd c.)
Pharmacia Corp.
Pharmavite Corp.
Pharos lighthouse at Alexandria (1 of 7 Wonders, Eg.)
Phazyme (med.)
Ph.D. (Doctor of Philosophy)
Pheasant Ridge Winery (US bus.)
Phelps Vineyards, Joseph (US bus.)
Phenaphen (med.)
Phenergan (med.)
Phenique, Campho- (med.)
Phenix City, AL
Phi Beta Kappa (honorary society; est. 1776)
Phi Beta Kappa key
Phidias (Gr. sculptor; c500-435 BC)
Phil(ip Joseph) Caputo (US writer; 1941-)
Phil Collins (ent.; 1951-)
Phil Donahue (ent.; 1935-)
Phil(ip Anthony) Esposito (hockey; 1942-)
Phil Everly (ent.; 1939-)
Phil Gramm (US cong.; 1942-)
Phil Harris (ent.; 1904-95)
Phil Hartman (ent.; 1948-98)
Phil(lip) Mahre (US skier; 1957-)
Phil Niekro (baseball; 1939-)
Phil Rizzuto (baseball; 1918-)
Phil Silvers (ent.; 1912-85)
Phil Spector (ent.; 1939-)
Phil Spitalny (cond.; 1890-1970)
Phil, Punxsutawney (groundhog)
Philadelphia 76ers (basketball team)
Philadelphia and Reading Railroad
Philadelphia Daily News (PA newspaper)
Philadelphia Eagles (football team)
Philadelphia Flyers (hockey team)
Philadelphia Inquirer (PA newspaper)
Philadelphia lawyer
Philadelphia Museum of Art
Philadelphia Phillies (baseball team)
Philadelphia, PA
Philbin, Regis (ent.; 1933-)
Philemon (rel., book of the New Testament)
Philip (Duke of Edinburgh, Prince of the UK, husband of Elizabeth II; 1921-)
Philip (Henry) Sheridan (US gen.; 1831-88)
Philip (Milton) Roth (US writer; 1933-)
Philip Barry (US writer; 1896-1949)
Philip Bosco (ent.; 1930-)
Philip Chesterfield, Lord (4th Earl of Chesterfield, Philip Dormer Stanhope)(Br. writer/pol.; 1694-1773)
Philip C. Jessup (US dipl.; 1897-1986)
Philip C(ortelyou) Johnson (US arch.; 1906-)
Philip D. Armour (US bus.; 1832-1901)
Philip Dormer Stanhope (4th Earl of Chesterfield, Lord Philip Chesterfield)(Br. writer/pol.; 1694-1773)
Philip Glass (US comp.; 1937-)

Philip II (king, Macedonia; 382-336 BC)
Philip II (king, Sp.; 1527-1598)
Philip II (Philip Augustus)(king, Fr.; 1165-1223)
Philip III (Philip the Bold)(king, Fr.; 1245-85)
Philip IV (Philip the Fair)(king, Fr.; 1268-1314)
Philip John Schuyler (US gen./pol.; 1733-1804)
Philip Kearny (US mil.; 1814-62)
Philip, King (aka Metacomet)(Wampanoag Indian chief; 1640-76)
Philip K. Wrigley (US bus., gum/baseball; 1895-1977)
Philip Larkin (Br. poet; 1922-85)
Philip Marlowe (fict. detective, R.T. Chandler)
Philip Michael Thomas (ent.; 1949-)
Philip Morris, Inc.
Philip Murray (US labor leader; 1886-1952)
Philip the Bold (Fr., duke, Burgundy; 1342-1404)
Philip the Bold (Philip III)(king, Fr.; 1245-85)
Philip the Fair (Philip IV)(king, Fr.; 1268-1314)
Philip the Good (Fr. duke, Burgundy; 1396-1467)
Philip the Tall (Philip V)(king, Fr.; c1294-1322)
Philip V (king, Sp.; 1683-1746)
Philip V (Philip the Tall)(king, Fr.; c1294-1322)
Philip VI (king, Fr.; 1293-1350)
Philip Weld (sailing; 1915-84)
Philipp Scheidemann (ex-chanc., Ger.; 1865-1939)
Philippe Entremont (pianist; 1934-)
Philippe Junot
Philippe, Louis ("Philippe Egalité" "the Citizen King")(king, Fr.; 1773-1850)
Philippians (rel., book of the New Testament)
Philippine Airlines (PAL)(airline)
Philippine mahogany (tree)
Philippines (Republic of the)(also Philippine Islands)(SE Asia)
Philippus Aureolus Paracelsus (b. Theophrastus Bombastus von Hohenheim)(Swiss phys./chem.; 1493-1541)
Philips Co., North American
Philips Electronics North America Corp.
Philips Magnavox (elec.)
Philistine (ancient people)
Phillies, Philadelphia (baseball team)
Phillip Seymour Hoffman (ent.; 1968-)
Phillippe, Ryan (ent.; 1974-)
Phillips curve (econ.)
Phillips head screw
Phillips Petroleum Co.
Phillips Screw Co.
Phillips screwdriver
Phillips 66 Co.
Phillips-Van Heusen Corp.
Phillips' Milk of Magnesia (med.)
Phillips, Bijou (ent.; 1980-)
Phillips, Chynna (ent.; 1968-)
Phillips, Lou Diamond (b. Lou Upchurch)(ent.; 1962-)
Phillips, Mackenzie (ent.; 1959-)
Phillips, Michelle (b. Holly Gilliam)(ent.; 1944-)
Phillis Wheatley (Afr./US poet; 1753-84)
Philly Joe Jones (US jazz; 1923-85)
Philo Remington (US inv./bus.; 1816-89)

Philo T. Farnsworth (US physt./TV pioneer; 1906-71)
Philosophy, Doctor of (also Ph.D., doctorate)
Phish (pop music)
pHisoDerm (med.)
pHisoHex (med.)
Phnom Penh, Cambodia
Phobos (Mars' moon; myth., personification of fear)
Phobos Mission (USSR uncrewed space probes)
Phoebe (Saturn moon; myth.)
Phoebe Cates (ent.; 1963-)
Phoebus (also Apollo)(myth., sun god)
Phoenicia (ancient Mediterranean kingdom; c1200-c332 BC)
Phoenician art
Phoenix (astron., phoenix/bird)
Phoenix (chicken)
Phoenix (US mil. missile)
Phoenix Cardinals (football team)
Phoenix Gazette (AZ newspaper)
Phoenix Home Life Mutual Insurance Company
Phoenix Republic (AZ newspaper)
Phoenix Suns (basketball team)
Phoenix, AZ
Phoenix, Joaquin (b. Joaquin Rafael Bottom) (ent.; 1974-)
Phoenix, River (b. River Jude Bottom)(ent.; 1970-93)
Phomvihan, Kaysone (ex-PM, Laos; 1920-92)
Phone-Mate
Phonemate, Inc.
Phonetic Alphabet, International (also IPA)
Phoolan Devi (aka the Bandit Queen)(Indian bandit/pol.; 1963-2001)
Photographic (mag.)
Photo-Mart (US bus.)
Photoshop, Adobe (compu.)
Photostat
Phoumsavan, Nouhak (ex-pres., Laos; 1914-)
Phrenilin (med.)
Phrygian cap (headwear)
Phyfe, Duncan (Scot./US furniture maker; c1768-1854)
Phylicia Rashad (ent.; 1948-)
Phyllis Curtin (soprano; 1927-)
Phyllis Diller (b. Phyllis Driver)(ent.; 1917-)
Phyllis George (US 1st woman sportscaster, ex-Miss America; 1949-)
Phyllis McGinley (US poet/writer; 1905-78)
Phyllis (Stewart) Schlafly (US activist; 1924-)
Physicians' Desk Reference
Physics, Nobel Prize for
Physiology or Medicine, Nobel Prize for
Phytin
Pia Zadora (b. Pia Schipani)(ent.; 1954-)
Piaf, Edith (b. Edith Giovanna Gassion)(Fr. ent.; 1915-63)
Piatigorsky, Gregor (Rus./US cellist; 1903-76)
Piazza, Marguerite (soprano; 1926-)
Picard, Jean (Fr. astron.; 1620-82)
Picard, Jean-Luc, Capt. (fict. chara., *Star Trek*)
Picardy (region, Fr.)
Picasso, Pablo (Ruiz y)(Sp. artist; 1881-1973)
Picasso, Paloma (US bus.; 1949-)
Picatinny Arsenal (NJ)

Piccadilly Circus (London)
Piccard, Auguste (Swiss physt.; 1884-1962)
Piccard, Jean Félix (Swiss chem./eng.; 1884-1963)
Piccone, Robin (fashion designer)
Pickens, T. Boone (US bus.; 1928-)
Pickering, Edward Charles (US astron./physt.; 1846-1919)
Pickering, William H(enry)(US astron.; 1858-1938)
Picket Fences (TV show)
Pickett, Cindy (ent.; 1947-)
Pickett, George E(dward)(US gen.; 1825-75)
Pickett, Wilson (ent.; 1941-)
Pickford, Mary (b. Gladys Marie Smith)(ent.; 1893-1979)
Pickles, Christina (ent.; 1935-)
Pickwick Papers, The (also *The Posthumous Papers of the Pickwick Club*)(C. Dickens novel)
Pickwick, Samuel (fict. chara., *Pickwick Papers*)
Pico Rivera, CA
Picon, Molly (ent.; 1898-1992)
Picone Hosiery, Evan- (US bus.)
Picone, Inc., Evan- (US bus.)
Pictionary (game)
Pictor (astron., painter)
Picts (ancient Scots)
Picture of Dorian Gray, The (Oscar Wilde novel)
Picturephone (used briefly in 1960s)
Pidgeon, Walter (ent.; 1897-1984)
Pidgin English (also pidgin English)
Pidgin Sign Lang.
Pied Piper of Hamelin, The (by Robert Browning)
Piedmont (region, It.)
Piedmont Plateau (region, E. US)
Piedmont, Greenville (SC newspaper)
Pier I Imports, Inc.
Pier Luigi Nervi (It. arch.; 1891-1979)
Pierce Brosnan (ent.; 1953-)
Pierce, David Hyde (ent.; 1959-)
Pierce, Fort, FL (city)
Pierce, Franklin (14th US pres.; 1804-69)
Pierce, Mildred (J.M. Cain novel)
Piercy, Marge (US writer; 1936-)
Piero de' Medici (It. pol.; 1416-69)
Piero della Francesca (It. artist; c1415-92)
Pierpont Morgan Library (NYC)
Pierre (or Peter) Abelard (Fr. phil.; 1079-1142)
Pierre Auguste Renoir (Fr. artist; 1841-1919)
Pierre Augustin Caron de Beaumarchais (Fr. writer; 1732-99)
Pierre Bérégovoy (ex-PM, France; 1925-93)
Pierre Bonnard (Fr. artist; 1867-1947)
Pierre Boulez (Fr. comp./cond.; 1925-)
Pierre Buyoya (pres., Burundi; 1949-)
Pierre Cardin (Fr. designer; 1922-)
Pierre Cecile Puvis de Chavannes (Fr. artist; 1824-98)
Pierre Charles (PM, Dominica; 1954-)
Pierre Charles L'Enfant (Fr./US arch./eng.; 1754-1825)
Pierre Corneille (Fr. dramatist; 1606-84)
Pierre Curie (Fr. physt., radium; 1859-1906)
Pierre de Fermat (Fr. math.; 1601-65)
Pierre de Ronsard (Fr. poet; 1524-85)

Pierre Joseph Proudhon (Fr. phil.; 1809-65)
Pierre Laval (ex-PM, Fr.; 1883-1945)
Pierre Monteux (cond.; 1875-1964)
Pierre-Paul Prud'hon (Fr. artist; 1758-1823)
Pierre Salinger (US TV jour./JFK press secy.; 1925-)
Pierre Samuel Du Pont (Fr. econ./pol.; 1739-1817)
Pierre Samuel du Pont (US bus.; 1870-1954)
Pierre S(imon) Laplace (aka Marquis de Laplace)(Fr. astron./math.; 1749-1827)
Pierre (Elliott) Trudeau (ex-PM, Can.; 1919-2000)
Pierre, SD
Pierrefonds, Quebec, Canada
Piers Anthony (b. Piers Anthony Jacob)(US writer; 1934-)
Piet Mondrian (b. Pieter Cornelis Mondriaan)(Dutch artist; 1872-1944)
Pieta (Michelangelo painting)
Pieter Brueghel, the Elder (also Breughel)(aka "Peasant Bruegel")(Flem. artist; 1525-69)
Pieter Brueghel, the Younger (also Breughel) (aka "Hell Bruegel")(Flem. artist; 1564-1638)
Pieter Oud, (Jacobus Johannes)(Dutch arch.; 1890-1963)
Pieter W. Botha (ex-pres., SAfr. pres.; 1916-)
Pieter Zeeman (Dutch physt.; 1865-1943)
Pietermaritzburg, South Africa
Pietism (rel.)
Pietro (de Cristoforo Vannucci) Perugino (It. artist; 1446-1523)
Pietro Belluschi (US arch.; 1899-1994)
Pietro Mascagni (It. comp.; 1863-1945)
Pietro Nenni (It. socialist leader/writer; 1891-1980)
pig Latin
Pig, Porky (cartoon chara.)
Piggledy, Higgledy- (play)
Piggy, Miss (Muppet)
Piglet (Winnie-the-Pooh)
Pigs, Bay of (Cuban inlet, invasion)
Pik Kommunizma (also Communism Peak) (formerly Mount Garmo, Mount Stalin)(Tajikisyan)
Pik-Nik Foods, Inc.
Pikachu (Pokémon chara.)
Pike, James A(lbert), Bishop (US rel.; 1913-69)
Pike, Zebulon Montgomery (US expl./mil.; 1779-1813)
Pikes Peak (CO)
Pikesville, MD
Pilate, Pontius (Roman mil./pol.; 1st c. AD)
Pileggi, Mitch (ent.; 1952-)
Pilgrim's Progress (J. Bunyan allegory)
Pilgrims (also Pilgrim Fathers)(settled MA; 1620)
Pilipino (also Filipino)(lang.)
Pillars of Hercules (rocks/entrance, Strait of Gibralter)
Pillowtex Corp.
Pillsbury Co., The
Pilobolus Dance Theater
Pilocar (med.)
Pilsener Bottling Co.
Pilsudski, Joseph (Pol. dictator; 1867-1935)
Piltdown man (anthrop. hoax)

Pima (Native Amer.)
Pimlico Race Course (Baltimore, MD)
Pinafore, H.M.S. *(or The Lass that Loved a Sailor)*(Gilbert/Sullivan opera)
Pinang (also Penang)(state, Malaysia)
Pinatubo, Mount (active volcano; Philippines)
Pincay, Laffit, Jr. (jockey; 1946-)
Pinchas Zuckerman (Isr. violinist/comp.; 1948-)
Pinchot, Bronson (ent.; 1959-)
Pinckney, Charles (US pol.; 1757-1824)
Pinckney, Charles Cotesworth (US pol.; 1746-1825)
Pinckney, Thomas (US pol.; 1750-1828)
Pindar (Gr. poet; c518-c438 BC)
Pindling, Lynden (Oscar)(ex-PM, Bahamas; 1930-2000)
Pine Bluff Arsenal (AR)
Pine Bluff, AR
Pine Tree State (nickname, ME)
Pine-Sol (cleaner)
Pinellas Park, FL
Ping-Pong (table tennis)
Pink Floyd (pop music)
Pink Panther Strikes Again, The (film, 1976)
Pink Panther, The (cartoon; film, 1964)
Pink Panther, The Return of the (film, 1975)
Pink Panther, The Revenge of the (film, 1978)
Pink Panther, Trail of the (film, 1982)
Pinkerton National Detective Agency
Pinkerton, Allan (US detective; 1819-84)
Pinkham, Lydia (Estes)(US bus.; 1819-83)
Pinkham's Vegetable Compound, Mrs. Lydia E. (med.)
Pinky Lee (b. Pinkus Leff)(ent.; 1908-93)
Pinocchio, The Adventures of (C. Collodi fantasy)
Pinochet (Ugarte), Augusto (ex-pres., Chile; 1915-)
Pinot Blanc (grape, wine)
Pinot Chardonnay (wine)
Pinot Noir (grape, wine)(also l.c.)
Pinsky, Robert (Neal)(US ex-poet laureate; 1940-)
Pinter, Harold (Br. writer; 1930-)
Pinto, Ford (auto.)
Pinyin (Ch. phonetic alphabet)
Pinza, Ezio (ent.; 1892-1957)
Pioneer (US uncrewed space probes)
Pioneer Electronics USA, Inc.
Pioneer Press, St. Paul (MN newspaper)
Pioneer Venus (US uncrewed space probes)
Pioneers, Sons of the (music group)
Piotr (or Pyotr, Peter)(Alekseevich) Kropotkin, Prince (Rus. anarchist; 1842-1921)
PIP Printing International (US bus.)
Piper Aircraft Corp.
Piper Cherokee
Piper-Heidsieck champagne
Piper Laurie (b. Rosetta Jacobs)(ent.; 1932-)
Piper of Hamelin, The Pied (by Robert Browning)
Piper Sonoma (US bus.)
Piper, Peter (fict. chara.)
Piper, Pied (fict. chara.)
Pippen, Scottie (basketball; 1965-)
Pippi Longstocking (fict. chara.)
Pippin (play; film, 1981)
Pips, Gladys Knight & the (pop music)

Piraeus, Greece
Pirandello, Luigi (It. writer; 1867-1936)
Piranesi, Giambattista (It. artist; 1720-78)
Pirates of Penzance, The (Gilbert & Sullivan operetta)
Pirates, Pittsburgh (baseball team)
Pirates, Terry & the (comic strip)
Pisa, Council of (Roman Catholic Church; 1409)
Pisa, Italy
Pisa, Leaning Tower of (It.)
Pisanello, (b. Antonio Pisano)(It. artist; c1395-1455)
Pisano, Andrea (b. Andrea da Pontadera)(It. sculptor; c1290-c1349)
Pisano, Giovanni (It. artist; c1250-c1314)
Pisano, Nicola (It. artist; c1220-84)
Piscataway, NJ
Pisces (zodiac, astron., fish)
Piscis Austrinius (astron., southern fish)
Piscopo, Joe (ent.; 1951-)
Pismo Beach, CA
Pissarro, Camille (Jacob)(Fr. artist; 1830-1903)
Pistoia, Italy
Piston, Walter (US comp.; 1894-1976)
Pistol Pete (Peter) Maravich (basketball; 1948-88)
Pistons, Detroit (basketball team)
Pitaka (rel.)
Pitaka, Abhidhamma (rel.)
Pitaka, Sutta (rel.)
Pitaka, Vinaya (rel.)
Pitcairn Island (Br. Polynesian island)
Pitcher, Molly (aka Mary [Ludwig Hays] McCauley)(US heroine; 1754-1832)
Pithecanthropus (anthrop.)
Pitkin, Walter (B.)(writer)
Pitman shorthand
Pitman, (Sir) Isaac (Br., inv. shorthand system; 1813-97)
Pitney-Bowes (office machines, postage meters)
Pitney Bowes, Inc.
Pitocin (med.)
Pitot-static tube/system (aeronautics)
Pitot tube (fluid flow)
Pitt, Brad (ent.; 1963-)
Pitt, William, the Elder (the "Great Commoner") (ex-PM, Br.; 1708-78)
Pitt, William, the Younger (ex-PM, Br.; 1759-1806)
Pitti Palace (It.)
Pitts, Zasu (ent.; 1898-1963)
Pittsburg Landing (also Battle of Shiloh)(US hist.; 1862)
Pittsburg, CA, KS
Pittsburgh Corning Corporation
Pittsburgh International Airport, Greater (PA)
Pittsburgh Penguins (hockey team)
Pittsburgh Pirates (baseball team)
Pittsburgh Post-Gazette (PA newspaper)
Pittsburgh Press (PA newspaper)
Pittsburgh Steelers (football team)
Pittsburgh Sun-Telegraph (PA newspaper)
Pittsburgh, PA
Pittsfield, MA
Piura, Peru

Pius II (b. Enea Silvio Piccolomini)(It., pope; 1405-64)

Pius IV (b. Giovanni Angelo Medici)(It., pope; 1499-1565)

Pius IX (b. Giovanni Maria Mastai-Ferretti)(It., pope; 1792-1878)

Pius V, St. (b. Antonio Ghislieri)(It., pope; 1504-72)

Pius VI (b. Giovanni Angelo Braschi)(It., pope; 1717-99)

Pius VII (b. Luigi Barnaba Chiaramonti)(It., (pope; 1742-1823)

Pius X, St. (b. Giuseppe Melchiorre Sarto)(It. pope; 1835-1914)

Pius XI (b. Ambrogio Damiano Achille Ratti)(It., pope; 1857-1939)

Pius XII (b. Eugenio Pacelli)(It., pope; 1876-1958)

Pius, Antoninus (emp., Rome; AD 86-161)

Piute (Native Amer.)

Pizarro, Francisco (Sp. mil./expl.; 1475?-1541)

Pizza Hut (US bus.)

Pizzetti, Ildebrando (It. comp./hist.; 1880-1968)

PKU (phenylketonuria)

P(amela) L. Travers (Austl. writer; 1906-96)

Place de la Concorde, (building/museum, Paris)

Placentia, CA

Placid, Lake, NY

Placido Domingo (Sp. tenor; 1941-)

Placidyl (med.)

Plager, Barclay (hockey; 1941-88)

Plain Dealer, Cleveland (OH newspaper)

Plain of Jezreel (also Esdraelon Plain)(Isr.)

Plain People (Mennonites, Amish, Dunkers)(rel.)

Plainfield, NJ

Plains Indians (NAmer.)

Plains of Abraham (Can.)

Plains, GA

Plainview, TX

Planck, Max (Karl Ernst Ludwig)(Ger. physt.; 1858-1947)

Planck's constant (physics)

Planck's (or Planck) radiation law/formula

Planet, Captain (TV show)

Planned Parenthood

Planned Parenthood Federation of America, Inc. (aka Planned Parenthood-World Population) (US org; est. 1921)

Plano, TX

Plant, Robert (ent.; 1947-)

Plantabbs Corp.

Plantagenet (or Anjou), House of (Br. ruling family; 1154-1399)

Plantagenet, Richard (Duke of York)(Br. mil.; 1411-60)

Plantation walking horse (also Tennessee walking horse)

Plantation, FL

Plante, Jacques (hockey; 1929-86)

Planters LifeSaver Co.

Plantin (type style)

plaster of Paris (synthetic gypsum)

Plasticine (modeling paste)

Plata, Rio de la (also River Plate)(SAmer.)

Plateau Indians

Plath, Sylvia (US writer; 1932-63)

Plato (Gr. phil.; c428-c347 BC)

Platonism (philosophy)

Platoon (film, 1986)

Platt Amendment (US hist.; 1901)

Platt, O(rville) H(itchcock)(US pol.; 1827-1905)

Platt/Hartex, Leggett & (US bus.)

Platte River (NE)

Platte River, South (CO/NE)

Platters, the (pop music)

Plattsburgh Air Force Base, NY

Plautus, Titus Maccius (Roman writer; c254-c184 BC)

Plavix (med.)

Plax (med.)

Playboy (mag.)

Playboy Enterprises, Inc.

Playboy of the Western World, The (John Millington Synge comedy)

Play-Doh

Player, Gary (golf; 1935-)

Playgirl (mag.)

Playskool (toys)

Playskool Baby, Inc.

Play Station (compu. game)

PlayStation2 (compu. game)

Playtex Apparel, Inc.

Plaza Hotel (NYC)

Plaza Suite (N. Simon play)

Pleasant Valley Wine Co.

Pleasence, Donald (ent.; 1919-95)

Pleiades (astron.; myth.)

Pleiku, Vietnam

Pleistocene epoch (2.5 million to 10,000 years ago)

Plekhanov, Georgi (Valentinovich)(Rus. phil., "Father of Russian Marxism"; 1857-1918)

Pleshette, Suzanne (ent.; 1937-)

Plessy v. Ferguson (US law; 1896)

Pleven, Bulgaria

Plexiglas (a plastic)

Plimpton, George (US writer; 1927-)

Plimpton, Martha (ent.; 1970-)

Pliny the Elder (Gaius Plinius Secundus)(Roman scholar; 23-79)

Pliny the Younger (Gaius Plinius Caecilius Secundus)(Roman writer; 62-113)

Pliocene epoch (12-2.5 million years ago)

Pliofilm

Plisetskaya, Maya Mikhaylovna (Rus. ballet; 1925-)

PLO (Palestine Liberation Organization)

Ploesti, Romania

Plott hound (dog)

Plough Corp., Schering-

Plovdiv, Bulgaria

Plowright, Joan (ent.; 1929-)

Plum, J. L. (clothing)

Plummer, Amanda (ent.; 1957-)

Plummer, Christopher (ent.; 1927-)

Plunkett, Jim (football; 1947-)

Plutarch (Gr. biographer; c46-120)

Pluto (planet; myth.)

Plutus (myth.)

Plymouth (auto.)

Plymouth Acclaim (auto.)

Plymouth Breeze (auto.)
Plymouth Colony (Br. colony in MA; 1620)
Plymouth Company (Br. hist.; 1606-35)
Plymouth Grand Voyager (now Chrysler)(auto.)
Plymouth Grand Voyager LE (auto.)
Plymouth Grand Voyager SE (now Chrysler)(auto.)
Plymouth Horizon (auto.)
Plymouth Neon (auto.)
Plymouth Neon Highline (auto.)
Plymouth Neon LX (auto.)
Plymouth Neon Sport (auto.)
Plymouth Prowler (now Chrysler)(auto.)
Plymouth Road Runner (auto.)
Plymouth Rock (chicken)
Plymouth Rock (Pilgrims landed)
Plymouth Sundance (auto.)
Plymouth Voyager (now Chrysler)(auto.)
Plymouth Voyager SE (now Chrysler)(auto.)
Plymouth Voyager STD (now Chrysler)(auto.)
Plymouth, CT, MA, MN
Plymouth, England
Plymouth, Montserrat
PM (also p.m.)(post meridiem, postmaster, prime minister)
PMG (paymaster general)
PMS (Pantone Matching System)(colors/ graphics)
PMS (premenstrual syndrome)
Pneumocystis carinii (med.)
PO (petty officer, post office [box])
Po (chem. sym., polonium)
Po River (It.)
Po, Li (Tai)(Ch. poet; 705-62)
POB (post office box)
Pocahontas (Rebecca Rolfe)(Native Amer. heroine; c1595-1617)
Pocatello, ID
PocketPC (compu.)
Poco (pop music)
Pocono Mountains (also Poconos)(PA)
Podesta, John David (US ex-White House chief of staff; 1949-)
Podgorica, Yugoslavia
Podgorny, Nikolay Viktorovich (USSR pol.; 1903-83)
Podhoretz, Norman (US writer; 1930-)
Podunk (any small, isolated town)
Poe, Edgar Allan (US writer; 1809-49)
Pogo (comic strip)
Pogue, William (astro.; 1930-)
Pohl, Frederik (US writer, sci-fi; 1919-)
Pohnpei, Micronesia
Pohnpeian (people)
Poincaré, Raymond (Nicolas Landry)(ex-pres., Fr.; 1860-1934)
Poindexter, Buster (aka David Johansen)(ent.; 1950-)
Poindexter, John F. (US pol.)
Poindexter, John M(arlan)(US adm.; 1936-)
Point Barrow, AK (northernmost point of US)
Point Mugu Nas, CA
point d'Alençon (also Alençon lace)
Pointe-a-Pitre, Guadeloupe
Pointe-aux-Trembles, Quebec, Canada (now part of Montreal)
Pointe-Claire, Quebec, Canada
Pointe-Noire, Congo
Pointillism (art)(also l.c.)
Poirot (TV show)
Poirot, Hercule (fict. detective, Agatha Christie)
Poison (pop music)
Poitier, Sidney (ent.; 1927-)
Poitou-Charentes (region, Fr.)
Pokémon (children's toy/game)
Pokémon: The First Movie (film, 1999)
Poker Alice (film, 1987)
Pokhara, Nepal
Pol Pot (also Saloth Sar)(Cambodian pol.; 1925-98)
Pola Negri (ent.; 1900-87)
Polack (slang)
Poland (Republic of)(E Eur.)
Polanski, Roman (ent.; 1933-)
Polaris (also North Star, Polestar)(astron.)
Polaroid camera
Polaroid Corp.
Pole (people)
Pole, North (N end of earth's axis)
Pole, South (S end of earth's axis)
Polestar (also North Star, Polaris)(astron.)
Police Gazette
Police Story (TV show)
Police, the (pop music)
Policy Development, Office of (US govt.)
Polident (health)
Polish (chicken)
Polish (lang./people)
Polish Airlines LOT
Polish Corridor (Pol. access to the Baltic)
Polish sausage
Politburo ("political bureau")(USSR)
Polk Audio, Inc.
Polk, Fort, LA (mil.)
Polk, James Knox (11th US pres.; 1795-1849)
Pollack, Sydney (ent.; 1934-)
Pollan, Tracy (ent.; 1960-)
Pollard, Michael J. (ent.; 1939-)
Pollenex (appliances)
Polley, Sara (ent.; 1979-)
Pollock v. Farmer's Loan and Trust Co. (US law; 1895)
Pollock, (Paul) Jackson (US artist; 1912-56)
Pollux, Castor and (astron.; myth., Gemini/ twins)
Polly Bergen (b. Nellie Paulina Burgin)(ent.; 1930-)
Pollyanna (E. Porter novel)
Pollyanna (foolishly optimistic person)
Polo, Marco (It. expl.; c1254-1324)
Polo/Ralph Lauren Leathergoods (US bus.)
Polonius (Hamlet chara.)
Poltava, Ukraine
Poltergeist (film, 1982)
Polybius (Gr. hist.; c200-c118 BC)
Polycarp, St. (Turk. rel.; 69?-155?)
Polycillin (med.)
Polyclitus (Gr. sculptor; 5th c. BC)
Polydorus (Gr. sculptor; 1st c. BC)
PolyGram Records, Inc.

Polyhymnia (myth.)
Polymox (med.)
Polynesia (islands, Pac.)
Polynesian (langs., people)
Polynesian, Malayo- (also Austronesian)(lang.)
Polynesian, Melanesian- (people)
PolyOne Corp.
Polyphemus (myth., Cyclops)
Polypodiophyta (ferns)
Polysporin (med.)
Pomerania (region, Pol.)
Pomeranian (dog)
Pomeranian (people)
Pomo (Native Amer.)
Pomona (myth.)
Pomona, CA
Pompadour, Marquise de (aka Jeanne
    Antoinette Poisson Le Normant d'Étioles)
    (mistress of Louis XV, Fr.; 1721-64)
Pompano Beach, FL
Pompeian red (also l.c.)(also dragon's blood)
Pompeii (ancient city, It.)
Pompey the Great (Gnaeus Pompeius Magnus)
    (Roman gen./pol.; 106-48 BC)
Pompidou, Georges (Jean Raymond)(ex-pres.,
    Fr.; 1911-74)
Pomus, Doc (b. Jerome Felder)(US comp.;
    1925-91)
Ponce de León, (Juan)(Sp. expl.; c1460-1521)
Ponce, Puerto Rico
Ponchartrain, Lake (LA)
Ponchielli, Amilcare (It. comp.; 1834-86)
Pond's (skin care)
Pond's, Inc., Chesebrough-
Ponderosa, Inc.
pons Varolii (also l.c.)(brain nerve fibers)
Pons, Lily (ent.; 1904-76)
Ponselle, Rosa (soprano; 1897-1981)
Ponstel (med.)
Pont de Nemours, E(leuthere) I. du (US bus.;
    1771-1834)
Pont l'Évêque (cheese)
Pont Neuf bridge (Paris)
Pont Pharmaceuticals, du (US bus.)
Pont, E(leuthere) I. du (US bus.; 1771-1834)
Pont, Henry (Belin) du (US bus.; 1899-1970)
Pont, Samuel Francis du (US mil.; 1803-65)
Pont, Thomas Coleman du (US bus./pol.; 1863-
    1930)
Ponti, Carlo (It. ent.; 1913-)
Pontiac (auto.)
Pontiac Aztek (auto.)
Pontiac Aztek GT (auto.)
Pontiac Bonneville (auto.)
Pontiac Bonneville SE (auto.)
Pontiac Bonneville SLE (auto.)
Pontiac Bonneville SSE (auto.)
Pontiac Bonneville SSEi (auto.)
Pontiac Firebird (auto.)
Pontiac Firebird Formula (auto.)
Pontiac Firebird Trans Am (auto.)
Pontiac Grand Am (auto.)
Pontiac Grand Am GT (auto.)
Pontiac Grand Am GT1 (auto.)
Pontiac Grand Am SE (auto.)

Pontiac Grand Am SE1 (auto.)
Pontiac Grand Am SE2 (auto.)
Pontiac Grand Prix (auto.)
Pontiac Grand Prix GT (auto.)
Pontiac Grand Prix GTP (auto.)
Pontiac Grand Prix SE (auto.)
Pontiac LeMans (auto.)
Pontiac Montana minivan (auto.)
Pontiac Sunbird (auto.)
Pontiac Sunfire (auto.)
Pontiac Sunfire GT (auto.)
Pontiac Sunfire SE (auto.)
Pontiac Trans Am
Pontiac Trans Sport (auto.)
Pontiac Trans Sport Montana (auto.)
Pontiac Trans Sport SE (auto.)
Pontiac, Chief (Native Amer./Ottawa; c1720-69)
Pontiac, IL, MI
Pontiac's Rebellion/Conspiracy (US hist.; 1763-
    66)
Pontianak, Indonesia
Pontius Pilate (Roman mil./pol.; 1st c. AD)
Pontocaine (med.)
Pontormo, Jacopo da (It. artist; 1492-1557)
Pony Express (mail service; 1860-61)
Pony League (baseball)
Ponzi scheme/game (also Ponzi)(investment
    swindle)
Pooh Bah (also poobah)
Pooh Corner, Welcome to (TV show)
Poole, England
Poona, India (also Pune)
Poor Richard's Almanac (by B. Franklin)
Pop Goes the Weasel (song)
Pop, Iggy (pop music)
Pop-Tarts
Popayán, Colombia
Popcorn, Faith (b. Faith Plotkin)(writer/trend
    analyst; 1943-)
Pope Air Force Base, NC
Pope Joan (card game)
Pope Valley Winery (US bus.)
Pope, Alexander (Br. poet; 1688-1744)
Pope, John Russell (US arch.; 1874-1937)
Popeye (cartoon)
Popeye Doyle (fict. chara., The French Connection)
Popeye the sailor-man (cartoon chara.)
Popeye's Famous Fried Chicken & Biscuits, Inc.
Popocatépetl, Mount (volcano, Mex.)
Popovich, Pavel R(omanovich)(cosmo.; 1930-)
Poppins, Mary (P. Travers novel)
Popsicle
Popular Mechanics (mag.)
Popular Photography (mag.)
Popular Science (mag.)
Populism (US hist.; late 19th c.)
Populist Party (also People's Party)(US pol.;
    1891-1908)
Populist Party of America (US pol.)
Porch of the Caryatids (Gr., female figures used
    for columns)
Porcupine River (AK/Can.)
Porgy and Bess (Gershwin operetta)
Porizkova, Paulina (model; 1965-)
Porky Pig (cartoon chara.)

Porky's (film, 1982)
Porsche (auto.)
Porsche 911 (auto.)
Porsche 911 Carrera (auto.)
Porsche 911 Carrera 4 (auto.)
Porsche 911 Carrera 4 S (auto.)
Porsche 911 Carrera S coupe (auto.)
Porsche 911 Carrera Targa (auto.)
Porsche 911 Turbo (auto.)
Porsche 911 Turbo S (auto.)
Porsche 928 GTS (auto.)
Porsche 968 (auto.)
Porsche Boxster (auto.)
Porsche Boxster Cabriolet (auto.)
Porsche Boxster roadster (auto.)
Porsche Boxster S (auto.)
Porsche Cars North America, Inc.
Porsche, Ferdinand (Ger. auto. eng.; 1875-1951)
Port Angeles, WA
Port Arthur, Ontario, Canada
Port Arthur, TX
Port-au-Prince, Haiti
Port Authority of New York and New Jersey
Port du Salut (also Port-Salut)(cheese)
Port Elizabeth, South Africa
Port Glaud, Seychelles
Port Harcourt, Nigeria
Port Huron, MI
Port Louis, Mauritius
Port Moresby, Papua New Guinea
Port-of-Spain, Trinidad
Port Richey, FL
Port Royal, Jamaica
Port Royal, SC
Port Said, Egypt
Port-Salut (also Port du Salut)(cheese)
Port Sudan, Sudan
Port Townsend, WA
Port-Vila, Vanuatu
Porter Wagoner (ent.; 1927-)
Porter, Cole (US comp.; 1893-1964)
Porter, Katherine Anne (US writer; 1890-1980)
Porter, Sylvia F(eldman)(US finan. writer;
   1914-91)
Porter, William Sydney (pseud. O Henry)(US
   writer; 1862-1910)
Porterville, CA
Portia de Rossi (b. Amanda Rogers)(ent.; 1973-)
Portinari de' Bardi, Beatrice (inspiration for
   Dante's Beatrice; 1266-90)
Portland Hoffa (ent.)
Portland Oregonian (OR newspaper)
Portland Press-Herald (ME newspaper)
Portland Telegram (ME newspaper)
Portland Trail Blazers (basketball team)
Portland, OR, ME, TX
Portman, John (US arch.; 1934-)
Portman, Natalie (ent./model; 1981-)
Portmeirion
Portmeirion (US bus.)
Portnoy's Complaint (P. Roth novel)
Pôrto Alegre, Brazil
Porto Novo, Benin
Porto, Portugal (also Oporto)
Portobello Road market (London)

Portofino, Italy
Portsmouth Naval Shipyard (NH)
Portsmouth, Dominica
Portsmouth, England
Portsmouth, NH, OH, RI, VA
Portugal (Republic of)(SW Eur.)
Portuguese (lang./people)
Portuguese man-of-war (sea animal)
Portuguese water dog
Posadas, Argentina
Poseidon (myth.)
Poseidon Adventure, The (film, 1972)
Posey, Parker (ent.; 1968-)
Post & Courier, Charleston (SC newspaper)
Post (cereals)
Post Co., Washington
Post-Dispatch, St. Louis (MO newspaper)
Post Exchange (PX)(mil. store)(also l.c.)
Post-Gazette, Pittsburgh (PA newspaper)
Post-Herald, Birmingham (AL newspaper)
Post-Intelligencer, Seattle (WA newspaper)
Post-it notes
Post Raisin Bran (cereal)
Post Standard, Syracuse (NY newspaper)
Post-Tribune, Gary (IN newspaper)
Post, Bridgeport (CT newspaper)
Post, Cincinnati (OH newspaper)
Post, Denver (CO newspaper)
Post, Emily (Price)(US writer, social etiquette;
   1873?-1960)
Post, George Browne (US arch.; 1837-1913)
Post, Houston (TX newspaper)
Post, Laurens (Jan) Van der (SAfr. writer;
   1906-96)
Post, Markie (ent.; 1950-)
Post, New York (NY newspaper)
Post, Washington (DC newspaper)
Post, West Palm Beach (FL newspaper)
Post, Wiley (US aviator; 1899-1935)
Postal Service, U.S. (USPS)(US govt. agcy.;
   est. 1865)
Postman Always Rings Twice, The (J.M. Cain
   novel; film, 1946, 1981)
Poston, Tom (ent.; 1927-)
Pot, Pol (also Saloth Sar)(Cambodian pol.;
   1925-98)
Potawatomi (Native Amer.)
Potemkin village/Village (showy facade)
Potemkin, Grigory Aleksandrovich, Prince (Rus.
   pol.; 1739-91)
Potok, Chaim (US writer; 1929-)
Potomac River (DC/MD/VA/WV)
Potomac, MD
Potosí, Bolivia
Potsdam Conference (US/UK/USSR; 1945)
Potsdam, Germany
Potsdam, NY
Pott's disease (tuberlosis)(med.)
Potter and the Chamber of Secrets, Harry (J.K.
   Rowling series, Book 2)
Potter and the Goblet of Fire, Harry (J.K.
   Rowling series, Book 4)
Potter and the Prisoner of Azkaban, Harry (J.K.
   Rowling series, Book 3)
Potter and the Sorcerer's Stone, Harry (J.K.

Rowling series, Book 1)
Potter Stewart (US jurist; 1915-85)
Potter, (Helen) Beatrix (Br. writer/artist; 1866-1943)
Potter, Harry (fict. chara.)
Potts, Annie (ent.; 1952-)
Pottstown, PA
Potvin, Denis Charles (hockey; 1953-)
Poughkeepsie, NY
Pouilly-Fuissé (wine)
Pouilly-Fumé (wine)
Poul Nyrup Rasmussen (PM, Den.; 1943-)
Poul Schlüter (Dan. pol.; 1929-)
Poulan (lawn care)
Poulan Pro (lawn care)
Poulenc Rorer Consumer Pharmaceuticals, Rhone- (US bus.)
Poulenc, Francis (Jean Marcel)(Fr. comp.; 1899-1963)
Pound, Ezra (Loomis)(US poet; 1885-1972)
Poundstone, Paula (ent.; 1959-)
Pourier, Miguel A. (PM, Netherlands Antilles)
Poussaint, Alvin F. (ent.; 1934-)
Poussin, Nicolas (Fr. artist; 1594-1665)
Povich, Maury (Maurice Richard)(US TV jour.; 1939-)
POW (prisoner of war)
Powder Puff Derby
Powell, Adam Clayton, Jr. (US pol./rel.; 1908-72)
Powell, Boog (John)(baseball; 1941-)
Powell, Bud (US jazz; 1924-66)
Powell, Colin L(uther), Gen. (US secy./state; 1937-)
Powell, Dick (ent.; 1904-63)
Powell, Eleanor (ent.; 1912-82)
Powell, Jane (ent.; 1928-)
Powell, John Wesley (US geol./ethnol.; 1834-1902)
Powell, Lake (AZ/UT)
Powell, Lewis F(ranklin), Jr. (US jurist; 1907-98)
Powell, Mike (track; 1963-)
Powell, (Sir) Robert Baden- (Br. gen., founded Boy Scouts; 1857-1941)
Powell, William (ent.; 1892-1984)
Power, Tyrone (ent.; 1913-58)
Powers Boothe (ent.; 1949-)
Powers: The Spy Who Shagged Me, Austin (film, 1999)
Powers: International Man of Mystery, Austin (film, 1997)
Powers, Francis Gary (US mil./U-2 spy pilot shot down over USSR in 1960; 1929-77)
Powers, Hiram (US sculptor; 1805-73)
Powers, Stefanie (b. Stefania Federkiewicz)(ent.; 1942-)
Powhatan (Native Amer.)
Poznan, Poland
PP (parcel post)
PPA (phenylpropanolamine)(med.)
PPG Industries, Inc.
PPO (preferred provider organization)
PR (public relations)
Prado (Madrid museum)
Praemium Imperiale (Imperial Prize)(Jap. art award)
Praetorian Guard (Roman bodyguards)
Prague, Czechoslovakia
Praia, Cape Verde
Prairie Provinces (Can.: Alberta, Manitoba, Saskatchewan)
Prairie State (nickname, IL)
Praise the Lord Network (PTL)(rel.)
Prati Wines, Inc., Martini &
Pratt, Kelly, Sharon (ex-DC mayor; 1944-)
Pravachol (med.)
Pravda (Rus. newspaper)
Praxiteles (Gr. sculptor; 400-330 BC)
Prayer of Manasses (rel., Apocrypha)
Prayer, World Day of
Preakness (horse racing)
Preakness Stakes (horse racing)
Precambrian era (4.6 billion-570 million years ago)
Precambrian Shield (also Laurentian [or Canadian] Plateau/Shield)(Can.)
pre-Columbian (art/arch.; pre-16th c. AD)
Pred Forte (med.)
Predstavnicki Dom (aka House of Representatives)(Bosnia-Hercegovina)
Preemption Act (US hist.; 1841)
Prefontaine, Steve (Roland)(runner; 1951-75)
Prego (sauce)
Preliminary Scholastic Aptitude Test (also PSAT)
Prelude, Honda (auto.)
Preludin (med.)
Premadasa, Ranasinghe (ex-pres., Sri Lanka; 1924-93)
Premarin (med.)
Premark International, Inc.
Premier Power (CAT system)
Premiere (mag.)
Preminger, Otto (Ludwig)(ent.; 1905-86)
Premium (saltines)
Prendergast, Maurice B(razil)(US artist; c1860-1924)
Prentice-Hall, Inc.
Prentiss, Paula (b. Paula Ragusa)(ent.; 1939-)
Preparation H (med.)
Pre-Raphaelite Brotherhood (PRB)(Br. art; 1848-53)
Pres (Lester Willis) Young (US jazz; 1909-59)
Presbyterian (rel.)
Presbyterian Church
Presbyterianism (rel.)
Prescott (Sheldon) Bush (US pol., grandfather of pres./father of ex-pres.; 1895-1972)
Prescott, William (Hickling)(US hist.; 1796-1859)
Preservation Hall Jazz Band
President and Vice President, Office of the (US govt.)
Presidential Medal of Freedom (US, highest civilian honor)
Presidents' Day
Presidio of San Francisco (US mil.)
Presidio, The (film, 1988)
Presley, Elvis (Aron)(ent.; 1935-77)
Presley, Lisa Marie (daughter of Elvis and Priscilla Presley; 1968-)
Presley, Priscilla (Beaulieu)(ent.; 1945-)

pre-Socratics (phil.)
Press & Sun-Bulletin, Binghamton (NY newspaper)
Press Association (Br. news org.; 1868)
Press International, United (UPS)(US news org.; est. 1958)
Press, Asbury Park (NJ newspaper)
Press, Associated (AP)(US news org.; est. 1848)
Press, Atlantic City (NJ newspaper)
Press, Evansville (IN newspaper)
Press, Grand Rapids (MI newspaper)
Press, Mobile (AL newspaper)
Press, Pittsburgh (PA newspaper)
Press, Savannah (GA newspaper)
Press-Democrat, Santa Rosa (CA newspaper)
Press-Enterprise, Riverside (CA newspaper)
Press-Gazette, Green Bay (WI newspaper)
Press-Herald, Portland (ME newspaper)
Press-Telegram, Long Beach (CA newspaper)
Presser, Jackie (US labor leader; 1927-88)
Pressler, Larry (Lee)(US pol.; 1942-)
Prester John (legendary priest-king; 12th-16th c.)
Preston Foster (ent.; 1901-70)
Preston Sturges (ent.; 1898-1959)
Preston, Billy (ent.; 1946-)
Preston, Robert (ent.; 1918-87)
Pretender, Old (aka James III, James [Francis] Edward Stuart)(Br. prince; 1688-1766)
Pretenders, the (pop music)
Pretoria, South Africa
Pretorius, Andries (SAfr. colonizer/mil.; 1799-1853)
Pretorius, Marthinus (Wessels)(SAfr. mil./pol.; 1819-1901)
Pretty Boy (Charles Arthur) Floyd (US bank robber; 1901-34)
Pretty Woman (film, 1990)
Prevacid (med.)
Préval, René Garcia (pres., Haiti; 1943-)
Prevention (mag.)
Previa, Toyota (auto.)
Previn, André (George)(US cond./comp.; 1929-)
Priam (myth.)
Priapus (myth.)
Price Co., The
Price Group, Inc., T. Rowe
Price Investment Services, Inc., T. Rowe
Price is Right, The (TV show)
Price/Stern/Sloan Publishers, Inc.
Price Toys, Fisher- (US bus.)
Price Waterhouse
Price, (Mary) Leontyne (opera; 1927-)
Price, George (Cadle)(ex-PM, Belize; 1919-)
Price, George (US cartoonist, *New Yorker*; 1901-95)
Price, Lloyd (ent.; 1933-)
Price, Mark (basketball; 1964-)
Price, Nick (golf; 1957-)
Price, Ray (ent.; 1926-)
Price, Reynolds (US writer; 1933-)
Price, Vincent (ent.; 1911-93)
Pride and Prejudice (J. Austin novel)
Pride, Charlie (ent.; 1938-)
Priest, Judas (rock group)
Priestley, J(ohn) B(oynton)(Br. writer; 1894-1984)

Priestley, Jason (ent.; 1969-)
Priestley, Joseph (Br. chem./writer; 1733-1804)
Prigg v. Pennsylvania (US law; 1842)
Prijedor, Bosnia-Hercegovina
Prilosec (med.)
Prima, Louis (ent.; 1911-78)
Primacor (med.)
Primakov, Yevgeny (Rus. pol.; 1929-)
Primatene (med.)
Prime of Miss Jean Brodie, The (film, 1969)
Primerica Corp.
PrimeTime Live (TV show)
Primitive Baptist
Primitive Friends
Primitive Methodist
Primo Carnera (boxing; 1907-67)
Primrose, William (violinist; 1904-82)
Prince (b. Prince Rogers Nelson)(ent.; 1960-)
Prince Albert (Br., husband of Queen Victoria; 1819-61)
Prince Albert (coat)
Prince Albert (prince, Monaco; 1958-)
Prince Albert, Saskatchewan, Canada
Prince and the Pauper, The (M. Twain novel)
Prince Andrew (Andrew Albert Christian Edward) (2nd son of Queen Elizabeth II; 1960-)
Prince Caspian (by C.S. Lewis)
Prince Charles (Charles Philip Arthur George, Prince of Wales)(eldest son of Queen Elizabeth II; 1948-)
Prince Charming
Prince Edward (Edward Anthony Richard Louis, Prince of the UK)(3rd son of Queen Elizabeth II; 1964-)
Prince Edward Island (province, Can.)
Prince Hans-Adam II (head of state, Liechtenstein; 1945-)
Prince Harry of Wales (Henry Charles Albert David Windsor)(youngest son of Prince Charles & Princess Diana; 1984-)
Prince Mbilini (ex-PM, Swaziland)
Prince Naruhito (Jap.; 1960-)
Prince of Darkness (the Devil)
Prince of Peace (Jesus)
Prince of Wales (Prince Charles Philip Arthur George)(eldest son of Queen Elizabeth II; 1948-)
Prince Otto (Eduard Leopold) von Bismarck ("Iron Chancellor")(ex-chanc., Ger.; 1815-98)
Prince Rainier III (aka Rainier Louis Henri Maxence Bertrand de Grimaldi)(head of state, Monaco; 1923-)
Prince Rupert, British Columbia, Canada
Prince Ulukalala Lavaka Ata (PM, Tonga; 1959-)
Prince Valiant (comic strip)
Prince Valiant (hairstyle)
Prince von Bülow Bernhard (ex-chanc., Ger.; 1849-1929)
Prince William of Wales (William Philip Arthur Louis Windsor)(eldest son of Prince Charles & Princess Diana; 1982-)
Prince William Sound (AK)
Prince, Bob (baseball announcer; 1917-85)
Princess Anne (Anne Elizabeth Alice Louise) (daughter of Queen Elizabeth II; 1950-)

Princess Beatrice of York (daughter of Prince Andrew and Sarah; 1988-)
Princess Caroline (princess, Monaco; 1957-)
Princess Diana (Princess of Wales, Lady Diana Spencer; 1961-97)
Princess Eugénie of York (daughter of Prince Andrew and Sarah; 1990-)
Princess Grace (b. Grace Patricia Kelly)(US actress; princess, Monaco; 1929-82)
Princess Margaret (Rose)(UK; 1930-)
Princess Masako (Owada)(Jap.; 1964-)
Princess Summerfall Winterspring (fict. chara., *Howdy Doody*)
Princeton University (Princeton, NJ)
Princeton, NJ
Principal, Victoria (ent.; 1950-)
Príncipe, São Tomé and (Democratic Republic of)(off W Afr. coast)
Principen (med.)
Principi, Anthony Joseph (US ex-secy./vet. affairs; 1944-)
Pringles (chips)
Prinivil (med.)
Prinze, Freddie (ent.; 1954-77)
Prinze, Freddie, Jr. (ent.; 1976-)
Priority Mail (USPS)
Priscilla (Beaulieu) Presley (ent.; 1945-)
Priscilla Lane (ent.; 1915-95)
Pritchett, V(ictor) S(awdon)(literary critic; 1900-97)
Pritikin diet
Prius, Toyota (auto.)
Privacy Act of 1974
Private Benjamin (film, 1980)
Private Ryan, Saving (film, 1998)
Prizm, Geo (Chevrolet)(auto.)
Prizzi's Honor (film, 1985)
Pro Bowl (football)
Pro-Banthine (med.)
Probe, Ford (auto.)
Procan SR (med.)
Procardia (med.)
ProCAT (CAT system)
Procol Harum (pop music)
Proconsul (Afr. prehistoric ape skull)
Procrustean bed (sociology)
Procrustes (also Damastes)(myth.)
Procter & Gamble Co.
Procter, William C. (US bus., soap; 1862-1934)
Proctor-Silex (kitchen appliances)
Proctor-Silex, Inc., Hamilton Beach/
Procyon (also Alpha Canis Minoris)(astron.)
Prodigy (compu. database)
Product 19, Kellogg's
Proell, Annemarie Moser (skiing; 1953-)
Professor Book Centers, Inc., Little
Professor Branestawm
Professor Moriarty (fict. chara., *Sherlock Holmes*)
Progressive-Conservative Party (Can. pol.)
Progressive Labor Party (US pol.)
Progressive Party (US pol.)
Progressivism (US hist.; late 1800s, early 1900s)
Progresso Quality Foods (US bus.)
Prohibition (US hist.; 1920-33)

Prohibition Party (US pol.)
Project Head Start (also Head Start)(educ.)
Prokofiev, Sergei (Sergeyevich)(Rus. comp.; 1891-1953)
Prolixin (med.)
Proloid (med.)
PROM (programmable read-only memory)(compu.)
Prometheus (myth.)
Promised Land (heaven)
Promised Land of Canaan (rel.)
Promises, Promises (play)
Promus Cos., Inc.
Pronestyl (med.)
Propa P.H. (med.)
Propecia (med.)
Prophet, The (by Kahlil Gibran)
Prophets (rel.)
Propine (med.)
Proscar (med.)
Prose Edda (also *Edda*)(Icelandic folk tales)
Proserpina (also Persephone)(myth.)
Prosky, Robert (ent.; 1930-)
ProSom (med.)
Prosper Mérimée (Fr. writer; 1803-70)
Prospero (fict. chara., *The Tempest*)
Prostaphlin (med.)
Protagoras (Gr. phil.; 480?-411? BC)
Protege, Mazda (auto.)
Proterozoic period (2.5 billion-570 million years ago)
Protestant (rel.)
Protestant Reformation (also Reformation)(Eur. rel./hist.; 16th c.)
Protestant Union
Protestant work ethic
Protestantism (rel.)
Proteus (myth.)
Proton (elec.)
Proton Corp.
Protozoa (1-celled organisms)
Proud, The Reincarnation of Peter (film, 1975)
Proudhon, Pierre Joseph (Fr. phil.; 1809-65)
Proulx, E(dna) Annie (US writer; 1935-)
Proust, Marcel (Fr. writer; 1871-1922)
Provençal (lang.)
Provence (region, Fr.)
Provence-Alpes-Côte d'Azur (region, Fr.)
Proventil (med.)
Provera (med.)
Proverbs (aka Book of Proverbs)(rel., book of the Old Testament)
Providence (rel.)
Providence Journal (RI newspaper)
Providence Journal-Bulletin (RI newspaper)
Providence, RI
Provincetown Players (MA/NYC; 1915-29)
Provincetown, MA
Provine, Dorothy (ent.; 1937-)
Provo, UT
Prowler, Chrysler (was Plymouth)(auto.)
Prowse, Juliet (ent.; 1936-96)
Proxima Centauri (astron.)
Proxmire, (Edward) William (US pol.; 1915-)
Prozac (med.)
Prudential Insurance Co. of America

Prudential Investment Management Services, LLC (US bus.)
Prudential Securities Inc.
Prudhoe Bay (AK)
Prudhomme, Paul (US chef; 1940-)
Prud'hon, Pierre-Paul (Fr. artist; 1758-1823)
Prussia (state, Ger.)
Prussian blue (color)
Prussian collar (clothing)
Prussian red (color)
Prussian War, Austro- (also Seven Weeks' War); 1866)
Prussian War, Franco- (also Franco-German War)(Fr./Ger.-Prussia; 1870-71)
Pryce, Jonathan (ent.; 1947-)
Pryor, David Hampton (US pol.; 1934-)
Pryor, Richard (ent.; 1940-)
Przhevalsk, Kyrgyzstan
Przhevalski's horse
PS (postscript)
Psalms (also Book of Psalms)(rel., book of the Old Testament)
Pseudepigrapha (rel.)
Psilocybe (hallucinogenic mushroom)
PSRO (Professional Standards Review Organization)
PST (Pacific Standard Time)
Psyche (myth.)
Psyche knot
Psycho (film, 1960)
Psycho II (film, 1983)
Psycho III (film, 1986)
Psychology Today (mag.)
Pt (chem. sym., platinum)
PTA (Parent-Teacher Association)
Ptah (myth.)
P(hineas) T(aylor) Barnum (ent., circus; 1810-91)
PT boat (US mil., patrol torpedo boat)
PT Cruiser, Chrysler (auto.)
PTL Club (Praise the Lord [J. Bakker])
Ptolemaic dynasty (Eg.; 323-30 BC)
Ptolemaic system (astron.)
Ptolemy (Claudius Ptolemaeus)(Eg. astron.; c100-170)
Ptolemy I (king, Eg.; c367-283 BC)
Ptolemy II (king, Eg.; 309-246 BC)
Ptolemy III (king, Eg.; 282?-221 BC)
Ptolemy V (king, Eg.; 210?-181 BC)
Ptolemy VI (king, Eg.; 186?-145 BC)
Ptolemy VII (king, Eg.; 184?-116 BC)
Ptolemy XIII (king, Eg.; 63-47 BC)
PT 109 (film, 1963)
Pu (chem. sym., plutonium)
Pu'uhonua o Honaunau National Historical Park (HI)
Puapua, Tomasi (gov.-gen., Tuvalu; 1938-)
Public Broadcasting System (PBS)(TV channel)
Public Enemy (pop music)
Public Works Administration (PWA)(US hist.; 1933-1943)
Public, John Q. (average US citizen)
Publishers Weekly (mag.)
Publius Cornelius Tacitus (Roman hist.; c55-c120)
Publix Super Markets, Inc.

Pucci Perfumes International, Inc., Emilio
Pucci, Emilio (It. designer; 1914-92)
Puccini, Giacomo (Antonio Domenico Michele Secondo Maria)(It. comp.; 1858-1924)
Puck (also Robin Goodfellow, Hobgoblin)(fict. chara., *A Midsummer Night's Dream*)
Puck of Pook's Hill (by Rudyard Kipling)
Puck, Wolfgang (chef)
Puckett and the Union Gap, Gary (pop music)
Puckett, Kirby (baseball; 1961-)
Puddleduck, Jemima
Puebla (de Zaragoza), Mexico
Pueblo (Native Amer.)
Pueblo, CO
Pueblo, U.S.S. (US ship./mil. incident, NKorea; 1968)
Puente, Tito (US jazz; 1923-2000)
Puerto Barrios, Guatemala
Puerto Cabello, Venezuela
Puerto Cabezas, Nicaragua
Puerto Cortés, Honduras
Puerto Limón, Costa Rica (also Limón)
Puerto Presidente Stroessner, Paraguay
Puerto Rico (Commonwealth of)(W Indies)
Puerto Sandino, Nicaragua
Puerto Vallarta, Mexico
Puffy (aka Sean Combs, aka Puff Daddy)(ent.; 1969-)
Puget Sound (WA)
Puget Sound Naval Shipyard (WA)
Puglia (also Apulia)(region, It.)
Pulaski, Count Casimir (Pol./Am. Revolutionary gen; 1748-79)
Pulitzer Prize (for literature, journalism, etc.)
Pulitzer, Joseph (US jour./publ./finan.; 1847-1911)
Pulitzer, Joseph, Jr. (US publ.; 1913-93)
Pulliam, Keshia Knight (ent.; 1979-)
Pullman car (railroad sleeping/parlor car)
Pullman, Bill (ent.; 1953-)
Pullman, George (Mortimer)(US inv./bus.; 1831-97)
Pulsar Time, Inc.
Pulver, Ensign (film, 1964)
Puma (sportswear)
Puma USA (US bus.)
Punakha, Bhutan
Punch-and-Judy show (Br. puppet show)
Punchinello (puppet show/chara.)
Pune, India (formerly Poona)
Punic Wars (Rome/Carthage; 264-241 BC, 218-201 BC, 149-146 BC)
Punisher, The (cartoon chara.)
Punjab (province, Pak.)
Punjab (state, India)
Punjabi (lang./people)
Punky Brewster (fict. chara.)
Punsalmaagiyn Ochirbat (ex-pres., Mongolia; 1943-)
Punta Arenas, Chile
Punta Gorda, Belize
Punta Gorda, FL
Puntsagiyn Jasray (ex-PM, Mongolia)
Punxsutawney Phil (groundhog)
Punxsutawney, PA

Puppis (astron., stern/deck)
Purcell, Henry (Br. comp.; 1658?-95)
Purdue University (West Lafayette, IN)
Pure Food and Drug Act (US hist.; 1906)
Pure Land Buddhism (rel.)
Purex Industries, Inc.
Purim (Jew. festival)
Purina (pet food)
Purina Cat Chow
Purina Co., Ralston (US bus.)
Purina Dog Chow
Purina Goat Chow
Purinethol (med.)
Puritan (rel.)
Puritan work ethic
Puritanism (rel.)
Purkinje, Johannes Evangelista (Czech. physiol.; 1787-1869)
Purkinje's cells/fibers (med.)
Purolator
Purolator Products Co.
Purple Heart, Order of the (US mil. metal)
Purple Rose of Cairo, The (film, 1985)
Pusan, South Korea (also Busan)
Pushkin, Aleksandr (Sergeyevich)(Rus. writer; 1799-1837)
Pushtu (also Pashto)(lang.)
Puss 'n Boots (fairy tale)
Putin, Vladimir V. (pres., Rus.; 1952-)
Putnam Publishing Group, The (US bus.)
Putt-Putt Golf Courses of America (US bus.)
Puyallup (Native Amer.)
Puyallup, WA
Puzo, Mario (US writer; 1920-99)
PVC (polyvinyl chloride)
P(amulaparti) V(enkata) Narasimha Rao (ex-PM, India; 1921-)
P-V-Tussin (med.)
PWA (Public Works Administration)
PX (post exchange, Post Exchange)(mil. store)
Pygmalion (G.B. Shaw play)
Pygmalion (myth.)
Pygmy (people)
Pyle, Denver (ent.; 1920-97)
Pyle, Ernest "Ernie" (US jour.; 1900-45)
Pyle, Gomer (fict. chara.)
Pym, John (Br. pol.; 1584-1643)
Pynchon, Thomas (US writer; 1937-)
Pyongyang, North Korea
Pyotr (or Piotr, Peter)(Alekseevich) Kropotkin, Prince (Rus. anarchist; 1842-1921)
Pyramid of Kafre (or Khafre)(Eg.)
Pyramid of Khufu (or Cheops), Great (Eg.)
Pyramus and Thisbe (myth.)
Pyrenees Mountains (Sp./Fr.)
Pyrenees, Great (dog)
Pyrex
Pyridium (med.)
Pyrrhic victory (not worth winning)
Pyrrhus (king, Gr.; c318-272 BC)
Pyrrophyta (algae)
Pythagoras (Gr. phil./math.; c580-c500 BC)
Pythagorean theorem/scale (math.)
Pythian Games (ancient Gr.)
Pythias, Damon and (myth., loyal friendship)

Pythias, Knights of (US benevolent secret society; founded 1864)
Python (myth.)
Python and the Holy Grail, Monty (film, 1975)
Python's Flying Circus, Monty (TV show)
Python's Life of Brian, Monty (film, 1979)
Pyxis (astron., compass)
PZI (protamine zinc)(med.)

-Q-

Q (aka Sir Arthur [Thomas] Quiller-Couch)(Br. writer; 1863-1944)
Qaboos (or Qabas) bin Said (sultan/PM, Oman; 1940-)
Qacentina/Constantine, Algeria
Qaddafi (or Khadafy), Colonel Muammar al- (pres., Libya; 1942-)
Qaida, Al- (aka al Qaeda)(network of radical groups under Osama bin Laden)
Qaiwain (or Qaywayn), Umm al (state, UAE)
Qamdo, China
Q & A (question[s] and answer[s])
Qantas Airways, Ltd.
Qarase, Laisenia (Fiji pol.; 1941-)
Qatar (State of)(Middle East)
Qattarah Depression (Eg.)
Qazvin (or Kazvin), Iran
QB (quarterback, qualified bidders)
QC (quality control)
Q clearance (highest nuclear security clearance)
Qin dynasty (also Ch'in)(Ch.; 221-206 BC)
Qing, Jiang (also Madame Mao, Chiang Ching, Jiang Ching, Lan Ping)(Ch. pol./ent., wife of Chairman Mao; 1914-91)
Qingdao, China (also Tsingtao)
Qinghai (also Tsinghai)(province, Ch.)
Qiyama (rel.)
QM (quartermaster)
Qom, Iran (also Qum)
Qormi, Malta
QT (keep secret ["on the QT"])
Q-Tips
Quaalude (med./sedative)
Quack Attack (cartoon)
Quad City Times, Davenport (IA newspaper)
Quadruple Alliance (Eur. hist.; 1718/1813/1834)
Quady Winery (US bus.)
Quaid, Dennis (ent.; 1954-)
Quaid, Randy (ent.; 1950-)
Quail Ridge Cellars & Vineyards (US bus.)
Quaker Oatmeal
Quaker Oats Co. The
Quaker State Corp.
Quaker State Oil Refining Corp.
Quakers (also [Religious] Society of Friends)(rel.)
Quakertown, PA
Quant, Mary (Br. designer; 1934-)
Quantico Marine Corps Development Command (VA)
Quantrill, William Clarke (US mil./outlaw; 1837-65)
Quantrill's Raiders (US Civil War guerrillas)
Quantum Corp.
Quantum Leap (TV show)
Quapaw (Native Amer.)
Quargel (cheese)
Quarles, Francis (Br. poet; 1592-1644)
Quartermaster Corps (US mil.)

Quarzan (med.)
Quasar (kitchen appliances)
Quasar Co.
Quasimodo (also Low Sunday)(1st Sunday after Easter)
Quasimodo (fict. chara., *The Hunchback of Notre Dame*)
Quasimodo, Salvatore (It. poet; 1901-68)
Quaternary period (2.5 million years ago to present)
Quatre Bornes, Mauritius
Quattro, Audi (auto.)
Quattrocento (It. art/lit.; 15th c.)
Quayle, Anthony (ent.; 1913-89)
Quayle, III, (James) Dan(forth)(ex-VP, US; 1947-)
Quayle, Marilyn (US atty., wife of ex-VP ; 1949-)
Que Que, Zimbabwe (also Kwekwe)
Quebec (province, Can.)
Quebec Nordiques (hockey team)
Quebec, Canada (province, Can.)
Quebec, Quebec, Canada
Quebecer (also Quebecker, Quebecois)(Quebec inhabitant)
Quechua (lang./people)
Queeg, Captain (fict. chara., *The Caine Mutiny*)
Queen (pop music)
Queen Anne style (arch./furn.; 1700-20)
Queen Anne's lace (flowering plant)
Queen Anne's War (Br./Fr. in Amer.; 1702-13)
Queen Beatrix (Wilhelmina Armgard)(queen, Netherlands; 1938-)
Queen Charlotte Islands (Br. Columbia)
Queen Elizabeth II (Elizabeth Alexandra Mary Windsor)(queen, Eng./UK; 1926-)
Queen Elizabeth Islands (Can.)
Queen Latifah (b. Dana Owens)(ent.; 1970-)
Queen Margrethe II (queen, Den.; 1940-)
Queen Maud Land (region, Antarctica)
Queen Maud Range (mountains, Antarctica)
Queen Mother, Her Majesty Queen Elizabeth the (b. the Honourable Elizabeth Angela Marguerite Bowes-Lyon)(1900-)
Queen of Hearts
Queen of Heaven (Virgin Mary)
Queen of Sheba (biblical, visited Solomon to test his wisdom)
Queen Victoria (b. Alexandrina Victoria)(queen, UK; 1819-1901)
Queen, Ellery (pseud. for US writers: Frederick Dannay, 1905-82; Manfred B. Lee, 1905-71)
Queen's (or King's) Bench (Br. law)
Queen's (or King's) Counsel (Br. law)
queen's (or king's) English (correct English)
Queenie Peavy (by Robert Burch)
Queens (borough, NYC)
Queensberry rules (also Marquis of Queensberry rules)(boxing)
Queensberry, John Sholto Douglas (Marquis of Queensberry; 1844-1900)
Queensborough Bridge (NYC)
Queensland (state, Austl.)
Queler, Eve (US cond.; 1936-)
Quennell, (Sir) Peter Courtney (Br. biographer; 1905-93)

Quentin Bell (writer/artist; 1910-96)
Quentin Massys (or Matsys)(Flem. artist;
    1466?-1530)
Quentin Tarantino (ent.; 1963-)
Querétaro, Mexico
Quesnay, Francois (Fr. econ.; 1694-1774)
Quest, Jonny (cartoon)
Quest, Nissan (auto.)
Questran (med.)
Quett (Ketumile Joni) Masire (ex-pres.,
    Botswana; 1925-)
Quetta, Pakistan (also Kwatah)
Quetzalcoatl (myth.)
Quezaltenango, Guatemala
Quezon City, Philippines
Quezon y Molina, Manuel Luis (ex-pres. Phil.;
    1878-1944)
Quibron (med.)
quiche Lorraine
Quick Draw McGraw (fict. chara.)
Quicken (compu.)
Quickie (mop)
Quik Print, Inc.
Quiller-Couch, (Sir) Arthur Thomas (aka "Q")
    (Br. writer; 1863-1944)
Quinaglute (med.)
Quincy Jones (US jazz; 1933-)
Quincy Patriot-Ledger (MA newspaper)
Quincy, IL, MA
Quindlen, Anna (US jour.; 1953-)
Quinidex (med.)
Quinlan, Kathleen (ent.; 1954-)
Quinn, Aidan (ent.; 1959-)
Quinn, Anthony (ent.; 1915-2001)
Quinn, Jane Bryant (US jour./finan.; 1939-)
Quinn, Martha (ent.; 1959-)
Quinn, Medicine Woman, Dr. (TV show)
Quintana Roo (state, Mex.)
Quintilian (Marcus Fabius Quintilianus)(Roman
    rhetorician; c35-c95)
Quintus Fabius Maximus Verrucosus
    ("Cunctator")(Roman pol./mil.; 275-03 BC)
Quisling, Vidkun (Nor. pol./traitor; 1887-1945)
Quito, Ecuador
Quivira, Gran (utopia)
Quixote de la Mancha, Don (by Cervantes)
Quixote, Don (film, 1935, 1957)
Qum, Iran (also Qom)
Qumran (also Khirbet Qumran)(Dead Sea
    Scrolls site)
Quo Vadis (H. Sienkiewicz novel)
Quonset hut
Quran (also Koran)(rel.)
Quthing, Lesotho
Qvale (auto.)
Qvale Mangusta (auto.)
QVC Shopping Network (TV channel)

Ra (also Re)(Eg. sun god)
Ra (chem. sym., radium)
Ra (T. Heyerdahl raft used to cross Atl.; 1969-70)
Ra Expeditions (crossing Atl.; 1969-70)
Ra, Sun (b. Herman Blount)(US jazz; 1916-93)
Rabat, Morocco
Rabaul, Papua New Guinea
Rabb, Ellis (ent.; 1930-98)
Rabbani, Burhanuddin (ex-pres., Afghan.; 1940-)
Rabbie Namaliu (ex-PM, Papua New Guinea; 1947-)
Rabbinical Judaism (rel.)
Rabbit, Brer (fict. chara., *Uncle Remus*)
Rabbit, Peter (fict. chara.)
Rabbit, Volkswagen (auto.)
Rabbit?, Who Framed Roger (film, 1988)
Rabbitt, Eddie (Edward Thomas)(ent.; 1944-98)
Rabe, David (US writer; 1940-)
Rabelais, François (Fr. writer; 1495-1553)
Rabi, Isidor Isaac (US physt.; 1899-1988)
Rabin, Yitzhak (ex-PM, Isr.; 1922-95)
Rabindranath Tagore, (Sir)(Indian poet; 1861-1941)
Rabinowitz, Solomon (aka Shalom [or Sholom] Aleichem)(Yiddish writer; 1859-1916)
Rabuka, Sitiveni (Ligamamada)(ex-PM, Fiji; 1948-)
Racan, Ivica (PM, Croatia; 1944-)
Rachel (Louise) Carson (US writer/biol.; 1907-64)
Rachel, Rachel (film, 1968)
Rachins, Alan (ent.; 1947-)
Rachmaninov, Sergei V(asilyevich)(Rus. comp./cond.; 1893-1943)
Racicot, Marc (ex-MT gov.; 1948-)
Racine, Jean (Baptiste)(Fr. writer; 1639-99)
Racine, WI
Radcliffe College (Cambridge, MA)
Radcliffe, Ann (Ward)(Br. writer; 1764-1823)
Raden Suharto (ex-pres., Indonesia; 1921-)
Radford University (Radford, VA)
Radford, VA
Radio City Music Hall (NYC)
Radio Corporation of America (RCA)
Radio Free Europe
Radio Liberty
Radio Shack (US bus.)
Radiohead (pop music)
Radisic, Zivko (co-pres., Bosnia-Hercegovina, Serb)
Radisson Hotels International (US bus.)
Radner, Gilda (ent.; 1946-89)
Radoje Kontic (ex-PM; Yug.; 1937-)
Radziwill (Ross), (Caroline) Lee (Bouvier)(sister of Jackie Kennedy Onassis; 1933-)
Rae Dawn Chong (ent.; 1962-)
Rae, Charlotte (b. Charlotte Lubotsky)(ent.; 1926-)
Rae, John (Scot. expl.; 1813-93)
Rae, Norma (film, 1979)

Rafael Angel Calderón Fournier (ex-pres., Costa Rica; 1949-)
Rafael Angel Calderón Guardia (ex-pres., Costa Rica; 1900-71)
Rafael Kubelik (cond.; 1914-96)
Rafael L. Trujillo Molina (ex-pres., Dom Rep.; 1891-1961)
Rafael Leonardo Callejas (ex-pres., Honduras; 1943-)
Rafer Johnson (decathlon; 1935-)
Raffi (Cavoukian)(ent.; 1948-)
Raffin, Deborah (ent.; 1953-)
Rafiq al-Hairi (ex-PM, Lebanon)
Rafiq Tarar, Mohammad (pres., Pak.; 1929-)
Rafsanjani, Hojatolisiam Ali Akbar Hashemi (ex-pres., Iran; 1935-)
Raft, George (ent.; 1895-1980)
Rage Against the Machine (pop music)
Raggedy Ann & Andy (fict. dolls)
Raggedy Ann doll
Ragheb, Ali Abu al- (PM, Jordan; 1946-)
Raglan, FitzRoy (James Henry) Somerset, Baron (Br. gen., raglan sleeve; 1788-1855)
Ragnarök (also Götterdämmerung)(myth.)
Ragú (spaghetti sauce)
Ragú Foods, Inc.
Rahal, Bobby (auto racing; 1953-)
Rahman, Mujibur (aka Sheik Mujib)(ex-PM, Bangladesh; 1920-75)
Rahman, Sheik Omar Abdel- (Muslim rel.; 1938-)
Rahman, Tunku Abdul (ex-PM, Malaysia; 1903-90)
Rahman, Ziaur (ex-pres., Bangladesh; 1935-81)
Rahu (myth.)
Raid (bug killer)
Raiders of the Lost Ark (film, 1981)
Raiders, Los Angeles (football team)
Raiders, Paul Revere and the (pop music)
Rain Man (film, 1988)
Rainbow Bridge (UT)
Rainbow Bridge National Monument (UT)
Rainer Maria Rilke (Ger. poet; 1875-1926)
Rainer Werner Fassbinder (Ger. ent.; 1946-82)
Raines, Ella (ent.; 1920-88)
Rainey, Joseph Hayne (US pol.; 1832-87)
Rainey, Ma (Gertrude)(US jazz; 1886-1939)
Rainier III, Prince (aka Rainier Louis Henri Maxence Bertrand de Grimaldi)(head of state, Monaco; 1923-)
Rainier National Park, Mount (WA)
Rains, Claude (ent.; 1890-1967)
Rainy Lake (US/Can.)
Raisa (Maksimova Titorenko) Gorbachev (wife of ex-Rus. pres./educ.; 1932-99)
Raisin Bran (cereal)
Raitt, Bonnie (ent.; 1949-)
Raitt, John (ent.; 1917-)
Rajasthan (state, India)
Rajiv Gandhi (ex-PM, India; 1944-91)
Rajkot, India
Rajneesh, Shree (or Osho)(aka Bhagwan)(b. Chaadra Mohan Jain)(Indian rel.; 1931-90)
Rajshahi, Bangladesh (formerly Rampur Boalia)
Rakhmanov, Ali (Tajikistan pol.)
Rakhmonov, Imomali (pres., Tajikistan; 1952-)

Raleigh News & Observer (NC newspaper)
Raleigh, NC
Raleigh, (Sir) Walter (Br. expl./writer; 1552?-1618)
Ralph Adams Cram (US arch.; 1863-1942)
Ralph Bakshi (ent.; 1938-)
Ralph Bellamy (ent.; 1904-91)
Ralph Boston (jumper; 1939-)
Ralph David Abernathy (US rel./civil rights leader; 1926-90)
Ralph Edwards (ent.; 1913-)
Ralph Ellison (Waldo)(US writer; 1914-94)
Ralph Fasanella (US artist; 1914-97)
Ralph Fiennes (ent.; 1962-)
Ralph Houk (baseball; 1919-)
Ralph Iron (aka Olive Schreiner)(SAfr. writer; 1855-1920)
Ralph J. Bunche (US dipl.; 1904-71)
Ralph Kiner (baseball; 1922-)
Ralph Kirkpatrick (US harpsichordist; 1911-84)
Ralph Kramden (fict. chara., *The Honeymooners*)
Ralph Lauren (b. Ralph Lifshitz)(US designer; 1939-)
Ralph Lauren (US bus.)
Ralph Lauren Leathergoods, Polo/ (US bus.)
Ralph Macchio (ent.; 1962-)
Ralph Meeker (ent.; 1920-88)
Ralph Nader (US atty./consumer advocate; 1934-)
Ralph Richardson, (Sir)(ent.; 1902-83)
Ralph Roister Doister (N. Udall comedy)
Ralph T. Walker (US arch.; 1889-1973)
Ralph Vaughan Williams (Br. comp.; 1872-1958)
Ralph Waite (ent.; 1929-)
Ralph Waldo Emerson (US writer/phil.; 1803-82)
Ralston Purina Co.
Ralston, Dennis (tennis; 1942-)
Ralston, Esther (ent.; 1902-94)
RAM (random access memory)(compu.)
Ram, Dodge (auto.)
Rama (rel.)
Rama IX (b. Bhumibol Adulyadej)(king, Thailand; 1927-)
Ramada International Hotels & Resorts (US bus.)
Ramadan (Muslim holy month)
Ramaema, Elias , Col. (Lesotho, mil.)
Ramakrishna (Hindu rel./educ.; 1834-86)
Ramapithecus (anthrop.)
Ramaswamy Venkataraman (ex-pres., India)
Ramat Gan, Israel
Ramayana (Sanskrit epic)
Rambeau, Marjorie (ent.; 1889-1970)
Rambert, Marie, Dame (b. Cyvia Rambam)(Br. ballet; 1888-1982)
Rambo (fict. Vietnam hero)
Ramcharger, Dodge (auto.)
Rameau, Jean Philippe (Fr. comp.; 1683-1764)
Ramey, Samuel (ent.; 1942-)
Ramiro de León Carpio (ex-pres., Guat.; 1942-)
Ramis, Harold (ent.; 1944-)
Ramism (phil.)
Ramiz, Alia (ex-pres., Albania; 1925-)
Ramon Hnatyshyn (ex-gov.-gen., Can.; 1934)
Ramon Novarro (ent.; 1899-1968)

Ramón (Jose) Velásquez (ex-pres., Venezuela; 1916-)
Ramones, the (pop music)
Ramos gin fizz (mixed drink)
Ramos, Fidel V. (ex-pres., Phil.; 1928-)
Rampal, Jean-Pierre (Fr. flutist; 1922-2000)
Rampling, Charlotte (ent.; 1946-)
Rampur Boalia (now Rajshahi, Bangladesh)
Rams, Los Angeles (football team)
Ramses II (Eg. king; 13th c. BC)
Ramses III (Eg. king; 12th c. BC)
Ramsey Lewis (US jazz; 1935-)
Ramsey, John (Bennett)(US news; 1943-)
Ramsey, JonBenet (Patricia)(US news; 1990-96)
Ramsey, Patsy (b. Patricia Ann Paugh)(US news; 1956-)
Ramsgate, England
Ranariddh, Norodom (ex-PM, Cambodia; 1944-)
Ranasinghe Premadasa (ex-pres., Sri Lanka; 1924-93)
Rancagua, Chile
Rancho Cordova, CA
Rancho Cucamonga, CA
Rancho Mirage, CA
Rancho Palos Verdes, CA
Rand Co., Ingersoll-
Rand Corp., Sperry
Rand International (US bus.)
Rand McNally & Co.
Rand McNally World Atlas
Rand, Ayn (b. Alisa Rosenbaum)(US writer/phil.; 1905-82)
Rand, Remington (former US bus., now Unisys)
Rand, the (also Witwatersrand)(SAfr. gold mining area)
Randall, Tony (b. Arthur Leonard Rosenberg) (ent.; 1920-)
R&B (rhythm & blues)
R&C (med. lotion/shampoo)
R&D (research & development)
Randers, Denmark
Randolph, A(sa) Philip (US labor leader; 1889-1979)
Randolph (Henry Spencer) Churchill, Lord (Br. pol., father of Winston; 1849-95)
Randolph Caldecott (Br. artist; 1846-86)
Randolph Scott (ent.; 1898-1987)
Randolph, Edmund (Jennings)(US atty.; 1753-1813)
Randolph, John (ent.; 1915-)
Randolph, John (of Roanoke)(US pol.; 1773-1833)
Randolph, Joyce (ent.; 1925-)
Randolph, MA
Random House Dictionary of the English Language, The
Random House, Inc.
R and R (or R&R)(rest and recreation, rest and recuperation, rest and relaxation, rock-'n'-roll, rock 'n' roll)
Randy Matson (shot putter; 1945-)
Randy Newman (ent.; 1943-)
Randy Quaid (ent.; 1950-)
Randy Travis (b. Randy Traywick)(ent.; 1959-)
Randy Weaver (US news, confrontation w/US marshals at Ruby Ridge, ID)

Range Rover (auto.)
Range Rover of North America, Inc.
Range Rover, Land Rover (auto.)
Rangel, Charles B. (US cong.; 1930-)
Ranger & Tonto, Lone (fict charas.)
Ranger (US uncrewed space probes)
Ranger Boat Co.
Ranger Rick (mag.)
Ranger Rick's Nature Club
Ranger, Ford (auto.)
Rangers, New York (hockey team)
Rangers, Texas (baseball team)
Rangoon (now called Yangon)
Rangoon, Burma (now Yangon, Myanmar)
Ranil Wickremasinghe (ex-PM, Sri Lanka)
Rankin, Jeannette (US pol.; 1880-1973)
Rankin, Judy (Torluemke)(golf; 1945-)
Ransom Eli Olds (US bus./auto.; 1864-1950)
Rantoul, IL
Rao, P(amulaparti) V(enkata) Narasimha (ex-
PM, India; 1921-)
Raoul Cédras, Lieut. Gen. (Haitian mil.)
Raoul Dufy (Fr. artist; 1877-1953)
Raoul Wallenberg (Swed. dipl.; 1912-47?)
Raoul Walsh (ent.; 1887-1980)
Raoult's law (chem.)
Rap Brown (b. Hubert Gerald Brown)(US
activist; 1943-)
Rapa Nui (also Easter Island)(S Pac.)
Rape of the Sabine Women, (G. da Bologna
sculpture, N. Poussin painting)
Raphael Sanzio (It. artist; 1483-1520)
Raphael Soyer (artist; 1899-1987)
Raphael, Sally Jessy (b. Sally Lowenthal)(TV
host; 1943-)
Rapid City, SD
Rapidograph (graphic design)
RAPIDTEXT (stenoscription system)
RapidTEXT, Inc.
RapidWrite (stenoscription system)
RapidWrite Pro (stenoscription system)
Rappahannock River (VA)
Rapture, the (rel.)
Rapunzel (fict. chara.)
Raquel Welch (b. Raquel Tejada)(ent.; 1940-)
Ras al Khaimah (or Khaymah)(state, UAE)
Ras Asir (also Cape Guardafui)(cape, Somalia)
Rascals, Little (TV show)
Rascals, the (pop music)
Raschi, Vic (baseball; 1919-88)
Rashad, Ahmad (b. Bobby Moore)(football,
sportscaster; 1949-)
Rashad, Phylicia (ent.; 1948-)
Rashid Al-Solh (ex-PM, Lebanon)
Rashomon (A. Ryunosuke short story)
Rasizade, Artur (PM. Azerbaijan; 1935-)
Rasmussen, Knud Johan Victor (Dan. expl.;
1879-1933)
Rasmussen, Poul Nyrup (PM, Den.; 1943-)
Rasputin, (Grigori Efimovich)(Rus. rel.; c1865-
1916)
Rastafarian (rel.)
Rastafarianism (rel.)
RasterOps (compu.)
Ratelle, (Joseph Gilbert Yvon) Jean (hockey;

1953-)
Rathbone, Basil (ent.; 1892-1967)
Rathenau, Walter (Ger. pol.; 1867-1922)
Rather, Dan (US TV jour.; 1931-)
Rather, The CBS Evening News With Dan (TV
show)
Ratnasiri Wickremanayake (PM, Sri Lanka; 1933-)
Ratsiraka, Didier (pres., Madagascar; 1936-)
Ratt (rock group)
Rattigan, (Sir) Terence (Mervyn)(Br. writer;
1911-77)
Ratu Josefa IIoilo (Fiji pol.)
Ratu Sir Penaia Ganilau (ex-pres., Fiji; 1918-)
Ratzenberger, John (ent.; 1947-)
Rau, Johannes (pres., Ger.; 1931-)
Rau, Santha Rama (Indian writer/astrol.; 1923-)
Raul Julia (ent.; 1940-94)
Rauschenberg, Robert (US artist; 1925-)
Rauwolfia serpentina (med. plant)
Ravana (myth.)
Rave (drug party)
Ravel, Maurice (Joseph)(Fr. comp.; 1875-1937)
Ravenna, Italy
Ravenna, OH
RAV4, Toyota (auto.)
Ravi River (S Asia)
Ravi Shankar (comp./sitarist, India; 1920-)
Ravony, Francisque (ex-PM, Madagascar)
Rawalpindi, Pakistan
Rawhide (TV show)
Rawis, Betsy (Elizabeth Earle)(golf; 1928-)
Rawlings, Jerry (John)(pres., Ghana; 1947-)
Rawlings, Marjorie Kinnan (US writer; 1896-
1953)
Rawls, Lou (ent.; 1936-)
Ray Bloch (ent.; 1902-82)
Ray Bolger (ent.; 1904-87)
Ray Bourque (hockey; 1960-)
Ray Bradbury (US writer, sci-fi; 1920-)
Ray Brown (US jazz; 1926-)
Ray Charles (b. Ray Charles Robinson)(ent.;
1930-)
Ray Conniff (ent.; 1916-)
Ray Conniff Orchestra
Ray Davies (ent., The Kinks; 1944-)
Ray Ewry (Olympics; 1873-1937)
Ray(mond A.) Kroc (US bus., founded
McDonald's; 1902-84)
Ray Lewis (football; 1975-)
Ray Liotta (ent.; 1955-)
Ray "Boom Boom" Mancini (boxing; 1961-)
Ray Milland (ent.; 1905-86)
Ray Price (ent.; 1926-)
Ray Romano (ent.; 1957-)
Ray Stevens (b. Harold Ray Ragsdale)(ent.;
1939-)
Ray Walston (ent.; 1914-2001)
Ray, Aldo (ent.; 1927-91)
Ray, Gene Anthony (ent.; 1963-)
Ray, James Earl (US, assassinated M.L. King;
1928-98)
Ray, John (Br. nat.; 1627-1705)
Ray, Johnnie (ent.; 1927-90)
Ray, Man (b. Emmanuel Radnitsky)(US artist;
1890-1976)

Ray, Satyajit (ent.; 1921-92)
Rayburn, Sam(uel Taliaferro)(US pol.; 1882-1961)
Raye, Martha (ent.; 1916-94)
Raymond Berry (football; 1933-)
Raymond Burr (ent.; 1917-93)
Raymond Chandler (US writer; 1888-1959)
Raymond Ditmars (US zool., writer; 1876-1942)
Raymond Duchamp-Villon (Fr. artist; 1876-1918)
Raymond Massey (ent.; 1896-1993)
Raymond Moody (writer, near-death experiences; 1944-)
Raymond (Nicolas Landry) Poincaré (ex-pres., Fr.; 1860-1934)
Raymond (Ames) Spruance (US mil.; 1886-1969)
Raymond Vineyard & Cellar (US bus.)
Raymond, Alex (cartoonist, *Flash Gordon, Jungle Jim*; 1909-56)
Raymond, Everybody Loves (TV show)
Raymond, Gene (ent.; 1908-98)
Raynaud's disease (med.)
Rayovac Corp.
Raytheon Co.
Raytown, MO
Razaf, Andy (US lyricist; 1895-1973)
Razanamasy, Guy (Willy)(ex-PM, Madagascar)
Rb (chem. sym., rubidium)
R(ichard) Buckminster Fuller (US eng./arch.; 1895-1983)
RCA Corp.
RCA Records (US bus.)
RCAF (Royal Canadian Air Force)
RCMP (Royal Canadian Mounted Police)
RCP (Royal College of Physicians)
RCS (Royal College of Surgeons)
RD (registered dietitian, rural delivery)
RDA (recommended daily [or dietary] allowance)
R(onald) D(avid) Laing (Scot. psych./writer; 1927-89)
RDR (Registered Diplomate Reporter)
Re (also Ra)(Eg. sun god)
Re (chem. sym., rhenium)
Rea, Stephen (ent.; 1943-)
Reach (health)
Reader's Digest (mag.)
Reader's Digest Association (publ.)
Reading Eagle (PA newspaper)
Reading Railroad, Philadelphia and
Reading Times (PA newspaper)
Reading, England
Reading, MA, OH, PA
Reagan, Nancy (b. Anne Francis Robbins, aka Nancy Davis)(wife of ex-US pres.; 1923-)
Reagan, Ronald (Wilson)(40th US pres.; 1911-)
Reaganomics (Reagan's economic policy)
Real Estate Brokers, National Association of
Real Stories of the Highway Patrol (TV show)
ReaLemon juice
Real-Kill (pesticide)
Realtor
Realtors, National Association of
Reason, Age of (phil.)
Reason, The Age of (by Thomas Paine; 1794-96)
Reasoner, Harry (US TV jour.; 1923-91)
Reb, Johnny (Confederate soldier, southerner)
Reba McEntire (ent.; 1954-)

Rebecca (D. DuMaurier novel)
Rebecca De Mornay (ent.; 1962-)
Rebecca of Sunnybrook Farm (film, 1917, 1938)
Rebecca Romijn-Stamos (model/ent.; 1972-)
Rebecca West, Dame (b. Cicily Isabel Fairfield) (Br. writer; 1892-1983)
Recamier day bed
Récamier, Juliette (b. Jeanne Françoise Julie Adélaide Bernard)(Fr. society; 1777-1849)
Recife, Brazil
Recklinghausen, Germany
Reconstruction (US hist.; 1865-77)
Record, Bergen County (NJ newspaper)
Record, Congressional (US Congress proceedings)
Record, Hackensack (NJ newspaper)
Record, Middletown (NY newspaper)
Record, York (PA newspaper)
Red (Arnold) Auerbach (basketball; 1917-)
Red Angus cattle
Red Army (USSR army until 1946)
Red Badge of Courage, The (Stephen Crane novel)
Red (Walter) Barber (ent.; 1908-92)
Red Bluff, CA
Red Buttons (b. Aaron Chwatt)(ent.; 1919-)
Red Carpet
Red Carpet Real Estate Services, Inc.
Red China (People's Republic of China)
Red Cloud, Chief (Sioux Native Amer.; 1822-1909)
Red Crescent (functioning as Red Cross in Muslim countries)
Red Cross (internat'l relief agcy.; est. 1864)
Red Cross, American National (US relief agcy.; est. 1881)
Red Delicious (apple)
Red Foley (ent.; 1910-68)
Red Garland (US jazz; 1923-84)
Red (Harold) Grange (football; 1903-91)
Red (Charles Roger) Grooms (US artist; 1937-)
Red Hot Chili Peppers (pop music)
Red Jacket (Sagoyewatha)(Seneca Native Amer. leader; c1756-1830)
Red (Leonard Patrick) Kelly (hockey; 1927-)
Red Light Bandit (Caryl Chessman)(US rapist; ?-1960)
Red Mass (rel., Catholic blessing for legal profession)
Red Nichols (US jazz; 1905-65)
Red (Kenneth) Norvo (US jazz; 1908-99)
Red No. 2 (dye banned by FDA as carcinogenic)
Red Ridinghood, Little (fairy tale)
Red River (of the North)(ND/MN/Can.)
Red River (S US)
Red River (SE Asia)
Red River Army Depot (TX)
Red River Rebellion (Can. hist.; 1869-70)
Red River Settlement (Can.)
Red Sea (NE Afr/SW Asia)
Red (Richard) Skelton (ent.; 1913-97)
Red (Walter) Smith (sports jour.; 1905-82)
Red Sox, Boston (baseball team)
Red Wing (Tantangamini)(Sioux leader; c1750-c1825)
Red Wings, Detroit (hockey team)
red Windsor (cheese)

Redbook (mag.)
Redd Foxx (b. John Elroy Sandford)(ent.; 1922-91)
Reddi-wip
Reddi-Wip, Inc.
Redding Products, Inc., Jheri
Redding, CA
Redding, Otis (ent.; 1941-67)
Reddy, Helen (ent.; 1941-)
Redeemer (Jesus Christ)
Redenbacher, Orville (popcorn)
Redenbacher, Orville (US bus.; 1907-95)
Redfield, Robert (US anthrop.; 1897-1958)
Redford, (Charles) Robert (ent.; 1937-)
Redgrave, Corin (ent.; 1939-)
Redgrave, Lynn (ent.; 1943-)
Redgrave, (Sir) Michael (Scudamore)(ent.; 1908-85)
Redgrave, Vanessa (ent.; 1937-)
Redha Malek (ex-PM, Algeria)
Redken (hair care)
Redken Laboratories, Inc.
Redlands, CA
Redman, Don (US jazz; 1900-64)
Redmond, WA
Redon, Odilon (Fr. artist; 1840-1916)
Redondo Beach, CA
Redoubt, Mount (active volcano, AK)
Reds, Cincinnati (baseball team)
Redskins, Washington (football team)
Redstone 3, Mercury- (also Liberty Bell 7)(1st US crewed space flight; May 5, 1961)
Redstone, Mercury- (US crewed space flights)
Redwood City, CA
Redwood National Park (CA)
Reebok (shoes)
Reebok International, Ltd. (US bus.)
Reed & Barton Silversmiths (US bus.)
Reed Army Medical Center, Walter (DC)
Reed Show, The Donna (TV show)
Reed Smoot (US pol.; 1862-1941)
Reed, Andre (football; 1964-)
Reed, Donna (ent.; 1921-86)
Reed, Dr. Walter (US phys.; 1851-1902)
Reed, Ishmael (US writer; 1938-)
Reed, Jack (US cong.; 1949-)
Reed, Jerry (ent.; 1937-)
Reed, Lou (b. Louis Firbank)(ent.; 1942-)
Reed, Oliver (ent.; 1938-99)
Reed, Rex (ent.; 1938-)
Reed, Robert (ent.; 1932-92)
Reed, (Sir) Carol (Br. ent.; 1906-76)
Reed, Willis (basketball; 1942-)
Reems, Harry (b. Herbert Streicher)(ent.; 1947-)
Reese Air Force Base, TX
Reese Finer Foods (US bus.)
Reese Witherspoon (ent.; 1976-)
Reese, Della (b. Deloreese Patricia Early)(ent.; 1931-)
Reese, Pee Wee (Harold)(baseball; 1918-99)
Reese's Peanut Butter Cups
Reese's Peanut Butter Puffs
Reese's Pieces
Reeve, Christopher (ent.; 1952-)
Reeves, George (ent.; 1914-59)

Reeves, "Gentleman" Jim (ent.; 1923-64)
Reeves, Keanu (Charles)(ent.; 1964-)
Reformation (also Protestant Reformation)(Eur. rel./hist.; 16th c.)
Reformation Sunday (rel.)
Reformation, Catholic (also Counter Reformation)(Eur. rel./hist.; 16th-17th c.)
Reformed Church in America
Regal, Buick (auto.)
Regel's tripterygium (plant)
Régence style (Fr. furn.; early 18th c.)
Regency style (Br. arch./furn.; early 19th c.)
Regency, Oldsmobile (auto.)
Regensburg, Germany
Regent's Park (London)
Regents of the University of California vs. Bakke (US law; 1978)
Reggie Jackson (baseball; 1946-)
Reggie Lewis (basketball; 1966-93)
Reggio de Calabria, Italy
Reggio Nell'emilia, Italy
Regina Resnik (ent.; 1924-)
Regina, Saskatchewan, Canada
Reginald Denny (ent.; 1891-1967)
Reginald Denny (US news)
Reginald Gardiner (ent.; 1903-80)
Reginald Marsh (US artist; 1898-1954)
Reginald Palmer (ex-gov.-gen., Grenada)
Regis & Kathie Lee (TV show)
Regis Philbin (ent.; 1933-)
Regis Toomey (ent.; 1898-1991)
Register-Guard, Eugene (OR newspaper)
Register Star, Rockford (IL newspaper)
Register, Des Moines (IA newspaper)
Register, Mobile (AL newspaper)
Register, New Haven (CT newspaper)
Register, Orange County (CA newspaper)
Reglan (med.)
Regnier de Graaf (Dutch phys.; 1641-73)
Regular Army (US army maintained in both peace and war)
Rehnquist, William H(ubbs)(US jurist; 1924-)
Rehoboam (king, Judah; 1st c. BC)
Rehoboth (Gebeit), Namibia
Rehoboth Beach, DE
Reich, First (Holy Roman Empire; 962-1806)
Reich, Robert (US ex-secy./labor; 1946-)
Reich, Second (Ger. empire; 1871-1918)
Reich, Steve (US comp.; 1936-)
Reich, Third (Nazi Germany; 1933-45)
Reich, Wilhelm (Aus. phys.; 1897-1957)
Reichstag (pre-WWII Ger. parliament)
Reichstag Fire (Ger. parliament bldg; 2/27/33)
Reid, Daphne Maxwell (ent.; 1948-)
Reid, Harry M. (US cong.; 1939-)
Reid, Tim (ent.; 1944-)
Reid, Wallace (ent.; 1891-1923)
Reign of Terror (Fr. hist.; 1793-94)
Reiki (med.)
Reilly, Charles Nelson (ent.; 1931-)
Reims Cathedral (also Rheims)
Reims, France (also Rheims)
Reincarnation of Peter Proud, The (film, 1975)
Reindeer Lake (W Can.)
Reiner, Carl (ent.; 1922-)

Reiner, Fritz (Hung. cond.; 1888-1963)
Reiner, Rob (ent.; 1945-)
Reinhardt, Django (US jazz; 1910-53)
Reinhardt, Max (b. Max Goldmann)(ent.; 1873-1943)
Reinhold Co., Inc., Van Nostrand
Reinhold Niebuhr (US rel.; 1892-1971)
Reinhold, Judge (Edward Ernest)(ent.; 1956-)
Reinking, Ann (ent.; 1949-)
Reiser, Paul (ent.; 1956-)
Reistertown, MD
REIT (real estate investment trust)
Rejang (lang.)
Relafen (med.)
Reliant Energy, Inc.
Religious Society of Friends (also Quakers, Society of Friends)(rel.)
Re/Max International, Inc.
REM (rapid eye movement)
Remarque, Erich Maria (Ger./US writer; 1898-1970)
Rembrandt (Harmenszoon) van Rijn (Dutch artist; 1606-69)
Rembrandt (health)
Rembrandt Peale (US artist; 1778-1860)
"Remember the Maine, to hell with Spain" (Sp.-Amer. War; 1898)
Remick, Lee (ent.; 1935-91)
Remington
Remington Arms Co.
Remington Rand (former US bus., now Unisys)
Remington Steele (TV show)
Remington, Eliphalet (US inv./bus.; 1793-1861)
Remington, Frederic (US artist; 1861-1909)
Remington, Philo (US inv./bus.; 1816-89)
Remnick, David (US writer; 1958-)
Remscheid, Germany
Remus, Romulus & (myth. twins raised by wolf/founded Rome)
Remus, Uncle (fict. narrator, J.C. Harris fables)
Remy Martin (cognac)
Remy Martin Amerique, Inc.
Renaissance (Eur. hist.; 1300-1600)
Renaissance (type style)
Renaissance art/arch. (Eur.; 1400-1600)
Renaissance man/woman
Renaldo Nehemiah (track; 1959-)
Renata Scotto (soprano; 1936-)
Renata Tebaldi (It. soprano; 1922-)
Renault (auto.)
Renault, Inc.
Rendezvous, Buick (auto.)
Rene Auberjonois (ent.; 1940-)
Rene Auguste Chouteau (US pioneer/fur trader; 1749-1829)
Rene Descartes (Fr. phil.; 1596-1650)
Rene Enriquez (ent.; 1932-90)
Rene Lalique (Fr. designer; 1860-1945)
Rene Lévesque (ex-premier, Quebec, Can.; 1922-87)
Rene Magritte (Belgian artist; 1898-1967)
Rene Russo (ent.; 1954-)
Rene Zellweger (ent.; 1969-)
René Garcia Préval (pres., Haiti; 1943-)
Réne Felber (ex-pres., Switz.)

Rene, France-Albert (pres., Seychelles; 1935-)
Renese (med.)
Renfrew, Scotland
Renfro, Brad (ent.; 1982-)
Rennes, France
Rennie, Michael (ent.; 1909-71)
Reno Gazette Journal (NV newspaper)
Reno, Janet (US ex-atty. gen.; 1938-)
Reno, NV
Reno, Shaw v. (US law; 1993)
Renoir, Jean (Fr. ent./writer; 1894-1979)
Renoir, Pierre Auguste (Fr. artist; 1841-1919)
Renoquid (med.)
Rent-A-Wreck of America, Inc.
Renta, Ltd., Oscar de la (US bus.)
Renta, Oscar de la (US designer; 1932-)
Renuzit Home Products, Inc.
Renwick, James, Jr. (US arch.; 1818-95)
REO Motor Car Co.
REO Speedwagon (pop music)
Repan (med.)
Replens (med.)
Repository, Canton (OH newspaper)
Republic Day (India)
Republic of Georgia (formerly part of the USSR) (SE Eur.)
Republic of the Congo (aka Congo Republic & Congo-Brazzaville)(W central Afr.)
Republic, Arizona (AZ newspaper)
Republic, Phoenix (AZ newspaper)
Republic, The (by Plato)
Republic, Third (Fr.; 1870-1940)
Republican Party (US pol.)
Republican River NE)
Republican, Springfield (MA newspaper)
Republika Srpska (Bosnia-Hercegovina entity)
Requiem (also Requiem Mass)(rel.)
Resch, Glenn "Chico" (hockey; 1948-)
Rescue 911 (TV show)
Reserve Officers Training Corps (ROTC)(US mil./educ.)
Resht, Iran
Resistencia, Argentina
Resnais, Alain (ent.; 1922-)
Resnik, Regina (ent.; 1924-)
Resolve (cleaner)
Respbid (med.)
Respect for the Aged Day (Jap.)
Respighi, Ottorino (It. comp.; 1879-1936)
Reston, James (Barrett) "Scotty" (US jour.; 1909-95)
Reston, VA
Restoration (Br. hist.; 1660)
Restoration comedy (Br. theater; 1660+)
Restoril (med.)
Resurrection (rel.)
Retin-A (med.)
Retrovir (med.)
Retton, Mary Lou (US gymnast; 1968-)
Return of the Jedi (film, 1983)
Return of the Pink Panther, The (film, 1975)
Reuben Lucius "Rube" Goldberg (US cartoonist, *Boob McNutt*; 1883-1970)
Reuben, Gloria (ent.; 1965-)
Reuben, Reuben (film, 1983)

Reuter, Paul Julius, Baron von (Ger., founded news agcy.; 1816-99)
Reuters (Br. news org.; est. 1851)
Reuther, Walter P(hilip)(US labor leader; 1907-70)
Revco, Inc.
Revelation (rel., book of the New Testament)
Revenge of Frankenstein, The (film, 1958)
Revenge of the Pink Panther, The (film, 1978)
Revere and the Raiders, Paul (pop music)
Revere Ware, Inc.
Revere, MA
Revere, Paul (Amer. patriot/silversmith; 1735-1818)
Reverence, Your (title)
Reverend (rel. title)
Revereware
Review-Journal, Las Vegas (NV newspaper)
Review of Books, the New York
Revised Standard Version (of the Bible)
Revised Version (of the Bible)
Revlon (cosmetics)
Revlon, Inc.
Revolution, American (also Revolutionary War; 1776-83)
Revolution, English (Eng. hist.; 1640-60)
Revolution, French (Fr. hist.; 1789-99)
Revolution, Russian (Rus. hist.; 1917)
Revolutionary Party, Socialist (Russian Populist Party; founded 1901)
Revson, Charles (US bus.; 1906-75)
Rex (cat)
Rex (Reginald Carey) Harrison (ent.; 1908-90)
Rex Reed (ent.; 1938-)
Rex Stout (US writer; 1886-1975)
Rex, Theodore (film, 1995)
Rexhep Mejdani (pres., Albania; 1944-)
Rey, Margaret E. (writer; 1906-96)
Reye's syndrome (med.)
Reykjavík, Iceland
Reynard the Fox (medieval epic)
Reynaud, Paul (ex-PM, Fr.; 1878-1966)
Reynolds Aluminum Supply Co.
Reynolds foil
Reynolds Foods, Inc., R. J. (RJR Foods, Inc.)
Reynolds Metals Co.
Reynolds Plastic Wrap
Reynolds Price (US writer; 1933-)
Reynolds Tobacco Co., R. J.
Reynolds Wrap
Reynolds, Albert (ex-PM, Ir.; 1932-)
Reynolds, Burt (ent.; 1936-)
Reynolds, Butch (Harry)(track; 1964-)
Reynolds, Debbie (ent.; 1932-)
Reynolds, Frank (US jour.; 1923-83)
Reynolds, Inc., Dean Witter
Reynolds, (Sir) Joshua (Br. artist; 1723-92)
Reynolds, Marjorie (b. Marjorie Goodspeed) (ent.; 1921-97)
Reynosa, Mexico
Reznor, Trent (ent., Nine Inch Nails; 1965-)
Rezso Nyers (Hung. pol.; 1923-)
RFD (rural free delivery)
Rh (chem. sym., rhodium)
Rh factor (also Rhesus factor)(med.)

Rh-negative (Rh-)(med.)
Rh-positive (Rh+)(med.)
Rhadamanthus (myth.)
Rhapsody in Blue (by G. Gershwin)
Rhea (Saturn moon; myth.)
Rhea Perlman (ent.; 1948-)
Rhee, Syngman (ex-pres., SKorea; 1875-1965)
Rheem Manufacturing Co.
Rheem water heater
Rheims Cathedral (also Reims)
Rheims, France (also Reims)
Rhesus factor (also Rh factor)(med.)
Rhesus monkey
Rhett Butler (fict. chara., *Gone With the Wind*)
Rheumatrex (med.)
Rhiannon (myth.)
Rhine (wine)
Rhine River (Eur.)
Rhine, Joseph Banks (US psych.; 1895-1980)
Rhineland (region, Ger,)
Rhineland-Palatinate (state, Ger.)
R. H. Macy & Co., Inc.
Rhoda (TV show)
Rhode Island (RI)
Rhode Island bent (flowering plant, grass)
Rhode Island Red (chicken)
Rhode Island White (chicken)
Rhodes (Gr. island)
Rhodes scholar/scholarship
Rhodes, Apollonius of (Gk. poet; c220-180 BC)
Rhodes, Cecil (John)(Br./SAfr. pol., est. Rhodes scholarships; 1853-1902)
Rhodes, Colossus of (statue of Apollo, fell in 224 BC)
Rhodes, Greece
Rhodesia, Northern (now Zambia)
Rhodesia, Southern (now Zimbabwe)
Rhodesian man (extinct Pleistocene human)
Rhodesian ridgeback (also African lion hound)(dog)
Rhonda Fleming (ent.; 1923-)
Rhondda, Wales
Rhone (wine)
Rhône-Alpes (region, Fr.)
Rhone-Poulenc Rorer Consumer Pharmaceuticals (US bus.)
Rhône River (S Eur.)
Rhue, Madlyn (ent.; 1934-)
RI (Rhode Island)
Ribbentrop, Joachim von (Ger. Nazi pol.; 1893-1946)
Ribeirão Preto, Brazil
Ric Ocasek (ent.; 1949-)
Ricardo Lagos Escobar (pres., Chile; 1938-)
Ricardo Montalban (ent.; 1920)
Ricardo, David (Br. econ.; 1772-1823)
Riccardo Muti (It. cond.; 1941-)
Riccardo Zandonai (It. comp.; 1883-1944)
Ricci Jewelry, Nina (US bus.)
Ricci, Christina (ent.; 1980-)
Rice Krispies (cereal)
Rice University (Houston, TX)
Rice, Anne (US writer; 1941-)
Rice, Condoleezza "Condi" (US nat'l security advisor; 1954-)

Rice, Donna (US news; 1958-)
Rice, Elmer (Leopold)(US writer; 1892-1967)
Rice, Grantland (US sports writer; 1880-1954)
Rice, Jerry (football; 1962-)
Rice, Jim (baseball; 1953-)
Rice-A-Roni
Rich Co., Louis
Rich "Goose" Gossage (baseball; 1951-)
Rich Little (ent.; 1938-)
Rich, Buddy (US jazz; 1917-87)
Rich, Charlie (ent.; 1932-)
Rich, Denise (US news, ex-wife of pardoned
    Marc Rich)
Rich, Frank (US drama critic)
Rich, Marc (b. Marc David Reich)(exiled US
    finan., pardoned in 2001; 1934-)
Rich, Ritchie (cartoon chara.)
Richard Adler (US comp.; 1921-)
Richard A. Gephardt (US cong.; 1941-)
Richard Aldington (Br. poet; 1892-1962)
Richard Anderson (ent.; 1926-)
Richard Anuszkiewicz (artist; 1930-)
Richard Arkwright, (Sir)(Br. inv.; 1732-92)
Richard Arlen (ent.; 1900-76)
Richard Attenborough, (Sir)(ent.; 1923-)
Richard Avedon (US photo.; 1923-)
Richard A. Whiting (US comp.; 1891-1938)
Richard B(ruce) "Dick" Cheney (US VP; 1941-)
Richard Bach (US writer)
Richard Basehart (ent.; 1914-84)
Richard Belzer (ent.; 1944-)
Richard Benjamin (ent.; 1938-)
Richard Berry (songwriter; 1935-97)
Richard Boone (ent.; 1917-81)
Richard B(rinsley) Sheridan (Ir. writer/pol.;
    1751-1816)
Richard B. Shull (ent.; 1929-)
Richard Burbage (Br. Shakespearean actor;
    1567-1619)
Richard Burton (b. Richard Walter Jenkins)
    (ent.; 1925-84)
Richard "Dick" Button (figure skating, ent.; 1929-)
Richard Carpenter (ent.; 1946-)
Richard Chamberlain (ent.; 1934-)
Richard Conte (ent.; 1911-75)
Richard Crenna (ent.; 1927-)
Richard D'Oyly Carte (Br. opera; 1844-1901)
Richard Dawson (ent.; 1932-)
Richard Dean Anderson (ent.; 1950-)
Richard Diebenkorn (US artist; 1922-93)
Richard Donner (ent.; 1939-)
Richard Dreyfuss (ent.; 1947-)
Richard Dysart (ent.; 1929-)
Richard E. Byrd, Adm. (US expl.; 1888-1957)
Richard E. Smalley (US chem.; 1943-)
Richard F. Gordon, Jr. (astro.; 1929-)
Richard Farnsworth (ent.; 1920-)
Richard (Phillips) Feynman (US physt.; 1918-88)
Richard Francis Burton, (Sir)(Br. expl.; 1821-90)
Richard (Jordan) Gatling (US inv.; 1818-1903)
Richard G(reen) Lugar (US cong.; 1932-)
Richard Gere (ent.; 1949-)
Richard Grenville (or Greynville), (Sir)(Br. mil.;
    1541-91)
Richard H. "Dick" Bryan (US pol.; 1937-)

Richard Harris (ent.; 1933-)
Richard Hatch (US TV "Survivor"; 1961-)
Richard (McGarrah) Helms (US ex-dir./CIA;
    1913-)
Richard Henry Tawney (Br. hist.; 1880-1962)
Richard Howe, Earl (Br. mil.; 1726-99)
Richard H. Rovere (US jour.; 1915-79)
Richard I (the Lion-Hearted or Coeur de Lion)
    (king, Eng.; 1157-99)
Richard II (king, Eng.; 1367-1400)
Richard III (king, Eng.; 1452-85)
Richard J. Durbin (US cong.; 1944-)
Richard Jaeckel (ent.; 1926-97)
Richard Jordan (ent.; 1938-)
Richard Joseph Daley (ex-mayor, Chicago;
    1902-76)
Richard K. "Dick" Armey (US econ./cong.; 1940-)
Richard Kiley (ent.; 1922-99)
Richard King (US rancher; 1825-85)
Richard LaClede Stockton (tennis; 1951-)
Richard Le Gallienne (US/Br. writer; 1866-1947)
Richard Leakey (Br. archaeol.; 1944-)
Richard Lewis (ent.; 1947-)
Richard Llewellyn (b. Richard David Vivian
    Llewellyn Lloyd)(Welsh writer; 1906-83)
Richard Long (ent.; 1927-77)
Richard Lovelace (Br. poet; 1618-58)
Richard M(entor) Johnson (ex-US VP; 1780-1850)
Richard M. Daley (Chicago mayor; 1942-)
Richard Marx (ent.; 1963-)
Richard Meier (US arch.; 1934-)
Richard Milhous Nixon (37th US pres.; 1913-94)
Richard Moll (ent.; 1943-)
Richard Mulligan (ent.; 1932-2000)
Richard (Joseph) Neutra (US arch.; 1892-1970
Richard Outcault (US cartoonist, *Buster Brown*;
    1863-1928)
Richard (Lee) Petty (auto racing; 1937-)
Richard Plantagenet (Duke of York)(Br. mil.;
    1411-60)
Richard Pryor (ent.; 1940-)
Richard Riordan (Los Angeles mayor; 1930-)
Richard (Charles) Rodgers (US comp.; 1902-79)
Richard Roundtree (ent.; 1942-)
Richard "Dick" Scobee, (Francis)(astro.,
    Challenger; 1939-86)
Richard (Craig) Shelby (US cong.; 1934-)
Richard Simmons (ent.; 1948-)
Richard Speck (US mass murderer; 1942-91)
Richard Stahl (ent.; 1932-)
Richard Steele (Br. writer; 1672-1729)
Richard Stern (US writer; 1928-)
Richard (Georg) Strauss (Ger. comp./cond.;
    1864-1949)
Richard the Lion-Hearted (or Coeur de Lion,
    Richard I)(king, Eng.; 1157-99)
Richard Thomas (ent.; 1951-)
Richard Todd (ent.; 1919-)
Richard Upjohn (US arch.; 1802-78)
Richard von Krafft-Ebing, Baron (Ger. phys.;
    1840-1902)
Richard von Weizsacker (ex-pres., Ger.; 1920-)
Richard (Wilhelm) Wagner (Ger. comp.; 1813-83)
Richard Widmark (ent.; 1914-)
Richard W(ilson) Riley (US ex-secy./educ.; 1933-)

Richard W. Sears (US bus.; 1863-1914)
Richard, Cliff (b. Harry Webb)(ent.; 1940-)
Richard, Keith (ent.; 1943-)
Richard, Little (b. Richard Penniman)(ent.; 1932-)
Richard, Maurice (Joseph Henri)("the Rocket")(hockey; 1921-2000)
Richards, Ann (Dorothy)(nee Willis)(ex-TX gov.; 1933-)
Richards, Denise (ent.; 1971-)
Richards, Michael (ent.; 1949-)
Richards-Gebaur Air Force Base (MO)
Richardson-Vicks USA (US bus.)
Richardson, Bill (William Blaine)(US ex-secy./ener.; 1947-)
Richardson, Elliot L. (US, ex-Cabinet member; 1920-99)
Richardson, Fort (AK)(mil.)
Richardson, Kevin (ent., Backstreet Boys; 1972-)
Richardson, Natasha (ent.; 1963-)
Richardson, (Sir) Ralph (ent.; 1902-83)
Richardson, Samuel (Br. writer; 1689-1761)
Richardson, Tony (ent.; 1928-91)
Richardson, TX
Richelieu, Armand Jean du Plessis, Duc de (Fr. rel.[cardinal]/pol.; 1585-1642)
Richey, Port (FL)
Richie Havens (ent./songwriter; 1941-)
Richie Rich (cartoon chara.)
Richie Sambora (ent.; 1959-)
Richie, Lionel (ent.; 1949-)
Richland, WA
Richmond Times-Dispatch (VA newspaper)
Richmond, British Columbia, Canada
Richmond, CA, IN, KY, VA
Richmond, Mitch (basketball; 1965-)
Richter scale (measures magnitude of earthquake)
Richter, Charles Francis (US seismol.; 1900-85)
Richter, Sviatoslav (Rus. pianist; 1915-97)
Rick (Richard) Barry (basketball; 1944-)
Rick James (b. James Johnson, Jr.)(ent.; 1948-)
Rick (Enrico Anthony) Lazio (US pol.; 1958-)
Rick (Richard Lionel) Martin (hockey; 1951-)
Rick Moranis (ent.; 1953-)
Rick(y) Nelson (ent.; 1940-85)
Rick Perry (TX gov.; 1950?-)
Rick Rockwell (TV's *Who Wants to Marry a Multimillionaire?* groom; 1957-)
Rick Santorum (US cong.; 1958-)
Rick Schroder (ent.; 1970-)
Rick Springfield (b. Richard Lewis Springthorpe)(ent.; 1949-)
Rickenbacker Air Force Base (OH)
Rickenbacker, Eddie (Edward Vernon), Capt. (US aviator; 1890-1973)
Rickey Bell (football; 1949-84)
Rickey, (Wesley) Branch (baseball; 1881-1965)
Ricki Lake (ent.; 1968-)
Rickie Lee Jones (ent./songwriter; 1954-)
Rickles, Don (ent.; 1926-)
Rickover, Hyman George, Adm. (US mil./A-bomb; 1900-86)
Ricky Martin (b. Enrique Jose Martin Morales)(ent.; 1971-)
Ricoh copier
Ricoh Corp.

Ridaura (med.)
Ridder, Inc., Knight- (US bus.)
Riddle, Nelson (US cond.; 1921-85)
Ride, Sally K(irsten)(astro.; 1952-)
Ridge Vineyards, Inc.
Ridge, Tom (Thomas Joseph)(PA gov.; 1945-)
Ridgemont High, Fast Times at (film, 1982)
Ridgway, Matthew Bunker (US gen.; 1895-1993)
Ridley Scott (ent.; 1937-)
Riegert, Peter (ent.; 1947-)
Riegle, Donald W., Jr. (US pol.; 1938-)
Riemann integral/sphere/surface
Riemann, (Georg Friedrich) Bernhard (Ger. math.; 1826-66)
Riemannian geometry
Riesling (grape, wine)
Riesling, Johannisberg (wine)
Riesman, David (US sociol./writer; 1909-)
Riessen, Martin (tennis; 1941-)
Rifadin (med.)
Riff (lang./people)
Rifle Association of America, National (NRA)
Rifleman (TV show)
Rift Valley, (Great)(SW Asia/SE Afr.)
Riga, Latvia
Rigby, Cathy (gymnast/ent.; 1952-)
Rigel (also Beta Orionis)(astron.)
Rigel Kentaurus (also Alpha Centauri)(astron.)
Rigg, Diana (ent.; 1938-)
Riggs, Bobby (tennis; 1918-95)
Right Guard (anti-perspirant)
Right Reverend (rel., form of address)
Right, Miss/Ms. (slang)
Right, Mr. (slang)
Right, Petition of (Br. hist.; 1628)
Righteous Brothers (pop music)
Rigney, William (baseball; 1918-)
Rigoletto (Verdi opera)
Rig-Veda (rel.)
Riis, Jacob (August)(US reformer; 1849-1914)
Rijeka, Croatia
Rijks Museum (also Ryks)(Amsterdam)
Rijn, Rembrandt (Harmenszoon) van (Dutch artist; 1606-69)
Riker, Commander William (fict. chara., *Star Trek*)
Riley, Fort, KS (mil.)
Riley, James Whitcomb (US poet; 1849-1916)
Riley, Jeannie C. (ent.; 1945-)
Riley, Pat (basketball; 1945-)
Riley, Richard W(ilson)(US ex-secy./educ.; 1933-)
Riley, The Life of (TV show, film)
Rilke, Rainer Maria (Aus. poet; 1875-1926)
Rimbaud, (Jean Nicolas) Arthur (Fr. poet; 1854-91)
Rimes, Leann (ent.; 1982-)
Rimini, Italy
Rimsky-Korsakov, Nicolay (Andreyevich)(Rus. comp.; 1844-1908)
Rin Tin Tin (dog)
Rin Tin Tin (TV show)
Rinehart, Mary Roberts (US writer; 1876-1958)
Ring Nebula (astron.)
Ring of the Nibelung, The (Richard Wagner

tetralogy)
Ring(gold Wilmer) Lardner (US writer; 1885-1933)
Ringadoo, Veerasamy (Mauritian pol.)
Ringer's solution
Ringling Brothers and Barnum & Bailey Circus
Ringling Brothers Circus
Ringling, Charles (US circus; 1863-1926)
Ringo Starr (aka Richard Starkey)(ent.; 1940-)
Ringwald, Molly (ent.; 1968-)
Rio de Janeiro, Brazil (also Rio)
Rio de la Plata (also River Plate)(SAmer.)
Rio Grande River (also Río Bravo)(CO to Mex.)
Rio Grande, Brazil
Rio Lobo (film, 1970)
Rio Rancho, NM
Rio, Kia (auto.)
Riobamba, Ecuador
Rioja (wine)
Riopan (med.)
Riopelle, Jean Paul (Can. artist; 1923-)
Riordan, Richard (Los Angeles mayor; 1930-)
Riot Act (English law; 1715)
RIP (rest in peace)
Rip Torn (b. Elmore Rual Torn, Jr.)(ent.; 1931-)
Rip Van Winkle (by W. Irving)
Ripken, Cal, Jr. (baseball; 1960-)
Ripley, Robert LeRoy (US cartoonist/collector; 1893-1949)
Ripley, The Talented Mr. (film, 1999)
Ripley's Believe It or Not!
Ripper, Jack the (London murderer; 1888)
Risë Stevens (ent.; 1913-)
Rit (dye)
Rita Coolidge (ent.; 1945-)
Rita Dove (US poet; 1952-)
Rita Hayworth (b. Margarita Carmen Cansino)(ent.; 1918-87)
Rita Moreno (b. Rosita Dolores Alverio)(ent.; 1931-)
Rita Rudner (ent.; 1955-)
Ritalin (med.)
Ritchard, Cyril (ent.; 1898-1977)
Ritchie Valens (b. Richard Valenzuela)(ent.; 1941-59)
Ritchie, Fort, MD (mil.)
Rite Aid Corp.
Rittenhouse, David (US astron./inv.; 1732-96)
Ritter, John (ent.; 1948-)
Ritter, Tex (Woodward Maurice)(ent.; 1907-74)
Ritter, Thelma (ent.; 1905-69)
Rituxan (med./cancer)
Ritz-Carlton
Ritz Crackers
Rive Gauche (also Left Bank)(Paris)
River Jordan (Pak.)
River Kwai, The Bridge on the (film, 1957)
River Phoenix (b. River Jude Bottom)(ent.; 1970-93)
River Styx (myth., underworld river)
Rivera, Chita (ent.; 1933-)
Rivera, Diego (Mex. artist; 1886-1957)
Rivera, (José) Fructuoso (ex-pres., Uruguay; 1784-1854)
Rivera, Geraldo (ent.; 1943-)
Rivera, José de (US sculptor; 1904-85)

Rivera, Uruguay
Rivers, Joan (ent.; 1933-)
Rivers, Johnny (b. John Ramistella)(ent.; 1942-)
Rivers, Larry (b. Vitzroch Loiza Grossberg)(US artist; 1923-)
Riverside Church (NYC)
Riverside Press-Enterprise (CA newspaper)
Riverside, CA
Riveter, Rosie the (WWII symbol)
Riviera (Fr./It. Mediterranean coast)
Riviera Beach, FL
Riviera, Buick (auto.)
Riyadh, Saudi Arabia
Riza Pahlavi (shah, Iran; 1877-1944)
Riza Pahlavi, Muhammad (shah, Iran; 1919-80)
Rizzo, Frank (ex-mayor, Phila.; 1921-91)
Rizzoli Bookstore
Rizzuto, Phil (baseball; 1918-)
R. James Woolsey (US ex-dir./CIA; 1941-)
RJR Nabisco (US bus.)
R. J. Reynolds Foods, Inc. (RJR Foods, Inc.)
R. J. Reynolds Tobacco Co.
R. Kelly, (Robert)(ent.; 1969-)
RKO Tape Corp.
R(obert) L(awrence) Stine (writer, *Goosebumps*; 1943-)
RMA (Royal Military Academy)
RMC (Royal Military College)
RMR (Registered Merit Reporter)
RMS (Royal Mail Service, Royal Mail Ship)
RN (registered nurse, Royal Navy)
Rn (chem. sym. radon)
RNA (ribonucleic acid)
RNR (Royal Naval Reserve)
Roach Motel
Roach, Hal (ent.; 1892-92)
Roach, Max (US jazz; 1925-)
Road & Track (mag.)
Road Runner, Plymouth (autó.)
Road to Morocco (film, 1942)
Road to Singapore (film, 1940)
Road to Utopia (film, 1946)
Road to Zanzibar (film, 1941)
Road Town, Tortola, British Virgin Islands
Roadmaster, Buick (auto.)
Roald Dahl (Br./US writer; 1916-90)
Roald Hoffmann (chem.; 1937-)
Roanoke Island, NC
Roanoke River (SE US)
Roanoke Times & World-News (VA newspaper)
Roanoke, VA
Roaring Twenties (also Roaring '20s)
Rob Lowe (ent.; 1964-)
Rob Morrow (ent.; 1962-)
Rob Reiner (ent.; 1945-)
Rob Roy (b. Robert MacGregor)(Scot. outlaw; 1671-1734)
Rob Roy (cocktail)
Rob Roy (W. Scott novel)
Robards, Jason, Jr. (ent.; 1922-2000)
Robards, Jason, Sr. (ent.; 1892-1963)
Robaxin (med.)
Robaxisal (med.)
Robb, Chuck (Charles S[pittal])(US pol.; 1939-)
Robb, Lynda Bird Johnson (US daughter ex-

pres.; 1944-)
Robbe-Grillet, Alain (Fr. writer; 1922-)
Robbia, Andrea della (It. sculptor; 1437-1528)
Robbia, Luca della (It. artist; 1400-82)
Robbie Knievel (US daredevil; 1960-)
Robbin, Cock
Robbins, Harold (US writer; 1916-97)
Robbins, Jerome (US ballet; 1918-98)
Robbins, Marty (ent.; 1925-82)
Robbins, Tim (ent.; 1958-)
Robby Benson (b. Robert Segal)(ent.; 1956-)
Robert A(nson) Heinlein (US writer, sci-fi;
   1907-88)
Robert Alda (ent.; 1914-86)
Robert Alexander Kennedy Runcie (Br. rel.;
   1921-2000)
Robert Altman (ent.; 1925-)
Robert Altman (US atty./banker; 1947)
Robert A(ndrews) Millikan (US physt.; 1868-
   1953)
Robert Anderson (playwright; 1917-)
Robert Armbruster (US cond.)
Robert Baden-Powell, (Sir)(Br. gen., founded
   Boy Scouts; 1857-1941)
Robert Benchley (US writer/humorist; 1889-
   1945)
Robert Bennett (US cong.; 1933-)
Robert Blake (b. Michael Gubitosi)(ent.; 1933-)
Robert Blake, Adm. (Br. mil.; 1599-1657)
Robert Bly (US poet/critic; 1926-)
Robert Bosch Corp.
Robert Boyle (Br. physt./chem.; 1627-91)
Robert "Bobby" Breen (ent.)
Robert Brown (Scot. botanist; 1773-1858)
Robert Browning (Br. poet, husband of
   Elizabeth; 1812-89)
Robert Burns (Scot. poet; 1759-96)
Robert Burns Woodward (US chem.; 1917-79)
Robert Carlyle (ent.; 1961-)
Robert Castlereagh (Br. pol.; 1769-1822)
Robert C. Atkins, Dr. (US, low-carb diet)
Robert Cavelier La Salle, (René)(aka Sieur de
   La Salle)(Fr. expl.; 1643-87)
Robert C(arlyle) Byrd (US cong.; 1917-)
Robert Charles Gallo (US scien.; 1937-)
Robert Clive (Br. leader in India; 1725-74)
Robert Cochran (skiing; 1951-)
Robert Conrad (ent.; 1935-)
Robert Crichton (US writer; 1925-93)
Robert Crumb (cartoonist, underground; 1943-)
Robert C. "Bob" Smith (US cong.; 1941-)
Robert Culp (ent.; 1930-)
Robert Cummings (ent.; 1908-90)
Robert De Niro (ent.; 1943-)
Robert Delaunay (Fr. artist; 1885-1941)
Robert Devereux (Earl of Essex)(Br. mil./pol.;
   1566-1601)
Robert "Bob" Dole (US pol.; 1923-)
Robert Donat (ent.; 1905-58)
Robert Downey, Jr. (ent.; 1965-)
Robert Duvall (ent.; 1931-)
Robert E. Armbruster (US gen.; 1949-)
Robert E(dward) Lee (US confed. gen.; 1807-70)
Robert E(dwin) Peary (US Arctic expl.; 1856-
   1920)

Robert E. Rubin (US ex-secy./treas.; 1938-)
Robert Englund (ent.; 1949-)
Robert Evans (ent.; 1930-)
Robert Falcon Scott (Br. expl.; 1868-1912)
Robert F. Bennett (US cong.; 1933-)
Robert F(rancis) Kennedy (US pol., bro. of ex-
   pres.; 1925-68)
Robert Flaherty (ent.; 1884-1951)
Robert Foxworth (ent.; 1941-)
Robert (Lee) Frost (US poet; 1874-1963)
Robert Fulton (US gunsmith/artist/eng./inv.
   steamship; 1745-1815)
Robert F(erdinand) Wagner, Jr. (ex-mayor;
   NYC; 1910-1991)
Robert F(erdinand) Wagner, Sr. (US pol.; 1877-
   1953)
Robert Ginty (ent.; 1948-)
Robert Gordon Menzies (ex-PM, Austl.; 1894-
   1978)
Robert Goulet (b. Stanley Applebaum)(ent.; 1933-)
Robert "Bob" Graham (US cong.; 1936-)
Robert (Ranke) Graves (Br. writer/hist.; 1895-
   1985)
Robert Guéi, Gen. (pres., Ivory Coast; 1941-)
Robert Guillaume (b. Robert Williams)(ent.;
   1937-)
Robert Guiscard (Robert de Hauteville)(Norman
   /It. mil.; c1015-85)
Robert (Philip) Hanssen (US traitor; 1944-)
Robert (Louis) Hass (US ex-poet laureate; 1941-)
Robert Hayes (ent.; 1947-)
Robert Henri (US artist; 1865-1926)
Robert Herrick (Br. poet; 1591-1674)
Robert H. Goddard (US physt., father of
   modern rocketry; 1882-1945)
Robert H(enry) Michel (US pol.; 1923-)
Robert Hooke (Br. physt./inv.; 1635-1703)
Robert James "Bobby" Fischer (US chess
   master; 1943-)
Robert James Lee "Bob" Hawke (ex-PM, Austl.;
   1929-)
Robert James Waller (US writer; 1939-)
Robert Jemison Van de Graaff (US physt.;
   1901-67)
Robert Joffrey (Abdullah Jaffa Bey Khan)(US
   ballet; 1930-88)
Robert John le Mesurier McClure, (Sir)(Br.
   expl.; 1807-73)
Robert Keenan Winery (US bus.)
Robert Klein (ent.; 1942-)
Robert Koch (Ger. phys./bacteriol.; 1843-1910)
Robert Kocharian (pres., Armenia; 1954-)
Robert Krups North America (US bus.)
Robert Lansing (b. Robert Howell Brown)(ent.;
   1928-94)
Robert Lansing (US atty./pol.; 1864-1928)
Robert L. Crippen (astro.; 1937-)
Robert LeRoy Ripley (US cartoonist/collector;
   1893-1949)
Robert Livingston (US pol.; 1654-1728)
Robert Loggia (ent.; 1930-)
Robert Louis (Balfour) Stevenson (Scot. writer;
   1850-94)
Robert Lowell (US poet; 1917-77)
Robert Ludlum (US writer; 1927-2001)

Robert MacNeil (jour.; 1931-)
Robert Malval (Haitian pol.)
Robert Mapplethorpe (US photo.; 1946-89)
Robert Marion La Follette (ex-gov., WI; 1855-1925)
Robert Marion La Follette, Jr. (US pol./publ., WI; 1895-1953)
Robert "Bob" Martinez (US pol.; 1934-)
Robert Maxwell, (Ian)(b. Jan Ludvik Hock) (Czech./Br. publ.; 1923-91)
Robert (Strange) McNamara (US bus./pol.; 1916-)
Robert Merrill (b. Moishe Miller)(ent.; 1919-)
Robert M. Gates (US ex-CIA dir.; 1943-)
Robert M. Hutchins (US educ.; 1899-1977)
Robert (Joseph) "Bob" Miller (ex-NV gov.; 1945-)
Robert Mills (US arch.; 1781-1855)
Robert Mitchum (ent.; 1917-97)
Robert Mondavi Winery (US bus.)
Robert Montgomery (ent.; 1904-81)
Robert Morley (Br. ent.; 1908-92)
Robert Morris (US pol./bus.; 1734-1806)
Robert Morris Page (US physt.; 1903-92)
Robert Morse (ent.; 1931-)
Robert Moses (US urban planner; 1888-1981)
Robert Moses "Lefty" Grove (baseball; 1900-75)
Robert (Burns) Motherwell (US artist; 1915-91)
Robert (Swan) Mueller, III (US FBI dir.; 1944-)
Robert (Gabriel) Mugabe (pres., Zimbabwe; 1925-)
Robert (David) Muldoon, (Sir)(ex-PM, NewZeal.; 1921-92)
Robert Musil (Aus. writer; 1880-1942)
Robert N. Noyce (US inv.; 1927-89)
Robert of Courtenay (emp., Constantinople; 13th c.)
Robert Oppenheimer, J(ulius)(US physt., atomic bomb; 1904-67)
Robert Owen (Br. phil./reformer; 1771-1858)
Robert Patrick Casey (ex-gov., PA; 1932-2000)
Robert Peel, (Sir)(ex-PM, Br.; 1788-1850)
Robert Penn Warren (US writer; 1905-89)
Robert (Neal) Pinsky (US ex-poet laureate; 1940-)
Robert Plant (ent.; 1947-)
Robert Preston (ent.; 1918-87)
Robert Prosky (ent.; 1930-)
Robert Q. Lewis (ent.; 1920-91)
Robert R. Livingston (US pol.; 1746-1813)
Robert Rauschenberg (US artist; 1925-)
Robert Redfield (US anthrop.; 1897-1958)
Robert Redford, (Charles)(ent.; 1937-)
Robert Reed (ent.; 1932-1992)
Robert Reich (US ex-secy./labor; 1946-)
Robert Richard Torrens, (Sir)(Br. pol. in Austl.; 1814-84)
Robert Robinson, (Sir)(Br. chem.; 1885-1975)
Robert Rodale (US publ./organic gardening; 1930-90)
Robert Russell Bennett (US comp.; 1894-1981)
Robert Ryan (ent.; 1909-73)
Robert Sanderson Mulliken (US chem./physt.; 1896-1986)
Robert Schuller (US rel.; 1926-)
Robert Schuman (ex-PM, Fr.; 1886-1963)

Robert (Alexander) Schumann (Ger. comp.; 1810-56)
Robert (Leslie) Shapiro (US atty.; 1942-)
Robert Shaw (chorale cond.; 1916-99)
Robert (Emmet) Sherwood (US writer; 1896-1955)
Robert S. Strauss (US dipl./pol.; 1918-)
Robert Stack (ent.; 1919-)
Robert Stirling (Scot. rel./inv.; 1790-1878)
Robert Stone (US writer; 1937-)
Robert (Alphonso) "Bob" Taft, II (OH gov.; 1942-)
Robert Taylor (ent.; 1911-69)
Robert Todd Lincoln (US atty., A. Lincoln's son; 1843-1926)
Robert Torricelli (US cong.; 1951-)
Robert Townsend (ent.; 1957-)
Robert Trout (b. Robert Albert Blondheim)(TV jour.; 1909-2000)
Robert Urich (ent.; 1946-)
Robert Vaughn (ent.; 1932-)
Robert (Charles) Venturi (US arch.; 1925-)
Robert Vesco (US finan./fugitive; 1935-)
Robert Wagner (ent.; 1930-)
Robert Walden (ent.; 1943-)
Robert Walker (ent.; 1914-51)
Robert Walpole (Earl of Oxford)(Br. pol.; 1676-1745)
Robert W. Bunsen (Ger. chem., invented Bunsen burner; 1811-99)
Robert William "Bob" Packwood (US pol.; 1932-)
Robert (Ellsworth) "Bob" Wise, Jr. (WV gov.; 1948-)
Robert W(illiam) Service (Can. writer; 1874-1958)
Robert Young (ent.; 1907-98)
Robert Zemeckis (ent.; 1952-)
Robert, Henry Martyn (US eng., wrote Robert's Rules of Order; 1837-1923)
Robert's Rules of Order (parliamentary procedure; compiled 1876)
Roberta Flack (ent.; 1939-)
Roberta Peters (ent.; 1930-)
Roberto Benigni (ent./writer; 1952-)
Roberto Clemente (baseball; 1934-72)
Roberto Danino (PM, Peru)
Roberto DeVicenzo (golf; 1923-)
Roberto Duran (boxing; 1951-)
Roberto Rossellini (It. ent.; 1906-77)
Roberts, Barbara (nee Hughey)(ex-OR gov.; 1936-)
Roberts, Cokie (b. Mary Martha Corinne Morrison Claiborne Boggs)(TV jour.; 1943-)
Roberts, Doris (ent.; 1929-)
Roberts, Eric (ent.; 1956-)
Roberts, Julia (ent.; 1967-)
Roberts, Mister (film, 1955)
Roberts, Oral (US rel.; 1918-)
Roberts, Pat (US cong.; 1936-)
Roberts, Pernell (ent.; 1930-)
Roberts, Tony (ent.; 1939-)
Roberts, Xavier (US bus., Cabbage Patch Kids; 1955-)
Robertson Davies, (William)(Can. writer; 1913-96)

Robertson, Cliff (ent.; 1925-)
Robertson, Dale (ent.; 1923-)
Robertson, Oscar (basketball; 1938-)
Robertson, Pat (Marion Gordon)(US pol./rel.;
    1930-)
Robeson, Paul (ent.; 1898-1976)
Robespierre, Maximilien (François Marie Isidore
    de)(Fr. mil./pol.; 1758-94)
Robin and the Seven Hoods (film, 1964)
Robin Cook (ophthalmologist/writer; 1940-)
Robin Givens (ent.; 1964-)
Robin Goodfellow (also Puck, Hobgoblin)(fict.
    chara., *A Midsummer Night's Dream*)
Robin Hood (legendary Eng. hero/outlaw; 13th-
    14th c.)
Robin Hood: Prince of Thieves (film, 1991)
Robin Hood's Merry Men
Robin Leach (ent.; 1941-)
Robin Piccone (fashion designer)
Robin Strasser (ent.; 1945-)
Robin the Boy Wonder (fict. chara.)
Robin Trower (ent.; 1945-)
Robin Williams (ent.; 1952-)
Robin Wright Penn (ent.; 1966-)
Robin, Christopher (fict. chara., *Winnie-the-
    Pooh*)
Robin, Leo (US lyricist; 1900-84)
Robinson and the Miracles, Smokey (pop music)
Robinson Crusoe (D. Defoe novel)
Robinson Jeffers, (John)(US writer; 1887-1962)
Robinson Peete, Holly (ent.; 1964-)
Robinson, Arnie (track; 1948-)
Robinson, Arthur N(apoleon) R. (pres.,
    Trinidad/Tobago; 1926-)
Robinson, Bill ("Bojangles")(US tap dancer;
    1878-1949)
Robinson, Brooks (baseball; 1937-)
Robinson, Charles (ent.)
Robinson, Charles (US pol.; 1818-94)
Robinson, David (basketball; 1965-)
Robinson, Edward G. (ent.; 1893-1973)
Robinson, Edwin Arlington (US poet; 1869-1935)
Robinson, Frank (baseball; 1935-)
Robinson, Jackie (John Roosevelt)(baseball;
    1919-72)
Robinson, James H. (US hist./educ.; 1863-1936)
Robinson, Larry (hockey; 1951-)
Robinson, Mary (ex-pres., Ir.; 1944-)
Robinson, (Sir) Robert (Br. chem.; 1885-1975)
Robinson, Smokey (William)(US comp.; 1940-)
Robinson, Sugar Ray (b. Walker Smith)(boxing;
    1920-89)
Robinson, The Swiss Family (J. Wyss novel)
Robinul (med.)
Robitaille, Luc (hockey; 1966-)
Robitussin (med.)
Robocop (film, 1987)
Robusti, Jacopo (aka Tintoretto)(It. artist;
    1518-94)
Rocaltrol (med.)
Roche-Bobois (US bus.)
Roche limit (astron.)
Roche, Eugene (ent.; 1928-)
Roche, Kevin (US arch.; 1922-)
Rochefoucauld, François, Duc de La (Fr. writer;

    1613-80)
Rochelle salt
Rochester Democrat & Chronicle (NY
    newspaper)
Rochester Times-Union (NY newspaper)
Rochester, England
Rochester, MN, NH, NY
"Rochester" Anderson, Eddie (ent.; 1905-77)
Rock and Roll Hall of Fame, The
Rock Cornish hen (also Rock Cornish game hen)
Rock Hill, SC
Rock Hudson (b. Roy Scherer, Jr.)(ent.; 1925-
    85)
Rock Island Arsenal (IL)
Rock Island, IL
Rock of Gibraltar (S coast of Sp.)
Rock Springs, WY
Rock, Chris (ent.; 1965-)
Rockefeller Center (NYC)
Rockefeller Foundation (est. 1913)
Rockefeller, David (US finan.; 1915-)
Rockefeller, John "Jay" D(avison), IV (US
    cong.; 1937-)
Rockefeller, John D(avison)(US bus./finan.;
    1839-1937)
Rockefeller, John D(avison), III (US finan.;
    1906-78)
Rockefeller, John D(avison), Jr. (US bus./
    finan.; 1874-1960)
Rockefeller, Laurance S(pelman)(US bus./
    finan.; 1910-)
Rockefeller, Nelson A(ldrich)(ex-US VP; 1908-79)
Rockefeller, oysters
Rockefeller, William (US bus./finan.; 1841-1922)
Rockefeller, Winthrop (ex-gov., AR; 1912-73)
Rockets, Houston (basketball team)
Rockettes, the (ent./dancers)
Rockford Files, The (TV show)
Rockford Register Star (IL newspaper)
Rockford, IL
Rockies, Colorado (baseball team)
Rockne, Knute (Kenneth)(football; 1888-1931)
Rockville, MD
Rockwell Corp., North American
Rockwell International Corp.
Rockwell Kent (US artist; 1882-1971)
Rockwell, Martha (skiing; 1944-)
Rockwell, Norman (US artist; 1894-1978)
Rockwell, Rick (TV's *Who Wants to Marry a
    Multimillionaire?* groom; 1957-)
Rocky (film, 1976)
Rocky (Rocco Domenico) Colavito (baseball;
    1933-)
Rocky Graziano (Thomas Rocco Barbella)
    (boxing, 1919-90)
Rocky Horror Picture Show, The (film, 1975)
Rocky II (film, 1979)
Rocky III (film, 1982)
Rocky IV (film, 1985)
Rocky Marciano (b. Rocco Francis Marchegiano)
    (boxing; 1923-69)
Rocky Mount, NC
Rocky Mountain Arsenal (CO)
Rocky Mountain goat (also mountain goat)
Rocky Mountain National Park (CO)

Rocky Mountain News, Denver (CO newspaper)
Rocky Mountain sheep (also bighorn sheep)
Rocky Mountain spotted fever (med.)
Rocky Mountains (also Rockies)(W NAmer.)
Rocky V (film, 1990)
Rococo style (art/arch., Eur.; 18th c.)
Rod Cameron (ent.; 1912-83)
Rod(ney Cline) Carew (baseball; 1945-)
Rod(rique) Gilbert (hockey; 1941-)
Rod(ney George) Laver (tennis; 1938-)
Rod McKuen (US writer/comp.; 1933-)
Rod(erick Raynor) Paige (US secy./educ.; 1933-)
Rod Serling (ent.; 1924-75)
Rod Steiger (ent.; 1925-)
Rod Stewart (ent.; 1945-)
Rod Taylor (ent.; 1930-)
Rodale Press, Inc.
Rodale, Robert (US publ./organic gardening; 1930-90)
Roddenberry, Gene (Eugene Wesley)(writer/producer, Star Trek; 1921-91)
Roddenbery Co., W. B.
Roddy McDowall (ent.; 1928-98)
Rodeo Drive (in Beverly Hills)
Rodeo, Isuzu (auto.)
Rodgers & Hart (comp./lyricist team)
Rodgers, Jimmie (James Charles)(ent.; 1897-1933)
Rodgers, Jimmy (James Frederick)(ent.; 1933-)
Rodgers, Richard (Charles)(US comp.; 1902-79)
Rodham Clinton, Hillary (US cong.; wife of ex-pres.; 1947-)
Rodham, Hugh (US atty./bro. of Hillary)
Rodham, Hugh (Ellsworth)(US father of Hillary; 1911-93)
Rodham, Tony (US bro. of Hillary)
Rodia, Simon (It. tile setter; 1875-1965)
Rodin, (François) Auguste (René)(Fr. sculptor; 1840-1917)
Rodman, Dennis (basketball; 1961-)
Rodney Crowell (ent.; 1950-)
Rodney Dangerfield (b. Jacob Cohen)(ent.; 1922-)
Rodney Earl Slater (US ex-secy./trans.; 1955-)
Rodney King (US news; 1965-)
Rodney Milburn, Jr. (US hurdler; 1950-)
Rodolphe Kreutzer (Fr. comp.; 1766-1831)
Rodrigo Carazo Odio (ex-pres., Costa Rica)
Rodrigo Diaz de Bivar (also El Cid, el Campeador)(Sp. mil.; 1040-99)
Rodríguez Echeverría, Miquel Angel (pres., Costa Rica; 1940-)
Rodríguez, Andrés (ex-pres., Paraguay; 1923-)
Rodriguez, Johnny (ent.; 1951-)
Rodríguez, Mireya Elisa Moscoso (pres., Panama; 1946-)
Rodzinski, Artur (US cond.; 1894-1958)
Roe vs. Wade (US law; 1973)
Roebuck & Co., Sears
Roeg, Nicolas (ent.; 1928-)
Roehm, Carolyne (writer)
Roemer, Olaus (or Ole)(Dan. astron.; 1644-1710)
Roentgen ray (also x-ray)(med.)
Roentgen, Wilhelm (Conrad)(Ger. physt., x-rays; 1845-1923)
Roethke, Theodore (US poet; 1908-1963)

Rogaine (med.)
Roger & Me (film, 1989)
Roger Bacon (Br. phil., scien.; 1214-94)
Roger (Gilbert) Bannister, (Sir)(Br. runner/phys.; 1929-)
Roger Brooke Taney (US jurist; 1777-1864)
Roger B(yron) Wilson (ex-MO gov.; 1948-)
Roger Clemens (baseball; 1962-)
Roger Clinton, Jr. (US half-brother of ex-pres.; 1956-)
Roger Daltrey (ent., The Who; 1944-)
Roger de Coverly, Sir (dance)
Roger Ebert (US critic; 1942-)
Roger (Eugene) Maris (baseball; 1934-85)
Roger "Jim" McGuinn (ent.; 1942-)
Roger Miller (ent.; 1936-92)
Roger Moore (ent.; 1927-)
Roger Mudd (TV jour.; 1928-)
Roger Rabbit?, Who Framed (film, 1988)
Roger (Huntington) Sessions (US comp.; 1896-1985)
Roger Sherman (US pol.; 1721-93)
Roger Staubach (football; 1942-)
Roger Tory Peterson (US nat./artist; 1908-96)
Roger Vadim (ent.; 1928-2000)
Roger Whittaker (ent.; 1936-)
Roger Williams (b. Louis Wertz)(ent.; 1925-)
Roger Williams (US rel.; c1603-83)
Roger, Jolly (the pirate flag)
Rogers Dry Lake, CA
Rogers Hornsby, (Rajah)(baseball; 1896-1963)
Rogers in the 21st Century, Buck (film, 1979)
Rogers, Buck (fict. chara.)
Rogers, Buddy (Charles)(ent.; 1904-99)
Rogers, Carl R(ansom)(US psych.; 1902-87)
Rogers, Formfit (US bus.)
Rogers, Fred (ent.; 1928-)
Rogers, Ginger (ent.; 1911-95)
Rogers, Kenny (ent.; 1938-)
Rogers, Mimi (ent.; 1956-)
Rogers, Roy (b. Leonard Slye)(ent./cowboy; 1912-98)
Rogers, Roy (nonalcoholic cocktail)
Rogers, Wayne (ent.; 1933-)
Rogers, Will(iam Penn Adair)(ent.; 1879-1935)
Rogers' Neighborhood, Mister (TV show)
Roget, Peter (Mark)(Br. phys./lexicographer, Roget's Thesaurus; 1779-1869)
Roget's Thesaurus (by Peter Mark Roget)
Rogier van der Weyden (Flem. artist; c1400-64)
Roh Tae Woo (ex-pres., SKorea; 1932-)
Rohe, Ludwig Mies van der (US arch.; 1886-1969)
Rohm and Haas Co.
Röhm, Ernst (Ger. Nazi; 1887-1934)
Rohmer, Sax (aka Arthur Sarsfield Ward)(Br. writer; 1886-1959)
Roister Doister, Ralph (Nicholas Udall comedy)
Roker, Al (TV host/meterol.; 1954-)
Rokina International, Inc.
Rokina lens
Rolaids (med.)
Roland (Eur. legendary hero; 8th c.)
Roland A. Wank (US arch.; 1898-1970)
Roland Barthes (Fr. critic; 1915-80)

Roland Petit (Fr. ballet; 1924-)
Roland, Chanson de (Fr. epic poem, *Song of Roland*)
Roland, Gilbert (b. Luis Antonio Damaso de Alonso)(ent.; 1905-94)
Rolex Watch USA, Inc.
Rolfe, John (Br. colonist in VA, husband of Pocahontas; 1585-1622)
Rolfing (massage)
Rolfs Leather Products (US bus.)
Rolland, Romain (Fr. writer; 1866-1944)
Rolle, Esther (ent.; 1920-98)
Rollei (photo. equip.)
Rollei of America, Inc.
Roller Derby (roller skating)
Rollerblade (in-line skates)
Rolling Stone (mag.)
Rolling Stones, the (pop music)
Rollins, Sonny (Theodore Walter)(US jazz; 1929-)
Rollo May (US psych.; 1909-94)
Rolls-Royce (auto.)
Rolls-Royce Corniche (auto.)
Rolls-Royce Motors, Inc.
Rolls-Royce Silver Seraph (auto.)
Rolodex (address files)
Rolodex Corp.
ROM (read-only memory)(compu.)
Roma Downey (ent.; 1960-)
Romain Rolland (Fr. writer; 1866-1944)
Roman alphabet (also Latin alphabet)
Roman art/arch. (ancient Rome; 4th c. BC-5th c. AD)
Roman brick
Roman calendar
Roman candle
Roman Catholic (rel.)
Roman Catholic Church (also Church of Rome)
Roman Catholicism (rel.)
Roman collar (also clerical collar)
Roman Curia (rel.)
Roman Empire (27 BC-5th c. AD)
Roman Gabriel (football; 1940-)
Roman Holiday (film, 1953)
Roman holiday (time of debauchery)
Roman law (ancient Rome)
Roman nose
Roman numerals (ancient Eur. number system, still used)
Roman Polanski (ent.; 1933-)
Roman sandal (footwear)
Roman senate
Roman wrestling, Greco-
Romana, Pax (peace imposed by strong nation on weaker one; e.g., ancient Rome over its dominions)
Romance Classics (TV channel)
Romance languages (Fr./It./Port./Romanian/Sp.)
Romancing the Stone (film, 1984)
Romanesque art/arch. (W Eur. arch.; 10th-12th c.)
Romania (SE Eur.)
Romanian (lang./people)
Romano, Ray (ent.; 1957-)
Romanoff and Juliet (film, 1961)
Romanoff, noodles

Romanov dynasty (Russian rulers; 1613-1917)
Romanov, Michael (or Mikhail) Fyodorovich (emp., Rus.; 1596-1645)
Romans (rel., book of the New Testament)
Romanticism (Eur./Amer. art, music, lit.; 19th c.)
Romany (lang./people)
Romberg, Sigmund (Hung. comp.; 1887-1951)
Rome (apple)
Rome, ancient (753 BC-AD 1453)
Rome, GA, NY
Rome, Georgia
Rome, Harold (US comp.; 1908-93)
Rome, Italy
Rome, Sack of (capture by Goths/end of Roman Empire; 410 AD)
Rome, See of (also Holy See)(Vatican)
Rome, Seven Hills of
Rome, the March on (It. hist.; 1922)
Romeo and Juliet (Shakespeare play)
Romeo Montague (fict. chara., *Romeo & Juliet*)
Romeo, Alfa (auto.)
Romer, Roy R. (ex-CO gov.; 1928-)
Romero, Cesar (ent.; 1907-94)
Romijn-Stamos, Rebecca (model/ent.; 1972-)
Rommel, Erwin (aka "Desert Fox")(Ger. gen. in NAfr.; 1891-1944)
Romney (sheep)
Romney, George (Br. artist; 1734-1802)
Romney, George (US pol./bus.; 1907-95)
Romulo, Carlos Pena (Phil. dipl./jour./educ.; 1899-1985)
Romulus & Remus (myth. twins raised by wolf/ founded Rome)
Romulus, MI
Romy Schneider (b. Rose-Marie Albach-Retty) (ent.; 1938-82)
Ron B. Kitaj (US artist; 1932-)
Ron(ald Harmon) Brown (US ex-secy./ commerce; 1941-96)
Ron Carey (ex-Teamsters pres.)
Ron Carter (US jazz; 1937-)
Ron Glass (ent.; 1945-)
Ron Howard (ent.; 1953-)
Ron(ald) Hubbard, L(afayette)(US writer/rel., Scientology; 1911-86)
Ron Leibman (ent.; 1937-)
Ron Moody (ent. 1924-)
Ron Perlman (ent.; 1950-)
Ron Silver (ent.; 1946-)
Ron Weasley (fict. chara., *Harry Potter*)
Ron Wyden (US cong.; 1949-)
Ron(ald) Ziegler (US ex-White House press secy.; 1939-)
Rona Barrett (b. Rona Burstein)(US gossip columnist; 1936-)
Ronald Ames Guidry (baseball; 1950-)
Ronald Colman (ent.; 1891-1958)
Ronald E. Evans (astro.; 1933-)
Ronald McDonald (fict. chara.)
Ronald McDonald House
Ronald (Wilson) Reagan (40th US pres.; 1911-)
Ronald Venetiaan (pres., Suriname; 1936-)
Rondec (med.)
Rondônia (state, Brazil)
Ronettes, the (pop music)

Rongji, Zhu (PM, Ch.; 1928-)
Ronnie Milsap (ent.; 1944-)
Ronnie Musgrove (MS gov.; 1956-)
Ronnie Ray Smith (sprinter; 1949-)
Ronnie Spector (b. Veronica Bennett)(ent.; 1943-)
Ronny Cox (ent.; 1938-)
Rono, Harry (track; 1952-)
Ronsard, Pierre de (Fr. poet; 1524-85)
Ronstadt, Linda (ent.; 1946-)
Röntgen (or Roentgen), Wilhelm Konrad (Ger.
    physt.; 1845-1923)
Ronzoni Foods, Inc.
Rookie of the Year (baseball)
Roone Arledge (US TV exec.; 1931-)
Rooney, Andy (Andrew Aitken)(US TV jour.;
    1919-)
Rooney, Art (football; 1901-88)
Rooney, Mickey (b. Joseph Yule, Jr.)(ent.; 1920-)
Roosa, Stuart A. (astro.; 1933-)
Roosevelt "Rosey" Grier (ent./football; 1932-)
Roosevelt Island (NY)
Roosevelt National Park, Theodore (ND)
Roosevelt, (Anna) Eleanor (wife of US pres., UN
    dipl.; 1884-1962)
Roosevelt, Franklin D(elano)(FDR)(32nd US
    pres.; 1882-1945)
Roosevelt, Franklin D(elano), Jr. (US pol.;
    1914-88)
Roosevelt, Teddy (Theodore)(26th US pres.;
    1858-1919)
Roosevelt's Rough Riders (US hist., Sp./Amer.
    War; 1898)
Rooster Cogburn (film, 1975)
Root, Elihu (US atty./pol.; 1845-1937)
Roots (A. Haley book)
Roper Poll
Roquefort (cheese)
Rorem, Ned (US comp.; 1923-)
Rorer Consumer Pharmaceuticals, Rhone-
    Poulenc (US bus.)
Rorschach test (inkblot psych. test)
Rory Calhoun (b. Francis Timothy Durgin)(ent.;
    1922-99)
Rosa Bonheur (Maria Rosalie)(Fr. artist; 1822-
    99)
Rosa Parks (US civil rights activist; 1913-)
Rosa Ponselle (soprano; 1897-1981)
Rosa, Julius La (ent.; 1930-)
Rosalind Russell (ent.; 1911-76)
Rosalyn Evette Bryant (track; 1956-)
Rosalynn (Smith) Carter (wife of US ex-pres.;
    1927-)
Rosalynn Sumners (figure skating; 1964-)
Rosanna Arquette (ent.; 1959-)
Rosanne Cash (ent.; 1955-)
Rosario, Antonio Gualberto do (PM, Cape Verde)
Rosario, Argentina
Rosarita Mexican Foods Co.
Roscoe Lee Browne (ent.; 1925-)
Roscoe Tanner, III, (Leonard)(tennis; 1951-)
Rose Bowl (CA)
Rose Bowl (college football)
Rose Elizabeth Kennedy (nee Fitzgerald)(US
    mother of ex-pres.; 1890-1995)
Rose Marie (Mazetta)(ent.; 1925-)

Rose of Cairo, The Purple (film, 1985)
Rose Parade
Rose Schneiderman (US labor leader; 1884-1972)
rose of Jericho (plant)
rose of Sharon (plant)
Rose, Audrey (film, 1977)
Rose, Axl (William Bailey)(ent.; 1962-)
Rose, Billy (ent.; 1899-1966)
Rose, Broadway Danny (film, 1984)
Rose, Charlie (US TV jour.; 1942-)
Rose, David (US comp.; 1910-90)
Rose, Jack (mixed drink)
Rose, Leonard (US cellist; 1918-84)
Rose, Pete(r Edward)(baseball; 1941-)
Rose, Vincent (US comp.; 1880-1944)
Roseanne Barr (ent.; 1952-)
Roseanne (TV show)
Roseanne Roseannadanna (fict. chara.;
    Saturday Night Live)
Roseau, Dominica
Rosecomb bantam (chicken)
Rosemary Casals (tennis; 1948-)
Rosemary Clooney (ent.; 1928-)
Rosemary De Camp (ent.; 1910-)
Rosemary Harris (ent.; 1930-)
Rosemary Kennedy (US sister of ex-pres.; 1918-)
Rosemary's Baby (film, 1968)
Rosenberg, Alfred (Ger. Nazi; 1893-1946)
Rosenberg, Ethel (Greenglass)(US, executed
    for treason; 1915-53)
Rosenberg, Julius (US, executed for treason;
    1918-53)
Rosenbloom, Maxie (boxing; 1904-76)
Rosenblum Cellars, Inc.
Rosencrantz & Guildenstern (T. Stoppard play)
Roses, Guns 'N (pop music)
Roses, War of the (Eng. hist.; 1455-85)
Rosetta Stone/stone (Eg., hieroglyphics; from
    197 BC)
Roseville, MI, MN
Rosewall, Ken (tennis; 1934-)
Rosey (Roosevelt) Grier (ent./football; 1932-)
Rosh Hashanah (High Holy Day, Yom Kippur,
    High Holiday)
Rosicrucian Fraternity (phil./rel.)
Rosicrucians (internat'l phil./rel. order)
Rosie O'Donnell (ent.; 1962-)
Rosie O'Grady, Sweet (film, 1943)
Rosie Perez (ent./choreographer; 1966-)
Rosie the Riveter (WWII symbol)
Rosollino, Frank (US jazz; 1926-78)
Ross Dependency (Antarctic)
Ross Ice Shelf (Antarctic)
Ross Island (Antarctic)
Ross Macdonald (aka Kenneth Millar)(US
    writer; 1915-83)
Ross Perot, H. (US bus./pol.; 1930-)
Ross Sea (arm of Antarctic Ocean)
Ross, Betsy (Griscom)(made 1st US flag; 1752-
    1836)
Ross, Diana (ent.; 1944-)
Ross, Elisabeth Kübler- (Swiss/US phys./writer;
    1926-)
Ross, (Sir) James Clark (Br. expl.; 1800-62)
Ross, (Sir) John (Br. expl.; 1777-1856)

Ross, John (aka Coowescoowe)(Cherokee Native Amer. chief; 1790-1866)
Ross, Katharine (ent.; 1942-)
Ross, Leonard Q. (pseud. Leo (Calvin) Rosten)(US humorist/sociol.; 1908-97)
Ross, Marion (ent.; 1928-)
Rossano Brazzi (It. ent.; 1916-94)
Rossdale, Gavin (ent., Bush; 1967-)
Rossellini, Isabella (It. ent.; 1952-)
Rossellini, Roberto (It. ent.; 1906-77)
Rossellino, Antonio (It. sculptor; 1427-79)
Rossellino, Bernardo (It. arch./sculptor; 1409-64)
Rossetti, Christina (Georgina)(Br. poet; 1830-94)
Rossetti, Dante Gabriel (Br. poet/artist; 1828-82)
Rossi Vineyards, Carlo (US bus.)
Rossi, Carlo (wine)
Rossignol Ski Co., Inc.
Rossini, Gioacchino (Antonio)(It comp.; 1792-1868)
Rostand, Edmond (Fr. writer; 1868-1918)
Rosten, Leo (Calvin)(pseud. Leonard Q. Ross)(US humorist/sociol.; 1908-97)
Rostenkowski, Dan(iel)(US pol.; 1928-)
Rostock, Germany
Rostov-on-Don, Russia
Rostow, Walt Whitman (US econ.; 1916-)
Rostropovich, Mstislav (Rus. cellist/cond.; 1927-)
Roswell, NM
Roswell: The U.F.O. Cover-Up (film, 1994)
Rotarian, The (mag.)
Rotary Club (bus./prof. club)
Rotary International (org. of bus./prof. clubs)
ROTC (Reserve Officers Training Corps)(US mil./educ.)
Rote, Kyle (football; 1928-)
Roth, David Lee (ent.; 1955-)
Roth, Henry (US writer; 1906-95)
Roth, Philip (Milton)(US writer; 1933-)
Roth, Tim (ent.; 1964-)
Roth, William Victor, Jr. (US pol.; 1921-)
Rothko, Mark (Rus./US artist; 1903-70)
Rothschild, Amschel Mayer (Ger. finan.; 1773-1855)
Rothschild, Anthony Gustav de (Br. finan.; 1887-1961)
Rothschild, Chateau Lafite- (Fr. wine)
Rothschild, Chateau Mouton- (Fr. wine)
Rothschild, James (Ger./Fr. finan.; 1792-1868)
Rothschild, Lionel de (Br. finan.; 1882-1942)
Rothschild, Lionel Nathan ("Lord Natty")(Br. finan./pol.; 1808-79)
Rothschild, Meyer A(nselm)(Ger. finan.; 1744-1812)
Rothschild, Nathan Mayer (Ger./Br. finan.; 1777-1836)
Rothschild, Nathaniel Mayer Victor (Br. scien./pol./finan.; 1910-90)
Rothschild, Salomon (Ger./Aus. finan.; 1774-1855)
Rothschild, (Sir) Nathan Mayer (Br. pol./baron; 1840-1915)
Rotisserie League (baseball)
Roto-Rooter
Rotterdam, NY
Rotterdam, the Netherlands

Rottweiler (dog)
Rouault, Georges (Henri)(Fr. artist; 1871-1958)
Rouen (duck)
Rouen Cathedral
Rouen, France
Rough Riders, Roosevelt's (US hist., Sp./Amer. War; 1898)
Round Hill Winery (US bus.)
Round Table, Knights of the (legendary King Arthur knights)
Roundhead (Br. hist.; 1640-60)
Roundtree, Richard (ent.; 1942-)
Rourke, Mickey (b. Philip Andre Rourke, Jr.) (ent.; 1956-)
Rous sarcoma (med.)
Rous, (Francis) Peyton (US phys.; 1879-1970)
Roush, Edd (baseball; 1893-1988)
Rousseau, (Pierre Étienne) Theodore (Fr. artist; 1812-67)
Rousseau, Henri (Julien Félix)("Le Douanier")(Fr. artist; 1844-1910)
Rousseau, Jean Jacques (Fr. phil./writer; 1712-78)
Rovaniemi, Finland
Rove, Karl (US White House pol. adviser; 1950-)
Rover (astron.)
Rover, Lunar (also l.c.)(also lunar roving vehicle)
Rover, Range (auto.)
Revere, Richard H. (US jour.; 1915-79)
Row Publishers, Inc., Harper &
Rowan and Martin's Laugh-In (TV show)
Rowan Atkinson (ent.; 1955-)
Rowan, Carl Thomas (US jour.; 1925-2000)
Rowan, Dan (ent.; 1922-87)
Rowasa (med.)
Rowe Price Group, Inc., T.
Rowe Price Investment Services, Inc., T.
Rowland, John G(rosvenor)(CT gov.; 1957-)
Rowlands, Gena (ent.; 1934-)
Rowling, J(oanne) K(athleen)(writer; 1965-)
Rowse, A(lfred) L(eslie)(Br. hist.; 1903-97)
Roxanne (film, 1987)
Roxicodone (med.)
Roxy Music (pop music)
Roy (Claxton) Acuff (ent.; 1903-1992)
Roy Bean, "Judge" (US frontier; 1825?-1903)
Roy Campanella (baseball; 1921-93)
Roy Clark (ent.; 1933-)
Roy Dotrice (ent.; 1923-)
Roy E(ugene) Barnes (GA gov.)
Roy Eldridge (US jazz; 1911-89)
Roy Emerson (tennis; 1936-)
Roy Harris (US comp.; 1898-1979)
Roy Haynes (US jazz; 1925-)
Roy Lichtenstein (US artist; 1923-97)
Roy Orbison (ent.; 1936-88)
Roy R. Romer (ex-CO gov.; 1928-)
Roy Rogers (b. Leonard Slye)(ent./cowboy; 1912-98)
Roy Rogers (nonalcoholic cocktail)
Roy Scheider (ent.; 1932-)
Roy Thinnes (ent.)
Roy Uwe Ludwig Horn, (illusionist, Siegfried and Roy; 1944-)

Roy Wilkins (US jour./reformer; 1901-81)

Roy, Rob (b. Robert MacGregor)(Scot. outlaw; 1671-1734)

Roy, Rob (cocktail)

Roy, Rob (W. Scott novel)

Royal Academy of Arts (Br. ; est. 1768)

Royal Air Maroc (airline)

Royal Ballet (formerly Sadler's Wells)(London)

Royal Canadian Mounted Police (RCMP, Mounties)(Can. police; est. 1873)

Royal Caribbean Cruise Line

Royal Copenhagen

Royal Copenhagen Porcelain, Inc.

Royal Crown Cos., Inc.

Royal Danish Ballet

Royal Dutch Shell Group

Royal Greenwich Observatory (London)(also Old Royal Observatory)

Royal Guard, Yeomen of the (beefeaters)

Royal Highlanders (also Royal Highland Regiment, Black Watch)(Scot. mil.)

Royal Highness (title)

Royal Jordanian Airline (airline)

Royal Majesty (title)

Royal Nepal Airline

Royal Oak, MI

Royal Shakespeare Company (RSC)(Br. theater; est. 1961)

Royal Society (also Royal Society of London for the Advancement of Science; est. 1645)

Royal Victoria Hall (also Old Vic Theatre) (London)

Royal, Port (Jamaica)

Royal, Port (SC)

Royall Tyler (US writer; 1757-1826)

Royals, Kansas City (baseball team)

Royce Motors, Inc., Rolls-

Royce, (Frederick) Henry (Br. eng./Rolls-Royce; 1863-1933)

Royce, Josiah (US phil.; 1855-1916)

Royce, Rolls- (auto.)

Royko, Mike (US jour.; 1932-97)

Roz Chast (cartoonist, *New Yorker*; 1954-)

Roz Ryan (ent.; 1951-)

Rozelle, Pete (Alvin Ray)(football exec.; 1926-96)

Rozonda Thomas (ent.; 1971-)

Rozsa, Miklos (US comp.; 1907-95)

RPR (Registerd Professional Reporter)

RR (railroad)

R. R. Bowker Co.

R. R. Donnelley & Sons (US bus.)

RSVP (repondez s'il vous plait [please respond])

RTF (rich text format)(compu.)

RTF/CRE (rich text format /court reporter extensions)

R2D2 (fict. chara., *Star Wars*)

Ru (chem. sym., ruthenium)

Rúa, Fernando de la (pres., Argentina; 1937-)

Ruanda (lang.)

Rubáiyát of Omar Khayyám, The (book of verses)

Rubbermaid (containers, etc.)

Rubbermaid, Inc.

Rubbia, Carlo (It. physt.; 1934-)

Rubble, Barney (cartoon chara.)

Rube (Reuben Lucius) Goldberg (US cartoonist, *Boob McNutt*; 1883-1970)

Rube Goldberg (complex/impractical inventions)

Ruben Blades (ent./songwriter; 1948-)

Rubens, Paul (b. Paul Rubenfeld)(aka Pee-Wee Herman)(ent.; 1952-)

Rubens, Peter Paul (Flem. artist; 1577-1640)

Rubicon (ancient river dividing Italy/Gaul; 49 BC)

Rubicon, cross the (take an irrevocable step)

Rubik, Erno (Hung. arch. 1944-)

Rubik's Cube (puzzle)

Rubin, Robert E. (US ex-secy./treas.; 1938-)

Rubinstein, Anton (Grigoryevich)(Rus. pianist/ comp.; 1829-94)

Rubinstein, Arthur (Pol./US pianist; 1887-1982)

Rubinstein, Helena (US bus.; 1871-1965)

Rubinstein, John (ent.; 1946-)

Ruby Dandridge (ent.)

Ruby Dee (ent.; 1924-)

Ruby Gentry (film, 1952)

Ruby Keeler (ent.; 1909-93)

Ruby Ridge, ID (US news, confrontation w/US marshals)

Ruby, Harry (US comp.; 1895-1974)

Ruby, Jack (US, murdered L.H. Oswald; 1911-67)

Rucker, Darius (ent./songwriter; 1966-)

Rucker, Fort (AL)(mil.)

Rudd (Rudolph Franz Marie) Lubbers (ex-PM, Netherlands; 1939-)

Rudd Weatherwax (Lassie's trainer; 1915?-85)

Rudel, Julius (cond.; 1921-)

Rudner, Rita (ent.; 1955-)

Rudolf Bing, (Sir)(opera; 1902-97)

Rudolf Diesel (Ger. eng.; 1858-1913)

Rudolf Firkusny (pianist; 1912-94)

Rudolf Friml (US comp.; 1879-1972)

Rudolf Hess (Walther Richard)(Ger. Nazi; 1894-1987)

Rudolf Mössbauer (Ger. physt.; 1929-)

Rudolf Nureyev (Rus. ballet; 1938-1993)

Rudolf Schuster (pres.; Slovakia; 1934-)

Rudolf Serkin (US pianist; 1903-91)

Rudolf (Ludwig Carl) Virchow (Ger. pathol.; 1821-1902)

Rudolf von Laban (Hung. ballet; 1879-1958)

Rudolph Arthur Marcus (chem.; 1923-)

Rudolph Carnap (US phil.; 1891-1970)

Rudolph Dirks (cartoonist, *Katzenjammer Kids*; 1877-1968)

Rudolph "Rudd" Franz Marie Lubbers (PM, Netherlands; 1939-)

Rudolph the Red-Nosed Reindeer (song; film, 1964)

Rudolph Valentino (b. Rodolpho d'Antonguolla) (ent.; 1895-1926)

Rudolph W. "Rudy" Giuliani (ex-mayor, NYC; 1944-)

Rudolph, Paul (Marvin)(US arch.; 1918-97)

Rudolph, Wilma (Glodean)(runner; 1940-)

Rudy (Rudolph W.) Giuliani (mayor, NYC; 1944-)

Rudy Vallee (ent.; 1901-86)

Rudy's Farm Co.

Rudyard Kipling, (Joseph)(Br. writer; 1865-1936)

Rue McClanahan, (Eddi-Rue)(ent.; 1935-)

Rue Morgue, The Murders in the (E.A. Poe story)
Ruehl, Mercedes (ent.; 1948-)
Rufen (med.)
Ruffin, Edmund (US agriculturist; 1794-1865)
Ruffo, Titta (baritone; 1878-1953)
Rufino Tamayo (Mex. artist; 1899-1991)
RU 486 (Mifeprex, mifepristone)(med.)
Rufus King (US pol.; 1755-1827)
Rufus Sewell (ent.; 1967-)
Rufus, the Red (William II)(king, Eng.; c1056-1100)
Rugby & Soccer Supply (US bus.)
Rugby football (also l.c.)
Rugby School (Rugby, Eng., founded 1567)
Rugby shirt (also l.c.)
Rugby, England
Ruggell, Liechtenstein
Ruggiero Leoncavallo (It. comp.; 1857-1919)
Ruggles, Carl (US comp.; 1876-1971)
Ruggles, Charlie (Charles)(ent.; 1886-1970)
Ruhengeri, Rwanda
Ruhollah Khomenei, Ayatollah (Iran, rel.; 1900-89)
Ruhr River (Ger.)
Ruidoso, NM
Ruisdael, Jacob (Isaackszoon) van (Dutch artist; c1628-82)
Rukeyser, Muriel (US poet; 1913-80)
Rules of Order, Robert's (parliamentary procedure; compiled 1876)
Rumer Godden, (Margaret)(Br. writer; 1907-98)
Rumpelstiltskin (fict. chara., *Grimms Fairy Tales*)
Rumpole of the Bailey (TV series)
Rumsfeld, Donald Henry (US secy./defense; 1932-)
Run D.M.C. (pop music)
Runcie, Robert Alexander Kennedy (Br. rel.; 1921-2000)
Rundgren, Todd (ent./songwriter; 1948-)
Rundi (also Kirundi)(lang.)
Rundu, Namibia
Runner's World (mag.)
Runnymede (meadow on Thames River, near London)
Runyon, (Alfred) Damon (US writer/jour.; 1880-1946)
Rupert Brooke (Br. poet; 1887-1915)
Rupert Everett (ent./model; 1959-)
Rupert Murdoch, (Keith)(Austl./US publ.; 1931-)
Rupert, Prince (Br. mil.; 1619-82)
Rupert's Land (Can.)
Ruse, Bulgaria
Rush (Hudson) Limbaugh, III (US radio commentator; 1951-)
Rush, Barbara (ent.; 1930-)
Rush, Benjamin (US phys./writer; 1745-1813)
Rush, Geoffrey (ent.; 1951-)
Rushdie, (Ahmed) Salman (Br. writer; 1947-)
Rushmore National Memorial, Mount (SD)
Rusk, (David) Dean (US pol.; 1909-94)
Ruskin, John (Br. writer/social reformer; 1819-1900)
Russ Columbo (ent.; 1908-34)
Russel Crouse (US writer; 1893-1966)
Russell Baker (US jour.; 1925-)

Russell Cave National Monument (AL)
Russell Corp.
Russell Crowe (ent.; 1964-)
Russell Feingold (US cong.; 1953-)
Russell L. (Rusty) Schweickart (astro.; 1935-)
Russell Myers (cartoonist, *Broom Hilda*; 1938-)
Russell Sage (US finan.; 1816-1906)
Russell Stover Candies, Inc.
Russell terrier, Jack (dog)
Russell, Bertrand (Arthur William)(Br. phil./math.; 1872-1970)
Russell, Bill (basketball; 1934-)
Russell, Bill (US jazz; 1905-92)
Russell, Charles M. (US arch.; 1866-1926)
Russell, Charles T(aze)(US, rel./Jehovah's Witnesses; 1852-1916)
Russell, Gail (ent.; 1924-61)
Russell, George (US jazz; 1923-)
Russell, Jane (ent.; 1921-)
Russell, John (ex-PM, Br.; 1792-1878)
Russell, Ken (ent.; 1927-)
Russell, Keri (ent.; 1976-)
Russell, Kurt (ent.; 1951-)
Russell, Leon (b. Hank Wilson)(ent./songwriter; 1941-)
Russell, Lillian (b. Helen Louise Leonard)(ent.; 1861-1922)
Russell, Mark (ent.; 1932-)
Russell, Nipsey (ent.; 1924-)
Russell, Pee Wee (US jazz; 1906-69)
Russell, Rosalind (ent.; 1911-76)
Russell, Theresa (ent.; 1957-)
Russell's viper (snake)
Russia (Russian Federation; since 1991) (formerly part of USSR)
Russia (USSR, Russian Empire; prior to 1991)
Russia Company (Rus./Eng. trading)
Russia Far East (formerly Soviet Far East)
Russian (lang./people)
Russian bank (card game)
Russian blouse
Russian Blue (formerly Archangel Blue)(cat)
Russian dressing
Russian Federation (also Russia)(N Asia/E Eur.)
Russian Information Telegraph Agency (RITA) (Rus. news agcy.)
Russian Orthodox (rel.)
Russian Orthodox Church
Russian owtchar (dog)
Russian Revolution (Rus. hist.; 1917)
Russian roulette
Russian Soviet Federated Socialist Republic (old Soviet Russia)
Russian Steppes, the (Rus. grasslands)
Russian thistle/tumbleweed (plant)
Russian wolfhound (now Borzoi)(dog)
Russo, Rene (ent.; 1954-)
Russo-Finnish War (Rus./Fin.; 1939-40)
Russo-Japanese War (Rus./Jap.; 1904-05)
Russo-Turkish Wars (Rus./Ottoman Turk.; 17th-19th c.)
Rustin, Bayard (US civil rights leader; 1910-87)
Rust-Oleum Corp.
Rustavi, Georgia
Rusty (Daniel) Staub (baseball; 1944-)

Rusty (Russell L.) Schweickart (astro.; 1935-)
Rutger Hauer (Neth. ent.; 1944-)
Rutgers University (NJ)
Rutgers University Press (US bus.)
Ruth (rel., book of the Old Testament)
Ruth Ann Minner (DE gov.; 1935-)
Ruth Bader Ginsburg (US jurist; 1933-)
Ruth Benedict (US anthrop.; 1887-1948)
Ruth Buzzi (ent.; 1936-)
Ruth Draper (ent.; 1889-1956)
Ruth Etting (ent.; 1897-1978)
Ruth Gordon (ent.; 1896-1985)
Ruth Hussey (ent.; 1914-)
Ruth Laredo (ent.; 1937-)
Ruth Montgomery (US writer/psychic; 1912-)
Ruth St. Denis (US dancer; 1877-1968)
Ruth Warrick (ent.; 1916-)
Ruth Westheimer, Dr. (b. Karola Ruth Siegal)
    (Ger./US sex therapist; 1928-)
Ruth, Babe (George Herman)(baseball; 1895-
    1948)
Rutherford atom/scattering
Rutherford B(irchard) Hayes (19th US pres.;
    1822-93)
Rutherford Hill Winery (US bus.)
Rutherford, Ann (ent.; 1920-)
Rutherford, Ernest, Baron (Br. physt.; 1871-
    1937)
Rutherford, Johnny (auto racing; 1938-)
Rutherford, Margaret, Dame (ent.; 1892-1972)
Rutland, VT
Rutledge, Ann (fianceé of Abraham Lincoln;
    1816-35)
Rutledge, Wiley Blount, Jr. (US jurist; 1894-
    1949)
Rutskoi, Alexander (Rus. pol.)
Ruttan, Susan (ent.; 1950-)
Rüütel, Arnold (ex-pres., Estonia)
Ruysdael, Salomon van (Dutch artist; c1600-70)
RV (recreation vehicle)
R. Walter Cunningham (astro.; 1932-)
Rwanda (lang.)
Rwanda (Republic of)(central Afr.)
R. W. Frookie (US bus.)
Rx (med.)
Ry(land) Cooder (ent./songwriter; 1947-)
Ryan O'Neal (ent.; 1941-)
Ryan Phillippe (ent.; 1974-)
Ryan White (US AIDS victim/activist; 1972-90)
Ryan, George H(omer)(IL gov.; 1934-)
Ryan, Irene (ent.; 1903-73)
Ryan, Jeri (b. Jeri Lynn Zimmerman)(ent.; 1968-)
Ryan, Meg (b. Margaret Hyra)(ent,; 1963-)
Ryan, Nolan (baseball; 1947-)
Ryan, Peggy (ent.; 1924-)
Ryan, Robert (ent.; 1909-73)
Ryan, Roz (ent.; 1951-)
Ryan, Saving Private (film, 1998)
Ryan, Thomas Fortune (US bus./finan.; 1851-
    1928)
Ryan's Daughter (film, 1970)
Rybinsk, Russia
Rybnik, Poland
Rydell, Bobby (ent.; 1942-)
Ryder Cup (US/Eur. golf tournament)

Ryder Systems, Inc.
Ryder Truck Rental, Inc.
Ryder, Albert Pickham (US artist; 1847-1917)
Ryder, Mitch (b. William Levise, Jr.)(ent.; 1945-)
Ryder, Winona (b. Winona Laura Horowitz)
    (ent.; 1971-)
Rye House Plot (Br. hist.; 1683)
Ryks Museum (also Rijks)(Amsterdam)
Ryman Auditorium (Grand Ole Opry)
Ryon, Luann (archery; 1953-)
Rysanek, Leonie (dramatic soprano; 1928-98)
Ryukyu Islands (Jap.)
Ryun, Jim (James Ronald)(runner; 1947-)
Ryunosuke, Akutagawa (Jap. writer; 1892-1927)
Rzeszów, Poland

S (chem. sym., sulfur)
SA (Salvation Army)
Saab (auto.)
Saab 9-3 (auto.)
Saab 9-3 HO Turbo SE (auto.)
Saab 9-3 HO Turbo Viggen (auto.)
Saab 9-3 SE (auto.)
Saab 9-3 Turbo (auto.)
Saab 9-3 Turbo SE (auto.)
Saab 9-3 Viggen (auto.)
Saab 9-5 (auto.)
Saab 9-5 Aero (auto.)
Saab 9-5 HO Turbo (auto.)
Saab 9-5 HO Turbo SE (auto.)
Saab 9-5 SE (auto.)
Saab 9-5 Turbo (auto.)
Saab 9-5 wagon (auto.)
Saab 900 (auto.)
Saab 900 Turbo (auto.)
Saab 900 Turbo S (auto.)
Saab 900 Turbo SE (auto.)
Saab 900S (auto.)
Saab 9000 (auto.)
Saab 9000CS (auto.)
Saab 9000CSE (auto.)
Saab 9000 LP Turbo CS (auto.)
Saab 9000 Turbo Aero (auto.)
Saab 9000 Turbo CSE (auto.)
Saab 9000CD (auto.)
Saab-Scania of America, Inc.
Saad al-Abdullah al-Salim al-Sabah, Sheik (PM,
  Kuwait; 1930-)
Saadia ben Joseph (al-Fayumi)(aka Saadia
  Gaon)(Jew. scholar; 882-942)
Saale River (Ger.)
Saami (lang.)
Saanen (goat)
Saar River (Fr./Ger.)
Saarinen, (Gottlieb) Eliel (US arch.; 1873-1950)
Saarinen, Eero (US arch.; 1910-61)
Saarland (state, Ger.)
Saavedra, Miguel de Cervantes (Sp. writer;
  1547-1616)
Saba (also Sheba)(ancient S Yemen)
Saba, the Netherlands Antilles
Sabah (state, Malaysia)
Sabah, Sheik Jaber al-Ahmad al-Jaber al-
  (emir, Kuwait; 1928-)
Sabah, Sheik Saad al-Abdullah al-Salim al-
  (PM, Kuwait; 1930-)
Sabatini, Gabriela (tennis; 1970-)
Sabbatai Zevi (Jew. rel.; 1626-76)
Sabbath (rel.)
Saberhagen, Bret (baseball; 1964-)
Sabin vaccine (med.)
Sabin, Albert Bruce (US phys./microbiol.; 1906-
  93)
Sabine (ancient people, It.)
Sabine River (S central US)

Sabine Women, Rape of the (G. da Bologna
  sculpture, N. Poussin painting)
Sable, Mercury (auto.)
Sabres, Buffalo (hockey team)
Sabrina (film, 1954)
Sabu (Dastagir)(ent.; 1924-63)
SAC (Strategic Air Command)(US mil.)
Sacagawea (or Sacajawea)(US Native Amer.,
  Lewis & Clark guide; 1787?-1812 or 1884)
Sac and Fox (also Sauk)(Native Amer.)
Sacco-Vanzetti Case (Nicola & Bartolomeo)(MA
  murder trial; 1920-27)
Sacha (Alexandre) Guitry (Fr. ent./dramatist;
  1885-1957)
Sacher torte (also Sachertorte)(also l.c)(dessert)
Sacheverell Sitwell, (Sir)(Br. writer; 1897-1988)
Sachs disease, Tay- (med.)
Sachs, Hans (Ger. writer; 1494-1576)
Sachs, Jeffrey D. (US econ./educ.; 1954-)
Sachs, Nelly (Leonie)(Ger. writer; 1891-1970)
Sack of Rome (capture by Goths/end of Roman
  Empire; 410 AD)
Sackville-West, Victoria Mary, Dame ("Vita")
  (Br. writer; 1892-1962)
Sacramento Bee (CA newspaper)
Sacramento Kings (basketball team)
Sacramento River (CA)
Sacramento Union (CA newspaper)
Sacramento, CA
Sacre-Coeur Church (Paris)
Sacred College of Cardinals (also College of
  Cardinals)(rel.)
Sacred Heart (heart of Jesus)
Sad Sack, The (comic strip)
Sada Thompson (ent.; 1929-)
Sadat, Anwar (el-)(ex-pres., Eg.; 1918-81)
SADD (Students Against Drunk Driving)
Saddam Hussein (al-Tikriti)(pres., Iraq; 1937-)
Sadducee (rel./pol.)
Sadducees, Pharisees & (opposing Hebrew
  grps; 2nd c.)
Sade (b. Helen Folasade Adu)(ent.; 1959-)
Sade, Marquis de (b. Donatien Alphonse François,
  Comte de Sade)(Fr. mil./writer; 1740-1814)
Sadie Hawkins dance
Sadie Hawkins Day
Sadie Thompson (film, 1929)
Sadie Thompson, Miss (film, 1953)
Sadler's Wells Ballet (now Royal Ballet)(London)
Sadou Hayatou (ex-PM, Cameroon)
SAE (self-addressed envelope)
Safari, GMC (auto.)
Safco Products Co.
SAFECO Corp.
SAFECO Insurance Co. of America
Safeguard (soap)
Safer, Morley (US TV jour.; 1931-)
Safety Council, National (est. 1913)
Safeway Stores, Inc.
Safire, William (US jour.; 1929-)
Saftee Glass Co., Inc.
Sag Harbor (clothes)
Sagal, Katey (ent.; 1954-)
Sagan, Carl (Edward)(US astron./writer; 1934-
  96)

Sagan, Françoise (b. Françoise Quoirez)(Fr. writer; 1935-)
Sage, Russell (US finan.; 1816-1906)
Sagebrush State (nickname, NV)
Saget, Bob (ent.; 1956-)
Saginaw Valley State University (University Center, MI)
Saginaw, MI
Sagitta (astron., arrow)
Sagittarius (zodiac, astron., archer)
Sahara Desert (N Afr.)
Sahara Resorts
Sahel (region, Afr.)
Sahl, Mort (ent.; 1927-)
Said Muhammad Djohar (ex-pres., Comoros; 1918-)
Said Musa (PM, Belize; 1944-)
Said, Port (Egypt)
Said, Qabus (or Qaboos) bin (sultan/PM, Oman; 1940-)
Saida, Lebanon (also Sayda, Sidon)
Saigon (now Ho Chi Minh City)
Saigon, Miss (play)
St. Agnes (Christian martyr; ?-304?)
St. Agnes's Eve (young woman may dream of future husband; 1/20)
St. Albans, Council of (Br. hist.)
St. Albans, England
St. Albans, VT
St. Albert the Great (also St. Albertus Magnus) (Ger. rel.; 1193-1280)
St. Ambrose (bishop of Milan; c340-397)
St. Andrew (patron saint of Scot.)
St. Andrew, Jamaica
St. Andrew's Cross/cross (X-shaped cross)
St. Andrews, Scotland
St. Anselm (archbishop of Canterbury; c1033-1109)
St. Anthony (Eg., founded monasticism; c251-356)
St. Anthony's Cross/cross (also tau cross)(T-shaped cross)
St. Anthony's fire (skin disease)(med.)
St. Athanasius (bishop of Alexandria; 298-373)
St. Augustine (1st archbishop of Canterbury; late 6th c.)
St. Augustine of Hippo (rel.; 354-430)
St. Augustine, FL
St. Barnabas ("Fellow Laborer")
St. Bartholomew (apostle)
St. Bartholomew's Day, Massacre of (Fr. hist.; 1572)
St. Bede ("the Venerable Bede")(Br. rel./hist.; c673-735)
St. Benedict (It., founded the Benedictines; c480-547)
St. Bernadette (aka Bernadette of Lourdes)(Fr.; 1844-79)
St. Bernard (dog)
St. Bonaventure (also Bonaventura)("the Seraphic Doctor")(It. rel./phil.; 1221-74)
St. Boniface (Br. rel. in Ger.; 680-754)
St. Cabrini, Frances Xavier (also Mother Cabrini)(US theologian/reformer; 1850-1917)
St. Caius (also Gaius)(pope; ?-296)
St. Calixtus

St. Catharines, Ontario, Canada
St. Catherine of Siena (It. mystic; 1347-80)
St. Celestine I (pope; ?-432)
St. Celestine II (Guido del Castello)(pope; ?-1144)
St. Celestine III (Giacinto Bobone)(It. pope; 1106?-98)
St. Celestine IV (Gofredo Castiglioni)(It. pope; ?-1241)
St. Celestine V (Pietro di Murrone [or Morone]) (pope; 1215-96)
Ste. Chapelle Winery, Inc.
Sainte-Chapelle (chapel, Paris)
St. Charles, MO
St. Christopher (patron saint of travelers)
St. Christopher-Nevis, (Federation of)(West Indies)
St. Clair Shores, MI
Saint Clair, Arthur (US gen.; 1736-1818)
St. Clair, Lake (US/Can.)
St. Clement Vineyards (US bus.)
St. Cloud State University (St. Cloud, MN)
St. Cloud, MN
St. Croix (US Virgin Island)
St. Cyprian (rel. in Africa; ?-258)
St. Denis, Ruth (US dancer; 1877-1968)
St. Dominic (Sp. rel, founded Dominican order; 1170-1221)
St. Elias National Park, Wrangell- (AK)
St. Elias, Mount (mountain, AK/Can.)
St. Elizabeth Ann (Bayley) Seton (also Mother Seton)(US rel.; 1774-1821)
St. Elmo's Fire (film, 1985)
St. Elmo's fire/light (visible electrical discharge)
Saint Emilion (Fr. wine district)
St.-Estèphe (also Saint-Estèphe)(Fr. wine region)
St. Eustatius, the Netherlands Antilles
Saint-Exupery, Antoine (Marie Roger) de (Fr. writer/aviator; 1900-44)
Sainte-Foy, Quebec, Canada
St. Frances Xavier Cabrini (also Mother Cabrini) (US rel./reformer; 1850-1917)
St. Francis of Assisi (It. rel., founded Franciscans; 1182-1226)
St. Francis Xavier (Francisco Javier)("the Apostle of the Indies")(Sp. rel.; 1506-52)
St. Gaius (also Caius)(pope; ?-296)
Saint-Gaudens, Augustus (US artist; 1848-1907)
Saint-John's-wort (plant)
St. George (by Donatello)
St. George (patron saint of Eng., legendary dragon slayer; ?-c303)
St. George's, Grenada
St. Gotthard (mountain, Switz.)
St. Gotthard Pass (Swiss Alps)
St. Gotthard Tunnel (Swiss Alps)
St. Gregory I ("the Great")(It., pope; c540-604)
St. Gregory II (It., pope; ?-731)
St. Gregory III (Syrian, pope; ?-741)
St. Gregory VII (aka Hildebrand)(It., pope; c1023-85)
St. Helena (Br. island[s], S Atl.)
St. Helens, Mount (active volcano, WA)
St. Hubert, Quebec, Canada
St. Ignatius of Loyola (aka Iñigo de Oñez y Loyola)(Sp. rel.; 1491-1556)

St. Ives (skin care)
St. Ives Laboratories, Inc.
St. Jacques, coquilles (scallop dish)
St. James, Court of (Br. royal court)
St. James, Susan (b. Susan Miller)(ent.; 1946-)
St. Jean, Inc., Chateau (wine)
St. Joan of Arc (also Jeanne d'Arc, Maid of
   Orléans)(Fr. rel./mil.; 1412?-31)
St. John (US Virgin Island)
St. John River (ME/Can.)
St. John the Baptist (Judean rel.; c6 BC-AD 27)
St. John the Divine, Cathedral of (NYC)
St. John, Jill (b. Jill Oppenheim)(ent.; 1940-)
St. John, New Brunswick, Canada
St. John's Bay (clothes)
St. John's-bread (herb/spice, tree)
St. John's College (Annapolis, MD; Santa Fe, NM)
St. John's Day (also Midsummer Day)(June 24)
St. John's University (Collegeville, MN;
   Jamaica, NY)
St. John's, Newfoundland, Canada
St. Johns (or John's), Antigua and Barbuda
St. Johns River (FL)
St. Johns, Adela Rogers (US writer; 1894-1988)
St. Joseph Cold Tablets (med.)
St. Joseph, MO
St. Jude (also St. Judas)(rel.; 1st c. AD)
St. Jude Children's Research Hospital
St.-Julien (also Saint-Julien)(Fr. wine region)
St. Justin Martyr (It. rel.; 100?-165)
St. Kitts-Nevis (officially Federation of St.
   Christopher-Nevis)(West Indies)
St.-Laurent SA, Yves (US bus.)
St. Laurent, French Guiana
St. Laurent, Louis S(tephen)(ex-PM, Can.;
   1882-1973)
Saint-Laurent, Quebec, Canada
Saint-Laurent, Yves (Henri Donat Mathieu)(Fr.
   designer; 1936-)
St. Lawrence Islands National Park (Can.)
St. Lawrence River (NY/Can.)
St. Lawrence Seaway (NE US/SE Can.)
Saint-Léonard, Quebec, Canada
St. Louis Blues (hockey team)
St. Louis Cardinals (baseball team)
St. Louis International Airport, Lambert- (MO)
St. Louis Post-Dispatch (MO newspaper)
St. Louis, MO
Saint-Louis, Senegal
St. Louis, Spirit of (C. Lindbergh plane,
   transatlantic flight)
St. Lucia (island nation)(West Indies)
St. Luke (rel.; 1st c. AD)
St. Maarten, the Netherlands Antilles
St. Malachy (Irish rel.; 1095-1148)
St. Marcellin (cheese)
Sainte-Marie, Buffy (Beverly)(ent.; 1941-)
St. Mark (b. John Mark)(rel.; 1st c. AD)
St. Mark's Basilica (Venice, It.)
St. Mark's fly (insect)
St. Martin (Fr. rel.; c316-401)
St. Martin (island, Leeward Islands, West Indies)
St. Martin's Press, Inc.
St. Mary-le-Bow Church (also Bow Church)
   (London)

St. Mary's Honor Center v. Hicks (US law; 1993)
St. Matthew (aka Levi)(a tax collector)
St. Matthew (rel.; 1st c. AD)
St. Matthias (chosen to replace Judas Iscariot)
Ste. Michelle Vintners, Chateau (US bus.)
St. Moritz Chocolatier (US bus.)
St. Moritz, Switzerland
St. Nicholas (also Santa Claus, Kriss Kringle)
St. Nicholas I (Nicholas the Great)(pope; 800?-
   67)
St. Patrick (Ir. rel.; 389?-461?)
St. Patrick's Cathedral (NYC)
St. Patrick's Day (3/17)
St. Paul (rel.; c3-c67)
St. Paul International Airport, Minneapolis- (MN)
St. Paul Pioneer Press (MN newspaper)
St. Paul, MN
St. Peter (also Simon Peter)(rel.; ?-AD c64)
St. Peter Damian (It. rel.; 1007-72)
St. Peter's Church (also St. Peter's Basilica)
   (Rome)
St. Petersburg Times (FL newspaper)
St. Petersburg, FL
St. Petersburg, Russia (formerly Leningrad)
St. Pierre and Miquelon (Fr. islands,
   Newfoundland)
St. Polycarp (Turk. rel.; 69?-155?)
St. Regis-Sheraton Hotel (NYC)
Saint-Saëns, (Charles) Camille (Fr. comp.;
   1835-1921)
St. Sebastian (Roman rel.; 3rd c.)
St. Siena, Catherine of (It. mystic; 1347-80)
Saint-Simon, Claude (Henri de Rouvoy), Comte
   de (Fr. phil.; 1760-1825)
Saint-Simon, Louis de Rouvroy, Duc de (Fr.
   mil./writer; 1675-1755)
Saint (or Santa) Sophia (also Hagia Sophia)
   (museum, Istanbul)
St. Stephen (1st Christian martyr; ?-AD 36?)
St. Teresa (of Ávila)(Sp. mystic; 1515-82)
St. Thérèse of Lisieux (Fr. rel.; 1873-97)
St. Thomas (US Virgin Island)
St. Thomas à Becket (Br. rel./pol.; 1118-70)
St. Thomas Aquinas ("the Angelic Doctor")(It.
   phil./rel.; 1225-74)
St. Thomas, Ontario, Canada
Saint-Tropez, France
St. Valentine (Roman rel.; ?-c270)
St. Valentine's Day (2/14)
St. Valentine's Day Massacre (US hist.; 1929)
St. Vincent and the Grenadines (island nation)
   (West Indies)
St. Vincent de Paul (Fr. rel.; 1576-1660)
St. Vincent Millay, Edna (US poet; 1892-1950)
St. Vitus (It. rel.; 3rd c.)
St. Vitus'(s) dance (nervous disorder)
St. Wenceslas (also "King Wenceslaus")(duke,
   Bohemia; 907-929)
Saint, Eva Marie (ent.; 1924-)
Saints, New Orleans (football team)
Saipan (island, Mariana Islands)
Saitoti, George (Kenya pol.)
Sajak, Pat (ent.; 1947-)
Sakharov, Andrei Dmitrievich (Rus. physt.;
   1921-89)

Saki (aka H[ector] H[ugh] Munro)(Br. writer; 1870-1916)
Sakigake (Jap. uncrewed space probe)
Sakrete (cement)
Sakrete, Inc.
Saks Fifth Avenue (US bus.)
Saks, Gene (ent.; 1921-)
Sakti (rel.)
Sal Mineo (ent.; 1939-76)
Salacia (myth.)
Salahuddin Abdul Aziz Shah, Sultan (paramount ruler, Malaysia; 1926-)
Salalah, Oman
Salamanca, Spain
Salamis (island, Gr.)
Salazar, Alberto (track; 1958-)
Salazar, Antonio de O(liveira)(ex-PM, Port.; 1899-1970)
Sale of the Century (TV show)
Sale v. Haitian Centers Council (US law; 1993)
Saleh, Ali Abdullah (pres., Yemen; 1942-)
Saleh, J. M. (gov., Netherlands Antilles)
Salem witchcraft trials (MA; 1692)
Salem, India
Salem, MA, OR, NH, VA, OH
Salerno, Anthony "Fat Tony" (US Mafia; 1912-92)
Salerno, Italy
Sales, Soupy (b. Milton Supman)(ent.; 1926-)
Sali Berisha (ex-pres., Albania; 1944-)
Salic law (excludes inheritances to females; from 6th c.)
Salieri, Antonio (It. comp./cond.; 1750-1825)
Salim al-Hoss (PM, Lebanon; 1929-)
Salim al-Sabah, Sheik Saad al-Abdullah al- (PM, Kuwait)
Salina, KS
Salinan (Native Amer.)
Salinas, CA
Salinger, J(erome) D(avid)(US writer; 1919-)
Salinger, Pierre (US TV jour./JFK press secy.; 1925-)
Salisbury Cathedral
Salisbury Plain, England (Stonehenge)
Salisbury steak
Salisbury, England
Salisbury, Harrison E. (US jour.; 1908-93)
Salisbury, MD, NC
Salish (also Flathead)(Native Amer.)
Salk vaccine (polio)
Salk, Jonas (Edward)(US phys./biol.; 1914-95)
Salk, Lee (US psych.; 1927-92)
Sallah (film, 1963)
Salle, (René) Robert Cavelier La (aka Sieur de La Salle)(Fr. expl.; 1643-87)
Sallie Mae (also Student Loan Marketing Association, SLMA)
Sallust (Gaius Sallustius Crispus)(Roman hist.; 86-34 BC)
Sally Field (ent.; 1946-)
Sally Hansen (US bus./cosmetics)
Sally Jessy Raphael (b. Sally Lowenthal)(TV host; 1943-)
Sally K(irsten) Ride (astro.; 1952-)
Sally Kellerman (ent.; 1937-)
Sally Lunn teacake

Sally Struthers (ent.; 1948-)
Sally, When Harry Met (film, 1989)
Salma Hayek (ent.; 1966-)
Salman Rushdie, (Ahmed)(Br. writer; 1947-)
Salmon P. Chase (US jurist; 1808-73)
Salmonella (bacteria)
Salome (danced for the head of John the Baptist; 1st c. AD)
Salomon Rothschild (Ger./Aus. finan.; 1774-1855)
Salomon Smith Barney Inc.
Salomon van Ruysdael (Dutch artist; c1600-70)
Salomon, Haym (Am. Revolution finan.; 1740-85)
Salon Selectives (hair care)
Salonen, Esa-Pekka (Fin. comp.; 1958-)
Saloth Sar (also Pol Pot)(Cambodian pol.; 1925-98)
Sal-Rei, Cape Verde
SALT (Strategic Arms Limitation Talks)(US/ USSR; 1969-89)
Salt Lake City Tribune (UT newspaper)
Salt Lake City, UT
Salt River (AZ)
Salt River Bay National Historical Park (VI)
Salten, Felix (b. Siegmund Salzman)(Aus. writer; 1869-1945)
Salto, Uruguay
Salton Sea (CA lake)
Salton, Inc.
Saluron (med.)
Salvador Dali (Sp. artist; 1904-89)
Salvador, Brazil (formerly Sao Salvador)
Salvador, El (Republic of)(CAmer.)
Salvador, San, Bahamas (also Watling Island) (1st Columbus landing?)
Salvador, San, El Salvador
Salvation Army (rel./charitable org.; est. 1865)
Salvatore Quasimodo (It. poet; 1901-68)
Salvatore Tonelli (captain-regent, San Marino)
Salween River (SE Asia)
Salyut (USSR crewed space flights)
Salzburg, Austria
Sam and Dave (pop music)
Sam Brownback (US cong.; 1956-)
Sam Browne belt (mil. sword belt)
San, Kang Song (ex-PM, NKorea)
Sam Cooke (ent.; 1935-64)
Sam Donaldson (US TV jour.; 1934-)
Sam Elliot (ent.; 1944-)
Sam Ervin, Jr. (US pol.; 1896-1985)
Sam "Momo" Giancana (US gangster; 1908-75)
Sam "Lightnin'" Hopkins (US jazz; 1912-82)
Sam(uel) Houston (US gen./pol.; 1793-1863)
Sam Houston State University (Huntsville, TX)
Sam (Robert Lee) Huff (football; 1934-)
Sam Jaffe (ent.; 1891-1984)
Sam Levene (ent.; 1905-80)
Sam Levenson (US humorist; 1911-80)
Sam Neill (b. Nigel Neill)(ent.; 1947-)
Sam Nujoma (pres., Namibia; 1929-)
Sam(uel Augustus) Nunn (US pol.; 1938-)
Sam Peckinpah (ent.; 1925-85)
Sam(uel Taliaferro) Rayburn (US pol.; 1882-1961)
Sam Shepard (b. Sam Rogers)(US writer/ent.; 1943-)

Sam Slick (aka Thomas Chandler Haliburton) (Can. writer/judge/hist.; 1796-1865)
Sam(uel Jackson) "Slamming Sammy" Snead (golf; 1912-)
Sam Spade (fict. detective, D. Hammett)
Sam Spiegel (ent.; 1903-85)
Sam S. Shubert (US theater; 1876-1905)
Sam (Moore) Walton (US bus., Wal-Mart; 1918-92)
Sam Wanamaker (ent.; 1919-93)
Sam Waterston (ent.; 1940-)
Sam, Kim Young (ex-pres., SKorea; 1927-)
Sam, Uncle (nickname, US govt.)
Sama-Veda (rel.)
Samantha Eggar (ent.; 1939-)
Samantha Fox (ent.; 1966-)
Samao National Park (Amer. Samoa)
Samara, Russia (formerly Kuybyshev)
Samaras, Lucas (US sculptor; 1936-)
Samaria (region, ancient Isr.)
Samaritan (ancient people)
Samarkand, Uzbekistan
Samarra, Great Mosque of
Samarra, Iraq
Samarrai, Ahmadal- (ex-PM, Iraq)
Sambora, Richie (ent.; 1959-)
Same Time, Next Year (play; film, 1978)
Sammo Hung (b. Samo Hung Kam-Bo)(ent.; 1952-)
Samms, Emma (ent.; 1960-)
Sammy (Samuel Adrian) Baugh (football; 1914-)
Sammy Cahn (b. Samuel Cohen)(US lyricist; 1913-93)
Sammy Davis, Jr. (ent.; 1925-90)
Sammy Fain (US comp.; 1902-89)
Sammy Kaye (US band leader; 1910-87)
Sammy Sosa (baseball; 1968-)
Samoa (Independent State of Western)(SW Pac.)
Samoa (volcanic islands, SW Pac.)
Samoa Standard Time
Samoa, American (SW Pac.)
Samoan (lang./people)
Samora Machel (ex-pres., Mozambique; 1933-86)
Samoyed (dog)(also l.c.)
Samoyed (lang./people)
Samoyedic (lang.)
Sampaio, Jorge (pres., Port.; 1939-)
Sampras, Pete (tennis; 1971-)
Samson (Isr. hero; 11th c. BC)
Samson & Delilah (rel.)
Samson Agonistes (by J. Milton)
Samsonite Corp.
Samsonov, Aleksandr (Rus. mil.; 1859-1914)
Samsung Electronics America, Inc.
Samuel (Finley Breese) Morse (US inv., telegraph; 1791-1872)
Samuel Adams (US patriot; 1722-03)
Samuel Barber (US comp.; 1910-81)
Samuel Beckett (Ir. writer; 1906-89)
Samuel (Richard) "Sandy" Berger (US ex-nat'l security advisor; 1945-)
Samuel Butler (Br. writer; 1835-1902)
Samuel Coleridge-Taylor (Br. comp.; 1875-1912)
Samuel Colt (US gunsmith; 1814-62)
Samuel Cunard (Can., trans-Atl. navigation; 1787-1865)
Samuel de Champlain (Fr. expl.; c1567-1635)
Samuel Eliot Morison (US hist.; 1887-1976)
Samuel Francis du Pont (US mil.; 1803-65)
Samuel Goldwyn (b. Samuel Goldfish)(ent.; 1882-1974)
Samuel Gompers (US labor leader; 1850-1924)
Samuel H. Kress (US bus.; 1863-1955)
Samuel H. Sheppard (US phys.; 1924-70)
Samuel Hinds (PM, Guyana; 1943-)
Samuel I(rving) Newhouse, Jr. (US publ.; 1895-1979)
Samuel Johnson ("Dr. Johnson")(Br. lexicographer/writer; 1709-84)
Samuel Johnson (US educ.; 1696-1772)
Samuel Langhorne Clemens (pseud. Mark Twain)(US writer; 1835-1910)
Samuel L(ewis) Warner (ent.; 1887-1927)
Samuel L. Jackson (ent.; 1948-)
Samuel Pepys (Br. writer; 1633-1703)
Samuel Pickwick (fict. chara., *Pickwick Papers*)
Samuel Ramey (ent.; 1942-)
Samuel Richardson (Br. writer; 1689-1761)
Samuel Sewall (US judge, witch trials; 1652-1730)
Samuel Taylor Coleridge (Br. poet; 1772-1834)
Samuel W. Yorty (ex-mayor, Los Angeles; 1909-98)
Samuel, I&II (rel., books of the Old Testament)
Samuelson, Joan Benoit (Olympic marathon; 1957-)
Samuelson, Paul A(nthony)(US econ.; 1915-)
Samurai, Suzuki (auto.)
San Andreas fault (CA)
San Angelo, TX
San Antonio Express News (TX newspaper)
San Antonio Light (TX newspaper)
San Antonio Metropolitan Transit Authority, Garcia v. (US law; 1985)
San Antonio Missions National Historical Park (TX)
San Antonio Spurs (basketball team)
San Antonio, TX
San Bernardino Sun (CA newspaper)
San Bernardino, CA
San Bruno, CA
San Clemente, CA
San Cristóbal, Venezuela
San Diego Chargers (football team)
San Diego Padres (baseball team)
San Diego Union-Tribune (CA newspaper)
San Diego, CA
S and L (also S&L)(savings and loan)
San Fernando Valley (CA)
San Fernando, Trinidad
San Francisco 49ers (football team)
San Francisco bomb (slang, cocaine/heroin/LSD)
San Francisco Chronicle (CA newspaper)
San Francisco Examiner
San Francisco Examiner (CA newspaper)
San Francisco Giants (baseball team)
San Francisco International Airport (CA)
San Francisco Maritime National Historical Park (CA)
San Francisco, CA
San Francisco, Presidio of (US mil.)

San Gabriel, CA
San Giacomo, Laura (ent.; 1962-)
San Jacinto River (TX)
San Joaquin River (CA)
San Joaquin Valley
San Jose Mercury-News (CA newspaper)
San Jose Sharks (hockey team)
San Jose, CA
San José, Costa Rica
San Juan Capistrano, CA (swallows return
    annually: March 19)
San Juan Hill, Cuba (captured by US forces,
    Spanish-American War)
San Juan Island National Historical Park (WA)
San Juan, Argentina
San Juan, Puerto Rico
San Leandro, CA
San Luis Obispo, CA
San Luis Potosi, Mexico
San Luis Rey, The Bridge of (film, 1944)
San Marino (Republic of)(It.)
San Marino, CA
San Marino, San Marino
San Mateo, CA
San Miguel, El Salvador
San Miguelite, Panama
San Miquel de Tucuman, Argentina
San-Pédro, Ivory Coast
San Pedro de Macorís, Dominican Republic
San Pedro Sula, Honduras
San Quentin Prison (CA)
San Rafael, CA
San Remo, Italy
San Salvador, Bahamas (also Watling Island)
San Salvador, El Salvador
San Sebastian, Spain
Sana, Yemen (also Sana'a)
Sancerre (wine)
Sanchez, Oscar Arias (ex-pres., Costa Rica;
    1941-)
Sancho Panza (fict. chara., *Don Quixote*)
Sanctus (also *Tersanctus*)(rel.)
Sanctus bell (rung during Mass)
Sand, George (aka Amandine Aurore Lucie
    Dupin)(Fr. writer; 1804-76)
Sandberg, Ryne (baseball; 1959-)
Sandburg, Carl (August)(US poet; 1878-1967)
Sander Vanocur (TV jour.; 1928-)
Sanders Show, The Larry (TV show)
Sanders, Barry (football; 1968-)
Sanders, Colonel (Harland)(US bus./chicken;
    1890-1980)
Sanders, Deion (baseball, football; 1967-)
Sanders, George (ent.; 1906-72)
Sanders, Lawrence (US writer; 1920-98)
Sanders, Summer (swimmer; 1972-)
Sanders, Wesberry v. (US law; 1964)
Sanderson, William (ent.; 1948-)
Sandi Patty (ent.; 1957-)
Sandiego, Carmen (TV show)
Sandiford, Erskine Lloyd (ex-PM, Barbados;
    1937-)
Sandinista (member, Sandinist National
    Liberation Front, Nicaragua)
Sandino, Augusto César (Nicaraguan mil.;

1893-1934)
Sandler, Adam (ent.; 1966-)
S&P (Standard & Poors)
Sandra Bernhard (ent.; 1955-)
Sandra Boynton (US writer)
Sandra Bullock (ent.; 1964-)
Sandra Day O'Connor (US jurist; 1930-)
Sandra Dee (b. Alexandra Zuck)(ent.; 1942-)
Sandra Haynie (golf; 1943-)
Sandrich, Jay (ent.; 1932-)
Sandro Botticelli (It. artist; 1444-1510)
Sands of Iwo Jima (film, 1949)
Sands, Tommy (ent.; 1937-)
Sandusky, OH
S & W Fine Foods, Inc.
Sandwich Islands (now Hawaii)
Sandwich, Earl of (John Montagu)(Br. pol.;
    1718-92)
Sandy (Samuel Richard) Berger (US ex-nat'l
    security advisor; 1945-)
Sandy Dennis (ent.; 1937-92)
Sandy Duncan (ent.; 1946-)
Sandy (Sanford) Koufax (baseball; 1935-)
Sandy, Gary (ent.; 1945-)
Sandy, UT
Sanford and Son (TV show)
Sanford B. Dole (ex-gov., HI; 1844-1921)
Sanford, Isabel (ent.; 1917-)
Sanforized (fabric treatment)
Sanger, Frederick (Br. biochem.; 1918-)
Sanger, Margaret (Higgins)(US reformer; 1883-
    1966)
Sangha (rel.)
Sangheli, Andrei (ex-PM, Moldova)
Sangho (lang.)
Sangre de Cristo Mountains (NM/CO)
Sanhedrin (Jew. hist./govt.)
Sani Abacha (ex-ruler, Nigeria; 1943-1998)
Sanibel Island, FL
Sanitas Wallcoverings (US bus.)
Sanka (coffee)
Sankhya yoga (rel.)
Sanmarinese (people)
Sansert (med.)
Sanskrit (lang.)
Sansom, Art (cartoonist, *The Born Loser*; 1920-
    91)
Sansovino, Andrea (It. sculptor; 1460-1529)
Sansovino, Jacopo (It. sculptor; 1486-1570)
Sansui Electronics Corp.
Santa (or Saint) Sophia (also Hagia
    Sophia)(museum, Istanbul)
Santa Ana winds (also Santa Anas)
Santa Ana, CA
Santa Ana, El Salvador
Santa Anita Derby
Santa Anita Park
Santa Anna, Antonio (López) de (ex-pres./gen.,
    Mex.; 1795?-1876)
Santa Barbara Islands (CA)
Santa Barbara, CA
Santa Catalina, CA (also Catalina Island)
Santa Clara, CA
Santa Clara, Cuba
Santa Clarita, CA

Santa Claus (also St. Nicholas, Kriss Kringle)
Santa Cruz, Bolivia
Santa Cruz, CA
Santa Fe Opera (NM)
Santa Fe Pacific Corp.
Santa Fe Springs, CA (oil wells)
Santa Fe Trail (trade route, MO/NM; c1820-1880)
Santa Fe, Argentina
Santa Fe, Hyundai (auto.)
Santa Fe, NM
Santa Gertrudis (cattle)
Santa Maria, Brazil
Santa Maria, CA
Santa Marta, Colombia
Santa Monica, CA
Santa Rosa Press-Democrat (CA newspaper)
Santa Rosa, Argentina
Santa Rosa, CA
Santali (lang.)
Santana (Martinez), Manuel (tennis; 1938-)
Santana (pop music)
Santana, Carlos (ent.; 1947-)
Santander, Spain
Sant'Angelo, Giorgio di (designer)
Santayana, George (Sp./US writer/phil.; 1863-1952)
Santee River (SC)
Sant'Elia, Antonio (It. arch.; 1888-1916)
Santer, Jacques (ex-PM, Luxembourg; 1937-)
Santeria (rel.)
Santha Rama Rau (Indian writer/astrol.; 1923-)
Santiago de Cuba, Cuba
Santiago de los Caballeros, Dominican Republic
Santiago, Chile
Santiago, Panama
Santini, The Great (film, 1980)
Santo Domingo, Dominican Republic
Santorum, Rick (US cong.; 1958-)
Santos, Brazil
Santos, José Eduardo dos (pres., Angola; 1942-)
Santos-Dumont, Alberto (Fr. aviator; 1873-1932)
Sanwa Bank, Ltd.
Sanyo Electric Co., Inc.
Sanyo Fisher USA Corp.
São Domingos, Guinea-Bissau
São Paulo, Brazil
São Tomé and Príncipe (Democratic Republic of)(off W Afr. coast)
São Tomé, São Tomé and Príncipe
Saparmurad A. Niyazov (pres., Turkmenistan; 1940-)
Sapir-Whorf hypothesis (linguistics)
Sapir, Edward (Ger./US anthrop.; 1884-1939)
Sappho (Gr. poet; c612-c580 BC)
Sapporo Breweries, Ltd.
Sapporo, Japan
Sar, Saloth (also Pol Pot)(Cambodian pol.; 1925-98)
Sara (people)
Sara Lee (desserts)
Sara Lee Corp.
Sara Polley (ent.; 1979-)
Sara Teasdale (US poet; 1884-1933)
Saracen (people)
Saragossa, Spain (also Zaragoza)

Sarah (or Sara)(rel.)
Sarah Bernhardt (ent.; 1844-1923)
Sarah Brady (US gun control advocate/Brady Bill; 1942-)
Sarah Caldwell (ent.; 1924-)
Sarah Churchill (Br., duchess of Marlboro; 1660-1744)
Sarah G. Blanding (US educ.; 1899-1985)
Sarah Jessica Parker (ent.; 1965-)
Sarah Lawrence College (Bronxville, NY)
Sarah Margaret "Fergie" Ferguson (Br., Duchess of York; 1959-)
Sarah McClendon (US jour.; 1910-)
Sarah McLachlan (ent.; 1968-)
Sarah Michelle Gellar (ent./model; 1977-)
Sarah Miles (ent.; 1941-)
Sarah (Kemble) Siddons (ent.; 1755-1831)
Sarah (Lois) Vaughan (US jazz; 1924-90)
Sarah, Plain and Tall (film, 1991)
Sarajevo, Bosnia-Hercegovina
Sarakole (people)
Saran Wrap
Saranac Lake, NY
Sarandon, Chris (ent.; 1942-)
Sarandon, Susan (b. Susan Abigail Tomaling) (ent.; 1946-)
Sarasota Herald-Tribune (FL newspaper)
Sarasota, FL
Sarasvati (myth.)
Saratoga National Historical Park (NY)
Saratoga Springs, NY
Saratoga Trunk (E. Ferber novel)
Saratoga trunk (luggage; 19th c.)
Saratoga, Battles of (US hist.; 1777)
Saratoga, CA
Saratov, Russia
Sarawak (state, Malaysia)
Sarazen, Gene (golf; 1902-99)
Sarbanes, Paul S(pyros)(US cong.; 1933-)
Sardi's restaurant
Sardinia (island, It.)
Sarelon (textile)
Sargasso Sea (N Atl.)
Sargent Shriver, (Robert), Jr. (US bus./pol.; 1915-)
Sargent, Dick (ent.; 1933-94)
Sargent, John Singer (US artist; 1856-1925)
Sargento (cheese)
Sarh, Chad
Sarkis, Elias (ex-pres., Lebanon)
Sarnath (archeol. site, India)
Sarnoff, David (US broadcasting pioneer, NBC; 1891-1971)
Sarnoff, Dorothy (ent.; 1917-)
Saroyan, William (US writer; 1908-81)
Sarrazin, Michael (ent.; 1940-)
Sarto, Andrea del (It. artist; 1486-1530)
Sartre, Jean-Paul (Fr. phil./writer; 1905-80)
SAS (Scandinavian Airlines System)
SASE (self-addressed stamped envelope)
Saskatchewan (province, Can.)
Saskatoon, Saskatchewan, Canada
Sasquatch (also Big Foot or Bigfoot)
Sasser, Jim (James Ralph)(US pol.; 1936-)
Sassoon & Co., Beverly

Sassoon, Beverly (Adams)(US bus.)
Sassoon, Inc., Vidal
Sassoon, Vidal (hair care)
Sassoon, Vidal (US bus.; 1928-)
Sassou-Nguesso, Denis (pres., Rep./Congo; 1943-)
Sassy (mag.)
SAT (Scholastic Aptitude Test, College Boards)
Satan (the devil)
Satanic Verses, The (S. Rushdie novel)
Satanism (devil worship)
Satchel (Leroy Robert) Paige (baseball; 1906-82)
Satcitananda (rel.)
Satellite TV Week (mag.)
Satie, Erik (Alfred Leslie)(Fr. comp.; 1866-1925)
Sato, Eisaku (ex-PM, Jap.; 1901-75)
Satsuma vase/pottery
Satsuma, Japan
Sattui Winery, V. (US bus.)
Saturday Evening Post, The (mag.)
Saturday Night Fever (film, 1977)
Saturday Night Live (TV show)
Saturday-night special (cheap handgun)
Saturn (auto.)
Saturn (planet; myth.)
Saturn Corporation
Saturn L-series (auto.)
Saturn LS (auto.)
Saturn LS1 (auto.)
Saturn LS2 (auto.)
Saturn LW (auto.)
Saturn LW1 (auto.)
Saturn LW2 (auto.)
Saturn rocket (US space program)
Saturn S-series (auto.)
Saturn SC (auto.)
Saturn SC1 (auto.)
Saturn SC2 (auto.)
Saturn SL (auto.)
Saturn SL1 (auto.)
Saturn SL2 (auto.)
Saturn SUV (auto.)
Saturn SW (auto.)
Saturn SW1 (auto.)
Saturn SW2 (auto.)
Saturn, Apollo- (US crewed space flights)
Saturn's rings (astron.)
Satyagraha (passive resistance)
Satyajit Ray (ent.; 1921-92)
Satyendranath Bose (Indian physt./chem./ math.; 1894-1974)
Sau-Sea Foods, Inc.
Saud (king, Saudi Arabia; 1902-69)
Saud, Ibn (also Abdul-Azaz Ibn-Saud)(king, Saudi Arabia; 1880-1953)
Saudi Arabia (Kingdom of)(SW Asia)
Sauk and Fox (also Sac)(Native Amer.)
Saul (king, Isr.; fl. 11th c BC)
Saul Baizerman (US/Rus. sculptor; 1899-1957)
Saul Bellow (US writer; 1915-)
Saul Steinberg (US artist; 1914-99)
Sault Ste. Marie Canals (also Soo Locks)(MI; Ontario, Can.)
Sault Ste. Marie, MI
Sault Ste. Marie, Ontario, Canada

Saunders Co., W. B.
Sausalito, CA
Saussure, Ferdinand de (Swiss linguist; 1857-1913)
Sauterne (wine)(also l.c.)
Sauvignon (grape)
Sauvignon Blanc (grape, wine)
Savage, Fred (ent.; 1976-)
Savage's Station (Civil War battle, VA)
Savalas, Telly (ent.; 1924-94)
Savana, GMC (auto.)
Savannah (clothing)
Savannah News (GA newspaper)
Savannah Press (GA newspaper)
Savannah, GA
Savannakhet, Laos
Savile Row cut (clothing)
Savimbi, Jonas (Angolan mil.; 1934-)
Savin copier
Savin Corp.
Saving Private Ryan (film, 1998)
Savion Glover (dancer/choreographer; 1973-)
Savior (Jesus Christ)
Savitch, Jessica (Beth)(US TV jour.; 1947-83)
Savonarola (or Dante) chair
Savonarola, Girolamo (It. rel./reformer; 1452-98)
Savonnerie (carpet)
Sav-On-Drugs, Inc.
Savoy (area, Fr.)
Savoy cabbage
Sawyer, Amos (ex-pres., Liberia; 1945-)
Sawyer, Diane (US TV jour.; 1945-)
Sawyer, The Adventures of Tom (M. Twain novel)
Sawyer, Tom (fict. Mark Twain chara.)
Sawyer, Youngstown Sheet and Tube Co. v. (US law; 1952)
Sawzall (constr.)
Sax Rohmer (aka Arthur Sarsfield Ward)(Br. writer; 1886-1959)
Saxe-Coburg-Gotha, House of (Br. ruling family; 1901-10)
Saxon (people)
Saxon, John (ent.; 1935-)
Saxony (state, Ger.)
Say's law (econ.)
Sayer, Leo (Gerard)(ent./songwriter; 1948-)
Sayers, Dorothy L(eigh)(Br. writer; 1893-1957)
Sayers, Gale (football; 1943-)
Sayles, John (ent.; 1950-)
Sayonara (film, 1957)
Sayyed Ali Khamenei, Ayatollah (rel. head, Iran; 1940-)
Sb (chem. sym., antimony)
SBA (Small Business Administration)
SBC Communications, Inc.
S-Blazer, Chevrolet (auto.)
SC (Security Council [UN], South Carolina)
Sc (chem. sym., scandium)
Scaggs, Boz (William Royce)(ent.; 1944-)
Scala, La (opera house, It.)
Scalfaro, Oscar Luigi (ex-pres., It.; 1918-)
Scalia, Antonin (US jurist; 1936-)
Scandinavian (lang./people)
Scandinavian (peninsula, NW Eur.)
Scandinavian Airlines System (SAS)

Scaramouche (fict. chara.)
Scaramouche (R. Sabatini novel)
Scarborough Fair (song)
Scarborough, Chuck (Charles)
Scarborough, England
Scarborough, ME
Scarborough, Ontario, Canada
Scarborough, Tobago
Scarlatti, (Pietro) Alessandro (Gaspare)(It. comp.; 1660-1725)
Scarlatti, (Giuseppe) Domenico (It. comp.; 1685-1757)
Scarlet Letter, The (Nathaniel Hawthorne novel)
Scarlet Pimpernel, The (film, 1934, 1982)
Scarlet, Will (fict. chara., *Robin Hood*)
Scarlett O'Hara (fict. chara., *Gone With the Wind*)
Scarsdale Diet (created by Herman Tarnower)
Scarsdale, NY
SCAT (cat system)
Scatman Crothers (ent.; 1910-86)
Scavullo, Francesco (photo.; 1929-)
Schaan, Liechtenstein
Schaap, Dick (TV sports jour.)
Schaefer, George (ent.; 1920-)
Schaefer, Jack (US writer; 1908-91)
Schaefer, William Donald (ex-MD gov.; 1921-)
Schafer, Edward T. (ex-ND gov.; 1946-)
Schallert, William (ent.; 1922-)
Schama, Simon (hist.; 1945-)
Schapiro, Meyer (US art hist.; 1904-96)
Schary, Dore (US writer/ent./reformer; 1905-80)
Schechter v. U.S. (US law; 1935)
Scheduled Castes (also Harijans, formerly Untouchables)(India)
Scheherazade (fict. chara., *Arabian Nights*)
Scheherazade (Rimski-Korsakov symphony)
Scheib, Inc., Earl (auto painting)
Scheidemann, Philipp (ex-chanc., Ger.; 1865-1939)
Scheider, Roy (ent.; 1932-)
Schell, Maria (ent.; 1926-)
Schell, Maximilian (ent.; 1930-)
Schelling, Friedrich Wilhelm Joseph von (Ger. phil.; 1775-1854)
Schempp, Abington Township v. (US law; 1963-)
Schenck v. U.S. (US law; 1919)
Schenectady, NY
Schenkel, Chris (ent.; 1923-)
Schering-Plough Corp.
Schering-Plough Healthcare Products (US bus.)
Schiaparelli, Elsa (Fr. designer; 1890-1973)
Schiaparelli, Giovanni (Virginio)(It. astron.; 1835-1910)
Schick (razors)
Schick test (diphtheria immunity test)
Schick USA, Inc.
Schickele, Peter (aka P. D. Q. Bach)(ent.; 1935-)
Schiele, Egon (Aus. artist; 1890-1918)
Schiff('s) reagent (aldehyde test)
Schiff, Dorothy (US publ.; 1903-89)
Schiffer, Claudia (model; 1970-)
Schildkraut, Joseph (ent.; 1895-1964)
Schiller, (Johann Christoph) Friedrich von (Ger. writer/hist.; 1759-1805)

Schindler's List (film, 1993)
Schipa, Tito (tenor; 1890-1965)
Schippers, Thomas (US cond.; 1930-77)
Schirra, Wally (Walter Marty), Jr. (US astro.; 1923-)
Schism of the West (also the Great Schism)(rel.)
Schlafly, Phyllis (Stewart)(US activist; 1924-)
Schlatter, George (ent.)
Schlegel, August Wilhelm von (Ger. writer; 1767-1845)
Schlegel, Friedrich von (Ger. phil./writer; 1772-1829)
Schleiermacher, Friedrich (Ernst Daniel)(Ger. rel.; 1768-1834)
Schlemmer & Co., Inc., Hammacher,
Schlesinger, Arthur M(eier), Jr. (US hist.; 1917-)
Schlesinger, Arthur M(eier)(US hist.; 1888-1965)
Schlessinger, Dr. Laura (radio talk show host; 1947-)
Schleswig-Holstein (state, Ger.)
Schliemann, Heinrich (Ger. archaeol.; 1822-90)
Schlossberg, Caroline Kennedy (US atty., daughter of JFK; 1957-)
Schlumberger, Ltd.
Schlüter, Poul (Dan. pol.; 1929-)
Schmeling, Max (Ger. boxing; 1905-)
Schmid Laboratories (US bus.)
Schmidt telescope/reflector (astron.)
Schmidt, Helmut (Heinrich Waldemar)(ex-chanc., WGer.; 1918-)
Schmidt, Mike (baseball; 1949-)
Schmitt, Jack (Harrison Hahen)(US pol./astro.; 1935-)
Schnabel, Artur (pianist/comp.; 1882-1951)
Schneider, John (ent.; 1954-)
Schneider, Maria (ent.; 1952-)
Schneider, Romy (b. Rose-Marie Albach-Retty)(ent.; 1938-82)
Schneiderman, Rose (US labor leader; 1884-1972)
Schoenberg, Arnold (Franz Walter)(Aus. comp.; 1874-1951)
Schofield Barracks (HI)(US mil.)
Schofield, John McAllister (US mil.; 1831-1906)
Scholastic Aptitude Test (SAT, College Boards)
Scholl's, Dr. (footware/care)
Schollander, Donald (swimming; 1946-)
Schomberg, Arthur (bibliophile, black lit./hist.; 1874-1938)
School District of Abington Township v. Schempp (US law; 1963)
School of Athens (by Raphael)
School/school of Paris (art)
Schopenhauer, Arthur (Ger. phil.; 1788-1860)
Schorr, Daniel (US jour.; 1916-)
Schramsberg Vineyards Co.
Schreiber, Avery (ent.; 1935-)
Schreiner, Olive (pseud. Ralph Iron)(SAfr. writer; 1855-1920)
Schroder, Rick (ent.; 1970-)
Schröder, Gerhard (chanc., Ger.; 1944-)
Schrödinger, Erwin (Aus. physt.; 1887-1961)
Schrödinger's cat
Schroeder, Patricia (Scott)(US pol.; 1940-)

Schubert, Franz (Peter)(Aus. comp.; 1797-1828)
Schulberg, Budd (Wilson)(US writer; 1914-)
Schuller, Robert (US rel.; 1926-)
Schulman, A. (rubber/plastic products co.)
Schultz, Theodore W. (US econ.; 1902-98)
Schulz, Charles M(onroe)(cartoonist, *Peanuts*; 1922-2000)
Schumacher, Joel (ent./writer; 1939-)
Schuman, Robert (ex-PM, Fr.; 1886-1963)
Schuman, William (Howard)(US comp.; 1910-92)
Schumann, Clara Josephine (Wieck)(Ger. pianist; 1819-96)
Schumann, Robert (Alexander)(Ger. comp.; 1810-56)
Schumann-Heink, Ernestine (opera; 1861-1936)
Schumer, Charles E. (US cong.; 1950-)
Schumpeter, Joseph (Alois)(US econ.; 1883-1950)
Schurz, Carl (Ger./US pol.; 1829-1906)
Schuschnigg, Kurt von (ex-chanc., Aus.; 1897-1977)
Schüssel, Dr. Wolfgang (chanc., Aus.; 1945-)
Schuster, Inc., Simon &
Schuster, Rudolf (pres.; Slovakia; 1934-)
Schuyler Colfax (ex-US VP; 1823-85)
Schuyler, Philip John (US gen./pol.; 1733-1804)
Schuylkill River (PA)
Schwab Corp., The Charles
Schwab, Charles M(ichael)(US bus.; 1862-1939)
Schwann cell (med.)
Schwann, Theodor (Ger. phys.; 1810-82)
Schwartz, Arthur (US comp.; 1900-84)
Schwarz, FAO (toy store/mail order)
Schwarzenegger, Arnold (ent.; 1947-)
Schwarzkopf, Elisabeth (Ger. opera; 1915-)
Schwarzkopf, H. Norman, Jr. ("Stormin' Norman")(US gen.; 1934-)
Schwarzschild radius (astron., physics)
Schweickart, Rusty (Russell L.)(astro.; 1935-)
Schweitzer, Dr. Albert (Ger. phys./phil./rel.; 1875-1965)
Schwenkfeld von Ossig, Kaspar (Ger. rel.; 1490-1561)
Schwenkfeldians (also Schwenkfelders)(rel.)
Schweppes (mixers)
Schweppes USA, Ltd. (US bus.)
Schwimmer, David (ent.; 1966-)
Schwinger, Julian (Seymour)(US physt.; 1918-94)
Schwinn Bicycle Co.
Schwitters, Kurt (Ger. artist; 1887-1948)
Science and Technology Policy, Office of (US govt.)
Science Applications International Corp.
Science Foundation, National (NSF)(US govt. agcy.; est. 1950)
Science, Doctor of (also Sc.D., Scientiae Doctor)
Sciences, National Academy of (org. 1863)
Scientific American (mag.)
Scientologist (rel.)
Scientology, Church of (rel.)
Sc-Fi Channel (TV channel)
Scilla rock (now Scylla)(rock in Strait of Messina off coast of Italy)
Scilly, Cornwall and Isles of (county, Eng.)

Scissorhands, Edward (film, 1990)
S. C. Johnson & Son, Inc.
SCLC (Southern Christian Leadership Conference)
Scobee, Dick (Francis Richard)(astro., Challenger; 1939-86)
Scofield, Paul (ent.; 1922-)
Scolari, Peter (ent.; 1954-)
Scone, Scotland
Scone, Stone of (Scot. kings' coronation seat)
Scooby Doo (fict. chara.)
Scoop Fresh (cat litter)
Scopas (Gr. sculptor/arch.; fl. 4th c. BC)
Scope (mouthwash)
Scopes Trial (also Monkey Trial)(US, evolution; 1925)
Scopes, John T(homas)(US educ./evolution; 1901-70)
SCORE (Service Corps of Retired Executives)
Scoresby Sound (Greenland)
Scoresby, William (Br. expl.; 1789-1857)
Scorpio (zodiac, scorpion)
Scorpius (astron., scorpion)
Scorsese, Martin (ent.; 1942-)
Scot (or Scott), Jock (fishing)
Scotch and Soda (mixed drink)
Scotch Blackface (sheep)
Scotch broom (plant)
Scotch broth
Scotch collie (dog)
Scotch egg
Scotch Highland (cattle)
Scotch pine (tree)
Scotch tape
Scotch whiskey
Scotchgard (cleaner, protective coating)
Scotland (part of UK)
Scotland Yard, New (Br. police)
Scotland, Church of
Scotsman/Scotswoman
Scott Adams (cartoonist; 1957-)
Scott Baio (ent.; 1961-)
Scott Bakula (ent.; 1954-)
Scott Carpenter, M(alcolm)(astro.; 1925-)
Scott Case/Decision, Dred (US law, pro-slavery; 1856-57)
Scott Glenn (ent.; 1942-)
Scott Hamilton (figure skating; 1958-)
Scott Joplin (US jazz; 1868-1917)
Scott LeFaro (US jazz; 1936-61)
Scott Paper Co.
Scott Turow (US writer; 1949-)
Scott Wolf (ent.; 1968-)
Scott, David R. (astro.; 1932-)
Scott, Dred (US slave; 1795?-1858)
Scott, George C(ampbell)(ent.; 1927-99)
Scott, Lizabeth (b. Emma Matzo)(ent.; 1922-)
Scott, Martha (ent.; 1914-)
Scott, Randolph (ent.; 1898-1987)
Scott, Ridley (ent.; 1937-)
Scott, Robert Falcon (Br. expl.; 1868-1912)
Scott, (Sir) Walter (Scot. writer; 1771-1832)
Scott, Willard (ent./meteor.; 1934-)
Scott, Winfield ("Old Fuss and Feathers")(US gen.; 1786-1866)
Scott, Zachary (ent.; 1914-65)

Scotties (tissues)
Scottish (people)
Scottish deerhound (dog)
Scottish language
Scottish terrier (dog)(also Scotch terrier)
Scotto, Renata (soprano; 1936-)
ScotTowels
Scotts (lawn care)
Scotts turf builder
Scottsboro Case (US law; 1931)
Scottsdale, AZ
Scoupe, Hyundai (auto.)
Scouting (mag.)
Scowcroft, Brent (US pol.; 1925-)
Scrabble (game)
Scranton Times (PA newspaper)
Scranton Tribune (PA newspaper)
Scranton, PA
Scratch (Satan)(also Old Scratch)
Scream, The (by Edvard Munch)
Screen Actors Guild
Scriabin, Alexander (Nikolayevich)(Rus. comp.; 1872-1915)
Scribe, (Augustin) Eugène (Fr. writer; 1791-1861)
Scriblerus Club (Br. lit. group; c1713-14)
Scribner, Charles, Jr. (US publ.)
Scribner, Charles, Sr. (US publ.)
Scribner's Sons, Charles (US bus.)
Scripps Co., E. W.
Scripps College (Claremont, CA)
Scripps Institution of Oceanography (CA)
Scripps, Edward (Wyllis)(US publ.; 1854-1926)
Scripps, James Edmund (US publ.; 1835-1906)
Scripto Tokai Corp.
Scripture(s)(also Holy Scripture[s])(rel.)
Scrooge McDuck (cartoon chara.)
Scrooge, Ebenezer (fict. chara., *A Christmas Carol*)
Scruggs, Earl (ent.; 1924-)
Scud (Soviet missile)
Sculley, John (US bus.; 1939-)
Scully, Vin (ent.; 1927-)
Sculptor (astron., sculptor)
Scutum (astron., shield)
Scylla and Charybdis (myth.)
Scylla rock (now Scilla)(off coast of It.)
Scyros (also Skiros, Skyros)(Gr. island)
Scythia (ancient region, Eur./Asia)
Scythians (ancient people)
SD (South Dakota)
SDI (Strategic Defense Initiative, Star Wars)(US mil.; 1983-)
Se (chem. sym., selenium)
Se Ri Pak (golf; 1977-)
Sea Gull, The (A. Chekhov play)
Sea Islands (off coast of SC/GA/FL)
Sea of Galilee (also Lake Tiberias)(Isr.)
Sea of Japan (Jap./Pac.)
Sea of Marmara (Turk.)
Sea of Okhotsk (N Pac.)
Sea of Tranquility (also Mare Tranquillitatus) (dark plain on Moon)
Sea World
Sea World of Florida

Seabee (also See-Bee)(large, ocean-going vessel)
Seabees (construction battalions of US Navy)
Seaborg, Dr. Glenn T(heodore)(US chem./chair, AEC; 1912-99)
Seagal, Steven (ent.; 1952-)
Seagate Technology, Inc.
Seagram & Sons, Inc., Joseph E.
Seagram Beverage Co., The
Seagram Co., Ltd.
Seagram Distillers Co.
Seagram's (beverages)
Seagren, Bob (Robert Lloyd)(pole vaulter; 1946-)
Seagull, Jonathan Livingston (R. Bach novel)
Seahawk (US Navy helicopter)
Seahawks, Seattle (football team)
Seal (b. Sealhenry Samuel)(ent.; 1963-)
Sealab (Navy habitats for aquanauts)
Seale, Bobby (cofounded Black Panther Party; 1936-)
Sealed Air Corp.
Seal-O-Matic Manufacturing Co.
SEALS (Sea, Air, and Land Soldiers)(US mil.)
Sealtest (dairy prod.)
Sealtest Foods (US bus.)
Sealy (mattress)
Sealy Posturepedic (mattress)
Sealy, Inc.
Sealyham terrier (dog)
Seamus Heaney (Ir. poet; 1939-)
Sean "Puffy" Combs (aka Puff Daddy)(ent.; 1969-)
Sean Connery (ent.; 1930-)
Sean Lennon (ent.; 1975-)
Sean O'Casey (Ir. writer; 1884-1964)
Sean Penn (ent.; 1960-)
Search for Bridey Murphy, The (film, 1956)
Sears Craftsman (tools)
Sears Tower (Chicago)(110 stories)
Sears, Richard W. (US bus.; 1863-1914)
Sears, Roebuck & Co.
Seasat (US space satellite)
Seashore test (music)
Seashore, Carl (US psych.; 1866-1949)
Seaside, CA
SEATO (Southeast Asia Treaty Organization) (1955-76)
Seattle Mariners (baseball team)
Seattle Post-Intelligencer (WA newspaper)
Seattle Seahawks (football team)
Seattle Slew (racehorse)
Seattle SuperSonics (basketball team)
Seattle Times (WA newspaper)
Seattle, Chief (also Seatlh)(Suquamish Native Amer.; c1790-1866)
Seattle, WA
Seaver, Tom (baseball; 1944-)
Sebastian (Newbold) Coe (track; 1956-)
Sebastian Cabot (ent.; 1918-77)
Sebastian Cabot (It. nav./expl.; 1474-1557)
Sebastian, Inc., Paul
Sebastian, John (ent.; 1944-)
Sebastian, (Sir) Cuthbert M. (gov.-gen., St. Kitts-Nevis; 1921-)
Sebastian, St. (Roman rel.; 3rd c.)
Sebastopol (goose)
Sebastopol, Crimea (also Sevastopol)

Seberg, Jean (ent.; 1938-79)
Sebring, Chrysler (auto.)
SEC (Securities and Exchange Commission)(US agcy.; est. 1934)
Secaucus, NJ
Secchi disk(s)(biology)
Secchi, Angelo (It. astron.; 1818-78)
Secession, War of (also American Civil War, War Between the States)(1861-65)
Seconal (med./sedative)
Second Coming (rel.)
Second Reich (Ger. empire; 1871-1918)
Second Temple (rel.)
Second Triumvirate (ancient Rome ruling board)
Second World War (also World War II, WWII)(1939-45)
Secret (anti-perspirant)
Secret Life of Walter Mitty, The (J. Thurber short story)
Secret Service, U.S. (US govt. agcy.; est. 1865)
Secretariat (of the UN)
Secretariat (racehorse)
Section Eight (also l.c.)(US Army discharge for unfitness/undesirable traits)
Sectral (med.)
Securities and Exchange Commission (SEC)(US agcy.; est. 1934)
Security Agency, National (NSA)(US govt.)
Security Council, National (NSC)(US govt. agcy.; est. 1947)
Security Council, United Nations
Sedaka, Neil (ent.; 1939-)
Seder (rel.)
Sedgwick, Kyra (ent.; 1965-)
Sedition Acts, Alien and (US hist.; 1798)
Seduction of Joe Tynan, The (film, 1979)
See-Bee (also Seabee)(large, ocean-going vessel)
See of Rome (also Holy See)(Vatican)
See, Holy (also See of Rome)(Vatican)
See's Candy Shop (US bus.)
Seeger, Pete(r) R. (ent.; 1919-)
Seeing Eye dog
Seenu, Maldives
Segal, Erich (US writer; 1937-)
Segal, George (ent.; 1934-)
Segal, George (US sculptor; 1924-2000)
Segar, Elzie C. (cartoonist, *Popeye*; 1894-1938)
Seger cone (ceramics)
Seger, Bob (ent./songwriter; 1945-)
Ségou, Mali
Segovia, Andrés (Sp. ent.; 1893-1987)
S. E. Hinton (US writer; 1948-)
Seidelman, Susan (ent.; 1952-)
Seidler, Maren (track; 1962-)
Seifert, Jaroslav (Czech. poet; 1902-86)
Seignoret, Clarence (Augustus)(pres., Dominica)
Seiji Ozawa (Jap./US cond.; 1935-)
Seiko Corp. of America
Seiko Epson Corp.
Seiko watch
Seine (river, Fr.)
Seinfeld (TV show)
Seinfeld, Jerry (ent.; 1954-)
Seingalt, Casanova de (also Giovanni Jacopo Casanova)(It. adventurer; 1725-98)

Seirra Leone (republic, W Afr.)
Seko (Kuku Ngbendu wa Zabanga), Mobutu Sese (b. Joseph Désiré Mobutu)(ex-pres., Congo/Zaire; 1930-97)
Sekondi-Takoradi, Ghana
Sela Ward (ent.; 1956-)
Selassie, Haile (Ras [Prince] Tafari, "the Lion of Judah")(emp., Eth.; 1891-1975)
Seldane (med.)
Selective Service Act (US mil.; 1917)
Selena (film, 1996)
Selena (b. Selena Quintanilla Perez)(ent.; 1971-95)
Selene (myth.)
Seles, Monica (tennis; 1973-)
Self (mag.)
Selke, Frank (hockey; 1893-1985)
Selkirk, Alexander (Scot. sailor; 1676-1721)
Sellecca, Connie (b. Concetta Sellecchia)(ent.; 1955-)
Selleck, Tom (ent.; 1945-)
Sellers, Peter (ent.; 1925-80)
Selma Diamond (ent.; 1920-85)
Selma, AL, CA
Selsun Blue (med. shampoo)
Selznick, David O(liver)(ent.; 1902-65)
Semarang, Indonesia
Semilente Iletin (med.)
Seminole (Native Amer.)
Semipalatinsk, Kazakhstan
Semite (people)
Semitic languages
Semyon (Konstantinovich) Timoshenko (USSR mil.; 1895-1970)
Sen, Hun (PM, Cambodia; 1950-)
Senate (of the U.S.)(US govt.)
Senate Finance Committee (US govt.)
Senate Judiciary Committee (US govt.)
Senators, Ottawa (hockey team)
Sendai, Japan
Sendak, Maurice (Bernard)(US writer; 1928-)
Seneca (lang.)
Seneca (Lucius Annaeus Seneca)(Roman phil./ writer; 4 BC-AD 65)
Seneca (Native Amer.)
Seneca Army Depot (NY)(US mil.)
Seneca Falls, NY
Senegal (Republic of)(W Afr.)
Sennett Studios, Mack (old Hollywood)
Sennett, Mack (b. Michael Sinnott)(ent.; 1880-1960)
Senokot (med.)
Senor Wences (b. Wenceslao Moreno) (ventriloquist; ?-1999)
Sensodyne (med.)
Sense & Sensibility (Jane Austen novel)
Sentinel, Milwaukee (WI newspaper)
Sentinel, Orlando (FL newspaper)
Sentra, Nissan (auto.)
Senufo (lang./people)
Seoul, South Korea
Sephardim (Sp./Port. Jews)
Sephia, Kia (auto.)
Sepoy Rebellion/Mutiny (also Indian Mutiny)(India/Br.; 1857-58)

Septra (med.)
Septuagint (rel.)
Sequoia National Park (CA)
Sequoia, Toyota (auto.)
Sequoya, Chief (aka George Guess)(Cherokee
    Native Amer., scholar; c1766-1843)
Serafin, Barry (US TV jour.)
Serax (med.)
Serb (people)
Serbia (republic. Yug.)
Serbian (people)
Serbian Orthodox (rel.)
Serbo-Croatian (aka Serbo-Croat)(lang.)
Serbs (people)
Serekunda, Gambia
Serena Williams (tennis; 1981-)
Serene Highness (title)
Serene Majesty (title)
Serengeti National Park (E Afr.)
Serengeti Plain (E Afr.)
Serenity pads (health)
Serentil (med.)
Serer (lang./people)
Seretse Khama (ex-pres., Botswana; 1921-80)
Serevent (med.)
Serge (Sergei Alexandrovich) Koussevitsky
    (Rus. cond.; 1874-1951)
Sergeant (Alvin Cullum) York (US mil.; 1887-
    1964)
*Sergeant Bilko (*also *Sgt. Bilko*)(TV show)
Sergeant York (film, 1941)
Sergei (Pavlovich) Diaghilev (Rus. ballet; 1872-
    1929)
Sergei Mironovich Kirov (Rus. pol.; 1886-1934)
Sergei (Sergeyevich) Prokofiev (Rus. comp.;
    1891-1953)
Sergei Tereshchenko (ex-PM, Kazakhstan)
Sergei V(asilyevich) Rachmaninov (Rus. comp./
    cond.; 1893-1943)
Sergio Franchi (ent.; 1933-90)
Sergio Mendes (ent.; 1941-)
Seria, Brunei
Series E bond (US Treasury)
Series H bond (US Treasury)
Series I bond (US Treasury)
Serkin, Peter (US pianist; 1947-)
Serkin, Rudolf (US pianist; 1903-91)
Serling, Rod (ent.; 1924-75)
Sermon on the Mount (Jesus' Beatitudes)
Serowe, Botswana
Serpasil (med.)
Serpens (astron., serpent)
Serpico (film, 1973)
Serra Junípero, Miguel José, Father (Sp. rel.;
    1713-84)
Serrano ham
Serta (mattress)
Serta, Inc.
Serutan (med.)
Service Cross, Distinguished (mil.)
Service Medal, Distinguished (mil.)
Service Merchandise, Inc.
Service Order, Distinguished (Br. mil.)
Service, Robert W(illiam)(Can. writer; 1874-1958)
ServiceMaster Co.

Servile Wars (Roman hist.; 1st-2nd c. BC)
Sesame Street (mag.)
Sesame Street (TV show)
Sesame Street Records (US bus.)
Sesotho (lang.)
Sessions, Jeff (US cong.; 1946-)
Sessions, Roger (Huntington)(US comp.; 1896-
    1985)
Sessions, William S(teele)(US, ex-dir./FBI; 1930-)
Sessue Hayakawa (ent.; 1890-1973)
Seth (rel.)
Seton Hall University (South Orange, NJ)
Seton, Mother (also St. Elizabeth Ann [Bayley]
    Seton)(US rel.; 1774-1821)
Setswana (lang.)
Setúbal, Portugal
Seurat, Georges (Fr. artist; 1859-91)
Seuss, Dr. (aka Theodore Seuss Geisel)(US
    writer/artist; 1904-91)
Sevareid, Eric (US TV jour.; 1913-92)
Sevastopol, Crimea (also Sebastopol)
Seve Ballesteros (golf; 1957-)
Seven against Thebes (Aeschylus tragedy)
Seven and Seven (mixed drink)
Seven Cities of Cibola (utopia)
Seven Hills of Rome
Seven Hills, City of (Rome)
Seven Sisters colleges (prestigious women's
    colleges)
Seven Weeks' War (also Austro-Prussian War)
    (1866)
Seven Wonders of the World
Seven Year Itch, The (film, 1955)
Seven Years' War (also French and Indian War)
    (Eur. hist.; 1756-63)
Seven Up, Inc., Dr Pepper/
7-Eleven (US bus.)
Seventeen (mag.)
1776 (play)
Seventh-Day Adventist (rel.)
76ers, Philadelphia (basketball team)
Severini, Gino (It. artist; 1883-1966)
Severinsen, Doc (Carl Hilding)(ent.; 1927-)
Severn bore (tidal wave)
Severn River (Wales/Eng.)
Sevigny, Chloe (ent.; 1974-)
Seville, Cadillac (auto.)
Seville, Spain
Seville, The Barber of (Beaumarchais play, G.
    Rossini opera)
Sèvres porcelain/ware
Sèvres, France
Sew News (mag.)
Sewall, Samuel (US judge, witch trials; 1652-
    1730)
Seward Peninsula (AK)
Seward, William Henry (US pol.; 1801-72)
Seward's Folly/folly (also Alaska Purchase)
    ($7.2 million; 1867)
Sewell, Anna (Br. writer; 1820-78)
Sewell, Joe (baseball; 1898-1990)
Sewell, Rufus (ent.; 1967-)
Sex Pistols (pop music)
Sextans (astron., sextant)
Sexton, Anne Harvey (US poet; 1928-74)

Seybou, Ali (ex-pres., Niger; 1940-)
Seychelles (Republic of)(islands, Indian Ocean)
Seydou Elimane Diarra (PM, Ivory Coast; 1933-)
Seyed Mohammed Khatami (pres., Iran; 1943-)
Seyfert galaxy (astron.)
Seymour, Jane (b. Joyce Frankenberg)(ent.; 1951-)
Seymour, Jane (queen, Eng., 3rd wife of Henry VIII; 1509?-37)
Seymour, Lynn (Can. ballet; 1939-)
Sezer, Ahmet Necdet (pres., Turk.; 1941-)
Sfax, Tunisia
Sforza, Carlo, Conte (It. pol./dipl.; 1873-1952)
Sforza, Francesco (It. pol.; 1401-66)
Sforza, Galeazzo Maria (It. pol.; 1444-76)
Sforza, Ludovico ("The Moor")(It. pol.; 1451-1508)
Sgt. Pepper's Lonely Hearts Club Band (Beatles album)
Shabazz, Betty (Sanders)(US civil rights activist; 1936-97)
Shabbat (Jew. Sabbath)
Shabuoth (also Shavuoth)(rel.)
Shackelford, Ted (ent.; 1946-)
Shackleton, (Sir) Ernest (Henry)(Br. expl.; 1874-1922)
Shaddai (also Shadai)(rel.)
Shadow, Dodge (auto.)
Shafer Vineyards (US bus.)
Shaffer, Paul (ent.; 1949-)
Shaffer, Peter (playwright; 1926-)
Shafi'i (Islamic law)
Shafi'ites (rel.)
Shafter, Fort, HI (mil.)
Shagari, Alhaji Shehu (ex-pres., Nigeria; 1925-)
Shaggy (b. Orville Richard Burrell)(Jam. ent.; 1968-)
Shah, Rajah Azlan Muhibuddin (ex-king, Malaysia)
Shahabuddin Ahmed (pres., Bangladesh; 1930-)
Shaham, Gil (violinist; 1971-)
Shaheen, (Cynthia) Jeanne (NH gov.; 1947-)
Shahn, Ben(jamin)(US artist; 1898-1969)
Shake 'N Bake (food)
Shaker Heights, OH
Shaker, Sharif Zaid ibn (ex-PM, Jordan)
Shakers (also United Society of Believers in Christ's Second Coming[Appearing], Millenial Church)
Shakespeare Company, Royal (RSC)(Br. theater; est. 1961-)
Shakespeare in Love (film, 1998)
Shakespeare, William (Br. writer; 1564-1616)
Shakespearean sonnet (also English sonnet, Elizabethan sonnet)
Shakur, Tupac (b. Lesane Parish Crooks)(ent.; 1971-96)
Shalala, Donna E(dna)(US ex-secy./HHS; 1941-)
Shales, Tom (US TV critic; 1958-)
Shalimar
Shalimar Accessories (US bus.)
Shalit, Gene (US critic; 1932-)
Shalom (or Sholom) Aleichem (aka Solomon Rabinowitz)(Yiddish writer; 1859-1916)
Shalom Harlow (model/ent.; 1973-)
Shamikh, Mubarak Abdullah al- (PM, Libia)

Shamir, Yitzhak (ex-PM, Isr.; 1915-)
Shamitoff Foods (US bus.)
Shamitoff's
Shamu (whale)
Shamus (film, 1972)
Shan (lang./people)
Shandling, Garry (ent.; 1949-)
Shandong (province, Ch.)
Shandong Peninsula (Ch.)
Shandy, Tristram (L. Sterne novel)
Shane (film, 1953)
Shang dynasty (Ch. hist.; 1766-1122 BC)
Shange, Ntozake (b. Paulette Williams)(US writer; 1948-)
Shanghai chicken
Shanghai, China
Shangkun, Yang (ex-pres., Ch.; 1907-)
Shangri-la (also Shangri-La)(utopia, from *Lost Horizon*)
Shania Twain (b. Eileen Regina Twain)(ent.; 1965-)
Shankar Dayal Sharma (ex-pres., India; 1918-99)
Shankar, Ravi (comp./sitarist, India; 1920-)
Shankar, Uday (dancer, India; 1900-77)
Shanker, Albert (US educ.; 1928-97)
Shannen Doherty (ent.; 1971-)
Shannon International Airport (Ir.)
Shannon River (also River Shannon)(Ir.)
Shannon, Del (ent.; 1940-90)
Shantung silk (also l.c.)
Shanxi (province, Ch.)
Shaoqi, Liu (also Liu Shao-chi)(Ch. pol.; 1898?-1969?)
SHAPE (also Shape)(Supreme Headquarters Allied Powers, Eur.)
Shape (mag.)
Shapiro, Karl (Jay)(US poet/editor; 1913-2000)
Shapiro, Robert (Leslie)(US atty.; 1942-)
Shapley, Harlow (US astron.; 1885-1972)
Shaquille O'Neal (basketball; 1972-)
Sharchop (lang./people)
Shari Belafonte (ent.; 1954-)
Shari Lewis (ent.; 1934-98)
Shari, Ubangi- (now Central African Republic)
Sharif Zaid ibn Shaker (ex-PM, Jordan)
Sharif, Nawaz (ex-PM, Pak.; 1948-)
Sharif, Omar (b. Michel Shalhoub)(ent.; 1932-)
Sharjah (state, UAE)
Sharkey, Jack (boxing; 1902-94)
Sharks, San Jose (hockey team)
Sharma, Shankar Dayal (ex-pres., India; 1918-99)
Sharon Gless (ent.; 1943-)
Sharon Lawrence (ent.; 1962-)
Sharon Pratt Kelly (ex-DC mayor; 1944-)
Sharon Stone (ent.; 1958-)
Sharon Tate (Polanski)(ent.; 1943-69)
Sharon, Ariel (Arik)(PM, Isr.; 1928-)
Sharon, PA
Sharon, rose of (plant)
Sharp Electronics Corp.
Sharp, Becky (fict. chara., *Vanity Fair*)
Sharpe Army Depot (CA)(US mil.)
Shar-Pei, Chinese (dog)

Sharpeville, South Africa
Sharpton, Al (clergyman/pol./activist; 1954-)
Shasta Beverages (US bus.)
Shasta daisy
Shasta, Mount (dormant volcano, CA)
Shastri, (Shri) Lal Bahadur (ex-PM, India; 1904-66)
Shatalov, Vladimir A. (cosmo.; 1927-)
Shatner, William (ent.; 1931-)
Shatt-al-Arab River (Iraq)
Shaun Cassidy (ent.; 1958-)
Shavuoth (also Shabuoth)(rel.)
Shaw Air Force Base, SC (US mil.)
Shaw Industries, Inc.
Shaw v. Reno (US law; 1993)
Shaw, Artie (b. Arthur Arshawsky)(US jazz; 1910-)
Shaw, George Bernard (Ir. writer/critic; 1856-1950)
Shaw, Henry Wheeler (pseud. Josh Billings)(US humorist; 1818-85)
Shaw, Irwin (US writer; 1913-84)
Shaw, Robert (chorale cond.; 1916-99)
Shaw, Robert (ent.; 1927-78)
Shaw, Vernon Lorden (pres., Dominica; 1930-)
Shawn Colvin (ent.; 1956-)
Shawn Fanning (aka Napster; 1981-)
Shawn, Ted (Edwin Myers)(US dancer/ choreographer; 1891-1972)
Shawn, Wallace (ent.; 1943-)
Shawnee (Native Amer.)
Shawnee, KS, OK
Shays' Rebellion (US hist.; 1786-87)
Shays, Daniel (US mil./pol.; 1747?-1825)
Shazam!
Shea Stadium (NYC)
Shea, John (ent.; 1949-)
Shean, (Ed) Gallagher & (Al)(ent.)
Shean, Al (b. Albert Schoenberg)(ent.; 1868-1949)
Shear Perfection (US bus.)
Shearer, Moira (ent.; 1926-)
Shearer, Norma (ent.; 1902-83)
Shearing, George (US jazz; 1919-)
Shearson Lehman Brothers, Inc.
Shearson Lehman Hutton Open
Sheba (also Saba)(ancient S Yemen)
Sheba, Queen of (biblical, visited Solomon to test his wisdom)
Shebat (also Shevat)(Jew. month)
Sheboygan, WI
Shecky Greene (b. Sheldon Greenfield)(ent.; 1926-)
Shedd's Food Products (US bus.)
Shedd's Spread
Sheedy, Ally (ent.; 1962-)
Sheehan, Patty (golf; 1956-)
Sheehy, Gail (US writer; 1937-)
Sheeler, Charles (US artist; 1883-1965)
Sheen, Charlie (ent.; 1965-)
Sheen, Fulton J(ohn), Bishop (US rel./writer/ educ.; 1895-1979)
Sheen, Martin (ent.; 1940-)
Sheena Easton (b. Sheena Orr)(ent.; 1959-)
Sheerness, England
Sheetrock (constr.)

Sheffield plate (copper/silver)
Sheffield, AL
Sheffield, England
Sheffield, Gary (baseball; 1968-)
Sheik (condoms)
Sheila MacRae (ent.; 1924-)
Sheila Young (speed skating; 1950-)
Sheilah Graham (gossip columnist; 1904-88)
Sheindlin, Judith (aka Judge Judy, Judy Blum) (TV judge; 1942-)
Shel Silverstein (US writer; 1932-99)
Shelby Foote (US hist.; 1916-)
Shelby Lynne (ent.; 1968-)
Shelby, Richard Craig (US cong.; 1934-)
Sheldon Harnick (US lyricist; 1924-)
Sheldon Leonard (ent.; 1907-97)
Sheldon, Sidney (US writer; 1917-)
Shell Oil Co.
Shelley Duvall (ent.; 1949-)
*Shelley Duvall's Bedtime Storie*s (TV show)
Shelley Fabares (ent.; 1942-)
Shelley Long (ent.; 1949-)
Shelley Winters (b. Shirley Schrift)(ent.; 1922-)
Shelley, Mary Wollstonecraft (Br. writer/ *Frankenstein*; 1797-1851)
Shelley, Percy Bysshe (Br. poet; 1792-1822)
Shelly Berman (ent.; 1926-)
Shelly Manne (US jazz; 1920-84)
Shema (rel.)
Shemp Howard (b. Samuel Horwitz)(ent.; 1895-1955)
Shem-Tov, Baal (also Israel ben Eliezer)(Jew. rel.; c1700-60)
Shenandoah Mountains (VA/MD)
Shenandoah National Park (VA)
Shenandoah River (SE US)
Shenandoah Valley (VA)
Shenandoah, VA
Shenyang, China (formerly Mukden)
Shenzen (econ. community, S Ch.)
Sheol (hell)
Shepard, Alan B(artlett), Jr. (astro.; 1923-98)
Shepard, Sam (b. Sam Rogers)(US writer/ent.; 1943-)
Shepherd, Cybill (ent.; 1950-)
Shepherd, Lee (auto racing; 1945-85)
Sheppard Air Force Base, TX (US mil.)
Sheppard, Samuel H. (US phys.; 1924-70)
Sheraton Corp.
Sheraton Grand Hotel
Sheraton hotels
Sheraton, Thomas (Br. furniture designer; 1751-1806)
Sherbrooke, Quebec, Canada
Shere Hite (US writer; 1942-)
Sheree North (ent.; 1933-)
Sheridan, Ann (ent.; 1915-67)
Sheridan, Fort (IL)(mil.)
Sheridan, Nicollette (ent./model; 1963-)
Sheridan, Philip (Henry)(US gen.; 1831-88)
Sheridan, Richard B(rinsley)(Ir. writer/pol.; 1751-1816)
Sheridan, WY
Sheriff of Nottingham (*Robin Hood*)
Sherlock Holmes (fict. detective)

Sherman Antitrust Act (US hist.; 1890)
Sherman Edwards (US comp.; 1919-81)
Sherman Hemsley (ent.; 1938-)
Sherman Silver Purchase Act (US hist.; 1890)
Sherman, James S(choolcraft)(ex-US VP; 1855-1912)
Sherman, John (US pol.; 1823-1900)
Sherman, Roger (US pol.; 1721-93)
Sherman, TX
Sherman, William T(ecumseh)(US gen.; 1820-91)
Shero, Fred (hockey; 1945-90)
Sherpas (Himalayan mountaineers)
Sherrill Milnes (ent.; 1935-)
Sherrington, (Sir) Charles (Scott)(Br. physiol.; 1857-1952)
Sherry Lee Lansing (ent.; 1944-)
Sherwin-Williams Co.
Sherwood Anderson (US writer; 1876-1941)
Sherwood Forest (Nottinghamshire, Eng.; R. Hood's home)
Sherwood, Robert (Emmet)(US writer; 1896-1955)
Sheryl Crow (ent.; 1962-)
Shetland Islands (Scot.)
Shetland pony
Shetland sheepdog (dog)
Shetland wool (fabric)
Shevardnadze, Eduard A. (pres., Georgia; 1928-)
Shevat (also Shebat)(Jew. month)
Shiba-Inu (dog)
Shield (soap)
Shields, Brooke (ent.; 1965-)
Shih Tzu (dog)
Shiite Muslim (also Shia)(rel., Islam)
Shik, Chung Won (ex-PM, SKorea)
Shikibu Murasaki, Lady (Jap. writer; c978-1031?)
Shikoku (island, Jap.)
Shilluk (lang.)
Shiloh (rel.)
Shiloh, Battle of (also Pittsburg Landing)(US hist.; 1862)
Shimon Peres (ex-PM, Isr.; 1923-)
Shinichi Suzuki (Jap. violinist/educ.; 1898-1998)
Shinto (rel.)
Shintoism (rel.)
Shiraz, Iran
Shire (draft horse)
Shire, Talia (b. Talia Rose Coppola)(ent.; 1946-)
Shirelles, the (pop music)
Shirer, William Lawrence (US writer/hist.; 1904-93)
Shires, the (Br. hunting counties)
Shirley Ann Grau (US writer; 1929-)
Shirley Babashoff (swimming; 1957-)
Shirley Bassey (ent.; 1937-)
Shirley Booth (ent.; 1907-92)
Shirley (Anita St. Hill) Chisholm (US pol.; 1924-)
Shirley Jackson (US writer; 1916-65)
Shirley Jones (ent.; 1934-)
Shirley MacLaine (ent.; 1934-)
Shirley Manson (ent.; 1966-)
Shirley Temple (non-alcoholic cocktail)
Shirley Temple Black (US ent./dipl.; 1928-)
Shirley Verrett (ent.; 1931-)

Shirley, Laverne & (TV show)
Shiseido Cosmetics America, Ltd. (US bus.)
Shiva (also Siva)(Hindu god)
Shkodër, Albania (also Shkodra)
Shmuel Yosef Agnon (b. Samuel Josef Czaczkes) (Isr. writer; 1888-1970)
SHO (Showtime)(TV channel)
Shockley, Dr. William B(radford)(US physt.; 1910-89)
Shoe (comic strip)
Shoe Corp., Inc., U.S.
Shoemaker, Willie (William Lee)(US jockey; 1931-)
Shofar Kosher Foods, Inc.
Shogun (J. Clavell book; TV miniseries, 1980)
Sholokhov, Mikhail (Aleksandrovich)(Rus. writer; 1905-84)
Sholom (or Shalom) Aleichem (aka Solomon Rabinowitz)(Yiddish writer; 1859-1916)
Shona (lang./people)
Shondells, Tommy James & the (pop music)
Shoney's (US bus.)
Shonin, Georgi S. (cosmo.; 1935-97)
Shoo-Fly Pie & Apple Pan Dowdy (song)
Shooting of Dan McGrew, The (R.W. Service ballad)
Shop 'Til You Drop (TV show)
Shop-Vac Corp.
Shopko Store
Shore, Dinah (ent.; 1917-94)
Shore, Eddie (hockey; 1902-85)
Shore, Pauly (ent.; 1968-)
Short, Bobby (ent.; 1924-)
Short, Martin (ent.; 1950-)
Shorter, Frank (runner; 1947-)
Shorthorn (cattle)
Shorty, Get (film, 1995)
Shoshone Falls (ID)
Shoshone National Forest (formerly Yellowstone Park Timber Reserve)
Shoshoni (also Shoshone)(Native Amer.)
Shostakovich, Dmitry (Dmitriyevich)(Rus. comp.; 1906-75)
Shotwell, James Thomson (Can/US hist.; 1874-1965)
Shout (spot remover)
Show Me State (nickname, MO)
Shower to Shower (health)
Showtime (SHO)(TV channel)
Showtime Networks, Inc.
Shredded Wheat, Nabisco (cereal)
Shredded Wheat, Spoonsize (cereal)
Shree (or Osho) Rajneesh (aka Bhagwan)(b. Chaadra Mohan Jain)(Indian rel.; 1931-90)
Shreveport Times (LA newspaper)
Shreveport, LA
Shrew, The Taming of the (Shakespeare play)
Shriner (member of Ancient Arabic Order of Nobles of the Mystic Shrine)
Shriner, Herb (ent.; 1918-70)
Shriner, Wil (ent.; 1953-)
Shriver, (Robert) Sargent, Jr. (US bus./pol.; 1915-)
Shriver, Eunice Kennedy (US wife of pol.; 1921-)
Shriver, Maria (US TV jour.; 1955-)

Shriver, Pam (tennis; 1962-)
Shropshire (county, Eng.)
Shropshire sheep
shroud of Turin (rel.)
Shrove Tuesday (also Mardi Gras)(rel.)
Shubert Alley (NYC)
Shubert Theater (NYC)
Shubert, Jacob J. (US theater; 1880-1963)
Shubert, Lee (US theater; 1875-1953)
Shubert, Sam S. (US theater; 1876-1905)
Shue, Andrew (ent.; 1967-)
Shue, Elisabeth (ent.; 1963-)
Shui-bia, Chen (pres., Taiwan; 1951-)
Shula, Don(ald Francis)(football; 1930-)
Shull, Richard B. (ent.; 1929-)
Shulman, Max (US writer; 1919-88)
Shultz, George P(ratt)(US pol./ex-secy./state;
    1920-)
Shushkevich, Stanislav S(tanislavavich)(ex-
    pres.; Belarus; 1934-)
Shuster, Joe (cartoonist, *Superman*; 1914-92)
Shute, Nevil (Br. writer/eng.; 1899-1960)
Shwe, Gen. Than (head of state/chairman,
    Myanmar; 1933-)
Shylock (fict. moneylender, *Merchant of Venice*)
Si (chem. sym., silicon)
Sialkot, Pakistan
Siam (now Thailand)
Siam (or Thailand), Gulf of
Siamese cat
Siamese fighting fish
Siamese twins
Sian, China (also Xian)
Siangtan, China (also Xiangtan)
Siauliai, Lithuania
Siba (fict. chara., *The Lion King*)
Sibelius, Jean (Julius Christian)(Fin. comp.;
    1865-1957)
Sibenik, Croatia
Siberia (region, N Asia)
Siberian husky (dog)
Siberian Railway, Trans- (>7,000 miles)
Sibomana, Adrien (ex-PM, Burundi)
Sica, Vittorio De (ent.; 1901-74)
Sichuan (also Szechwan)(province, Ch.)
Sichuan cuisine (also Szechwan)
Sicilian Vespers rebellion (It./Fr. hist.; 1282)
Siciliano, Angelo (aka Charles Atlas)(US body
    builder; 1894-1972)
Sicily, Italy (largest Mediterranean island)
Sickert, Walter Richard (Br. artist; 1860-1942)
Sid and Nancy (film, 1986)
Sid Caesar (ent.; 1922-)
Sid (El Sid) Fernandez (baseball; 1962-)
Sid Krofft (puppeteer; 1931-)
Sid Luckman (football; 1916-98)
Sid Vicious (b. John Simon Ritchie)(ent.; 1957-79)
Sidamo (people)
Siddhartha, Gautama (Buddha)(Indian phil.,
    founded Buddhism; c563-c483 BC)
Siddons, Sarah (Kemble)(ent.; 1755-1831)
Sidekick, Suzuki (auto.)
Sidewinder (missile)
Sidi Mohamed Ould Boubacar (ex-PM,
    Mauritania)

Sidibe, Mande (PM, Mali)
Sidimé, Lamine (PM, Guinea; 1944-)
Sidney (James) Webb (Br. reformer/writer;
    1859-1947)
Sidney Bechet (US jazz; 1897-1959)
Sidney Catlett ("Big Sid")(US jazz; 1910-51)
Sidney Hook (US phil.; 1902-89)
Sidney Kingsley (b. Sidney Kirschner)(US
    playwright; 1906-95)
Sidney Lanier (US poet; 1842-81)
Sidney Lumet (ent.; 1924-)
Sidney Poitier (ent.; 1927-)
Sidney Sheldon (US writer; 1917-)
Sidney, Sylvia (ent.; 1910-99)
Sidon, Lebanon (also Sayda, Saida)
Sidonie Gabrielle Colette (Fr. writer; 1873-1954)
Sidqi, Atef (ex-PM, Eg.)
SIDS (sudden infant death syndrome)(med.)
Siege of Yorktown (US hist.; 1781, 1862)
Siege Perilous (Arthurian)
Siegel, Benjamin "Bugsy" (US gangster/Las
    Vegas gambling; 1906-47)
Siegel, Jerry (cartoonist, *Superman*; 1914-96)
Siegelman, Don(ald)(Eugene)(AL gov.; 1946-)
Siegfried (also Sigurd)(legendary Ger. hero;
    c700)
Siegfried and Roy (illusionists, Siegfried
    Fischbacher and Roy Horn)
Siegfried Fischbacher (illusionist, Siegfried and
    Roy; 1939-)
Siemaszko, Casey (ent.; 1961-)
Siemens Components, Inc.
Siemens Hearing Instruments, Inc.
Siena, Italy
Siena, St. Catherine of (It. mystic; 1347-80)
Sienna, Toyota (auto.)
Siepi, Cesare (basso; 1923-)
Sierra (mag.)
Sierra Club (conservation org.; est. 1892)
Sierra Club Books (US bus.)
Sierra Club Legal Defense Fund
Sierra Leone (Republic of)(W Afr.)
Sierra Madre (CO/WY mountain range)
Sierra Madre (Mex. mountain range)
Sierra Madre, CA
Sierra Nevada (CA mountain range)
Sierra Nevada (Sp. mountain range)
Sierra Vista Winery (US bus.)
Sierra, GMC (auto.)
Siewert, Jake (US ex-White House press secy.)
Sigismund (Augustus) II (king, Pol.; 1520-72)
Sigismund (Holy Roman emp.; 1368-1437)
Sigismund I ("The Old")(king, Pol.; 1467-1548)
Sigismund III (king, Pol.; 1566-1632)
Sigmund Freud (Aus. phys., founder of
    psychoanalysis; 1856-1939)
Sigmund Romberg (Hung. comp.; 1887-1951)
Sign (or sign) English
Signac, Paul (Fr. artist; 1863-1935)
Signal (mouthwash)
Signe Hasso (Swed. ent.; 1910-)
Signorelli, Luca (d'Egidio di Ventura de')(It.
    artist; c1445-1523)
Signoret, Simone (ent.; 1921-85)
Sigourney Weaver (ent.; 1949-)

Sigurd (also Siegfried)(legendary Ger. hero; c700)
Sihanouk, Norodom (king, Cambodia; 1922-)
S(amuel) I(chiye) Hayakawa (US educ./pol./ linguist; 1906-92)
Sikh (rel.)
Sikh Wars (India; 1845-49)
Sikhism (rel.)
Si-Kiang River (also Xi Jiang)(Ch.)
Sikkim (state, India)
Sikking, James B. (ent.; 1934-)
Sikorsky, Igor I. (Rus./US aeronautical eng.; 1889-1972)
Silas Atopare (gov.-gen., Papua New Guinea)
Silas Marner (G. Eliot novel)
Silent Spring (R. Carson book)
Silent, William the (Dutch, Prince of Orange; 1533-84)
Silenus (myth.)
Silesia (region, Eur.)
Silex, Inc., Hamilton Beach/Proctor-
Silhouette, Oldsmobile (auto.)
Silicon Valley (nickname, Santa Clara Co., CA)
Silius (Roman poet; c25-101)
Silivas, Daniela (gymnast; 1970-)
Silkie (chicken)
Silkwood (film, 1983)
Silkwood, Karen (US nuclear safety advocate; 1946-74)
Sill, Fort, OK (mil.)
Sills, Beverly (b. Belle Silverman)(US opera; 1929-)
Sills, Milton (ent.; 1882-1930)
Silly Putty
Silone, Ignazio (Secondo Tranquilli)(It. writer; 1900-78)
Silurian period (430-395 million years ago)
Silva, Aníbal Cavaco (ex-PM, Port.; 1939-)
Silvadene (med.)
Silver Seraph, Rolls-Royce (auto.)
Silver Spring, MD
Silver Springs, FL
Silver Star medal/Medal (mil.)
Silver State (nickname, NV)
Silver, Ron (ent.; 1946-)
Silverado Vineyards, The (US bus.)
Silverado, Chevrolet (auto.)
Silverheels, Jay (b. Harry Jay Smith)(ent.; 1919-80)
Silverman, Fred (ent.; 1937-)
Silvers, Phil (ent.; 1912-85)
Silverstein, Shel (US writer; 1932-99)
Silverstone, Alicia (ent.; 1976-)
Silvester, Jay (discus thrower; 1937-)
Silvestre Siale Bileka (ex-PM, Equatorial Guinea)
Silvio Berlusconi (ex-PM, It.; 1936-)
Simba (film, 1955)
Simenon, Georges (Georges Sim)(mystery writer; 1903-89)
Simi Valley (CA)
Simi Winery, Inc.
Simitas, Costas (or Kostis)(PM, Gr.; 1936-)
Simmel, George (Ger. sociol./phil.; 1858-1918)
Simmonds, Kennedy A(Iphonse)(ex-PM, St. Kitts-Nevis; 1936-)
Simmons Beautyrest (mattress)

Simmons, Al (baseball; 1902-56)
Simmons, Gene (b. Chaim Witz)(ent.; 1949-)
Simmons, Jean (ent.; 1929-)
Simmons, Richard (ent.; 1948-)
Simon & Schuster, Inc.
Simon Achidi Achu (ex-PM, Cameroon)
Simon and Garfunkel (pop music)
Simon Bolivar ("El Libertador")(SAmer. pol.; 1783-1830)
Simon Guggenheim (US finan./bus.; 1867-1941)
Simon Le Bon (ent.; 1958-)
Simon Legree (fict. chara., *Uncle Tom's Cabin*)
Simon Museum of Art, Norton (CA)
Simon Peter (also St. Peter)(rel.; ?-AD c64)
Simon Rodia (It. tile setter; 1875-1965)
Simon Schama (hist.; 1945-)
Simon Templar (fict. chara., *The Saint*)
Simon Wiesenthal (Aus. reformer; 1908-)
Simon, Carly (ent.; 1945-)
Simon, (Marvin) Neil (US writer; 1927-)
Simon, Norton (US bus.; 1907-93)
Simon, Paul (ent.; 1942-)
Simon, Paul (Martin)(US pol.; 1928-)
Simon, Simple (nursery rhyme chara.)
Simon, St.
Simone de Beauvoir (Fr. writer; 1908-86)
Simone Signoret (ent.; 1921-85)
Simone, Nina (ent.; 1933-)
Simonides (Gr. poet; 556-c468 BC)
Simoniz (car wax)
Simoniz Co.
Simons, Menno (Dutch rel.; c1496-c1561)
Simple Simon (nursery rhyme chara.)
Simplesse (fat substitute)
Simplesse Co., The
Simplicity Pattern Co., Inc.
Simplon pass (Switz./It.)
Simpson, Alan K. (US pol.; 1931-)
Simpson, Bart (cartoon chara.)
Simpson, George Gaylord (US paleontol.; 1902-84)
Simpson, Jessica (ent.; 1980-)
Simpson, Nicole (Brown)(US news; 1959-94)
Simpson, O(renthal) J(ames)(football; 1947-)
Simpson, Sudie and (film, 1990)
Simpson, Wallis "Wally" Warfield (Duchess of Windsor)(US socialite, m. Edward VIII; 1896-1986)
Simpsons, The (cartoon)
Sims, Billy (football; 1955-)
Sims, Zoot (John Haley)(US jazz; 1925-85)
Sinai Medical Center, Cedars-
Sinai Peninsula (Eg.)
Sinai, Mount (NE Eg.; Moses, 10 Commandments)
Sinanthropus (anthrop.)
Sinarest (med.)
Sinatra, Frank (Francis Albert)(ent.; 1915-98)
Sinbad (b. David Adkin)(ent.; 1956-)
Sinbad the Sailor (also Sindbad)(fict. chara., *Arabian Nights)*
Sinclair Lewis, (Harry)(US writer; 1885-1951)
Sinclair, Upton (Beall)(US writer/reformer; 1878-1968)
Sinde bele (lang.)

Sindhi (lang./people)
Sinéad O'Connor (ent.; 1966-)
Sine-Aid (med.)
Sinemet (med.)
Sine-Off (med.)
Sinequan (med.)
Sing Sing (state prison, NY)
Singapore (Republic of)(SE Asia)
Singapore Airlines, Ltd. (US bus.)
Singapore City, Singapore
Singapore sling (mixed drink)
Singapore, Road to (film, 1940)
Singer Co., The
Singer, Isaac B(ashevis)(Pol./US writer; 1904-91)
Singer, Isaac M(errit)(US, inv. sewing machine; 1811-75)
Singh, Vishwanath Pratap (ex-PM, India; 1931-)
Singhalese (also Sinhalese)(lang./people)
Singletary, Mike (football; 1958-)
Singleton, John (ent./writer; 1968-)
Singleton, Penny (ent.; 1908-)
Singleton, Zutty (US jazz; 1898-1975)
Sining, China (also Xining)
Sinise, Gary (ent.; 1955-)
Sinkiang Uighur (also Xinjiang Uygur)(region, Ch.)
Sinn Fein (Ir. pol. party)
Sino-Japanese Wars (Jap./Ch.; 1894-95, 1931-45)
Sino-Soviet
Sino-Tibetan languages
Sinsiang, China (also Xinxiang)
Sinuiju, North Korea
Sinutab (med.)
Sioux (also Dakota)(Native Amer.)
Sioux City Sue (film, 1946)
Sioux City, IA
Sioux Falls, SD
Sioux State (nickname, ND)
Siphandon, Khamtai (pres., Laos; 1924-)
Sippie Wallace (b. Beulah Thomas)(ent.; 1898-1986)
Siqueiros, David Alfaro (Mex. artist; 1896-1974)
Sir Bedivere (Arthurian knight)
Sir Bors (Arthurian knight)
Sir Galahad (Arthurian knight)
Sir Gawain (Arthurian knight)
Sir Percivale (also Parsifal)(Arthurian knight)
Sir Roger de Coverly (dance)
Sir Speedy (printing)
Sir Speedy, Inc.
Siren (myth.)
Sirhan B(ishara) Sirhan (assassinated R.F. Kennedy; 1944-)
Sirica, John (US judge; 1904-92)
Sirimavo Bandaranaike (ex-PM, Sri Lanka; 1916-2000)
Sirius (astron., part of Canis Major [or Great Dog])
Sirtis, Marina (ent.; 1959-)
Sisavat Keobounphan (PM, Laos; 1928-)
Siskel & Ebert (US critics)
Siskel, Gene (ent.; 1946-99)
Sisler, George (Harold)(baseball; 1893-1973)
Sisley, Alfred (Fr. artist; 1840?-99)
Sisophon, Cambodia
Sisqo (b. Mark Andrews)(ent.; 1975-)
Sissela Bok (b. Sissela Ann Myrdal)(US phil./ writer; 1934-)
Sissy (Mary Elizabeth) Spacek (ent.; 1949-)
Sister (Elizabeth) Kenny (Austl. nurse; 1886-1952)
Sisters (TV show)
Sisters, The Lennon (pop music)
Sistine Chapel (Vatican)(Michelangelo frescoes)
Sisyphus (myth.)
Sitiveni (Ligamamada) Rabuka (ex-PM, Fiji; 1948-)
Sitka National Historical Park (AK)
Sitka, AK
Sitting Bull, Chief (Tatanka Yotanka)(Sioux Native Amer.; c1831-90)
Sitwell, Dame Edith (Br. writer; 1887-1964)
Sitwell, (Sir Francis) Osbert Sacheverell (Br. writer; 1892-1969)
Sitwell, (Sir) Sacheverell (Br. writer; 1897-1988)
Siuslaw National Forest
Siva (also Shiva)(Hindu god)
Sivan (Jew. month)
Six-Day War (Arab/Isr.; 1967)
Sixto Durán Bellén (ex-pres., Ecuador; 1921-)
$64,000 Question (TV show)
60 Minutes (TV show)
Sizzler (steaks)
Sizzler Restaurants International (US bus.)
S(idney) J(oseph) Perelman (US writer; 1904-79)
Skeet Ulrich (ent./model; 1970-)
Skeeter Davis (b. Mary Frances Penick)(ent.; 1931-)
Skelton, Red (Richard)(ent.; 1913-97)
Skerritt, Tom (ent.; 1933-)
Skiing (mag.)
Skilcraft (US bus.)
Skilsaw (constr.)
Skin-So-Soft (skin care)
Skinner box (psych.)
Skinner, B(urrhus) F(rederic)(US psych./writer; 1903-90)
Skinner, Cornelia Otis (US writer/ent.; 1901-79)
Skinner, Otis (US writer/ent.; 1858-1942)
Skippy (peanut butter)
Skippy Homeier (ent.)
Skiros (also Scyros, Skyros)(Gr. island)
Skjoldungs of Denmark, House of the (Br. ruling family; 1016-42)
Skokie, IL
Skopje, Macedonia
Skouras, Spyros (Panagiotes)(ent.; 1893-1971)
Skowron, Bill "Moose" (baseball; 1930-)
Sky Harbor International Airport (Phoenix AZ)
Skye (island, Scot.)
Skye terrier (dog)
Skylab (US space station)
Skylark (film, 1993)
Skylark, Buick (auto.)
Skyline Corp.
Skynyrd, Lynyrd (pop music)
Skyros (also Skiros, Scyros)(Gr. island)
Skywalker, Luke (fict. chara., *Star Wars*)
Skywest Airlines
Slade Gorton (US cong.; 1928-)
Slam (Leroy Elliot) Stewart (ent.; 1914-87)
Slaney, Mary Decker (US runner; 1958-)

Slater, Christian (b. Christian Hawkins)(ent.;
1969-)
Slater, Helen (ent.; 1965-)
Slater, Rodney Earl (US ex-secy./trans.; 1955-)
Slatkin, Leonard (US cond.; 1944-)
Slaughter, Frank G. (US writer; 1908-)
Slav(ic)(lang./people)
Slave Coast (slavery traffic, W Afr.; 17th-19th c.)
Slayton, Donald Kent "Deke" (astro.; 1924-93)
Sledge, Percy (ent.; 1941-)
Sleepinal (med.)
Sleeping Beauty (fict. chara.)
Sleeping Gypsy, The (Rousseau)
Sleepy Hollow, The Legend of (W. Irving tale)
Sleuth (play; film, 1972)
Slezak, Erika (ent.; 1946-)
Slezak, Walter (ent.; 1902-83)
Slezevicius, Adolfas (ex-PM, Lith.; 1948-)
Slick, Grace (b. Grace Wing)(ent.; 1939-)
Slick, Sam (aka Thomas Chandler Haliburton)
(Can. writer/judge/hist.; 1796-1865)
Slidell, John (US pol.; 1793-1871)
Slim (Bulee) Gaillard (ent.; 1916-91)
Slim Jim, Inc.
slim Jim
Sliwa, Curtis (founder, Guardian Angels; 1954-)
Sloan Publishers, Inc., Price/Stern/
Sloan, Alfred Pritchard (US bus.; 1875-1966)
Sloan, John F(rench)(US artist; 1871-1951)
Sloan-Kettering Cancer Center (NYC)
Sloan-Kettering Institute for Cancer Research
(NYC)
Slo-bid (med.)
Slobodan Milosevic (Serbian pol.; 1941-)
Slo-Phyllin (med.)
Slovak (lang./people)
Slovakia (Czech. republic)
Slovene (lang./people)
Slovenia (republic. Yug.)(SE Eur.)
Slovenian (lang.)
Slovik, The, Execution of Private (film, 1974)
Slovo, Joe (b. Yossel Mashel)(SAfr. pol.; 1926-
95)
Slow-K (med.)
Sly and the Family Stone (pop music)
Sly Stone (b. Sylvester Stewart)(ent.; 1944-)
Sm (chem. sym., samarium)
SMA Infant Formula
Small Business Administration (SBA)(US govt.
agcy.; est. 1953)
Smalley, Richard E. (US chem.; 1943-)
SMART Yellow Pages
Smart, Maxwell (fict. TV chara.)
SmartWriter (steno writer)
Smetana, Bedrich (Czech. comp.; 1824-84)
Smirnoff Beverage & Import Co.
Smirnoff, Yakov (b. Yakov Pokhis)(ent.; 1951-)
Smith & Wesson (US bus.)
Smith College (Northampton, MA)
Smith Corona (typewriters)
Smith Corona Corp.
Smith Goes to Washington, Mr. (film, 1939)
Smith, Adam (Br. econ.; 1723-90)
Smith, Alexis (ent.; 1921-93)
Smith, Alfred E(manuel)(NY gov.; 1873-1944)

Smith, Allison (ent.; 1969-)
Smith, Barney, Harris Upham and Co.
Smith, Bessie (US jazz; 1894-1937)
Smith, Billy (hockey; 1950-)
Smith, Bob (Robert C.)(US cong.; 1941-)
Smith, Bruce (football; 1963-)
Smith, Bubba (Charles Aaron)(football; 1945-)
Smith, Buffalo Bob (b. Robert Schmidt)(ent.;
1917-98)
Smith, (Sir) C. Aubrey (ent.; 1863-1948)
Smith, Clarence "Pinetop" (US jazz; 1904-29)
Smith, David (Roland)(US sculptor; 1906-65)
Smith, Dean (basketball; 1931-)
Smith, Emmitt (football; 1969-)
Smith, Fort (AR)(city)
Smith, Gordon (US cong.; 1952-)
Smith, Harry (TV jour.; 1951-)
Smith, Hedrick (US writer; 1933-)
Smith, Howard K. (TV news jour.; 1914-)
Smith, Ian (Douglas)(ex-PM, Rhodesia; 1919-)
Smith, Jaclyn (ent.; 1947-)
Smith, Jada Pinkett (ent.; 1971-)
Smith, Jean Ann (nee Kennedy)(US dipl., sister
of ex-pres.; 1928-)
Smith, Jeff (US chef/writer; 1939-)
Smith, Jennifer (premier, Bermuda)
Smith, John (Br. colonist in Amer., Pocahontas;
1580-1631)
Smith, John Maynard (Br. biol.; 1920-)
Smith, Joseph (US rel., founded Mormons;
1805-44)
Smith, Kate (Kathryn)(ent.; 1909-86)
Smith, Keely (ent.; 1935-)
Smith, Lane (US illus./writer; 1959-)
Smith, Liz (US jour.; 1923-)
Smith, Maggie (ent.; 1934-)
Smith, Margaret Chase (US pol.; 1897-1995)
Smith, Ozzie (baseball; 1954-)
Smith, Patti (ent.; 1946-)
Smith, Red (Walter)(sports jour.; 1905-82)
Smith, Ronnie Ray (sprinter; 1949-)
Smith, Snuffy (cartoon chara.)
Smith, Stanley Roger (tennis; 1946-)
Smith, Thorne (US writer; 1892-1934)
Smith, Tommie (sprinter; 1944-)
Smith, Will (ent.; 1969-)
Smith, William Kennedy (US phys.; 1960-)
Smith, Willie "The Lion" (US jazz; 1897-1973)
Smithereens, the (pop music)
Smithfield Ham & Products Co., The
Smithfield ham
Smithfield, Ltd., Gwaltney of (US bus.)
SmithKline Beecham Consumer Brands (US
bus./med.)
SmithKline Beecham, Inc.
Smithsonian (mag.)
Smithsonian Astrophysical Observatory (MA)
Smithsonian Environmental Research Center
(MD)
Smithsonian Institution (DC)
Smithsonian Tropical Research Institute
(Panama)
Smits, Jimmy (ent.; 1955-)
Smoke, Marcia Jones (canoeing; 1941-)
Smokey (Joseph) Wood (baseball; 1890-1985)

Smokey (William) Robinson (US comp.; 1940-)
Smokey and the Bandit (film, 1977)
Smokey Robinson and the Miracles (pop music)
Smokey the Bear (fict. chara.)
Smoky Mountains National Park, Great (NC/TN)
Smoky Mountains, Great (NC/TN)
Smollett, Tobias (Br. writer; 1721-71)
Smoot Tariff Act, Hawley- (US hist.; 1930)
Smoot, Reed (US pol.; 1862-1941)
Smothers Brothers Comedy Hour (TV show)
Smothers, Dick (ent.; 1939-)
Smothers, Tom (ent.; 1937-)
Smucker Co., The J. M.
Smucker's (jams/jellies)
Smurf doll
Smurfit-Stone Container Corp.
Smurfs (TV show)
Smuts, Jan C(hristian)(ex-PM, SAfr.; 1870-1950)
Smyrna, Turkey (now Izmir)
Smyth, Ethel, Dame (Br. comp.; 1858-1944)
Smyth, Patty (ent.; 1957-)
Smytington, Fife (AZ gov.; 1945-)
Sn (chem. sym., tin)
Snap-On Tools Corp.
Snapper (lawn care)
S(amuel) N(athaniel) Behrman (US writer; 1893-1973)
Snead, Sam(uel Jackson) "Slamming Sammy" (golf; 1912-)
Snegur, Mircea (Ion)(ex-pres., Moldova; 1940-)
Snell (van Royen), Willebrod (Dutch math./ physt.; 1581-1626)
Snell's law (physics)
Sneva, Tom (auto racing; 1948-)
SNF (skilled nursing facility)
Snickers (candy)
Snider, Duke (Edwin)(baseball; 1926-)
Snipes, Wesley (ent.; 1962-)
SNL (*Saturday Night Live*)(TV show)
Snodgrass, Carrie (ent.; 1946-)
Snodgrass, W(illiam) D(eWitt)(US poet; 1926-)
Snooks, Baby (fict. chara, radio)
Snooky Lanson (b. Roy Landman)(ent.; 1914-90)
Snoop Dogg (b. Cordozar "Calvin" Broadus) (ent.; 1971-)
Snoopy (fict. dog, *Peanuts*)
Snoqualmie Falls, WA
Snoqualmie Pass, WA
Snoqualmie, WA
Snow White (fict. chara.)
Snow White and the Seven Dwarfs (fairy tale)
Snow, Baron C(harles) P(ercy)(Br. writer/ physt.; 1905-80)
Snow, Hank (ent.; 1914-99)
Snowdon, Earl of (Anthony Armstrong-Jones) (Br. photo.; 1930-)
Snowe, Olympia J. (US cong.; 1947-)
The Snows of Kilimanjaro (film, 1952)
Snowy bleach
Snowy Mountains (Austl. Alps)
Snuffy (DeWitt) Jenkins (ent.; 1908-90)
Snuffy Smith (cartoon chara.)
Snuggle (clothes softener)
Snyder, Jimmy "the Greek" (oddsmaker; 1919-96)

Snyder, Mitch (US reformer/homeless; 1944-90)
Snyder, Tom (ent.; 1936-)
Snyders, Frans (Flem. artist; 1579-1657)
Soap Box Derby
Soap Opera Digest (mag.)
Soares, Mário (Alberto Nobre Lopes)(ex-pres., Port.; 1924-)
SOB (son of a bitch)
Sobieski, Leelee (ent./model; 1982-)
Soccer League, North American (also NASL)
Social and Liberal Democrats (Br. pol. party)
Social Democratic Party (Br. pol. party; 1981-90)
Social Democrats (US pol. party)
Social Gospel movement (also l.c.)
Social Register
Social Security
Social Security Administration (SSA)(US govt. agcy.; est. 1946)
Social/social Darwinism
Socialist Labor Party (US pol.)
Socialist Party U.S.A. (US pol.)
Socialist Revolutionary Party (Russian Populist Party; founded 1901)
Socialist Workers Party (US pol.)
Society of Believers in Christ's Second Coming(Appearing), United (also Shakers, Millenial Church)
Society of Friends, (Religious)(also Quakers)(rel.)
Society of Jesus (Jesuits)(rel.)
Society, Royal (also Royal Society of London for the Advancement of Science; est. 1645)
Socks (Clintons' cat)
Socorro, NM
Socrates (Gr. phil.; 469-399 BC)
Socratic method (phil./educ.)
Soddy, Frederick (Br. chem.; 1877-1956)
Soderbergh, Steven (US ent./director; 1963-)
Sodium Pentothal (barbiturate)
Sodom and Gomorrah (ancient cities destroyed for wickedness)
Sofia, Bulgaria
Soft & Dri (anti-perspirant)
Soft Scrub (cleaner)
Softsoap (liquid soap)
Softsoap Enterprises, Inc.
Sogavare, Manasseh (PM, Solomon Islands; 1954-)
Soglo, Nicéphore (ex-pres., Benin; 1934-)
Soglow, Otto (US cartoonist, *Little King*; 1900-75)
SoHo (NYC)(also Soho)
Soho (London)
Sojourner Truth (US reformer; c1797-1883)
Sokodé, Togo
Sokoloff, Nikolai (Rus./US cond.; 1886-1965)
Sokolova, Lydia (Br. ballet; 1896-1974)
Sokolow, Anna (US dancer/choreographer; 1915-2000)
Sol (Roman sun god)
Sol Estes, Billy (US bus./scandal)
Sol(omon) Hurok (Rus./US impresario; 1884-1974)
Sol, Armando Calderon (ex-pres., El Salvador; 1948-)
Solarcaine (med.)
Solarian (floor vinyl)

Solchiro Hondo (Jap. bus./auto.; 1907-91)
Soldier, Unknown (Arlington National Cemetery [VA])
Solectron Corp.
Soleri, Paolo (US arch.; 1919-)
Solh, Rashid Al- (ex-PM, Lebanon)
Solidarity (Pol. labor org.)
Solingen, Germany
Solo Cup Co.
Solo, Han (fict. chara., *Star Wars*)
Solomon (king, Isr.; fl. 10th c BC)
Solomon Islands (SW Pac.)
Solomon Mamaloni (ex-PM, Soloman Islands; 1943-)
Solomon R(obert) Guggenheim (US bus./finan.; 1861-1949)
Solomon R. Guggenheim Museum (NYC)
Solomon Rabinowitz (pseud. Shalom [or Shalom] Aleichem)(Yiddish writer; 1859-1916)
Solomon West Ridgeway Dias Bandaranaike (ex-PM, Sri Lanka; 1899-1959)
Solomon, Harold (tennis; 1952-)
Solomon, Knights of the Temple of (also Templar)(rel./mil. order; 1119-1307)
Solomon, Song of (rel., aka Song of Songs, Canticle of Canticles)(rel., book of the Old Testament)
Solomon, Wisdom of (rel., Apocrypha)
Solomon's Mines, King (film, 1937, 1950, 1985)
Solomon's seal (plant)
Solon (Gr. pol.; c640-c560 BC)
Solovyov, Vladimir (Sergeyevich)(Rus. phil.; 1853-1900)
Solti, (Sir) Georg (Br. cond.; 1912-97)
Solvang, CA
Solvay process (sodium carbonate)
Solvay, Ernest (Belgian chem.; 1838-1922)
Solyman (or Suleiman)("the Magnificent," "the Lawgiver")(sultan, Ottoman Empire; 1494-1566)
Solzhenitsyn, Alexander (or Aleksandr) Isayevich (Rus. writer; 1918-)
Soma (med.)
Soma Compound (med.)
Somali (cat)
Somali (lang./people)
Somalia (Somali Democratic Republic)(NE Afr.)
Somaliland (region, E Afr.)
Somba (lang.)
Some Like it Hot (film, 1959)
Somers, Suzanne (b. Suzanne Mahoney)(ent.; 1946-)
Somerset (county, Eng.)
Somerset Maugham, W(illiam)(Br. writer; 1874-1965)
Somerset Raglan, FitzRoy (James Henry), Baron (Br. gen., raglan sleeve; 1788-1855)
Somerville, MA, NJ
Somes, Michael (ballet; 1917-94)
Sominex (med.)
Sommer, Elke (b. Elke Schletz)(ent.; 1940-)
Somnus (myth.)
Somophyllin (med.)
Somoza (Debayle), Anastasio (ex-pres., Nicaragua; 1925-80)
Somoza (Debayle), Luis (ex-pres., Nicaragua; 1922-67)
Somoza (Garcia), Anastasio (ex-pres., Nicaragua; 1896-1956)
Son (Jesus)
Son of God (Jesus Christ)
Son of Man (Jesus Christ)
Sonata, Hyundai (auto.)
Sonatine (film, 1996)
Sondheim, Stephen (Joshua)(US comp./lyricist; 1930-)
Sondra Locke (ent.; 1947-)
Song of Bernadette, The (film, 1943)
Song of Roland (Fr. epic poem, *Chanson de Roland*)
Song of Solomon (rel., aka Song of Songs, Canticle of Canticles)(rel., book of the Old Testament)
Songhai Empire (NW Afr.; 8th-16th c.)
Songhua (also Sungari)(river, Ch.)
Sonja Henie (figure skating/ent.; 1912-69)
Sonnenfeld, Barry (ent.; 1953-)
Sonny (Ralph) Barger (founder, Hell's Angels; 1938-)
Sonny (Salvatore) Bono (ent./pol.; 1935-98)
Sonny Jurgensen (football; 1934-)
Sonny (Charles) Liston (boxing; 1933-71)
Sonny (Theodore Walter) Rollins (US jazz; 1929-)
Sonny Stitt (US jazz; 1924-82)
Sonny's Real Pit Bar-B-Q (US bus.)
Sonoma Vineyards (US bus.)
Sonoma, GMC (auto.)
Sonoma, Piper (US bus.)
Sonoma, Williams- (US bus.)
Sonoma-Cutrer Vineyards (US bus.)
Sonora (state, Mex.)
Sons of Katie Elder (film, 1965)
Sons of Liberty (US hist.; 1765-66)
Sons of the Pioneers (music group)
Sontag, Susan (US writer; 1933-)
Sony Corp. of America
Sony PlayStation
Sony Walkman
Soon-Yi Farrow Previn (M. Farrow's daughter; 1971-)
Sooner State (nickname, OK)
SOP (standard operating procedure)
Sopé, Barak T. (PM, Vanuatu)
Sophia Loren (b. Sophia Scicoloni)(It. ent.; 1934-)
Sophia, Saint (or Santa)(also Hagia Sophia) (museum, Istanbul)
Sophie Marceau (ent.; 1966-)
Sophie Tucker (b. Sophie Abruza)(ent.; 1884-1966)
Sophie (Rhys-Jones) Wessex, Countess of Wessex, wife of Eng. Prince Edward; 1965-)
Sophie's Choice (W. Styron novel)
Sophists (ancient Gr. teachers/scholars)
Sophocles (Gr. drama.; c496-406 BC)
Sopranos, The (TV show)
Sopwith Camel biplane
Sopwith, (Sir) Thomas (Br. aircraft designer; 1888-1989)
Sorbian (lang.)
Sorbitrate (med.)
Sorbo, Kevin (ent.; 1958-)

Sorbonne (University of Paris)
Sören (or Søren) Kierkegaard (Dan. phil.;
   1813-55)
Sorrell Booke (ent.; 1930-94)
Sorrento, Italy
Sorrows, Man of (Jesus)
Sorvino, Mira (ent.; 1967-)
Sorvino, Paul (ent.; 1939-)
SOS (save our ship [distress signal])
Sosa, Sammy (baseball; 1968-)
Soss Manufacturing Co.
Sosuke, Uno (ex-PM, Jap.; 1922-)
Sotheby's auction house
Sothern, Ann (b. Harriette Lake)(ent.; 1909-)
Sotho (lang./people)
Soto, Hernando (or Fernando) de (Sp. expl.;
   c1496-1542)
Sotto, Sotto (film, 1985)
Soul, David (b. David Solberg)(ent.; 1943-)
Sound of Music, The (play; film, 1965)
Sounder (film, 1972)
Soundesign Corp.
Soundesign radio
Soupy Sales (b. Milton Supman)(ent.; 1926-)
Sousa, John Philip (US comp.; 1854-1932)
Sousse, Tunisia
Soussous (people)
Souter, David H(ackett)(US jurist; 1939-)
South Africa (Republic of)
South Africa, Union of (now Republic of South
   Africa)
South African Airways (airline)
South African War (also Boer War)(Boers/Br.;
   1899-1902)
South America
South American Indians
South Australia (state, Austl.)
South Bend Tribune (IN newspaper)
South Bend, IN
South Carolina (SC)
South China Sea (also China Sea)(off SE Asia)
South Dakota (SD)
South Dartmouth, MA
South Gate, CA
South Korea (Republic of Korea)(E Asia)
South Lake Tahoe, CA
South Orkney Islands
South Pacific (play; film, 1958)
South Platte River (CO/NE)
South Pole (S end of earth's axis)
South Sea Bubble (Br. hist.; 1720)
South Seas
South Tipperary (county, Ir.)
South Weymouth Naval Air Station (MA)
South Yemen (now part of Yemen)
South, the (US region)
Southampton, England
Southampton, NY
Southeast Asia (region, Asia)
Southeast Asia Treaty Organization (SEATO)
   (1954-77)
Southern Alps (NewZeal.)
Southern Bell
Southern Cone Common Market (Argentina/
   Brazil/Paraguay/Uruguay; 1991-)

Southern Cross (also Stars and Bars)
   (Confederate flag)
Southern Hemisphere
Southern Illinois University (Carbondale/
   Edwardsville, IL)
Southern Illinois University Press (US bus.)
Southern Living (mag.)
Southern Methodist University (SMU)(Dallas, TX)
Southern Rhodesia (now Zimbabwe)
Southern Triangle (astron., Triangulum Australe)
Southern Yemen (now Yemen)
Southerner
Southfield, MI
Southgate, MI
Southhampton, Earl of (Henry Wriothesley)(Br.
   scholar; 1573-1624)
Southside Johnny and the Asbury Jukes (pop
   music)
South-West Africa (now Namibia)
Southwest Airlines Co.
Southwestern Bell Corp.
Southwestern Indians
Soutine, Chaim (Fr. artist; 1893-1943)
Souverain, Chateau (US bus.)
Soviet Far East (now Russia Far East)
Soviet Socialist Republics, Union of (USSR)
   (disbanded 1991)
Soviet Union (also Union of Soviet Socialist
   Republics, USSR)(disbanded 1991)
Soviet, Sino-
Sow, Abdoulaye Sekou (ex-PM, Mali)
Soweto, South Africa (*South West Township*)
Soyer, Raphael (artist; 1899-1987)
Soyinka, Wole (Nigerian writer; 1934-)
Soylent Green (film, 1973)
Soyuz (USSR crewed space flights)
Spaak, Paul Henri (Belgium pol.; 1899-1972)
Spaatz, Carl (US mil.; 1891-1974)
Space Age (also l.c.)
Spacek, Sissy (Mary Elizabeth)(ent.; 1949-)
Spacelab (space station)
Spacemaster Home Products (US bus.)
Spacesaver Corp.
Spacey, Kevin (ent.; 1959-)
Spackle (constr.)
Spade (Donnell Clyde) Cooley (ent.; 1910-69)
Spade, David (ent.; 1964-)
Spade, Sam (fict. detective, D. Hammett)
Spader, James (ent.; 1960-)
Spahn, Warren (Edward)(baseball; 1921-)
Spain (SW Eur.)
Spalding
Spalding Sports Worldwide (US bus.)
Spalding, Albert (Goodwill)(baseball; 1850-1915)
Spam
Span, Spic & (cleaner)
Spaniard
Spanier, Muggsy (Francis Joseph)(US jazz;
   1906-67)
Spanish (lang./people)
Spanish American War (Sp./US; 1898)
Spanish Armada (Invincible Armada)(fleet of
   ships; 1588)
Spanish Civil War (1936-39)
Spanish fly (aphrodisiac)

Spanish Guinea (now Equatorial Guinea)
Spanish Inquisition
Spanish mackerel (fish)
Spanish Main (Caribbean/N SAmer.; 16th-17th c.)
Spanish moss (air plant)
Spanish ocher (color)
Spanish onion
Spanish paprika
Spanish rice
Spanish Steps (Rome)
Spanish Town, Jamaica
Spanish Wells, the Bahamas
Spanky (George) McFarland (ent.; 1928-93)
Spano, Joe (ent.; 1946-)
Spar (also SPAR)(women's U.S. Coast Guard
   reserve; WWII)
Spark, Muriel (writer; 1918-)
Sparkletts Water Co.
Sparks, NV
Sparky (George) Anderson (baseball; 1934-)
Sparta (also Lacedaemon)(ancient Gr.)
Spartacists (also Spartacus Party)(Ger. hist.;
   early 1900's)
Spartacus (film, 1960)
Spartacus (Thracian slave/gladiator; ?-73 BC)
Spartanburg, SC
Spasoje Tusevljak (pol., Bosnia-Hercegovina)
SPCA (Society for the Prevention of Cruelty to
   Animals)
SPCC (Society for the Prevention of Cruelty to
   Children)
Speaker of the House (US govt.)
Speaker, Tris(tram)(baseball; 1888-1958)
Spears, Britney (ent.; 1981-)
Special Astrophysical Observatory (USSR)
Special Forces (also Green Berets)(US mil.)
Special K (cereal)
Special Olympics (for handicapped)
Speck, Richard (US mass murderer; 1942-91)
Spectazole (med.)
Specter, (J.) Arlen (US cong.; 1930-)
Spector, Phil (ent.; 1939-)
Spector, Ronnie (b. Veronica Bennett)(ent.;
   1943-)
Spectra, Kia (auto.)
Spectrobid (med.)
Speed Queen (US bus.)
Speed Stick (deodorant)
Speedee Oil Change and Tune-Up (US bus.)
Speedo (sportswear)
Speedo America (US bus.)
Speedvision (TV channel)
Speedy Transmission Centers (US bus.)
Speer, Albert (Ger. arch./Nazi pol.; 1905-81)
Speightstown, Barbados
Speke, John Hanning (Br. expl. in Afr.; 1827-64)
Spelke, Elizabeth (US psych.; 1949-)
Spelling, Aaron (ent.; 1928-)
Spelling, Tori (Victoria Davey)(ent.; 1973-)
Spencer (steak)
Spencer-Churchill, Baroness Clementine (wife
   of ex-Br. PM; 1885-1977)
Spencer Davis (ent.; 1942-)
Spencer Davis Group (pop music)
Spencer Gifts, Inc.

Spencer Tracy (US ent.; 1900-67)
Spencer, Abraham (Edmund)(US secy./ener.;
   1952-)
Spencer, Brian (hockey; 1949-88)
Spencer, Herbert (Br. phil.; 1820-1903)
Spencer, John (ent.; 1946-)
Spencer's, Inc.
Spencer's Mountain (film, 1963)
Spender, Stephen (Br. poet/critic; 1909-95)
Spengler, Oswald (Ger. phil./hist.; 1880-1936)
Spenser: For Hire (TV show)
Spenser, Edmund (Br. poet; 1552-99)
Sperry Rand Corp.
Sperry Univac (US bus.)
Sperry, Elmer Ambrose (US eng./inv.; 1860-
   1930)
Spetznaz (mil.)
Spewack, Bella (playwright; 1899-1990)
Sphinx (myth.)
Sphinx, the Great (Eg.; c2500 BC)
Spic and Span (cleaner)
Spice Islands (also Moluccas)(Indonesia)
Spice Islands (seasoning)
Spider Woman, Kiss of the (film, 1985)
Spider, Alfa Romeo (auto.)
Spider-Man, The Amazing (cartoon chara.)
Spiegel catalog
Spiegel, Der (*The Mirror,* Ger. news mag.)
Spiegel, Inc.
Spiegel, Sam (ent.; 1903-85)
Spiegelman, Art (cartoonist; 1948-)
Spielberg, Steven (ent./writer; 1947-)
Spike (Shelton Jackson) Lee (ent.; 1957-)
Spike Jones (ent.; 1911-1965)
Spillane, Mickey (b. Frank Morrison Spillane)
   (US writer; 1918-)
Spin (mag.)
Spin City (TV show)
Spiner, Brent (ent.; 1949-)
Spinks, Leon (boxing; 1953-)
Spinks, Michael (boxing; 1956-)
Spinoza, Benedict de (also Baruch)(Dutch phil.;
   1632-77)
Spirit (Holy Spirit)
Spirit of St. Louis (Charles Lindbergh plane,
   transatlantic flight)
Spirit, Dodge (auto.)
Spiro T(heodore) Agnew (ex-US VP; 1918-96)
Spitalny, Phil (cond.; 1890-1970)
Spitz, Mark (Andrew)(US swimmer; 1950-)
Spivak, Charlie (ent.)
Spivak, Lawrence (ent.; 1900-94)
Spivey, Victoria (ent.; 1906-76)
Split, Croatia
Spock, Dr. Benjamin (McLane)(US phys./educ.;
   1903-98)
Spock, Mr. (fict. chara., *Star Trek*)
Spode china (also Spode ware)
Spode, Josiah (Br. potter, father; 1733-97)
Spode, Josiah (Br. potter, son; 1754-1827)
Spokane Spokesman-Review (WA newspaper)
Spokane, WA
Spokesman-Review, Spokane (WA newspaper)
Spoleto Festival (also Festival of the Two
   Worlds)(It. and SC)

Spoon River Anthology (by Edgar Lee Masters)
Spooner, William Archibald, Rev. (spoonerism)
Sport (mag.)
Sportage, Kia (auto.)
Sporting News, The (mag.)
Sports Afield (mag.)
Sports Illustrated (mag.)
Sports Illustrated for Kids (mag.)
Sportside, Chevrolet (auto.)
Sportvan, Chevrolet (auto.)
Spotsylvania, PA
Sprachgefühl (linguistics)
Spray'n Wash (stain remover)
Spring Air Bedding, Inc.
Spring Bank Holiday (Br.)
Spring Byington (ent.; 1893-1971)
Spring Valley (vitamins)
Springdale, AR
Springer, Jerry (Gerald)(ent./pol.; 1944-)
Springfield News-Leader (MO newspaper)
Springfield Republican (MA newspaper)
Springfield rifle
Springfield State Journal-Register (IL
    newspaper)
Springfield Union-News (MA newspaper)
Springfield, Buffalo (pop music)
Springfield, Dusty (b. Mary O'Brien)(ent.;
    1939-99)
Springfield, IL, MA, MO, OH, OR, PA, TN, VT
Springfield, Rick (b. Richard Lewis
    Springthorpe)(ent.; 1949-)
Springsteen, Bruce (ent.; 1949-)
Sprint Communications Co.
Sprint Corp. (US bus.)
Sprint PCS (US bus.)
Sprite (soda)
Spruance, Raymond (Ames)(US mil.; 1886-1969)
Spruce Goose (plane)
Spud (Spurgeon Ferdinand) Chandler (baseball;
    1907-90)
Spuds MacKenzie (dog)
Spurs, San Antonio (basketball team)
Sputnik (USSR space satellite, world's 1st)
Spy (mag.)
Spyri, Johanna (Swiss writer; 1827-1901)
Spyros (Panagiotes) Skouras (ent.; 1893-1971)
Squanto (aka Tisquantum)(Wampanoag Native
    Amer./interpreter for Pilgrims; c1590-1622)
Squanto: A Warrior's Tale (film, 1994)
Square One Television (TV show)
Squaw Valley, CA
Squeaky (Lynette) Fromme (US, shot Pres. Ford)
Squeeze (pop music)
Squibb Co., Bristol-Myers
Squirrel Nutkin (fict. chara., The Tale of
    Squirrel Nutkin by Beatrix Potter)
Sr (chem. sym., strontium)
Sranantonga (lang.)
Sri Lanka (Democratic Socialist Republic
    of)(formerly Ceylon)(island, Indian Ocean)
S. R. Nathan (pres., Singapore; 1924-)
SRO (standing room only)
Srpska, Republika (Bosnia-Hercegovina entity)
SS (Schutzstaffel [mil. unit, Nazi party], social
    security)

SSA (Social Security Administration)
S.S. Andrea Doria (steamship, sank 1956)
S. S. Kresge (US bus.; 1867-1966)
S.S. Lusitania (Br. ship sunk by Ger.; 1915)
SSS (Selective Service System)
SST (supersonic transport)
S.S. Titanic (Br. luxury liner; sunk 1912)
St. (see Saint)
Stabenow, Debbie A. (US cong.; 1950-)
Stabler, Kenneth (football; 1945-)
Stack, Robert (ent.; 1919-)
Stacy Keach (ent.; 1941-)
Stade, Frederica Von (ent.; 1945-)
Stadol (med.)
Stafford Cripps, (Sir)(Br. pol.; 1889-1952)
Stafford, Jim (ent.; 1944-)
Stafford, Jo (ent.; 1918-)
Stafford, Thomas P. (astro.; 1930-)
Staffordshire (also Stafford)(county, Eng.)
Staffordshire bull terrier (dog)
Stag's Leap Wine Cellars (US bus.)
Stags' Leap Winery (US bus.)
Stagg, Amos Alonzo (football; 1862-1965)
Stahl, Lesley (US TV jour.; 1941-)
Stahl, Richard (ent.; 1932-)
StairMaster (US bus.)
Stalag 17 (film, 1973)
Stalin, Joseph (b. Iosif Vissarionovich
    Dzhugashvili)(ex-dictator, USSR; 1879-1953)
Stalingrad (now Volgograd)
Stallone, Sylvester "Sly" (ent.; 1946-)
Stamford, CT
Stamos, John (ent.; 1963-)
Stamp Act (Br./US hist.; 1765)
Stamp Act Congress (US hist.; 1765)
Stamp, Terence (ent.; 1938-)
Stan Drake (cartoonist; 1921-97)
Stan Freberg (ent.; 1926-)
Stan(ley) Getz (US jazz; 1927-91)
Stan Kenton (US jazz; 1912-79)
Stan Laurel (b. Arthur Stanley Jefferson)(ent.;
    1890-1965)
Stan Lee (b. Stanley Lieber)(cartoonist, Marvel
    Comics; 1922-)
Stan Mikita (hockey; 1940-)
Stan(ley Frank) Musial ("Stan the Man")
    (baseball; 1920-)
Standard & Poor's 500 (finan.)
Standard & Poor's Corp.
Standard Book Number, International (ISBN)
Standard Oil Co.
Standard Oil Co. of California
Standard Oil Co. of Indiana
Standard Oil Co. of New Jersey
Standard Oil Co. of New Jersey, et al. v. U.S.
    (US law; 1911)
Standardbred (also American trotter)(horse)
Standards, National Bureau of (NBS)(US govt.
    agcy.; est. 1901)
Stander, Lionel (ent.; 1908-94)
Standish, Miles (Br./Amer. settler/mil.; c1584-
    1656)
Stanford-Binet test (intelligence test)
Stanford Linear Accelerator Center (CA)
Stanford University (Stanford, CA)

Stanford White (US arch.; 1853-1906)
Stanford, A(masa) Leland (US bus./finan./pol.;
    1824-93)
Stang, Arnold (ent.; 1925-)
Stanhome, Inc.
Stanhope, Philip Dormer (4th Earl of
    Chesterfield, Lord Philip Chesterfield)(Br.
    writer/pol.; 1694-1773)
Stanislaus James (ex-gov.-gen., St. Lucia)
Stanislaus National Forest
Stanislav S(tanislavavich) Shushkevich (ex-
    pres.; Belarus; 1934-)
Stanislavsky, Konstantin (Sergeivich)(Rus.
    ent.; 1863-1938)
Stanley & Co. Inc., Morgan
Stanley and Iris (film, 1990)
Stanley and (Dr. David) Livingstone, (Sir Henry)
Stanley-Bostitch Inc.
Stanley Cup (ice hockey)
Stanley Dancer (harness racing; 1927-)
Stanley Dean Witter & Co., Morgan
Stanley Dean Witter Online Inc., Morgan
Stanley Donen (ent.; 1924-)
Stanley DW Inc., Morgan
Stanley Elkin (US writer; 1930-)
Stanley Kramer (ent.; 1913-2001)
Stanley Kubrick (ent.; 1928-99)
Stanley (Jasspon) Kunitz (US poet laureate;
    1905-)
Stanley Roger Smith (tennis; 1946-)
Stanley Steemer Carpet Cleaner (US bus.)
Stanley Works (US bus.)
Stanley, (Sir) Henry M(orton)(aka John
    Rowlands)(Br. jour./expl.; 1841-1904)
Stanley, Kim (ent.; 1925-)
Stanton, Edwin M(cMasters)(US mil./pol.;
    1814-69)
Stanton, Elizabeth Cady (US suffragist; 1815-
    1902)
Stanton, Harry Dean (ent.; 1926-)
Stanwyck, Barbara (ent.; 1907-90)
Stanza, Nissan (auto)
Staples, Inc.
Stapleton International Airport (Denver, CO)
Stapleton, Jean (b. Jeanne Murray)(ent.; 1923-)
Stapleton, Maureen (ent.; 1925-)
Star (mag.)
Star-Bulletin, Honolulu (HI newspaper)
Star Chamber, Court of (Br. hist.; 1487-1641)
Star-Ledger, Newark (NJ newspaper)
Star of Bethlehem (rel.)
Star-of-Bethlehem (plant)
Star of David (also Magen David)(6 points, Jew.
    symbol)
Star Search (TV show)
Star-Spangled Banner, The (US national
    anthem by Francis Scott Key)
Star-Telegram, Fort Worth (TX newspaper)
Star Trek (TV show)
Star Trek: Deep Space Nine (TV show; film,
    1993)
Star Trek: First Contact (film, 1996)
Star Trek Generations (film, 1994)
Star Trek II: The Wrath of Khan (film, 1982)

Star Trek III: The Search for Spock (film, 1984)
Star Trek IV: The Voyage Home (film, 1986)
Star Trek: The Motion Picture (film, 1979)
Star Trek: The Next Generation (TV show; film,
    1987)
Star Trek V: The Final Frontier (film, 1989)
Star Trek VI: The Undiscovered Country (film,
    1991)
Star-Tribune, Minneapolis (MN newspaper)
Star Wars (film, 1977)
Star Wars (Strategic Defense Initiative, SDI)
    (US mil.;1983-)
Starwood Hotels & Resorts Worldwide, Inc.
Star, Indianapolis (IN newspaper)
Star, Kansas City (MO newspaper)
Star, Lincoln (NE newspaper)
Starbucks Corp.
Starbucks Coffee Co.
Starfire, Buick (auto.)
Stargell, Willie (baseball; 1941-2001)
Stark, Koo (Br. news)
StarKist Foods, Inc.
Starkist tuna
Starr, Bart (football; 1934-)
Starr, Belle (b. Myra Belle Shirley)(US outlaw;
    1848-89)
Starr, Brenda (comic strip)
Starr, Kay (ent.; 1922-)
Starr, Ken(neth Winston)(US atty./Clinton
    hearings; 1946-)
Starr, Ringo (aka Richard Starkey)(ent.; 1940-)
Starry Night, The (Vincent van Gogh)
Stars and Bars (also Southern Cross)
    (Confederate flag)
Stars and Stripes (also Old Glory)(US flag)
START (Strategic Arms Reduction Talks)(US/
    USSR; 1982-)
Starwood Hotels & Resorts Worldwide, Inc.
STARZ! (TV channel)
STARZ! Cinema (TV channel)
STARZ! Family (TV channel)
STARZ! Theater (TV channel)
Stash Tea Co.
Stassen, Harold (Edward)(US pol.; 1907-2001)
State Farm Insurance
State Farm Life and Accident Assurance Co.
State Farm Life Insurance Co.
State Farm Mutual Automobile Insurance Co.
State Indemnity Co.
State Journal, Madison (WI newspaper)
State-Journal, Lansing (MI newspaper)
State Journal-Register, Springfield (IL
    newspaper)
State of the Union message/address (US govt.)
State, Columbia (SC newspaper)
State, Department of (US govt.)
Staten Island (borough, NYC)
Staten Island Advance (NY newspaper)
Stater Brothers, Inc.
States, War Between the (also War of
    Secession, American Civil War)(1861-65)
Staticin (med.)
Stations of the Cross (rel.)
Statius (Roman poet; c45-c96)
Statler Brothers, The

Statler Hotel
Statue of Liberty (NYC)
Statue of Liberty play (football)
Staub, Rusty (Daniel)(baseball; 1944-)
Staubach, Roger (football; 1942-)
Staudinger, Hermann (Ger. chem.; 1881-1965)
Stavanger, Norway
Stayfree (health)
STD (sexually transmitted disease)(med.)
Stead, Christina (Austl. writer; 1903-83)
steak Diane
Stealth, Dodge (auto.)
Steamboat Springs, CO
Steber, Eleanor (soprano; 1916-90)
Stedman's Medical Dictionary
Steed, John (fict. chara., *The Avengers*)
Steegmuller, Francis (biographer; 1906-94)
Steel Workers of America, United (USWA)
    (union; est. 1942)
Steel, Danielle (writer; 1947-)
Steelcase (office furniture)
Steelcase, Inc.
Steele, Remington (TV show)
Steele, (Sir) Richard (Br. writer; 1672-1729)
Steele, Tommy (ent.; 1936-)
Steelers, Pittsburgh (football team)
Steely Dan (pop music)
Steen, Jan (Havickszoon)(Dutch artist; 1626-79)
Steenburgen, Mary (ent.; 1953-)
Stefan Edberg (tennis; 1966-)
Stefan Milenkovic (also Milenkovich)(violinist;
    1977-)
Stefan Wyszynski, Cardinal (Pol. rel.; 1901-81)
Stefan Zweig (Aus. writer; 1881-1942)
Stefani, Gwen (ent.; 1969-)
Stefanie Powers (b. Stefania Federkiewicz)
    (ent.; 1942-)
Steffens, (Joseph) Lincoln (US writer; 1866-1926)
Steffi (Stephanie Maria) Graf (tennis; 1969-)
Stegner, Wallace (US writer; 1909-93)
Steichen, Edward (US photo.; 1879-1973)
Steig, William (cartoonist, *New Yorker*; 1907-)
Steiger, Janet D. (US ex-chair/FTC; 1939-)
Steiger, Rod (ent.; 1925-)
Stein, Clarence S. (US arch.; 1882-1975)
Stein, Gertrude (US writer; 1874-1946)
Steinbeck, John (Ernst)(US writer; 1902-68)
Steinberg, David (ent.; 1942-)
Steinberg, Saul (US artist; 1914-99)
Steinberg, William (cond.; 1899-1978)
Steinbrenner, George (Michael), III (US bus./
    baseball; 1930-)
Steinem, Gloria (US jour./feminist; 1934-)
Steinkraus, William C. (equestrian; 1925-)
Steinmetz, Charles P(roteus)(Ger./US eng.;
    1865-1923)
Steinway & Sons (US bus.)
Steinway Musical Properties, Inc.
Steinway piano
Steinway, Henry Engelhard (b. Steinweg)(US
    piano manufacturer; 1797-1871)
Stelazine (med.)
Stella Adler (US acting teacher; 1901-1992)
Stella Dallas (film, 1937)
Stella D'oro Biscuit Co., Inc.

Stella McCartney (Br. designer; 1971-)
Stella Stevens (b. Estelle Eggleston)(ent.; 1936-)
Stella, Frank (US artist; 1936-)
Sten gun
Stendhal (aka Marie Henri Beyle)(Fr. writer;
    1783-1842)
StenEd (Stenotype Educational Products, Inc.)
Stenerud, Jan (football; 1942-)
Stengel, Casey (Charles)(baseball; 1890-1975)
Stenmark, Ingemar (skiing; 1956-)
StenoCAT (CAT system)
StenoCAT by Gigatron (US bus.)
Stenograph Corp.
StenoRAM (stenowriter)
StenoRam ULTRA (steno writer)
Stenotype Educational Products, Inc. (StenEd)
Stenovations (US bus.)
Stenoware, Inc.
Stentura (steno writer)
Steny H(amilton) Hoyer (US cong.; 1939-)
Step Saver (cleaner)
Stepford Wives, The (film)
Stephane Grappelli (US jazz; 1908-97)
Stéphane Mallarmé (Fr. poet; 1842-98)
Stephanie Zimbalist (ent.; 1956-)
Stephanopoulos, Constantinos (or
    Konstantinos)(pres., Gr.; 1926-)
Stephanopoulos, George (US pol./jour.; 1961-)
Stephen A. Douglas (US pol./orator; 1813-61)
Stephen Baldwin (ent.; 1966-)
Stephen Biko (b. Stephen Bantu)(SAfr. civil
    rights leader; 1946-77)
Stephen Boyd (b. Stephen Millar)(ent.; 1928-77)
Stephen Collins Foster (US comp.; 1826-64)
Stephen Coonts (US writer; 1946-)
Stephen Crane (US writer; 1871-1900)
Stephen Decatur (US mil.; 1779-1820)
Stephen F. Austin State University
    (Nacagdoches, TX)
Stephen Fuller Austin (Texas colonizer; 1793-
    1836)
Stephen G. Breyer (US jurist; 1938-)
Stephen Girard (US finan.; 1750-1831)
Stephen (William) Hawking (Br. physt./math./
    writer; 1942-)
Stephen Jay Gould (US paleontol./writer; 1941-)
Stephen J. Cannell (ent.; 1942-)
Stephen (Watts) Kearny (US mil.; 1794-1848)
Stephen King (US writer; 1947-)
Stephen Lang (ent.; 1952-)
Stephen (Butler) Leacock (Can. writer/
    humorist; 1868-1944)
Stephen M. "Steve" Case (US bus./AOL; 1958-)
Stephen R. Covey (US writer; 1932-)
Stephen Rea (ent.; 1943-)
Stephen Samuel Wise (Hung./US rabbi/Zionist
    leader; 1874-1949)
Stephen Spender (Br. poet/critic; 1909-95)
Stephen Stills (ent.; 1945-)
Stephen (Joshua) Sondheim (US comp./lyricist;
    1930-)
Stephen Vincent Benét (US writer; 1898-1943)
Stephen Wozniak (US bus./compu.; 1950-)
Stephen, St. (1st Christian martyr; ?-AD 36?)
Stephens, Darren (fict. chara., *Bewitched*)

Stephens, James (ent.; 1951-)
Stephens, James (Ir. writer; 1882-1950)
Stepin Fetchit (b. Lincoln Perry)(ent.; 1898-1985)
Steppenwolf (pop music)
Steppes, the Russian (Rus. grasslands)
Steptoe, Patrick (US phys.; 1914-88)
Sterapred (med.)
Stereo Review (mag.)
Sterling Drug, Inc.
Sterling Hayden (ent.; 1916-86)
Sterling Heights, MI
Sterling Holloway (ent.; 1905-1992)
Sterling Optical (US bus.)
Sterling Vineyards (US bus.)
Stern, David J. (basketball; 1942-)
Stern, Howard (ent.; 1954-)
Stern, Isaac (Rus. violinist; 1920-)
Stern, Richard (US writer; 1928-)
Stern/Sloan Publishers, Inc., Price/
Sterne, Laurence (Ir. writer; 1713-68)
Sternhagen, Frances (ent.; 1930-)
Stetson (cologne)
Stetson (hat)
Stetson Hat Co., Inc.
Stetson, John B(atterson)(US bus.; 1830-1906)
Stettinius, Edward R., Jr. (US bus./pol.; 1900-49)
Steuben glass
Steuben, Friedrich Wilhelm (Ludolf Gerhard
    Augustin) von, Baron (Prussian/US gen.;
    1730-94)
Steubenville, OH
Steve Allen (ent.; 1921-2000)
Steve Austin, "Stone Cold" (b. Steven Williams)
    (wrestling; 1964-)
Steve Buscemi (ent.; 1957-)
Steve Canyon (comic strip)
Steve(n Norman) Carlton (baseball; 1944-)
Steve (Stephen M.) Case (US bus./AOL; 1958-)
Steve Cauthen (jockey)
Steve Ditko (cartoonist, *Spider-Man*; 1927-)
Steve Earle (ent./songwriter; 1955-)
Steve(nson), Forbes, Jr., (Malcolm)(US publ.,
    pol.; 1947-)
Steve Forrest (ent.; 1924-)
Steve Garvey (baseball; 1948-)
Steve Guttenberg (ent.; 1958-)
Steve Harvey (ent.; 1960-)
Steve(n) Jobs (US bus./Apple.; 1955-)
Steve Kanaly (ent.; 1946-)
Steve Kroft (TV jour.; 1945-)
Steve Lawrence (ent.; 1935-)
Steve(n) Mahre (US skier; 1957-)
Steve Marriott (ent.; 1947-)
Steve Martin (ent.; 1945-)
Steve(n) McQueen, (Terrence)(ent.; 1930-80)
Steve (Stephen) Merrill (ex-NH gov.; 1946-)
Steve Ovett (track; 1955-)
Steve (Roland) Prefontaine (runner; 1951-75)
Steve Reich (US comp.; 1936-)
Steve Winwood (ent.; 1948-)
Steven Bochco (ent.; 1943-)
Steven Halpern (ent./writer; 1947-)
Steven Seagal (ent.; 1952-)
Steven Soderbergh (US ent./director; 1963-)
Steven Spielberg (ent./director/writer; 1947-)

Steven Tyler (b. Steven Tallarico)(ent.; 1948-)
Steven Wright (ent.; 1955-)
Stevens International, Inc., Patricia
Stevens, Andrew (ent.; 1955-)
Stevens, Cat (aka Steven Georgiou, Yusuf
    Islam)(ent.; 1948-)
Stevens, Connie (b. Concetta Ann Ingolia)(ent.;
    1938-)
Stevens, Inger (ent.; 1934-70)
Stevens, John Paul (US jurist; 1920-)
Stevens, Ray (b. Harold Ray Ragsdale)(ent.;
    1939-)
Stevens, Risë (ent.; 1913-)
Stevens, Stella (b. Estelle Eggleston)(ent.; 1936-)
Stevens, Ted (US cong.; 1923-)
Stevens, Wallace (US poet; 1879-1955)
Stevenson, Adlai E(wing)(US pol.; 1835-1914)
Stevenson, Adlai E(wing), II (US pol./IL gov.;
    1900-65)
Stevenson, Adlai E(wing), III (US pol.; 1930-)
Stevenson, McLean (ent.; 1929-96)
Stevenson, Parker (ent.; 1952-)
Stevenson, Robert Louis (Balfour)(Scot. writer;
    1850-94)
Stevie Nicks (ent.; 1948-)
Stevie Ray Vaughan (ent.; 1956-90)
Stevie Wonder (b. Steveland Judkins Morris)
    (ent.; 1950-)
Stewart Alsop (jour.; 1914-74)
Stewart Granger, (James)(ent.; 1913-93)
Stewart L(ee) Udall (US ex-secy./interior; 1920-)
Stewart, Dave (baseball; 1957-)
Stewart, Jackie (auto racing; 1939-)
Stewart, James "Jimmy" (ent.; 1908-97)
Stewart, Jon (b. Jonathan Stewart Leibowitz)
    (ent.; 1962-)
Stewart, Martha (US bus.; 1941-)
Stewart, Patrick (ent.; 1940-)
Stewart, Potter (US jurist; 1915-85)
Stewart, Rod (ent.; 1945-)
Stewart, Slam (Leroy Elliot)(ent.; 1914-87)
Stich, Otto (ex-pres., Switz.; 1927-)
Stick Ups (air freshener)
Stick*Free (gum)
Stieff Co., Kirk
Stieglitz, Alfred (US photo.; 1864-1946)
Stiers, David Ogden (ent.; 1942-)
Stijl, de (Dutch art, early 20th c.)
Stiller, Ben (ent.; 1965-)
Stiller, Jerry (ent.; 1929-)
Stills, Stephen (ent.; 1945-)
Stillson wrench (constr.)
Stillwater, OK, MN
Stilphostrol (med.)
Stilton cheese
Stilwell, Joseph W(arren)("Vinegar Joe")(US
    gen.; 1883-1946)
Stimson Doctrine (US denouncement of
    Japanese invasion of Manchuria)
Stimson, Henry L(ewis)(US pol.; 1867-1950)
Stine, R(obert) L(awrence)(writer,
    Goosebumps; 1943-)
Sting (b. Gordon Sumner)(ent.; 1951-)
Stinger (antiaircraft missile)
Stipe (or Stjephan) Mesic (pres., Croatia; 1934-)

Stipe, Michael (ent., R.E.M.; 1960-)
Stirling engine
Stirling, Robert (Scot. rel./inv.; 1790-1878)
Stitt, Sonny (US jazz; 1924-82)
Stock Market Crash (US; 10/24/29)
Stockard Channing (ent.; 1944-)
Stockhausen, Karlheinz (Ger. comp.; 1928-)
Stockholm, Sweden
Stockton, CA
Stockton, Frank (Francis Richard)(US writer; 1834-1902)
Stockton, John (basketball; 1962-)
Stockton, Richard LaClede (tennis; 1951-)
Stockwell, Dean (ent.; 1936-)
Stoicism (phil.)
Stoke-on-Trent, England (also Stoke-upon-Trent)
Stokely Carmichael (aka Kwame Ture)(activist; 1941-98)
Stokely USA, Inc.
Stoker, Bram (Abraham)(Br. writer; 1847-1912)
Stokes respiration/psychosis, Cheyne- (med.)
Stokes, Carl (US TV jour.; 1927-96)
Stokowski, Leopold (Antoni Stanislaw)(US cond.; 1882-1977)
Stolojan, Theodor (ex-PM, Romania)
Stoltenberg, Jens (PM, Nor.; 1959-)
Stoltz, Eric (ent.; 1961-)
Stolz, Mary (Slattery)(US writer; 1920-)
Stone Age (2 million to 4,500 years ago)
Stone Age, Middle (Mesolithic period; 15,000 to 10,000 years ago)
Stone Age, New (Neolithic period; 10,000 to 4,500 years ago)
Stone Age, Old (Paleolithic period; 2 million to 15,000 years ago)
Stone Mill Winery, Inc.
Stone Mountain Memorial (GA)
Stone of Scone (Scot. kings' coronation seat)
Stone, Edward Durell (US arch.; 1902-75)
Stone, Harlan Fiske (US jurist; 1872-1946)
Stone, I. F. (US jour.; 1908-89)
Stone, Irving (US writer; 1903-89)
Stone, Lucy (US suffragist; 1818-93)
Stone, Milburn (ent.; 1904-80)
Stone, Oliver (ent./writer; 1946-)
Stone, Robert (US writer; 1937-)
Stone, Sharon (ent.; 1958-)
Stone, Sly (b. Sylvester Stewart)(ent.; 1944-)
Stonehenge (Salisbury Plain, Eng.)(monument; c2500 BC)
Stoner, Lucy (married woman who keeps maiden name)
Stones, Dwight Edwin (track; 1953-)
Stonewall (Thomas Jonathan) Jackson (US gen.; 1824-63)
Stonewall Jackson (ent.; 1932-)
Stony Hill Vineyard (US bus.)
Stony Point, NY
Stony Ridge Winery (US bus.)
Stooges, Three (Curly, Moe, Larry)
Stookey, Paul (ent.; 1937-)
Stoppard, Tom (b. Thomas Straussler)(Br. writer; 1937-)
Storage Technology Corp.
Storch, Larry (ent.; 1923-)

Storey, David Malcolm (Br. writer; 1933-)
Storm Jameson, (Margaret) (writer; 1897-1986)
Storm, Gale (b. Josephine Owaissa Cottle) (ent.; 1922-)
Story Vineyard (US bus.)
Story, Fort (VA)(mil.)
Story, Joseph (US jurist; 1779-1845)
Storybook Mountain Vineyards (US bus.)
Stossel, John (TV jour.; 1947-)
Stouffer Foods Corp.
Stouffer Hotels & Resorts (US bus.)
Stouffer's frozen food
Stouffer's Lean Cuisine
Stout, Rex (US writer; 1886-1975)
Stove Top dressing
Stover Candies, Inc., Russell
Stow-A-Way Industries (US bus.)
Stowaway Sports Industries, Inc.
Stowe, Harriet Beecher (US writer/abolitionist; 1811-96)
Stowe, Madeleine (ent.; 1958-)
Stoyanov, Petar (pres., Bulgaria; 1952-)
STP (standard temperature and pressure)
STP Corp.
Strabo (Gr. hist./geographer; c63 BC-AD 21)
Strachey, (Giles) Lytton (Br. writer; 1880-1932)
Stradella, Alessandro (It. comp.; 1642-82)
Stradivarius violin
Stradivarius, Antonius (also Antonio Stradivari) (It. violin maker; 1644-1737)
Straight, Beatrice (ent.; 1918-)
Strait of Belle Isle (Labrador/Newfoundland)
Strait of Dover (Eng./Fr.)
Strait of Gibralter (NAfr./Sp.)
Strait of Hormuz (or Ormuz)(Iran)
Strait of Juan de Fuca (also Juan de Fuca Strait)(WA/Can.)
Strait of Magellan (tip of SAmer.)
Strait of Malacca (Indian Ocean/China Sea)
Strait of Messina (channel, Mediterranean)
Strait of Ormuz (or Hormuz)(Iran)
Strait, George (ent.; 1952-)
Straits of Mackinac (Lake Huron/Lake Michigan)
Straits Settlements (Br. colony, SE Asia; 1867-1946)
Strange, Curtis (golf; 1955-)
Strangelove: or, How I Learned to Stop Worrying and Love the Bomb, Dr. (film, 1964)
Strasberg, Lee (US ent./educ.; 1901-82)
Strasberg, Susan (ent.; 1938-99)
Strasbourg, France
Strasky, Jan (ex-PM, Czech.)
Strasser, Robin (ent.; 1945-)
Strasser, Valentine (Esegragbo Melvine)(ex-pres., Sierra Leone; 1965?-)
Stratas, Teresa (soprano; 1938-)
Strategic Air Command (SAC)(US mil.)
Strategic Arms Limitation Talks (SALT)(US/USSR; 1969-89)
Strategic Arms Reduction Talks (START)(US/USSR; 1982-)
Strategic Defense Initiative (SDI, Star Wars)(US mil.;1983-)
Stratemeyer, Edward (US writer; 1862-1930)
Stratford-on-Avon, England (also Stratford-

upon-Avon)(Shakespeare home)
Stratford, CT
Stratford, Ontario, Canada
Strathclyde (region, Scot.)
Strathmore Paper Co.
Stratus, Dodge (auto.)
Straub, Peter (US writer; 1943-)
Straus, Nathan (Ger./US bus./finan.; 1848-1931)
Straus, Oskar (Aus. comp.; 1870-1954)
Straus/Jordan Marsh Co., Abraham &
Strauss Co., Levi
Strauss, Claude Lévi- (Fr. anthrop.; 1908-1990)
Strauss, Franz Joseph (WGer. pol.; 1915-88)
Strauss, Johann (the Elder)(Aus.comp./cond.;
    1804-49)
Strauss, Johann (the Younger)("The Waltz
    King")(Aus. comp.; 1825-99)
Strauss, Josef (Aus. comp.; 1827-70)
Strauss, Levi (US bus.; c1829-1902)
Strauss, Peter (ent.; 1947-)
Strauss, Richard (Georg)(Ger. comp./cond.;
    1864-1949)
Strauss, Robert S. (US dipl./pol.; 1918-)
Stravinsky, Igor F(ederovich)(Rus./US comp.;
    1882-1971)
Strawberry, Darryl (baseball; 1962-)
Strawbridge & Clothier (US bus.)
Strayer University (Washington, DC)
Strayhorn, Billy (US jazz; 1915-67)
Streep, Meryl (ent.; 1949-)
Street, John F. (Phila. mayor; 1943-)
Strega (liqueur)
Streicher, Julius (Ger. Nazi/publ.; 1885-1946)
Streisand, Barbra (ent.; 1942-)
Stresemann, Gustav (ex-chanc., Ger.; 1878-
    1929)
Stresstabs (med.)
Stri-Dex (med.)
Stride Rite (shoes)
Stride Rite Corp.
Strieber, Louis Whitley (US writer; 1945-)
Strindberg, (Johan) August (Swed. writer;
    1849-1912)
Stripes, Stars and (also Old Glory)(US flag)
Stritch, Elaine (ent.; 1926-)
Stroessner, Alfredo (ex-pres., Paraguay; 1912-)
Stroganoff, beef (also beef stroganoff)
Stroh Brewery Co., The
Stroh's beer
Stroheim, Erich Von (ent.; 1885-1957)
Strom Thurmond, J(ames)(US cong.; 1902-)
Stromboli Island (active volcano, It.)
Strouse, Charles (US comp.; 1928-)
Struthers, Sally (ent.; 1948-)
Stuart A. Roosa (astro.; 1933-)
Stuart Davis (US artist; 1894-1964)
Stuart Elliot Eizenstat (US atty./pol.; 1943-)
Stuart Hall Co., Inc.
Stuart Little (E.B. White novel)
Stuart Symington (US pol.; 1901-88)
Stuart, Charles Edward (aka the Young
    Pretender, Bonnie Prince Charles [or
    Charlie])(prince, Br.; 1720-88)
Stuart, Gilbert (Charles)(US artist; 1755-1828)
Stuart, House of (Br. ruling family; 1603-49,

1660-88, 1702-14)
Stuart, J(ames) E(well) B(rown)(US mil.; 1833-
    64)
Stuart, James (Francis) Edward ("Old
    Pretender")(prince, Br.; 1688-1766)
Stuart, Mary (aka Mary, Queen of Scots)
    (queen, Scot.; 1542-87)
Stubbs, George (Br. artist; 1724-1806)
Stubby Kaye (ent.; 1918-97)
Stuckey's Corp.
Studebaker (auto.)
Studebaker, Clement (US bus.; 1831-1901)
Studebaker-Packard Corp.
Student Loan Marketing Association (also
    SLMA, Sallie Mae)
Studio 54 (NYC nightclub)
Studs (Louis) Terkel (US writer; 1912-)
Stunt Dawgs (cartoon)
Sturbridge, MA
Sturgeon, Theodore (aka Edward Hamilton
    Waldo)(US writer; 1918-85)
Sturges, John (ent.; 1910-92)
Sturges, Preston (ent.; 1898-1959)
Sturm und Drang (Storm and Stress)(Ger. lit.;
    18th c.)
Stuttgart Ballet
Stuttgart, Germany
Stutz Bearcat (auto.)
Stutz Motor Car Co. of America
Stuyvesant, Bedford- (Brooklyn neighborhood)
Stuyvesant, Peter (Dutch gov. of NY; 1592-1672)
Styne, Jule (Br./US comp.; 1905-94)
Styrofoam
Styron, William (Clark), Jr. (US writer; 1925-)
Styx (myth. underground river)
Styx (pop music)
Suárez González, Adolfo (ex-PM, Sp.; 1933-)
Suárez, Hugo Banzer (pres., Bolivia; 1926-)
Suave (hair care)
Subaru (auto.)
Subaru Forester (auto.)
Subaru Forester L (auto.)
Subaru Forester S (auto.)
Subaru Impreza (auto.)
Subaru Impreza 2.5RS (auto.)
Subaru Impreza Brighton (auto.)
Subaru Impreza L (auto.)
Subaru Impreza LX (auto.)
Subaru Impreza Outback Sport wagon (auto.)
Subaru Impreza RS (auto.)
Subaru Impreza WRX (auto.)
Subaru Legacy (auto.)
Subaru Legacy Brighton (auto.)
Subaru Legacy GT (auto.)
Subaru Legacy GT Limited (auto.)
Subaru Legacy L (auto.)
Subaru Legacy LS (auto.)
Subaru Legacy LSi (auto.)
Subaru Legacy Outback (auto.)
Subaru Legacy Outback H6-3.0 VDC (auto.)
Subaru Legacy Outback L.L. Bean (auto.)
Subaru Legacy Outback Limited (auto.)
Subaru Legacy Outback wagon (auto.)
Subaru of America, Inc.
Subaru Outback (auto.)

Subaru Outback Limited (auto.)
Subaru SVX (auto.)
Subotica, Serbia
Suburban, Chevrolet/GMC (auto.)
Success (mag.)
Success (rice)
Suchocka, Hanna (ex-PM, Pol.)
Suckling, (Sir) John (Br. poet; 1609-42)
Sucre, Bolivia
Sucrets (med.)
Sudafed (med.)
Sudan (Democratic Republic of)(NE Afr.)
Sudan, French (now Republic of Mali)(NW Afr.)
Sudan, Port (Sudan)
Sudanic tribal (lang.)
Sudanic tribes
Sudbury Consumer Products, Inc.
Sudbury, MA
Sudbury, Ontario, Canada
Sudie and Simpson (film, 1990)
Sue, Sioux City (film, 1946)
SueBee (honey)
Suetonius (Gaius Suetonius Tranquillus)(Roman
    hist.; c69-c140)
Suez Canal (Eg.)
Suez Crisis (mil.; 1956)
Suez, Egypt
Suez, Gulf of (Eg.)
Suffolk (county, Eng.)
Suffolk draft horse
Suffolk sheep
Suffolk, VA
Sufi (rel.)
Sufism (rel.)
Sugar Babies (play)
Sugar Bowl (college football)
Sugar Daddy
Sugar Loaf Mountain (Rio de Janeiro, Brazil)
Sugar Ray Leonard (boxing; 1956-)
Sugar Ray Robinson (b. Walker Smith)(boxing;
    1920-89)
Suharto, Raden (ex-pres., Indonesia; 1921-)
Sui dynasty (Ch. hist.; 589-618)
Suisei (Jap. uncrewed space probe)
Suisse (Fr. for Switz.)
Suk, Josef (Czech. comp.; 1874-1935)
Sukarno, Achmed (ex-pres., Indonesia; 1901-70)
Sukhumi, Georgia
Sukkoth (also Feast of Tabernacles)(rel.)
Sukkur, Pakistan
Sukuma, Nyamwezi- (lang.)
Sulawesi (formerly Celebes)(Indonesian island)
Suleiman (or Solyman)("the Magnificent," "the
    Lawgiver")(sultan, Ottoman Empire; 1494-1566)
Suleyman Demirel (ex-PM, Turk.; 1924-)
Sullavan, Margaret (ent.; 1911-60)
Sullivan, (Sir) Arthur S(eymour)(Br. comp.;
    1842-1900)
Sullivan, Barry (ent.; 1912-94)
Sullivan, Ed(ward Vincent)(ent.; 1902-74)
Sullivan, Francis L. (ent.; 1903-56)
Sullivan, Frank (Francis John)(US humorist;
    1892-1976)
Sullivan, Gilbert & (created comic operas)
Sullivan, Gordon R. (US mil.; 1937-)

Sullivan, Harry Stack (US psych.; 1892-1949)
Sullivan, John (US mil./pol.; 1740-95)
Sullivan, John L(awrence)(boxing; 1858-1918)
Sullivan, Kathleen (ent.)
Sullivan, Louis Henry (US arch.; 1856-1924)
Sullivan, Mike (Michael John)(ex-WY gov.; 1939-)
Sullivan, New York Times v. (US law; 1964)
Sullivan, Susan (ent.; 1944-)
Sullivanian theory (psych.)
Sullivans, The Fighting (film, 1942)
Sully, Thomas (US artist; 1783-1872)
Sultan (chicken)
Sultan of Brunei (Muda Hassanal Bolkiah
    Mu'izzaddin Waddaulah)
Sultanov, Utkir T. (PM, Uzbekistan; 1939-)
Sulu Archipelago (volcanic islands, SW
    Philippines)
Sulu Sea (E of Philippines)
Sulzberger, Arthur Hays (US publ.; 1881-1968)
Sulzberger, Arthur Ochs (US publ.; 1926-)
Sulzberger, Iphigene Ochs (US publ.; 1883-1990)
Sumac, Yma (Peru. ent.; 1927-)
Sumatra (chicken)
Sumatra (island, Indonesia)
Sumaye, Frederick Tluway (PM, Tanzania; 1950-)
Sumer (ancient country, SW Asia)
Sumerian (lang.)
Sumerian civilization (SW Asia; c3500BC)
Sumgait, Azerbaijan
Summer Olympics (also Summer Games)
Summer, Donna (b. LaDonna Gaines)(ent.; 1948-)
Summer's Eve douche
Summerall, Pat (US sportscaster; 1930-)
Summerfall Winterspring, Princess (fict. chara.,
    Howdy Doody)
Summerhill (Eng. school)
Summers, Larry (Lawrence Henry)(US ex-
    secy./treas.; 1954-)
Sumner Locke Elliott (Austl. writer; 1917-91)
Sumner, Charles (US pol.; 1811-74)
Sumners, Rosalynn (figure skating; 1964-)
Sumter, Fort, SC (fort)
Sumter, SC
Sumycin (med.)
SUN (Sunshine Network)(TV channel)
Sun Belt (also Sunbelt, also l.c.)(S/SW US)
Sun Company, Inc.
Sun-Diamond Growers of California (US bus.)
Sun-Lite, Inc.
Sun-Maid Growers of California (US bus.)
Sun Microsystems, Inc.
Sun Myung Moon, Rev. (Korean rel.; 1920-)
Sun Oil Co.
Sun Ra (b. Herman Blount)(US jazz; 1916-93)
Sun-Sentinel, Fort Lauderdale (FL newspaper)
Sun-Telegraph, Pittsburgh (PA newspaper)
Sun-Times, Chicago (IL newspaper)
Sun Tzu (Chinese writer/mil. strategist; c500-
    320 BC)
Sun Valley, ID
Sun Yat-sen (Ch. pol./mil.; 1866-1925)
Sun, Baltimore (MD newspaper)
Sun, Gainesville (FL newspaper)
Sun, Las Vegas (NV newspaper)
Sun, San Bernardino (CA newspaper)

Sun, Toronto (Can. newspaper)
Sun, Vancouver (Can. newspaper)
Sunapee trout (fish)
Sunbeam Appliance Co.
Sunbeam Oster Corp.
Sunbelt (S US)
Sunbird, Pontiac (auto.)
Sunburst Fruit Juices (US bus.)
Sundance Channel (TV channel)
Sundance Kid, Butch Cassidy and the (film, 1969)
Sundance Television, Ltd.
Sundance, Plymouth (auto.)
Sundance: The Early Days, Butch and (film, 1979)
Sundanese (lang./people)
Sunday Afternoon on the Island of La Grande Jatte, A (by Seurat)
Sunday best/clothes
Sunday drive
Sunday-go-to-meeting clothes
Sunday Mirror (Br. newspaper)
Sunday Night Movie, CBS (TV show)
Sunday punch (knockout punch)
Sunday school (also Sabbath school)(rel.)
Sunday, Billy (William Ashley)(US rel.; 1862-1935)
Sunday, Bloody (Rus. hist., 1905; NIre. hist., 1972)
Sundlun, Bruce G. (RI gov.; 1920-)
Sundown Vitamins, Inc.
Sundquist, Don (Kenneth)(TN gov.; 1936-)
Sunfire, Pontiac (auto.)
Sunflower State (nickname, KS)
Sung dynasty (Ch. hist.; 960-1280)
Sung, Kim Il (ex-pres., NKorea; 1912-94)
Sungari (also Songhua)(river, Ch.)
Sunkist (citrus)
Sunkist Growers, Inc.
Sunni Muslim (rel.)
Sunnites (rel.)
Sunny (Martha) von Bulow (US news; 1932-)
Sunny Delight (drink)
Sunnyvale, CA
Sunray Products (US bus.)
Sunrise, FL
Suns, Phoenix (basketball team)
Sunset (mag.)
Sunset Magazine & Books (US bus.)
Sunshine Krispy (crackers)
Sunshine Network (SUN)(TV channel)
Sunshine State (nickname, FL)
Sunshine State (nickname, SD)
Sunsweet prunes
Sununu, John E. (US cong.; 1964-)
Sununu, John H. (US pol./ex-White House chief of staff; 1939-)
Sunyata (rel.)
Super 8 Motels, Inc.
Super Bowl (football)
Super Glue
Superboy (cartoon chara.)
Supercuts (US bus.)
Superdome, the (New Orleans)
Superfund (US govt.)

Supergirl (cartoon chara.)
Superior, Lake (US/Can.)
Superior, Mother (head nun of convent)
Superior, WI
Superman (fict. chara.)
Superman (comics; TV show; film, 1978)
Superman II (film, 1980)
Superman III (film, 1983)
Superman IV (film, 1987)
SuperSonics, Seattle (basketball team)
Supervalu, Inc.
Supper, Last (rel.)
Supper, The Last (da Vinci)
Supper, Lord's (also Holy Communion, Eucharist)(rel.)
Supra, Toyota (auto.)
Suprax (med.)
Suprematism (Rus. art; 1913-18)(also l.c.)
Supreme Being (God)
Supreme Council (also Supreme Soviet)(former USSR govt.)
Supreme Court, U.S. (also High Court)
Supreme Soviet (also Supreme Council)(former USSR govt.)
Supremes, the (pop music)
Sur, Lebanon (site of ancient port of Tyre)
Surabaya, Indonesia
Surat Huseynov (ex-PM, Azerbaijan)
Sure & Natural (health)
Surfak (med.)
Surgeon General (of the US)
Surgeon General's Report (smoking)
Suribachi, Mount (marine flag raising on Iwo Jima)
Surinam toad
Suriname (Republic of)(also Surinam)(formerly Dutch Guiana)(N SAmer.)
Surmontil (med.)
Surrealism (art, lit.; mid 1990s)(also l.c.)
Surrey (county, Eng.)
Surveyor (US uncrewed space probes)
Survivor: The Australian Outback (TV show)
Surya (myth.)
Susan Anspach (ent.; 1939-)
Susan Anton (ent.; 1950-)
Susan B(rownell) Anthony (US reformer/suffragist; 1820-1906)
Susan Cheever (US writer; 1943-)
Susan Clark (ent.; 1940-)
Susan Dey (ent.; 1952-)
Susan Faludi (US writer; 1959-)
Susan Hayward (ent.; 1917-75)
Susan Isaacs (US writer; 1943-)
Susan Love (US phys./activist; 1948-)
Susan Lucci (ent.; 1948-)
Susan Maxwell Berning (golf; 1941-)
Susan McDougal (Whitewater)
Susan M. Collins (US cong.; 1952-)
Susan Ruttan (ent.; 1950-)
Susan Sarandon (b. Susan Abigail Tomaling)(ent.; 1946-)
Susan Seidelman (ent.; 1952-)
Susan Sontag (US writer; 1933-)
Susan St. James (b. Susan Miller)(ent.; 1946-)
Susan Strasberg (ent.; 1938-99)
Susan Sullivan (ent.; 1944-)

Susann, Jacqueline (US writer; 1921-74)
Susanna, Oh! (song)
Susannah (Fletcher) York (ent.; 1942-)
Susquehanna Pfaltzgraff Co.
Susquehanna River (MD/PA/NY)
Susquehanna University (Selinsgrove, PA)
Susquehanna, PA
Sussex cattle
Sussex chicken
Sussex spaniel (dog)
Sussex, East (county, Eng.)
Sussex, West (county, Eng.)
Susskind, David (ent.; 1920-87)
Sustaire (med.)
Sustrisno, Try (Indonesia, pol.)
Susu (people)
Sutherland, Donald (ent.; 1934-)
Sutherland, Graham (Vivian)(Br. artist; 1903-80)
Sutherland, Joan, Dame (opera; 1926-)
Sutherland, Kiefer (ent.; 1966-)
Sutra, Kama (also Kamasutra)(Indian/Sanskrit
   treatise on love)
Sutra, Lotus (rel.)
Sutta Pitaka (rel.)
Sutter Home Winery, Inc.
Sutter, John A(ugustus)(US pioneer, gold;
   1803-80)
Sutter's Mill, CA (gold discovered; 1848)
Sutton, Don(ald Howard)(baseball; 1945-)
Sutton, Willie (US bank robber; 1901-80)
SUV (sport utility vehicle)
Suva, Fiji
Suvari, Mena (ent.; 1979-)
Suvero, Mark di (US artist; 1933-)
Suwannee River (also Swanee)(GA/FL)
Suzanne Farrell (b. Roberta Sue Ficker)(ballet;
   1945-)
Suzanne Pleshette (ent.; 1937-)
Suzanne Somers (b. Suzanne Mahoney)(ent.;
   1946-)
Suzanne Vega (ent.; 1959-)
Suze Orman (finan. writer; 1951-)
Suzette, crepes (also l.c.)
Suzie Wong, The World of (film, 1960)
Suzuki (auto.)
Suzuki Esteem (auto.)
Suzuki Esteem GL (auto.)
Suzuki Esteem GLX (auto.)
Suzuki Esteem GLX+ (auto.)
Suzuki Grand Vitara (auto.)
Suzuki Grand Vitara JLS (auto.)
Suzuki Grand Vitara JLS+ (auto.)
Suzuki Grand Vitara JLX (auto.)
Suzuki Grand Vitara JLX+ (auto.)
Suzuki Grand Vitara JS (auto.)
Suzuki Grand Vitara Limited (auto.)
Suzuki Grand Vitara XL-7 (auto.)
Suzuki Harunobu (Jap. artist; 1725-70)
Suzuki of America Automotive Corp.
Suzuki Samurai (auto.)
Suzuki Sidekick (auto.)
Suzuki Sidekick JLX Sport (auto.)
Suzuki Sidekick JS (auto.)
Suzuki Sidekick JS Sport (auto.)
Suzuki Sidekick JX (auto.)

Suzuki Sidekick JX Sport (auto.)
Suzuki Swift (auto.)
Suzuki Swift GA (auto.)
Suzuki Swift GL (auto.)
Suzuki Vitara (auto.)
Suzuki Vitara JLS (auto.)
Suzuki Vitara JLX (auto.)
Suzuki Vitara JS (auto.)
Suzuki Vitara JS+ (auto.)
Suzuki Vitara JX (auto.)
Suzuki Vitara JX+ (auto.)
Suzuki X-90 (auto.)
Suzuki Zenko (ex-PM, Jap; 1911-)
Suzuki, Daisetz Teitaro (Jap. rel.; 1870-1966)
Suzuki, Ichiro (baseball; 1973-)
Suzuki, Pat (ent.; 1931-)
Suzuki, Shinichi (Jap. violinist/educ.; 1898-1998)
Suzy Parker (model/ent.; 1933-)
Svengali (dominating fict. chara., *Trilby*)
Svenson, Bo (ent.; 1941-)
Sverdlovsk (now Ekaterinburg)
Svetlana (Iosifovna) Alliluyeva, (daughter of J.
   Stalin; 1927-)
Svetovid (myth.)
Sviatoslav Richter (Rus. pianist; 1915-97)
Swabia (region, Ger.)
Swabian League (Ger. hist.; 14th-15th c.)
Swados, Elizabeth (US comp./playwright; 1951-)
Swaggart, Jimmy, Rev. (US rel.; 1935-)
Swahili (also Kiswahili)(lang.)
SWAK (sealed with a kiss)
Swakopmund, Namibia
Swammerdam, Jan (Dutch biol./nat.; 1637-80)
Swamp Fox, the (Francis Marion)(US mil/pol.
   c1732-95)
Swan, John (ex-premier, Bermuda; 1935-)
Swank, Hilary (ent.; 1974-)
*Swann vs. Charlotte-Mecklenburg County Board
   of Education* (US law; 1971)
Swann, Lynn (football; 1952-)
Swansea, MA
Swansea, Wales
Swanson frozen foods
Swanson, Gloria (b. Gloria Josephine Mae
   Svenson)(ent.; 1899-1983)
S.W.A.T. team (also SWAT)(Special Weapons
   and Tactics)(law enforcement)
Swarthmore College (Swarthmore, PA)
Swarthout, Gladys (US opera; 1904-69)
Swatch Watch USA (US bus.)
Swayze, John Cameron (US TV jour.; 1906-95)
Swayze, Patrick (ent.; 1952-)
Swazi (lang./people)
Swaziland (Kingdom of)(SE Afr.)
Sweatt v. Painter (US law; 1950)
Sweden (Kingdom of)(N Eur.)
Swedenborg, Emanuel (Swed. phil./rel.; 1688-
   1772)
Swedenborgians (also Church of the New
   Jerusalem)
Swedes (people)
Swedish (lang./people)
Swedish massage (med.)
Swedish turnip (rutabaga)
Sweeney Todd (play)

Sweeney, D(aniel) B(ernard)(ent.; 1961-)
Sweet Adeline (film, 1926, 1935)
Sweet 'N Low
Sweet Home, OR
Sweet Lorraine (film, 1987)
Sweet Rosie O'Grady (film, 1943)
Sweetheart Cup Co., Inc.
Sweetwater, TX
Swenson, Inga (ent.; 1932-)
Swift and Co. v. U.S. (US law; 1905)
Swift-Eckrich, Armour (US bus.)
Swift, Gustavus (US pioneer meat packer; 1839-1903)
Swift, Jonathan (b. Isaac Bickerstaff)(Br. writer; 1667-1745)
Swift, Kay (US comp.; 1908-93)
Swift, Suzuki (auto.)
Swigert, John L. "Jack," Jr. (astro.; 1931-82)
Swinburne, Algernon (Charles)(Br. poet; 1837-1909)
Swingline stapler
Swingline, Inc.
Swiss (people)
Swiss account (econ.)
Swiss Alps
Swiss army knife
Swiss chard (plant)
Swiss cheese
Swiss Colony Stores, Inc.
Swiss Family Robinson, The (J. Wyss novel)
Swiss Guards (Swiss guards of the pope)
Swiss Miss (pudding)
Swiss steak
Swissair (airline)
Swit, Loretta (ent.; 1937-)
Switzerland (Swiss Confederation)(W Eur.)
Swoosie Kurtz (ent.; 1944-)
Swope, Gerard (US bus./econ.; 1872-1957)
Swope, Herbert Bayard (US jour.; 1882-1958)
Sword/sword of Damocles
Sy (Seymour) Barry (cartoonist; 1928-)
Sy Oliver (US jazz; 1910-88)
Sybarite (wealthy inhabitant, ancient Sybaris) (also l.c.)
Sybil (film, 1975)
Sybil Thorndike, (Agnes), Dame (ent.; 1882-1976)
Sycamore Creek Vineyards (US bus.)
Sydenham, Thomas (Br. phys.; 1624-89)
Sydenham's chorea/disease (med.)
Sydney Boehm (screenwriter)
Sydney Greenstreet (ent.; 1879-1954)
Sydney Omarr (b. Zelig Kimmelman)(astrol.)
Sydney Pollack (ent.; 1934-)
Sydney silky (dog)
Sydney, New South Wales, Australia
Sydney, Nova Scotia, Canada
Sydow, Max Von (Swed. ent.; 1929-)
Sylphide, La (ballet)
Sylphides, Les (ballet)
Sylva, Buddy De (US lyricist; 1895-1950)
Sylvaner (wine)
Sylvania (light bulb)
Sylvania Electric Products, Inc.
Sylvester "Sly" Stallone (ent.; 1946-)

Sylvester the Cat (cartoon chara.)
Sylvestre Nsanzimana (ex-PM, Rwanda)
Sylvia (comic strip)
Sylvia Browne (US psychic)
Sylvia F(eldman) Porter (US finan. writer; 1914-91)
Sylvia Miles (ent.; 1934-)
Sylvia Plath (US writer; 1932-63)
Sylvia Sidney (ent.; 1910-99)
Sylvia Syms (ent.; 1918-92)
Sylvie Kinigi (ex-PM, Burundi)
Symbionese Liberation Army (US urban guerrillas; early '70s)
Symbolism (Fr. art/lit.; late 19th c.)
Symington, Fife (ex-AZ gov.; 1945-)
Symington, Stuart (US pol.; 1901-88)
Symmetrel (med.)
Symons, Arthur (poet/critic; 1865-1945)
Symphonie Fantastique (by H. Berlioz)
Syms Corp.
Syms, Sylvia (ent.; 1918-92)
Synalar (med.)
Synalgos (med.)
Synanon (place, therapy)
Synarel (med.)
Syncom (US space satellite)
Syndecrete (constr.)
Synge, John M(illington)(Ir. writer; 1871-1909)
Synkayvite (med.)
Synoptic Gospels (rel.)
Synthroid (med.)
Syr Darya River (W central Asia)
Syracuse Herald-American (NY newspaper)
Syracuse Herald-Journal (NY newspaper)
Syracuse Post Standard (NY newspaper)
Syracuse watch glass (chem.)
Syracuse, Italy
Syracuse, NY
Syria (Syrian Arab Republic)(SW Asia)
Syriac language
Syrian bear
Syrinx (myth.)
SYSCO Corp.
System of Units, International (also SI, Système Internationale d'Unités)
Szczecin, Poland
Szechwan (also Sichuan)(province, Ch.)
Szechwan cuisine (also Sichuan)
Szeged, Hungary
Szell, George (US cond.; 1897-1970)
Szilard, Leo (US/Hung. physt.; 1898-1964)

-T-

T, Mr. (Lawrence Tero)(ent.; 1952-)
Ta (chem. sym., tantalum)
Taal, the (lang.)
Tab Hunter (b. Arthur Gelien)(ent.; 1931-)
Tabasco (state, Mex.)
Tabasco sauce
Taber's Cyclopedic Medical Dictionary
Tabernacles, Feast of (also Sukkoth)(rel.)
Tabone, Vincent (Censu)(ex-pres., Malta; 1913-)
Tabriz (Pers. rug)
Tabriz, Iran
TACA International Airlines
T account (econ.)
TACE (med.)
Tacitus, Publius Cornelius (Roman hist.; c55-c120)
Taco Bell restaurant
Taco Bell, Inc.
Taco Time International, Inc.
Tacoma News-Tribune (WA newspaper)
Tacoma, Toyota (auto.)
Tacoma, WA
TacoTime restaurant
Tadd Dameron (US jazz; 1917-65)
Tadeusz Mazowiecki (ex-PM, Pol.; 1927-)
Tadjik (also Tajik, Tadzhik)(lang./people)
Tadjoura, Gulf of (Djibouti)
Tadmor (also Palmyra)(ancient city, Syria)
Taegu, South Korea
Taejon, South Korea
Taft-Hartley Act (Labor-Management Relations Act of 1947)
Taft, Bob (Robert Alphonso), II (OH gov.; 1942-)
Taft, Lorado (US sculptor; 1860-1936)
Taft, William Howard (27th US pres.; 1857-1930)
Tagalog (lang./people)
Tagamet (med.)
Taglioni, Maria (It. ballet; 1804-84)
Tagore, (Sir) Rabindranath (Indian poet; 1861-1941)
Tahiti (island, Fr. Polynesia)
Tahitian (lang./people)
Tahoe, Chevrolet (auto.)
Tahoe, Lake (CA/NV)
Tahoua, Niger
Tai (lang./people)
Taichung, Taiwan
Taif, Saudi Arabia
Tailhook Association (Navy/Marine pilot assoc.)
Tailhook sex scandal (US news)
Tainan, Taiwan
Taine, Hippolyte (Adolphe)(Fr. hist.; 1828-93)
Taipei, Taiwan (also Taibei)
Taiping Rebellion (Ch. hist.; 1850-64)
Taiwan (lang.)
Taiwan (Republic of China)(also Formosa)(E Asia)
Taiwanese (people)
Taiyuan, China

Taj Mahal (mausoleum, India)
Tajik (also Tadjik, Tadzhik)(lang./people)
Tajikistan (Republic of)(formerly part of USSR)(central Asia)
Takei, George (ent.; 1939-)
Takeshita, Noboru (ex-PM, Jap.; 1924-2000)
Taking of Pelham One Two Three, The (film, 1974)
Talbot, J(ames) Thomas (US finan./insider trading)
Talbot, William Henry Fox (Br. photo.; 1800-77)
Talbot's (clothing)
Talbots, Inc.
Tale of Mrs. Tiggy-Winkle, The (B. Potter story)
Tales From the Crypt (TV show, comic book)
Tales of Hoffmann, The (Jacques Offenbach opera)
Talia Shire (b. Talia Rose Coppola)(ent.; 1946-)
Taliban (Islamic militia)
Taliban movement, Islamic (mil., Afghan.)
Taliesen West (F. L. Wright)
Talking Heads (pop music)
Talented Mr. Ripley, The (film, 1999)
Tall, Philip the (Philip V)(king, Fr.; c1294-1322)
Talladega National Forest
Tallahassee Democrat (FL newspaper)
Tallahassee, FL
Tallchief, Maria (US ballet; 1925-)
Talleyrand(-Périgord), Charles (Maurice) de (Fr. pol.; 1754-1838)
Tallinn, Estonia
Tallis, Thomas (Br. comp.; c1510-85)
Tallulah Bankhead (ent.; 1902-68)
Talmadge, Constance (ent.; 1897-1973)
Talmadge, Norma (ent.; 1893-1957)
Talmud, the (rel.)
Talon, Eagle (auto.)
Taltos (A. Rice novel)
Talvela, Martti (basso; 1935-89)
Talwin (med.)
Tamale, Ghana
Tamara Karsavina (Rus. ballet; 1885-1978)
Tamayo, Rufino (Mex. artist; 1899-1991)
Tambo, Mr. (slang)
Tambo, Oliver (SAfr. pol.; 1917-93)
Tambocor (med.)
Tambrands, Inc.
Tamburlaine (also Tamerlane)(Mongol mil.; 1336-1405)
Tamil (lang./people)
Taming of the Shrew, The (Shakespeare play)
Tamirat Layne (ex-PM, Ethiopia)
Tamiroff, Akim (ent.; 1899-1972)
Tammany bosses (US hist.)
Tammany Hall (US pol. hist.; 1800-1930s)
Tammany Society (also Columbian Order of NYC)
Tammuz (Jew. month; myth.)
Tammy and the Bachelor (film, 1957)
Tammy and the Doctor (film, 1963)
Tammy Faye (LaValley) Bakker (ex-wife of Jim Bakker; 1942-)
Tammy Grimes (ent.; 1934-)
Tammy Wynette (ent.; 1942-98)
Tampa Bay Buccaneers (football team)
Tampa Bay Lightning (hockey team)

Tampa Times (FL newspaper)
Tampa Tribune (FL newspaper)
Tampa, FL
Tampax (tampons)
Tampax, Inc.
Tampere, Finland
Tampico, Mexico
Tamuning, Guam
Tan, Amy (US writer; 1952-)
Tanaka, Kakuei (ex-PM, Jap.; 1918-93)
Tanaka, Tomoyuki (ent.; 1910-97)
Tandem Computers, Inc.
Tandja Mamadou (pres., Niger; 1938-)
Tandjungpriok, Indonesia
Tandy (compu.)
Tandy Corp.
Tandy, Jessica (ent.; 1909-94)
Taney, Roger Brooke (US jurist; 1777-1864)
T'ang (or Tang) dynasty (Ch. hist.; 618-907)
Tanga, Tanzania
Tanganyika, Lake (E Afr.)
Tangier, Morocco
Tangier, VA
Tanglewood Festival (MA)
Tangshan, China
Tanguay, Eva (ent.; 1878-1947)
Tanguy, Yves (Fr. artist; 1900-55)
Tannenbaum, O (Ger., Christmas tree)
Tannenbaum, O (song)
Tanner, (Leonard) Roscoe, III (tennis; 1951-)
Tanner, Beatrice (aka Mrs. Patrick Campbell)
    (ent.; 1865-1940)
Tannhäuser (Ger. poet; 13th c.)
Tannhäuser (R. Wagner opera)
Tansu Ciller (PM, Turk.)
Tantalus (myth.)
Tantely Andrianarivo (PM, Madagascar; 1954-)
Tantra (rel.)
Tanumafili II, Malietoa (head of state, Samoa;
    1913-)
Tanya Tucker (ent.; 1958-)
Tanzania (United Republic of)(E Afr.)
Tao-te Ching (rel.)
Taoism (rel.)
Taoist (rel.)
Taos, NM
Tapazole (med.)
Tappan (appliances)
Tappan Co., The
Tar Heel State (nickname, NC)
Tara (hill, Ir.)
Tara (plantation, Gone With the Wind)
Tara Lipinski (figure skating; 1982-)
Tarantino, Quentin (ent.; 1963-)
Tarar, Mohammad Rafiq (pres., Pak.; 1929-)
Tarascan (Native SAmer.)
Tarawa atoll (central Pac.)
Tarawa, Kiribati
Tar-baby (fict. chara.)
Tarbell, Ida Minerva (US writer; 1857-1944)
Targa Accessories, Inc.
Targa car radio
Target (stores)
Target Brands, Inc.
Tarif, Sheik Amin (Islamic rel.; 1898-1993)

Tarja Halonen (pres., Fin.; 1943-)
Tarkenton, Fran(cis Asbury)(football; 1940-)
Tarkett, Inc.
Tarkington, (Newton) Booth (US writer; 1869-
    1946)
Tarmidi, Bianrifi (PM, Comoros)
Tarnower, Herman (US phys., Scarsdale Diet;
    1911-80)
Tarpon Springs, FL
Tarrytown, NY
Tarsus, Turkey
Tartabull, Danny (baseball; 1962-)
Tartar (also Tatar)(people)
Tartarstan (E Russia)
Tartarus (myth., lowest region of Hades)
Tartikoff, Brandon (ent.; 1949-97)
Tartu, Estonia
Tartuffe, Le (Molière comedy)
Tarzan (fict. chara.)
Tarzan of the Apes (by Edgar Rice Burroughs)
Tarzan, The Ape Man (film, 1932, 1981)
Tasaday (people)
Tashkent, Uzbekistan
Taslima Nasrin (phys./writer; 1962-)
Tasman Sea (S Pac.)
Tasman, Abel Janszoon (Dutch expl./nav.;
    1603?-59)
Tasmania (state, Austl.)
Tasmanian devil (marsupial)
Tass (Telegrafnoye Agentstvo Sovyetskovo
    Soyuza)(Rus. news agcy.)
Tass, ITAR- (Rus. news org.)
Tasso, Torquato (It. poet; 1544-95)
Tastee-Freez International, Inc.
Taster's Choice (coffee)
Tastykake (pastries)
Tastykake, Inc.
Tatanka Yotanka (Chief Sitting Bull)(Sioux
    Native Amer.; c1831-90)
Tatar (also Tartar)(people)
Tate, (John Orley) Allen (US poet/critic/editor;
    1899-1979)
Tate (Polanski), Sharon (ent.; 1943-69)
Tate Co., Ashton-
Tate Gallery (London)
Tatiana perfume
Tatiana Troyanos (ent.; 1938-)
Tatum O'Neal (ent.; 1963-)
Tatum, Art(hur)(US jazz; 1910-56)
Tatum, Edward Lawrie (US biochem.; 1909-75)
Tatum, Goose (Reese)(basketball; 1921-67)
Tatung (compu.)
Tatung Co. of America, Inc.
Taufa'ahau Tupou IV (king, Tonga; 1918-)
Taupin, Bernie (lyricist; 1950-)
Taurus (zodiac, astron., bull)
Taurus, Ford (auto.)
Taussig, Frank W. (US econ./educ.; 1859-1940)
Taussig, Helen Brooke (US phys.; 1898-1986)
Tavist-1 (med.)
Tavist-D (med.)
Tawney, Richard Henry (Br. hist.; 1880-1962)
Taxco, Mexico
Taxol (med.)
Tay Pay (Thomas Power) O'Connor (Ir. jour./

pol.; 1848-1929)

Taya, Maaouya Ould Sidi Ahmed (pres., Mauritania; 1943-)

Tayback, Vic (b. Victor Tabback)(ent.; 1930-90)

Taye Diggs (ent.; 1971-)

Taylor Caldwell (writer; 1900-85)

Taylor Wine Co., Inc., The

Taylor, A(lan) J(ohn) P(ercivale)(Br. hist.; 1906-89)

Taylor, Ann (designer)

Taylor, (James) Bayard (US jour.; 1825-78)

Taylor, Billy (US jazz; 1921-)

Taylor, Cecil (US jazz; 1933-)

Taylor, Charles (Ghankay)(pres., Liberia; 1948-)

Taylor, Deems (US comp.; 1885-1966)

Taylor, Elizabeth (Rosemond)(ent.; 1932-)

Taylor, Frederick Winslow (US inv.; 1856-1915)

Taylor, James (ent.; 1948-)

Taylor, Laurette (b. Laurette Cooney)(ent.; 1884-1946)

Taylor, Lawrence (football; 1959-)

Taylor, Lord & (US bus.)

Taylor, Maxwell Davenport (US gen.; 1901-87)

Taylor, Niki (model; 1975-)

Taylor, Peter (US writer; 1917-94)

Taylor, Robert (ent.; 1911-69)

Taylor, Rod (ent.; 1930-)

Taylor, Samuel Coleridge- (Br. comp.; 1875-1912)

Taylor, Zachary ("Old Rough and Ready")(12th US pres.; 1784-1850)

Tay-Sachs disease (med.)

Taystee Bakeries (US bus.)

TB (tuberlosis)(med.)

Tb (chem. sym., terbium)

TBA (to be announced)

T-bar (also tee)(constr.)

T(homas) Berry Brazelton II (pediatrician/ writer; 1918-)

Tbilisi, Georgia (formerly Tiflis)

T-bill (Treasury bill)

T-Bird (Thunderbird)(auto.)

TBN (Turner Broadcast Network)(TV channel)

T-bone steak

T-Bone Walker (ent.; 1910-75)

T. Boone Pickens (US bus.; 1928-)

TBS (Turner Broadcast System)(TV channel)

Tc (chem. sym., technetium)

T cell (also T lymphocyte)(med.)

Tchaikovsky, Peter I(lyich)(Rus. comp.; 1840-93)

TCM (Turner Classic Movies)(TV channel)

TD (touchdown)

Te (chem. sym., tellurium)

Tea Leoni (b. Elizabeth Tea Pantaleoni)(ent.; 1966-)

Teach, Edward (also Thatch, Thach, Blackbeard)(pirate; ?-1718)

Teachers Insurance and Annuity Association of America

Teagarden, Jack (Weldon John)(US jazz; 1905-64)

Teamsters Union (International Brotherhood of Teamsters, Chauffeurs, Warehousemen, and Helpers of America)(trade union; est. 1903)

Teaneck, NJ

Teannaki, Teatao (ex-pres., Kiribati)

Teapot Dome scandal (US hist.; 1920s)

Teasdale, Sara (US poet; 1884-1933)

Teatao Teannaki (ex-pres., Kiribati)

Tebaldi, Renata (It. soprano; 1922-)

Tebbetts, Birdie (George R.)(baseball; 1914-99)

Tebet (also Tevet)(Jew. month)

Teburoro Tito (pres., Kiribati; 1953-)

Tech Data Corp.

Technicolor (color process)

Technics (US bus.)

Tecumseh Chief (also Tecumtha)(Shawnee Native Amer.; 1768-1813)

Ted & Alice, Bob & Carol & (film, 1969)

Ted Bundy (US serial killer; 1946-89)

Ted Danson (ent.; 1947-)

Ted DeCorsia (ent.; 1904-73)

Ted Healy (b. Charles Earnest Nash)(ent.; 1896-1937)

Ted (Edward James) Hughes (Br. poet; 1930-98)

Ted Husing (US sportscaster; 1901-62)

Ted (Edward Moore) Kennedy (US cong., bro. of ex-pres.; 1932-)

Ted Key (cartoonist, *Hazel*; 1912-)

Ted Kluszewski (baseball; 1924-88)

Ted Knight (ent.; 1923-86)

Ted Koppel (US TV jour.; 1940-)

Ted Kwalik, (Thaddeus John)(football; 1947-)

Ted Nugent (ent.; 1948-)

Ted Shackelford (ent.; 1946-)

Ted (Edwin Myers) Shawn (US dancer/ choreographer; 1891-1972)

Ted Stevens (US cong.; 1923-)

Ted Turner (US bus./media; 1938-)

Ted (Theodore Samuel) Williams (baseball; 1918-)

Teddy Pendergrass (ent.; 1950-)

Teddy (Theodore) Roosevelt (26th US pres.; 1858-1919)

Teddy Wilson (US jazz; 1912-86)

Tedral (med.)

Teen (mag.)

Teenage Mutant Ninja Turtles (cartoon; film, 1990)

Teflon (nonstick plastic)

Tegopen (med.)

Tegretol (med.)

Tegrin (med.)

Tegucigalpa, Honduras

Tehachapi Mountains (CA)

Tehachapi, CA

Tehran Conference (FDR/Churchill/Stalin; 1943)

Tehran, Iran (also Teheran)

Teicher, Ferrante & (US piano duet)

Te Kanawa, Kiri (soprano; 1944-)

Teke (lang./people)

Tektronix, Inc.

Tel Aviv, Israel (also Tel Aviv-Jaffa)

T(homas) E(dward) Lawrence (of Arabia)(Br. mil.; 1888-1935)

Teledyne Water Pik (US bus.)

Teledyne, Inc.

Telegram Gazette, Worcester (MA newspaper)

Telegram, Portland (ME newspaper)

Telegraph, Macon (GA newspaper)

Telegraph, Worcester (MA newspaper)
Telemann, Georg Philipp (Ger. comp.; 1681-1767)
Teleme (cheese)
Telephoto (comm.)
TelePrompTer
Telescopium (astron., telescope)
Teletype Corp.
Television and Radio Announcers, National Association of (also NATRA)
Television Arts and Sciences, National Academy of (NATAS, Emmy Awards)
Telex (comm.)(also l.c.)
Telex Corp., The
Tell, William (legendary Swiss patriot; 14th c.)
Teller, Dr. Edward (US physt., A-bomb/H-bomb; 1908-)
Telluride, CO
Telly Savalas (ent.; 1924-94)
Telstar (US space satellite)
Telugu (lang./people)
Tema, Ghana
Temne (lang./people)
Tempe, AZ
Tempest, The (Shakespeare play)
Tempestt Bledsoe (ent.; 1973-)
Templar (Knights of the Temple of Solomon) (rel./mil. order; 1119-1307)
Templar, Simon (fict. chara., *The Saint*)
Temple Black, Shirley (US ent./dipl.; 1928-)
Temple of Amen (or Amon)(Karnak, Eg.; built 13th-20th c. BC)
Temple of Artemis at Ephesus (also Artemision)
Temple of Athena (Gr.)
Temple of Athena Nike (Gr.)
Temple of Athena Parthenos (also Parthenon, Gr.)
Temple of Jerusalem (rel.)
Temple of Solomon, Knights of the (also Templar)(rel./mil. order; 1119-1307)
Temple University (Philadelphia, PA)
Temple, Shirley (non-alcoholic cocktail)
Temple, TX
temples of Karnak (Eg., built 21st-1st c. BC)
Templeton Distributors, Inc., Franklin
Templeton Investments, Franklin (US bus.)
Templeton, Alec Andrew (pianist/comp.; 1910-63)
Tempo, Ford (auto.)
Tempra (med.)
Temptations, the (pop music)
Tempter (Satan)
Temuco, Chile
Ten Commandments (also Decalog[ue])(rel.)
Ten Years' War (Cuba/Sp.; 1868-78)
Tenderloin district (city district noted for corruption)
Tenerife (Canary island)
Tenerife (lace)
Tenet, George (US dir./CIA; 1953-)
Tenex (med.)
Teng Hsiao-ping (also Deng Xiaoping)(Ch. pol.; 1904-97)
Tenghui, Lee (ex-pres., Taiwan; 1923-)
Tenneco, Inc.
Tennessean, Nashville (TN newspaper)

Tennessee (Thomas Lanier) Williams (US writer; 1914-83)
Tennessee (TN)
Tennessee Ernie Ford (ent.; 1919-91)
Tennessee River (SE US)
Tennessee Valley Authority (TVA)(US govt. corp.; est. 1933)
Tennessee Valley Authority, Ashwander v. (US law; 1936)
Tennessee walking horse (also Plantation walking horse)
Tenniel, (Sir) John, (Br. artist; 1820-1914)
Tennille, Captain & (Daryl & Toni)(pop music)
Tennille, Toni (ent.; 1943-)
Tennis (mag.)
Tennyson, Alfred, Lord (Br. poet; 1809-92)
Tenoretic (med.)
Tenormin (med.)
Tenskwatawa (Shawnee prophet; c1770-c1835)
Tenuate (med.)
Tenure of Office Act (US hist.; 1867)
Tenzing Norkey (Sherpa mountaineer; climbed Mt. Everest with Sir Edmund Hillary)
Teodoro Obiang Nguema Mbasogo (pres., Equatorial Guinea; 1942-)
Teotihuacán (ancient Mex. city)
Tepe Gawra, Iraq (archeological site)
Terazol (med.)
Terbrugghen, Hendrick (Dutch artist; 1588-1629)
Tercel, Toyota (auto.)
Terence (Mervyn) Rattigan, (Sir)(Br. writer; 1911-77)
Terence (Roman drama.; 185-c159 BC)
Terence Stamp (ent.; 1938-)
Terence Trent D'Arby (ent.; 1962-)
Teresa (of Ávila), St. (Sp. mystic; 1515-82)
Teresa (of Calcutta), Mother (b. Agnes Gonxha Bojaxhiu)(Albanian rel.; 1910-97)
Teresa Brewer (ent.; 1931-)
Teresa Stratas (soprano; 1938-)
Teresa Wright (ent.; 1918-)
Tereshchenko, Sergei (ex-PM, Kazakhstan)
Tereshkova, Valentina (Vladimirovna)(cosmo., 1st woman in space; 1937-)
Terhune, Albert Payson (US writer; 1872-1942)
Teri Garr (ent.; 1949-)
Teri Hatcher (ent.; 1964-)
Terkel, Studs (Louis)(US writer; 1912-)
Termagant (myth.)
Terminator, The (film, 1984)
Terminator 2: Judgment Day (film, 1991)
Terminix International, Inc.
Ter-Petrosyan, Levon (ex-pres., Armenia; 1943-)
Terpsichore (myth.)
Terramycin (med.)
Terre Haute, IN
Terror, Reign of (Fr. hist.; 1793-94)
Terry & the Pirates (comic strip)
Terry Anderson (US jour./former hostage; 1947-)
Terry Bradshaw (football; 1948-)
Terry Drinkwater (US TV jour.; 1936-)
Terry E(dward) Branstad (ex-IA gov.; 1946-)
Terry Fox Story, The (film, 1983)
Terry McAuliffe (US finan./pol.; 1957?-)
Terry Melcher (ent.; 1942-)

Terry Moore (b. Helen Koford)(aka Judy Ford, Jan Ford)(ent.; 1929-)

Terry (Lynn) Nichols (Oklahoma City bombing; 1955-)

Terry-Thomas (b. Thomas Terry Hoar Stevens)(ent.; 1912-90)

Terry (Terence Hardy) Waite (Br. rel., hostage; 1939-)

Terry, Dame Ellen (Alicia)(ent.; 1847-1928)

Terry, Paul (cartoonist, *Mighty Mouse*; 1887-1971)

Tersanctus (also *Sanctus*)(rel.)

Tertiary period (65-2.5 million years ago)

Terylene (polyester fiber)

Tesh, John (ent.; 1952-)

Tesla coil/transformer (elec.)

Tesla, Nikola (Croatian/US elec.eng.; 1856-1943)

Teslac (med.)

Tess Harper (b. Tessie Jean Washam)(ent.; 1950-)

Tess of the D'Urbervilles (T. Hardy novel)

Test Ban Treaty (US/USSR/UK; 1963)

Tet (Viet. holiday)

Tet Offensive (Viet.; 1968)

Tethys (Saturn moon; myth.)

Teton Range (Rocky Mts., WY)

Tetrazzini, chicken (food)

Tetrazzini, Luisa (It. opera; 1874-1940)

Teutonic Knights (Knights of the Teutonic Order)(Ger. mil./rel.; est. 1190)

Tevet (also Tebet)(Jew. month)

Tex (Woodward Maurice) Ritter (ent.; 1907-74)

Tex Avery (cartoonist, *Bugs Bunny, Porky Pig, Daffy Duck*; 1908-80)

Texaco, Inc.

Texarkana Gazette (AR newspaper)

Texarkana, AR, TX

Texas (TX)

Texas Instruments, Inc.

Texas leaguer (baseball)

Texas Longhorn/longhorn (cattle)

Texas Monthly (mag.)

Texas Rangers (baseball team)

Texas Rangers (law enforcement corps; est. 1835)

Texas two-step (dance)

Texas v. White (US law; 1869)

Texasware (US bus.)

Tex-Mex (culture/food/lang./music)

Texsport (US bus.)

Textron, Inc.

Teyateyaneng, Lesotho

T formation (football)

TGIF (thank God it's Friday)

T-group (psych.)

Th (chem. sym., thorium)

Thabo Mbeki (pres. SAfr; 1942-)

Thackeray, William Makepeace (Br. writer; 1811-63)

Thad Cochran (US cong.; 1937-)

Thad Jones (US jazz; 1923-86)

Thaddeus Kosciusko (Tadeusz Andrzej Bonawentura Kosciuszko)(Pol./US mil.; 1746-1817)

Thai (lang./people)

Thai Airways International (airline)

Thai cuisine

Thai stick (slang, marijuana from Thailand)

Thailand (Kingdom of)(formerly Siam)(SE Asia)

Thailand (or Siam), Gulf of

Thalberg, Irving (Grant)(ent.; 1899-1936)

Thales (Gr. phil.; c634-c546 BC)

Thalia (myth.)

Thames River (Eng.)

Than Shwe, Gen. (head of state/chairman, Myanmar; 1933-)

Thanatos (myth.)

Thang, Ton Duc (ex-pres., NViet.; 1888-1980)

Thani, Abdullah bin Khalifa al- (PM, Qatar)

Thani, Sheik Hamad bin Khalifa al- (emir, Qatar; 1950-)

Thani, Sheik Khalifa bin Hamad al- (ex-emir, Qatar; 1932-)

Thanksgiving Day (US)

Thant, U (Burmese dipl./UN; 1909-74)

Tharp, Twyla (US dancer; 1941-)

Tharsis ridge (astron.)

Thatch (or Thach)(aka Edward Teach, Blackbeard)(pirate; ?-1718)

Thatcher, Margaret (Hilda Roberts)(ex-PM, Br.; 1925-)

Thaves, Bob (cartoonist, *Frank and Ernest*; 1924-)

The Hague, Netherlands

Thebes (cities, ancient Gr., ancient Eg.)

Thebes, Seven against (Aeschylus tragedy)

Thebom, Blanche (mezzo-soprano; 1919-)

Theda Bara (b. Theodosia Goodman)(ent.; 1890-1955)

Theismann, Joe (football; 1946-)

Thelma & Louise (film, 1991)

Thelma Ritter (ent.; 1905-69)

Thelonious (Sphere) Monk (US jazz; 1920-82)

Themis (myth.)

Themistocles (Gr. pol./mil.; 527?-460? BC)

Theo van Doesburg (Dutch artist/writer; 1883-1931)

Theo, Vincent & (film, 1990)

Theobid (med.)

Theocritus (Gr. poet; c310-c250 BC)

Theodor Mommsen (Ger. hist.; 1817-1903)

Theodor Schwann (Ger. phys.; 1810-82)

Theodor Stolojan (ex-PM, Romania)

Theodorakis, Mikis (comp.; 1925-)

Theodore Bikel (ent.; 1924-)

Theodore Dreiser (US writer; 1871-1945)

Theodore H. White (US jour.; 1915-86)

Theodore "Ted" Kaczynski (US news, Unabomber)

Theodore M. Hesburgh (US educ.; 1917-)

Theodore N. Vail (US bus.; 1845-1920)

Theodore Rex (film, 1995)

Theodore Roethke (US poet; 1908-1963)

Theodore "Teddy" Roosevelt (26th US pres.; 1858-1919)

Theodore Roosevelt National Park (ND)

Theodore Rousseau, (Pierre Étienne)(Fr. artist; 1812-67)

Theodore Seuss Geisel (pseud. Dr. Seuss)(US writer/artist; 1904-91)

Theodore Sturgeon (aka Edward Hamilton Waldo (US writer; 1918-85)

Theodore W. Schultz (US econ.; 1902-98)

Theo-Dur (med.)

Theognis (Gr. poet; fl. 6th c. BC)
Theolair (med.)
Theology, Doctor of (also D.Th., D.Theol.)
Theophrastus (Gr. phil.; c372-c287 BC)
Theosophical Society (mystical rel.)
Theosophy (rel.)
Theo-24 (med.)
Theovent (med.)
TheraFlu (med.)
Theragran (med.)
Theravada Buddhism (rel.)
Theresa Russell (ent.; 1957-)
Theresa, Maria (empress, Austria; 1717-80)
Therese & Isabelle (film, 1967)
Thérèse of Lisieux, St. (Fr. rel.; 1873-97)
Thermador/Waste King (US bus.)
Thermo Electron Corp.
Thermofax
Thermos
Theron, Charlize (ent./model; 1975-)
Theroux, Paul (US writer; 1941-)
Theseus (myth.)
Thespis (Gr. poet; 6th c. BC)
Thessalonians, I&II (rel., books of the New
  Testament)
Thessaloniki, Greece
Thessaly (region, Gr.)
Thiam, Habib (ex-PM, Senegal)
Thicke, Alan (ent.; 1947-)
Thiès, Senegal
Thieu, Nguyen Van (ex-pres., SViet; 1923-)
Thimbu, Bhutan (also Thimphu)
Thinnes, Roy (ent.)
Thinsulate (fabric)
Thiokol (synthetic rubber)
Thiong'o, Ngugi wa (Kenyan writer; 1938-)
Thiosulfil Forte (med.)
Third of May, 1808 (by Goya)
Third Reich (Nazi Germany; 1933-45)
Third Republic (Fr.; 1870-1940)
Third Rock From the Sun (TV show)
Third World (less developed nations)
Thirteen Colonies (original US states)
Thirty Years' War (Eur.; 1618-48)
Thirtysomething (TV show)
This is Your Life (TV show)
This Morning (TV show)
This Week (TV show)
This Week with David Brinkley (TV show)
Thisbe, Pyramus and (myth.)
Thívai, Greece (formerly Thebes)
Tho, Le Duc (aka Phan Dinh Khai)(NViet pol.;
  1911-90)
Thoeni, Gustavo (skiing; 1951-)
Thom McAn Shoe Co.
Thomas à Becket, St. (Br. rel./pol.; 1118-70)
Thomas A(ndrew) Daschle (US cong.; 1947-)
Thomas A. Dooley (US phys.; 1927-61)
Thomas A(ndrews) Hendricks (ex-US VP; 1819-
  85)
Thomas à Kempis (Gr. rel.; c1380-1471)
Thomas Alva Edison (US inv.; 1847-1931)
Thomas Ambroise (Fr. comp.; 1811-96)
Thomas Andrew Dorsey (father of gospel
  music; 1899-1993)

Thomas Aquinas, St. ("the Angelic Doctor")(It.
  phil./rel.; 1225-74)
Thomas Bailey Aldrich (US writer; 1836-1907)
Thomas Barnardo (Br. reformer; 1845-1905)
Thomas Beecham, (Sir)(Br. cond.; 1879-1961)
Thomas Berger (US writer; 1924-)
Thomas B(abington) Macauley, Baron (Br. hist./
  pol.; 1800-59)
Thomas Bodley, (Sir)(Br. scholar/dipl., founded
  Bodleian Library; 1545-1613)
Thomas Bowdler (Shakespeare editor; 1754-1825)
Thomas Carew (Br. poet; 1595?-1640?)
Thomas Carlyle (Scot. hist.; 1795-1881)
Thomas C. Durant (US indust./finan.; 1820-85)
Thomas Chandler Haliburton (pseud. Sam
  Slick)(Can. writer/judge/hist.; 1796-1865)
Thomas Chatterton (Br. poet; 1752-70)
Thomas Chippendale (Br. furniture designer;
  c1718-79)
Thomas Cole (US artist; 1801-48)
Thomas Coleman du Pont (US bus./pol.; 1863-
  1930)
Thomas Cook (Br. travel agent; 1808-92)
Thomas Cranmer (Br. rel./writer; 1489-1556)
Thomas Crown Affair, The (film, 1999)
Thomas Decker (or Dekker)(Br. writer; 1572?-
  1632?)
Thomas Eakins (US artist; 1844-1916)
Thomas E(dmund) Dewey (ex-gov., NY; 1902-71)
Thomas Fortune Ryan (US bus./finan.; 1851-
  1928)
Thomas (Franklin) "Mack" McLarty, III (US ex-
  White House chief of staff; 1946-)
Thomas G(arrigue) Masaryk (ex-pres., Czech.;
  1850-1937)
Thomas Gage (Br. gen./colonial gov.; 1721-87)
Thomas Gainsborough (Br. artist; 1727-88)
Thomas Gallaudet (US rel./educ. for the deaf;
  1822-1902)
Thomas George "Tommy" Thompson (US secy./
  HHS, ex-WI gov.; 1941-)
Thomas Graham (Scot. chem.; 1805-69)
Thomas Gray (Br. poet; 1716-71)
Thomas Gresham, (Sir)(Br. finan.; 1519?-79)
Thomas Hardy (Br. writer; 1840-1928)
Thomas Harris (US writer, *Silence of the
  Lambs*; 1940-)
Thomas Hart Benton (US artist; 1889-1975)
Thomas Hart Benton (US pol.; 1782-1858)
Thomas Hastings (US arch.; 1860-1929)
Thomas Hearns ("Hit Man")(boxing; 1958-)
Thomas Hobbes (Br. writer/phil.; 1588-1679)
Thomas Hobson (Br. bus.; 1544-1631)
Thomas Hopkins Gallaudet (US educ. for the
  deaf; 1787-1851)
Thomas Hunt Morgan (US geneticist; 1866-1945)
Thomas J(ohn) Watson (US bus.; 1874-1956)
Thomas J(ohn) Watson, Jr. (US bus.; 1914-93)
Thomas J(ohnstone) Lipton, (Sir)(Scot. bus.,
  tea; 1850-1931)
Thomas J. Lipton, Inc.
Thomas Jefferson (3rd US pres.; 1743-1826)
Thomas Jefferson Memorial (DC)
Thomas Jonathan "Stonewall" Jackson (US
  gen.; 1824-63)

Thomas (Michael) Keneally (Austl. writer; 1935-)
Thomas Kennerly, Jr. (pseud. Tom Wolfe)(US writer; 1931-)
Thomas Kid (or Kyd)(Br. writer; c1557-95)
Thomas Kinkade (US art.,"Painter of Light")
Thomas Klestil (pres., Aus.; 1932-)
Thomas K. Mattingly (astro.; 1936-)
Thomas Lawrence, (Sir)(Br. artist; 1769-1830)
Thomas Malory, (Sir)(Br. writer; c1400-71)
Thomas Mann (Ger. writer; 1875-1955)
Thomas McGuane (US writer; 1939-)
Thomas Merton (US rel.; 1915-68)
Thomas Mitchell (ent.; 1892-1962)
Thomas Moore (Ir. poet; 1779-1852)
Thomas More, (Sir)(Br. writer/pol.; 1478-1535)
Thomas Nashe (Br. writer; 1567-1601)
Thomas Nast (US artist/cartoonist; 1840-1902)
Thomas "Tom" Paine (US writer; 1737-1809)
Thomas Pelham-Holles Newcastle (ex-PM, Br.; 1693-1768)
Thomas Penfield Jackson (US atty./judge)
Thomas Pinckney (US pol.; 1750-1828)
Thomas P. "Tip" O'Neill, Jr. (US pol.; 1912-1994)
Thomas P. Stafford (astro.; 1930-)
Thomas Power "Tay Pay" O'Connor (Ir. jour./pol.; 1848-1929)
Thomas Pynchon (US writer; 1937-)
Thomas R(ichard) "Tom" Carper (US cong./ex-DE gov.; 1947-)
Thomas R. Harkin (US cong.; 1939-)
Thomas (Joseph) "Tom" Ridge (PA gov.; 1945-)
Thomas R(obert) Malthus (Br. econ.; 1766-1834)
Thomas R(iley) Marshall (ex-US VP; 1854-1925)
Thomas Schippers (US cond.; 1930-77)
Thomas S. Foley (US pol.; 1929-)
Thomas Sheraton (Br. furniture designer; 1751-1806)
Thomas Sopwith, (Sir)(Br. aircraft designer; 1888-1989)
Thomas Sully (US artist; 1783-1872)
Thomas Sydenham (Br. phys.; 1624-89)
Thomas Tallis (Br. comp.; c1510-85)
Thomas Tryon (writer/ent.; 1926-91)
Thomas "Fats" Waller (US comp./US jazz; 1904-43)
Thomas (Clayton) Wolfe (US writer; 1900-38)
Thomas Wolsey, Cardinal (Br. rel./pol.; 1475-1530)
Thomas' English muffins
Thomas, Clarence (US jurist; 1948-)
Thomas, Craig (US cong.; 1933-)
Thomas, Danny (ent.; 1912-91)
Thomas, Debi (figure skating/phys.; 1967-)
Thomas, Derrick (football; 1967-2000)
Thomas, doubting
Thomas, Dylan (Marlais)(Welsh poet; 1914-53)
Thomas, Frank (baseball; 1968-)
Thomas, George H(enry)(US mil.; 1816-70)
Thomas, Isiah (basketball; 1961-)
Thomas, Jay (ent.; 1948-)
Thomas, Jonathan Taylor (b. Jonathan Weiss) (ent.; 1981-)
Thomas, Kristin Scott (ent.; 1960-)
Thomas, Lowell (US newscaster/expl.; 1892-1981)

Thomas, Marlo (Margaret)(ent.; 1938-)
Thomas, Michael Tilson (cond.; 1944-)
Thomas, Philip Michael (ent.; 1949-)
Thomas, Richard (ent.; 1951-)
Thomas, Rozonda (ent.; 1971-)
Thomas, Terry- (b. Thomas Terry Hoar Stevens)(ent.; 1912-90)
Thomas, Thurman (football; 1966-)
Thomas, Norman M(attoon)(US pol.; 1884-1968)
Thomason, Harry (ent.)
Thomason, Linda Bloodworth- (ent.)
Thomasville Furniture Industries, Inc.
Thomism (phil.)
Thompson & Formby, Inc.
Thompson seedless grapes
Thompson submachine gun (also Tommy gun)
Thompson, David (basketball; 1954-)
Thompson, Dorothy (US writer; 1894-1961)
Thompson, Emma (ent.; 1959-)
Thompson, Fred D. (US cong.; 1942-)
Thompson, Hunter S. (US jour.; 1939-)
Thompson, James Walter (US bus.; 1847-1928)
Thompson, John (basketball; 1941-)
Thompson, John Taliaferro (US mil./inv.; 1860-1940)
Thompson, Lea (ent.; 1961-)
Thompson, Miss Sadie (film, 1953)
Thompson, Sada (ent.; 1929-)
Thompson, Sadie (film, 1929)
Thompson, Tommy (Thomas George)(US secy./HHS, ex-WI gov.; 1941-)
Thomson effect, Joule- (thermodynamics)
Thomson Newspapers Holding, Inc. (Can.)
Thomson, James (US scien./stem cells; 1958-)
Thomson, (Sir) J(oseph) J(ohn)(Br. physt.; 1856-1940)
Thomson, Kenneth R(oy)(Can. bus.; 1923-)
Thomson, Virgil (Garnett)(US comp.; 1896-1989)
Thor (myth.)
Thor Heyerdahl (Nor. expl./anthrop.; 1914-)
Thorazine (med.)
Thoreau, Henry David (US writer/phil./nat.; 1817-62)
Thorndike, (Agnes) Sybil, Dame (ent.; 1882-1976)
Thorne Smith (US writer; 1892-1934)
Thorne-Smith, Courtney (ent.; 1967-)
Thornton (Niven) Wilder (US writer; 1897-1975)
Thornton, Billy Bob (ent.; 1955-)
Thorogood, George (ent.; 1951-)
Thoroughbred (horse)
Thoroughly Modern Millie (film, 1967)
Thorpe, Jim (James Francis)(athlete; 1888-1953)
Thorstein B(unde) Veblen (US econ.; 1857-1929)
Thoth (myth.)
Thousand and One Nights, The (also *Arabian Nights, The Arabian Nights' Entertainments*)(myth.)
Thousand Island dressing
Thousand Islands (St. Lawrence River, US/Can.)
Thousand Oaks, CA
Thrace (ancient empire, SE Eur.)
Three Dog Night (pop music)

Three Emperors' League (Aus.-Hung./Ger./
  Rus.; 1872)
Three Faces of Eve, The (film, 1957)
Three Kingdoms period (Korean hist.; began
  3rd c.)
Three Kings of the Orient (also Wise Men of the
  East, Magi, Three Wise Men)(rel.)
3M (Minnesota Mining & Manufacturing Co.)
Three Men and a Baby (film, 1987)
Three Mile Island (PA)(nuclear accident; 1979)
Three Musicians (by Picasso)
Three Musketeers, The (A. Dumas novel)
Three Musketeers, The (Athos, Porthos, Aramis)
Three Stooges (Curly, Moe, Larry)
Three Suns, The
321 Contact (mag.)
Three Wise Men (also Wise Men of the East,
  Magi, Three Kings of the Orient)(rel.)
three R's, the (reading, 'riting, 'rithmetic)
Three's Company (TV show)
3Com Corp.
Thrift Drug Co.
Thrifty Rent-A-Car System, Inc.
Thucydides (Gr. hist.; c455-c400 BC)
Thugs (former sect of murders/robbers, India)
Thule (northernmost land)
Thule, Greenland
Thumb Tom, Gen. (aka Charles Sherwood
  Stratton)(US circus midget; 1838-83)
Thumb, Tom (fairy tale)
Thumbelina (fairy tale)
Thunder Bay, Ontario, Canada
Thunderbird, Ford (T-Bird)(auto.)
Thurber, James (Grover)(US writer/humorist;
  1894-1961)
Thurgood Marshall (US jurist; 1908-93)
Thuringia (former state, Ger.)
Thurman Munson (baseball; 1947-79)
Thurman, Uma (ent.; 1970-)
Thurmond, J(ames) Strom (US cong.; 1902-)
Thutmose I, II, III (Eg. kings; 1524-1450 BC)
T(erence) H(anbury) White (Br. writer; 1906-64)
Ti (chem. sym., titanium)
Ti, Mo (also Mo-tze, Mo Tzu, Mo-tse, Mo Tse)
  (Ch. phil.; 5th c. BC)
TIAA-CREF (Teachers Insurance and Annuity
  Association-College Retirement Equities Fund)
Tiahuanacu (also Tiahuanaco)(pre-Incan culture)
Tian Tian (panda)
Tiananmen Square (Beijing, Ch.)
Tianjin, China (formerly Tientsin)
Tibbett, Lawrence (Mervil)(ent.; 1896-1960)
Tibbs, Casey (rodeo)
Tiber River (It.)
Tiberius Claudius Drusus Nero Germanicus
  (Claudius I)(emp., Rome; 10 BC-AD 54)
Tiberius, Claudius Nero (Caesar)(emp., Rome;
  42 BC-AD 37)
Tibet (SW Ch.)
Tibetan (lang./people)
Tibetan Book of the Dead, The (rel.)
Tibetan Buddhism
Tibetan languages, Sino-
Tibetan mastiff (dog)
Tibetan spaniel (dog)

Tibetan terrier (dog)
Tibullus (Roman poet; c55-19 BC)
Tiburon, Hyundai (auto.)
Tic Tac Dough (TV show)
Ticketmaster Corp.
Ticlid (med.)
Ticonderoga (ship, nuclear accident off Jap.
  coast; 1965)
Ticonderoga, Fort (NY)(fort)
Ticonderoga, NY
Tide (detergent)
Tiegs, Cheryl (model/ent.; 1947-)
Tientsin (rug)
Tientsin, China (also Tianjin)
Tiepolo ceiling
Tiepolo, Giovanni Battista (It. artist; 1696-1770)
Tierney, Gene (ent.; 1920-91)
Tierra del Fuego (island grp., Chile/Argentina)
Tiffany & Co.
Tiffany (b. Tiffany Renee Darwish)(ent.; 1971-)
Tiffany Chin (figure skating; 1967-)
Tiffany lamp
Tiffany, Charles Lewis (US bus.; 1912-1902)
Tiffany, Louis (Comfort)(US artist/glassmaker;
  1848-1933)
Tiffany's, Breakfast at (film, 1961)
Tiflis (now Tbilisi)
Tigan (med.)
Tiger (Eldrick) Woods (US golf; 1975-)
Tiger Moth airplanes
Tiger? The Lady or the (F.R. Stockton short story)
Tigers, Detroit (baseball team)
Tigger (fict. chara., *Winnie-the-Pooh*)
Tiggy-Winkle, The Tale of Mrs. (B. Potter story)
Tigré (lang./people)
Tigré (region, Ethiopia)
Tigrinya (lang.)
Tigris River (Tur./Iraq)
Tiit, Vahl (ex-PM, Estonia)
Tijuana Brass, Herb Alpert and The (pop music)
Tijuana, Mexico
Tiki, Kon (T. Heyerdahl raft used to cross Pac.;
  1947)
Tiki, Kon- (myth.)
Tilade (med.)
Tilden, Big Bill (William Tatem), Jr. (tennis;
  1893-1953)
Till Eulenspiegel (Ger. legend/practical jokes;
  14th c.)
Tillamook cheese
Tillamook, OR
Tillich, Paul (US rel./phil.; 1886-1965)
Tillis, Mel (ent.; 1932-)
Tillis, Pam (ent.; 1957-)
Tilly, Meg (ent.; 1960-)
Tilsit cheese
Tilton, Charlene (ent.; 1958-)
Tilzer, Albert von (US comp.; 1878-1956)
Tilzer, Harry von (US comp.; 1872-1946)
Tim Allen (b. Timothy Allen Dick)(ent.; 1953-)
Tim Burton (ent.; 1958-)
Tim Conway (ent.; 1933-)
Tim Curry (ent.; 1946-)
Tim Hutchinson (US cong.; 1949-)
Tim Johnson (US cong.; 1946-)

Tim Matheson (ent.; 1947-)
Tim McCarver (ent.; 1941-)
Tim McGraw (ent.; 1966-)
Tim O'Brien (US writer; 1946-)
Tim Reid (ent.; 1944-)
Tim Robbins (ent.; 1958-)
Tim Roth (ent.; 1964-)
Tim Russert (US TV jour.)
Tim White (US anthrop.; 1950-)
Tim, Tiny (b. Herbert Khaury)(ent.; 1923-96)
Timakata, Fred(erick)(ex-pres., Vanuatu; 1936-)
Timberlake, Justin (ent., 'N Sync; 1981-)
Timberwolves, Minnesota (basketball team)
Timbuktu, Mali (also Tombouctou)
Time (mag.)
Time-Life Books (US bus.)
Time Life Libraries, Inc.
Time Life, Inc.
Time Trax (TV show)
Time Warner Communications, Inc.
Time Warner Entertainment Co., L.P.
Time Warner, Inc., AOL
Time, Inc.
Times & World-News, Roanoke (VA newspaper)
Times Book Review, New York
Times-Dispatch, Richmond (VA newspaper)
Times Herald, Middletown (NY newspaper)
Times Mirror Co., The
Times-Picayune, New Orleans (LA newspaper)
Times Roman (type style)
Times Square (NYC)
Times-Union, Albany (NY newspaper)
Times-Union, Jacksonville (FL newspaper)
Times-Union, Rochester (NY newspaper)
Times, Cape Cod (MA newspaper)
Times, Chattanooga (TN newspaper)
Times, El Paso (TX newspaper)
Times, Erie (PA newspaper)
Times, Huntsville (AL newspaper)
Times, Lake County (IN newspaper)
Times, Los Angeles (CA newspaper)
Times, New York (NY newspaper)
Times, Reading (PA newspaper)
Times, Scranton (PA newspaper)
Times, Seattle (WA newspaper)
Times, Shreveport (LA newspaper)
Times, St. Petersburg (FL newspaper)
Times, Tampa (FL newspaper)
Times, Washington (DC newspaper)
Timex Corp.
Timisoara, Romania
Timolide (med.)
Timon (Gr. phil.; c320-c230 BC)
Timon of Athens (by Shakespeare)
Timoptic (med.)
Timoshenko, Semyon (Konstantinovich)(USSR mil.; 1895-1970)
Timothy, I&II (rel., books of the New Testament)
Timothy Bottoms (ent.; 1951-)
Timothy Busfield (ent.; 1957-)
Timothy Dalton (ent.; 1944-)
Timothy Daly (ent.; 1956-)
Timothy Hutton (ent.; 1960-)
Timothy Leary (US educ./writer; 1920-96)
Timothy (James) McVeigh (Oklahoma City

bomber; 1968-2001)
Timurids dynasty (founded by Tamerlane [or Timur], Tartar conqueror)
Tin Pan Alley (district where pop music is published, esp. NYC)
Tina Louise (ent.; 1937-)
Tina Turner (b. Anna Mae Bullock)(ent.; 1938-)
Tina Wesson (TV survivor; 1960-)
Tina Yothers (ent.; 1973-)
Tinactin (med.)
Tindal (med.)
Tinker, Grant (ent.; 1926-)
Tinkertoy
Tinseltown (Hollywood)
Tintoretto, Il (the Little Dyer)(b. Jacopo Robusti)(It. artist; 1518-94)
Tiny Tim (b. Herbert Khaury)(ent.; 1923-96)
Tiny Tim Cratchit (fict. chara., *A Christmas Carol*)
Tiny Toons (cartoon)
Tiomkin, Dimitri (Rus./US comp.; 1899-1979)
Tionne Watkins (ent.; 1970-)
Tip (Thomas P.) O'Neill, Jr. (US pol.; 1912-94)
Tippecanoe (nickname, Wm. Henry Harrison)
Tippecanoe River (IN)
Tippecanoe, Battle of (US hist.; 1811)
Tipper Gore (b. Mary Elizabeth Aitcheson)(US wife of ex-VP; 1948-)
Tipperary, North (county, Ir.)
Tipperary, South (county, Ir.)
Tippett, (Sir) Michael (Kemp)(Br. comp.; 1905-98)
Tippi (Nathalie) Hedren (ent.; 1928-)
Tippy's Taco House, Inc.
Tirana, Albania (also Tiranë)
Tiraspol, Moldova
Tire, General (US bus.)
Tiro (US space satellite)
Tirolean (also Tyrolean, Tyrolese, Tirolese) (clothing style, people)
Tirpitz, Alfred von (Ger. mil.; 1849-1930)
Tirthankara (rel.)
Tisarana (rel.)
Tisha Campbell (ent.; 1970-)
Tishri (Jew. month)
Tissot, J(ames) J(oseph Jacques)(Fr. artist; 1836-1902)
Titan (Saturn moon; myth.)
Titan (US uncrewed space probe)
Titan crane (films)
Titan rocket (US space program)
Titania (queen of fairyland, *Midsummer Night's Dream*)
Titania (Uranus moon)
Titanic (film, 1953, 1997)
Titanic, S.S. (Br. luxury liner; sunk 1912)
TitanSports, Inc.
Titian (b. Tiziano Vecellio)(It. artist; c1477-1576)
Titicaca, Lake (SAmer.)
Tito and Me (film, 1992)
Tito (Toriano) Jackson (ent.; The Jacksons; 1953-)
Tito Puente (US jazz; 1923-2000)
Tito Schipa (tenor; 1890-1965)

Tito, Marshal (Josip Broz)(ex-pres., Yug.; 1892-1980)
Tito, Teburoro (pres., Kiribati; 1953-)
Titograd, Yugoslavia
Titov, Gherman (or Herman) S(tepanovich) (cosmo.; 1935-)
Titralac (med.)
Titta Ruffo (baritone; 1878-1953)
Tittle, Y(elberton) A(braham)(football; 1926-)
Titus (rel., book of the New Testament)
Titus Andronicus (Shakespeare play)
Titus Flavius Sabinus Vespasian(us)(Roman emp.; AD 9-79)
Titus Livius Livy (Roman hist.; 59 BC-AD 17)
Titus Lucretius (Carus)(Roman poet/phil.; c99-c55 BC)
Titus Maccius Plautus (Roman writer; c254-c184 BC)
Titus, Arch of (statue)
Titusville, FL, PA
Tivoli Gardens (It.)
Tivoli, Italy
Tizard, Dame Catherine (Anne)(nee Maclean) (ex-gov.-gen., NewZeal.; 1931-)
TJX Companies, Inc.
Tl (chem. sym., thallium)
Tlaloc (myth.)
TLC (tender, loving care)
TLC (The Learning Channel)(TV channel)
Tlingit (Native Amer.)
TM (trademark, transcendental meditation)
Tm (chem. sym., thulium)
TMC (Movie Channel, The)(TV channel)
TN (Tennessee)
TNN (The National Network)(TV channel)
TNT (trinitrotoluene)(explosive)
TNT (Turner Network Television)(TV channel)
Toad of Toad Hall, Mr. (fict. chara., *The Wind in the Willows*)
Toamasina, Madagascar
Toaripi Lauti (ex-gov.-gen., Tuvalu)
Toastmaster, Inc.
Toastmaster, The (mag.)
Tobacco Road (E. Caldwell novel)
Tobago (Republic of Trinidad and)(West Indies)
Tobey Maguire (ent.; 1975-)
Tobias Smollett (Br. writer; 1721-71)
Tobias Wolff (US writer; 1945-)
Tobin, James (US econ.; 1918-)
Tobit (rel., Apocrypha)
Tobrex (med.)
Tobruk, Libya
Toby Belch, (Sir)(fict. chara., *Twelfth Night*)
Tocqueville, Alexis (Charles Henri Maurice Clérel) de (Fr. hist.; 1805-59)
Today (med.)
Today (TV show)
Today, Melbourne (FL newspaper)
Today, USA (newspaper)
Todd Bridges (ent.; 1965-)
Todd Rundgren (ent./songwriter; 1948-)
Todd, Michael (ent.; 1909-58)
Todd, Richard (ent.; 1919-)
Todd, Sweeney (play)
Todor Zhivkov (ex-pres.; Bulgaria; 1911-98)

Toffler, Alvin (US sociol./writer; 1928-)
Tofilau Eti Alesana (ex-PM, WSamoa; 1921-99)
Tofranil (med.)
Tofutti (US bus.)
Toggenburg (goat)
Togliatti, Palmiro (It. pol.; 1893-1964)
Togo (Republic of)(W Afr.)
Togo D. West, Jr. (US ex-secy./vet. affairs; 1942-)
Togo Heihachiro, Marquis (Jap. mil.; 1847-1934)
Tojo Hideki (ex-PM, Jap.; 1884-1948)
Tokai Corp., Scripto
Tokaj, Hungary (also Tokay)
Tokay (grape, wine)
Tokayev, Kasymzhomart (PM, Kazakhstan; 1953-)
Tokelau Islands (NewZeal.)
Tokina Optical Corp.
Toklas, Alice B. (US writer; 1877-1967)
Toklas!, I Love You, Alice B. (film, 1968)
Tokugawa (Jap. shogun family; 1603-1867)
Tokushima, Japan
Tokyo, Japan
Toledo Blade (OH newspaper)
Toledo, Alejandro (pres., Peru; 1946-)
Toledo, OH
Toledo, Spain
Toliary, Madagascar
Tolinase (med.)
Tolkien, J(ohn) R(onald) R(euel)(Br. writer/educ.; 1892-1973)
Toll House (chocolate chips)
Tolstoy, Leo (Nikolaievich), Count (Rus. writer; 1828-1910)
Toltec (Native Amer./Mex.)
Tom and Jerry (cartoon)
Tom and Jerry (cocktail)
Tom Arnold (ent.; 1959-)
Tom Batiuk (cartoonist; 1947-)
Tom Berenger (b. Thomas Michael Moore)(ent.; 1950-)
Tom Bosley (ent.; 1927-)
Tom Bradley (ex-mayor, Los Angeles, CA; 1917-98)
Tom Brokaw (US TV jour.; 1940-)
Tom (Thomas Richard) Carper (US cong./ex-DE gov.; 1947-)
Tom Carvel (Ger./US bus.; 1908-90)
Tom Clancy (Ir. ent.; 1923-90)
Tom Clancy (US writer; 1947-)
Tom Collins (mixed drink)
Tom Conti (Scot. ent.; 1941-)
Tom Courtenay (ent.; 1937-)
Tom Cruise (b. Thomas Cruise Mapother, IV) (ent.; 1962-)
Tom (Thomas Dale) DeLay (US cong.; 1947-)
Tom Dooley (song)
Tom Ewell (ent.; 1909-94)
Tom Fogarty (ent.; 1942-90)
Tom Gardner (US finan./Motley Fool)
Tom Green (ent.; 1971-)
Tom Hanks (ent.; 1956-)
Tom (Thomas E.) Hayden (US pol.; 1941-)
Tom Hulce (ent.; 1953-)
Tom Jarriel (TV jour.; 1934-)
Tom Jones (H. Fielding novel)

Tom Jones (b. Thomas Jones Woodward)(ent.; 1940-)

Tom Landry (football; 1924-2000)

Tom Mboya (Kenyan pol.; 1930-69)

Tom (Thomas Edwin) Mix (ent.; 1880-1940)

Tom Okker (tennis; 1944-)

Tom (Thomas) Paine (US writer; 1737-1809)

Tom Petty (ent.; 1953-)

Tom Petty and the Heartbreakers (pop music)

Tom Poston (ent.; 1927-)

Tom (Thomas Joseph) Ridge (PA gov.; 1945-)

Tom Sawyer (fict. Mark Twain chara.)

Tom Sawyer, The Adventures of (M. Twain novel)

Tom Seaver (baseball; 1944-)

Tom Selleck (ent.; 1945-)

Tom Shales (US TV critic; 1958-)

Tom Skerritt (ent.; 1933-)

Tom Smothers (ent.; 1937-)

Tom Sneva (auto racing; 1948-)

Tom Snyder (ent.; 1936-)

Tom Stoppard (b. Thomas Straussler)(Br. writer; 1937-)

Tom T. Hall (ent.; 1936-)

Tom Thumb (fairy tale)

Tom Thumb, Gen. (aka Charles Sherwood Stratton)(US circus midget; 1838-83)

Tom Udall (US cong.; 1948-)

Tom Vilsack (IA gov.; 1950-)

Tom Waits (ent.; 1949-)

Tom Watson (golf; 1949-)

Tom Weiskopf (golf; 1942-)

Tom Wilson (cartoonist, Ziggy; 1931-)

Tom Wolfe (aka Thomas Kennerly, Jr.)(US writer; 1931-)

Tom Wopat (ent.; 1951-)

Tom, Dick, and Harry (the ordinary person)

Tom, Long (WWII weapon)

Tom, Peeping

Tom, Uncle (fict. chara., Uncle Tom's Cabin; slang, subservient black)

Tom's Cabin, Uncle (H.B. Stowe novel)

Tomasi Puapua (gov.-gen., Tuvalu; 1938-)

Tomba, Alberto (skiing; 1966-)

Tombaugh, Clyde (discoverer of Pluto; 1906-97)

Tombouctou, Mali (also Timbuktu)

Tombstone, AZ

Tomei, Marisa (ent.; 1964-)

Tomlin, Lily (ent.; 1939-)

Tommaso Guidi (Masaccio)(It. artist; 1401-28?)

Tommie Smith (sprinter; 1944-)

Tommy (Br. slang, army private)

Tommy Aaron (baseball; 1939-84)

Tommy Atkins (slang, Br. army private)

Tommy (Thomas) Chong (ent.; 1938-)

Tommy Dorsey (US cond.; 1905-56)

Tommy gun (also Thompson submachine gun)

Tommy Hilfiger (designer; 1951-)

Tommy James & the Shondells (pop music)

Tommy Lasorda (baseball/ent.; 1927-)

Tommy Lee (b. Thomas Lee Bass)(ent.; 1962-)

Tommy Lee Jones (ent.; 1946-)

Tommy Mottola (ent.; 1949-)

Tommy Sands (ent.; 1937-)

Tommy Steele (ent.; 1936-)

Tommy (Thomas George) Thompson (US secy./

HHS, ex-WI gov.; 1941-)

Tommy Tune (b. Thomas James Tune)(ent.; 1939-)

Tomoyuki Tanaka (ent.; 1910-97)

Tompkins, Daniel D. (ex-US VP; 1774-1825)

Tomsk, Siberia

Ton Duc Thang (ex-pres., NViet; 1888-1980)

Tone Loc (b. Anthony Smith)(ent.; 1966-)

Tone, Franchot (ent.; 1903-68)

Tonelli, Salvatore (captain-regent, San Marino)

Tong, Goh Chok (PM, Singapore; 1941-)

Tonga (Kingdom of)(also Friendly Islands)(SW Pac.)

Tongan (lang./people)

Toni Braxton (ent.; 1966-)

Toni Morrison (b. Chloe Anthony Wofford)(US writer/poet; 1931-)

Toni Tennille (ent.; 1943-)

Tonight (TV show)

Tonight Show with Jay Leno, The (TV show)

Tonight Show, The (TV show)

Tonkin Gulf (also Gulf of Tonkin)(Viet./Ch.)

Tonkin Gulf resolution (US hist.; 1964)

Tonocard (med.)

Tonto, Lone Ranger & (fict. charas.)

Tony Award (theater)

Tony Bennett (b. Anthony Dominick Benedetto) (ent.; 1926-)

Tony Blair (PM, Br.; 1953-)

Tony Conigliaro (baseball; 1945-90)

Tony Curtis (b. Bernard Schwartz)(ent.; 1925-)

Tony Danza (b. Antonio Iadanza)(ent.; 1951-)

Tony Dorsett (football; 1954-)

Tony Dow (ent.; 1945-)

Tony (Anthony) Franciosa (b. Anthony Papaleo) (ent.; 1928-)

Tony Gwynn (baseball; 1960-)

Tony Knowles (Anthony)(AK gov.; 1943-)

Tony (William Anthony) Lake (US ex-nat'l security advisor; 1939-)

Tony Martin (b. Alvin Morris)(ent.; 1913-)

Tony Musante (ent.; 1936-)

Tony (Pedro) Oliva (baseball; 1940-)

Tony Orlando (b. Michael Anthony Orlando Cassivitis)(ent.; 1944-)

Tony Orlando and Dawn (pop music)

Tony (Antonio) Pastor (ent.; 1837-1908)

Tony (Anthony) Perkins (ent.; 1932-92)

Tony Randall (b. Arthur Leonard Rosenberg)(ent.; 1920-)

Tony Richardson (ent.; 1928-91)

Tony Roberts (ent.; 1939-)

Tony Rodham (US bro. of Hillary)

Tony (Anthony Allen) Williams (DC mayor; 1951-)

Tonya Harding (US figure skating/US news; 1970-)

Tooele Army Depot (UT)(US mil.)

Toomey, Regis (ent.; 1898-1991)

Toomey, William (decathlon; 1939-)

TOON (Toon Disney)(TV channel)

Toon Disney (TOON)(TV channel)

Toonerville trolley (dilapidated train/trolley)

Tootsie (film, 1982)

Tootsie Pop (candy)

Tootsie Roll (candy)

Tootsie Roll Industries, Inc.

Toowoomba, Queensland, Australia
Top Forty (also Top 40, top forty)
Top Gun (film, 1986)
Top of the Mark (Mark Hopkins Hotel, San
 Francisco)
Top-Sider (shoe)
Topaz, Mercury (auto.)
Topeka, KS
Tophet(h)(place of punishment after death)
Topicort (med.)
Topicycline (med.)
Topol (toothpaste)
Tora! Tora! Tora! (film, 1970)
Toradol (med.)
Torah (also Pentateuch)(1st 5 books of Bible)
Torch Song Trilogy (play)
Tori (Myra Ellen) Amos (ent.; 1963-)
Tori (Victoria Davey) Spelling (ent.; 1973-)
Tormak, Kyrgyzstan
Torme, Mel (ent.; 1925-99)
Torn, Rip (b. Elmore Rual Torn, Jr.)(ent.; 1931-)
Tornalate (med.)
Toro (lawn care)
Toro Co., The
Toronado, Oldsmobile (auto.)
Toronto Blue Jays (baseball team)
Toronto Globe & Mail (Can. newspaper)
Toronto Maple Leafs (hockey team)
Toronto SkyDome
Toronto Sun (Can. newspaper)
Toronto, Ontario, Canada
Torquato Tasso (It. poet; 1544-95)
Torrance, CA
Torremolinos, Spain
Torrens Act (Austl. hist.; 1857)
Torrens, (Sir) Robert Richard (Br. pol. in Austl.;
 1814-84)
Torrey pine (tree)
Torricelli, Robert (US cong.; 1951-)
Torrid Zone (also Tropical Zone, Tropics)
 (between tropics of Cancer and Capricorn)
Torrijos Herrera, Omar (Panamanian gen./pol.;
 1929-81)
Tors, Ivan (ent.; 1916-83)
Tortilla Flat (John Steinbeck novel)
Tortola (Br. Virgin Island)
Tortuga (island, Haiti)
Torvill, Jayne (figure skating; 1957-)
Tory Party (Br. pol. party; c1680-1830)
Tosca (Giacomo Puccini opera)
Toscanini, Arturo (It. cond.; 1867-1957)
Toshiba (elect.)
Toshiba America Business Solutions, Inc.
Toshiba America, Inc.
Toshiba American Information Systems, Inc.
Toshiki, Kaifu (ex-PM, Jap.; 1931-)
Toshiro, Mifune (Jap. actor; 1920-97)
Tostitos
Totacillin (med.)
Totally Different Pauly (TV show)
Totenberg, Nina (US jour.; 1944-)
Totie Fields (ent.; 1931-78)
Totino's Pizza Co.
Toto (dog, *Wizard of Oz*)
Toucouleur (people)

Tough, Dave (US jazz; 1908-48)
Toulouse (goose)
Toulouse, France
Toulouse-Lautrec, Henri (Marie Raymond) de
 (Fr. artist; 1864-1901)
Tour de France (Fr. bicycle race)
Toure, Amadou Toumani (ex-pres., Mali)
Tourette's syndrome/disease (med.)
Touring America (mag.)
Tournament of Roses Parade
Tours, France
Tov, Baal Shem- (also Israel ben Eliezer)(Jew.
 rel.; c1700-60)
Tovah Feldshuh (ent.; 1952-)
Tower Books
Tower of Babel (Babylon, different languages)
Tower of London (fortress; built 1078)
Tower Records/Video
Tower, John G. (US pol.; 1926-91)
Towle Manufacturing Co.
Town & Country (mag.)
Town Car, Lincoln (auto.)
Town & Country, Chrysler (auto.)
Townes, Charles Hard (US physt./educ.; 1915-)
Townsend plan (pension plan, never enacted)
Townsend, Francis E(verett)(US phys./
 reformer; 1867-1960)
Townsend, Port (WA)
Townsend, Robert (ent.; 1957-)
Townshend Acts (Br./Amer. hist.; 1767)
Townshend, Charles (Br. pol., Townshend Acts;
 1725-67)
Townshend, Charles, Viscount ("Turnip")(Br.
 pol./agr.; 1675-1738)
Townshend, George, Marquis (Br. mil.; 1724-
 1807)
Townshend, Pete(r Dennis Blandford)(ent./The
 Who; 1945-)
Townsville, Queensland, Australia
Towson University (Towson, MD)
Towson, MD
Toynbee, Arnold (Joseph)(Br. hist.; 1889-1975)
Toyota (auto.)
Toyota Avalon (auto.)
Toyota Avalon XL (auto.)
Toyota Avalon XLS (auto.)
Toyota Camry (auto.)
Toyota Camry CE (auto.)
Toyota Camry DX (auto.)
Toyota Camry LE (auto.)
Toyota Camry SE (auto.)
Toyota Camry Solara (auto.)
Toyota Camry Solara SE (auto.)
Toyota Camry Solara SLE (auto.)
Toyota Camry XLE (auto.)
Toyota Celica (auto.)
Toyota Celica GT (auto.)
Toyota Celica GT Limited (auto.)
Toyota Celica GT-S (auto.)
Toyota Celica ST (auto.)
Toyota Celica ST Limited (auto.)
Toyota Corolla (auto.)
Toyota Corolla CE (auto.)
Toyota Corolla DX (auto.)
Toyota Corolla LE (auto.)

Toyota Corolla S (auto.)
Toyota Corolla VE (auto.)
Toyota Echo (auto.)
Toyota 4Runner (auto.)
Toyota 4Runner Limited (auto.)
Toyota 4Runner SR4 (auto.)
Toyota 4Runner SR5 (auto.)
Toyota Highlander (auto.)
Toyota Land Cruiser (auto.)
Toyota Motor Sales, U.S.A., Inc.
Toyota MR2 (auto.)
Toyota MR2 Spyder (auto.)
Toyota Paseo (auto.)
Toyota Previa (auto.)
Toyota Previa DX minivan (auto.)
Toyota Previa LE minivan (auto.)
Toyota Prius (auto.)
Toyota RAV4 (auto.)
Toyota Sequoia (auto.)
Toyota Sequoia Limited (auto.)
Toyota Sequoia SR5 (auto.)
Toyota Sienna CE minivan (auto.)
Toyota Sienna LE minivan (auto.)
Toyota Sienna minivan (auto.)
Toyota Sienna XLE minivan (auto.)
Toyota Supra (auto.)
Toyota Supra Turbo (auto.)
Toyota T100 (auto.)
Toyota Tacoma Double Cab (auto.)
Toyota Tacoma pickup (auto.)
Toyota Tacoma PreRunner (auto.)
Toyota Tacoma S-Runner (auto.)
Toyota Tacoma Xtracab (auto.)
Toyota Tercel (auto.)
Toyota Tercel CE (auto.)
Toyota Tercel DX (auto.)
Toyota Tercel Limited (auto.)
Toyota Tundra Access Cab (auto.)
Toyota Tundra pickup (auto.)
Toyota Tundra regular cab (auto.)
Toys "R" Us (US bus.)
TPN (total parenteral nutrition)(med.)
Trabzon, Turkey (also Trebizond)
Tracer, Mercury (auto.)
Tracey Gold (ent.; 1969-)
Tracey Ullman (ent.; 1959-)
Traci Lords (b. Nora Louise Kuzma)(ent.; 1968-)
Tracker, Chevrolet (auto.)
Tracker, Geo (Chevrolet)(auto.)
Tracy Austin (tennis; 1962-)
Tracy Caulkins (swimming; 1963-)
Tracy Chapman (ent.; 1964-)
Tracy Keenan Wynn (ent./screenwriter)
Tracy Nelson (ent.; 1963-)
Tracy Pollan (ent.; 1960-)
Tracy, Dick (fict. chara.)
Tracy, Spencer (US ent.; 1900-67)
Trade Representative, Office of the U.S. (US govt.)
Trade Unions Congress (TUC)(Br.)
Trader Vic's (restaurant)
Trader Vic's Food Products, Inc.
Trafalgar Square (London)
Trafalgar, Battle of (Eng./Fr.-Sp.; 1805)
Traffic (pop music)

Tragedy of Othello, The Moor of Venice, The (Shakespeare play)
Trail of the Pink Panther (film, 1982)
Trailblazer (US bus.)
TrailBlazer, Chevrolet (auto.)
Trail Blazers, Portland (basketball team)
Trailways bus
Trajkovski, Boris (pres., Macedonia; 1956-)
Trakehner (horse)
Tralee, Ireland
Tran Duc Luong (pres., Viet.; 1937-)
Trandate (med.)
Trane (air conditioner)
Tranquility, Sea of (also Mare Tranquillitatus) (dark plain on Moon)
Trans African Airline
Trans-Alaskan Pipeline (oil transport; 1977-)
Trans Am, Pontiac (auto.)
Trans-Amazonian Highway (also Transamazonica)(Brazil; 1970-)
Transamerica Corp.
Transamerica Pyramid
Transbrasil Airlines
Transderm Scop (med.)
Transderm-Nitro (med.)
Transjordan (area, Jordan)
Transportation Safety Board, National (US govt. agcy.; est. 1975)
Transportation, Department of (DOT)(US govt.)
Trans-Siberian Railway (>7,000 miles)
Trans Sport, Pontiac (auto.)
Transvaal, South Africa
Trans World Airlines, Inc. (TWA)
Transylvania (region, Romania)
Transylvanian Alps
Tranxene (med.)
Trapp Family Singers
Trapp, Baroness Maria Von (b. Maria Augusta Kutschera)(Aus. singer; 1905-87)
Trapper John, M.D. (TV show, fict. chara.)
Trapper Keeper notebook
Trappist (monk/nun order; est. 1664)
Trappist cheese (also Gethsemane cheese)
Traubel, Helen (US opera; 1903-72)
Travanti, Daniel J. (ent.; 1940-)
Travel & Leisure (mag.)
Travel Channel (TV channel)
Travel Holiday (mag.)
Travelers Aid Association of America (est. 1917)
Travelers Corp.
Travelocity
Travelodge International, Inc.
Travers, Mary (ent.; 1936-)
Travers, P(amela) L. (Austl. writer; 1906-96)
Traviata, La (G. Verdi opera)
Travis Air Force Base, CA (US mil.)
Travis Tritt (ent.; 1963-)
Travis, Merle (ent.; 1917-83)
Travis, Randy (b. Randy Traywick)(ent.; 1959-)
Travolta, John (ent.; 1954-)
Treacher, Arthur (ent.; 1894-1975)
Treacher's Fish & Chips, Arthur (US bus.)
Treadway Hotels & Resorts (US bus.)
Treasure Island (R. L. Stevenson novel)
Treasure Island Naval Station (CA)

Treasure Island, FL, TN
Treasure State (nickname, MT)
Treasurer of the United States
Treasury, Department of the (US govt.)
Treat (Richard) Williams (ent.; 1951-)
Treaty of Amiens (Br. & Fr./Sp./Batavia; 1802)
Treaty of Cambrai (Rome/Fr.; 1529)
Treaty of Ghent (US/Br.; 1814)
Treaty of Guadalupe Hidalgo (ended Mexican
    War; 1848)
Treaty of London (Br./Fr./Rus./It.; 1915)
Treaty of Paris (various peace treaties)
Treaty of Versailles (Allies/Ger.; 1919)
Trebek, Alex (ent.; 1940-)
Trebizond Empire (c1204-1461)
Trebizond, Turkey (also Trabzon)
Treblinka (Nazi concentration camp, Pol.)
Tree of Life, Inc.
Tree Top, Inc.
Tree, Ellen (Kean)(ent.; 1806-80)
Tree, (Sir) Herbert (b. Herbert Beerbohm)(ent.;
    1853-1917)
Treeing Walker coonhound (dog)
Trekkie (*Star Trek* fan)
Tremayne, Les (ent.; 1913-)
Trenary, Jill (figure skating; 1968-)
Trent Affair (Br./US; 1861)
Trent Lott (US cong.; 1941-)
Trent Reznor (ent., Nine Inch Nails; 1965-)
Trent River (Eng.)
Trent, Council of (rel. hist.; 1545-63)
Trental (med.)
Trenton Times (NJ newspaper)
Trenton, MI, NJ
Trenton, Ontario, Canada
Trentonian (NJ newspaper)
Trevelyan, George Macaulay (Br. hist.; 1876-
    1962)
Trevelyan, (Sir) George (Otto)(Br. hist.; 1838-
    1928)
Trevi Fountain (Rome)
Trevino, Lee (golf; 1939-)
Trevor, Claire (ent.; 1909-2000)
T-Rex
Triad (Ch. secret society; est. AD 36)
Triaminic (med.)
Triaminicin (med.)
Triaminicol (med.)
Triangle Shirtwaist Factory fire (NYC)(lead to
    labor reform; 1911)
Triangulum (astron., triangle)
Triangulum Australe (astron., Southern Triangle)
Trianon, Le Petit (built for Mme. de Pompadour
    by Louis XV)
Triassic period (225-195 million years ago)
Triavil (med.)
TriBeCa (NYC)(also Tribeca)
Tribes of Israel
Triborough Bridge (NYC)
Tribune Co.
Tribune-Review, Greensburg (PA newspaper)
Tribune, Albuquerque (NM newspaper)
Tribune, Chicago (IL newspaper)
Tribune, Oakland (CA newspaper)
Tribune, Salt Lake City (UT newspaper)

Tribune, Scranton (PA newspaper)
Tribune, South Bend (IN newspaper)
Tribune, Tampa (FL newspaper)
Tribute, Mazda (auto.)
Trichomonas (med.)
Tricia (Patricia) Nixon Cox (daughter of ex-US
    pres.; 1946-)
Tricon Global Restaurants, Inc.
Trident (US nuclear missile)
Trident gum
Tridesilon (med.)
Tridil (med.)
Trier (wine glass)
Trier, Germany
Trieste, Italy
Trifari (US bus.)
Trigère, Pauline (US designer; 1912-)
Trigesic (med.)
Trigger (Roy Rogers' horse)
Trilafon (med.)
Tri-Levlen (med.)
Trilisate (med.)
Trillin, Calvin (US writer; 1935-)
Trilling, Diana (US writer; 1905-96)
Trilling, Lionel (US writer/educ.; 1905-75)
Trimox (med.)
Trimurti (rel.)
Trinalin (med.)
Trincomalee, Sri Lanka
Trini Lopez (ent.; 1937-)
Trinidad and Tobago (Republic of)(West Indies)
Trinity College (Hartford, CT; Washington, DC;
    Dunedin, FL; Deerfield, IL; Burlington, VT;
    Dublin, Ir.)
Trinity Industries, Inc.
Trinity Sunday (Sunday after Pentecost)(rel.)
Trinity University (San Antonio, TX)
Trinity, the (also Holy Trinity)(Father, Son, Holy
    Ghost/Spirit)(rel.)
Tri-Norinyl (med.)
Triphasil (med.)
Tripitaka (also Pali Canon)(rel.)
Triple Alliance (Eur. hist.; various countries/dates)
Triple Crown (baseball)
Triple Crown (horse racing)
Triple Entente (Br./Fr./Rus.; 1907-17)
Tripoli, Lebanon
Tripoli, Libya
Tripolitan War (US/Tripoli; 1801-5)
Tripp, Linda Rose (nee Carotenuto)(US news;
    1949-)
Tris(tram) Speaker (baseball; 1888-1958)
Triscuit, Nabisco (crackers)
Trisha Brown (choreographer; 1936-)
Trisha Yearwood (ent.; 1964-)
Tristan and Isolde (also Tristam, Iseult)(Celtic
    legend)
Tristan da Cunha (Br. volcanic islands, S Atl.)
Tristano, Lennie (US jazz; 1919-78)
Tristesse, Bonjour (F. Sagan novel)
Tristram Shandy (Laurence Sterne novel)
Triton (Neptune moon; myth.)
Tritt, Travis (ent.; 1963-)
Triumvirate, First/Second (ancient Rome ruling
    board)

Trivandrum, India
Trivial Pursuit (game)
Trix cereal
Troilus and Cressida (Shakespeare play)
Trois-Rivières, Quebec, Canada (Three Rivers)
Trojan (condom)
Trojan Horse (myth.)
Trojan War (Asia Minor; mid 13th c. BC)
Trojan Women, The (Euripides tragedy)
Troll Magazine (mag.)
Trollope, Anthony (Br. writer; 1815-82)
Trombe wall (constr.)
Trondheim, Norway
Tronothane (med.)
Trooper, Isuzu (auto.)
Tropic of Cancer (H. Miller novel)
Tropic of Capricorn (H. Miller novel)
tropic of Cancer (23° 27′ N of equator)
tropic of Capricorn (23° 27′ S of equator)
Tropical Zone (also Tropics, Torrid Zone)
  (between tropics of Cancer and Capricorn)
Tropicana Products, Inc.
Trotsky, Léon (b. Lev Davidovich Bronstein)
  (USSR pol.; 1879-1940)
Trotskyism (pol. phil.)
Trottier, Bryan (hockey; 1956-)
Trout, Robert (b. Robert Albert Blondheim)(TV
  jour.; 1909-2000)
Trovatore, Il (Verdi opera)
Trovoada, Miguel (pres., São Tomé/Príncipe;
  1936-)
T. Rowe Price Group, Inc.
T. Rowe Price Investment Services, Inc.
Trower, Robin (ent.; 1945-)
Troy (ancient city, Asia Minor)
Troy-Bilt (garden equip.)
Troy Donahue (b. Merle Johnson)(ent.; 1936-
  2001)
Troy, AL, MI, NY, OH
Troyanos, Tatiana (ent.; 1938-)
Truckee, CA
Trudeau, Garry (Can./US cartoonist,
  Doonesbury; 1948-)
Trudeau, Margaret (Can., ex-wife of ex-PM)
Trudeau, Pierre (Elliott)(ex-PM, Can.; 1919-
  2000)
True Grit (film, 1969)
True Story (mag.)
True Story Plus (mag.)
Truex, Ernest (ent.; 1890-1973)
Truffaut, François (Fr. ent.; 1932-84)
Trujillo, César Gaviria (ex-pres., Colombia; 1947-)
Trujillo, Peru
Trukese (people)
Truman Bradley (ent.; 1905-74)
Truman Capote (US writer; 1924-84)
Truman Doctrine (US hist.; 1947)
Truman Show, The (film, 1998)
Truman, Bess (Wallace)(wife of ex-US pres.;
  1885-1982)
Truman, Harry S (33rd US pres.; 1884-1972)
Truman, (Mary) Margaret (daughter of ex-US
  pres.; 1924-)
Trumbull, John (US artist; 1756-1843)
Trumbull, John (US poet/atty.; 1750-1831)

Trumbull, Jonathan (US pol.; 1710-85)
Trump (Mazzucchelli), Ivana (nee Zelnicek)(US
  bus./ex-wife of D. Trump; 1949-)
Trump, Donald (John)(US bus.; 1946-)
Truro, Nova Scotia, Canada
Trustees of Dartmouth College v. Woodward
  (US law; 1819)
Truth or Consequences (radio/TV show)
Truth or Consequences, NM
Truth, Sojourner (US reformer; c1797-1883)
TRW, Inc.
Try Sustrisno (Indonesia, pol.)
Trygve H(alvdan) Lie (Nor. pol./UN; 1896-1968)
Tryon, Thomas (writer/ent.; 1926-91)
Tse, Mo (also Mo Ti, Mo-tze, Mo Tzu, Mo-tse)
  (Ch. phil.; 5th c. BC)
T(homas) S(terns) Eliot (US/Br. poet; 1888-1965)
Tse-tung, Mao (also Mao Zedong, Chairman
  Mao)(Ch. pol.; 1893-1976)
T-shirt (also tee shirt, tee, T)
Tshisekedi, Etienne (premier, Zaire)
Tshombe, Moise K(apenda)(ex-PM, Congo/
  Zaire; 1919-69)
Tsimshian (Native Amer.)
Tsinghai (also Qinghai)(province, Ch.)
Tsingtao, China (also Qingdao)
Tsiolkovsky, Konstantin E. (Rus., father of
  cosmonautics; 1857-1935)
Tsongas, Paul (US pol.; 1941-97)
T square (T-shaped ruler)
T-stop (hockey, photo.)
T-strap (shoe)
Tsuen Wan, Hong Kong
Tswana (lang./people)
Tuareg (people)
Tuatha Dé Danann (myth.)
Tubb, Ernest (ent.; 1914-84)
Tubman, Harriet (b. Araminta Ross)(US
  reformer; c1820-1913)
Tuborg beer
Tucana (astron., toucan)
Tuchman, Barbara W(ertheim)(US writer/hist.;
  1912-89)
Tuck, Friar (fict. chara., *Robin Hood*)
Tucker, Chris (ent.; 1971-)
Tucker, Forrest (ent.; 1919-86)
Tucker, Jim (James) Guy, Jr. (ex-AR gov.; 1943-)
Tucker, Michael (ent.; 1944-)
Tucker, Sophie (b. Sophie Abruza)(ent.; 1884-
  1966)
Tucker, Tanya (ent.; 1958-)
Tucson Citizen (AZ newspaper)
Tucson Star (AZ newspaper)
Tucson, AZ
Tucuman, Argentina
Tucumcari, NM
Tudjman, Franjo (ex-pres., Croatia; 1922-99)
Tudor style (art/arch.; 1485-1603)
Tudor, Antony (choreographer; 1909-87)
Tudor, House of (Br. ruling family; 1485-1603)
Tudor, Margaret (Eng., wife of James IV, Scot.;
  1489-1541)
Tudor, Mary (also Mary I, "Bloody
  Mary")(queen, Eng.; 1516-58)
Tuesday (Susan) Weld (ent.; 1943-)

Tuftex Industries
Tufts University (Medford, MA)
Tu Fu (Ch. poet; 710-770)
Tugboat Annie
Tuilaepa Sailele Malielegaoi (PM, Samoa; 1945-)
Tuileries Gardens (Paris)
Tuinal (med.)
Tukulor (lang./people)
Tulane University (New Orleans, LA)
Tull, Jethro (Br. agr.; 1674-1741)
Tull, Jethro (pop music)
Tulsa World (OK newspaper)
Tulsa, OK
Tultex Apparel Group (US bus.)
Tumacacori National Historical Park (AZ)
Tumbling Tumbleweeds (song)
Tums (med.)
Tumwater, WA
Tunbridge Wells, England
Tundra, Toyota (auto.)
Tune, Tommy (b. Thomas James Tune)(ent.;
    1939-)
Tung Chee Hwa (or Tung Chee-hwa)(chief
    exec., Hong Kong; 1937-)
Tunis, Tunisia
Tunisia (Republic of)(N Afr.)
Tunku Abdul Rahman (ex-PM, Malaysia; 1903-
    90)
Tunney, Gene (b. James Joseph
    Tunney)(boxing; 1898-1978)
Tupac Shakur (b. Lesane Parish Crooks)(ent.;
    1971-96)
Tupelo, MS
Tupou IV, Taufa'ahau (king, Tonga; 1918-)
Tupperware Co.
Tupperware party
Turandot (G. Puccini opera)
TurboCAT (CAT system)
TurboTax (compu.)
Turgenev, Ivan (Sergeievich)(Rus. writer;
    1818-83)
Turgut Ozal (ex-pres., Turk.; 1927-93)
Turin, Italy
Turin, shroud of (rel.)
Turk (horse)
Turk (lang./people)
Turk (Melvin Edward Alton) Murphy (US jazz;
    1915-87)
Turken (chicken)
Turkey (Republic of)(SE Eur./SW Asia)
Turkic (lang.)
Turkish (lang./people)
Turkish bath
Turkish delight (also Turkish paste)(candy)
Turkish skirt
Turkish swimming (cat)
Turkish tobacco
Turkish towel (also l.c.)
Turkish van (cat)
Turkish Wars, Russo- (Rus./Ottoman Turk.;
    17th-19th c.)
Turkman (also Turkoman)(lang./people)
Turkmenistan (Republic of)(formerly part of
    USSR)(central Asia)
Turko-Persian war

Turkoman (also Turkman)(lang./people)
Turkoman (rug)
Turk's-head (knot)
Turks and Caicos Islands (Br. West Indies)
Turku, Finland
Turlington, Christy (model; 1969-)
Turner and Hooch (film, 1989)
Turner Broadcast Network (TBN)(TV channel)
Turner Broadcast System (TBS)(TV channel)
Turner Classic Movies (TCM)(TV channel)
Turner Network Television (TNT)(TV channel)
Turner, Big Joe (ent.; 1911-85)
Turner, Frederick J(ackson)(US hist./educ.;
    1861-1932)
Turner, Ike (ent.; 1931-)
Turner, Janine (ent.; 1962-)
Turner, J(oseph) M(allord) W(illiam)(Br. artist;
    1774-1851)
Turner, John (Napier)(ex-PM, Can.; 1929-)
Turner, Kathleen (ent.; 1954-)
Turner, Lana (ent.; 1920-95)
Turner, Nat (US slave/reformer; 1800-31)
Turner, Ted (US bus./media; 1938-)
Turner, The Confessions of Nat (W. Styron book)
Turner, Tina (b. Anna Mae Bullock)(ent.; 1938-)
Turner's syndrome (genetics)(med.)
Turnquest, (Sir) Orville A(lton)(gov.-gen.,
    Bahamas; 1929-)
Turow, Scott (US writer; 1949-)
TURP (transurethral prostatectomy)(med.)
Turpin, Ben (ent.; 1874-1940)
Turpin, Dick (Richard)(Br. highwayman; 1706-39)
Tursenbek Chyngyshev (ex-PM, Kyrgyzstan)
Turtle Wax, Inc.
Turturro, John (ent.; 1957-)
Tuscaloosa, AL
Tuscan column (arch.)
Tuscany (region, It.)
Tuscarora (Native Amer.)
Tusevljak, Spasoje (pol., Bosnia-Hercegovina)
Tuskegee National Forest
Tuskegee University (Tuskegee, AL)
Tussaud, Madame (Anne) Marie
    (Grosholtz)(Swiss wax modeler; 1760-1850)
Tussaud's Exhibition, Madame (wax museum,
    London)
Tussy Cosmetics, Inc.
Tut, King (Tutankhamen)(king, Eg.; 1343-25 BC)
Tutong, Brunei
Tuttle, Frank Wright (ent.; 1892-1963)
Tutu, Desmond (Mpilo)(SAfr. rel.; 1931-)
Tutume, Botswana
Tutwiler, Margaret D. (US ambassador/
    Morocco; 1950-)
Tuvalu (South West Pac. State of)(W Pac.)
Tuvaluan (lang.)
Tuzla, Bosnia-Hercegovina
TV Guide (mag.)
TV Guide Channel, The (TVG)(TV channel)
TV Land (TV channel)
TVA (Tennessee Valley Authority)
Tver, Russia (formerly Kalinin)
TVG (The TV Guide Channel)(TV channel)
TWA (Trans World Airlines)
Twa (people)

Twagiramungu, Faustin (ex-PM, Rwanda; 1945-)
Twain, Mark (aka Samuel Langhorne Clemens)(US writer; 1835-1910)
Twain, Shania (b. Eileen Regina Twain)(ent.; 1965-)
Tweed Ring (corrupt NYC politicians)
Tweed, William M(arcy)("Boss Tweed")(US pol.; 1823-78)
Tweedledum & Tweedledee (2 almost identical people/things)
Twelfth Day (12 days after Christmas [Jan. 6], Epiphany)
Twelfth Night (rel.)
Twelfth Night, Or What You Will (Shakespeare play)
Twelve Tables, Law of the (Roman law; est. 451-50 BC)
Twelve Tribes (rel.)
Twelve, the (12 apostles chosen by Christ)
Twenties, Roaring (also Roaring '20s)
20th Century Plastics Co.
20th Century-Fox Film Co.
20th Century-Fox Record Corp.
Twentynine Palms, CA
20/20 (TV show)
Twiggy (aka Leslie Hornby)(model; 1949-)
Twilight of the Gods (also Götterdämmerung) (Ger. myth.)
Twilight Zone (TV show, film; 1983)
Twin Cities (Minneapolis & St. Paul, MI)
Twin Falls, ID
Twin Peaks (TV show)
Twining, Nathan F. (US Air Force gen.; 1897-1982)
Twinkies
Twins, Minnesota (baseball team)
Twist, Oliver (Dickens novel)
Twisted Sister (pop music)
Twittering Machine (by Klee)
Twitty, Conway (ent.; 1933-93)
Twix candy
Two Gentlemen of Verona, The (Shakespeare play)
2 Live Crew (pop music)
Two Sicilies (former kingdom, Sicily and S. Italy)
2001: A Space Odyssey (film, 1968)
Twyla Tharp (US dancer; 1941-)
TX (Texas)
TXU Corp.
Ty(rus Raymond) Cobb (baseball; 1886-1961)
Tyana, Apollonius of (Gr. phil.; 1st c. AD)
Tyche (myth.)
Tycho Brahe (Dan. astron.; 1546-1601)
Tyco (toys)
Tyco Industries, Inc.
Tylenol (med.)
Tyler, Anne (US writer; 1941-)
Tyler, John (10th US pres.; 1790-1862)
Tyler, Liv (ent.; 1977-)
Tyler, Royall (US writer; 1757-1826)
Tyler, Steven (b. Steven Tallarico)(ent.; 1948-)
Tyler, TX
Tyler, Wat (Walter)(Br. rebel; ?-1381)
Tynan, The Seduction of Joe (film, 1979)

Tyne Daly, (Ellen)(ent.; 1946-)
Tyner, McCoy (US jazz; 1938-)
Type A personality
Type B personality
Typhoid Mary (b. Mary Mallon)(Ir. cook, typhoid carrier; ?-1938)
Typhon (myth.)
Tyra Banks (model/ent.; 1973-)
Tyre, Apollonius of (fict. Gr. hero)
Tyre, Lebanon
Tyrian purple (color)
Tyrol, Austria (also Tirol)
Tyrolean (also Tirolean, Tyrolese, Tirolese)(clothing style, people)
Tyrone (William) Guthrie, (Sir)(Br. ent.; 1900-71)
Tyrone Power (ent.; 1913-58)
Tyrrhenian Sea (arm, Mediterranean)
Tyson Foods, Inc.
Tyson, Cicely (ent.; 1933-)
Tyson, Laura D'Andrea (US ex-chair/council econ. advisers; 1947-)
Tyson, Mike (Michael Gerald)(boxing; 1966-)
Tyus, Wyomia (track; 1945-)
Tzekung, China (also Zigong)
Tzu, Mo (also Mo-tze, Mo Ti, Mo-tse, Mo Tse) (Ch. phil.; 5th c. BC)

UAE (United Arab Emirates)
UAL Corp.
UAW (United Automobile Workers)
Ubangi River (central Afr.)
Ubangi-Shari (now Central African Republic)
Übermensch (Ger., superman)
U-boat
U bolt
UCC (Uniform Commercial Code)
Uccello, Paolo (b. Paolo di Dono)(It. artist; 1397-1475)
Udall, Mark (US cong.; 1950-)
Udall, Mo (Morris King)(US pol.; 1922-98)
Udall, Stewart L(ee)(US ex-secy./interior; 1920-)
Udall, Tom (US cong.; 1948-)
Uday Shankar (dancer, India; 1900-77)
Udon Thani, Thailand
Ueberroth, Peter (US bus./sports; 1937-)
Uecker, Bob ("Mr. Baseball")(ent.; 1935-)
Uffizi Gallery (Florence, It.)
Uffizi Palace (Florence, It.)
UFO (unidentified flying object)
Uganda (Republic of)(E Afr.)
Ugarte, Augusto Pinochet (ex-pres., Chile; 1915-)
Uggams, Leslie (ent.; 1943-)
Ugly American
Ugly Duckling Rent-A-Car (US bus.)
U-Haul
UHF (ultrahigh frequency)
Uhuru (US space satellite)
Uigur (people)
Uitzilopochtli (also Huitzilopochtli)(myth.)
Ukraine (E central Eur.)(formerly part of USSR)
Ukrainian (lang./people)
Ukrainian Catholic (rel.)
ul-Adha, Eid (Muslim festival)
Ulan Bator, Mongolia (also Ulaanbaatar)
Ulanova, Galina (ballet; 1910-98)
Ulbricht, Walter (Ger. pol.; 1893-1873)
ul-Fitr, Eid (Muslim festival)
ul-Haq, Muhammad Zia ("President Zia")(ex-pres., Pak.; 1924-88)
Ullman, Tracey (ent.; 1959-)
Ullmann, Liv (ent.; 1939-)
Ulmanis, Guntis (ex-pres., Latvia)
Ulrich (or Huldreich) Zwingli (Swiss rel.; 1484-1531)
Ulrich, Skeet (ent./model; 1970-)
Ulster (area, NIre.; province, Ir.)
Ultra/brite (toothpaste)
Ultracef (med.)
Ultra Downy (clothes softener)
Ultralente Iletin (med.)
Ultra Slim Fast
Ultrasuede (synthetic leather)
Ulukalala Lavaka Ata, Prince (PM, Tonga; 1959-)
Ulysses (J. Joyce novel)
Ulysses S(impson) Grant (18th US pres.; 1822-85)

Ulysses, king of Ithaca (also Odysseus)(myth.)
Uma Thurman (ent.; 1970-)
Umar Arteh Ghalib (ex-PM, Somalia)
Umberto Boccioni (It. artist; 1882-1916)
Umberto Giordano (It. comp.; 1867-1948)
Umberto Mastroianni (It. artist; 1910-98)
Umbrella Tree, Under the (TV show)
Umbriel (astron.)
Umm al Qaiwain (or Qaywayn)(UAE)
UN (United Nations)
Unabomber (US news, Theodore "Ted" Kaczynski)
Un-American Activities, House Committee on (HUAC)(US govt. comm.; 1938-75)
Una Merkel (ent.; 1903-86)
Uncle Remus (fict. narrator, J.C. Harris fables)
Uncle Sam (nickname, US govt.)
Uncle Tom (fict. chara., *Uncle Tom's Cabin*; slang, subservient black)
Uncle Tom's Cabin (H.B. Stowe novel)
Uncle Vanya (A. Chekhov play)
UNCTAD (United Nations Conference on Trade and Development)(est. 1964)
Under the Umbrella Tree (TV show)
Under the Yum Yum Tree (film, 1963)
Underground Railroad (US hist., for escaping slaves)
Underwood Deviled Ham
Underwood, Blair (ent.; 1964-)
Underwood, Cecil H(arland)(ex-WV gov.; 1922-)
Underwood's Fine Foods (US bus.)
Underwriters Laboratories, Inc.
UNDP (United Nations Development Program)(est. 1965)
UNESCO (United Nations Educational, Scientific, and Cultural Organization)(est. 1945)
UNHCR (United Nations Office of High Commissioner for Refugees)(est. 1951)
Uniate Church
Unicap (med.)
UNICEF (United Nations Children's Fund, formerly United Nations International Children's Emergency Fund)(est. 1946)
UNIDO (United Nations Industrial Development Organization)(est. 1966)
Unifax (UPI wire service)
Unification Church (also Moonies; est. 1954)
Unilever PLC (US bus.)
Unimog, DaimlerChrysler (universal motorized machine)(auto.)
Union Carbide Corp.
Union Gap, Gary Puckett and the (pop music)
Union Jack (Br. flag)
Union News, Springfield (MA newspaper)
Union of Concerned Scientists
Union of South Africa (now Republic of South Africa)
Union of Soviet Socialist Republics (USSR)(disbanded 1991)
Union Pacific Corp.
Union-Tribune, San Diego (CA newspaper)
Union, Sacramento (CA newspaper)
Unipen (med.)
Uniroyal Chemical Co., Inc.
Uniroyal Goodrich Tire Co.
Unisom (med.)

Unisys Corp.
UNITAR (United Nations Institute for Training and Research)(est. 1963)
Unitarian Universalist Association (rel.)
Unitarianism (rel.)
Unitas, Johnny (John Constantine)(football; 1933-)
United Airlines
United Arab Emirates (UAE)(SW Asia)
United Arab Republic (Egypt/Syria; 1958-61)
United Artists Corp. (UA)(film co.)
United Automobile Workers of America (UAW) (union, est. 1935)
United Brethren in Christ, Church of the
United Church of Canada
United Church of Christ
United Colonies of New England (New England Confederation)(US his.)
United Kingdom (of Great Britain and Northern Ireland)(Eng./Scot./Wales/NIre.)(UK)(NW Eur.)
United Methodist Church
United Mine Workers of America (UMWA) (union, est. 1890)
United Nations (internat'l org.; est. 1945)
United Nations Children's Fund (UNICEF) (formerly United Nations International Children's Emergency Fund)(est. 1946)
United Nations Conference on Environment and Development (Earth Summit)(June 1992)
United Nations Conference on Trade and Development (UNCTAD)(est. 1964)
United Nations Day
United Nations Development Program (UNDP) (est. 1965)
United Nations Educational, Scientific, and Cultural Organization (UNESCO)(est. 1945)
United Nations Industrial Development Organization (UNIDO)(est. 1966)
United Nations Institute for Training and Research (UNITAR)(est. 1963)
United Nations Office of High Commissioner for Refugees (UNHCR)(est. 1951)
United Nations Permanent Court of International Justice (World Court)(est. 1945)
United Nations Security Council
United Negro College Fund
United Parcel Service (UPS)
United Press International (UPI)(US news org.; est. 1958)
United Service Organizations, Inc. (USO)(est. 1941)
United Society of Believers in Christ's Second Coming(Appearing)(also Shakers, Millenial Church)
United States (U.S., US)
United States Air Force (US mil.)
United States Air Force Academy (Colorado Springs, CO)(est. 1954)
United States Army (US mil.)
United States Coast Guard (US mil.)
United States Coast Guard Academy (New London, CT)(est. 1876)
United States Department of Agriculture (USDA)
United States District Court (USDC)(US law)
United States Geological Survey (USGS)

United States Information Agency (USIA)
United States Marine Corps (US mil.)
United States Merchant Marine (US bus./mil.)
United States Merchant Marine Academy (Kings Point, NY)
United States Military Academy (West Point, NY)(est. 1802)
United States Naval Academy (Annapolis, MD) (est. 1845)
United States Navy (US mil.)
United States of America (USA, U.S.A.)
United States Pharmacopeia (USP)
United States Postal Service (USPS)
United Steel Workers of America (USWA) (union; est. 1942)
United Steelworkers Union
United Technologies Corp.
United Van Lines, Inc.
United Way (charitable org.; est. 1918)
UnitedHealth Group Corp.
Univac, Sperry (US bus.)
Univar Corp.
Univers (type style)
Universal City Studios (US bus.)
Universal Corp.
Universal Foods Corp.
Universal machines (med.)
Universal Pictures (US bus.)
Universal Product Code (also UPC)
Universal Studios (US bus.)
Universalism (rel.)
University of California Press (US bus.)
University of Chicago Press (US bus.)
University of Illinois Press (US bus.)
University of Michigan Press (US bus.)
University of Missouri Press (US bus.)
University of Nebraska Press (US bus.)
University of New Mexico Press (US bus.)
University of Notre Dame (South Bend, IN)
University of Oklahoma Press (US bus.)
University of Paris (aka Sorbonne)
University of Tennessee Press (US bus.)
University of Utah Press (US bus.)
Univision (TV channel)
Unix (compu.)
Unknown Soldier (Arlington National Cemetery [VA])
Uno Sosuke (ex-PM, Jap; 1922-)
Unocal Corp.
Unser, Al (auto racing; 1939-)
Unser, Al, Jr. (auto racing; 1962-)
Unser, Bobby (auto racing; 1934-)
Unsinkable Molly Brown, The (film, 1964)
Unsolved Mysteries (TV show)
Untermeyer, Louis (US anthologist/poet; 1885-1977)
Untouchables (TV show; film, 1987)
U (Thakin) Nu (ex-PM, Myanmar; 1907-95)
Upanishads (rel.)
UPC (Universal Product Code)
Updike, John (Hoyer)(US writer; 1932-)
UPI (United Press International)
UPI Cable News
UPI Radio Network
Upjohn Co.

Upjohn, Richard (US arch.; 1802-78)
Upland, CA
Upper Volta (now Burkina Faso)
Uppsala, Sweden
UPS (United Parcel Service)
Upson board (constr.)
Upton (Beall) Sinclair (US writer/reformer; 1878-1968)
Uptown Comedy Club (TV show)
Ur (ancient city, Mesopotamia)
Ural Mountains (Eur./Asia)
Ural River (Eur./Asia)
Urania (myth.)
Uranus (planet; myth.)
Urban Cowboy (film, 1980)
Urban League, National (org. 1910)
Urbana, IL
Urdu (lang./people)
Urecholine (med.)
Urey, Harold C. (US chem.; 1893-1981)
Uri Geller (Isr. psychic; 1946-)
Uriah Heep (villain, *David Copperfield*)
Urich, Robert (ent.; 1946-)
Uris, Leon (US writer; 1924-)
Urispas (med.)
Urogesic (med.)
Ursa Major (astron., great bear; part of Big Dipper)
Ursa Minor (astron., little/lesser bear; part of Little Dipper)
Ursula Andress (Swiss ent.; 1936-)
Ursula LeGuin (US writer; 1929-)
Uruguay (Republic of)(S Amer.)
US (also U.S., United States)
US (mag.)
U.S. (also US, United States)
US Airways, Inc.
U.S. Air Force (US mil.)
U.S. Air Force Academy (Colorado Springs, CO) (est. 1954)
U.S. Army (US mil.)
U.S. Coast Guard (USCG)(US mil.)
U.S. Coast Guard Academy (New London, CT) (est. 1876)
U.S. Court of Appeals
U.S. Department of Agriculture (USDA)
U.S. District Court (USDC)(US law)
U.S. Geological Survey (USGS)
U.S. Gulf States (AL/FL/LA/MS/TX)
U.S. Information Agency (USIA)
U.S. Marine Corps (US mil.)
U.S. Marine Corps War Memorial (also Iwo Jima Memorial)(VA)
U.S. Merchant Marine (US bus./mil.)
U.S. Merchant Marine Academy (Kings Point, NY)
U.S. Military Academy (West Point, NY)(est. 1802)
U.S. National Guard (US mil.)
U.S. Naval Academy (Annapolis, MD)(est. 1845)
U.S. Navy (US mil.)
U.S. News & World Report (mag.)
U.S. Open (golf tournament)
U.S. Pharmacopoeia (USP)
U.S. Postal Service (USPS)(US govt. agcy.; est. 1865)

U.S. Shoe Corp., Inc.
U.S. Steel Group, USX- (US bus.)
U.S. Trade Representative, Office of the (US govt.)
U.S. v. American Tobacco Co. (US law; 1911)
U.S. v. Butler (US law; 1936)
U.S. v. Classic (US law; 1941)
U.S. v. Darby Lumber Co. (US law; 1941)
U.S. v. Dixon (US law; 1993)
U.S. v. E. C. Knight Co. (US law; 1895)
U.S. v. Gouveja (US law; 1984)
U.S. v. Nixon (US law; 1974)
U.S. West, Inc.
U.S,. Austin v. (US law; 1993)
U.S., Abrams v. (US law; 1919)
U.S., Addyston Pipe and Steel Co. v. (US law; 1899)
U.S., Dennis et al v. (US law; 1951)
U.S., Heart of Atlanta Motel, Inc. v. (US law; 1964)
U.S., Hylton v. (US law; 1796)
U.S., Korematsu v. (US law; 1944)
U.S., Northern Securities Co. v. (US law; 1904)
U.S., Olmsted v. (US law; 1928)
U.S., Schechter v. (US law; 1935)
U.S., Schenck v. (US law; 1919)
U.S., Standard Oil Co. of New Jersey, et al. v. (US law; 1911)
U.S., Swift and Co. v. (US law; 1905)
USA (also U.S.A., United States of America)
USA Network (TV channel)
USA Today (newspaper)
USA Today Crosswords (mag.)
USAF (United States Air Force)
USAir Group, Inc.
USAir, Inc. (airline)
USB port (compu.)
USCG (United States Coast Guard)
USDA (United States Department of Agriculture)
USES (United States Employment Service)
USGS (United States Geological Survey)
Usher (b. Usher Raymond, IV)(ent.; 1978-)
Usher, The Fall of the House of (E.A. Poe short story)
Ushuaia, Argentina
USIA (United States Information Agency)
USM (United States Mail, United States Mint)
USMC (United States Marine Corps)
USN (United States Navy)
USNG (United States National Guard)
USO (United Service Organizations, Inc.)(est. 1941)
USP (United States Pharmacopoeia)
USPS (United States Postal Service)
USS (United States Senate)
U.S.S (a;so USS)(United States Ship)
U.S.S. Chesapeake (US frigate, War of 1812)
U.S.S. Cole (Navy warship bombed in Aden, Yemen; 10/12/2000)
U.S.S. Greeneville (US sub that collided with Japanese fishing vessel near Hawaii, 2/9/2001)
U.S.S. Pueblo (US ship./mil. incident, NKorea; 1968)
U.S.S. Vincennes (US ship/mil. incident, Iran; 1987)
USSR (Union of Soviet Socialist Republics)

(disbanded 1991)
UST, Inc.
Ustinov, (Sir) Peter (Alexander)(ent.; 1921-)
USX-U.S. Steel Group (US bus.)
UT (Utah)
Uta Hagen (ent.; 1919-)
Utah (UT)
Utah Jazz (basketball team)
Ute (Native Amer.)
Uteem, Cassam (pres., Mauritius; 1941-)
U Thant (Burmese dipl./UN; 1909-74)
Uther Pendragon (King Arthur's father)
Utica (ancient city, N Afr.)
Utica, NY
Uticort (med.)
Utilicare (utility assistance, low-income elderly)
UtiliCorp United, Inc.
Utkir T. Sultanov (PM, Uzbekistan; 1939-)
Utley, Garrick (TV jour.)
Utopia (imaginary, ideal land)
Utopia (T. More book)
Utopia, Road to (film, 1946)
Utrecht, Netherlands
Utrillo, Maurice (Fr. artist; 1883-1955)
U-turn
U-2 (US spy plane)
U2 (pop music)
UV (ultraviolet)
Uxmal (ancient city, Mex.)
Uzbek (lang./people)
Uzbekistan (Republic of)(formerly part of
   USSR)(central Asia)
Uzi submachine gun

V (chem. sym., vanadium)
VA (Virginia)
Vacarolu, Nicolae (ex-PM, Romania)
Vacaville, CA
Vaccaro, Brenda (ent.; 1939-)
Vachel Lindsay, (Nicholas)(US poet; 1879-1931)
Vacherin (cheese)
Václav Havel (pres./writer, Czech.; 1936-)
Václav Klaus (ex-PM, Czech.; 1941-)
Vader, Darth (fict. chara., *Star Wars*)
Vadim Medvedev (Rus. pol.)
Vadim, Roger (ent.; 1928-2000)
Vaduz, Liechtenstein
Vaea, Baron (ex-PM, Tonga)
Vagistat (med.)
Vahl Tiit (ex-PM, Estonia)
Vail, CO
Vail, Theodore N. (US bus.; 1845-1920)
Vaira Vike-Freiberga (pres., Latvia; 1937-)
Vajpayee, A(tal) B(ihari)(PM, India; 1924-)
Val Bisoglio (ent.; 1926-)
Val Dufour (ent.; 1927-2000)
Val Kilmer (ent.; 1959-)
Val Wine Co., Ltd., The Clos du
Valachi Papers, The (film, 1972)
Valance, The Man Who Shot Liberty (film, 1962)
Valdas Adamkus (pres., Lith.; 1926-)
Valdepeas (wine)
Valdez, AK
Valdez, Exxon (US tanker, oil spill; 1989)
Valdis Birkavs (ex-PM, Latvia; 1942-)
Valdosta State University (Valdosta, GA)
Valdosta, GA
Vale, Jerry (b. Genaro Louis Vitaliano)(ent.; 1932-)
Valencia oranges
Valencia, CA
Valencia, Spain
Valencia, Venezuela
Valencian (people)
Valenciennes (lace)
Valenciennes, France
Valens, Ritchie (b. Richard Valenzuela)(ent.; 1941-59)
Valenti, Jack (US writer/ent.; 1921-)
Valentic, Nikica (ex-PM, Croatia)
Valentin (Vitalyevich) Lebedev (cosmo.; 1942-)
Valentin Paniagua (Peruvian pol.)
Valentina (Vladimirovna) Tereshkova (cosmo., 1st woman in space; 1937-)
Valentine (Esegragbo Melvine) Strasser (ex-pres., Sierra Leone; 1965?-)
Valentine, Karen (ent.; 1947-)
Valentine, St. (Roman rel.; ?-c270)
Valentine's Day, St. (2/14)
Valentino (b. Valentino Garavani)(It. designer; 1932-)
Valentino, Rudolph (b. Rodolpho Guglielmi) (ent.; 1895-1926)

Valenzuela, Fernando (baseball; 1960-)
Valera, Eamon de (ex-PM/pres., Ir.; 1882-1975)
Valeri Brumel (jumper; 1942-)
Valeria Messalina (Roman empress; c22-48)
Valerie Bertinelli (ent.; 1960-)
Valerie Harper (ent.; 1940-)
Valerie Perrine (ent.; 1943-)
Valéry F. Bykovsky (cosmo.; 1934-)
Valéry Giscard d'Estaing (ex-pres., Fr.; 1926-)
Valéry N(ikolayevich) Kubasov (cosmo.; 1935-)
Valéry, Paul (Ambroise)(Fr. writer; 1871-1945)
Valhalla (myth.)
Valiant, Prince (comic strip)
Valisone (med.)
Valium (med.)
Valjean, Jean (fict. chara., *Les Miserables*)
Valkyrie (myth.)
Vallee, Rudy (ent.; 1901-86)
Vallejo, CA
Valletta, Malta
Valley Forge (PA)
Valley Forge National Historical Park (PA)
Valli, Frankie (b. Frank Castelluccio)(ent.; 1937-)
Valli, June (ent.; 1930-93)
Valois, Margaret of (also Queen Margot)(Fr.; 1553-1615)
Valparaiso, IN
Valparaíso, Chile
Valpin (med.)
Valpolicella (wine)
Valsalva maneuver (med.)
Value Rent-A-Car
ValueVision (TV channel)
Valvoline
Valvoline Instant Oil Change (US bus.)
Vampire Armand, The (A. Rice novel)
Vampire Lestat, The (A. Rice novel)
Van Allen, James Alfred (US space physt.; 1914-)
Van Allen radiation belts (regions surrounding earth)
Van Allsburg, Chris (US writer/artist; 1949-)
van Alstyne, Egbert (US comp.; 1882-1951)
Van Ark, Joan (ent.; 1943-)
van Beethoven, Ludwig (Ger. comp.; 1770-1827)
Van Brocklin, Norm (football; 1926-83)
Van Buren, Abigail (Dear Abby)(b. Pauline Esther Friedman)(US advice columnist; 1918-)
Van Buren, Martin (8th US pres.; 1782-1862)
Van Camp Sea Food Co., Inc.
Van Camp's Beanee Weenee
Van Cleef & Arpels, Inc.
Van Cleef, Lee (ent.; 1925-89)
Van Cliburn (Harvey Lavan Cliburn, Jr.)(ent.; 1934-)
Van Conversion, Inc.
Van Damme, Jean-Claude (b. Jean-Claude Van Varenberg)(ent.; 1960-)
Van de Graaff generator (also electrostatic generator)
Van de Graaff, Robert Jemison (US physt.; 1901-67)
Van de Kamp's Frozen Foods (US bus.)
Van Der Beek, James (ent.; 1977-)
Van der Post, Laurens (Jan)(SAfr. writer; 1906-96)

van der Rohe, Ludwig Mies (US arch.; 1886-1969)

van der Weyden, Rogier (Flem. artist; c1400-64)

van Doesburg, Theo (Dutch artist/writer; 1883-1931)

Van Dong, Pham (ex-PM, NViet.; 1906-2000)

Van Doren, Carl (US writer/educ.; 1885-1950)

Van Doren, Charles (US educ./TV scandal; 1926-)

Van Doren, Mamie (b. Joan Lucile Olander)(ent.; 1933-)

Van Druten, John (William)(US writer; 1901-57)

van Dunem, Fernando (PM, Angola)

van Dyck, (Sir) Anthony (Flem. artist; 1599-1641)

Van Dyke, Dick (ent.; 1925-)

Van Dyke, Jerry (ent.; 1931-)

van Eyck, Hubert (or Huybrecht)(Flem. artist; 1366-1426)

van Eyck, Jan (Flem. artist; 1385?-1441?)

Van Fleet, Jo (ent.; 1919-96)

van Gogh, Vincent (Dutch artist; 1853-90)

Van Halen, Eddie (ent.; 1957-)

van Hamel, Martine (ballet; 1945-)

Van Heflin (ent.; 1910-71)

Van Heusen Corp., Phillips-

Van Heusen, Jimmy (James)(US comp.; 1913-90)

Van Houten & Zoon, Inc., C. J.

Van Impe, Jack (TV show)

Van Johnson (ent.; 1916-)

van Leeuwenhoek, Anton (Dutch, father of microbiology; 1632-1723)

Van Lingo Mungo (baseball; 1911-85)

Van Morrison (ent.; 1945-)

Van Nostrand Reinhold Co., Inc.

Van Nuys, CA

van Ostade, Adriaen (Dutch artist; 1610-85)

Van Patten, Dick (ent.; 1928-)

Van Peebles, Melvin (US playwright; 1932-)

van Rijn, Rembrandt (Harmenszoon)(Dutch artist; 1606-69)

van Ruisdael, Jacob (Isaackszoon)(Dutch artist; c1628-82

van Ruysdael, Salomon (Dutch artist; c1600-70)

Van Slyke, Andy (baseball; 1960-)

Van Thieu, Nguyen (ex-pres., SViet; 1923-)

Van Vogt, A(lfred) E(lton)(US writer; 1912-2000)

Van Winkle, Rip (by W. Irving)

Van Wyck Brooks (US hist.; 1886-1963)

Vance Air Force Base, OK

Vance Brand (astro.; 1931-)

Vance Packard (US writer; 1914-96)

Vance, Cyrus R(oberts)(US pol.; 1917-)

Vance, Vivian (ent.; 1911-79)

Vancenase (med.)

Vanceril (med.)

Vancocin (med.)

Vancouver Canucks (hockey team)

Vancouver Island (Can.)

Vancouver Sun (Can. newspaper)

Vancouver, British Columbia, Canada

Vancouver, WA

Vandellas, Martha and the (pop music)

Vandenberg Air Force Base, CA

Vandenberg, Arthur H(endrick)(US pol.; 1884-1951)

Vanderbilt University (Nashville, TN)

Vanderbilt, Amy (US writer/manners; 1908-74)

Vanderbilt, Cornelius (US bus./finan.; 1794-1877)

Vanderbilt, Cornelius (US bus./finan.; 1843-99)

Vanderbilt, Gloria (perfume/clothing)

Vanderbilt, Gloria (US bus.; 1924-)

Vanderbilt, William Henry (US bus./finan.; 1821-85)

Vanderbilt's Complete Book of Etiquette, Amy

Vanderlyn, John (US artist; 1775-1852)

Vandross, Luther (ent.; 1951-)

Vandyke (beard)(also l.c.)

Vandyke brown (also Cassel brown, Cassel earth)(color)

Vandyke collar

Vanessa Harwood (ballet)

Vanessa Redgrave (ent.; 1937-)

Vanessa Williams (ent.; 1963-)

Vanguard (US space satellite)

Vanguard Group, Inc., The

Vanguard Marketing Corporation

Vanilla Ice (b. Robert Van Winkle)(ent.; 1968-)

Vanilli, Milli (pop music/lip-sync)

Vanir (myth.)

Vanity Fair (mag.)

Vanna White (b. Vanna Rosich)(ent.; 1957-)

Vannevar Bush (US eng.; 1890-1974)

Vanocur, Sander (TV jour.; 1928-)

Vanquish (med.)

Vanquish, Aston Martin (auto.)

Vanuatu (Republic of)(SW Pac.)

Vanya, Uncle (A. Chekhov play)

Vanzetti Case, Sacco- (Nicola & Bartolomeo)(MA murder trial; 1920-27)

VAR (visual-aural range)

Varathane (constr.)

Varden, Dolly (clothing style)

Varden, Dolly (fict. chara.)

Vardhamana Mahavira (legendary educ./rel.; ?-480? BC)

Vargas, Virgilio Barco (ex-pres., Columbia; 1921-)

Varig Brazilian Airlines

Varna, Bulgaria

Varolii, pons (also l.c.)(brain nerve fibers)

Varona, Donna De (swimming/sportscaster; 1947-)

Vasco da Gama (Port. nav.; c1460-1524)

Vasco Núñez de Balboa (Sp. expl., discovered Pac.; 1475-1519)

Vaseline (med.)

Vaseline Intensive Care (med.)

Vaseretic (med.)

Vasili (or Wassily, Vasily) Kandinsky (Rus. artist; 1866-1944)

Vaslav (or Waslaw) Nijinsky (Rus. ballet; 1890-1950)

Vasodilan (med.)

Vasotec (med.)

Vassar College (Poughkeepsie, NY)

Vassar, Matthew (Br./US bus./educ.; 1792-1868)

Vassilou, George (ex-pres., Cyprus; 1931-)

Västeras, Sweden

Vatican (govt. of the pope)

Vatican City (The Holy See)(independent state

in Rome)
Vatican Councils (rel. hist.; 1869-70, 1962-65)
Vatican Library (Rome)
Vatican Palace (also Vatican)(pope's residence)
Vaughan Williams, Ralph (Br. comp.; 1872-1958)
Vaughan, Sarah (Lois)(US jazz; 1924-90)
Vaughan, Stevie Ray (ent.; 1956-90)
Vaughn Monroe (ent.; 1911-73)
Vaughn, Robert (ent.; 1932-)
Vaughn, Vince (ent.; 1970-)
Vaxholm, Sweden
VC (vice chairman, vice consul, Victoria Cross, Viet Cong)
V(irginia) C. Andrews (US writer)
V-Cillin K (med.)
VCR (videocassette recorder)
VD (venereal disease)
V-Day (Victory Day)
VDT (video display terminal)(compu.)
VDU (video display unit)
V-E Day (WWII Allies victory in Eur.; 5/8/45)
Veblen, Thorstein B(unde)(US econ.; 1857-1929)
Veda(s)(sacred Hindu books)
Veda, Atharva- (rel.)
Veda, Rig- (rel.)
Veda, Sama- (rel.)
Veda, Yajur- (rel.)
Vedanta Society (rel.)
Vee, Bobby (b. Robert Velline)(ent.; 1943-)
Veerasamy Ringadoo (Mauritian pol.)
Vega (Carpio), Lope (Félix) de (Sp. writer; 1562-1635)
Vega (USSR uncrewed space probes)
Vega, Chevrolet (auto.)
Vega, Suzanne (ent.; 1959-)
Vegetarian Times (mag.)
VehiCROSS, Isuzu (auto.)
Veidt, Conrad (ent.; 1893-1943)
Veiga, Carlos (ex-PM, Cape Verde)
V8 (juice)
Vela (astron., sail)
Velásquez, Ramón (Jose)(ex-pres., Venezuela; 1916-)
Velázquez, Diego (Rodríguez de Silva y)(Sp. artist; 1599-1660)
Velcro
Velcro USA, Inc.
Velosef (med.)
Velosulin (med.)
Velox (graphic design)
Velux (windows)
Velveeta (cheese)
Velvet Underground, the (pop music)
Venatici, Canes (astron., hunting dogs)
Vendela (Kirsebom)(model; 1967-)
Veneman, Ann M. (US secy./agr.; 1949-)
Venera (USSR uncrewed space probes)
Venerable Bede, the (aka St. Bede)(Br. rel./ hist.; c673-735)
Venetiaan, Ronald (pres., Suriname; 1936-)
Venetian blue (color)
Venetian cloth (fabric)
Venetian lamp
Venetian point (lace)
Venetian red (color)

Venezuela (Republic of)(N SAmer.)
Venice, CA, FL
Venice, Italy
Venizelos, Eleutherios (Gr. pol.; 1864-1936)
Venkataraman, Ramaswamy (ex-pres., India)
Venn diagram (math.)
Ventarama Skylight Corp.
Venter, J(ohn) Craig (US genet./human genome; 1946-)
Ventolin (med.)
Ventspils, Latvia
Ventura, CA
Ventura, Jesse (b. James George Janos)(MN gov.; 1951-)
Ventura: Pet Detective, Ace (film, 1993)
Ventura: When Nature Calls, Ace (film, 1995)
Venture, Chevrolet (auto.)
Venturi, Robert (Charles)(US arch.; 1925-)
Venus (planet; myth.)
Venus de Milo (also *Venus of Melos, Aphrodite of Melos*)(Gr. statue; c200 BC)
Venus Williams (tennis; 1980-)
Venus('s) flytrap (plant)
Venuta, Benay (b. Benvenuta Rose Crooke) (ent.; 1911-95)
Venuti, Joe (US jazz; 1904-78)
VePesid (med.)
Vera-Ellen (ent.; 1926-81)
Vera Miles (b. Vera Ralston)(ent.; 1930-)
Vera Sportswear (US bus.)
Vera Wang (designer; 1949-)
Veracruz, Mexico
Verbatim Corp.
Verdi Travelwear (US bus.)
Verdi, Giuseppe (Fortunino Francesco)(It. comp.; 1813-1901)
Verdon, Gwen (ent.; 1925-2000)
Verdun, France
Verdun, Quebec, Canada
Vere C(ornwall) Bird (ex-PM, Antigua and Barbuda; 1910-99)
Vereen, Ben (ent.; 1946-)
Verelan (med.)
Vergil (Publius Vergilius Maro)(also Virgil) (Roman poet; 70-19 BC)
Verhofstadt, Guy (PM, Belgium; 1953-)
VeriSign, Inc.
Verizon Communications (US bus.)
Verizon Wireless (US bus./GTE & Bell Atlantic merge)
Verlaine, Paul (Fr. poet; 1844-96)
Vermeer, Jan (Dutch artist; 1632-75)
Vermont (VT)
Verne, Jules (Fr. writer; 1828-1905)
Vernon Castle (US dancer; 1887-1918)
Vernon Corp., Lillian
Vernon Duke (US comp.; 1903-69)
Vernon E. Jordan, Jr. (US atty.)
Vernon Lorden Shaw (pres., Dominica; 1930-)
Vernon, Mount (G. Washington's home)(VA)
Vero Beach, FL
Verona, Italy
Verona, NJ
Veronese, Paolo (It. artist; 1528-88)
Veronica Cartwright (ent.; 1950-)

Veronica Hamel (ent.; 1943-)
Veronica Lake (ent.; 1919-73)
Veronica Webb (ent./model/writer; 1965-)
Verrazano-Narrows Bridge (NYC)
Verrazano, Giovanni da (It. navigator; c1485-1528)
Verrett, Shirley (ent.; 1931-)
Verrocchio, Andrea del (b. Andrea di Michele di Francesco di Cioni)(It. artist; 1435-88)
Verrucosus, Quintus Fabius Maximus ("Cunctator")(Roman pol./mil.; 275-03 BC)
Versace, Donatella (designer; 1955-)
Versace, Gianni (It. fashion designer; 1946-97)
Versailles, France
Versailles, Palace of (Fr.)
Versailles, Treaty of (Allies/Ger.; 1919)
Verwoerd, Hendrik F. (ex-PM, SAfr; 1901-66)
Vesalius, Andreas (Flem. anatomist; 1515-64)
Vesco, Robert (US finan./fugitive; 1935-)
Vespa motor scooter
Vespasian(us), Titus Flavius Sabinus (Roman emp.; AD 9-79)
Vesprin (med.)
Vespucius, Americus (also Amerigo Vespucci)(It. nav./expl.; 1451?-1512)
Vesta (astron.; myth.)
Vesuvius, Mount (active volcano, It.)
Veterans Administration (now Department of Veterans Affairs)
Veterans Affairs, Department of (US govt.)
Veterans Day (formerly Armistice Day)
Veterans of Foreign Wars of the United States (VFW)(est. 1899)
VF Corp.
VFR (visual flight rules)
VFW (Veterans of Foreign Wars)
VHF (very high frequency)
VH1 Music First (TV channel)
VHS (video home system)
VI (Virgin Islands)
Viacom International, Inc.
Viadent, Inc.
Viagra (med.)
Vibeke Larsen (High Comm., Faeroe Islands)
Vibramycin (med.)
Vic Damone (b. Vito Farinola)(ent.; 1928-)
Vic Dickenson (US jazz; 1906-84)
Vic (Victor Herbert) Fazio, Jr. (US pol.; 1942-)
Vic Morrow (ent.; 1932-82)
Vic Raschi (baseball; 1919-88)
Vic Tayback (b. Victor Tabback)(ent.; 1930-90)
Vic Theatre, Old (also Royal Victoria Hall) (London)
Vicar of (Jesus) Christ (pope)
Vicara (fiber)
Vicente Aleixandre (Sp. poet; 1898-1984)
Vicente Fox (Quesada)(pres., Mex.; 1942-)
Vicenza, Italy
Vichy government (WWII regime; 1940-44)
Vichy Springs Mineral Water Corp.
Vichy, France (health resort)
Vicious, Sid (b. John Simon Ritchie)(ent.; 1957-79)
Vickers Petroleum Corp.
Vickers, Jon (ent.; 1926-)

Vicki Lawrence (ent.; 1949-)
Vicki! (TV show)
Vicks (med.)
Vicks DayQuil (med.)
Vicks Formula 44 (med.)
Vicks NyQuil (med.)
Vicks Sinex (med.)
Vicks USA, Richardson- (US bus.)
Vicks VapoRub (med.)
Vicksburg, Campaign of (US hist.; 1862-63)
Vicksburg, MS
Vico, Giovanni (Battista)(It. hist./phil.; 1668-1744)
Vicodin (med.)
Victor Borge (b. Boerge Rosenbaum)(Dan./US ent./musician; 1909-2000)
Victor E. Frankl (US psych.; 1905-97)
Victor Franz Hess (Aus. physt.; 1883-1964)
Victor Hasselblad, Inc.
Victor Herbert (Ir./US comp./cond.; 1859-1924)
Victor (Marie) Hugo (Fr. writer; 1802-85)
Victor Jory (ent.; 1902-82)
Victor Mature (ent.; 1913-99)
Victor McLaglen (ent.; 1907-71)
Victor Milan (aka Richard Austin, Robert Baron) (writer; 1954-)
Victor Moore (ent.; 1876-1962)
Victor Paz Estenssoro (ex-pres., Bolivia; 1907-)
Victor/Victoria (film, 1982)
Victoria (b. Alexandrina Victoria)(queen, UK; 1819-1901)
Victoria (mag.)
Victoria (myth.)
Victoria (state, Austl.)
Victoria & Albert Museum (London)
Victoria Beckham (aka Posh Spice)(ent.; 1974-)
Victoria Claflin Woodhull (US publ./reformer; 1838-1927)
Victoria Cross (Br. mil. award)
Victoria Falls (Afr.)
Victoria Hall, Royal (also Old Vic Theatre)(London)
Victoria Jackson (ent.; 1959-)
Victoria Mary Sackville-West, Dame ("Vita")(Br. writer; 1892-1962)
Victoria Principal (ent.; 1950-)
Victoria Spivey (ent.; 1906-76)
Victoria, British Columbia, Canada
Victoria, Guadalupe (b. Manuel Félix Fernández)(ex-pres., Mex.; 1789-1843)
Victoria, Hong Kong (also Hong Kong City)
Victoria, Lake (Afr.)
Victoria, Seychelles
Victoria, TX
Victoria's Secret (US bus.)
Victorian Age (Br.; 1837-1901)
Victorian style (arch./lit.; mid- to late 19th c.)
Victory Garden, The (TV show)
Vida Blue (baseball; 1949-)
Vidal Sassoon (hair care)
Vidal Sassoon (US bus.; 1928-)
Vidal Sassoon, Inc.
Vidal, Gore (b. Eugene Luther Vidal)(US writer/ critic; 1925-)
Video (mag.)

Video Hits One (VH-1)
Vidkun Quisling (Nor. pol./traitor; 1887-1945)
Vidmar, Peter (US gymnast; 1961-)
Vidor, King (Wallis)(ent.; 1895-1982)
Vieira, João Bernardo (ex-pres., Guinea-Bissau;
    1939-)
Vienna Sausage Manufacturing Co.
Vienna sausage
Vienna, Austria
Vienna, Congress of (Eur. hist.; 1814-15)
Vienna, VA, WV
Vientiane, Laos
Vietcong (National Front for the Liberation of
    SViet.; 1960-75?)
Vietminh (Vietnam Independence League;
    1941-54?)
Vietnam (Socialist Republic of)(SE Asia)
Vietnam War (NViet./SViet.; 1954-75. US
    involvement; 1964-75)
Vietnam War Memorial
Vietnamese (lang./people)
Vietnamization (US mil. policy, Vietnam War)
Vigdís Finnbogadóttir (ex-pres., Iceland; 1930-)
Vigo, Spain
Vigoda, Abe (ent.; 1921-)
Vigor, Acura (auto.)
Vijaya Lakshmi Pandit (dipl., India; 1900-90)
Vike-Freiberga, Vaira (pres., Latvia; 1937-)
Viking (ancient Scandinavian sea warrior)
Viking (US uncrewed space probes)
Viking Penguin Inc.
Vikings, Minnesota (football team)
Vikki Carr (ent.; 1941-)
Viktor I(vanovich) Patsayev (cosmo.; 1933-71)
Viktor Orbán (PM, Hung.; 1963-)
Viktor S. Chernomyrdin (ex-PM, Rus.)
Viktor V(asilyevich) Gorbatko (cosmo.; 1934-)
Viktor Yushchenko (PM, Ukraine; 1954-)
Vila, Efate, Vanuatu
Vilas, Guillermo (tennis; 1952-)
Villa Mt. Eden (US bus.)
Villa, Pancho (Villa, Francisco, b. Doroteo
    Arango)(Mex. gen.; c1877-1923)
Villa-Lobos, Heitor (Brazilian comp.; 1881-1959)
Village Voice
Villager, Mercury (auto.)
Villanova, PA
Villanova University (Villanova, PA)
Villechaize, Herve (ent.; 1943-93)
Villella, Edward (ballet; 1936-)
Villeroy & Boch Tableware, Ltd. (US bus.)
Villon, François (Fr. poet; 1431-65?)
Villon, Jacques (b. Gaston Duchamp)(Fr. artist;
    1875-1963)
Villon, Raymond Duchamp- (Fr. artist; 1876-
    1918)
Vilnius, Lithuania
Vilsack, Tom (IA gov.; 1950-)
Vin Diesel (ent.; 1967-)
Vin Scully (ent.; 1927-)
Viña del Mar, Chile
Vinaya Pitaka (rel.)
Vince Gill (ent.; 1957-)
Vince(nt Thomas) Lombardi (football; 1913-70)
Vince Vaughn (ent.; 1970-)

Vincennes, France
Vincennes, IN
Vincennes, U.S.S. (US ship/mil. incident, Iran;
    1987)
Vincent and the Grenadines, St. (island
    nation)(West Indies)
Vincent & Theo (film, 1990)
Vincent d'Indy, (Paul Marie Théodore)(Fr.
    comp.; 1851-1931)
Vincent D'Onofrio (ent.; 1959-)
Vincent de Paul, St. (Fr. rel.; c1581-1660)
Vincent Edwards (b. Vincent Edward Zoino)
    (ent.; 1928-96)
Vincent Foster, Jr. (US atty/pol.; 1945-93)
Vincent Gardenia (ent.; 1921-92)
Vincent Lopez (US band leader; 1895-1975)
Vincent Millay, Edna St. (US poet; 1892-1950)
Vincent Price (ent.; 1911-93)
Vincent Rose (US comp.; 1880-1944)
Vincent (Censu) Tabone (ex-pres., Malta; 1913-)
Vincent van Gogh (Dutch artist; 1853-90)
Vincent Youmans (US comp.; 1898-1946)
Vincent, Gene (ent.; 1935-71)
Vincent, Jan-Michael (ent.; 1945-)
Vincente Minnelli (ent.; 1910-86)
Vincenzo Bellini (It. comp.; 1801-35)
Vinci, Leonardo da (It. artist/scien.; 1452-1519)
Vindicator, Youngstown (OH newspaper)
Vineland, NJ
Vinny, My Cousin (film, 1992)
Vinton, Bobby (ent.; 1935-)
Vinylite (constr.)
Viola, Frank (baseball; 1960-)
Violeta Barrios de Chamorro (ex-pres.,
    Nicaragua; 1939-)
Vioxx (med.)
Viper, Dodge (auto.)
Virazole (med.)
Virchow, Rudolf (Ludwig Carl)(Ger. pathol.;
    1821-1902)
Viren, Lasse (track; 1949-)
Virgil (Publius Vergilius Maro)(also
    Vergil)(Roman poet; 70-19 BC)
Virgil I. "Gus" Grissom (astro.; 1926-67)
Virgil (Garnett) Thomson (US comp.; 1896-1989)
Virgilio Barco Vargas (ex-pres., Columbia; 1921-)
Virgilio Godoy (Nicaragua, pol.)
Virgin Gorda (Br. Virgin Island)
Virgin Islands National Park (St. John Island)
Virgin Islands, British (West Indies)
Virgin Islands, U.S. (West Indies)
Virgin Mary (also the Madonna, Holy Mother,
    Mary, Our Lady)(rel.)
Virginia (VA)
Virginia Beach, VA
Virginia City, NV
Virginia Company (Br. colonization cos. in
    Amer.; 1606)
Virginia creeper (plant)
Virginia Dare (1st Eng. child born in Amer.;
    1587-?)
Virginia deer (white-tailed deer)
Virginia E(shelman) Johnson, Dr. (US psych.,
    Masters & Johnson; 1925-)
Virginia fence (also Virginia rail fence, snake

fence)
Virginia Graham (ent.; 1912-98)
Virginia ham
Virginia Mayo (ent.; 1920-)
Virginia pepperwood (plant)
Virginia reel (dance)
Virginia Resolutions, Kentucky and (US hist.; 1798)
Virginia tobacco
Virginia Wade (tennis; 1945-)
Virginia (Stephen) Woolf, (Adeline)(Br. writer; 1882-1941)
Virginia Woolf?, Who's Afraid of (film, 1966)
Virginia, Loving v. (US law; 1967)
Virginie Ledoyen (ent./model; 1976-)
Virgo (astron., zodiac, virgin/maiden)
Viroptic (med.)
Visa (credit card)
Visalia, CA
Vishnevskaya, Galina (soprano; 1926-)
Vishnu (rel.)
Vishwanath Pratap Singh (ex-PM, India; 1931-)
Visigoth (people)
Visine (med.)
Vision 486 (CAT system/writer)
Vision, Eagle (auto.)
Visken (med.)
Visnijc, Goran (Croatian ent.; 1972-)
VISTA (Volunteers in Service to America)
Vistaril (med.)
Vitale, Dick (ent.; 1940-)
Vitalis (hair tonic)
Vitara, Suzuki (auto.)
Vitas Gerulaitis (tennis; 1954-94)
Vitebsk, Belarus
Viterbo, Italy
Vito Genovese (US Mafia; 1898-1969)
Vitold Fokin (Ukrainian pol.)
Vitruvius (Pollio), (Marcus)(Roman arch.; 1st c. BC)
Vittadini, Adrienne (clothing)
Vittel/USA (US bus.)
Vitti, Monica (ent.; 1931-)
Vittorio (A. Rice novel)
Vittorio De Sica (ent.; 1901-74)
Vittorio Gassman (ent.; 1922-2000)
Vitus'(s) dance, St. (nervous disorder)
Vitus, St. (It. rel.; 3rd c.)
Viva paper towels
Viva Zapata! (film, 1952)
Vivactil (med.)
Vivaldi, Antonio (Lucio)(It. comp.; 1678-1741)
Vivarin (med.)
Vivian Blaine (ent.; 1921-95)
Vivian Vance (ent.; 1911-79)
Vivica A. Fox (ent.; 1964-)
Vivien Leigh (ent.; 1913-67)
Vivienne Della Chiesa (ent.; 1920-)
Vivitar Corp.
Vizsla (dog)
V-J Day (WWII Allies victory over Japan; 8/15/45)
Vlaams (lang.)
Vladimir A. Shatalov (cosmo.; 1927-)
Vladimir Ashkenazy (Rus. pianist/cond.; 1937-)
Vladimir Feltsman (Rus. pianist; 1952-)
Vladimir Horowitz (Rus./US pianist; 1904-89)

Vladimir Ilyich (Ulyanov) Lenin (USSR leader; 1870-1924)
Vladimir Mayakovsky (Rus. writer; 1893-1930)
Vladimir Meciar (ex-pres., Slovakia; 1942-)
Vladimir M(ikhalovich) Komarov (cosmo.; 1927-67)
Vladimir (Vladomirovich) Nabokov (Rus./US writer; 1899-1977)
Vladimir V. Putin (pres., Rus.; 1952-)
Vladimir (Sergeyevich) Solovyov (Rus. phil.; 1853-1900)
Vladimir Yermoshin (or Yarmoshyn)(PM, Belarus)
Vladimir (Kosma) Zworykin ("Father of Television")(Rus./US physt./eng./inv.; 1889-1982)
Vladimir, Russia
Vladislav N. Volkov (cosmo.)
Vladivostok, Russia
Vlaminck, Maurice de (Fr. artist; 1876-1958)
Vlasic (pickles)
Vlasic Foods, Inc.
VLF (very low frequency)
Vlore, Albania
VMD (Doctor of Veterinary Medicine)
V neck (clothing)
Vo Chi Cong (ex-pres., Viet.)
Vo Van Kiet (ex-PM, Viet.; 1922-)
VO5 (hair care)
Vodaphone (Br. bus.)
Vogt, A(lfred) E(lton) Van (US writer; 1912-2000)
Vogue (mag.)
Vogue Pattern Service (US bus.)
Voice of America (US broadcasting service)
Voight, Jon (ent.; 1938-)
Voinovich, George (Victor)(US cong./ex-OH gov.; 1936-)
Voit Sports, Inc.
Vojislav Kostunica (Yug. pres.; 1944-)
Vojvodina (province, Yug.)
Vol, Frank De (US comp.; 1911-99)
Volans (astron., flying fish)
Volcker, Paul A. (US econ.; 1927-)
Volga River (Eur.)
Volgograd, Russia (formerly Stalingrad)
Volkov, Vladislav N. (cosmo.)
Volkswagen (auto.)(also Bug, Beetle, VW)
Volkswagen Cabrio (auto.)
Volkswagen Cabrio GL (auto.)
Volkswagen Cabrio GLS (auto.)
Volkswagen Cabrio GLX (auto.)
Volkswagen Cabrio Highline (auto.)
Volkswagen Corrado (auto.)
Volkswagen EuroVan (auto.)
Volkswagen EuroVan GLS (auto.)
Volkswagen EuroVan MV (auto.)
Volkswagen Golf (auto.)
Volkswagen Golf GL (auto.)
Volkswagen Golf GL TDI (auto.)
Volkswagen Golf GLS (auto.)
Volkswagen Golf GLS 1.8T (auto.)
Volkswagen Golf GLS GTI (auto.)
Volkswagen Golf GLS TDI (auto.)
Volkswagen Golf GLX GTI (auto.)
Volkswagen Golf GTI (auto.)

Volkswagen Golf K2 (auto.)
Volkswagen Golf Trek (auto.)
Volkswagen Golf Wolfsburg (auto.)
Volkswagen Jetta (auto.)
Volkswagen Jetta GL (auto.)
Volkswagen Jetta GL TDI (auto.)
Volkswagen Jetta GLS (auto.)
Volkswagen Jetta GLS TDI (auto.)
Volkswagen Jetta GLX (auto.)
Volkswagen Jetta GT (auto.)
Volkswagen Jetta K2 (auto.)
Volkswagen Jetta TDI (auto.)
Volkswagen Jetta Wolfsburg (auto.)
Volkswagen New Beetle (auto.)
Volkswagen New Beetle GL (auto.)
Volkswagen New Beetle GLS (auto.)
Volkswagen New Beetle GLX (auto.)
Volkswagen New Beetle TDI (auto.)
Volkswagen of America, Inc.
Volkswagen Passat (auto.)
Volkswagen Passat GLS (auto.)
Volkswagen Passat GLX (auto.)
Volkswagen Passat TDI (auto.)
Volkswagen Rabbit (auto.)
Volkswagenwerke
Volpone (B. Jonson play)
Volstead Act (Prohibition; 1919)
Volstead, Andrew (US pol.; 1860-1947)
Volsunga Saga (also *Volsungasaga*)(myth.)
Volta River (Ghana)
Volta, Alessandro, Count (It. physt.; 1745-1827)
Voltaic languages
Voltaire (b. Françoise Marie Arouet)(Fr. phil./
    writer; (1694-1778)
Voltaren (med.)
Volunteer State (nickname, TN)
Volvo (auto.)
Volvo 240 (auto.)
Volvo 850 (auto.)
Volvo 850 GLT (auto.)
Volvo 850 R (auto.)
Volvo 850 T5 (auto.)
Volvo 940 (auto.)
Volvo 960 (auto.)
Volvo C70 (auto.)
Volvo C70 HT (auto.)
Volvo C70 LT (auto.)
Volvo Cars of North America, Inc.
Volvo GM Heavy Truck Corp.
Volvo S40 (auto.)
Volvo S60 (auto.)
Volvo S60 T5 (auto.)
Volvo S70 (auto.)
Volvo S70 GLT (auto.)
Volvo S70 GLT SE (auto.)
Volvo S70 GT (auto.)
Volvo S70 SE (auto.)
Volvo S70 T5 (auto.)
Volvo S80 (auto.)
Volvo S80 Executive (auto.)
Volvo S80 T6 (auto.)
Volvo S90 (auto.)
Volvo V40 (auto.)
Volvo V70 (auto.)
Volvo V70 GLT (auto.)

Volvo V70 GT (auto.)
Volvo V70 R (auto.)
Volvo V70 SE (auto.)
Volvo V70 T5 (auto.)
Volvo V70 XC (auto.)
Volvo V90 (auto.)
Volyanov, Boris V. (cosmo.)
von Behring, Emil (Ger. bacteriol.; 1854-1917)
von Bismarck, Otto (Eduard Leopold), Prince
    ("Iron Chancellor")(ex-chanc., Ger.; 1815-98)
von Blücher, Gebhard (Ger. gen.; 1742-1819)
von Braun, Werner (or Wernher)(Ger./US eng.;
    1912-77)
von Bulow, Claus (US news; 1926-)
von Bülow, Bernhard, Prince (ex-chanc., Ger.;
    1849-1929)
von Bulow, Sunny (Martha)(US news; 1932-)
von Clausewitz, Karl (Ger. mil.; 1780-1831)
von Dohnányi, Ernst (or Ernö)(Hung. pianist/
    comp.; 1877-1960)
von Flotow, Friedrich (Ger. comp.; 1812-83)
von Fraunhofer, Joseph (Ger. optician/physt.;
    1787-1826)
von Furstenberg Importing Co., Diane
von Furstenberg, Betsy (ent.; 1935-)
von Furstenberg, Diane (Halfin)(US bus.; 1946-)
von Gluck, Christoph W(illibald)(Ger. comp.;
    1714-87)
von Goethe, Johann Wolfgang (Ger. writer/
    phil.; 1749-1852)
von Humboldt, (Friedrich Heinrich) Alexander,
    Baron (Ger. expl.; 1769-1859)
von Karajan, Herbert (Aus. cond.; 1908-89)
von Kleist, Heinrich (Ger. writer; 1777-1811)
von Kluck, Alexander (Ger. gen.; 1846-1934)
von Krafft-Ebing, Richard, Baron (Ger. phys.;
    1840-1902)
von Laban, Rudolf (Hung. ballet; 1879-1958)
von Leibnitz, Gottfried Wilhelm, Baron (Ger.
    phil./math; 1646-1716)
von Liebig, Justus, Baron (Ger. chem.; 1803-73)
von Mannerheim, Carl Gustaf Emil, Baron (Fin.
    gen./pol.; 1867-1951)
von Ossig, Kaspar Schwenkfeld (Ger. rel.;
    1490-1561)
von Papen, Franz (Ger. pol.; 1879-1969)
von Ribbentrop, Joachim (Ger. Nazi pol.; 1893-
    1946)
Von Ryan's Express (film, 1965)
von Schelling, Friedrich Wilhelm Joseph (Ger.
    phil.; 1775-1854)
von Schiller, (Johann Christoph) Friedrich (Ger.
    writer/hist.; 1759-1805)
von Schlegel, August Wilhelm (Ger. writer;
    1767-1845)
von Schlegel, Friedrich (Ger. phil./writer; 1772-
    1829)
von Schuschnigg, Kurt (ex-chanc., Aus.; 1897-
    1977)
Von Stade, Frederica (ent.; 1945-)
Von Stroheim, Erich (ent.; 1885-1957)
Von Sydow, Max (Swed. ent.; 1929-)
von Steuben, Friedrich Wilhelm (Ludolf Gerhard
    Augustin), Baron (Prussian/US gen.; 1730-94)
von Tilzer, Albert (US comp.; 1878-1956)

von Tilzer, Harry (US comp.; 1872-1946)
von Tirpitz, Alfred (Ger. mil.; 1849-1930)
Von Trapp family (singers)
Von Trapp, Baroness Maria (b. Maria Augusta
    Kutschera)(Aus. singer; 1905-87)
von Wassermann, August (Ger. phys./
    bacteriol.; 1866-1925)
von Weber, Carl Maria (Friedrich Ernst), Baron
    (Ger. comp.; 1786-1826)
von Weizsacker, Richard (ex-pres., Ger.; 1920-)
Von Zell, Harry (ent.; 1906-81)
von Zeppelin, Ferdinand Graf, Count (Ger. mil./
    aeronaut; 1838-1917)
V1, V2 (Ger. flying bombs; WWII)
Vonnegut, Kurt, Jr. (US writer; 1922-)
Vontrol (med.)
Vorlage (Ger., skiing)
Voskhod (USSR crewed space flights)
Vostok (USSR crewed space flights)
Voto, Bernard A. De (US hist.; 1897-1955)
Vouvray (wine)
Voyager (US uncrewed space probes)
Voyager, Chrysler (was Plymouth)(auto.)
Voyageurs National Park (MN)
VP (vice president)
Vranitzky, Franz (ex-chanc., Aus.; 1937-)
Vreeland, Diana (Fr./US editor/designer; 1903-
    89)
Vries, Hugo De (Dutch botanist; 1848-1935)
Vries, Peter De (US writer; 1910-93)
VS (veterinary surgeon)
V. Sattui Winery (US bus.)
V(ictor) S(awdon) Pritchett (literary critic;
    1900-97)
VT (variable time, Vermont)
Vuarnet-France (US bus.)
Vuillard, (Jean) Édouard (Fr. artist; 1868-1940)
Vukovar, Croatia
Vulcan (mil. weapon)
Vulcan (myth.)
Vulcan Materials Co.
Vulgar Latin
Vulgate (rel.)
Vulpecula (astron., fox)
VU/TEXT (compu. database)
VW (see Volkswagen)(auto.)
Vyacheslav F. Kebich (ex-PM, Belarus)
Vyacheslav M(ikhailovich) Molotov (ex-PM,
    Rus.; 1890-1986)
Vyatka, Russia (formerly Kirov)
Vytautas Landsbergis (ex-pres., Lith.; 1932-)

W (chem. sym., tungsten)
WA (Washington)
Wabash (railroad slang)
Wabash Cannonball (A.P. Carter song)
Wabash River (central US)
Wabash, IN
WAC (Women's Army Corps)
Waco, TX
Waddaulah, Muda Hassanal Bolkiah Mu'izzaddin (sultan, Brunei)
Wade Boggs (baseball; 1958-)
Wade-Giles system (Eng. representation of Ch.)
Wade, Abdoulaye (pres., Senegal; 1926-)
Wade, Benjamin Franklin (US pol.; 1800-78)
Wade, Roe vs. (US law; 1973)
Wade, Virginia (tennis; 1945-)
Wadi Medani, Sudan
WAF (Women in the Air Force)
Waffle House, Inc.
Wagadugu, Burkina Faso (also Ouagadougou)
Wages and Hours Act (also Fair Labor Standards Act; 1938)
Waggoner, Lyle (ent.; 1935-)
Wagnalls Corp., Funk & (US bus.)
Wagnalls encyclopedias, Funk &
Wagnalls, Adam Willis (US publ.; 1843-1924)
Wagner, (John Peter) Honus (baseball; 1867-1955)
Wagner, Lindsay (ent.; 1949-)
Wagner, Richard (Wilhelm)(Ger. comp.; 1813-83)
Wagner, Robert (ent.; 1930-)
Wagner, Robert F(erdinand), Jr. (ex-mayor, NYC; 1910-1991)
Wagner, Robert F(erdinand), Sr. (US pol.; 1877-1953)
Wagoner, Porter (ent.; 1927-)
Wahabi (rel.)
Wahid, Abdurrahman (pres., Indonesia; 1940-)
Wahl, Ken (ent. 1956-)
Wahlberg, Donnie (ent.; 1969-)
Wahlberg, Mark (ent./model; 1971-)
Wahran, Algeria
Waihee, John D(avid), III (ex-HI gov.; 1946-)
Waikiki Beach (Honolulu, HI)
Wailer, Bunny (b. Neville O'Riley Livingston)(ent.; 1947-)
Wailing Wall (also Western Wall)(Jerusalem)(rel.)
Waimea, HI
Wain, Bea (ent.; 1917-)
Wainwright, Fort (AK)(mil.)
Wainwright, Gideon v. (US law; 1963)
Wainwright, Jonathan M(ayhew)(US gen.; 1883-1953)
Waipahu, HI
Waite, Ralph (ent.; 1929-)
Waite, Terry (Terence Hardy)(Br. rel., hostage; 1939-)
Waiting for Godot (S. Beckett play)

Waits, Tom (ent.; 1949-)
Waitz, Grete (Andersen)(runner; 1953-)
Wake Forest, NC
Wake Island (US air base, central Pac.)
Wakefield, Dick (baseball; 1921-85)
Wakefield, England
Wakefield, MA, VA
Wal-Mart Stores, Inc.
Walcott, Jersey Joe (b. Arnold Raymond Cream)(boxing; 1914-)
Waldemar Pawlak (ex-PM, Pol.; 1959-)
Walden Pond (MA)(Thoreau's inspiration)
Walden, Robert (ent.; 1943-)
Waldenbooks
Waldheim, Kurt (ex-pres., Aus./UN dipl.; 1918-)
Waldorf salad
Waldorf-Astoria Hotel (NYC)
Waler (horse)
Wales (Principality of)(part of UK)
Wales Conference (hockey)
Wales, Prince of (Prince Charles Philip Arthur George)(eldest son of Queen Elizabeth II; 1948-)
Wales, The Outlaw Josey (film, 1976)
Walesa, Lech (ex-pres., Pol.; 1943-)
Walgreen Co.
Walgreen, Charles R. (US bus.; 1873-1939)
Walgreens (drug stores)
Walhalla (also Valhalla, Walhall, Valhall)(myth.)
Walken, Christopher (ent.; 1943-)
Walker & Sons, Inc., Hiram
Walker, Alice (US writer; 1944-)
Walker, Jimmy (James John)(ex-mayor, NYC; 1881-1946)
Walker, Johnnie (whiskey)
Walker, Larry (baseball; 1966-)
Walker, Matthew (knot)
Walker, Mort (cartoonist; *Beetle Bailey*; 1923-)
Walker, Nancy (ent.; 1922-92)
Walker, Ralph T. (US arch.; 1889-1973)
Walker, Robert (ent.; 1914-51)
Walker, T-Bone (ent.; 1910-75)
Walker: Texas Ranger (TV show)
Walkman (music)
Wall of China, Great (1,450 miles; built 214 BC)
Wall Street (NYC)(US financial center)
Wall Street Journal (newspaper)
Walla Walla, WA
Wallace Beery (ent.; 1889-1949)
Wallace K. Harrison (US arch.; 1895-1981)
Wallace Reid (ent.; 1891-1923)
Wallace Shawn (ent.; 1943-)
Wallace Stegner (US writer; 1909-93)
Wallace Stevens (US poet; 1879-1955)
Wallace, Alfred Russel (Br. nat.; 1823-1913)
Wallace, Christopher (aka The Notorious B.I.G.)(ent.; 1972-97)
Wallace, DeWitt (US publ.; 1889-1981)
Wallace, George C(orley)(ex-gov., AL; 1919-98)
Wallace, Henry A(gard)(ex-US VP; 1888-1965)
Wallace, Irving (US writer; 1916-90)
Wallace, Lila (Acheson)(US publ.; 1889-1984)
Wallace, Mike (US TV jour.; 1918-)
Wallace, Sippie (b. Beulah Thomas)(ent.; 1898-1986)
Wallach, Eli (ent.; 1915-)

Wallawalla (Native Amer.)
Wallbanger, Harvey (mixed drink)
Wallenberg, Raoul (Swed. dipl.; 1912-47?)
Wallenda, Karl (Ger. circus; 1905-78)
Wallenstein, Alfred (US cond.; 1898-1983)
Waller, Fats (Thomas Wright)(US comp./jazz;
    1904-43)
Waller, Robert James (US writer; 1939-)
Wallis "Wally" Warfield Simpson (Duchess of
    Windsor)(US socialite, m. Edward VIII;
    1896-1986)
Wallis and Futuna Islands (SW Pac.)
Wallis, Hal (Harold Brent)(ent.; 1899-1986)
Walloon (lang./people)
Wallop, Malcolm (US pol.; 1933-)
Wally Cox (ent.; 1924-73)
Wally (Walter J.) Hickel (ex-AK gov.; 1919-)
Wally (Walter Marty) Schirra, Jr. (US astro.;
    1923-)
Walnut Creek, CA
Walpole, Horace (Horatio)(Earl of Oxford)(Br.
    writer; 1717-97)
Walpole, Robert (Earl of Oxford)(Br. pol.; 1676-
    1745)
Walpurgis Night (May 1)
Walsh, Adam (football; 1902-85)
Walsh, Bill (football; 1931-)
Walsh, Joe (ent.; 1947-)
Walsh, Raoul (ent.; 1887-1980)
Walston, Ray (ent.; 1914-2001)
Walt(er Elias) Disney (US bus./ent.; 1901-66)
Walt Disney Co., The
Walt Frazier (basketball; 1945-)
Walt Kelly (cartoonist, *Pogo*; 1913-73)
Walt(er) Whitman (US poet; 1819-92)
Walt Whitman Rostow (US econ.; 1916-)
Waltari, Mika (writer; 1903-79)
Walter Alston (baseball; 1911-84)
Walter Annenberg (US publ./finan.; 1908-)
Walter Bagehot (Br. econ./jour.; 1826-77)
Walter Brennan (ent.; 1894-1974)
Walter Camp (football; 1859-1925)
Walter Corp., Jim
Walter Cronkite (US TV jour.; 1916-)
Walter Cunningham, R. (astro.; 1932-)
Walter de la Mare (Br. poet; 1873-1956)
Walter D(ale) Miller (ex-SD gov.; 1925-)
Walter Donaldson (US comp.; 1893-1947)
Walter F(rederick) "Fritz" Mondale (US pol.;
    1928-)
Walter F. Kerr (US writer/critic; 1913-96)
Walter F(rancis) White (US reformer; 1893-
    1955)
Walter Gilbert (US chemist; 1932-)
Walter (Adolf) Gropius (US arch.; 1883-1969)
Walter Hagen (golf; 1892-1969)
Walter Houser Brattain (US physt./inv.; 1902-87)
Walter Huston (ent.; 1884-1950)
Walter J. "Wally" Hickel (ex-AK gov.; 1919-)
Walter (Perry) "Big Train" Johnson (baseball;
    1887-1946)
Walter Johannes Damrosch (cond.; 1862-1950)
Walter Koenig (ent./writer; 1936-)
Walter Lantz (cartoonist, *Woody Woodpecker*;
    1900-94)

Walter Lippmann (US jour.; 1889-1974)
Walter L. Jacobs (US bus.; 1898-1985)
Walter Matthau (ent.; 1920-2000)
Walter Mitty, The Secret Life of (J. Thurber
    short story)
Walter O'Malley (baseball exec.; 1903-79)
Walter (Horatio) Pater (Br. writer; 1839-94)
Walter Payton (football; 1954-99)
Walter P(ercy) Chrysler (US car bus.; 1875-1940)
Walter Pidgeon (ent.; 1897-1984)
Walter Piston (US comp.; 1894-1976)
Walter (B.) Pitkin (writer)
Walter P(hilip) Reuther (US labor leader; 1907-
    70)
Walter P. Webb (US hist.; 1888-1963)
Walter Raleigh, (Sir)(Br. expl./writer; 1552?-
    1618)
Walter Rathenau (Ger. pol.; 1867-1922)
Walter Reed Army Medical Center (DC)
Walter Reed, Dr. (US phys.; 1851-1902)
Walter Richard Sickert (Br. artist; 1860-1942)
Walter Scott, (Sir)(Scot. writer; 1771-1832)
Walter Slezak (ent.; 1902-83)
Walter Ulbricht (Ger. pol.; 1893-1873)
Walter Wanger (b. Walter Feuchtwanger)(US
    ent.; 1894-1968)
Walter Winchell (US newscaster; 1897-1972)
Walter, Bruno (b. Bruno Walter Schlesinger)
    (cond.; 1876-1962)
Walter, Jessica (ent.; 1944-)
Walters, Barbara (US TV jour.; 1931-)
Walters, David (ex-OK gov.; 1951-)
Walton Beach, Fort (FL)(city)
Walton, Bill (basketball; 1952-)
Walton, Izaak (Br. writer; 1593-1683)
Walton, Sam (Moore)(US bus./Wal-Mart; 1918-
    92)
Walton, (Sir) William (Turner)(Br. comp.;
    1902-83)
Waltons, The (TV show)
Wambaugh, Joseph (US writer; 1937-)
Wanamaker, Inc., John
Wanamaker, John (US bus.; 1838-1922)
Wanamaker, Sam (ent.; 1919-93)
Wanamaker's (department store)
Wanda, A Fish Called (film, 1988)
Wandering Jew (legendary Jew condemned to
    wander)
wandering Jew (plant)
Wanderjahr (Ger., year of travel)
Wang An-Shih (Ch. pol.; 1021-86)
Wang Laboratories, Inc.
Wang School, Lu- (Ch. phil.)
Wang Wei (Ch. poet/artist; 699-759)
Wang, An (Ch./US inv./bus.; 1920-90)
Wang, Vera (designer; 1949-)
Wangchuk, Jigme Singye (king, Bhutan; 1955-)
Wanger, Walter (b. Walter Feuchtwanger)(US
    ent.; 1894-1968)
Wank, Roland A. (US arch.; 1898-1970)
Wankel engine (auto.)
Wankel, Felix (Ger., inv.; 1902-88)
Wapner, Judge Joseph (*People's Court*; 1919-)
War Between the States (also American Civil
    War, War of Secession)(1861-65)

War of 1812 (US/Br.; 1812-15)
War of Jenkin's Ear (Br./Sp.; 1739-41)
War of Secession (also American Civil War, War Between the States)(1861-65)
War of the Nations (also World War I, First World War, Great War)(1914-18)
War of the Pacific (Chile/Bolivia, Peru; 1879-83)
War of the Roses (Eng. hist.; 1455-85)
War Powers Act (US hist.; 1973)
War, Department of (US govt.)
Warbeck, Perkin (Flem. pretender to Br. throne; 1474-99)
Ward Bond (ent.; 1903-60)
Ward, Aaron Montgomery (US bus.; 1843-1913)
Ward, Barbara (Baroness Jackson of Lodsworth)(Br. econ.; 1914-81)
Ward, Fred (ent.; 1942-)
Ward, Sela (ent.; 1956-)
Warden, Jack (b. Jack Warden Lebzelter)(ent.; 1920-)
Warfield, William (ent.; 1920-)
Warhol, Andy (b. Andrew Warhola)(US artist; 1927-87)
Waring Products (US bus.)
Waring, Fred M. (US cond., designed Waring blender; 1900-84)
Warnaco Group, Inc.
Warner Books (US bus.)
Warner Brothers (WB)(TV channel)
Warner Brothers Records, Inc.
Warner Brothers, Inc.
Warner Cable Corp.
Warner Communications, Inc., Time
Warner-Lambert Co.
Warner-Lambert Consumer Group (US bus.)
Warner Oland (ent.; 1880-1938)
Warner, Albert (ent.; 1884-1967)
Warner, Harry M(orris)(ent.; 1881-1958)
Warner, Inc., Time
Warner, Jack L(eonard)(ent.; 1892-1978)
Warner, John W. (US cong.; 1927-)
Warner, Malcolm-Jamal (ent.; 1970-)
Warner, Samuel L(ewis)(ent.; 1887-1927)
Warnes, Jennifer (ent.; 1947-)
Warren Beatty (ent.; 1937-)
Warren Berlinger (ent.; 1937-)
Warren Bridge, Charles River Bridge v. (US law; 1837)
Warren Buffett (investment expert; 1930-)
Warren (Earl) Burger (US jurist; 1907-95)
Warren Commission (US hist.; 1963-64)
Warren "Baby" Dodds (US jazz; 1898-1959)
Warren G(amaliel) Harding (29th US pres.; 1865-1923)
Warren Giles (baseball exec.; 1896-1979)
Warren Report (US hist.; 1964)
Warren (Edward) Spahn (baseball; 1921-)
Warren Zevon (ent./songwriter; 1947-)
Warren, Christopher (US ex-secy./state; 1925-)
Warren, Earl (US jurist; 1891-1974)
Warren, Harry (US comp.; 1893-1981)
Warren, Lesley Ann (ent.; 1946-)
Warren, MI, OH
Warren, Robert Penn (US writer; 1905-89)

Warri, Nigeria
Warrick, Ruth (ent.; 1916-)
Warriors, Golden State (basketball team)
Warsaw Pact (also Warsaw Treaty Organization)(USSR/E Eur.; 1955-91)
Warsaw, IN
Warsaw, Poland
Wart-Off (med.)
Warwick, Dionne (b. Marie Warrick)(ent.; 1940-)
Warwick, England
Warwick, RI
Warwickshire (county, Eng.)
Wasatch Range (ID/UT)
Washington (WA)
Washington Allston (US artist; 1779-1843)
Washington and Lee University (VA)
Washington Bullets (basketball team)
Washington Capitals (hockey team)
Washington Irving (US writer/hist.; 1783-1859)
Washington Journalism Review
Washington Monument (DC)
Washington pie
Washington Post (DC newspaper)
Washington Post Co.
Washington Redskins (football team)
Washington thorn (tree)
Washington Times (DC newspaper)
Washington, Booker T(aliaferro)(US educ./reformer; 1856-1915)
Washington, DC (District of Columbia, US capital)
Washington, Denzel (ent.; 1954-)
Washington, Dinah (ent.; 1924-63)
Washington, George (1st US pres.; 1732-99)
Washington, Harold (ex-mayor, Chicago; 1922-87)
Washington, Martha (Dandridge)(wife of ex-US pres.; 1732-1802)
Washington's Birthday (February 22)
Washingtonia (tree)
Washingtonian (mag.)
Waslaw (or Vaslav) Nijinsky (Rus. ballet; 1890-1950)
Wasmosy, Juan Carlos (ex-pres., Paraguay; 1942-)
WASP (white Anglo-Saxon Protestant)
Wassail (mixed drink)
Wasserman, Lew (ent.; 1913-)
Wassermann test/reaction (for syphilis)
Wassermann, August von (Ger. phys./bacteriol.; 1866-1925)
Wasserstein, Wendy (playwright; 1950-)
Wassily (or Vasili, Vasily) Kandinsky (Rus. artist; 1866-1944)
Waste King, Thermador/ (US bus.)
Wat (Walter) Tyler (Br. rebel; ?-1381)
Water Pik
Waterbury, CT
Waterfield, Bob (football; 1921-83)
Waterford Glass, Inc.
Waterford glass/crystal
Waterford, CT
Waterford, Ireland
Watergate (US hist.; 1972-74)
Watergate Hotel/apartments (DC)

Waterloo Bridge (film, 1940)
Waterloo, Battle of (Napoleon's defeat; 1815)
Waterloo, Belgium
Waterloo, IA
Waterloo, Ontario, Canada
Waterman, Willard (ent.)
Waters, Ethel (ent.; 1900-77)
Waters, John (ent./writer; 1946-)
Waters, Muddy (aka McKinley Morganfield) (ent.; 1915-83)
Watership Down (R. Adams novel)
Waterston, Sam (ent.; 1940-)
Watertown, MA, NY, SD
Waterville, ME
Watervliet Arsenal (NY)
Watervliet, NY
Watkins, Carlene (ent.; 1952-)
Watkins, Tionne (ent.; 1970-)
W. Atlee Burpee Co.
Watley, Jody (ent.; 1959-)
Watling Island, Bahamas (also San Salvador)
WATS (Wide Area Telecommunications Service) (comm.)
Watson-Crick model (3-D structure of DNA)
Watson, Dr. (fict. chara. w/Sherlock Holmes)
Watson, Emily (ent.; 1967-)
Watson, James Dewey (US biol.; 1928-)
Watson, Martha Rae (track; 1946-)
Watson, Thomas J(ohn)(US bus.; 1874-1956)
Watson, Thomas J(ohn), Jr. (US bus.; 1914-93)
Watson, Tom (golf; 1949-)
Watt, James E. (Scot. eng./inv.; 1736-1819)
Watt, James G. (US ex-secy./interior; 1938-)
Watteau back (clothing)
Watteau hat
Watteau, Jean Antoine (Fr. artist; 1684-1721)
Watterson, Bill (cartoonist, Calvin and Hobbes; 1958-)
Wattleton, Faye (US reformer; 1943-)
Watts riots (Los Angeles; 1965)
Watts, Andre (pianist; 1946-)
Watts, George Frederic (Bt. artist; 1817-1904)
Watusi (people)
Waugh, Alec (Alexander Raban)(Br. writer; 1898-1981)
Waugh, Evelyn (Arthur St. John)(Br. writer; 1903-66)
Waukegan, IL
Waukesha, WI
Wausau Insurance Companies
Wausau Paper Mills Co.
Wausau, WI
Wauwatosa, WI
Wavell, Archibald (Percival)(Br. mil.; 1883-1950)
Waves (also WAVES)(Women's Reserve, US Navy)
Waxman, Franz (Ger./US comp.; 1906-67)
Way, Middle (rel.)
Wayans, Damon (ent.; 1960-)
Wayans, Keenan Ivory (ent.; 1958-)
Waylon Jennings (ent.; 1937-)
Wayne Allard (US cong.; 1943-)
Wayne Gretzky (hockey; 1961-)
Wayne Knight (ent.; 1955-)
Wayne L. Hays (US pol.; 1912-89)

Wayne Morse (US pol.; 1900-74)
Wayne Newton (ent.; 1942-)
Wayne Rogers (ent.; 1933-)
Wayne State College (Wayne, NE)
Wayne State University (Detroit, MI)
Wayne, Anthony (Mad Anthony)(US gen.; 1745-96)
Wayne, Bruce (ent.)
Wayne, David (ent.; 1914-95)
Wayne, Fort (IN)(city)
Wayne, John (b. Marion Michael Morrison, aka "the Duke")(ent.; 1907-79)
Wayne's World (film, 1992)
Ways and Means Committee, House (US govt.)
Wazed, Sheik Hasina (PM, Bangladesh; 1947-)
WB (Warner Brothers)(TV channel)
W. B. Roddenbery Co., Inc. (Roddenbery's)
W. B. Saunders Co.
W(illiam) B(utler) Yeats (Ir. writer; 1865-1939)
WCC (World Council of Churches)
W. C. Fields (b. William Claude Dukenfield) (ent.; 1880-1946)
W(illiam) C(hristopher) Handy (US jazz; 1873-1958)
WCTU (Woman's Christian Temperance Union)
W(illiam) D(eWitt) Snodgrass (US poet; 1926-)
Wealthy apple
Weasley, Ron (fict. chara., Harry Potter)
Weather Channel, The (TV channel)
Weather Service, National (US govt.; est.1870)
Weatherwax, Rudd (Lassie's trainer; 1915?-85)
Weaver, Charlie (aka Cliff Arquette)(ent.; 1905-74)
Weaver, Dennis (ent.; 1924-)
Weaver, Doodles (Winstead)(ent.; 1912-83)
Weaver, Earl (baseball; 1930-)
Weaver, Fritz (ent.; 1926-)
Weaver, Randy (US news, confrontation w/US marshals at Ruby Ridge, ID)
Weaver, Sigourney (ent.; 1949-)
Web, the (Internet)
Webb Hotels, Del (US bus.)
Webb, (Martha) Beatrice (Potter)(Br. reformer/ writer; 1858-1943)
Webb, Chick (US jazz; 1902-39)
Webb, Clifton (ent.; 1891-1966)
Webb, Jack (ent.; 1920-82)
Webb, Jimmy (US comp.; 1946-)
Webb, Sidney (James)(Br. reformer/writer; 1859-1947)
Webb, Veronica (ent./model/writer; 1965-)
Webb, Walter P. (US hist.; 1888-1963)
Webber, Andrew Lloyd (Br. comp.; 1948-)
Webber, Chris (basketball; 1973-)
W(illiam) E(dward) B(urghardt) Du Bois (US educ./writer, NAACP; 1868-1963)
Weber Food Products Co.
Weber State University (Ogden, UT)
Weber, Carl Maria (Friedrich Ernst) von, Baron (Ger. comp.; 1786-1826)
Weber, Max (Ger. econ./hist.; 1864-1920)
Weber, Max (US artist; 1881-1961)
Webster Hubbell (US atty., Whitewater)
Webster University (St. Louis, MO)
Webster, Alex (football; 1931-)

Webster, Ben (US jazz; 1909-73)
Webster, Daniel (US orator/pol.; 1782-1852)
Webster, The Devil and Daniel (film, 1941)
Webster, Margaret (ent.; 1905-73)
Webster, Noah (US lexicographer; 1758-1843)
Webster, Paul Francis (US lyricist; 1907-84)
Webster's Collegiate Dictionary, Merriam-
Webster's Dictionary, Merriam-
Webster's New World Dictionary of American
  English
Wechsler Scales (intelligence tests)
Weddell Sea (S Atl.)
Wedgewood USA, Inc.
Wedgwood blue (color)
Wedgwood china
Wedgwood, Josiah (Br. potter; 1730-95)
Wedtech scandal (US news; mid-1980s)
Wee Kim Wee (ex-pres., Singapore; 1914-)
Wee Willie Winkie (fict. chara.)
Wee, Wee Kim (ex-pres., Singapore; 1914-)
Weeb (Wilbur Charles) Ewbank (football; 1907-
  98)
Weed Eater, Inc.
Weed, CA
Week in Review (TV show)
Weeki Wachee Springs (FL)
Wegener, Alfred L(othar)(Ger. meteor.; 1880-
  1930)
Wei, Wang (Ch. poet/artist; 699-759)
Weibel Vineyards (US bus.)
Weicker, Lowell Palmer, Jr. (ex-CT gov.; 1931-)
Weight Watchers International, Inc.
Weight Watchers Magazine
Weil, Andrew (US phys./writer, alternative med.)
Weil, Cynthia (US comp.; 1937-)
Weill, Kurt (Julian)(Ger./US comp.; 1900-50)
Weimar Republic (Ger. hist.; 1919-33)
Weimar, Germany
Weimaraner (dog)
Weinberg principle/law/distribution, Hardy-
  (genetics)
Weinberger, Caspar "Cap" W(illard)(US ex-
  secy./defense; 1917-)
Weiner, Norbert (US math.; 1894-1964)
Weir, Peter (ent.; 1944-)
Weis Markets, Inc.
Weiskopf, Tom (golf; 1942-)
Weiss, George (baseball exec.; 1895-1972)
Weissmuller, Johnny (Peter John)(US swimmer/
  ent.; 1903-84)
Weitz, Bruce (ent.; 1943-)
Weitz, Paul J. (astro.; 1932-)
Weizman, Ezer (ex-pres., Isr.; 1924-)
Weizmann, Chaim (ex-pres., Isr.; 1874-1952)
Weizsacker, Richard von (ex-pres., Ger.; 1920-)
Welby, M.D., Marcus (TV show)
Welch Foods, Inc.
Welch, Jack (US bus.; 1935-)
Welch, Raquel (b. Raquel Tejada)(ent.; 1940-)
Welcome Back, Kotter (TV show)
Welcome to Pooh Corner (TV show)
Welcome Wagon (to welcome newcomers)
Weld, Philip (sailing; 1915-84)
Weld, Tuesday (Susan)(ent.; 1943-)
Weld, William F(loyd)(ex-MA gov.; 1945-)

Weldon Roberts Rubber Co.
Welk, Lawrence (US cond.; 1903-92)
Well-Tempered Clavier (by Johann S. Bach)
Welland Ship Canal (Lake Erie/Lake Ontario)
Wellbutrin (med.)
Welles, Gideon (US pol./jour.; 1802-78)
Welles, (George) Orson (ent.; 1915-85)
Wellesley College (Wellesley, MA)
Wellesley, Arthur (Duke of Wellington)(Br. mil.;
  1769-1852)
Wellesley, MA
Wellington boots (also l.c.)
Wellington, (Arthur Wellesley), Duke of (Br.
  mil.; 1769-1852)
Wellington, beef
Wellington, New Zealand
Wells Fargo & Co.
Wells Fargo Bank
Wells, H(erbert) G(eorge)(Br. writer; 1866-1946)
Wells, Ida Bell (Barnett)(US jour./civil rights
  leader; 1862-1931)
Wells, Kitty (b. Muriel Deason)(ent.; 1919-)
Wells, Mary (ent.; 1943-92)
Wellstone, Paul (David)(US cong.; 1944-)
Welsh (lang./people)
Welsh cob (pony)
Welsh corgi (dog)
Welsh pony
Welsh rabbit (also Welsh rarebit)(cheese dish)
Welsh springer spaniel (dog)
Welsh terrier (dog)
Weltanschauung (Ger., world-view)
Weltgeist (Ger., spirit of the times)
Weltschmerz (also l.c.)(Ger., world-pain,
  sentimental pessimism)
Welty, Eudora (US writer; 1909-2001)
Wembley (district, London)
Wen Ho Lee (Taiwan/US eng./scien., nuclear
  weapons; 1939-)
Wenatchee National Forest
Wences, Senor (b. Wenceslao Moreno)
  (ventriloquist; ?-1999)
Wenceslas (emp., Rome; king, Ger./Bohemia;
  1361-1419)
Wenceslas, Good King (also Wenceslaus)(song)
Wenceslas, St. (also "King Wenceslaus")(duke,
  Bohemia; 907-929)
Wendell Corey (ent.; 1914-68)
Wendell Hampton Ford (US pol.; 1924-)
Wendell L(ewis) Willkie (US pol.; 1892-1944)
Wendt, George (ent.; 1948-)
Wendy Hiller, Dame (ent.; 1912-)
Wendy O(rlean) Williams (ent.; 1949-98)
Wendy Wasserstein (playwright; 1950-)
Wendy's International, Inc.
Wendy's restaurant
Wenner, Jann (US publ., *Rolling Stone*; 1946-)
Wenrich, Percy (US comp.; 1887-1952)
Wensleydale (cheese)
Wente Brothers (US bus.)
Wenzel, Hanni (skiing; 1956-)
Werfel, Franz (Aus. writer; 1890-1945)
Werner Carl Heisenberg (Ger. physt.; 1901-76)
Werner Herzog (Ger. ent.; 1942-)
Werner Klemperer (Ger. ent.; 1920-2000)

Werner, Oskar (b. Josef Schliessmayer)(ent.; 1922-84)

Werner (or Wernher) von Braun (Ger./US eng.; 1912-77)

Wertheimer, Linda (radio jour.; 1943-)

Wertheimer, Max (Czech. psych./phil.; 1880-1943)

Werther's Original (candy)

Wertmüller, Lina (It. ent.; 1926?-)

Wes(ley Earl) Craven (ent.; 1939-)

Wes Montgomery (US jazz; 1925-68)

Wesberry v. Sanders (US law; 1964)

Wesley Crusher, Ensign (fict. chara., *Star Trek*)

Wesley Snipes (ent.; 1962-)

Wesley, John (Br. rel., founded Methodism; 1703-91)

Wesleyan College (Macon, GA)

Wesleyan University (Middletown, CT)

Wessex (Eng. kingdom; 6th-9th c.)

Wesson Fire Arms Co.

Wesson, Inc., Hunt-

Wesson, Tina (TV survivor; 1960-)

West Bank (of Jordan River)(disputed area, SW Asia)

West Bend Co., The

West Bengal (state, India)

West Bromwich, England

West Chester, PA

West Flanders (province, Belgium)

West Germany (now part of Germany)

West Hartford, CT

West Haven, CT

West Highland (cattle)

West Highland white terrier (dog)

West Indian (people)

West Indies (Bahamas, Greater Antilles, Lesser Antilles)

West Jordan, UT

West Orange, NJ

West Pakistan (now Republic of Pakistan)

West Palm Beach Post (FL newspaper)

West Palm Beach, FL

West Point (fort., NY)

West Point, US Military Academy at (NY)

West Point-Pepperell Mill Store (US bus.)

West Siberian Plain (region, Siberia)

West Side Story (film, 1961)

West Sussex (county, Eng.)

West Valley City, UT

West Virginia (WV)

West Virginia State Board of Education v. Barnette (US law; 1943)

West, American (west of Mississippi River)

West, Benjamin (US artist; 1738-1820)

West, Dottie (ent.; 1932-91)

West, Jerry (basketball; 1938-)

West, Jessamyn (US writer; 1903-84)

West, Mae (ent.; 1892-1980)

West, Mae (life jacket)

West, Nathanael (aka Nathan Wallenstein Weinstein)(US writer; 1904-40)

West, Rebecca, Dame (b. Cicily Isabel Fairfield) (Br. writer; 1892-1983)

West, Togo D., Jr. (US ex-secy./vet. affairs; 1942-)

West, Dame Victoria Mary Sackville- ("Vita") (Br. writer; 1892-1962)

WestAir Airlines

Westbrook Pegler, (James)(US jour.; 1894-1969)

Westchester, NY, IL

Westclox (US bus.)

Westerlies (winds)

Western Australia (state, Austl.)

Western Auto Supply (US bus.)

Western blot (med.)

Western Conference (basketball)

Western Hemisphere

Western saddle (also stock saddle)

Western Samoa (Independent State of)(SW Pac.)

Western Tsin (or Chin) dynasty (also Chin)(Ch.; 265-316)

Western Union (comm.)

Western Union Corp.

Western Wall (also Wailing Wall)(Jerusalem)(rel.)

Westerner

Westfalia (Volkswagen van)

Westheimer, Dr. Ruth (b. Karola Ruth Siegal) (Ger./US sex therapist; 1928-)

Westin Hotels & Resorts

Westinghouse (appliances)

Westinghouse break (rr.)

Westinghouse Electric Corp.

Westinghouse, George (US bus.; 1846-1914)

Westlake, Donald E. (US writer; 1933-)

Westlaw (compu. database, law)

Westminster Abbey (also Collegiate Church of St. Peter)(London)

Westminster Palace (Houses of Parliament)(London)

Westminster, CA, CO

Westmoreland, William (Childs)(US gen.; 1914-)

Weston, Jack (ent.; 1924-96)

Westover Air Force Base, MA

Westphalia (region, Ger.)

Westphalian ham

WestPoint Stevens, Inc.

Westvaco Corp.

Westworld (film, 1973)

Wet 'n' Wild (cosmetics)

Wexford (county, Ir.)

Weyden, Rogier van der (Flem. artist; c1400-64)

Weyerhaeuser Co.

Weyerhaeuser lumber

Weymouth, MA

Wff'n Proof Learning Games Associates (US bus.)

WGN (TV channel)

Whalers, Hartford (hockey team)

Wharton, Edith (Newbold Jones)(US writer; 1862-1937)

What's Happening Now!! (TV show)

What's Happening!! (TV show)

What's My Line? (TV show)

Whatever Happened to Baby Jane? (film, 1962)

W(ystan) H(ugh) Auden (Br. poet; 1907-73)

Wheaties cereal

Wheatley, Phillis (Afr./US poet; 1753-84)

Wheaton, IL, MD

Wheaton, Wil (ent.; 1972-)

Wheatstone bridge (elect.)
Wheel of Fortune (TV show)
wheel of Fortune (gambling)
Wheeler Air Force Base, HI
Wheeler, William A(lmon)(ex-US VP; 1819-87)
Wheeling, IL, WV
When Harry Met Sally (film, 1989)
Whidbey Island Naval Air Station (WA)
Whiffenpoof Song, The
Whig Party (UK/US hist.)
Whipple Observatory, (Fred Lawrence)(AZ)
Whipple, Fred Lawrence (US astron.; 1906-)
Whirlpool (appliances)
Whirlpool Corp.
Whirlpool Gold (appliances)
Whiskas cat food
Whiskey Rebellion (US hist.; 1794)
Whiskey Ring (US hist./scandal)
Whistler, James (Abbott) McNeill (US artist; 1834-1903)
Whitaker, Forest (ent.; 1961-)
Whitaker, Pernell (boxing; 1964-)
Whitchurch-Stouffville, Ontario, Canada
White Castle Systems, Inc.
White Christmas (song)
White Fang (film, 1991)
White Foods, Inc., Martha
White Friar (Carmelite friar)
White House, the (also Executive Mansion)(US pres. residence)(DC)
White Leghorn (chicken)
White Plains, NY
White Rain (hair care)
White Russian (cocktail)
White Sands Missile Range, NM
White Slave Traffic Act (also Mann Act)(US hist.; 1910)
White Sox, Chicago (baseball team)
White, Betty (ent.; 1922-)
White, Bill (baseball; 1934-)
White, Byron R(aymond)("Whizzer")(US jurist; 1917-)
White, Devon (baseball; 1962-)
White, E(lwyn) B(rooks)(US writer; 1899-1985)
White, Edmund (US writer; 1940-)
White, Edward H(iggins), II (astro., 1st Amer. to walk in space; 1930-67)
White, Jaleel (ent.; 1976-)
White, Jesse (ent.; 1919-97)
White, Margaret Bourke- (US photo./writer; 1906-71)
White, Reggie (football; 1961-)
White, Ryan (US AIDS victim/activist; 1972-90)
White, Stanford (US arch.; 1853-1906)
White, T(erence) H(anbury)(Br. writer; 1906-64)
White, Texas v. (US law; 1869)
White, Theodore H. (US jour.; 1915-86)
White, Vanna (b. Vanna Rosich)(ent.; 1957-)
White, Tim (US anthrop.; 1950-)
White, Walter F(rancis)(US reformer; 1893-1955)
White, Willye B. (jumper; 1936-)
Whitechapel district (London)
Whitefriars district (London)
Whitehall Laboratories, Inc.
Whitehall Palace (London)

Whitehead, Alfred North (Br. phil./math.; 1861-1947)
Whitehorse, Yukon Territory, Canada
Whiteman Air Force Base, MO
Whiteman, Paul ("Pops")(US cond.; 1891-1967)
Whitesnake (pop music)
Whitewater (US pol. scandal; 1994)
Whitey (Edward Charles) Ford ("Duke of Paducah")(baseball; 1928-)
Whiting Field Naval Air Station, FL
Whiting, Margaret (ent.; 1924-)
Whiting, Richard A. (US comp.; 1891-1938)
Whitman Corp.
Whitman, Christine "Christie" Todd (US adm./ EPA, ex-NJ gov.; 1946-)
Whitman, Meg (Margaret C.)(US bus./eBay; 1957-)
Whitman, Walt(er)(US poet; 1819-92)
Whitman's Candies, Inc.
Whitmore, James (ent.; 1921-)
Whitney Houston (ent.; 1963-)
Whitney Museum of American Art (NYC)
Whitney M(oore) Young, Jr. (US reformer; 1921-71)
Whitney v. California (US law; 1927)
Whitney, Eli (US inv./bus.; 1765-1825)
Whitney, John Hay (US publ./finan.; 1905-82)
Whitney, Mount (CA)
Whitsunday (also Pentecost)(rel.)
Whittaker, Roger (ent.; 1936-)
Whittier, CA
Whittier, John Greenleaf (US poet/jour.; 1807-92)
Whitworth, Kathy (golf; 1939-)
WHO (World Health Organization [UN])
Who Framed Roger Rabbit? (film, 1988)
Who Wants to be a Millionaire? (TV show)
Who, the (pop music)
Who, Doctor (film, 1996)
Who's Afraid of Virginia Woolf? (film, 1966)
Who's Harry Crumb? (film, 1989)
Who's the Boss (TV show)
Whoopi Goldberg (b. Caryn Johnson)(ent.; 1950-)
Whyte classification (rr.)
WI (West Indies, Wisconsin)
WIA (wounded in action)
Wichita (Native Amer.)
Wichita Eagle (KS newspaper)
Wichita Falls, TX
Wichita State University (Wichita, KS)
Wichita, KS
Wickes Cos., Inc.
Wicklow (county, Ir.)
Wickremanayake, Ratnasiri (PM, Sri Lanka; 1933-)
Wickremasinghe, Ranil (ex-PM, Sri Lanka)
Wicks 'N Sticks (US bus.)
Wide Area Telecommunications Service (also WATS)(comm.)
Wideman, John Edgar (US writer; 1941-)
Widing, Juha (hockey; 1948-85)
Widmark, Richard (ent.; 1914-)
Wiener schnitzel (veal dish)
Wienerschnitzel International, Inc.
Wiesbaden, Germany
Wiesel, Elie(zer)(US writer/reformer; 1928-)

Wiesenthal, Simon (Aus. reformer; 1908-)
Wiest, Dianne (ent.; 1948-)
Wiffle Ball, Inc., The
Wigglesworth, Michael (US rel./writer; 1631-1705)
Wiggs of the Cabbage Patch, Mrs. (film, 1942)
Wight, Isle of (island/county, Eng.)
Wigraine (med.)
Wigwam Mills, Inc.
Wijetunge, Dingiri Banda (ex-pres., Sri Lanka; 1922-)
Wil Shriner (ent.; 1953-)
Wil Wheaton (ent.; 1972-)
Wilander, Mats (tennis; 1964-)
Wilberforce, William (Br. reformer; 1759-1833)
Wilbur D. Mills (US pol.; 1910-92)
Wilbur Wright (US aviator/inv.; 1867-1912)
Wilcox, Ella Wheeler (US poet; 1850-1919)
Wild Bill (James Butler) Hickok (US frontier/law; 1837-76)
Wild Bill Davison (US jazz; 1906-89)
Wild Eights (also Crazy Eights)(card game)
Wild Kingdom (TV show)
Wild West (also old West)
Wild, Wild West, The (TV show)
Wilde, Brandon De (ent.; 1942-72)
Wilde, Cornel (ent; 1915-89)
Wilde, L(awrence) Douglas (ex-VA gov.; 1931-)
Wilde, Oscar (Fingal O'Flahertie Wills)(Ir. writer; 1854-1900)
Wilder, (Lawrence) Douglas (ex-gov., VA; 1931-)
Wilder, Billy (Samuel)(ent./writer; 1906-)
Wilder, Gene (ent.; 1935-)
Wilder, Laura Ingalls (US writer; 1867-1957)
Wilder, Thornton (Niven)(US writer; 1897-1975)
Wilderness of Zin
Wilderness Road (route for settlers of old West)
Wilderness, Battle of the (US hist.; 1864)
Wilding, Michael (ent.; 1912-79)
Wiley Blount Rutledge, Jr. (US jurist; 1894-1949)
Wiley Post (US aviator; 1899-1935)
Wilford Brimley (ent.; 1934-)
Wilfredo Lam (Cuban artist; 1902-82)
Wilfried Martens (ex-PM, Belgium; 1936-)
Wilhelm Friedemann Bach (Ger. comp.; 1710-84)
Wilhelm (Karl) Grimm (Ger. writer/linguist; 1786-1859)
Wilhelm Mauser (Ger. inv.; 1834-82)
Wilhelm Ostwald (Ger. chem.; 1853-1932)
Wilhelm Reich (Aus. phys.; 1897-1957)
Wilhelm (Conrad) Roentgen (Ger. physt., x-rays; 1845-1923)
Wilhelmina I (Wilhelmina Helena Pauline Maria [of Orange-Nassau])(queen, Netherlands; 1880-1962)
Wilhelmshaven, Germany
Wilkens, Mac Maurice (track; 1950-)
Wilkes-Barre, PA
Wilkins, Domique (basketball; 1960-)
Wilkins, Lennie (basketball; 1937-)
Wilkins, Roy (US jour./reformer; 1901-81)
Wilkinson Sword, Inc.
Wilkinson, Bud (Charles Burnham)(football; 1916-94)
Will & Baumer Candle Co., Inc.

Will and Grace (TV show)
Will Durant (US hist.; 1885-1981)
Will Ferrell (US ent./SNL; 1967-)
Will Geer (ent.; 1902-78)
Will Hunting, Good (film, 1997)
Will K. Kellogg (US bus.; 1860-1951)
Will(iam Penn Adair) Rogers (ent.; 1879-1935)
Will Scarlet (fict. chara., *Robin Hood*)
Will Smith (ent.; 1969-)
Will, George F. (US jour.; 1941-)
Willa (Sibert) Cather (US writer; 1873-1947)
Willamette Industries, Inc.
Willamette National Forest
Willamette River (OR)
Willard Scott (ent./meteor.; 1934-)
Willard Waterman (ent.)
Willard, Archibald M. (US artist; 1836-1918)
Willard, Emma (Hart)(US educ.; 1787-1870)
Willard, Frances E(lizabeth Caroline)(US educ./reformer; 1839-98)
Willard, Frank (cartoonist, *Moon Mullins*; 1893-1958)
Willard, Nancy (writer/artist; 1936-)
Willebrod Snell (Dutch math./physt.; 1581-1626)
Willem Dafoe (ent.; 1955-)
Willem de Kooning (US artist; 1904-97)
Willemstad, Netherlands Antilles
Willi Baumeister (Ger. artist; 1889-1955)
William A. Anders (astro.; 1933-)
William and Mary, College of (Williamsburg, VA)
William Atherton (ent.; 1947-)
William A(lmon) Wheeler (ex-US VP; 1819-87)
William Baffin (Br. nav.; 1584-1622)
William Baldwin (ent.; 1963-)
William Barclay "Bat" Masterson (US marshal; 1853-1921)
William Baziotes (US artist; 1912-63)
William Beebe, (Charles)(US nat./expl./writer; 1877-1962)
William Bendix (ent.; 1906-64)
William Blackstone, (Sir)(Br. jurist; 1723-80)
William Blake (Br. poet/artist; 1757-1827)
William Bligh (Br. captain, H.M.S. *Bounty*; 1754-1817)
William Booth ("General Booth")(Br., founded Salvation Army; 1829-1912)
William Boyce (comp.; 1710-79)
William Boyd (aka Hopalong Cassidy)(ent.; 1898-1972)
William Bradford (1st gov., Pilgrim colony; 1590-1657)
William Brewster (Br., Pilgrim leader; 1567-1644)
William B(radford) Shockley, Dr. (US physt.; 1910-89)
William Butler Yeats (Ir. writer; 1865-1939)
William Byrd (Br. comp.; 1543-1623)
William Carlos Williams (US poet; 1883-1963)
William Caslon (Br. typographer; 1692-1766)
William Caxton (1st English printer; c1422-91)
William C. Bullitt (US dipl.; 1891-1967)
William C. Durant (US bus./auto.; 1861-1947)
William C. Gargas (US phys.; 1854-1920)
William Chambers, (Sir)(Br. arch.; 1723-96)
William Christopher (ent.; 1932-)
William Claire Menninger (US psych.; 1899-1966)

William Clark (US explorer; 1770-1838)
William Clarke Quantrill (US mil./outlaw; 1837-65)
William Colgate (US bus.; 1783-1857)
William Congreve (Br. writer; 1670-1729)
William Conrad (ent.; 1920-94)
William Cowper (Br. judge; 1665?-1723)
William Cowper (Br. phys.; 1666-1709)
William Cowper (Br. poet; 1731-1800)
William C. Procter (US bus./soap; 1862-1934)
William Crookes, (Sir)(Br. physt./chem.; 1832-1919)
William C. Steinkraus (equestrian; 1925-)
William Cullen Bryant (US poet/jour.; 1794-1878)
William Daniel Leahy (US adm.; 1875-1959)
William Daniels (ent.; 1927-)
William Demarest (ent.; 1892-1983)
William Devane (ent.; 1939-)
William Donald Schaefer (ex-MD gov.; 1921-)
William Douglas-Home (Br. writer; 1912-92)
William Dudley Haywood (US labor leader; 1869-1928)
William E. Borah (US pol.; 1865-1940)
William Edward Parry, (Sir)(Br. expl.; 1790-1855)
William E(wart) Gladstone (ex-PM, Br.; 1809-98)
William Ellery Channing (US rel.; 1780-1842)
William Faulkner (US writer; 1897-1962)
William F. Buckley, Jr. (US editor/writer; 1925-)
William F(rederick) Cody, (Buffalo Bill)(Amer. scout/ent.; 1846-1917)
William F(rederick) Halsey (US mil.; 1882-1959)
William Foxwell Albright (US archaeol.; 1891-1971)
William Franklin "Billy" Graham, Rev. (US rel.; 1918-)
William Frawley (ent.; 1887-1966)
William Friedkin (ent.; 1939-)
William "Bill" Frist (US cong.; 1952-)
William F(loyd) Weld (ex-MA gov.; 1945-)
William Gaddis (US writer; 1922-98)
William "Bill" Gates (US bus./Microsoft; 1955-)
William George Fargo (US bus.; 1818-81)
William George Hayden (ex-gov.-gen., Austl.; 1933-)
William Gilbert, (Sir)(Br. physt./phys.; 1540-1603)
William (James) Glackens (US artist; 1870-1938)
William G. McGowan (US bus.; 1928-92)
William (Gerald) Golding (US writer; 1912-93)
William Goldman (US writer; 1931-)
William (Preston) "Bill" Graves (KS gov.; 1953-)
William Green (US labor leader; 1873-1952)
William Gregg (US bus.; 1800-67)
William Gropper (US artist; 1897-1977)
William Harrison Ainsworth (Br. writer; 1805-82)
William Harvey (Br. phys.; 1578-1657)
William Haughton (harness racing; 1923-86)
William Henry "Bill" Mauldin (US writer/cartoonist; 1921-)
William Henry Bonney ("Billy the Kid")(US outlaw; 1859-81)
William Henry Bragg, (Sir)(Br. physt.; 1862-1942)
William Henry Fox Talbot (Br. photo.; 1800-77)
William Henry Harrison (9th US pres.; 1773-1841)
William Henry Seward (US pol.; 1801-72)

William Henry Vanderbilt (US bus./finan.; 1821-85)
William Hewlett (US bus.; 1913-2001)
William Hill Winery (US bus.)
William H. Macy (ent.; 1950-)
William H(owell) Masters, Dr. (US phys./writer; 1915-2001)
William H(olmes) McGuffey (US educ.; 1800-73)
William H(enry) Pickering (US astron.; 1858-1938)
William H(ubbs) Rehnquist (US jurist; 1924-)
William Hogarth (Br. artist; 1697-1764)
William Howard Taft (27th US pres.; 1857-1930)
William Howe, (Sir)(Br. mil.; 1729-1814)
William Hurt (ent.; 1950-)
William I (b. Friedrich Wilhelm Viktor Albert)(emp., Ger.; 1859-1941)
William I (b. Willem Frederik)(king, Netherlands; 1772-1843)
William I (the Conqueror)(king, Eng.; 1027-87)
William II (b. Wilhelm Friedrich Ludwig)(emp., Ger.; 1797-1888)
William II (b. Willem Frederik George Lodewijk)(king, Netherlands; 1792-1849)
William II (Rufus, the Red)(king, Eng.; c1056-1100)
William III (b. Willem Alexander Paul Frederik Lodewijk)(king, Netherlands; 1817-90)
William III (of Orange)(king, Br./Ir.; 1650-1702)
William (Motter) Inge (US writer; 1913-73)
William (Ralph) Inge (Br. rel.; 1860-1954)
William IV (king, Br./Ir.; 1765-1837)
William James (US phil./psych.; 1842-1910)
William J(oseph) Brennan, Jr. (US jurist; 1906-97)
William J(oseph) Casey (ex-dir./FBI; 1914-87)
William Jefferson "Bill" Clinton (42nd US pres.; 1946-)
William Jenner (Br. phys.; 1815-98)
William Jennings Bryan (US pol./orator; 1860-1925)
William J(ohn) "Bill" Janklow (SD gov.; 1939-)
William J(ames) Mayo (US surgeon; 1861-1939)
William J. Perry (US ex-secy./defense; 1927-)
William Katt (ent.; 1950-)
William Kennedy (US writer; 1928-)
William Kennedy Smith (US phys.; 1960-)
William Kidd (aka Captain Kidd)(Scot. pirate; 1645?-1701)
William Kunstler (US atty.; 1919-95)
William Lawrence Bragg, (Sir)(Br. physt.; 1890-1971)
William Lawrence Shirer (US writer/hist.; 1904-93)
William Lily(e)(Br. scholar; c1468-1522)
William Lloyd Garrison (US reformer; 1805-79)
William Lyon Mackenzie King (ex-PM, Can.; 1874-1950)
William Makepeace Thackeray (Br. writer; 1811-63)
William Manchester (US writer; 1922-)
William Maxwell Beaverbrook, Baron (aka Lord Beaverbrook)(Br. finan./pol.; 1879-1964)
William McKinley (25th US pres.; 1843-1901)

William M(ichael) "Bill" Daley (US ex-secy./ commerce; 1948-)
William M. Gaines (US publ.; 1922-92)
William Morris (Br. designer; 1834-96)
William Morris Agency, Inc.
William Moses (ent.; 1959-)
William M(arcy) Tweed ("Boss Tweed")(US pol.; 1823-78)
William O(rville) Douglas (US jurist; 1898-1980)
William of Occam (Br. phil.; c1285-c1349)
William of Orange (William III)(king, Br./Ir.; 1650-1702)
William Osler, (Sir)(Can. phys./educ.; 1849-1919)
William "Bill" Owens (CO gov.; 1950-)
William Paley (Br. rel.; 1743-1805)
William Paterson College (Wayne, NJ)
William Patrick Deane, (Sir)(gov.-gen., Austl.; 1931-)
William Penn (Br. Quaker, founded PA; 1644-1718)
William Pereira (US arch.; 1909-85)
William Philip Arthur Louis, Prince (eldest son of Prince Charles & Princess Diana; 1982-)
William Pitt, the Elder (the "Great Commoner")(ex-PM, Br.; 1708-78)
William Pitt, the Younger (ex-PM, Br.; 1759-1806)
William Pogue (astro.; 1930-)
William Powell (ent.; 1892-1984)
William Primrose (violinist; 1904-82)
William (Hickling) Prescott (US hist.; 1796-1859)
William Proxmire, (Edward)(US pol.; 1915-)
William Putnam Bundy (US editor; 1917-2000)
William Randolph Hearst (US publ.; 1863-1951)
William Randolph Hearst, Jr. (US publ.; 1908-93)
William R. Higgins (US mil./murdered by Lebanese terrorists; 1945-90)
William (Blaine) "Bill" Richardson (US ex-secy./ ener.; 1947-)
William Rigney (baseball; 1918-)
William Riker, Commander (fict. chara., *Star Trek*)
William Rockefeller (US bus./finan.; 1841-1922)
William R(ufus De Vane) King (ex-US VP; 1786-1853)
William Safire (US jour.; 1929-)
William Sanderson (ent.; 1948-)
William Saroyan (US writer; 1908-81)
William S. Burroughs (US writer; 1914-97)
William Schallert (ent.; 1922-)
William (Howard) Schuman (US comp.; 1910-92)
William Schwenck Gilbert, Sir (Br. librettist; 1836-1911)
William S(ebastian) Cohen (US ex-secy./ defense; 1940-)
William Scoresby (Br. expl.; 1789-1857)
William Shakespeare (Br. writer; 1564-1616)
William S(hakespeare) Hart (ent.; 1870?-1946)
William Shatner (ent.; 1931-)
William S. Knudsen (US bus.; 1879-1848)
William S. Paley (US TV exec.; 1901-90)
William S(teele) Sessions (US, ex-dir./FBI; 1930-)
William Steig (cartoonist, *New Yorker*; 1907-)
William Steinberg (cond.; 1899-1978)
William (Clark) Styron, Jr. (US writer; 1925-)

William Sydney Porter (pseud. O Henry)(US writer; 1862-1910)
William Tell (legendary Swiss patriot; 14th c.)
William the Conqueror (William I)(king, Eng.; 1027-87)
William the Lion (king, Scot.; 1143-1214)
William the Silent (Dutch, Prince of Orange; 1533-84)
William Thomas Cosgrave (Ir. pol.; 1880-1965)
William Thomson Kelvin, Lord (Br. physt./ math.; 1824-1907)
William (Tatem) "Big Bill" Tilden, Jr. (tennis; 1893-1953)
William Toomey (decathlon; 1939-)
William T(ecumseh) Sherman (US gen.; 1820-91)
William Victor Roth, Jr. (US pol.; 1921-)
William (Turner) Walton, (Sir)(Br. comp.; 1902-83)
William Warfield (ent.; 1920-)
William (Childs) Westmoreland (US gen.; 1914-)
William Wilberforce (Br. reformer; 1759-1833)
William Windom (ent.; 1923-)
William Wordsworth (Br. poet; 1770-1850)
William Wrigley, Jr. (US bus., gum/baseball; 1861-1932)
William Wrigley, Jr. Co.
William Wurster (US arch.; 1895-1973)
William Wyler (ent.; 1902-81)
William Wyndham Grenville, Baron (Br. pol.; 1759-1834)
William, pear (liqueur)
William of Wales, Prince (William Philip Arthur Louis Windsor)(eldest son of Prince Charles & Princess Diana; 1982-)
Williams Co., Sherwin-
Williams, Andy (ent.; 1930-)
Williams, Anthony A(llen) "Tony" (DC mayor; 1951-)
Williams, Billy Dee (ent.; 1937-)
Williams, Charles "Cootie" (US jazz; 1908-85)
Williams, Cindy (ent.; 1947-)
Williams, Del (football; 1945-84)
Williams, Dick (baseball; 1929-)
Williams, Edward Bennett (US atty.; 1920-88)
Williams, Emlyn (ent./playwright; 1905-87)
Williams, Esther (ent., swimmer; 1923-)
Williams, Gluyas (US cartoonist; 1888-1982)
Williams, Gunther Gebel- (Ger. animal trainer)
Williams, Guy (ent.; 1924-89)
Williams, Hal (ent.; 1938-)
Williams, Hank (ent.; 1923-53)
Williams, Hank, Jr. (ent.; 1949-)
Williams, JoBeth (ent.; 1948-)
Williams, Joe (b. Joseph Goreed)(ent.; 1918-99)
Williams, John (US comp./cond.; 1932-)
Williams, Mary Lou (US jazz; 1914-81)
Williams, Matt (baseball; 1965-)
Williams, Michelle (ent.; 1980-)
Williams, Mitch (baseball; 1964-)
Williams, Montel (ent.; 1956-)
Williams, Paul (ent.; 1940-)
Williams, Ralph Vaughan (Br. comp.; 1872-1958)
Williams, Robin (ent.; 1952-)
Williams, Roger (b. Louis Wertz)(ent.; 1925-)
Williams, Roger (US rel.; c1603-83)

Williams, Serena (tennis; 1981-)
Williams, (Sir) Daniel C. (gov.-gen., Grenada; 1935-)
Williams, Ted (Theodore Samuel)(baseball; 1918-)
Williams, Tennessee (Thomas Lanier)(US writer; 1914-83)
Williams, Treat (Richard)(ent.; 1951-)
Williams, Vanessa (ent.; 1963-)
Williams, Venus (tennis; 1980-)
Williams, Wendy O(rlean) (ent.; 1949-98)
Williams, William Carlos (US poet; 1883-1963)
Williamsburg, VA
Williamson, Nicol (ent.; 1938-)
Williamsport, PA
Williams-Sonoma (US bus.)
Willie Davenport (track; 1943-)
Willie (William R.) Horton, Jr. (US murd. in 1988 pol. ad)
Willie Ley (science writer; 1906-69)
Willie (Howard) Mays (baseball; 1931-)
Willie McCovey (baseball; 1938-)
Willie Mosconi (billiards; 1913-93)
Willie Nelson (ent.; 1933-)
Willie (William Lee) Shoemaker (US jockey; 1931-)
Willie "The Lion" Smith (US jazz; 1897-1973)
Willie Stargell (baseball; 1941-2001)
Willie Sutton (US bank robber; 1901-80)
Willie Winkie, Wee (fict. chara.)
Willie, BoxCar (b. Lecil Martin)(ent.; 1931-99)
Willig, George (ent.; 1949-)
Willis Reed (basketball; 1942-)
Willis, Bruce (ent.; 1955-)
Willkie, Wendell L(ewis)(US pol.; 1892-1944)
Willow Bay (model, TV jour.; 1963-)
Wills (Moody), Helen Newington (tennis; 1906-98)
Wills, Chill (ent.; 1903-78)
Wills, Maury (baseball; 1932-)
Willson, Meredith (US comp.; 1902-84)
Willy (Herbert Ernst Karl Frahm) Brandt (ex-chanc., WGer.; 1913-92)
Willy Loman (fict. chara., *Death of a Salesman*)
Willy (Wilhelm) Messerschmitt (Ger. airplane designer; 1898-1978)
Willy Wonka & the Chocolate Factory (film, 1971)
Willy Wonka Brands (US bus.)
Willy, Chilly (cartoon chara.)
Willy, Free (film, 1993)
Willy 2: The Adventure, Free (film, 1995)
Willy 3: The Rescue, Free (film, 1997)
Willye B. White (jumper; 1936-)
Wilma (Glodean) Rudolph (runner; 1940-)
Wilmington News Journal (DE newspaper)
Wilmington, DE, MA, NC, OH
Wilmot Proviso (US hist.; 1846)
Wilson Pickett (ent.; 1941-)
Wilson Sporting Goods Co.
Wilson, August (b. Frederick August Kittel)(US writer; 1945-)
Wilson, Brian (ent.; 1942-)
Wilson, Carl (ent.; 1946-98)
Wilson, Carnie (ent.; 1968-)
Wilson, Cassandra (US jazz/comp.; 1955-)

Wilson, Demond (ent.; 1946-)
Wilson, Dooley (ent.; 1894-1953)
Wilson, Edmund (US writer/critic; 1895-1972)
Wilson, Edward O. (US zool.; 1929-)
Wilson, Elizabeth (ent.; 1925-)
Wilson, Flip (Clerow)(ent.; 1933-98)
Wilson, Gahan (US cartoonist; 1930-)
Wilson, (Sir James) Harold (ex-PM, Br.; 1916-95)
Wilson, Henry (ex-US VP; 1812-75)
Wilson, Jackie (ent.; 1934-84)
Wilson, Lanford (US writer; 1937-)
Wilson, Marie (ent.; 1917-72)
Wilson, Nancy (ent.; 1937-)
Wilson, Pete(r Barton)(ex-CA gov.; 1933-)
Wilson, Roger B(yron)(ex-MO gov.; 1948-)
Wilson, Teddy (US jazz; 1912-86)
Wilson, Tom (cartoonist, *Ziggy*; 1931-)
Wilson, (Thomas) Woodrow (28th US pres.; 1856-1924)
Wilt (Norman) Chamberlain (Wilt the Stilt) (basketball; 1936-99)
Wilton (carpet)
Wilton Corp.
Wilton Industries, Inc.
Wiltshire (county, Eng.)
Wim Kok (PM, Netherlands; 1938-)
Wimbledon (tennis, London)
Wimsey, Lord Peter (fict. chara., D. Sayers)
Win, Ne (b. Maung Shu Maung)(ex-pres., Myanmar; 1911-)
Winchell, Walter (US newscaster; 1897-1972)
Winchester Cathedral (Eng.)
Winchester drive/disk (compu.)
Winchester rifle
Winchester, England
Winchester, MA, VA
Wind Cave National Park (SD)
Wind in the Willows, The (by K. Grahame)
Wind Song (perfume)
Windbreaker (jacket)
Windemere Press, Inc.
Windermere, Lake (Eng.)
Windex (cleaner)
Windhoek, Namibia
Winding, Kai (US jazz; 1922-83)
Windmere (appliances)
Windmere Corp.
Windom, William (ent.; 1923-)
Window Rock, AZ
Windows (compu.)
Windows Computer Magazine (mag.)
Windows Me (compu.)
Windows Millennium (compu.)
Windows 95 (compu.)
Windows 98 (compu.)
Windows NT (compu.)
Windows 2000 (compu.)
Windscale (now Sellafield)(Cumbria, Eng.) (nuclear accident; 1957)
Windsor Castle (residence, Br. royalty)
Windsor chair
Windsor knot
Windsor tie
Windsor Vineyards & Great River Winery (US bus.)

Windsor, CT
Windsor, Duchess of (Wallis "Wally" Warfield Simpson)(US socialite, m. Edward VIII; 1896-1986)
Windsor, Duke of (Edward VIII)(abdicated Br. throne; 1894-1972)
Windsor, England (officially Windsor and Maidenhead)
Windsor, House of (Br. ruling family; 1910-present)
Windsor, Ontario, Canada
Windstar, Ford (auto.)
Windward Islands, Lesser Antilles (Grenada, Barbados, St. Vincent, St. Lucia, Martinque, Dominica, Guadeloupe)
Windward Passage (channel, Haiti/Cuba)
Windy City (Chicago)
Winesap (apple)
Winfield Scott ("Old Fuss and Feathers")(US gen.; 1786-1866)
Winfield, Dave (baseball; 1951-)
Winfield, Paul (ent.; 1941-)
Winfrey, Oprah (ent.; 1954-)
Wing, Red (Tantangamini)(Sioux leader; c1750-c1825)
Winger, Debra (ent.; 1955-)
Wings (TV show)
Wingti, Paias (ex-PM, Papua New Guinea; 1951-)
Wink (Winston Conrad) Martindale (ent.; 1934-)
Winkerbean, Funky (comic strip)
Winkie, Wee Willie (fict. chara.)
Winkle, Rip Van (by W. Irving)
Winkle, The Tale of Mrs. Tiggy- (B. Potter story)
Winkler, Henry (ent.; 1945-)
Winn-Dixie Stores, Inc.
Winnebago (Native Amer.)
Winnebago Industries, Inc.
Winnebago RV
Winnebago, Lake (WI)
Winnemucca, NV
Winnetka, IL
Winnie (Nomzamo) Mandela (SAfr. pol./reformer; 1934-)
Winnie-the-Pooh (A. A. Milne children's stories)
Winningham, Mare (ent.; 1959-)
Winnipeg (Can. river)
Winnipeg Free Press
Winnipeg Jets (hockey team)
Winnipeg, Lake (Can.)
Winnipeg, Manitoba, Canada
Winona Ryder (b. Winona Laura Horowitz)(ent.; 1971-)
Winslet, Kate (ent.; 1975-)
Winslow Homer (US artist; 1836-1910)
Winslow, AZ
Winston (Leonard Spencer) Churchill, (Sir)(ex-PM, Br.; 1874-1965)
Winston Churchill (US writer; 1871-1947)
Winston, Harry (US bus./diamonds; ?-1978)
Winston, Inc., Harry
Winston-Salem Journal (NC newspaper)
Winston-Salem, NC
Winter Haven, FL
Winter King, the (Frederick V)(king, Bohemia

for one winter; 1596-1632)
Winter of Our Discontent, The (J. Steinbeck novel)
Winter Olympics
Winter Park, FL
Winter, Edgar (ent.; 1946-)
Winter, Johnny (ent.; 1944-)
Winter's Tale, The (Shakespeare play)
Winterbourne, Mrs. (film, 1996)
Winters, Jonathan (ent.; 1925-)
Winters, Shelley (b. Shirley Schrift)(ent.; 1922-)
Winthrop Rockefeller (ex-gov., AR; 1912-73)
Winthrop, John (Br./Amer., ex-gov., MA; 1588-1649)
Winthrop, John (ex-gov., CT; 1606-76)
Winthrop, John (or Fitz-John)(ex-gov., CT; 1638-1707)
Winthrop, John (US astron./math./physt.; 1714-79)
Winwood, Steve (ent.; 1948-)
Wirephoto (comm.)
Wisconsin (WI)
Wisconsin Cheese (US bus.)
Wisconsin v. Mitchell (US law; 1993)
Wisdom of Solomon (rel., Apocrypha)
Wise Foods (US bus.)
Wise Men of the East (also Magi, Three Kings of the Orient, Three Wise Men)(rel.)
Wise, Bob (Robert Ellsworth), Jr. (WV gov.; 1948-)
Wise, Stephen Samuel (Hung./US rabbi/Zionist leader; 1874-1949)
Wisk detergent
Witches of Eastwick, The (film, 1987)
Witching Hour, The (A. Rice novel)
Wite-Out Products, Inc.
Withers, Jane (ent.; 1926-)
Witherspoon, John (US rel.; 1723-94)
Witherspoon, Reese (ent.; 1976-)
Witness Protection Program (US govt.)
Witt, James Lee (US ex-dir./FEMA; 1944-)
Witt, Katarina (Ger. figure skating; 1965-)
Witt, Paul Junger (ent.; 1943-)
Witter & Co., Morgan Stanley Dean
Witter Online Inc., Morgan Stanley Dean
Witter Reynolds Inc., Dean
Wittgenstein, Ludwig (Josef Johann)(Aus. phil.; 1889-1951)
Wittig, Georg F. K. (Ger. chem.; 1897-1987)
Witwatersrand (also the Rand)(SAfr. gold mining area)
Wiz, The (play; film, 1978)
Wizard (air freshener)
Wizard of Id (comic strip)
Wizard of Oz, The (by L.F. Baum)
Wizard's World, Mr. (TV show)
WKRP in Cincinnati (TV show)
W(enzel) L(othar) Metternich, Clemens (Prince von Metternich)(ex-chanc., Aus.; 1773-1859)
WO (warrant officer)
Wobblies (members Industrial Workers of the World)
Wobegon, Lake (fict. town, G. Keillor)
Wodan (also Woden, Odin, Wotan)(myth.)
Wodehouse, (Sir) P(elham) G(renville)(US

writer/humorist; 1881-1975)
Woden (also Odin, Wotan, Wodan)(myth.)
Wofford, Harris (US educ./pol.; 1926-)
Wojceich Jaruzelski (ex-pres., Pol.; 1923-)
Wojtyla, Karol (Pope John Paul II)(Pol. pope;
 1920-)
Wole Soyinka (Nigerian writer; 1934-)
Wolf-Ferrari, Ermanno (It. comp.; 1876-1948)
Wolf Trap Farm Park for the Performing Arts
 (VA)
Wolf, Burt (US chef/writer)
Wolf, Hugo (Aus. comp.; 1860-1903)
Wolf, Scott (ent.; 1968-)
Wolfe, Billy De (ent.; 1907-74)
Wolfe, Nero (fict. detective)
Wolfe, Thomas (Clayton)(US writer; 1900-38)
Wolfe, Tom (b. Thomas Kennerly Wolfe, Jr.)(US
 writer; 1931-)
Wolff Industries, Inc.
Wolff Shoe Co.
Wolff, Tobias (US writer; 1945-)
Wolfgang Amadeus Mozart (Aus. comp.; 1756-
 91)
Wolfgang Pauli (Aus. physt.; 1900-58)
Wolfgang Puck (chef)
Wolfgang Schüssel, Dr. (chanc., Aus.; 1945-)
Wolfman Jack (b. Robert Weston Smith)(disc
 jockey, *American Graffiti*; 1939-95)
Wollongong, New South Wales, Australia
Wollstonecraft, Mary (Br. reformer; 1759-97)
Wolof (lang./people)
Wolper, David L. (ent.)
Wolsey, Thomas, Cardinal (Br. rel./pol.; 1475-
 1530)
Wolverine (cartoon chara.)
Wolverine State (nickname, MI)
Wolverine World Wide Corp.
Woman's Christian Temperance Union, National
 (WCTU)
Woman's Day (mag.)
Woman's World (mag.)
Women of Brewster Place, The (TV show)
Women Voters, League of
Women's Army Corps (WAC)(US mil.; est. 1942)
Women's Wear Daily (trade paper/garment
 industry)
Wonder Bar Products, Inc.
Wonder State (nickname, AR)
Wonder Woman (comic, TV show)
Wonder Years, The (TV show)
Wonder, Stevie (b. Steveland Judkins Morris)
 (ent.; 1950-)
Wong, Anna May (b. Lu Tsong Wong)(ent.;
 1907-61)
Wong, The World of Suzie (film, 1960)
Wonka & the Chocolate Factory, Willy (film,
 1971)
Wonka Brands, Willy (US bus.)
Wonsan, North Korea
Woo, John (ent./writer; 1946-)
Woo, Roh Tae (ex-pres., SKorea; 1932-)
Wood Reading Dynamics, Evelyn (US bus.)
Wood, Danny (ent.; 1969-)
Wood, Ed(ward Davis), Jr. (ent.; 1924-78)
Wood, Elijah (ent.; 1981-)

Wood, Fort Leonard (MO)(mil.)
Wood, Grant (US artist; 1891-1942)
Wood, Kimba (US atty.; 1944-)
Wood, Natalie (ent.; 1938-81)
Wood, Peggy (ent.; 1892-1978)
Wood, Smokey (Joseph)(baseball; 1890-1985)
Woodard, Alfre (ent.; 1953-)
Wooden, John R. (basketball; 1910-)
Woodhead, Cynthia (swimming; 1964-)
Woodhouse, Barbara (Br. dog trainer; writer;
 1910-88)
Woodhull, Victoria Claflin (US publ./reformer;
 1838-1927)
Woodiwiss, Kathleen (writer; 1939-)
Woodpecker, Woody (cartoon)
Woodrow Wilson, (Thomas)(28th US pres.;
 1856-1924)
Woodruff, Judy (US TV jour.; 1946-)
Woods Hole Oceanographic Institution (MA)
Woods, James (ent.; 1947-)
Woods, Lake of the (Ontario, Can.)
Woods, Tiger (Eldrick)(golf; 1975-)
Woodson, Carter G. (US hist.; 1875-1950)
Woodstock Festival (also Woodstock Music &
 Art Fair)(NY rock festival; 1969)
Woodstock, NY
Woodward & Bernstein (Watergate reporters)
Woodward, Bob (US jour.; 1943-)
Woodward, Edward (ent.; 1930-)
Woodward, Joanne (ent.; 1930-)
Woodward, Robert Burns (US chem.; 1917-79)
Woodward, Trustees of Dartmouth College v.
 (US law; 1819)
Woody Allen (b. Allen Stewart
 Konigsberg)(ent.; 1935-)
Woody (Woodrow Wilson) Guthrie (ent.; 1912-
 67)
Woody Harrelson (ent.; 1961-)
Woody Hayes (football; 1913-87)
Woody Woodpecker (cartoon)
Woolco (stores)
Woolery, Chuck (ent.)
Woolf, (Adeline) Virginia (Stephen)(Br. writer;
 1882-1941)
Woolf, Leonard Sidney (Br. writer; 1880-1969)
Woolf?, Who's Afraid of Virginia (film, 1966)
Woolite (soap)
Woollcott, Alexander (US writer; 1887-1943)
Woolley, Monty (ent.; 1888-1963)
Woolsey, R. James (US ex-dir./CIA; 1941-)
Woolworth Building (NYC)
Woolworth Co., F. W.
Woolworth, Frank W(infield)(US bus.; 1852-
 1919)
Woolworth's (stores)
Woonsocket, RI
Wopat, Tom (ent.; 1951-)
Worcester china/porcelain (also Royal Worcester)
Worcester Telegram Gazette (MA newspaper)
Worcester Telegraph (MA newspaper)
Worcester, England
Worcester, MA
Worcestershire sauce
Word of God, the
Word, Microsoft (compu.)

Worden, Alfred M. (astro.; 1932-)
WordPerfect (compu.)
WordPerfect Corp.
WordStar (compu.)
WordStar International, Inc.
Wordsworth, Dorothy (Br. writer; 1771-1855)
Wordsworth, William (Br. poet; 1770-1850)
Worf, Lieutenant (fict. chara., *Star Trek*)
Workbasket, The (mag.)
Workbench (mag.)
Working Mother (mag.)
Working Woman (mag.)
Works Projects Administration (WPA)(also
 Works Progress Administration)(US hist;
 1935-43)
World According to Garp, The (J. Irving novel)
World Bank (International Bank for Reconstruction
 and Development)(UN; est. 1945)
World Council of Churches (WCC)(est. 1945)
World Court (also United Nations Permanent
 Court of International Justice)(est. 1945)
World Cup (soccer)
World Day of Prayer
World Ecology Report (mag.)
World Health Day (UN)
World Health Organization (WHO)(UN; est. 1946)
World Intellectual Property Organization
 (WIPO)(UN; est. 1974)
World Meteorological Organization (WMO)(UN;
 est. 1947)
World of Henry Orient, The (film, 1964)
World of Suzie Wong, The (film, 1960)
World Savings & Loan Association
World Series (baseball)
World Trade Center (NYC)
World War I (also WWI, First World War)(1914-
 18)
World War I Allies (chiefly Fr., Br., Rus., US)
World War I Central Powers (Ger., Aus-Hung.,
 Turk.)
World War II (also WWII, Second World War)
 (1939-45)
World War II Allies (chiefly Br., US, USSR, Ch.)
World War II Axis Powers (Ger., Jap., It.)
World Wide Fund for Nature (WWF)(formerly
 World Wildlife Fund)(est. 1961)
World Wildlife Fund (WWF)(aka World Wide
 Fund for Nature outside US)(est. 1961)
World Wrestling Federation (WWF)
World, Third (less developed nations)
World-Herald, Omaha (NE newspaper)
WorldCom, Inc.
Worldwatch Institute
Worley, Jo Anne (ent.; 1937-)
Worms, Diet of (rel. hist.; 1521)
Worms, Germany
Worship, Your (title)
Worth, Fort (TX)(city)
Worth, Mary (cartoon chara.)
Worthy, James (basketball; 1961-)
Wotan (also Woden, Odin, Wodan)(myth.)
Wottle, David James (runner; 1950-)
Wouk, Herman (US writer; 1915-)
Woulff bottle (chem.)
Wounded Knee (SD)(US Army/Sioux conflict;
 1890)
Wovoka (Jack Wilson)(Paiute Native Amer./
 originator, ghost dance rel.; c1858-1932)
Wozniak, Stephen (US bus./compu.; 1950-)
WPA (Works Projects Administration)
WPM (also wpm)(words per minute)
WRAC (Women's Royal Army Corps)
WRAF (Women's Royal Air Force)
Wrangell-St. Elias National Park (AK)
Wrangler Co.
Wrangler, Jeep (auto.)
Wrather, Jack (US bus.; 1918-84)
Wray, Fay (ent.; 1907-)
Wreck of the Hesperus, The (by. H.W.
 Longfellow)
Wren, (Sir) Christopher (Br. arch./astron./
 math.; 1632-1723)
Wrexham, Wales
W. R. Grace & Co.
Wright brothers (Wilbur & Orville)
Wright Morris (US writer; 1910-98)
Wright Patterson Air Force Base, OH
Wright State University (Dayton, OH)
Wright, Frank Lloyd (US arch.; 1867-1959)
Wright, Martha (ent.; 1926-)
Wright, Mickey (Mary Kathryn)(golf; 1935-)
Wright, Orville (US aviator/inv.; 1871-1948)
Wright, Steven (ent.; 1955-)
Wright, Teresa (ent.; 1918-)
Wright, Wilbur (US aviator/inv.; 1867-1912)
Wrigley Field (Chicago)
Wrigley, Jr. Co., William
Wrigley, Philip K. (US bus., gum/baseball;
 1895-1977)
Wrigley, William, Jr. (US bus., gum/baseball;
 1861-1932)
Wrigley's gum
Wrinkle in Time, A (book)
Wriothesley, Henry (Earl of Southhampton)(Br.
 scholar; 1573-1624)
Writer, The (mag.)
Writer's Digest (mag.)
Writers Guild of America
Wroclaw, Poland
W(illiam) S(chwenck) Gilbert (Br. writer; 1836-
 1911)
W(illiam) Somerset Maugham (Br. writer;
 1874-1965)
Wu (lang.)
Wuhan, China (also Han Cities)
Wuppertal, Germany
Wurlitzer Co., The
Wurster, William (US arch.; 1895-1973)
Wurtsmith Air Force Base, MI
Wuthering Heights (E. Brontë novel)
WV (West Virginia)
WWF (World Wildlife Fund)(aka World Wide
 Fund for Nature outside US)(est. 1961)
WWF (World Wrestling Federation)
WWI (World War I, First World War)(1914-18)
WWII (World War II, Second World War)(1939-
 45)
WY (Wyoming)
Wyandotte (chicken)
Wyandotte, MI

Wyatt (Berry Stapp) Earp (US frontier; 1848-1929)

Wyatt, Jane (ent.; 1912-)

Wyclef Jean (ent.; 1969-)

Wycliffe, John (Br. rel.; c1320-84)

Wyden, Ron (US cong.; 1949-)

Wyeth, Andrew N(ewell)(US artist; 1917-)

Wyeth, James Browning (US artist; 1946-)

Wyeth, N(ewel) C(onvers)(US artist; 1882-1945)

Wygesic (med.)

Wyle, Noah (ent.; 1971-)

Wyler, William (ent.; 1902-81)

Wylie, Elinor (US poet; 1885-1928)

Wyman, Jane (b. Sarah Jane Fulks)(ent.; 1914-)

Wyndham Lewis, (Percy)(Br./US artist/writer; 1884-1957)

Wynette, Tammy (ent.; 1942-98)

Wynken, Blynken & Nod (E. Field poem)

Wynn, Ed (ent.; 1886-1966)

Wynn, Keenan (ent.; 1916-86)

Wynn, Tracy Keenan (ent./screenwriter)

Wynonna Judd (b. Christina Claire Ciminella) (ent.; 1964-)

Wynton Marsalis (US jazz; 1961-)

Wyomia Tyus (track; 1945-)

Wyoming (WY)

WYSIWYG (compu., what you see is what you get)

Wyss, Johann David (Swiss writer; 1743-1818)

Wyss, Johann Rudolf (Swiss writer; 1782-1830)

Wyszynski, Stefan, Cardinal (Pol. rel.; 1901-81)

Wytensin (med.)

Wythe, George (US jurist; 1726-1806)

X, Malcolm (b. Malcolm Little)(US black-rights
   activist; 1926-65)
X-Acto knife
X-Acto, Inc.
Xanadu (film, 1980)
Xanadu (legendary utopian city)
Xanax (med.)
Xanthippe (wife of Socrates; late 5th c BC)(ill-
   tempered)
Xavier Cugat (Sp./US cond.; 1920-90)
Xavier Roberts (US bus., Cabbage Patch Kids;
   1955-)
Xavier, Francis, St. (Francisco Javier)("the
   Apostle of the Indies")(Sp. rel.; 1506-52)
X chromosome (med.)
Xe (chem. sym., xenon)
XEC5 (CAT system)
XEC-2001 (CAT system)
Xenocrates (Gr. phil.; 396-14 BC)
Xenophanes (Gr. phil./poet; c570-c480 BC)
Xenophon (Gr. hist.; c434-c355 BC)
Xerox (copiers)
Xerox Corp.
Xerxes I (king, Persia; c519-465 BC)
X-Files, The (TV show)
Xhosa (lang./people)
Xi Jiang River (also Si-Kiang)(Ch.)
Xia dynasty (also Hsia)(Ch.; 2205-1766 BC)
Xian, China (also Sian)
Xiang (lang.)
Xiang, Mei (panda)
Xiangtan, China (also Siangtan)
Xiaoping, Deng (also Teng Hsiao-ping)(Ch.
   pol.; 1904-97)
Xingú (region, Brazil)
Xining, China (also Sining)
Xinjiang Uygur (also Sinkiang Uighur)(region, Ch.)
Xinxiang, China (also Sinsiang)
Xipe (myth.)
Xmas (abbrev., Christmas)
X-Men, The (cartoon charas.)
Xochipilli (myth.)
X-Prep (med.)
Xscribe Corp. (former US bus.)
Xterra, Nissan (auto.)
Xylocaine (med.)
XYZ Affair (US hist.; 1797-98)

-Y-

Y (chem. sym., yttrium)
Yaacov Agam (Isr. artist; 1928-)
Yablonski, Joseph A. (US labor leader; ?-1969)
Yaga, Baba (myth. monster, eats children)
Yahoo (fict. chara./race, *Gulliver's Travels*)
   (lower case as lout, yokel)
Yahoo (Internet search engine)
Yahoo! Inc. (or Yahoo Inc.)
Yahtzee (game)
Yahweh (Jehovah)(rel.)
Yahya Jammeh, Colonel (pres., Gambia; 1965-)
Yajur-Veda (rel.)
Yakima (Native Amer.)
Yakima, WA
Yakov Smirnoff (b. Yakov Pokhis)(ent.; 1951-)
Yakovlev, Aleksandr N. (Rus. pol.)
Yakovlev, Aleksandr S. (Rus. airplane designer;
   1905-89)
Yakut (people)
Yalá, Kumba (pres., Guinea-Bissau; 1953?-)
Yale University (New Haven, CT)
Yale, Elihu (US bus./finan.; 1649-1721)
Yalta Conference (Churchill [UK]/Roosevelt
   [US]/Stalin [USSR]; 1945)
Yalta, Crimea
Yalu River (Korea/Ch.)(also Amnok)
Yama (Hindu god of the dead)
Yamaguchi, Kristi (figure skating; 1971-)
Yamaha Corp. of America
Yamaha Motor Corp. USA
Yamasaki, Minoru (US arch.; 1912-86)
Yamassoum, Nagoum (PM, Chad)
Yamoussoukro, Ivory Coast
Yanbu al-Bahr, Saudi Arabia
Yancey, Jimmy (US jazz; 1894-1951)
Yang Shangkun (ex-pres., Ch.; 1907-)
Yang, Chen Ning (Ch./US physt.; 1922-)
Yang, Lee and (Ch. physicists)
Yangon, Myanmar (formerly Rangoon)
Yangtze Kiang River (also Chang Jiang)(Ch/)
Yankee (US northerner)
Yankee Doodle (song)
Yankee Doodle Dandy (song; film, 1942)
Yankee screwdriver (constr.)
Yankee Stadium (Bronx, NY)
Yankees, New York (baseball team)
Yankovic, Weird Al (ent.; 1959-)
Yanni (b. Yanni Chrysomallis)(ent.; 1954-)
Yanomano (also Yanomama)(lang./people)
Yao (lang./people)
Yaoundé, Cameroon
Yaphet Kotto (ent.; 1937-)
Yaqui Indians/lang.)
Yaqui River (Mex.)
Yarborough (card game term)
Yarborough, (William) Cale(b)(auto racing;
   1939-)
Yarborough, Barton (ent.; 1900-51)
Yarborough, Glenn (ent.; 1930-)

Yarbro, Chelsea Quinn (US writer; 1942-)
Yard, Molly (Mary Alexander)(US reformer, ex-
   pres./NOW; 1912-)
Yardbirds, the (pop music)
Yardley of London, Inc.
Yaren, Nauru
Yarrow, Peter (ent.; 1938-)
Yasir Arafat (PLO Chairman; 1929-)
Yasmin (Aga) Khan, Princess (1949-)
Yasmine Bleeth (ent.; 1968-)
Yastrzemski, Carl (baseball; 1939-)
Yasuhiro, Nakasone (ex-PM, Jap.; 1917-)
Y(elberton) A(braham) Tittle (football; 1926-)
Yat-sen, Sun (Ch. pol./mil.; 1866-1925)
Yawkey, Jean R. (US bus./baseball; 1908-92)
Yazoo River (MS)
Yb (chem. sym., ytterbium)
Y chromosome (med.)
Yeager, Chuck (Charles Elwood), Col. (US
   aviator; 1923-)
Yearwood, Trisha (ent.; 1964-)
Yeats, W(illiam) B(utler)(Ir. writer; 1865-1939)
Yegorov, Boris B. (cosmo.; 1937-)
Yehudi Menuhin, (Sir)(Br. violinist; 1916-99)
Yeliseyev, Aleksei (cosmo.; 1934-)
Yellen, Jack (US lyricist; 1892-1991)
Yeller, Old (F. Gipson novel)
Yellow Brick Road
Yellow Christ (by Gauguin)
Yellow Pages
Yellow River (also Huang He)(Ch.)
Yellow Sea (also Huang Hai)(Ch./Korea)
Yellowknife, Northwest Territories, Canada
Yellowstone Falls (Yellowstone Nat'l Park)
Yellowstone Lake (Yellowstone Nat'l Park)
Yellowstone National Park (ID/MT/WY)
Yellowstone River (W US)
Yeltsin, Boris (Nikolayevich)(ex-pres., Rus.;
   1931-)
Yemen (Republic of)(SW Asia)
Yemen Airways
Yemen, North (now part of Yemen)
Yemen, South (now part of Yemen)
Yemenites (people)
Yenisei River (Rus.)
Yentl (film, 1983)
Yerby, Frank (US writer; 1916-92)
Yerevan, Armenia
Yermoshin (or Yarmoshyn), Vladimir (PM,
   Belarus)
YES (clothing)
Yes (pop music)
Yes Clothing Co.
Yes, Giorgio (film, 1982)
Yeshey Zimba (PM, Bhutan)
Yevgeny Aleksandrovich Yevtushenko (Rus.
   poet; 1933-)
Yevgeny Primakov (Rus. pol.; 1929-)
Yevgeny V(asilyevich) Khrunov (cosmo.; 1933-)
Yevtushenko, Yevgeny Aleksandrovich (Rus.
   poet; 1933-)
Yggdrasil (myth.)
Yhombi-Opango, Jacques-Joachim (ex-PM,
   Congo; 1940-)
Yi (lang./people)

Yichun (province, Ch.)
Yiddish (lang.)
Yield House, Inc.
Yip (E. Y.) Harburg (US lyricist; 1898-1981)
Yitzhak Rabin (ex-PM, Isr.; 1922-95)
Yitzhak Shamir (ex-PM, Isr.; 1915-)
YM (mag.)
Yma Sumac (Peru. ent.; 1927-)
YMCA (Young Men's Christian Association)
YMHA (Young Men's Hebrew Association)
Yo-Yo Ma (US cellist; 1955-)
Yoakam, Dwight (ent.; 1956-)
Yogi & Friends (cartoon)
Yogi (Lawrence Peter) Berra (baseball; 1925-)
Yogi Bear (cartoon)
Yogi Bear Bunch (cartoon)
Yogi Bear's Jellystone Park Camp-Resort (US bus.)
Yogi, Maharishi Mahesh (Hindu guru)
Yoko Ono (Lennon)(ent.; 1933-)
Yokohama, Japan
Yom Kippur (Day of Atonement)(rel.)
Yom Kippur War (Eg., Syria/Isr.; 1973)
Yon Hyong Muk (ex-premier, NKorea)
Yonkers, NY
Yonli, Paramango Ernest (PM, Burkina Faso)
Yoo-Hoo Chocolate Beverage Corp.
Yoplait (yogurt)
Yoplait USA, Inc.
York Candies (US bus.)
York Dispatch (PA newspaper)
York News (PA newspaper)
York Record (PA newspaper)
York, Dick (ent.; 1929-92)
York, England
York, House of (Br. ruling family; 1461-70, 1471-85)
York, Michael (ent.; 1942-)
York, Ontario, Canada
York, PA
York, Sergeant (Alvin Cullum)(US mil.; 1887-1964)
York, Susannah (Fletcher)(ent.; 1942-)
Yorkin, Bud (ent.; 1926-)
Yorkshire chair (also Derbyshire chair)
Yorkshire dresser
Yorkshire ham/hog
Yorkshire pudding
Yorkshire terrier (dog)
Yorktown Naval Weapons Station (VA)
Yorktown, Siege of (US hist.; 1781, 1862)
Yorty, Samuel W. (ex-mayor, Los Angeles; 1909-98)
Yoruba (lang./people)
Yosemite Falls (Yosemite Nat'l Park)
Yosemite National Park (CA)
Yoshiro Mori (PM, Jap.; 1937-)
Yosuke Matsuoka (Jap. pol.; 1880-1946)
Yotanka, Tatanka (Chief Sitting Bull)(Sioux Native Amer.; c1831-90)
Yothers, Tina (ent.; 1973-)
You Bet Your Life (radio/TV show)
You Can't Do That on Television (TV show)
You Can't Go Home Again (T. Wolfe novel)
Youmans, Vincent (US comp.; 1898-1946)

Young and Rubicom, Inc.
Young and the Restless (TV soap)
Young Frankenstein (film, 1974)
Young Memorial Museum, M. H. de (San Francisco)
Young Men's Christian Association (YMCA)(est. 1844)
Young Riders, The (TV show)
Young Turk (young rebel)
Young Women's Christian Association (YMCA) (est. 1855)
Young, Alan (ent.; 1919-)
Young, Andrew Jackson, Jr. (US dipl./pol.; 1932-)
Young, Art (pol. cartoonist; 1866-1943)
Young, Brigham (US rel./Mormon; 1801-77)
Young, Burt (ent.; 1940-)
Young, Chic (Murat Bernard)(cartoonist, *Blondie*; 1901-73)
Young, Coleman (Detroit mayor; 1918-97)
Young, Cy (Denton True)(baseball; 1867-1955)
Young, Dean (cartoonist, *Blondie*)
Young, Faron (ent.; 1932-96)
Young, Gig (b. Byron Ellsworth Barr)(ent.; 1913-78)
Young, Inc., Ernst &
Young, John W(atts)(astro.; 1930-)
Young, Karen (ent.)
Young, Loretta (ent.; 1913-2000)
Young, Neil (ent.; 1945-)
Young, Pres (Lester Willis)(US jazz; 1909-59)
Young, Robert (ent.; 1907-98)
Young, Sheila (speed skating; 1950-)
Young, (Sir) Colville N(orbert)(gov.-gen., Belize; 1932-)
Young, Steve (football; 1961-)
Young, Whitney M(oore), Jr. (US reformer; 1921-71)
Younger, (Thomas) Cole(man)(US outlaw; 1844-1916)
Youngman, Henny (ent.; 1906-98)
Youngstown Sheet and Tube Co. v. Sawyer (US law; 1952)
Youngstown State University (Youngstown, OH)
Youngstown Vindicator (OH newspaper)
Youngstown, OH
Your Cheatin' Heart (H. Williams song)
Your Eminence (title)
Your Excellency (title)
Your Grace (title)
Your Highness (title)
Your Holiness (title)
Your Honor (title)
Your Majesty (title)
Your Money (mag.)
Your Reverence (title)
Your Worship (title)
Youssouf Ouedraogo (ex-PM, Burkina Faso)
Youssoufi, Abderrahmane El- (PM, Morocco; 1924-)
Yoweri Kaguta Museveni (pres., Uganda; 1944-)
Ypsilanti, MI
Y2K (Year 2000)
Yüan (or Mongol) dynasty (Ch. ruling house; 1279-1368)
Yuban coffee

Yucatán (state, Mex.)
Yucatán peninsula (CAmer.)
Yue (lang.)
Yuga, Kali- (rel.)
Yugo (auto.)
Yugoslavia (Federal Republic of)(SE Eur.)
Yukio, Mishima (aka Hiraoka Kimitake)(Jap.
    writer; 1925-70)
Yukon Denali, GMC (auto.)
Yukon River (NAmer.)
Yukon Territory (Can.)
Yukon, Fort (AK)(city)
Yukon, GMC (auto.)
Yul Brynner (ent.; 1915-85)
Yum Yum Tree, Under the (film, 1963)
Yuma (Native Amer.)
Yuma Proving Ground (AZ)
Yuma, AZ
Yun-Fat Chow (ent.; 1955-)
Yunnan (province, Ch.)
Yuppie
Yuri A(lexeyevich) Gagarin (cosmo.; 1st to orbit
    earth; 1934-68)
Yuri Andropov (ex-pres., Rus.; 1914-84)
Yushchenko, Viktor (PM, Ukraine; 1954-)
Yutang, Lin (Ch. writer; 1895-1976)
Yutopar (med.)
Yvan Serge Cournoyer (hockey; 1943-)
Yves Montand (Fr. ent.; 1921-91)
Yves (Henri Donat Mathieu) Saint-Laurent (Fr.
    designer; 1936-)
Yves St.-Laurent SA (US bus.)
Yves Tanguy (Fr. artist; 1900-55)
Yvette Mimieux (ent.; 1939?-)
Yvonne DeCarlo (ent.; 1922-)
YWCA (Young Women's Christian Association)
YWHA (Young Women's Hebrew Association)
Yzerman, Steve (hockey; 1965-)

-Z-

Z particle (phys.)

Zabanga, Mobutu Sese Seko Kuku Ngbendu wa (b. Joseph Désiré Mobutu)(ex-pres., Congo/ Zaire; 1930-97)

Zabrze, Poland (also Hindenburg)

Zaca Mesa Winery (US bus.)

Zacatecas purple (slang, Mexican purple marijuana)

Zachary Scott (ent.; 1914-65)

Zachary Taylor ("Old Rough and Ready")(12th US pres.; 1784-1850)

Zack's Famous Frozen Yogurt, Inc.

Zacky Foods Co.

Zadar, Croatia

Zadkine, Ossip (Rus. artist; 1890-1967)

Zadora, Pia (b. Pia Schipani)(ent.; 1954-)

Zafy, Albert (ex-pres., Madagascar; 1927?-)

Zagreb, Croatia

Zagros Mountains (Iran)

Zaharias, Babe (Mildred) Didrikson (US athlete; 1914-56)

Zahn, Paula (US TV jour.; 1956-)

Zaid bin Sultan al-Nahayan, Sheik (pres., UAE; 1923-)

Zaire (now Democratic Republic of the Congo)(central Afr.)

Zambezi River (Afr.)

Zambia (Republic of)(formerly Northern Rhodesia)(S central Afr.)

Zambia Airways

Zamboanga, Philippines

Zamboni machine (hockey)

Zamfir, Gheorghe (Romanian ent./panflutist; 1941-)

Zamora, Jaime Paz (ex-pres., Bolivia)

Zandonai, Riccardo (It. comp.; 1883-1944)

Zane Grey (US writer; 1875-1939)

Zane, Billy (William George Zane, Jr.)(ent.; 1966-)

Zanesville, OH

Zantac (med.)

Zanuck, Darryl F(rancis)(ent.; 1902-79)

Zanzibar, Road to (film, 1941)

Zanzibar, Tanzania

Zapata, Emiliano (Mex. mil./agr.; c1879-1919)

Zaporozhye, Ukraine

Zapotec (Native Amer./Mex.)

Zappa, Dweezil (ent.; 1969-)

Zappa, Frank (ent.; 1940-1993)

Zappa, Moon Unit (ent.; 1967-)

Zaragoza, Spain (also Saragossa)

Zarathustra (also Zoroaster)(Persian rel./educ.; 6th c. BC)

Zaria, Nigeria

Zarontin (med.)

Zaroxolyn (med.)

Zarqa, Jordan

Zasu Pitts (ent.; 1898-1963)

Zayak, Elaine (US figure skating; 1965-)

Zbigniew Brzezinski (US ex-pres. adviser; 1928-)

ZCMI Department Store

Zealot (rel.)

Zebulon Montgomery Pike (US expl./mil.; 1779-1813)

Zechariah (rel.)

Zedekiah (king, Judah; 6th c. BC)

Zedong, Mao (also Mao Tse-tung, Chairman Mao)(Ch. pol.; 1893-1976)

Zeebrugge, Belgium

Zeeland (province, Netherlands)

Zeeman effect/splitting (optics)

Zeeman, Pieter (Dutch physt.; 1865-1943)

Zeffirelli, Franco (ent.; 1923-)

Zeist, Netherlands

Zeitgeist (Ger., spirit of the time)

Zelig (film, 1983)

Zell Miller (US cong./ex-GA gov.; 1932-)

Zell, Harry Von (ent.; 1906-81)

Zellerbach (US bus.)

Zellweger, Rene (ent.; 1969-)

Zeman, Milos (PM, Czech; 1944-)

Zemeckis, Robert (ent.; 1952-)

Zemin, Jiang (pres., Ch.; 1926-)

Zen Buddhism (rel.)

Zena Enterprises, Inc.

Zenawi, Meles (PM., Ethiopia; 1955-)

Zend-Avesta (rel.)

Zener cards (ESP)

Zener diode (elec.)

Zenica, Bosnia-Hercegovina

Zenith (TV's, etc.)

Zenith Electronics Corp.

Zenko, Suzuki (ex-PM, Jap; 1911-)

Zeno of Citium (Gr. phil.; late 4th early 3rd c. BC)

Zeno of Elea (Gr. phil./math.; c490-430 BC)

Zephaniah (rel., book of the Old Testament)

Zephyr Hills Water Co.

Zephyrus (myth.)

Zeppelin, Ferdinand von, Graf (Ger. mil./ aeronaut; 1838-1917)

Zeppelin, Graf (Ger. airship)

Zeppelin, Led (pop music)

Zeppo (Herbert) Marx (ent.; 1901-79)

Zerbe, Anthony (ent.; 1936-)

Zerit (med.)

Zermatt, Switzerland

Zero (Samuel Joel) Mostel (ent.; 1915-77)

Zeron Group

Zest soap

Zestoretic (med.)

Zestril (med.)

Zeta-Jones, Catherine (ent.; 1969-)

Zetar (med.)

Zeus (myth.)

Zeus (sculpture by Phidias, 1 of 7 Wonders)

Zevi, Sabbatai (Jew. rel.; 1626-76)

Zevon, Warren (ent./songwriter; 1947-)

Zhangjiakou, China (also Changchiakow)

Zhao Ziyang (Ch. pol.; 1918-)

Zhejiang (also Chekiang)(province, Ch.)

Zhelev, Zhelyu (ex-pres., Bulgaria; 1936-)

Zhengzhou, China (also Chengchow)

Zhivago, Doctor (B. Pasternak novel)

Zhivkov, Todor (ex-pres.; Bulgaria; 1911-98)

Zhou Enlai (also Chou En-Lai)(ex-PM, Ch.; 1898-1976)
Zhu Rongji (PM, Ch.; 1928-)
Zhuang (lang./people)
Zhukov, Georgi (Konstantinovich)(USSR mil.; 1895-1974)
Zia ul-Haq, Muhammad ("President Zia")(ex-pres., Pak.; 1924-88)
Zia, Begum Khaleda (ex-PM, Bangladesh; 1944-)
Ziac (med.)
Ziaur Rahman (ex-pres., Bangladesh; 1935-81)
Ziegfeld Follies, The
Ziegfeld, Flo(renz)(ent.; 1869-1932)
Ziegler, Karl (Ger. chem.; 1898-1973)
Ziegler, Ron(ald)(US ex-White House press secy.; 1939-)
Ziggy (cartoon)
Ziggy (David) Marley (ent.; 1968-)
Ziggy Elman (b. Harry Finkelman)(1914-68)
Zigong, China (also Tzekung)
Zimba, Yeshey (PM, Bhutan)
Zimbabwe (Republic of)(formerly Rhodesia)(S central Afr.)
Zimbalist, Efrem, Jr. (ent.; 1923-)
Zimbalist, Efrem, Sr. (US violinist/comp.; 1889-1985)
Zimbalist, Stephanie (ent.; 1956-)
Zimmer, Kim (ent.; 1955-)
Zina Garrison (tennis; 1963-)
Zindel, Paul (US writer; 1936-)
Zinder, Niger
Zine el-Abidine Ben Ali (pres., Tunisia; 1936-)
Zinka (Kunc) Milanov (Yug. opera; 1906-89)
Zinnemann, Fred(erick)(ent.; 1907-97)
Zino Francescatti (Fr. violinist; 1902-91)
Zinsser, Hans (US bacteriol.; 1878-1940)
Zion National Park (UT)
Zion, Mount (Jerusalem)
Zionism (Jew. pol. movement)
ZIP + 4
ZIP Code
Zip-a-dee-doo-dah (song)
Ziploc (storage bags)
Zippo Manufacturing Co.
Zivko Radisic (co-pres., Bosnia-Hercegovina, Serb)
Ziyang, Zhao (Ch. pol.; 1918-)
Zn (chem. sym., zinc)
Zocor (med.)
Zoe Caldwell (ent.; 1933-)
Zoë Baird (US atty.; 1952-)
Zoeller, Fuzzy (Frank Urban)(golf; 1951-)
Zog I (b. Ahmed Bey Zogu)(king, Albania; 1895-1961)
Zohar (rel.)
Zola Budd (SAfr. athlete; 1966-)
Zola, Émile (Édouard Charles Antoine)(Fr. writer; 1840-1902)
Zollinger-Ellison syndrome/tumor (med.)
Zoltán Kodály (Hung. comp.; 1882-1967)
Zomba, Malawi
Zona Gale (US writer; 1874-1938)
Zond (Soviet space probes)
Zoot (John Haley) Sims (US jazz; 1925-85)
Zora Neale Hurston (US writer; 1901-60)
Zorach v. Clausen (US law; 1952)

Zoran Djindjic (PM, Serbia; 1952)
Zoran Lilic (ex-pres., Yug.)
Zorba the Greek (film, 1964)
Zorn, Anders (Leonhard)(Swed. artist; 1860-1920)
Zoroaster (also Zarathustra)(Persian rel./educ.; 6th c. BC)
Zoroastrianism (also Mazdaism)(rel.)
Zorro (TV show)
Zorro, the Gay Blade (film, 1981)
Zouave (also l.c.)(mil.)
Zouave jacket
Zouérate, Mauritania
Zovirax (med.)
ZPG (zero population growth)
Zr (chem. sym., zirconium)
Zrenjanin, Yugoslavia
Zsa Zsa (Sari) Gabor (ent.; 1917?-)
Zubi, Mahmoud (ex-PM, Syria)
Zubin Mehta (India, cond.; 1936-)
Zuckerman Unbound (P. Roth novel)
Zuckerman, Pinchas (Isr. violinist/comp.; 1948-)
Zuider Zee (former sea inlet, Holland)
Zukor, Adolph (ent.; 1873-1976)
Zulfikar Ali Bhutto (ex-pres./PM, Pak.; 1928-79)
Zulu (lang./people)
Zululand (region, SAfr.)
Zumwalt, Elmo R(ussell), Jr. (US adm.; 1920-2000)
Zuni (Native Amer.)
Zuni (pueblo, NM)
Zuni-Cibola National Historical Park (NM)
Zürich, Switzerland
Zutty Singleton (US jazz; 1898-1975)
Zweig, Stefan (Aus. writer; 1881-1942)
Zviad Gamsakhurdia (ex-pres., Georgia)
Zwickau, Germany
Zwingli, Huldreich (or Ulrich)(Swiss rel.; 1484-1531)
Zwinglianism (rel.)
Zwolle, Netherlands
Zworykin, Vladimir (Kosma)("Father of Television")(Rus./US physt./eng./inv.; 1889-1982)
Zyban (med.)
Zyloprim (med.)
ZymoGenetics, Inc.
Zyrtec (med.)
ZZ Top (pop music)